Science

CBSE Class 10

As Per Latest CBSE Syllabus 2022-23
Issued on 21 April, 2022

Science
CBSE Class 10

Authors
Sonal Singh & Ruchi Kapoor *(Physics)*
Imran Ahmad *(Chemistry)*
Sanubia & Rashmi Gupta *(Biology)*

ARIHANT PRAKASHAN (School Division Series)

ARIHANT PRAKASHAN
(School Division Series)
All Rights Reserved

ॐ © PUBLISHER

No part of this publication may be re-produced, stored in a retrieval system or by any means, electronic, mechanical, photocopying, recording, scanning, web or otherwise without the written permission of the publisher. Arihant has obtained all the information in this book from the sources believed to be reliable and true. However, Arihant or its editors or authors or illustrators don't take any responsibility for the absolute accuracy of any information published and the damage or loss suffered thereupon.

All disputes subject to Meerut (UP) jurisdiction only.

ॐ ADMINISTRATIVE & PRODUCTION OFFICES

Regd. Office
'Ramchhaya' 4577/15, Agarwal Road, Darya Ganj, New Delhi -110002
Tele: 011- 47630600, 43518550; Fax: 011- 23280316

ॐ Head Office

Kalindi, TP Nagar, Meerut (UP) - 250002, Tel: 0121-7156203, 7156204

ॐ SALES & SUPPORT OFFICES

Agra, Ahmedabad, Bengaluru, Bareilly, Chennai, Delhi, Guwahati, Hyderabad, Jaipur, Jhansi, Kolkata, Lucknow, Nagpur & Pune.

PO No. : TXT-59-T047921-7-22

Published By Arihant Publications (India) Ltd.

For further information about the books published by Arihant, log on to www.arihantbooks.com or e-mail at info@arihantbooks.com

Follow us on

ॐ **PRICE** ₹ 550.00

PRODUCTION TEAM

Publishing Managers
Mahendra Singh Rawat &
Keshav Mohan

Project Coordinator
Yojna Sharma

Cover Designer
Shanu Mansoori

Inner Designer
Ankit Saini

Page Layouting
Rajbhaskar Rana

Proof Readers
Princi Mittal
Vivek Chaudhary

A WORD
WITH THE READERS

All in one Science Class 10th has been written keeping in mind the needs of students studying in Class 10th CBSE. This book has been made in such a way that students will be fully guided to prepare for the exam in the most effective manner, securing higher grades.

The purpose of this book is to equip any CBSE student with a sound knowledge of Science at Class 10th Level. It covers the whole syllabus of class 10th Science divided into chapters as per the NCERT Textbook. This book will give you support during the course as well as guide you on Revision and Preparation for the exam itself. The material is presented in a Clear & Concise form and there are questions for you to practice.

KEY FEATURES

- To make the students understand the chapter completely, each chapter has easy to understand theory, supported by Solved Examples, Related Figures, Notes, Tables, etc., followed by NCERT Folder having detailed solutions of all the Exercises of NCERT Textbook.

- Exam Practice Section of each chapter contains questions in that format in which these are asked in the examinations. Questions have been divided into Multiple Choice Questions, Very Short Answer Type Questions, Short Answer Type Questions and Long Answer Type Questions. All the questions given here having Detailed Answers.

- There are 3 Sample Question Papers to make the students' practise for the examination as well.

- At the end of book, New features like– Statewise NTSE Questions, Junior Science Olympiad Questions are added.

All-in-One Science for CBSE Class 10th has all the material required for Learning, Understanding, Practice and Assessment, and will surely guide the students on the Path to Success.

We are highly thankful to ARIHANT PRAKASHAN, MEERUT for giving us such an excellent opportunity to write this book. The role of Arihant DTP Unit and Proofreading team is praiseworthy in the making of this book.

Huge efforts have been made from our side to keep this book error free, but inspite of that if any error or whatsoever is skipped in the book then that is purely incidental, apology for the same, please write to us about that so that it can be corrected in the further edition of the book. Suggestions for further improvement of the book will also be welcomed.

In the end, we would like to wish **BEST OF LUCK** to our readers!

Sonal Singh & Ruchi Kapoor (Physics)
Imran Ahmad (Chemistry)
Sanubia & Rashmi Gupta (Biology)

All in one PREVIEW
COMPLETE STUDY | COMPLETE PRACTICE | COMPLETE ASSESSMENT

CHAPTER THEORY
Contains the necessary study material well supported by Definitions, Facts, Examples, Figures etc. This section is totally in sync with NCERT Textbook and provides all the essentials needed to prepare you for the exam.

NCERT FOLDER
To make the students fully familiar with the NCERT Textbook (the most important books for CBSE examinations), solutions of all the Exercises of NCERT Textbook have been provided with each chapter.

CHAPTER 01

Chemical Reactions and Equations

We came across a variety of changes around us which may be physical or chemical changes. A physical change can be easily reversed but a chemical change cannot be reversed easily. Evaporation, melting of wax, freezing of water etc., are physical changes whereas conversion of milk to curd, rusting of iron, digestion of food etc., are chemical changes.

All chemical changes are accompanied by chemical reactions and these are represented with the help of chemical equations. In this chapter, we will study about the various types of chemical reactions and the chemical equations which represent chemical changes.

Chapter Checklist
- Chemical Reaction
- Chemical Equations
- Types of Chemical Reactions
- Effect of Oxidation Reactions in Everyday Life

Chemical Reactions

A chemical reaction is a change in which one or more substance(s) or reactant(s) react(s) to form new substance(s) with entirely different properties.

The reacting species (molecule, atom, ion) are known as **reactants** (the substances that undergo chemical change in the chemical reaction) and the new species formed as a result of the reaction are called **products** (the new substances formed during reaction).

e.g. $Na(s) + H_2O(l) \longrightarrow NaOH(aq) + H_2(g)\uparrow$
Sodium   Water   Sodium   Hydrogen
Reactants   hydroxide
                       Products

In the above chemical reaction, sodium hydroxide and hydrogen are the products and sodium and water are the reactants.

Identification of Chemical Reaction
A chemical reaction can be identified by either of the following observations:
(i) Change in state
(ii) Change in colour
(iii) Evolution of a gas
(iv) Change in temperature
(v) Formation of a precipitate

Check Point 01
1. What is the name given for the substance that reacts and forms in a chemical reaction?
2. State the law of conservation of mass.
3. Write the skeletal equation and balanced equation for the following reaction:
   Potassium bromide (aq) + Barium iodide (aq) ⟶ Potassium iodide (aq) + Barium chloride (s)   CBSE 2014
4. Balance the following chemical equations:
   (i) $MgCO_3 + HCl \longrightarrow MgCl_2 + H_2O$
   (ii) $N_2 + H_2 \longrightarrow NH_3$
   (iii) $P_4 + O_2 \longrightarrow P_2O_5$

2. Decomposition Reaction
A reaction in which a single reactant breaks down to form two or more products, is known as decomposition reaction. This reaction is opposite to combination reaction. On the basis of the form of energy required for the reaction, these reactions are of three types:

(i) **Thermal decomposition** These reactions use the energy in the form of heat for decomposition of the reactant, e.g.

(a) Calcium carbonate on heating, decomposes to give calcium oxide and carbon dioxide. Calcium oxide is used for manufacturing of cement.

CHECK POINT
To assess your step-by-step learning of chapter, Check Point Questions are incorporated in between the theory.

NCERT FOLDER

Intext Questions

1. **Why should a magnesium ribbon be cleaned before burning in air?**   Pg 6
   Sol. Magnesium ribbon reacts with oxygen present in air to form a protective and inert layer of magnesium oxide on its surface. This layer is unreactive and prevents the ribbon from burning. Hence, it needs to be cleaned with sand paper before burning in air.

2. **Write the balanced equation for the following chemical reactions:**   Pg 6
   (i) Hydrogen + Chlorine ⟶ Hydrogen chloride
   (ii) Barium chloride + Aluminium sulphate ⟶ Barium sulphate + Aluminium chloride
   (iii) Sodium + Water ⟶ Sodium hydroxide + Hydrogen
   Sol. (i) $H_2 + Cl_2 \longrightarrow 2HCl$
   (ii) $3BaCl_2 + Al_2(SO_4)_3 \longrightarrow 3BaSO_4 + 2AlCl_3$
   (iii) $2Na + 2H_2O \longrightarrow 2NaOH + H_2$

3. **Write a balanced chemical equation with state symbols for the following reactions:**   Pg 6
   (i) Solutions of barium chloride and sodium sulphate in water react to give insoluble barium sulphate and the solution of sodium chloride.
   (ii) Sodium hydroxide solution (in water) reacts with hydrochloric acid solution (in water) to produce sodium chloride solution and water.
   Sol. (i) $BaCl_2(aq) + Na_2SO_4(aq) \longrightarrow BaSO_4(s)\downarrow + 2NaCl(aq)$
   (ii) $NaOH(aq) + HCl(aq) \longrightarrow NaCl(aq) + H_2O(l)$

4. **A solution of a substance 'X' is used for white washing.**
   (i) Name the substance 'X' and write its formula.

5. **Why is the amount of gas collected in one of the test tubes in activity 1.7 (electrolysis of water) double of the amount collected in the other? Name this gas.**   Pg 10
   Sol. The composition of water, i.e. the chemical formula H_2O, suggests that the molar ratio of hydrogen and oxygen is 2 : 1. Therefore, when water is electrically decomposed, the constituent gases hydrogen and oxygen are produced in the same molar ratio, 2 : 1. Thus, the amount (volume) of hydrogen gas is double that of oxygen gas. So, this gas is hydrogen.

6. **Why does the colour of copper sulphate solution change when an iron nail is dipped in it?**   Pg 13
   Sol. The colour of copper sulphate solution changes when an iron nail is dipped in it because iron being more reactive than copper, displaces copper metal from aqueous copper sulphate solution. Thus, blue colour of copper sulphate fades away to give green colour solution of ferrous sulphate.
   $Fe(s) + CuSO_4(aq) \longrightarrow FeSO_4(aq) + Cu(s)$
   Grey   Blue   Green   Brown

7. **Give an example of a double displacement reaction other than the reaction of barium chloride with sodium sulphate.**   Pg 13
   Sol. The following reaction is an example of a double displacement reaction:
   $2NaOH(aq) + H_2SO_4(aq) \longrightarrow Na_2SO_4(aq) + 2H_2O(l)$
   Sodium   Sulphuric acid   Sodium sulphate   Water
   hydroxide

8. **Identify the substances that are oxidised and the substances that are reduced in the following reactions.**   Pg 13
   (i) $4Na(s) + O_2(g) \longrightarrow 2Na_2O(s)$
   (ii) $CuO(s) + H_2(g) \longrightarrow Cu(s) + H_2O(l)$

SUMMARY
- A **chemical reaction** is a change in which one or more substance(s) (reactant(s)) react(s) to form new substance(s) (product(s)) with entirely different properties.
- The symbolic representation of a chemical reaction is chemical equation.
- A **balanced chemical equation** is that in which the total number of atoms of each element are equal on both sides of the equation.
- A reaction in which two or more reactants combine to form a single product is called **combination reaction**.
- A reaction in which a single reactant breaks down to form two or more products, is known as **decomposition reaction**.
- In **displacement reactions** a more active element displaces a less active element from its compound.
- In **double displacement reactions**, two different atoms or groups of atoms are exchanged.
- **Oxidation** is the process of addition of oxygen to a substance or removal of hydrogen from a substance.
- **Reduction** is the process of removal of oxygen from a substance or addition of hydrogen to a substance.
- Those reactions in which oxidation and reduction takes place simultaneously are called **redox reactions**.
- The reactions which are accompanied by the evolution of heat are called **exothermic reactions**. e.g. respiration.
- The reactions which occur by the absorption of heat/energy are called **endothermic reactions**. e.g. photosynthesis.
- **Corrosion** is the phenomenon due to which metals are slowly eaten away by the reaction of air, water and chemicals present in the atmosphere, is called corrosion. The corrosion of iron is called rusting.
- **Rancidity** is the process of slow oxidation of oils and fats present in the food materials resulting in the change of smell and taste in them.

SUMMARY
For complete revision of each chapter, Summary is given. It contains crux of the chapter theory.

"for CBSE Class 10th Examination is a complete book which can give you all Study, Practice & Assessment. It is hoped that this book will reinforce and extend your ideas about the subject and finally will place you in the ranks of toppers."

EXAM PRACTICE

It contains questions in that format in which these are asked in the examinations, i.e., Multiple Choice Questions, Very Short Answer Type Questions, Short Answer Type Questions, Long Answer Type Questions. All the questions are fully explained. The explanations given here teach the students, how to write the explanations in the examinations to get full marks. Students can use these questions for practice and assess their understanding & recall of the chapter.

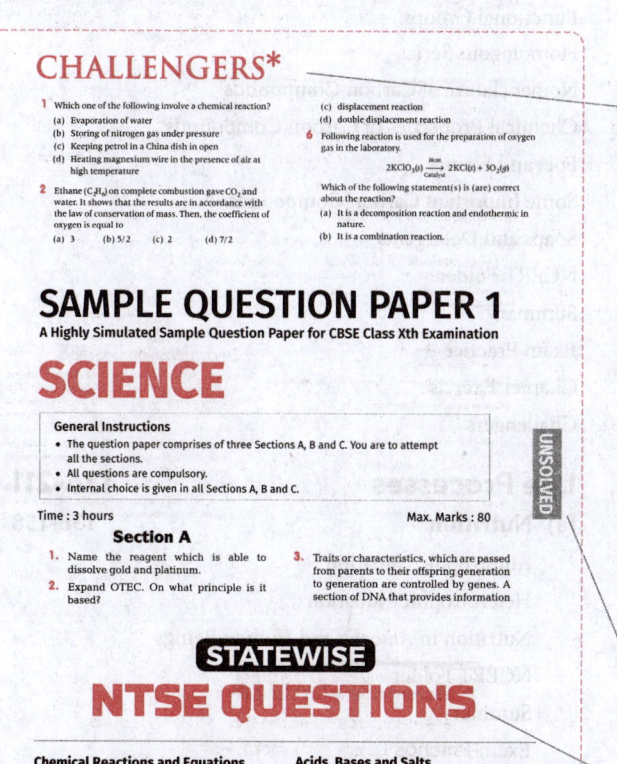

CHALLENGERS

At the end of the chapter, challenger questions are given. These questions may be or may not be asked in the examination, have been given just for additional practice.

CHAPTER EXERCISE

At the end of the chapter, these unsolved questions are for practice and assessment of students. By practising these questions, students can assess their preparation level for the chapter.

SAMPLE QUESTION PAPER

To give the student a look of real examination Question Paper, we have provided 3 Sample Question Papers.

NTSE AND JUNIOR SCIENCE OLYMPIAD

At the end of the book, these are Statewise NTSE Questions and Junior Science Olympiad Chapterwise Questions. These Questions will help you to integrate your school studies with competitive exams at this level.

CONTENTS

1. **Chemical Reactions and Equations**   1-29
   - Chemical Reactions and Chemical Equations
   - Types of Chemical Reactions
   - Effect of Oxidation Reactions in Everyday Life
   - NCERT Folder
   - Summary
   - Exam Practice
   - Chapter Exercise
   - Challengers

2. **Acids, Bases and Salts**   30-58
   - Acids and Bases
   - Indicators
   - Strength of an Acid or Base
   - pH Scale
   - Salts
   - Water of Crystallisation
   - NCERT Folder
   - Summary
   - Exam Practice
   - Chapter Exercise
   - Challengers

3. **Metals and Non-metals**   59-88
   - Metals and Non-metals
   - Reaction Between Metals and Non-Metals
   - Occurrence and Refining of Metals
   - Corrosion
   - NCERT Folder
   - Summary
   - Exam Practice
   - Chapter Exercise
   - Challengers

4. **Carbon and Its Compounds**   89-135
   - Covalent Bond in Carbon Compounds
   - Allotropes of Carbon and their Properties
   - Versatile Nature of Carbon
   - Hydrocarbons
   - Isomerism
   - Functional Groups
   - Homologous Series
   - Nomenclature of Carbon Compounds
   - Chemical Properties of Carbon Compounds
   - Fuel and Flames
   - Some Important Carbon Compounds
   - Soaps and Detergents
   - NCERT Folder
   - Summary
   - Exam Practice
   - Chapter Exercise
   - Challengers

5. **Life Processes**   136-211
   - (a) **Nutrition**   136-158
     - Autotrophic Nutrition
     - Heterotrophic Nutrition
     - Nutrition in *Amoeba* and *Human* Beings
     - NCERT Folder
     - Summary
     - Exam Practice
     - Chapter Exercise
     - Challengers
   - (b) **Respiration**   159-176
     - Respiration and Its Types

Exchange of Gases in Plant and Animals
Human Respiratory System
NCERT Folder
Summary
Exam Practice
Chapter Exercise
Challengers

(c) **Transportation** 177-194
Transportation in Human Beings
Transportation in Plants
NCERT Folder
Summary
Exam Practice
Chapter Exercise
Challengers

(d) **Excretion** 195-211
Excretion in Human Beings
Excretion in Plants
NCERT Folder
Summary
Exam Practice
Chapter Exercise
Challengers

6. **Control and Coordination** 212-236
Nervous System
Divisions of Nervous System
Coordination in Plants
Chemical Communication
NCERT Folder
Summary
Exam Practice
Chapter Exercise
Challengers

7. **How Do Organisms Reproduce?** 237-265
The Fundamentals of Reproduction
Types of Reproduction
Modes of Asexual Reproduction
Modes of Sexual Reproduction
Sexual Reproduction in Flowering Plants
Sexual Reproduction in Human Beings
Significance of Sexual Reproduction
Reproductive Health
NCERT Folder
Summary
Exam Practice
Chapter Exercise
Challengers

8. **Heredity and Evolution** 266-281
Variation
Sex Determination
NCERT Folder
Summary
Exam Practice
Chapter Exercise
Challengers

9. **Light: Reflection and Refraction** 282-327
Reflection of Light
Mirror
Image Formation by Spherical Mirrors
Mirror Formula
Refraction of Light
Lens
Image Formation in Lenses Using Ray Diagram
Lens Formula
Power of a Lens

NCERT Folder
Summary
Exam Practice
Chapter Exercise
Challengers

10. Human Eye and the Colorful World — 328-355
The Human Eye
Defects of Vision and their Correction
Refraction of Light through a Prism
Dispersion of White Light by a Glass Prism
Atmospheric Refraction
Scattering of Light
NCERT Folder
Summary
Exam Practice
Chapter Exercise
Challengers

11. Electricity — 356-399
Electric Charge and Current
Electrical Potential and Potential Difference
Electric Circuit
Ohm's Law
Resistance
Resistance of a System of Resistors
Heating Effect of Electric Current
Electric Power
NCERT Folder
Summary
Exam Practice
Chapter Exercise
Challengers

12. Magnetic Effects of Electric Current — 400-421
Magnetic Field
Force on a Current Carrying Conductor in a Magnetic Field
Domestic Electric Circuits
NCERT Folder
Summary

Exam Practice
Chapter Exercise
Challengers

13. Our Environment — 422-447
Ecosystem
Trophic Levels
Human Impact on the Natural Environment
Managing the Garbage We Produce
Waste Types and their Effects on Our Environment
NCERT Folder
Summary
Exam Practice
Chapter Exercise
Challengers

*14. Management of Natural Resources — 448-469
Management and Conservation of Natural Resources
Forests
Water for All
Coal and Petroleum
An Overview of Natural Resource Management
NCERT Folder
Summary
Exam Practice
Chapter Exercise
Challengers

- **Experiments** — 470-514
- **Periodic Tests** — 515-521
- **Sample Papers (1-3)** — 525-542
- **Statewise NTSE Questions** — 543-552
- **Junior Science Olympid Chapterwise Questions** — 553-560

*This chapter will not be assessed in the year end examination.

Course Structure
Science

Unit No.	Unit	Marks
I	Chemical Substances- Nature and Behaviour	25
II	World of Living	25
III	Natural Phenomena	12
IV	Effects of Current	13
V	Natural Resources	05
	Total	**80**
	Internal Assessment	20
	Grand Total	**100**

THEME Materials
UNIT I : Chemical Substances-Nature and Behaviour

Chemical Reactions Chemical equation, Balanced chemical equation, implications of a balanced chemical equation, types of chemical reactions: combination, decomposition, displacement, double displacement, precipitation, endothermic exothermic reactions, oxidation and reduction.

Acids, Bases and Salts Their definitions in terms of furnishing of H^+ and OH^- ions. General properties, examples and uses, neutralisation, concept of pH scale (Definition relating to logarithm not required), importance of pH in everyday life; preparation and uses of sodium hydroxide, bleaching powder, baking soda, washing soda and Plaster of Paris.

Metals and Non-metals Properties of metals and non-metals, reactivity series, formation and properties of ionic compounds, basic metallurgical processes, corrosion and its prevention.

Carbon Compounds Covalent bonding in carbon compounds. Versatile nature of carbon. Homologous series. Nomenclature of carbon compounds containing functional groups (halogens, alcohol, ketones, aldehydes, alkanes and alkynes), difference between saturated hydrocarbons and unsaturated hydrocarbons. Chemical properties of carbon compounds (combustion, oxidation, addition and substitution reaction). Ethanol and Ethanoic acid (only properties and uses), soaps and detergents.

THEME The World of the Living
UNIT II : World of Living

Life Processes "Living Being". Basic concept of nutrition, respiration, transportation and excretion in plants and animals.

Control and Coordination in Animals and Plants Tropic movements in plants; Introduction of plant hormones; control and coordination in animals : nervous system; voluntary, involuntary and reflex action; chemical coordination: animal hormones.

Reproduction Reproduction in animals and plants (asexual and sexual) reproductive health-need and methods of family planning. Safe sex *vs* HIV/AIDS. Child bearing and women's health.

Heredity and Evolution Heredity; Mendel's contribution- Laws for inheritance of traits: Sex determination: brief introduction: (Topics excluded-evolution; evolution and classification and evolution should not be equated with progress).

THEME Natural Phenomena
UNIT III : Natural Phenomena

Reflection of light by curved surfaces, Images formed by spherical mirrors, Centre of curvature, principal axis, principal focus, focal length. mirror formula (derivation not required), magnification.

Refraction; laws of refraction, refractive index.

Refraction of light by spherical lens, image formed by spherical lenses, lens formula (derivation not required), magnification. Power of a lens.

Functioning of a lens in human eye, defects of vision and their corrections, applications of spherical mirrors and lenses.

Refraction of light through a prism, dispersion of light, scattering of light, applications in daily life. (excluding colour of the sun at sunrise and sunset).

THEME How Things Work
UNIT IV : Effects of Current

Electric current, potential difference and electric current. Ohm's law; Resistance, Resistivity. Factors on which the resistance of a conductor depends. Series combination of resistors, parallel combination of resistors and its applications in daily life. Heating effect of electric current and its applications in daily life. Electric power, Interrelation between P, V, I and R.

Magnetic Effects of Current Magnetic field, field lines, field due to a current-carrying conductor, field due to current-carrying coil or solenoid; force on current-carrying conductor, Fleming's Left-Hand Rule, Direct current. Alternating current : frequency of AC. Advantage of AC over DC. Domestic electric circuits.

THEME Natural Resources
UNIT V : Natural Resources

Our Environment Eco-system, environmental problems, ozone depletion, waste production and their solutions. Biodegradable and non-biodegradable substances.

NOTE FOR THE TEACHERS

1. The chapter Management of Natural Resources (NCERT Chapter 16) will not be assessed in the year-end examination. However, learners may be assigned to read this chapter and encouraged to prepare a brief write up to any concept of this chapter in their Portfolio. This may be for Internal Assessment and credit may be given Periodic Assessment/Portfolio).

2. The NCERT text books present information in boxes across the book. These help students to get conceptual clarity. However, the information in these boxes would not be assessed in the year-end examination.

PRACTICALS

Practical should be conducted alongside the concepts taught in theory classes

LIST OF EXPERIMENTS

1. **A. Finding the pH of the following samples by using pH paper/universal indicator.** UNIT I
   - (a) Dilute Hydrochloric Acid
   - (b) Dilute NaOH solution
   - (c) Dilute Ethanoic Acid solution
   - (d) Lemon juice
   - (e) Water
   - (f) Dilute Hydrogen Carbonate Solution

   B. Studying the properties of acids and bases (HCl and NaOH) on the basis of their reaction with UNIT I
   - (a) Litmus solution (Blue/Red)
   - (b) Zinc metal
   - (c) Solid sodium carbonate

2. **Performing and observing the following reactions and classifying them into** UNIT I
   - (a) Combination reaction
   - (b) Decomposition reaction
   - (c) Displacement reaction
   - (d) Double displacement reaction
     - i. Action of water on quicklime
     - ii. Action of heat on ferrous sulphate crystals
     - iii. Iron nails kept in copper sulphate solution
     - iv. Reaction between sodium sulphate and barium chloride solutions

3. **Observing the action of Zn, Fe, Cu and Al metals on the following salt solutions** UNIT I
   - i. $ZnSO_4 (aq)$
   - ii. $FeSO_4 (aq)$
   - iii. $CuSO_4 (aq)$
   - iv. $Al_2(SO_4)_3 (aq)$

   Arranging Zn, Fe, Cu and Al (metals) in the decreasing order of reactivity based on the above result.

4. Studying the dependence of potential difference (V) across a resistor on the current (I) passing through it and determine its resistance (R). Also plotting a graph between V and I. UNIT IV

5. Determination of the equivalent resistance of two resistors when connected in series and parallel. UNIT IV

6. Preparing a temporary mount of a leaf peel to show stomata. UNIT II

7. Experimentally show that carbon dioxide is given out during respiration. UNIT II

8. **Studying of the following properties of acetic acid (ethanoic acid):**
   - (a) odour
   - (b) solubility in water
   - (c) effect on litmus
   - (d) reaction with sodium hydrogen carbonate UNIT I

9. Study of the comparative cleaning capacity of a sample of soap in soft and hard water. UNIT I

10. **Determination of the focal length of**
    - (a) concave mirror
    - (b) convex lens

    by obtaining the image of a distant object. UNIT III

11. Tracing the path of a ray of light passing through a rectangular glass slab for different angles of incidence. Measure the angle of incidence, angle of refraction, angle of emergence and interpret the result. UNIT III

12. Studying (a) binary fission in *Amoeba*, and (b) budding in yeast and *Hydra* with the help of prepared slides. UNIT II

13. Tracing the path of the rays of light through a glass prism. UNIT III

14. Identification of the different parts of an embryo of a dicot seed (Pea, gram or red kidney bean). UNIT II

Question Paper Design
SCIENCE (CLASS 10)

Time : 3 Hours **Max. Marks : 80**

Competencies	
Demonstrate Knowledge and Understanding	46%
Application of Knowledge Concepts	22%
Formulate, Analyze, Evaluate and Create	32%
	100%

Note

- Typology of Questions: VSA including Objective Type Questions, Assertion – Reasoning Type Questions; SA; LA; Source-based/ Case-based/ Passage-based/ Integrated Assessment Questions.
- An internal choice of approximately 33% would be provided.

Internal Assessment (20 Marks)

- **Periodic Assessment** - 05 marks + 05 marks
- **Subject Enrichment** (Practical Work) - 05 marks
- **Portfolio** - 05 marks

CHAPTER 01

Chemical Reactions and Equations

In our daily life, we came across a variety of changes which may be physical or chemical changes. A **physical change** can be easily reversed but a **chemical change** cannot be reversed easily. Evaporation, melting of wax, freezing of water etc., are physical changes whereas conversion of milk to curd, rusting of iron, digestion of food etc., are chemical changes.

All chemical changes are accompanied by chemical reactions and these are represented with the help of chemical equations.

In this chapter, we will study about the various types of chemical reactions and the chemical equations which represent chemical changes.

Chapter Checklist

- Chemical Reactions
- Chemical Equations
- Types of Chemical Reactions
- Effects of Oxidation Reactions in Everyday Life

Chemical Reactions

A chemical reaction is a change in which one or more substance(s) or reactant(s) react(s) to form new substances with entirely different properties.

The reacting species (molecule, atom, ion) are known as **reactants** (the substances that undergo chemical change in the chemical reaction) and the new species formed as a result of the reaction are called **products** (the new substances formed during reaction).

e.g.

$$2Na(s) + 2H_2O(l) \longrightarrow 2NaOH(aq) + H_2(g)\uparrow$$

Sodium, Water (Reactants) — Sodium hydroxide, Hydrogen (Products)

In the above chemical reaction, sodium hydroxide and hydrogen are the products and sodium and water are the reactants.

Identification of Chemical Reaction

A chemical reaction can be identified by either of the following observations:

(i) Change in state
(ii) Change in colour
(iii) Evolution of a gas
(iv) Change in temperature
(v) Formation of a precipitate

Chemical Equations

A chemical equation is the symbolic representation of a chemical reaction. Symbols and formulae of the reactants and products are used for the same. e.g. the reaction of burning of methane gas can be written in words as:

Methane + Oxygen ⟶ Carbon dioxide + Water
(Reactants) (Products)

This equation is called **word equation**. The word equation can be changed into a chemical equation by writing symbol and formulae of the substance in place of their name.

$$CH_4(g) + 2O_2(g) \xrightarrow{\Delta} CO_2(g) + 2H_2O(l)$$
Methane Oxygen Carbon dioxide Water

Writing a Chemical Equation

A chemical equation shows a change of reactants to products through an arrow (→) placed between them.

On the **left hand side** (LHS) of the arrow, reactants are written with a plus sign (+) between them. Similarly, on the **right hand side** (RHS), products are written with a plus sign (+) between them.

The arrow head points towards the products and shows the direction of the reaction, e.g. the reaction between magnesium (Mg) and oxygen (O_2) resulting into the formation of magnesium oxide can be written as:

$$Mg + O_2 \longrightarrow MgO$$
(Reactants)   (Product)

In the above equation, number of magnesium and oxygen atoms are not same on both sides of an equation. Such an unbalanced equation is called **skeletal chemical equation**.

Balanced Chemical Equations

A balanced chemical equation is that in which the total number of atoms of each element are equal on both sides of the equation.

The balancing of a chemical equation is based on law of conservation of mass. According to the law of conservation of mass, '*mass can neither be created nor be destroyed during a chemical reaction*.' In the same way, the number of atoms of each element remains the same, before and after a chemical reaction.

The method used for balancing chemical equations is called **hit and trial method** as we make trials to balance the equation by using the smallest whole number coefficient. In this method, the number of atoms of each element remains the same, before and after a chemical reaction.

Balancing of a Chemical Equation

Several steps are involved in balancing a chemical equation. These steps are as follows:

Step (a) Writing unbalanced equation and enclosing the formulae in brackets.

$$(Na) + (H_2O) \longrightarrow (NaOH) + (H_2)$$
Sodium Water Sodium hydroxide Hydrogen

Step (b) Making list of number of atoms of different elements as present in unbalanced equation.

Element	Number of Atoms in Reactants (LHS)	Number of Atoms in Products (RHS)
Na	1	1
H	2	3
O	1	1

Step (c) Balancing first element From the table shown above, it is clear that it is only the hydrogen atoms, which are unbalanced. So, firstly we try to balance it.

Atoms of H	In Reactants	In Products
Initially	2 (in H_2O)	3 (1 in NaOH and 2 in H_2)
To balance	2 × 2	2 × 1 in NaOH, 2 in H_2 = 4H-atoms

Thus, the equation now becomes
$$(Na) + 2(H_2O) \longrightarrow 2(NaOH) + (H_2)$$

Step (d) Balancing second element We examine the obtained equation and select another element which is still unbalanced. In the above equation, Na is still unbalanced. To balance the number of Na-atoms,

Atoms of Na	In Reactants	In Products
Initially	1 (in Na)	2 (in NaOH)
To balance	2 × 1	2

Thus, after balancing Na and removing the brackets, we get the equation:
$$2Na + 2H_2O \longrightarrow 2NaOH + H_2$$

Step (e) Balancing other elements If we further examine the reaction, no element is found to be unbalanced. This method of balancing chemical equation is called hit-and-trial method.

Step (f) Checking the correctness of equation To check the correctness of the equation, we further tabulate the number of atoms of each element separately.

Element	Number of Atoms in Reactants	Number of Atoms in Products
Na	2	2
H	4	4
O	2	2

The above table clearly reveals that the obtained equation is a balanced chemical equation.

Chemical Reactions and Equations

Example 1. *Balance the following equation.*
$$C_2H_6 + O_2 \longrightarrow CO_2 + H_2O$$

Sol. *Step* I First of all, enclose all the formulae in brackets.
$$(C_2H_6) + (O_2) \longrightarrow (CO_2) + (H_2O)$$

Step II Count the number of atoms of each element on the reactant and product side of the equation.

Elements	Number of Atoms in Reactants (LHS)	Number of Atoms in Products (RHS)
C	2	1
H	6	2
O	2	3

Step III From the table, it is clear that hydrogen possesses maximum number of atoms. So, first of all to balance hydrogen atom multiply H_2O molecules by 3.
$$(C_2H_6) + (O_2) \longrightarrow (CO_2) + 3(H_2O)$$

Step IV Count further the number of atoms of each element on both sides.

Elements	Number of each Atoms in Reactants (LHS)	Number of Atoms in Products (RHS)
C	2	1
H	6	6
O	2	3

Now, to balance carbon atom multiply CO_2 molecules by 2.
$$(C_2H_6) + (O_2) \longrightarrow 2(CO_2) + 3(H_2O)$$

There are 7 O-atoms on RHS. To make 7 O-atoms at LHS, we have to write 7/2 before O_2 but we can use only whole number to balance the equation, so we write 7/2 before O_2 and multiply the whole equation by 2.

$$\left[C_2H_6 + \frac{7}{2}O_2 \longrightarrow 2CO_2 + 3H_2O\right] \times 2$$

Thus, on removing the brackets from equation, then the equation becomes $2C_2H_6 + 7O_2 \longrightarrow 4CO_2 + 6H_2O$ which is a balanced chemical equation.

Example 2. *Balance the following skeletal equation.*
$$Fe + H_2O \longrightarrow Fe_3O_4 + H_2$$

Sol. *Step* I First of all, enclose all the formulae in brackets.
$$(Fe) + (H_2O) \longrightarrow (Fe_3O_4) + (H_2)$$

Step II Count the number of atoms of each elements on the reactant and product side of the equation.

Elements	Number of Atoms in Reactants (LHS)	Number of Atoms in Products (RHS)
Fe	1	3
H	2	2
O	1	4

Step III From the table, it is clear that oxygen possesses maximum number of atoms. So, first of all to balance oxygen atom multiply H_2O molecules by 4.
$$(Fe) + 4(H_2O) \longrightarrow (Fe_3O_4) + (H_2)$$

Step IV Count further the number of atoms of each elements on both sides.

Elements	Number of Atoms in Reactants (LHS)	Number of Atoms in Products (RHS)
Fe	1	3
H	8	2
O	4	4

Now, to balance hydrogen atom multiply H_2 molecule by 4.
$$(Fe) + 4(H_2O) \longrightarrow (Fe_3O_4) + 4(H_2)$$

There are 3 Fe-atoms on RHS. To make 3 Fe-atoms at LHS, multiply Fe-atom by 3 on LHS.
$$3(Fe) + 4(H_2O) \longrightarrow Fe_3O_4 + 4(H_2)$$

Thus, on removing the brackets from equation, the equation becomes
$$3Fe + 4H_2O \longrightarrow Fe_3O_4 + 4H_2$$

Making a Chemical Equation More Informative

The following facts remains unexplained in a chemical equation shown in step (d).

(*i*) Physical states of substances (*ii*) Reaction conditions
(*iii*) Evolution/absorption of energy

Some of these limitations of a chemical equation can be overcome by adding the following symbols or information as discussed below:

(*i*) The physical states of the reactants and products can be represented by using the symbols, (*s*) for solid, (*l*) for liquid, (*g*) for gas and (*aq*) for aqueous solution, alongwith their respective formulae. The word aqueous (*aq*) is written if the reactant or product is present as a solution in water.

$$2Na(s) + 2H_2O(l) \longrightarrow 2NaOH(aq) + H_2(g)$$

Precipitate can also be represented by using an arrow pointing downwards (↓) instead of using symbol (*s*).

In the same way, the gaseous state of an evolved gas can be represented by using an arrow pointing upward direction (↑) instead of using symbol (*g*), e.g. magnesium reacting with dilute sulphuric acid is represented by the chemical equation

$$\underset{\text{Magnesium}}{Mg(s)} + \underset{\substack{\text{Sulphuric}\\\text{acid}}}{H_2SO_4(aq)} \longrightarrow \underset{\substack{\text{Magnesium}\\\text{sulphate}}}{MgSO_4(aq)} + \underset{\text{Hydrogen}}{H_2\uparrow}$$

(ii) The specific conditions of the reaction like temperature, pressure, catalyst etc., are written above or below the arrow in the chemical equation.

$$CO(g) + 2H_2(g) \xrightarrow{340 \text{ atm}} CH_3OH(l)$$
Carbon monoxide, Hydrogen, Methanol

(iii) Evolution of heat or absorption of heat can be indicated by writing [+Heat] on the right hand side or left hand side of the equation, respectively e.g. Burning of carbon in the presence of air.

$$C(s) + O_2(g) \longrightarrow CO_2(g) + \text{Heat}$$
Carbon, Oxygen, Carbon dioxide

Note Although it is not always necessary to mention the physical states and reaction conditions in a balanced chemical equation. So, you can left this step until it is asked in the question.

Check Point 01

1. What are the name given for the substance that reacts and formed in a chemical reaction?
2. State the law of conservation of mass.
3. Write the skeletal equation and balanced equation for the following reaction :
   Potassium bromide (aq) + Barium iodide (aq) ⟶
                   Potassium iodide (aq) + Barium bromide (s)
4. Fill in the blanks:
   The symbol (aq) and (s) indicates …… and …… respectively in any chemical equation.
5. State True or False for the following sentence:
   The number of atoms of each element is conserved in any chemical reaction.
6. Balance the following chemical equations:
   (i) $Mg(OH)_2 + HCl \longrightarrow MgCl_2 + H_2O$
   (ii) $N_2 + H_2 \longrightarrow NH_3$
   (iii) $P_4 + O_2 \longrightarrow P_2O_5$

Types of Chemical Reactions

The chemical reactions are classified into different classes depending upon the type of chemical changes taking place. These reactions are as follows:

1. Combination Reaction

A reaction in which two or more reactants combine to form a single product, is called **combination** reaction, e.g.

(i) Calcium oxide (quick lime) reacts vigorously with water to form calcium hydroxide (slaked lime). The reaction is highly exothermic, as a lot of heat is produced during the reaction.

$$CaO(s) + H_2O(l) \longrightarrow Ca(OH)_2(aq) + \text{Heat}$$
Calcium oxide (Quick lime), Water, Calcium hydroxide (Slaked lime)

Note Solution of calcium hydroxide (slaked lime) is used for white washing walls. Calcium hydroxide reacts slowly with carbon dioxide in air to form a thin layer of calcium carbonate, on the walls which gives a shiny appearance to the walls. Calcium carbonate is formed after two to three days of white washing.

$$Ca(OH)_2(aq) + CO_2(g) \longrightarrow CaCO_3(s) + H_2O(l)$$
Calcium hydroxide, Calcium carbonate

(ii) Burning of coal.

$$C(s) + O_2(g) \longrightarrow CO_2(g)$$
Carbon, Oxygen, Carbon dioxide

(iii) Reaction between hydrogen gas and oxygen gas to form water.

$$2H_2(g) + O_2(g) \longrightarrow 2H_2O(l)$$
Hydrogen, Oxygen, Water

2. Decomposition Reaction

A reaction in which a single reactant breaks down to form two or more products, is known as **decomposition reaction**. This reaction is opposite to combination reaction. On the basis of the form of energy required for the reaction, these reactions are of three types:

(i) **Thermal decomposition** These reactions use the energy in the form of heat for decomposition of the reactant, e.g.

(a) Calcium carbonate on heating, decomposes to give calcium oxide and carbon dioxide. Calcium oxide is used for manufacturing of cement.

$$CaCO_3(s) \xrightarrow{\text{Heat}} CaO(s) + CO_2(g)$$
Calcium carbonate (Limestone), Calcium oxide (Quick lime), Carbon dioxide

(b) Ferrous sulphate, the green colour crystals $FeSO_4 \cdot 7H_2O$ on heating lose water of crystallisation and forms dehydrated $FeSO_4$, which on decomposition gives ferric oxide, sulphur dioxide, SO_2 and sulphur trioxide, SO_3. Ferric oxide is a solid, while SO_2 and SO_3 are gases.

$$2FeSO_4(s) \xrightarrow{\text{Heat}} Fe_2O_3(s) + SO_2(g) + SO_3(g)$$
Ferrous sulphate, Ferric oxide, Sulphur dioxide, Sulphur trioxide

(c) On heating lead nitrate, it decomposes to give yellow lead monoxide, nitrogen dioxide and oxygen gas.

$$2Pb(NO_3)_2(s) \xrightarrow{\text{Heat}} 2PbO(s) + 4NO_2(g) + O_2(g)$$
Lead nitrate (Colourless), Lead oxide (Yellow), Nitrogen dioxide (Brown fumes), Oxygen

(ii) **Electrolysis** These reactions involve the use of electrical energy for the decomposition of the reactant molecules. e.g.

(a) When electric current is passed through water, it decomposes to give oxygen and hydrogen.

$$2H_2O(l) \xrightarrow{\text{Electric current}} 2H_2(g) + O_2(g)$$
Water — Hydrogen Oxygen

(b) When electric current is passed through molten sodium chloride, it decomposes to give sodium metal and chlorine gas.

$$2NaCl(l) \xrightarrow{\text{Electric current}} 2Na(s) + Cl_2(g)$$
Molten sodium chloride — Sodium Chlorine

(iii) **Photolysis or photochemical decomposition** These reactions involve the use of light energy for the purpose of decomposition, e.g.

(a) When silver chloride is exposed to sun light, it decomposes to give silver metal and chlorine gas.

$$2AgCl(s) \xrightarrow{\text{Sunlight}} 2Ag(s) + Cl_2(g)$$
Silver chloride (White) — Silver (Greyish white) Chlorine (Yellowish green)

(b) Similarly, silver bromide gives silver metal and bromine gas in the presence of sunlight.

$$2AgBr(s) \xrightarrow{\text{Sunlight}} 2Ag(s) + Br_2(g)$$
Silver bromide (Pale yellow) — Silver (Greyish white) Bromine (Brown)

(The reaction of decomposition of silver halides are used in black and white photography).

3. Exothermic and Endothermic Reactions

Depending upon whether heat is evolved or absorbed during a reaction, the reaction can be exothermic or endothermic

(i) **Exothermic reactions** The reactions which are accompanied by the evolution of heat, are called exothermic reactions (combustion reaction) or the reactions in which heat is released alongwith the formation of products are called exothermic reactions. Respiration is an exothermic process. The decomposition of vegetable matter into compost is also an example of an exothermic reaction.

e.g.

(a) Burning of natural gas (combustion reaction).

$$CH_4(g) + 2O_2(g) \longrightarrow CO_2(g)$$
Methane Oxygen Carbon dioxide
$$+ 2H_2O(g) + \text{Heat}$$
Water

(b) Burning of magnesium ribbon

$$2Mg(s) + O_2(g) \longrightarrow 2MgO(s) + \text{Heat}$$
Magnesium Oxygen Magnesium oxide

(c) The decomposition of vegetable matter into compost is also an example of exothermic reaction.

(ii) **Endothermic reactions** The reactions which occur by the absorption of heat/energy (either in the form of light or electricity), are called endothermic reactions.

Photosynthesis is an endothermic process. All decomposition reactions are endothermic reactions as such reactions requires energy either in the form of heat, light or electricity for breaking down the reactants.

e.g.

(a) $6CO_2(aq) + 12H_2O(l) \xrightarrow[\text{Chlorophyll}]{\text{Sunlight}} C_6H_{12}O_6$
Glucose
$+ 6O_2 + 6H_2O$

(b) $2HgO(s) + \text{Heat} \longrightarrow 2Hg(l) + O_2(g)$
Mercuric oxide — Mercury Oxygen

(c) $NH_4Cl(s) + \text{Heat} \longrightarrow NH_3(g) + HCl(g)$
Ammonium chloride — Ammonia Hydrochloric acid

(d) $Ba(OH)_2 + NH_4Cl \xrightarrow{\Delta} BaCl_2 + 2NH_3 + 2H_2O$

4. Displacement Reaction

When a more reactive element displaces less reactive element from its compound, it is called **displacement reaction**.

This reaction is of two types :

(i) **Single displacement reaction** It is a type of chemical reaction where an element reacts with a compound and takes the place of another element in that compound is called single displacement.

(a) Zinc being more reactive than Cu, displaces Cu from $CuSO_4$ solution and forms new product, zinc sulphate and Cu metal.

$$Zn(s) + CuSO_4(aq) \longrightarrow ZnSO_4(aq) + Cu(s)$$
Zinc metal (Grey) — Copper sulphate solution (Blue) — Zinc sulphate solution (Colourless) — Copper metal (Brown)

(b) Similarly, iron being more reactive than Cu displaces copper from aqueous solution of copper sulphate.

$$Fe(s) + CuSO_4(aq) \longrightarrow FeSO_4(aq) + Cu(s)$$
Iron — Copper sulphate (Blue) — Ferrous sulphate or Iron (II) sulphate (Green) — Copper metal

(c) Also, lead is more reactive than copper so, it displaces copper from its solution and white coloured lead chloride gets formed.

$$Pb(s) + CuCl_2(aq) \longrightarrow PbCl_2(aq) + Cu(s)$$
Copper chloride — Lead chloride

(ii) **Double displacement reaction** The reaction in which two different ions or group of atoms in the reactant molecules are displaced by each other is called **double displacement reaction**. It is also called **precipitation reaction** as precipitate is produced in such reactions.

e.g.

(a) On adding sodium sulphate to barium chloride, a curdy white precipitate of barium sulphate and a solution of sodium chloride are formed.

$$Na_2SO_4(aq) + BaCl_2(aq) \longrightarrow$$
Sodium sulphate — Barium chloride
$$BaSO_4 \downarrow + 2NaCl(aq)$$
Barium sulphate (White ppt.) — Sodium chloride

(b) On adding silver nitrate solution to sodium bromide, a yellow precipitate of silver bromide and solution of sodium nitrate are formed.

$$AgNO_3(aq) + NaBr(aq) \longrightarrow AgBr \downarrow$$
Silver nitrate — Sodium bromide — Silver bromide (Yellow ppt.)
$$+ NaNO_3(aq)$$
Sodium nitrate

Note The reaction in which acid or acidic oxide react with base or basic oxide to form salt and water are called neutralisation reactions. e.g.

$$2NaOH + H_2SO_4 \longrightarrow Na_2SO_4 + H_2O$$
Sodium hydroxide — Sulphuric acid — Sodium sulphate — Water

5. Oxidation and Reduction Reactions

Oxidation

It can be defined as:

The process in which oxygen is added to a substance.

Or

The process in which hydrogen is removed from a substance.

Or

The process in which a substance loses electron(s).

e.g.

(i) $2Cu + O_2 \xrightarrow{Heat} 2CuO$
Copper — Oxygen — Copper oxide

(ii) $2H_2S + O_2 \longrightarrow 2S + 2H_2O$
Hydrogen sulphide — Oxygen — Sulphur — Hydrogen oxide

(iii) $Zn \longrightarrow Zn^{2+} + 2e^-$
Zinc

Reduction

It can be defined as:

The process in which oxygen is removed from a substance.

Or

The process in which hydrogen is added to a substance.

Or

The process in which a substance gains electron(s).

e.g. (i) $2KClO_3(s) \xrightarrow{\Delta} 2KCl(s) + 3O_2(g)$
Potassium chlorate — Potassium chloride — Oxygen

(ii) $2Na + H_2 \longrightarrow 2NaH$
Sodium — Hydrogen — Sodium hydride

(iii) $Zn^{2+} + 2e^- \longrightarrow Zn$
Zinc

Note If a substance gains oxygen during a reaction, it is said to be oxidised. If a substance loses oxygen during a reaction, it is said to be reduced.

Oxidising agent The substance which can bring about oxidation of other substances is called an oxidising agent.

Reduction agent The substance which can bring about reduction of other substance is called a reducing agent.

Redox Reactions

Those reactions in which oxidation and reduction take place simultaneously, are called **redox reactions**. e.g.

(i) In the following reaction, the copper (II) oxide is losing oxygen and is being reduced. Whereas, oxygen is added to hydrogen and is being oxidised.

Reduction
$$CuO + H_2 \xrightarrow{Heat} Cu + H_2O$$
Copper oxide — Hydrogen — Copper — Water
Oxidation

(ii) In the following reaction, HCl is oxidised to Cl_2 whereas, MnO_2 is reduced to $MnCl_2$.

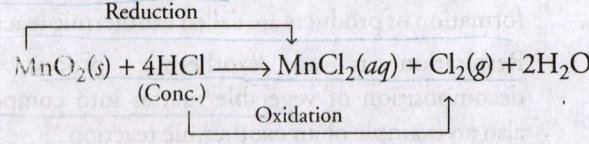

Effects of Oxidation Reactions in Everyday Life

Corrosion

The phenomenon due to which open surface of the metals are slowly eaten away by the reaction of air, water and chemicals present in the atmosphere, is called corrosion.

e.g. Iron articles are shiny when new, but get coated with a reddish brown powder when left for some time.

The process of corrosion of iron is called **rusting**. The rusting of iron is a redox reaction. The black coating on silver and the green coating on copper are other examples of corrosion.

Painting, galvanising, electroplating are some of the methods to prevent corrosion.

Effects of Corrosion

The effects of corrosion are :

(i) Corrosion causes damage to car bodies, bridges, iron railings, ships and all objects made up of metals, specially those which are made up of iron.

(ii) Corrosion is a wasteful process in most of cases. Every year tones of various metals especially iron get wasted in the country. Hence, it is quite necessary to prevent corrosion.

Note In case of aluminium, corrosion is not proved to be wasteful.

Rancidity

It is the process of slow oxidation of oil and fat (which are volatile in nature) present in the food materials resulting in the change of smell and taste in them.

The methods to prevent rancidity are:

(i) Keeping food materials in air-tight containers.

(ii) Refrigeration of cooked food at low temperatures.

(iii) Packing of food items like potato wafers etc., in packets containing nitrogen gas instead of air.

(iv) Avoid keeping the cooked food and food materials in direct sunlight.

(v) By adding antioxidants, e.g. BHA (Butylated Hydroxy Anisole) and BHT (Butylated Hydroxy Toluene).

Check Point 02

1. Identify the type of reaction:
   (i) $CH_4(g) + 2O_2(g) \longrightarrow CO_2(g) + 2H_2O(g)$
   (ii) $2NaCl(l) \xrightarrow{\text{Electric current}} 2Na(s) + Cl_2(g)$
   (iii) $MnO_2 + 4HCl \longrightarrow MnCl_2 + 2H_2O + Cl_2$

2. State True or False for the following sentence:
   When hydrogen gas is added to copper oxide, the oxidising agent is H_2.

3. Name one reaction which is accompanied by the evolution of heat.

4. Name the type of reaction for the following:
   (i) Vegetable matter changing into compost.
   (ii) Burning of natural gas.

5. Write the four factors responsible for the corrosion of iron.

6. Fill in the blank:
   A reaction that produces water from two ions is known as…. .

NCERT FOLDER

Intext Questions

1 Why should a magnesium ribbon be cleaned before burning in air? **Pg 6**

Sol. Magnesium ribbon reacts with oxygen present in air to form a protective and inert layer of magnesium oxide on its surface. This layer is unreactive and prevents the ribbon from burning. Hence, it needs to be cleaned with sand paper before burning in air.

2 Write the balanced equation for the following chemical reactions: **Pg 6**

(i) Hydrogen + Chlorine $\longrightarrow$ Hydrogen chloride

(ii) Barium chloride + Aluminium sulphate $\longrightarrow$ Barium sulphate + Aluminium chloride

(iii) Sodium + Water $\longrightarrow$ Sodium hydroxide + Hydrogen

Sol. (i) $H_2 + Cl_2 \longrightarrow 2HCl$

(ii) $3BaCl_2 + Al_2(SO_4)_3 \longrightarrow 3BaSO_4\downarrow + 2AlCl_3$

(iii) $2Na + 2H_2O \longrightarrow 2NaOH + H_2$

3 Write a balanced chemical equation with state symbols for the following reactions: **Pg 6**

(i) Solutions of barium chloride and sodium sulphate in water react to give insoluble barium sulphate and the solution of sodium chloride.

(ii) Sodium hydroxide solution (in water) reacts with hydrochloric acid solution (in water) to produce sodium chloride solution and water.

Sol. (i) $BaCl_2(aq) + Na_2SO_4(aq) \longrightarrow BaSO_4(s)\downarrow + 2NaCl(aq)$

(ii) $NaOH(aq) + HCl(aq) \longrightarrow NaCl(aq) + H_2O(l)$

4 A solution of a substance 'X' is used for white washing.

(i) Name the substance 'X' and write its formula.

(ii) Write the reaction of the substance 'X' named in (i) above with water. **Pg 10**

Sol. (i) Substance X is calcium oxide or quicklime. Its formula is CaO

(ii) Quicklime reacts with water as:

$\underset{X}{CaO(s)} + \underset{Water}{H_2O(l)} \longrightarrow \underset{\substack{Slaked\ lime\\(Calcium\ hydroxide)}}{Ca(OH)_2(aq)}$

5 Why is the amount of gas collected in one of the test tubes in activity 1.7 (electrolysis of water) double of the amount collected in the other? Name this gas. **Pg 10**

Sol. The composition of water, i.e. the chemical formula H_2O, suggests that the molar ratio of hydrogen and oxygen is 2 : 1. Therefore, when water is electrically decomposed, the constituent gases hydrogen and oxygen are produced in the same molar ratio, 2 : 1. Thus, the amount (volume) of hydrogen gas is double than that of oxygen gas. So, this gas is hydrogen.

6 Why does the colour of copper sulphate solution change when an iron nail is dipped in it? **Pg 13**

Sol. The colour of copper sulphate solution changes when an iron nail is dipped in it because iron being more reactive than copper, displaces copper metal from aqueous copper sulphate solution. Thus, blue colour of copper sulphate fades away to give green colour solution of ferrous sulphate.

$\underset{Grey}{Fe(s)} + \underset{Blue}{CuSO_4(aq)} \longrightarrow \underset{Green}{FeSO_4(aq)} + \underset{Brown}{Cu(s)}$

7 Give an example of a double displacement reaction other than the reaction of barium chloride with sodium sulphate. **Pg 13**

Sol. The following reaction is an example of a double displacement reaction:

$\underset{\substack{Sodium\\hydroxide}}{2NaOH(aq)} + \underset{Sulphuric\ acid}{H_2SO_4(aq)} \longrightarrow \underset{Sodium\ sulphate}{Na_2SO_4(aq)} + \underset{Water}{2H_2O(l)}$

8 Identify the substances that are oxidised and the substances that are reduced in the following reactions. **Pg 13**

(i) $4Na(s) + O_2(g) \longrightarrow 2Na_2O(s)$

(ii) $CuO(s) + H_2(g) \longrightarrow Cu(s) + H_2O(l)$

Sol. (i) $4Na(s) + O_2(g) \longrightarrow 2Na_2O(s)$

Na has gained oxygen and forms Na_2O. So, Na is oxidised and O_2 is reduced

(ii) $CuO(s) + H_2(g) \longrightarrow Cu(s) + H_2O(l)$

CuO has lost oxygen and forms Cu.

So, Cu is reduced while H_2 has gained oxygen, hence, it is oxidised.

All in one Chemical Reactions and Equations

Exercises
(On Pages 14, 15 and 16)

1 Which of the statements about the reaction below are incorrect?

$2PbO(s) + C(s) \longrightarrow 2Pb(s) + CO_2(g)$

(i) Lead is getting reduced
(ii) Carbon dioxide is getting oxidised
(iii) Carbon is getting oxidised
(iv) Lead oxide is getting reduced

Sol. The given reaction can be written in the form of two separate reactions:

$2PbO(s) \xrightarrow[\text{Loss of oxygen}]{\text{Reduction}} 2Pb(s)$

and $C(s) \xrightarrow[\text{Gain of oxygen}]{\text{Oxidation}} CO_2(g)$

Therefore, (i) and (ii) are incorrect, while (iii) and (iv) are correct statements.

2 $Fe_2O_3 + 2Al \longrightarrow Al_2O_3 + 2Fe$

The above reaction is an example of a
(i) combination reaction
(ii) double displacement reaction
(iii) decomposition reaction
(iv) displacement reaction

Sol. (iv) In the above reaction, Al is more reactive than Fe. So, it displaces Fe from Fe_2O_3 to form Al_2O_3. Hence, it is a displacement reaction.

3 What happens when dilute hydrochloric acid is added to iron filings? Tick the correct answer.
(i) Hydrogen gas and iron chloride are produced
(ii) Chlorine gas and iron hydroxide are produced
(iii) No reaction takes place
(iv) Iron salt and water are produced

Sol. (i) Iron being more reactive than hydrogen, displaces hydrogen from the dilute hydrochloric acid. Thus, hydrogen gas and iron chloride a salt of iron are formed.

$Fe(s) + 2HCl(aq) \longrightarrow FeCl_2(aq) + H_2(g)\uparrow$

4 What is a balanced chemical equation? Why should chemical equations be balanced?

Sol. A chemical change is represented by a chemical equation. When the number of atoms of different elements on reactant and product side are equal, then the chemical equation is called a balanced chemical equation.

It is important to balance a chemical equation because
(i) to validate the **law of conservation of mass** which states that the mass of reactants should be equal to the mass of the products. The total mass of a system is thus conserved.

This law holds true only if number of atoms of reactants reacting together is equal to number of product atoms formed.

(ii) a balanced chemical equation tells us about the physical state of the reactants and products whether they are solid (s), liquid (l) or gas (g) or aqueous (aq).

(iii) it tells us about heat changes that can take place in a chemical reaction. Δ is the symbol of heat. Hence, it is endothermic or exothermic can be deduced from a balanced chemical equations.

5 Translate the following statements into chemical equations and then balance them:
(i) Hydrogen gas combines with nitrogen to form ammonia.
(ii) Hydrogen sulphide gas burns in air to give water and sulphur dioxide.
(iii) Barium chloride reacts with aluminium sulphate to give aluminium chloride and a precipitate of barium sulphate.
(iv) Potassium metal reacts with water to give potassium hydroxide and hydrogen gas.

Sol. (i) $3H_2(g) + N_2(g) \longrightarrow 2NH_3(g)$
(ii) $2H_2S(g) + 3O_2(g) \longrightarrow 2H_2O(l) + 2SO_2(g)$
(iii) $3BaCl_2(aq) + Al_2(SO_4)_3(aq) \longrightarrow$
$2AlCl_3(aq) + 3BaSO_4(s)\downarrow$
(iv) $2K(s) + 2H_2O(l) \longrightarrow 2KOH(aq) + H_2(g)$

6 Balance the following chemical equations:
(i) $HNO_3 + Ca(OH)_2 \longrightarrow Ca(NO_3)_2 + H_2O$
(ii) $NaOH + H_2SO_4 \longrightarrow Na_2SO_4 + H_2O$
(iii) $NaCl + AgNO_3 \longrightarrow AgCl + NaNO_3$
(iv) $BaCl_2 + H_2SO_4 \longrightarrow BaSO_4 + HCl$

Sol. (i) $\underset{\text{Nitric acid}}{2HNO_3} + \underset{\text{Calcium hydroxide}}{Ca(OH)_2} \longrightarrow \underset{\text{Calcium nitrate}}{Ca(NO_3)_2} + \underset{\text{Water}}{2H_2O}$

(ii) $\underset{\text{Sodium hydroxide}}{2NaOH} + \underset{\text{Sulphuric acid}}{H_2SO_4} \longrightarrow \underset{\text{Sodium sulphate}}{Na_2SO_4} + \underset{\text{Water}}{2H_2O}$

(iii) $\underset{\text{Sodium chloride}}{NaCl} + \underset{\text{Silver nitrate}}{AgNO_3} \longrightarrow \underset{\text{Silver chloride}}{AgCl} + \underset{\text{Sodium nitrate}}{NaNO_3}$

(iv) $\underset{\text{Barium chloride}}{BaCl_2} + \underset{\text{Sulphuric acid}}{H_2SO_4} \longrightarrow \underset{\text{Barium sulphate}}{BaSO_4} + \underset{\text{Hydrochloric acid}}{2HCl}$

7 Write the balanced chemical equations for the following reactions:

(i) Calcium hydroxide + Carbon dioxide $\longrightarrow$
Calcium carbonate + Water

(ii) Zinc + Silver nitrate $\longrightarrow$
Zinc nitrate + Silver

(iii) Aluminium + Copper chloride $\longrightarrow$
Aluminium chloride + Copper

(iv) Barium chloride + Potassium sulphate $\longrightarrow$
Barium sulphate + Potassium chloride

Sol. (i) $Ca(OH)_2 + CO_2 \longrightarrow CaCO_3 + H_2O$
(ii) $Zn + 2AgNO_3 \longrightarrow Zn(NO_3)_2 + 2Ag$
(iii) $2Al + 3CuCl_2 \longrightarrow 2AlCl_3 + 3Cu$
(iv) $BaCl_2 + K_2SO_4 \longrightarrow BaSO_4 + 2KCl$

8. Write the balanced chemical equation for the following and identify the type of reaction in each case:
(i) Potassium bromide (aq) + Barium iodide (aq) $\longrightarrow$ Potassium iodide (aq) + Barium bromide (s)
(ii) Zinc carbonate (s) $\longrightarrow$ Zinc oxide (s) + Carbon dioxide (g)
(iii) Hydrogen (g) + Chlorine (g) $\longrightarrow$ Hydrogen chloride (g)
(iv) Magnesium (s) + Hydrochloric acid (aq) $\longrightarrow$ Magnesium chloride (aq) + Hydrogen (g)

Sol. (i) $2KBr(aq) + BaI_2(aq) \longrightarrow 2KI(aq) + BaBr_2(s)$
Type: Double displacement reaction
(ii) $ZnCO_3(s) \xrightarrow{\Delta} ZnO(s) + CO_2(g)$
Type: Thermal decomposition reaction
(iii) $H_2(g) + Cl_2(g) \longrightarrow 2HCl(g)$
Type: Combination reaction
(iv) $Mg(s) + 2HCl(aq) \longrightarrow MgCl_2(aq) + H_2(g)$
Type: Displacement reaction

9. What does one mean by exothermic and endothermic reactions? Give examples.

Sol. Exothermic reactions These reactions proceed with the evolution (or release) of heat or energy, e.g.
(i) $H_2SO_4(aq) \xrightarrow{Water} 2H^+(aq) + SO_4^{2-}(aq) + Heat$
(ii) $\underset{Methane}{CH_4(g)} + \underset{Oxygen}{2O_2(g)} \longrightarrow \underset{Carbon\ dioxide}{CO_2(g)} + \underset{Water}{2H_2O(l)} + Heat$
(iii) $\underset{Glucose}{C_6H_{12}O_6(aq)} + \underset{Oxygen}{6O_2(g)} \longrightarrow$
$\underset{Carbon\ dioxide}{6CO_2(g)} + \underset{Water}{6H_2O(l)} + Energy$

Endothermic reactions These reactions involve the absorption of heat or energy, e.g.
(i) $\underset{Mercuric\ oxide}{2HgO(s)} + Heat \longrightarrow \underset{Mercury}{2Hg(l)} + \underset{Oxygen}{O_2(g)}$
(ii) $NH_4Cl(aq) + Heat \rightleftharpoons NH_4^+(aq) + Cl^-(aq)$
(iii) $N_2(g) + O_2(g) + Heat \longrightarrow 2NO(g)$

10. Why is respiration considered an exothermic reaction? Explain.

Sol. The food taken by the living beings is ultimately broken down to glucose by the digestive system. The glucose so formed is slowly oxidised to carbon dioxide and water with the release of heat energy. Thus, respiration is an exothermic reaction.
$\underset{(Glucose)}{C_6H_{12}O_6(aq)} + 6O_2(g) \longrightarrow 6CO_2(g)$
$+ 6H_2O(l) + energy$

11. Why are decomposition reactions called the opposite of combination reactions? Write equations for these reactions. **CBSE 2010**

Sol. In a decomposition reaction, single reactant breaks down to produce two or more products, whereas in a combination reaction, two or more reactants combine to give a single product. Thus, these reactions are supposed to be opposite of each other, e.g.
(i) $2H_2 + O_2 \xrightarrow{(Combination)} 2H_2O$
or Electroytic
$2H_2O \xrightarrow[\text{(Decomposition)}]{\text{Electric current or electrolyte}} 2H_2 + O_2$
(ii) $CaCO_3 + H_2O + CO_2 \xrightarrow{(Combination)} Ca(HCO_3)_2$
$Ca(HCO_3)_2 \xrightarrow[\text{(Decomposition)}]{\Delta} CaCO_3 + H_2O + CO_2$

12. Write one equation each for decomposition reactions where energy is supplied in the form of heat, light or electricity.

Sol. (i) Heat : $CaCO_3(s) \xrightarrow{Heat} CaO(s) + CO_2(g)$
(ii) Light : $2AgCl(s) \xrightarrow{Light} 2Ag(s) + Cl_2(g)$
(iii) Electricity :
$\underset{(Acidulated)}{2H_2O(l)} \xrightarrow{Electric\ current} 2H_2(g) + O_2(g)$

13. What is the difference between displacement and double displacement reactions? Write equations for these reactions. **CBSE 2012, 11, 10**

Sol. In a displacement reaction, a more reactive element displaces a less reactive element from its salt solution. But in a double displacement reaction, two atoms or groups from different compounds displace each other.
Chemical equation for single displacement,
$Zn(s) + CuSO_4(aq) \longrightarrow ZnSO_4(aq) + Cu(s)$
Here, Zn displaces Cu from its salt solution ($CuSO_4$).
Chemical equation for double displacement,
$BaCl_2(aq) + K_2SO_4(aq) \longrightarrow BaSO_4(s) + 2KCl(aq)$
Here, Ba and K displace each other.

14 In the refining of silver, the recovery of silver from silver nitrate solution involved displacement by copper metal. Write down the reaction involved.

Sol. The reaction involved is:

$$2AgNO_3(aq) + Cu(s) \longrightarrow$$
$$\underset{\text{Silver nitrate}}{} \quad \underset{\text{Copper metal}}{}$$

$$Cu(NO_3)_2(aq) + 2Ag(s)$$
$$\underset{\text{Copper nitrate}}{} \quad \underset{\text{Silver metal}}{}$$

15 What do you mean by a precipitation reaction? Explain by giving examples.

Sol. The reaction which is accompanied by the formation of an insoluble solid mass (called precipitate) is known as precipitation reaction, e.g.

(i) When barium chloride solution is added to an aqueous solution of sodium sulphate, a white precipitate of barium sulphate is obtained.

$$BaCl_2(aq) + Na_2SO_4(aq) \longrightarrow$$

$$\underset{\text{(White ppt.)}}{BaSO_4(s)\downarrow} + 2NaCl(aq)$$

(ii) When silver nitrate is added to an aqueous solution of sodium chloride, a white precipitate of silver chloride (AgCl), which is soluble in NH$_4$OH is obtained.

$$AgNO_3(aq) + NaCl(aq) \longrightarrow$$

$$\underset{\text{(White ppt.)}}{AgCl(s)\downarrow} + NaNO_3(aq)$$

16 Explain the following in terms of gain or loss of oxygen with two examples each.
(i) Oxidation (ii) Reduction

Sol. (i) **Oxidation** It is a process in which a substance gains oxygen, e.g.

(a) $4Na + O_2 \longrightarrow 2Na_2O$
$\underset{\text{Sodium}}{} \quad \underset{\text{Oxygen}}{} \quad \underset{\text{Sodium oxide}}{}$

(b) $2H_2 + O_2 \longrightarrow 2H_2O$
$\underset{\text{Hydrogen}}{} \quad \underset{\text{Oxygen}}{} \quad \underset{\text{Water}}{}$

In the above reactions, Na and H$_2$ gains oxygen to form Na$_2$O and H$_2$O respectively.

(ii) **Reduction** It is a process in which a substance loses oxygen.
e.g.

(a) $CuO + H_2 \longrightarrow Cu + H_2O$
CuO loses oxygen to form Cu.

(b) $2KClO_3(s) \xrightarrow{\Delta} 2KCl(s) + 3O_2(g)$
$\underset{\text{Potassium chlorate}}{} \quad \underset{\text{Potassium chloride}}{} \quad \underset{\text{Oxygen}}{}$

KClO$_3$ loses oxygen to form KCl and O$_2$.

17 A shiny brown coloured element X on heating in air becomes black in colour. Name the element X and the black coloured compound formed.

Sol. Element X is copper and the black coloured compound is copper (II) oxide.

$$2\underset{\underset{\text{(Brown)}}{X}}{Cu(s)} + O_2(g) \xrightarrow{\text{Heat}} 2\underset{\underset{\text{oxide (Black)}}{\text{Copper (II)}}}{CuO(s)}$$

18 Why do we apply paint on iron articles?

Sol. By applying paint on iron articles, they can be prevented from corrosion (rusting). Paint does not allow oxygen (from air) and water (moisture) to come in contact with the surface of iron.

19 Oil and fat containing food items are flushed with nitrogen. Why? **CBSE 2014**

Sol. Nitrogen is unreactive gas as compared to oxygen. Oil and fat present in the food items get oxidised and become rancid in the presence of air or oxygen. But such reaction is prevented in the presence of nitrogen. Therefore, food items like potato chips etc., are packed with nitrogen gas to prevent them from rancidity for a long time.

20 Explain the following terms with one example of each:
(i) Corrosion
(ii) Rancidity

Sol. Refer to text on page 7.

SUMMARY

- A **chemical reaction** is a change in which one or more substance(s) (reactant(s)) react(s) to form new substances(s) (product(s)) with entirely different properties.
- The symbolic representation of a chemical reaction is chemical equation.
- A **balanced chemical equation** is that in which the total number of atoms of each element are equal on both sides of the equation.
- A reaction in which two or more reactants combine to form a single product is called **combination reaction**.
- A reaction in which a single reactant breaks down to form two or more products, is known as **decomposition reaction**.
- In **displacement reactions** a more active element displaces a less active element from its compound.
- In **double displacement reactions**, two different atoms or groups of atoms are exchanged.
- **Oxidation** is the process of addition of oxygen to a substance or removal of hydrogen from a substance.
- **Reduction** is the process of removal of oxygen from a substance or addition of hydrogen to a substance.
- Those reactions in which oxidation and reduction takes place simultaneously are called **redox reactions**.
- The reactions which are accompanied by the evolution of heat are called **exothermic reactions**. e.g. respiration.
- The reactions which occur by the absorption of heat/energy are called **endothermic reactions**. e.g. photosynthesis.
- **Corrosion** is the phenomenon due to which metals are slowly eaten away by the reaction of air, water and chemicals present in the atmosphere, is called corrosion. The corrosion of iron is called rusting.
- **Rancidity** is the process of slow oxidation of oils and fats present in the food materials resulting in the change of smell and taste in them.

Exam Practice

Objective Type Questions

Multiple Choice Questions

1 Which of the following is a physical change?
CBSE (All India) 2020
(a) Formation of curd from milk
(b) Ripening of fruits
(c) Getting salt from sea water
(d) Burning of wood

Sol. (c) The changes, which can give back the reactants by physical means are called physical changes. Hence, getting of salt from sea water is a physical change.

2 When $Ca(NO_3)_2$ is heated, it gives CaO, $NO_2(g)$ and $O_2(g)$. The correct number of moles of $Ca(NO_3)_2$, CaO, $NO_2(g)$ and $O_2(g)$ are present in the reaction are respectively
(a) 2, 1, 3, 2   (b) 2, 2, 4, 1
(c) 2, 2, 2, 1   (d) 1, 2, 4, 1

Sol. (b) $Ca(NO_3)_2$ on heating gives CaO, $NO_2(g)$ and $O_2(g)$. The balanced chemical equation is as follows:

$$2Ca(NO_3)_2 \longrightarrow 2CaO + 4NO_2(g) + O_2(g)$$

Hence, number of moles of reactant $Ca(NO_3)_2$ and products CaO, $NO_2(g)$ and $O_2(g)$ are present 2, 2, 4 and 1 respectively.

3 Which of the following correctly represents a balanced chemical equation?
CBSE SQP (Term-I)
(a) $Fe(s) + 4H_2O(g) \longrightarrow Fe_3O_4(s) + 4H_2(g)$
(b) $3Fe(s) + 4H_2O(g) \longrightarrow Fe_3O_4(s) + 4H_2(g)$
(c) $3Fe(s) + H_2O(g) \longrightarrow Fe_3O_4(s) + H_2(g)$
(d) $3Fe(s) + 4H_2O(g) \longrightarrow Fe_3O_4(s) + H_2(g)$

Sol. (b) In chemcial equation (a), the number of Fe atoms in reactants and products is not equal. In chemical equation (b), the number of all atoms in reactants and products is equal. In chemical equation (c), the number of O-atoms in reactants and products is not equal.
In chemical equatants (d), the number of H-atoms is not equal in reactants and products.

4 Electrolysis of water is a decomposition reaction. The mole ratio of hydrogen and oxygen gases liberated during electrolysis of water is **NCERT Exemplar**
(a) 1 : 1   (b) 2 : 1   (c) 4 : 1   (d) 1 : 2

Sol. (b) The water decomposes during electrolysis to form hydrogen and oxygen gases in the molar ratio 2 : 1 by volume.

$$2H_2O(l) \xrightarrow{\text{Electric current}} 2H_2(g) + O_2(g)$$
Water ———— Hydrogen Oxygen
                    2 : 1

5 The chemical reaction between copper and oxygen can be categorised as
(a) displacement reaction
(b) decomposition reaction
(c) combination reaction
(d) double displacement reaction

Sol. (c) The chemcial reaction between copper and oxygen can be written as

$$2Cu + O_2 \longrightarrow 2CuO$$

As oxygen and copper combines to form copper oxide, hence this given reaction is a combination reaction.

6 Which among the following statements is/are true? Exposure of silver chloride to sunlight for a long duration turns grey due to
(i) the formation of silver by decomposition of silver chloride.
(ii) sublimation of silver chloride.
(iii) decomposition of chlorine gas from silver chloride.
(iv) oxidation of silver chloride.
NCERT Exemplar
(a) (i) Only
(b) (i) and (iii)
(c) (ii) and (iii)
(d) Only (iv)

Sol. (a) Decomposition of silver chloride takes place in the presence of sunlight.

$$2AgCl \xrightarrow{\text{Sunlight}} 2Ag(s) + Cl_2$$
Silver ——————— Sliver
chloride   (grey)

In this reaction, the white colour of silver chloride changes greyish white due to the formation of silver metal.

7 Which among the following is/are double displacement reaction(s)?
(i) $Pb + CuCl_2 \longrightarrow PbCl_2 + Cu$
(ii) $Na_2SO_4 + BaCl_2 \longrightarrow BaSO_4 + 2NaCl$
(iii) $C + O_2 \longrightarrow CO_2$
(iv) $CH_4 + 2O_2 \longrightarrow CO_2 + 2H_2O$

(a) (i) and (iv) (b) Only (ii)
(c) (i) and (ii) (d) (iii) and (iv)
NCERT Exemplar

Sol. (b) In double displacement reaction, two compounds exchange their ions to form two new compounds.
Only in reaction (ii), exchange of ions is taking place (cations and anions of both reactants are exchanged).
$$Na_2SO_4 + BaCl_2 \longrightarrow \underset{\text{White ppt.}}{BaSO_4} + 2NaCl$$

8 Reema took 5 mL of lead nitrate solution in a beaker and added approximately 4 mL of potassium iodide solution to it. What would she observe? **CBSE SQP (Term-I)**
(a) The solution turned red
(b) Yellow precipitate was formed
(c) White precipitate was formed
(d) The reaction mixture became hot

Sol. (b) The chemcial reaction involved in given statement is
$$\underset{\substack{\text{Potassium}\\\text{iodide}}}{KI} + \underset{\substack{\text{Lead}\\\text{nitrate}}}{Pb(NO_3)_2} \to \underset{\substack{\text{Potassium}\\\text{nitrate}}}{KNO_3} + \underset{\substack{\text{Lead iodide}\\\text{(Yellow)}}}{PbI_2\downarrow}$$

This reaction is an example of precipitation and double displacement reaction because of the formation of yellow precipitate of lead iodide.

9 Limestone $\xrightarrow[\text{Step 1}]{\text{Heated}}$ X + CO$_2$
$\downarrow$ + H$_2$O Step 2
Slaked lime

Identify the correct option from the given table which represents the type of reactions occurring in step 1 and step 2.
CBSE SQP (Term-I)

	Endothermic	Exothermic
(a)	✗	✓
(b)	✓	✗
(c)	✓	✓
(d)	✗	✗

Sol. (c) In step 1, when limestone is heated, it absorbs heat which is an endothermic process and decomposes to form calcium oxide (✗) and carbon dioxide. In step 2, when water is added to calcium oxide (✗), then slaked lime is formed with the evolution of heat which is exothermic process.

10 Which of the following statements about the given reaction are correct?
$$3Fe(s) + 4H_2O(g) \longrightarrow Fe_3O_4(s) + 4H_2(g)$$
(i) Iron metal is getting oxidised.
(ii) Water is getting reduced.
(iii) Water is acting as reducing agent.
(iv) Water is acting as oxidising agent.
(a) (i), (ii) and (iii) (b) (iii) and (iv)
(c) (i), (ii) and (iv) (d) (ii) and (iv)
NCERT Exemplar

Sol. (c) Fe is gaining oxygen to give Fe$_3$O$_4$. H$_2$O is losing oxygen to give H$_2$. The substance which oxidises the other substance in a chemical reaction is known as an oxidising agent. So, water is acting as oxidising agent.

11 In the reaction of iron with copper sulphate solution,
$$CuSO_4 + Fe \longrightarrow Cu + FeSO_4$$
Which option in the given table correctly represents the substance oxidised and the reducing agent ?

	Substance oxidised	Reducing agent
(a)	Fe	Fe
(b)	Fe	FeSO$_4$
(c)	Cu	Fe
(d)	CuSO$_4$	Fe

CBSE SQP (Term-I)

Sol. (a) The given chemical reaction is as follows

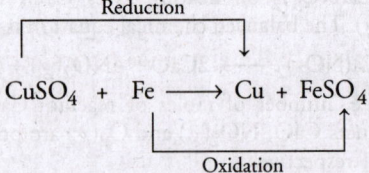

In the above reaction, oxygen is being removed from CuSO$_4$ and added to Fe. Therefore, Fe undergoes oxidation and becomes oxidised substance and acts as reducing agent.

12 The following reaction is an example of a
$$4NH_3(g) + 5O_2(g) \to 4NO(g) + 6H_2O(g)$$
(i) displacement reaction
(ii) combination reaction
(iii) redox reaction
(iv) neutralisation reaction
(a) (i) and (iv) (b) (ii) and (iii)
(c) (i) and (iii) (d) (iii) and (iv)
NCERT Exemplar

Sol. (d) It is a redox reaction because oxidation and reduction both take place simultaneously in this reaction. Also, it is a displacement reaction because H of NH$_3$ has been displaced by oxygen.

13 A dilute ferrous sulphate solution was gradually added to the beaker containing acidified permanganate solution. The light purple colour of the solution fades and finally disappears. Which of the following is the correct explanation for the observation?

Chemical Reactions and Equations

(a) $KMnO_4$ is an oxidising agent, it oxidises $FeSO_4$.
(b) $FeSO_4$ acts as an oxidising agent and oxidises $KMnO_4$.
(c) The colour disappears due to dilution, no reaction is involved.
(d) $KMnO_4$ is an unstable compound and decomposes in the presence of $FeSO_4$ to a colourless compound. **NCERT Exemplar**

Sol. (a) Potassium permanganate ($KMnO_4$) in presence of dil H_2SO_4, i.e., in acidic medium acts as strong oxidising agent. In acidic medium, $KMnO_4$ oxidises ferrous sulphate to ferric sulphate.

$$2KMnO_4 + 8H_2SO_4 + 10\underset{\text{Ferrous sulphate}}{FeSO_4} \longrightarrow$$

$$K_2SO_4 + 5\underset{\text{Ferric sulphate}}{Fe_2(SO_4)_3} + 2MnSO_4 + 8H_2O$$

14 Which of the following are exothermic processes?
(i) Reaction of water with quick lime
(ii) Dilution of an acid
(iii) Evaporation of water
(iv) Sublimation of camphor (crystals)
(a) (i) and (ii) (b) (ii) and (iii)
(c) (i) and (iv) (d) (iii) and (iv).

NCERT Exemplar

Sol. (a) When quicklime reacts with water, a large amount of heat is released along with the formation of calcium hydroxide. Similarly, the process of dissolving an acid or base in water is a highly exothermic reaction. Evaporation of water and sublimation of camphor are endothermic reactions.

15 Solid calcium oxide reacts vigorously with water to form calcium hydroxide accompanied by liberation of heat. This process is called slaking of lime. Calcium hydroxide dissolves in water to form its solution called lime water. Which among the following is are true about slaking of lime and the solution formed?
(i) It is an endothermic reaction.
(ii) It is exothermic reaction.
(iii) The pH of the resulting solution will be more than seven.
(iv) The pH of the resulting solution will be less than seven. **NCERT Exemplar**
(a) (i) and (ii) (b) (ii) and (iii)
(c) (i) and (iv) (d) (iii) and (iv)

Sol. (b) It is an exothermic reaction because heat is given out and the resulting compound is $Ca(OH)_2$ which is basic in nature so, the pH of the resulting solution will be more than seven.

$$\underset{\text{Calcium oxide}}{CaO} + H_2O \longrightarrow \underset{\substack{\text{Calcium} \\ \text{hydroxide} \\ \text{(basic)}}}{Ca(OH)_2} + \text{heat}$$

$Ca(OH)_2$ turns red litmus solution to blue. So, its pH value is greater than seven.

16 Food items made up of oils or fats are generally flushes with some inert gas :
I. To protect them from corrosion.
II. To enhance their flavour.
III. To protect them from being rancid.
IV. To protect their taste.

The correct statement is **CBSE 2021 (Term-I)**
(a) II, III, IV (b) III and IV
(c) only III (d) All of these

Sol. (b) Nitrogen gas is filled inside food items to prevent rancidity and spoilage of food due to its taste.

17 Two gases 'Z' having suffocating odour are obtained when a green solid 'X' is heated, alongwith a residue 'Y'. These gases are major air pollutants. When the vapours of the gases are collected and dissolved in water, the solution turns blue litmus to red. The colour of the residue becomes red.

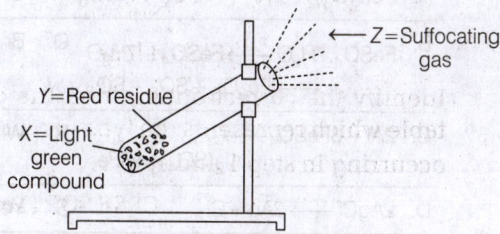

What would be X, Y, Z.
(a) $Pb(NO_3)_2, PbO_2, NO_2, N_2O_4$
(b) $Fe(OH)_2, FeO, H_2O, H_2O_2$
(c) $FeSO_4, Fe_2O_3, SO_2, SO_3$
(d) $PbSO_4, Pb_2O_3, SO_2, SO_3$

Sol. (c) $2\underset{\substack{\text{Green} \\ (X)}}{FeSO_4} \longrightarrow \underset{\substack{\text{Reddish} \\ \text{brown} \\ (Y)}}{Fe_2O_3} + \underbrace{SO_2\uparrow + SO_3\uparrow}_{\substack{\text{Suffocating} \\ \text{Smell} \\ (Z)}}$

$2SO_2 + 2H_2O \longrightarrow 2\underset{\substack{\text{Sulphurous} \\ \text{acid}}}{H_2SO_3}$ (turns blue litmus to red)

Fill in the Blanks

18 The precipitation reactions produce ...... salts.

Sol. insoluble

19 When ammonium chloride is heated with caustic soda, the gas evolved is ....

Sol. NH_3 (ammonia)

20 A complete chemical equation represents the reactants, product and their ....

Sol. physical state

True and False

21 Rusting is a double decomposition reaction.

Sol. False; Rusting is a redox reaction.

22 In decomposition reaction, one reactant produce two or more products.

Sol. True

23 When a strip of copper is introduced in a solution of zinc sulphate, zinc is precipitated out.

Sol. False; Copper is less reactive than Zn, it cannot displace zinc from its solution.

Match the Column

24. Match the following Columns.

	Column I (Reaction)		Column II (Colour of precipitate)
A.	$Pb(NO_3)_2 + 2KI \longrightarrow PbI_2 + KNO_3$	P.	Grey
B.	$FeSO_4 \cdot 7H_2O \xrightarrow{\Delta} FeSO_4 + 7H_2O$ $\longrightarrow Fe_2O_3 + SO_2 + SO_3$	Q.	Brown
C.	$2Al + 3FeSO_4 \longrightarrow Al_2(SO_4)_3 + 3Fe$	R.	White
D.	$2AgCl \longrightarrow 2Ag + Cl_2$	S.	Yellow

Sol. A→S, B→Q, C→R, D→P

Assertion–Reason

Direction (Q. Nos. 25-30) *In each of the following questions, a statement of Assertion is given by the corresponding statement of Reason. Of the statements, mark the correct answer as.*

(a) Both Assertion and Reason are true and Reason is the correct explanation of Assertion.
(b) Both Assertion and Reason are true, but Reason is not the correct explanation of Assertion.
(c) Assertion is true, but Reason is false.
(d) Assertion is false, but Reason is true.

25 Assertion The following chemical equation,

$$2C_6H_6 + \frac{7}{2}O_2 \longrightarrow 4CO_2 + 3H_2O$$

is a balanced chemical equation.

Reason In a balanced chemical equation, the total number of atoms of each element is equal on both side of the equation.

Sol. (d) Assertion is false but reason is true. In a balanced chemical equation, the total number of atoms of each element are equal on both sides of the equation. Moreover, the correct balanced chemical equation is,

$$2C_2H_6 + 7O_2 \longrightarrow 4CO_2 + 6H_2O$$

26 Assertion $Fe_2O_3 + 2Al \longrightarrow Al_2O_3 + 2Fe$

The above chemical equation is an example of displacement reaction.

Reason Aluminium being more reactive than iron, displaces Fe from its oxide.

CBSE 2021 (Term-I)

Sol. (a) Both Assertion and Reason are true and Reason is the correct explanation of Assertion.

$Fe_2O_3 + 2Al \longrightarrow Al_2O_3 + 2Fe$

is a displacement reaction. Here, a highly reactive element (Al) displaces Fe from Fe_2O_3.

27 Assertion Decomposition of vegetable matter into compost is an endothermic reaction.

Reason Decomposition reaction involves breakdown of a single reactant into simpler products.

CBSE SQP (Term-I)

(a) Both A and R are true and R is the correct explanation of A.
(b) Both A and R are true, but R is not the correct explanation of A.
(c) A is true, but R is false.
(d) A is false, but R is true.

Sol. (d) The decomposition of vegetable matter into compost is an example of an exothermic reaction, not of endothermic reaction. Hence, given assertion is false and reason is true as decomposition reaction involves breakdown of a single reaction into simpler products.

28 Assertion In the following chemical equation,

$$CuO(s) + Zn(s) \longrightarrow ZnO(s) + Cu(s)$$

Zinc is getting oxidised and copper oxide is getting reduced.

Reason The process in which oxygen is added to a substance is called oxidation whereas the process in which oxygen is removed from a substance is called reduction.

Sol. (a) Both Assertion and Reason are true and Reason is the correct explanation of Assertion. The reaction involves both oxidation and reduction in which, CuO is reduced to Cu and Zn is oxidised to ZnO.

29 Assertion Quicklime reacts vigorously with water releasing a large amount of heat.

Reason The above chemical reaction is an exothermic reaction.

Sol. (a) Both Assertion and Reason are true and Reason is the correct explanation of Assertion. In exothermic reactions, heat is released alongwith the formation of products.

30 Assertion Photosynthesis is considered as an endothermic reaction.

Reason Energy gets released in the process of photosynthesis.

Sol. (c) Assertion is true but Reason is false. Photosynthesis is considered as an endothermic reaction because energy in the form of sunlight is absorbed by the green plants.

Case Based Questions

Direction (Q. Nos. 31-34) *Answer the questions on the basis of your understanding of the following passage and related studied concepts:*

During a chemical reaction atoms of one element do not change into those of another element. Nor do atoms disappear from the mixture or appear from elsewhere. Actually, chemical reactions involve the breaking and making of bonds between atoms to produce new substances. There are different types of chemical reactions occurring during this process. We have observed the effect of these chemical reactions in our everyday life also. Redox reaction, photochemical reaction, precipitation reaction are some of the types of chemical reactions.

31 Which decomposition reaction followed by two combination reactions are involved in white wash of walls?

Sol. Decomposition of limestone ($CaCO_3$) gives quicklime which combine with water to form slaked lime $Ca(OH)_2$, which after putting on the walls, combine with CO_2 of the air to form $CaCO_3$.

Decomposition reaction :

$$CaCO_3(s) \longrightarrow \underset{\text{Quick lime}}{CaO(s)} + CO_2(g)$$

Combination reaction :

(a) $CaO + H_2O \longrightarrow \underset{\text{Slaked lime}}{Ca(OH)_2}$

(b) $Ca(OH)_2 + CO_2(g) \longrightarrow \underset{\text{Calcium carbonate}}{CaCO_3(s)} + H_2O$

32 How photochemical reactions have played an important role in photography?

Sol. A photographic film used in black and white photography is a celluloid filon coating with silver chloride. Its working is based on the decomposition of silver chloride in the presence of sunlight.

$$2AgCl \xrightarrow[\text{Decomposition}]{\text{Sunlight}} 2Ag + Cl_2(g)$$

33 Copper nitrate gives a test of nitrate ion, but if we heat a small amount of it in a boiling tube, it does not give test of nitrate ion. Why?

Sol. Initially copper nitrate contains NO_3^- ions. Thus, the presence of this ion can be confirmed by test. On heating copper nitrate decomposes according to the following equation.

$$2Cu(NO_3)_2 \xrightarrow{\Delta} 2CuO(s) + 4NO_2(g) + O_2(g)$$

Thus, according to the above equation there is no NO_3^- ion available after heating. Therefore, resulting solid CuO will not give test for NO_3^- ion.

34 Give one example of oxidation reaction in everyday life.

Sol. Iron particles are shiny when new but get coated with a reddish brown powder when left for some time. This process is commonly known as rusting of iron which is an example of oxidation reaction.

Direction (Q. Nos. 35-39) *Answer the questions on the basis of your understanding of the following passage and related studied concepts:*

Marble's popularity began in ancient Rome and Greece, where white and off-white marble were used to construct a variety of structures, from hand-held sculptures to massive pillars and buildings. **CBSE (All India) 2020**

35 The substance not likely to contain $CaCO_3$ is
(a) dolomite (b) a marble statue
(c) calcined gypsum (d) sea shells

Sol. *(c)* The substance not likely to contain $CaCO_3$ is calcined gypsum. The composition of gypsum is $CaSO_4 \cdot 2H_2O$. It does not have $CaCO_3$. Marble is composed of recrystallised carbonate minerals, most commonly calcite $(CaCO_3)$ or dolomite $(CaMg(CO_3)_2)$ Hence, option (c) is correct.

36 A student added 10 g of calcium carbonate in a rigid container, secured it tightly and started to heat it. After some time, an increase in pressure was observed, the pressure reading was then noted at intervals of 5 min and plotted against time, in a graph as shown below. During which time interval did maximum decomposition took place?

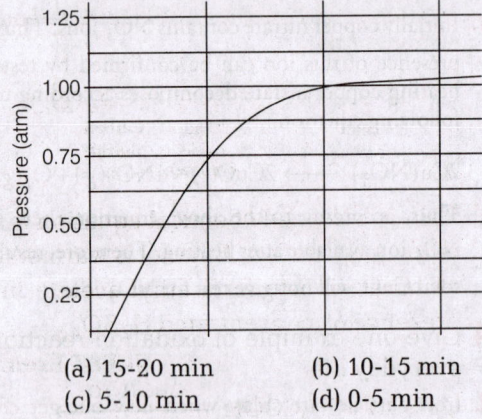

(a) 15-20 min (b) 10-15 min
(c) 5-10 min (d) 0-5 min

Sol. *(d)* The pressure reading was noted at intervals of 5 min and plotted against time of the reaction which involved:

$$CaCO_3 \xrightarrow{\Delta} CaO + CO_2 \uparrow$$

formation of CO_2 gas increases pressure and is maximum in (0-5) min graph as shown sharp curve in (0-5) min.
Hence, option (d) is correct.

37 Gas A, obtained above is a reactant for a very important biochemical process which occurs in the presence of sunlight. Identify the name of the process.
(a) Respiration
(b) Photosynthesis
(c) Transpiration
(d) Photolysis

Sol. *(b)* Gas A (CO_2), for a very important biochemical process which occurs in the presence of sunlight, the name of the process is photosynthesis. The reactants for photosynthesis are light energy, water, carbon dioxide and chlorophyll, while the products are glucose, oxygen and water.

38 Marble statues are corroded or stained when they repeatedly come into contact with polluted rain water. Identify the main reason.

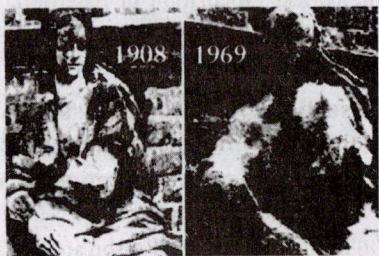

(a) Decomposition of calcium carbonate to calcium oxide
(b) Polluted water is basic in nature, hence it reacts with calcium carbonate
(c) Polluted water is acidic in nature, hence it reacts with calcium carbonate
(d) Calcium carbonate dissolves in water to give calcium hydroxide.

Sol. *(c)* Marble statues are corroded or stained when they repeatedly come into contact with polluted rain water. Polluted rain water is acidic in nature. Hence, it reacts with calcium carbonate.

$$CaCO_3(s) + H_2SO_4(aq) \longrightarrow CaSO_4(s) + CO_2(g) + H_2O$$

Hence, option (c) is correct.

39 Calcium oxide can be reduced to calcium, by heating with sodium metal. Which compound would act as an oxidising agent in the above process?
(a) Sodium (b) Sodium oxide
(c) Calcium (d) Calcium oxide

Sol. *(d)* Calcium oxide can be reduced to calcium by heating with sodium metal and calcium oxide acts as an oxidising agent because it oxidises other substance, i.e. sodium and its gets reduced.

Direction (Q. Nos. 40-43) *Answer the questions on the basis of your understanding of the following passage, table and related studied concepts:*

A magnesium ribbon 'X' was taken by four students P, Q, R and S and they cleaned it by sand paper. 2 cm of 'X' and a piece of coal 'Y' were taken in a watch glass by four students. On burning two 'X' and 'Y' by using burner following observation were recorded in the form of table as given below:

Chemical Reactions and Equations

Observations by	Item	Flame's colour	Residue obtained
P	X	Dazzling white	Greyish ash
	Y	Yellowish	Black ash
Q	X	Dazzing White	White powder
	Y	Sooty	Blackish grey ash
R	X	White flame	Grey powder
	Y	White flame	Black coke
S	X	Yellowish	Greyish ash
	Y	Sooty	Black ash

40 The correct observation was made by the student
(a) P   (b) Q
(c) R   (d) S

Sol. (b) Magnesium ribbon burns with Dazzling white flame and sooty fumes. The correct observation was made by the student Q.

41 When magnesium ribbon burnt it produce
(a) magnesium hydroxide
(b) magnesium oxide
(c) magnesium chloride
(d) magnesium carbonate

Sol. (b) When magnesium ribbon burns, it reacts with oxygen present in the air and form a powdery ash called magnesium oxide (MgO).

42 Why magnesium ribbon must be cleaned before burning in air?

Sol. Magnesium ribbon must be cleaned before burning in the air, so as to remove the layer of MgO formed due to reaction between magnesium and air.

43 Name the type of reaction occur during this experiment.

Sol. Combustion reaction:
$Mg(s) + H_2SO_4(aq) \longrightarrow MgO(s) + H_2(g)\uparrow$

Very Short Answer Type Questions

44 Identify the oxidising agent in the following:
$MnO_2(s) + 4HCl \longrightarrow MnCl_2(aq) + Cl_2(g) + 2H_2O$

Sol. MnO_2 is the oxidising agent in the given reaction.

45 In the reaction,
$Be_2C + xH_2O \longrightarrow yBe(OH)_2 + CH_4$
write the values of x and y.

Sol. On balancing the given equation,
$\underset{\text{Beryllium carbide}}{Be_2C} + 4H_2O \longrightarrow \underset{\text{Beryllium hydroxide}}{2Be(OH)_2} + \underset{\text{Methane}}{CH_4}$
Hence, $x = 4$ and $y = 2$.

46 Complete the missing component / variable given as X and Y in the following reaction.
$Zn(s) + H_2SO_4(aq) \longrightarrow ZnSO_4(X) + H_2(Y)$ **NCERT Exemplar**

Sol. $\underset{\text{Zinc}}{Zn(s)} + \underset{\text{Sulphuric acid}}{H_2SO_4(aq)} \longrightarrow \underset{\text{Zinc sulphate}}{ZnSO_4(aq)} + \underset{\text{Hydrogen}}{H_2(g)}$
$\therefore X = (aq)$ and $Y = (g)$

47 The carbonate of metal X is a white solid. It decomposes when heated to form carbon dioxide and a yellow solid oxide. What is metal X?

Sol. Metal X is lead(Pb). The name of metal carbonate is lead carbonate ($PbCO_3$).
$\underset{\text{Lead carbonate}}{PbCO_3(s)} \xrightarrow{\Delta} \underset{\substack{\text{Lead oxide}\\\text{(Yellow)}}}{PbO(s)} + \underset{\text{Carbon dioxide}}{CO_2(g)}$

48 Write a balanced chemical equation for the following reaction; Ethanol is warmed with ethanoic acid to form ethyl acetate in the presence of concentrated H_2SO_4. **NCERT Exemplar**

Sol. $\underset{\text{Ethanol}}{C_2H_5OH} + \underset{\text{Ethanoic acid}}{CH_3COOH} \xrightarrow[\text{Esterification}]{\text{Conc. } H_2SO_4}$
$\underset{\substack{\text{Ethyl ethanoate}\\\text{(Ester)}}}{CH_3COOC_2H_5} + H_2O$

49 What is the difference between the following two reactions?
(i) $Mg + 2HCl \longrightarrow MgCl_2 + H_2$
(ii) $NaOH + HCl \longrightarrow NaCl + H_2O$

Sol. (i) Here, Mg is more reactive than H. Hence, displaces hydrogen. Therefore, it is a displacement reaction.
(ii) In this reaction, exchange of ions between the reactants occur. Hence, it is a double displacement reaction.

50 Identify the reducing agent in the following reaction. **NCERT Exemplar**
$Fe_2O_3 + 3CO \longrightarrow 2Fe + 3CO_2$

Sol. CO, i.e. carbon monoxide is the reducing agent in the given reaction as it removes oxygen from Fe_2O_3 and causes its reduction.

51 Why do not a wall immediately acquire a1z white colour when a coating of slaked lime is applied on it?

Sol. When a solution of slaked lime is applied on the wall, CO_2 gas present in air slowly reacts with thin layer of calcium hydroxide to form a thin layer of calcium carbonate, that is quite white.

Therefore, the newly formed calcium carbonate impart white look to the walls.

$$Ca(OH)_2(aq) + CO_2(g) \rightarrow CaCO_3(s) + H_2O(l)$$

52 Consider the following reaction:

$$2FeSO_4(s) \longrightarrow Fe_2O_3(s) + SO_2(g) + SO_3(g)$$

Is it a redox reaction or not? If yes, why?

Sol. It is a redox reaction because ferrous (Fe^{2+}) is getting oxidised to ferric ion (Fe^{3+}) whereas SO_4^{2-} is getting reduced to SO_2.

Short Answer (SA) Type Questions

1 State one example each characterised by the following alongwith the chemical equation:
(i) Change in state   (ii) Evolution of gas
(iii) Change in temperature   **CBSE 2016**

Sol. (i) Burning of coal
$$C(s) + O_2(g) \longrightarrow CO_2(g)$$
(ii) Evolution of gas
$$Zn(s) + 2HCl(aq) \longrightarrow ZnCl_2(s) + H_2(g)\uparrow$$
(iii) Change in temperature
$$CaO(s) + H_2O(l) \longrightarrow Ca(OH)_2(aq) + \text{Heat}$$

2 Write the balanced chemical equations for the following and identify the type of chemical reactions.
(i) Hydrogen iodide on reacting with chlorine gas gives iodine and hydrochloric acid.
(ii) Methane gas burns in oxygen of air to form carbon dioxide and water.
(iii) On passing electric current through molten aluminium oxide, it decomposes to form aluminium metal and oxygen gas.   **CBSE 2015**

Sol. (i) $2HI(aq) + Cl_2(g) \longrightarrow I_2(g) + 2HCl(aq)$
It is a displacement reaction.
(ii) $CH_4(g) + O_2(g) \longrightarrow CO_2(g) + 2H_2O(g)$
(From air) $+ \text{Heat}$
It is an exothermic reaction.
(iii) $2Al_2O_3(l) \xrightarrow{\text{Electrolysis}} 4Al(s) + 3O_2(g)$
It is a decomposition reaction.

3 Balance the following chemical equations. Write the symbols of physical states of all the reactants and the products.
(i) $Pb_3O_4 + HNO_3$
$\longrightarrow Pb(NO_3)_2 + PbO_2 + H_2O$

(ii) $C_2H_5OH + O_2$
$\longrightarrow CO_2 + H_2O + \text{Heat}$
(iii) $Pb_3O_4 + HCl \longrightarrow PbCl_2 + Cl_2 + H_2O$

Sol. (i) $Pb_3O_4(s) + 4HNO_3(aq) \longrightarrow$
$2Pb(NO_3)_2(aq) + PbO_2(s) + 2H_2O(l)$
(ii) $C_2H_5OH(l) + 3O_2(g)$
$\longrightarrow 2CO_2(g) + 3H_2O(l) + \text{Heat}$
(iii) $Pb_3O_4(s) + 8HCl(aq)$
$\longrightarrow 3PbCl_2(aq) + Cl_2(g) + 4H_2O(l)$

4 Write the balanced chemical equations for the following reactions and identify the type of reaction in each case.
(i) In thermite reaction, iron (III) oxide reacts with aluminium and gives molten iron and aluminium oxide.
(ii) Magnesium ribbon is burnt in an atmosphere of nitrogen gas to form solid magnesium nitride.
NCERT Exemplar

Sol. (i) $\underset{\text{Iron (III) oxide}}{Fe_2O_3(s)} + \underset{\text{Aluminium}}{2Al(s)} \xrightarrow{\Delta} \underset{\text{Molten iron}}{2Fe(l)} + \underset{\text{Aluminium oxide}}{Al_2O_3(s)}$

It is a displacement reaction.

(ii) $\underset{\text{Magnesium}}{3Mg(s)} + \underset{\text{Nitrogen}}{N_2(g)} \xrightarrow{\Delta} \underset{\text{Magnesium nitride}}{Mg_3N_2(s)}$

It is a combination reaction.

5 Write chemical equations for the reactions taking place when
(i) Magnesium reacts with dilute HNO_3
(ii) Sodium reacts with water.
(iii) Zinc reacts with dilute hydrochloric acid.   **CBSE 2016**

Sol. (i) $Mg(s) + 2HNO_3(aq) \longrightarrow Mg(NO_3)_2(aq) + H_2(g)$

(ii) $2Na(s) + 2H_2O(l) \longrightarrow H_2(g) + 2NaOH(aq)$

(iii) $Zn(s) + 2HCl(aq) \longrightarrow ZnCl_2(aq) + H_2(g)$

6. A metal salt MX when exposed to light, split up to form metal M and a gas X_2. Metal M is used in making ornaments whereas gas X_2 is used in making bleaching powder. The salt MX is itself used in black and white photography.

(i) Identify metal M and gas X_2.

(ii) Mention the type of chemical reaction involved when salt MX is exposed to light. **CBSE 2018**

Sol. (i) The metal (M) is silver (Ag) and gas (X_2) is chlorine (Cl_2).

(ii) The chemical reaction involved is decomposition reaction.

$$2AgCl(s) \xrightarrow{Light} 2Ag(s) + Cl_2(g)$$
(Silver chloride)

7. Decomposition reactions require energy either in the form of heat or light or electricity for breaking down the reactants. Write one equation each for decomposition reactions where energy is supplied in the form of heat, light and electricity. **CBSE 2018**

Sol. Decomposition reaction A reaction in which a single reactant breaks down to form two or more products, is known as decomposition reaction.

(i) When a decomposition reaction is carried out by heating, then it is known as thermal **decomposition reaction**.

$$CaCO_3(s) \xrightarrow{Heat} CaO(s) + CO_2(g)$$
Calcium carbonate (Limestone) — Calcium oxide (Quick lime) — Carbon dioxide

(ii) A decomposition reaction in which energy is supplied in the form of light, is known as **photochemical decomposition reaction**.

$$2AgCl(s) \xrightarrow{Sunlight} 2Ag(s) + Cl_2$$
Silver chloride (White) — Silver (Greyish white) — Chlorine (Yellowish green)

(iii) A decomposition reaction in which energy is supplied in the form of electricity, is known as **electrolytic decomposition reaction**.

$$2H_2O(l) \xrightarrow{Electrical\ current} 2H_2(g) + O_2(g)$$
Water — Hydrogen, Oxygen

8. What happens when a piece of

(i) zinc metal is added to copper sulphate solution?

(ii) aluminium metal is added to dilute hydrochloric acid?

(iii) silver metal is added to copper sulphate solution? Also, write the balanced chemical equation if the reaction occurs. **NCERT Exemplar**

Sol. (i) Blue colour of copper sulphate solution gets fade away.

Reason Zinc being more reactive than copper reacts with copper sulphate to form colourless zinc sulphate solution and a solid brown copper gets deposited.

$$Zn(s) + CuSO_4(aq) \longrightarrow ZnSO_4(aq) + Cu(s)$$
Zinc (Grey) — Copper sulphate (Blue) — Zinc sulphate (Colourless) — Copper (Brown)

(ii) Hydrogen gas is evolved.

Reason Aluminium reacts with dilute hydrochloric acid to form aluminium chloride and hydrogen gas.

$$2Al(s) + 6HCl(aq) \longrightarrow 2AlCl_3(aq) + 3H_2(g)\uparrow$$
Aluminium — Hydrochloric acid — Aluminium chloride — Hydrogen

(iii) No reaction occurs.

Reason Silver metal is less reactive than copper, therefore, it cannot displace copper from copper sulphate solution.

$$Ag(s) + CuSO_4(aq) \longrightarrow No\ reaction$$
Silver — Copper sulphate

9. Write a balanced chemical equation for each of the following reactions and also classify them.

(i) Lead acetate solution is treated with dilute hydrochloric acid to form lead chloride and acetic acid solution.

(ii) A piece of sodium metal is added to absolute ethanol to form sodium ethoxide and hydrogen gas.

(iii) Hydrogen sulphide gas reacts with oxygen gas to form solid sulphur and liquid water. **NCERT Exemplar**

Sol. (i) $(CH_3COO)_2Pb(aq) + 2HCl \longrightarrow PbCl_2(aq) + 2CH_3COOH(aq)$
(Double displacement reaction)

(ii) $2Na(s) + 2C_2H_5OH(l) \longrightarrow 2C_2H_5ONa(l) + H_2(g)\uparrow$
(Displacement reaction)

(iii) $2H_2S(g) + O_2(g) \longrightarrow 2S(s) + 2H_2O(l)$
(Displacement reaction)

10 State the type of chemical reactions with chemical equations that take place in the following.
(i) Magnesium wire is burnt in air.
(ii) Electric current is passed through water.
(iii) Ammonia and hydrogen chloride gases are mixed. **CBSE 2016**

Sol. (i) Magnesium wire is burnt in air to produce magnesium oxide and heat
$$2Mg(s) + O_2(g) \longrightarrow 2MgO(s) + Heat$$
(Combination reaction)

(ii) Electric current is passed through water to evolve hydrogen and oxygen gases.
$$2H_2O(l) \xrightarrow{\text{Electric current}} 2H_2(g) + O_2(g)$$
(Decomposition reaction)

(iii) Ammonia and hydrogen chloride gases are mixed to form ammonium chloride
$$NH_3 + HCl \longrightarrow NH_4Cl$$
(Combination reaction)

11 On heating blue coloured powder of copper (II) nitrate in a boiling tube, copper oxide (black), oxygen gas and a brown gas X is formed. **NCERT Exemplar**
(i) Write a balanced chemical equation of the reaction.
(ii) Identify the brown gas X evolved.
(iii) Identify the type of reaction.
(iv) What could be the pH range of the aqueous solution of the gas X?

Sol. (i) $2Cu(NO_3)_2(s) \xrightarrow{\text{Heat}} 2CuO(s) + 4NO_2(g) + O_2(g)$
Copper (II) nitrate — (Black) (Brown) (X) Oxygen

(ii) The brown gas X evolved is nitrogen dioxide, NO_2.
(iii) Thermal decomposition.
(iv) pH < 7
Reason NO_2 dissolves in water to form acidic solution (pH lies below 7).

12 When solutions of silver nitrate and sodium chloride are mixed, a white precipitate forms. The ionic equation for the reaction is
$$Ag^+(aq) + Cl^- \longrightarrow AgCl(s)$$

(i) (a) What is the name of the white precipitate?
(b) Is it a soluble or insoluble compound?
(ii) Is the precipitation of silver chloride a redox reaction?

Sol. (i) (a) Silver chloride (AgCl) is the white precipitate formed.
(b) Silver chloride (AgCl) is an insoluble compound.
(ii) It is not a redox reaction.
$$\underset{\text{Sodium chloride}}{NaCl(aq)} + \underset{\text{Silver nitrate}}{AgNO_3(aq)} \longrightarrow \underset{\text{Silver chloride}}{AgCl(s)} + \underset{\text{Sodium nitrate}}{NaNO_3(aq)}$$

In this reaction, cations Ag^+ and Na^+ have exchanged their anions NO_3^- and Cl^- and a precipitate of AgCl has been formed. It is an example of double displacement and precipitation reactions.

13 (i) Give an example for a combination reaction which is exothermic.
(ii) Identify the oxidising agent and reducing agent in the following reaction.
$$H_2S(g) + Cl_2(g) \longrightarrow 2HCl(g) + S(s)$$
(iii) Name the phenomenon due to which the taste and smell of oily food changes when kept for a long time in open. Suggest one method to prevent it.

Sol. (i) $\underset{\text{Calcium oxide}}{CaO(s)} + \underset{\text{Water}}{H_2O(g)} \longrightarrow \underset{\text{Slaked lime}}{Ca(OH)_2(aq)} + Heat$

It is a combination reaction because two compounds reacts to give single product.
As heat is also evolved during the process, thus it is also an example of exothermic reaction.

(ii) $\underset{\text{Hydrogen sulphide}}{H_2S(g)} + \underset{\text{Chlorine}}{Cl_2(g)} \longrightarrow \underset{\text{Hydrochloric acid}}{2HCl(g)} + \underset{\text{Sulphur}}{S(s)}$

Oxidising agent - Cl_2, Reducing agent - H_2S

(iii) This is known as rancidity.
Prevention Oily food must be kept in airtight containers.

14 On adding a drop of barium chloride solution to an aqueous solution of sodium sulphite, white precipitate is obtained.
(i) Write a balanced chemical equation of the reaction involved.
(ii) What other name can be given to this precipitation reaction?

Chemical Reactions and Equations

(iii) On adding dilute hydrochloric acid to the reaction mixture, white precipitate disappears. Why? **NCERT Exemplar**

Sol. (i) $\underset{\text{Sodium sulphite}}{Na_2SO_3(aq)} + \underset{\text{Barium chloride}}{BaCl_2(aq)} \longrightarrow$
$\underset{\text{Barium sulphite}}{BaSO_3(s)} + \underset{\text{Sodium chloride}}{2NaCl(aq)}$

(ii) Double displacement reaction

(iii) $\underset{\text{(White ppt.)}}{BaSO_3(s)} + \underset{\text{Dil. hydrochloric acid}}{2HCl(aq)} \longrightarrow$
$\underset{\substack{\text{Barium chloride}\\\text{(Soluble)}}}{BaCl_2(aq)} + \underset{\text{Water}}{H_2O(l)} + \underset{\text{Sulphur dioxide}}{SO_2(g)}$

As the reaction product, barium chloride, is water soluble thus, the white precipitate disappears.

15. A metal 'X' acquires a green colour coating on its surface on exposure to air.
(i) Identify the metal 'X' and name the process involved in it.
(ii) Name and write chemical formula of the green coating formed.
(iii) List two important methods to prevent the process.

Sol. (i) The metal 'X' is copper (Cu) and the process involved is corrosion.
(ii) Green coating formed is basic copper carbonate i.e. $CuCO_3.Cu(OH)_2$.
(iii) Two important methods to prevent the process are painting and galvanising (Coating of iron surface with zinc metal).

16. (i) Classify the following reactions into different types:
(a) $AgNO_3(aq) + NaCl(aq) \longrightarrow AgCl(s) + NaNO_3(aq)$
(b) $CaO(s) + H_2O(l) \longrightarrow Ca(OH)_2(aq)$
(c) $2KClO_3(s) \longrightarrow 2KCl(aq) + 3O_2(g)$
(d) $Zn + CuSO_4 \longrightarrow ZnSO_4 + Cu$

(ii) Translate the following statement into a balanced chemical equation.
"Barium chloride reacts with aluminium sulphate to give aluminium chloride and barium sulphate." **CBSE 2019**

Sol. (i) (a) Double displacement reaction and precipitation reaction
(b) Combination reaction
(c) Thermal decomposition reaction
(d) Metal displacement reaction.
(ii) Refer to NCERT Folder, page-8, Q-2(ii).

17. When potassium iodide solution is added to a solution of lead (II) nitrate in a test tube, a precipitate is formed. **CBSE 2019**
(i) What is the colour of this precipitate? Name the compound precipitated.
(ii) Write the balanced chemical equation for this reaction.
(iii) List two types of reactions in which this reaction can be placed.

Sol. (i) A yellow precipitate of lead iodide (PbI_2) is formed.

(ii) $\underset{\text{Lead nitrate}}{Pb(NO_3)_2(aq)} + \underset{\text{Potassium iodide}}{2KI(aq)} \longrightarrow$
$\underset{\substack{\text{Lead iodide}\\\text{(Yellow ppt.)}}}{PbI_2(s)} + \underset{\text{Potassium nitrate}}{2KNO_3(aq)}$

(iii) Precipitation reaction or double displacement reaction.

18. (i) Which of the following reaction(s) is/are an endothermic reaction(s) where decomposition also happens? **CBSE SQP 2020-21**
• Respiration
• Heating of lead nitrate
• Decomposition of organic matter
• Electrolysis of acidified water

(ii) Silver chloride when kept in the open turns grey. Illustrate this with a balanced chemical equation.

Sol. (i) Heating of lead nitrate – Endothermic and decomposition reaction
Electrolysis of acidified water – Decomposition

(ii) Silver chloride when kept in the open turns grey. This is due to decomposition of silver chloride into silver and chlorine.
$$2AgCl \longrightarrow 2Ag + Cl_2$$

19. A metal X generally turns black when kept in open for several days. The metal when rubbed with toothpaste again start shining.
(i) Identify the metal X.
(ii) Why do the metal X turns balck. Name the phenomenon involved.
(iii) Name the black substance formed and write its formula. **NCERT Exemplar**

Sol. (i) X = Ag (Silver)
(ii) Silver reacts with some sulphur compounds as hydrogen sulphide to form black layer of silver sulphide.

$$\underset{\text{Silver}}{2Ag} + \underset{\substack{\text{Hydrogen}\\\text{sulphide}}}{H_2S} \longrightarrow \underset{\substack{\text{Silver}\\\text{sulphide}}}{Ag_2S} + H_2\uparrow$$

This phenomenon is known as corrosion.

(iii) Ag_2S (Silver sulphide).

20 A yellowish coloured compound 'X' is a photosensitive material. On exposure to sunlight, it gives a greyish substance 'Y' and brown fumes of a gas 'Z'. Identify X, Y and Z. How will you obtain 'X' from the nitrate salt of 'Y'?

Sol. $\underset{X}{2AgBr} \longrightarrow \underset{Y}{2Ag} + \underset{\substack{Z(\text{Brown}\\\text{fumes})}}{Br_2\uparrow}$

On exposure to sunlight AgBr undergoes decomposition reaction.

To obtain AgBr, add sodium bromide solution into the test tube containing silver nitrate solution.

$AgNO_3(aq) + NaBr(aq) \longrightarrow$

$+ NaNO_3(aq)$ $\underset{\substack{\text{Silver}\\\text{bromide}\\(\text{Yellow ppt.})}}{AgBr\downarrow}$

Long Answer (LA) Type Questions

1 Identify the type of chemical reaction taking place in each of the following:

(i) Barium chloride solution is mixed with copper sulphate solution and a white precipitate is observed.

(ii) On heating copper powder in air in a China dish, the surface of copper powder turns black.

(iii) On heating green coloured ferrous sulphate crystals, reddish brown solid is left and smell of a gas having odour of burning sulphur is experienced.

(iv) Iron nails when left dipped in blue copper sulphate solution become brownish in colour and the blue colour of copper sulphate fades away.

(v) Quicklime reacts vigorously with water releasing a large amount of heat.

Sol. (i) Double displacement and precipitation reactions.
(ii) Combination and oxidation reactions.
(iii) Thermal decomposition reaction.
(iv) Displacement reaction.
(v) Combination and exothermic reactions.

2 (i) Identify the type of reactions taking place in each of the following cases and write the balanced chemical equations for the reactions

(a) Barium chloride solution is mixed, with copper sulphate solution and a white precipitate is obtained.

(b) On heating copper powder in air, the surface of the copper powder turns black.

(ii) What happens when hydrogen gas is passed over the heated copper oxide? Write the chemical equation involved in this reaction. **CBSE 2016**

Sol. (i) (a) $BaCl_2(aq) + CuSO_4(aq)$
$\longrightarrow BaSO_4(s) + CuCl_2(aq)$
Double decomposition reaction

(b) $2Cu(s) + O_2(g) \xrightarrow{\text{Heat}} 2CuO(l)$
Redox reaction

(ii) If hydrogen gas is passed over heated material (CuO) the black coating on the surface turns brown as the reaction takes place and copper is obtained.

$\underset{(\text{Black})}{CuO(s)} + H_2(g) \xrightarrow{\text{Heat}} \underset{(\text{Brown})}{Cu(s)} + H_2O(l)$

3 Define rancidity. What kind of substances are used to prevent rancidity? Explain any three methods to prevent rancidity.

Sol. It is the process of slow oxidation of oils and fats present in food materials resulting in the production of foul odour and taste in them. Antioxidants like BHA and BHT are used to prevent rancidity.

Methods by which rancidity can be prevented are as follows:

(i) Keeping the food materials in air-tight containers.

(ii) Refrigeration of cooked food at low temperature.

(iii) Packing of food like wafers, potato chips in packets containing nitrogen gas instead of air.

4 There are different types of chemical reactions occurring around us or being carried out for the benefit of mankind, e.g. combination reactions, decomposition reactions, displacement reactions, precipitation reactions, reduction-oxidation (redox) reactions, photochemical reactions etc.

Now, answer the following questions:

(i) Combustion of coke is a combination reaction. CO_2 formed during reaction is not a pollutant. Then why is combustion of coke harmful?

(ii) Which reaction followed by two combination reactions are involved in white wash of walls?

(iii) Give one use of tin plating in daily life.

(iv) How photochemical reactions have played an important role in photography?

Sol. (i) CO_2 is not a pollutant when present in the atmosphere upto a certain percent. Rather, it helps to maintain the temperature of the Earth. Combustion of coke is harmful as it increases the concentration of CO_2 in the atmosphere which causes global warming (greenhouse effect).

(ii) Reaction of calcium with oxygen gives quicklime (CaO) which combines with water to form slaked lime, $Ca(OH)_2$ which after putting on the walls, combines with CO_2 of the air to form $CaCO_3$.

$$2Ca(s) + O_2(g) \longrightarrow \underset{\text{Quicklime}}{2CaO(s)}$$

$$CaO(s) + H_2O(l) \longrightarrow \underset{\text{Slaked lime}}{Ca(OH)_2(aq)}$$

$$Ca(OH)_2(aq) + CO_2(g) \longrightarrow \underset{\substack{\text{Calcium}\\ \text{carbonate}}}{CaCO_3(s)} + H_2O(l)$$

(iii) Tiffin boxes made up of steel are either tin plated or nickel plated to protect them from rusting. However, tin-plating is preferred because tin is non-poisonous and hence, does not contaminate the food kept in them.

(iv) A photographic film used in black and white photography is a celluloid film coated with silver chloride.
Its working is based on the decomposition of silver chloride in the presence of sunlight.

$$2AgCl(s) \xrightarrow[\text{(Decomposition)}]{\text{Sunlight}} \underset{\substack{\text{Silver}\\ \text{(Grey)}}}{2Ag(s)} + Cl_2(g)$$

5 You are provided with two containers made up of copper and aluminium. You are also provided with solutions of dil. HCl, dil. HNO_3, $ZnCl_2$ and H_2O. In which of the above containers, these solutions can be kept? **NCERT Exemplar**

Sol. The container made up of copper or aluminium is suitable for storing these solutions.
This can be decided by studying their reactions with Cu and Al (which also depend on the respective position in activity series).

(i) **Reactions of copper with**

(a) **Dil. HCl** $Cu + \underset{\text{(Dil.)}}{HCl} \longrightarrow$ No reaction,

So, it can be stored in Cu container.

(b) **Dil. HNO_3** Being a strong oxidising agent, dil. HNO_3 reacts with copper, so it cannot be stored in copper container.

(c) **$ZnCl_2$** Copper is less reactive than zinc, so it does not react with $ZnCl_2$ solution. Therefore, it can be stored in copper container.

(d) **H_2O** Copper does not react with water. So, its container can be used to store H_2O.

(ii) **Reactions of aluminium with**

(a) **Dil. HCl** Al reacts with dil. HCl, so it cannot be kept in aluminium container.
$$2Al + 6HCl \longrightarrow 2AlCl_3 + 3H_2 \uparrow$$

(b) **Dil. HNO_3** When dil. HNO_3 is kept in Al container, it forms a protective layer of aluminium oxide on it, which prevents aluminium from further reaction therefore it can be kept in Al container.

(c) **$ZnCl_2$** Al is more reactive than zinc, so $ZnCl_2$ solution cannot be kept in aluminium container.
$$2Al(s) + 3ZnCl_2(aq) \longrightarrow 2AlCl_3(g) + 3Zn(s)$$

(d) **H_2O** Aluminium does not react with water (hot or cold). Therefore, water can be kept in aluminium container. Aluminium is attacked by steam to form aluminium oxide and hydrogen.
$$2Al(s) + 3H_2O(g) \longrightarrow Al_2O_3(g) + 3H_2(g)$$

6 (i) A student mixes sodium sulphate powder in barium chloride. What change would the student observe on mixing the two powder. Justify your answer and explain how he can obtaned the desired change?

(ii) (a) Arrange the following metals in the increasing order reactivities.
Copper, zinc, aluminium and iron.

(b) List two observations you would record in your 30 minutes after adding iron filings to copper sulphate solution. **CBSE 2019**

Sol. (i) When the student mixes sodium sulphate powder in barium chloride in a dry state, no change would be observed. But when he dissolved them in water, barium sulphate precipitates out and sodium chloride remains in solution. This is called a double displacement reaction.
Refer to text on page 6 (Double displacement reaction).

(ii) (a) Copper < iron < zinc < aluminium
(b) Refer to NCERT Folder page 8, Q-6.

CHAPTER EXERCISE

Multiple Type Questions

1. In which of the following chemical equations, the abbreviations represent the correct states of the reactants and products involved at reaction temperature? **NCERT Exemplar**
   (a) $2H_2(l) + O_2(l) \longrightarrow 2H_2O(g)$
   (b) $2H_2(g) + O_2(l) \longrightarrow 2H_2O(l)$
   (c) $2H_2(g) + O_2(g) \longrightarrow 2H_2O(l)$
   (d) $2H_2(g) + O_2(g) \longrightarrow 2H_2O(g)$

2. Which of the following is not a combination reaction?
   (a) Reaction of hydrogen with nitrogen
   (b) Reaction of quicklime with water
   (c) Combustion of magnesium in air
   (d) Heating of limestone

3. Which among the following is getting reduced in the following reaction:
   $$Fe_2O_3 + 3CO \longrightarrow 2Fe + 3CO_2$$
   (a) CO   (b) Fe
   (c) CO_2 (d) Fe_2O_3

4. The following reaction is used for the preparation of oxygen gas in the laboratory **NCERT Exemplar**
   $$2KClO_3(s) \xrightarrow[\text{Catalyst}]{\text{Heat}} 2KCl(s) + 3O_2(g)$$
   Which of the following statements is/are correct about the reaction?
   (a) It is a decomposition reaction and endothermic in nature.
   (b) It is a combination reaction.
   (c) It is a decomposition reaction and accompanied by release of heat.
   (d) It is a photochemical decomposition reaction and exothermic in nature.

5. In the double displacement reaction between aqueous potassium iodide and aqueous lead nitrate, a yellow precipitate of lead iodide is formed. While performing the activity if lead nitrate is not available, which of the following can be used in place of lead nitrate? **NCERT Exemplar**
   (a) Lead sulphate (insoluble)
   (b) Lead acetate
   (c) Ammonium nitrate
   (d) Potassium sulphate

Fill in the Blanks

6. The chemical formula of slaked lime is ....

7. The colour of ferrous sulphate crystals before heating is ....

True and False

8. On adding ammonium chloride to the barium hydroxide, boiling tube becomes warm.

9. The white precipitate of $BaSO_4$ is formed by the reaction of SO_4^{-2} and Ba^{+2}.

10. Combustion can takes place even without oxygen.

Match the Columns

11. Match the following Columns.

	Column I (Reaction)		Column II (Gas evolved)
A.	Zinc granules are treated with dilute H_2SO_4.	P.	O_2
B.	Calcium carbonate on reaction with HCl.	Q.	CO_2
C.	Lead nitrate is heated strongly in a hard glass test tube	R.	H_2
D.	Decomposition of $KClO_3$	S.	NO_2

Assertion–Reason

Direction (Q. Nos. 12-13) *In each of the following questions, a statement of Assertion is given by the corresponding statement of Reason. Of the statements, mark the correct answer as.*
(a) Both Assertion and Reason are true and Reason is the correct explanation of Assertion.
(b) Both Assertion and Reason are true, but Reason is not the correct explanation of Assertion.
(c) Assertion is true, but Reason is false.
(d) Assertion is false, but Reason is true.

12. **Assertion** The following chemical equation is an example of thermal decomposition reaction.
$$2KClO_3(s) \xrightarrow[\text{Catalyst}]{\text{Heat}} 2KCl(s) + 3O_2(g)$$
Reason Heat gets released in the decomposition reactions.

13 Assertion $2Na + H_2 \longrightarrow 2NaH$

In the above chemical equal, sodium is getting oxidised and H_2 is getting reduced.

Reason The chemical reaction in which oxidation and reduction take place simultaneously, are called redox reactions.

Case Based Questions

Direction (Q.Nos. 14-17) *Answer the questions on the basis of your understanding of the following passage and related studied concepts:*

Rancid fats are formed in human diet in places such as cooking oils and fats, deep fried foods and some ethnic foods that are purposely made rancid. However, any fat, given the right conditions and amount of time, can go rancid. It means that any food containing fat can become rancid.

For instance, India, 1992, a group of 45 children were hospitalised with vomiting, abdominal pain, and diarrhoea, which prompted an investigation. The investigation turned up a total of 71 children and 9 adults who were affected by eating rancid cream-filled biscuits which the children had found in the street and shared with their families. Most children ate 0.5 to 2 biscuits and were discharged from the hospitals within 24 hours, one girl ate 12 biscuits and remained in the hospital for 7 days. All the hospitalised children were treated successfully and the researchers decided that the cause of illness was the oxidative rancidity of the cream inside the biscuits presence of antioxidants is an antidote for rancidity.

14 Some food items are given below:
 I. Potato wafers.
 II. Dark green vegetables.
 III. Biscuits (butter)
 IV. Fried peanuts.

Which of these become oxidised and inedible if placed for a few hours in open?
(a) I, II, III (b) III and IV
(c) I, III, IV (d) All of these

15 Here are some steps that you can do to protect yourself from the effect of rancid fats.
 I. Avoid fat or fat containing products that have a rancid or stale smell.
 II. Store oils and fats correctly.
 III. Consume antioxidants containing foods such as dark green vegetables.

The correct things are
(a) I, II and III (b) II and III
(c) Only II (d) All of these

16 Why does fresh food become stale and tasteless when exposed to air?

17 What role does refrigerator play in keeping food stuffs fresh?

Direction (Q. Nos. 18-21) *Answer the questions on the basis of your understanding of the following passage, table and related studied concepts:*

The method used for balancing chemical equation is called hit and trial method. In this method, the number of atoms of each elements remaine the same, before and after a chemical reaction.

Zn metal reacts with dilute sulphuric acid to form 'X' and hydrogen gas.

Count the number of atoms of all the elements in the reactants and products separately.

Elements	In reactant	In Product
Zn	1	1
H	2	2
S	1	1
O	4	4

18 Identify the 'X'.

19 Write the balanced chemical equation when Zn metal react with dil H_2SO_4.

20 Name the type of reaction occur when Zn metal react with dil. H_2SO_4.

21 Balance the given reaction:

$BaCl_2(aq) + Na_2SO_4(aq) \rightarrow BaSO_4(s)\downarrow + NaCl$

Very Short Answer (VSA) Type Questions

22 What is breaking and making of bonds in chemical reaction called? **CBSE 2009**

23 Which product is formed when carbon dioxide and water react in the same ratio?

24 Nickel (II) nitrate is prepared by heating nickel metal with liquid dinitrogen tetraoxide. In addition to the nitrate, gaseous nitrogen monoxide is formed. Write the balanced equation.

25 Which kind of chemical reaction takes place when electric current is passed through fused lead bromide?

26 Silver article gets black coating. Name the phenomenon.

Answers

1. (c) 2. (d) 3. (d) 4. (a) 5. (a)
6. $Ca(OH)_2$ 7. Green 8. False
9. True 10. False
11. $A \rightarrow R, B \rightarrow Q, C \rightarrow S, D \rightarrow P$
12. (c) 13. (b) 14. (c) 15. (d)

Short Answer (SA) Type Questions

27 Complete the missing components/variables given as reactant and product in the following reactions:

(i) $BaCl_2 + 'X' \longrightarrow + BaSO_4 \downarrow$

(ii) $Cu + AgNO_3 \longrightarrow Cu(NO_3)_2 + 'Y'$

(iii) $CaCO_3 \xrightarrow{'Z'} CaO + CO_2$

28 Zinc oxide reacts with carbon, on heating to form zinc metal and carbon monoxide. Write a balanced chemical equation for this reaction. Name (i) oxidising agent (ii) reducing agent in this reaction.

29 Iron fillings are put in different test tubes A, B, C, and D containing $ZnSO_4, CuSO_4, Al_2(SO_4)_3, CaCl_2$ solutions respectively. In which of the following test-tubes will change be observed?

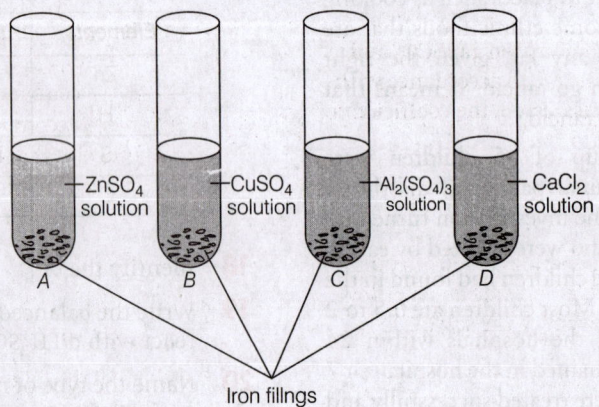

Long Answer (LA) Type Questions

30 With the help of an activity, demonstrate how do we know that a chemical reaction has taken place?

31 A water insoluble substance X on reaction with dilute hydrochloric acid released a colourless and odourless gas accompanied by brisk effervescence.

When the gas passed through water, the solution obtained turns blue litmus red.

On bubbling the gas through lime water, it initially became milky and milkiness disappeared when the gas was passed in excess. Identify the substance X. Write the chemical equation of the reaction involved.

Challengers*

1. Which one of the following involve a chemical reaction?
   (a) Evaporation of water
   (b) Storing of nitrogen gas under pressure
   (c) Keeping petrol in a China dish in open
   (d) Heating magnesium wire in the presence of air at high temperature

2. Ethane (C_2H_6) on complete combustion gave CO_2 and water. It shows that the results are in accordance with the law of conservation of mass. Then, the coefficient of oxygen is equal to
   (a) 3   (b) 5/2
   (c) 2   (d) 7/2

3. A powdered salt (X) in a dry test tube was heated that evolves brown fumes of nitrogen dioxide and a yellow residue of lead oxide is also formed. The salt (X) is
   (a) $MgCO_3$ (b) $Pb(NO_3)_2$
   (c) $(NH_4)_2SO_4$ (d) $CaCO_3$

4. A reddish brown coloured metal used in electric wires, when powdered and heated strongly in an open China dish, its colour turns black. When hydrogen gas is passed over this black substances, it regain its original colour. Based on this information, the metal and black coloured substances are
   (a) copper and copper nitrate
   (b) silver and silver oxide
   (c) copper and copper oxide
   (d) aluminium and aluminium oxide

5. When dilute sulphuric acid is added to pieces of iron sulphide, hydrogen sulphide gas is produced and soluble ferrous sulphate is formed. The type of chemical reaction involved is
   (a) decomposition reaction
   (b) combination reaction
   (c) displacement reaction
   (d) double displacement reaction

6. Following reaction is used for the preparation of oxygen gas in the laboratory.
   $$2KClO_3(s) \xrightarrow[\text{Catalyst}]{\text{Heat}} 2KCl(s) + 3O_2(g)$$
   Which of the following statement(s) is (are) correct about the reaction?
   (a) It is a decomposition reaction and endothermic in nature.
   (b) It is a combination reaction.
   (c) It is a decomposition reaction and accompanied by the release of heat.
   (d) It is a photochemical decomposition reaction and exothermic in nature.

7. A metal 'M' reacts with an acid according to the equation.
   $$M + H^+ \longrightarrow M^{3+} + H_2$$
   Which of the following is correct for metal M?
   (a) Calcium   (b) Aluminium
   (c) Barium   (d) Potassium

8. Which among the following statement(s) is/are true? Exposure of silver chloride to sunlight for a long duration turns grey due to   **NCERT Exemplar**
   (i) the formation of silver by decomposition of silver chloride.
   (ii) sublimation of silver chloride.
   (iii) evolution of chlorine gas from silver chloride.
   (iv) oxidation of silver chloride.
   (a) (i) only   (b) (i) and (iii)
   (c) (ii) and (iii)   (d) (iv) only

Answer Key

1.	(d)	2.	(d)	3.	(b)	4.	(c)	5.	(d)
6.	(a)	7.	(c)	8.	(a)				

*These questions may or may not be asked in the examination, have been given just for additional practice.

CHAPTER 02

Acids, Bases and Salts

All the chemical compounds can be classified on the basis of their chemical properties as acids, bases and salts. They have certain definite properties which distinguish these compounds from each other. Most of the digestive fluids of humans and animals contain acids. The bitter taste of substances like bitter gourd, cucumber etc., is due to the bases present in them.

Acids

Acids are those chemical substances which have a sour taste and change the colour of blue litmus to red. Some common fruits such as unripe mango, lemon, orange, tamarind etc., are sour in taste. This suggests that these fruits contain acids. Some commonly used acids are hydrochloric acid (HCl), sulphuric acid (H_2SO_4), nitric acid (HNO_3) etc.

Some naturally occurring acids are:

Natural source	Acid
Vinegar	Acetic acid
Orange and lemon	Citric acid
Tamarind	Tartaric acid
Tomato	Oxalic acid
Curd	Lactic acid
Antsting	Methanoic acid

Chapter Checklist

- Acids
- Bases
- Indicators
- Strength of an Acid or Base
- pH Scale
- Importance of pH in Everyday Life
- Salts
- Water of Crystallisation

Chemical Properties of Acids

(i) **Reaction with metals** Acids like dilute HCl and dilute H_2SO_4, react with certain active metals like zinc (Zn), iron (Fe) etc., to form salt and evolves H_2 gas. Thus, these acids or substances containing these kind of acids should not be kept in metal containers.

Metal + Dilute acid $\longrightarrow$ Salt + Hydrogen gas

e.g., $Zn + H_2SO_4 \longrightarrow ZnSO_4 + H_2 \uparrow$

(ii) Reaction with metal carbonate and hydrogen carbonate Limestone, chalk and marble are different forms of calcium carbonate. Acids react with metal carbonates and hydrogen carbonates (bicarbonate) to produce their corresponding salts, carbon dioxide gas and water.

Metal carbonate / Metal hydrogen carbonate + Acid
$\longrightarrow$ Salt + Carbon dioxide + Water

e.g., $CaCO_3 + 2HCl \longrightarrow CaCl_2 + H_2O + CO_2 \uparrow$

The carbon dioxide gas is released with a brisk effervescence.

Test for CO_2 gas When CO_2 gas is passed through lime water, it turns milky due to the formation of white precipitate of $CaCO_3$.

But if CO_2 is passed in excess, milkiness disappears due to the formation of $Ca(HCO_3)_2$ which is soluble in water.

$\underset{\text{Lime water}}{Ca(OH)_2(aq)} + \underset{\text{Carbon dioxide}}{CO_2(g)} \longrightarrow \underset{\substack{\text{Calcium carbonate}\\\text{(White ppt.)}}}{CaCO_3(s)} + \underset{\text{Water}}{H_2O(l)}$

$\underset{\substack{\text{Calcium carbonate}\\\text{(Milkiness)}}}{CaCO_3(s)} + \underset{\text{Water}}{H_2O(l)} + \underset{\substack{\text{Carbon dioxide}\\\text{(Excess)}}}{CO_2(g)} \longrightarrow \underset{\substack{\text{Calcium bicarbonate}\\\text{(Soluble in water)}}}{Ca(HCO_3)_2(aq)}$

(iii) Reaction with metal oxides Acids react with certain metal oxides (being basic in nature also called basic oxides) to form salt and water.

Metal oxide + Acid $\longrightarrow$ Salt + Water

e.g. $CuO + 2HCl \longrightarrow CuCl_2 + H_2O$

Bases

Bases are those chemical substances which are bitter in taste, soapy to touch and turn red litmus to blue. e.g. sodium hydroxide (NaOH), calcium hydroxide $Ca(OH)_2$ etc.

Chemical Properties of Bases

(i) Reaction with metals Strong bases react with active metals to produce hydrogen gas. Thus, these bases should not be kept in metal container (active metals).

Metal + Base $\longrightarrow$ Salt + Hydrogen gas

e.g. $\underset{\text{Zinc}}{Zn(s)} + \underset{\substack{\text{Sodium}\\\text{hydroxide}}}{2NaOH(aq)} \longrightarrow \underset{\text{Sodium zincate}}{Na_2ZnO_2(s)} + \underset{\substack{\text{Hydrogen}\\\text{gas}}}{H_2(g)}$

(ii) Reaction with non-metallic oxide Bases react with non-metallic oxides (being acidic in nature also called acidic oxides) to produce salt and water.

This reaction proves that non-metallic oxides are acidic in nature.

Base + Non-metallic oxide $\longrightarrow$ Salt + Water

e.g. $\underset{\substack{\text{Carbon}\\\text{dioxide}}}{CO_2(g)} + \underset{\text{Slaked lime}}{Ca(OH)_2(aq)} \longrightarrow \underset{\substack{\text{Calcium}\\\text{carbonate}}}{CaCO_3(s)} + \underset{\text{Water}}{H_2O(l)}$

Acids/ Bases in Water Solution

In presence of water, all acids give H^+ ion. As H^+ ion cannot exist alone so it combines with water molecules and form H_3O^+ (Hydronium ion). So, we can say in **presence of water, all acids give H^+ ion or H_3O^+ ion.**

In the same way, **in presence of water, all the bases give OH^- ion.**

e.g. $HCl + H_2O \longrightarrow H_3O^{\oplus} + Cl^-$

$H^+ + H_2O \longrightarrow H_3O^+$

$NaOH(s) \xrightarrow{H_2O} Na^{\oplus}(aq) + OH^-(aq)$

$KOH \xrightarrow{H_2O} K^+(aq) + OH^-(aq)$

$Mg(OH)_2 \longrightarrow Mg^{2+}(aq) + 2OH^-(aq)$

Note All bases do not dissolves in water. An alkali is a base that dissolves in water. Both acids and bases conduct electric current in their aqueous solutions due to the presence of free ions.

Reaction between Acids and Bases

Acids react with bases to produce salt and water. In this reaction, an acid neutralises a base, i.e. acid nullifies or reduces the effect of a base or *vice-versa*, thus the reaction is known as **neutralisation reaction**.

In general, neutralisation reaction can be written as :

Base + Acid $\longrightarrow$ Salt + Water

$H \boxed{X + M} OH \longrightarrow MX + HOH$

Here, H represents hydrogen atom and M represents metal atom.

$H^+(aq) + OH^-(aq) \longrightarrow H_2O(l)$

e.g. $\underset{\substack{\text{Sodium}\\\text{hydroxide}}}{NaOH(aq)} + \underset{\substack{\text{Hydrochloric}\\\text{acid}}}{HCl(aq)} \longrightarrow \underset{\substack{\text{Sodium}\\\text{chloride}}}{NaCl(aq)} + \underset{\text{Water}}{H_2O(l)}$

Effect of Dilution on an Acid or Base

Mixing of an acid or base with water is called **dilution**. It results in decrease in the concentration of ions (H_3O^+/OH^-) per unit volume and the acid or base is said to be diluted.

When acid or base is added to water, their molecules dissociate to form ions.

$$HCl + H_2O \longrightarrow H_3O^+ + Cl^-$$
$$\text{Acid}$$

$$H_2O + H^+ \longrightarrow H_3O^+ \text{(Hydronium ion)}$$

Or $NaOH(s) \xrightarrow{H_2O} Na^+(aq) + OH^-(aq)$
Base

Dissolving an acid or a base in water is a highly exothermic (heat generating) reaction, so care must be taken while doing it. The acids must always be added slowly to water with constant stirring.

Warning sign displayed on containers containing concentrated acids and bases (showing their corrosive nature)

Water should not be added to concentrated acid because if water is added, the heat generated may cause the mixture to splash out and cause burns.

Check Point 01

1. Which type of chemical compound found in citrus fruits?
2. Fill in the blank:
   All alkali are bases but all bases are .... alkali?
3. Bases should not be kept in active metal container. Why?
4. Give a chemical reaction to prove that non-metallic oxides are acidic in nature.
5. State True or False for the following statement:
   Everything that tastes sour contains an acid.
6. How H_3O^+ ion is formed in water solution?
7. What is the effect of dilution on an acid or base?

Indicators

Indicators are the substances that change their colour or odour when added into an acid or an alkaline solution to indicate the presence of acid or base.

Indicators can be classified in the following ways:

Natural Indicators

These indicators are found in nature in the plants, e.g. litmus solution is a purple colour dye extracted from the lichen plant belonging to the division "Thallophyta".

Some Natural Indicators with Characteristic Colours

Indicator	Colour in Acidic Medium	Colour in Alkaline Medium
Litmus	Red	Blue
Red cabbage juice (from leaves)	Red	Green
Turmeric juice (haldi)	Yellow	Reddish brown
Flowers of *Hydrangea* plant	Blue	Pink

Synthetic Indicators

The indicators which are synthesised in the laboratory or industry are known as synthetic indicators, e.g. methyl orange, phenolphthalein, methylene blue and methyl red are synthetic indicators.

Some Synthetic Indicators with Characteristic Colours

Indicator	Colour in Acidic Solution	Colour in Basic Solution	Colour in Neutral Solution
Phenolphthalein	Colourless	Pink	Colourless
Methyl orange	Red	Yellow	Orange

Olfactory Indicators

Those substances whose odour changes in acidic or basic medium are called olfactory indicators. Vanilla extract and onion can be used as olfactory indicators. The smell of these two indicators can be detected in presence of acid only but not in the presence of base.

Universal Indicators

To judge how strong a given acid or base is, a **universal indicator** is used, which is a mixture of several indicators. It shows different colours at different concentrations of hydrogen ion in a solution.

Strength of an Acid or Base

Strength of an acid or base depends on the number of H^+ ions or OH^- ions produced by them respectively. Larger the number of H^+ ions produced by an acid, stronger is the acid. Similarly, larger the number of OH^- ions produced by a base, stronger is the base.

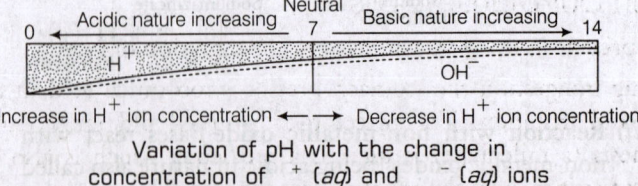
Variation of pH with the change in concentration of $H^+(aq)$ and $OH^-(aq)$ ions

Acids, Bases and Salts

The pH Scale

It is a scale used for measuring hydrogen ion concentration. The **p** in pH stands for *potenz* which means **power** in German.

It has values ranging from 0 (very acidic) to 14 (very alkaline). **pH is a number which indicates the acidic or basic nature of a solution.**

Higher the hydronium ion concentration present in the solution, lower is its pH value [pH means power of hydrogen ions].

- If pH > 7, solution is basic.
- If pH < 7, solution is acidic.
- If pH = 7, solution is neutral.

Pure water is neutral because of the absence of free ions. A paper impregnated with the universal indicator is used for measuring pH.

Now-a-days, pH meter, an electronic device, is used to measure the pH value.

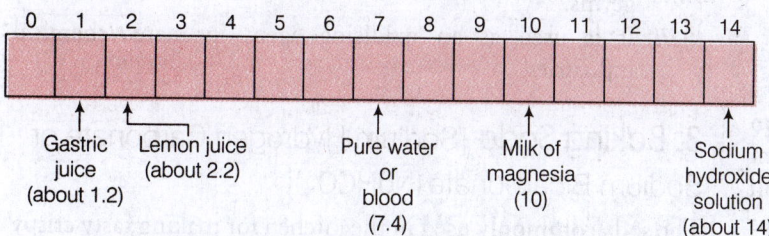

pH of some common substances shown on a pH paper

Importance of pH in Everyday Life

Following are the examples showing importance of pH in everyday life:

Plants and Animals are pH Sensitive

Living organisms can survive only in a narrow range of pH change, our body works normally within a pH range of 7.0 to 7.8.

When pH of rain water goes below 5.6, it is called acid rain. When acid rain flows into the rivers, it lowers the pH of the river water and makes survival of aquatic life difficult.

pH of the Soil

Every type of plant requires a specific pH range for healthy growth. Therefore, the nature of soil is known first by testing its pH and then a particular crop is grown in it. It is also suitable for selecting the fertiliser for a particular crop by knowing the pH of the soil.

pH in Our Digestive System

HCl present in the stomach helps in the digestion of food.

During indigestion the stomach produces too much acid, it causes pain and irritation. To correct the disturbed pH range, milk of magnesia (a mild base) is used as a medicine, which is also called **antacid** as it reduces the effect of acid (or acidity).

pH Change Leads to Tooth Decay

Tooth enamel is made up of calcium phosphate and is the hardest substance in the body. If the pH inside the mouth decreases below 5.5 (acidic), the decay of tooth enamel begins.

The bacteria present in the mouth degrades the sugar and left over food particles and produce acids that remains in the mouth after eating.

The best way to prevent this is to clean the mouth after eating food. To prevent tooth decay, toothpastes (basic) are used which neutralise the excess acid.

Self Defence by Animals and Plants through Chemical Warfare

When insects like honeybee, ant etc., bite, they inject an acid into the skin, that causes pain and irritation. If a mild base like baking soda is applied on the affected area, it gives relief.

pH in Plants

Stinging hair of nettle leaves injects methanoic acid in the skin which causes burning pain. It is cured by rubbing the affected area with the leaves of dock plant, which often grows beside the nettle plant.

Check Point 02

1. Which indicator gives pink colour in basic solution?
2. In which pH range our body works?
3. Fill in the blank:
   To prevent tooth decay, toothpaste are used which are .... in nature.
4. Name the chemical which is injected into the skin of a person during wasp's sting and during the nettle leaf hair sting.
5. State True or False for the following statement:
   The colour of gastric juice on pH paper is blue.
6. Write the role of HCl present in the stomach.

Salts

Salts are produced by the **neutralisation reaction** between acid and base. Salts of strong acid and a strong base are neutral with pH value of 7.

Salts of a strong acid and weak base are acidic with pH value less than 7. Salts of strong base and weak acid are basic in nature with pH value more than 7. Now, we will study about preparation and properties of some salts.

Common Salt [Sodium Chloride (NaCl)]

Common salt is formed by the combination of hydrochloric acid and sodium hydroxide solution. It is the salt that we use in food. Sea water contains many salts dissolved in it. It is obtained on large scale from sea water by separating other salts from it. It may also be obtained from rock salt.

Deposits of solid salt are also found in several parts of the world. These large crystals are often brown due to impurities. This is called rock salt. Beds of rock salt were formed when seas of bygone ages dried up. Rock salt is mined like coal.

Common salt is an important raw material for various materials of daily use, like sodium hydroxide, baking soda, washing soda, bleaching powder etc.

1. Caustic Soda [Sodium Hydroxide (NaOH)]

When electricity is passed through an aqueous solution of sodium chloride (called brine), it decomposes to form sodium hydroxide. This process is called **chlor-alkali process** because of the products formed, i.e. chlor for chlorine and alkali for sodium hydroxide.

$$2NaCl(aq) + 2H_2O(l) \xrightarrow{\text{Electric current}} 2NaOH(aq)$$
Sodium chloride   Water   Sodium hydroxide

$$+ Cl_2(g) + H_2(g)$$
Chlorine   Hydrogen

In this process, chlorine gas is given off at the anode and hydrogen gas at the cathode and sodium hydroxide solution is formed near the cathode. The following three products produced in this process are very useful.

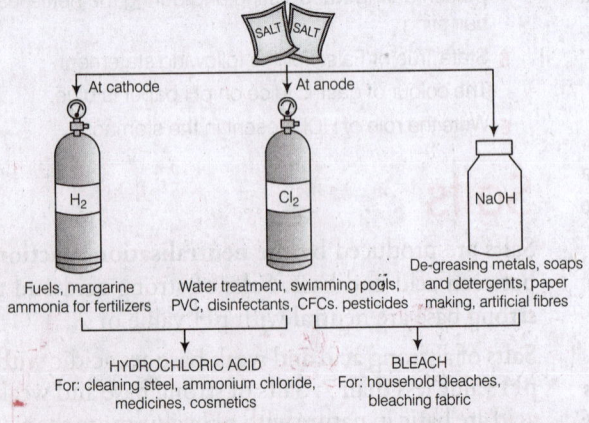

Important products from the chlor-alkali process

2. Bleaching Powder [Calcium Oxychloride (CaOCl₂)]

It is produced by the action of chlorine on dry slaked lime. It is represented as $CaOCl_2$, though the actual composition is quite complex.

$$Ca(OH)_2 + Cl_2 \longrightarrow CaOCl_2 + H_2O$$
Slaked lime   Chlorine   Bleaching powder   Water

On standing for a longer time, it undergoes auto-oxidation due to which bleaching action decreases.

Uses of Bleaching Powder

(i) It is used for bleaching cotton and linen in textile industry, for bleaching wood pulp in paper industry and for bleaching washed clothes in laundry.

(ii) It is also used as a disinfectant for water to make it free of germs.

(iii) It is used as an oxidising agent in many chemical industries.

3. Baking Soda [Sodium Hydrogen Carbonate or Sodium Bicarbonate (NaHCO₃)]

The soda commonly used in the kitchen for making tasty crispy pakoras is baking soda. It is a mild non-corrosive base. It is the major constituent of baking powder. Sometimes, it is added for fast cooking. Chemically, it is sodium hydrogen carbonate. It is produced by using sodium chloride as one of the raw material.

Manufacture of baking soda is shown in reaction given below:

$$NaCl(aq) + H_2O(l) + CO_2(g) + NH_3(g)$$
Brine   Carbon dioxide   Ammonia

$$\longrightarrow NH_4Cl(g) + NaHCO_3(s)$$
Ammonium chloride   Sodium hydrogen carbonate

The following reaction takes place when it is heated during cooking :

$$2NaHCO_3 \xrightarrow{\text{Heat}} Na_2CO_3 + H_2O + CO_2\uparrow$$
Sodium hydrogen carbonate   Sodium carbonate

Uses of Baking Soda

(i) For making baking powder, which is a mixture of baking soda (sodium hydrogen carbonate) and a mild edible acid such as tartaric acid. When baking powder is heated or mixed in water, the following reaction takes place:

$$NaHCO_3 + H^+ \longrightarrow CO_2 + H_2O$$
Sodium hydrogen carbonate   (From any acid)   Carbon dioxide   Water

$$+ \text{Sodium salt of acid}$$

Acids, Bases and Salts

Carbon dioxide produced during the reaction causes bread or cake to rise making them soft and spongy.

(ii) Sodium hydrogen carbonate is also an ingredient of antacids. Being alkaline, it neutralises excess acid in the stomach and provides relief.

$$\underset{\text{Sodium hydrogen carbonate}}{NaHCO_3(s)} + \underset{\text{Hydrochloric acid}}{HCl(l)} \longrightarrow \underset{\text{Sodium chloride}}{NaCl(aq)} + \underset{\text{Water}}{H_2O(l)} + \underset{\text{Carbon dioxide}}{CO_2(g)}$$

(iii) It is also used in soda-acid fire extinguishers.

Note Baking soda is also acts as a preservative for milk. In summer, it is added to the milk, as milk decompose and release lactic acid which makes milk sour. Added $NaHCO_3$ reacts with acid to form salt and water. It neutralises the acidic effect and milk does not become sour.

4. Washing Soda
[Sodium Carbonate ($Na_2CO_3 \cdot 10H_2O$)]

Sodium carbonate is a white crystalline solid. Its solution in water is alkaline in nature (turns red litmus blue).

It has the property to remove dirt and grease from dirty clothes, thus it is called washing soda.

Sodium carbonate can be obtained by heating baking soda. The recrystallisation of sodium carbonate gives washing soda. It is also a **basic salt**.

$$Na_2CO_3(s) + 10H_2O(l) \longrightarrow Na_2CO_3 \cdot 10H_2O(s)$$

Uses of Washing Soda

(i) It is used in glass, soap and paper industries.
(ii) It is used for the manufacture of sodium compounds like borax.
(iii) It also removes permanent hardness of water.
(iv) It is used as a cleansing agent (detergent) in houses and laundries.

5. Plaster of Paris [Calcium Sulphate Hemihydrate ($CaSO_4 \cdot 1/2H_2O$)]

It is obtained by heating gypsum ($CaSO_4 \cdot 2H_2O$) at 373 K. At this temperature, gypsum loses water molecules and forms plaster of Paris.

$$\underset{\text{Gypsum}}{CaSO_4 \cdot 2H_2O} \xrightarrow[\text{Heat}]{373\ K} \underset{\text{Plaster of Paris}}{CaSO_4 \cdot \frac{1}{2}H_2O} + 1\frac{1}{2}H_2O$$

When gypsum is heated above 400 K, dead burnt plaster (anhydrous $CaSO_4$) is obtained which does not have the property of hardening.

Plaster of Paris is a white powder and on mixing with water, it changes to gypsum giving a hard solid mass.

$$\underset{\text{Plaster of Paris}}{CaSO_4 \cdot \frac{1}{2}H_2O} + 1\frac{1}{2}H_2O \longrightarrow \underset{\text{Gypsum}}{CaSO_4 \cdot 2H_2O}$$

Uses of Plaster of Paris

(i) It is used by doctors for joining the fractured bones at right position, i.e. for making plaster to support fractured bones.
(ii) It is also used for making decorative pieces and for making designs on ceilings.

Water of Crystallisation

Crystals of some compounds seem to be dry (or anhydrous) but actually contain some water molecules attached to them. This water is called water of crystallisation and such salts are called **hydrated salts**.

Water of crystallisation is the fixed number of water molecules present in one formula unit of a salt. Five water molecules are present in one formula unit of copper sulphate (blue vitriol; $CuSO_4 \cdot 5H_2O$). Other salt which possesses water of crystallisation is gypsum ($CaSO_4 \cdot 2H_2O$). It has two water molecules as water of crystallisation. This water is removed by heating the crystals of the hydrated salt. Plaster of Paris possesses 1/2 molecule of water of crystallisation.

Check Point 03

1. Fill in the blank:
   The salt that we used in food is a .... salt.
2. State True or False for the following statement:
   Sodium hydrogen carbonate is used in fire extinguisher.
3. Name the chemical compound which is used as a disinfectant for water.
4. When a sodium compound X which is also used in soda-fire extinguisher is heated, gives a sodium compound Y alongwith water and carbon dioxide. Y on crystallisation forms compound Z. Identify X, Y and Z.
5. Write the chemical formula of blue vitriol.

NCERT FOLDER

INTEXT QUESTIONS

1. You have been provided with three test tubes. One of them contains distilled water and the other two contain an acidic solution and a basic solution, respectively. If you are given only red litmus paper, how will you identify the contents of each test tube? **Pg 18**

Sol. We take a small amount of each of the given liquids in three separate test tubes (test tube no.1, 2, 3). Now, we dip red litmus paper strips separately in all the three test tubes. The liquid which turns red litmus blue is a basic solution. By removing this test tube (no. 1), we have now remaining two. Now, add one drop from each solution one by one on this above blue litmus paper (which turns blue due to basic solution). The solution which turns the blue litmus paper red is acidic and which do not able to change the colour is distilled water.

2. Why should curd and sour substances not be kept in brass and copper vessels? **Pg 22**

Sol. Curd and sour substances contain acids which react with copper and brass to form certain salts that are poisonous in nature and can cause food poisoning. Hence, sour substances like curd, pickles etc., should not be kept in brass and copper vessels.

3. Which gas is usually liberated when an acid reacts with a metal? Illustrate with an example. How will you test for the presence of this gas? **Pg 22**

Sol. Hydrogen gas is usually liberated when an acid reacts with metal.

e.g. $Zn(s) + H_2SO_4(aq) \longrightarrow ZnSO_4(aq) + H_2 \uparrow$

4. Metal compound A reacts with dilute hydrochloric acid to produce effervescence. The gas evolved extinguishes a burning candle. Write a balanced chemical equation for the reaction, if one of the compounds formed is calcium chloride. **Pg 22**

Sol. CO_2 is the gas that extinguishes a burning candle.
CO_2 is produced when metal carbonate reacts with acid. Since, one of the products is calcium chloride.
Thus, the compound A should be calcium carbonate. The balanced chemical equation is

$CaCO_3(s) + 2HCl(aq) \longrightarrow CaCl_2(aq)$
$+ CO_2(g) + H_2O(l)$

5. Why do HCl, HNO₃, etc., show acidic characters in aqueous solutions while solutions of compounds like alcohol and glucose do not show acidic character?

Sol. Acidic character of a compound is due to the presence of replaceable H^+ ions, which are released in aqueous solution and are responsible for acidic properties. As HCl, HNO_3 etc have replaceable H^+ ions, they show acidic character while glucose and alcohol do not have replaceable H^+ ions, hence, no acidic character is shown by them.

6. Why does an aqueous solution of an acid conduct electricity?

Sol. An acid molecule dissociates in an aqueous solution to produce H^+ (or H_3O^+) ions and corresponding anions A^-. These free ions carry the electrical charge from one place to other, hence conduct electricity.

7. Why does dry HCl gas not change the colour of dry litmus paper?

Sol. Dry HCl gas does not contain any H^+ or H_3O^+ ions, so it does not show any acidic property. Hence, it does not change the colour of dry litmus paper. To show its acidic behaviour, it needs wet litmus paper.

8. While diluting an acid, why is it recommended that the acid should be added to water and not water to the acid? **Pg 25**

Sol. Dilution of a concentrated acid is a highly exothermic reaction and a lot of heat is generated. Care must be taken while mixing concentrated acid with water. The acid must always be added slowly to water with constant stirring. If water is added to the concentrated acid, the heat generated may cause the mixture to splash out and cause burns. The glass container may also break due to excessive local heating.

9. How is the concentration of hydronium ions H_3O^+ affected when a solution of an acid is diluted? **Pg 25**

Sol. An acid dissociates into hydronium ions (H_3O^+) and anions when dissolved in water. When a solution is diluted, the volume of the solution increases but the number of ions remains the same, so concentration of hydronium ions (H_3O^+) per unit volume decreases.

Acids, Bases and Salts

10 How is the concentration of hydroxide ions (OH⁻) affected when excess base is dissolved in a solution of sodium hydroxide? **Pg 25**

Sol. Sodium hydroxide is a strong base. When excess base is dissolved in the solution of NaOH, the concentration of hydroxide ions (OH⁻) per unit volume increases due to dissociation of NaOH as well as the other base in aqueous solution.

$$NaOH \xrightleftharpoons{H_2O} Na^+ + OH^-$$

Any other base

e.g. $M(OH)_x \xrightleftharpoons{H_2O} M^+ + xOH^-$

11 You have two solutions A and B. The pH of solution A is 6 and pH of solution B is 8.
 (i) Which solution has more H⁺ ion concentration?
 (ii) Which solution is acidic and which is basic? **Pg 28**

Sol. (i) pH = 6 has more H⁺ ion concentration.
 (ii) Solution A having pH 6 is acidic.
 Solution B having pH 8 is basic.

12 What effect does the concentration of H⁺(aq) ions have on the nature of the solution? **Pg 28**

Sol. Higher the concentration of H⁺ ions in a solution, more acidic is the solution.

13 Do basic solutions also have H⁺(aq) ions? If yes, then why are these basic? **Pg 28**

Sol. Yes, basic solutions also contain H⁺(aq) ions but they are basic because in these solutions, concentration of OH⁻ is much higher than that of H⁺ ions.

14 Under what soil condition do you think a farmer would treat the soil of his fields with quicklime (calcium oxide) or slaked lime (calcium hydroxide) or chalk (calcium carbonate)? **Pg 28**

Sol. These fertilisers [CaO, Ca(OH)₂, CaCO₃] are of basic nature. Therefore, their use will be beneficial, if the soil is acidic. The purpose is to neutralise or decrease the acidity of the soil.

15 What is the common name of the compound CaOCl₂? **Pg 33**

Sol. Bleaching powder.

16 Name the substance which on treatment with chlorine yields bleaching powder. **Pg 33**

Sol. Calcium hydroxide (or slaked lime) in dry state.

17 Name the sodium compound which is used for softening hard water. **Pg 33**

Sol. Sodium carbonate.

18 What will happen if a solution of sodium hydrogen carbonate is heated? Give the equation of the reaction involved. **Pg 33**

Sol. When sodium hydrogen carbonate is heated, carbon dioxide gas is produced alongwith sodium carbonate.

$$2NaHCO_3(s) \xrightarrow{Heat} Na_2CO_3(s) + H_2O(l) + CO_2(g)\uparrow$$

19 Write an equation to show the reaction between plaster of Paris and water. **Pg 33**

Sol. $CaSO_4 \cdot \frac{1}{2}H_2O(s) + 1\frac{1}{2}H_2O(l) \longrightarrow CaSO_4 \cdot 2H_2O(s)$ (Gypsum)

or $(CaSO_4)_2 \cdot H_2O(s) + 3H_2O(l) \longrightarrow 2CaSO_4 \cdot 2H_2O(s)$

EXERCISES
(On Pages 34 and 35)

1 A solution turns red litmus blue, its pH is likely to be
 (a) 1 (b) 4 (c) 5 (d) 10

Sol. (d) If a solution turns red litmus blue then the solution is basic in nature and its pH value is likely to be greater than 7.

2 A solution reacts with crushed egg-shells to give a gas that turns lime water milky. The solution contains
 (a) NaCl (b) HCl
 (c) LiCl (d) KCl

Sol. (b) The crushed egg-shells consist of layer of calcium carbonate which reacts with dil. HCl to evolve CO₂(g). The CO₂ gas turns lime water milky.

3 10 mL of a solution of NaOH is found to be completely neutralised by 8 mL of a given solution of HCl. If we take 20 mL of the same solution of NaOH, the amount of HCl solution required to neutralise it will be
 (a) 4 mL (b) 8 mL
 (c) 12 mL (d) 16 mL

Sol. (d) If we take double the amount of same NaOH solution, the amount of the same HCl solution required to neutralise it is also doubled.
Hence, 16 mL of HCl solution will be required to neutralise 20 mL NaOH solution.

4 Which one of the following types of medicines is used for treating indigestion?
(a) Antibiotic (b) Analgesic
(c) Antacid (d) Antiseptic

Sol. (c) Antacid contains solution of mild bases and hence, they are used for treating indigestion.

5 Write word equations and then balanced equations for the reaction taking place when
(i) dilute sulphuric acid reacts with zinc granules.
(ii) dilute hydrochloric acid reacts with magnesium ribbon.
(iii) dilute sulphuric acid reacts with aluminium powder.
(iv) dilute hydrochloric acid reacts with iron filings.

Sol. (i) Dilute sulphuric acid + Zinc (Granules) $\longrightarrow$ Zinc sulphate + Hydrogen gas

$H_2SO_4(aq)$ (Dilute) + $Zn(s)$ (Granulated) $\longrightarrow ZnSO_4(aq) + H_2(g)$

(ii) Dilute hydrochloric acid + Magnesium $\longrightarrow$ Magnesium chloride + Hydrogen gas

$2HCl(aq)$ (Dilute) + $Mg(s) \longrightarrow MgCl_2(aq) + H_2(g)$

(iii) Dilute sulphuric acid + Aluminium $\longrightarrow$ Aluminium sulphate + Hydrogen gas

$3H_2SO_4(aq)$ (Dilute) + $2Al(s) \longrightarrow Al_2(SO_4)_3(aq) + 3H_2(g)$

(iv) Dilute hydrochloric acid + Iron $\longrightarrow$ Iron (II) chloride + Hydrogen gas

$2HCl(aq)$ (Dilute) + $Fe(s) \longrightarrow FeCl_2(aq) + H_2(g)$

6 Compounds such as alcohols and glucose also contain hydrogen but are not categorised as acids. Describe an activity to prove it.

Sol. Alcohols and glucose contain hydrogen but are not categorised as acids because they do not ionise in the solution to produce $H^+(aq)$ ions and hence can't conduct electricity.

Activity Set the apparatus as shown below and test for the solution of HCl, alcohol and glucose.

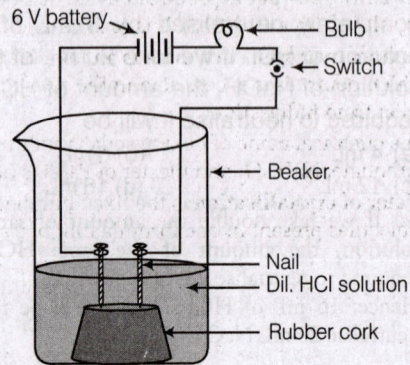

Observation
(i) The bulb glows when dil. HCl was added to beaker.
(ii) The bulb did not glow when alcohol and glucose solution was added to the beaker.

Conclusion
(i) Alcohol and glucose cannot form ions in solution and hence, can't conduct electricity.
(ii) Dil. HCl solution forms $(aq)H^+$ ions and hence, can conduct electricity suggesting that electric current is carried through the solution by ions formed by them.

7 Why does distilled water not conduct electricity, whereas rain water does?

Sol. Distilled water does not contain any ions and have no electrolytes. Hence, it does not conduct electricity. But in rain water, a small amount of electrolyte is present in the form of acids. These acids are produced due to dissolution of acidic oxides (e.g. SO_2, NO_2) in rain water and make it a better conductor of electricity.

8 Why do acids not show acidic behaviour in the absence of water?

Sol. Ions are produced only in aqueous medium and presence of H^+ ions are responsible for the existence of acidic properties. Hence, acids show acidic behaviour only in the presence of water and not in its absence.

9 Five solutions A, B, C, D and E when tested with universal indicator showed pH as 4, 1, 11, 7 and 9 respectively. Which solution is (i) neutral (ii) strongly alkaline (iii) strongly acidic (iv) weakly acidic (v) weakly alkaline? Arrange the pH in increasing order of H^+ion concentration. **CBSE 2010**

Sol.

Solution	A	B	C	D	E
pH Value	4	1	11	7	9

(i) D (ii) C (iii) B (iv) A (v) E

pH in increasing order of H^+ion concentration is $C < E < D < A < B$

10 Equal lengths of magnesium ribbons are taken in test tubes A and B. Hydrochloric acid (HCl) is added to test tube A, while acetic acid (CH_3COOH) is added to test tube B. Amount and concentration taken for both the acids are same. In which test tube, will the fizzing occur more vigorously and why?

Sol. (i) Reaction occurs in test tube A

$2HCl(aq) + Mg(s) \longrightarrow MgCl_2(aq) + H_2(g)$

Acids, Bases and Salts

(ii) Reaction occurs in test tube B
$$2CH_3COOH(aq) + Mg(s) \longrightarrow (CH_3COO)_2Mg(aq) + H_2(g)$$

Fizzing occurs in both the test tubes due to the evolution of H_2 gas but it is faster in test tube A because of the greater extent of dissociation of HCl (strong acid) as compared to B as CH_3COOH is not completely dissociated (weak acid).

11 Fresh milk has a pH of 6. How do you think the pH will change as it turns into curd? Explain.
CBSE 2012, 11, 10, 09

Sol. pH will decrease from 6 because during curd formation, lactic acid is produced which makes it acidic. When milk changes into curd, its pH changes and becomes less than 6.

12 A milkman adds a very small amount of baking soda to fresh milk.
(i) Why does he shift the pH of the fresh milk from 6 to slightly alkaline?
(ii) What do you expect to observe when milk comes to boil?
Or What is the effect of addition of baking soda to milk?
(iii) Why does this milk take a longer time to set as a curd? **CBSE 2012, 11**

Sol. (i) Alkaline medium does not allow milk to turn sour easily.

(ii) When milk is about to boil, there must be more effervescence due to the presence of baking soda.

(iii) When milk is set to curd, the presence of alkali does not allow it to become acidic easily. Hence, this milk take a longer time to set as a curd.

13 Plaster of Paris should be stored in moisture proof containers. Explain why?

Sol. Plaster of Paris (POP) is chemically calcium sulphate hemihydrate $(CaSO_4 \cdot \frac{1}{2}H_2O)$. When it comes in contact with water it sets into a hard solid mass, called gypsum.

$$\underset{\text{Plaster of Paris}}{CaSO_4 \cdot \frac{1}{2}H_2O} + 1\frac{1}{2}H_2O \longrightarrow \underset{\text{Gypsum}}{CaSO_4 \cdot 2H_2O}$$

To prevent this, POP must be stored in moisture-proof containers.

14 What is a neutralisation reaction? Give two examples.

Sol. The reaction between an acid and base to form salt and water is called neutralisation reaction.

Acid + Base $\longrightarrow$ Salt + Water

e.g. $HNO_3(aq) + KOH(aq) \longrightarrow KNO_3(aq) + H_2O(l)$

$HCl(aq) + NaOH(aq) \longrightarrow NaCl(aq) + H_2O(l)$

15 Give two important uses of washing soda and baking soda.

Sol. Uses of washing soda are:
(i) It is used as a cleansing agent (detergents).
(ii) It is used to remove permanent hardness of water.

Uses of baking soda are:
(i) It is used in bakery.
(ii) It is used for extinguishing fire (in soda-acid fire extinguishers).

SUMMARY

- **Acids** are those chemical substances which are sour in taste and change the colour of blue litmus solution to red.
- **Bases** are those chemical substances which are bitter in taste, soapy to touch and turn red litmus solution to blue.
- Acids react with bases to produce salt and water.
- In presence of water, acids give H^+ ions.
- **Indicators** are the substances that change their colour or odour when added into an acid or an alkaline solution.
- **Litmus solution** is a purple dye, which is extracted from lichen, a plant belonging to the division thallophyta, and is commonly used as an indicator.
- **Olfactory indicators** are the substances whose odour changes in acidic or basic media.
- Strength of an acid or base depend on the number of H^+ ions or OH^- ions produced by them respectively.
- Larger the number of H^+ ions produced by an acid, stronger is the acid and *vice-versa*.
- **pH** is a number which indicates the acidic or basic nature of a solution.
- **Salts** are produced by the neutralisation reaction between acid and base.
- **Bleaching powder** is produced by the action of chlorine on dry slaked lime $[Ca(OH)_2]$. It is represented as $CaOCl_2$.
- **Sodium hydrogen carbonate** is an ingredient of antacids, which neutralises excess acid in the stomach and provides relief from indigestion.
- The chemical name of baking soda is sodium hydrogen carbonate, $NaHCO_3$ and plaster of Paris is $CaSO_4 \cdot 1/2H_2O$.
- **Water of crystallisation** is the fixed number of water molecules present in one formula unit of a salt.

Exam Practice

Objective Type Questions

Multiple Choice Questions

1 Incorrect statement about acids is/are
(a) they have sour taste
(b) they may change the colour of indicator
(c) they changes the colour of blue litmus to red
(d) they change the colour of red litmus to blue

Sol. (d) Acids will change the colour of blue litmus to red but makes no effect on red litmus. Hence, statement (d) is incorrect.

2 When aqueous sodium carbonate (Na_2CO_3) reacts with HCl(aq), it gives
(a) NaOH, $H_2(g)$ and $CO_2(g)$
(b) NaCl, H_2O and $CO_2(g)$
(c) $NaHCO_3$, $H_2(g)$ and $CO_2(g)$
(d) $NaHCO_3$, $H_2O(l)$ and $CO_2(g)$

Sol. (b) It is an example of acid (HCl) and base (Na_2CO_3) reaction, because Na_2CO_3 is basic in nature. Thus, the reaction gives salt (NaCl), water (H_2O) and $CO_2(g)$.
$Na_2CO_3(aq) + 2HCl(aq) \longrightarrow$
$\qquad 2NaCl(s) + H_2O(l) + CO_2(g)$

3 Which of the following gives the correct increasing order of acid strength?
(a) Water < acetic acid < hydrochloric acid
(b) Water < hydrochloric acid < acetic acid
(c) Acetic acid < water < hydrochloric acid
(d) Hydrochloric acid < water < acetic acid
NCERT Exemplar

Sol. (a) Hydrochloric acid is a mineral acid and ionises completely in water, that's why it is a strong acid. Acetic acid is an organic acid and ionises only partially in water, hence, it is a weak acid. Water has some what neutral nature. Thus, the order of acidity is, water < acetic acid < hydrochloric acid.

4 Concentrated H_2SO_4 is diluted by adding drop by drop
(a) water to acid with constant stirring
(b) acid to water with constant stirring
(c) water to acid followed by a base
(d) base to acid followed by cold water

Sol. (b) Dilution of concentrated H_2SO_4 is done by adding concentrated H_2SO_4 to water dropwise with constant stirring because mixing of water to an acid is highly exothermic in nature.

5 If a few drops of a concentrated acid accidentally spills over the hand of a student, what should be done?
NCERT Exemplar
(a) Wash the hand with saline solution.
(b) Wash the hand immediately with plenty of water and apply a paste of sodium hydrogen carbonate.
(c) After washing with plenty of water apply solution of sodium hydroxide on the hand.
(d) Neutralise the acid with a strong alkali.

Sol. (b) Wash the hand immediately with plenty of water to wash away most of the acid and then apply a paste of baking soda ($NaHCO_3$) to neutralise the little acid left. Here a strong base cannot be used to neutralise the acid due to its **corrosive nature**.

6 On prolong supply of $CO_2(g)$ in lime solution (lime-water), it is observed that
(a) lime solution changes to gaseous state
(b) the milkiness of lime water disappears
(c) the colour of lime water changes from white to red
(d) the colour of lime water becomes black

Sol. (b) On prolong supply of $CO_2(g)$ in lime solution, the milky solution becomes colourless due to formation of $CaCO_3(s)$.
$\underset{\text{Lime water}}{Ca(OH)_2(aq)} + \underset{\text{(in excess)}}{CO_2(g)} \longrightarrow \underset{\text{Salt}}{CaCO_3(s)} + H_2O(l)$

7 When $Ca(OH)_2$ reacts with $CO_2(g)$, it will give $CaCO_3(s)$ and $H_2O(l)$. The nature of $CaCO_3$ is
(a) acidic
(b) basic
(c) neutral
(d) All are possible

Sol. (b) $CaCO_3$ is basic in nature, as it is the salt of strong base. $Ca(OH)_2$ (calcium hydroxide) and a weak acid, H_2CO_3 (carbonic acid).

Acids, Bases and Salts

8 The table given below shows the reaction of a few elements with acids and bases to evolve hydrogen gas.

Which of these elements form amphoteric oxides?

Element	Acid	Base
A	✗	✗
B	✓	✓
C	✓	✗
D	✓	✓

CBSE SQP (Term-I)

(a) A and D (b) B and D
(c) A and C (d) B and C

Sol. (b) Amphoteric oxides are those oxides which can act as both acid and base.
So, the elements B and D form amphoteric oxides as they react with both acid and base and evolve H_2 gas.

9 A solution gives yellowish orange colour when a few drops of universal indicator are added to it. This solution is of

(a) lemon juice
(b) sodium chloride
(c) sodium hydroxide
(d) milk of magnesia

Sol. (a) The given solution is lemon juice because only lemon juice is acidic among others. So, it turns yellowish orange colour if an universal indicator is added to it.

10 Which one of the following can be used as an acid-base indicator by a visually impared student?

(a) Litmus (b) Turmeric
(c) Vanilla essence (d) Petunia leaves

NCERT Exemplar

Sol. (c) Vanilla essence is an olfactory indicator. So, its smell is different in acid and basic media which can be detected easily by a visually impared student. Vanilla extract has a characteristic pleasant smell.
If a basic solution like sodium hydroxide solution is added to vanilla extract then we cannot detect the characteristic smell of vanilla extract. An acidic solution like hydrochloric acid, however, does not destroy the smell of vanilla extract.

11 An aqueous solution 'A' turns phenolphthalein solution pink. On addition of an aqueous solution 'B' to 'A', the pink colour disappears. The following statement is true for solutions 'A' and 'B'.

CBSE (All India) 2020

(a) A is strongly basic and B is a weak base
(b) A is strongly acidic and B is a weak acid
(c) A has pH greater than 7 and B has pH less than 7
(d) A has pH less than 7 and B has pH greater than 7

Sol. (c) A has pH greater than 7 and B has pH less than 7. This is because, phenolphthalein is a synthetic indicator which turns pink in basic solution and colourless in acidic or neutral solution.

12 If 10 mL of H_2SO_4 is mixed with 10 mL of $Mg(OH)_2$ of the same concentration, the resultant solution will give the following colour with universal indicator:

CBSE (All India) 2020

(a) Red (b) Yellow
(c) Green (d) Blue

Sol. (c) The colour of the resulting solution of 10 mL of H_2SO_4 and 10 mL of $Mg(OH)_2$ with universal indicator will be green. Because, H_2SO_4 is an acid and $Mg(OH)_2$ is base. Thus, they both produces a neutral salt which shows green colour on universal indicators.

13 Calcium phosphate is present in tooth enamel. Its nature is

(a) basic (b) acidic
(c) neutral (d) amphoteric

NCERT Exemplar

Sol. (a) Calcium phosphate $Ca_3(PO_4)_2$ is basic salt, as it is a salt of weak acid (phosphoric acid) and slightly stronger base (calcium hydroxide). Also when pH of our mouth falls below 5.5 due to eating of sweets etc., i.e., mouth is acidic, the dissolution of enamel (calcium phosphate) starts which shows that calcium phosphate is basic in nature.

14 The graph given below depicts a neutralisation reaction (acid + alkali → salt + water). The pH of a solution changes as we add excess of acid to an alkali.

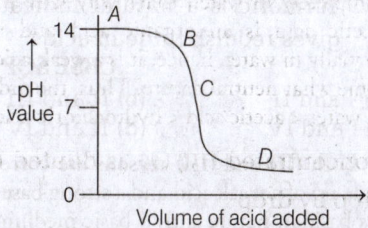

Which letter denotes the area of the graph where both acid and salt are present?

CBSE SQP (Term-I)

(a) A (b) B (c) C (d) D

Sol. (d) Acid and base reacts with each other to form salt and water, this reaction is known as neutralisation reaction.

$$\text{Acid} + \text{Base} \longrightarrow \text{Salt} + H_2O$$

As the pH of acid is below 7, so the letter which donates the area of the graph where both acid and salt are present after addition of excess acid to an alkali is (D).

15 Sodium hydrogen carbonate when added to acetic acid evolves a gas. Which of the following statements are true about the gas evolved? **NCERT Exemplar**

(i) It turns lime water milky.
(ii) It extinguishes a burning splinter.
(iii) It dissolves in a solution of sodium hydroxide.
(iv) It has a pungent odour.
(a) (i) and (ii)   (b) (i), (ii) and (iii)
(c) (ii), (iii) and (iv)   (d) (i) and (iv)

Sol. (b) When sodium hydrogen carbonate is added to acetic acid then carbon dioxide (CO_2) gas is evolved.

$$\underset{\substack{\text{Sodium}\\\text{hydrogen}\\\text{carbonate}}}{NaHCO_3} + \underset{\substack{\text{Acetic}\\\text{acid}}}{CH_3COOH} \longrightarrow \underset{\substack{\text{Sodium}\\\text{acetate}}}{CH_3COONa}$$
$$+ CO_2 + H_2O$$

CO_2 turns lime water milky, it is a non-supporter of combustion and is absorbed by strong alkalies like NaOH.

16 Vinay observed that the stain of curry on a white shirt becomes reddish-brown when soap is scrubbed on it, but it turns yellow again when the shirt is washed with plenty of water. What might be the reason for his observation?

I. Soap is acidic in nature.
II. Soap is basic in nature.
III. Turmeric is a natural indicator which gives reddish tinge in bases.
IV. Turmeric is a natural indicator which gives reddish tinge in acids.
CBSE SQP (Term-I)
(a) I and II   (b) II and III
(c) I and IV   (d) II and IV

Sol. (b) Both (II) and (III) reasons are correct. Soap is made up of a weak acid and a strong base, therefore, it is basic in nature and in basic medium, turmeric (natural indicator) gives reddish tinge.

17 A sample of soil is mixed with water and allowed to settle. The clear supernatant solution turns the pH paper yellowish-orange. Which of the following would change the colour of this pH paper to greenish-blue? **NCERT Exemplar**

(a) Lemon juice
(b) Vinegar
(c) Common salt
(d) An antacid

Sol. (d) As pH paper turns greenish blue for weakly basic compound and antacids contain weak base like $Mg(OH)_2$. So, an antacid would change the colour of this pH paper to greenish-blue. Other options (a) and (b) contain acids and option (c) is a neutral salt.

18 Salt 'A' commonly used in food products, is a reactant to produce salt 'B', used in the kitchen for making tasty, crispy pakoras. Salt 'B' on heating converts into another salt 'C', which is used in the manufacturing of glass. Salts 'A', 'B' and 'C' respectively are **CBSE 2021 (Term-I)**

(a) $NaHCO_3$, $NaCl$, Na_2CO_3
(b) Na_2CO_3, $NaHCO_3$, $NaCl$
(c) Na_2CO_3, $NaCl$, $NaHCO_3$
(d) $NaCl$, $NaHCO_3$, Na_2CO_3

Sol. (d) Salt 'A' is common salt, i.e. NaCl, Salt 'B' is sodium bicarbonate ($NaHCO_3$) and is also known as baking soda. Salt 'C' is sodium carbonate (Na_2CO_3).

19 Given below is a reaction showing chlor-alkali process

$$2NaCl(aq) + 2H_2O(l) \longrightarrow$$
$$\underset{(A)}{2NaOH(aq)} + \underset{(B)}{Cl_2(g)} + \underset{(C)}{H_2(g)}$$

The products A, B and C are produced respectively

(a) at the anode, at the cathode, near the cathode
(b) near the cathode, at the anode, at the cathode
(c) at the cathode, near the cathode, at the anode
(d) at the anode, near the cathode, at the cathode **CBSE 2021 (Term-I)**

Sol. (b) In the chlor-alkali process, the product A (NaOH) produced near the cathode, product B (Cl_2 gas) at the anode and product C (H_2 gas) at the cathode.

20 Several factories were pouring their wastes in rivers A and B. Water samples were collected from these two rivers. It was observed that sample collected from river A was acidic while that of river B was basic. The factories located near A and B are **CBSE (All India) 2020**

Acids, Bases and Salts

(a) soaps and detergents factories near *A* and alcohol distillery near *B*
(b) soaps and detergents factories near *B* and alcohol distillery near *A*
(c) lead storage battery manufacturing factories near *A* and soaps and detergents factories near *B*
(d) lead storage battery manufacturing factories near *B* and soaps and detergents factories near *A*

Sol. (*b*) The wastes of soaps and detergents factories are basic in nature, while the wastes from the alcohol distillery are acidic in nature. Therefore, the soap and detergent industries are located near river *B* and alcohol distillery industries are located near to river *A*.

Fill in the Blanks

21 .... colour of the solution is due to the formation of copper chloride in the reaction.

Sol. Blue-green; Acid reacts with certain metal oxides to form salt and water.
$CuO + 2HCl \longrightarrow CuCl_2 + H_2O$

22 Mixing of an acid or base with water results in .... in the concentration of ions per unit volume.

Sol. decrease; During dilution of an acid or base concentration of ions per unit volume decrease.

23 The atmosphere of venus is made up of thick white and yellowish coluds of ....

Sol. Sulphuric acid

24 The strength of an acid or an alkali can be tested by using a ....

Sol. pH scale; It gives the measure of hydrogen ion concentration in a solution.

True and False

25 On heating plaster of Paris, it loses water molecules and becomes calcium sulphate.

Sol. True; On heating plaster of Paris, it loses water of crystallisation.
$CaSO_4 \cdot \frac{1}{2} H_2O \longrightarrow CaSO_4 + \frac{1}{2} H_2O$

26 The chemical name of bleaching powder is calcium chloride.

Sol. False; Chemical name of bleaching powder is calcium hypochlorite (Calcium oxychloride) or lime of chloride.

27 An acidic solution does not destroy the smell of onion.

Sol. True; Onion juice act as a olfactory indicator whose odour get diminished in basic solutions.

28 Calcium hydroxide is used to make soaps and in glass industry.

Sol. False; Na_2CO_3 is used to make soaps and glass industry.

29 Antacid is a medicine used to treat indigestion.

Sol. True

30 When a oxide of a non-metal reacts with water base is formed.

Sol. False; A non-metal oxide forms acid on treatment with water.
$$CO_2 + H_2O \longrightarrow \underset{\text{Carbonic acid}}{H_2CO_3}$$

Match the Columns

31 Match the following columns.

	Column A (Compound)		Column B (In Solution)
A.	Sodium carbonate	(i)	Contain ions and molecules
B.	Ammonium hydroxide solution	(ii)	Contain only ions
C.	Dilute hydrochloric acid	(iii)	Basic salt
D.	Carbon tetrachloride	(iv)	Contain only molecules

Sol. A→ (iii), B→ (i) C→ (ii) D→ (iv).
A→ (iii) Na_2CO_3 is a salt of strong base and weak acid.
B→ (i) NH_4OH is a weak base, so it remains in undissociated form in aqueous solution.
C→ (ii) HCl is a strong acid and ionise completely in water. It contains H^+ and Cl^- ions only.
D→ (iv) Carbon tetrachloride is a molecule of a compound.

Assertion-Reason

Direction (Q. Nos. 32-37) *In each of the following questions, a statement of Assertion is given by the corresponding statement of Reason. Of the statements, mark the correct answer as.*

(a) Both Assertion and Reason are true and Reason is the correct explanation of Assertion.

(b) Both Assertion and Reason are true, but Reason is not the correct explanation of Assertion.

(c) Assertion is true, but Reason is false.

(d) Assertion is false, but Reason is true.

32 Assertion HCl produces hydronium ions (H_3O^+) and chloride ions (Cl^-) in aqueous solution.

Reason In presence of water, basic give H^+ ions.

Sol. (c) Assertion is correct but Reason is false.

HCl produces H^+ ions in aqueous solution because in presence of water, acids give H^+ ions. As H^+ ions cannot exist alone so it combines with water molecules and form H_3O^+.

33 Assertion Sodium hydroxide reacts with zinc to produce hydrogen gas.

Reason Acids reacts with active metals to produce hydrogen gas.

Sol. (b) Both Assertion and Reason are true but reason is not the correct explanation of assertion.

Sodium hydroxide being an strong base, reacts with active metal (zinc) to produce H_2 gas. The reaction is given as follows:

$$Zn(s) + 2NaOH(aq) \longrightarrow Na_2ZnO_2(aq) + H_2(g)$$

34 Assertion While dissolving an acid or base in water, the acids must always be added slowly to water with constant stirring.

Reason Dissolving an acid on a base in water is highly exothermic reaction.

Sol. (a) Both Assertion and Reason are true and Reason is the correct explanation of Assertion.

35 Assertion Phenolphthalein gives pink colour in basic solution.

Reason Phenolphthalein is a natural indicator.

Sol. (c) Assertion is true but Reason is false. Phenolphthalein is a synthetic indicator.

36 Assertion If the pH inside the mouth decreases below 5.5, the decay of tooth enamel begins.

Reason The bacteria present in mouth degrades the sugar and left over food particles and produce acids that remains in the mouth after eating.

Sol. (a) Both Assertion and Reason are true and Reason is the correct explanation of Assertion. Tooth enamel is calcium phosphate, which gets affected when pH of our mouth falls below 5.5

It happens because the bacteria present in our mouth breakdown sugar and food particles into acids which damage our teeth by corroding them.

37 Assertion Fresh milk in which baking soda is added, takes a longer time to set as curd.

Reason Baking soda decreases the pH value of fresh milk to below 6.
CBSE SQP (Term-I)

Sol. (c) Assertion is true, but Reason is false because baking soda, being a base, increase the pH value of fresh milk to above 6.

Case Based Questions

Direction (Q. Nos. 38-41) *Answer the questions on the basis of your understanding of the following passage and related studied concepts:*

Sodium is a very important element Many of its compound are widely used by us, even in our food as well as for washing clothes. Sodium carbonate decahydrate ($Na_2CO_3 \cdot 10H_2O$) is called washing soda and is widely used for washing clothes. When it is saturate with dioxide of carbon in moist environemnt, it given a product called baking soda.

$$Na_2CO_3 + H_2O + CO_2 \xrightarrow{\Delta} NaHCO_3$$

Baking soda is used in small amount in making bread and cake. It helps to make these soft and spongy. An aqueous solution of baking soda turns red litmus blue. It is also used in soda-acid fire extinguisher.

38 Baking powder helps in making cakes and bread soft and spongy by

(a) providing hydrogen gas
(b) releasing carbon monoxide gas
(c) releasing carbon dioxide gas
(d) reacting dough of cakes and bread

Sol. (c) $NaHCO_3 \xrightarrow{\Delta} Na_2CO_3 + H_2O + CO_2$

$NaHCO_3 + H^+ \longrightarrow CO_2 + H_2O^+$(Sodium salt of acid)

Both the above reactions take place on adding baking powder while making cakes or bread.

The released CO_2 gas makes the cakes or bread soft and spongy.

39 Which reaction is used in soda-acid fire extinguishers?

(a) $NaHCO_3 \xrightarrow{\Delta} Na_2CO_3 + H_2O + CO_2$

Acids, Bases and Salts

(b) $NaHCO_3 + H^+ \longrightarrow CO_2 + H_2O$
　　　　(Sodium salt of acid).
(c) Both (a) and (b)
(d) None of the above

Sol. (b) In soda-acid fire extinguishers, CO_2 is released by the reaction of sodium bicarbonate with acid.

40 What is the approximate pH value of baking soda solution?

Sol. Baking soda ($NaHCO_3$) is a salt of strong base and weak acid, so its pH value must be greater than 7.

41 Flow many water of crystallisation present in wasing soda. What happen when we heat the crystals?

Sol. 10 water of crystallisation present in wasing soda. When we heat the compound loses its water of crystallisation (efflorescent occur) and become anhydrous.

Direction (Q. Nos. 42-45) *Answer the questions on the basis of your understanding of the following passage and related studied concepts:*

The salt pans in Marakkanam, a port town about 120 km from Chennai are the third largest producer of salt in Tamil Nadu. Separation of salt from water is a laborious process and the salt obtained is used as raw materials for manufacture of various sodium compounds. One such compound is sodium hydrogen carbonate, used in baking, as an antacid and in soda acid fire extinguishers.

The table shows the mass of various compounds obtained when 1 L of sea water is evaporated.

Compound	Formula	Mass of solid present/g
Sodium chloride	NaCl	28.0
Magnesium chloride	$MgCl_2$	8.0
Magnesium sulphate	$MgSO_4$	6.0
Calcium sulphate	$CaSO_4$	2.0
Calcium carbonate	$CaCO_3$	1.0
Total amount of salt obtained		45.0

CBSE SQP (Term-I)

42 Which compound in the table reacts with acids to release carbon dioxide?
(a) NaCl　　　(b) $CaSO_4$
(c) $CaCO_3$　　(d) $MgSO_4$

Sol. (c) Metal carbonates on treating with acids, releases carbon dioxide and water along with corresponding metal salt.

Hence, when calcium carbonates, $CaCO_3$ reacts with acid like HCl, then calcium chloride, $CaCl_2$, carbon dioxide and water will be formed.
$$CaCO_3(s) + HCl(aq) \longrightarrow CaCl_2(aq) + H_2O(l) + CO_2(g)$$

43 How many grams of magnesium sulphate are present in 135 g of solid left by evaporation of sea water?
(a) 6 g　(b) 12 g　(c) 18 g　(d) 24 g

Sol. (c) Mass of magnesium sulphate present in per gram solid = 6.0 g
Total amount of salt obtained = 45 g
So, in 135 g of solid,
Mass of magnesium sulphate = $\frac{135}{45} \times 6 = 18$ g

44 What is the saturated solution of sodium chloride called?
(a) Brine　　　(b) Lime water
(c) Slaked lime　(d) Soda water

Sol. (a) Brine is a high-concentration solution of salt, sodium chloride in water or it is the saturated solution of sodium chloride.

45 What is the pH of the acid which is used in the formation of common salt?
(a) Between 1 to 3　(b) Between 6 to 8
(c) Between 8 to 10　(d) Between 11 to 13

Sol. (a) Common salt is formed from hydrochloric acid and sodium hydroxide base.
$$HCl + NaOH \longrightarrow NaCl + H_2O$$
So, the acid used is strong acid which has pH value between 1 to 3.

Direction (Q. Nos. 46-49) *Answer the questions on the basis of your understanding of the following passage and related studied concepts:*

One day Kamal saw that her mother was roasting peanuts in a pan (kadahi) in the kitchen and she had taken ordinary salt to roast the peanuts. She was suprised to observe that in spite of very high temperature, the salt does not melt and the peanuts also get roasted.

46 The chemical name of common salt is
(a) potassium chloride
(b) sodium carbonate
(c) sodium hydrogen carbonate
(d) sodium chloride

Sol. (d) Sodium chloride (NaCl) is the chemical name of common salt.

47 Common salt is
(a) a covalent compound
(b) an ionic compound formed by sharing electrons

(c) an ionic compound formed by the transfer of electrons
(d) soluble in organic solvents

Sol. (c) Common salt (NaCl) is an ionic compound in which Na and Cl-atoms are bonded by transfer of electrons.

48. Common salt is not a raw material for
(a) bleaching powder (b) plaster of paris
(c) baking soda (d) caustic soda

Sol. (b) Common salt is used as raw material for bleaching powder, baking soda and caustic soda.

49. Common salt is used as a raw material in the preparation of washing soda in which the number of molecules of water of crystallisation is
(a) 10 (b) 7 (c) 5 (d) 2

Sol. (a) Washing soda crystals contain 10 molecules of water of crystallisation. It's chemical formula is $Na_2CO_3 \cdot 10H_2O$.

Very Short Answer Type Questions

50 If a few drops of concentrated acid accidentally spills over the hand of a student, what should be done? **NCERT Exemplar**

Sol. Wash the hand immediately with plenty of water and apply a paste of baking soda ($NaHCO_3$). Baking soda is a mild base. Here, a strong base cannot be used to neutralise the acid due to its corrosive nature.

51 A few drops of liquid X were added to distilled water. It was observed that the pH of the water decreased. What could be the liquid sample X?

Sol. Distilled water has pH = 7
X could be any acid like HCl, therefore when it is added to distilled water, pH becomes less than 7.

52 What happens when nitric acid is added to egg shell? **NCERT Exemplar**

Sol. Egg shells contain calcium carbonate. On reacting it with nitric acid, a brisk effervescence of carbon dioxide gas is produced.
The reaction involved is
$CaCO_3(s) + 2HNO_3(aq) \longrightarrow Ca(NO_3)_2(aq) + H_2O(l) + CO_2(g)$

53 During the preparation of hydrogen chloride gas on a humid day, the gas is usually passed through the guard tube containing calcium chloride. What is the role of calcium chloride taken in the guard tube? **NCERT Exemplar**

Sol. The role of calcium chloride ($CaCl_2$) is to absorb moisture from the gas because calcium chloride is a good dehydrating agent.

54 Why does 1M HCl solution have a higher concentration of H^+ ions than 1M CH_3COOH solution?

Sol. 1 M HCl solution will have a higher concentration of H^+ ions than 1 M CH_3COOH because HCl molecules dissociate completely into H^+ ions and Cl^- ions, hence, more H^+ ions are produced. Being a weaker acid, molecules of CH_3COOH do not dissociate completely, thus, less H^+ ions are produced.

55 How does the flow of acid rain water into a river makes the survival of aquatic life in the river difficult?

Sol. Acid rain water, if mixed with river water, will lowers its pH below 5.6, i.e. makes river water acidic. While the living body works normally within a pH range of 7-7.8. That's why, flow of acid rain water into a river makes the survival of aquatic life in the river difficult.

56 Arrange the following in an increasing order of their pH values: NaOH solution, blood, lemon juice.

Sol. Lemon juice (pH = 2.2) < Blood (pH = 7.4) < NaOH (pH = 14)

57 How does a strong acid differ from a concentrated acid?

Sol. The strength of an acid depends upon its dissociation power whereas, concentration depends on water content in the acid.

58 An aqueous solution turns red litmus solution blue. Excess addition of which solution would reverse the change?

Sol. The given solution is alkaline as it changes red litmus blue. When acid is added to the given alkaline solution, first it neutralises the base and further addition of acid makes the solution acidic that turns blue litmus red.

59 Write the name and chemical formula of the products formed by heating gypsum at 373 K.

Sol. The products formed by heating gypsum at 373 K are:
(i) Plaster of Paris or calcium sulphate hemihydrate $\left(CaSO_4 \cdot \frac{1}{2} H_2O\right)$
(ii) Water (H_2O)

Acids, Bases and Salts

60 A solution has pH of 7. Explain how would you
  (i) increase its pH   (ii) decrease its pH?
Sol. (i) pH is increased by adding any alkali to solution.
(ii) pH is decreased by adding any mineral acid to solution.

61 Name two crystalline substances which do not contain water of crystallisation.
Sol. (i) Common salt (NaCl)
(ii) Sugar ($C_{12}H_{22}O_{11}$)

62 Write the chemical name and chemical formual of the salt used to remove permanent hardness of water.
Sol. Sodium carbonate decahydrate is the chemical name with its chemical formual $Na_2CO_3 \cdot 10H_2O$, is used to remove permanent hardness of water.

Short Answer (SA) Type Questions

1 (i) Name one natural source of each of the following acids :
  (a) Citric acid   (b) Oxalic acid
  (c) Lactic acid   (d) Tartaric acid
(ii) Which ion is commonly produced by all acids?

Sol. (i)

Acid	Sources
(a) Citric acid	Lemon juice
(b) Oxalic acid	Tomato
(c) Lactic acid	Curd
(d) Tartaric acid	Tamarind

(ii) All acids produced H^+ ions in an aqueous solution.

2 How the following substances will dissociate to produce ions in their solutions?
  (i) Hydrochloric acid
  (ii) Nitric acid
  (iii) Sulphuric acid
  (iv) Sodium hydroxide
  (v) Potassium hydroxide
  (vi) Magnesium hydroxide   **CBSE 2014**

Sol. Dissociation of various compounds in their solutions
(i) Hydrochloric acid (HCl) (aq)
$$HCl(aq) \rightleftharpoons H^+(aq) + Cl^-(aq)$$
(ii) Nitric acid (HNO_3)
$$HNO_3(aq) \rightleftharpoons H^+(aq) + NO_3^-(aq)$$
(iii) Sulphuric acid (H_2SO_4)
$$H_2SO_4(aq) \rightleftharpoons 2H^+(aq) + SO_4^{2-}(aq)$$
(iv) Sodium hydroxide (NaOH)
$$NaOH(aq) \rightleftharpoons Na^+(aq) + OH^-(aq)$$
(v) Potassium hydroxide (KOH)
$$KOH(aq) \rightleftharpoons K^+(aq) + OH^-(aq)$$
(vi) Magnesium hydroxide [$Mg(OH)_2$]
$$Mg(OH)_2(aq) \rightleftharpoons Mg^{2+}(aq) + 2OH^-(aq)$$

3 Account for the following:
(i) Antacid tablets are used by a person suffering from acidity.
(ii) Toothpaste is used for cleaning teeth.
(iii) Which acid is stinging hair of nettle leaves?

Sol. (i) Antacid tablets generally consist of magnesium hydroxide and aluminium hydroxide which are mild bases. They react chemically with the excess hydrochloric acid produced in stomach and neutralise its effect.
(ii) The toothpastes contain some basic ingredients and they help in neutralising the effect of the acid and also in increasing the pH of the mouth. These toothpastes help in checking corrosion of enamel and decay of teeth.
(iii) Methanoic acid

4 What is observed when sulphur dioxide is passed through (i) water? (ii) lime water? Also write chemical equations for the reactions that takes place.

Sol. (i) When SO_2 is passed through water, sulphurous acid is formed. The aqueous solution of SO_2 turns blue litmus red.
$$\underset{\text{Sulphur dioxide}}{SO_2(g)} + \underset{\text{Water}}{H_2O(l)} \rightleftharpoons \underset{\text{Sulphurous acid}}{H_2SO_3(aq)}$$
(ii) But when SO_2 is passed through lime water, calcium sulphite (white ppt.) is formed, which reacts with excess SO_2 to form calcium hydrogen sulphite.
The chemical equation for the reactions are:
$$\underset{\text{Lime water}}{Ca(OH)_2} + \underset{\text{Sulphur dioxide}}{SO_2} \longrightarrow \underset{\text{Calcium sulphite}}{CaSO_3} + \underset{\text{Water}}{H_2O}$$
$$\underset{\text{Calcium sulphite}}{CaSO_3} + \underset{\text{Water}}{H_2O} + \underset{\text{(Excess)}}{SO_2} \longrightarrow \underset{\text{Calcium bisulphite}}{Ca(HSO_3)_2}$$

5 2 mL of sodium hydroxide solution is added to a few pieces of granulated zinc metal taken in a test tube. When the contents are warmed, a gas evolves which is bubbled through a soap solution before testing. Write the equation of the chemical reaction involved and the test to detect the gas. Name the gas which will be evolved when the same metal reacts with dilute solution of a strong acid. **CBSE 2018**

Sol. 2 mL of sodium hydroxide (NaOH) solution is added to a few pieces of granulated zinc metal taken in a test tube and then contents are warmed. The evolved gas can be identified by bringing a burning splinter near the gas (mouth of the reaction vessel). The gas burns with a pop sound, hence it is a hydrogen gas.

The reaction involved as:

$$\underset{\text{Zinc}}{Zn(s)} + \underset{\substack{\text{Sodium hydroxide}\\(\text{Strong base})}}{2NaOH(aq)} \longrightarrow \underset{\substack{\text{Sodium}\\\text{zincate}}}{Na_2ZnO_2(s)} + \underset{\text{Hydrogen gas}}{H_2(g)\uparrow}$$

If same metal (Zn) reacts will dilute solution of a strong acid then hydrogen gas evolved.

$$\underset{\text{Zinc}}{Zn(s)} + \underset{\text{Hydrochloric acid}}{2HCl(aq)} \longrightarrow \underset{\text{Zinc chloride}}{ZnCl_2} + \underset{\text{Hydrogen gas}}{H_2(g)\uparrow}$$

$$\underset{\text{Zinc}}{Zn(s)} + \underset{\text{Sulphuric acid}}{H_2SO_4(aq)} \longrightarrow \underset{\text{Zinc sulphate}}{ZnSO_4} + \underset{\text{Hydrogen gas}}{H_2(g)\uparrow}$$

6 The pH of a salt used to make tasty and crispy pakoras is 14. Identify the salt and write a chemical equation for its formation. List its two uses. **CBSE 2018**

Sol. The pH of a salt used to make tasty and crispy pakoras is 14. The salt is sodium bicarbonate or sodium hydrogen carbonate. Its formula is $NaHCO_3$. This is also known as baking soda.

The chemical reaction involved as:

$$2NaHCO_3(s) \xrightarrow{\text{Heat}} Na_2CO_3 + H_2O(l) + CO_2\uparrow$$

Uses (i) For making baking powder.
(ii) It is also an ingredient in antacids.

7 What pH do you expect for the following salt solutions and why?

$$NaCl, CuSO_4 \text{ and } Na_2CO_3$$

Sol. NaCl is a salt of strong acid (HCl) and a strong base (NaOH). Therefore, its solution is neutral with pH = 7.

$CuSO_4$ is a salt of strong acid (H_2SO_4) and weak base [$Cu(OH)_2$]. Therefore, its solution is acidic with pH < 7.

Na_2CO_3 is a salt of strong base (NaOH) and weak acid (H_2CO_3). Therefore, its solution is basic with pH > 7.

8 What is tooth enamel chemically? State the condition when it starts corroding. What happens when food particles left in the mouth after eating degrades? Why do doctors suggest use of tooth powder/ toothpaste to prevent tooth decay? **CBSE 2011**

Or Tooth enamel is one of the hardest substances in our body. How does it undergo damage due to the eating of chocolates and sweets? What should we do to prevent it? **CBSE 2012, 10**

Sol. White tooth enamel is calcium phosphate though a very hard substance, which gets affected when the pH of our mouth falls below 5.5.

It happens because the bacteria present in our mouth breakdown sugar and food particles into acids which damage our teeth by corroding them. To prevent the tooth decay, after eating one should clean mouth thoroughly with tooth powder or toothpaste, which is basic in nature. It neutralises the excess of acid produced in the mouth.

9 In the electrolysis of water
(a) Name the gases liberated at anode and cathode.
(b) Why is it that the volume of a gas collected on one electrode is two times that on the other electrode?
(c) What would happen if dil. H_2SO_4 is not added to water?

Sol. (a) The gases liberated at anode and cathode are respectively oxygen gas and hydrogen gas.
(b) The volume of hydrogen liberated at cathode during the electrolysis of water is almost double to that oxygen liberated at anode. This is because, 2 moles of H_2 is liberate at cathode whereas only one mole of O_2 is liberated at anode. The reactions are as follows:

At anode : $2H_2O \longrightarrow O_2 + 4H^+ + 4e^-$

At cathode : $4H_2O + 4e^- \longrightarrow 2H_2 + 4OH^-$

(c) If dilute H_2SO_4 is not added during the electrolysis, then pure water will not be able to ionise completely, as it does not carry enough charge due to lack of ions.

10 Answer the following:
(i) Why is sodium hydrogen carbonate an essential ingredient in most antacids?
(ii) When electricity is passed through an aqueous solution of sodium

chloride, three products are obtained. Why is the process called chlor-alkali process?

Sol. (i) Sodium hydrogen carbonate is an essential ingredient in most antacids because it is slightly alkaline in nature.

(ii) When electricity is passed through an aqueous solution of sodium chloride, the three products are obtained which is hydrogen, chlorine and sodium hydroxide. But this process is called chlor-alkali process because here, chlor stands for chlorine and alkali for sodium hydroxide. The amount of hydrogen obtained is very less, thus, it is not given in the name of the process.

11. (i) A chemical compound X is used in glass and soap industry. Identify the compound and give its chemical formula.

(ii) How many molecules of water of crystallisation are present in compound X?

(iii) How will you prepare the above compound starting from sodium chloride? Write all relevant equations involved in the process. **CBSE 2015**

Sol. (i) The compound (X) is sodium carbonate which is used in glass and soap industry.
Its chemical formula is Na_2CO_3.

(ii) Ten molecules of water of crystallisation (i.e. $10H_2O$) are present in this compound.

(iii) Ammonia and carbon dioxide gas is passed through brine solution (or sodium chloride solution). As a result, a mixture of $NaHCO_3$ and NH_4Cl formed.

$NaCl(s) + NH_3(g) + CO_2(g) + H_2O(l)$
$\longrightarrow NaHCO_3(s) + NH_4Cl(g)$

On heating $NaHCO_3$, sodium carbonate, water and carbon dioxide are formed.

$2NaHCO_3(s) \xrightarrow{\Delta} Na_2CO_3(s) + H_2O(l)$
$+ CO_2(g)$

Anhydrous sodium carbonate is dissolved in water. The solution is concentrated and upon cooling, it gives hydrated sodium carbonate (called washing soda).

$\underset{\text{Soda ash}}{Na_2CO_3(s)} + 10H_2O(l) \longrightarrow \underset{\text{Washing soda}}{Na_2CO_3 \cdot 10H_2O(s)}$

12. A substance X is used as a building material and insoluble in water. When reacts with dil. HCl, it produces a gas which turns lime water milky. Predict the substance and write the chemical equation involved.

Sol. The substance X is $CaCO_3$, used as a building material and insoluble in water. The reaction involve with dil. HCl is:

$\underset{\substack{\text{Calcium} \\ \text{carbonate} \\ (X)}}{CaCO_3(s)} + \underset{\text{Dil.}}{2HCl(aq)} \longrightarrow \underset{\substack{\text{Calcium} \\ \text{chloride}}}{CaCl_2(aq)}$
$+ H_2O(l) + CO_2 \uparrow$

CO_2 when passed through lime water, the lime water turns milky. Due to the formation of white precipitate of $CaCO_3$.

$Ca(OH)_2(aq) + CO_2(g) \longrightarrow CaCO_3(s) + H_2O(l)$

13. During electrolysis of brine, a gas 'G' is liberated at anode. When this gas 'G' is passed through slaked lime, a compound 'C' is formed, which is used for disinfecting drinking water.

(a) Write formula of 'G' and 'C'.
(b) State the chemical equation involved.
(c) What is common name of compound 'C'? Give its chemical name.
CBSE (All India) 2020

Sol. (a) During electrolysis of brine, gas $Cl_2(G)$ is liberated at anode. When Cl_2 reacts with slaked lime, $Ca(OH)_2$ compound $CaOCl_2(C)$ is formed which is used for disinfecting drinking water.
Thus, G and C are respectively Cl_2 and $CaOCl_2$.

(b) The chemical equation involved is as follows
$Ca(OH)_2 + Cl_2 \rightarrow CaOCl_2 + H_2O$

(c) The common name of compound C is bleaching powder and its chemical name is calcium oxychloride $(CaOCl_2)$.

14. Answer the following:

(i) What happens when crystals of washing soda are left open in dry air?
(ii) Name the change that takes place. Which two industries are based on the use of washing soda?
(iii) With the help of balanced chemical equation, state the reaction that takes place when sodium hydrogen carbonate is heated during cooking.
CBSE 2012

Sol. (i) When crystals of washing soda is left open in dry air, it loses water of crystallisation.

(ii) Dehydration takes place and we get anhydrous salt. Sodium carbonate is used in glass and paper industries.

(iii) $2NaHCO_3 \xrightarrow{\text{Heat}} Na_2CO_3 + H_2O + CO_2 \uparrow$

Sodium hydrogen carbonate changes into sodium carbonate with the release of CO_2 gas.

15 (i) Explain how anhydrous copper sulphate can be used to detect the presence of moisture in a liquid?
(ii) What is meant by amphoteric oxide?
(iii) Give the chemical name and formula of chloride of lime.

Sol. (i) Anhydrous copper sulphate is white in colour but turns blue when comes in contact with water. Thus, it can be used to detect the presence of moisture.
(ii) Oxide which can act both as an acid and as a base is called amphoteric oxides.
(iii) Calcium oxychloride ($CaOCl_2$)

16 A dry pellet of a common base B when kept in open absorbs moisture and turns sticky. The compound is also a by-product of chlor-alkali process.
(i) Identify B.
(ii) What type of reaction occurs when B is treated with an acidic oxide?
(iii) Write a balanced chemical equation for one such solution.   **NCERT Exemplar**

Sol. (i) B is sodium hydroxide (NaOH).
(ii) Neutralisation reaction occurs when B is treated with an acidic oxide.
(iii) $2NaOH(s) + CO_2(g) \longrightarrow Na_2CO_3(s) + H_2O(l)$
  (B) Sodium hydroxide   Carbon dioxide (Acidic oxide)   Sodium carbonate (Salt)   Water

17 In one of the industrial processes used for the manufacture of sodium hydroxide, a gas X is formed as by-product.
The gas X reacts with lime water to give a compound Y which is used as a bleaching agent in chemical industry. Identify X and Y by giving the chemical equation of the reactions involved.   **NCERT Exemplar**

Sol. X = Chlorine (Cl_2)
Y = Bleaching powder ($CaOCl_2$)
Equations involved are:
(i) $2NaCl(aq) + 2H_2O(l) \longrightarrow 2NaOH(aq) + Cl_2(g) + H_2(g)$
  Sodium chloride   Water   Sodium hydroxide   Chlorine (X)   Hydrogen gas
(ii) $Cl_2 + Ca(OH)_2 \longrightarrow CaOCl_2 + H_2O$
  Chlorine (X)   Slaked lime (Lime water)   Bleaching powder (Y)   Water

18 A chemical compound 'X' is used in the soap and glass industry. It is prepared from brine.
(a) Write the chemical name, common name and chemical formula of 'X'.
(b) Write the equation involved in its preparation.
(c) What happens when it is treated with water containing Ca or Mg salts?
    CBSE (All India) 2020

Sol. (a) The chemical name of compound 'X' is sodium carbonate. Its common name is washing soda and its chemical formula is $Na_2CO_3 \cdot 10H_2O$.
(b) The equation of its formation are as follows:
$NaCl(aq) + H_2O(l) + CO_2(g) + NH_3(g) \longrightarrow NH_4Cl(g) + NaHCO_3$
  Brine   Carbon dioxide   Ammonium chloride   Sodium bicarbonate

$2NaHCO_3 \xrightarrow{\Delta} Na_2CO_3 + H_2O + CO_2 \uparrow$
  Sodium hydrogen carbonate   Sodium carbonate

(c) When washing soda is treated with water containing Ca or Mg salts, it results into permanent hardness of water.

19 State reason for the following:
(i) Dry HCl gas does not change the colour of the dry blue litmus paper.
(ii) Alcohol and glucose also contain hydrogen, but do not conduct electricity.
(iii) Concentration of H_3O^+ ions is affected when a solution of an acid is diluted.

Sol. (i) Dry HCl gas does not contains free H^+ ions. Hence, it does not change the colour of the dry blue litmus paper.
(ii) Alcohol and glucose contain hydrogen but are not categorised as acids because they do not ionise in the solution to produce H^+ ions and can not conduct electricity.
(iii) When a solution is diluted, the volume of the solution increases but the number of ions remains the same, so concentration of H_3O^+ per unit volume decreases.

20 Identify the acid and base which form sodium hydrogen carbonate. Write chemical equation in support of your answer. State whether this compound is acidic, basic or neutral. Also, write its pH value.   **CBSE 2019**

Sol. Acid = Carbonic acid (H_2CO_3)
Base = Sodium hydroxide (NaOH)

Acids, Bases and Salts

$NaHCO_3 + H_2O \longrightarrow \underset{\text{Strong base}}{NaOH} + \underset{\text{Weak acid}}{H_2CO_3}$

So, sodium hydrogen carbonate is weakly alkaline or basic. Its pH value is 9.

21. A white powder is used by doctors to support fractured bones.
(i) Write the name and chemical formula of the powder.
(ii) How is this powder prepared?
(iii) When this white powder is mixed with water, a hard solid mass is obtained. write a balanced chemical equation for the change.
(iv) Give one more use of this white powder.
CBSE 2019

Sol. (i) Plaster of Paris
(Calcium sulphate hemihydrate)
($CaSO_4 \cdot ½ H_2O$)
(ii) It is obtained by heating gypsum
($CaSO_4 \cdot 2H_2O$) at 373 K.
At this temperature, gypsum loses water molecules and forms plaster of Paris.

$\underset{\text{Gypsum}}{CaSO_4 \cdot \frac{1}{2} H_2O} \xrightarrow[\text{Heat}]{373 K} \underset{\text{Plaster of Paris}}{CaSO_4 \cdot \frac{1}{2} H_2O} + 1\frac{1}{2} H_2O$

(iii) Plaster of Paris is a white powder and on mixing with water, it changes to gypsum giving a hard solid mass.

$\underset{\text{Plaster of Paris}}{CaSO_4 \cdot \frac{1}{2} H_2O} + 1\frac{1}{2} H_2O \longrightarrow \underset{\text{Gypsum}}{CaSO_4 \cdot 2H_2O}$

(iv) It is also used for making decoative pieces and for making designs on ceilings.

22. How is plaster of Paris chemically different from gypsum? How can they be interconverted? Write two uses of Plaster of Paris. **CBSE 2016**

Sol. Plaster of Paris is chemically $CaSO_4 \cdot ½ H_2O$ but gypsum is $CaSO_4 \cdot 2H_2O$. On heating gypsum ($CaSO_4 \cdot 2H_2O$) at 373K, it loses water molecules and becomes calcium sulphate hemihydrate $\left(CaSO_4 \cdot \frac{1}{2} H_2O\right)$.

On mixing with water, plaster of Paris changes to gypsum once again leaving a hard solid mass.
Uses
(i) It is used for making ceiling designs.
(ii) It is used for joining the fractured bones.

23. (i) What happen, when bleaching powder is kept open in air?
(ii) When soap is scrubbed on a stain of curry on a white cloth, why does it become reddish brown and turns yellow again when the cloth is washed with plenty of water.

Sol. (i) We get smell of chlorine because CO_2 present in air reacts with bleaching powder.
$CaOCl_2 + CO_2 \longrightarrow CaCO_3 + CO_2 \uparrow$
(ii) Curry contain turmeric which act as acid-base indicator. Soap is basic in nature. Turmeric turns reddish brown in basic medium. On washing with plenty of water reddish brown colour is removed and yellow turmeric is left.

Long Answer (LA) Type Questions

1. What is water of crystallisation? Write the common name and chemical formula of a commercially important compound which has ten water molecules as water of crystallisation. How is this compound obtained? Write the chemical equation also. List any two uses of this compound.
CBSE 2014

Sol. Water of crystallisation Refer to text on Page 35.
The common name for compound containing ten molecules of water of crystallisation is washing soda and its chemical formula is $Na_2CO_3 \cdot 10 H_2O$.

Preparation
$NaCl(s) + H_2O(l) + CO_2(g) + NH_3(g) \longrightarrow$
$NH_4Cl(g) + NaHCO_3(s)$
$2NaHCO_3(s) \xrightarrow{\text{Heat}} Na_2CO_3(s) + H_2O(l) + CO_2(g) \uparrow$
$Na_2CO_3(s) + 10H_2O(l) \longrightarrow Na_2CO_3 \cdot 10H_2O(s)$

Uses
(i) Used in glass, soap and paper industries.
(ii) Used for removing permanent hardness of water.

2. Give one example in each case:
(i) A basic oxide which is soluble in water.
(ii) A basic oxide which is insoluble in water.
(iii) A weak mineral acid.
(iv) A base which is not an alkali.

(v) A hydrogen containing compound which is not an acid.

Sol. (i) Sodium oxide, Na$_2$O
(ii) Copper (II) oxide, CuO
(iii) Carbonic acid, H$_2$CO$_3$
(iv) Copper (II) hydroxide, Cu(OH)$_2$
(v) Methane, CH$_4$

3 (i) Write three physical properties each of acids and bases. (ii) How will you show with an example that metal oxides are basic in nature? Give chemical equation also.

Sol. (i) **Properties of acids**
(a) Acids are sour in taste.
(b) Acids turns blue litmus to red.
(c) Acids are corrosive in nature.

Properties of bases
(a) Bases have bitter taste.
(b) Bases feels soapy to touch.
(c) Bases turn red litmus to blue.

(ii) The reaction between copper oxide and dil. hydrochloric acid:

$$\underset{\text{Copper oxide}}{CuO(s)} + 2HCl(aq) \longrightarrow \underset{\substack{\text{Copper chloride} \\ \text{(Blue-Green)}}}{CuCl_2(aq)} + \underset{\text{Water}}{H_2O(l)}$$

The colour of the solution becomes blue-green due to the formation of copper (II) chloride.
Metallic oxide, i.e. CuO behaves as a base and forms salt and water when it reacts with an acid like HCl. Hence, metallic oxides are basic in nature.

4 (i) Define a universal indicator. Mention its one use.

(ii) Solution A gives pink colour when a drop of phenolphthalein indicator is added to it.
Solution B gives red colour when a drop of methyl orange is added to it. What type of solutions are A and B and which one of the solutions A and B will have higher pH value.

(iii) Name one salt whose solution has pH more than 7 and one salt whose solution has pH less than 7.

Sol. (i) Universal indicator is a solution of many indicators which shows different colour changes for solutions with different pH values. It is used to test whether a solution is acid or a base. It changes colour according to the pH of the acidic or basic medium.

(ii) As solution A turns pink when phenolphthalein indicator is added, i.e. it is a basic solution. Solution B is acidic as it gives red colour after adding a drop of methyl orange.

The pH value of A is higher as compared to B because basic solution has higher pH value.

(iii) Sodium carbonate (Na$_2$CO$_3$) solution has a pH more than 7 and ammonium chloride (NH$_4$Cl), solution has a pH less than 7.

5 (i) What is meant by pH?

(ii) Two solutions A and B have pH values of 3.0 and 9.5 respectively. Which of these will turn litmus solution from blue to red and which will turn phenolphthalein from colourless to pink?

(iii) Water is a neutral substance. What colour will you get when you add a few drops of universal indicator to a test tube containing distilled water?

Sol. (i) The p in pH stands for potenz which means power in German. pH is a number which indicates the acidic or basic nature of a solution.

(ii) As the pH value of solution A is 3.0, i.e. acidic in nature hence, it turn litmus solution from blue to red and phenolphthalein indicator in basic medium change its colour to pink.

(iii) It turns the universal indicator solution green as its pH value is 7.

6 In the following schematic diagram for the preparation of hydrogen gas as shown in the figure, what would happen if the following changes are made?
NCERT Exemplar

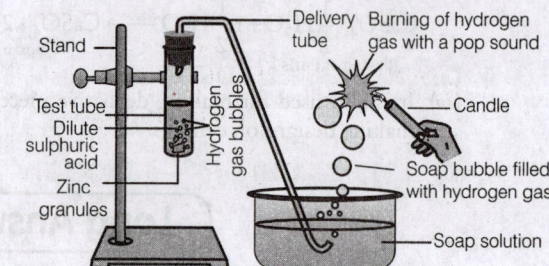

(i) In place of zinc granules, same amount of zinc dust is taken in the test tube.

(ii) Instead of dilute sulphuric acid, dilute hydrochloric acid is taken.

(iii) In place of zinc, copper turnings are taken.

(iv) Sodium hydroxide is taken in place of dilute sulphuric acid and the test tube is heated.

Sol. (i) If same amount of zinc dust is taken in the test tube then the reaction will be comparatively faster and hydrogen gas will evolve with greater speed. It is because zinc dust has larger surface area than zinc granules.

(ii) With dilute hydrochloric acid, almost same amount of gas is evolved.

(iii) With copper turnings, hydrogen gas will not evolve because copper is less reactive, so, it does not react with dil. H_2SO_4 or dil. HCl. Hence, no reaction will take place.

(iv) Zinc also reacts with NaOH. So, if sodium hydroxide is taken, then hydrogen gas will be evolved.

$$\underset{\text{Zinc}}{Zn(s)} + \underset{\text{Sodium hydroxide}}{2NaOH(aq)} \longrightarrow \underset{\text{Sodium zincate}}{Na_2ZnO_2(aq)} + \underset{\text{Hydrogen gas}}{H_2(g)\uparrow}$$

7 A metal carbonate X on heating with an acid gives a gas which when passed through a solution Y gives the carbonate back. On the other hand, a gas G that is obtained at anode during electrolysis of brine is passed on dry Y, it gives a compound Z, used for disinfecting drinking water. Identify X, Y, G and Z. **NCERT Exemplar**

Sol. X is calcium carbonate ($CaCO_3$).
Y is slaked lime [$Ca(OH)_2$].
G is chlorine (Cl_2) gas.
Z is bleaching powder ($CaOCl_2$).
The reactions involved are:

(i) $\underset{(X)}{CaCO_3} + 2HCl \longrightarrow CaCl_2 + \underset{\text{(Acidic gas)}}{CO_2} + H_2O$

(ii) $\underset{(Y)}{CO_2(g) + Ca(OH)_2(aq)} \longrightarrow \underset{(X)}{CaCO_3(s)} + H_2O(g)$

(iii) $2NaCl(aq) + 2H_2O(l) \longrightarrow 2NaOH(aq) + \underset{(G)}{Cl_2(g)} + H_2(g)$

(iv) $\underset{(G)}{Cl_2(g)} + \underset{\substack{\text{(Dry)}\\(Y)}}{Ca(OH)_2(s)} \longrightarrow \underset{(Z)}{CaOCl_2(s)} + H_2O(l)$

8 (i) Identify the acid and the base from which NaCl is obtained. Which type of salt is it? When is it called rock salt? How is rock salt formed?

(ii) Blue litmus solution is added to two test tubes A and B containing dilute HCl and NaOH solution respectively. In which test tube, a colour change will be observed? State the colour change and give its reason.

Or

What is observed when 2 mL of dilute hydrochloric acid is added to 1 g of sodium carbonate taken in a clean and dry test tube? Write chemical equation for the reaction involved. **CBSE 2019**

Sol. (i) Refer to text on page 34 (Common salt).

(ii) Refer to text on page 32 (Some natural indicator with characteristic colours).

Reason As dil. HCl is acidic in nature which turns blue litmus solution to red but dil. NaOH is alkaline in nature and thus, it does not change the colour fo blue litmus solution. (it changes red litmus solution to blue).

Or

Observation CO_2 gas evolves from the reaction mixture. Chemical equation is given as follow:

$$2HCl + Na_2CO_3 \longrightarrow 2NaCl + H_2O + CO_2$$

9 Write the main difference between an acid and a base. With the help of suitable examples, explain the term neutralisation and the formation of **CBSE 2019**

(i) acidic   (ii) basic and
(iii) neutral salts

Sol. Refer to text on pages 30 and 31 (Acids, bases)
(i), (ii), (iii) Refer to text on pages 31, 32, 33 and 34 (Salts).

10 (i) Salt 'P', commonly used in bakery products, on heating gets converted into another salt 'Q' which itself is used for the removal of hardness of water and a gas 'R' is evolved. The gas 'R' when passed through freshly prepared lime water turns milky. Identify 'P', 'Q' and 'R', giving chemical equation for the justification of your answer.

(ii) A solution 'X' gives orange colour when a drop of it falls on pH paper, while another solution 'Y' gives bluish colour when a drop of its falls on pH paper. What is the nature of both the solutions? Determine the pH of solutions 'X' and 'Y'. **CBSE 2019**

Sol. (i) Since, the gas 'R' evolved turned lime water milky. Therefore, it must be carbon dioxide. Moreover, salt 'Q' produced is used for removal of hardness of water, it must be washing soda.
Chemical equations as follow :

$$\underset{'P'}{2NaHCO_3(s)} \xrightarrow{\Delta} \underset{\substack{\text{Sodium carbonate}\\ 'Q'}}{Na_2CO_3(s)} + H_2O(l) + \underset{'R'}{CO_2(g)\uparrow}$$

$$Na_2CO_3(s) + 10H_2O \longrightarrow \underset{'Q'}{Na_2CO_3 \cdot 10H_2O}$$

P : Sodium hydrogen carbonate (Baking soda)
Q : Sodium carbonate (washing soda)
R : Carbon dioxide (CO_2)

(ii) Solution X has pH value around 4 and acidic in nature.
Solution Y has pH value around 10 and basic in nature.

Explanation According to pH colour chart orange colour corresponds to the pH value 4 and bluish colour represent pH value 10. Also, compounds having pH value less than 7 are acidic in nature and which have pH value greater than 7 are basic in nature.

11 Match the following pH values 1, 7, 10, 13 to the solutions given below:
- Milk of magnesia
- Gastric juices
- Brine
- Aqueous sodium hydroxide

Amit and Rita decided to bake a cake and added baking soda to the cake batter.

Explain with a balanced reaction, the role of the baking soda. Mention any other use of baking soda.

Or (i) Four samples A, B, C and D change the colour of pH paper or solution to Green, reddish-pink, blue and Orange. Their pH was recorded as 7, 2, 10.5 and 6 respectively. Which of the samples has the highest amount of Hydrogen ion concentration? Arrange the four samples in the decreasing order of their pH.

(ii) Rahul found that the Plaster of Paris, which he stored in a container, has become very hard and lost its binding nature. What is the reason for this? Also, write a chemical equation to represent the reaction taking place.

(iii) Give any one use of Plaster of Paris other than for plastering or smoothening of walls. **CBSE SQP 2020-21**

Sol. Match of the solutions to their pH values.

Solutions	pH
Milk of magnesia	10
Gastric juices	1
Brine	7
Aqueous sodium hydroxide	13

To bake the cake, we add baking soda into cake batter. It's role is to make the cake pluffy and soft. When cake batter get heated, baking soda get decomposes to form sodium carbonate, water and carbon dioxide. Carbon dioxide makes the cake pluffy.

$$\underset{\text{Baking soda}}{NaHCO_3} \xrightarrow{\Delta} \underset{\substack{\text{Sodium} \\ \text{bicarbonate}}}{Na_2CO_3} + \underset{\text{Water}}{H_2O} + \underset{\substack{\text{Carbon} \\ \text{dioxide}}}{CO_2}$$

Some other uses of baking soda:
(i) It used in fire extinguishers.
(ii) It used as an antacid to neutralise excess acid in stomach.
(iii) It also used to neutralise the effect of acid in insect string.

Or
(i) Recorded pH ⇒ 7, 2, 10.5, 6
of samples ⇒ A B C D

Highest pH value shows the lowest amount of H^+ ions concentration.

Sample B has the highest amount of H^+ ions concentration, as it pH value is the lowest.

The decreasing order of pH values of samples is
C > A > D > B.
10.5 7   6   2

(ii) The Plaster of Paris should be kept in air-tight container. Because on the contracting with moisture, it become hard.

$$\underset{\text{Plaster of Paris}}{CaSO_4 \cdot \frac{1}{2}H_2O} + 1\frac{1}{2}H_2O \longrightarrow \underset{\text{Gypsum}}{CaSO_4 \cdot 2H_2O}$$

(iii) It is used for making decorative pieces and for making designs on ceilings.

CHAPTER EXERCISE

Multiple Type Questions

1. Which of the following statements is not correct?
   NCERT Exemplar
   (a) All metal carbonates react with acid to give a salt, water and carbon dioxide.
   (b) All metal oxides react with water to give salt and acid.
   (c) Some metals react with acids to give salt and hydrogen.
   (d) Some non-metal oxides react with water to form an acid.

2. Equal volumes of hydrochloric acid and sodium hydroxide solutions of same concentration are mixed and the pH of the resulting solution is checked with a pH paper. What would be the colour obtained? (You may use colour guide given in figure of NCERT Book (Science Class X) on page 26). **NCERT Exemplar**
   (a) Red   (b) Yellow
   (c) Yellowish green (d) Blue

3. Common salt besides being used in kitchen can also be used as the raw material for making
   NCERT Exemplar
   (i) washing soda   (ii) bleaching powder
   (iii) baking soda   (iv) slaked lime
   (a) (i) and (ii)
   (b) (i), (ii) and (iv)
   (c) (i), (ii) and (iii)
   (d) (i), (iii) and (iv)

Fill in the Blanks

4. In plaster of Paris .... formula units of $CaSO_4$ share .... molecule of water.

5. The chemical composition of milk of magnesia is ....

6. A blend of several indicators is called a ....

True and False

7. The gas produced when either metal carbonate or bicarbonate are treated with dilute hydrochloric acid extinguishes the lightning splinter.

8. pH of rain water is more than distilled water.

Match the Columns

9. Match the chemical substances given in Column I with their appropriate application given in Column II.

	Column I (Chemical substance)		Column II (Application)
A.	Bleaching powder	1.	Preparation of glass
B.	Baking soda	2.	Production of H_2 and Cl_2
C.	Washing soda	3.	Decolourisation
D.	Sodium chloride	4.	Antacid

Codes   **NCERT Exemplar**
    A B C D   A B C D
(a) 2 1 4 3   (b) 3 2 4 1
(c) 3 4 1 2   (d) 2 4 1 3

Assertion–Reason

Direction (Q. Nos. 10-11) *In each of the following questions, a statement of Assertion is given by the corresponding statement of Reason. Of the statements, mark the correct answer as.*

(a) Both Assertion and Reason are true and Reason is the correct explanation of Assertion.
(b) Both Assertion and Reason are true, but Reason is not the correct explanation of Assertion.
(c) Assertion is true, but Reason is false.
(d) Assertion is false, but Reason is true.

10. **Assertion** The pH of sodium chloride solution is seven.
    Reason Salt of strong acid and a strong base are acidic in nature.

11. **Assertion** On heating, gypsum gets converted into plaster of Paris.
    Reason Gypsum loses water molecules on heating at 373 K temperature.

Case Based Questions

Direction (Q. Nos. 12-15) *Answer the questions on the basis of your understanding of the following passage, table and related studied concepts:*

Nick and Jody were classmates. They both are keen of performing experiment to prove known facts. Their science teacher told them about the tooth decay by the acidic substances. They both tried to prove it separately.

Nick knew that human teeth and eggshells are made of similar substances so he set up an investigation using eggshells.

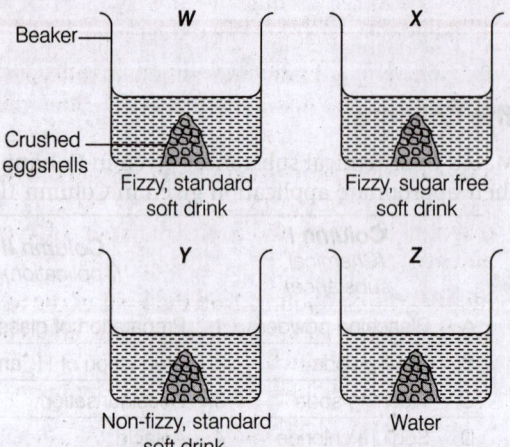

Nick found that the mass of the eggshells in beakers W and X decreased but the mass of the eggshells in beakers Y and Z did not. Jody was investigating the effect of different types of soft drink on human teeth. She used identical shells to model teeth. She put one shell in each type of soft drink for two weeks. To find out how much of the shell has dissolved, Jody measured the mass of the shell before and after the investigation and calculated the change in the mass of the shells.

The table shows the changes in the mass of the shells.

Type of soft drink	Change in mass of shells (g)			
	Trial 1	Trial 2	Trial 3	Trial 4
Cola	2.01	2.03	2.34	2.01
Orange	2.10	2.51	2.16	2.15
Lemonade	1.04	1.06	1.05	1.03
Cream soda	1.07	1.08	1.07	1.07

12 Which of the following is supported by these observations?
(a) Soft drinks cause tooth decay
(b) The sugar in soft drinks causes tooth decay
(c) Children should not be allowed to drink soft drinks
(d) The substance that makes the soft drink fizzy may contribute to tooth decay

13 Why did Nick crush the eggshells?
(a) To increase the surface area of eggshells in contact with the liquid
(b) To make sure that the eggshells were completely covered by liquid
(c) To make it easier to compare the amounts of eggshells in the beaker
(d) To make the eggshells in all the beakers appear to have the same colour

14 According to Jody's table, which type of soft drink will cause the most damage to teeth?

15 What is the best way to prevent tooth decay.

Direction (Q. Nos. 16-19) *Answer the questions on the basis of your understanding of the following passage and related studied concepts:*

If chlorine is passed for a considerable time over solid (slaked lime), the product formed is bleaching powder. Bleaching powder is represented as $CaOCl_2$. It has greater available chlorine than sodium hypochloride NaClo (liquid bleach). If contains about 36% of available chlorine. Bleaching powder deteriorates, if left in contact with the air and smells of chlorine because of action of CO_2 in atmosphere.

It is widely used as a bleaching agent for bleaching clothes. It is used for disinfection of drinking water or swimming pool water. For use in outdoor swimming pool, $CaOCl_2$ can be used as a sanitizer in combination, with cyanuric acid stabilizer. Two stabilizer will reduce the loss of chloride because of VV.

16 How is bleaching powder prepared?

17 Why bleaching powder smell of chlorine?

18 Why $CaOCl_2$ use as an oxidising agent in many chemical industries?

19 How much amount of chlorine is present in bleaching powder?

Answers

1. (b)   **2.** (c)   **3.** (c)   **4.** two, one
5. $Mg(OH)_2$ **6.** universal indicator
7. True   **8.** False   **9.** (c)   **10.** (c)
11. (a)   **12.** (d)   **13.** (a)   **14.** (b)

Very Short Answer Type Questions

20 Name the ion other than ammonium ion formed when ammonia dissolves in water.

21 Name one oxidising agent which is used in many chemical industries.

22 Give two examples of salt belonging to the chloride family.

23 The colour of pH paper changed to light green when a drop of compound is put on it. What will be the colour of pH paper when a pinch of common salt dissolved in a compound?

24 What are the constituents of baking powder?

Acids, Bases and Salts

25 What is the name of the concentrated solution of sodium chloride?

26 Write down the net ionic equation for the reaction of sodium hydroxide with hydrochloric acid.

Short Answer (SA) Type Questions

27 What happens when an acid or a base is added to the water? Why does the beaker appear warm? Why should we always add acid or base to the water and not water to the acid or base?

28 Give reasons:
(i) Use of a mild base like baking soda provides relief on the area stung by honeybee.
(ii) Baking powder is added to make the cakes spongy and soft.
(iii) The colour of blue copper sulphate crystals changes to white on heating.

29 Among sulphurous acid and sulphuric acid, which is stronger and why?

30 (i) State the colour of phenolphthalein in soap solution.
(ii) Name the by-product of chlor-alkali process which is used for the manufacture of bleaching powder.
(iii) Name one indicator which specifies the various level of H^+ ion concentration. **CBSE 2016**

31 Give reason why solution of sulphuric acid conduct electricity whereas, alcohol does not.

Long Answer (LA) Type Questions

32 Answer the following:
(i) What happens when a concentrated solution of sodium chloride is electrolysed? Write the equation of the reaction involved.
(ii) Why is the electrolysis of a concentrated solution of sodium chloride known as chlor-alkali process?
(iii) Name three products of the chlor-alkali process. State two uses of each product.

33 Explain why is hydrochloric acid is called, a strong acid and acetic acid, a weak acid? How can it be verified?

34 State in brief the method of preparation of bleaching powder. Write a balanced chemical equation for the reaction involved and state the uses of bleaching powder.

35 Identify the compound X on the basis of the reactions given below. Also, write the name and chemical formula of A, B and C.

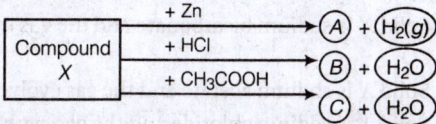

36 Fill in the missing data in the given table.

	Name of the salt	Formula	Salt obtained from Base	Salt obtained from Acid
(i)	Ammonium chloride	NH_4Cl	NH_4OH	—
(ii)	Copper sulphate	—	—	H_2SO_4
(iii)	Sodium chloride	$NaCl$	$NaOH$	—
(iv)	Magnesium nitrate	$Mg(NO_3)_2$	—	HNO_3
(v)	Potassium sulphate	K_2SO_4	—	—
(vi)	Calcium nitrate	$Ca(NO_3)_2$	$Ca(OH)_2$	—

Challengers*

1. Aqueous solution of copper sulphate reacts with aqueous ammonium hydroxide solution to give:
   (a) brown precipitate (b) pale blue precipitate
   (c) white precipitate (d) green precipitate

2. Acetic acid was added to a solid X kept in a test tube. A colourless and odourless gas was evolved. The gas was passed through lime water which turned milky. It was concluded that:
   (a) Solid X is sodium hydroxide and the gas evolved is CO_2
   (b) Solid X is sodium bicarbonate and the gas evolved is CO_2
   (c) Solid X is sodium acetate and the gas evolved is CO_2
   (d) Solid X is sodium chloride and the gas evolved is CO_2

3. Consider the following reaction :

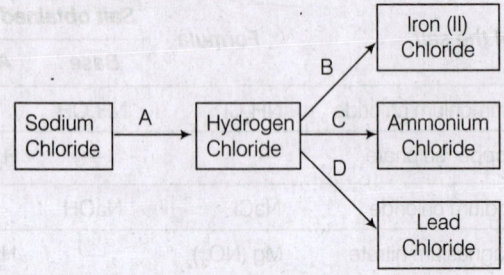

   Here, A, B, C and D respectively are :
   (a) A = Conc. HCl; B = Fe; C = NH_4OH; D = PbO
   (b) A = Conc. H_2SO_4; B = Fe; C = NH_4OH; D = $Pb(NO_3)_2$
   (c) A = Conc. H_2SO_4; B = Fe; C = NH_3; D = $Pb(NO_3)_2$
   (d) A = Conc. HCl; B = Fe; C = NH_3; D = PbO

4. In one of the industrial processes used for manufacture of sodium hydroxide, a gas X is formed as by-product. The gas X reacts with lime water to give a compound Y which is used as a bleaching agent in chemical industry. The compound X and Y could be
   (a) H_2 and $NaHCO_3$ respectively.
   (b) CO_2 and $CaOCl_2$ respectively.
   (c) Cl_2 and $CaOCl_2$ respectively.
   (d) Cl_2 and $NaHCO_3$ respectively.

5. The organic acid present in tomato is
   (a) oxalic acid (b) lactic acid
   (c) malic acid (d) tartaric acid

6. You are having five solutions A, B, C, D and E with pH values as follows :
   A = 1.8, B = 7, C = 8.5, D = 8 and E = 5
   Which solution would be most likely to liberate hydrogen with magnesium powder?
   (a) Solution A and B (b) Solution A
   (c) Solution C (d) All of these

7. The reagent used to distinguish iron (II) chloride and iron (III) chloride is
   (a) distilled water (b) NaOH
   (c) dil. HCl (d) Warm water

8. An acid (A) with sodium hydrogencarbonate is used in making the cakes fluffy and spongy. It is due to the release of (B) gas in the reaction. Here, X and Y are
   (a) A : Oxalic acid (:) B : CO_2
   (b) A : Tartaric acid (:) B : O_2
   (c) A : succinic acid (:) B : H_2
   (d) A : Tartaric acid (:) B : CO_2

9. The pH of a solution is 4.0. What should be the change in the hydrogen ion concentration of the solution, if its pH is to be increased to 5.0.
   (a) decreases to 1/10 of its original concentration
   (b) halved
   (c) doubled
   (d) increases by 10 times

10. The pH of a solution is 5.0. Its hydrogen ion concentration is decreased by 100 times, the solution will be :
    (a) more acidic (b) basic
    (c) neutral (d) unaffected

Answer Key

1.	(b)	2.	(b)	3.	(c)	4.	(c)	5.	(a)
6.	(b)	7.	(b)	8.	(d)	9.	(a)	10.	(c)

*These questions may or may not be asked in the examination, have been given just for additional practice.

- **Melting and boiling points** Metals generally have high melting and boiling points. Tungsten has the highest melting point among metals, while gallium and caesium have very low melting points. These two metals will melt if we keep them on our palm.
- *iii)* **Sonority** The metals that produce a sound on striking a hard surface are said to be sonorous. Using this property, school bells are made up of metals.

Note All metals (except mercury) exist as solid at room temperature.

Chemical Properties of Metals

The different chemical properties of metals are as follows:

1. Reaction of Metals with Oxygen
(Burning in Air or Formation of Oxides)

Almost all metals combine with oxygen (or air) to form metal oxides.

$$\text{Metal} + \text{Oxygen} \longrightarrow \text{Metal oxide}$$

e.g. Aluminium forms aluminium oxide, when heated in air.

$$4Al(s) + 3O_2(g) \xrightarrow{\Delta} 2Al_2O_3(s)$$
Aluminium Oxygen   Aluminium oxide

Similarly, when copper is heated in air, it combines with oxygen to form copper (II) oxide, a black oxide.

$$2Cu(s) + O_2(g) \xrightarrow{\Delta} 2CuO(s)$$
Copper Oxygen   Copper (II) oxide
                       (Black)

Generally, metal oxides are basic in nature.

Exception Some metal oxides such as aluminium oxide, zinc oxide show both acidic and basic behaviour, such metal oxides which react with both acids as well as bases to produce salt and water are called **amphoteric oxides**.

e.g. Aluminium oxide reacts with acids and bases in the following manner:

$$Al_2O_3(s) + 6HCl(aq) \longrightarrow 2AlCl_3(aq) + 3H_2O(l)$$
(Acting as   Hydrochloric acid   Aluminium   Water
basic oxide)   chloride

$$Al_2O_3(s) + 2NaOH(aq) \longrightarrow 2NaAlO_2(aq) + H_2O(l)$$
(Acting as   Sodium   Sodium   Water
acidic oxide) hydroxide   aluminate

Metallic oxides are insoluble in water but some of these dissolve in water to form hydroxides known as **alkali**.

e.g. Sodium oxide and potassium oxide dissolve in water to produce alkalies as follows:

$$Na_2O(s) + H_2O(l) \longrightarrow 2NaOH(aq)$$
Sodium   Water   Sodium hydroxide
oxide   (Alkali)

$$K_2O(s) + H_2O(l) \longrightarrow 2KOH(aq)$$
Potassium oxide Water   Potassium hydroxide
                          (Alkali)

Note Alkalies are the bases that dissolve in water. The aqueous solution of a metallic (basic) oxide turns red litmus solution blue.

Order of Reactivity of Metals with Oxygen

Different metals react with oxygen at different rates, e.g. sodium (Na) and potassium (K) react so vigorously with oxygen that they catches fire if left in the open. Hence, these are the most reactive metals. Therefore, to prevent accidental fires, these metals are kept immersed in kerosene oil. At room temperature, the surfaces of magnesium and aluminium are covered with a thin layer of oxide which prevents the metal from further oxidation. Magnesium (Mg) and aluminium burns in air only by heating.

Zinc (Zn) burns only on strong heating while iron (Fe) does not burn in the form of rod or block but burns in the form of filing only. Copper (Cu) does not burn on heating but blister copper burns. Silver and gold do not react with oxygen even at high temperatures. Hence, the order of reactivity of these metals with oxygen is

$$Na > Mg > Zn > Fe > Cu > Ag$$

Anodising

It is the process of forming a thick oxide layer on the surface of aluminium. Aluminium develops a thin layer of oxide, when left in air. This oxide layer is protective and prevents the metal from further oxidation. This layer can be made more thick by anodising. In this process, clean aluminium article is taken as anode and dil. H_2SO_4 as an electrolyte. When electric current is passed, O_2 gas get liberated, which reacts with metal aluminium to form a thicker layer of oxide on its surface.

2. Reaction of Metals with Water

Metals react with water and produce a metal oxide and hydrogen gas. Metal oxides that are soluble in water dissolves in it further to form metal hydroxide. All metals do not react with water as the metals placed lower in the reactivity series are less reactive towards water.

$$\text{Metal} + \text{Water} \longrightarrow \text{Metal oxide} + \text{Hydrogen gas}$$
$$\text{Metal oxide} + \text{Water} \longrightarrow \text{Metal hydroxide}$$

CHAPTER 03

Metals and Non-Metals

All elements and their large number of compounds are very important in our everyday life. At present about 118 chemical elements are known. On the basis of their properties, all of them can be divided into two main groups, i.e. **metals** and **non-metals**. Apart from these, some elements show properties of both metals and non-metals. These are called **metalloids**.

Chapter Checklist
- Metals
- The Reactivity Series of Metals
- Non-Metals
- Reaction between Metals and Non-Metals (Ionic Bond Formation)
- Occurrence of Metals
- Corrosion

Metals

Those elements which form positive ions by losing electrons are called **metals**. e.g. copper, iron, aluminium, sodium etc.

Physical Properties of Metals

The various physical properties of metals are as follows :

(i) **Metallic lustre** In pure state, metals have a bright shining surface. This property is called metallic lustre. Metals like gold, silver and platinum are known for their shining surface.

(ii) **Hardness** Most of the metals are hard. The hardness varies from metal to metal. Some alkali metals like lithium, sodium and potassium are so soft that they can be easily cut with a knife.

(iii) **Ductility** Metals are generally ductile. It is the property due to which a metal can be drawn into thin wires. Gold is the most ductile metal.

(iv) **Malleability** Most of the metals are malleable. It is the property of metal due to which it can be beaten into thin sheets. Gold and silver are the most malleable metals.

(v) **Electrical conductivity** Most of the metals are good conductors of electricity in solid state. However, conductivity may vary from one metal to another.
The conduction of electricity or flow of electric current occurs due to the flow of free electrons present in the metal.

(vi) **Good conductor of heat** Generally metals are good conductors of heat, except lead and mercury, which are poor conductors of heat. Metals like copper and silver are the best conductors of heat.

CHAPTER 03

Metals and Non-Metals

All elements and their large number of compounds are very important in our everyday life. At present about 118 chemical elements are known. On the basis of their properties, all of them can be divided into two main groups, i.e. **metals** and **non-metals**. Apart from these, some elements show properties of both metals and non-metals. These are called **metalloids**.

Chapter Checklist
- Metals
- The Reactivity Series of Metals
- Non-Metals
- Reaction between Metals and Non-Metals (Ionic Bond Formation)
- Occurrence of Metals
- Corrosion

Metals

Those elements which form positive ions by losing electrons are called **metals**.
e.g. copper, iron, aluminium, sodium etc.

Physical Properties of Metals

The various physical properties of metals are as follows :

(i) **Metallic lustre** In pure state, metals have a bright shining surface. This property is called metallic lustre. Metals like gold, silver and platinum are known for their shining surface.

(ii) **Hardness** Most of the metals are hard. The hardness varies from metal to metal. Some alkali metals like lithium, sodium and potassium are so soft that they can be easily cut with a knife.

(iii) **Ductility** Metals are generally ductile. It is the property due to which a metal can be drawn into thin wires. Gold is the most ductile metal.

(iv) **Malleability** Most of the metals are malleable. It is the property of metal due to which it can be beaten into thin sheets. Gold and silver are the most malleable metals.

(v) **Electrical conductivity** Most of the metals are good conductors of electricity in solid state. However, conductivity may vary from one metal to another.
The conduction of electricity or flow of electric current occurs due to the flow of free electrons present in the metal.

(vi) **Good conductor of heat** Generally metals are good conductors of heat, except lead and mercury, which are poor conductors of heat. Metals like copper and silver are the best conductors of heat.

(vii) **Melting and boiling points** Metals generally have high melting and boiling points. Tungsten has the highest melting point among metals, while gallium and caesium have very low melting points. These two metals will melt if we keep them on our palm.

(viii) **Sonority** The metals that produce a sound on striking a hard surface are said to be sonorous. Using this property, school bells are made up of metals.

Note All metals (except mercury) exist as solid at room temperature.

Chemical Properties of Metals

The different chemical properties of metals are as follows :

1. Reaction of Metals with Oxygen
(Burning in Air or Formation of Oxides)

Almost all metals combine with oxygen (or air) to form metal oxides.

$$\text{Metal} + \text{Oxygen} \longrightarrow \text{Metal oxide}$$

e.g. Aluminium forms aluminium oxide, when heated in air.

$$\underset{\text{Aluminium}}{4Al(s)} + \underset{\text{Oxygen}}{3O_2(g)} \xrightarrow{\Delta} \underset{\text{Aluminium oxide}}{2Al_2O_3(s)}$$

Similarly, when copper is heated in air, it combines with oxygen to form copper (II) oxide, a black oxide.

$$\underset{\text{Copper}}{2Cu(s)} + \underset{\text{Oxygen}}{O_2(g)} \xrightarrow{\Delta} \underset{\substack{\text{Copper (II) oxide}\\\text{(Black)}}}{2CuO(s)}$$

Generally, metal oxides are basic in nature.

Exception Some metal oxides such as aluminium oxide, zinc oxide show both acidic and basic behaviour, such metal oxides which react with both acids as well as bases to produce salt and water are called **amphoteric oxides**.

e.g. Aluminium oxide reacts with acids and bases in the following manner:

$$\underset{\substack{\text{(Acting as}\\\text{basic oxide)}}}{Al_2O_3(s)} + \underset{\text{Hydrochloric acid}}{6HCl(aq)} \longrightarrow \underset{\substack{\text{Aluminium}\\\text{chloride}}}{2AlCl_3(aq)} + \underset{\text{Water}}{3H_2O(l)}$$

$$\underset{\substack{\text{(Acting as}\\\text{acidic oxide)}}}{Al_2O_3(s)} + \underset{\substack{\text{Sodium}\\\text{hydroxide}}}{2NaOH(aq)} \longrightarrow \underset{\substack{\text{Sodium}\\\text{aluminate}}}{2NaAlO_2(aq)} + \underset{\text{Water}}{H_2O(l)}$$

Metallic oxides are insoluble in water but some of these dissolve in water to form hydroxides known as **alkali**.

e.g. Sodium oxide and potassium oxide dissolve in water to produce alkalies as follows :

$$\underset{\substack{\text{Sodium}\\\text{oxide}}}{Na_2O(s)} + \underset{\text{Water}}{H_2O(l)} \longrightarrow \underset{\substack{\text{Sodium hydroxide}\\\text{(Alkali)}}}{2NaOH(aq)}$$

$$\underset{\text{Potassium oxide}}{K_2O(s)} + \underset{\text{Water}}{H_2O(l)} \longrightarrow \underset{\substack{\text{Potassium hydroxide}\\\text{(Alkali)}}}{2KOH(aq)}$$

Note Alkalies are the bases that dissolve in water. The aqueous solution of a metallic (basic) oxide turns red litmus solution blue.

Order of Reactivity of Metals with Oxygen

Different metals react with oxygen at different rates, e.g. sodium (Na) and potassium (K) react so vigorously with oxygen that they catches fire if left in the open. Hence, these are the most reactive metals. Therefore, to prevent accidental fires, these metals are kept immersed in kerosene oil. At room temperature, the surfaces of magnesium and aluminium are covered with a thin layer of oxide which prevents the metal from further oxidation. Magnesium (Mg) and aluminium burns in air only by heating.

Zinc (Zn) burns only on strong heating while iron (Fe) does not burn in the form of rod or block but burns in the form of filing only. Copper (Cu) does not burn on heating but blister copper burns. Silver and gold do not react with oxygen even at high temperatures. Hence, the order of reactivity of these metals with oxygen is

$$Na > Mg > Zn > Fe > Cu > Ag$$

Anodising

It is the process of forming a thick oxide layer on the surface of aluminium. Aluminium develops a thin layer of oxide, when left in air. This oxide layer is protective and prevents the metal from further oxidation. This layer can be made more thick by anodising. In this process, clean aluminium article is taken as anode and dil. H_2SO_4 as an electrolyte. When electric current is passed, O_2 gas get liberated, which reacts with metal aluminium to form a thicker layer of oxide on its surface.

2. Reaction of Metals with Water

Metals react with water and produce a metal oxide and hydrogen gas. Metal oxides that are soluble in water dissolves in it further to form metal hydroxide. All metals do not react with water as the metals placed lower in the reactivity series are less reactive towards water.

$$\text{Metal} + \text{Water} \longrightarrow \text{Metal oxide} + \text{Hydrogen gas}$$

$$\text{Metal oxide} + \text{Water} \longrightarrow \text{Metal hydroxide}$$

Metals and Non-Metals

e.g.

(i) Metals like potassium and sodium react violently with cold water. In case of sodium and potassium, the reaction is very violent and exothermic.

$$2K(s) + 2H_2O(l) \longrightarrow 2KOH(aq) + H_2(g) + Heat$$
Potassium (Cold) — Potassium hydroxide — Hydrogen

$$2Na(s) + 2H_2O(l) \longrightarrow 2NaOH(aq) + H_2(g) + Heat$$
Sodium (Cold) — Sodium hydroxide — Hydrogen

The heat evolved is sufficient for hydrogen to catch fire. That's why, Na and K catch fire when kept in water. Therefore, both these metals are kept in 'kerosene' in order to avoid contact with both air and water.

(ii) The reaction of calcium with water is less violent. The heat evolved is not sufficient for the hydrogen to catch fire.

$$Ca(s) + 2H_2O(l) \longrightarrow Ca(OH)_2(aq) + H_2(g)$$
Calcium Water (Cold) — Calcium hydroxide — Hydrogen

Calcium (Ca) floats over water because the bubbles of hydrogen gas formed stick on the surface of the metal.

(iii) Metals like aluminium, iron and zinc do not react either with cold or hot water. They react with steam and form the metal oxide and hydrogen.

$$2Al(s) + 3H_2O(g) \longrightarrow Al_2O_3(s) + 3H_2(g)$$
Aluminium (Steam) — Aluminium oxide — Hydrogen

$$3Fe(s) + 4H_2O(g) \longrightarrow Fe_3O_4(s) + 4H_2(g)$$
Iron (Steam) — Ferrous oxide — Hydrogen

(iv) Lead, copper, silver and gold do not react with water at all. Thus, the reactivity order of metals toward water is

K > Na > Ca > Mg > Al > Fe > Pb > Cu > Ag > Au

3. Reaction of Metals with Acids

(i) **Reaction of metals with dil. HCl** Except a few less reactive metals (such as Cu, Hg, Ag, Au, Pt etc), all metals react with dilute sulphuric acid and hydrochloric acid to produce salt and hydrogen gas.

Metal + Dilute acid ⟶ Salt + Hydrogen

e.g. $Zn(s) + 2HCl(aq) \longrightarrow ZnCl_2(aq) + H_2(g)\uparrow$
Zinc (Dil.) — Zinc chloride — Hydrogen gas

Note The rate of formation of hydrogen gas bubbles decreases in the order Mg > Al > Zn > Fe. This shows the decreasing chemical reactivity of the given metals with dilute hydrochloric acid.

(ii) **Reaction of metals with dil. HNO$_3$** Hydrogen gas is not evolved when a metal reacts with nitric acid. This is due to strong oxidising nature of nitric acid. It oxidises the H$_2$ produced to water and itself get reduced to any of the nitrogen oxide (N$_2$O, NO, NO$_2$). But magnesium (Mg) and manganese (Mn) react with very dil. HNO$_3$ to evolve H$_2$ gas.

$$Metal + HNO_3 \longrightarrow Salt + NO_2/N_2O\uparrow + H_2O$$
(Dil.)

Exceptional case (Only for Mn and Mg)

$$Metal\,(Mn/Mg) + HNO_3 \longrightarrow Salt + H_2\uparrow$$
(Dil.)

> **Aqua-regia** (Latin for 'royal water')
> It is a freshly prepared mixture of concentrated hydrochloric acid and concentrated nitric acid in the ratio of 3 : 1. It can dissolve gold, even though neither of these acids can do so alone. *Aqua-regia* is a highly corrosive, fuming liquid. It is one of the few reagents that is able to dissolve gold and platinum.

4. Reaction of Metals with Solutions of Other Metal Salts

Reactive metals can displace a comparatively less reactive metal from its compounds in aqueous salt solution or in molten form. General equation is,

Metal A + Salt solution of B
⟶ Salt solution of A + Metal B

e.g. $Cu(s) + 2AgNO_3(aq) \longrightarrow Cu(NO_3)_2(aq) + 2Ag(s)$
Copper — Silver nitrate — Copper nitrate — Silver

This type of reaction is called displacement reaction.

Check Point 01

1. What are metalloids?
2. State True or False for the following statements:
   Metalloids are the elements which shows properties of both metals and non-metal.
3. Fill in the blank:
   Among the metals, ... have the highest melting point.
4. Some metals melt on keeping them on palm. Why? Also give an example.
5. An element X is soft and can be cut with a knife easily. This is very reactive with air and cannot be kept open with air. It reacts vigorously with water. Name the element X.
6. Write a chemical reaction for metals with dil. HCl.
7. Name the reagent which is able to dissolve gold and platinum.

The Reactivity Series of Metals

The reactivity series is a list of metals arranged in the order of their decreasing activities. On the basis of their relative tendency to lose electron and their reactive nature, metals are arranged in a series, this series is called **activity series** or **reactivity series of metals**.

The metals that are placed above hydrogen are called **most reactive metals** (e.g. K, Na, Ca etc.) and the metals that are placed below hydrogen are called **least reactive metals** (e.g. noble metals, i.e. gold and platinum).

Reactivity Series (activity series) of Metals

These metals are more reactive than hydrogen	K	Potassium	(Most reactive metal)
	Na	Sodium	
	Ca	Calcium	
	Mg	Magnesium	
	Al	Aluminium	
	Zn	Zinc	
	Fe	Iron	
	Sn	Tin	
	Pb	Lead	
	H	Hydrogen	
These metals are less reactive than hydrogen	Cu	Copper	
	Hg	Mercury	
	Ag	Silver	
	Au	Gold	(Least reactive metal)

(Decreasing chemical reactivity)

Note Hydrogen also have non-metallic properties but, due to its electropositive nature, it has been placed in the reactivity series.

Non-Metals

Those elements which form negative ions by gaining electrons are called **non-metals**, e.g. iodine, sulphur, oxygen, hydrogen etc. The non-metals are either solids or gases except bromine which is a liquid.

Physical Properties of Non-metals

The various physical properties of metals are as follows :
(i) **Malleability and ductility** Non-metals are neither malleable nor ductile, i.e. they cannot be beaten into thin sheets or drawn into wires.

(ii) **Brittleness** Non-metals are brittle in nature. For instance, sulphur is a brittle solid. If it is hammered, it breaks into pieces.

(iii) **Physical state** Most of the non-metals are soft (if solid). Only diamond, an allotropic form of carbon is the hardest known substance.

(iv) **Lustre** Non-metals do not have lustre, i.e. shining surface. However, diamond, graphite (the allotropic forms of carbon) and iodine have lustre, even though they are non-metals.

(v) **Electrical and thermal conductivity** Non-metals are generally poor conductors of heat and electricity. Graphite, an allotrope of carbon, is a good conductor of electricity.

(vi) **Melting and boiling points** Generally, non-metals have low melting and boiling points. But non-metals that are solids have comparatively higher boiling points, e.g. B, Si, C etc.

Note The non-metals are either solids or gases except bromine (liquid).
The gases like nitrogen, oxygen, carbon dioxide etc., which constitute air are all poor conductors of electricity.

Chemical Properties of Non-metals

Non-metals do not react with water, steam or dilute acids to evolve hydrogen gas.

The reason is that they act as an electron acceptor and cannot supply electrons to the H^+ ions of acids to reduce them to hydrogen gas. But on heating, readily form oxides or salts with conc. acids.

$$S(s) + 2H_2SO_4 \text{ (conc.)} \xrightarrow{\text{Heat}} 3SO_2(g) + 2H_2O(l)$$

$$S(s) + 6HNO_3 \text{ (conc.)} \xrightarrow{\text{Heat}} H_2SO_4(aq) + 6NO_2(g) + 2H_2O(aq)$$
(Reddish brown vapour)

Non-metals also show displacement reaction like metals.

e.g. $\underset{\text{Chlorine}}{Cl_2(g)} + \underset{\text{Sodium bromide}}{2NaBr(l)} \longrightarrow \underset{\text{Sodium chloride}}{2NaCl(l)} + \underset{\text{Bromine}}{Br_2(g)}$

Note Most of the non-metal produces acidic oxides when dissolved in water.

Check Point 02

1. Fill in the blank:
   Iron is a .... reactive metal than tin.
2. Do non-metals possess lustre? Give two exceptions of this property of non-metal.
3. Give an example of a non-metal which is
   (i) hardest known substance.
   (ii) a good conductor of heat and electricity.
4. Non-metals do not evolve hydrogen gas when react with water, steam or dilute acids. Why?
5. Write the product by giving balanced chemical equation :
   (i) When sulphur reacts with conc. nitric acid.
   (ii) When phosphorus reacts with conc. sulphuric acid.
   (iii) When phosphorus reacts with conc. nitric acid.

Reaction between Metals and Non-Metals (Ionic Bond Formation)

Each element wants to have a completely filled valence shell, i.e. it wants to have either 2 or 8 electrons in their outermost shell.

Metals have a tendency to loose electrons to form **cations** (+ve ions) and non-metals have a tendency to gain electrons to form **anions** (-ve ions). When metals and non-metals react with each other then both of them tries to achieve completely filled outermost shell by the transfer of electrons.

This type of chemical bond formed by the complete transfer of electrons from one atom to another is called **ionic bond**. Such compounds are called **ionic compounds**.

e.g. electronic configuration of **sodium** (which is a metal) is $\begin{smallmatrix}K&L&M\\2,&8,&1\end{smallmatrix}$ and in order to complete its octet, (i.e. 8 electrons in the outermost shell), it is easier for sodium to loose one electron from the M-shell rather than accepting 7 electrons in it.

Thus, it has a tendency to loose one electron to have completely filled valence shell. Similarly, if we see the electronic configuration of **chlorine** (configuration $\begin{smallmatrix}K&L&M\\2,&8,&7\end{smallmatrix}$, a non-metal), we found that it is easier for chlorine to gain one electron in its M-shell rather than losing 7 electrons from it. So, it has a tendency to gain electrons to have completely filled orbitals.

If sodium and chlorine reacts with each other then electron lost by sodium (Na^+) is gained by chlorine (Cl^-). Na^+ and Cl^- ions being oppositely charged, attract each other and held by strong electrostatic forces of attraction to exist as NaCl. Thus, an **ionic bond** is formed between them.

$$Na_{(2,8,1)} \longrightarrow Na^+_{(2,8)} + e^-$$
(Sodium cation)

$$Cl + e^-_{(2,8,7)} \longrightarrow Cl^-_{(2,8,8)}$$
(Chloride anion)

$$Na^{\bullet} + {}^{\times}_{\times}\overset{\times\times}{\underset{\times\times}{Cl}}{}^{\times} \longrightarrow [Na^+] \left[{}^{\times}_{\times}\overset{\times\times}{\underset{\times\times}{Cl}}{}^{\times} \right]^-$$

or $\quad Na^+ Cl^-$ or NaCl

Thus, it is also clear that ionic compounds (like sodium chloride) do not exist as discrete molecules but indeed they are the aggregates of oppositely charged ions.

Formation of ionic bond can further be understood by taking an another example of magnesium chloride (where magnesium is a metal and chlorine is a non-metal).

$$Mg_{(2,8,2)} \longrightarrow Mg^{2+}_{(2,8)} + 2e^-$$
(Magnesium cation)

$$Cl + e^-_{(2,8,7)} \longrightarrow Cl^-_{(2,8,8)}$$
(Chloride anion)

$$Mg^{\bullet}_{\bullet} + \overset{\times\times}{\underset{\times\times}{Cl}}{}^{\times}_{\times} \;\; \overset{\times\times}{\underset{\times\times}{Cl}}{}^{\times}_{\times} \longrightarrow (Mg^{2+}) \left[{}^{\times}_{\times}\overset{\times\times}{\underset{\times\times}{Cl}}{}^{\times} \right]^-_2$$

Properties of Ionic Compounds

(i) **Physical nature** Ionic compounds are hard crystalline solids because of strong forces of attraction between the positive and negative ions. These compounds are generally brittle and break into pieces when pressure is applied.

(ii) **Melting and boiling points** These compounds have high melting and boiling points as large amount of energy is required to break strong inter-ionic attraction.

(iii) **Solubility** These compounds are soluble in water (polar solvent) and insoluble in organic solvents (non-polar solvent) like kerosene, benzene, ether, petrol etc. As water is polar in nature it helps in separation of oppositely charged ions from their ionic compound.

(iv) **Conduction of electricity** The conduction of electricity through a solution involves movement of charged particles. Ionic or electrovalent compounds are good conductors of electricity, but they conduct electricity either in molten form or in their aqueous solution. A solution of an ionic compound in water contain ions, which move to the oppositely charged electrode when electricity is passed through it.

In molten form, the electrostatic forces of attraction between oppositely charged ions are overcome due to heat. This is the reason due to which ions move freely and conduct electricity. They do not conduct electricity in solid form because movement of ions in the solid state is not possible due to their rigid structure.

Check Point 03

1. A non-metal gains electrons to form anions. What do you mean by this statement?
2. State True or False for the following statements:
   Ionic bonds are formed only by the partial transfer of electrons from one atom to another.
3. Water helps in separation of oppositely charged ions from their ionic compound. Give reason.
4. Ionic compounds are crystalline solids and brittle. Why?
5. Why ions move freely and conduct electricity in the molten form?

Occurrence of Metals

The earth's crust is the major source of metals. Sea water also contains soluble salts like sodium chloride, magnesium chloride, etc.

The elements or compounds which occur naturally in the earth crust are known as **minerals**. Those minerals from which metals can be extracted profitably are called **ores**.

Extraction of Metals

The process of obtaining pure metal from its ore is called **extraction of metals**. Some metals are found in earth's crust in free state while some are found in the form of their compounds.

The metals present at the bottom of the reactivity series are least reactive, so they are found in free state, e.g. gold, silver, platinum, copper etc. Copper and silver are also found in the form of combined state as their sulphide or oxide ores. The metals at the top of the reactivity series (K, Na, Ca, Mg and Al) are highly reactive, so they are not found in nature as free elements.

The metals in the middle of the reactivity series (Zn, Fe, Pb, etc.) are moderately reactive and they are found as oxides, sulphides or carbonates in the earth's crust. Ores of many metals are oxide, as oxygen is very reactive element and is very abundant on the earth.

Thus, the different techniques used for extraction of metals depend upon their position in the activity series and is divided into three categories :

(i) Metals of low reactivity
(ii) Metals of medium reactivity
(iii) Metals of high reactivity

Summary of several steps involved in the extraction of pure metal from their ores is given below in the form of flow chart followed by their detailed description:

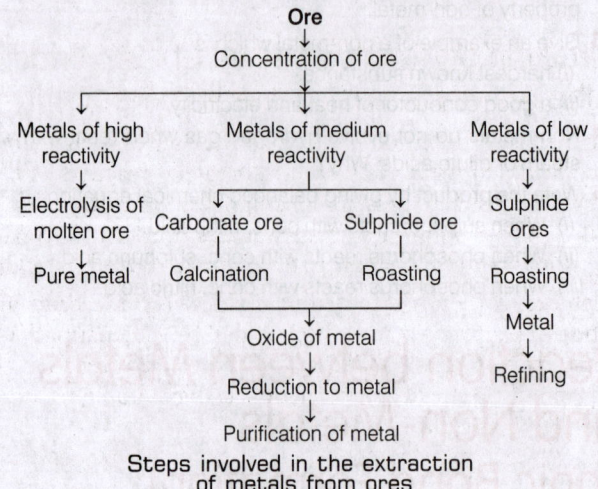

Steps involved in the extraction of metals from ores

Enrichment of Ores

The undesirable impurities like soil, sand, etc., found in ore are called **gangue or matrix**. Removal of gangue from the ore is called enrichment or concentration of ore.

The processes used for the removing the gangue from an ore are based on the differences between the physical and chemical properties of the gangue and the ore.

Depending upon the nature of impurities, different-separation techniques for enrichment of ores are employed.

Extraction of Metals (Present at the Bottom of the Activity Series) of Low Reactivity

These metals, being less reactive, can be obtained by reducing their oxides to metals by heating alone.

(i) **Cinnabar** (HgS) It is an ore of mercury. When heated in air, it first changes into its oxide, HgO and then reduced into mercury metal on further heating.

e.g. $\underset{\text{Cinnabar}}{2HgS(s)} + \underset{\text{(From air)}}{3O_2(g)} \xrightarrow{\Delta} \underset{\substack{\text{Mercury}\\\text{oxide}}}{2HgO(s)} + \underset{\substack{\text{Sulphur}\\\text{dioxide}}}{2SO_2(g)}$

$\underset{\text{Mercury (II) oxide}}{2HgO(s)} \xrightarrow{\Delta} \underset{\substack{\text{Mercury}\\\text{metal}}}{2Hg(l)} + \underset{\text{Oxygen}}{O_2(g)}$

(ii) **Copper glance** (Cu_2S) When it is heated in air, partially gets oxidised and then the oxidised product reacts with the remaining copper glance to give copper metal.

Metals and Non-Metals

e.g. $\underset{\text{Copper glance}}{2Cu_2S(s)} + \underset{\text{(From air)}}{3O_2(g)} \xrightarrow{\Delta} \underset{\text{Copper oxide}}{2Cu_2O(s)} + \underset{\substack{\text{Sulphur}\\\text{dioxide}}}{2SO_2(g)}$

$\underset{\text{Copper oxide}}{2Cu_2O(s)} + \underset{\substack{\text{Copper}\\\text{sulphide}}}{Cu_2S(s)} \xrightarrow{\Delta} \underset{\text{Copper metal}}{6Cu(s)} + \underset{\substack{\text{Sulphur}\\\text{dioxide}}}{SO_2(g)}$

Extraction of Metals (Present at the Middle of the Activity Series) of Medium Reactivity

The metals in the middle of the activity series such as iron, zinc, lead, copper, etc., are moderately reactive. These metals are usually present as sulphides or carbonates in nature. These sulphides or carbonates are first converted into oxides because it is easy to extract metals from its oxide.

Sulphides are converted into oxides by roasting and carbonates are converted into oxides by calcination. The metal oxides thus obtained are then reduced to the corresponding metals by reduction using suitable reducing agents such as carbon.

Chemical reactions involved in the roasting and calcination of zinc ores are as follows:

(i) **Roasting** It is the process in which a sulphide ore is heated below its melting point in the presence of excess air to convert it into metal oxide.

e.g. $\underset{\substack{\text{Zinc}\\\text{sulphide}}}{2ZnS(s)} + \underset{\substack{\text{Oxygen}\\\text{(from air)}}}{3O_2(s)} \xrightarrow[\Delta]{\text{Roasting}} \underset{\substack{\text{Zinc}\\\text{oxide}}}{2ZnO(s)} + \underset{\substack{\text{Sulphur}\\\text{dioxide}}}{2SO_2(g)}$

(ii) **Calcination** It is a process in which a carbonate ore is heated below its melting point in the absence of air to convert it into metal oxide.

e.g. $\underset{\substack{\text{Zinc}\\\text{carbonate}}}{ZnCO_3(s)} \xrightarrow[\Delta]{\text{Calcination}} \underset{\substack{\text{Zinc}\\\text{oxide}}}{ZnO(s)} + \underset{\substack{\text{Carbon}\\\text{dioxide}}}{CO_2(g)}$

(iii) **Reduction of oxide ore** It is the process of conversion of metal oxide ore into metal. It can be done by heating the oxides with suitable reducing agents like carbon in the form of coke.

$\underset{\text{Zinc oxide}}{ZnO(s)} + \underset{\text{Coke}}{C(s)} \longrightarrow \underset{\text{Zinc}}{Zn(s)} + \underset{\substack{\text{Carbon}\\\text{monoxide}}}{CO(g)}$

Sometime displacement reactions can also be used to reduce metal oxides to metals. The highly reactive metals such as sodium, calcium, aluminium etc., are used as reducing agents because they can displace metals of lower reactivity from their compounds,

e.g. Reaction of manganese dioxide with aluminium powder.

$\underset{\substack{\text{Manganese}\\\text{oxide}}}{3MnO_2(s)} + \underset{\text{Aluminium}}{4Al(s)} \longrightarrow \underset{\text{Manganese}}{3Mn(l)} + \underset{\substack{\text{Aluminium}\\\text{oxide}}}{2Al_2O_3(s)} + \text{Heat}$

These displacement reactions are highly exothermic. The amount of heat produced is so high that the metals are produced in the molten state. The reaction of iron (III) oxide (Fe_2O_3) with aluminium to produce iron is used to join railway tracks or cracked machine parts. This process is called **thermite welding**.

$\underset{\text{Ferric oxide}}{Fe_2O_3(s)} + \underset{\text{Aluminium}}{2Al(s)} \longrightarrow \underset{\text{Iron}}{2Fe(l)} + \underset{\substack{\text{Aluminium}\\\text{oxide}}}{Al_2O_3(s)} + \text{Heat}$

This reaction of metal oxide to form metal by using aluminium powder as a reducing agent is known as **thermite reaction**.

Extraction of Metals (At the Top of the Activity Series) of High Reactivity

The metallic compounds at the top of the activity series cannot be reduced by carbon or any other reducing agent due to their high affinity with oxygen. Therefore, electrolytic reduction is employed for metals like Na, Mg, Ca etc.

Electrolytic reduction The salts of these metals like chlorides in molten form are electrolysed. Metal is deposited at the cathode (the negative electrode) and chlorine is liberated at the anode (the positive electrode).

The reactions are as follows :

At cathode $Na^+ + e^- \longrightarrow Na$ (Reduction)

At anode $2Cl^- \longrightarrow Cl_2 + 2e^-$ (Oxidation)

Similarly, aluminium is obtained by the electrolytic reduction of molten aluminium oxide also (called **alumina**).

Refining of Metals

It is the process of purification of the metal obtained after reduction. Various methods for refining are employed, but the most common one is the **electrolytic refining**.

Electrolytic Refining

Many metals like Cu, Zn, Ni, Ag, Au etc., are refined electrolytically.

Process In this process, a thick block of impure metal is used as anode and a thin strip of pure metal is used as cathode. A solution of metal salt (to be refined) is used as an electrolyte. When electric current is passed, metal ions from the electrolyte are reduced as metal which get deposited on the cathode. An equivalent amount of pure metal from the anode gets oxidised to metal ion and goes into the electrolyte and from there it goes to cathode and deposit.

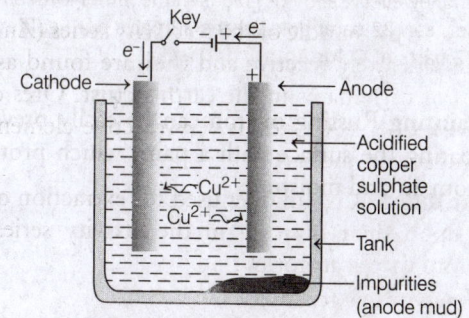

Electrolytic refining of copper

This cycle is repeated until whole of the metal ion from impure block is dissolved and deposited on cathode. The soluble impurities go into the solution, whereas the insoluble impurities settle down below anode and are known as **anode mud**, e.g. in electrolytic refining of crude copper. Here, anode is impure copper whereas cathode is a strip of pure copper. The electrolyte is a solution of acidified $CuSO_4$. On passing electric current, pure copper is deposited on the cathode.

Corrosion

It is the slow process of eating away of metals by the reaction of atmospheric air and moisture, e.g. rusting of iron, tarnishing of silver, formation of green coating over copper etc.

Prevention of Corrosion

Rusting of iron is prevented by galvanising, by making alloys, painting, greasing or oiling and tin-plating and chrome plating (chromium plating) which are explained below :

- **Galvanisation** It is the process of coating iron and steel objects with a thin layer of zinc. It is done by dipping the object in molten zinc. The galvanised article is protected against rusting even if the zinc coating is broken.
- **Alloying** It is the method of improving the properties of a metal by mixing the metal with another metal or non-metal.
- **Alloying of iron** Pure iron is very soft and stretches easily when hot. It is mixed with a small amount of carbon (about 0.05%) and it becomes hard and strong. Iron is mixed with many metals to form different alloys. For e.g. when iron is mixed with nickel and chromium, stainless steel is obtained, which is hard and does not rust.

Alloying of gold

Pure gold is very soft. It is called 24 carat gold. To increase the strength and hardness of gold and to make it suitable for making jewellery, alloy of gold is made either with silver or copper, e.g. 22 carat gold means 22 parts pure gold mixed with 2 parts of Cu or Ag.

- **Painting** Rusting of iron can be easily prevented by coating the surface with a paint which protects iron from air and moisture.

- **Greasing or Oiling** When grease or oil is applied to the surface of an iron object then air and moisture cannot come in contact with it and hence, rust is prevented, e.g. tools and machine parts made up of iron are smeared with grease.
- **Tin Plating and Chromium Plating** Tin and chromium metals are resistant to corrosion. So, when a thin layer of tin metal is deposited on iron object by electro-plating, then iron and steel objects are protected from rusting.

Note When the coating of metal is done with the help of electricity by making the use of other metal, it is known as electro-plating.

Alloy

An alloy is a homogeneous mixture of two or more metals or a metal and a non-metal. It is prepared by mixing the metals in molten form and then cooling the mixture.

The electrical conductivity and melting point of an alloy is less than that of pure metals, e.g. brass, an alloy of copper and zinc (Cu and Zn) and bronze, an alloy of copper and tin (Cu and Sn) are not good conductors of electricity whereas copper is used for making electrical circuits. Solder, an alloy of lead and tin has a low melting point and is used for welding electrical wires together. If an alloy contains mercury as one of its components, it is called **amalgam**, e.g. sodium-mercury amalgam, silver-mercury amalgam etc.

The Wonder of Ancient Indian Metallurgy

The Iron Pillar near Qutub Minar in Delhi was built more than 1600 years ago by the iron workers of India. They had developed a process which prevented iron from rusting. This is due to the presence of thin layer of magnetic oxide, Fe_3O_4 on their surface. For its quality of rust resistance, it has been examined by scientists from all parts of the world. The Iron Pillar is 8 m high and weighs 6 tonnes (6000 kg).

Check Point 04

1. State True or False for the following statements:
   (i) Cinabar is an ore of mercury.
   (ii) Roasting is a process in which a carbonate ore is heated below its melting point in the absence of air.
2. Which type of metals are extracted by electrolytic reduction method?
3. Fill in the blanks:
   In electrolytic reduction of NaCl, metal is deposited at the ...... and chlorine is liberated at the ....
4. What is galvanisation? Name the element used in the process.
5. What is the special quality of iron pillar near Qutub Minar?

NCERT FOLDER

INTEXT QUESTIONS

1 Give an example of a metal which **Pg 40**
  (i) is a liquid at room temperature.
  (ii) can be easily cut with a knife.
  (iii) is a good conductor of heat.
  (iv) is a poor conductor of heat.

Sol. (i) Mercury (ii) Sodium (iii) Silver (iv) Lead

2 Explain the meanings of malleable and ductile. **Pg 40; CBSE 2016**

Sol. Malleable A substance or material, which can be beaten into thin sheets is called malleable, e.g. metals like Ag (silver), Au (gold) etc.
Ductile A substance capable of being drawn into thin wires is called ductile, e.g. metals like Ag, Au etc.

3 Why is sodium kept immersed in kerosene oil? **Pg 46**

Sol. Sodium metal being reactive highly reacts so vigorously with oxygen that it catches fire if kept in open air. Therefore, to protect it from accidental fires, sodium is kept immersed in kerosene oil.

4 Write equations for the reactions of
  (i) iron with steam.
  (ii) calcium and potassium with water. **Pg 46**

Sol. (i) $3Fe(s) + 4H_2O(g) \longrightarrow Fe_3O_4(s) + 4H_2(g)$
(Iron) (Steam) (Iron oxide) (Hydrogen)

(ii) (a) $Ca(s) + 2H_2O(l) \longrightarrow Ca(OH)_2(aq) + H_2(g)$
(Calcium) (Water) (Calcium hydroxide) (Hydrogen)

(b) $2K(s) + 2H_2O(l) \longrightarrow 2KOH(aq) + H_2(g)$
(Potassium) (Water) (Potassium hydroxide) (Hydrogen)

5 Samples of four metals A, B, C and D were taken and added to the following solution one by one. The results obtained have been tabulated as follows:

Metal	Iron (II) Sulphate	Copper (II) Sulphate	Zinc Sulphate	Silver Nitrate
A	No reaction	Displacement	—	—
B	Displacement	—	No reaction	—
C	No reaction	No reaction	No reaction	Displacement
D	No reaction	No reaction	No reaction	No reaction

Use the given table to answer the following questions about metals A, B, C and D.
  (i) Which is the most reactive metal?
  (ii) What would you observed if B is added to a solution of Copper (II) sulphate?
  (iii) Arrange the metals A, B, C and D in the order of decreasing reactivity. **Pg 46**

Sol. (i) B is the most active metal as it displaces iron from its salt solution.
(ii) B will displace Cu from $CuSO_4$ solution because B is more reactive than copper.
(iii) B > A > C > D.

6 Which gas is produced when dilute hydrochloric acid is added to a reactive metal? Write the chemical reaction when iron reacts with dil. H_2SO_4. **Pg 46**

Sol. Hydrogen gas is produced when dilute hydrochloric acid is added to a reactive metal.

$Fe(s) + H_2SO_4(aq) \longrightarrow FeSO_4(aq) + H_2(g)$
(Iron) (Dil. Sulphuric acid) (Ferrous sulphate) (Hydrogen)

7 What would you observe when zinc is added to a solution of iron (II) sulphate? Write the chemical reaction that takes place. **Pg 46**

Sol. Zinc being more reactive than iron displaces iron from iron (II) sulphate solution. Thus, the green colour of the solution fades and iron metal gets deposited.

$Zn(s) + FeSO_4(aq) \longrightarrow ZnSO_4(aq) + Fe(s)$
(Zinc) (Green) (Colourless) (Iron Deposited)

8. (i) Write the electron dot structures for sodium, oxygen and magnesium.
(ii) Show the formation of Na_2O and MgO by the transfer of electrons.
(iii) What are the ions present in these compounds? **Pg 49**

Sol. (i) The electron dot structures of sodium, oxygen and magnesium are tabulated below:

Element	Atomic Number	Electronic Configuration	Electron dot Structure
Na	11	2, 8, 1	Na•
O	8	2, 6	:Ö:
Mg	12	2, 8, 2	:Mg

(ii) Ionic bond is formed in Na_2O and MgO.

(a) Na₂O $2Na_{(2,8,1)} \longrightarrow 2Na^+_{(2,8)} + 2e^-$

$O_{(2,6)} + 2e^- \longrightarrow O^{2-}_{(2,8)}$

$Na \atop Na$ + :Ö: ⟶ 2[Na⁺] [:Ö:]²⁻ or Na₂O

(b) MgO $Mg_{(2,8,2)} \longrightarrow Mg^{2+}_{(2,8)} + 2e^-$

$O_{(2,6)} + 2e^- \longrightarrow O^{2-}_{(2,8)}$

Mg + :Ö: ⟶ [Mg²⁺] [:Ö:]²⁻ or MgO

(iii) Na₂O has Na⁺ and O²⁻ ions.
MgO has Mg²⁺ and O²⁻ ions.

9 Why do ionic compounds have high melting points? **Pg 49**

Sol. In ionic compounds, strong electrostatic forces of attraction are present between the oppositely charged ions. When these compounds are heated, a lot of heat energy is consumed to break these strong electrostatic forces of attraction during melting. Therefore, ionic compounds have high melting and boiling points.

10 Define the following terms:
(i) Mineral (ii) Ore (iii) Gangue **Pg 53**

Sol. (i) The naturally occurring elements or compounds of metals present in the earth's crust are called **minerals**.
(ii) **Ores** are those minerals from which a particular metal can be extracted profitably.
(iii) The undesirable impurities present in the ore are called **gangue** or **matrix**.

11 Name two metals which are found in nature in the free state. **Pg 53**

Sol. Gold and platinum are the two metals that are found in nature in free state.

12 What chemical process is used for obtaining a metal from its oxide? **Pg 53**

Sol. Metal is obtained from its oxide by reduction. This reduction can be done either by heating with carbon (coke) or by using highly reactive metals such as sodium, calcium, aluminium etc.

e.g. $ZnO(s) + C(s) \longrightarrow Zn(s) + CO(g)$
   Zinc oxide Coke   Zinc   Carbon monoxide

This reaction is highly exothermic. The heat produced is so large that metal is produced in the molten form.

13 Metallic oxides of zinc, magnesium and copper were heated with the following metals:

Metal	Zinc	Magnesium	Copper
Zinc oxide			
Magnesium oxide			
Copper oxide			

In which cases will you find displacement reactions taking place? **Pg 55**

Sol. Zinc will react with copper oxide to displace copper. Magnesium will also displace zinc from zinc oxide and copper from copper oxide. Copper, being least reactive will not react with any of the given oxides.

Metal	Zinc	Magnesium	Copper
Zinc oxide	—	✓	—
Magnesium oxide	—	—	—
Copper oxide	✓	✓	—

14 Which metals do not corrode easily? **Pg 55**

Sol. Metals present at the bottom of the reactivity series do not corrode easily, e.g. gold, silver, platinum etc.

15 What are alloys? **Pg 55**

Sol. An alloy is a homogeneous mixture of two or more metals or a metal and a non-metal. It is prepared by mixing the metals in molten form and then cooling the mixture. The electrical conductivity and melting point of an alloy is less than that of pure metals.

e.g.

Alloy	Composition	Uses
Brass	Copper and zinc	Utensils and taps
Bronze	Copper and tin	Medals, statues and valves

EXERCISES
(On Pages 56 and 57)

1 Which of the following pairs will give displacement reactions?
(i) NaCl solution and copper metal
(ii) MgCl₂ solution and aluminium metal
(iii) FeSO₄ solution and silver metal
(iv) AgNO₃ solution and copper metal

Sol. (iv) AgNO₃ solution will give displacement reaction with copper (Cu) because copper is placed above silver in the activity series, i.e. copper is more reactive than silver.

$2AgNO_3(aq) + Cu(s) \longrightarrow Cu(NO_3)_2(aq) + 2Ag(s)$

Metals and Non-Metals

2 Which of the following methods is suitable for preventing an iron frying pan from rusting?
  (i) Applying grease
  (ii) Applying paint
  (iii) Applying a coating of zinc
  (iv) All of the above

Sol. (iv) Applying a coating of zinc will prevent an iron frying pan from rusting.

3 An element reacts with oxygen to give a compound with a high melting point. This compound is also soluble in water. The element is likely to be
  (i) calcium (ii) carbon (iii) silicon (iv) iron

Sol. (i) The compound is likely to be calcium (Ca) because it combines with oxygen to give CaO (calcium oxide) with very high melting point. Calcium oxide dissolves in water to form calcium hydroxide.

$$2Ca(s) + O_2(g) \longrightarrow 2CaO(s)$$
$$CaO(s) + H_2O(l) \longrightarrow 2Ca(OH)_2(aq)$$
Calcium hydroxide

Note Although iron can also combine with oxygen to form Fe_2O_3 as ionic compound with high melting point but it is not soluble in water.

4 Food cans are coated with tin and not with zinc because
  (i) zinc is costlier than tin
  (ii) zinc has a higher melting point than tin
  (iii) zinc is more reactive than tin
  (iv) zinc is less reactive than tin

Sol. (iii) Food cans are not coated with zinc because it being more reactive than tin, can react with organic acids present in the food.

5 You are given a hammer, a battery, a bulb, wires and a switch.
  (i) How would you use them to distinguish between samples of metals and non-metals?
  (ii) Assess the usefulness of these tests in distinguishing between metals and non-metals.

Sol. (i) (a) Take the given samples of metals and non-metals; and strike them with the hammer. If it converts into a sheet, it is a metal and if not, it is non-metal. Metals are malleable, non-metals are not.
  (b) If it produces sound when struck with the hammer, it is a metal. Metals are sonorous. But if it does not produce a sound, it is non-metal.
  (c) Now arranging the given objects to form an electric circuit.
  Insert any one sample between clips A and B. If the bulb glows, it is a metal (good conductor of electricity). If the bulb does not glows, it is a non-metal.

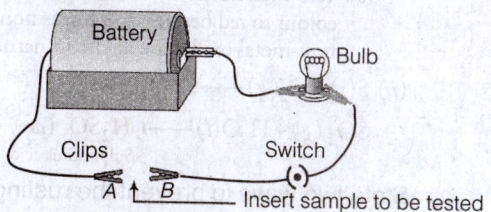

Electrical circuit diagram to show conductivity of metals

(ii) From the above tests, it is clear that metals are generally malleable, sonorous and good conductors of electricity, while non-metals are generally non-malleable/brittle, non-sonorous and poor conductors of electricity.

6 What are amphoteric oxides? Give two examples of amphoteric oxides.

Sol. The metallic oxides which show the properties of acids as well as bases are called amphoteric oxides. It means that they react with both bases and acids to form salt and water.
e.g. ZnO and Al_2O_3

$$\underset{\substack{\text{Zinc oxide} \\ \text{(As a base)}}}{ZnO(s)} + \underset{\substack{\text{Hydrochloric} \\ \text{acid}}}{2HCl(aq)} \longrightarrow \underset{\text{Zinc chloride}}{ZnCl_2(aq)} + \underset{\text{Water}}{H_2O(l)}$$

$$\underset{\substack{\text{Zinc oxide} \\ \text{(As an acid)}}}{ZnO(s)} + \underset{\text{Sodium hydroxide}}{2NaOH(aq)} \longrightarrow \underset{\text{Sodium zincate}}{Na_2ZnO_2(aq)} + \underset{\text{Water}}{H_2O(l)}$$

7 Name two metals which will displace hydrogen from dilute acids, and two metals which will not.

Sol. Zinc and magnesium displace H_2 from dilute acids while copper and silver do not.

8 In the electrolytic refining of a metal M, what would you take as the anode, the cathode and the electrolyte?

Sol. **Anode** (positively charged) Block of the impure metal M.
Cathode (negatively charged) Strip of the pure metal M.
Electrolyte Aqueous solution of a salt of the metal M.

9 Pratyush took sulphur powder on a spatula and heated it. He collected the gas evolved by inverting a test tube over it, as shown in the figure below.

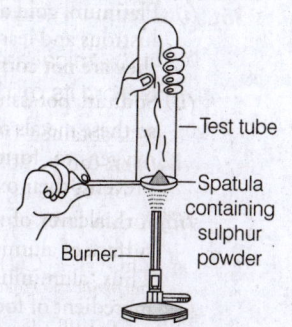

(i) What will be the action of the gas on
  (a) dry blue litmus paper?
  (b) moist blue litmus paper?
(ii) Write a balanced chemical equation for the reaction taking place.

Sol. (i) (a) No change in colour will take place in case of dry blue litmus.

(b) The moist blue litmus paper will change its colour to red because sulphur is non-metal and non-metal oxides are acidic in nature.

(ii) $S(s) + O_2(g) \longrightarrow SO_2(g)$

$SO_2(g) + H_2O(l) \longrightarrow \underset{\text{Sulphurous acid}}{H_2SO_3(aq)}$

10 State two ways to prevent the rusting of iron.

Sol. Ways to prevent rusting of iron

(i) By painting or greasing the surface of iron, it can be prevented from rusting because in this condition iron will not be in the direct contact with air.

(ii) By galvanising the iron surface. In glavanisation a layer of zinc is coated on the iron surface. Zinc is more reactive than iron, so it will be rusted in preference of iron.

11 What type of oxides are formed when non-metals combine with oxygen?

Sol. Non-metals form acidic oxides, i.e. their aqueous solution turns blue litmus solution red.

$\underset{\underset{\text{(Non-metal)}}{\text{Carbon}}}{C(s)} + \underset{\text{Oxygen}}{O_2(g)} \longrightarrow \underset{\text{Carbon dioxide}}{CO_2(g)}$

$\underset{\underset{\text{dioxide}}{\text{Carbon}}}{CO_2(g)} + \underset{\text{Water}}{H_2O(l)} \longrightarrow \underset{\text{Carbonic acid}}{H_2CO_3(aq)} \xrightarrow[\text{solution}]{\text{Blue litmus}} \text{Red}$

12 Give reasons:

(i) Platinum, gold and silver are used to make jewellery.

(ii) Sodium, potassium and lithium are stored under oil.

(iii) Aluminium is a highly reactive metal, yet it is used to make utensils for cooking.

(iv) Carbonate and sulphide ores are usually converted into oxides during the process of extraction.

Sol. (i) Platinum, gold and silver are highly malleable, lustrous and least reactive, i.e. noble metals, so they are not corroded by air and water easily.

(ii) Sodium, potassium and lithium are very reactive, so these metals react vigorously with atmospheric oxygen to form oxides. Storing them in oil prevents their oxidation.

(iii) A thin layer of aluminium oxide formed on the surface of aluminium prevents it from corrosion. Thus, aluminium vessels do not react with any ingredient of food and are suitable for cooking.

(iv) It is easier to obtain metal from its oxide rather than its carbonates and sulphides. Therefore, these ores are first converted to oxide and then reduced to metal.

13 You must have seen tarnished copper vessels being cleaned with lemon or tamarind juice. Explain, why these sour substances are effective in cleaning the vessels?

Sol. A layer of basic copper carbonate is formed by the reaction of air on copper metal.

$2Cu(s) + \underbrace{O_2(g) + H_2O(l) + CO_2(g)}_{\text{(From air)}}$

$\longrightarrow \underbrace{CuCO_3 \cdot Cu(OH)_2(s)}_{\text{Basic copper carbonate}}$

This layer being insoluble in water, cannot be cleaned with water alone. But, it is soluble in acids so lemon containing citric acid, tamarind containing tartaric acid or any other sour substance containing acid can be effective in cleaning the vessels. As these acids neutralises the basic copper carbonate and dissolves the layer. Hence, surface of copper vessels are cleaned with lemon or tamarind juice to give the surface of copper vessel its characteristics lustre.

14 Differentiate between metals and non-metals on the basis of their chemical properties.

Sol.

Chemical Properties	Metals	Non-metals
Formation of ions	They are electropositive elements, lose electron(s) and form cations, e.g. $Na \longrightarrow Na^+ + e^-$	They are electronegative elements, gain electron(s) and form anions. $Cl + e^- \longrightarrow Cl^-$
Discharge of ions	Discharge at the cathode during electrolysis of their compound. At cathode, $\underset{\text{Cation}}{Na^+ + e^- \longrightarrow Na}$	Liberated at anode during electrolysis. **Except** hydrogen, liberated at cathode. At cathode, $2H^+ + 2e^- \longrightarrow H_2 \uparrow$
Reducing or Oxidising agent	They are reducing agents as they donate electrons during chemical reaction.	They are oxidising agents, as they accept electrons during chemical reaction.
Nature of oxides	Metallic oxides are basic. Some of them dissolves in water forming alkaline solution, e.g. Basic oxide : K_2O, Na_2O, CaO, MgO and CuO Amphoteric oxide : Al_2O_3, PbO and ZnO	Non-metallic oxides are acidic in nature. Acidic oxide : CO_2, SO_2, SO_3, NO_2 and P_2O_5 Neutral oxide : CO, NO, N_2O and H_2O
Reaction with acids	Active metals react with dil. HCl/H_2SO_4 to yield H_2 gas and salts. $M + 2HCl \longrightarrow MCl_2 + H_2$	Non-metals do not react with dilute acids, as they cannot replace H^+ ion from an acid to form salt.

Metals and Non-Metals

15. A man went door to door posing as a goldsmith. He promised to bring back the glitter of old and dull gold ornaments. An unsuspecting lady gave a set of gold bangles to him which he dipped in a particular solution. The bangles sparkled like new but their weight was reduced drastically. The lady was upset but after a futile argument, the man beat a hasty retreat. Can you play the detective to find out the nature of the solution he had used?

Sol. The man used aqua-regia, a mixture of conc. HCl and conc. HNO_3 in the ratio of 3 : 1. This is the only solution, that can dissolve gold. As the gold from the bangles was dissolved in aqua-regia, their weight was reduced drastically.

16. Give reasons, why copper is used to make hot water tanks and not steel (an alloy of iron)?

Sol. Iron (or steel) is more reactive than copper when in contact with steam formed from hot water to form Fe_3O_4.

$$3Fe(s) + 4H_2O(g) \longrightarrow Fe_3O_4(s) + H_2O(l)$$

So, the body of tank is made of copper but not steel as copper does not react with water.

SUMMARY

- At present about **118 elements** are known.
- Elements can be divided into two main groups: metals and non-metals.
- Elements which form positive ions by losing electrons are called **metals**.
- Metals are lustrous, ductile, malleable and good conductors of heat and electricity. They are solids at room temperature except mercury which is a liquid.
- Almost all the metals combine with oxygen (or air) to form metal oxides that are basic in nature except aluminium oxide and zinc oxide which are amphoteric in nature.
- **Metallic oxides** are insoluble in water but some of them dissolve in water to form hydroxides known as **alkalis**.
- Metals react with water and produce a metal hydroxide and hydrogen gas.
- Except a few less reactive metals (such as Cu, Hg, Ag, Au, Pt, etc), all metals react with dil. sulphuric acid, hydrochloric acid to produce salt and hydrogen gas.
- **Aqua-regia** is a freshly prepared mixture of concentrated hydrochloric acid and concentrated nitric acid in the ratio of 3:1.
- Reactive metal can displace a comparatively less reactive metal from its compounds in aqueous salt solution or in molten form.
- Metals above hydrogen in the reactivity series can displace hydrogen from dilute acids.
- Hydrogen also have non-metallic properties but, due to its electropositive nature, it has been placed in the reactivity series.
- **Non-metals** are those which form negative ions by gaining electrons.
- Non-metals do not react with water or steam to evolve hydrogen gas.
- Non-metals do not react with dilute acids to release hydrogen gas. Thet react with hydrogen to form hydrides.
- **Ionic compounds** (like sodium chloride) do not exist as discrete molecules but indeed they are the aggregates of oppositely charged particles.
- The elements or compounds which occur naturally in the earth crust are known as **minerals**.
- Minerals from which metals can be extracted profitably are called **ores**.
- Removal of unwanted material (gangue) from the ore is called **enrichment** or **concentration of ore**.
- The process of purification of the metal obtained after reduction is called refining of metals.
- Many metals like Cu, Sn, Ni, Ag, etc, are refined electrolytically.
- **Corrosion** is the slow process of eating away of metals by the reaction of atmospheric air and moisture.
- **Rusting of iron** is prevented by galvanising, by making alloys, painting, greasing or oiling and tin-plating and chromium plating.
- An **alloy** is a homogeneous mixture of two or more metals or a non-metal.

Exam Practice

Objective Type Questions

Multiple Choice Questions

1 Which of the following metal has highest melting point?
   (a) Copper   (b) Silver
   (c) Sodium   (d) Tungsten

Sol. (d) Tungsten has the highest melting point among the metals.

2 The ability of metals to be drawn into thin wire is known as   **NCERT Exemplar**
   (a) ductility   (b) malleability
   (c) sonorousity   (d) conductivity

Sol. (a) These are all physical properties of metals. The ability of metals to be drawn into thin wire is known as ductility.

3 Which of the following is a characteristic of metals?
   (a) They have one to three valence electrons
   (b) They have 4 to 8 valence electrons
   (c) They are brittle
   (d) They are capable to form anions easily

Sol. (a) Metal can easily given up their electrons and form electropositive ions. They have one to three valence electrons. They are not brittle and do not form anions.

4 A cable manufacturing unit tested few elements on the basis of their physical properties.

Properties	W	X	Y	Z
Malleable	Yes	No	No	Yes
Ductile	Yes	No	No	Yes
Electrical conductivity	Yes	Yes	Yes	No
Melting point	High	Low	Low	High

Which of the above elements were discarded for usage by the company?
CBSE SQP (Term-I)
   (a) W, X, Y   (b) X, Y, Z
   (c) W, X, Z   (d) W, Y, Z

Sol. (b) The elements X, Y and Z were discarded for usage by the company because for a cable manufacturing, the element should be ductile, malleable, good conductor of electricity and should have high melting point and the elements X, Y and Z do not have all these properties. Hence, X, Y and Z are discarded.

5 Which of the following reaction shows that the given oxide is amphoteric in nature?
   (a) $2Zn + O_2 \xrightarrow{\Delta} 2ZnO$
   (b) $ZnO + H_2SO_4 \longrightarrow ZnSO_4 + H_2O(l)$
   (c) $ZnO + 2NaOH \longrightarrow Na_2ZnO_2 + H_2O(l)$
   (d) (b) and (c) together   **NCERT Exemplar**

Sol. (d) Metals when react with the oxygen, give basic-oxides/ amphoteric oxides. ZnO is an amphoteric oxide.
Option (b) and (c) indicates that, ZnO react with the acid (H_2SO_4) as well as with the base (NaOH).
Hence, (b) and (c) together gives the nature of oxide.

6 What happens when calcium is treated with water?   **NCERT Exemplar**
   (i) It does not react with water.
   (ii) It reacts violently with water.
   (iii) It reacts less violently with water.
   (iv) Bubbles of hydrogen gas formed stick to the surface of calcium.
   (a) (i) and (iv)   (b) (ii) and (iii)
   (c) (i) and (ii)   (d) (iii) and (iv)

Sol. (d) Calcium reacts less violently with water and the bubbles of hydrogen gas produced stick to the surface of calcium. Due to which it floats over water surface.
$Ca(s) + 2H_2O(l) \longrightarrow Ca(OH)_2(aq) + H_2(g)\uparrow$
Calcium hydroxide

Much less heat is produced in this reaction due to which hydrogen gas formed does not catch fire.

7 A reactive metal (M) is treated with H_2SO_4 (dil). The gas is evolved and is collected over the water as shown in the figure:

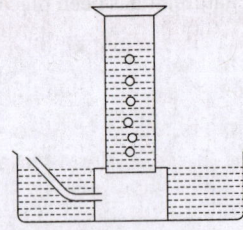

The correct conclusion drawn is/are
(a) the gas is hydrogen
(b) the gas is lighter than air
(c) the gas is SO_2 and is lighter than air
(d) Both (a) and (b)

Sol. (d) When any reactive metal (M) reacts with the acid H_2SO_4 (dil.), it evolves hydrogen gas (H_2). It is lighter than air.

$$M(s) + H_2SO_4 (dil.) \longrightarrow M\text{-sulphate} + H_2(g)$$

8 The composition of aqua-regia is
(a) Dil. HCl : Conc. HNO_3
　　　3 : 1
(b) Conc. HCl : Dil. HNO_3
　　　3 : 1
(c) Conc. HCl : Conc. HNO_3
　　　3 : 1
(d) Dil. HCl : Dil. HNO_3
　　　3 : 1

Sol. (c) Conc. HCl and conc. HNO_3 in 3 : 1 ratio form *aqua-regia*. *Aqua-regia* is a highly corrosive, fuming liquid. It can dissolve all metals even gold and platinum also.

9 Which of the following only contain non-metals?
(a) Carbohydrates
(b) Proteins
(c) Alloys
(d) Both (a) and (b)

Sol. (d) Carbohydrates contain carbon (C), hydrogen (H) and oxygen (O) as their components, while proteins contain carbon (C), nitrogen (N), hydrogen (H) and oxygen (O) but alloys are mixture of metals and may be some non-metals. Hence, option (d) is the correct answer.

10 Which of the following is not a property of non-metals?
(a) They are neither malleable nor ductile
(b) They are brittle
(c) They are sonorous
(d) They are poor conductor of heat and electricity (except graphite)

Sol. (c) Almost all the non-metals produce no metallic sound on hitting. Thus, they are not sonorous.

11 In the following diagram, what would happen if same amount of sodium hydroxide is taken in place of sulphuric acid and the test tube is heated.

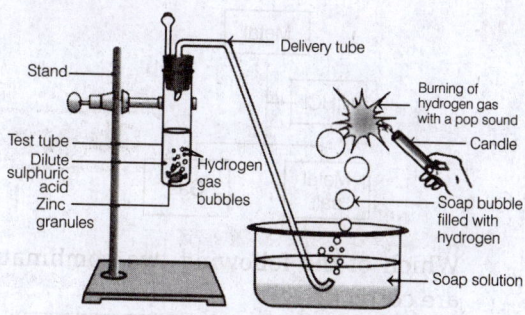

CBSE 2021 (Term-I)

(a) Same amount of H_2 gas is evolved
(b) H_2 gas is not evolved
(c) The amount of H_2 gas evolved is much less
(d) In place of H_2 gas, O_2 gas evolves

Sol. (a) If same amount of sodium hydroxide is taken in place of dilute sulphuric acid, then same amount of H_2 gas is evolved and sodium zincate is produced.

$$Zn + 2NaOH \longrightarrow Na_2ZnO_2 + H_2\uparrow$$

12 Which of the following metal will not give $H_2(g)$ with H_2O ?
(a) Na $(s) + 2H_2O \longrightarrow$　(b) Mg$(s) + H_2O \longrightarrow$
(c) Zn$(s) + H_2O \longrightarrow$　(d) Cu $+ H_2O \longrightarrow$

Sol. (d) Metals placed below the hydrogen in reactivity series, will not give $H_2(g)$ with water (H_2O).
Decreasing order of reactivity of metals is
Na > Mg > Zn > Cu

13 Identify gas A in the following experiment.

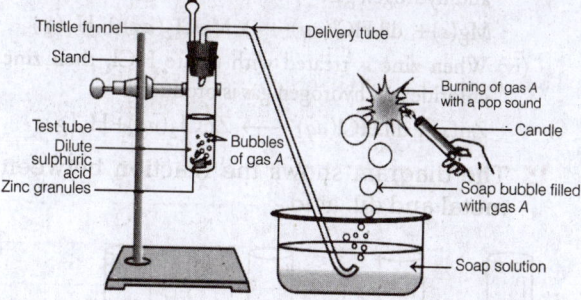

(a) Nitrogen　　(b) Hydrogen
(c) Oxygen　　(d) Carbon dioxide

CBSE SQP (Term-I)

Sol. (b) When zinc granules react with dilute sulphuric acid, then hydrogen gas is produced.

$$\underset{\text{Zinc}}{Zn} + \underset{\text{Dil sulphuric acid}}{H_2SO_4} \longrightarrow \underset{\text{Zinc sulphate}}{ZnSO_4} + \underset{\text{Hydrogen}}{H_2\uparrow}$$

This hydrogen makes a pop sound on burning due to the reaction between hydrogen and oxygen present in air.

14

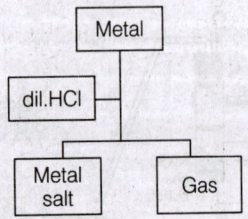

Which of the following two combinations are correct?

	Metal	Gas evolved
(i)	Copper	Yes
(ii)	Iron	Yes
(iii)	Magnesium	No
(iv)	Zinc	Yes

CBSE SQP (Term-I)

(a) (i) and (iii) (b) (i) and (iv)
(c) (ii) and (iii) (d) (ii) and (iv)

Sol. (d)
(i) When copper metal reacts with dilute hydrochloric acid, then no reaction occurs because copper cannot displace hydrogen from HCl to evolve H_2 gas as it is less reactive than hydrogen.
(ii) When iron reacts with dilute hydrochloric acid, then iron chloride and hydrogen gas is formed.
$Fe(s) + dil.HCl(aq) \longrightarrow FeCl_2(aq) + H_2(g)$
(iii) The reaction between magnesium and dilute hydrochloric acid produces magnesium chloride and hydrogen gas.
$Mg(s) + dil.HCl(aq) \longrightarrow MgCl_2(aq) + H_2(g)$
(iv) When zinc is treated with dilute HCl, then zinc chloride and hydrogen gas is produced.
$Zn(s) + dil.HCl(aq) \longrightarrow ZnCl_2(aq) + H_2(g)$

15 The diagram shows the reaction between metal and dil. acid.

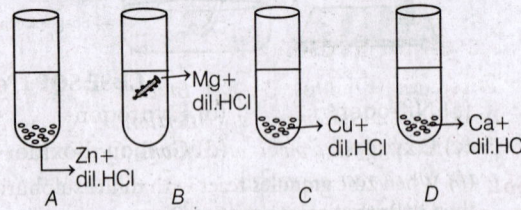

What is the reason for different behaviour of Mg in test tube B? **CBSE SQP (Term-I)**

(a) Mg is lighter element than dil. HCl
(b) Mg reacts with dil. HCl to produce H_2 gas which helps in floating
(c) Mg reacts with dil. HCl to produce N_2 gas which helps in floating
(d) Mg reacts with dil. HCl to produce CO_2 gas which helps in floating

Sol. (b) When magnesium reacts with dil.HCl in test tube B, then there is formation of salt, i.e. $MgCl_2$ and hydrogen gas comes out as bubbles. This hydrogen gas bubbles are responsible for the floating of magnesium metal.
$$Mg + 2HCl \underset{(dil.)}{\longrightarrow} MgCl_2 + H_2 \uparrow$$

16 Metals are refined by using different methods. Which of the following metals are refined by electrolytic refining?
(i) Au (ii) Cu
(iii) Na (iv) K
(a) (i) and (ii) (b) (i) and (iii)
(c) (ii) and (iii) (d) (ii) and (iv)

Sol. (a) Electrolytic refining is used for metals like Cu, Zn, Ag, Au etc.
The method to be used for refining an impure metal depends on the nature of the metal as well as on the nature of impurities present in it.

17 Silver articles become black on prolonged exposure to air. This is due to the formation of
(a) Ag_3N (b) Ag_3O
(c) Ag_2S (d) Ag_2S and Ag_3N

Sol. (c) Silver article become black because silver reacts with H_2S gas present in air to form black coating of Ag_2S. The reaction is
$$\underset{\text{Silver}}{Ag} + \underset{\substack{\text{Hydrogen}\\\text{sulphide}}}{H_2S} \longrightarrow \underset{\substack{\text{Silver}\\\text{sulphide}\\\text{(black)}}}{Ag_2S} + H_2 \uparrow$$

18 Match the metal (Column I) with its reaction with oxygen (Column II).

Column I	Column II
A. Potassium	1. Does not react even at high temperatures
B. Zinc	2. Gets coated with black-coloured layer of oxide
C. Copper	3. Does not burn at ordinary temperature
D. Silver	4. Burns vigorously

CBSE 2021 (Term-I)

Codes
	A B C D		A B C D
(a)	4 3 2 1	(b)	4 2 1 3
(c)	3 2 1 4	(d)	4 2 3 1

Sol. (a) A → 4, B → 3, C → 2, D → 1.
A. Potassium being very reactive, burns vigorously when it comes in contact with oxygen.

B. Zinc does not burn at ordinary temperature, however it reacts with oxygen in moist air.
C. When copper comes in contact with oxygen, it gets coated with black-coloured layer of oxide.
D. Silver does not react with oxygen even at high temperatures.

19 Galvanisation is a method of protecting iron from rusting by coating it with a thin layer of
(a) gallium (b) aluminium
(c) zinc   (d) silver

Sol. (c) Galvanisation is a method of protecting iron from rusting by coating it with a thin layer of zinc (Zn) metal.

20 An alloy is
(a) an element
(b) a compound
(c) a homogeneous mixture
(d) a heterogeneous mixture

Sol. (c) An alloy is a homogeneous mixture of different metals or a metal and a non-metal.

Fill in the Blanks

21. .... is the only metal that exist as liquid at room temperature.

Sol. Mercury

22. The elements having a tendency to .... electrons are called non-metals.

Sol. gain

23. The most abundant metal in the earth's crust is........

Sol. aluminium

24. Removal of gangue from the ore is known as........

Sol. concentration of ore

True and False

25. The best conductor of heat are silver and gold.

Sol. False; Copper and silver are the best conductor of heat.

26. When aluminium is treated with hot water, a gas is released which burns with, 'pop' sound.

Sol. False; Metals like aluminium, iron and zinc donot react with either cold or hot water.

27. Non-metals can be solids, liquids or gases.

Sol. True

28. Metals high in reactivity series are obtained by roasting and refining of the ore.

Sol. False; Electrolytic reduction method is employed for the metallic compounds present at the top of the activity series.

29. Metals are converted into their alloys to make them less brittle, hard and corrosion resistant.

Sol. True.

Match the Columns

30. Match the terms given in column A (related to metals) with their meaning example given in column B.

Column A	Column B
P. Malleability	I. Bright shine
Q. Ductility	II. Alkali metal
R. Sonority	III. Tendency to drawn into wires
S. Softness	IV. Tendency to beaten into thin sheets
T. Lustre	V. Bells

Sol. (P)→(IV); Q→(III), R→(V); S→(II), T→(I), P→(IV).

Property of a metal due to which it can be beaten into thin sheets.

Q→(III)-Property of a metal due to which it can be drawn into thin wires.

R→(V)-Using the property of sonority, school bells are made up of metals.

S→(II)-Some alkali metals like lithum, sodium and potassium are very soft.

T→(I)-In pure state, metals have a bright shining surface. This property is called metallic lustre.

Assertion-Reason

Direction (Q. Nos. 31-35) *In each of the following questions, a statement of Assertion is given by the corresponding statement of Reason. Of the statements, mark the correct answer as.*

(a) Both Assertion and Reason are true and Reason is the correct explanation of Assertion.
(b) Both Assertion and Reason are true, but Reason is not the correct explanation of Assertion.
(c) Assertion is true, but Reason is false.
(d) Assertion is false, but Reason is true.

31 **Assertion** Electrical wires cannot be made by copper.

Reason Copper is a bad conductor of electricity.

Sol. (c) Assertion is true but Reason is false. Electrical wires are made up of copper as copper is very good conductor of electricity.

32 **Assertion** When zinc is added to a solution of iron (II) sulphate, no change is observed.

Reason Zinc is more reactive than iron.

Sol. (d) Assertion is false but Reason is true. Zinc being more reactive than iron displaces iron from iron (II) sulphate solution.

Thus, the green colour of the solution fades and iron metal gets deposited.

$$\underset{\text{Zinc}}{Zn(s)} + \underset{\text{Green}}{FeSO_4(aq)} \longrightarrow \underset{\text{(Colourless)}}{ZnSO_4(aq)} + \underset{\text{(Iron deposited)}}{Fe(s)}$$

33 **Assertion** Food cans are coated with tin and not with zinc.

Reason Zinc is more reactive than tin.

Sol. (a) Both Assertion and Reason are true and Reason is the correct explanation of Assertion. Food cans are coated with tin not with zinc because zinc is more reactive than tin, it can react with organic acids present in food.

34 **Assertion** Carbon reacts with oxygen to form carbon dioxide which is an acidic oxide.

Reason Non-metals form acidic oxides.

Sol. (a) Both Assertion and Reason are true and Reason is the correct explanation of Assertion. Carbon being a non-metal form acidic oxides, i.e. their aqueous solution turns blue litmus solution red.

35 **Assertion** Alloys are commonly used in electrical heating devices like electric iron and heater.

Reason Resistivity of an alloy is generally higher than that of its constituent metals but the alloys have lower melting points than their constituent metals.

Sol. (c) (A) is true but (R) is false. Hence, the correct statement is resistivity and melting point of alloys are higher than their constituent metals, so alloys are commonly used in electrical heating devices like electric iron and heater.

Case Based Questions

Direction (Q. Nos. 36-39) *Answer the questions on the basis of your understanding of the following passage and related studied concepts:*

The reactivity series is a list of metals arranged in the order of their decreasing activities. Copper and silver, both being placed lower than hydrogen in the reactivity series are easily displaced out of a solution of their ions by reactive metals higher up in the reactivity series. Iron, however cannot displace Na^+ and Ca^{2+} as it below Na and Ca in the reactivity series.

36 Name the metals that can be displaced, when excess of iron fillings is added to a solution containing a mixture of ions Pb^{2+}, Zn^{2+}, Hg^{2+} and Mg^{2+}.

Sol. Iron can displace lead (Pb) and mercury (Hg) from their solutions as iron is more reactive than lead and mercury. This is because it is placed about them in the reactivity series of the metals.

37 Zinc is used in the galvanisation of iron and not copper.

Sol. Zinc is placed above iron in the activity series. When deposited over its surface (galvanisation), zinc gets corroded and not iron. But copper is placed below iron and therefore, does not participate the corrosion. In this case, iron is corroded or rusted.

38 5 mL each of concentrated HCl, HNO_3 and a mixture of concentrated HCl (15 mL) and concentrated HNO_3 (5 mL) were taken in a test tube labelled as *A*, *B* and *C*. A small pieces of metal was put in each test tube. No change occurred in test tube *A* and *B* but the metal got dissolved in the tube *C*. Identity of metal present in test tube *C*.

Sol. Gold dissolved in *aqua-regia*

39 Name two metals which will displace hydrogen from dilute acids.

Sol. Zine and magnesium

Direction (Q. Nos. 40-43) *Answer the questions on the basis of your understanding of the following passage and related studied concepts:*

The reactivity series is a list of metals arranged in the order of their decreasing activities.

Metals and Non-Metals

On the basis of their reactive tendency to lose electron and their reactive nature, metals are arranged in a seires, this series is called activity series or reactivity series of metals.

The metals that are placed above hydrogen are called most reactive metals and the metals that are placed below hydrogen are called least reactive metals. The most reactive metals can displaces less rectives metals from its salts solution.

K	Potassium	Most reactive
Na	Sodium	
Ca	Calcium	
Mg	Magnesium	
Al	Aluminium	
Zn	Zinc	Reactivity decrease
Fe	Iron	
Pb	Lead	
H	Hydrogen	
Cu	Copper	
Hg	Mercury	
Ag	Silver	
Au	Gold	Least reactive

40 Metal which exist in their native states in nature is/are
(a) Cu and Au (b) Au and Ag
(c) Zn and Cu (d) Cu and Ag

Sol. (b) Au and Ag are least reactive.

41 The method is used to extract metal present at the top of the series will be
(a) electrolytic refining
(b) calcination
(c) electrolytic reduction
(d) roasting

Sol. (c) Due to high affinity with oxygen, electrolytic reduction is employed for metals, like Na, Mg, Ca etc.

42 Name the metals which react with stream but not hot water.

Sol. Aluminium, iron and zinc.

43 What happen when calcium react with nitric acid?

Sol. Calcium reacts with nitric acid to form calcium nitrate, dinitrogen monoxide and water.

44 Which of the following metals will melt at body temperature (37°C)? Gallium, magnesium, caesium and aluminium.

Sol. Gallium and caesium melt at body temperature (37°C).

45 Name two metals which react with dil.HNO_3 to evolve hydrogen gas.

Sol. Manganese (Mn) and magnesium (Mg) are the examples of two metals that react with dil. HNO_3 to evolve hydrogen gas.

46 Arrange the following metals in the decreasing order of reactivity Na, K, Cu and Ag.

Sol. The decreasing order of reactivity of the given metals is
K > Na > Cu > Ag.

47 Although, metals form basic oxides, name one metal which forms an amphoteric oxide. **NCERT Exemplar**

Sol. Aluminium is a metal which forms an amphoteric oxide.

48 Name one metal which reacts neither with cold water, nor with hot water, but reacts with steam to produce hydrogen gas. **NCERT Exemplar**

Sol. Iron is the metal which does not react with cold and hot water but reacts with steam to produce hydrogen gas.

49 A piece of granulated zinc was dropped into copper sulphate solution. After sometime, the colour of the solution changed from blue to colourless. Why?

Sol. Blue copper sulphate is converted to colourless zinc sulphate, as zinc, being more reactive, displaces copper from $CuSO_4$ solution and forms a colourless solution of zinc sulphate.

$$Zn(s) + CuSO_4(aq) \longrightarrow ZnSO_4(aq) + Cu(s)$$

50 A cleaned aluminium foil was placed in an aqueous solution of zinc sulphate. When the aluminium foil was taken out of the zinc sulphate solution after 15 minutes, its surface was found to be coated with a silvery grey deposit. From the given observation, what can be concluded?

Sol. Aluminium being more reactive than zinc displaces zinc from zinc sulphate solution.

$$\underset{\text{Zinc sulphate}}{3ZnSO_4(aq)} + \underset{\text{Aluminium}}{2Al(s)} \longrightarrow \underset{\text{Aluminium sulphate}}{Al_2(SO_4)_3(aq)}$$
$$+ \underset{\text{Zinc}}{3Zn(s)}$$

51 Show the electron transfer in the formation of $MgCl_2$ from its elements.

Sol. The electron transfer in the formation of $MgCl_2$ from its elements is shown below:

$$Mg : \begin{matrix} \times Cl \times \\ \times Cl \times \end{matrix} \longrightarrow [Mg^{2+}] \left[\times Cl \times^- \right]_2 \text{ or } MgCl_2$$

52 Show the formation of MgO by the transfer of electrons in the two elements using electron dot structures. **CBSE 2012**

Or Atomic number of Mg is 12 and of oxygen is 8. Show the formation of MgO from its elements. **CBSE 2010**

Or Using the electronic configurations, explain how magnesium atom combines with oxygen atom to form magnesium oxide by transfer of electrons. **CBSE 2011**

Sol. Refer to NCERT folder (Intext Questions) Q. 8 (ii) on page no. 67 and 68.

53 Name one property which is not shown by ionic compounds. **NCERT Exemplar**

Sol. Ionic compounds do not conduct electricity in the solid state.

54 Metals are refined by using different methods. Which of the following metals are refined by electrolytic refining?
Au, Cu, Na and K

Sol. Electrolytic refining is used for metals like Cu, Zn, Ag, Au etc. This method to be used for refining an impure metal that depends on the nature of the metal as well as on the nature of impurities present in it. Cu and Au are refined by electrolytic refining.

55 A green layer is gradually formed on a copper plate when left exposed to air for a week in a bathroom. What could this green substance be?

Sol. This green substance is basic copper carbonate $CuCO_3 \cdot Cu(OH)_2$.

56 Name two metals that are obtained by electrolysis of their chlorides in molten form. **NCERT Exemplar**

Sol. Sodium and calcium are obtained by electrolysis of their chlorides in molten form.

57 Name an alloy that contains a non-metal as one of its constituents. **NCERT Exemplar**

Sol. Steel (iron + carbon) is an alloy that contains a non-metal as one of its constituents.

58 Name an alloy which has mercury as one of its constituents. **NCERT Exemplar**

Sol. Zinc amalgam is an alloy that has mercury as one of its constituents.

59 Explain what happens if bauxite containing iron and silica as impurities is directly subjected to the process of electrolytic reduction without prior purification.

Sol. Crude bauxite contains iron oxide and silica as impurities. If any amount of iron is present in the bauxite, it will get deposited at the cathode in preference to aluminium because iron is less electropositive than aluminium.

Short Answer (SA) Type Questions

1 Explain the reactions of different metals with hot water, cold water and steam. Give one example with a proper balanced chemical equation. Name two metals which do not react with any form of water. **CBSE 2012**

Sol. Reaction of metal with water

(i) With cold water
$$2Na(s) + 2H_2O(l) \longrightarrow 2NaOH(aq) + H_2(g)$$
Sodium (Cold)   Sodium hydroxide   Hydrogen

(ii) With hot water
$$Mg(s) + 2H_2O(l) \longrightarrow Mg(OH)_2(aq) + H_2(g)\uparrow$$
Magnesium (Hot)   Magnesium hydroxide   Hydrogen

(iii) With steam
$$Fe(s) + H_2O(g) \longrightarrow FeO(s) + H_2(g)\uparrow$$
Iron (II) or ferrous (Steam)   Iron (II) oxide

$$2Fe(s) + 3H_2O \longrightarrow Fe_2O_3(s) + 3H_2(g)\uparrow$$
Iron (III) or ferric (Steam)   Iron (III) oxide

$$3Fe(s) + 4H_2O(l) \longrightarrow Fe_3O_4(s) + 4H_2(g)\uparrow$$
Iron (II, III) oxide

- The increasing order of reactivity of these metals is Fe < Mg < Na
- Gold and silver do not react with any form of water.

Metals and Non-Metals

2 (a) By the transfer of electrons, illustrate the formation of bond in magnesium chloride and identify the ions present in this compound.
(b) Ionic compounds are solids. Give reasons.
(c) With the help of a labelled diagram show the experimental set up of action of steam on a metal. **CBSE (All India) 2020**

Sol. (a) The formation of bond in magnesium chloride is as follows:
Refer to text on page 63.
The ions present in this compound are Mg^{2+} and Cl^-.
(b) Refer to text on page 63.
(c) The diagram that shows the experimental set up of action of steam on metal is given below

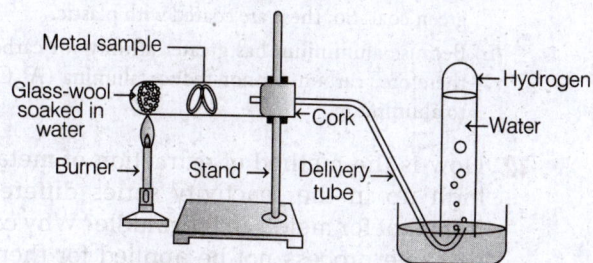

3 Cheshta, a 10th class student was asked to identify iron, copper, zinc and aluminium only by observing the effect of action of concentrated nitric acid and caustic soda on each metal. How did she put the reactions of these metals with each of the reagents?

Sol.

Action of Concentrated Nitric Acid	Action of Caustic Alkali	Inference
No characteristic change	No characteristic change	Iron
Liberates brown coloured NO_2 gas	No characteristic change	Copper
Liberates brown coloured NO_2 gas	Liberates hydrogen gas	Zinc
No characteristic change	Liberates hydrogen gas	Aluminium

4 State the property utilised in the following:
(i) Graphite in making electrodes.
(ii) Electrical wires are coated with Polyvinyl Chloride (PVC) or a rubber-like material.
(iii) Metal alloys are used for making bells and strings of musical instruments. **CBSE 2012**

Sol. (i) Graphite is an allotrope of carbon which is a good conductor of electricity so it is cheap, insoluble in water, do not react with acids and bases and is non-corrosive material. Due to these properties, it is used in making electrodes.
(ii) Polyvinyl Chloride (PVC) or a rubber-like material are insulators and hence do not allow electrons to flow. Hence, these are used in coating the electrical wires.
(iii) Metals and metal alloys are generally sonorous in nature, i.e. they produce sound. Due to this property, they are used for making bells and strings of musical instruments.

5 A student was given Mg, Zn, Fe and Cu metals. He puts each of them in dil. HCl contained in different test tubes. Identify which of them
(i) will not displace H_2 from dil. HCl?
(ii) will give H_2 with 5% HNO_3?
(iii) will be displaced from its salt solution by all other metals?

Sol. (i) Cu metal will not displace H_2 from dil. HCl.
(ii) Mg will give H_2 with 5% HNO_3.
(iii) Cu metal will be displaced from its salt solution by all other metals.

6 (i) Write any two properties of ionic compounds.
(ii) Show the formation of aluminium chloride by the transfer of electrons between the atoms. (Atomic number of aluminium and chlorine are 13 and 17 respectively). **CBSE 2015**

Sol. (i) Properties of ionic compounds are:
(a) They are hard crystalline solids.
(b) These compounds have high melting and boiling points as large amount of energy is required to break strong electrostatic forces of attraction.

(ii) Al = 2, 8, 3 $Al \longrightarrow Al^{3+} + 3e^-$,
Cl = 2, 8, 7 $3Cl + 3e^- \longrightarrow 3Cl^-$

$:\overset{..}{\underset{..}{Cl}}: + \overset{\times}{Al}\overset{\times}{\times} + :\overset{..}{\underset{..}{Cl}}: \longrightarrow [Al^{3+}][:\overset{..}{\underset{..}{\overset{\times}{Cl}}}:^-]_3$
$:\overset{..}{\underset{..}{Cl}}:$

7 P, Q and R are 3 elements which undergo chemical reactions according to the following equations:
(a) $P_2O_3 + 2Q \longrightarrow Q_2O_3 + 2P$

(b) $3RSO_4 + 2Q \longrightarrow Q_2(SO_4)_3 + 3R$
(c) $3RO + 2P \longrightarrow P_2O_3 + 3R$ **CBSE 2014**

Answer the following questions:
(i) Which element is most reactive?
(ii) Which element is least reactive?
(iii) State the type of reaction listed above.

Sol. (i) Most reactive metal is Q as it has replaced both P and R from their compounds.
(ii) Element R is least reactive as it has been replaced by both P and Q.
(iii) Displacement reaction

8 State which of the following chemical reactions will take place or which will not, giving suitable reason for each?
(i) $Zn(s) + CuSO_4(aq) \longrightarrow ZnSO_4(aq) + Cu(s)$
(ii) $Fe(s) + ZnSO_4(aq) \longrightarrow FeSO_4(aq) + Zn(s)$
(iii) $Zn(s) + FeSO_4(aq) \longrightarrow ZnSO_4(aq) + Fe(s)$

Sol. (i) Zinc displaces copper from copper sulphate because zinc is more reactive than copper as it is placed above copper in the reactivity series of metals.
(ii) This reaction will not occur as iron is less reactive than zinc.
(iii) Zinc displaces iron because zinc is more reactive than iron.

9 A metal A, which is used in thermite process, when heated with oxygen gives an oxide B, which is amphoteric in nature. Identify A and B. Write down the reactions of oxide B with HCl and NaOH.
NCERT Exemplar

Sol. Metal A is aluminium (Al) which is used in thermite reaction. Al reacts with oxygen to form aluminium oxide, Al_2O_3 (B), which is amphoteric in nature.
$$4Al(s) + 3O_2(g) \longrightarrow 2Al_2O_3(s)\ (B)$$
(i) $\underset{\text{Aluminium oxide}}{Al_2O_3(s)} + \underset{\text{Hydrochloric acid}}{6HCl(aq)} \longrightarrow$
$\underset{\text{Aluminium chloride}}{2AlCl_3(aq)} + 3H_2O(l)$
(ii) $\underset{\text{Aluminium oxide}}{Al_2O_3(s)} + \underset{\text{Sodium hydroxide}}{2NaOH(aq)} \longrightarrow$
$\underset{\text{Sodium aluminate}}{2NaAlO_2(aq)} + H_2O(l)$

10 A metal acts as a good reducing agent. It reduces Fe_2O_3 and MnO_2. The reaction with Fe_2O_3 is used for joining broken railway tracks. Identify the metal and write all the chemical reactions.

Sol. Metal which reduces Fe_2O_3 and MnO_2 is aluminium Al.
$3MnO_2(s) + 4Al(s) \longrightarrow 3Mn(l) + 2Al_2O_3(s) + $ Heat
$Fe_2O_3(s) + 2Al(s) \longrightarrow 2Fe(l) + Al_2O_3(s) + $ Heat

11 Account for the following :
(i) Electrical wires are coated with plastic.
(ii) Carbon is not used for reducing aluminium from aluminium oxide.
CBSE 2016

Sol. (i) Electrical wires are made-up of copper. Copper reacts with moist carbon dioxide in the air and solwly loses its shiny brown surface and gains a green coat. So, these are coated with plastic.
(ii) Because aluminium has greater affinity for carbon therefore, carbon cannot reduce alumina (Al_2O_3) to aluminium.

12 How is the method of extraction of metals high up in the reactivity series different from that for metals in the middle? Why can be same process not be applied for them? Name the process used for the extraction of these metals.   **CBSE 2019**

Sol. The metals in the middle of the reactivity series (such as iron, zinc, lead, copper etc.) is moderately reactive. Thus, to obtain such metals from their compounds, their sulphides and carbonates are first converted into their oxides by the process of roasting and clacination respectively and then the metal oxides are reduced to corresponding metal by using suitable reducing agents such as carbon.
On the other hand, metals which is high up in the reactivity series (such as sodium, magnesium, calcium, aluminium, etc.) is very reactive and cannot be obtained from its compound by heating with carbon. Therefore, such metals are obtained by electrolytic reduction of their molten salt.

13 Two ores A and B were taken. On heating, ore A gives CO_2, whereas ore B gives SO_2. What steps will you take to convert them into metals?   **NCERT Exemplar**

Sol. (i) Ore A is a carbonate ore.
The steps involved in extraction of A are:
(a) **Calcination** The carbonate ore is heated strongly in the limited supply of air to produce metal oxide.
$$ACO_3(s) \xrightarrow{\Delta} AO(s) + CO_2(g)$$

(b) **Reduction to metal** The oxide ore is reduced with C (coke).
$$AO(s) + C(s) \longrightarrow A(s) + CO(g)$$

(ii) Ore B is a sulphide ore.
Following steps are involved in its extraction:

(a) **Roasting** The sulphide ore is heated strongly in the presence of excess of air to produce metal oxide.
$$2BS(s) + 3O_2(g) \xrightarrow{\Delta} 2BO(s) + 2SO_2(g)$$

(b) **Reduction** Oxide of metal B is reduced by carbon to obtain the corresponding metal.
$$\underset{\text{Carbon}}{BO(s) + C(s)} \longrightarrow \underset{\text{Metal}}{B(s)} + CO_2/CO(g)$$

14 A metal X, which is used in thermite process, when heated with oxygen gives an oxide Y which is amphoteric in nature. Identify X and Y. Write balanced chemical equations of the reactions of oxide Y with hydrochloric acid and sodium hydroxide.
CBSE 2019

Sol. Since, the metal 'X' is used in thermite process, therefore,
'X' is aluminium and 'Y' is aluminium oxide, Al_2O_3 (amphoteric in nature).
Balanced chemical equation is as follow :

(i) $\underset{\text{Aluminium oxide}}{Al_2O_3(s)} + 6HCl(aq) \longrightarrow \underset{\text{Aluminium chloride}}{2AlCl_3(aq)} + 3H_2O(l)$

(ii) $\underset{\text{Aluminium oxide}}{Al_2O_3(s)} + \underset{\text{Sodium hydroxide}}{2NaOH(aq)} \longrightarrow \underset{\text{Sodium aluminate}}{2NaAlO_2(aq)} + H_2O(l)$

15 What is meant by electrolytic reduction? How is sodium obtained from its molten chloride? Explain. **CBSE 2010**

Sol. In electrolytic reduction, the metals are extracted by the electrolysis of their salts. Sodium obtained by the electrolysis of their molten chlorides. The metals are deposited at the cathode (the negatively charged electrode), whereas chlorine is liberated at the anode (the positively charged electrode).

At cathode $Na^+ + e^- \longrightarrow Na$

At anode $2Cl^- \longrightarrow Cl_2 + 2e^-$

Reaction $NaCl \longrightarrow Na^+ + Cl^-$

16 Why sodium forms sodium hydroxide when react with water whereas aluminium forms only aluminium oxide?

Sol. The metals placed lower in the reactivity series are less reactive towards water. Sodium metal placed above aluminium reacts with water to form sodium oxide which further dissolves in water to give sodium hydroxide solution. Whereas, aluminium reacts with oxygen to form aluminium oxide which does not dissolve in water to form aluminium hydroxide.

17 What happens, when
(i) $ZnCO_3$ is heated in the absence of oxygen?
(ii) a mixture of Cu_2O and Cu_2S is heated?
NCERT Exemplar

Sol. (i) Zinc oxide and carbon dioxide are produced.

$\underset{\text{Zinc carbonate}}{ZnCO_3(s)} \xrightarrow[\text{Calcination}]{\text{Heat}} \underset{\text{Zinc oxide}}{ZnO(s)} + \underset{\text{Carbon dioxide}}{CO_2(g)}$

Moisture and volatile impurities are also expelled out during the process of calcination.

(ii) Copper metal and sulphur dioxide gas are produced.

$\underset{\substack{\text{Cuprous}\\\text{oxide}}}{2Cu_2O(s)} + \underset{\substack{\text{Cuprous}\\\text{sulphide}}}{Cu_2S(s)} \xrightarrow[\text{Reduction}]{\text{Heat}} \underset{\text{Copper}}{6Cu(s)} + \underset{\substack{\text{Sulphur}\\\text{dioxide}}}{SO_2(g)}$

18 Hydrogen is not a metal but it has been assigned a place in the reactivity series of metals. Explain.

Sol. Although, hydrogen is not a metal yet it has been assigned a place in the reactivity series of metals. The reason is that like metal, hydrogen also has a tendency to lose electron and forms a positive ion H^+.

The metals which lose electrons less readily than hydrogen are placed below it and the metals which lose electrons more readily than hydrogen are placed above it in the reactivity series of metals.

19 During extraction of metals, electrolytic refining is used to obtain pure metals.
(i) Which material will be used as anode and cathode for refining of silver metal by this process?
(ii) Suggest a suitable electrolyte also.
(iii) In this electrolytic cell, where do we get pure silver after passing electric current? **NCERT Exemplar**

Sol. (i) **Anode** Impure block of silver metal
Cathode Pure thin strip of silver metal
(ii) Aqueous solution of a silver salt like $AgNO_3$ can be used as an electrolyte.
(iii) We get pure silver at cathode, because at cathode, reduction reaction will take place.
$$Ag^+(aq) + e^- \longrightarrow Ag(s)$$

20 Explain the process of electrolytic refining for copper with the help of a labelled diagram. **CBSE 2016**

Sol.

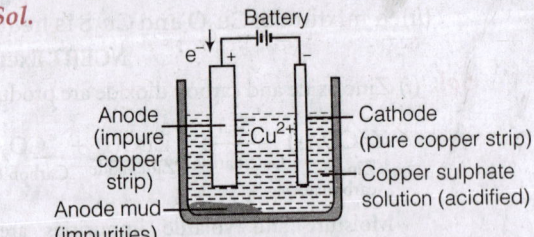

In electrolytic process, the impure metal is made the anode and a thin strip of pure metal is made the cathode. A solution of the metal salt is used as an electrolyte. On passing the current through the electrolyte, the pure metal from the anode dissolves into the electrolyte. An equivalent of pure metal from the electrolyte is deposited on the cathode.

At cathode $Cu^{2+} + 2e^- \longrightarrow Cu$ (deposited)
At anode $Cu(s) \longrightarrow Cu^{2+}(aq) + 2e^-$
(Impure metal) (Dissolved)

21 An element A reacts with water to form a compound B which is used in white washing.
The compound B on heating forms an oxide C which on treatment with water gives back B. Identify A, B and C and give the reactions involved. **NCERT Exemplar**

Sol. Element A is calcium (Ca). When it reacts with water, it forms calcium hydroxide. Thus, compound B is calcium hydroxide $[Ca(OH)_2]$, which is used in white washing.
$$\underset{(A)}{Ca(s)} + 2H_2O(l) \longrightarrow \underset{(B)}{Ca(OH)_2(aq)} + H_2(g)$$

Compound B on heating gives CaO.
$$\underset{(B)}{Ca(OH)_2(aq)} \xrightarrow{\Delta} \underset{(C)}{CaO(s)} + H_2O(l)$$

Thus, C is calcium oxide (CaO).
C(CaO) on treatment with water gives back B $[Ca(OH)_2]$.
$$\underset{(C)}{CaO(s)} + H_2O(l) \longrightarrow \underset{(B)}{Ca(OH)_2(aq)}$$

22 An alkali metal A gives a compound B (molecular mass = 40) on reacting with water. The compound B gives a soluble compound C on treatment with aluminium oxide. Identify A, B and C and give the reactions involved. **NCERT Exemplar**

Sol. Let the atomic weight of alkali metal A be x. When it reacts with water, it forms a compound B having molecular mass 40. Let the reaction be
$$2A + 2H_2O \longrightarrow \underset{(B)}{2AOH} + H_2\uparrow$$

According to the question,
$x + 16 + 1 = 40$ (Given)
$\therefore \quad x = 40 - 17 = 23$
It is the atomic weight of Na (sodium).
Therefore, the alkali metal (A) is Na and the reaction is
$$\underset{(A)}{2Na(s)} + 2H_2O(l) \longrightarrow \underset{(B)}{2NaOH(aq)} + H_2(g)$$

So, compound B is sodium hydroxide (NaOH).
Sodium hydroxide reacts with aluminium oxide (Al_2O_3) to give sodium aluminate $(NaAlO_2)$. Thus, C is sodium aluminate $(NaAlO_2)$. The reaction involved is
$$Al_2O_3(s) + \underset{(B)}{2NaOH(aq)} \longrightarrow$$
$$\underset{\substack{\text{Sodium aluminate}\\(C)}}{2NaAlO_2(aq)} + H_2O(l)$$

Long Answer (LA) Type Questions

1 (i) Predict the reaction, if any, between
(a) zinc and silver nitrate solution.
(b) magnesium and iron (II) chloride solution.
(c) copper and magnesium sulphate solution.
Write the equations, with its physical form and symbols, for the reaction.

(ii) A lump of element X can be cut by a knife. During its reaction with water, X floats and melts. What is X? Explain.

Sol. (i) (a) Zinc is more reactive than silver. It will displace silver from silver nitrate solution.
$$Zn(s) + 2AgNO_3(aq) \longrightarrow Zn(NO_3)_2(aq) + 2Ag(s)$$

(b) Magnesium is more reactive than iron. It will displace iron from iron (II) chloride solution.
$$Mg(s) + FeCl_2(aq) \longrightarrow MgCl_2(aq) + Fe(s)$$

Metals and Non-Metals

(c) Copper is less reactive than magnesium. It will not displace magnesium from magnesium sulphate solution. Thus, no reaction will take place.

$$Cu(s) + MgSO_4(aq) \longrightarrow \text{No reaction}$$

(ii) X is potassium (K).

Potassium being soft can be cut with a knife and being lighter than water floats at the surface. The heat produced during reaction with water will melt it.

2 With the help of a suitable example, explain how ionic compounds are formed? State any three general properties of ionic compounds.

Sol. Ionic compounds are formed by the transfer of electrons from one atom to another. These compounds are composed of positively charged metal cations and negative charged anion, e.g. sodium oxide Na_2O.

$$\underset{(2,8,1)}{2Na} \longrightarrow \underset{(2,8)}{2Na^+} + 2e^-$$

$$\underset{(2,6)}{O} + 2e^- \longrightarrow \underset{(2,8)}{O^{2-}}$$

$$\begin{matrix} Na \cdot \\ Na \cdot \end{matrix} \overset{\times\times}{\underset{\times\times}{O_{\times}^{\times}}} \longrightarrow 2[Na^+] \left[\overset{\times\times}{\underset{\cdot\cdot}{O_{\times}^{\times}}} \right]^{2-} \text{ or } Na_2O$$

Properties of ionic compounds are :
(i) These compounds are water soluble.
(ii) These compounds have high melting and boiling points.
(iii) These compounds conduct electricity in molten form or in the form of aqueous solution.

3 Give reasons for the following:
(i) Ionic compounds have higher melting and boiling points.
(ii) Sodium is kept immersed in kerosene.
(iii) Reaction of calcium with water is less violent.
(iv) Prior to reduction the metal sulphides and carbonates must be converted into metal oxides for extracting metals. **CBSE 2014**

Sol. (i) Refer to Q.9 of NCERT Folder Intext Questions on Pg. 68.
(ii) Refer to Q.3 of NCERT Folder Intext Questions on Pg. 67.
(iii) Calcium reacts with water to form calcium hydroxide and hydrogen. The heat produced in this reaction is less which is insufficient to burn the hydrogen gas which is formed. Hence, the reaction of calcium with water is less violent.

(iv) It is easier to obtain metal from its oxide rather than its carbonates and sulphides. Therefore, these ores are first converted to oxide and then reduced to metal.

4 Explain the following :
(i) Sodium chloride is an ionic compound which does not conduct electricity in solid state whereas it does conduct electricity in molten state as well as in aqueous solution.
(ii) Reactivity of aluminium decrease if it is dipped in nitric acid.
(iii) Metals like calcium and magnesium are never found in their free state in nature. **CBSE 2019**

Sol. (i) Refer to text on pages 63 and 64 (Conduction of electricity).
(ii) When aluminium is dipped in nitric acid, a layer of aluminium oxide is formed on the metal. This happens because nitric acid is a strong oxidising agent. The layer of aluminium oxide prevents further reaction of aluminium. Due to this, the reactivity of aluminium decreases.
(iii) Ca and Mg are alkaline earth metals. They are most reactive metals and readily reacts with atmospheric oxygen and other gases. Therefore, they are found in nature in the form of their compounds.

5 Give reasons for the following:
(i) Generally no hydrogen gas is evolved when metals react with dilute nitric acid.
(ii) Sodium hydroxide solution cannot be kept in aluminium containers.
(iii) Silver metal does not combine easily with oxygen but silver jewellery tarnishes after some time.
(iv) Sodium is obtained by the electrolysis of its molten chloride and not from its aqueous solution.
(v) Aluminium reacts with dilute hydrochloric acid slowly in the beginning. **CBSE 2014**

Sol. (i) Nitric acid (HNO_3) is a strong oxidising agent. So, as soon as hydrogen gas is formed in the reaction between a metal and dilute nitric acid. The nitric acid oxidises this hydrogen to water and itself gets reduced to NO_2 or NO or N_2O.

So, in the reaction of metals (except Mn and Mg) with dilute nitric acid, no hydrogen gas is evolved.

(ii) Sodium hydroxide reacts with Al thereby corroding the metal and produces highly flammable hydrogen gas. Hence, it cannot be kept in Al containers.

(iii) Silver is a highly unreactive metal. So, it does not react with the oxygen of air easily. But silver jewellery tarnishes after some time (turns black) due to the formation of a thin sulphide layer on their surface by the action of hydrogen sulphide (H_2S) gas present in air.

(iv) We cannot use an aqueous solution of sodium chloride to obtain sodium metal because if we electrolyse an aqueous solution of NaCl, then as soon as sodium metal is produced at cathode, it will react with water present in the aqueous solution to form sodium hydroxide. So, the electrolysis of aqueous solution of NaCl will produce NaOH instead of Na metal.

(v) Al metal reacts with dilute HCl slowly in the beginning due to the presence of a tough protective layer of aluminium oxide on its surface.

6 (i) Write chemical equations for the following reactions :
(a) Calcium metal reacts with water.
(b) Cinnabar is heated in the presence of air.
(c) Manganese dioxide is heated with aluminium powder.

(ii) What are alloys ? List two properties of alloys. **CBSE 2019**

Sol. (i) (a) Refer to text on page no. 60 and 61 (Reaction of metals with water).
(b) Refer to text on page no. 64 (Extraction of metals of low reactivity).
(c) As aluminium is more reactive than magnesium so it displace it from its oxide. The following reaction takes place.
$$3MnO_2 + 4Al \longrightarrow 3Mn + 2Al_2O_3$$

(ii) Refer to text on page no. 66 (Alloy).

7 (i) Given below are the steps for extraction of copper from its ore. Write the reaction involved. **NCERT Exemplar**
(a) Roasting of copper (I) sulphide.
(b) Reduction of copper (I) oxide with copper (I) sulphide.
(c) Electrolytic refining.

(ii) Draw a neat and well labelled diagram for electrolytic refining of copper.

Or How is copper obtained from its ore (Cu_2S)? Write only the chemical equations. How is copper thus obtained refined? Name and explain the process alongwith a labelled diagram. **CBSE 2014**

Sol. (i) (a) $2Cu_2S(s) + 3O_2(g) \xrightarrow{Heat} 2Cu_2O(s) + 2SO_2(g)$

(b) $2Cu_2O(s) + Cu_2S(s) \xrightarrow{Heat} 6Cu(s) + SO_2(g)$

(c) Copper is refined electrolytically. The reactions are as follows:
At cathode $Cu^{2+}(aq) + 2e^- \longrightarrow Cu(s)$
At anode $Cu(s) \longrightarrow Cu^{2+}(aq) + 2e^-$

(ii) The diagram shown below is of electrolytic refining of copper

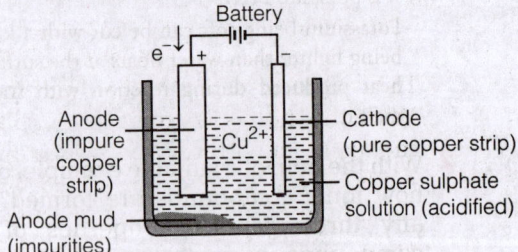

8 (i) Give differences between roasting and calcination with suitable examples.

(ii) Explain how the following metals are obtained from their compounds by the reduction process.
(a) Metal M which is in the middle of the reactivity series.
(b) Metal N which is high up in the reactivity series.
Give one example of each type.

Sol. (i)

Roasting	Calcination
Ore is heated in excess of air.	Ore is heated in the absence or limited supply of air.
This is used for sulphide ores.	This is used for carbonate ores.
SO_2 is produced along with metal oxide.	CO_2 is produced along with metal oxide.
e.g. $2ZnS(s) + 3O_2(g)$ $\xrightarrow{\Delta} 2ZnO(s) + 2SO_2(g)$	e.g. $ZnCO_3(s) \xrightarrow{\Delta}$ $ZnO(s) + CO_2(g)$

(ii) (a) The metal M which is in the middle of the reactivity series (such as iron, zinc, lead, copper etc) is moderately reactive. Thus, to obtain such metals from their compounds, their sulphides and carbonates (in which they are present in nature) are first converted into their oxides by the process of roasting and calcination respectively.

The metal oxides (MO) are then reduced to the corresponding metals by using suitable reducing agents such as carbon, e.g. zinc metal can be obtained from its oxide as follows:
$$\underset{\text{Zinc oxide}}{ZnO(s)} + \underset{\text{Carbon}}{C(s)} \longrightarrow \underset{\text{Zinc}}{Zn(s)} + \underset{\substack{\text{Carbon} \\ \text{monoxide}}}{CO(g)}$$

(b) The metal N which is high up in the reactivity series (such as sodium, magnesium, calcium, aluminium etc) is very reactive and cannot be

Metals and Non-Metals

obtained from its compound by heating with carbon. Therefore, such metals are obtained by electrolytic reduction of their molten salt, e.g. sodium is obtained by the electrolysis of molten sodium chloride (NaCl).

At cathode $\quad Na^+ + e^- \longrightarrow Na$

At anode $\quad 2Cl^- \longrightarrow Cl_2 + 2e^-$

9 In what forms are metals found in nature? With the help of examples, explain how metals react with oxygen, water and dilute acids. Also, write chemical equations for the reactions. **CBSE 2011, 10**

Sol. Metals are found in both free and combined states.

Reaction of metals with oxygen All metals combine with oxygen at different rates to form metal oxides, e.g. sodium forms sodium oxide at room temperature on reacting with oxygen.

$$4Na + O_2 \longrightarrow 2Na_2O$$

But copper forms copper oxide when it is heated in the presence of air.

$$2Cu + O_2 \xrightarrow{\Delta} 2CuO$$

Reaction of metals with water Metals like sodium react with cold water, magnesium with hot water to form their hydroxides and evolve hydrogen gas. But iron reacts with steam to form oxides and evolve hydrogen gas.

$$2Na(s) + 2H_2O(l) \longrightarrow 2NaOH(aq) + H_2(g)$$
$$Mg(s) + 2H_2O(l) \longrightarrow Mg(OH)_2(aq) + H_2(g)$$
$$3Fe(l) + 4H_2O(l) \longrightarrow Fe_3O_4(s) + 4H_2(g)$$

Reaction of metals with acids Metals react with acids to form salt and evolve hydrogen gas.

e.g. magnesium reacts with dilute hydrochloric acid to form magnesium chloride and evolve H_2.

$$Mg(s) + 2HCl(aq) \longrightarrow MgCl_2(aq) + H_2(g)\uparrow$$

10 (i) Write the steps involved in the extraction of pure metals in the middle of the activity series from their carbonate ores.

(ii) How is copper extracted from its sulphide ore? Explain the various steps supported by chemical equations. Draw labelled diagram for the electrolytic refining of copper. **CBSE 2018**

Sol. (i) Steps involved in the extraction of pure metals in the middle of the activity series from their carbonate ores.

Carbonate ore
↓
Calcination
(Carbonate ores are changes into oxides by heating strongly in limited supply of air)
↓
Reduction of metal
(Metal oxides are reduced to the corresponding metals by using siutable reducing agent)
↓
Purification of metal
(Removal of impurities)

(ii) Refer to Long Answer Type Questions Q. 7 on Page 84.

11 Two ores X and Y were taken. On heating these ores, it was observed that

(a) ore X gives CO_2 gas, and
(b) ore Y gives SO_2 gas.

Write steps to convert these ores into metals, giving chemical equations of the reactions that take place.
CBSE (All India) 2020

Sol. (a) The ore X which gives CO_2 gas is a carbonate ore.

(b) The ore Y which gives SO_2 gas is a sulphide ore.

The steps involves in the conversion of these ores into metals is given as below:

(i) **Enrichment of ores** Removal of unwanted material (gangue) from the ore is called enrichment or concentration of ore. The undesirable impurities like soil, sand etc. are gangue or matrix.

(ii) **Conversion of ores into oxides**

$$\underset{(X)}{ZnCO_3} \xrightarrow{\text{Calcination}} ZnO + CO_2\uparrow$$

$$\underset{(Y)}{2ZnS} + 3O_2 \xrightarrow{\text{Roasting}} 2ZnO + 2SO_2\uparrow$$

(iii) Reaction of oxide ore (smelting) follows as:

$$\underset{\text{Zinc oxide}}{ZnO} + \underset{\text{Carbon}}{C} \longrightarrow \underset{\text{Zinc}}{Zn} + \underset{\substack{\text{Carbon}\\\text{monoxide}}}{CO}$$

(iv) **Refining** It is the process of purification of the metal obtained after reduction. Various methods for refining are employed but most common method is electrolytic refining.

12 (a) With the help of a diagram explain the method of refining of copper by electrolysis.

(b) How are broken railway tracks joined? Give the name of the process and the chemical equation of the reaction involved. **CBSE (All India) 2020**

Sol. (a) Refer to text on pages 65 and 66.

(b) The broken railway tracks are joined by the reaction of iron (III) oxide with aluminium. This process is called thermite welding. The chemical equation involved is given as follows:

$$\underset{\text{Ferric oxide}}{Fe_2O_3(s)} + \underset{\text{Aluminium}}{2Al(s)} \longrightarrow \underset{\text{Iron}}{2Fe(l)}$$
$$+ \underset{\text{Aluminium oxide}}{Al_2O_3(s)} + \text{Heat}$$

CHAPTER EXERCISE

Multiple Type Questions

1. An element A is soft and can be cut with a knife. This is very reactive to air and cannot be kept open in air. It reacts vigorously with water. Identify the element from the following.
   (a) Mg   (b) Na
   (c) P   (d) Ca

2. Which one of the following four metals would be displaced from the solution of its salts by other three metals?
   (a) Mg   (b) Ag
   (c) Zn   (d) Cu

3. An electrolytic cell consists of
   (i) positively charged cathode
   (ii) negatively charged anode
   (iii) positively charged anode
   (iv) negatively charged cathode
   (a) (i) and (ii)
   (b) (iii) and (iv)
   (c) (i) and (iii)
   (d) (ii) and (iv)

Fill in the Blanks

4. Potassium oxide dissolves in water to produce......
5. Non-metal......is considered to be a brittle solid.
6. The reaction of metal oxide to form metal by using aluminium powder as a reducing agent is known as......

True and False

7. Aluminium can replace zinc from zinc sulphate salt but opposite reaction does not take place.
8. In the conversion of copper oxide into copper metal, copper sulphide acts as a reductant.
9. Solder, a lead alloy, is used for soldering wire and electronic components.

Match the Columns

10. Match the alloys given in **column A** with their composition given in **column B**.

	Column A		Column B
P.	Brass	I.	Na–Hg
Q.	Bronze	II.	Cu + Zn
R.	Solder	III.	Cu + Sn
S.	Amalgam	IV.	Pb + Sn

Assertion-Reason

Direction (Q. Nos. 11-12) *In each of the following questions, a statement of Assertion is given by the corresponding statement of Reason. Of the statements, mark the correct answer as.*

(a) Both Assertion and Reason are true and Reason is the correct explanation of Assertion.
(b) Both Assertion and Reason are true, but Reason is not the correct explanation of Assertion.
(c) Assertion is true, but Reason is false.
(d) Assertion is false, but Reason is true.

11. **Assertion** Hydrogen is not a metal but it has been assigned a place in the reactivity series of metals.
    Reason Hydrogen has a tendency to lose electron and forms a positive ion H^+.

12. **Assertion** When lead vessel is kept in a solution of $ZnSO_4$, lead will remain unaffected.
    Reason Lead is more electropositive than zinc.

Passage based Questions

Direction (Q.Nos. 13 to 16) *Answer the questions on the basis of your understanding of the following passage, table and related studied concepts:*

Generally, the metals form basic oxides whereas non-metals form acidic oxides. Only a few metals form hydrides with hydrogen and these hydrides are unstable while the non-metals form stable hydrides. Metal atom can donate electrons easily hence they act as reducing agents and the non-metals can accept electrons readily, therefore they act as oxidising agent. Thermal conductivity is the ability of an element to allow heat to pass through it. Generally, all metals are good conductors of heat except lead and mercury. The table shows the thermal conductivity values of some elements expressed in Watt/centimeter Kelvin (W/cm-K).

Element	Symbol	Thermal conductivity (W/cm-K)
Lead	Pb	0.34
Copper	Cu	4.01
Aluminium	Al	2.37
Iron	Fe	0.802
Selenium	Se	0.0204
sulphur	S	0.00269
Phosphorus	P	0.00235

All in one Metals and Non-Metals

13. Name a metal which is a best conductor of heat.
14. Which reducing agent can be used in the extraction of metals placed at the top of the reactivity series?
15. Name a metal which combines with hydrogen gas. Name the compound formed.
16. An element forms an oxide A_2O_3 which is acidic in nature. Identify A as metal or non-metal.

Direction (Q. Nos. 17-20) *Answer the questions on the basis of your understanding of the following passage and related studied concepts:*

Refining is the process of purification of metals. One of the important method of refining is electrolysis. In electrolysis, electrical energy is used to bring about a non-spontaneous redox reaction. This is done by passing an electric current through a liquid containing ions, known as electrolyte. In contrast to metals, the current in electrolytes is carried by the movement of ions rather than the movement of electrons. The soild conductors inserted into the liquid are called the electrodes, the one with positive charge is called the anode and the one with the negative charge is called cathode.

17. Which of the following metal is present in the anode mude during refining of copper?
    (a) Sodium (b) Aluminium
    (c) Gold (d) Iron
18. The metal which is not refined by electrolytic method is
    (a) Na (b) Al (c) Zn (d) Cu
19. Name the elecrolyte used in refining of copper?
20. What is anode mude?

Answers

1. (b) 2. (b) 3. (b)
4. Alkali (potassium hydroxide) 5. Sulphur
6. Thermite reaction 7. True
8. True 9. True
10. P→(II), Q→(III), R→(IV), S→(I)
17. (c) 18. (a)

Very Short Answer Type Questions

21. Which of the following elements is a metal?
    $^{7}_{3}X$, $^{3}_{1}Y$, $^{10}_{9}Z$
22. Name one metal and one non-metal which are obtained on a large scale from sea water.
23. Name the process used for the concentration of the sulphide ore.   **CBSE 2008**

24. For the reduction of metal oxide to metal, suggest a reducing agent cheaper than aluminium.

Short Answer (SA) Type Questions

25. Answer the following:
    (i) Name a metal which does not stick to glass.
    (ii) What is the nature of zinc oxide?
    (iii) What is deposited at the cathode, a pure or impure metal?
    (iv) Will carbon monoxide (CO) change the colour of blue litmus?
26. Zn is more electropositive than Fe. Therefore, it should get corroded faster than Fe. But it does not happen. Instead, it is used to galvanise iron. Explain why does it happen so?   **CBSE 2007**
27. Write the equations for the reactions of
    (i) iron with steam
    (ii) calcium with water
    (iii) potassium with water
28. Why Al metal cannot be obtained by the reduction of Al_2O_3 with coke? Explain.
29. A solution of $CuSO_4$ was kept in an iron pot. After few days, the iron pot was found to have a number of holes in it. Explain the reason in terms of reactivity. Write the equation of the reaction involved.   **NCERT Exemplar**
30. List three properties of sodium in which it differs from the general physical properties of most of the metals.

Long Answer (LA) Type Questions

31. (i) An ore, on heating in air, give sulphur dioxide gas. Name the method in each metallurgical step, that will be required to extract this metal from its ore.
    (ii) State which of the following reactions will take place or which will not, giving suitable reason for each?
    $Zn(s) + CuSO_4(aq) \longrightarrow ZnSO_4(aq) + Cu(s)$
    $Fe(s) + ZnSO_4(aq) \longrightarrow FeSO_4(aq) + Zn(s)$ **CBSE 2015**
32. A non-metal A which is the largest constituent of air, when heated with H_2 in 1 : 3 ratio in the presence of catalyst (Fe) gives a gas B. On heating with O_2, it gives an oxide C. If this oxide is passed into water in the presence of air, it gives an acid D which acts as a strong oxidising agent.
    (i) Identify A, B, C and D.
    (ii) To which group of the periodic table, does this non-metal belongs?   **NCERT Exemplar**

Challengers*

1. In each test tubes A, B, C and D, 2mL of solution of $Al_2(SO_4)_3$ in water was filled. Clean pieces of zinc was placed in test tube A, clean iron nail was put in test tube B, silver (Ag) was placed in test tube C and a clean copper wire was placed in test tube D.

   Which of the following option (s) is/are correct about above experiment?

   (a) Zinc is more reactive than aluminium
   (b) Copper is more reactive than aluminium
   (c) Zinc is more reactive than copper
   (d) Zinc, iron, silver and copper are less reactive than aluminium.

2. On the basis of the sequence of the given reactions identify the most and least reactive elements:

   $X + YA \longrightarrow XA + Y$ ...(i)
   $X + YB \longrightarrow XB + Y$ ...(ii)
   $Z + XA \longrightarrow ZA + X$

   (a) X and Z
   (b) Y and Z
   (c) Z and X
   (d) Z and Y

3. A metal M has electronic configuration 2,8,3 and occurs in earth's crust and its oxide M_2O_3. It is more reactive than zinc. Which of the following options (s) is/are correct?

   (a) The metal M is iron
   (b) The metal M is lead
   (c) The ore from which metal M is extracted is haematite.
   (d) The ore from which metal M is extracted is bauxite.

4. Metal M reacts with oxygen to form metallic oxide MO. This oxide reacts with moisture and carbon dioxide of the atmosphere to form a basic carbonate metal M. The metal 'M' is

   (a) Cu
   (b) Fe
   (c) Zn
   (d) Cr

5. Beakers A, B and C contain zinc sulphate, silver nitrate and iron (II) sulphate solutions respectively. Copper pieces are added to each beaker. Blue colour will appear in case of

   (a) beaker A
   (b) beaker B
   (c) beaker C
   (d) all the beakers.

6. A student puts one big iron nail each in four test tubes containing solutions of zinc sulphate, aluminium sulphate, copper sulphate and iron sulphate. A reddish brown coating was observed only on the surface of iron nail which was put in the solution of

   (a) zinc sulphate
   (b) iron sulphate
   (c) copper sulphate
   (d) aluminium sulphate

7. Which of the following reactions not occur?

   (a) $2AgNO_3(aq) + Zn(s) \longrightarrow Zn(NO_3)_2(aq) + 2Ag(s)$
   (b) $CuSO_4(aq) + Zn(s) \longrightarrow ZnSO_4(aq) + Cu(s)$
   (c) $2AgNO_3(aq) + Fe(s) \longrightarrow Fe(NO_3)_2(aq) + 2Ag(s)$
   (d) $CuSO_4(aq) + 2Ag(s) \longrightarrow Cu(s) + Ag_2SO_4(aq)$

8. Hydrogen gas is not widely used as a reducing agent because

   (a) hydrogen decomposes to atomic hydrogen at higher temperature
   (b) it has risk of explosion with water
   (c) hydrogen isomerises to ortho hydrogen at higher temperature.
   (d) many metals form hydrides at lower temperatures.

9. Alloys are homogeneous mixtures of a metal with a metal or non-metal. Which among the following alloys contain non-metal as one of its constituents?

   (a) Brass
   (b) Bronze
   (c) Amalgam
   (d) Steel

10. E is an element that's ore is rich in E_2O_3. E_2O_3 is not affected by water. It forms two chlorides, ECl_2 and ECl_3. The element E is

    (a) copper
    (b) zinc
    (c) aluminium
    (d) iron

Answer Key

1.	(d)	2.	(d)	3.	(d)	4.	(a)	5.	(b)
6.	(c)	7.	(d)	8.	(b)	9.	(d)	10.	(d)

*These questions may or may not be asked in the examination, have been given just for additional practice.

CHAPTER 04

Carbon and Its Compounds

Carbon is the third most important element after oxygen and hydrogen, for the existence of life on the earth. The name carbon is derived from the Latin word '*Carbo*' which means 'coal'.

The earth crust has only 0.02% carbon which is present in the form of minerals (like carbonates, hydrogen-carbonates, coal and petroleum) and the atmosphere has 0.03% of carbon dioxide. Fuels (like wood, kerosene, coal, LPG, CNG, petrol etc.), clothing material (like cotton, nylon, polyester), paper, rubber, plastics, leather, drugs and dyes are all made up of carbon, also all living structures are carbon based.

In this chapter, we will study the properties of carbon compounds which makes them very important to us.

Chapter Checklist
- Covalent Bonding in Carbon Compounds
- Allotropes of Carbon and Their Properties
- Versatile Nature of Carbon
- Organic Compounds
- Hydrocarbons
- Isomerism
- Functional Groups
- Homologous Series
- Nomenclature of Carbon Compounds
- Chemical Properties of Carbon Compounds
- Fuels and Flames
- Some Important Carbon Compounds
- Soaps and Detergents

Covalent Bonding in Carbon Compounds

The bonds which are formed by the sharing of an electron pair between the atoms (either same or different atoms) are known as **covalent bonds**.

Atomic number of carbon (C) is 6. So, its electronic configuration = $\begin{matrix} K & L \\ 2, & 4 \end{matrix}$.

Thus, there are 4 electrons in its outermost shell and its octet can be completed by the following two ways:

(*i*) It could gain 4 electrons and form C^{4-} anion. But for a nucleus having 6 protons, it would be difficult to hold on 10 electrons, i.e. 4 extra electrons.

(*ii*) It could lose 4 electrons and form C^{4+} cation. But a large amount of energy is required to remove 4 electrons leaving behind a carbon cation with 6 protons in its nucleus holding on just two electrons together, which is not possible.

Therefore, in order to overcome this problem, carbon shares its valence electrons with other atoms of carbon or with atoms of other elements. These shared electrons belong to the outermost shells of both atoms and in this way, both atoms attain the nearest noble gas configuration. This type of bonding is called **covalent bonding**.

The number of electrons shared between two atoms to complete their octet (except hydrogen which shows duplet) is known as the **covalency** of that atom. Thus, the covalency of hydrogen is 1, oxygen is 2, nitrogen is 3 and carbon is 4. Other atoms also exhibit similar type of bonding.

Some Examples Depicting Covalent Bonding

1. Formation of Hydrogen Molecule (H₂)

Atomic number of H = 1

Electronic configuration = $\dfrac{K}{1}$

It has 1 electron in its K-shell and needs 1 more electron to fill the K-shell completely.

Thus, two H-atoms share their electrons to form a molecule of H_2. This allows each H-atom to attain the nearest noble gas configuration, i.e. configuration of helium (having two electrons in its K-shell). Valence electrons are depicted by using crosses.

The shared pair of electrons constitute a single bond between the two H-atoms, which is represented by a single line between the two atoms.

2. Formation of Chlorine Molecule (Cl₂)

Atomic number of Cl = 17

Electronic configuration = $\dfrac{K\ L\ M}{2,\ 8,\ 7}$

It has 7 electrons in its outermost shell and thus require 1 more electron to fulfill its outermost shell. This is achieved by sharing 1 electron with another Cl-atom, forming a chlorine diatomic molecule (Cl_2).

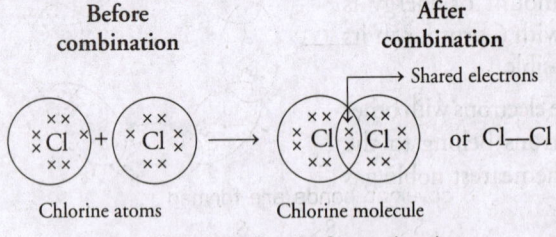

Covalent bonding in Cl₂ molecule

3. Formation of Oxygen Molecule (O₂)

Atomic number of O = 8

Electronic configuration = $\dfrac{K\ L}{2,\ 6}$

It has 6 electrons in its outermost shell thus, require 2 electrons to complete its octet for attaining noble gas configuration. This is achieved by sharing 2 electrons with another oxygen atom.

The two electrons contributed by each oxygen atom give rise to two shared pairs of electrons.

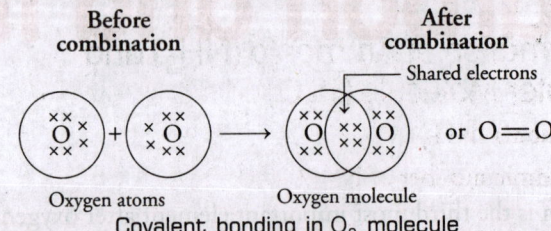

Covalent bonding in O₂ molecule

Here, a double bond is formed between two oxygen atoms thereby forming an oxygen molecule. The above figure represents the sharing of 4 electrons.

4. Formation of Nitrogen Molecule (N₂)

Atomic number of N = 7.

Electronic configuration = $\dfrac{K\ L}{2,\ 5}$

Nitrogen needs 3 more electrons to attain noble gas configuration. Thus, in order to attain octet each nitrogen atom in nitrogen molecule contributes three electrons giving rise to three shared pair of electrons.

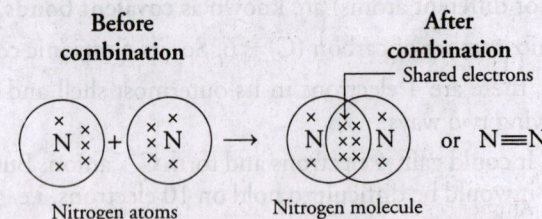

Covalent bonding in N₂ molecule

Here, a triple bond is formed between the two nitrogen atoms.

5. Formation of Methane (CH₄)

In the formation of a methane molecule, one carbon atom shares its 4 electrons with four hydrogen atoms (one electron of each hydrogen atom). It shows carbon is tetravalent because it possesses 4 valence electrons and hydrogen is **monovalent** because it has only 1 valence electron.

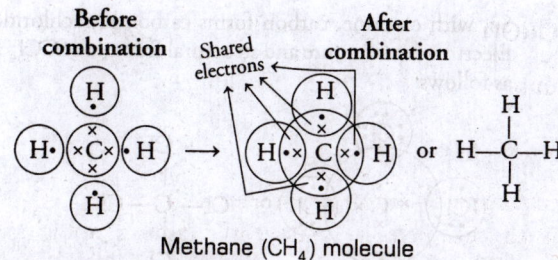

Methane (CH₄) molecule

Note Methane is a carbon compound which is also called marsh gas. It is used as a fuel and a major component of CNG (Compressed Natural Gas) and biogas. It is one of the simplest compounds formed by carbon.

6. Formation of Ammonia (NH₃) and Water Molecule (H₂O)

- **Ammonia** (NH₃)

  Atomic number of N = 7

  Electronic configuration = $\begin{array}{cc} K & L \\ 2, & 5 \end{array}$

  Atomic number of H = 1

  Electronic configuration = $\begin{array}{c} K \\ 1 \end{array}$

  To attain the electronic configuration of the nearest noble gas, nitrogen needs 3 electrons and hydrogen needs 1 electron. When a molecule of ammonia is to be formed, one atom of nitrogen shares its three electrons, one with each of the three atoms of hydrogen.

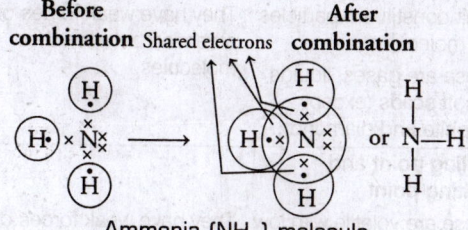

Ammonia (NH₃) molecule

Note Ammonia gas (NH₃) can be used as refrigerant.

- **Water** (H₂O)

  Atomic number of O = 8

  Electronic configuration = $\begin{array}{cc} K & L \\ 2, & 6 \end{array}$

  Atomic number of H = 1

  Electronic configuration = $\begin{array}{c} K \\ 1 \end{array}$

  To attain the stable electronic configuration of the nearest noble gas, hydrogen needs 1 electron and oxygen needs 2 electrons.

In case of a water molecule, two hydrogen atoms share an electron pair with the oxygen atom such that hydrogen acquires a duplet configuration and oxygen an octet, resulting in the formation of two single covalent bonds.

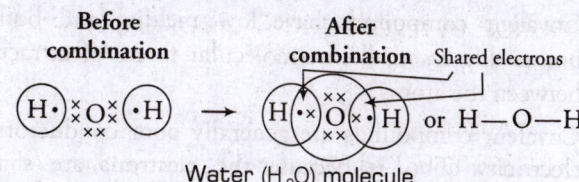

Water (H₂O) molecule

7. Formation of Carbon Dioxide (CO₂)

Atomic number of C = 6

Electronic configuration = $\begin{array}{cc} K & L \\ 2, & 4 \end{array}$

Atomic number of O = 8

Electronic configuration = $\begin{array}{cc} K & L \\ 2, & 6 \end{array}$

To attain the stable electronic configuration, carbon needs 4 electrons, while oxygen needs 2 electrons. So, in CO₂, each of oxygen atom share two electrons from carbon. Thus, oxygen and carbon both attain octet.

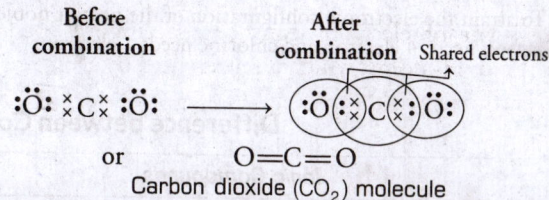

Carbon dioxide (CO₂) molecule

8. Formation of Sulphur Molecule (S₈)

Atomic number of sulphur (S) = 16

Electronic configuration = $\begin{array}{ccc} K & L & M \\ 2, & 8, & 6 \end{array}$

To attain the electronic configuration of the nearest noble gas, each sulphur needs 2 electrons.

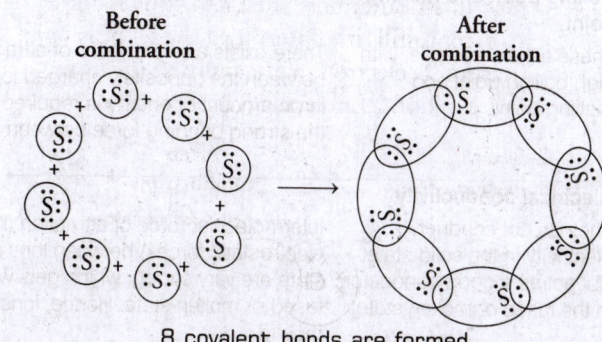

8 covalent bonds are formed

Crown shaped (S₈) molecule

Properties of Covalent Compounds

The compounds containing covalent bonds are called **covalent compounds**. It has the following properties:

(i) Covalent compounds have low melting and boiling points due to small intermolecular forces of attraction between the atoms.

(ii) Covalent compounds are generally poor conductors of electricity. This is because the electrons are shared between atoms and no charged particles are formed in these compounds.

(iii) Covalent compounds are generally volatile in nature.

Example 1. *Carbon a group (14) element in the periodic table, is known to form compounds with many elements. Write an example of a compound formed with*
(i) *chlorine (group 17 of periodic table)*
(ii) *oxygen (group 16 of periodic table)* **NCERT Exemplar**

Sol. (i) Electronic configuration of carbon, C(6) is $\overset{K}{2}, \overset{L}{4}$

Electronic configuration of chlorine, Cl(17) is $\overset{K}{2}, \overset{L}{8}, \overset{M}{7}$

To attain the electronic configuration of the nearest noble gas, carbon needs 4 electron and chlorine needs 1 electron.

So, with chlorine, carbon forms carbon tetrachloride. Electron dot structure and structural formula of CCl_4 is as follows:

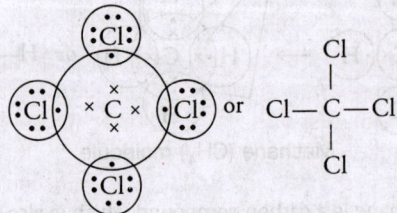

Carbon tetrachloride (CCl_4)

(ii) Electronic configuration of oxygen, O(8) is $\overset{K}{2}, \overset{L}{6}$

With oxygen, carbon forms carbon dioxide. To attain the electronic configuration of the nearest noble gas, carbon needs 4 electrons and oxygen needs 2 electrons. Therefore, in CO_2, each oxygen atom shares 2 electrons with carbon. Electronic configuration of carbon (6) is $\overset{K}{2}, \overset{L}{4}$. The electron dot structure and structural formula of CO_2 is as follows:

Carbon dioxide (CO_2)

Difference between Covalent and Ionic Compounds

	Ionic Compounds		Covalent Compounds	
	Property	*Reason*	*Property*	*Reason*
1.	**Nature** (i) Their constituent particles are ions. (ii) They are hard solids consisting of ions.	These have strong intermolecular forces of attraction between their ions, which cannot be separated easily.	**Nature** Their constituent particles are molecules. These are gases, liquids or soft solids (except graphite and diamond).	They have weak forces of attraction between their molecules.
2.	**Boiling point and melting point** These are non-volatile, with high boiling point and melting point.	There exists a strong force of attraction between the oppositely charged ions, so a large amount of energy is required to break the strong bonding force between ions.	**Boiling point and melting point** These are volatile with low boiling and low melting point.	They have weak forces of attraction between the binding molecules, thus less energy is required to break the force of bonding.
3.	**Electrical conductivity** They do not conduct electricity in the solid state. But act as a good conductor in the fused or molten state.	Intermolecular force of attraction (i.e. electrostatic forces) between ions in the solid state are very strong, which gets weaken in fused or molten state. Hence, ions become mobile.	**Electrical conductivity** They are non-conductors of electricity in solid, molten or aqueous state.	Due to the absence of free ions or charged particles.
4.	**Solubility** These are soluble in water but insoluble in organic solvents.	Water is a polar solvent, it decreases the intermolecular forces of attraction, resulting in free ions in aqueous solution. Hence, they dissolve.	**Solubility** These are insoluble in water but dissolve in organic solvents.	As organic solvents are non-polar, hence, these dissolve in non-polar covalent compounds.

Check Point 01

1. What do you mean by covalent bonding?
2. An element X which has 6 electrons in its outermost shell, require 2 electrons to complete its octet for attaining noble gas configuration. X is an essential element for the survival of all living beings. What is X?
3. Fill in the blanks:
   (i) The main constituent of marsh gas is ....
   (ii) In case of a water molecule, hydrogen acquires a .... configuration.
4. Write the covalent bonding in nitrogen.
5. Why covalent compound are volatile in nature with low boiling and low melting point?
6. State True or False for the following statements:
   Covalent compounds shows large melting point and boiling point?

Allotropes of Carbon and Their Properties

Allotropy is the property by virtue of which an element exists in more than one form and each form has different physical properties but identical chemical properties. These different forms are called allotropes. Carbon exists in different allotropic forms; some of them are:
(i) Crystalline form, e.g. diamond, graphite and fullerene.
(ii) Micro-crystalline form or amorphous form, e.g. coal, lampblack and charcoal.

Diamond

General Properties

- It is a colourless transparent substance with extra ordinary brilliance due to its high refractive index.
- It is quite heavy and extremely hard (hardest natural substance known).
- It does not conduct electricity (because of the absence of free electrons) but it has high thermal conductivity and high melting point.

Structure

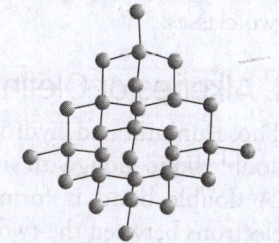

The structure of diamond

It is a giant molecule of carbon atoms in which each carbon atom is bonded to four other carbon atoms forming a rigid three-dimensional network structure, which is responsible for its hardness. Moreover, a lot of energy is required to break the network of strong covalent bonds in the diamond crystal. Therefore, its melting point is very high.

Note Diamond can be prepared artificially by subjecting pure carbon to very high pressure and temperature. These synthetic diamonds are small but are indistinguishable from natural diamonds.

Graphite

General Properties

- It is a greyish black, opaque substance.
- It is lighter than diamond, smooth and slippery to touch.
- It is a good conductor of electricity (due to the presence of free electrons) but bad conductor of heat.

Structure

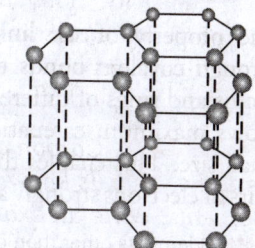

The structure of graphite

A graphite crystal consists of layers of carbon atoms or sheets of carbon atoms. Each carbon atom in a graphite layer is joined to three other carbon atoms by strong covalent bonds to form flat hexagonal rings. However, the fourth electron of each carbon atom is free which makes it a good conductor of electricity. The various layers of carbon atoms in graphite are held together by weak van der Waals' forces so these can slide over one another and therefore, graphite is slippery to touch.

Fullerenes

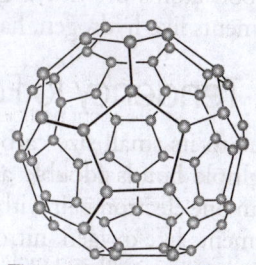

The structure of C-60 Buckminster fullerene

These are recently discovered allotropic forms of carbon which were prepared for the first time by **H W Kroto, Smalley** and **Robert Curt** by the action of laser beam on the vapours of graphite. The first known fullerene was C_{60} which contains 60 carbon atoms (C_{60}) arranged in the shape of a football with smaller proportion of (C_{70}) and traces of compounds containing even upto 370 carbon atoms. Fullerene (C_{60}) was named **Buckminster fullerene** due to their resemblance (in structure) with geodesic domes, designed and built by the American Architect Robert Buckminster Fuller.

Check Point 02

1. Write the two examples of crystalline form of carbon.
2. Draw the structure of diamond.
3. Fill in the blank:
   Graphite is a .... conductor of electricity.
4. How do diamond can be prepared artificially?
5. Give two differences between ionic and covalent compounds.
6. State True or False for the following statements:
   Diamond is a covalent solid, yet has a high melting point.

Versatile Nature of Carbon

The estimated number of carbon compounds known today is about three million. But now the question is, which property or properties of carbon is/are responsible for the formation of such a large number of carbon compounds. Main factors that enables carbon to form large number of compound are:

1. Catenation

The property of self linking of elements mainly C-atoms through covalent bonds to form long, straight or branched chains and rings of different sizes is called *catenation*. Carbon shows maximum catenation in the periodic table due to its small size. This enables the nucleus to hold on to the shared pairs of electrons strongly and C — C bond becomes strong.

> **Note** Elements other than carbon like sulphur, silicon also have a tendency to show the property of self linking, i.e. catenation but to a much lesser extent, due to less bond energy or strength. The bond formed by elements having bigger atoms are much weaker.

2. Tetravalency of Carbon

Carbon belongs to group 14 of the periodic table. Its atomic number is 6 and the electronic configuration is 2, 4. Thus, it has four electrons in the outermost shell. Hence, its valency is four, i.e. it is capable of bonding or pairing with four other carbon atoms or with the atoms of some other monovalent elements like hydrogen, halogen (chlorine, bromine) etc.

3. Tendency to Form Multiple Bonds

Due to its small size carbon has a strong tendency to form multiple bonds (double and triple bonds) by sharing more than one electron pair with its own atoms or with the atoms of elements like oxygen, nitrogen, sulphur etc. As a result, it can form a variety of compounds that are exceptionally stable.

Organic Compounds

The compounds of carbon except for carbides its oxides of carbon, carbonates and hydrogen carbonate salts, are known as **organic compounds**. These compounds were initially extracted from natural substances and it was thought that these carbon compounds could only be formed within a living system. Thus, it was postulated that a 'vital force' was necessary for their synthesis.

In 1828, German chemist **Friedrich Wohler** accidently prepared urea from ammonium cyanate when he was trying to prepare ammonium cyanate by heating ammonium sulphate and potassium cyanate. Thus, synthesis of urea discarded the vital force theory.

Hydrocarbons

The organic compounds containing only carbon and hydrogen are called hydrocarbons. e.g. CH_4, C_2H_6, C_2H_4 and C_2H_2. These are the simplest organic compounds and are regarded as parent organic compounds. All other compounds are considered to be derived from them by the replacement of one or more hydrogen atoms by other atoms or group of atoms.

The hydrocarbons can be classified as :

(*i*) Saturated hydrocarbons

(*ii*) Unsaturated hydrocarbons

Saturated Hydrocarbons

The hydrocarbons in which all the carbon atoms are linked by only single covalent bonds are called **saturated hydrocarbons** or **alkanes** or **paraffins.**

The general formula of these compounds is C_nH_{2n+2}, where, n = number of carbon atoms in one molecule of a hydrocarbon.

e.g. if there is only one carbon atom then, its formula should be $C_1H_{2 \times 1 + 2} = CH_4$ (methane).

Similarly, if there are two carbon atoms in the saturated hydrocarbon (alkane), its formula must be

$$C_2H_{2 \times 2 + 2} = C_2H_6 \text{ (ethane)}$$

Unsaturated Hydrocarbons

The hydrocarbons in which atleast one double or triple bond (or multiple bond) is present alongwith single bonds are called **unsaturated compounds**. These compounds generally burn with sooty or smoky flame due to their incomplete combustion. These are more reactive than saturated hydrocarbons and generally undergo addition reactions (which are discussed later in the chapter).

Unsaturated compounds are further divided into following two classes:

1. Alkenes or Olefins

Those unsaturated hydrocarbons which have atleast one double bond alongwith single bonds are called alkenes. (A double bond is formed by sharing of two pairs of electrons between the two carbon atoms).

General formula of these compounds is C_nH_{2n}.

e.g. if an alkene have 2 carbon atoms, i.e. $n = 2$, its formula is $C_2H_{2 \times 2} = C_2H_4$ (ethene).

2. Alkynes

Those unsaturated hydrocarbons which have one or more triple bonds alongwith the single bonds are called alkynes. (A **triple bond** is formed by the sharing of 3 pairs of electrons between two carbon atoms).

General formula of these compounds is C_nH_{2n-2}.

e.g. if an alkyne have two carbon atoms, then its formula is $C_2H_{2\times 2-2} = C_2H_2$ (ethyne). If there are three carbon atoms in the alkyne then its formula must be $C_3H_{2\times 3-2} = C_3H_4$ (propyne).

> **Note** The minimum number of carbon atoms present in an unsaturated compound is two because formation of double or triple bonds is possible only between two carbon atoms.

Structure of Saturated and Unsaturated Compounds

Steps to draw the structure of carbon compound:

Step I First connect all the carbon atoms together with a single bond.

Step II After that use the hydrogen atoms to satisfy the remaining valencies of carbon (as carbon forms 4 bonds due to its 4 valency).

Step III If number of available H-atoms are less than what is required, satisfy the remaining valency by using double or triple bond.

1. Structure of Ethane (C_2H_6)

In ethane, two carbon atoms are present. To find the structure of simple carbon compounds, the first step is to link the two C-atoms together with a single bond,
i.e.   C — C   [Step I]

Here, only 1 valency of carbon is satisfied and the 3 valencies of each carbon atom remain unsatisfied.

Each of these unsatisfied valencies is satisfied by using H-atoms.

```
    H   H
    |   |
H — C — C — H      [Step II]
    |   |
    H   H
```

Now, the tetravalency of carbon in ethane is satisfied.

Electron dot structure of ethane (C_2H_6)

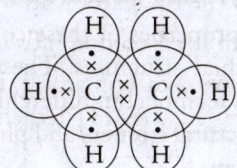

2. Structure of Propane (C_3H_8)

Same rules are followed here as in case of ethane. Here, the three carbon atoms are linked together with a single bond.

C — C — C   [Step I]

To satisfy the remaining valencies of carbon atoms, hydrogen atoms are linked with them.

```
    H   H   H
    |   |   |
H — C — C — C — H      [Step II]
    |   |   |
    H   H   H
```

2 carbon atoms are bonded to 3 hydrogen atoms and 1 carbon atom is bonded to 2 hydrogen atoms.

Electron dot structure of propane (C_3H_8)

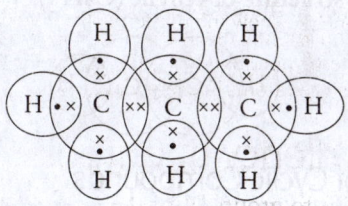

3. Structure of Ethene (C_2H_4)

Link the two carbon atoms by single bond.

C — C   [Step I]

Link the four hydrogen atoms with carbon atom to satisfy the unsatisfied valencies of carbon.

```
H       H
 \     /
  C — C           [Step II]
 /     \
H       H
```

But in this case, even after linking the available hydrogen atoms with carbon atoms, still one valency of each carbon remains unsatisfy. To satisfy it, a double bond is used between the two carbon atoms.

```
H       H
 \     /
  C = C           [Step III]
 /     \
H       H
```

Now, all the four valencies of carbon are satisfied.

Electron dot structure of ethene

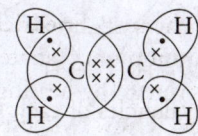

4. Structure of Ethyne (C_2H_2)

Link the two carbon atoms by single bond.

$$C—C \quad [Step\ I]$$

Link the two hydrogen atoms with unsatisfied valencies of carbon.

$$H—C—C—H \quad [Step\ II]$$

But in this case even after linking the available hydrogen atoms with carbon atoms, still two valencies of each carbon is unsatisfy. To satisfy it, a triple bond is used between the two carbon atoms.

$$H—C≡C—H \quad [Step\ III]$$

In ethyne, the two carbon atoms share three pairs of electrons among themselves to form a carbon-carbon triple bond. Each carbon atom shares one electron with each hydrogen atom to form two carbon-hydrogen single bonds.

Electron dot structure of ethyne (C_2H_2)

Structure of Cyclic Compounds

Some carbon compounds also exist in cyclic or ring structure.

To draw the structure of cyclic or ring compounds:

Step I   First connect the available carbon atoms by a single bond in the cyclic form.

Step II Try to satisfy the tetravalency of each carbon with the available hydrogen atoms.

Step III Now, check the valency of each carbon. If it is found unsatisfied, use double or triple bond to satisfy it.

e.g.

(i) Structure of Cyclohexane (C_6H_{12})

Step I Linking of carbon atoms by single bond.

Step II Linking of H-atoms with unsatisfied valencies of carbon.

As all the 4 valencies of each C-atom are satisfied. Therefore, there is no need to draw double or triple bond.

(ii) Structure of Benzene (C_6H_6)

Step I Linking of carbon atoms by single bond.

Step II Linking of hydrogen atoms with unsatisfied valencies of carbon.

But in this case, even after linking the available H-atoms with C-atoms, still one valency of each carbon remains unsatisfied. To satisfy it, a double bond is used between the two C-atoms.

Now, all the four valencies of each C-atom are satisfied.

Check Point 03

1. State True or False for the following statements:
   Catenation is the combining capacity of an element.
2. Why does carbon forms a large number of compounds?
3. Differentiate between saturated and unsaturated hydrocarbons.
4. Write the electron dot structure of C_3H_8.
5. Fill in the blank:
   Synthesis of urea .... the vital force theory.

Isomerism

Organic compounds with same molecular formula but different chemical and physical properties are called **isomers**. This phenomenon is called **isomerism**.

The difference in properties of these compounds is due to the difference in their structures. These compounds have identical molecular formula but different structures. Hence, they are called **structural isomers** and phenomenon is called **structural isomerism**.

e.g. Two structural isomers are possible for butane (C_4H_{10}).

Straight chain structure   Branched chain structure

In some compounds, carbon atoms are arranged in the form of ring. For example, cyclohexane (C_6H_{12}) and benzene (C_6H_6).

C_6H_{12} (Cyclohexane) C_6H_6 (Benzene)

Example 2. *Write the structural formulae of all the isomers of an alkane with six C-atoms (C_6H_{14}).*

Sol. Hexane has the following five isomers:

(i) $CH_3—CH_2—CH_2—CH_2—CH_2—CH_3$

(ii) $\overset{1}{C}H_3—\overset{2}{C}H—\overset{3}{C}H_2—\overset{4}{C}H_2—\overset{5}{C}H_3$
         |
         CH_3

[Here, 5 carbon atoms are arranged in straight line, one is branch at 2 C-atom]

(iii) $\overset{1}{C}H_3—\overset{2}{C}H_2—\overset{3}{C}H—\overset{4}{C}H_2—\overset{5}{C}H_3$
                      |
                      CH_3

[Here, branch is at 3C-atom]

(iv) $\overset{1}{C}H_3—\overset{2}{C}H—\overset{3}{C}H—\overset{4}{C}H_3$
                 | |
                 CH_3 CH_3

[Here, branches are at C-2 and C-3 atoms]

(v) $\overset{1}{C}H_3—\overset{2}{C}—\overset{3}{C}H_2—\overset{4}{C}H_3$
                |
         CH_3 (above) CH_3 (below)

[Here, branches are at C-2 carbon atom only]

Functional Groups

Carbon can also forms bonds with other elements such as halogens, oxygen, nitrogen, sulphur etc. These are called **heteroatoms.** Heteroatoms are also present in form of group of atoms. These atoms or the group of atoms, replace one or more hydrogen atoms of the hydrocarbon and are responsible for the chemical reactivity of the compound.

Hence, these are called **functional groups**.

Thus, functional groups may be defined as an 'atom' or a 'group of atoms' which makes a carbon compound (or organic compound) reactive and decide its properties (or functions) regardless of the length and nature of carbon chain.

Some important functional groups are tabulated below.

Some Functional Groups in Carbon Compounds

Hetero atom	Functional Group	Formula of Functional Group
Cl, Br, F, I	Halo (chloro/bromo fluoro/Ido)	—Cl, —Br, —F, —I [substitutes for H- atom]
Oxygen	1. Alcohol	—OH
	2. Aldehyde	—CHO
	3. Ketone	$—\overset{\overset{\displaystyle}{\|\|}}{\underset{O}{C}}—$
	4. Carboxylic acid	$—\overset{\overset{O}{\|\|}}{C}—OH$

Note Free valency or valencies of the carbon atoms of functional group are shown by the single line.

Homologous Series

A series of similarly constituted compounds in which the members present have the same functional group and similar chemical properties and any two successive members in a particular series differ in their molecular formula by a —CH_2— unit, is called a homologous series.

e.g. $CH_4, C_2H_6, C_3H_8, C_4H_{10}$ are the members of alkane family.

Characteristics of a Homologous Series

- All the members of a homologous series can be represented by the same general formula.
- Any two adjacent homologues differ by 1 carbon atom and 2 hydrogen atoms in their molecular formula.
- All the compounds of a homologous series show similar chemical properties.

- With increase in the molecular mass, a gradual change in the physical properties is seen, e.g. **the melting and boiling points increase with increasing molecular mass.**
- The difference in the molecular masses of any two adjacent homologues or members is 14 u.

Nomenclature of Carbon Compounds

Generally, organic compounds have two names, i.e. IUPAC and common names. The IUPAC names have been adopted by the International Union of Pure and Applied Chemistry and are based on certain rules. The common names (also known as trivial names) have no proper system for naming.

In general, IUPAC name of organic compounds are based on the name of parent carbon chain modified by a prefix (phrase before) or suffix (phrase after) indicating the name (or nature) of the functional group.

Writing IUPAC Name of a Compound

Following steps are used to write the name of an organic compound:

Step I   Count the number of carbon atoms in the given compound and write the root word for it. Root words upto 10 carbon atoms are tabulated below.

Root Words for Carbon Atoms

Number of C-atom(s)	Root Word	Number of C-atom(s)	Root Word
1 (C_1)	Meth	6 (C_6)	Hex
2 (C_2)	Eth	7 (C_7)	Hept
3 (C_3)	Prop	8 (C_8)	Oct
4 (C_4)	But	9 (C_9)	Non
5 (C_5)	Pent	10 (C_{10})	Dec

Step II If the compound is saturated, add suffix 'ane' to the root word, but if it is unsaturated, add suffix 'ene' and 'yne' for double and triple bonds respectively.

e.g. $CH_3CH_2CH_3$ contains three C-atoms, so the root word is 'prop' and it contains only single bonds, thus, suffix used is 'ane'. Hence, the name of this compound is propane.

Similarly, the compound $CH_3CH=CH_2$ is named as propene as here suffix 'ene' is used for double bond.

Step III If functional group is present in the compound, it is indicated in the name of the compound with either a prefix or a suffix (which are given in the table).

Prefix and Suffix of Different Functional Groups

Functional Group	Prefix/Suffix	Example	IUPAC Name
Halogen	Prefix-chloro, bromo etc.	CH_3Cl or H–C(H)(H)–Cl CH_3CH_2Br or H–C(H)(H)–C(H)(H)–Br	Chloromethane Bromoethane
Alcohol	Suffix-ol	H–C(H)(H)–C(H)(H)–C(H)(H)–H CH_3—CH_2—CH_2OH	Propane $\xrightarrow[-e]{+ol}$ Propanol
Aldehyde	Suffix-al	H–C(H)(H)–C(H)=O or CH_3CHO	Ethane $\xrightarrow[-e]{+al}$ Ethanal
Ketone	Suffix-one	H–C(H)(H)–C(=O)–C(H)(H)–H or CH_3COCH_3	Propane $\xrightarrow[-e]{+one}$ Propanone
Carboxylic acid	Suffix-oic acid	H–C(H)(H)–C(=O)–OH or CH_3COOH	Ethane $\xrightarrow{+oic}$ Ethanoic acid
Double bond (alkenes)	Suffix-ene	H–C(H)(H)–C(H)=C(H)(H) or CH_3—CH $=$ CH_2	Propene
Triple bond (alkynes)	Suffix -yne	H–C(H)(H)–C≡C–H or CH_3—C $≡$ CH	Propyne

Note
- If the functional group is named as a suffix, and the suffix of the functional group begins with a vowel *a, e, i, o, u*, then the final 'e' of alkane (or alkene or alkyne) is substituted by appropriate suffix.
- If the functional group and substituents are not present at first carbon, then their location is indicated by digits 2,3,4....

Carbon and Its Compounds

Example 3. *Give the formula and IUPAC names of next two members of homologous series given below.*
(i) C_2H_6 (ii) CH_3OH (iii) $HCOOH$

Sol. (i) C_2H_6; IUPAC name – Ethane
The general formula of alkane is C_nH_{2n+2}.
On adding CH_2 and $(CH_2)_2$ to C_2H_6, we get the next two members which are:
C_3H_8;   IUPAC name – Propane
C_4H_{10};   IUPAC name – Butane

(ii) CH_3OH;   IUPAC name – Methanol
The general formula of an alcohol can be written as $R—OH$ (where, R is an alkyl group).
Here, also CH_2 and $(CH_2)_2$ are added to CH_3OH the next two members are:
$C_2H_5—OH$;   IUPAC name – Ethanol
$C_3H_7—OH$;   IUPAC name – Propanol

(iii) $HCOOH$;   IUPAC name – Methanoic acid
Next two members are (in the same manner as before)
CH_3COOH;   IUPAC name – Ethanoic acid
$C_2H_5—COOH$;   IUPAC name – Propanoic acid

Example 4. *Identify and name the functional groups present in the following compounds. Also, write the IUPAC name of each compound.*

(i) H—C—C—C—OH (with H atoms on each C)

(ii) H—C—C—C—OH (with =O on middle/third C)

(iii) H—C—C—C—C—C—H (with =O on third C)

(iv) H—C—C—C=C—H

Ans.

	Functional group	IUPAC name
(i)	—OH (alcohol)	Propanol
(ii)	—C—OH (carboxylic acid) $\parallel$ O	Propanoic acid
(iii)	—C— (ketone) $\parallel$ O	Pent-3-one
(iv)	—C=C— (alkene)	But-1-ene or butene

Check Point 04

1. Write the structural formulae of all the isomers of an alkane with seven C-atoms (C_7H_{16}).
2. What is meant by homologous series?
3. Fill in the blanks:
   (i) The gradual change in the physical properties occurs with increase in the ....
   (ii) IUPAC stands for ....
4. What are primary and secondary suffixes as applied to IUPAC nomenclature?
5. State True or False for the following statements:
   $\begin{matrix} R \\ H \end{matrix} \!\!>\!\! C = O$ represents carboxylic group.

Chemical Properties of Carbon Compounds

Some of the important chemical properties of carbon compounds are as follows:

Combustion

All the carbon compounds (including its allotropic forms also) burn in oxygen to give carbon dioxide and water vapours. Heat and light are also released during this process. This reaction is called as **combustion**.

e.g. $C + O_2 \longrightarrow CO_2 + Heat + Light$
$CH_4 + 2O_2 \longrightarrow CO_2 + 2H_2O + Heat + Light$
$2CH_3CH_2OH + 6O_2 \longrightarrow 4CO_2 + 6H_2O$
$+ Heat + Light$

Further, once carbon and its compounds ignite, they keep on burning without the requirement of additional energy. That's why, these compounds are used as fuels.

Saturated hydrocarbons give a clean blue flame due to their complete combustion whereas, unsaturated hydrocarbons give a yellow flame with lots of black smoke as they do not undergo complete combustion.

Even saturated hydrocarbons undergoes incomplete combustion in the limited supply of air and gives a sooty flame. The gas stoves used at home has inlets for air so that a sufficiently oxygen-rich mixture is burnt to give a clean blue flame. But sometimes the bottoms of cooking vessels get blackened because the air holes present at the bottom of the vessels gets blocked and fuel [or LPG] do not get enough oxygen. Therefore, it does not burn properly and undergoes incomplete combustion producing sooty flames which blackened the bottom of the vessels.

Oxidation

It is the reaction involving the addition of oxygen and removal of hydrogen. Alcohols can be oxidised to carboxylic acid by heating them either in presence of oxidising agents like alkaline $KMnO_4$ (potassium permanganate) or acidified $K_2Cr_2O_7$ (potassium dichromate).

e.g. $\underset{\text{Ethanol}}{CH_3CH_2OH} \xrightarrow[+ \text{ Heat}]{\text{Alkaline } KMnO_4 + \text{Heat or acidified } K_2Cr_2O_7} \underset{\substack{\text{Acetic acid} \\ \text{(Ethanoic acid)}}}{CH_3\overset{\overset{O}{\|}}{C}-OH}$

Substances that are capable of adding oxygen to other substances are called **oxidising agents**.

In general, Alcohol $\xrightarrow{[O]}$ Aldehyde $\xrightarrow{[O]}$ Carboxylic acid

Alcohols are converted into carboxylic acid only under complete oxidation. In partial oxidation, alcohols are converted into aldehydes.

Addition Reactions

The reaction in which a reagent completely add to a reactant without the removal of small molecules are called **addition reactions**.

e.g. addition of hydrogen (hydrogenation) in the presence of catalysts like palladium or nickel, to unsaturated hydrocarbons yield saturated hydrocarbons. Catalysts are the substances that cause a reaction to occur or proceed at a different rate without the reaction itself being affected.

$$\underset{R}{\overset{R}{>}}C=C\underset{R}{\overset{R}{<}} \xrightarrow[H_2,\ 200°C]{\text{Nickel catalyst}} R-\underset{\underset{R}{|}}{\overset{\overset{H}{|}}{C}}-\underset{\underset{R}{|}}{\overset{\overset{H}{|}}{C}}-R$$

The above reaction is commonly used in the hydrogenation of vegetable oils [that are unsaturated compounds] using a nickel catalyst.

Note
- Saturated fatty acids which are generally present in animal fats are harmful for health.
- Oils containing unsaturated fatty acids should be chosen for cooking.

Substitution Reactions

The reactions in which a reagent replaces an atom or a group of atoms from the reactant (substrate) are called **substitution reactions**. These are generally shown by saturated compounds.

Most of the saturated hydrocarbons are fairly inert and unreactive in the presence of most reagents. However, these reactions take place readily in the presence of sunlight. e.g.

In the presence of sunlight, chlorine is added to hydrocarbons at a rapid rate. In this reaction, Cl replaces H-atom one by one. A number of products are usually formed with the higher homologues of alkanes

$$CH_4 + Cl_2 \xrightarrow{\text{Sunlight}} CH_3Cl + HCl$$

$$CH_3Cl + Cl_2 \xrightarrow{\text{Sunlight}} CH_2Cl_2 + HCl$$

$$CH_2Cl_2 + Cl_2 \xrightarrow{\text{Sunlight}} CHCl_3 + HCl$$

$$CHCl_3 + Cl_2 \xrightarrow{\text{Sunlight}} CCl_4 + HCl$$

Fuels and Flames

Fuels

Those carbon compounds which have energy stored in them and burn with heat and light are called fuels. The released energy (heat or light) is utilised for various purposes like for cooking food, running machines in factories etc.

In fuels, the carbon can be in free state as present in coal, coke and charcoal or in combined state as present in petrol, LPG (Liquefied petroleum gas whose main constituent is butane), CNG (Compressed natural gas, main constituent of which is methane), kerosene, petroleum, natural gas etc.

Those fuels which were formed by the decomposition of the remains of the pre-historic plants and animals (fossils) buried under the earth long ago are called **fossil fuels**. e.g. coal, petroleum and natural gas.

Coal

It is a complex mixture of compounds of carbon, hydrogen and oxygen and some free carbon along with traces of nitrogen and sulphur. It is formed by the decomposition of plants, ferns and trees which got buried under the earth millions of years ago.

Petroleum

It is a dark viscous foul smelling oil and is also known as **rock oil** or **black gold.** It is formed by the decomposition of the remains of extremely small plants and animals buried under the sea millions of years ago.

Carbon and Its Compounds

Flame

The coal or charcoal in an angithi sometimes just glows red and gives out heat without a flame. This is because a flame is only produced when combustion (or burning) of gaseous substances takes place. When wood or charcoal is ignited, the volatile substances present vapourise and burn with a flame in the begining. Depending upon the amount of oxygen available and burning of fuels, flames are of the following two types :

Blue or Non-luminous Flame

When the oxygen supply is sufficient, the fuels burn completely producing a blue flame and no light is produced. e.g. burning of LPG in gas stove.

Yellow or Luminous Flame

In the insufficient supply of air, the fuels burn incompletely and produce yellow flame because of the presence of unburnt carbon particles, e.g. burning of wax vapours.

Check Point 05

1. Which type of hydrocarbon gives sooty flame after burning?
2. Fill in the blanks:
   (i) Alcohols are converted into carboxylic acid only under ....
   (ii) In partial oxidation; alcohols are converted into ....
3. State True or False for the following statements:
   In the presence of sunlight methane form alcohol.
4. Why compounds like petrol, coal, etc. generate heat or light or both on combustion?

Some Important Carbon Compounds

Ethanol

Its common name is ethyl alcohol and formula is C_2H_5OH or CH_3CH_2OH.

$$\begin{array}{c} H \;\; H \\ | \;\;\; | \\ H-C-C-O-H \\ | \;\;\; | \\ H \;\; H \end{array}$$

Preparation

Alcohol (ethanol) is obtained by the fermentation of molasses which are obtained from sugarcane juice.

Physical Properties

It is a liquid at room temperature. Its melting point is 156 K and boiling point is 351 K. It is soluble in water in all proportions.

Chemical Properties

(i) **Reaction with Sodium** Ethyl alcohol reacts with sodium metal leading to the evolution of hydrogen gas alongwith the formation of sodium ethoxide.

$$2\underset{\text{Sodium}}{Na} + 2\underset{\text{Ethanol}}{CH_3CH_2OH} \longrightarrow$$
$$2\underset{\text{Sodium ethoxide}}{CH_3CH_2\overset{-}{O}\overset{+}{Na}} + \underset{\text{Hydrogen gas}}{H_2\uparrow}$$

Note Hydrogen gas burns with a pop sound.

(ii) **Dehydration** Removal of water molecules from a compound is known as dehydration reaction.

When ethanol is heated at 443 K with excess conc. H_2SO_4, the water molecules get removed from it and ethene is obtained.

$$\underset{\text{Ethanol}}{CH_3-CH_2OH} \xrightarrow[\substack{H_2SO_4, \\ 170°C}]{\text{Hot conc.}} \underset{\text{Ethene}}{CH_2=CH_2} + \underset{\text{Water}}{H_2O}$$

Thus, in the above reaction, conc. H_2SO_4 act as a dehydrating agent.

Uses

Uses of ethanol are:
- It is used as an active ingredient in all alcoholic drinks.
- It is useful in medicines like tincture of iodine, cough syrups and many other tonics.

Alcohol as a fuel Alcohol is used as an additive in petrol, since it is a cleaner fuel and give rise to only CO_2 and H_2O when burnt in sufficient air.

Effect of Ethanol on Living Beings

When large quantities of alcohol/ethanol are consumed, it tends to slow metabolic processes and depress the central nervous system which in turn results in lack of coordination, drowsiness, mental confusion, lowering of the normal inhibitors and finally stupor.

The individual may be relaxed but does not realise that his sense of judgement and muscular coordination have been seriously impaired. Therefore, in order to stop the misuse of ethanol, it is made unfit for drinking by adding poisonous substances like methanol, copper sulphate, pyridine etc. and coloured substance like dyes. Such alcohol is called denatured alcohol.

Unlike ethanol, intake of methanol in very small quantities can cause death. In liver, methanol is oxidised to methanal which reacts readily with the components of cells and causes coagulation of protoplasm. It also affects optic nerves, causing blindness.

Ethanoic Acid

It is commonly known as acetic acid. Its formula is CH_3COOH. 5-8% solution of ethanoic acid in water is known as **vinegar**.

Physical Properties

Physical properties of ethanoic acid are:
- Its melting point is 290 K.
- During winters it often freezes in cold climates and forms ice like flakes, so it is also called **glacial acetic acid**. Glacial acetic acid is a trivial name for water free (anhydrous) acetic acid.
- It is a weaker acid than HCl but stronger than alcohol.

Chemical Reactions

(i) **Acidity** Weak acidity of acetic acid as compared to HCl is because of its low ionisation but is more acidic than alcohol is because of the more stability of ion formed after the removal of a proton (H^+). It evolves hydrogen gas when reacts with sodium metal.

$$2CH_3COOH + 2Na \longrightarrow 2CH_3CO\bar{O}Na^+ + H_2\uparrow$$
(Acetic acid) (Sodium metal) (Sodium acetate)

(ii) **Reaction with a base** It reacts with a base such as sodium hydroxide to give a salt (sodium ethanoate or sodium acetate) and water.

$$CH_3COOH + NaOH \longrightarrow CH_3CO\bar{O}Na^+ + H_2O$$
(Acetic acid) (Sodium hydroxide) (Sodium acetate)

(iii) **Esterification** When ethanol (an alcohol) reacts with acetic acid (a carboxylic acid) in the presence of an acid as catalyst, a fruity (sweet) smelling liquid called **ester** is obtained. This reaction is called esterification.

$$CH_3COOH + CH_3CH_2OH \xrightarrow[-H_2O]{Conc.\, H_2SO_4}$$
(Ethanoic acid) (Ethanol)

$$CH_3-\underset{\underset{O}{\|}}{C}-O-CH_2CH_3$$
(Ester)

Note Here, H_2SO_4 act as dehydrating agent, i.e. it removes water formed, otherwise ester formed will get converted into acid.

The ester gets converted back into alcohol and sodium salt of acid when treated with alkali like sodium hydroxide. This reaction is called **saponification**, as it is used for the preparation of soap.

$$CH_3COOCH_2CH_3 \xrightarrow{NaOH} CH_3CH_2OH$$
(Ethyl acetate) (Ethyl alcohol)

$$+ CH_3CO\bar{O}Na^+$$
(Sodium acetate)

(iv) **Reaction with carbonates and hydrogen carbonates** In the reaction of acetic acid with carbonates or hydrogen carbonates, carbon dioxide gas is obtained. It is an example of acid-base reaction.

$$CH_3COOH + NaHCO_3 \longrightarrow CH_3CO\bar{O}Na^+$$
(Sodium acetate)
$$+ H_2O + CO_2\uparrow$$

$$2CH_3COOH + Na_2CO_3 \longrightarrow 2CH_3CO\bar{O}Na^+$$
(Sodium acetate)
$$+ H_2O + CO_2\uparrow$$

Uses of Acetic Acid

Use of ethanoic or acetic acid are as given below:
(i) It is used for making vinegar.
(ii) It is widely used as a preservative in pickles.
(iii) It is used for the synthesis of other compounds like esters.

Soaps and Detergents

Soaps are sodium or potassium salts of long chain carboxylic acids and have general formula $RCO\bar{O}Na^+$.
where, $R = C_{15}H_{31}, C_{17}H_{35}$ etc.

Detergents are usually ammonium or sulphonate salts of long chain carboxylic acids. They are also called as **soapless soap**.

Manufacture of Soaps and Detergents

Soaps are made from animal fats or vegetable oils by heating it with sodium hydroxide. This process of preparation of soap is called **saponification**.

Fat or Oil + Alkali $\xrightarrow{Heat}$ Soap + Glycerol
(Ester)   (Sodium hydroxide)   (Sodium salt of fatty acid)   (An alcohol)

Structure of a Soap Molecule

A soap molecule is made up of two parts–a long hydrocarbon part (or non-ionic part) and a short ionic part containing $—CO\bar{O}Na^+$ group.

Carbon and Its Compounds

The long hydrocarbon part is hydrophobic and therefore insoluble in water but soluble in oil.

The ionic portion of the soap molecule is hydrophilic so, soluble in water and insoluble in oil.

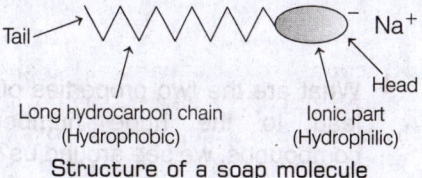
Structure of a soap molecule

Cleansing Action of Soaps (Micelle Formation)

Soap molecules have different properties at their two ends. Its one end is **hydrophilic** (soluble in water) and other is **hydrophobic** (soluble in fats or oils).

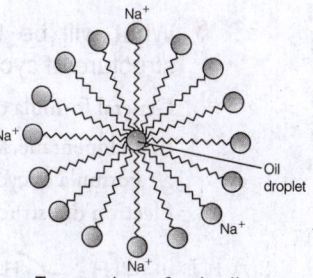
Formation of micelles

At the surface of water, the hydrophobic end or tail of soap will be insoluble in water and the soap will align along the surface of water with the ionic end in water and the hydrocarbon 'tail' protruding out of water.

Inside water, these molecules show a unique orientation that keeps the hydrocarbon portion out of the water. This is done by forming clusters of molecules in which the hydrophobic tails are in the interior of the cluster and on the surface of cluster, ionic ends are present.

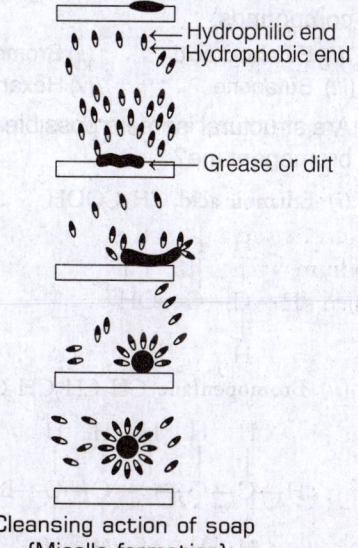
Cleansing action of soap (Micelle formation)

This formation of cluster of molecules is called **micelle**. To wash away the loosened dirt particles in the form of micelles from the surface of the cloth, it is either scrubbed mechanically or beaten or agitated in washing machine.

In the form of a micelle, soap is able to clean, since the oily dirt is being collected in the centre of micelle.

Micelles stay as colloids in the solution and does not come together to precipitate due to ion-ion repulsion. Hence, the dirt suspended in the micelles is also easily rinsed away.

Note Soap solution appears cloudy because the ion aggregate to form spherical clustures which forms micelles that are large enough to scatter light.

Detergents

Sometime while bathing that foam is formed with difficulty and an insoluble substance (scum) remains after washing with water. This is caused by the reaction of soap with the calcium and magnesium salts, which cause the hardness of water. Hence, a large amount of soap get wasted. This problem is overcome by using another class of compounds called detergents as cleansing agents. Detergents are generally sodium salts of sulphonic acids or ammonium salts wtih chlorides or bromides ions etc. Both have long hydrocarbon chain.

The charged ends of these compounds do not form insoluble precipitates with the calcium and magnesium ions in hard water. Thus, they remain effective in hard water. Detergents are usually used to make shampooos and products for cleaning clothes.

Check Point 06

1. State True or False for the following statements:
   Saponification is the reverse of esterification reaction.
2. What happens, when ethyl alcohol reacts with sodium metal?
3. Give any two examples of chemicals that are added to denature the alcohol.
4. Mention two uses of ethanoic acid.
5. Fill in the blank:
   Soap help in forming .... of oil and water by acting as a bridge between the two.

NCERT FOLDER

Intext Questions

1 What would be the electron dot structure of carbon dioxide which has molecular formula CO_2? **Pg 61**

Sol. Refer to text on Pg. 85.

2 What would be the electron dot structure of a molecule of sulphur which is made up of 8 atoms of sulphur? **Pg 61**

Sol. Refer to text on Pg. 85.

3 How many structural isomers can you draw for pentane? **Pg 68**

Sol. Pentane (C_5H_{12}) has a skeleton of five carbon atoms which can be arranged in straight chain or in the form of chain containing one or two branches.
Molecular formula C_5H_{12} accounts for the following isomers:

```
    H   H   H   H   H
    |   |   |   |   |
H — C — C — C — C — C — H
    |   |   |   |   |
    H   H   H   H   H
```
or $CH_3—CH_2—CH_2—CH_2—CH_3$
Straight chain structure

```
    H   H   H   H                  H
    |   |   |   |                  |
H — C — C — C — C — H           H — C — H
    |   |   |   |                  |
    H   H   |   H       or     H   H
        H — C — H                  |   |
            |               H — C — C — C — H
            H                   |   |   |
                                H   H   H
                                    |
                                H — C — H
                                    |
                                    H
```
or or
$CH_3—CH_2—CH—CH_3$ $\quad CH_3 \underset{CH_3}{\overset{CH_3}{-\underset{|}{\overset{|}{C}}-}} CH_3$
$\quad\quad\quad\quad |$
$\quad\quad\quad CH_3$
Branched chain structures

4 What are the two properties of carbon which lead to the huge number of carbon compounds, we see around us? **Pg 68**

Sol. Two main properties which led the carbon to form a huge number of carbon compounds are:
(i) catenation
(ii) tetravalency of carbon

5 What will be the formula and electron dot structure of cyclopentane? **Pg 68**

Sol. General formula of cycloalkane = C_nH_{2n}
In cyclopentane, $n = 5$
∴ Formula of cyclopentane, $C_{5}H_{5 \times 2} = C_5H_{10}$
Electron dot structure of cyclopentane

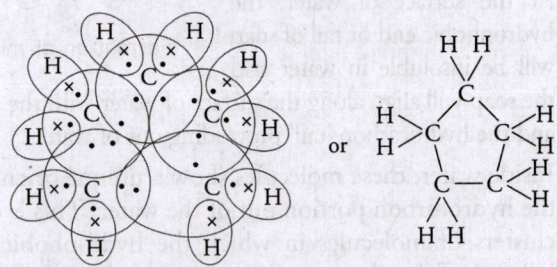

6 Draw the structures of the following compounds:
(i) Ethanoic acid   (ii) Bromopentane
(iii) Butanone   (iv) Hexanal
Are structural isomers possible for bromopentane? **Pg 69**

Sol. (i) Ethanoic acid, CH_3COOH

```
    H   O
    |   ||
H — C — C — OH
    |
    H
```

(ii) Bromopentane, $CH_3CH_2CH_2CH_2CH_2Br$

```
    H   H   H   H   H
    |   |   |   |   |
H — C — C — C — C — C — Br
    |   |   |   |   |
    H   H   H   H   H
```

All in one Carbon and Its Compounds

(iii) **Butanone,** $CH_3CH_2\overset{\overset{O}{\|}}{C}-CH_3$

$$H-\underset{H}{\overset{H}{C}}-\underset{H}{\overset{H}{C}}-\overset{\overset{O}{\|}}{C}-\underset{H}{\overset{H}{C}}-H$$

(iv) **Hexanal,** $CH_3CH_2CH_2CH_2CH_2CHO$

$$H-\underset{H}{\overset{H}{\underset{6}{C}}}-\underset{H}{\overset{H}{\underset{5}{C}}}-\underset{H}{\overset{H}{\underset{4}{C}}}-\underset{H}{\overset{H}{\underset{3}{C}}}-\underset{H}{\overset{H}{\underset{2}{C}}}-\overset{\overset{O}{\|}}{\underset{1}{C}}-H$$

Yes, isomers of bromopentane are possible. They are as follows :

(a) $CH_3CH_2CH_2CH_2CH_2Br$
   1- bromopentane

(b) $CH_3CH_2CH_2\underset{Br}{\overset{|}{C}H}CH_3$
   2- bromopentane

(c) $CH_3CH_2\underset{Br}{\overset{|}{C}H}CH_2CH_3$
   3- bromopentane

(d) $CH_3CH_2\underset{CH_3}{\overset{|}{C}H}CH_2Br$
   1- bromo- 2- methylbutane

(e) $CH_3-\underset{CH_3}{\overset{\overset{CH_3}{|}}{C}}-CH_2Br$
   1- bromo-2, 2- dimethylpropane

(f) $CH_3CH_2-\underset{Br}{\overset{\overset{CH_3}{|}}{C}}-CH_3$
   2- bromo -2- methylbutane

7 How would you name the following compounds?

(i) CH_3-CH_2-Br (ii) $H-\overset{\overset{H}{|}}{C}=O$

(iii) $H-\underset{H}{\overset{H}{C}}-\underset{H}{\overset{H}{C}}-\underset{H}{\overset{H}{C}}-\overset{}{C}\equiv C-H$

Pg 69

Sol. (i) CH_3-CH_2-Br, bromoethane (because for two carbons, root word is 'eth' and for bromine group, prefix used is 'bromo').

(ii) $H-\overset{\overset{H}{|}}{C}=O$, methanal (because for single carbon, root word is 'meth' and for functional group $-\overset{\overset{O}{\|}}{C}-$, suffix is 'al').

(iii) $\overset{6}{C}H_3\overset{5}{C}H_2\overset{4}{C}H_2\overset{3}{C}H_2\overset{2}{C}\equiv\overset{1}{C}H$

1-hexyne (because for 6 carbons, root word is 'hex' and for triple bond, suffix is 'yne'). Also triple bond is located at first position so position of triple bond is indicated in IUPAC name.

8 Why is conversion of ethanol to ethanoic acid an oxidation reaction? **Pg 71**

Sol. Oxidation is the addition of oxygen and removal of hydrogen from any compound. During the conversion of ethanol to ethanoic acid, we are actually removing two hydrogens and adding one oxygen to ethanol, so it is an oxidation reaction.

$$\underset{\text{Ethanol}}{CH_3CH_2OH} \xrightarrow[\text{Or acidified } K_2Cr_2O_7 + \text{Heat}]{\text{Alk. } KMnO_4 + \text{Heat}} \underset{\text{Ethanoic acid}}{CH_3\overset{\overset{O}{\|}}{C}-OH + H_2O}$$

9 A mixture of oxygen and ethyne is used for welding. Can you tell why a mixture of ethyne and air is not used? **Pg 71**

Sol. We need a high temperature for welding but when ethyne is burnt in air, it undergoes incomplete combustion and releases a lot of smoke and the temperature is also not very high.

In order to ensure complete oxidation and to obtain the high temperature needed for welding, a mixture of ethyne and oxygen is used.

$2CH \equiv CH + 5O_2 \longrightarrow 4CO_2 + 2H_2O$
$\qquad\qquad\qquad\qquad\qquad + \text{Heat} + \text{Light}$

10 How would you distinguish experimentally between an alcohol and a carboxylic acid? **Pg 74**

Sol. Alcohol and carboxylic acid can be distinguished experimentally by two reactions:

(i) **Reaction with Base**

Alcohols do not react with base like NaOH, KOH while carboxylic acids react with base to form salt and water.

e.g. $CH_3COOH + NaOH \longrightarrow$
$CH_3COO^-Na^+ + H_2O$
$CH_3CH_2OH + NaOH \longrightarrow$ No reaction

(ii) **Reaction with Sodium bicarbonate**
Carboxylic acids react with sodium bicarbonate rapidly to give brisk effervescence of CO_2 gas while alcohols do not react.
e.g. $CH_3COOH + NaHCO_3 \longrightarrow$
$CH_3COONa + H_2O + CO_2 \uparrow$
$CH_3CH_2OH + NaHCO_3 \longrightarrow$ No reaction

11 What are oxidising agents? **Pg 74**

Sol. Substances that are capable of providing oxygen to other substances are called oxidising agents.
Alkaline potassium permanganate ($KMnO_4$) or acidified potassium dichromate ($K_2Cr_2O_7$) act as an oxidising agent in oxidising alcohols into acids.

12 Would you be able to check if water is hard by using a detergent? **Pg 76**

Sol. No, because detergent does not form scum with hard water.

13 People use a variety of methods to wash clothes. Usually, after adding soap, they 'beat' the clothes on a stone or beat it with a paddle scrub with a brush or agitate the mixture in a washing machine. Why is this agitation necessary to get clean clothes? **Pg 76**

Sol. When soap solution is made and dirty clothes are soaked in it then micelles formation occurs. This results in the formation of an emulsion (a stable suspension of small droplets of one liquid in another with which it is immiscible). To wash away the loosen dirt particles in the form of micelles from the surface of the cloth, it is either scrubbed mechanically or beaten or agitated in washing machine.

EXERCISE
(On Pages 77 and 78)

1 Ethane with molecular formula C_2H_6 has
(i) 6 covalent bonds   (ii) 7 covalent bonds
(iii) 8 covalent bonds (iv) 9 covalent bonds

Sol. (ii) Structure formula of ethane (C_2H_6) is

```
    H  H
    |  |
H — C — C — H
    |  |
    H  H
```

It is clear that it has 7 covalent bonds.

2 Butanone is a four carbon compound with functional group
(i) carboxylic acid
(ii) aldehyde
(iii) ketone
(iv) alcohol

Sol. (iii) In butanone, the functional group is ketone (one) $>C=O$.

3 While cooking, if the bottom of the vessel is getting blackened on the outside, it means that
(i) food is not cooked completely
(ii) the fuel is not burning completely
(iii) fuel is wet
(iv) fuel is burning completely

Sol. (ii) If the bottom of the vessel is getting blackened, it means that the air holes are blocked and fuel is getting wasted as it is not burning completely.

4 Explain the nature of the covalent bond using the bond formation in CH_3Cl.

Sol. Carbon has 4 electrons in its valence shell. To complete its octet, it either needs to gain 4 electrons or lose 4 electrons to the other atom. Both these processes are impossible. Therefore, carbon atom achieve noble gas configuration by sharing 4 electrons with other atoms of itself or atoms of other elements. The bonds that are formed by sharing electrons are known as covalent bond. In covalent bonding, both atoms share the valence electrons, i.e. the shared electrons belong to the valence shells of both the atoms. CH_3Cl is called chloromethane, which contains 1 carbon atom, 3 hydrogen atoms and 1 chlorine atom.

Electronic configuration of carbon, $6 = \overset{K}{2}, \overset{L}{4}$

Electronic configuration of hydrogen, $1 = \overset{K}{1}$

Electronic configuration of chlorine, $17 = \overset{K}{2}, \overset{L}{8}, \overset{M}{7}$

Carbon atom has four outermost electrons, each hydrogen atom has one electron and chlorine has seven outermost electrons. Carbon shares its four outermost electrons with 3 hydrogen atoms and 1 chlorine atom to form CH_3Cl as follows:

5 Draw the electron dot structures for :
(a) Ethanoic acid
(b) H_2S
(c) Propanone
(d) F_2

Sol. (a) Ethanoic acid

$$H-\underset{\underset{H}{|}}{\overset{\overset{H}{|}}{C}}-\overset{\overset{O}{\|}}{C}-O-H$$

(b) Electron dot structure for H₂S

or H—S—H

(c) Propanone

or CH₃COCH₃

(d) Electron dot structure for F₂

or :F̈—F̈:

6. What is a homologous series? Explain with an example. **CBSE 2013**

Sol. A series of similarly constituted compounds in which the members present have the same functional group and similar chemical properties and any two successive members in a particular series differ in their molecular formula by (— CH₂) unit, is called a homologous series. e.g. alkane series C_nH_{2n+2}

CH₄	Methane	C₂H₆	Ethane
C₃H₈	Propane	C₄H₁₀	Butane
C₅H₁₂	Pentane		

7. How can ethanol and ethanoic acid can be differentiated on the basis of their physical and chemical properties?

Sol. (i) Distinction based on physical properties:
(a) **Smell** Ethanoic acid has a pungent smell. Ethanol has a pleasant smell.
(b) **Melting point** Ethanol has lower melting point (156 K) than ethanoic acid (290 K).
(c) **Physical state** Ethanoic acid is solid (glacial acetic acid) in winters but ethanol is always a liquid.

(ii) Distinctions based on chemical properties:
(a) **Reaction with sodium hydrogen carbonate** On adding a small amount of sodium hydrogen carbonate to ethanoic acid, carbon dioxide gas is evolved with brisk effervescence. However, no such reaction noticed in case of ethanol.

$$\underset{\text{Ethanoic acid}}{CH_3COOH} + NaHCO_3 \longrightarrow$$
$$CH_3COO^-Na^+ + CO_2\uparrow + H_2O$$

$$\underset{\text{Ethanol}}{C_2H_5OH} + NaHCO_3 \longrightarrow \text{No reaction}$$

(b) **Reaction with caustic alkalies** Ethanoic acid reacts with both sodium hydroxide (NaOH) and potassium hydroxide (KOH) to form corresponding salt and water. Ethanol fails to react with either of these.

$$CH_3COOH + NaOH \longrightarrow CH_3COO^-Na^+ + H_2O$$

$$CH_3COOH + KOH \longrightarrow CH_3COO^-K^+ + H_2O$$

8. Why does micelle formation take place when soap is added to water? Will a micelle be formed in other solvents such as ethanol also?

Sol. When soap is at the surface of water, the hydrophobic 'tail' of soap will not be soluble in water and the soap will align along the surface of water with the ionic end in water and the hydrocarbon 'tail' protruding out of water. Inside water, these molecules have a unique orientation that keeps the hydrocarbon portion out of the water. This is achieved by forming clusters of molecules in which the hydrophobic tails are in the interior of the cluster and the ionic ends are on the surface of the cluster. This formation is called micelle.

Micelle will not form in all types of solvents. It will form in such type of solvent in which soap is soluble. e.g. soap is insoluble in ethanol, hence, no micelle formation takes place.

9. Why are carbon and its compounds used as fuel for most applications?

Sol. Carbon burns in oxygen (air) to form carbon dioxide and water. During this reaction, a large amount of heat and light is released. Further once ignited, carbon and its compounds keep on burning without the requirement of additional energy. Hence, they are used as fuels.

$$C + O_2 \longrightarrow CO_2 + \text{Heat} + \text{Light}$$

10. Explain the formation of scum when hard water is treated with soap.

Sol. Hard water contains calcium and magnesium ions. Soap is basically sodium or potassium salt of higher fatty acids. When soap is added to hard water, corresponding calcium and magnesium salts are formed, which being insoluble gets precipitated. These precipitates are called scum.

Reactions taking place are shown as:

$$\underset{\text{Hard water}}{Ca^{2+}} + \underset{\text{Soap}}{2RCOONa} \longrightarrow \underset{\text{Calcium salt precipitate}}{(RCOO)_2Ca\downarrow} + 2Na^+$$

$$\underset{\text{Hard water}}{Mg^{2+}} + \underset{\text{Soap}}{2RCOONa} \longrightarrow \underset{\text{Magnesium salt precipitate}}{(RCOO)_2Mg\downarrow} + 2Na^+$$

11. What change will you observe if you test soap with litmus paper (red or blue)?

Sol. Soap is alkaline in nature. Hence, it turns red litmus paper blue and have no effect on the blue litmus paper.

12 What is hydrogenation? What is its industrial application?

Sol. Hydrogenation The addition of hydrogen to unsaturated hydrocarbons in the presence of catalyst is known as hydrogenation.

Industrial application When hydrogen gas is made to pass through vegetable oil in the presence of nickel catalyst, it changes to solid fat (ghee).

$$\underset{\text{Unsaturated}}{\text{Vegetable oils}} + H_2 \xrightarrow[\text{Heat}]{Ni} \underset{\text{Saturated}}{\text{Fat (ghee)}}$$

13 Which of the following hydrocarbons undergo addition reaction?

$C_2H_6, C_3H_8, C_3H_6, C_2H_2$ and CH_4

Sol. Unsaturated hydrocarbons like alkenes and alkynes (containing double and triple bond respectively) undergo addition reactions and their general formula are C_nH_{2n} and C_nH_{2n-2} respectively.

C_2H_6, (C_nH_{2n+2})

$$H-\underset{\underset{H}{|}}{\overset{\overset{H}{|}}{C}}-\underset{\underset{H}{|}}{\overset{\overset{H}{|}}{C}}-H \quad \text{(alkane)}$$

C_3H_6, (C_nH_{2n})

$$H-\underset{\underset{H}{|}}{\overset{\overset{H}{|}}{C}}-\overset{\overset{H}{|}}{C}=\overset{\overset{H}{|}}{C}-H \quad \text{(alkene)}$$

C_3H_8, (C_nH_{2n+2})

$$H-\underset{\underset{H}{|}}{\overset{\overset{H}{|}}{C}}-\underset{\underset{H}{|}}{\overset{\overset{H}{|}}{C}}-\underset{\underset{H}{|}}{\overset{\overset{H}{|}}{C}}-H \quad \text{(alkane)}$$

C_2H_2, (C_nH_{2n-2})

$$H-C\equiv C-H \quad \text{(alkyne)}$$

CH_4, (C_nH_{2n+2})

$$H-\underset{\underset{H}{|}}{\overset{\overset{H}{|}}{C}}-H \quad \text{(alkane)}$$

Thus, C_3H_6 and C_2H_2 will undergo addition reactions.

14 Give a test that can be used to differentiate between butter and cooking oil.

Sol. Butter contains saturated compounds while cooking oil contains unsaturated compounds. Since, unsaturated compounds are oxidised by alk. $KMnO_4$ with disappearance of its pink colour. Therefore, when cooking oil is treated with a few drops of alk. $KMnO_4$, pink colour of $KMnO_4$ disappears. With butter, however, the pink colour of $KMnO_4$ does not disappear.

15 Explain the mechanism of the cleansing action of soaps.

Sol. Refer to text on Pg. 96.

SUMMARY

- Inspite of its small amount available in nature, carbon is a versatile element as it form basis of all living organisms and many things which we use.
- **Covalent bonds** are formed by sharing of electrons between two atoms, so that both can achieve a completely filled outermost shell.
- **Organic compounds** are the compounds of carbon except its carbides, oxides, carbonates and hydrogen carbonate salts.
- **Hydrocarbons** are the compounds of carbon and hydrogen only. They are of two types, i.e. saturated hydrocarbon having only one single bond between two carbon atoms and another is unsaturated hydrocarbon, they have atleast one multiple bond (i.e. double or triple bond) between two carbon atoms alongwith the single bonds.
- **Alkenes or olefins** These have carbon-carbon double bonds alongwith single bonds. Their general formula is C_nH_{2n}.
- **Alkynes** These have atleast one carbon-carbon triple bond alongwith single bonds. Their general formula is C_nH_{2n-2}.
- Organic compounds with same molecular formula but different structural formula are called **isomers**. The phenomenon is called **isomerism**.
- The functional groups such as alcohol $(R-OH)$, aldehydes $(R-CHO)$, ketones $(R-\overset{\overset{O}{\|}}{C}-R')$ and carboxylic acid $(R-COOH)$ decide characteristic properties of the carbon compounds that contain them.
- A series of compounds having same functional group but a difference of $-CH_2$ unit (14 unit mass) between two successive members is called **homologous series**.
- **Oxidation** It is the process of addition of oxygen and removal of hydrogen. The substances which provide oxygen to other substances are called oxidising agents.
- **Combustion** It is the reaction in which CO_2 and H_2O are obtained by burning organic compound. Saturated hydrocarbons burn with blue flame due to their complete combustion.
- **Addition reaction** In this reaction, the reagents add completely to the substrate, e.g. hydrogenation to vegetable oil to obtain ghee.
- **Substitution reaction** In this reaction, an atom or group of atoms replace another atom or group from the substrate.
- Carbon and its compounds are some of the major sources of **fuel**, e.g. coal, petroleum etc.
- **Flame** is the region where combustion of gases occur. It is of two type : blue flame (or non-luminous flame) and yellow flame (or luminous flame).
- Ethanol, C_2H_5OH is soluble in water. It gives ethene on reaction with conc. H_2SO_4 at 160°C. It gives sodium ethoxide with Na.
- Ethanoic acid, CH_3COOH also called acetic acid. Its 5-8% aqueous solution is called vinegar. It gives CO_2 gas with sodium carbonate and bicarbonates.
- **Soaps** are sodium or potassium salts of long chain fatty acid $(RCOONa)$, here, $R=C_{15}H_{31}, C_{17}H_{35}$.
- **Detergents** are ammonium or sulphonate salts of long chain carboxylic acids.

Exam Practice

Objective Type Questions

Multiple Choice Questions

1 Carbon exists in the atmosphere in the form of
(a) only carbon monoxide
(b) carbon monoxide in traces and carbon dioxide
(c) only carbon dioxide
(d) coal **NCERT Exemplar**

Sol. (c) Carbon exists in the atmosphere in the form of carbon dioxide gas (CO_2) in air (only 0.03%). Carbon also occurs in the earth's crust in the form of minerals likes carbonates.

2 A molecule of ammonia (NH_3) has
(a) only single bonds
(b) only double bonds
(c) only triple bonds
(d) two double bonds and one single bond **NCERT Exemplar**

Sol. (a) A molecule of ammonia (NH_3) has only single bonds and these are covalent bonds.

3 Which of the following will contain covalent double bond between its atoms?
(a) H_2 (b) O_2 (c) NaCl (d) Cl_2

Sol. (b) Oxygen atom has six (6) valence electrons. Thus, to complete its octet, it forms double bond with another oxygen atom to get O_2 molecule.

4 Which of the following is not a property of carbon?
(a) Carbon compounds are good conductor of heat and electricity
(b) Carbon compounds are poor conductor of heat and electricity
(c) Most of the carbon compounds are covalent compounds
(d) Boiling and melting point of carbon compounds are relatively lower than those of ionic compounds

Sol. (a) Carbon compounds are covalently bonded and are poor conductor of heat and electricity. Due to covalent bonds, their boiling and melting points are relatively lower than those of ionic compounds.

5 Which of the following is not the use of graphite?
(a) It is used as lubricant
(b) It is used in manufacturing of lead-pencils
(c) It is used in manufacturing of artificial diamond
(d) It is used for making insulated plates

Sol. (d) Graphite can not be used for making insulated plates, as it is a good conductor of electricity.

6 Buckminsterfullerene is an allotropic form of **NCERT Exemplar**
(a) phosphorus (b) sulphur
(c) carbon (d) tin

Sol. (c) Buckminsterfullerene is an allotrope of carbon containing clusters of 60 carbon atoms joined together to form spherical molecules. Its formula is C_{60} (C-Sixty).

7 Which among the following are unsaturated hydrocarbons?
(i) $H_3C—CH_2—CH_2—CH_3$
(ii) $H_3C—C≡C—CH_3$
(iii) $H_3C—CH—CH_3$
          |
          CH_3
(iv) $H_3C—C=CH_2$
          |
          CH_3
  NCERT Exemplar
(a) (i) and (iii) (b) (ii) and (iii)
(c) (ii) and (iv) (d) (iii) and (iv)

Sol. (c) Unsaturated hydrocarbons have double or triple bond in the structure. Both (ii) and (iv) structures have triple and double carbon-carbon bonds respectively.

8 Which of the following are correct structural isomers of butane?

(i) 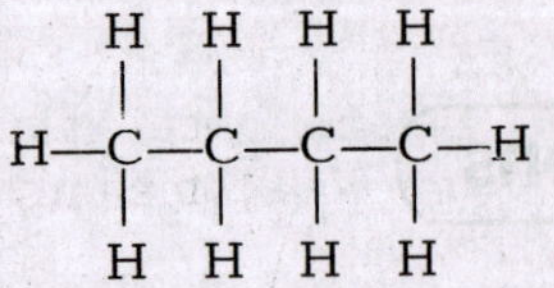
```
    H   H   H   H
    |   |   |   |
H—C—C—C—C—H
    |   |   |   |
    H   H   H   H
```

(ii) 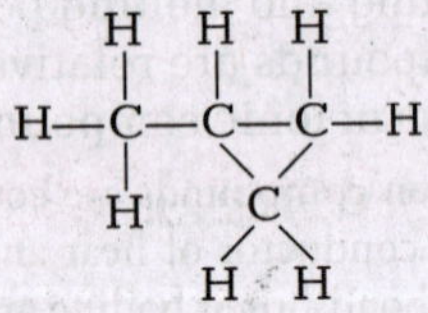
```
    H   H   H
    |   |   |
H—C—C—C—H
    H   C   H
        H H
```

(iii) 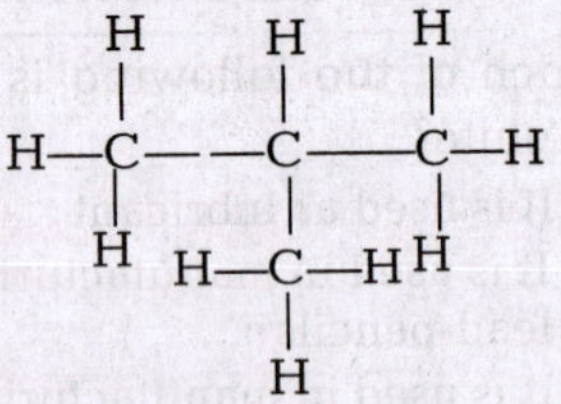
```
    H   H   H
    |   |   |
H—C—C—C—H
    H   |   H
      H—C—H
        |
        H
```

(iv) 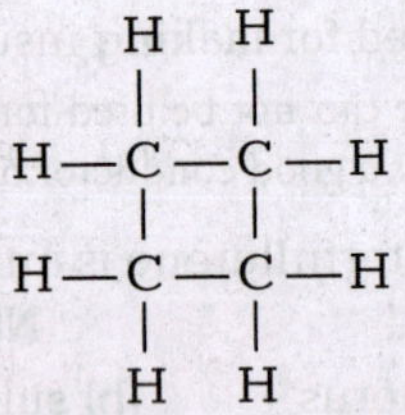
```
    H   H
    |   |
H—C—C—H
    |   |
H—C—C—H
    |   |
    H   H
```
NCERT Exemplar

(a) (i) and (iii)   (b) (ii) and (iv)
(c) (i) and (ii)   (d) (iii) and (iv)

Sol. (a) Structure (i) is *n*-butane
Structure (iii) is *iso*-butane
Since, molecular formula is same, only structures are different. So, (i) and (iii) are isomers while structure (ii) and (iv) have molecular formula C_4H_8.

9 Which of the following is not the property of homologous series?
(a) They differ by —CH_2 units
(b) They differ by – 14 units by mass
(c) They all contain double bond
(d) They can be represented by a general

Sol. (c) It is not necessary for a homologous series that it must contain the double bond.

10 Which of the following does not belong to the same homologous series?
(a) CH_4 (b) C_2H_6
(c) C_3H_8 (d) C_4H_8
NCERT Exemplar

Sol. (d) Because succesive members of a homologous series differ by —CH_2 unit.

So, homologous series of alkanes is
Methane CH_4,   Ethane C_2H_6,
Propane C_3H_8,   Butane C_4H_{10}
So, C_4H_8 does not belong to the homologous series.

11 Correct formula for propanoic acid is
(a) CH_3COOH (b) $CH_3—CH_2—COOCH_3$
(c) $HOOCCH_2CH_3$ (d) CH_3COOCH_3

Sol. (c) The correct formula for propanoic acid is as follows :
$$CH_3—CH_2—\underset{\underset{O}{\|}}{C}—OH$$

12 Which of the following can show addition reaction?
(a) C_2H_4 (b) C_2H_6
(c) C_2H_5OH (d) $CH_3CH_2CH_3$

Sol. (a) Presence of double bond between two carbon atoms is the necessary condition to show addition reaction. Thus, only $C_2H_4 (CH_2 = CH_2)$ can show the addition reaction.

13 Which one is an example of substitution reaction?
(a) $CH_2 = CH_2 + H_2 \xrightarrow{h\nu} CH_3—CH_3$
(b) $CH_3CH_2OH \xrightarrow{KMnO_4 \text{ (alk.)}} CH_3COOH$
(c) $CH_4 + Cl_2 \xrightarrow{h\nu} CH_3Cl + HCl$
(d) $CH \equiv CH + H_2 \xrightarrow{h\nu} CH_2 = CH_2$

Sol. (c) When one atom or group of atoms is replaced by some other atom or group of atoms, it is known as substitution reaction.
Option (c) is an example of substitution reaction, in which one of the hydrogen atom is replaced by chlorine (Cl) atom.

14 $CH_3—CH_2—OH \xrightarrow{\text{Alkaline } KMnO_4 + \text{Heat}} CH_3—COOH$

In the above given reaction, alkaline $KMnO_4$ acts as **NCERT Exemplar**
(a) reducing agent   (b) oxidising agent
(c) catalyst   (d) dehydrating agent

Sol. (b) $KMnO_4$ acts as oxidising agent because it removes hydrogen from CH_3CH_2OH and adds one oxygen to it.

15 The soap molecule has a
(a) hydrophilic head and a hydrophobic tail
(b) hydrophobic head and a hydrophilic tail
(c) hydrophobic head and a hydrophobic tail
(d) hydrophilic head and a hydrophilic tail
NCERT Exemplar

Sol. (a) A soap molecule is made up of two parts:
A long hydrocarbon part and a short ionic part —COO⁻Na⁺ group. The long hydrocarbon chain is hydrophobic (water repelling) and ionic portion is hydrophilic (water attracting).

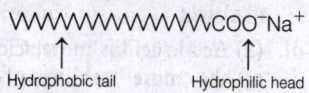

Hydrophobic tail — Hydrophilic head

Fill in the Blanks

16 Newly discovered allotrope of carbon is called ....

Sol. Buckminster fullerene

17 .... is the catalyst generally used in the hydrogenation of oils.

Sol. Nickel (Ni)
Catalysts are the substances that causes a reaction to occur or proceed at a different rate without the reaction itself being affected.

18 Saturated hydrocarbons will generally give a .... flame while unsaturated carbon compounds will gives a .... flame.

Sol. clean, yellow or blue
When the oxygen supply is sufficient, the fuels burn completely producing a blue flame. In the insufficient supply of air, the fuels burns incompletely and produce yellow flame.

19 Fuels such as coal and petroleum have some amount of .... and .... in them, oxides of which are major pollutants in the environment.

Sol. sulphur and nitrogen.

True and False

20 Graphite acquires some double bond character.

Sol. True;
In graphite, each carbon atom is bonded to three other carbon atoms in the same plane giving a hexagonal array. One of these bonds is a double bond and thus, the valency of carbon is satisfied.

21 The concentrated sulphuric acid can be regarded as a dehydrating agent while removes water from ethanol.

Sol. True;

22 If a hydrocarbon has double or triple covalent bond, it is saturated?

Sol. False;
Unsaturated compounds contains double or triple bond.

23 Soap solutions are true solution.

Sol. False;
Soap solutions are colloidal solution.

24 Methane undergoes substitution reactions.

Sol. True;

25 Ethanoic acid reacts with carbonates to form salt commonly called sodium acetate.

Sol. True;
$$2CH_3COOH + Na_2CO_3 \longrightarrow 2CH_3COONa + H_2O + CO_2\uparrow$$
Sodium acetate

Match the Column

26 Match the following column A (Type) and B (Reaction).

Column A (Type)		Column B (Reaction)
A. Combustion reaction	(i)	$C_3H_8 + Cl_2 \xrightarrow{UV\ light} C_3H_7Cl + HCl$
B. Oxidation reaction	(ii)	$CH_2=CH_2 + H_2 \xrightarrow{Ni/Pd} CH_3—CH_3$
C. Addition reaction	(iii)	$2CH_4 + 2O_2(g) \longrightarrow CO_2 + 2H_2O + Heat + Light$
D. Substitution reaction	(iv)	$CH_3CH_2OH \xrightarrow{Alkaline\ KMnO_4 + Heat}$ $CH_3—\underset{\underset{O}{\parallel}}{C}—OH$

Sol. A→ (iii), B→ (iv) C→ (ii) D→ (i).
A→ (iii), During combustion heat and light are produced.
B→ (iv), Removal of hydrogen atom and addition of oxygen atom is oxidation.
C→ (ii), Addition of atoms of reagent by breaking of double or triple bond is addition reaction.
D→ (i), Chlorine atom replace H-atom from propane. So, it is substitution reaction.

Assertion-Reason

Direction (Q. Nos. 27-32) *In each of the following questions, a statement of Assertion is given by the corresponding statement of Reason. Of the statements, mark the correct answer as.*

(a) Both Assertion and Reason are true and Reason is the correct explanation of Assertion.

(b) Both Assertion and Reason are true, but Reason is not the correct explanation of Assertion.

(c) Assertion is true, but Reason is false.

(d) Both Assertion and Reason are false

27. Assertion Carbon has a strong tendency to either lose or gain electrons to attain noble gas configuration.
Reason Carbon has four electrons in its outermost shell and has the tendency to share electrons with carbon or other elements. **CBSE (All India) 2020**
Sol. (d) Carbon has strong tendency to show catenation due to its small size and strong C—C bond.

28. Assertion Carbon shows maximum catenation property in the periodic table.
Reason Carbon has small size and thus, forms strong C—C bond.
Sol. (a) Catenation is the bonding of atoms of the same element into a series, called as chain. Catenation occurs more readily with carbon, which forms strong covalent bond with other C-atoms to form long chains and structures.

29. Assertion Graphite is slippery to touch.
Reason The various layers of carbon atoms in graphite are held together by weak van der Waal's forces.
Sol. (a) A graphite crystal consists of various layers of carbon atoms in which each carbon atom is joined to three other atoms by strong covalent bonds. The various layers of carbon atoms in graphite are held together by weak van der Waal's forces making it slippery to touch.

30. Assertion Following are the members of a homologous series:
$CH_3OH, CH_3CH_2OH, CH_3CH_2CH_2OH$
Reason A series of compounds with same functional group but differing by —CH_2— unit is called a homologous series. **CBSE (All India) 2020**
Sol. The alchohols have general formula of $C_nH_{2n+1}OH$. So, the alchohols have the series of formula from the different compounds with different between the succeeding and preceding molecules being a —CH_2— unit.

31. Assertion When ethanol is heated at 443 K with exces conc. H_2SO_4, ethene is obtained.
Reason Conc. H_2SO_4 acts as a dehydrating agent.
Sol. (a) When ethanol is heated with conc. sulphuric acid [H_2SO_4] at 443 K, dehydration takes place and ethene is obtained. In this, conc. H_2SO_4 acts as a dehydrating agent.

32. Assertion Acetic acid is less acidic than alcohol.
Reason The ion formed after the removal of proton from acetic acid is less stable.
Sol. (d) Acetic acid is more acidic than alcohol because of the more stability of ion formed after the removed of a proton.

Case Based Questions

Direction (Q. Nos. 33-36) *Answer the questions on the basis of your understanding of the following passage, table and related studied concepts:*

Esters are wonderfully odoriferous compounds. In the simplest terms, esters can be defined as the reaction products of acids and alcohols. They are derived from carboxylic acids. A carboxylic acid contains the —COOH group and in an ester, the hydrogen in this group is replaced by a hydrocarbon group.

Many fragrances contain a group of compounds called esters.

The table gives information about some esters and the fragrance they produce.

Ester	Structural formula of molecule	Fragrance
Ethyl methanoate	H—C(=O)—O—CH$_2$—CH$_3$	Rum
Methyl butanoate	CH$_3$—CH$_2$—CH$_2$—C(=O)—O—CH$_3$	Apple
Ethyl butanoate	CH$_3$—CH$_2$—CH$_2$—C(=O)—O—CH$_2$—CH$_3$	Pineapple
Propyl ethanoate	CH$_3$—C(=O)—O—CH$_2$—CH$_2$—CH$_3$	Pear

Animal and vegetable fats and oils are composed of long chain, complicated esters. The physical differences observed between fat (like butter) and oil (like sunflower oil) are due to differences in melting points of the mixture of esters they contain. If the melting point of the substance is below room temperature, it will be a liquid-oil. If the melting point is above room temperature, it will be a solid-a fat.

A greater number of double bonds or degree of unsaturation in the molecules results in a lower melting point because the van der Waals' forces are less effective.

Carbon and Its Compounds

33 Which structure do the ester compounds in the table have in common?

(a) CH$_3$—C(=O)—O— (b) —CH$_2$—CH$_2$—

(c) —O—CH$_2$— (d) —C(=O)—O—

Sol. (d) The given compounds have ester group (—C(=O)—O—) in common.

34 Structures of some molecules are shown below :

I. II. III. IV.

The correct order of their melting point is
(a) IV < I < II < III (b) III < I < IV < II
(c) III < I < IV < II (d) II < IV < I < III

Sol. (d) Melting point increases with increase in chain length but decreases with unsaturation. Thus, the correct order of melting point is II < IV < I < III.

35 The photograph shows a model of an ester molecule.

Which fragrance is produced by this ester?

Sol. The model shows that the structure of the given compound is

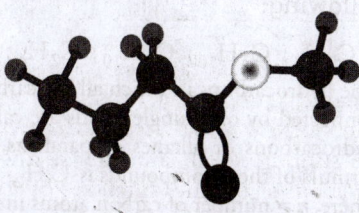

Thus, it produces fragrance of apple.

36 The formulae of an ester is

Write the structural farmula of the corrosponding alcohol and the acid?

Sol.

So Alcohol = CH$_3$OH

Acid = C$_6$H$_5$—C(=O)—OH

Direction (Q. Nos. 37-40) *Answer the questions on the basis of your understanding of the following passage and related studied concepts:*

Chemistry in Automobiles

For an internal combustion engine to move a vehicle down the road, it must convert the energy stored in the fuel into mechanical energy to drive the wheels.

In your car, the distributor and battery provide this starting energy by creating an electrical "spark", which helps in combustion of fuels like gasoline. Below is the reaction depicting complete combustion of gasoline in full supply of air   **CBSE Question Bank**

$$2C_8H_{18}(l) + 25O_2(g) \longrightarrow 6X + Y$$

37 Which of the following are the products obtained from the reaction mentioned in the above case?

	Product 'X'	Product 'Y'
(a)	CO$_2$	H$_2$O$_2$
(b)	H$_2$O	CO
(c)	CH$_3$OH	H$_2$O
(d)	CO$_2$	H$_2$O

Sol. (d) The balanced combustion reaction for octane (gasoline) burning in oxygen is

$$2C_8H_{18}(l) + 25\,O_2(g) \longrightarrow 16\,CO_2(g)$$
(Volatile and flammable alkane) (X)

$$+ 18\,H_2O(g)$$
(Y)

Here 'X' is CO$_2$ and Y is H$_2$O.
Hence, option (d) is correct.

38 Identify the types of chemical reaction occurring during the combustion of fuel.
(a) Oxidation and endothermic reaction
(b) Decomposition and exothermic reaction
(c) Oxidation and exothermic reaction
(d) Combination and endothermic reaction

Sol. (c) During the combustion of fuel, oxidation and exothermic reaction occur. Octane is the compound which is widely used in gasoline and thus the reaction with oxygen release energy.

Octane (isooctane) reacts with oxygen to give CO_2 and water thus this reaction is the combustion reaction and is exothermic in nature.

39 On the basis of evolution/absorption of energy, which of the following processes are similar to combustion of fuel?
I. Photosynthesis in plants.
II. Respiration in the human body.
III. Decomposition of vegetable matter.
IV. Decomposition of ferrous sulphate.
(a) II and III (b) I and II
(c) III and IV (d) II and I

Sol. (a) Respiration and burning uses oxygen and produce energy. Both give out CO_2 as the end product and the decomposition of vegetable matter into compost is an example of exothermic reaction, hence, both process are similar to combustion of fuel. So, option (a) is correct.

40 'A student while walking on the road observed that a cloud of black smoke belched out from the exhaust stack of moving trucks on the road.' Choose the correct reason, for the production of black smoke.
(a) Limited supply of air leads to incomplete combustion of fuel.
(b) Rich supply of air leads to complete combustion of fuel.
(c) Rich supply of air leads to a combination reaction.
(d) Limited supply of air leads to complete combustion of fuel.

Sol. (a) A cloud of black smoke belched out from the exhaust stack of moving trucks on the road. Due to limited supply of air leads to incomplete combustion of fuel. During incomplete combustion, part of the carbon is not completely oxidised and producing soot or carbon monoxide.

Or

'Although nitrogen is the most abundant gas in the atmosphere, it does not take part in combustion'. Identify the correct reason for this statement.

(a) Nitrogen is a reactive gas
(b) Nitrogen is an inert gas
(c) Nitrogen is an explosive gas
(d) Only hydrocarbons can take part in combustion

Sol. (b) Nitrogen gas is not highly reactive i.e. does not support combustion with other molecules in the atmosphere and is mainly present in air as N_2 (78%).

The unreactive behaviour results from the powerful triple bonds that formed by sharing of three pairs of electrons between two nitrogen atoms, which requires more energy to break. Nitrogen becomes more reactive at higher temperature.

Very Short Answer Type Questions

41 How are covalent bonds formed? **CBSE (All India) 2020**

Sol. Covalent bonds are formed by the sharing of an electron-pair between the atom (either same or different atoms). For example, H_2, Cl_2, CH_4, NH_3, etc., have covalent bonds.

42 Which of the following is not observed in a homologous series? Give reason for your choice. **CBSE SQP 2020-21**
(a) Change in chemical properties
(b) Difference in —CH_2 and 14u molecular mass
(c) Gradation in physical properties
(d) Same functional group

Sol. Homologous series does not show changes in chemical properties. Chemical properties remain similar in homologous series it is due to the presence of same functional group.
e.g. CH_3OH, C_2H_5OH, C_3H_6OH, etc.

43 Select saturated hydrocarbons from the following: **CBSE 2016**

C_3H_6 ; C_5H_{10} ; C_4H_{10} ; C_2H_4 ; C_6H_{14}

Sol. The hydrocarbons in which all the carbon atoms are connected by only single bonds are called saturated hydrocarbons or alkanes or paraffins. The general formula of these compounds is C_nH_{2n+2}, where, n = number of carbon atoms in one molecule of a hydrocarbon.

Amongst, the given compounds, only C_4H_{10} and C_6H_{14} belongs to the formula of C_nH_{2n+2}. Therefore, C_4H_{10} and C_6H_{14} are saturated hydrocarbons.

44 Write the name and formula of the second member of the carbon compounds having functional group —OH. **CBSE 2012**

Sol. First member is : CH_3OH — Methanol
Second member is : CH_3CH_2OH — Ethanol

All in one Carbon and Its Compounds

45 A compound 'X' on heating with excess conc. sulphuric acid at 443K gives an unsaturated compound 'Y'. 'X' also reacts with sodium metal to evolve a colourless gas 'Z'. Identify 'X', 'Y' and 'Z'. Write the equation of the chemical reaction for the formation of 'Y' and also write the role of sulphuric acid in the reaction. **CBSE 2018**

Sol. Compound 'X' reacts with excess of conc. H_2SO_4 at temperature of 443 K to form unsaturated compound 'Y'. Thus, compound 'X' is alcohol.

$$CH_3-CH_2-OH \underset{\text{Ethanol}}{(X)} \xrightarrow[443K]{\text{Excess conc. } H_2SO_4} \underset{\text{Ethene}}{CH_2=CH_2}_{(Y)} + \underset{\text{Water}}{H_2O}$$

Here, conc. H_2SO_4 is used as dehydrating agent which removes water molecule from ethanol and ethene is obtained. This is called as a dehydration reaction. When compound 'X' (CH_3-CH_2-OH) reacts with sodium metal, then it leads to evolution of hydrogen. Following reaction takes place when ethanol 'X' reacts with sodium (Na)

$$\underset{\substack{\text{Sodium}\\\text{metal}}}{2Na} + \underset{\substack{(X)\\\text{Ethanol}}}{2CH_3-CH_2-OH} \longrightarrow$$
$$\underset{\text{Sodium ethoxide}}{2CH_3-CH_2-O^-Na^+} + \underset{\substack{\text{Hydrogen}\\\text{gas }(Z)}}{H_2 \uparrow}$$

46 Write molecular formula of alcohol which can be derived from butane. **CBSE 2015**

Sol. Butanol ($CH_3-CH_2-CH_2-CH_2-OH$)

47 Write the name and structure of an alcohol with three carbon atoms in its molecule. **CBSE 2016**

Sol. Structure

$$\begin{bmatrix} & H & H & H \\ & | & | & | \\ H- & C- & C- & C-OH \\ & | & | & | \\ & H & H & H \end{bmatrix}$$

IUPAC Name Propanol

48 Atom of an element contains five electrons in its valence shell. This element is major component of air. It exist as a diatomic molecule. Identify the element. Draw the electron dot structure of this molecule.

Sol. For electron dot structure of nitrogen :
Refer to page 90 (Formation of nitrogen molecule).

49 A colourless gas 'X' has a formula C_3H_6. It decolourises bromine water. Write the chemical name of 'X'.

Sol. X = propene, $CH_3-CH=CH_2$

The structural formula of citric acid is shown below :

$$\begin{array}{c} COOH \\ | \\ CH_2 \\ | \\ H_3C-C-COOH \\ | \\ CH_2 \\ | \\ COOH \end{array}$$

50 State the name of —COOH functional group in citric acid.

Sol. Carboxylic acid

51 State the part of soap molecule that attaches itself to dirt when soap is dissolved in water. **CBSE 2013**

Sol. Hydrophobic end also called as tail, i.e. hydrocarbon chain.

52 How is scum formed? **CBSE 2012**

Sol. When soap reacts with hard water, a white curdy precipitate is formed which is called scum.

53 What do you mean by the term soapless soaps?

Sol. Detergents are also called 'soapless soaps' because though they act like a soap in having the cleansing properties but they do not contain the composition of usual soaps like sodium stearate etc.

54 What would be the disadvantage of detergents over soaps?

Sol. An important disadvantage of detergents over soaps is that some of the detergents are non-biodegradable, i.e. they cannot be decomposed by microorganisms like bacteria, hence causes water pollution in lakes and rivers.

Short Answer (SA) Type Questions

1. The table shows the electronic structures of four elements.

Element	Electronic structure
P	2, 6
Q	2, 8, 1
R	2, 8, 7
S	2, 8, 8

(i) Identify which element(s) will form covalent bonds with carbon.

(ii) "Carbon reacts with an element in the above table to form several compounds." Give suitable reason.
CBSE SQP (Term-II)

Sol. (i) The elements P and R will form covalent bond with carbon because both the elements are electronegative in nature and share their electrons with carbon to complete their octet.

While element Q (2, 8, 1) is an electropositive element (metal) and element 'S' (2, 8, 8) is stable due to complete octet in valence shell. Hence, they do not form covalent bond with carbon.

(ii) Carbon reacts with an element in table to form several compounds because of
(a) **Tetravalency of carbon** Carbon has electronic structure of (2, 4). Thus, it has four electrons in outermost shell. It is capable of bonding with four other elements.
(b) **Catenation** Due to small size, C—C bond in strong. This allow carbon to form long chain compound of different size.

2. Give a test that can be used to confirm the presence of carbon in a compound.

With a valency of 4, how is carbon able to attain noble gas configuration in its compounds? **CBSE SQP 2020-21**

Sol. This test can be used to confirm the presence of carbon in a compound. First burn the given compound in presence of oxygen. The gas evolved. Allow this gas to pass through the lime water. If this gas contains carbon then it will turn lime water milky. This happens due to the formation of white ppt. of calcium carbonate.

$$\underset{\text{Carbon}}{C(s)} + \underset{\text{Oxygen}}{O_2(g)} \longrightarrow \underset{\text{Carbon dioxide}}{CO_2(g)}$$

$$\underset{\text{Lime water}}{Ca(OH)_2(l)} + \underset{\text{Carbon dioxide}}{CO_2(g)} \longrightarrow \underset{\text{Calcium carbonate}}{CaCO_3(l)} + \underset{\text{Water}}{H_2O(l)}$$

With a valency of 4, carbon is able to attain noble gas configuration in its compounds by sharing its four valence electrons with atoms of the other elements.

These shared electrons belongs to the outermost shells of both atoms, both atoms attain the nearest noble gas configuration. This is known as covalent bonding.

3. The number of carbon compounds is more than those formed by all other elements put together. Justify the statement by giving two reasons. **CBSE SQP 2020-21**

Sol. The number of carbon compounds are more than those formed by all other elements put together because, (i) carbon shows catenation and (ii) it has a valancy of four.

Carbon shares its four valence electrons with other atoms of carbon, this is called catenation. It has valency of four. So, it can form bonds with four other atoms of carbon or atoms of some other monovalent element (which shows vatency of one).

4. What is covalent bond? What type of bond exists in
(i) CCl_4 (ii) $CaCl_2$
(iii) CH_4 (iv) NH_3 **CBSE 2013**

Sol. The chemical bonds formed between two atoms by the sharing of electrons between them is known as covalent bond.

The sharing of electrons between the two atoms take place in such a way that both the atoms acquire stable electronic configuration of their nearest noble gas.

(i) CCl_4 : Covalent bond (ii) $CaCl_2$: Ionic bond
(iii) CH_4 : Covalent bond (iv) NH_3 : Covalent bond

5. Choose the kind of chemical bonding (ionic bond, covalent bond, both ionic and covalent bonds) present in the following compounds. Potassium chloride, magnesium oxide, sulphuric acid, ammonium hydroxide, zinc sulphide, phosphorus trichloride (PCl_3).

Sol.

	Ionic bond	Covalent bond	Both ionic and covalent bond
(i)	Potassium chloride	Phosphorus trichloride	Sulphuric acid Ammonium hydroxide
(ii)	Magnesium oxide		
(iii)	Zinc sulphide		

6. A compound has the formula H_2Y (Y=non-metal). State the following:
(i) The outer electronic configuration of Y.
(ii) The valency of Y.
(iii) The bonding present in H_2Y.

All in One Carbon and Its Compounds

Sol. (i) For compound H_2Y

Valency of Y is $2(8-6=2)$ and it is a non-metal which shows that it belongs to oxygen family, have 6 electrons in its valence shell.

Thus, outer electronic configuration of Y is

$$\begin{array}{cc} K & L \\ 2, & 6 \end{array}$$

(ii) Valency of Y is 2.

(iii) As bond formation is through sharing of electrons. These shared electrons belong to the outermost shells of both the atoms and in this way, both atom attain the noble gas configuration. This type of bonding is called covalent bonding.

7 Give answers to the following statements.
  (i) An allotrope of carbon which has a two dimensional layered structure consisting of fused benzene rings.
  (ii) An allotrope of carbon which looks like a soccer ball.
  (iii) An allotrope of carbon which contains both single and double bonds.

Sol. (i) Graphite (ii) Buckminster fullerene
  (iii) Graphite

8 Diamond and graphite show different physical properties although they are made up of carbon. Name this relationship between diamond and graphite. Give the basis of this relationship also.

Sol. This relationship is called allotropy. The physical properties are different because the carbon-carbon bonding in both the allotropes varies.

Diamond is hard because in it one carbon atom is bonded with four other carbon atoms with strong covalent bond, while graphite is soft in which each C-atom is joined to three other C-atoms by strong covalent bonds to form flat hexagonal rings.

The various layers of C-atoms in graphite are quite far apart, so that covalent bonds can exist between them. The various layers of carbon atom in graphite are held together by weak van der Waals' forces, they can slide over one another.

9 (a) Explain the formation of calcium chloride with the help of electron dot structure. (Atomic numbers : Ca = 20; Cl =17)
  (b) Why do ionic compounds not conduct electricity in solid state but conduct electricity in molten and aqueous state?
  CBSE SQP 2020-21

Sol. (a) The formation of calcium chloride with the help of electron dot structure.

Element	Atomic number	Electronic configuration
Calcium (Ca)	20	2, 8, 8, 2
Chlorine (Cl)	17	2, 8, 7

$$Ca: + \begin{array}{c} \ddot{Cl} \\ \ddot{Cl} \end{array} \longrightarrow Ca^{2+} \left[:\ddot{Cl}: \right]_2^-$$

$$Ca^{2+} + 2Cl^- \longrightarrow CaCl_2$$

Two valence electrons of calcium attack the valency of two chlorine to attain the noble gas configuration.

(b) Ionic compounds do not conduct electricity in solid state but conduct electricity in molten and aqueous state because in solid state, there is no free ion to move and pass electricity. Whereas in the molten and aqueous state, there is free ions to move and pass electricity.

10 Give the molecular formula and electron dot structure of ethyne and ethene.
CBSE 2013

Sol. For ethyne refer to text on page 96.
For ethene refer to text on page 95.

11 Draw the possible isomers of the compound with molecular formula C_3H_6O and also give their electron dot structures.
NCERT Exemplar; CBSE 2013

Sol. There are four isomers possible for the molecular formula C_3H_6O. These are as follows:

(i) CH_3CH_2CHO or $CH_3CH_2-\underset{\underset{O}{\|}}{\overset{H}{C}}$
Propanal

(ii) $CH_3-\underset{\underset{O}{\|}}{C}-CH_3$
Propan-2-one

(iii) $CH_3-CH=CH-OH$
Prop-1-enol

(iv) $CH_2=CH-CH_2-OH$
Prop-2-enol

Hence, the isomers are propanal, propan-2-one, prop-1-enol and prop-2-enol.

12 (i) How many isomers are possible for the compound with the molecular formula C_4H_8? Draw the electron dot structure of branched chain isomer.

(ii) How will you prove that C_4H_8 and C_5H_{10} are homologues?
CBSE SQP (Term-II)

Sol. (i) Isomers are the compounds having same molecular formula but different structural formula.
The isomers of C_4H_8 are

$$CH_3-CH=CH-CH_3,$$
But-2-ene

$$CH_3-CH_2-\underset{\underset{H}{|}}{C}=CH_2$$
But-1-ene

$$CH_3-\underset{\underset{CH_3}{|}}{C}=CH_2$$
2-methyl-prop-1-ene

$$\begin{array}{c} CH_2-CH_2 \\ | \quad\quad | \\ CH_2-CH_2 \end{array}$$
Cyclobutane

∴ There are 4 isomers of compound with molecular formula C_4H_8.

The electron dot structure of branched isomer of C_4H_8, i.e. (2-methylpropene) is

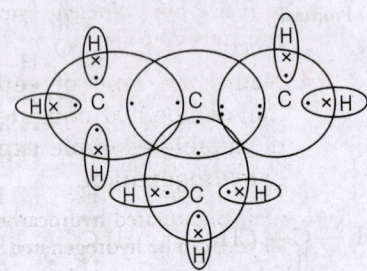

(ii) C_4H_8 is an alkene with general formula C_nH_{2n}, where $n = 4$.
The next homologues will have value of $n = 5$.
∴ Its molecular formula will be $C_5H_{2\times 5}$, i.e. C_5H_{10}.
Also, both have same functional group (alkane) and differ by "—CH_2—" group.

13 A carbon compound 'A' having melting point 156 K and boiling point 351K, with molecular formula C_2H_6O is soluble in water in all proportions.

(i) Identify 'A' and draw its electron dot structure.

(ii) Give the molecular formulae of any two homologues of 'A'.
CBSE SQP (Term-II)

Sol. (i) The compound with molecular formula C_2H_6O can be

$$\underset{\text{Ethanol}}{CH_3CH_2-OH}, \underset{\text{Ether}}{CH_3-O-CH_3}$$

Out of above compound, ethanol will have high melting and boiling point with high solubility in water due to hydrogen bonding.
∴ Compound 'A' is ethanol.
The electron dot structure of ethanol is

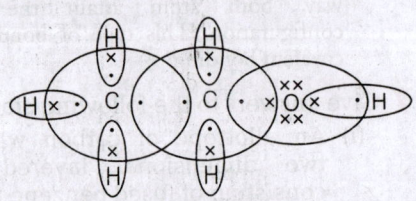

(ii) The general molecular formula for alcohol is $C_nH_{2n+1}OH$.
The homologues series with $n = 3$ and $n = 4$ are
$C_3H_{2\times 3+1}OH$, i.e. C_3H_8O
$C_4H_{2\times 4+1}OH$, i.e. $C_4H_{10}O$

14 Name the following compounds :

(i) CH_3-CH_2-Br (ii) $H-\underset{\underset{H}{|}}{C}=O$

(iii) $H-\underset{\underset{H}{|}}{\overset{\overset{H}{|}}{C}}-\underset{\underset{H}{|}}{\overset{\overset{H}{|}}{C}}-\underset{\underset{H}{|}}{\overset{\overset{H}{|}}{C}}-\underset{\underset{H}{|}}{\overset{\overset{H}{|}}{C}}-C\equiv C-H$

CBSE 2013

Sol. (i) Bromoethane (ii) Methanal
(iii) Hex-1-yne or hexyne

15 Consider the molecular formula of the carbon compounds (i) and (ii) given below:
(i) C_3H_8O
(ii) $C_3H_6O_2$
(a) Identify the functional groups in (i) and (ii) and write their structures.
(b) Are (i) and (ii) isomers? Give reason.
(c) What happens when alkaline $KMnO_4$ is added, drop by drop, into a test tube containing warm propanol? Write the chemical equation for the reaction and state the role of alkaline $KMnO_4$ in this reaction.
CBSE (All India) 2020

Sol. (a) (i) C_3H_8O contains alcoholic functional groups.
(ii) $C_3H_6O_2$ contains carboxylic acid functional group. Their structures are as follows:

Carbon and Its Compounds

(An Alcohol)
$$H-\underset{\underset{H}{|}}{\overset{\overset{H}{|}}{C}}-\underset{\underset{H}{|}}{\overset{\overset{H}{|}}{C}}-\underset{\underset{H}{|}}{\overset{\overset{H}{|}}{C}}-OH$$

(A carboxylic acid)
$$H-\underset{\underset{H}{|}}{\overset{\overset{H}{|}}{C}}-\underset{\underset{H}{|}}{\overset{\overset{H}{|}}{C}}-\overset{\overset{O}{\|}}{C}-O-H$$

(b) No, (i) and (ii) are not isomers. Isomers isomers are the organic compounds with same molecular formula but different chemical and physical properties. But, here molecular formula of (i) and (ii) are different.

(c) When alkaline $KMnO_4$ is added drop by drop into test tube containing warm propanol, it converts propanol to propanoic acid. The reaction is as follows :

$$CH_3CH_2CH_2OH \xrightarrow{[O], \text{ Alkaline } KMnO_4} CH_3CH_2COOH$$
Ethanol → Propanoic acid

Here, alkaline $KMnO_4$ acts as an oxidising agent.

16 Name the following compounds :

(i) $H-\underset{\underset{H}{|}}{\overset{\overset{H}{|}}{C}}-\underset{\underset{H}{|}}{\overset{\overset{H}{|}}{C}}-\underset{\underset{H}{|}}{\overset{\overset{H}{|}}{C}}-OH$

(ii) $H-\underset{\underset{H}{|}}{\overset{\overset{H}{|}}{C}}-\underset{\underset{H}{|}}{\overset{\overset{H}{|}}{C}}-\overset{\overset{O}{\|}}{C}-OH$

(iii) $H-\underset{\underset{H}{|}}{\overset{\overset{H}{|}}{C}}-\underset{\underset{H}{|}}{\overset{\overset{H}{|}}{C}}-\underset{\underset{H}{|}}{\overset{\overset{H}{|}}{C}}-Cl$

(iv) $H-\underset{\underset{H}{|}}{\overset{\overset{H}{|}}{C}}-\underset{\underset{H}{|}}{\overset{\overset{H}{|}}{C}}-\overset{}{C}=O$ (with H on the last C)

(v) $H-\underset{\underset{H}{|}}{\overset{\overset{H}{|}}{C}}-C\equiv CH$

(vi) $H-\underset{\underset{H}{|}}{\overset{\overset{H}{|}}{C}}-\overset{\overset{H}{|}}{C}=\underset{\underset{H}{|}}{\overset{\overset{O}{|}}{C}}-\underset{\underset{H}{|}}{\overset{\overset{H}{|}}{C}}-H$

Sol. (i) Propan-1-ol or propanol
(ii) Propanoic acid
(iii) chloropropane
(iv) Propanal
(v) Prop-1-yne or propyne
(vi) Butan-2-one

17 An aldehyde as well as a ketone can be represented by the same molecular formula, say C_3H_6O. Write their structures and name them. State the relation between the two in the language of science. **CBSE 2016**

Sol. An aldehyde as well as a ketone can be represented by the same molecular formula, say C_3H_6O. Their structures are as follows:

- Structure $CH_3CH_2-\overset{\overset{O}{\|}}{C}-H$
  IUPAC name Propanal

- Structure $CH_3-\overset{\overset{O}{\|}}{C}-CH_3$
  IUPAC name Propanone

Such compounds with identical molecular formula but different structures are called structural isomers.

18 Name the type of carbon compounds that can be hydrogenated. With the help of suitable example explain the process of hydrogenation. **CBSE 2013**

Sol. Only unsaturated hydrocarbons, i.e. alkenes and alkynes can be hydrogenated.

e.g. in the presence of a catalyst Ni/Pd, ethyne is hydrogenated into ethane.

$$H-C\equiv C-H \xrightarrow[H_2]{Ni/Pd} \underset{H}{\overset{H}{>}}C=C\underset{H}{\overset{H}{<}}$$
Ethyne → Ethene

$$\xrightarrow[H_2]{Ni/Pd} H-\underset{\underset{H}{|}}{\overset{\overset{H}{|}}{C}}-\underset{\underset{H}{|}}{\overset{\overset{H}{|}}{C}}-H$$
Ethane

119

19 Complete the following reactions and name the main product formed in each case:

(i) $CH_3COOH + NaOH \longrightarrow ...... + ...$

(ii) $C_2H_5OH + O_2 \longrightarrow ...... + ...$

(iii) $(CH_3)_2C=C(CH_3)_2 + H_2 \xrightarrow{Ni\ Catalyst} ...$

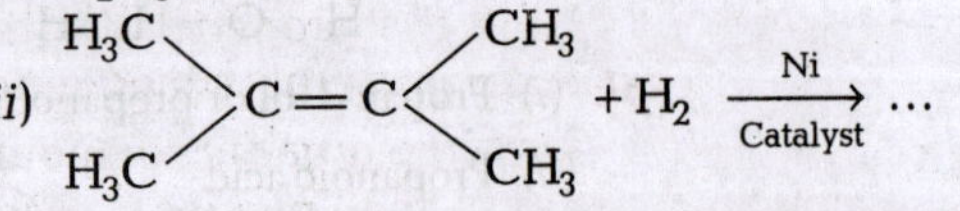

CBSE 2013

Sol. (i) $CH_3COOH + NaOH \longrightarrow \underset{\text{Sodium ethanoate}}{CH_3COONa} + H_2O$

(ii) $2C_2H_5OH + 6O_2 \longrightarrow \underset{\text{Carbon dioxide}}{4CO_2\uparrow} + 6H_2O + \text{Heat} + \text{Light}$

(iii) $(CH_3)_2C=C(CH_3)_2 + H_2 \xrightarrow{Ni\ Catalyst}$

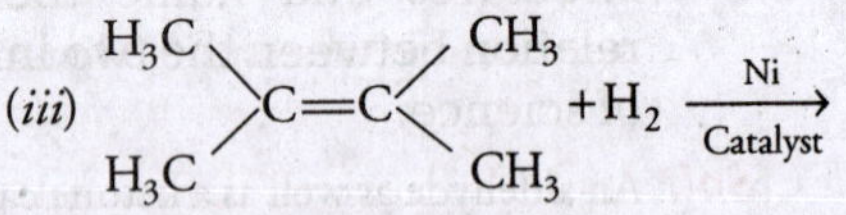

2,3-dimethylbut-2-ene

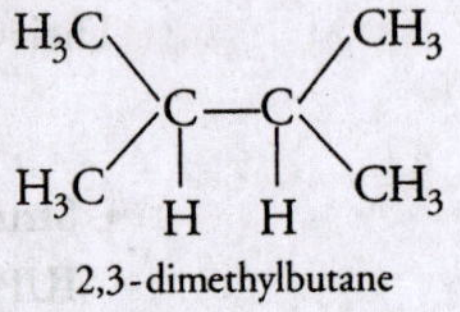

$\underset{\text{2,3-dimethylbutane}}{(CH_3)_2CH-CH(CH_3)_2}$

20 Name the compound formed when ethanol is heated in excess of concentrated sulphuric acid at 443 K. Also write the chemical equation of the reaction stating the role of concentrated sulphuric acid in it. What would happen, if hydrogen is added to the product of this reaction in the presence of catalyst such as palladium or nickel? **CBSE 2016**

Sol. When ethanol is heated in excess of concentrated sulphuric acid at 443 K, ethene is formed.

Reaction involved

$\underset{\text{Ethanol}}{CH_3CH_2OH} \xrightarrow[\text{443 K}]{\text{Conc.}H_2SO_4} \underset{\text{Ethene}}{CH_2=CH_2} + H_2O$

Conc. H_2SO_4 act as dehydrating agent, it remove water molecules from a compound. If hydrogen is added to the product, i.e. ethene, ethane is formed.

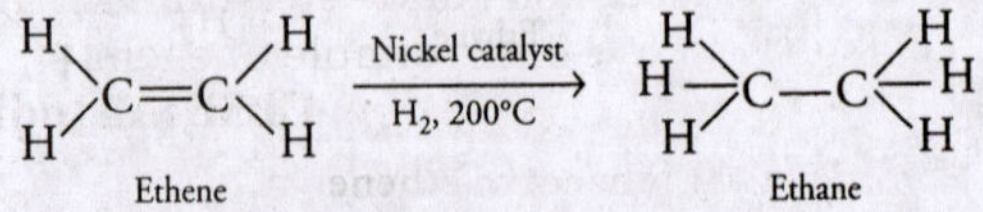

$\underset{\text{Ethene}}{H_2C=CH_2} \xrightarrow[H_2, 200°C]{\text{Nickel catalyst}} \underset{\text{Ethane}}{H_3C-CH_3}$

21 Answer the following questions :
(i) State the functional group present in alcohols.
(ii) Give the general formula of alcohol.
(iii) What is meant by denatured alcohol?

Sol. (i) —OH

(ii) $C_nH_{2n+1}OH$

(iii) To prevent the misuse of alcohols produced for industrial purposes, it is made unfit for drinking by adding poisonous substances like methanol to it. This is called denatured alcohol.

22. (i) Why are most carbon compounds poor conductors of electricity?

(ii) Write the name and structure of a saturated compound in which the carbon atoms are arranged in a ring. Give the number of single bonds present in this compound. **CBSE 2018**

Sol. (i) Carbon mainly forms covalent compounds in which molecules are present instead of ions. In other words, the bonding present in these compounds does not give rise to any ions.

(ii) Cyclopropane

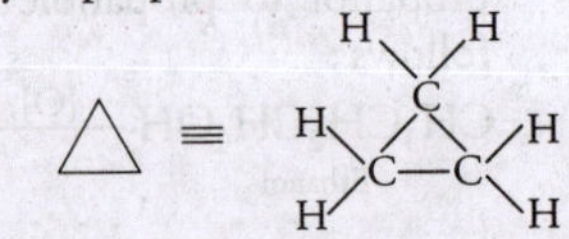

△ ≡ (structure of cyclopropane with H atoms)

Cyclopropane contains three C–C single bond and six C–H single bond.
Total 9 single bonds are present in cyclopropane.

23 A student reports the police about the illegal vending of alcohol near his school. He also knew about denatured alcohol.
(i) What is denatured alcohol?
(ii) What would happen if somebody consumes denatured alcohol?

Sol. (i) When poisonous substances such as methanol, copper sulphate etc., are added to ethanol, then it is known as denatured alcohol.

(ii) If somebody consumes denatured alcohol, it results in coagulation of protoplasm causing acute nausea, blindness and even death.

24 Some esters are added to food items for special smells. An ester can be made from ethanol and ethanoic acid. **CBSE 2015**

(i) Name the ester which is obtained due to the chemical reaction between ethanol and ethanoic acid in the presence of concentrated sulphuric acid and write the chemical equation.
(ii) Name the process.

Sol. (i) Ethyl ethanoate

$\underset{\text{Ethanoic acid}}{CH_3COOH} + \underset{\text{Ethanol}}{CH_2CH_3OH} \xrightarrow{\text{Conc. }H_2SO_4} \underset{\text{Ethyl ethanoate}}{CH_3COOCH_2CH_3} + H_2O$

(ii) The process is called esterification.

All in one Carbon and Its Compounds

25 Name the product formed when an organic acid and alcohol react in the presence of acid catalyst. Write the equation and give two uses of the product formed. **CBSE 2013**

Sol. Refer Chemical Reactions (iii) on page 102
Ester is used in preparing perfumes and flavouring agents.

26 Ethyl ethanoate smells like pears and is used for flavouring sweets. **CBSE 2015**
(i) Write the chemical formula of ethyl ethanoate.
(ii) Write the chemical reaction between ethanoic acid and ethanol in the presence of concentrated sulphuric acid.
(iii) Suggest the function of concentrated sulphuric acid in the reaction.

Sol. (i) $CH_3COOCH_2CH_3$
(ii) Refer to Ans. 24 (i)
(iii) Sulphuric acid acts as dehydrating agent, i.e. it removes water formed, otherwise ester formed will get hydrolysed and get converted into acid.

27 When ethanol reacts with ethanoic acid in the presence of conc. H_2SO_4, a substance with fruity smell is produced. Answer the following:
(i) State the class of compounds to which the fruity smelling compounds belong. Write the chemical equation for the reaction and write the chemical name of the product formed.
(ii) State the role of conc. H_2SO_4 in this reaction. **CBSE 2016**

Sol. (i) Refer to ans 21.
(ii) Conc. H_2SO_4 act as a dehydrating agent.

28 (i) The formula of an ester is $CH_3COOC_2H_5$. Write the structural formulae of the corresponding alcohol and the acid.
(ii)(a) Mention the experimental conditions involved in obtaining ethene from ethanol.
(b) Write the chemical equation for the above reaction. **CBSE 2011**

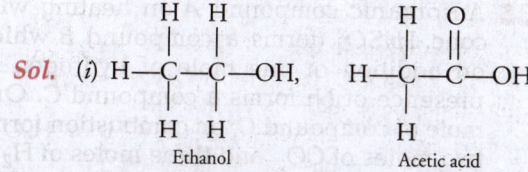

Sol. (i) Ethanol, Acetic acid

(ii) (a) Heating ethanol at 443 K in the presence of excess of conc. H_2SO_4 (which act as dehydrating agent,) converts into ethene.

(b) $CH_3-CH_2OH \xrightarrow[443 K]{Hot\ conc.\ H_2SO_4} CH_2=CH_2 + H_2O$

29 (i) Name the property of ethanol which makes it useful in medicines.
(ii) Name the organic compound which is used in pickles. Mention its composition.
(iii) Mention any two uses of alcohol in medicines. **CBSE 2013**

Sol. (i) Ethanol is a good solvent, so it is used to make medicines.
(ii) Vinegar is widely used as a preservative in pickles. It is 5-8% solution of ethanoic acid in water.
(iii) Alcohol is used in tincture of iodine and cough syrups.

30 (a) Define isomerism. Draw all possible isomers of butane.
(b) "A compound 'X' on combustion gives a yellow flame with lots of smoke." What inference would you draw from this statement?
(c) State the role of alkaline $KMnO_4$ in the reaction involving conversion of an alcohol to corresponding carboxylic acid. **CBSE (All India) 2020**

Sol. (a) Refer to text on pages 96 and 97.
(b) A compound 'X' is an unsaturated compound, because they do not undergo complete combustion. Therefore, these produces yellow flame with lots of black smoke.
(c) Alkaline $KMnO_4$ acts as an oxidising agent in the conversion of an alcohol to corresponding carboxylic acid.

e.g. $\underset{Alcohol}{CH_3CH_2OH} \xrightarrow[Alkaline\ KMnO_4]{[O]} \underset{Carboxylic\ acid}{CH_3COOH}$

31 (a) Carry out the following conversions:
(i) Ethanol to ethene
(ii) Ethanol to ethanoic acid
(b) Differentiate between addition reaction and substitution reaction. Give one example of each. **CBSE (All India) 2020**

Sol. (a) (i) Ethanol to ethene

$\underset{Ethanol}{CH_3CH_2OH} \xrightarrow[H_2SO_4, 443\ K]{Hot\ conc.} \underset{Ethene}{CH_2=CH_2} + \underset{Water}{H_2O}$

(ii) Ethanol to ethanoic acid

$\underset{Ethanol}{CH_3CH_2OH} \xrightarrow[K_2Cr_2O_7]{[O]} \underset{Ethanoic\ acid}{CH_3COOH}$

121

(b) Difference between addition reaction and substitution reaction is as follows:

	Addition reaction	Substitution reaction
(i)	The reaction in which a reagent completely add to a reactant without the removal of small molecules are called addition reactions.	The reaction in which a reagent replaces an atom or a group of atoms from the reactant are called substitution reactions.
(ii)	These reactions are shown by unsaturated compounds. e.g. Hydrogenation of alkene. $$\underset{R}{\overset{R}{>}}C=C\underset{R}{\overset{R}{<}} \xrightarrow[H_2, 200°C]{Ni}$$ $$R-\underset{\underset{H}{|}}{\overset{\overset{H}{|}}{C}}-\underset{\underset{H}{|}}{\overset{\overset{H}{|}}{C}}-R$$ Alkane	These reactions are generally shown by saturated compounds. e.g. $\underset{Methane}{CH_4} + Cl_2 \xrightarrow{Sunlight}$ $\underset{Chloro-methane}{CH_3Cl} + HCl$

32 An organic compound A is a constituent of many medicines and used as an antifreeze and has the molecular formula C_2H_6O. Upon reaction with alk. $KMnO_4$, the compound A is oxidised to another compound B with formula $C_2H_4O_2$. Identify the compounds A and B. Write the chemical equation for the reaction which leads to the fomation of B.

Sol. The organic compound A which is a constituent of many medicines and act as antifreeze with the molecular formula C_2H_6O is ethanol (CH_3CH_2OH). Ethanol is oxidised to ethanoic acid (B) upon reaction with alk. $KMnO_4$.

$$\underset{\underset{(A)}{Ethanol}}{CH_3CH_2OH} \xrightarrow{Alk.\ KMnO_4 + Heat} \underset{\underset{(B)}{Ethanoic\ acid}}{CH_3COOH}$$

33 A compound X is used in cough syrups and many tonics. It is also soluble in water in all proportions.
(i) Name the compound X. Write its chemical formula.
(ii) Which gas is evolved when the compound X reacts with sodium? How will you test the presence of this gas? Write the chemical equation involved in reaction of X with sodium.
(iii) Complete the following equation for X and identify Y.

$$X \xrightarrow[Heat]{Alk.\ KMnO_4} Y \quad \text{CBSE 2012}$$

Sol. (i) The compound X is ethanol CH_3CH_2OH as it is soluble in water in all proportions and used in cough syrups.

(ii) Hydrogen gas is evolved when ethanol reacts with sodium. On bringing a burning matchstick near to the gas, it burns with a pop sound.

$$2C_2H_5OH + 2Na \longrightarrow 2C_2H_5\overset{-}{O}\overset{+}{Na} + H_2\uparrow$$

(iii) $\underset{'X'}{CH_3CH_2OH} \xrightarrow[Heat]{Alk.\ KMnO_4} \underset{'Y'}{CH_3COOH}$

The compound Y is ethanoic acid.

34 On dropping a small piece of sodium in a test tube containing carbon compound X with molecular formula C_2H_6O, a brisk effervescence is observed and a gas Y is produced. On bringing a burning splinter at the mouth of the test tube the gas evolved burns with a pop sound. Identify X and Y. Also write the chemical equation for the reaction. Write the name and structure of the product formed, when you heat X with excess concentrated sulphuric acid.
CBSE 2016

Sol. Since, compound X (molecular formula, C_2H_6O) contains one O-atom, therefore most probably it may be an alcohol, i.e. ethanol (CH_3CH_2OH).

Since, given compound (i.e. alcohol) react with Na metal to evolve a gas hydrogen (Y) which burns with a pop sound along with the formation of compound sodium ethoxide (i.e. $CH_3CH_2\overset{-}{O}Na^+$).

Reaction involved

$$\underset{\underset{metal}{Sodium}}{2Na} + \underset{\underset{(X)}{Ethanol}}{2CH_3CH_2OH} \longrightarrow \underset{\underset{ethoxide}{Sodium}}{2CH_3CH_2\overset{-}{O}Na^+}$$
$$+ \underset{\underset{(Y)}{Hydrogen\ gas}}{H_2\uparrow}$$

When ethanol is reacted with excess of conc. H_2SO_4, the water molecule get removed from it and ethene is obtained.

$$\underset{Ethanol}{CH_3CH_2OH} \xrightarrow[170°C]{Excess\ conc.\ H_2SO_4}$$
$$\underset{Ethene}{CH_2=CH_2} + \underset{Water}{H_2O}$$

35 An organic compound A on heating with conc. H_2SO_4 forms a compound B which on addition of one mole of hydrogen in presence of Ni forms a compound C. One mole of compound C, on combustion forms two moles of CO_2 and three moles of H_2O. Identify the compounds A, B and C. Write the chemical equation of the reactions involved.
NCERT Exemplar

All in one Carbon and Its Compounds

Sol. Since, compound C on combustion forms two moles of CO_2 and 3 moles of H_2O, therefore, compound C must contain two carbon atoms and six hydrogen atoms. Thus, compound C must be ethane (C_2H_6).

$$\underset{\underset{(C)}{\text{Ethane}}}{C_2H_6} + \underset{\text{Oxygen}}{7/2\,O_2} \xrightarrow{\text{Heat}} \underset{\text{Carbon dioxide}}{2CO_2} + \underset{\text{Water}}{3H_2O}$$

Since, compound C is obtained by addition of 1 mole of H_2 in presence of Ni to compound B, therefore, B must be ethene (C_2H_4).

$$\underset{\underset{(B)}{\text{Ethene}}}{CH_2=CH_2} + H_2 \xrightarrow{\text{Ni, Heat}} \underset{\underset{(C)}{\text{Ethane}}}{CH_3-CH_3}$$

Since, compound B is formed by heating compound A with conc. H_2SO_4, therefore, compound A must be ethanol (C_2H_5OH).

$$\underset{\underset{(A)}{\text{Ethanol}}}{CH_3CH_2OH} \xrightarrow[\text{Dehydration}]{\text{Conc. }H_2SO_4,\,443\,K} \underset{\text{Ethene }(B)}{CH_2=CH_2} + H_2O$$

Hence, A is ethanol (CH_3CH_2OH), B is ethene ($CH_2=CH_2$) and C is ethane (CH_3-CH_3).

36 An organic acid X is a liquid which often freezes during winter time in cold countries. It has molecular formula $C_2H_4O_2$. On warming with ethanol in the presence of a few drops of conc. H_2SO_4, a compound Y with sweet smell is formed.
(i) Identify X and Y.
(ii) Write the chemical equation for the reaction involved. **CBSE 2011**

Sol. (i) Compound X is ethanoic acid (CH_3COOH) and Y is ethyl ethanoate ($CH_3COOCH_2CH_3$).

(ii) $CH_3COOH + CH_3CH_2OH \xrightarrow{\text{Conc. }H_2SO_4}$
$CH_3COOCH_2CH_3 + H_2O$

37 A compound X is formed by the reaction of a carboxylic acid $C_2H_4O_2$ and an alcohol in the presence of a few drops of H_2SO_4. The alcohol on oxidation with alk. $KMnO_4$ followed by acidification gives the same carboxylic acid as used in this reaction. Give the names and structures of (i) carboxylic acid, (ii) alcohol and (iii) the compound X. Also write the reaction.
NCERT Exemplar; CBSE 2013

Sol. (i) Carboxylic acid having molecular formula $C_2H_4O_2$ is acetic acid or ethanoic acid. Its structure is $CH_3-\underset{\underset{O}{\parallel}}{C}-OH$.

(ii) Since, an alcohol which on oxidation with alk. $KMnO_4$ followed by acidification gives ethanoic acid. Therefore, it must be ethanol. Its structure is CH_3CH_2-OH.

$$CH_3CH_2OH \xrightarrow[\text{(ii) Dil. }H_2SO_4]{\text{(i) Alk. }KMnO_4} CH_3-\underset{\underset{\text{acid}}{\text{Ethanoic}}}{\underset{\parallel}{\underset{O}{C}}}-OH$$

(iii) Since compound X is formed by the reaction of ethanoic acid with ethanol in presence of a few drops of conc. H_2SO_4. Therefore, compound X must be an ester, i.e. ethyl ethanoate. Its structure is $CH_3-\underset{\underset{O}{\parallel}}{C}-O-C_2H_5$.

The reaction is

$$\underset{\text{Ethanoic acid}}{CH_3COOH} + \underset{\text{Ethanol}}{C_2H_5OH} \xrightarrow{\text{Conc. }H_2SO_4}$$
$$\underset{\underset{(X\text{ - an ester})}{\text{Ethyl ethanoate}}}{CH_3COOC_2H_5} + H_2O$$

38 'Conversion of ethanol to ethanoic acid is an oxidation reaction." Justify this statement giving the relevant equation for the chemical reaction involved. **CBSE 2019**

Sol. The chemical reaction for the conversion of ethanol to ethanoic acid are given below:

(i) $\underset{\text{Ethanol}}{CH_3-CH_2OH} + [O] \longrightarrow \underset{\text{Ethanal}}{CH_3CHO} + H_2O$

(ii) $CH_3CHO + [O] \longrightarrow \underset{\text{Ethanoic acid}}{CH_3COOH}$

As, in the first reaction H_2 is given out from ethanol. We know that removal of hydrogen is oxidation. So, this reaction is an oxidation reaction.
Similarly, is second equation an oxygen atom is added to ethanal to form ethanoic acid. As we know, addition of oxygen is called oxidation. So, the second reaction is also an oxidation reaction.

39 What happens, when 5% alkaline potassium permanganate solution is added drop by drop to warm propyl alcohol (propanol) taken in a test tube? Explain with the help of a chemical equation.
CBSE 2019

Sol. When 5% alkaline potassium parmanganate solution is added drop by drop to warm propanol then oxidation reaction occurs and propanoic acid is formed.

$$\underset{\text{Propanol}}{CH_3CH_2CH_2-OH} \xrightarrow[\text{Heat}]{\text{Alk. }KMnO_4} \underset{\text{Propanoic acid}}{CH_3CH_2COOH}$$

40 Write the name and molecular formula of a carbon compound having its name suffixed with "-ol" and having two carbon atoms in its molecule. With the help of a chemical equation indicate what happens, when this compound is heated with excess conc. H_2SO_4? **CBSE 2019**

Sol. Name of the compound : Ethanol
Molecular formula : CH_3CH_2OH
Ethanol is treated at 443 K with excess conc. H_2SO_4, the water molecules gets removed from it and ethene is obtained.

$$CH_3-CH_2OH \xrightarrow[\text{Conc.} H_2SO_4, 443K]{\text{Hot}} CH_2=CH_2 + H_2O$$
(Ethanol) (Ethene) (Water)

41 Take about 3 mL of ethanol in a test tube and warm it gently in a water bath. Add a 5% solution of alkaline potassium permanganate drop by drop to the solution.
(i) What is the colour of $KMnO_4$ solution.
(ii) Which acid is formed when excess of $KMnO_4$ is added to the ethanol.
(iii) What happens to the colour of $KMnO_4$ added initially and then in excess. Give reason.

Sol. (i) Purple
(ii) Ethanoic acid (CH_3COOH)
(iii) The purple colour of alkaline $KMnO_4$ solution gets initially discharged. On adding the reagent in excess, the purple colour persists. Actually, $KMnO_4$ is an oxidising agent. It provides oxygen to oxidise ethanol to ethanoic acid. Once the oxidation complete the further addition of $KMnO_4$ imparts the purple colour to the solution.

$$CH_3CH_2OH \xrightarrow[\text{Heat}]{\text{Alk. } KMnO_4} CH_3COOH$$

42 In three test tubes A, B and C are three different liquids namely, distilled water, underground water and distilled water in which a pinch of calcium sulphate is dissolved, respectively are taken. Equal amount of soap solution is added to each test tube and the contents are shaken. In which test tube will the length of the foam (lather) be longest? Justify your answer. **CBSE 2019**

Sol. (i) In test tube A containing distilled water, the length of foam will be longer.
(ii) In test tube B under ground water, smaller length of foam will be observed.
In test tube C distilled water + pinch of calcium sulphate, minimum length of the foam will be observed as the soap solution is wasted in reacting with calcium ions present in test tube C to form insoluble precipitate called scum.

43 What are soaps chemically? How do they differ from synthetic detergents? Also, mention their uses? **CBSE 2019**

Sol. Soaps are chemically sodium or potassium salts of long chain carboxylic acids. In contrast, detergents are ammonium or sulphonate salts of long chain carboxylic acids. Both soaps and detergents are used as cleansing agents.

Soaps are used for washing clothes only in soft water. i.e. water which do not contain Mg^{2+} and Ca^{2+} ions, while detergents are used to make shampoos and products for cleaning clothes even in hard water.

Long Answer (LA) Type Questions

1 State the reason why carbon can neither form C^{4+} cations nor C^{4-} anions but forms covalent compounds? **CBSE 2014**
Also, state the reasons to explain why covalent compounds
(i) are bad conductors of electricity?
(ii) have low melting and boiling points?

Sol. Atomic number of carbon is six. This means that it has four electrons in its outermost shell and it needs four more electrons to attain noble gas electronic configuration. It does not form C^{4+} cation, as the removal of four valence electrons will require a huge amount of energy.

The cation formed will have six protons and two electrons. This makes it highly unstable. Carbon is unable to form C^{4-} anion as its nucleus with six protons will not be able to hold ten electrons due to its small size. Thus, carbon achieves noble gas electronic configuration by sharing its four electrons either with same or different other atoms, i.e. it forms covalent compounds.

(i) Covalent compounds does not have free ions, due to this they are bad conductors of electricity in solid, molten or aqueous state.

(ii) Covalent compounds are formed by covalent bonds and it has been found that the intermolecular force of attraction in covalent compounds are weak.

Thus, low amount of energy is required to break these force of attraction. Hence, their melting and boiling points are quite low.

2 Define structural isomer and draw the isomeric structures of butane. Compare the structure of benzene and cyclohexane by drawing them. **CBSE 2015**

Sol. Carbon compounds having same molecular formula but different structural formula are called structural isomers.

e.g. butane (C_4H_{10}) shows the following two structural isomers.

n-butane
Straight chain structure
I

2-methyl propane
Branched chain structure
II

Structure of benzene and cyclohexane are as follows:

Benzene (C_6H_6)   Cyclohexane (C_6H_{12})

Benzene (C_6H_6) has six C-atoms and six H-atoms, it contains three double bonds alternately between two C-atoms. Cyclohexane (C_6H_{12}) has six C-atoms each possessing two H-atoms, thus twelve H-atoms in total. It does not consist of any double bond.

3 Give an example of each of the following :

(i) A carbon compound containing two double bonds.

(ii) A molecule in which central atom is linked to three other atoms.

(iii) A compound containing both ionic and covalent bonds.

(iv) An organic compound which is soluble in water.

(v) A carbon compound which burns with a sooty flame.

Sol. (i) Carbon dioxide (CO_2)

$$:\!\ddot{O}\!: = C = :\!\ddot{O}\!:$$

(ii) Ammonia molecule (NH_3) H—N̈—H
                                      |
                                      H

(iii) Ammonium chloride (NH_4Cl) contains both ionic and covalent bonds.

$$\begin{bmatrix} H \\ | \\ H-N-H \\ | \\ H \end{bmatrix}^+ Cl^-$$

(iv) Ethanol (CH_3CH_2OH) or ethanoic acid (CH_3COOH) is soluble in water.

(v) Unsaturated compounds, e.g. ethene, ethyne, benzene etc., burn with a sooty flame.

4 (i) What are hydrocarbons? Give examples.

(ii) Give the structural differences between saturated and unsaturated hydrocarbons with two examples each.

(iii) What is functional group? Give examples of four different functional groups. **NCERT Exemplar**

Sol. (i) The compounds that are made up of carbon and hydrogen atoms are called hydrocarbons. e.g. methane (CH_4), ethene ($CH_2 = CH_2$). Ethyne (C_2H_2), cyclohexane (C_6H_{12}), benzene (C_6H_6) etc.

(ii) In saturated hydrocarbons, all the four valencies of carbon are satisfied by a single covalent bond while in unsaturated hydrocarbons, double or triple bonds are required to satisfy the valencies of carbon. e.g.

(a) Saturated hydrocarbons
  Methane (CH_4), Ethane ($CH_3 — CH_3$)

(b) Unsaturated hydrocarbons
  Ethene ($H_2C = CH_2$), Ethyne ($HC \equiv CH$)

(iii) A functional group is an atom or group of atoms that defines the structure (or the properties) of organic compounds. The four examples are:
(a) —OH   Alcohol
(b) —COOH Carboxylic acid
(c) —CHO   Aldehyde
(d) —X   Halogens

5 What is the difference between combustion and oxidation? Under what condition an oxidation reaction can be called as combustion? Illustrate your answer with one example in each case.

Sol. Addition of oxygen or removal of hydrogen from any substance is called oxidation.

e.g. when ethanol is burnt in air, it produces CO_2 and water.

$$CH_3CH_2OH + 3O_2 \longrightarrow 2CO_2\uparrow + 3H_2O$$
Ethanol, Carbon dioxide
+ heat + light

However, when ethanol is heated with alk. $KMnO_4$ or acidified $K_2Cr_2O_7$, it gives ethanoic acid.

$$CH_3CH_2OH + 2[O] \xrightarrow[\text{Acid } K_2Cr_2O_7/H_2SO_4]{\text{Alk. }KMnO_4} CH_3COOH + H_2O$$

Both these reactions are oxidation reactions. In both the cases, oxygen has been added or hydrogen has been removed. But complete oxidation of an organic compound to form CO_2 and H_2O is called combustion. Therefore, oxidation of ethanol to form CO_2 and H_2O can also be called combustion reaction.

Thus, complete oxidation of an organic compound to form CO_2 and H_2O is also called combustion while partial oxidation of a compound to give a compound other than CO_2 and H_2O is called oxidation.

6 Describe the addition reaction of carbon compounds with its application. State the function of catalyst in this reaction. How this reaction is different from a substitution reaction? Explain with an example.
CBSE 2015

Sol. The addition of hydrogen to an unsaturated molecule to make it saturated is known as hydrogenation or addition reaction.

e.g. $CH_2=CH_2 + H_2 \xrightarrow[\text{Ni}]{200°C} CH_3—CH_3$
Ethene, Ethane

This reaction is applied to convert unsaturated vegetable oil to saturated ghee.

$$\text{Vegetable oil (Unsaturated)} \xrightarrow[200°C]{H_2/Ni} \text{Ghee (Saturated)}$$

The rate of reaction increases in the presence of catalyst (Ni or Pt). This is an addition reaction.

In substitution reaction, a reagent substitutes on atom or a group of atoms from the reactant instead of addition.

e.g. $CH_4 + Cl_2 \xrightarrow{\text{Sunlight}} CH_3Cl + HCl$

7 (i) Give a chemical test to distinguish between saturated and unsaturated hydrocarbon.
(ii) Name the products formed when ethane burns in air. Write the balanced chemical equation for the reaction showing the types of energies liberated.
(iii) Why is reaction between methane and chlorine in the presence of sunlight considered a substitution reaction?
CBSE 2016

Sol. (i) Saturated hydrocarbon burn with blue and non-smoky flame due to their complete combustion and unsaturated hydrocarbons generally burn with sooty flame due to their incomplete combustion.

Another test
Unsaturated compounds decolourises bromine colour.

e.g. $CH_2=CH_2 + Br_2(aq) \longrightarrow \underset{\substack{\text{1, 2-dibromoethane}\\\text{(Colourless)}}}{CH_2—CH_2}$
Ethene, Bromine (Brown), Br Br

But, saturated compounds does not decolourise the bromine water.

(ii) Carbon dioxide and water are formed when ethane burns in air.

$$CH_3CH_3 + \frac{7}{2}O_2 \longrightarrow 2CO_2 + 3H_2O + \text{light} + \text{heat}$$

(iii) The reactions in which a reagent substitutes (replace) atom or a group of atoms form the reactant (substrate) are called substitution reactions.

These are generally shown by saturated compounds and benzene. When chlorine is added to hydrocarbons in the presence of sunlight, Cl replaces H-atoms one by one to give carbon tetrachloride as final product.

$$CH_4 + Cl_2 \xrightarrow{\text{Sunlight}} CH_3Cl + HCl$$
$$CH_3Cl + Cl_2 \xrightarrow{\text{Sunlight}} CH_2Cl_2 + HCl$$
$$CH_2Cl_2 + Cl_2 \xrightarrow{\text{Sunlight}} CHCl_3 + HCl$$
$$CHCl_3 + Cl_2 \xrightarrow{\text{Sunlight}} CCl_4 + HCl$$

8 (i) Write the names of the functional groups in

(a) $\underset{R}{\overset{R}{>}}C=O$ (b) $\underset{H}{\overset{R}{>}}C=O$

(ii) Describe a chemical test to distinguish between ethanol and ethanoic acid.
(iii) Write a chemical equation to represent what happens when hydrogen gas is passed through an unsaturated hydrocarbons in the presence of nickel as a catalyst?
CBSE 2009

Sol. (i) (a) Ketone   (b) Aldehyde
(ii) Distinguish between ethanol and ethanoic acid :
• Ethanol does not react with metal carbonate while ethanoic acid reacts with metal carbonates to form salt, water and CO_2.

Carbon and Its Compounds

e.g. $2CH_3COOH + Na_2CO_3 \longrightarrow$
$2CH_3\overset{-}{COO}\overset{+}{Na} + CO_2 + H_2O$

- Ethanol does not react with NaOH while ethanoic acid reacts with NaOH to form sodium ethanoate and water.
  e.g. $CH_3COOH + NaOH \longrightarrow$
  $CH_3\overset{-}{COO}\overset{+}{Na} + H_2O$

- Ethanol is oxidised to give ethanoic acid in presence of alkaline $KMnO_4$, while no reaction takes place with ethanoic acid in presence of alkaline $KMnO_4$.

(iii) Saturated hydrocarbon is obtained.

$$\underset{\substack{\text{Ethene}\\(\text{Unsaturated}\\\text{hydrocarbon})}}{CH_2=CH_2} + H_2 \xrightarrow{\text{Ni}\atop\text{Catalyst}} \underset{\substack{\text{Ethane}\\(\text{Saturated}\\\text{hydrocarbon})}}{CH_3-CH_3}$$

9 Explain the given reactions with the examples.
(i) Hydrogenation reaction
(ii) Oxidation reaction
(iii) Substitution reaction
(iv) Saponification reaction
(v) Combustion reaction   **NCERT Exemplar**

Sol. (i) **Hydrogenation reaction** The addition of hydrogen to an unsaturated molecule to make it saturated is known as hydrogenation.

e.g. $\underset{\text{Ethene}}{CH_2=CH_2} + H_2 \xrightarrow[\text{Ni}]{200°C} \underset{\text{Ethane}}{CH_3-CH_3}$

(ii) **Oxidation reaction** The reaction in which an oxygen is added to the substance or removal of hydrogen is called oxidation reactions.

e.g. $CH_3CH_2OH \xrightarrow[K_2Cr_2O_7]{[O]} CH_3COOH$

In the above reaction oxygen is added to ethanol, CH_3CH_2OH therefore it is an oxidation reaction.

(iii) **Substitution reaction** The reaction in which a reagent substitutes (or replaces) an atom or a group of atoms from the reactant (substrate) are called substitution reactions.

e.g. $CH_4 + Cl_2 \xrightarrow{\text{Sunlight}} CH_3Cl + HCl$

(iv) **Saponification reaction** When esters are hydrolysed in the presence of a base (NaOH) to get back an alcohol and sodium salt of an acid then reaction is called saponification reaction. It is used in the preparation of soaps.

e.g. $CH_3COOCH_3 + NaOH \longrightarrow$
$CH_3\overset{-}{COO}\overset{+}{Na} + CH_3OH$

(v) **Combustion reaction** Organic compounds burn in oxygen and yield CO_2 and water vapours. Heat and light are also released during this process. This reaction is known as combustion reaction.

e.g. $C_2H_5OH + 3O_2 \longrightarrow$
$2CO_2 + 3H_2O + \text{Energy}$

10 (i) How is vinegar made?   **CBSE 2012**
(ii) What is glacial acetic acid? What is its melting point?
(iii) Why is butanoic acid a weak acid?
(iv) Write the name and the formula of the two compounds formed when the ester, $CH_3COOC_2H_5$ undergoes saponification.

Sol. (i) 5-8% solution of acetic acid in water is called vinegar. It is obtained by dissolving 5 g acetic acid in 100 mL water.
(ii) Pure ethanoic acid is called glacial acetic acid. Its melting point is 290 K.
(iii) Butanoic acid is a weak acid because it does not ionise completely.
(iv) Ethanol (C_2H_5OH) and sodium ethanoate (CH_3COONa).

11 A salt X is formed and a gas is evolved when ethanoic acid reacts with sodium hydrogen carbonate. Name the salt X and the gas evolved. Describe an activity and draw the diagram of the apparatus to prove that the evolved gas is the one which you have named. Also, write the chemical equation of the reaction involved.
NCERT Exemplar

Sol. X is sodium ethanoate.
Gas evolved is carbon dioxide (CO_2).

Activity
1. Take $NaHCO_3$ in a test tube and add 2 mL ethanoic acid.
2. CO_2 gas is evolved with brisk effervescence.
3. Pass the gas through freshly prepared lime water, it will turn milky.

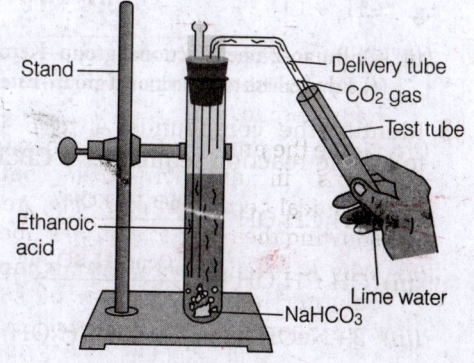

This shows that the evolved gas is carbon dioxide. The reaction involved is:

$$CH_3COOH + NaHCO_3 \longrightarrow CH_3COO^-Na^+ \text{ (X)}$$
Ethanoic acid
$$+ H_2O + CO_2\uparrow$$
$$CO_2 + Ca(OH)_2 \longrightarrow CaCO_3\downarrow + H_2O$$
Lime water — White ppt.

12 (i) Complete the following reactions and name the main product formed in each case.

(a) $CH_3CH_2CH_2OH + 2[O] \xrightarrow[K_2Cr_2O_7]{\text{Acidified}}$

(b) $C_2H_5COOH + NaHCO_3 \longrightarrow$

(c) $C_3H_7COOC_2H_5 + NaOH \longrightarrow$

(ii) Write the names of the following compounds.

(a) H—C—C—C—C—H (with H, H, O, H structure)

(b) H—C—C—O—C—C—H (with H, O, H, H structure)

State the functional group present in each compound. **CBSE 2011**

Sol. (i) (a) $CH_3CH_2CH_2OH + 2[O] \xrightarrow[K_2Cr_2O_7]{\text{Acidified}}$
$$CH_3CH_2COOH + H_2O$$
Propanoic acid

(b) $C_2H_5COOH + NaHCO_3 \longrightarrow C_2H_5COO^-Na^+$
Sodium propanoate
$$+ H_2O + CO_2$$

(c) $C_3H_7COOC_2H_5 + NaOH \longrightarrow C_2H_5OH$
Ethanol
$$+ C_3H_7COO^-Na^+$$

(ii) (a) Butan-2-one functional group–Ketone
(b) Ethyl ethanoate, functional group–Ester

13 Identify the compounds A to E in the following reaction sequence. **CBSE 2012**

(i) $CH_3CH_2OH \xrightarrow{KMnO_4 + KOH} A$

(ii) $CH_3CH_2OH + A \xrightarrow[\Delta]{\text{Conc. } H_2SO_4} B$

(iii) $B + NaOH \longrightarrow C + CH_3CH_2OH$

(iv) $A + NaHCO_3 \longrightarrow C + D + H_2O$

(v) $CH_3CH_2OH + E \longrightarrow CH_3CH_2ONa + H_2$

Sol. (i) A : CH_3COOH (Acetic acid)

(ii) B : $CH_3-\overset{\overset{O}{\|}}{C}-OC_2H_5$ (Ethyl ethanoate)

(iii) C : $CH_3COO^-Na^+$ (Sodium ethanoate)

(iv) D : CO_2 (Carbon dioxide)

(v) E : Na (Sodium)

14 (i) State the litmus test to distinguish between an alcohol and a carboxylic acid.

(ii) Give the equation for the reaction of a carboxylic acid with an alcohol. State the condition for the reaction and name the product formed. What is this reaction known as?

(iii) Write a reaction which is reverse of this reaction? Mention the conditions required for the reaction. Name and write the use of this reaction.

Sol. (i) Take 2mL of alcohol and carboxylic acid in two test tube A and B. Put 1 drop of blue litmus in each of the test tubes, the liquid which shows no effect is alcohol whereas the liquid which turns it into red is carboxylic acid.

(ii) When ethanol (an alcohol) reacts with acetic acid (a carboxylic acid), a fruity smelling liquid called ester is obtained. This reaction is called esterification.

$$CH_3COOH + CH_3CH_2OH \xrightarrow[-H_2O]{\text{Conc. } H_2SO_4}$$
Ethanoic acid — Alcohol

$$CH_3-\underset{\overset{\|}{O}}{C}-O-CH_2CH_3$$
Ester

(iii) The reverse of esterification is saponification. In this, ester is converted back to alcohol and salt of carboxylic acid by treating the ester with an alkali.

$$CH_3COOC_2H_5 \xrightarrow{NaOH} C_2H_5OH + CH_3COONa$$

The above reaction is used in the preparation of soap.

15 (i) What are fatty acids?
(ii) Which process is used for manufacture of soaps?
(iii) What kind of solution is formed by dirt and grease with water-free solution or emulsion?
(iv) What are soap forming structures?
(v) Soaps are biodegradable or non-biodegradable?

Sol. (i) Carboxylic acids containing more than 15 C-atoms.
(ii) Saponification (iii) Emulsion
(iv) Micelles (v) Biodegradable

16 Look at the figure and answer the following questions.

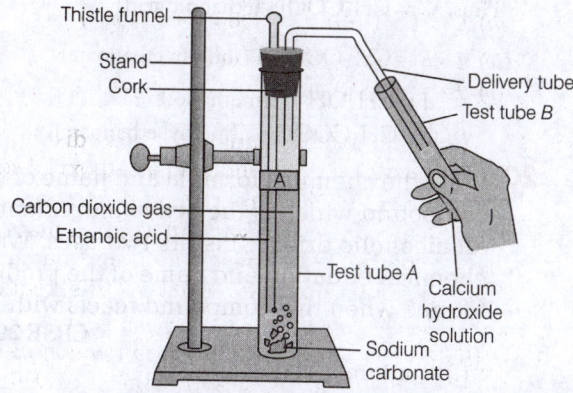

(i) What change would you observe in the calcium hydroxide solution taken in test tube B?
(ii) Write the reactions involved in test tube A and B respectively.
(iii) If ethanol is given instead of ethanoic acid, would you expect the same change?
(iv) How can a solution of lime water be prepared in the laboratory?
NCERT Exemplar

Sol. (i) The calcium hydroxide solution taken in test tube B will turn milky due to the reaction with carbon dioxide.
(ii) In test tube A,
$$2CH_3COOH + Na_2CO_3 \longrightarrow 2CH_3\overset{-}{COO}\overset{+}{N}a + H_2O + CO_2 \uparrow$$
(Ethanoic acid) (Sodium carbonate)

In test tube B,
$$CO_2 + Ca(OH)_2 \longrightarrow \underset{\text{Milky ppt.}}{CaCO_3 \downarrow} + H_2O$$

(iii) No, the same change would not be expected.
(iv) Lime water is obtained when quicklime (CaO) is dissolved in water. It produces $Ca(OH)_2$ which is a white powder and the resulting solution of calcium hydroxide in water is filtered. The filtrate is called lime water.
$$CaO + H_2O \longrightarrow Ca(OH)_2 + Heat$$

17 An organic compound A is widely used as a preservative in pickles and has a molecular formula $C_2H_4O_2$. This compound reacts with ethanol to form a sweet smelling compound B.

(i) Identify the compound A.
(ii) Write the chemical equation for its reaction with ethanol to form compound B.
(iii) How can we get compound A from B?
(iv) Name the process and write corresponding chemical equation.
(v) Which gas is produced when compound A reacts with washing soda? Write the chemical equation. **CBSE 2011**

Sol. (i) A is ethanoic acid (CH_3COOH).
(ii) $$\underset{(A)}{CH_3COOH} + \underset{\text{Ethanol}}{C_2H_5OH} \xrightarrow{\text{Conc. } H_2SO_4}$$
$$\underset{(B)}{CH_3COOC_2H_5} + H_2O$$

(iii) Compound A can be obtained from compound B by the action of a base.
(iv) Saponification.
$$CH_3COOC_2H_5 \xrightarrow{NaOH} C_2H_5OH + CH_3\overset{-}{COO}\overset{+}{N}a$$

(v) CO_2 gas is produced.
$$2CH_3COOH + \underset{\text{Washing soda}}{Na_2CO_3} \longrightarrow$$
$$2CH_3\overset{-}{COO}\overset{+}{N}a + H_2O + CO_2 \uparrow$$

18 An organic compound A of molecular formula C_2H_4 on reduction gives another compound B of molecular formula C_2H_6. B on reaction with chlorine in the presence of sunlight gives C of molecular formula C_2H_5Cl.

(i) Name the compounds A, B and C.
(ii) Write chemical equation for the conversion of A to B.

Sol. (i) The compound A of molecular formula C_2H_4 is an alkene. Upon reduction with hydrogen, it gives B of molecular formula C_2H_6.
The compound B upon chlorination gives C of molecular formula C_2H_5Cl.

$$\underset{\underset{(A)}{\text{Ethene}}}{CH_2=CH_2} + H_2 \xrightarrow[573 K]{Ni} \underset{\underset{(B)}{\text{Ethane}}}{CH_3-CH_3}$$

$$\underset{(B)}{CH_3-CH_3} + Cl_2 \xrightarrow{\text{Sunlight}}$$
$$\underset{\underset{(C)}{\text{Chloroethane}}}{CH_3-CH_2Cl} + HCl$$

(ii) $$\underset{\underset{(A)}{\text{Ethene}}}{CH_2=CH_2} + H_2 \xrightarrow[573 K]{Ni} \underset{\underset{(B)}{\text{Ethane}}}{CH_3-CH_3}$$

19. A compound C (molecular formula, $C_2H_4O_2$) reacts with Na metal to form a compound R and evolves a gas which burns with a pop sound. Compound C on treatment with an alcohol A in the presence of an acid forms a sweet smelling compound S (molecular formula = $C_3H_6O_2$).

On addition of NaOH to C, it also gives R and water. S on treatment with NaOH solution gives back R and A.

Identify C, R, A, S and write down the reactions involved. **NCERT Exemplar**

Sol. Since, compound C (Molecular formula $C_2H_4O_2$) contains two oxygen atoms, therefore most probably it may be a carboxylic acid, i.e. ethanoic acid (CH_3COOH). Ethanoic acid reacts with a metal (Na), to evolve a gas which burns with a pop sound alongwith the formation of compound R, therefore, R must be a salt, i.e. sodium ethanoate and the gas which burns with a pop sound must be H_2 gas.

$$2CH_3-\underset{\text{Ethanoic acid (C)}}{\underset{||}{\overset{O}{C}}}-OH + 2\underset{\text{Sodium}}{Na} \longrightarrow 2CH_3-\underset{\text{Sodium ethanoate (R)}}{\underset{||}{\overset{O}{C}}}-\bar{O}Na^+ + \underset{\text{Burns with a pop sound}}{H_2}$$

(Molecular formula = $C_2H_4O_2$)

H_2 gas burns with pop sound.

Compound R is sodium ethanoate. This is also supported by the observation that when ethanoic acid reacts with NaOH, it gives R, (sodium ethanoate) and water.

$$CH_3-\underset{\text{Ethanoic acid (C)}}{\underset{||}{\overset{O}{C}}}-OH + NaOH \longrightarrow CH_3-\underset{\text{Sodium ethanoate (R)}}{\underset{||}{\overset{O}{C}}}-\bar{O}Na^+ + H_2O$$

$$\underset{(C)}{CH_3COOH} + \underset{(A)}{CH_3OH} \xrightarrow{\text{Conc. }H_2SO_4} \underset{(S)}{CH_3COOCH_3} + H_2O$$

Since, compound C on treatment with an alcohol A in presence of acid forms a sweet smelling compound S(Molecular formula $C_3H_6O_2$), therefore, S is methyl ethanoate (ester).

Since, ester S has three carbon atoms and the acid C has two carbon atoms, therefore alcohol A must contain one C atom, i.e. A is methanol.

$$\underset{\text{Methyl ethanoate (S)}}{CH_3COOCH_3} + NaOH \longrightarrow \underset{(R)}{CH_3COO^-Na^+} + \underset{(A)}{CH_3OH}$$

Thus, $C = CH_3COOH$ (ethanoic acid)

$R = CH_3COO^-Na^+$ (sodium ethanoate)

$A = CH_3OH$ (methanol)

$S = CH_3COOCH_3$ (methyl ethanoate)

20. Write the chemical formula and name of the compound which is the active ingredient of all alcoholic drinks. List its two uses. Write chemical equation and name of the product formed when this compound reacts with **CBSE 2019**

(i) sodium metal.

(ii) hot concentrated sulphuric acid.

Sol. Refer to page no. 101 (Ethanol).

21. What is methane? Draw its electron dot structure. Name the type of bonds formed in this compound.

Why are such compounds

(i) poor conductors of electricity?

(ii) have low melting and boiling points? What happens, when this compound burns in oxygen? **CBSE 2019**

Sol. Refer to Pg. 90 and 91 (Formation of methane).

(i), (ii) Refer to Pg. 92 (Properties of covalent compounds) and Refer to Pg. 99 (Combustion).

22. (i) Distinguish between esterification and saponification reactions with the help of chemical equations for each.

(ii) With a labelled diagram describe in brief an activity to show the formation of an ester. **CBSE 2019**

Sol. (i) **Esterification** When ethanol (an alcohol) reacts with acetic acid (a carboxylic acid) in the presence of an acid as catalyst, a fruity (sweet) smelling liquid called **ester** is obtained.

This reaction is called esterification.

$$\underset{\text{Ethanoic acid}}{CH_3COOH} + \underset{\text{Ethanol}}{CH_3CH_2OH} \xrightarrow[-H_2O]{\text{Conc. }H_2SO_4} CH_3-\underset{||}{\underset{O}{C}}-O-CH_2CH_3$$

Ester

Carbon and Its Compounds

Soaps are made from animal fats or vegetable oils by heating it with sodium hydroxide. This process of preparation of soap is called **saponification**.

$$\underset{\text{(Ester)}}{\text{Fat or Oil}} + \underset{\substack{\text{(Sodium} \\ \text{hydroxide)}}}{\text{Alkali}} \xrightarrow{\text{Heat}} \underset{\substack{\text{(Sodium salt} \\ \text{of fatty acid)}}}{\text{Soap}} + \underset{\text{(An alcohol)}}{\text{Glycerol}}$$

(ii) **Activity**
1. Take 1 mL ethanol and 1 mL glacial acetic acid alongwith a few drops of concentrated sulphuric acid in a test tube.
2. Warm the contents in a water bath for atleast 5 min.
3. Pour into a beaker containing 20-50 mL of water and smell the resulting mixture.
4. Sweet smell would be observed.

Reaction

$$\underset{\text{Ethanoic acid}}{CH_3COOH} + \underset{\text{Alcohol}}{CH_3CH_2OH} \xrightarrow{\text{Conc. } H_2SO_4}$$

$$\underset{\text{Ester}}{CH_3-\underset{\underset{O}{\|}}{C}-OC_2H_5} + H_2O$$

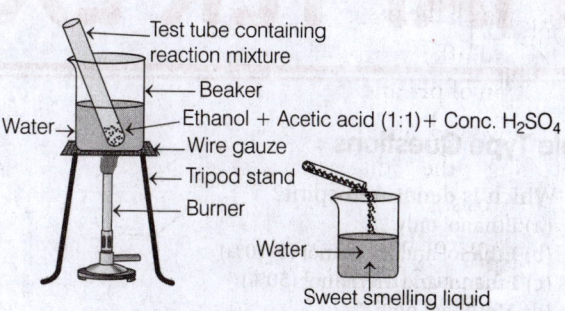

23 What is the difference between soaps and detergents? State in brief the cleansing action of soaps in removing an oily spot from a fabric. Why are soaps not very effective when a fabric is washed in hard water? How is this problem resolved?

CBSE 2019

Sol. Refer to Pg. 103. Cleansing action of soaps (micelle formation).

CHAPTER EXERCISE

Multiple Type Questions

1. Which is denatured spirit?
   (a) Ethanol only
   (b) Ethanol and methanol (5-10%)
   (c) Ethanol and methanol (50%)
   (d) Methanol only

2. Which of the following can be used for the denaturation of ethyl alcohol?
   (a) Pyridines (b) Dyes
   (c) Methyl alcohol (d) All of these

3. Vinegar is a solution of
   (a) 5-8% acetic acid in water
   (b) 5-8% acetic acid in alcohol
   (c) 30-40% acetic acid in water
   (d) 30-40% acetic acid in alcohol

Fill in the Blanks

4. The molecular formula of benzene and cyclohexane are .... and .... respectively.

5. Absolute alcohol contains .... amount of water.

True and False

6. HCHO generally mixed with alcohol to make it denatured.

7. Sugarcane juice can be used to prepare molasses which is fermented to give alcohol.

Match the Column

8. Match the Column (A) with Column (B).

Column (A)		Column (B)
A. Diamond	(i)	Dry lubricant
B. Graphite	(ii)	Super batteries
C. Graphene	(iii)	Interlocked hexagonal and pentagonal rings.
D. Fullerene	(iv)	Knives for cutting marbles.

Assertion-Reason

Direction (Q. Nos. 9-10) *In each of the following questions, a statement of Assertion is given by the corresponding statement of Reason. Of the statements, mark the correct answer as.*
   (a) Both Assertion and Reason are true and Reason is the correct explanation of Assertion.
   (b) Both Assertion and Reason are true, but Reason is not the correct explanation of Assertion.
   (c) Assertion is true, but Reason is false.
   (d) Assertion is false, but Reason is true.

9. **Assertion** Diamond does not conduct electricity.
   Reason Diamond has high refractive index.

10. **Assertion** Alcohol can not be used as an additive in petrol.
    Reason Alcohol give rise to CO_2 and H_2O when burnt in sufficient air.

Case Based Questions

Direction (Q. Nos.11-14) *Answer the questions on the basis of your understanding of the following passage, table and related studied concepts:*

The table shows some information about compounds in a homologous series.

Name of compound	Molecular formula	Relative molecular mass	Boiling point/°C
Methanol	CH_3OH	32	65
Ethanol	C_2H_5OH	46	78
Propan-1-ol	C_3H_7OH	60	97
Butan-1-ol	C_4H_9OH	74	117
Pentan-1-ol	$C_5H_{11}OH$	88	138

A lot of ethyl alcohol (ethanol) is used in industry for manufacturing various products. For industrial purposes, ethyl alcohol is supplied 'duty free' (without charging production tax) by the government.

This makes the industrial alcohol much cheaper than its market rate. To prevent the misuse of industrial purposes is denatured by adding small amount of poisonous substances like methanol, pyridine, copper sulphate etc. The addition of small amount of $CuSO_4$ imparts a blue colour to industrial ethyl alcohol so that it can be identified easily.

11. Predict the relative molecular mass of the compound, in the same series, which has seven carbon atoms in one molecule.

12. Write the general formula for a compound in this homologous series.

13. State the use of ethanol, other than in drinks.

Carbon and Its Compounds

14 Predict the boiling point of hexan-1-ol which has six carbon atom in one molecule.

Direction (Q. Nos. 15-18) *Answer the questions on the basis of your understanding of the following passage and related studied concepts:*

Compounds which contain only carbon and hydrogen are called hydro carbon. Among these the compounds containing all single covalent bonds are called saturated hydrocarbons while the compounds containing atleast one double or triple bond are called unsaturated hydrocarbons. Saturated hydrocarbons after combustion give a clean flame while unsaturated hydrocarbons given a yellow sooty flame. Unsaturated hydrocarbons are more reactive than saturated hydrocarbons. Unsaturated hydrocarbons add hydrogen in the presence of catalysts such as palladium or nickel to give saturated hydrocarbons.

15 The reaction given below is
$$CH_3CH_2CH=CH_2 \xrightarrow[H_2]{Ni} CH_3CH_2CH_3 (X)$$
(a) combustion (b) oxidation
(c) hydrogenation (d) substitution

16 The CH_3CHCH_2 is called
(a) saturated (b) unsaturated
(c) alcoholic (d) carboxylic

17 Between $CH_3CH_2CH_3$ and CH_3CHCH_2 which is more reactive?

18 Write two difference between saturated and unsaturated hydrocarbons.

Very Short Answer Type Questions

19 Which property of diamond allows it to be used in knives for cutting marble?

20 Which of the following are alkenes?
$CH_4, C_2H_6, C_2H_4, C_3H_6$ and C_3H_8

21 In order to form a branched organic compound, what should be the minimum number of carbon atoms?

22 Which of the following two organic compounds belong to the same homologous series?
$C_2H_6, C_2H_6O, C_2H_6O_2, CH_4O$

23 How two successive members of a homologous series differ from each other?

24 What is the common name of this compound

```
    H   H   H
    |   |   |
H — C — C — C — Cl  or (C_3H_7Cl)?
    |   |   |
    H   H   H
```

25 Draw the structural formula of ethyl ethanoate.

26 Which functional group can be detected by using sodium hydrogen carbonate test?

27 If water contains dissolved calcium hydrogen carbonate then out of soaps and synthetic detergents, which one will you use for cleaning the dirt of clothes?

28 Which is common in all the members of a family?

29 Draw the structure of simplest ketone.

30 Out of butter and ground nut oil, which is unsaturated in nature.

31 Which functional groups are present in the family of
(i) alcohols
(ii) aldehydes
(iii) carboxylic acids.

32 Which ions are responsible for making water hard?

Answers
1. (b) 2. (c) 3. (c)
4. C_6H_6 and C_6H_{12}
5. Zero 6. False 7. True
8. A→(iii), B→(i), C→(ii), D→(iii)
9. (b) 10. (d) 11. (a) 12. $C_nH_{2n+1}OH$
14. 160° 15. (c) 16. (b)

Short Answer (SA) Type Questions

33 Give reasons for the following :
(i) Unsaturated hydrocarbons show addition reaction.
(ii) Alcohol supplied for industrial purpose is mixed with copper sulphate.

34 Name the following compounds.

(i)
```
            H
            |
        H — C — H
            |
    H   H   |   H   H
    |   |   |   |   |
H — C — C — C — C — C — H
    |   |   |   |   |
    H   H   H   H   H
```

(ii)
```
    H   H   H   H
    |   |   |   |
H — C — C — C — C — O — H
    |   |   |   ||
    H   H   H   O
```

35 (i) What is black gold and how is it formed?
(ii) Why coal and petroleum are considered as air pollutants?

36 A substance (X) be oxidised to acetic acid (CH_3COOH)? Name substance (X) and write two tests to demonstrate acidic nature of acetic acid.

37 An organic compound X which is sometimes used as an antifreeze has the molecular formula C_2H_6O. X on oxidation gives a compound Y which gives effervescence with a baking soda solution. Identify X and Y. Write the chemical equation of reaction. **CBSE 2013**

38 (i) What indicates the non-sooty flame of alcohol and smoky flame of camphor or napthalene ?
(ii) What is a micelle ?

39 (i) How do the melting and boiling points of the hydrocarbons change with increase in molecular mass. Give reason.
(ii) Give the name of the following :
(a) An aldehyde derived from methane.
(b) Ketone derived from butane.
(iii) Give a chemical test to distinguish between soaps and detergents.

Long Answer (LA) Type Questions

40 Give a detailed explanation on the following :
(i) Properties of acetic acid
(ii) Versatile nature of carbon

41 How are the following pairs related?
(i) 2, 2-dimethylpropane and 2-methylbutane
(ii) Ethane and propane
(iii) C_2H_5Cl and C_3H_7Cl
(iv) C_3H_4 and C_2H_4

42 Draw the structures of
(i) chlorohexane   (ii) butanol
(iii) propanone   (iv) sodium ethanoate
(v) butanoic acid   (vi) butyraldehyde
(vii) sodium ethoxide (viii) sodium stearate
(ix) glycerol   (x) sodium acetate

43 Give the reaction for the hydrogenation of unsaturated carbon compounds. Define the term catalyst and name the catalyst used in this reaction. Which oil should be chosen for cooking and why? **CBSE 2013**

44 Give account of chemical properties?
(i) combustion of ethanol
(ii) oxidation of ethanol
(iii) reaction of C_2H_5OH with sodium metal
(iv) dehydration of C_2H_5OH
(v) reaction of C_2H_5OH with ethanoic acid

45 An organic compound A with molecular formula $C_4H_8O_2$ on alkaline hydrolysis gives two compound B and C. C on acidification with dil. HCl gives D. Oxidation of B with $K_2Cr_2O_7/H_2SO_4$ also gives D. Identify A, B, C and D and explain all the reactions involved.

Challengers*

1 Consider the following statements related to diamond and graphite.
  I. Both diamond and graphite are used as abrasives.
  II. Diamond and graphite have different arrangements of carbon atoms.
  III. The carbon atoms in graphite have a different number of neutrons from those in diamond.
  IV. The carbon atoms in both graphite and diamond have four single covalent bonds.
  The incorrect statement(s) is/are
  (a) I and III
  (b) II and IV
  (c) I, III and IV
  (d) All of the above

2 What would happen if graphene is heated in sufficient supply of air?
  (a) It aggregates to form graphite
  (b) It gets converted into diamond
  (c) Carbon dioxide gas is released
  (d) It becomes a non-conductor

3 C^{4+} does not exist but Pb^{4+} exists although both belong to the same group. This is because
  I. size of carbon is much smaller than Pb.
  II. large amount of energy is needed in case of carbon.
  III. of inert pair effect.
  IV. nucleus cannot hold such a large number of electrons.
  The correct statement(s) is/are
  (a) Only I
  (b) I and II
  (c) Only III
  (d) II, III and IV

4 The structures of three hydrocarbons are given below.

$H-\underset{\underset{H}{|}}{\overset{\overset{H}{|}}{C}}-\underset{\underset{H}{|}}{\overset{\overset{H}{|}}{C}}-H$ $H-\underset{\underset{H}{|}}{\overset{\overset{H}{|}}{C}}-\underset{\underset{H}{|}}{\overset{\overset{H-C-H}{|}}{C}}-\underset{\underset{H}{|}}{\overset{\overset{H}{|}}{C}}-H$

$H-\underset{\underset{H}{|}}{\overset{\overset{H}{|}}{C}}-\underset{\underset{H}{|}}{\overset{\overset{H}{|}}{C}}-\underset{\underset{H}{|}}{\overset{\overset{H}{|}}{C}}-\underset{\underset{H}{|}}{\overset{\overset{H}{|}}{C}}-H$

Which statement is correct for all the above three compounds?

  (a) They are isomers of each other
  (b) They have the same general formula
  (c) They have the same physical properties
  (d) They react with aqueous bromine

5 The diagram shows the molecule, ethyl propanoate.

$CH_3-CH_2-C\underset{O-CH_2-CH_3}{\overset{O}{\lVert}}$

How many bonding pairs of electrons are there in the molecule?
  (a) 13
  (b) 16
  (c) 17
  (d) 20

6 Which compound has an addition reaction with chlorine?
  (a) C_2H_4
  (b) C_2H_5OH
  (c) C_2H_6
  (d) CH_3CO_2H

7 One mole of a hydrocarbon X reacted completely with one mole of hydrogen gas in the presence of a heated catalyst.
  What could be the formula of X?
  (a) C_2H_6
  (b) C_5H_{10}
  (c) C_3H_8
  (d) C_7H_{16}

8 Compound X is a six carbon compound. When it is burnt, light is generated. Here, the colour of the flame is yellow because of the presence of carbon particles.
  Compound X cannot be
  (a) C_6H_{12}
  (b) C_6H_{14}
  (c) C_6H_6
  (d) C_6H_{10}

9 A reaction scheme is shown below:

Ethene + Steam $\xrightarrow{\text{Catalyst}}$ X $\xrightarrow[\text{potassium dichromate}]{\text{Acidified}}$ Y $\xrightarrow{X}$ Z
$\quad\quad\quad\quad\quad\quad\quad\quad\quad\quad\quad\quad\quad$ (VI)

What is the final product Z?
  (a) A carboxylic acid
  (b) An alcohol
  (c) An alkene
  (d) An ester

Answer Key

1.	(c)	2.	(c)	3.	(b)	4.	(b)	5.	(c)
6.	(a)	7.	(b)	8.	(b)	9.	(d)		

*These questions may or may not be asked in the examination, have been given just for additional practice.

CHAPTER 05 a

Life Processes : Nutrition

The process that all living organism perform to maintain their life are called life processes. The basic life processes common to all living organisms are nutrition, respiration, transportation and excretion. Out of these processes, nutrition is discussed in this chapter.

Nutrition

It is a process by which an organism obtains nutrients from food and utilises them to obtain energy and for building repairing their tissues. Nutrients are defined as the substances required for proper growth and maintenance of a living body, i.e. the materials, which provide energy to an organism.

All living organisms do not obtain food by the same process, e.g. plants and some bacteria have the green pigment chlorophyll to help synthesise food by the process called **photosynthesis**. Likewise animals, fungi and other bacteria depend on plants and other organisms for food. Based on this, there are two main modes of nutrition, i.e. **autotrophic** and **heterotrophic**.

Autotrophic Nutrition

The mode of nutrition in which organisms synthesise their food from simple inorganic substances like carbon dioxide and water (present in environment) in the presence of sunlight is called autotrophic, e.g. green plants and some bacteria. This mode of nutrition is called **autotrophic mode of nutrition**.

Note In chemosynthetic mode of nutrition, chemical energy is utilised by the organisms to prepare food, e.g. chemosynthetic bacteria.

Chapter Checklist
- Nutrition
- Autotrophic Nutrition
- Heterotrophic Nutrition
- Nutrition in *Amoeba*
- Nutrition in Human Beings

Plant Nutrition : Photosynthesis

It is a complex process by which green parts of the plant synthesise organic food. This food is prepared by green plants from carbon dioxide and water in the presence of sunlight and chlorophyll. It involves the given reaction

$$\underset{\text{Carbon dioxide}}{6CO_2} + \underset{\text{Water}}{12H_2O} \xrightarrow[\text{Chlorophyll}]{\text{Sunlight}} \underset{\text{Glucose}}{C_6H_{12}O_6} + \underset{\text{Water}}{6H_2O} + \underset{\text{Oxygen}}{6O_2} \uparrow$$

The equation clearly indicates that the raw materials for photosynthesis are carbon dioxide and water. The end products of photosynthesis are **glucose** (carbohydrate) and **oxygen**.

Carbohydrates are utilised for providing energy to the plant. The remaining carbohydrates, which are not used immediately are stored in the form of starch. It serves as the internal energy reserve and it is used by the plant whenever required. Similarly, glycogen serves as an internal energy reserve to be used when required in humans.

Site of Photosynthesis : Chloroplasts

The organelles in the cells of green plant which contains chlorophyll are called **chloroplasts**.

Chloroplasts are the site of photosynthesis as they contain **chlorophyll pigment**. These are the organelles present in the photosynthetic cells (or mesophyll cells) of green plants. These contain the light absorbing green pigment, chlorophyll. Chloroplast can be seen as disc-like structure in the cross-section of leaf using a microscope.

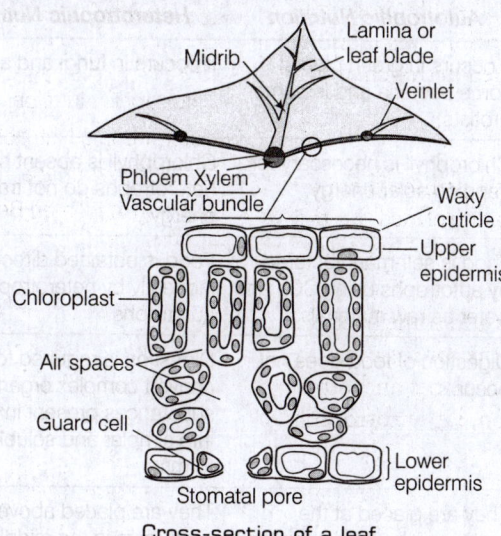

Cross-section of a leaf

Raw Materials for Photosynthesis

Following raw materials are essential to carry out the process of photosynthesis in plants :

(i) **Carbon Dioxide** It is released into the atmosphere during cellular respiration by organisms and enters the leaf through stomata. Later are tiny pores present on the surface of leaves through which massive amount of gaseous exchange takes place. Apart from this, surface of stems, leaves and roots also contribute in the gaseous exchange.

(ii) **Water** It is absorbed by roots from the soil and transported upward through xylem to the leaves and then to the photosynthetic cells. These water molecules split in the presence of sunlight to form hydrogen and oxygen. This is called photolysis of water. Hydrogen ions are used to reduce CO_2 and O_2 is given off as a byproduct.

Note Aquatic plants (e.g. *Hydrilla, Vallisnaria*) use CO_2 dissolved in water for photosynthesis.

(iii) **Other Materials** Mineral nutrients like nitrogen, phosphorus, iron and magnesium are also taken up from the soil. Nitrogen is an essential element used in the synthesis of proteins and other compounds. It is taken up in the form of inorganic nitrates (or nitrites) or as organic compounds prepared by symbiotic bacteria like *Rhizobium* from atmospheric nitrogen.

Conditions Necessary for Photosynthesis

Various experiments have shown that the presence of sunlight and chlorophyll are necessary for photosynthesis. They are discussed below

(i) **Sunlight** Intensity, quality and duration of sunlight affect the rate of photosynthesis.

(ii) **Chlorophyll** A green coloured photosynthetic pigment found in chloroplast of a plant. It is responsible for trapping solar energy.

Events in Photosynthesis

Major events that occur during the process of photosynthesis are

(i) **Absorption** of light energy by chlorophyll.

(ii) **Conversion** of light energy into chemical energy and splitting of water molecules into hydrogen and oxygen.

(iii) **Reduction** of carbon dioxide to carbohydrates.

The above steps need not take place one after the other immediately, e.g. desert plants take up carbon dioxide at night and prepare an intermediate compound. This intermediate compound is acted upon by the energy absorbed during the day by the chlorophyll.

Opening and Closing of Stomata
(Singular : Stoma)

Stomata are the tiny pores present on the surface of the leaves. They allow gases to enter and exist the leaf rapidly between the plant and atmosphere.

Opening and closing of stomata are an important event in the process of photosynthesis. Along with gaseous exchange, large amount of water loss (i.e. transpiration) also occurs through stomata. So, plants close stomata when they do not need carbon dioxide and want to conserve water. The opening and closing of stomata are caused by the change in the turgidity of guard cells.

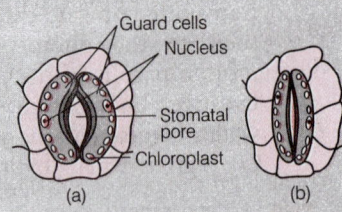

Stomatal pore (a) Open (b) Closed

Guard cells are bean-shaped cells that frame the stomatal openings. They contain chloroplasts and have cell wall.

A plant cell is said to be turgid when it is fully inflated with water due to high sugar content in it. When guard cells are turgid stomatal pore open and when guard cell losses water (shrinks), the stomatal pore close.

Check Point 01

1. Identify the mode of nutrition of organisms in which sunlight is used along with CO_2 and water to prepare food.
2. State the photosynthetic reaction and where does it occur?
3. Which cell organelle acts as the site of photosynthesis?
4. State True or False for the following statement:
   Hydrilla and *Vallisnaria* use CO_2 dissolved in water for photosynthesis.
5. Fill in the blank:
   ...... is an essential element used in the synthesis of proteins and other compuonds.

Heterotrophic Nutrition

In heterotrophic mode of nutrition, organisms cannot prepare food on their own. These organisms are termed as heterotrophs, e.g. humans, animals, non-green plants, etc. Heterotrophs obtain energy from organic molecules already produced by the autotrophs. The heterotrophic forms of nutrition differ in various organisms depending on the type, availability and process of obtaining food materials by an organism.

Accordingly, there are herbivores, carnivores, omnivores, saprotrophs and parasites, included in heterotrophs. Heterotrophic mode of nutrition can be of following three main types

(i) **Holozoic Nutrition** Herbivores (plant-eaters), carnivores (meat-eaters) and omnivores (both plant and meat-eaters) possess the holozoic mode of nutrition. In this type of nutrition, complex food molecules are taken in and then broken down into simpler and soluble molecules e.g. *Amoeba*, cow, goat, dog, cat, human being, etc.

(ii) **Saprotrophic Nutrition** (Saprophytic nutrition) Saprotrophs are the organisms which feed upon dead organic matter, these organisms breakdown complex materials outside the body and then absorb it, e.g. fungi like bread moulds, mushrooms, yeast and bacteria.

(iii) **Parasitic Nutrition** Parasites are the organisms having parasitic nutrition. These organisms live either on or inside the body of other organism (host) to obtain their nutrition without killing them, e.g. *Plasmodium*, ticks, lice, leech, tapeworm, flatworm, plants like *Cuscuta* (amarbel), etc.

Differences between Autotrophic and Heterotrophic Nutrition

Autotrophic Nutrition	Heterotrophic Nutrition
It occurs in green plants, some bacteria and in some protists.	It occurs in fungi and animals.
Chlorophyll is necessary for trapping solar energy.	Chlorophyll is absent hence, heterotrophs do not trap solar energy.
Food is self-manufactured by autotrophs using CO_2 and water as raw materials.	Food is obtained directly or indirectly by heterotrophs from autotrophs.
Digestion of food does not occur.	Digestion is required to convert complex organic substances present in food into simpler and soluble forms.
They are placed at the bottom of the food chain as producers.	They are placed above producers in the middle of food chain as consumers.

Nutrition in Different Organisms

The type of food and the way of obtaining it varies from one organism to another. Due to this, different organisms possess different types of digestive system. In single-celled organisms, like *Amoeba*, the food may be taken in by the entire surface. On the other hand, in complex (multicellular) organisms, there are specialised parts or organs for the complete process of digestion.

Nutrition in *Amoeba*

Amoeba is a unicellular and omnivore organism. The mode of nutrition in *Amoeba* is **holozoic**. It has no mouth or adher organ for intake of food. It ingests food particles by formis temporary finger–like projections pseudopodia. Pseudopodia fuse over the food particle to form a food vacuole.

Inside the food vacuole, complex food breaks into small soluble molecules, i.e. **digestion** and gets readily absorbed by the cytoplasm, i.e. **absorption**. The remaining undigested food material is removed by the cell membrane, which ruptures suddenly at any place and eliminates out the undigested food, i.e. **egestion**.

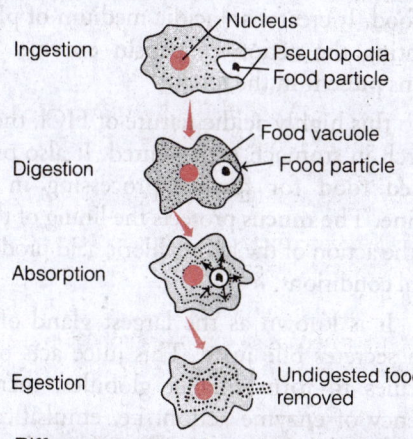

Different stages of nutrition in *Amoeba*

Note *Paramecium* is another unicellular organism, which has definite shape. Food is taken in at a specific spot in it. Food is moved to this spot by the movement of cilia, which cover the entire surface of the cell.

Check Point 02

1. What type of nutrition occurs in fungi?
2. How do parasitic organisms derive their nutrition?
3. State True or False for the following statement:
   The mode of nutrition in *Amoeba* is autotrophic.
4. Explain the term ingestion.
5. What are pseudopodia?

Nutrition in Human Beings

In human beings, the process of intake of essential nutrients in the form of food takes place through an entire system known as **digestive system**.

Digestion is a catabolic process, in which complex and large components of food are broken down into their respective simpler and smaller forms with the help of various hydrolytic enzymes. These simpler forms are finally absorbed and are further taken up by different parts of body.

The human digestive system constitutes a long tubular structure called **alimentary canal** and various **digestive glands** associated with it. These glands secrete different digestive enzymes.

Alimentary Canal

It is a long tube (about 7-8 m), where the entire process of digestion takes place. The complete process of ingestion, digestion, absorption, assimilation and egestion of food material is done within the alimentary canal itself.

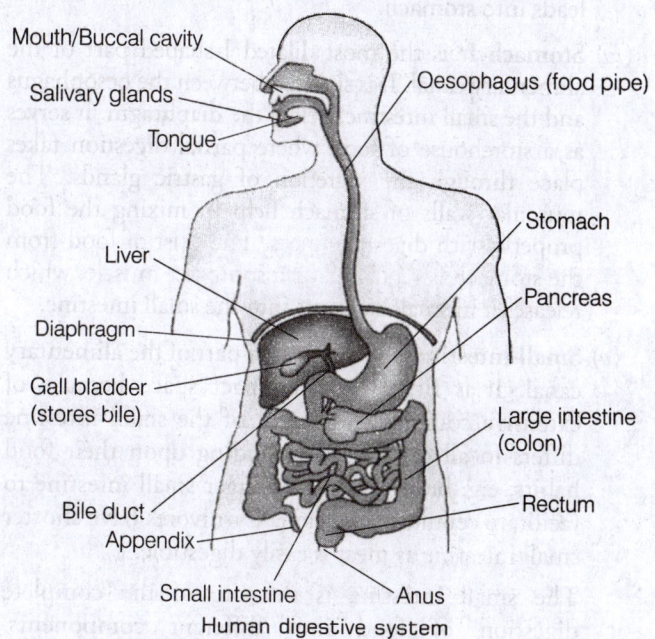

Human digestive system

The major portions of alimentary canal are discussed below

(i) **Mouth** It is the first part of the digestive system from where the food enters into the alimentary canal. It is mainly comprised of two major parts

- **Tongue** It is a highly muscular sensory organ present at the floor of buccal cavity. It bears several taste buds and helps in mixing of food with saliva. Apart from this, it is also helpful in producing speech.
- **Teeth** These are hard structures present on the bones of both lower and upper jaw. Teeth are basically used for the purpose of **grinding**, **cutting** and **chewing** of food.

Dental Caries (Tooth Decay)

It is a condition, which causes gradual softening of enamel and dentine. It usually begins when bacteria acting on sugars produce acids and soften or demineralise the enamel. Masses of bacterial cells together with food particles stick to the teeth to form dental plaque. Due to this, the saliva fails to reach the tooth surface to neutralise the acid because plaque covers the teeth. Brushing the teeth after eating removes the plaque before the bacteria produce acids. If untreated, microorganisms may invade the pulp, causing inflammation and infection.

(ii) **Pharynx** It is a small funnel-shaped chamber located behind the oral cavity. It communicates with both oesophagus and trachea (windpipe).

(iii) **Oesophagus** It is a thin and long muscular tube that leads into stomach.

(iv) **Stomach** It is the most dilated J-shaped part of the alimentary canal. It is situated between the oesophagus and the small intestine, below the diaphragm. It serves as a storehouse of food where partial digestion takes place through the secretion of gastric glands. The muscular walls of stomach help in mixing the food properly with digestive juices. The exist of food from the stomach is regulated by a sphincter muscle, which releases it in small amounts into the small intestine.

(v) **Small Intestine** It is the longest part of the alimentary canal. It is fitted in a compact space because of extensive coiling. The length of the small intestine differs in all organisms depending upon their food habits, e.g. herbivores have longer small intestine to facilitate cellulose digestion. Carnivores have shorter small intestine as meat is easily digestible.

The small intestine is the site of the complete digestion of food into different components. Secretions from liver and pancreas enter the intestine to help the digestion process. The inner lining of the small intestine has numerous finger-like projections called villi, which increase the surface area for absorption.

(vi) **Large Intestine** Although shorter, but is called **large intestine** because it is wider in diameter than the small intestine. Appendix is the part of large intestine.

(vii) **Rectum** It is the last and broad chamber-like structure that serves to store faecal matter temporarily.

(viii) **Anus** It is the end point of the alimentary canal, which helps in exit of waste materials. This process is regulated by **anal sphincter**.

Digestive Glands

Various glands are associated with alimentary canal serving the process of digestion of food. These are given below

(i) **Salivary Glands** These glands are of three types porotial glands, sub-mandibular glands and sub-maxillary glands and secrete saliva containing an enzyme called **salivary amylase** (ptyalin). It converts starch into sugars at an optimum pH of about 7. It is due to these salivary glands that our mouth waters when we eat or smell something we like.

(ii) **Gastric Glands** These are found in the wall of the stomach. These glands release digestive juice containing HCl, pepsin, mucus, etc.

Hydrochloric Acid (HCl) kills the bacteria ingested with food. It creates an acidic medium of pH about 2, facilitating the action of **pepsin** enzyme. It acts on proteins present in the food.

Due to this highly acidic nature of HCl, the digestion of starch in stomach is prevented. It also prepares the ingested food for further processing in the small intestine. The **mucus** protects the lining of the stomach from the action of the hydrochloric acid produced under normal conditions.

(iii) **Liver** It is known as the largest gland of the body, which secretes bile juice. This juice acts on large fat molecules to form smaller globules, increasing the efficiency of enzyme action, i.e. emulsification. Gall bladder stores bile juices for the further use.

(iv) **Intestinal Glands** The walls of the small intestine contain numerous glands that secrete intestinal juice containing amylolytic, proteolytic and **lipolytic enzymes**.

(v) **Pancreas** It secretes pancreatic juice, which contains enzymes like amylase, trypsin and lipase. It is connected to the small intestine through its main duct called **pancreatic duct**.

Mechanism of Digestion of Food

The food we eat contains various components like carbohydrates, proteins, fats, vitamins, minerals, etc.

Various steps involved in digestion of these nutrients is given below

1. Ingestion

It is the process of intake of food by mouth. Food is moistened by saliva, before swallowing, masticated by teeth into smaller particles.

2. Digestion

The process of breaking down large organic molecules (like carbohydrates) into smaller molecules (like simple sugars) is called **digestion**. It is done with the help of enzymes. It is completed in following main steps

Carbohydrates digestion initiates inside the mouth. Starch is converted to simple sugars by **salivary amylase**.

Proteins are converted into peptones with the help of **pepsin and rennin**.

Emulsification of fats with the help of **bile juices**.

Breakdown of emulsified fats by **lipase**.

Complete conversion of proteins to amino acids, complex carbohydrates into glucose and fats into fatty **acids** and **glycerol**.

3. Absorption

It is the process by which digested food passes from the alimentary canal into the blood. All the digested food is taken up by the walls of **intestine**, which has numerous **villi** and **lacteals** (small lymph capillaries found in the villi of the small intestine).

Peristalsis

It is the necessary action of digestive process and is essential for moving food in a regulated manner along the digestive tube. The lining of the alimentary canal has muscles, which contract rhythmically in order to push the food forward. These movements are called **peristaltic movements**. These occur all along the gut, e.g. it occurs in oesophagus when food is moved into the stomach.

4. Assimilation

It is the distribution of digested food products to various cells of the body. The villi in the small intestine are richly supplied with blood vessels, which take up the absorbed food to each and every cell of the body. It is then utilised for obtaining energy, building up new tissues and repairing the older ones.

5. Egestion

The elimination of undigested food formed in the colon of the large intestine through anus is called egestion. Peristalsis gradually pushes the undigested food from the small intestine to large intestine. The remaining material after reabsorption of water and ions is stored in the rectum for sometime and is ultimately removed from the body through anus.

Check Point 03

1. State the location of salivary glands.
2. Why carnivores have shorter small intestine?
3. How do villi increase the surface area?
4. Explain the significance of peristalsis.
5. What is the function of anal sphincter?
6. State True or False for the following statement:
   Food is moistened by gastric juice before swallowing.

NCERT FOLDER

Intext Questions

1. Why is diffusion insufficient to meet the oxygen requirements of multicellular organisms like humans? *Pg 95*

Sol. Multicellular organisms such as human beings have complex body designs and large body size. They bear specialised cells and tissues for performing various necessary functions of the body such as intake of food and oxygen, etc.

Unlike, unicellular organisms, multicellular organisms do not have all the cells of the body in direct contact with the environment. Hence, diffusion cannot meet their oxygen requirements as per their body needs.

2. What criteria do we use to decide whether something is alive? *Pg 95*

Sol. The different criteria that can be used to decide whether something is alive are the various features of living organisms, which are as follows

Movement, growth, metabolism, nutrition, respiration, transportation, excretion, response to stimuli, etc.

3. What are outside raw materials used by an organism? *Pg 95*

Sol. Carbon based molecules, i.e. **food** is used by body from outside to meet its energy need. **Oxygen** is used to oxidise food which release energy. **Water** is required for operating most of the functions inside the body. So, food, water and oxygen are the basic raw materials used by an organism.

4. What processes would you consider essential for maintaining life? *Pg 95*

Sol. Four basic processes that are essential for maintaining life are

(i) **Nutrition** It is the process of transferring source of energy from outside to the body of an organism.

(ii) **Respiration** It is the process of acquiring oxygen from outside into the body and using it for the breakdown of food sources to release energy for cellular needs.

(iii) **Transportation** It is the process of carrying food and oxygen from one place to another in the body.

(iv) **Excretion** It is the process of removing byproducts and waste products from body which are formed during energy generating reactions.

5. What are the differences between autotrophic and heterotrophic nutrition? *Pg 101*

Sol. The differences between autotrophic and heterotrophic nutrition are as follows

Features	Autotrophic Nutrition	Heterotrophic Nutrition
Food	In this mode of nutrition, food is prepared by organism itself.	In this mode of nutrition, food is obtained from other organisms (autotrophs).
Inorganic substances	The raw materials are required by autotrophs.	The raw materials are not required by heterotrophs.
Digestion	This process is absent.	This process is required for the conversion of complex molecules into simpler and more soluble ones.
Chlorophyll	It is present in autotrophs for trapping light.	It is absent.
Status	They are known as producers.	They are known as consumers.

6. Where do plants get each of the raw materials required for photosynthesis? *Pg 101*

Sol. The raw materials for photosynthesis are carbon dioxide and water. These are taken up by the plants in the following ways

(i) CO_2 is taken up through the stomata from the atmosphere in case of land plants, while the aquatic plants take up CO_2 dissolved in water.

(ii) Water is taken up or is absorbed by the roots through the process of osmosis and is transported to the leaves containing photosynthetic cells by the xylem vessels.

7. What is the role of acid in our stomach? *Pg 101*

Sol. Hydrochloric acid (HCl) is the acid secreted inside the stomach and plays the following roles

(i) It makes medium inside the stomach acidic, which is necessary for the activation of enzyme called pepsin. It converts inactive pepsin into active pepsin.

(ii) It also kills any bacteria, entering the stomach along with the food.

8. What is the function of digestive enzymes? *Pg 101*

Sol. Digestive enzymes help to breakdown large and insoluble food molecules into small soluble molecules, e.g. enzyme, amylase breaks down starch and enzyme, trypsin breaks down proteins.

Life Processes : Nutrition

9 How is small intestine designed to absorb digested food?   CBSE 2016; Pg 101

Sol. The small intestine is the main region for the absorption of digested food. The inner lining of the small intestine is covered by millions of tiny finger-like projections called villi. The presence of villi gives the inner walls of the small intestine a very large surface area for the absorption of digested food.

Exercises (On Page 113)

1 The autotrophic mode of nutrition requires
   (a) carbon dioxide and water   (b) sunlight
   (c) chlorophyll   (d) All of these

Sol. (d) The autotrophic mode of nutrition requires carbon dioxide, water, chlorophyll and sunlight.

2 How are fats digested in our bodies? Where does this process take place?

Sol. The small intestine is the site of the complete digestion of fats. The upper part of the small intestine receives bile juice, which contains bile salts for breakdown of fats into smaller globules thereby, increasing the efficiency of the enzyme action. This process is known as **emulsification**. Bile also makes the medium alkaline. The walls of the small intestine secrete intestinal juice containing enzyme lipase. It finally converts the emulsified fats into fatty acids and glycerol.

3 What is the role of saliva in the digestion of food?

Sol. Saliva is secreted by the salivary glands in the mouth. It contains the enzyme salivary amylase, which breaks down starch into maltose. It lubricates the mouth and food.

4 What are the necessary conditions for autotrophic nutrition and what are its byproducts?

Sol. The necessary conditions for autotrophic nutrition are :
   (i) water   (ii) carbon dioxide
   (iii) sunlight   (iv) chlorophyll
The byproduct of autotrophic nutrition is oxygen, which is released into the atmosphere through stomata.

SUMMARY

- **Nutrition** is the process of transfer of energy source from outside to the body of living organisms, providing energy necessary for performing basic life processes like nutrition, respiration, reproduction, etc.
- **Nutrients** are the energy providing substances which are consumed by living beings.
- **Autotrophic nutrition** is the mode of nutrition performed by green plants; some bacteria etc., for manufacturing their own food from inorganic sources, i.e. CO_2 and water. These organisms are called autotrophs.
- **Photosynthesis** is the process by which green plants synthesise organic food as carbohydrates in the presence of sunlight, chlorophyll, water, CO_2 and some other raw materials.
- **Chloroplasts** are the site of photosynthesis, present in leaves of a plant. They contain a green coloured pigment, chlorophyll that traps solar energy from the Sun.
- **Heterotrophic Nutrition** The heterotrophs cannot synthesise their own food, but are dependent on the autotrophs for their nutrition. It can be of three types
  Holozoic nutrition (e.g. *Amoeba*, humans), **saprotrophic nutrition** (e.g. fungi) and **parasitic nutrition** (e.g. ticks, lice, leech, etc.)
- **Nutrition in *Amoeba*** which is a unicellular omnivores gathers and ingests food with the help of pseudopodia. It lacks special organs for nutrition.
  Nutrition in human beings involves the breakdown of complex substances ingested from outside in the body by different parts of the alimentary canal.
- **Human digestive system** consists of the alimentary canal, i.e. a tube-like structure consisting of mouth, pharynx, oesophagus, stomach, small intestine and large intestine and digestive juices.
- **Mouth** is the first part of digestive system which helps in intake of food. Tongue is a muscular organ which bears taste buds. It also helps in mixing the chewed food with saliva. Teeth help in chewing of food. Mouth opens into buccal cavity that further opens into pharynx.
- **Oesophagus** or the food pipe helps in the transfer of food from mouth down to the stomach.
- **Stomach** is a J-shaped organ which stores and partially digest the food entering through the food pipe.
- **Intestine** is the main organ of digestion and absorption. Small intestine is longer in length compared to large intestine.
- **Anus** is the end point of the alimentary canal from where the waste is removed out from the body.
- **Digestive glands** are the salivary, gastric, intestinal glands along with pancreas and liver.
  Salivary glands (in mouth) secrete saliva containing **salivary amylase** which helps in the digestion of starch.
  Gastric glands present in stomach secrete digestive juice containing pepsin, HCl and mucus.
  Intestinal glands present in the walls of the small intestine secrete intestinal juice containing amylolytic, proteolytic and lipolytic enzymes.
  Liver is the largest gland of our body and it secretes bile juice for emulsification of fats.
  Pancreas secretes pancreatic juice containing trypsin, amylase and lipase enzyme.
- The process of digestion in all involves **ingestion**, i.e. intake of food by mouth, **digestion**, **absorption**, i.e. passage of digested food from alimentary canal to blood, **assimilation**, i.e. distribution of digested food to cells of the body and **egestion**, i.e. the elimination of undigested food (waste) from the body.

Exam Practice

Objective Type Questions

Multiple Choice Questions

1 What is the final product of photosynthesis?
(a) Protein (b) Fat
(c) Starch (d) Mineral salt

Sol. (c) The final product of photosynthesis in plants is glucose. The glucose produced is stored as starch in storage organs of the plants.

2 From which structure, the free oxygen gas produced during photosynthesis is released?
(a) Epidermis (b) Stomata
(c) Cortex (d) Guard cell

Sol. (b) The oxygen gas produced during photosynthesis is released into the surroundings through stomata.

3 In the following flow chart showing autotrophic nutrition in green plants, A and B respectively are **CBSE 2021 (Term-I)**

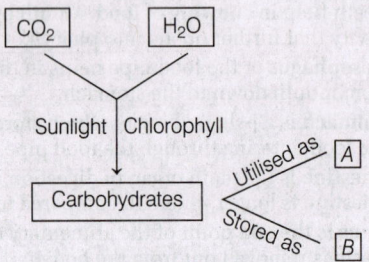

(a) oxygen and energy (b) starch and oxygen
(c) energy and starch (d) oxygen and water

Sol. (c) In autotrophic mode of nutrition in green plants, carbohydrates formed are utilised in the form of energy and stored as starch.

4 Opening and closing of stomatal pore depends on **CBSE SQP (Term-I)**
(a) atmospheric temperature
(b) oxygen concentration around stomata
(c) carbon dioxide concentration around stomata
(d) water content in the guard cells

Sol. (d) Opening and closing of guard cells depends on the water content in the cells.
When guard cells have enough water, the cells become turgid and open. These pores close when water moves out, thus closing the stomata.

5 What is the mode of nutrition in fungi?
(a) Autotrophic
(b) Heterotrophic
(c) Saprophytic
(d) Parasitic

Sol. (c) Fungal organisms feed on dead and decaying matter. They release chemicals to break complex organic matter into simple forms and absorb them. This is called saprophytic mode of nutrition.

6 In which of the following groups of organisms, food material is broken down outside the body and absorbed?
(a) Mushroom, green plants, *Amoeba*
(b) Yeast, mushroom, bread mould
(c) *Paramecium, Amoeba, Cuscuta*
(d) *Cuscuta*, lice, tapeworm
NCERT Exemplar, CBSE SQP (Term-I)

Sol. (b) Yeast, mushroom and bread mould are saprophytes. They breakdown and convert complex organic molecules present in dead and decaying matter into simpler substances outside their body. These simpler substances are then absorbed by them, i.e. saprotrophic nutrition.

7 In human alimentary canal, the specific enzyme/ juice secreted in locations (i), (ii) and (iii) are

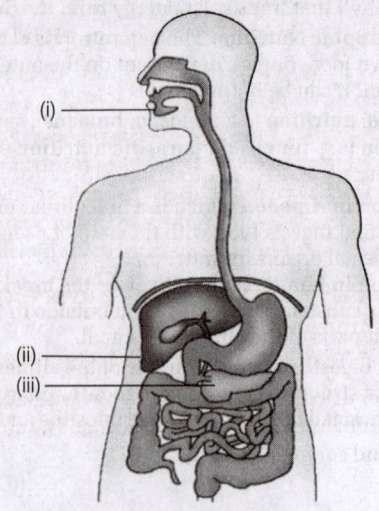

(a) (i) Amylase (ii) Pepsin (iii) Bile
(b) (i) Amylase (ii) Bile (iii) Trypsin
(c) (i) Lipase (ii) Amylase (iii) Pepsin
(d) (i) Trypsin (ii) Bile (iii) Amylase
CBSE 2021 (Term-I)

Sol. (b) Location (i) salivary glands, secrete salivary amylase which converts starch into sugars at a pH of about 7. Location (ii) liver secretes bile juice which acts on large fat molecules to form smaller glolules.
Location (iii)- Pancreas, secretes pancreatic juice containing enzymes like trypsin, amylase and lipase.

8 In which part of the alimentary canal food is finally digested?
(a) Stomach
(b) Mouth cavity
(c) Large intestine
(d) Small intestine **NCERT Exemplar**

Sol. (d) The small intestine in human beings is the site of complete digestion of food. The food gets semidigested in stomach to form a semisolid paste with the help of secretions from liver and pancreas. Undigested remains then pass into the large intestine.

9 Villi present on the internal wall of intestine help in the
(a) emulsification of fats
(b) breakdown of proteins
(c) absorption of digested food
(d) digestion of carbohydrates

Sol. (c) The small finger-like projections, i.e. villi present on the internal wall of intestine increase the surface area for better absorption of digested food.

10 The function not performed by villi is
CBSE 2021 (Term-I)
(a) to increase the surface area for absorption
(b) to ensure rich supply of blood vessels
(c) absorption of food
(d) egestion of food

Sol. (d) Walls of the small intestine have numerous villi which increase the surface area for absorption of food and also ensures rich supply of blood vessels. However, egestion of food in not vessel. However, egestion of food is not carried out by villi.

11 How many pairs of salivary glands are found in humans?
(a) Two (b) Three (c) Six (d) Four

Sol. (b) There are three pairs of salivary glands present in humans, namely the parotid glands, submandibulars and sublingual glands.

12 Observe the diagram of human digestive system.   **CBSE SQP (Term-I)**

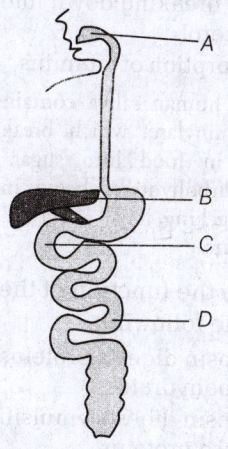

Match the labelling referred in Column I and correlate with the function in Column II.

Column I		Column II
A	1.	The length of this depends on food the organism eats.
B	2.	Initial phase of starch digestion
C	3.	Increases the efficiency of lipase enzyme action.
D	4.	This is the site of the complete digestion of carbohydrates, proteins and fats.

Codes
  A B C D   A B C D
(a) 1 2 3 4   (b) 2 3 4 1
(c) 2 4 3 1   (d) 4 1 2 3

Sol. (b) Parts labelled A, B, C and D with their respective functions are

A — Mouth-The digestion of starch begins with ptyalin secreted in mouth

B — Liver- Bile secreted from the liver helps in emulsification of fats. It also activates lipases, thus increasing efficiency of enzymatic action.

C— Duodenum - Breakdown of macromolecules occur here. It is the site of complete digestion of proteins, fats and carbohydrates.

D —Small intestine-is a long tube like organ having finger like projections called villi. Its length depends upon the type of food eaten by organism.

13 If salivary amylase is lacking in the saliva, which of the following events in the mouth cavity will be affected?

(a) Proteins breaking down into amino acids
(b) Starch breaking down into sugars
(c) Fats breaking down into fatty acids and glycerol
(d) Absorption of vitamins **NCERT Exemplar**

Sol. (b) The human saliva contains an enzyme called salivary amylase, which breaks down the starch present in food into sugar. The digestion of starch (carbohydrates) begins in the mouth. In case, saliva is lacking, it will affect the breakdown of starch into sugars.

14 Choose the function of the pancreatic juice from the following.
(a) Trypsin digests proteins and lipase carbohydrates
(b) Trypsin digests emulsified fats and lipase proteins
(c) Trypsin and lipase digest fats
(d) Trypsin digests proteins and lipase emulsified fats **NCERT Exemplar**

Sol. (d) Pancreas secretes pancreatic juice which contains digestive enzymes like amylase, lipase, trypsin. Amylase breaks down the starch, trypsin digests the proteins and lipase breaks down the emulsified fats.

15 Proteins $\xrightarrow{A}$ Peptones

Identify the enzyme A involved in the above reaction.
(a) Salivary amylase (b) Bile juice
(c) Pepsin (d) Lipase

Sol. (c) Proteins present in food are converted to peptones with the help of pepsin enzyme. It is secreted by gastric glands found in stomach wall.

Fill in the Blanks

16 Nutrients provides .... to the body.
Sol. energy

17 The opening and closing of stomata is regulated by ....
Sol. guard cells

18 The oral cavity opens into the ....
Sol. oesophagus

19 Pancreatic juice contains .... for the breakdown of fat.
Sol. lipase

20 Herbivores have longer small intestine to digest ....
Sol. cellulose

True and False

21 Carbon and energy requirements of the autotrophic organisms are fulfilled by photosynthesis.
Sol. True

22 Bile produced by liver is acidic in nature.
Sol. False; bile produced by liver is alkaline in nature.

23 Carnivores like tigers have a shorter small intestine because meat is easier to digest.
Sol. True

24 Stomach serves as a storehouse of food where complete digestion takes place.
Sol. False; stomach serves as a storehouse of food where partial digestion takes place.

25 Carbon dioxide is released during photosynthesis.
Sol. False; oxygen is released during photosynthesis.

Match the Columns

26 Match the following columns.

	Column I		Column BII
1.	Chlorophyll	(A)	Food reserve in plants
2.	Heterotrophic nutrition	(B)	Parasite
3.	*Cuscuta*	(C)	Photosynthesis
4.	Starch	(D)	Consumers

Sol. (1) → (C), (2) → (D), (3) → (B), (4) → (A)

27 Match the following columns.

	Column I		Column II
1.	Amoeba	(A)	Extensive coiling
2.	Trypsin	(B)	Pseudopodia
3.	Liver	(C)	Pancreatic juice
4.	Small intestine	(D)	Bile

Sol. (1) → (B), (2) → (C), (3) → (D), (4) → (A)

Assertion–Reason

Direction (Q. Nos. 28-32) *In each of the following questions, a statement of Assertion is given by the corresponding statement of Reason. Of the statements, mark the correct answer as*

(a) If both Assertion and Reason are true and Reason is the correct explanation of Assertion

(b) If both Assertion and Reason are true, but Reason is not the correct explanation of Assertion
(c) If Assertion is true, but Reason is false
(d) If Assertion is false, but Reason is true

28. **Assertion** Raw materials needed for photosynthesis are carbon dioxide, water and minerals.
Reason Nutrients provide energy to an organism.
Sol. (b) Raw materials needed for photosynthesis are carbon dioxide, water and minerals like nitrogen, phosphorus, iron and magnesium.
Nutrients are the substances required for proper growth and maintenance of a living body as they provide energy to an organism.
Hence, both Assertion and Reason are true, but Reason is not the correct explanation of Assertion.

29. **Assertion** Autotrophic nutrition occurs in green plants.
Reason Green plants self-manufacture their food.
Sol. (a) Autotrophic nutrition occurs in green plants. Food is self-manufactured by them using CO_2, light energy trapped by chlorophyll and water as raw materials.
Both Assertion and Reason are true and Reason is the correct explanation of Assertion.

30. **Assertion** *Amoeba* is an omnivore organism.
Reason Lion is a carnivore organism.
Sol. (b) *Amoeba* is an omnivore organism, its mode of nutrition is holozoic. Lion is a carnivore organism because it eats other animals (meat eaters).
Both Assertion and Reason are true, but Reason is not the correct explanation of Assertion.

31. **Assertion** Liver is known as the smallest gland of the body.
Reason It secretes bile juice.
Sol. (d) Liver is known as the largest gland of the body, which secretes bile juice.
Assertion is false, but Reasons is true.

32. **Assertion** Walls of the intestine has numerous villi.
Reason These villi increase the surface area of digestion.
Sol. (c) All the digested food is taken up by the walls of intestine, which has numerous villi. These increase the surface area of absorption.
Assertion is true, but Reason is false.

Case Based Questions

Direction (Q. Nos. 33-36) *Answer the questions on the basis of your understanding of the following passage and related studied concepts:*

Take a healthy potted plant with elongated leaves. Select a leaf and insert about one half of this leaf in a test tube containing KOH and make it air tight. Place the set-up in Sun for two hours.

Take out the leaf from the test tube and dip it in boiling water for a few minutes.

Put this leaf in a beaker with alcohol and boil it in a water bath. Wash the leaf with water and then dip the leaf in iodine solution for a few minutes. The portion of the leaf dipped in KOH solution will not show any change when dipped in iodine solution. **CBSE 2021 (Term-I)**

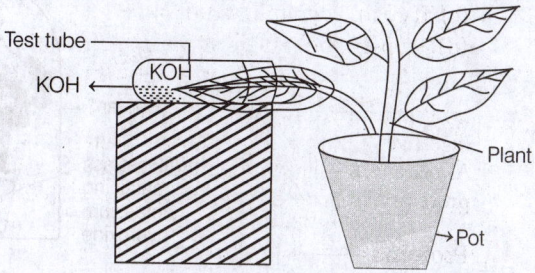

33. The function of KOH taken in the test tube is to absorb
(a) released water vapours
(b) released CO_2
(c) released O_2
(d) chlorophyll
Sol. (b) KOH (Potassium hydroxide) absorbs CO_2 released in the reaction.

34. On the basis of this activity, we may conclude that the essential factor for photosynthesis is
(a) carbon dioxide   (b) oxygen
(c) chlorophyll   (d) water vapour
Sol. (a) Photosynthesis is the process by which green plants synthesize their own food using CO_2, carbon dioxide, sunlight and water from the atmosphere. Thus, carbon dioxide is an essential factor for photosynthesis.

35. The event that does not occur in photosynthesis is
(a) absorption of light energy by chlorophyll
(b) reduction of carbon dioxide to carbohydrates
(c) oxidation of carbon to carbon dioxide
(d) conversion of light energy to chemical energy

Sol. (c) Photosynthesis involves conversion of light energy into chemical energy by chlorophyll. During this process, carbon dioxide is reduced to carbohydrates and no oxidation of carbon takes place.
Thus, option (c) is correct.

36. Iodine solution gives blue-black colour with
(a) starch (b) proteins (c) glucose (d) fats

Sol. (a) Iodine is an indicator of starch and can be used for testing the presence of starch in a sample. In the presence of starch, iodine gives blue-black colouration.

Direction (Q. Nos. 37-40) *Answer the questions on the basis of your understanding of the following passage and related studied concepts:*

The figure shown alongside represents an activity to prove the requirements for photosynthesis. During this activity, two healthy potted plants were kept in the dark for 72 hours. After 72 hours, KOH is kept in the watch glass in setup X and not in setup Y.

Both these setups are air tight and have been kept in light for 6 hours. Then, iodine test is performed with one leaf from each of the two plants X and Y.

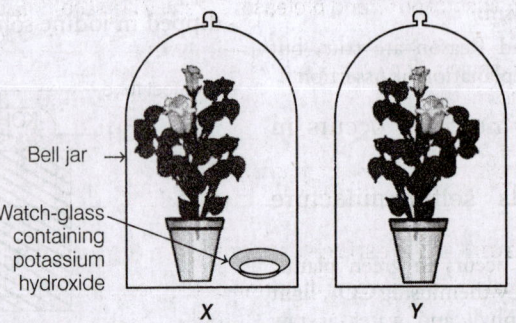

CBSE SQP (Term-I)

37. This experimental setup is used to prove essentiality of which of the following requirements of photosynthesis?
(a) Chlorophyll (b) Oxygen (c) Carbon dioxide (d) Sunlight

Sol. (c) This experimental set up is used to prove the essentiality of carbon dioxide for photosynthesis.

38. The function of KOH is to absorb
(a) oxygen (b) carbon dioxide (c) moisture (d) sunlight

Sol. (b) KOH absorbs carbon dioxide

39. Which of the following statements shows the correct results of Iodine Test performed on the leaf from plant X and Y respectively?
(a) Blue - black colour would be obtained on the leaf of plant X and no change in colour on leaf of plant Y
(b) Blue - black colour would be obtained on the leaf of plant Y and no change in colour on leaf of plant X
(c) Red colour would be obtained on the leaf of plant X and brown colour on the leaf of plant Y
(d) Red colour would be obtained on the leaf of plant Y and brown colour on the leaf of plant X

Sol. (b) Starch is produced during photosynthesis. In plant X, CO_2 which is essential for photosynthesis is not available as it gets absorbed by KOH. In plant Y, since, KOH is not present, the availability of CO_2 will help the plant photosynthesize and thus make starch. Iodine test would depect blue black colouration in Y plant only.

40. Which of the following steps can be followed for making the apparatus air tight?
   I. Placing the plants on glass plate.
   II. Using a suction pump.
   III. Applying vaseline to seal the bottom of jar.
   IV. Creating vacuum.

(a) I and II (b) II and III (c) I and III (d) II and IV

Sol. (*b*) In order to make an apparatus air tight, the plants are placed on a glass plate and vaseline can be applied to seal the jar bottom.

Direction (Q. Nos. 41-44) *Answer the questions on the basis of your understanding of the following table and related studied concepts:*

Parts of the human digestive system	Main function	Main type of enzyme acting	Source of the enzyme	Substance on which enzymes act	Product of digestion
Mouth, teeth, tongue and salivary glands	Food broken down into smaller pieces, some digestion of starch	Amylase	Salivary glands	Starch	Complex sugars
Oesophagus	Transports food to stomach	—	—	—	—
Stomach	Digestion of protein	Protease	Gastric glands	Proteins	Protein fragments and some amino acids
Small intestine	Final digestion, followed by absorption of nutrients	Amylase, lipase and protease	Pancreas and small intestine	Complex sugars, fats and protein fragments	Simple sugars, fatty acids, glycerol and amino acids
Large intestine	Salts, vitamins and water absorbed from wastes, undigested wastes collected	—	—	—	—
Anus	Elimination of wastes	—	—	—	—

41 Name the parts of the human digestive system where digestion of food does not take place.

Sol. In the human alimentary canal, the parts where digestion of food does not take place is the oesophagus, the large intestine and the anus.

42 Compare the function of the small intestine and the function of the large intestine.

Sol. In the small intestine, the complete digestion of food takes place followed by the absorption of nutrients. However, in the large intestine, salts, vitamins and water are absorbed from the undigested food and is stored till it is not removed through the anus.

43 Based on the information in the table, which substance breaks down starch?
 (a) Lipase (b) Amylase
 (c) Complex sugars (d) Trypsin

Sol. (*b*) Amlyase is a carbohydrate digestive enzyme, which is responsible for the breakdown of starch into smaller units.

44 Which of the following would be found in greater amounts than usual in the undigested waste as a consequence of removal of part of the small intestine where much of the absorption takes place?
 (a) Protein fragments (b) Complex sugars
 (c) Starch (d) Amino acids

Sol. (*d*) Most of the products of digestion are absorbed into the blood from the small intestine. For medical reasons, if their occurs removal of a part of the small intestine, then amino acids would be found in greater amounts than usual in the undigested waste as a consequence of such an operation.

Direction (Q. Nos. 45-48) *Answer the questions on the basis of your understanding of the following passage and related studied concepts:*

The digestion in stomach is taken care of by the gastric glands present in the wall of the stomach. These release HCl, pepsin and mucus. The hydrochloric acid creates an acidic medium which facilitates the action of the enzyme, pepsin. The mucus protects the inner lining of the stomach from the action of the acid under normal conditions.

45 What is the composition of gastric juice?

Sol. The gastric juice secreted by the gastric glands of the stomach includes HCl (hydrochloric acid), pepsin and mucus.

46 What is the function of the enzyme pepsin?

Sol. Pepsin is a protein digestive enzyme. It is responsible for the breakdown of proteins into peptones.

47 What would happen, if HCl is not secreted?

Sol. If HCl is not secreted by the gastric glands, then pepsin will not be activated. This will inhibit the process of digestion of proteins in the stomach.

48 Hydrochloric acid is very acidic (pH~2), but does not erode the inner lining of the stomach wall. Why?

Sol. Hydrochloric acid is very acidic (pH~2), but does not erode the inner lining of the stomach wall because the mucus protects the inner lining of the stomach from the action of acid under normal conditions.

Very Short Answer Type Questions

49 Energy is required by an organism even during sleep. Why?

Sol. While asleep, all biological activities are continuously occurring, which require energy.

50 Chemosynthetic mode of nutrition is different from photosynthetic mode in which way?

Sol. In chemosynthetic mode of nutrition, an organism utilises chemical energy to synthesise organic materials, whereas in photosynthetic mode, autotrophs require light energy.

51 Some organisms derive nutrition from plants or animals without killing them. What are these organisms called? Give one example.

Sol. Parasites derive nutrition from host body without killing them, e.g., plant like *Cuscuta* (amarbel) and animals like *Plasmodium, Ascaris,* leeches, etc.

52 In an experiment, saliva is added to the test tube containing pieces of bread (powdered). What will be the result?

Sol. Salivary amylase present in saliva will breakdown carbohydrate present in powdered bread into simple sugars.

53 Name the enzyme, which initiates the protein digestion in infants.

Sol. Rennin is the enzyme, which initiates the protein digestion in stomach in infants.

54 Why does acidity problem occur?

Sol. Problem of acidity occurs when cells of the inner lining of stomach produce large amounts of acid then is actually needed by our stomach. This causes burning sensation just above and below the stomach.

55 What is the primary requirement for pancreatic enzymes to act?

Sol. The primary requirement for pancreatic enzymes to act is the presence of alkaline medium in the small intestine. This is aided by bile which is alkaline in nature.

56 How is the wall of small intestine adapted for performing the function of absorption of food? **CBSE SQP 2020-21**

Or Out of a goat and a tiger, which one will have a longer small intestine? Justify your answer.

Sol. The primary function of the small intestine is the absorption of nutrients and minerals found in food with the help of numerous finger-like projection called villi present in the inner lining of small intestine, which increase the surface area of absorption.

Or

Herbivores like goat, need longer small intestine to facilitates the digestion of cellulose, meat is easier to digest hence carnivores like tiger have small intestine.

57 State the role of pancreas in digestion of food. **CBSE SQP 2020-21**

Sol. The pancreas produces digestive juice which contains enzymes like trypsin, chymotrypsin, pancreatic lipase and amylase for the breakdown of emulsified fats.

58 Name the movement of food all along the gut.

Sol. The lining of the alimentary canal has muscles which contract rhythmically to push the food forward. This movement is known as peristalsis.

59 A patient in hospital had his gall bladder removed and needs a special diet. Which nutrient free diet would be suitable for this patient?

Sol. The diet free from fat would be suitable for the patient whose gall bladder is removed. It is because bile stored in the gall bladder help in the digestion of fat.

60 What do you mean by emulsification of fat?

Sol. Large fat globules are broken down into small uniformly distributed fat particles by the action of bile salts present in bile juice. This is called emulsification of fat.

Short Answer (SA) Type Questions

1 Name the following. **NCERT Exemplar**
  (i) The process in plants that links light energy with chemical energy.
  (ii) Organisms that can prepare their own food.
  (iii) The cell organelle where photosynthesis occurs.
  (iv) Cells that surround a stomatal pore.
  (v) Organisms that cannot prepare their own food.
  (vi) An enzyme secreted from gastric glands in stomach that acts on proteins.

Sol. (i) **Photosynthesis** It is a process by which green plants having chlorophyll can synthesise simple sugar (glucose) from water and CO_2 using the energy of sunlight. The absorbed energy causes splitting of water molecules into hydrogen and oxygen. During this process, the light energy gets converted into chemical energy.
  (ii) **Autotrophs** These organisms can synthesise their own food from inorganic substances present in the environment, e.g. green plants, autotrophic bacteria, etc.
  (iii) **Chloroplast** The cells of the leaves contain special organelles called chloroplasts, which are the main sites of photosynthesis.
  (iv) **Guard cells** Each stomatal pore is surrounded by a pair of guard cells that control their opening and closing by the inflow and outflow of water.
  (v) **Heterotrophs** These organisms which cannot make their own food from inorganic substances and depend on other organisms for their food, e.g. all animals, yeast, most bacteria, etc.
  (vi) **Pepsin** It is a protein digesting enzyme secreted from the gastric glands present in the walls of stomach.

2 What are the adaptations of leaf for photosynthesis?

Sol. The adaptations of leaf for photosynthesis are as follows
  (i) Large surface area for maximum light absorption.
  (ii) Presence of chlorophyll containing chloroplasts.
  (iii) Presence of numerous stomata on the surface of leaf for gaseous exchange.

3 What is photosynthesis? Explain its mechanism. **CBSE Delhi 2019**

Sol. Photosynthesis is a process by which green plants, having chlorophyll, synthesise the simple sugar (glucose) from the simple raw materials, water and carbon dioxide using the energy of sunlight. Oxygen is released in this process.

The major events that occur during the process of photosynthesis are as follows
1. Light energy is first absorbed by chlorophyll molecules found inside the chloroplasts.
2. The absorbed energy causes spilitting of water molecules into hydrogen and oxygen. During this process, the light energy gets converted into chemical energy.
3. Finally, carbon dioxide is reduced to carbohydrate (the end product of photosynthesis).

4 State the events occurring during the process of photosynthesis. Is it essential that these steps take place one after the other immediately? **CBSE SQP 2020-21**

Sol. The photosynthesis takes place in the following three steps
  (i) Absorption of sunlight energy of chlorophyll.
  (ii) Conversion of light energy into chemical energy and splitting of water into hydrogen and oxygen by light energy.
  (iii) Reduction of carbon dioxide by hydrogen to form carbohydrate like glucose by utilising the chemical energy.

$$6CO_2 + 6H_2O \xrightarrow[\text{Chlorophyll}]{\text{Sunlight}} C_6H_{12}O_6 + 6O_2$$
Carbon dioxide · Water · Glucose · Oxygen

The steps not need to take place one after the other immediately For example, desert plants take up carbon dioxide at night and prepare intermediate which is acted upon by the energy absorbed by the chlorophyll during the day.

5 In each of the following situations what happens to the rate of photosynthesis?
   (i) Cloudy days **NCERT Exemplar**
   (ii) No rainfall in the area
   (iii) Good manuring in the area

Sol. (i) **Cloudy Days** The rate of photosynthesis will decrease because sunlight is necessary for photosynthesis. On a cloudy day, there will be less sunlight.
(ii) **No Rainfall in the Area** The rate of photosynthesis will decrease because water is one of the raw material needed by plants for photosynthesis. If there is no rainfall in an area, there will be less water available to plants.
(iii) **Good Manuring in the Area** The rate will increase because plants need raw minerals such as N, P, Fe, Mg, etc., for their growth and take these minerals from the soil. Good manuring in the area will increase the amount of these minerals in the soil, thus increasing the rate of photosynthesis.

6 Two green plants are kept separately in oxygen free containers, one in the dark and other in the continuous light. Which one will live longer? Give reasons.

Sol. The plant which is kept in the dark is unable to carry out photosynthesis and hence, the container would be filled with CO_2 within a very short span of time. Lack of oxygen in the container would kill the plant. On the other hand, the plant kept in light would be able to carry out photosynthesis and thus, converts CO_2 into oxygen. Hence, this plant would live for a longer duration.

7 Write a short note on different types of heterotrophic nutrition.

Sol. Heterotrophic nutrition is of the following types
(i) **Saprotrophic Nutrition** In this mode of nutrition, organisms obtain nutrients from dead and decaying organic matter, e.g. fungi, yeast and bacteria.
(ii) **Parasitic Nutrition** It refers to the mode of obtaining nutrition from the body of other organims. The organisms which obtain food is called parasite, while the organism from which food is absorbed is called host, e.g. *Cuscuta* (amarbel), *Plasmodium*, ticks, etc.

(iii) **Holozoic Nutrition** In this type of nutrition, organisms obtain complex organic matter in the form of solid food which is digested and then absorbed into the cells for its utilisation, e.g. *Amoeba*, frog and human beings.

8 Explain with the help of neat and well-labelled diagrams the different steps involved in the nutrition in *Amoeba*.
NCERT Exemplar
Sol. Refer to text 'Nutrition of *Amoeba*' on Pg. 139.

9 Why is small intestine in herbivores longer than in carnivores? **NCERT Exemplar**

Sol. Cellulose forms the largest part of the herbivore's food. Digestion of cellulose takes longer time, because the enzymes for its digestion are produced by the ruminant bacteria that live in the gut of the herbivores. Long length of the small intestine ensures that the food stays for a longer duration and proper digestion is possible. In the case of carnivores, cellulose is not present in the diet, thus the length of the small intestine is smaller.

10 (i) Write the function of the following in the human alimentary canal.
   (a) Saliva   (b) HCl in stomach
   (c) Bile juice   (d) Villi
(ii) Write one function each of the following enzymes. **CBSE (All India) 2019**
   (a) Pepsin   (b) Lipase

Sol. (i) (a) Saliva has salivary amylase that breaks down starch into maltose and also lubricates the mouth and food.
(b) HCl in stomach makes the medium inside the stomach acidic which is necessary for the activation of enzyme called pepsin.
(c) Bile juice contains bile salts which breakdown large fat globules into smaller globules to increase the efficiency of enzyme action.
(d) Villi increase the surface area for absorption of the food in the small intestine.

(ii) (a) Pepsin, a protein digestive enzyme breaks down proteins into peptones and polypeptides.
(b) Lipase, a fat digestive enzyme breaks down emulsified fats into fatty acids and glycerol.

11 (a) State the role played by the following in the process of digestion.
   (i) Enzyme trypsin
   (ii) Enzyme lipase
(b) List two functions of finger-like projections present in the small intestine. **CBSE 2020**

Sol. (a) (i) **Trypsin** It digests proteins in the stomach.

(ii) **Lipase** It digests lipids into glycerol and fatty acids.

(b) The finger-like projections present in the small intestine increase the surface area for digestion. It also helps the absorption of nutrients through wall of intestine.

12 State the function of the following in the alimentary canal **CBSE 2015**

(i) Liver (ii) Gall bladder (iii) Villi

Sol. (i) The cells of liver secrete bile juice which helps in emulsification of fats. It also makes the acidic food coming from the stomach alkaline thus, facilitating the action of pancreatic enzymes.

(ii) Gall bladder stores and concentrates the bile juice produced by the liver.

(iii) The villi increase the intestinal absorptive surface area. This ensures that there is more space for the food and its components to be absorbed.

13 Name the correct substrates for the following enzymes. **NCERT Exemplar**

(a) Trypsin (b) Amylase (c) Pepsin (d) Lipase

Sol. The correct substrates for the following enzymes are

	Enzymes	Substrates
A.	Trypsin	Proteins (peptides)
B.	Amylase	Starch
C.	Pepsin	Proteins
D.	Lipase	Emulsified fats

14 Bile juice does not have any digestive enzyme but still plays a significant role in the process of digestion. Justify the statement. **CBSE SQP 2020-21**

Sol. Bile juice makes the acidic food coming from the stomach alkaline before stomach content enter the duodenum. Although no enzymes are present in bite itself, the bile salts that it contains emulsify fats present in the intestinal lumen, increasing the surface available for interaction with the pancreatic lipases.

Hence, this is important for the proper digestion and absorption of all fats including the lipid-soluble vitamins.

Long Answer (LA) Type Questions

1 (i) Why is nutrition a necessity for an organism? State three reasons.

(ii) What is likely to happen if green plants disappear from Earth? **NCERT Exemplar**

Sol. (i) Nutrition is necessary because

(a) it helps in the growth of new cells and repair of older ones.

(b) it is needed to develop resistance against diseases.

(c) it provides energy for metabolic processes.

(ii) Disappearance of green plants from Earth would mean a total disaster for the ecosystem. Green plants are the source of energy for all organisms. All other organisms directly or indirectly depend on them for food. So, if they disappear from the Earth, all the herbivores will die due to starvation and so will the carnivores. It would result in the extinction of life from the Earth.

2 The graph shows how the amount of carbon dioxide taken in by a plant varies through a 24 hour period.

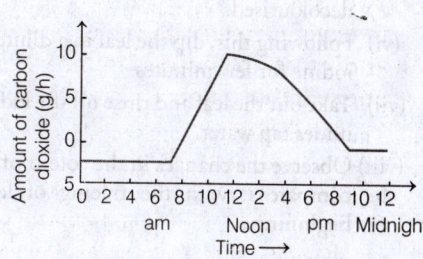

(i) At what time did photosynthesis start?

(ii) At what time was the rate of photosynthesis greatest?

(iii) At what time of the day did it get dark?

(iv) (a) How does plant obtain CO_2?

(b) What happens to this CO_2?

(v) What other factors could affect the rate of photosynthesis?

Sol. (i) Photosynthesis starts at 7.00 am.

(ii) The rate of photosynthesis was greatest at 12 (noon) as the amount of carbon dioxide taken in was greatest at that time.

(iii) At 9.00 pm, it was dark.
(iv) (a) Plants obtain CO_2 through stomata.
(b) CO_2 is reduced to carbohydrates.
(v) Factors which affect the rate of photosynthesis are light, humidity, temperature and concentration level of carbon dioxide in the air. There are optimum levels for each factor above which the rate of photosynthesis will start to decrease.

3 Design an activity to show that chlorophyll is essential for photosynthesis. **CBSE 2020**

Sol. **Plan of an Activity**
To show that chlorophyll is essential for photosynthesis.

Materials Required
A potted plant of variegated leaves such as money plant or crotons, white paper sheet, pencil, beaker, water, water bath, iodine solution and alcohol.

Procedure
(i) Keep the plant in a dark room for three days so that all the starch gets used up (destarching).
(ii) Now, keep this plant in sunlight for about six hours.
(iii) Pluck a variegated leaf from the plant. Mark the green areas in it and trace them on a sheet of paper.
(iv) Dip the leaf in boiling water for few minutes and then immerse it in a beaker containing alcohol.
(v) Boil the beaker in a water bath till the leaf gets decolourised.
(vi) Following this, dip the leaf in a dilute solution of iodine for few minutes.
(vii) Take out the leaf and rinse off the iodine solution under tap water.
(viii) Observe the changes in the colour of the leaf and compare it with the tracing of leaf done in beginning.

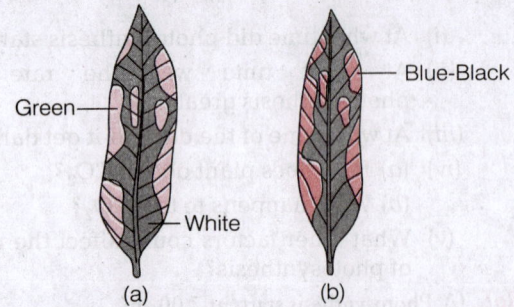

Variegated leaf : (a) before and (b) after starch test

Observation
(i) The leaf will show two types of patches, i.e. bluish-black and white. The bluish-black areas contain starch and the white areas are without starch.
(ii) Bluish-black areas are the ones, which were green previously while, non-green areas remain pale coloured.

Conclusion
This experiment proves that only chlorophyll containing areas, i.e. green parts of the leaf produces starch, which is a product of photosynthesis. Thus, chlorophyll is essential for photosynthesis.

4 Describe holozoic nutrition in *Amoeba* with well-labelled diagram.

Sol. Refer to text 'nutrition in *Amoeba*' on Pg. 139.

5 (i) What are herbivores, carnivores and omnivores? Give two examples of each.
(ii) Classify the following into herbivores, carnivores and omnivores:
Lion, man, dog, goat, crow, elephant, snake, hawk, rabbit, deer.
(iii) Name the five steps which occur in the process of nutrition in animals.

Ans. (i) Herbivores are those animals which only eat plants. Some of the examples are buffalo, monkey and camel.
Carnivores are those animals which eat only other animals as food. Some of the examples are frog, lizard and tiger.
Omnivores are those animals which eat both, plants and animals as food.
Some of the examples are bear, sparrow and ant.
(ii) Herbivores– Goat, elephant, rabbit and deer
Carnivores– Lion, snake and hawk
Omnivores– Man, dog and crow
(iii) Refer to text 'mechanism of digestion of food', on page 140 and 141.

6 Explain the process of digestion of food in mouth, stomach and small intestine in human body.

Sol. Digestion of food occurs in following steps
(i) **Mouth** (Buccal cavity) The mouth contains teeth, which crush the food into small particles. Salivary glands present in the mouth secrete saliva, which moistens the food. It also contains enzyme salivary amylase that acts as follows

$$\text{Starch (Complex sugar)} \xrightarrow{\text{Salivary amylase or ptyalin}} \text{Maltose (Simpler sugar)}$$

(ii) **Stomach** Gastric glands are present in the wall of the stomach which release following secretions
(a) **Hydrochloric acid** To make the medium acidic for the action of enzyme pepsin.
(b) **Mucus** To protect the inner lining of stomach from the action of acid.

(c) **Pepsin** A protein digesting enzyme which acts as follows

$$\text{Proteins} \xrightarrow{\text{Pepsin}} \text{Peptones and proteases}$$
$$\text{(Simple proteins)}$$

(iii) **Small intestine** It is the site of complete digestion of carbohydrates, proteins and fats. It receives secretions from liver and pancreas.

(a) **Bile juice** It is secreted by liver and temporarily stored in the gall bladder. It makes the medium alkaline for the pancreatic enzymes to act. It also breaks down large fat globules into smaller globules.

(b) **Pancreatic juice** It is secreted by pancreas. It contains enzymes like amylase for digesting starch, trypsin for digesting proteins and lipase for breaking down emulsified fats.

(c) **Intestinal juice** It is secreted by the walls of the small intestine. It contains a number of enzymes such as maltase, lipase, etc., for the complete digestion of food.

7 (i) Draw a diagram depicting human alimentary canal and label the components gall bladder, liver and pancreas in it.

(ii) State the role of liver and pancreas.

(iii) Name the organs which perform the following functions in humans.
- Absorption of digested food
- Absorption of water

Sol. (i) For fig. refer to Pg. 139.

(ii) Liver secretes bile juice for the digestion of fats present in food and **pancreas** secretes pancreatic enzymes to digest proteins, carbohydrates and fats.

(iii) Absorption of food occurs in the small intestine, while water gets absorbed in the large intestine.

8 Figure A shows the human alimentary canal.

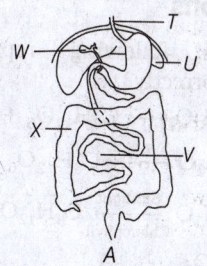

(i) In figure. A, label structures T, U and V.

(ii) Name the secretion, which passes down tube W and explain how it helps in fat digestion.

(iii) In case of diarrhoea, name the major process in region X, which is no longer occurring normally.

Sol. (i) T – Oesophagus, U – Liver,
V – Small intestine

(ii) The secretion which passes down tube W is bile. Role of bile in fat digestion

(a) It makes the acidic food alkaline to facilitate the action of enzyme lipase on it.

(b) Bile salts breakdown fats present in food into small globules for enzymes to act.

(iii) In case of diarrhoea the process of absorption of water will not occur normally in region X (large intestine).

CHAPTER EXERCISE

Multiple Type Questions

1. Which of the following represents the photosynthesis correctly?
   (a) $6CO_2 + 12H_2O \longrightarrow C_6H_{12}O_6 + 6H_2O + 6O_2$
   (b) $6CO_2 + 12H_2O \xrightarrow{\text{Sunlight}} C_6H_{12}O_6 + O_2 + 6H_2O$
   (c) $6CO_2 + 12H_2O \xrightarrow[\text{Chlorophyll}]{\text{Sunlight}} C_6H_{12}O_6 + 6H_2O + 6O_2$
   (d) $6CO_2 + 12H_2O \xrightarrow[\text{Chlorophyll}]{\text{Sunlight}} C_6H_{12}O_6 + 6CO_2 + 6H_2O$

2. Which cell bundle is involved in the process of formation of glucose?
   (a) Golgi body
   (b) Mitochondria
   (c) Endoplasmic reticulum
   (d) Plastids

3. Chloroplasts are the site of photosynthesis because
   (a) they contain carotenoids
   (b) they contain xanthophylls
   (c) they contain chlorophyll
   (d) they fix atmospheric carbon dioxide

4. The opening and closing of stomata are regulated by
   (a) turgidity of guard cells
   (b) availability of solar radiations
   (c) biological clock of plants
   (d) concentration of atmospheric CO_2

5. Bile juice is stored in which organ of human body?
   (a) Kidney
   (b) Gall bladder
   (c) Pancreas
   (d) Liver

Fill in the Blanks

6. Since autotrophic plants are able to produce food, they are also called ………… .

7. ………… is the muscular partition between the chest cavity and the abdominal cavity.

8. The digested food is taken up by the walls of the ………… .

True and False

9. The small intestine receives the secretions of liver and pancreas.

10. Gastric glands are present in the small intestine.

11. Carbon dioxide is not essential for photosynthesis.

12. Match the following columns.

Column I		Column II
A. Leech	1.	Peptic ulcer
B. Gastric glands	2.	Parasitic nutrition
C. Villi	3.	Inner lining of small intestine
D. Stomach	4.	Pepsin

Assertion–Reason

Direction (Q. Nos. 13-15) *In each of the following questions, a statement of Assertion is given by the corresponding statement of Reason. Of the statements, mark the correct answer as*
   (a) If both Assertion and Reason are true and Reason is the correct explanation of Assertion
   (b) If both Assertion and Reason are true, but Reason is not the correct explanation of Assertion
   (c) If Assertion is true, but Reason is false
   (d) If Assertion is false, but Reason is true

13. **Assertion** Leaves are the major photosynthetic organs of a plant.
    Reason They contain chloroplasts.

14. **Assertion** Nutrition in *Amoeba* takes place with the help of pseudopodia.
    Reason Different stages of nutrition in *Amoeba* are ingestion, digestion, absorption and egestion.

15. **Assertion** Tongue is a part of mouth that bears several taste buds.
    Reason It is helpful in producing speech.

Case Based Questions

Direction (Q. Nos. 16-19) *Answer the questions on the basis of your understanding of the following passage and related studied concepts:*

Masses of bacterial cells together with food particles stick to the teeth to form dental plaque. Saliva cannot reach the tooth surface to neutralise the acid as plaque covers the teeth. Brushing the teeth after eating removes the plaque before the bacteria produce acids.
If untreated, microorganisms may invade the pulp, causing inflammation and infection.

16. What do you understand by dental plaque?

17. Name the microorganism present at the region where dental plaque is present.

All in one Life Processes : Nutrition 157

18 What happens, if the teeth are not cleaned regularly?

19 The following table shows the pH value of the plaque surrounding the teeth of a girl over 4hrs.

Time/h	0	1	2	3	4
pH	7.0	7.0	7.1	7.2	4.1

State the time during the day when condition are most favourable for the process of tooth decay.

Answers

1. (c) 2. (d) 3. (c) 4. (a) 5. (b)
6. autotrophs 7. Diaphragm 8. intestine
9. True 10. False 11. False
12. (A) → (2), (B) → (4), (C) → (3), (D) → (1),
13. (a) 14. (b) 15. (b)

Very Short Answer Type Questions

20 Which raw material is responsible for the release of O_2 in photosynthesis?

21 What happens to extra glucose or carbohydrate in an animal body?

22 What is mainly digested by stomach of man?

Short Answer (SA) Type Questions

23 (i) Write the reaction that represents the chemical changes which take place during photosynthesis.
(ii) State the function of chlorophyll.

24 Which feature(s) help the plants to make food by the process of photosynthesis?

Long Answer (LA) Type Questions

25 (i) Give the steps involved in photosynthesis.
(ii) Write the difference between nutrition in plants and animals.

26 (i) Draw a labelled diagram of stomata. List two functions of stomata.
(ii) What are the raw materials required for photosynthesis to occur? Write the chemical equation of the process.

27 Explain the digestion of chapati in human beings. Draw a diagram depicting the human alimentary canal.

Challengers*

1. In photosynthesis, which substances are used up, which are produced and which are necessary, but remain unchanged after the reaction?

	Used up	Produced	Remain Unchanged
(a)	Carbon dioxide	Water	Oxygen
(b)	Chlorophyll	Carbon dioxide	Water
(c)	Oxygen	Starch	Cellulose
(d)	Water	Oxygen	Chlorophyll

2. The diagram shows the arrangement of cells inside the leaf of a green plant (No cell contents are shown). Which cells normally contain chloroplasts?

   (a) 1 and 2   (b) 1 and 4
   (c) 2 and 3   (d) 2 and 4

3. Choose the forms in which most plants absorb nitrogen.
   I. Proteins
   II. Nitrates and nitrites
   III. Urea
   IV. Atmospheric nitrogen
   Choose the correct option.

   (a) I and II   (b) II and III
   (c) III and IV   (d) I and IV

4. A plant is kept in the dark for two days. A leaf is used in an experiment to investigate the effect of two factors on photosynthesis as shown in the diagram.

   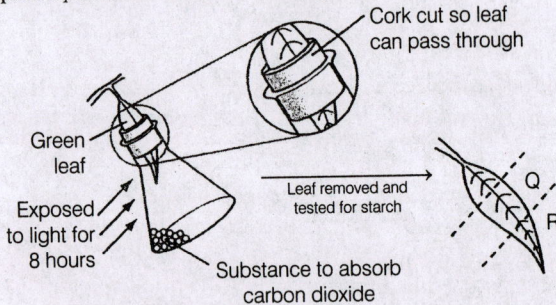

   What are the colours of Q and R, when the leaf is tested for starch, using iodine solution?

	Q	R
(a)	Blue/black	Brown
(b)	Brown	Brown
(c)	Blue/black	Blue/black
(d)	Brown	Blue/black

5. The diagram represents a section through the small intestine.

   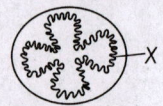

   What is the role of the structure labelled X?
   (a) They help to move the food along
   (b) They make a large surface area for absorption
   (c) They protect against bacteria
   (d) They move mucus over the surface

6. When a person eats some egg white, proteins and water enter the stomach. Which substances are found leaving the stomach and leaving the small intestine?

	Leaving the Stomach	Leaving the Small Intestine
(a)	Amino acids and water	Amino acids and water
(b)	Fatty acids, glycerol and water	Fatty acids, glycerol and water
(c)	Protein and water	Fatty acids and glycerol
(d)	Protein, amino acids and water	Water

7. In which order do these events occur in human nutrition?
   (a) Digestion → ingestion → absorption → assimilation
   (b) Digestion → ingestion → assimilation → absorption
   (c) Ingestion → digestion → absorption → assimilation
   (d) Ingestion → digestion → assimilation → absorption

8. The diagram shows the human gut. Which numbered structures secrete digestive enzymes?

   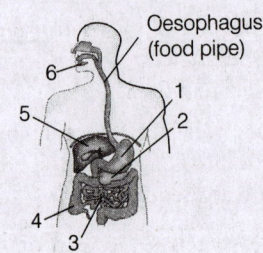

   (a) 1, 2, 3 and 4   (b) 1, 2, 3 and 6
   (c) 2, 3, 4 and 5   (d) 2, 3, 5 and 6

9. Only two of the following statements accurately describe what happens in the mouth.
   1. Amylase breaks down large starch molecules into smaller maltose molecules.
   2. Chewing increases the surface area of food for digestion.
   3. Saliva emulsifies fats into smaller droplets.
   4. Teeth breakup large insoluble molecules into smaller soluble molecules.

   Which statements are correct?
   (a) 1 and 2   (b) 2 and 3   (c) 3 and 4   (d) 1 and 4

Answer Key

1.	(d)	2.	(d)	3.	(b)	4.	(b)	5.	(b)
6.	(d)	7.	(c)	8.	(b)	9.	(a)		

*These questions may or may not be asked in the examination, have been given just for additional practice.

CHAPTER 05 b

Life Processes : Respiration

Respiration is the process by which food taken through the process of nutrition gets oxidised and release energy for performing various activities. During this process, oxygen acquired by organisms from outside the body is used to breakdown the food materials to provide energy.

Chapter Checklist
- Respiration
- Exchange of Gases in Plants
- Exchange of Gases in Animals
- Human Respiratory System

Respiration

It is defined as the process of biochemical oxidation of nutrients at cellular level. It occurs in the presence of specific enzymes at optimum temperature in the cells to release energy for various metabolic activities.

It is a catabolic process, in which exchange of gases (*viz* oxygen and carbon dioxide) takes place between the body and the outside environment. The process in a complete way can be written in the form of equation as

$$\text{Food} + \text{Oxygen} \longrightarrow \text{Carbon dioxide} + \text{Water} + \text{Energy}$$

The organic substances undergoing oxidative breakdown during respiration are called **respiratory substrates**, e.g. glucose.

The biochemical oxidation of nutrients takes place in different ways in different organisms. Some organisms use oxygen to breakdown glucose completely into carbon dioxide and water, while others do not require oxygen and carry it out in the absence of oxygen. Based on this, we have two types of respiration, i.e. aerobic respiration and anaerobic respiration.

1. Aerobic Respiration

It is the process, in which large amount of energy is released in the presence of oxygen (air) from the breakdown of food substances. Aerobic respiration can be summarised in the form of the equation is given below

$$\underset{\text{(6 carbon molecule)}}{\text{Glucose}} \xrightarrow{\text{Glycolysis}} \underset{\text{(2 molecules)}}{\text{Pyruvate} + \text{Energy}} \xrightarrow[\text{In mitochondria}]{\text{Oxygen}} \underset{\text{(6 molecules)}}{\text{Carbon dioxide}} + \underset{\text{(6 molecules)}}{\text{Water}} + \underset{\text{(Energy)}}{38 \text{ ATP}}$$

This process starts in the cytoplasm and continues in the mitochondria of the cell.

Water and carbon dioxide are produced as the waste products. The energy released during this process is used for all other life processes. The release of energy in aerobic process is much more than in anaerobic process.

2. Anaerobic Respiration

It is the process, in which small amount of energy is released in the absence of oxygen (air) from the breakdown of food substances. It takes place in yeast, bacteria and in human muscles.

> **Note** Muscle cells become temporarily anaerobic, when there is lack of enough oxygen supply during active excercise.

Anaerobic respiration is termed as fermentation in microorganisms. On the basis of the products formed, it is categorised as two types

(i) Alcoholic Fermentation

An incomplete breakdown of sugar into ethanol and carbon dioxide to release energy is called as **alcoholic fermentation**. This process occurs mainly in yeast, which is used to produce beer, wine, toddy, cheese etc. by brewing. It can be summarised as:

Glucose (6 molecules) $\xrightarrow{\text{In cytoplasm}}$ Pyruvate (2 molecules) + Energy $\xrightarrow[\text{In yeast}]{\text{Absence of oxygen}}$

Ethanol (2 molecules) + Carbon dioxide (2 molecules) + 2 ATP (Energy)

(ii) Lactic Acid Fermentation

It is the process of incomplete breakdown of sugar into lactic acid and energy in some bacteria, e.g. in yogurt some bacteria cause milk to turn sour. These bacteria feed on sugar and break it into lactic acid.

In human muscles, during vigorous physical exercise, glucose is metabolised to form lactic acid. The accumulation of **lactic acid** causes fatigue and muscle cramps after prolonged exercises. It can be summarised as

Glucose (6 molecules) $\longrightarrow$ Pyruvate (2 molecules) + Energy $\xrightarrow[\text{In muscle cells}]{\text{Lack of oxygen}}$

Lactic acid (2 molecules) + 2 ATP (Energy)

The overall process of breakdown of glucose in both aerobic and anaerobic respiration can be summarised as follows:

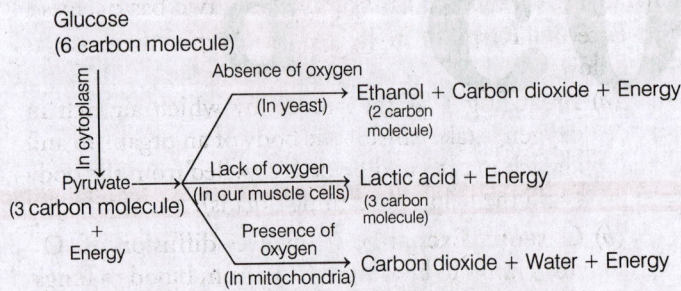

Breakdown of glucose by various pathways

Differences between Aerobic and Anaerobic Respiration

Aerobic Respiration	Anaerobic Respiration
Occurs in the presence of oxygen, releases large amount of energy.	Occurs in the absence of oxygen, releases relatively small amount of energy.
Each glucose molecule produces 38 molecules of ATP.	Each glucose molecule produces 2 molecules of ATP.
Begins in the cytoplasm and continues in the mitochondria, e.g. most of plants and animals.	Occurs only in the cytoplasm, e.g. anaerobic bacteria, yeast.

ATP

The word 'ATP' stands for Adenosine Triphosphate, also known as the **energy currency of the cell**. The energy released during the process of respiration is used to build-up an ATP molecule from ADP and inorganic phosphate (Pi). This can be summarised as the equation given below:

$$ADP + Pi \xrightarrow{\text{Energy}} ADP \sim Pi = ATP$$

The energy equivalent to 30.5 kJ/mol is released, when the terminal phosphate linkage in ATP is broken down using water. The energy thus, produced is eventually used as a fuel to drive the endothermic reactions taking place during the cellular activities such as contraction of muscles, conduction of nerve impulses, protein synthesis etc.

Check Point 01

1. What are respiratory substrates? Give one example.
2. Where does aerobic respiration occur? How many molecules of ATP are released during it?
3. The end products of a process are ethanol and carbon dioxide with the release of energy. Name this process and write the pathway involved in the reaction.
4. Fill in the blank:
   The accumulation of .... causes fatigue and muscle cramps after prolonged exercises.
5. State the function of ATP.

Stages of Respiration

Generally, respiration consists of following two basic stages:

(i) **External Respiration** It is of two types there are as follows

  (a) **Breathing** It is the process by which air rich in oxygen is taken inside the body of an organism and air rich in carbon dioxide is expelled from the body (with the help of breathing organs).

  (b) **Gaseous Exchange** It involves diffusion of O_2 from lungs to blood and CO_2 from blood to lungs. In plants, gaseous exchange takes place through stomata of leaf with the environment.

(ii) **Internal Respiration** It refers to the gaseous exchange between the arterial blood and the body cells.

Exchange of Gases In Plants

In plants, exchange of gases occurs through stomata and large intercellular spaces present throughout the plant body ensure that all cells are in contact with air. Roots, stems and leaves are involved in the gaseous exchange of plants.

1. In Leaves

In leaves, gaseous exchange takes place by diffusion of oxygen through stomata into the cells of the leaf. Stomata (Gk. *Stoma*–mouth) are the aerating pores present on the epidermis of the leaf. The direction of diffusion mainly depends upon environmental conditions and requirements of plants.

During daytime, when photosynthesis occurs, carbon dioxide is rapidly used up, while oxygen release is the major event. Thus, the net gas exchange in leaves during day time is: O_2 diffuses in; CO_2 diffuses out.

On the other hand during night, elimination of carbon dioxide takes place. Thus, the net gas exchange in leaves at night is O_2 diffuses in; CO_2 diffuses out.

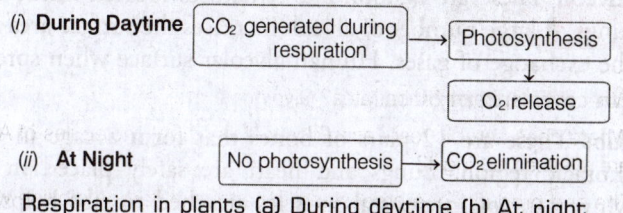

Respiration in plants (a) During daytime (b) At night

2. In Roots

Exchange of gases in the roots of a plant takes place by the process of **diffusion** from the air present in between soil particles.

Oxygen diffuses into the root hair and passes into the root cells, from where carbon dioxide moves out into the soil.

3. In Stems

In woody plants, gaseous exchange occurs through the small pores found on stems called **lenticels**. On the other hand, in herbaceous plants, stomata on the stem aids in exchange of respiratory gases.

In certain aspects, respiration in plants is different from that in animals. For example, all the parts of a plant (like root, stem and leaves) perform respiration individually. However an animal performs respiration as a single unit. In plants, respiration occurs at a much slower rate than in animals. Also, there is little transport of gases from one part of the plant to another, unlike in animals.

Check Point 02

1. What is the difference between external and internal respiration?
2. List the factors on which diffusion in plants depends.
3. What happens with CO_2 and O_2 in plants during daytime?
4. State True or False for the following statement:
   Gaseous exchange occurs through the small pores called lenticels on leaves.

Exchange of Gases in Animals

Animals have evolved different organs for the uptake of oxygen from the environment and for getting rid of the carbon dioxide produced in body during respiration. These organs work together and constitute the **respiratory system** of an organism.

For efficient gaseous exchange, respiratory surface should be

(i) thin-walled
(ii) moist to speed up diffusions
(iii) large surface area
(iv) rich in blood supply

1. In Aquatic Organisms

The rate of breathing in aquatic organisms is much faster than that seen in terrestrial organisms. This happens because aquatic organisms utilise oxygen dissolved in water for respiration where the amount of dissolved oxygen is fairly low than the amount of oxygen in the air.

The aquatic organisms breathe more rapidly to accumulate more and more oxygen. Fishes take in water through their mouth and force it to pass into the gills where the dissolved oxgyen is taken up by blood flowing in blood vessels.

2. In Terrestrial Organisms

Terrestrial organisms use atmospheric oxygen for respiration. This oxygen is absorbed by different organs in different animals. All these organs have a structure that increases their surface area and present in contact with the oxygen rich atmosphere.

Since, the exchange of oxygen and carbon dioxide has to take place across this surface, the surface is very fine and delicate.

To protect this surface, it is usually placed within the body well-protected, so there have to be numerous passages that will take air to this area. In addition, there is a mechanism for moving air in and out of this area where the oxygen is absorbed. The respiratory surfaces in different animals are given below in a tabular form

Respiratory Surface in Different Animals

Animals	Respiratory Surface
Amoeba and Planaria	Cell membrane
Earthworm and leech	Moist skin (cutaneous respiration)
Fish, prawn, mussel and tadpole (aquatic animals)	Gills
Frog	Moist skin and lungs
Grasshopper, mosquito and housefly	Spiracles and air tubes
Birds, lizards and terrestrial animals	Lungs

Check Point 03

1. Fill in the blank:
   In small animals, the exchange of gases occurs through the ....
2. Respiratory surface of animals must always be moist. Why?
3. Why does the rate of breathing in aquatic animals is faster than others?
4. What is the essential feature of respiratory organ of different terrestrial animals?
5. State True or False for the following statement:
   The surface across which breathing in animals occurs is very fine and delicate.

Human Respiratory System

Like other animals, respiratory system in human beings serves to provide fresh oxygen to all body cells and removes harmful carbon dioxide from the body.

The well-labelled diagram of the human respiratory system is as follows

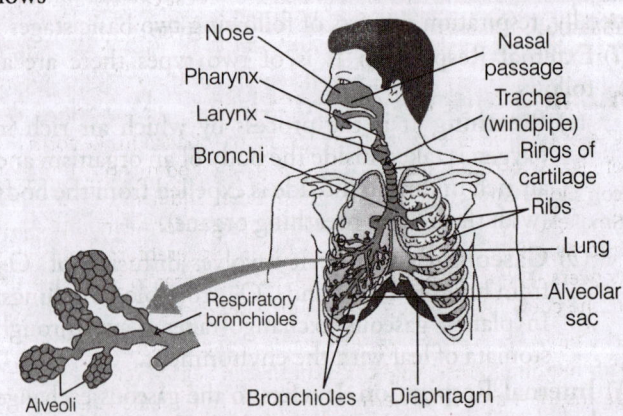

Human respiratory system

The parts of the human respiratory system and their respective functions are as follow

- **Nostrils** Air is taken into the body through the nostrils. It is lined by fine hair and mucus which helps to filter the air entering through it.
- **Nasal Passage** Air entering the nostrils leads to the nasal passage. It is mainly the conducting zone for air.
- **Pharynx** Nasal chamber opens into the pharynx. It passes air to the larynx.
- **Larynx** (or sound box) is located in the neck region and in front of trachea. It also produces sound.
- **Trachea** (windpipe) The air passes from the pharynx and goes into trachea. Incomplete rings of cartilage keep trachea open allowing the passage of air to the lungs. These ensure that the air passage does not collapse.
- **Bronchi** Trachea divides into two smaller tubes called bronchi after entering the thoracic cavity, which further extends into each lung.
- **Bronchioles** Bronchi are subdivided into smaller tubes called bronchioles. Each bronchiole finally terminates into many alveoli.
- **Alveoli** These are balloon-like structures located inside the lungs. A large number of alveoli increases the surface area for the exchange of gases. Human alveolar surface when spread can cover area of 80 m^2.
- **Ribs** These are 12 pairs of bones that form a cage in the thoracic region. Lungs and heart are safely placed in it. Movement of intercostal muscles attached to ribs helps in breathing.
- **Lungs** These are primary organs for respiration, which are located on the two sides of heart. These transport O_2 from the atmosphere into blood and release CO_2 from blood to atmosphere. They are enclosed by the protective membranes called **pleura**.

- **Diaphragm** It is a muscular partition between the thorax and the abdomen and forms the base of chest cavity. During inhalation, it flattens and increases chest cavity.

Smoking and Lung Cancer

Use of tobacco directly or any product of tobacco in the form of cigar, cigarettes, gutkha, etc., is harmful and most commonly affects the tongue, lungs, heart and liver. Smokeless tobacco is also a major risk factor for heart attacks, strokes, pulmonary diseases and several forms of cancers. There is a high incidence of oral cancer in India due to the chewing of tobacco in the form of gutkha.

The upper part of respiratory tract is provided with small hair like structures called cilia. These cilia help to remove germs, dust and other harmful particles from inhaled air. Smoking destroys these hair due to which germs, dust, smoke and other harmful chemicals enter lungs and cause infection, cough and even lung cancer.

Mechanism of Gaseous Exchange in Humans

Human beings take in oxygen from the atmosphere (inspiration) and release carbon dioxide in return (expiration). This complete process occurs in breathing. A breath means 'one inhalation plus one exhalation'. The mechanism for moving the oxygen and carbon dioxide out in human beings is termed as gaseous exchange.

It gets completed in three main steps as discussed below

1. Inhalation

The process of taking in oxygen from the atmosphere. It occurs are as follows

Air is taken in into the body through nostrils where it is filtered by hair and mucus.
↓
Air then passes down through the trachea.
↓
Chest cavity becomes larger due to flattened diaphragm and lifted ribs.
↓
Expansion of the chest cavity creates a partial vacuum in the chest cavity.
↓
Air is sucked in into the lungs and fills the expanded alveoli.

2. Exchange of Oxygen and Carbon Dioxide in Alveoli

The walls of alveoli contain an extensive network of blood vessels. The sequence of exchange of oxygen and carbon dioxide, which occurs between blood vessels and alveoli is listed below:

Oxygen is taken up by blood from alveoli to blood vessels.
↓
Blood releases carbon dioxide into alveoli that it brings from the whole body.
↓
Haemoglobin in blood takes up oxygen and carries it to tissues, which are deficient in oxygen.
↓
Oxygen is then transported to all cells in the body by respiratory pigment and due to diffusion pressure.

During the breathing cycle, when air is taken in and thrown out, the lungs always contain a residual volume of air.

Respiratory Pigment

Diffusion pressure alone cannot take care of oxygen delivery to all body parts in large sized animals because if diffusion were to move oxygen in our body, then it is estimated that it would take 3 years for a molecule of oxygen to get to our toes from our lungs. So, respiratory pigments take up oxygen from the air in the lungs and carry it to tissues.

Haemoglobin is the respiratory pigment in human beings. It has very high affinity for oxygen and is present in RBCs (responsible for the red colour of RBCs). CO_2 being more soluble in water than O_2 is mostly transported in the dissolved form in our blood. Haemoglobin shows more affinity to carbon monoxide than oxygen.

3. Exhalation

It is process of giving out carbon dioxide from lungs to the atmosphere. It occurs as follows:

Carbon dioxide is transported in dissolved form in blood.
↓
From blood, carbon dioxide passes to the alveoli.
↓
Chest cavity is compressed due to relaxation of ribs and diaphragm.
↓
Air is forced out of lungs to the atmosphere.

Check Point 04

1. In human beings, where does the gaseous exchange take place?
2. How does the air necessary for breathing enter the body of a human being?
3. Why do we need a respiratory pigment to perform respiration?
4. State True or False for the following statement:
   CO_2 being less soluble in water than O_2 is mostly transported in the precipitated form in the blood.
5. Name the substance which is oxidised in body during respiration.

NCERT FOLDER

Intext Questions

1 What advantage over an aquatic organism does a terrestrial organism have with regard to obtaining oxygen for respiration? **Pg 105**

Sol. A terrestrial organism can obtain oxygen directly from the air and has a slow breathing rate, whereas an aquatic organism has to obtain oxygen dissolved in water and so, it has a high breathing rate. The amount of oxygen dissolved in water is fairly low as compared to the amount of oxygen present in the air. So, aquatic organisms have high breathing rate. Therefore, terrestrial organisms have much easier access to oxygen and have an advantage over aquatic organisms.

2 What are the different ways in which glucose is oxidised to provide energy in various organisms? **Pg 105**

Sol. Utilisation of glucose for the production of energy depends upon the availability of oxygen. In the presence of oxygen (aerobic respiration), glucose is broken down aerobically in mitochondria, whereas in the absence of oxygen (anaerobic respiration), glucose is broken down anaerobically in cytoplasm to produce comparatively lesser amount of energy.

3 How is oxygen and carbon dioxide transported in human beings? **CBSE 2019; Pg 105**

Sol. When we inhale air, oxygen reaches the alveoli in lungs, which are surrounded by thin capillaries. These capillaries carry blood in them. The oxygen diffuses from the alveoli walls to the blood in capillaries. This blood travels through the body. Haemoglobin binds with oxygen and carries it along with blood.

Carbon dioxide is produced as a waste product in respiration in the cells of tissues. CO_2 is more soluble in water. Hence, it is more transported from body tissues in the dissolved in our blood plasma to lungs where it diffuses from blood to air in the lungs and then expelled out through nostrils.

4 How are the lungs (alveoli) designed in human beings to maximise the area for exchange of gases? **CBSE 2015; Pg 105**

Sol. In lungs, balloon-like structures called alveoli are present that provide maximum surface area for the exchange of gases. The alveoli have very thin walls and contain an extensive network of blood vessels to facilitate the exchange of gases.

Exercises
(On Page 113)

1 The breakdown of pyruvate to give carbon dioxide, water and energy takes place in
(a) cytoplasm
(b) mitochondria
(c) chloroplast
(d) nucleus

Sol. (b) The breakdown of pyruvate to give carbon dioxide, water and energy requires the presence of oxygen and takes place in mitochondria.

2 What are the differences between aerobic and anaerobic respiration? Name some organisms that use the anaerobic mode of respiration.

Sol. Refer to text "Differences between Aerobic respiration and Anaerobic respiration on Pg. 177 and 178.
Organisms using anaerobic mode of respiration are anaerobes. e.g. yeast, bacteria, etc.

3 How are the alveoli designed to maximise the exchange of gases?

Sol. The bronchi, within the lungs divide into smaller tubes called bronchioles and finally terminate in balloon-like structures called 'alveoli'. The alveoli are made up of thin moist membranes which are richly supplied with blood and provide a very large surface area for the gaseous exchange.

SUMMARY

- **Respiration** is the process by which food is oxidised to release energy at cellular level. As a catabolic process, it causes biochemical oxidation of nutrients such as glucose.
- **Aerobic respiration** is the complete breakdown of food in the presence of oxygen. It releases large amount of energy in the form of ATP molecules.
- **ATP** (Adenosine Triphosphate) is the energy currency of every cell.
- **Anaerobic respiration** is incomplete breakdown of food occurring in the absence of oxygen, releasing small amount of energy. It can be alcoholic fermentation, i.e. sugar breaks into ethanol and CO_2 or lactic acid fermentation, i.e. sugar breaks into lactic acid.
- **Exchange of gases in plants** The energy produced in plants by respiration is utilised in growth and life functions.
- **In leaves**, exchange of gases occurs through diffusion of oxygen through stomata into the cells of the leaf.
- **In roots**, exchange of gases occurs by diffusion from air present in soil particles to the roots.
- **In stems**, exchange of gases occurs through small pores present in the stems called lenticels.
- **Exchange of gases in animals** may occur through their skin or through specific respiratory organs.
  These organs have structures that increase the surface area and are in contact with oxygen rich atmosphere.
- **In aquatic organisms** The rate of breathing is higher as compared to terrestrial organisms as these organisms utilise oxygen dissolved in water which is present in lesser amount compared to others. Respiration occurs through gills and body surfaces.
- **In terrestrial organisms** These organisms use atmospheric oxygen for respiration.
- **Human Respiratory System** consists of a nose, larynx, trachea, lungs with bronchi and bronchioles and alveoli.
- **Nostrils and nasal passage** initiate the process of respiration by breathing in the air.
- **Larynx** is located in neck and helps in the sound production.
- **Trachea**, a non-collapsible air conducting tube, exhibits the presence of incomplete rings of cartilages; which also helps keep it open.
- **Bronchi and bronchioles** are the branches into which trachea further divides. Bronchioles are formed by repeated branching of bronchi.
- **Alveoli** are the functional units of kidney. These provide surface area for gaseous exchange in humans.
- **Lungs** are the primary organs for respiration, present in the thoracic cavity.
- **Ribs** are 12 pairs of bones, helps in respiration by movement of intercoastal muscles attached to them.
- **Diaphragm** is a muscular partition between thorax and abdomen. It forms the base of chest cavity and helps in breathing.
- **Gaseous Exchange in Humans** Oxygen is absorbed *via* inhalation. Exchange of oxygen and carbon dioxide occurs between blood and alveoli. Carbon dioxide is exhaled through lungs, i.e. exhalation and oxygen is assimilated in the body.
- **Haemoglobin** is the pigment present in Red Blood Cells (RBCs) which takes up the oxygen from the air in lungs and carries it to the tissues.

Exam Practice

Objective Type Questions

Multiple Choice Questions

1. The process of conversion of glucose into pyruvic acid occurs in
   (a) mitochondria
   (b) cytoplasm
   (c) outside the cell
   (d) chloroplast

   Sol. (b) During aerobic respiration, the glucose is converted into pyruvic acid in the cytoplasm of respiring cells.

2. Which cell organelle is involved in breakdown of glucose to produce energy for metabolic activities?
   (a) Mitochondria
   (b) Chloroplast
   (c) Endoplasmic reticulum
   (d) Golgi body

   Sol. (a) Mitochondria perform the cellular respiration, in which the glucose is broken down to liberate energy in the form of ATP for other metabolic activities.

3. During vigorous physical exercise, lactic acid is formed from glucose inside the muscle cells because
   (a) there is lack of oxygen
   (b) there is lack of water
   (c) there is excess of carbon dioxide
   (d) None of the above

   Sol. (a) During vigorous physical exercise, lactic acid is formed from glucose inside the muscle cells because there is lack of oxygen. Muscle cells respire anaerobically to produce lactic acid.

4. The correct sequence of anaerobic reaction in yeast is
   (a) Glucose $\xrightarrow{\text{Cytoplasm}}$ Pyruvate $\xrightarrow{\text{Mitochondria}}$ Ethanol + Carbon dioxide
   (b) Glucose $\xrightarrow{\text{Cytoplasm}}$ Pyruvate $\xrightarrow{\text{Cytoplasm}}$ Lactic acid
   (c) Glucose $\xrightarrow{\text{Cytoplasm}}$ Pyruvate $\xrightarrow{\text{Mitochondria}}$ Lactic acid
   (d) Glucose $\xrightarrow{\text{Cytoplasm}}$ Pyruvate $\xrightarrow{\text{Cytoplasm}}$ Ethanol + Carbon dioxide
   NCERT Exemplar

   Sol. (d) Glucose is converted into pyruvate (glycolysis) in the cytoplasm of the cell. It is the first stage of respiration. After glycolysis, pyurvate breaks down to release ethanol, CO_2 and small amount of ATP.

5. During anaerobic alcoholic fermentation by yeast, alcohol is formed
   (a) in the yeast cell vacuole
   (b) in the yeast cell mitochondrion
   (c) outside the yeast cell
   (d) within the yeast cell

   Sol. (d) During anaerobic alcoholic fermentation by yeast, alcohol is formed within the yeast cell. It is an incomplete breakdown of sugar into ethanol and carbon dioxide to release energy.

6. The sequence of anaerobic respiration in our muscle cells during heavy exercise is :
   (a) Glucose $\xrightarrow{\text{Cytoplasm}}$ Pyruvate $\xrightarrow{\text{Muscle cells}}$ Lactic acid + Energy
   (b) Glucose $\xrightarrow{\text{Mitochondria}}$ Pyruvate $\xrightarrow{\text{Muscle cells}}$ Carbon dioxide + Water
   (c) Glucose $\xrightarrow{\text{Cytoplasm}}$ Pyruvat $\xrightarrow{\text{Muscle cells}}$ Ethanol + Carbon dioxide
   (d) Glucose $\xrightarrow{\text{Mitochondria}}$ Pyruvate $\xrightarrow{\text{Muscle cells}}$ Ethanol + Lactic acid
   CBSE 2021 (Term-I)

   Sol. (d) Conversion of glucose into Pyruvate takes place in mitochondria. This pyruvate convert to ethanol and lactic acid in human muscle cells. This causes muscle cramps after prolonged exercise.

7. The energy released during cellular respiration is used to synthesise
   CBSE 2021 (Term-I)
   (a) ribosomes   (b) RBC
   (c) ATP   (d) mitochondria

   Sol. (c) During cellular respiration, the energy released is immediately used to synthesize ATP. This ATP further fuels all other activities in the cell.

8. When air is blown from mouth into a test-tube containing lime water, the lime water turned milky due to the presence of
   NCERT Exemplar

Life Processes : Respiration

(a) oxygen (b) carbon dioxide
(c) nitrogen (d) water vapour

Sol. (b) When air is blown from mouth into test tube, the lime water turned milky because the air we breathe out has more CO_2.

9 Which of the following structures is involved in gaseous exchange in woody stem of a plant?
(a) Stomata (b) Lenticel
(c) Guard cell (d) Epidermis

Sol. (b) In the stems of woody plants, the exchange of respiratory gases takes place through lenticels. These are small openings in the pits of the bark.

10 What is the function of guard cells?
(a) To regulate the flow of respiratory gases
(b) To regulate the opening and closing of stomata
(c) To regulate the exchange of photosynthetic gases
(d) All of the above

Sol. (d) The guard cells regulate the opening and closing of stomata to maintain the flow of respiratory as well as photosynthetic gases (CO_2 and O_2) in the plants.

11 Carefully study the diagram of the human respiratory system with labels (i), (ii), (iii) and (iv). Select the option which gives correct identification and main function and /or characteristic.

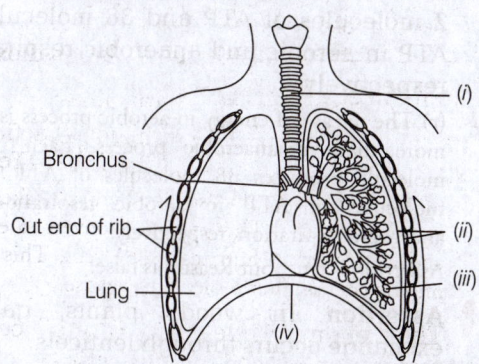

(a) (i) Trachea: It is supported by bony rings for conducting inspired air
(b) (ii) Ribs: When we breathe out, ribs are lifted
(c) (iii) Alveoli: Thin walled sac-like structures for exchange of gases
(d) (iv) Diaphragm: It is pulled up when we breathe in
CBSE SQP (Term-I)

Sol. (c) Alveoli are balloon like structures located inside the lungs. These are meant for gaseous exchange.

12 Which is the correct sequence of air passage during inhalation?
(a) Nostrils → Larynx → Pharynx → Trachea → Lungs
(b) Nasal passage → Trachea → Pharynx → Larynx → Alveoli
(c) Larynx → Nostrils → Pharynx → Lungs
(d) Nostrils → Pharynx → Larynx → Trachea → Alveoli
NCERT Exemplar

Sol. (d) The air for respiration is drawn into our body through the nostrils, into nasal passage. From there, air enters into pharynx, larynx, then into the windpipe (or trachea), bronchi, lungs and finally to the alveoli where gaseous exchange takes place.

13 The function of the lining of mucus in the nasal passage of human beings is to
(a) increase the temperature of inhaled air
(b) move the air in and out
(c) filter the air that we breathe in
(d) absorb oxygen from the air
CBSE 2021 (Term-I)

Sol. (c) Mucus lining in the nasal passage filter the air that we breathe in.

14 Which of the following statements are true about respiration?
(i) During inhalation, ribs move inward and diaphragm is raised.
(ii) In the alveoli, exchange of gases takes place, i.e., oxygen from alveolar air diffuses into blood and carbon dioxide from blood into alveolar air.
(iii) Haemoglobin has greater affinity for carbon dioxide than oxygen.
(iv) Alveoli increases surface area for exchange of gases. **NCERT Exemplar**
(a) (i) and (iv) (b) (ii) and (iii)
(c) (i) and (iii) (d) (ii) and (iv)

Sol. (d) Statements (ii) and (iv) are correct. Incorrect statements (i) and (iii) can be corrected as follows
(i) During inhalation, ribs lift up and diaphragm flattens to increase the size of chest cavity.
(iii) Haemoglobin present in RBCs has a very high affinity for oxygen.

Fill in the Blanks

15. ATP is the .... for most cellular processes.
Sol. energy currency

16. In plants, respiration occurs at a much .... rate than in animals.
Sol. slower

17. Terrestrial animals use .... of the atmosphere for respiration.

Sol. oxygen

18. From the larynx air goes to ....

Sol. trachea

19. Reptiles, birds and .... have lungs for the exchange of gases.

Sol. mammals

True or False

20. Glycolysis takes place in the cytoplasm of the cell.

Sol. True

21. Anaerobic reactions after glycolysis produce lactic acid or ethanol.

Sol. True

22. As compared to aerobic respiration, anaerobic respiration produces more energy.

Sol. False; As compared to aerobic respiration, anaerobic respiration produces less energy.

23. ATP is formed in the cytoplasm.

Sol. False; ATP is formed inside the mitochondria.

24. The build up of ethanol in our muscles causes cramps.

Sol. False; The build up of lactic acid in our muscles causes cramps.

Match the Columns

25. Match the following columns.

	Column I		Column II
1.	Glycolysis	A.	3–Carbon compound
2.	Human muscles	B.	ATP Synthesis
3.	Mitochondria	C.	Lactic acid
4.	Yeast	D.	Fermentation
5.	Pyruvate	E.	Cytoplasm

Sol. 1. → (E), 2. → (C), 3. → (B), 4. → (D), 5. → (A)

26. Match the following columns.

	Column I		Column II
1.	Fish	A.	Epiglottis
2.	Larynx	B.	Cartilage rings
3.	Trachea	C.	Balloon like structures
4.	Mammals	D.	Lungs
5.	Alveoli	E.	Gills

Sol. 1. → (E), 2. → (A), 3. → (B), 4. → (D), 5. → (C)

Assertion–Reason

Direction (Q. Nos. 27-32) In each of the following questions, a statement of Assertion is given by the corresponding statement of Reason. Of the statements, mark the correct answer as

(a) If both Assertion and Reason are true and Reason is the correct explanation of Assertion

(b) If both Assertion and Reason are true, but Reason is not the correct explanation of Assertion

(c) If Assertion is true, but Reason is false

(d) If Assertion is false, but Reason is true

27 Assertion Respiration is a biochemical process opposite to photosynthesis.

Reason Energy is released during respiration.

Sol. (a) Respiration is defined as the process of biochemical oxidation of nutrients at cellular level. It occurs in the presence of specific enzymes at optimum conditions in the cells to release energy for various metabolic activities. However, it is opposite to photosynthesis where energy is stored in the bonds of carbohydrates.

Both Reason and Assertion are true and Reason is the correct explanation of Assertion.

28 Assertion The release of energy in aerobic process is much more than in anaerobic process.

Reason Each glucose molecule produces 2 molecules of ATP and 38 molecules of ATP in aerobic and anaerobic respiration, respectively.

Sol. (c) The release of energy in aerobic process is much more than in anaerobic process. Each glucose molecule produces 38 molecules of ATP and 2 molecules of ATP in aerobic respiration and anaerobic respiration, respectively.

Assertion is true, but Reason is false.

29 Assertion In woody plants, gaseous exchange occurs through lenticels.

Reason Lenticels are specialised cells found along with stomata on the stem of woody plants.

Sol. (c) In woody plants, gaseous exchange occurs through the small pores found on stems called lenticels. Stomata on the stem aid in gaseous exchange, in herbaceous plants.

Assertion is true, but Reason is false.

30 Assertion The rate of breathing in aquatic organisms is much slower than that seen in terrestrial organisms.

Reason The amount of oxygen dissolved in water is very low as compared to the amount of oxygen in air.

CBSE 2021 (Term-I)

Sol. (d) Assertion is false but Reason is true and Assertion can be corrected as

The rate of breathing in aquatic organisms is much faster than that seen in terrestrial animals due to the lesser amount of dissolved oxygen in water.

31. Assertion Lungs always contain a residual volume of air.

Reason It provides sufficient time for oxygen to be absorbed and for carbon dioxide to be released.

Sol. (a) During the breathing cycle, when air is taken in and thrown out, the lungs always contain a residual volume of air. It provides sufficient time for oxygen to be absorbed and for carbon dioxide to be released.

Both Reason and Assertion are true and Reason is the correct explanation of Assertion.

32. Assertion Haemoglobin is the respiratory pigment in human beings.

Reason It transports oxygen in the human body.

Sol. (a) Haemoglobin is the respiratory pigment in human beings. It takes up oxygen from the air in the lungs and carries it to tissues.

Both Assertion and Reason are true and Reason is the correct explanation of Assertion.

Case Based Questions

Direction (Q. Nos. 33-36) *Answer the questions on the basis of your understanding of the following table and related studied concepts:*

Physiological Adjustment to Altitude

Effect	Minutes	Days	Weeks
Increased heart rate			
Increased breathing	←——→		
Concentration of blood	←——→	←——→	
Increased red blood cell production			
increased capillary density		←——→	←——→

33. Refer to the table showing physiological adjustment to altitude. Identify one short term physiological adaptation that humans make to high altitude.

Sol. One short term physiological adaptation that humans make to high altitude is increased heart rate.

34. What is the aim of the physiological adjustments to altitude?

Sol. The physiological adjustments to altitude are all aimed at improving the rate of supply of oxygen to the body tissues.

35. Sudden exposure to an altitude of 2000 m would make a person breathless on exertion.

The effect of altitude on physiology is related to…… .
(a) lower oxygen availability.
(b) higher oxygen availability.
(c) lower carbon dioxide availability.
(d) Both (b) and (c)

Sol. (a) Sudden exposure to an altitude of 2000 m would make a person breathless on exertion. The effect of altitude on physiology is related to lower oxygen availability.

36. When we climb a mountain, the breathing rate becomes.
(a) Faster
(b) Slower
(c) does not change
(d) zero

Sol. (a) When we climb up a mountain, the breathing rate becomes faster. It occurs because increased physical activity or exercise needs more energy.

Direction (Q. Nos. 37-40) *Answer the questions on the basis of your understanding of the following passage and related studied concepts:*

Regardless of the gas exchange system present, the amount of oxygen that can be carried in solution in the blood is small. The efficiency of gas exchange in animals is enhanced by the presence of **respiratory pigments**. All respiratory pigments consist of proteins complexed with iron or copper. They combine reversibly with oxygen and greatly increase the capacity of blood to transport oxygen and deliver it to the tissues.

For example, the amount of oxygen dissolved in the plasma in mammals is only about $2 \text{ cm}^3 O_2$ per liter. However the amount carried bound to haemoglobin is 100 times this. Haemoglobin is the most widely distributed respiratory pigment and is characteristic of all vertebrates and many invertebrate taxa.

37. Why does the small and single-celled animals such as *Amoeba*, not require any respiratory pigment?

Sol. The small and single celled animals such as *Amoeba* do not require any respiratory pigment because the volume of their body is so small that oxygen can be introduced quickly into the whole body by the process of diffusion.

38. What are the consequences of binding of haemoglobin with carbon monoxide?

Sol. Carbon monoxide binds very strongly with haemoglobin in the blood and prevents it from carrying oxygen to the brain and other parts of the body.

39. Why do the respiratory pigments combine reversibly with oxygen?

Sol. Respiratory pigments are coloured proteins capable of combining reversibly with oxygen, hence increasing the amount of oxygen that can be carried by the blood.

40. Where do you find the respiratory pigment (haemoglobin) in human bodies?

Sol. Haemoglobin is present in the red blood corpuscles in the human blood.

Direction (Q. Nos. 41-45) *Answer the questions on the basis of your understanding of the following table and related studied concepts:*

All living cells require energy for various activities. This energy is available by the breakdown of simple carbohydrates either using oxygen or without using oxygen.

41. Energy in the case of higher plants and animals is obtained by
(a) Breathing
(b) Tissue respiration
(c) Organ respiration
(d) Digestion of food

Sol. (b) **Tissue Respiration** Internal respiration (tissue respiration) is the exchange of oxygen and carbon dioxide between blood and cells in different tissues of on animal body.

42. The graph below represents the blood lactic acid concentration of an athlete during a race of 400 m and shows a peak at point D.

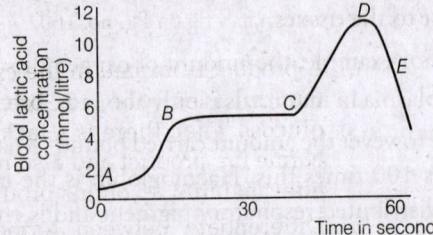

Lactic acid production has occurred in the athlete, while running in the 400 m race. Which of the following processes explains this event?
(a) Aerobic respiration
(b) Anaerobic respiration
(c) Fermentation
(d) Breathing

Sol. (b) **Anaerobic Respiration** happens in muscles during hard exercise and there is a build up of lactic acid instead of glucose, unlike aerobic respiration.

43. Study the graph below that represents the amount of energy supplied with respect to the time while an athlete is running at full speed.

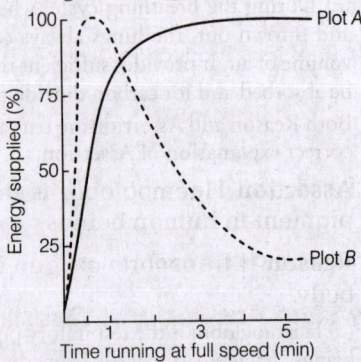

Choose the correct combination of plots and justification provided in the following table.

	Plot A	Plot B	Justification
(a)	Aerobic	Anaerobic	Amount of energy is low and inconsistent in aerobic and high in anaerobic
(b)	Aerobic	Anaerobic	Amount of energy is high and consistent in aerobic and low in anaerobic
(c)	Anaerobic	Aerobic	Amount of energy is high and consistent in aerobic and low in anaerobic
(d)	Anaerobic	Aerobic	Amount of energy is high and inconsistent in anaerobic and low in aerobic

Sol. (b)

Plot A	Plot B	Justification
Aerobic	Anaerobic	Amount of energy high and consistent in aerobic and low in anaerobic

All in one Life Processes : Respiration

44. The characteristic processes observed in anaerobic respiration are
   I. presence of oxygen
   II. release of carbon dioxide
   III. release of energy
   IV. release of lactic acid
   (a) I and II   (b) I, II and III
   (c) I, III and IV   (d) Only IV

Sol. (c) The characteristic processes observed in anaerobic respiration are release of carbon dioxide release of energy release of lactic acid

45. Study the table given below and select the row that has the incorrect information.

		Aerobic	Anaerobic
(a)	Location	Cytoplasm	Mitochondria
(b)	End Product	CO_2 and H_2O	Ethanol and CO_2
(c)	Amount of ATP	High	Low
(d)	Oxygen	Needed	Not needed

Sol. (a) Location Aerobic Anaerobic
                     Cytoplasm Mitochondria
has the incorrect information.

Very Short Answer Type Questions

46 Name the cell organelle in which breakdown of pyruvate to give CO_2, water and energy takes place. **CBSE 2015**

Sol. Breakdown of pyruvate to give CO_2, water and energy takes place in mitochondria.

47 Name the intermediate and end products of breakdown of glucose in aerobic respiration.

Sol. **Intermediate products** of breakdown of glucose in aerobic respiration are pyruvic acid and energy.
End products of breakdown of glucose in aerobic respiration are CO_2, H_2O and energy.

48 One point which is common for both aerobic and anaerobic respiration.

Sol. The respiratory substrate is the same for both aerobic and anaerobic respiration, which is glucose.

49 Why does the air passage not collapse when there is no air in it? **CBSE 2016**

Sol. The air passage, i.e. trachea is supported by incomplete C-shaped cartilaginous rings, which prevent its collapsing in the absence of air.

50 While breathing out, point out the changes you think occur in diaphragm and intercostal muscles.

Sol. The diaphragm and intercostal muscles relax when we breathe out. This compresses the chest cavity forcing the air out of lungs.

51 Give the path travelled by a molecule of oxygen when it enters the body.

Sol. The following pathway is travelled by a molecule of oxygen when it enters the body:
Nostrils → Trachea → Bronchus → Bronchiole → Alveolus → Blood → Tissues.

52 Why carbon dioxide is mostly transported in dissolved form?

Sol. Carbon dioxide is mostly transported in dissolved form because it is more soluble in water than oxygen.

Short Answer (SA) Type Questions

1 Write two different ways in which glucose is oxidised to provide energy in human body. Write the products formed in each case. **CBSE Delhi 2019**

Sol. Glucose utilisation in our body depends upon oxygen availability, i.e.
(i) In the presence of oxygen (aerobic respiration)
Glucose $\xrightarrow{\text{(Presence of oxygen)}}_{\text{(In mitochondria)}}$ Pyruvate + energy
$6CO_2 + 6H_2O + 38\,ATP$

(ii) In the lack of oxygen (lactic acid fermentation)
Glucose ⟶ Pyruvate + Energy $\xrightarrow{\text{(Lack of oxygen)}}_{\text{(In muscle cells)}}$ Lactic acid + 2ATP (2 molecules)

2 Draw a flowchart to show the breakdown of glucose by various pathways. **CBSE 2016**

Sol. Refer to text and fig on Pg. no. 160.

3 (i) A product is formed in the cytoplasm of our muscles due to breakdown of glucose when there is a lack of oxygen. Name the product and also mention the effect of build up of this product.

(ii) Differentiate between fermentation in yeast and aerobic respiration on the basis of end products formed.

Sol. (i) Lactic acid is formed in the cytoplasm of our muscle cells when there is a lack of oxygen. Formation and accumulation of lactic acid in muscles causes cramps and muscle fatigue.

(ii) During fermentation in yeast, ethanol is formed, while in aerobic respiration, carbon dioxide and water are formed. The energy (ATP) released in the process of fermentation is very less as compared to energy released in the aerobic respiration.

4 What is the logic behind the heavy breathing as we climb up a mountain?

Sol. When we climb up a mountain, the breathing rate becomes faster. As we continue to climb, we start breathing deeper and heavier, i.e. start gasping. This occurs because increased physical activity or exercise needs more energy.

Thus, to fulfil this need, the rate of respiration increases. However at higher altitudes, lesser oxygen is available. To ensure the oxygen availability, we start breathing faster. Some parts of the body also start respiring anaerobically to compensate the increasing oxygen demand. As a result, lactic acid accumulation also starts in the muscles due to which we experience muscle fatigue.

5 State the role of the following in human respiratory system.

(i) Nasal hair
(ii) Diaphragm
(iii) Alveoli
(iv) Nasal cavity

Sol. (i) **Nasal hairs** These are fine hairs present in the inner lining of the nasal passage. These hairs help in filtering the air passing through nostrils, so that germ free air could reach the lungs.

(ii) **Diaphragm** It is a muscular partition between the thoracic and abdominal region in our body. Movement of diaphragm helps in the breathing process.

(iii) **Alveoli** These are balloon-like structures, which increase the surface area for the gaseous exchange in lungs.

(iv) **Nasal cavity** Nasal passage warm and moisturises the air entering through it, while nostrils filter the air before it reaches lungs.

6 (a) In the process of respiration, state the function of alveoli.

(b) Rate of breathing in aquatic organisms is much faster than that in terrestrial organisms. Give reasons.

(c) Complete the following pathway showing the breakdown of glucose:

Glucose (6-carbon molecules) $\xrightarrow{\text{in cytoplasm}}$ (i) $\dfrac{?}{(3\text{-carbon molecules} + \text{energy})}$

$\xrightarrow{\text{Presence of } O_2 \text{ in mitochondria}}$ (ii) $\dfrac{?}{} + H_2O + \text{energy}$

Sol. (a) The exchange of gases (CO_2 out, O_2 in) takes place through the walls of lung alveoli.

(b) Rate of breathing in aquatic organism is much faster than that of terrestrial organism because the water has less dissolved O_2 content, so these organisms breathe fast to obtain more O_2.

(c) (i) Pyruvic acid
(ii) CO_2

7 Identify the parts correctly matched with description given below. **CBSE 2016**

(i) Small pores present in woody plants for gaseous exchange.
(ii) Respiratory surface in humans.
(iii) Respiratory surface of earthworms.
(iv) Primary organ of respiration.
(v) Cartilaginous flap.
(vi) Contraction and relaxation of these changes the thoracic volume.

Sol. (i) Lenticels (ii) Alveoli
(iii) Skin (iv) Lungs
(v) Epiglottis (vi) Intercostal muscles

8 What is the role of respiratory pigment in respiration? Give one example.

Sol. Animals have large body size due to which the diffusion pressure alone cannot deliver oxygen to all parts of the body.

Therefore, the respiratory pigments take up oxygen from the lungs and carry it to the tissues, which are deficient in oxygen.

Haemoglobin is one such respiratory pigment found in the Red Blood Cells (RBCs) of human beings.

Long Answer (LA) Type Questions

1. What are the different ways in which glucose is oxidised to provide energy in various organisms? **CBSE 2015**

Or Explain the three pathways of breakdown of glucose in living organisms. **NCERT Exemplar**

Sol. In the first step of breakdown of a 6 carbon molecule of glucose 2 molecules of pyruvate are formed. This process takes place in the cytoplasm of the cell.

Further, oxidation of pyruvate depends on the absence or presence of oxygen as follows:

(i) In yeast, pyruvate is converted into ethanol and carbon dioxide in the absence of oxygen.

$$\text{Glucose (1 molecule)} \xrightarrow{\text{Cytoplasm}} \text{Pyruvate (2 molecules)} \xrightarrow[\text{Yeast}]{\text{Absence of oxygen}} \text{Ethanol (2 molecules)} + 2CO_2 + \text{Energy (2 ATP)}$$

(ii) In our skeletal muscles, pyruvate is converted into lactic acid, when there is deficiency/lack of oxygen.

$$\text{Glucose (1 molecules)} \xrightarrow{\text{Cytoplasm}} \text{Pyruvate (2 molecules)} \xrightarrow[\text{Absence of oxygen}]{\text{(In muscle cells)}} \text{Lactic acid (2 molecules)} + \text{Energy (2 ATP)}$$

(iii) The aerobic oxidation of pyruvate occurs in the mitochondria; where the complete oxidation of glucose gives rise to carbon dioxide and water along with release of energy.

$$\text{Glucose (1 molecules)} \xrightarrow{\text{Cytoplasm}} \text{Pyruvate (2 molecules)} \xrightarrow[\text{In oxygen}]{\text{Mitochondria}} 6CO_2 + 6H_2O + \text{Energy (38 ATP)}$$

2. During respiration in an organism A, one molecule of glucose produces 2 ATP molecules whereas in respiration of another organism B, one molecule of glucose produces 38 ATP molecules.

(i) Which organism is undergoing aerobic respiration?
(ii) Which organism is undergoing anaerobic respiration?
(iii) Which type of organism A or B can convert glucose into alcohol?
(iv) Name one organism which behaves like A.
(v) Name one organism which behaves like B.

Sol. (i) Organism B (ii) Organism A (iii) Organism A
(iv) Yeast (v) Human being

3. Describe the process of breathing in human beings. **NCERT Exemplar**

Sol. Breathing in human involves three following steps:

(i) **Inspiration** When we breathe in, ribs move up and flatten the diaphragm, due to which the chest cavity becomes larger. Expansion of the chest cavity creates a partial vacuum in the chest cavity. As a result, air is sucked into the lungs and fills the expanded alveoli.

(ii) **Gaseous exchange** Haemoglobin binds with oxygen and carries it along the blood in the body. As blood passes through the tissues of the body, oxygen from the blood diffuses into the cell, whereas carbon dioxide which is produced during respiration diffuses into the blood from tissues. It is then carried to lungs for expiration.

(iii) **Expiration** Ribs move down and diaphragm becomes dome-shaped decreasing the chest cavity. Thus, pushing the air out from lungs.

4. Carefully observe the figure given below and answer the following questions:

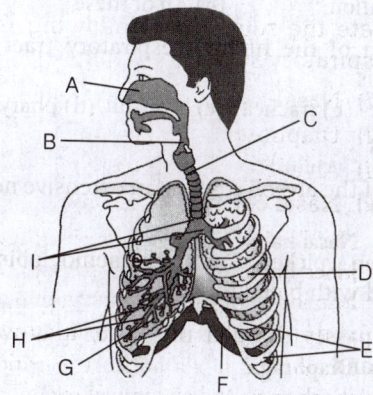

(i) Identify the part from the above diagram which flattens during inhalation.
(ii) Identify the part from the above diagram which terminates in balloon–like structure.
(iii) Identify the part from the above diagram which protects the lungs.
(iv) What would be the consequences of deficiency of haemoglobin in our bodies?

Sol. (i) F (Diaphragm) (ii) H (Bronchioles)
(iii) E (Ribs)
(iv) The deficiency of haemoglobin in the blood of a person reduces the oxygen carrying capacity of blood resulting in breathing problems, tiredness and lack of energy. The person look pale and loses height.

CHAPTER EXERCISE

Multiple Choice Questions

1. How does the exchange of gases occur in roots of a plant?
   (a) Through lenticels
   (b) Through root stomata
   (c) Through root hairs
   (d) None of these

2. Which of the following is the first site for the exchange of inhaled air?
   (a) Blood capillaries of lungs
   (b) Alveoli of lungs
   (c) Blood capillaries adjacent to body cells
   (d) Left auricle of the heart

3. Which breathing organ is helpful in initialising the process of inspiration and expiration of air?
   (a) Diaphragm (b) Alveoli (c) Larynx (d) Nostrils

4. The mechanism of human body which facilitates the exchange of respiratory gases is called
   (a) exhalation   (b) breathing
   (c) circulation   (d) All of these

5. The portion of the human respiratory tract called sound box is
   (a) larynx (b) trachea (c) bronchi (d) pharynx

Fill in the Blanks

6. The walls of the alveoli contain an extensive network of ....

7. The oxygen picked up by haemoglobin gets transported with blood to various......... .

8. When air passes through the nose, it is warmed, moistured and ....

True and False

9. Rings of cartilage are present in the throat.

10. All alveoli are not covered by web of blood capillaries.

11. The lungs always contain residual volume of air.

12. Match the following columns.

Column I		Column II
1. ATP	A.	Aerobic respiration
2. Complete oxidation of food	B.	Energy currency
3. Lungs	C.	Carbon monoxide
4. Haemoglobin	D.	Spiracles
5. Insects	E.	Residual volume

Assertion–Reason

Direction (Q. Nos. 13-15) *In each of the following questions, a statement of Assertion is given by the corresponding statement of Reason. Of the statements, mark the correct answer as*

(a) If both Assertion and Reason are true and Reason is the correct explanation of Assertion.
(b) If both Assertion and Reason are true, but Reason is not the correct explanation of Assertion
(c) If Assertion is true, but Reason is false
(d) If assertion is false, but Reason is true

13. **Assertion** Larynx passes air to the pharynx.
    Reason Pharynx produces sound.

14. **Assertion** During inhalation, diaphragm flattens and increases chest cavity.
    Reason Comparison of the chest Cavity creates a partial vacuum in the chest cavity.

15. **Assertion** Exchange of oxygen and carbon dioxide occurs between blood vessels and alveoli.
    Reason Oxygen diffuses from alveoli to blood vessels and carbon dioxide diffuses from blood vessels to alveoli.

Case Based Questions

Direction (Q. Nos. 16-19) *Answer the questions on the basis of your understanding of the following passage and related studied concepts:*

Tobacco smoking has only recently been accepted as a major health hazard, despite its practice in Western countries for more than 400 years, and much longer elsewhere. Cigarettes became popular at the end of World War I because they were cheap, convenient, and easier to smoke than pipes and cigars. The milder smoke can be more readily inhaled, allowing nicotine (a powerful addictive poison) to be quickly absorbed into the bloodstream.

Lung cancer is the most widely known and most harmful effect of smoking: 98% of cases are associated with cigarette smoking. The damaging components of cigarette smoke include tar, carbon monoxide, nitrogen dioxide, and nitric oxide. Many of these harmful chemicals occur in greater concentrations in side stream smoke (passive smoking) than in mainstream smoke (inhaled) due to the presence of a filter in the cigarette.

16. Why is passive smoking more dangerous than active smoking?

17 Give any one short term effect of smoking.

18 Name the constituent of cigarette which is responsible for cigarette and smoking addiction.

19 Other than lung cancer, what are the types of cancers which occur due to tobacco smoking?

Answers

1. (c) **2.** (b) **3.** (a) **4.** (b) **5.** (a)
6. blood capillaries **7.** body tissues **8.** cleaned
9. True **10.** False **11.** True
12. (1) → (B), (2) → (A); (3) → (E), (4) → (C), (5) → (D)
13. (d) **14.** (a) **15.** (a) **18.** Nicotine
19. Mouth cancer, pharynx cancer, oesophageal cancer.

Very Short Answer Type Questions

20 Write the events that occur during the process of breathing in humans.

21 What will happen if a human being starts inhaling air with mouth instead of nose?

Short Answer (SA) Type Questions

22 'Aerobic respiration produces more ATP than anaerobic respiration'. Justify this statement.

23 Tabulate adaptations of terrestrial respiration in human being.

24 Each and every respiratory organ is structurally specialised in its function. Justify with examples.

Long Answer (LA) Type Questions

25 Distinguish between aquatic and terrestrial respiration.

26 With a schematic diagram, explain the overall process of respiration in animals.

27 Breathing cycle is an essential process for the exchange of gases'. Justify this statement.

28 If a person holds his breath after expiration for about 25 sec, would there be occurrence of any exchange of respiratory gases in the lungs during this period? Explain.

Challengers*

1. Which process occurring in human body does not involve energy from respiration?
   (a) Contraction of heart muscle
   (b) Diffusion of oxygen from the alveoli into the blood
   (c) Digestion of bread
   (d) Maintaining a constant body temperature

2. **Assertion** (A) In the daytime, CO_2 generated during respiration is used up for photosynthesis.
   Reason (R) There is no CO_2 release during day.
   (a) Both A and R are true and R is the correct explanation of A
   (b) Both A and R are true, but R is not the correct explanation of A
   (c) A is true, but R is false
   (d) A is false, but R is true

3. Which substances are produced by anaerobic respiration in yeast?

	Carbon dioxide	Alcohol	Lactic Acid	Water
(a)	✓	✓	✗	✗
(b)	✓	✗	✓	✗
(c)	✗	✓	✗	✓
(d)	✗	✗	✓	✓

   Key ✓ = produced, ✗ = not produced

4. The following changes take place in an athlete's body during a 100 m race. Which change occurs first?
   (a) Increased availability of oxygen to muscles
   (b) Increased breathing rate
   (c) Increased carbon dioxide concentration in the blood
   (d) Increased production of carbon dioxide by muscles

5. The diagram shows part of the human gas exchange system.

   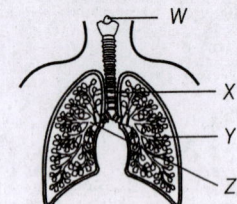

   What are W, X, Y and Z?

	Bronchus	Bronchiole	Larynx	Trachea
(a)	W	X	Z	Y
(b)	X	Z	Y	W
(c)	Y	W	X	Z
(d)	Z	Y	W	X

6. An experiment is set up as shown. Flasks 1 and 2 contain lime water. Air is pumped through the flasks.

   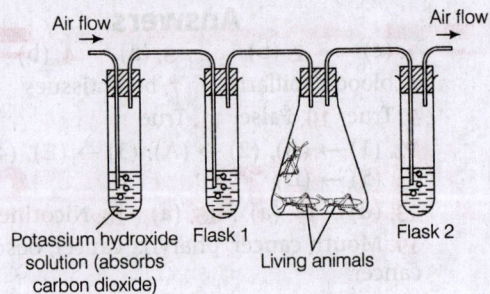

   What is the appearance of lime water in flasks 1 and 2 after a period of ten minutes?

	Flask 1	Flask 2
(a)	Clear	Clear
(b)	Clear	White/Cloudy
(c)	White/Cloudy	Clear
(d)	White/Cloudy	White/Cloudy

7. The diagram shows the ribs and some of the muscles used in breathing.

   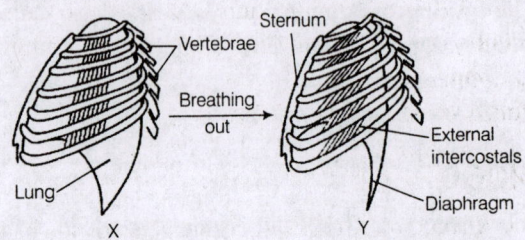

   Which muscles relax in moving from position X to position Y?

	Diaphragm	External Intercostals
(a)	No	No
(b)	No	Yes
(c)	Yes	No
(d)	Yes	Yes

Answer Key

| 1. | (b) | 2. | (b) | 3. | (a) | 4. | (d) | 5. | (d) |
| 6. | (b) | 7. | (d) | | | | | | |

*These questions may or may not be asked in the examination, have been given just for additional practice.

CHAPTER 05

Life Processes : Transportation

During metabolism, cell produces some useful and some waste products. The substances that are useful, need to be transported to other cells, while harmful substances are to be eliminated. Circulatory system is formed in higher animals which transports both useful and waste products, to and fro to their target parts within the body.

Transportation in Human Beings

The transport system of human beings also called the circulatory system, comprises of a **blood vascular system** and a **lymphatic system**. The blood vascular system has three components—blood, blood vessels and the heart. The lymphatic system includes lymph, lymph vessels and lymph nodes.

Blood

It is a red coloured fluid connective tissue, which circulates in our body. Blood is red because it contains a red pigment called haemoglobin in its red cells. It supplies nutrients and oxygen, etc., to all living cells and collects waste products and carbon dioxide to be thrown out of the body.

Blood consists of two main components

(i) **Plasma** is the straw-coloured liquid (or fluid) part of the blood. It constitutes about 55% of blood volume. It is made up of water with various substances dissolved in it. These include proteins, salts, glucose, nitrogenous compounds, and so on. Blood cells are suspended in the plasma. It transports carbon dioxide and nitrogenous wastes in dissolved form.

(ii) **Blood cells or corpuscles** constitute about 45% of the blood. These include Red Blood Corpuscles (RBCs), White Blood Corpuscles (WBCs) and Platelets. RBCs transport oxygen to all cells. WBCs help to destroy foreign particles and germs in the body. Platelets help in blood clotting at the site of injury.

Chapter Checklist

- Transportation in Human Beings
- Blood
- Heart
- Lymph (Tissue Fluid) Transportation in Plants
- Transport of Water
- Transport of Food and Other Substances

Functions of Blood

The important functions of blood in our body are as follows

(i) It helps in transport of nutrients to all parts of the body for storage, oxidation and synthesis of new substances.

(ii) It is involved in the transport of excretory products like urea, uric acid and ammonia.

(iii) It helps in the transport of oxygen and carbon dioxide to all the tissues of body for respiration.

(iv) It acts as buffer system in our body. It helps in the regulation of pH and body temperature.

(v) It is involved in protection against diseases by engulfing the disease causing microbes by phagocytosis.

(vi) The plasma of blood helps to transport hormones from their place of synthesis to the target organs.

(vii) Platelets present in the blood form a clot at the site of injury to prevent further loss of blood.

(viii) It maintains proper water balance in the body to a required constant level.

(ix) Nutrients absorbed in the small intestine enter the blood capillaries. Blood carries these nutrients and distributes them to all parts of the body.

Maintenance by Platelets (Blood Clotting)

In case of any injury when bleeding occurs, loss of blood from the system has to be minimised. Leakage leads to a loss of pressure which reduces the efficiency of pumping system. To prevent this, blood has platelet cells which circulate around the body and form a mesh-like network or clot at the site of injury.

Hence, **blood clotting** is a mechanism that prevents the loss of blood from the site of an injury or wound by forming a blood clot.

Check Point 01

1. Give one function of plasma.
2. What are the main components of blood?
3. Name the type of cells that help in preventing infection.
4. State True or False for the following statement:
   Platelets stop the blood at injury site by clotting it.

The Heart

It is a muscular organ that plays the role of a pump in the circulatory system. Its pumping action maintains the circulation of blood. The size of our heart is as big as our fist. It is situated in between the lungs slightly tilted towards left. A sheath of tissue called 'pericardium' protects the muscular heart. Between the heart and the pericardium is a fluid which reduces the friction produced during heartbeat.

The human heart is four-chambered. Its four different chambers are meant to prevent the mixing of oxygenated or oxygen rich and deoxygenated or carbon dioxide rich blood.

The different chambers of the heart are as follows

(i) **Atria** (Upper chambers) There are two atria, i.e. left atrium and right atrium, separated by an **interauricular septum**. The walls of atria are thin to receive the blood through veins.

(ii) **Ventricles** (Lower chambers) The two inferior chambers of the heart are right ventricle and left ventricle separated by an **interventricular septum**. Since, ventricles have to pump blood into various organs with high pressure, they have thicker walls as compared to atria.

The schematic representation of the sectional view of the human heart is as follows

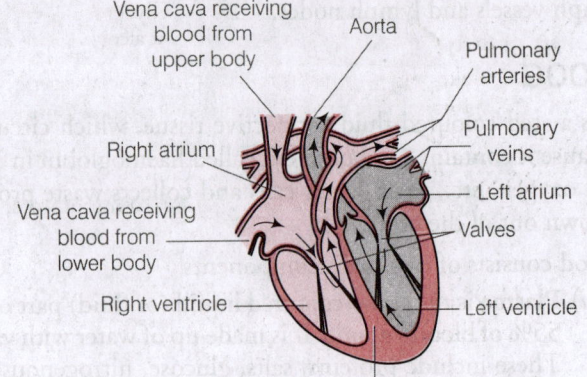

Schematic sectional view of the human heart

Pumping Action of Heart

Left atrium receives oxygenated blood from the lungs *via* pulmonary vein. During this collection, the left atrium relaxes. It then contracts, while the next chamber, the left ventricle expands, so that the blood is transferred to it.

Life Processes : Transportation

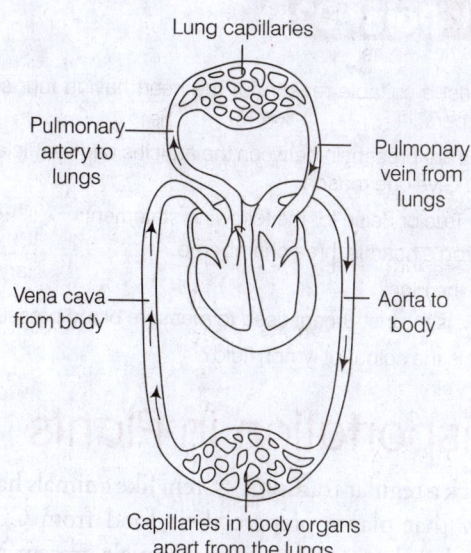

Schematic representation of transport and exchange of oxygen and carbon dioxide

As the left ventricle contracts, the blood is then pumped out for circulation in the body. Deoxygenated blood collected from the body enters to the right atrium as it expands. When the right atrium contracts, the corresponding lower chamber, i.e. the right ventricle dilates.

Deoxygenated blood thus, enters in it which inturn is pumped to the lungs for oxygenation. This whole process is repeated continuously.

Valves are the muscular flaps which ensure that blood does not flow backwards when the atria or ventricles contract.

Blood Vessels

The tubes (or pipes) through which the blood flows are called blood vessels. There are three main types of blood vessels involved in blood circulation, i.e. arteries, veins and capillaries. These are all connected to form one continuous closed system.

Characteristics and Functions of Blood Vessels

Blood Vessels	Characteristics	Functions
Arteries	They have thick, muscular and elastic walls to withstand the high pressure of the blood emerging from the heart. They do not have valves.	They carry oxygenated blood from the heart to various organs of the body except pulmonary artery.
Veins	They have thin walls than the arteries and carry blood at low pressure. They have valves to prevent the backflow of blood (to maintain unidirectional flow).	They collect deoxygenated blood from different organs of the body and bring it back to the heart except pulmonary vein.
Capillaries	Artery divides into smaller vessels known as capillaries on reaching an organ or tissue. The walls of capillaries are one cell thick. They also have valves to prevent the backflow of blood.	They help in exchange of materials between blood and surrounding cells that takes place across the thin walls of capillaries.

Blood Pressure

The pressure at which the blood is pumped against the wall of a vessel is called blood pressure. This pressure is much greater in arteries than in veins. The pressure of blood inside the artery during ventricular systole or contraction phase, is called the **systolic pressure**. The pressure of blood in the artery during ventricular diastole or relaxation phase is called the **diastolic pressure**. The normal systolic pressure is about 120 mm of Hg and diastolic pressure is 80 mm of Hg.

Blood pressure is measured by **sphygmomanometer**. High blood pressure is known as hypertension and is caused by the constriction of arterioles. It results in increased resistance to the flow of blood which may lead to the rupture of an artery and causes internal bleeding.

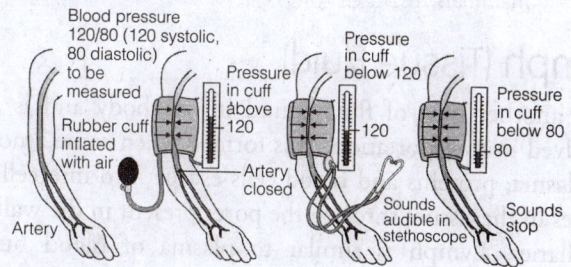

Note
- One cycle of contraction (systole) and relaxation (diastole) constitutes the cardiac cycle.
- Disorders of circulatory system are atherosclerosis, heart attack, arteriosclerosis, angina, etc.
- The average number of heart beats of a person at rest is about 70 to 72 per minute, but the number of heart beats increases too much after a physical exercise or when a person is excited.

Circulation of Blood in Animals

(i) **In birds and mammals**, heart is four-chambered. There is separation of oxygenated blood from deoxygenated blood in all including human. This allows a highly efficient supply of oxygen to the body. This is because these animals have high energy needs. They use this energy to maintain their body temperature. They are called warm-blooded animals.

All animals having four chambered hearts have **double circulation** in which the blood passes through the heart 'twice' in one complete cycle of the body. In the human circulatory system, the pathway of blood from the heart to the lungs and back to the heart is called **pulmonary circulation** and the pathway of blood from the heart to the rest of the body and back to the heart is called the **systemic circulation**. These two types of circulation are collectively called double circulation.

(ii) **In fishes**, two chambered heart is present and the blood is pumped to the gills, where it gets oxygenated and supplied directly to rest of the body. Blood goes only once through the heart during one cycle of circulation (single circulation).

(iii) **In amphibians and reptiles**, temperature of the body depends upon the temperature of the environment (cold-blooded animals). They have three-chambered heart (two atria and single ventricle) and possess a **double circulation**. They can tolerate some mixing of oxygenated and deoxygenated blood. They do not use energy to maintain their body temperature.

Note Mostly reptiles have a three chambered heart. However, crocodiles heart is four chambered like that of birds and mammals.

Lymph (Tissue Fluid)

It is another type of fluid found in our body and is also involved in transportation. It is formed when some amount of plasma, proteins and blood cells escape into intercellular spaces in the tissues through the pores present in the walls of capillaries. Lymph is similar to plasma of blood but is colourless and contains less proteins. Lymph from the intercellular spaces drains into lymphatic capillaries which further join to form large lymph vessels that finally open into larger veins.

Functions of Lymph

The important functions of lymph are as follows

(i) It is involved in transportation of substances where blood vessels do not reach.

(ii) It carries digested and absorbed fat from intestine and drains excess fluid from extracellular space back into the blood.

(iii) It maintains the balance between tissue fluid and blood.

(iv) Lymph nodes produce WBCs that prevent infection.

Check Point 02

1. Suggest a suitable reason for the heart having four separate chambers.
2. Valves are present in between the auricles and ventricles of the heart. Give one reason.
3. State True or False for the following statement:
   The frog's heart is three chambered.
4. Fill in the blank:
   .... is the instrument used to measure blood pressure.
5. What is the colour of lymph fluid?

Transportation in Plants

Plants lack a regular transport system like animals have. We all know that plants prepare their food from CO_2 and water in their leaves. The other materials present in plant body like nitrogen, phosphorus and other minerals are taken directly from the soil. The conduction of some materials to short distances, occurs through diffusion, while for longer distances a need of proper transportation system arises.

Therefore, two pathways have developed in plants independently which comprise of

(i) Xylem tissues   (ii) Phloem tissues

Both xylem and phloem carry substances from one part of the plant body to another. Xylem transports water and minerals obtained from the soil. Phloem transports products of photosynthesis from leaves to other parts of the plant.

Transport of Water and Minerals

Xylem tissues of plants have interconnected network of **vessels** and **tracheids** of roots, stems and leaves. They form continuous system of water conducting channels which reaches all parts of the plant. At the roots, cells in contact with the soil actively take up ions, creating a difference in the concentration of these ions between the roots and soil (root pressure).

The water that enters into roots from soil eliminate this difference, i.e. making the concentrations equal. Hence, there is a steady movement of water into root xylem from the soil that creates a column of water pushing it upwards. Another strategy used by plants to move water upwards in xylem over highest points of plant is **transpiration** (loss of water from stomata).

Transpiration

The loss of water in the form of vapours from the aerial parts of the plant is called transpiration. It takes place mainly through stomata. The water which is lost through the stomata is replaced by water from the xylem vessels in the leaf. Evaporation of water molecules from leaf's cells creates a suction (transpiration pull) which pulls water from the xylem cells of the root.

It has following advantages

(*i*) It helps in the absorption and upward movement of water and minerals dissolved in it from roots to the leaves.
(*ii*) It helps in the regulation of temperature.
(*iii*) It maintains a constant supply of ions to the leaves.
(*iv*) It removes excess water from the plant.

The diagrammatic representation of relationship between transpiration and absorption in a tree are as follows

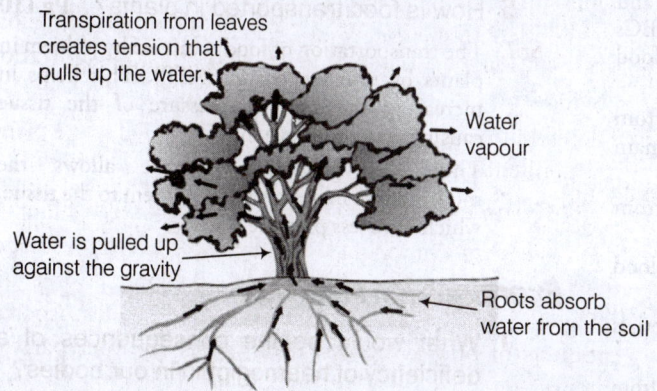

Movement of water during transpiration a tree

Note The effect of root pressure in transport of water is more important at night. During the daytime, when the stomata are open, the transpiration pull becomes the major driving force in the movement of water in the xylem.

Transport of Food and Other Substances

The transport or movement of soluble products (sugar) of photosynthesis from leaves to other parts of the plant is termed as **translocation**. It occurs in the part of vascular tissue known as **phloem**. Besides the product of photosynthesis, phloem also transports amino acids and other substances (such as plant hormones). These substances are especially delivered to storage organs of roots, fruits, seeds and growing organs.

Translocation of substances takes place in the **sieve-tubes** with the help of adjacent **companion cells**, both in upward and downward directions.

The translocation in phloem is mainly achieved by utilising energy. Material like sucrose is transferred into phloem tissue using energy from ATP, which increases the osmotic pressure of the tissue causing water to move into it.

The pressure then moves the material in the phloem to tissues with less pressure. This allows phloem to move material according to the plants needs. For example, in the spring, sugar stored in roots or stems tissues would be transported to the buds which need more energy to grow.

Check Point 03

1. Why do we need a proper transportation system in plants?
2. Fill in the blank:
   Xylem tissues of plants have interconnected network of .... of roots, stems and leaves.
3. State True or False for the following statement:
   Translocation is the loss of water through stomata.
4. Define root pressure.
5. Name the cells involved in translocation.

NCERT FOLDER

Intext Questions

1. What are the components of the transport system in human beings? What are the functions of these components? **Pg 110**

Sol. The components of the transport system in human beings includes :

(i) **Heart** It pumps the blood to be circulated and also receives the blood from different body parts.

(ii) **Blood** It is a fluid connective tissue consisting of two main components
  (a) **Plasma** It transports food, carbon dioxide nitrogenous wastes and hormones, etc., in dissolved form.
  (b) **Blood corpuscles** These include RBCs, WBCs and platelets. RBCs transport respiratory gases, WBCs protect body from harmful pathogens and blood platelets help in blood clotting.

(iii) **Blood vessels** These carry blood to and fro from different parts of the body. These are of three main types
  (a) **Arteries** These transport oxygenated blood from heart to different body parts.
  (b) **Veins** These transport deoxygenated blood towards heart from various body parts.
  (c) **Capillaries** These allows exchange of materials between blood and tissues.

(iv) **Lymph** It carries digested and absorbed fat from intestine and drains the excess fluid from the extracellular spaces back into the blood.

2. Why is it necessary to separate oxygenated and deoxygenated blood in mammals and birds? **CBSE 2016, Pg 110**

Sol. Mammals and birds are warm-blooded animals, so they constantly need energy in order to maintain their body temperature. Due to this high energy demand, they require more oxygen. Thus, it is important that their oxygenated blood should not get mixed up with deoxygenated blood in order to make circulatory system much more efficient.

3. What are the components of the transport system in highly organised plants? **Pg 110**

Sol. The main components of the transport system in highly organised plants are xylem and phloem. Xylem consists of tracheids and vessels which conduct water and minerals (obtained from the soil) to the leaves. Phloem consists of sieve tubes and companion cells. It helps to transport food, amino acids, hormones, etc., from leaves to various parts of the plant.

4. How are water and minerals transported in plants? **Pg 110**

Sol. Water and minerals are transported through xylem in plants. The cells in roots that are in contact with soil actively take up ions, creating a difference in concentration of ions between the cell sap of roots and soil water.

Water moves into the roots to eliminate this difference of concentration forming a steady movement of water in the root xylem. This creates a column of water that is steadily pushed upwards. Loss of water from leaves creates a suction that pulls water from the xylem of the roots to the aerial parts of the body.

5. How is food transported in plants? **Pg 110**

Sol. The transportation of food is carried by phloem in plants by utilising energy (ATP). This helps in increasing the osmotic pressure of the tissue causing water to move into it.

Thus, the generated pressure allows the movement of materials from phloem to the tissue, which have less pressure.

Exercises (On Page 113)

1. What would be the consequences of a deficiency of haemoglobin in our bodies?

Sol. Haemoglobin efficiently binds with oxygen and transports it to various parts of the body. Deficiency of haemoglobin is referred to as **anaemia**. The consequence of such condition is that the blood is unable to carry sufficient amount of oxygen as required by the body and would cause less respiration.

Also, less energy would be liberated. In anaemia, the person feels weak, skin becomes pale, person feel lethargic and is unable to perform heavy physical tasks.

2. Describe double circulation in human beings. Why is it necessary?

Or Why is blood circulation in human heart called double circulation? **NCERT Exemplar**

Sol. During double circulation in human beings, blood passes the through heart twice for completing one cycle of circulation.

All in one Life Processes : Transportation

183

The double circulation includes the following processes

(i) **Pulmonary circulation** In this circulation, the deoxygenated blood is pushed by right ventricle to the lungs for oxygenation through pulmonary artery. This oxygenated blood is then brought back to the left atrium of the heart through pulmonary veins.

(ii) **Systemic circulation** In this circulation, oxygenated blood brought to left atrium goes to the left ventricle. It is then passed on to different body parts of body through aorta.

Such separation allows a highly efficient supply of oxygen to the body. This is usefull in animals that have high energy needs, such as birds and mammals, which constantly, use energy to maintain their body temperature.

3 The xylem in plants are responsible for
(a) transport of water
(b) transport of food
(c) transport of amino acid
(d) transport of oxygen

Sol. (a) Xylem in plants is responsible for the transport of water and minerals which are obtained from the soil.

4 What are the differences between the transport of materials in xylem and phloem?

Sol. The differences between transport of materials in xylem and phloem are as follows :

Transport in Xylem	Transport in Phloem
Xylem transports water and minerals in plants.	Phloem transports the products of photosynthesis, amino acids and other organic substances in plants.
The movement of water is unidirectional in xylem.	The movement of substances can be multidirectional.
Major operating forces are diffusion and transpirational pull.	Energy (ATP) is required for translocation.
It is not influenced by metabolic inhibitors.	Phloem transport is inhibited by metabolic inhibitors.
It is carried out by xylem vessels and tracheids.	It is carried out by sieve tubes with the help of adjacent companion cells.

SUMMARY

- **Transportation** is the life process in which a substance (Made or absorbed) in one part of the body of an organism is carried to other parts of its body.
- **Human circulatory system** consists of blood, the heart and network of blood vessels.
- **Blood** is a specialised connective tissue consisting of plasma and formed elements (i.e RBC, WBC and platelets). It helps in the transport of nutrients, gases, waste products, etc. It also regulates body temperature and pH.
- **Heart** is present between the lungs in the thoracic cavity slightly tilted to left. Human heart is four-chambered consisting of two auricles and two ventricles each separated by septum.
- **Blood vessels** associated with circulatory system include arteries, veins and capillaries.
- **Arteries** take oxygenated blood from the heart to various body parts. They are thick-walled and have no valves.
- **Veins** transport deoxygenated blood from body tissues to the heart. They are thin-walled with valves to prevent the backflow of blood.
- **Capillaries** are thin, narrow tubes which connect arteries to veins, allowing exchange of materials between blood and body cells.

- **Blood Pressure** (BP) is the force exerted by blood on the walls of a blood vessel. It is measured by **sphygmomanometer**. The normal range of BP in human body is 120/80 mm Hg.
- **Lymph** is similar to plasma with less proteins. It carries digested and absorbed fat from intestine and drains back excess fluid to blood.
- **Transportation in plants** consists of two pathways using two different conducting tissues.
- **Xylem** transports water and minerals obtained from the soil.
- **Phloem** transports food prepared from the leaves to other parts of plant, i.e translocation.
- **Transport of water** occurs due to transpiration pull and root pressure.
- **Transpiration** is the loss of water in the form of vapour from aerial parts of plant. The pressure exerted by transpiration on the walls of xylem is called transpiration pull. It causes upward movement of water and minerals.
- **Transport of food** The products of photosynthesis are transported from the leaves to other parts by using energy derived from ATP.

Exam Practice

Objective Type Questions

Multiple Choice Questions

1. Which of the following statement (s) is (are) true about heart?
   (i) Left atrium receives oxygenated blood from different parts of body while right atrium receives deoxygenated blood from lungs.
   (ii) Left ventricle pumps oxygenated blood to different body parts while right ventricle pumps deoxygenated blood to lungs.
   (iii) Left atrium transfers oxygenated blood to right ventricle which sends it to different body parts.
   (iv) Right atrium receives deoxygenated blood from different parts of the body while left ventricle pumps oxygenated blood to different parts of the body.
   NCERT Exemplar
   (a) Only (i)   (b) Only (ii)
   (c) (ii) and (iv)   (d) (i) and (iii)
   Sol. (c) Statement (ii) and (iv) are correct about heart.
   Route of blood circulation in heart is as follows

   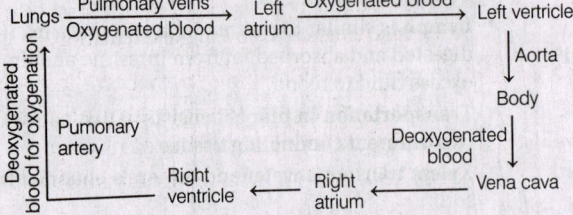

2. Identify the phase of circulation which is represented in the diagram of heart given below. Arrows indicate contraction of the chambers shown.
   CBSE SQP (Term-I)

   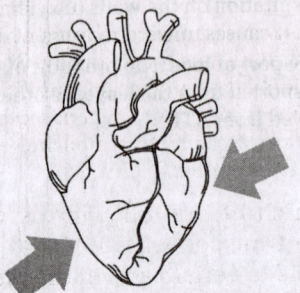

   (a) Blood transferred to the right ventricle and left ventricle simultaneously
   (b) Blood is transferred to lungs for oxygenation and is pumped into various organs simultaneously
   (c) Blood transferred to the right auricle and left auricle simultaneously
   (d) Blood is received from lungs after oxygenation and is received from various organs of the body
   Sol. (b) The diagram shows ventricular systole. Through ventricular systole, blood gets transferred to the lungs for oxygenation and is then pumped into various organs simultaneously.
   Thus, option (b) is correct.

3. What prevents backflow of blood inside the heart during contraction?
   (a) Valves in heart
   (b) Thick muscular walls of ventricles
   (c) Thin walls of atria
   (d) All of the above   **NCERT Exemplar**
   Sol. (a) Valves present in the heart ensures that blood does not flow backwards when the atria or ventricles contracts.

4. The figure given below shows a schematic plan of blood circulation in humans with labels. Identify the correct label with its functions.   **CBSE SQP (Term-I)**

   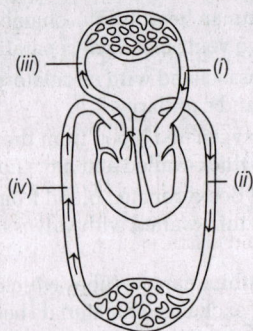

   (a) (i) Pulmonary vein - takes impure blood from body parts
   (b) (ii) Pulmonary artery - takes blood from lungs to heart
   (c) (iii) Aorta - takes blood from heart to body parts

Life Processes : Transportation

(d) (iv) Vena cava - takes blood from body parts to right auricle

Sol. (d) (iv) Vena cava- takes blood from body parts to right auricle is the correct match. Vena cava is a large vein that carries deoxygenated blood from body parts to the right atrium of the heart.

5 The blood leaving the tissues becomes richer in
   (a) carbon dioxide   (b) water
   (c) haemoglobin   (d) oxygen
   NCERT Exemplar

Sol. (a) The blood leaving the tissues becomes richer in carbon dioxide (CO_2). When the oxygenated blood passes through the capillaries of the body organs/tissues, it gives oxygen to the body cells.

At the same time, carbon dioxide produced during respiration enters into blood. Thus, deoxygenated blood (carrying CO_2) leaves the tissues and enters the vena cava, from where they are again passed to the lungs for oxygenation.

6 Choose the correct statement that describes arteries.
   (a) They have thick elastic walls, blood flows under high pressure; collect blood from different organs and bring it back to the heart
   (b) They have thin walls with valves inside, blood flows under low pressure and carry blood away from the heart to various organs of the body
   (c) They have thick elastic walls, blood flows under low pressure carry blood from the heart to various organs of the body
   (d) They have thick elastic walls without valves inside, blood flows under high pressure and carry blood away from the heart to different parts of the body
   NCERT Exemplar

Sol. (d) Statement (d) is correct about arteries. Arteries carry oxygenated blood away from the heart to various organs of the body. Since, the blood emerges from the heart under high pressure, the arteries have thick and elastic walls.

7 Instrument used to measure blood pressure is
   (a) barometer   (b) potometer
   (c) thermometer   (d) sphygmomanometer

Sol. (d) Blood pressure is measured by the instrument named sphygmomanometer. Two readings of blood pressire are taken : systolic pressure and diastolic pressure.

8 Which one indicates hypertension or high Blood Pressure (BP)?
   (a) 120/80   (b) 110/70   (c) 130/80   (d) 140/90

Sol. (d) Person having blood pressure 140/90, shows hypertension or high blood pressure. The normal blood pressure for humans is 120/80.

9 Single circulation, i.e. blood flows through the heart only once during one cycle of passage through the body, is exhibited by
   (a) *Labeo, Chameleon, Salamander*
   (b) *Hippocampus, Exocoetus, Anabas*
   (c) *Hyla, Rana, Draco*
   (d) whale, dolphin, turtle   **NCERT Exemplar**

Sol. (b) Fishes (*Hippocampus*, *Exocoetus* and *Anabas*) have 2-chambered heart and blood flows through the heart only once during one cycle of passage through the body, i.e. single circulaton.

10 In which of the following groups of organisms, blood flows through the heart only once during one cycle of passage through the body?
   (a) Rabbit, parrot, turtle
   (b) Frog, crocodile, pigeon
   (c) Whale, *Labeo*, penguin
   (d) Shark, dog fish, sting ray
   CBSE SQP (Term-I)

Sol. (d) Organisms like shark, dog fish and sting ray have a two chambered heart -one atrium and one ventricle. Thus, one cycle of blood passage through the heart to the body is found in such organisms i.e. they are characterised by single circulation.

11 What is common between extensive network of blood vessels around walls of alveoli and in glomerulus of nephron?
   (a) Thick walled arteries richly supplied with blood
   (b) Thin walled veins poorly supplied with blood
   (c) Thick walled capillaries poorly supplied with blood
   (d) Thin walled capillaries richly supplied with blood   **CBSE SQP (Term-I)**

Sol. (d) Alveoli are present in lungs whereas glomerules of nephron is present in kideny, Both of these organs perform the function of purification of blood *via* gaseous and toxic material exchange. Thus, to perform exchange thin capillaries are required to ease the transfet process.

12 Which of the following is responsible for the transport of water and minerals from roots to aerial parts of the plant?

(a) Xylem (b) Phloem
(c) Cortex (d) Both (a) and (b)

Sol. (a) In plants, transport of water and minerals occurs through xylem from roots to aerial parts of the plant.

13 The process of carrying food from the leaves to other parts of a plant is called
(a) transpiration
(b) transportation
(c) translocation
(d) transformation

Sol. (c) The process of carrying food from the leaves to other parts of a plant is called translocation. It occurs in the part of vascular tissue known as phloem.

14 Which of the following is accomplished in a plant by utilising the energy stored in ATP?
(a) Transport of food
(b) Transport of oxygen
(c) Transport of water and minerals
(d) Transport of water, minerals and food

Sol. (a) Transport of food is accomplished in a plant by utilising the energy stored in ATP. Transport of water and minerals is accomplished by diffusion and transpiration pull.

Fill in the Blanks

15 Heart is situated in the middle of the ...... cavity.

Sol. thoracic

16 .... surrounds the heart.

Sol. Pericardium

17 Cardiac cycle is divided into .... and ...... phase.

Sol. systolic; diastolic

18 ...... helps in the obsorption and upward movement of water and minerals.

Sol. Transpiration

19 ...... and .... cells are involved in translocation.

Sol. Sieve tubes; Companion cells

True and False

20 Arteries are more muscular than veins.

Sol. True

21 Pericardial fluid is called lymph.

Sol. False; Pericardial fluid is present between the double membranous covering of the heart called pericardium.

22 In fish, the heart receives only pure blood.

Sol. False; In fish, the heart receives only impure blood.

23 Plants lack a regular transport system like animals have.

Sol. True

24 The translocation in phloem is mainly achieved by diffusion process.

Sol. False; The translocation in phloem is mainly achieved by utilising energy in form of ATP.

Match the Columns

25 Match the following columns.

	Column I		Column II
1.	Platelets	A.	Size of Fist
2.	Heart	B.	Warm blooded animals
3.	Veins	C.	Translocation
4.	Birds	D.	Valves
5.	Sieve tubes	E.	Blood clotting

Sol. 1. → E, 2. → A, 3. → D, 4. → B, 5. → C

26 Match the following columns.

	Column I		Column II
1.	Xylem	A.	Night
2.	Phloem	B.	Sucrose
3.	Root pressure	C.	Necessary evil
4.	Transpiration	D.	Minerals
5.	Translocation	E.	Companion cells

Sol. 1. → D, 2. → B, 3. → A, 4. → C, 5. → E

Assertion–Reason

Direction (Q. Nos. 27-31) *In each of the following questions, a statement of Assertion is given by the corresponding statement of Reason. Of the statements, mark the correct answer as*

(a) If both Assertion and Reason are true and Reason is the correct explanation of Assertion
(b) If both Assertion and Reason are true, but Reason is not the correct explanation of Assertion
(c) If Assertion is true, but Reason is false
(d) If Assertion is false, but Reason is true

27 Assertion Interauricular septum separates left atrium from right atrium.

Reason Interventricular septum separates left ventricle from right ventricle.

Sol. (b) There are four chambers of the human heart. The left atria and right atria are separated by an **interauricular septum**. The two inferior chambers of the heart, i.e., right and left ventricles are separated by an **interventricular septum**.

Both Assertion and Reason are true but Reason is not the correct explanation of Assertion.

28 **Assertion** All the arteries carry oxygenated blood from the heart to various organs.

Reason Pulmonary vein carries deoxygenated blood to the heart.

Sol. (d) The arteries carry oxygenated blood from the heart to various organs, except for pulmonary artery.

The veins collect deoxygenated blood from different organs and bring it back to the heart, except for pulmonary vein. Assertion is false but Reason is true.

29 **Assertion** Lymph, also known as tissue fluid is colourless.

Reason It lacks erythrocytes.

Sol. (a) Lymph is similar to plasma of blood but is colourless. Erythrocytes contain haemoglobin, which imparts red colour to blood. Due to its absence, lymph is colourless.

Both Assertion and Reason are true and Reason is the correct explanation of Assertion.

30 **Assertion** Resins and gums are stored in old xylem tissue in plants.

Reason Resins and gums facilitate transport of water molecules.

Sol. (c) Resins and gums are stored in old xylem tissue in plants as waste products.

Since, resins and gums are waste products, they play no role in facilitating the transport of water molecules.

Thus Assertion is true, but Reason is false.

31 **Assertion** Translocation of sugar occurs through the phloem.

Reason It is achieved by diffusion of sugars through phloem.

Sol. (c) The transport or movement of soluble products (sugar) of photosynthesis from leaves to other parts of the plant is termed as translocation. It occurs in the part of vascular tissue known as phloem. The translocation in phloem is mainly achieved by utilising energy by expenditure of ATP.

Assertion is true, but Reason is false.

Case Based Questions

Directions (Q. Nos. 32-35) *Answer the questions on the basis of your understanding of the following table and related studied concepts:*

Comparison between Blood and Lymph

Feature	Blood	Lymph
Cells	RBCs, WBCs and platelets	Lymphocytes (WBCs)
Proteins	Hormones and plasma proteins	Few proteins
Fats	Some transported as lipoproteins	More than in blood (absorbed from lacteals in small intestine)
Glucose	80-120 mg per 100 cm^3	Less than in blood
Amino acids	More than in other fluids	Less than in blood
Oxygen	More than in other fluids	Less than in blood
Carbon dioxide	Little	More

32 Refer to the table showing comparison between blood and lymph. Give the comparison of cells present in blood and cells present in lymph.

Sol. Cells present in blood are RBCs, WBCs and platelets. However, lymph mainly has lymphocytes (a type of WBCs) only.

33 How is lymph formed?

Sol. Lymph is formed when some amount of plasma, proteins and blood cells escape into intercellular spaces in the tissues through the pores present in the wall of capillaries.

34 What is common in blood and lymph?
(a) Protection against diseases
(b) Unidirectional flow in the body
(c) Clotting of blood
(d) None of the above

Sol. (a) Both blood and lymph are responsible for protection against diseases because these fluids contain lymphocytes which engulf the disease causing microbes by phagocytosis.

35 The relatively clear liquid medium which carries the other cells of blood is called as
(a) lymph (b) serum
(c) plasma (d) blood vessel

Sol. (c) The relatively clear liquid medium which carries the other cells of blood is called as plasma. It constitutes about 55% of blood volume.

Direction (Q. Nos. 36-39) *Answer the questions on the basis of your understanding of the following passage and related studied concepts:*

Plants loss water all the time, despite all the adaptations they have to help prevent it (e.g. waxy leaf cuticle). Approximately 99% of the water a plant absorbs from the soil is lost by evaporation from the leaves and stem.

This loss, mostly through stomata, is called **transpiration** and the flow of water through the plant is called the **transpiration stream**. A number of processes contribute to water movement up the plant transpiration pull, cohesion and root pressure. Transpiration may seem to be a wasteful process, but it has benefits.

36 What pulls up water through the xylem vessels in a plant?

Sol. The continuous loss of water through stomata (transpiration) pulls up water through the xylem vessels in a plant.

37 What is the role of transpiration stream?

Sol. The transpiration stream helps the plant to maintain on adequate mineral uptake, as many essential minerals occur in low concentrations in the soil.

38 State the significance of the root pressure.

Sol. The pressure with which water is pushed into the xylem tubes of the root is called root pressure. The water moving upwards forms a column, which is maintained upto a certain height due to root pressure.

39 Give one adaptation of plants that helps them to prevent excess loss of water through stomata.

Sol. Waxy leaf cuticle helps plants to prevent transpiration (loss of water through stomata).

Very Short Answer Type Questions

40 State the role and functions of the following
  (i) Blood   (ii) WBCs

Sol. (i) Blood circulates in our body. Its function is to transport nutrients, oxygen, carbon dioxide, urea and hormones to different parts of the body.
  (ii) WBCs are the type of blood corpuscles found in blood. It kills germs present in blood and tissues.

41 What will happen if platelets were absent in the blood? **NCERT Exemplar**

Sol. If platelets are not present in the blood, then clotting at the site of injury will not take place. Blood will continue to flow which could be fatal to an organism.

42 Write the functions of two upper chambers of human heart.

Sol. The functions of two upper chambers, i.e. left atrium and right atrium of human heart are given below:
  (i) Left atrium receives oxygenated blood from pulmonary vein and transfers it to left ventricle.
  (ii) Right atrium receives deoxygenated blood from vena cava and transfers it to right ventricle.

43 Why are the walls of ventricles thicker than the walls of atria?

Sol. Ventricles have to pump blood into various organs with high pressure, so they have thicker walls than atria.

44 What is special about blood capillaries?

Sol. The capillaries are thin walled (one cell thick) and extremely fine tubules which connect arteries to veins.

45 Veins are thin walled and have valves. Justify. **CBSE SQP 2020-21**

Sol. Veins are thin walled because they handle very less pressure of blood that flows from different organs to the heart and they have valves to ensure blood how is unidirectional.

46 Why have plants low energy needs?

Sol. Plants have low energy needs as they do not perform physical movements and have a large proportion of dead-cells in many tissues.

47 Which mechanism plays an important role in transportation of water in plants?
  (i) During daytime   (ii) At night

Sol. (i) During daytime, transpiration pull plays an important role in transportation of water in plants.
  (ii) At night, root pressure plays an important role in transportation of water in plants.

48 Out of xylem and phloem, which one carries materials
  (i) Upwards as well as downwards?
  (ii) Only upwards?

Sol. (i) Phloem carries materials upwards as well as downwards.
  (ii) Xylem carries materials only upwards.

Life Processes : Transportation

Short Answer (SA) Type Questions

1 Write down any six functions of blood.

Sol. Refer to text 'Functions of Blood' on Pg no. 178.

2 Write three types of blood vessels. Give one important feature of each. **CBSE Delhi 2019**

Sol. The three types of blood vessels are arteries, veins and capillaries.

Rest, refer to text 'Characteristics and functions of blood vessels' on Pg. no. 179.

3 Why do veins have thin walls as compared to arteries? **NCERT Exemplar**

Sol. Arteries are thick-walled blood vessels, which carry oxygenated blood from heart to all parts of the body. They have thick walls because blood emerges from the heart under high pressure. In comparison, veins are thin-walled blood vessels, which carry deoxygenated blood from all parts of the body back to the heart. They do not need thick walls because blood flowing through them is no longer under high pressure. Instead, they have valves, which prevent the backflow of blood.

4 Give the appropiate one word answer for the following :

(i) Blood vessel entering from lower parts of body into right atrium.

(ii) Blood vessel leaving the right ventricles to lungs.

(iii) Blood vessel entering into right atrium from upper parts of body.
CBSE 2016

Sol. (i) Posterior vena cava

(ii) Pulmonary artery

(iii) Anterior vena cava.

5 Differentiate between an artery and a vein. **NCERT Exempler**

Sol. Refer to table "characteristics and functions of blood vessels" on Pg. no. 179.

6 Write the function of each of the following components of the transport system in human beings: **CBSE 2015**

(i) Blood vessels

(ii) Lymph

(iii) Heart

Sol. Refer to Ans 1 of intext questions on Pg no. 182.

7 In birds and mammals the left and right side of the heart are separated. Give reasons. **CBSE SQP 2020-21**

Sol. Heart of mammals and birds is four-chambered and it helps them in various ways as these are warm-blooded animals and their metabolism is complex and the body temperature is to be maintained throughout and for all above the energy is constantly required. The separation keeps oxygenated and deoxygenated blood from mixing allowing a highly efficient supply of oxygen to the body.

8 Why and how does water enter continuously into the root xylem? **NCERT Exemplar**

Sol. Plants require water to carry out photosynthesis and other processes. The continuous flow of water in root xylem is due to transpirational pull.

The water which is lost through the stomata is replaced by water from the xylem vessels.

Evaporation of water molecules from the cells of leaf creates a suction which pulls water from the xylem of roots to leaves.

Thus, transpiration helps in absorption and upward movement of water and minerals dissolved in soil from roots to leaves.

Cells of roots are in close contact with soil and so they actively take up ions by diffusion. The ion-concentration increases inside the root and hence, osmotic pressure increases the movement of water from soil into the roots and this process occurs continuously.

9 Define the term transpiration. Design an experiment to demonstrate this process.
CBSE Delhi 2019

Sol. The loss of water in the form of vapours from the aerial parts of the plants is called transpiration. It is also called a necessary evil.

The experiment to demonstrate the process of transpiration is as follows

Take a healthy potted plant, well-watered; cover the pot with rubber sheet (only aerial parts should remain uncovered). Place the potted plant on a glass plate and cover it with a bell jar. Keep the whole set up in sunlight for sometime and observe.

Water droplets will appear inside the wall of the bell jar. Thus, it can be concluded that the water drops are seen due to transpiration from the aerial parts of plant.

10 (i) Transport of food in plants requires living tissues and energy. Justify this statement.

(ii) Name the components of food that are transported by the living tissues.

Sol. (i) Food is transported by sieve tubes (phloem) at the expense of ATP. As phloem is largely composed of living cells thus, it shows that food transport requires living tissues and energy.

(ii) Components of food that are transported by the living tissues are:
(a) Photosynthetic products or sucrose
(b) Amino acids and plant hormones.

11 What is 'translocation'? Why is it essential for plants? Where in plants are the following synthesised?
(i) Sugar   (ii) Hormones

Sol. **Translocation** Transport of food prepared in the leaves to other parts of the plants is known as translocation.

It is essential for the plants to supply food to all parts of the plants. Food is needed for producing energy, which in turn is required by all parts of the plants to perform their activities.

(i) **Sugars** are synthesised in leaves and then transported to storage organs like roots, fruits and seeds.

(ii) **Plant hormones** are synthesised at the tip of the stems and roots.

Long Answer (LA) Type Questions

1 (i) Draw a schematic representation of transport and exchange of oxygen and carbon dioxide during transportation of blood in human beings and label following parts on it. Lungs to capillaries, pulmonary artery to lungs, aorta to body, pulmonary veins from lungs.

(ii) What is the advantage of having separate channels of heart for oxygenated and deoxygenated blood in mammals and birds?

Or

What is the advantage of having four-chambered heart? **NCERT Exemplar**

Sol. (i) For figure refer to Pg. no. 179.

(ii) Separation of oxygenated blood from deoxygenated blood allows a highly efficient supply of oxygen to the body. These animals have constant high energy requirements in order to perform various activities and maintain their body temperature.

2 The diagram given below is the longitudinal section of human heart.

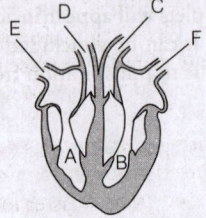

(i) What is the difference in composition of blood in parts C and F?

(ii) What is the function of part D?

(iii) Name the structure which separates part A and part B?

(iv) Describe the circulation of blood in amphibians and reptiles.

Sol. (i) The blood vessel C (pulmonary artery) has got deoxygenated blood, while the blood vessel F (pulmonary vein) has got oxygenated blood.

(ii) The blood vessel D (aorta) receives oxygen rich blood from the left ventricle and circulates it to different parts of the body.

(iii) Interventricular septum separates part A (right ventricle) and part B (left ventricle).

(iv) Refer to text 'Circulation of Blood in Animals' on Pg. no. 179 and 180.

3 (i) Mention any two components of blood.

(ii) Trace the movement of oxygenated blood in the body.

(iii) Write the function of valves present in between atria and ventricles.

(iv) Write one structural difference between the composition of artery and veins. **CBSE 2018**

Sol. (i) Blood consists of two main components viz plasma and blood corpuscles.

(ii) The movement of blood from lungs to the heart constitutes the pulmonary circulation. Movement of blood in pulmonary circulation occurs in the following ways

All in One Life Processes : Transportation

Oxygenated blood from lungs comes
back to the left auricle of heart through
four pulmonary veins, i.e. two from
each lung
↓
From left auricle, blood is
poured into left ventricle
↓
As the left ventricle fills up, it contracts forcing
blood out
↓
The blood is finally pumped to the
whole body via aorta as the
muscular left ventricle contracts

(iii) The valves present in between atria and ventricle regulate the unidirectional flow of blood from atria to ventricles.

(iv) Arteries have thick, muscular and elastic walls, while the veins have thin walls and possess valves.

4 Describe the flow of blood through the heart of human beings. **NCERT Exemplar**

Sol. The flow of blood through human heart is as follows

Oxygen rich blood from the lungs comes to the thin-walled upper chamber of the heart on the left, i.e. **left atrium**. The left atrium relaxes when it is collecting the blood. It then contracts and the blood is allowed to enter in the next chamber i.e. **left ventricle**, as it expands. When the muscular left ventricle contracts, the blood is pumped out to the body via aorta.

Deoxygenated blood reaches from the body to the upper chamber on the right namely **right atrium** and it expands. As the right atrium contracts, the corresponding lower chamber, the **right ventricle**, dilates. This transfers the blood to right ventricle, which in turn pumps it to the **lungs** for oxygenation.

This whole process is repeated continuously. In this way, the blood keeps on circulating in our body without stopping due to which all the body parts keep on getting oxygen, digested food and other materials all the time.

5 The figure given below represents the set-up at the start of a certain experiment to demonstrate an activity of plants.

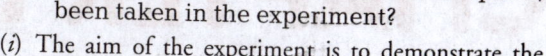

(i) What is the aim of the experiment?
(ii) Why has oil been put in each test tube?
(iii) What will be the observation in two test tubes after about 2-3 days?
(iv) Give reason to explain any change observed as answered in (iii).

(v) Why has the test tube B without the plant, been taken in the experiment?

Sol. (i) The aim of the experiment is to demonstrate the process of transpiration.
(ii) Oil has been put to avoid any evaporation from the water surface in the tube.
(iii) The level of water in the test tube 'A' will fall, while the level of water in the test tube 'B' will remain the same on observing after 2-3 days.
(iv) The fall in the water level in the test tube 'A' is because of transpiration through aerial parts of the plant.
(v) Test tube 'B' without the plant clearly shows that no evaporation of water takes place through oil layer present on the surface.

6 (i) What is the role of transpiration in transportation? Explain with diagram.
(ii) Which plant part helps in unidirectional flow of water?
(iii) Write a short note on translocation.

Sol. (i) The loss of water in transpiration creates a suction which pulls water from the xylem cells of roots. Thus, water reaches to the upper parts of the plant by transpirational pull.
For figure refer to Pg. no. 181.
(ii) Xylem of plants help in upward unidirectional flow of water.
(iii) Refer to text on Pg. no.181.

7 Give reasons:
(a) Ventricles have thicker muscular walls than atria.
(b) Transport system in plants is slow.
(c) Circulation of blood in aquatic vertebrates differs from that in terrestrial vertebrates.
(d) During the daytime, water and minerals travel faster through xylem as compared to the night.
(e) Veins have valves whereas arteries do not. **CBSE 2020**

Sol. (a) Ventricles have to pump blood into the body and towards lungs. For this their walls are thick in order to propel blood out of the heart with high pressure.
(b) Transport system in plant is slow because it is simple and is based on physical forces (diffusion, osmosis, transpiration).
(c) The blood circulation in aquatic animal is different from terrestrial because these have to absorb O_2 from water which is low in content in water as compared to air.
(d) During daytime, due to transpiration process, more water is absorbed by roots due to transpiration pull so absorption is faster in daytime.
(e) Veins have valves to prevent back flow of blood due to less pressure. In arteries, the pressure of flow is fast.

CHAPTER EXERCISE

Multiple Type Questions

1. The number of chamber(s) present in human heart is
   (a) one
   (b) two
   (c) three
   (d) four

2. Right atrium receives blood from
   (a) pulmonary aorta
   (b) pulmonary veins
   (c) inferior vena cava
   (d) superior and inferior vena cava

3. Which one of the following statements related to capillaries is correct?
   (a) These act as connective link between arteries and veins
   (b) These are deeply penetrated inside the tissues
   (c) These help in exchange of materials between blood and surrounding cells
   (d) All of the above

4. All reptiles have a three-chambered heart except
   (a) snake
   (b) crocodile
   (c) lizard
   (d) Both (b) and (c)

5. The value of normal systolic and diastolic blood pressure in human is
   (a) 120 mm Hg and 80 mm Hg, respectively
   (b) 80 mm Hg and 120 mm Hg, respectively
   (c) 100 mm Hg and 90 mm Hg, respectively
   (d) 130 mm Hg and 85 mm Hg, respectively

Fill in the Blanks

6. Crocodiles have ...... heart.

7. Heart is largely composed of ...... muscles.

8. The .... tissue transports water and minerals.

True and False

9. The blood vascular system comprises of blood, blood vessels and lymph.

10. Blood has platelet cells which circulate around the body and form a clot at the site of injury.

11. Translocation of substances takes place in the sieve tubes in downward direction only.

Match the Columns

12. Match the following

	Column I		Column II
1.	Lymph	A.	Hypertension
2.	RBCs	B.	Colourless
3.	Blood pressure	C.	Vessels
4.	Tracheids	D.	Haemoglobin
5.	Hormones	E.	Phloem

Assertion–Reason

Direction (Q. Nos. 13-15) *In each of the following questions, a statement of Assertion is given by the corresponding statement of Reason. Of the statements, mark the correct answer as*
   (a) If both Assertion and Reason are true and Reason is the correct explanation of Assertion
   (b) If both Assertion and Reason are true, but Reason is not the correct explanation of Assertion
   (c) If Assertion is true, but Reason is false
   (d) If Assertion is false, but Reason is true

13. **Assertion** Blood clotting prevents the leakage of blood from the site of an injury.
    Reason It reduces the loss of blood from the system.

14. **Assertion** Left atrium receives oxygenated blood from the lungs by pulmonary vein.
    Reason In the lungs, deoxygenated blood is purified and oxygenated blood is carried in pulmonary artery.

15. **Assertion** Translocation of solutes takes place across the phloem.
    Reason Solutes can be translocated both in upward and downward directions.

Case Based Questions

Direction (Q. Nos. 16-19) *Answer the questions on the basis of your understanding of the following passage and related studied concepts:*

Double circulation systems occur in all vertebrates other than fish. The blood is pumped through a pulmonary circuit to the lungs, where it is oxygenated. The blood returns to the heart which pump the oxygenated blood, through a systemic circuit, to the body. In amphibians and most reptiles, the heart is not completely divided and there is some mixing of oxygenated and deoxygenated blood. In birds and mammals, the heart is fully divided and there is no mixing.

16 Name the animals in which double circulation occurs?

17 What is the need of separation of oxygenated blood from deoxygenated blood in human?

18 Why a circulatory system is required in larger and more complex organisms?

19 Name the site in fishes where oxygenation of blood takes place.

Answers

1. (d) 2. (d) 3. (d) 4. (b) 5. (a)
6. four chambered 7. cardiac 8. xylem
9. False 10. True 11. False
12. (1) → (B), (2) → (D), (3) → (A), (4) → (E), (5) → (C)
13. (b) 14. (c) 15. (b)

Very Short Answer Type Questions

20 The blood leaving the tissues becomes richer in a component. Name it.

21 When the right atrium contracts, blood flows from it to which part of the heart?

Short Answer (SA) Type Questions

22 Blood is a fluid connective tissue. Explain.

23 Platelets help in clotting of blood at injured site. Draw a flow diagram of this process.

24 Blood does not clot in the blood vessels. Give reason.

25 How is double circulation different from single circulation?

Long Answer (LA) Type Questions

26 Name a circulatory fluid in the human body other than blood. State its functions. How does it differ from blood?

27 Explain how deoxygenated blood travels from body to lung for purification. Draw well-labelled diagram in support of your answer.

28 Plants absorb water from the soil. How does this water reach to the top of the tree? Explain in detail.

29 (i) How does food prepared by leaves is utilised by roots? Explain.
(ii) Water is absorbed by roots and lost through leaves. How does this happen?

Challengers*

1. The diagram represents a part of human circulatory system. Where is the blood pressure highest?

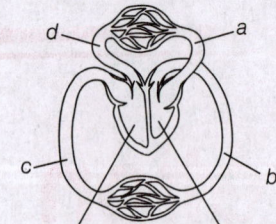

2. The diagram shows a vertical section through the heart.

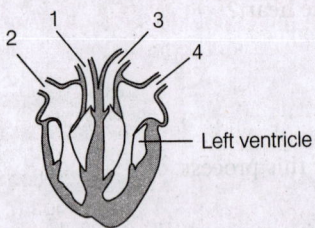

   What are the functions of the numbered blood vessels?

	Carries blood to body	Carries blood to lungs	Carries blood from lungs	Carries blood from body
(a)	1	2	3	4
(b)	1	3	4	2
(c)	2	4	3	1
(d)	3	1	4	2

3. What is the correct route for blood flow in a human?
   (a) Left atrium → Left ventricle → Lungs → Right ventricle → Right atrium
   (b) Left atrium → Left ventricle → Right ventricle → Right atrium → Lungs
   (c) Right atrium → Right ventricle → Left ventricle → Left atrium → Lungs
   (d) Right atrium → Right ventricle → Lungs → Left atrium → Left ventricle

4. What may happen if a young plant is dug up and re-planted in another place?
   (a) The leaves lose less water
   (b) The roots cannot take up mineral salts
   (c) The stem cannot transport water
   (d) The surface area of the root is reduced

5. Which of the following is not a purpose of transpiration?
   (a) Supplies water for photosynthesis
   (b) Helps in translocation of sugar in plants
   (c) Cools leaf surface
   (d) Transports minerals from the soil to all the parts of the plant

6. The table shows the characteristics of blood in one blood vessel of the body.

Oxygen concentration	Carbon dioxide concentration	Pressure
High	Low	High

   Which blood vessel contains blood with these characteristics?
   (a) Aorta   (b) Pulmonary artery
   (c) Pulmonary vein (d) Vena cava

7. What are the functions of the Xylem?

	Carrying sugars	Carrying water	Carrying mineral ions	Giving support
(a)	✓	✗	✗	✓
(b)	✓	✓	✗	✗
(c)	✗	✓	✓	✗
(d)	✗	✓	✓	✓

   Key
   ✓ = a function of xylem, ✗ = not a function of xylem.

8. The diagram shows parts of a flowering plant. Where does the most transpiration take place?

   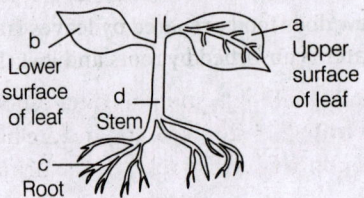

9. Which chambers of human heart contain oxygenated blood?
   (a) Left atrium and left ventricle
   (b) Left atrium and right ventricle
   (c) Right atrium and left ventricle
   (d) Right atrium and right ventricle

Answer Key

1.	(b)	2.	(d)	3.	(d)	4.	(d)	5.	(b)
6.	(a)	7.	(d)	8.	(b)	9.	(a)		

*These questions may or may not be asked in the examination, have been given just for additional practice.

CHAPTER 05 d

Life Processes : Excretion

Excretion is the biological process by which an organism removes harmful metabolic wastes (nitrogenous materials) from the body. The mode of excretion is completely different in unicellular (single-celled) and multicellular (many celled) organisms, which is discussed below

- **Unicellular Organisms** Waste products produced by cellular metabolism are diffused into the surrounding water through the body surface, e.g. *Amoeba* and *Paramecium*.
- **Multicellular Organisms** Specialised organs perform the function of excretion, e.g. flame cells (*Planaria*), nephridia (earthworm), uric acid (birds), kidneys (birds and humans), etc. Ammonia is water soluble waste product excreted by aquatic animals.

Chapter Checklist

- Excretion in Human Beings
- Kidney : Structure and Function
- Artificial Kidney (Haemodialysis)
- Excretion in Plants

Excretion in Human Beings

The main function of human excretory system is to remove nitrogenous wastes such as urea from the body. It includes a pair of kidneys, a pair of ureters, a urinary bladder and a urethra. Kidneys are located in the abdomen, one on either side of the backbone.

The purpose of making urine is to filter out waste products from the blood. These wastes are removed from blood by kidneys and are passed down to the urinary bladder by a pair of ureters. The urethra further releases the urine out of the body.

The diagrammatic representation of the human excretory system is as follows

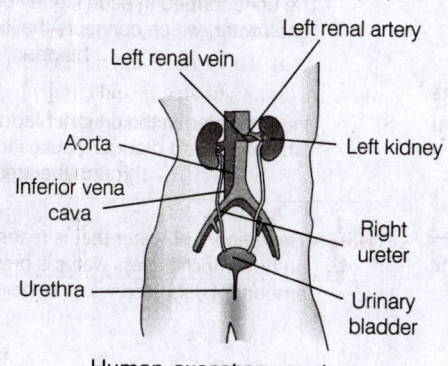

Human excretory system

Note Egestion and excretion are two different processes which occur in the body. Egestion is the discharge of undigested matter from the digestive tract *via* anus in the form of faeces, while excretion is the removal of nitrogenous waste products from the body.

Kidney : Structure and Function

The main organ of human excretory system is kidney. It is reddish-brown and bean-shaped structure, located towards the back of abdominal cavity, one on each side of the backbone. The left kidney is placed a little higher than the right kidney to adjust in the abdominal cavity. This asymmetry is caused due to the positioning of liver.

The internal structure of kidney is diagrammatically shown below

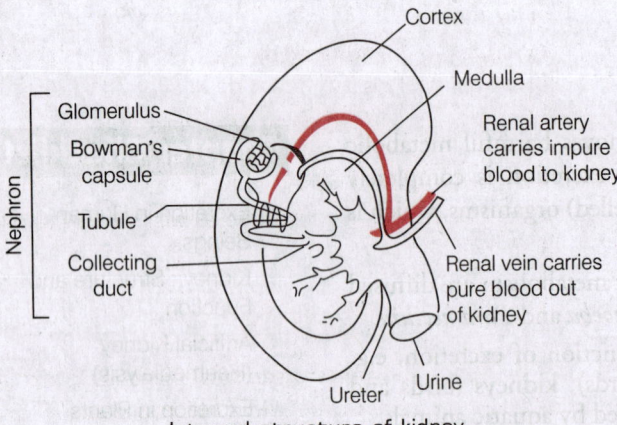

Internal structure of kidney

The major functions performed by kidneys are as follows
 (*i*) Removing excess of water from the body (osmoregulation) and nitrogenous wastes (urea and uric acid) from blood in the form of urine. Urea is the product of nitrogen metabolism occurring in the liver.
 (*ii*) Maintaining the constant concentration of blood plasma.
 (*iii*) Regulating the pH of blood.
 (*iv*) Homeostasis.

Structure of Nephron

Each kidney contains large number of tiny filtration units called **nephrons**. These are the structural and functional units of kidney.

The nephron has a cup-like capsule called **Bowman's capsule** at its upper end and the lower end is tube-like structure called **tubule**. Thus, the Bowman's capsule and the tubule taken together constitute a **nephron**.

Blood at high pressure flows into these tubules by blood capillaries called **glomerulus**, which are surrounded by Bowman's capsule. The structure of a nephron is diagrammatically shown below

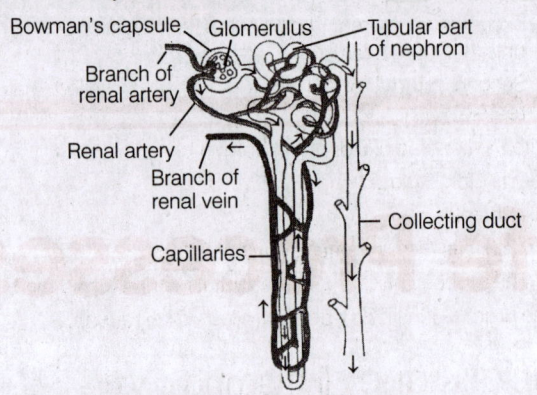

Structure of a nephron

This cup-shaped structure is followed by long tubular structure, which is convoluted and twisted. It finally leads to the collecting duct that collect the filtered urine. On an average, 1-2L of urine is produced by human body in 24 hours.

Formation and Removal of Urine

It takes place by the following processes

Ultrafiltration occurs in glomerulus under high pressure forcing many of the substances dissolved in blood into the Bowman's capsule.

↓

The blood then passes through the tubular part of nephron where useful substances such as glucose, amino acids, salts and major amount of water are **selectively reabsorbed.**

↓

Same nitrogenous waste products like creatinine and K^+ are removed from the blood by the tubule and are then added to the urine (tubular secretion).

↓

The urine formed in each kidney enters a long tube called the **ureter**, which connects the kidneys with the urinary bladder.

↓

Urine is stored in the urinary bladder until the pressure of the expanded bladder causes the urge to pass it out through the urethra.

Note The amount of water that is reabsorbed in the body depends on how much excess water is present in the body and the amount of dissolved waste to be excreted.

Check Point 01

1. How do unicellular organisms perform excretion?
2. State True or False for the following statements:
   (i) Excretion is different in multicellular organisms compared to unicellular organisms.
   (ii) Second stage of urine formation is called selective reabsorption.
3. Write the location of kidneys in human body.
4. What is glomerulus?
5. Fill in the blanks:
   (i) .... is the fundamental unit of kidney.
   (ii) The process of .... is essential in urine formation.
6. 'The urge to urinate can be controlled'. Give reason.

Artificial Kidney (Haemodialysis)

Our kidneys act as the vital organs for survival. Several factors such as infections, injury or restricted blood flow to kidneys reduce the normal activities of kidneys. This leads to accumulation of poisonous wastes in the body that can even lead to death. Kidney failures can be managed by **artificial kidney**. Artificial kidney is a device used to remove nitrogenous waste products from the blood through dialysis.

Artificial kidney contains a number of tubes with a semipermeable lining suspended in a tank filled with a dialysing fluid. This fluid has the same osmotic pressure as that of blood except that it is devoid of nitrogenous wastes such as urea.

During the procedure of dialysis, patient's blood is passed through these tubes. As the blood passes, the waste products from the blood move into dialysing fluid by diffusion and the purified blood is pumped back into the patient's body. The dialysis unit allows the blood to run along one side of a cellophane membrane and dialysis fluid in opposite direction. This is generally done to maintain the concentration gradient between the patient's blood and the dialysis fluid. The schematic representation of the process of dialysis is as follows

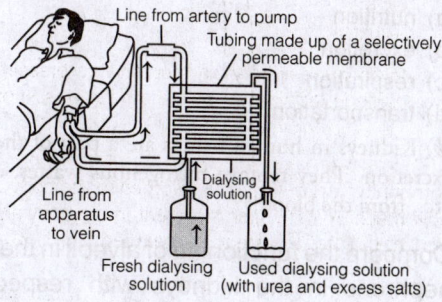

Process of dialysis

Difference between Artificial Kidney and Natural Kidney

Artificial kidney is different from natural kidney as the process of reabsorption does not occur in artificial kidney. Normally, in a healthy adult, the initial filtrate in the kidneys is about 180 L daily. However, the volume actually excreted is only 1-1.8 L a day. This happens because the remaining filtrate is reabsorbed in the tubules of the kidney.

Note In organ transplantation, the organ is surgically removed from one person (organ donor) and transplanted to another person (the recipient). Common transplantations include corneas, Kidneys, heart, liver, pancreas, etc.

Check Point 02

1. Fill in the blank:
   Kidney failures can be managed by ....
2. Explain the term dialysis.
3. State True or False for the following statements:
   Artificial kidney is different from natural kidney as ultrafiltration does not occur in artificial kidney.
4. In the artificial kidneys, the tubes are all with semipermeable lining. Why?

Excretion in Plants

Like human beings and other organisms, plants also excrete various waste products during their life processes. These waste products are excreted by plants in completely different forms than those of animals as follows

1. Gaseous Waste Products

Plants release gaseous wastes such as carbon dioxide and water vapour produced during respiration at night and oxygen produced during photosynthesis in daytime through **stomata** in leaves and **lenticels** found in stems.

2. Liquid Waste Products

Plants get rid of excess water produced as a waste during respiration by the process of transpiration. Some species of plants exude water through stomata, while others through hydathodes.

Plants also store waste substances in old xylem as resins and gums. Gums are the degradation products of internal plant tissues (mostly cellulose), while resins are formed as the oxidation products of various essential oils.

Rubber plant is the common example of a plant which exudes latex (used in tyre industry) as an excretory product. Plants also excrete some essential oils like sandalwood oil, clove oil, etc., as excretory products.

3. Solid Waste Products

Some plants store waste substances in the cellular vacuoles and in tissues with dead cells, e.g. in heartwood.

Waste products may also be stored within leaves, barks, etc., which fall off or get rid of by plants, e.g. deciduous plants. Plants excrete some solid waste substances into the soil around them.

Useful Plant Wastes

- Plants like oak store their excretory products as **tannin** in their trunk, which is used in treatment of leather.
- **Essential oils** excreted by plants such as sandalwood oil, olive oil, etc., are widely used in various household purposes.
- **Gums** from plants are widely used to make adhesives.
- **Resins** are used to make varnishes, glazing agents, etc.
- **Natural rubber** is used as raw material in tyre industry.

Check Point 03

1. Fill in the blanks:
   (i) .... are two gaseous waste products secreted by plants.
   (ii) Excess of water is removed by the plants by ....
   (iii) The useful plant waste used to make tyres is ....
2. Some plants excrete wastes through stomata, others through hydathodes. Name the processes occurring in them.
3. State True or False for the following statements:
   Latex is used in treatment of leather.
4. In what forms, apart from water, do plants excrete out liquid waste?

NCERT FOLDER

Intext Questions

1 Describe the structure and functioning of nephron.
Pg 112

Sol. **Structure of nephron** Nephron is the basic filtering unit found in kidney. It is a long coiled tubule whose one end is connected to the double walled cup-shaped structure called Bowman's capsule and the other end to a urine collecting duct. Bowman's capsule contains a bundle of blood capillaries, known as glomerulus that is followed by the tubular part of nephron, which forms loops at some places. For figure refer to "Structure of a nephron" on Pg. 188.

Functioning of nephron
(i) Glomerulus filters the blood passing through it.
(ii) It also ensures to remove only harmful substances from the body that includes nitrogenous materials.
(iii) The useful substances like glucose, amino acids, salts and a major amount of water are selectively reabsorbed by the tubular part of nephron.
(iv) Some substances like K^+ are actively secreted into the urine through the tubule.
(v) The collecting duct collects the urine and passes it to the ureter.

2 What are the methods used by plants to get rid of excretory products? **Pg 112**

Sol. Some of the methods employed by plants to get rid of excretory products are as follows
(i) Gaseous wastes (i.e. carbon dioxide and oxygen) are removed through stomata in leaves and lenticels in stems into the atmosphere.
(ii) Plants get rid of excess water by transpiration.
(iii) Some waste products are stored as resins and gums.
(iv) Plants also excrete some waste substances into the soil around them.
(v) Waste products may be stored in leaves, bark or any other plant part, which fall off .

3 How is the amount of urine produced regulated?
Pg 112

Sol. The amount of urine produced is regulated by the selective reabsorption in the tubule of nephron as urine flows along the tube. The amount of water reabsorbed (or urine formed) depends on how much excess of water is there in the body and on how much of dissolved wastes is there which is to be excreted.

Exercises (On Page 113)

1 The kidneys in human beings are a part of the system for
(a) nutrition
(b) excretion
(c) respiration
(d) transportation

Sol. (b) Kidneys in human beings are a part of the system for excretion. They remove nitrogenous wastes, excess water etc., from the blood.

2 Compare the functioning of alveoli in the lungs and nephrons in the kidneys with respect to their structure and functioning.

Sol. The functioning of alveoli in the lungs and nephrons in the kidneys is compared below

Alveoli in the Lungs	Nephrons in the Kidneys
These are balloon-like structures found within the lungs.	These are long, coiled tubule-like structures present within the kidneys.
The thin-walled alveoli contain an extensive network of blood vessels.	Nephrons contain a bundle of blood capillaries called glomerulus. The tubular part of nephron also contains blood vessels for reabsorption of useful substances.
Alveoli provide a large surface area, where exchange of gases can take place.	Nephrons help in filtering waste from blood, so that only harmful products are eliminated.
The phenomenon of diffusion is employed in exchange of gases in alveoli.	Nephrons apply selective reabsorption of useful substances into the blood capillaries.
A large number of alveoli are present in lungs.	Nephrons are very small in size, but are large in number in each kidney.

SUMMARY

- **Excretion** is a biological process by which an organism removes harmful metabolic wastes from the body.
- In **unicellular organisms**, wastes are excreted *via* diffusion through cell surface, while **multicellular organisms** have developed specialised organs for the function of excretion.
- **Human excretory system** includes a pair of kidneys, ureters, a urinary bladder and a urethra. It removes nitrogenous waste products from the body.
- **Kidneys** are primary organs of the excretory system. These are bean-shaped, located towards the back of the abdominal cavity.
- **Nephrons** are the structural and functional unit of kidneys.
- **Ureter** are paired, thin, muscular tubes coming from each kidney which carry urine to urinary bladder.
- **Urinary bladder** is a muscular, pear-shaped bag where urine is temporarily stored.
- **Urethra** is a duct which transmits the urine stored in the bladder to the exterior of the body.
- **Formation of urine** occurs to filter out waste products from the blood. It involves three stages, i.e. ultrafiltration in glomerulus, selective reabsorption of useful substances like glucose, amino acids, etc., in tubular part and tubular secretion, i.e. active secretion of ions, metabolites, etc., from blood into urine.
- **Urine** is the end product of filtration process containing urea, uric acid, ammonium salts and urochrome pigment (imparts yellow colour to urine).
- **Removal of urine** Urine remains stored in the bladder until the pressure expands too much and control the urge to urinate.
- **Kidney disorders** occur when one or both kidneys stop functioning or malfunctions.
- **Haemodialysis** is the process used in case of kidney failures. It acts as an artificial kidney and removes nitrogenous waste products from the body.
- **Excretion in plants** occurs to remove the wastes produced by them.
- **Gaseous waste products** are carbon dioxide during respiration and oxygen during photosynthesis. These are excreted out through stomata and lenticels.
- **Liquid waste products** are excess water, gums, i.e. degradation product of internal tissues, resins, etc. These are excreted *via* stomata or hydathodes (guttation).
- **Solid waste products** are stored waste substances in cell vacuoles and tissues with dead cells. Plants get rid of them by dropping their leaves.
- Some plant wastes are useful products for human beings, e.g. essential oils, gums (used to make adhesives), resins, natural rubber (tyre industry) and tannin (for leather treatment), etc.

Exam Practice

Objective Type Questions

Multiple Choice Questions

1. Flame cells are the excretory structures in
   (a) arthropods
   (b) platyhelminths
   (c) annelids
   (d) crustaceans

   Sol. (b) Flame cells are the excretory structures of organisms belonging to phylum Platyhelminthes.

2. Main excretory organ of humans is
   (a) kidney   (b) lungs
   (c) skin   (d) liver

   Sol. (a) Kidney is the main excretory organ of human beings, while lungs, skin and liver act as accessory excretory organs.

3. In the given diagram, A, B, C and D respectively are **CBSE 2021 (Term-I)**

   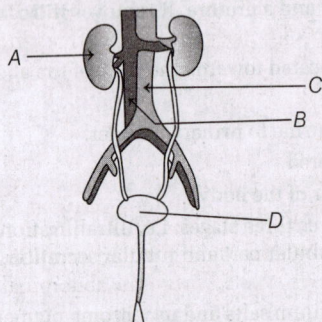

   (a) A - Left kidney; B - Aorta; C - Vena cava; D - Urethra
   (b) A - Left kidney; B - Vena cava; C - Aorta; D - Urinary bladder
   (c) A - Right kidney; B - Aorta; C - Ureter; D - Urethra
   (d) A - Right kidney; B - Vena cava: C - Aorta; D - Urinary bladder

   Sol. (d) A- Right kidney is smaller in size and is located slightly lower than the left kidney
   B- Vena cava carries blood directly to the heart
   C- Aorta supplies blood to the kidneys for filtration
   D-Urinary bladder stores urine temporarily

4. Structural and functional unit of kidney is
   (a) renal pelvis   (b) nephridia
   (c) nephron   (d) hilum

   Sol. (c) Nephron is the structural and functional unit of kidney.

5. An adult human on an average produces
   (a) 1-2 L of urine per day
   (b) 1-5 L of urine per day
   (c) 2-5 L of urine per day
   (d) 4-5 L of urine per day **NCERT Exemplar**

   Sol. (a) An adult human on an average produces 1-2 L of urine in 24 hours. This volume depends of intake of fluids, physical activities, etc.

6. Choose the correct path of urine in our body.
   (a) Kidney → Ureter → Urethra → Urinary bladder
   (b) Kidney → Urinary bladder → Urethra → Ureter
   (c) Kidney → Ureter → Urinary bladder → Urethra
   (d) Urinary bladder → Kidney → Ureter → Urethra **NCERT Exemplar**

   Sol. (c) The correct path of urine in our body is Kidney → Ureter → Urinary bladder → Urethra.

7. Choose the incorrect pair.
   (a) Ultrafiltration – Glomerulus
   (b) Concentration of urine – Collecting duct
   (c) Transport of urine – Ureter
   (d) Storage of urine – Urinary bladder

   Sol. (b) The pair in option (b) is incorrect as concentration of urine takes place in Henle's loop and not in collecting duct.
   Rest of the pairs are correct.

8. In a person, the tubule part of the nephron is not functioning at all. What will be its effect on urine formation?
   CBSE SQP (Term-I)
   (a) The urine will not be formed
   (b) Quality and quantity of urine is unaffected
   (c) Urine is more concentrated
   (d) Urine is more diluted

   Sol. (d) Tubule part of the nephron is associated with the reabsorption.
   If this part of the nephron shows improper functioning, water will not be reabsorbed and thus, the urine formed will be dilute.

Life Processes : Excretion

9. Dialysing unit (artificial kidney) contains a fluid which is almost same as plasma except that it has
(a) high glucose
(b) high urea
(c) no urea
(d) high uric acid

Sol. (c) The dialysing fluid has the same composition as that of blood plasma except that it is devoid of nitrogenous waste such as urea.

10. The major gaseous excretory product of plants is
(a) carbon dioxide
(b) oxygen
(c) alkaloids
(d) gums

Sol. (b) The only major gaseous excretory product of plants is oxygen. Other excretory products of plants include resins, gums, alkaloids, etc.

11. Plants use completely different process for excretion as compared to animals. Which one of the following processes is not followed by plants for excretion?
CBSE SQP (Term-I)
(a) They can get rid of excess water by transpiration
(b) They selectively filter toxic substances through their leaves
(c) Waste products are stored as resins and gums in old xylem
(d) They excrete waste substances into the soil around them

Sol. (b) Plants use completely different process for excretion as compared to animals. They have different mechanisms like transpiration (for excess water), storage (waste products) or direct excretion into soil. However, plants cannot selectively filter toxic substances through their leaves.

12. Example(s) of liquid waste product in plants is/are
(a) rubber
(b) clove oil
(c) gum
(d) All of these

Sol. (d) Examples of liquid waste products in plants are rubber, clove oil and gum.

13. Which of the following is used in manufacturing of varnishes, glazing agents, etc?
(a) Tannin
(b) Resins
(c) Essential oil
(d) Rubber

Sol. (b) Resins are used in manufacturing of varnishes, glazing agents, etc.

Fill in the Blanks

14. The unit of kidney is called ....
Sol. nephron

15. The bunch of blood capillary in nephron is called ....
Sol. glomerulus

16. The duct that emerges from kidney is called ....
Sol. ureter

17. .... is the reabsorption of water to maintain the balance of water in human body.
Sol. Osmoregulation

18. The dialyser works as kidney except does not perform ....
Sol. selective reabsorption

True and False

19. Kidney produces RBCs.
Sol. False, kidney filters the blood and produces urine.

20. The main function of human excretory system is to remove nitrogenous wastes from the body.
Sol. True

21. The right kidney is placed a little higher than the left kidney to adjust in the abdominal cavity.
Sol. False; the left kidney is placed a little higher than the right kidney to adjust in the abdominal cavity.

22. Artificial kidney is used to remove glucose from the blood through dialysis.
Sol. False: artificial kidney is used to remove nitrogenous waste products from the blood through dialysis.

23. The patients are advised kidney transplantation when kidney failure cannot be treated by dialysis.
Sol. True.

Match the Columns

24. Match the following columns.

Column I		Column II
1. Nephridia	A.	Glomerulus
2. Bowman's capsule	B.	Kidney
3. Osmoregulation	C.	Dialysis
4. Kidney failure	D.	Pale yellow
5. Urine	E.	Earthworm

Sol. 1. → E, 2. → A, 3. → B, 4. → C, 5. → D.

25 Match the following columns.

	Column I		Column II
1.	Initial filtrate	A.	Respiration
2.	Carbon dioxide	B.	180 L
3.	Urine	C.	Tannin
4.	Latex	D.	Rubber
5.	Oak	E.	1-2 L per day

Sol. 1. → B, 2. → A, 3. → E, 4. → D, 5. → C.

Assertion–Reason

Direction (Q. Nos. 26-30) *In each of the following questions, a statement of Assertion is given by the corresponding statement of Reason. Of the statements, mark the correct answer as*

(a) If both Assertion and Reason are true and Reason is the correct explanation of Assertion

(b) If both Assertion and Reason are true, but Reason is not the correct explanation of Assertion

(c) If Assertion is true, but Reason is false

(d) If Assertion is false, but Reason is true

26 Assertion Excretion is the biological process by which harmful wastes are removed from an organism's body.

Reason The mode of excretion is completely same in both unicellular and multicellular organisms.

Sol. (c) Excretion is the biological process by which harmful metabolic wastes are removed from an organism's body. The mode of excretion is completely different in unicellular and multicellular organisms. In unicellular organisms, waste products are diffused into surrounding water through body surface. While, in multicellular organisms, specialised organs perform the function of excretion.
Thus, Assertion is true, but Reason is false.

27 Assertion Egestion is the removal of nitrogenous waste products from the body.

Reason In human beings, the excretory products in the form of soluble nitrogen compounds are removed by the nephrons in the kidneys.

Sol. (d) Egestion is the discharge of undigested matter from the digestive tract *via* anus, while excretion is the removal of nitrogenous waste products from the body. In human beings, the excretory products in the form of soluble nitrogen compounds are removed by the nephrons in the kidneys.
Assertion is false, but Reason is true.

28 Assertion The main organ of human excretory system is kidney.

Reason Kidneys perform the function of removing excess water and nitrogenous wastes from the body.

Sol. (a) The main organ of human excretory system is kidney. The major function performed by kidneys is to remove excess water and nitrogenous wastes from blood in the form of urine. Thus, both Assertion and Reason are true and Reason is the correct explanation of Assertion.

29 Assertion Artificial kidney is a device used to remove nitrogenous waste products from the blood through dialysis.

Reason Reabsorption does not occur in artificial kidney.

Sol. (b) Kidney failure can be managed by artificial kidney. It is a device used to remove nitrogenous waste products from the blood through dialysis.
Artificial kidney is different from natural kidney as the process of reabsorption does not occur in artificial kidney.
Both Assertion and Reason are true, but Reason is not the correct explanation of Assertion.

30 Assertion Plants excrete various waste products during their life processes.

Reason They produce urea just like humans.

Sol. (c) Like human beings and other organisms, plants also excrete various waste products during their life processes. The waste prodcuts include gums, CO_2, O_2, resins, rubber, etc.
Plants do not produce urea.
Thus, Assertion is true, but Reason is false.

Case Based Questions

Direction (Q. Nos. 31- 34) *Answer the questions on the basis of your understanding of the following table and related studied concepts:*

Substances	Organ(s) of Excretion
Carbon dioxide	Lungs, skin
Water	Lungs, kidneys, skin
Bile pigments	Gut
Urea	Kidneys, skin
Ions (K^+, H^+)	Kidneys, skin
Hormones	Kidneys, skin
Poisons	Kidneys, skin
Drugs	Kidneys

31 Refer to the table showing substances and their respective organs of excretion.
Explain the role of the liver in excretion, even though it is not an excretory organ itself.

Sol. Liver produces urea from ammonia in the urea cycle. The breakdown of haemoglobin in the liver produces the bile pigments, e.g. bilirubin.

32 Based on your understanding, state the main organ of excretion in mammals.

Sol. In mammals, the kidney is the main organ of excretion, although the skin, gut and lungs also play important roles.

33 Which of the following does not come under excretion in mammals?
(a) Removal of faeces (b) Removal of drugs
(c) Removal of urea   (d) Removal of CO_2

Sol. Removal of faeces does not come under excretion in mammals. It comes under egestion.

34 Which of the normal constituent of urine?
(a) RBCs   (b) Urea
(c) Salts   (d) Drugs

Sol. RBCs are not normally found in the urine. In case, kidneys do not perform the ultrafiltration then RBCs, proteins, etc., can be found in urine.

Direction (Q. Nos. 35-38) *Answer the questions on the basis of your understanding of the following passage and related studied concepts:*

A dialysis machine is a machine designed to remove wastes from the blood. It is used when the kidney fail, or when blood acidity, urea, or potassium levels increase much above normal. In kidney dialysis, blood flows through a system of tubes composed of partially permeable membranes.

Dialysis fluid (dialysate) has a composition similar to blood except that the concentration of wastes is low. It flows in the opposite direction to the blood on the outside of the dialysis tubes. Consequently, waste products like urea diffuses from the blood into the dialysis fluid, which is constantly replace. The dialysis fluid flows at a rate of several 100 cm^3 per minute over a large surface area. For some people dialysis is an ongoing procedure, but for others dialysis just allows the kidneys to rest and recover.

35 In kidney dialysis, explain why the dialysing solution is constantly replaced rather than being recirculated?

Sol. The dialysing solution is constantly replaced because it already contained the waste products of metabolism. It is not recirculated because the kidneys do not have the capability to filter the dialysate.

36 Give a reason why the dialysing solution flows in the opposite direction to the blood.

Sol. The dialysing solution flows in the opposite direction to the blood to maintain the concentration gradient between the patient's blood and the dialysis fluid.

37 What is the best long term solution for kidney failure?

Sol. The best long term solution for kidney failure is the kidney transplant.

38 How is artificial kidney different from natural kidney?

Sol. Artificial kidney is different from natural kidney as the process of reabsorption does not occur in artificial kidney.

Very Short Answer Type Questions

39 Name the process used by single-celled organisms for taking in food, exchange of gases or removal of wastes. **CBSE 2016**

Sol. Diffusion from the body surface into surrounding is used by single-celled organisms for all vital life processes, e.g. nutrition, respiration, excretion, etc.

40 Which nitrogenous waste product is most soluble in water?

Sol. Ammonia is the most soluble nitrogenous waste in water.

41 The left kidney is placed a little higher than the right kidney. Give suitable reason for this statement.

Sol. Left kidney is positioned a little higher than right kidney due to the presence of liver just above it.

42 What causes the liquid part of blood to filter out from glomerulus into the renal tubule?

Sol. The high pressure of the blood causes the liquid part of blood to filter out from glomerulus into the renal tubule.

43 The volume of glomerular filtrate produced is 180 L, but the volume of urine excreted is just 1-2 L. Give suitable reason for this statement.

Sol. Only 1.5-2 L of fluid filtered by kidneys is excreted as urine. The remaining 168.5 L of fluid is reabsorbed into the blood by the renal tubules.

44 Name the substance which is present at a higher concentration in renal artery than in renal vein.

Sol. Urea is present at higher concentration in renal artery than in renal vein.

45 Why is it said that kidneys help in the process of osmoregulation? Explain.

Sol. Osmoregulation is the phenomenon of maintenance of optimum concentration of water and salts in the body fluids. Since, the reabsorption of water from filtrate occurs in the kidney tubule and maintains the water balance and thus, helps in osmoregulation.

46 In artificial kidney, which substance passes from the blood to the dialysis fluid?

Sol. Urea passes from blood to the dialysis fluid in artificial kidney.

47 What is the key step in the process of organ transplantation?

Sol. In organ transplantation, the organ is surgically removed from one person (organ donor) and transplanted to another person (the recipient).

48 Name two excretory products in plants other than oxygen and carbon dioxide.

Sol. The two excretory products in plants other than oxygen and carbon dioxide are resins and gums.

Short Answer (SA) Type Questions

1 Define excretion. Write two vital functions of kidney. **CBSE 2016**

Sol. The biological proces by which an organism removes harmful metabolic wastes from the body is called excretion.

The two vital functions of kidney are as follows
(i) Removing excess water from the body, i.e. helps in osmoregulation and homeostasis.
(ii) Removing nitrogenous wastes (urea and uric acid) from blood in the form of urine.

2 Name the filtering unit of kidney and why is it called so?

Sol. Nephron is the filtering unit of kidney. It is so called because it filters the blood and removes nitrogenous wastes from it.

The harmful products get filtered and useful products are reabsorbed by the tubular part of nephron.

3 Differentiate between:
(i) Excretion and Egestion
(ii) Urea and Urine

Sol. (i) Differences between excretion and egestion are as follows

Excretion	Egestion
It is the removal of metabolic wastes from the body.	It is the removal of undigested food material from the body.
It is associated with kidneys.	It is associated with alimentary canal.

(ii) Differences between urea and urine are as follows

Urea	Urine
It is a chemical compound.	It is a mixture of metabolic wastes.
It is formed in liver.	It is formed in kidneys.

4 In what way is kidney a homeostatic organ?

Sol. Homeostasis means maintenance of constant internal environment of an organism. Kidney helps to maintain a steady internal environment by excreting waste products and reabsorbing useful components like water ans salts of sodium and potassium and also maintaining the water contents of blood.

5 Draw a diagram of human excretory system and label the following
(i) Urinary bladder
(ii) Left kidney
(iii) Left ureter **CBSE (All India) 2019**

Sol. Refer to fig. 'Human excretory system' on pg. no. 195.

6 (i) Write the important functions of the structural and functional unit of kidney.
(ii) Write any one function of an artificial kidney.

Sol. (i) Nephron is the structural and functional unit of kidney.
It has following functions
(a) Filtration
(b) Selective reabsorption
(c) Secretion

All in One Life Processes : Excretion

(a) Helps to remove harmful wastes, extra salts and water.
(b) Maintains the balance of ions in a patient whose kidneys fail to function properly.

7 Explain where and how urine is produced?
CBSE SQP 2020-21

Sol. Our body produces waste chemical compounds like urea and uric acid. These waste compounds are filtered out from blood in the kidney. So, kidney is filtration unit for blood. Nephrons are the basic structures present in the kidney that helps in the filtration of blood. It has two parts Bowman's capsule and Renal tubule. Bowman's capsule is a cup-shaped and consists of the coiled tube have blood capillary and glomerulus, helps in filtering out of blood. The filtrate goes to the renal tubule, glucose, amino acids, salts get absorbed selectively along with major amount of water in the capillaries surrounding the renal tubule, as it passes through it.

The rest of the liquid moves through the collecting duct towards the urinary bladdar to get stored, before micturition.

8 Observe the following table carefully and match the components of part I with part II of the table. Write them in complete sentences.

Part I	Part II
Unicellular organism	Transpiration
Human beings	Diffusion
Plants	Urination

Sol. (i) **Unicellular organisms** excrete out wastes accumulated in body through the process of **diffusion**.
(ii) **Human beings** excrete out nitrogenous wastes generated by various metabolic activities through the process of **urination**.
(iii) **Plants** remove excess water through the process of **transpiration**.

9 What is the role of following in excretion by various organisms?
(i) Leaves (ii) Glomerulus (iii) Ureter

Sol. (i) **Leaves** Plants can accumulate some of their wastes in leaves. These leaves fall off and the plant gets rid of the waste.
(ii) **Glomerulus** in nephrons filters the blood passing through it.
(iii) **Ureter** Transports urine from kidney to urinary bladder.

Long Answer (LA) Type Questions

1 (i) Define excretion.
(ii) Name the basic filtration unit present in the kidney.
(iii) Draw excretory system in human beings and label the following organs of excretory system which perform following functions
(a) Form urine.
(b) Is a long tube which collects urine from kidney.
(c) Stores urine until it is passed out.
CBSE 2018

Sol. (i) Excretion is the biological process by which an organism removes harmful metabolic wastes from the body.
(ii) Nephron is the basic filtration unit present in the kidney.
(iii) The diagram of excretory system in human beings with the respective parts is as follows

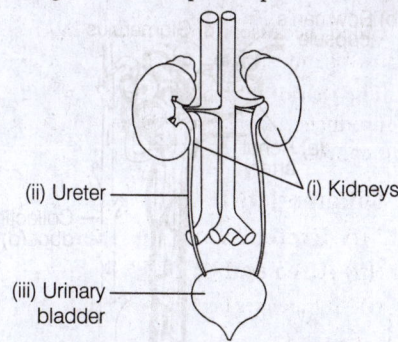

(a) **Kidney** – forms urine.
(b) **Ureter** – is a long tube which collects urine from kidney.
(c) **Urinary bladder** – stores urine until it is passed out.

2 Explain the location, structure and functions of kidney in human beings. Also draw an appropriate diagram supporting your answer.

Sol. **Location** Human beings have a pair of kidneys found in the abdomen, one on either side of the backbone.

Structure Each kidney is bean-shaped and reddish-brown coloured organ. The renal artery brings the impure blood containing waste substances into the kidneys, while renal vein carries away the pure blood from the kidneys. They contain nephron as their structural and functional unit in large number.

For figure refer to Pg. 196.

The main functions of kidney are as follows

(i) Nephrons remove harmful substances such as urea and other salts along with excess of water from the blood and form urine.

(ii) It helps to regulate the osmotic pressure/water balance of the blood.

(iii) It also regulates the optimum pH of the blood.

3 (i) Draw the structure of a nephron and label the following parts on it.

(a) Renal artery (b) Bowman's capsule
(c) Glomerulus (d) Collecting duct

(ii) Name four substances in the initial filtrate which are selectively reabsorbed as the filtrate floor along the tubule.

Sol. (i) The structure of a nephron with the labelled parts is as follows

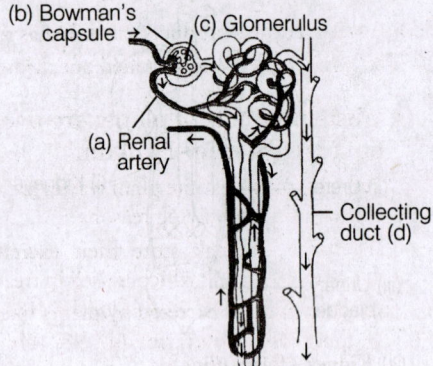

Structure of a nephron

(ii) Glucose, amino acids, salts and major amount of water are useful substances. When blood passes through the tubular part of nephron, these substances are selectively reabsorbed as the urine flows along the tubule.

4 (i) Draw a neat diagram of the human excretory system and label the following parts.

(a) Urethra (b) Kidney
(c) Ureter (d) Urinary bladder

(ii) What are nephrons? How is a nephron involved in the filtration of blood and formation of urine?

Sol. (i) For figure refer to Pg. 195.

(ii) Nephrons are the structural and functional units of kidneys. Nephron helps to filter the blood and forms urine. When the blood at high pressure flows into the tubules by glomerulus, it forces out many substances dissolved in the blood through thin capillary walls. Its tubular part reabsorbs the major amount of water and useful substances as amino acids, glucose, salts, etc. Ultimately, the excretory product called urine is formed containing urea as the major nitrogenous waste.

5 A figure given below shows a diagram of a kidney and its associated structures. The table list the percentage of certain components found within the structures A and B.

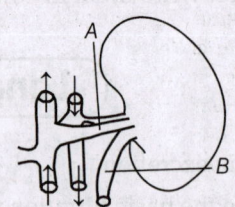

In Structure A	
Components	Concentration %
Urea	0.03
Glucose	0.10
Amino acids	0.05
Salts	0.72
Proteins	8.00
In Structure B	
Components	Concentration %
Urea	2.00
Glucose	0.00
Amino acids	0.00
Salts	1.50
Proteins	0.00

Life Processes : Excretion

(i) Using only the information given in the tables, deduce the functions of the kidney.

(ii) Explain how the proportions of components present in part *B* would change if a person is suffering from diabetes mellitus.

Sol. (i) The urea content is higher in structure *B*, whereas the concentration of useful components such as glucose is low. This shows that kidney performs the function of filtration. It filters out useful substances, e.g. glucose, amino acids into the blood, while throwing out nitrogenous waste, e.g. urea and salts.

(ii) There would be glucose in *B* as without insulin, blood glucose would not be converted to glycogen for storage. The kidney attempts to reduce the blood glucose level by excreting it in urine.

6 Describe the process of urine formation in kidneys. **NCERT Exemplar**

Sol. Urine is formed in the nephrons of kidneys. Nephron is the structural and functional unit of kidney. Blood at high pressure flows into these tubules by the tuft of blood capillaries called glomerulus contained in the Bowman's capsule.

The following steps are involved in the process of urine formation

(i) **Filtration** Blood enters the glomerulus through the afferent arterioles. It passes under high pressure that results in filtration of blood. Water and small molecules are forced out of glomerular capillary walls and Bowman's capsule. Large molecules remain in the blood of the glomerulus.

(ii) **Selective Reabsorption** Some molecules are selectively reabsorbed into the blood. The glomerular filtrate flows through the tubular parts of U-shaped Henle's loop. The useful substances such as glucose, amino acids and salts which require energy are reabsorbed by a process called selective reabsorption. Hence, the filtrate now contains urea, some salts and water. Reabsorption of solutes increases the water concentration of the filtrate. Water is then reabsorbed into blood by osmosis.

(iii) **Tubular secretion** Some nitrogenous waste products and some other substances are removed from blood by parts of Henle's loop and are passed to blood. The urine thus, formed is collected in the urinary bladder.

7 (i) Suggest some waste products obtained from metabolic processes occurring in our body and for each waste product, state an organ which removes it from the blood.

(ii) Why is the removal of faeces from the alimentary canal not considered to be excretion?

Sol. (i) The waste products of metabolism and their excretory organs are as follows

Metabolic Waste Products	Excretory Organs
Carbon dioxide and water	Lungs
Urea, other nitrogenous substances and water	Kidneys
Poisons, such as alcohol	Liver
Urea, salts and water	Skin

(ii) Excretion is the removal of metabolic or nitrogenous waste products which are formed by chemical reactions occurring in the cells. The removal of faeces (defecation) from the body is the removal of undigested or indigestible substances from the alimentary canal through the anus. Since, faecal matter is not produced by metabolism, removal of faeces cannot be considered as excretion.

8 Plants excrete waste products from their body by various means. Justify the above statement.

Sol. Plants follow different strategies to get rid of the wastes produced by various activities.

Some of the strategies involved are as follows

(i) Excess water is removed by plant through the process of transpiration.

(ii) Wastes are also accumulated in the dead cells of plants.

(iii) Some wastes are stored in leaves that fall off from plants.

(iv) Many plant waste products are stored in cellular vacuoles.

(v) Some waste products are stored as resins and gums.

(vi) CO_2 and O_2 are expelled out through stomata.

9 Waste products of plants are useful for human beings. Is it true? Explain.

Sol. Yes, it is true that some plant wastes are useful for human beings for the following reasons

(i) Plants like oak store their excretory products as tannin in trunk which is used in treatment of leather.

(ii) Essential oils excreted by plants like sandalwood oil, olive oil, *Eucalyptus* oil, etc., are widely used in household purposes.

(iii) Gums from plants are widely used to make adhesives.

(iv) Resins are used to make varnishes, glazing agents, etc.

(v) Natural rubber obtained from rubber plant is used as raw material in tyre industry.

10 (a) How do leaves of plants help in excretion? Explain briefly.

(b) Describe the structure and function of a nephron. **CBSE 2020**

Sol. (a) Like human beings and other organisms, plants also excrete various waste products during their life process.
  (i) The excretory metabolites get deposited in the leaf tissue as secondary metabolites. The plants shed off leaves and thus get rid of excretory products.
  (ii) The gaseous excretory products (CO_2 in respiration, O_2 in photosynthesis) gets diffused out of leaves through stomata by simple diffusion methods.

(b) Nephron is structural and functional unit of kidney nearly one lakh nephrons are found in kidney.

Structure of Nephron

Each kidney is made up of thousands of tiny filtration units or tubules called nephron. It is the structural and functional unit of kidney. Blood at high pressure travels into these tubules by blood capillaries called glomerulus, which are surrounded by a cup-shaped capsule called Bowman's capsule.

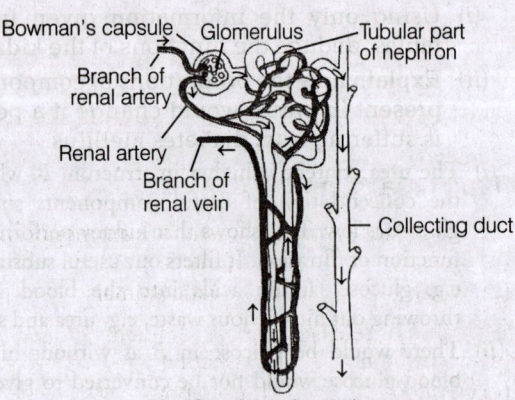

Structure of a nephron

This cup-shaped structure is followed by long tubular structure. It is convoluted, twisted and known as **Henle loop**. It finally leads to the collecting duct that collects the filtered urine. 1-2L of urine is produced by human body in 24 hours.

CHAPTER EXERCISE

Multiple Type Questions

1. Which of the following organisms are ammonotelic?
   (a) Birds (b) Humans
   (c) Reptiles (d) Aquatic animals

2. The process of release of urine is called
   (a) micturition (b) sweating
   (c) egestion (d) excretion

3. An organism which does not have loop of Henle will excrete
   (a) no urine (b) dilute urine
   (c) concentrated urine (d) no change in urine

4. Which of the following is/are the respiratory organs of the plant?
   (a) Bark (b) Hydathodes
   (c) Stomata (d) Both (a) and (c)

5. The liquid waste product of plants formed due to oxidation of various essential oils is
   (a) gums (b) latex
   (c) resins (d) tannin

Fill in the Blanks

6. The cup-like capsule in a nephron is called ....

7. The bag in which urine is collected is called ....

8. Each kidney is connected to the urinary bladder by a tube called......... .

True and False

9. The process of excretion may be divided into three stages, i.e., filtration, selective reabsorption and tubular secretion.

10. The lungs help in getting rid of urea formed as a result of cellular respiration, through exhalation.

11. Some organs such as kidney, part of a liver, lungs, etc., and the tissues can be donated, while the donor is alive.

Match the Column

12. Match the following

	Column I		Column II
1.	Kidneys	A.	Urea
2.	Renal vein	B.	No nitrogenous wastes
3.	Liver	C.	Aquatic animals
4.	Dialysing fluid	D.	Impure blood
5.	Ammonia	E.	Birds and humans

Assertion–Reason

Direction (Q. Nos. 13-15) *In each of the following questions, a statement of Assertion is given by the corresponding statement of Reason. Of the statements, mark the correct answer as*

(a) If both Assertion and Reason are true and Reason is the correct explanation of Assertion
(b) If both Assertion and Reason are true, but Reason is not the correct explanation of Assertion
(c) If Assertion is true, but Reason is false
(d) If Assertion is false, but Reason is true

13. **Assertion** Urine formed enters the ureter through the kidneys.
    Reason It is temporarily stored in the urinary bladder.

14. **Assertion** Ultrafiltration involves the filtration of blood under high pressure.
    Reason Reabsorption of major amount of water occurs in the tubular part of the nephron.

15. **Assertion** Useful plant wastes are essential oils, tannin, gums, resins, natural rubber, etc.
    Reason Rubber plant is the common example of a plant which exudes latex (used in tyre industry) as an excretory product.

Case Based Questions

Directions (Q.Nos. 16-19) *Answer the questions on the basis of your understanding of the following passage and related studied concepts:*

Compared to animals, plants do not have a well-developed excretory system to remove nitrogenous waste materials. This is because of the differences in their physiology. Therefore, plants use different strategies for excretion.

The gaseous waste materials produced during respiration (CO_2) and photosynthesis (O_2) diffuse out through stomata in the leaves and through lenticels in other parts of the plant. Many plants store organic waste products in their permanent tissues that have dead cells, e.g. in heartwood. The leaves of many plants, like *Eucalyptus*, lemon, etc., contain essential oils.

16. Based on the data given, write about transpiration in your own words.

17. How are solid waste products removed from the plants?

18. What does Heartwood in trees store?

19. Name any two useful plant wastes.

Answers

1. (d) 2. (a) 3. (b) 4. (c) 5. (c)
6. Bowman's capsule 7. Urinary bladder 8. Ureter
9. True 10. False 11. True
12. 1. → E, 2. → D, 3. → A, 4. → B, 5. → C.
13. (b) 14. (b) 15. (b)

Very Short Answer Type Questions

20. Name the excretory organs in unicellular organisms.
21. What are the major constituents of urine?
22. State the process by which chemical from blood enters the dialysing fluid.
23. Name the substance which is present in the blood, but not in the urine of a healthy person.

Short Answer (SA) Type Questions

24. Explain, how the blood system carries waste products from liver to the kidneys?
25. Explain the principle of haemodialysis.
26. How do plants get rid of their excretory products?

Long Answer (LA) Type Questions

27. What is the difference between excretion and defaecation? Explain the process of excretion in humans.
28. Outline the functioning of kidney dialysis machine.

Challengers*

1 Observe the figure given below which represents the control of water concentration in the blood.

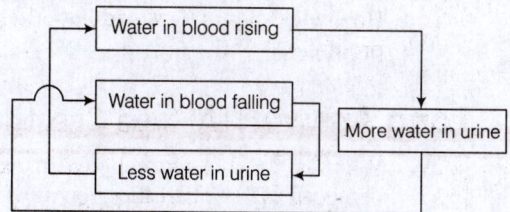

This is a negative feedback system because
(a) it decreases the amount of water in the blood
(b) it increases any change occurring in the amount of water in the blood
(c) it reverses any change occurring in the amount of water in the blood
(d) it increases the amount of water in the blood

2 The diagram given along side shows the human excretory system.

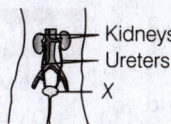

Identify the function of part labelled as X.
(a) To excrete urea   (b) To produce urea
(c) To produce urine   (d) To store urine

3 In the figure given along side, the structures associated with human kidneys are marked (X, Y and Z).
The relative concentrations of urea in these structures is
(a) X is sometimes higher than Y
(b) Y is always higher than Z
(c) Y is always lower than Z
(d) Z is sometimes lower than X

4 The diagram given below represents the liver, kidney and some associated blood vessels. Identify the vessel from the labelled parts A-D in which the blood will contain the lowest concentration of urea.
(a) A   (b) B   (c) C   (d) D

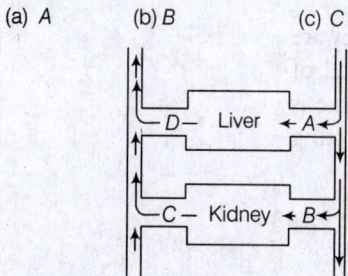

5 A healthy woman consumes a litre of water at once.
(i) How will be the internal environment of her body affected by this?
(ii) A corrective measure to bring the arising condition to normal state is.
Select the correct option for (i) and (ii) from those given below

	(i)	(ii)
(a)	Plasma becomes diluted.	Concentration of the urine formed.
(b)	Osmotic pressure of the plasma decreases.	Increase in the volume of urine formed.
(c)	The body cells undergo shrinkage.	Less water is reabsorbed by the kidneys.
(d)	Osmotic pressure of the plasma increases.	Formation of dilute urine occurs.

6 Which substances will be present in the glomerular filtrate from the kidneys of a mammal?

	Glucose	Protein	Salts
(a)	✓	✓	✗
(b)	✗	✓	✓
(c)	✓	✗	✓
(d)	✗	✗	✓

Key ✓ = present, ✗ = absent

7 Most often during a kidney disorder, the colour of urine changes from yellow to others. A patient is secreting dark coloured urine which turns to blue or black later. This is due to the presence of which of the following?
(a) Homogentisic acid   (b) Methaemoglobin
(c) Coproporphyrin   (d) Both (a) and (b)

8 Figure given below is representing the dialysis machine for removing nitrogenous wastes in patient with a kidney failure.

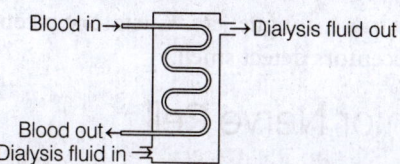

Which substances out of the following in the dialysis fluid should be at a lower concentration than in the blood of patient?
(a) Glucose and urea   (b) Glucose and amino acids
(c) Salts and urea   (d) Glucose and salts

Answer Key

1.	(c)	2.	(d)	3.	(c)	4.	(c)	5.	(b)
6.	(c)	7.	(a)	8.	(c)				

*These questions may or may not be asked in the examination, have been given just for additional practice.

CHAPTER 06

Control and Coordination

Chapter Checklist
- Nervous System
- Divisions of Nervous System
- Coordination in Plants
- Chemical Communication

The working together of various organs of a living organism in a systematic, controlled and efficient way to produce proper response to various stimuli is known as **coordination**.

All living organisms have a well-organised system, which provides them with control and coordination. Due to the general principles of body organisation, multicellular organisms have specialised tissues, which provide control and coordination.

Animals have **nervous system** and **hormones** to control and coordinate their body activities. Plants lack the nervous system, but coordinate *via* the hormones.

Nervous System

In animals including humans, the nervous system along with muscular tissue is the control centre of the body. It consists of highly specialised cells called **neurons**, **nerves** and **neural organs** that link, coordinate and control the activities of different organs in the body. Information from environment is detected through receptors, present in sense organs such as inner ear, nose, tongue, etc. **Gustatory receptors** are meant to detect **taste**, while the **olfactory receptors** detect **smell**.

Neuron or Nerve Cell

The information from environment is detected by the nerve cells called **neurons**. They are structural and functional unit of the nervous system. A neuron is the longest cell of human body (the length of some nerve cells may be 90-100 cm). The nervous tissue is made up of network of nerve cells or neurons. These are specialised for conducting information through electrical impulses from one part of the body to another.

Control and Coordination

Structure of Neuron or Nerve Cell

Neuron is composed of following main parts:
- (i) **Cell body or Cyton** It is the broad rounded part of neuron. It has a central nucleus, abundant cytoplasm and various cell organelles except centrioles.
- (ii) **Dendrites** These are the protoplasmic, branched processes of the cell body, which receive and transmit stimulus.
- (iii) **Axon** These are long, fibre-like cytoplasmic process. They conduct impulses away from the cell body. The axon may be covered by a protective sheath called **myelin sheath**.
- (iv) **Nerve Ending** These are the fine branch-like termination of neurons.

The structure of a neuron is shown below:

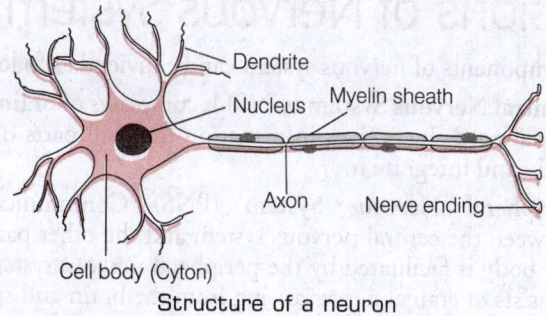
Structure of a neuron

Synapse
A small gap between two adjacent neurons, where the nerve impulse passes from one neuron to another in one direction.

Transmission of a Nerve Impulse

The transmission of a nerve impulse in the body has a general scheme of flow. All the information from the environment is detected by the **receptors** (sense organs) present in the body, which transfer it to sensory neuron.

The information acquired at the end of the **dendritic tip** of a neuron causes a chemical reaction that produces an **electrical impulse**.

This impulse, travels from the **dendrite** of sensory neuron to its **cell body** (cyton) and then along the **axon** to its end. At the end of axon, the electrical impulse causes the release of some chemicals (neurotransmitters).

These chemicals cross the gap (synapse) and start a similar electrical impulse in dendrite of next neuron.

A similar synapse allows the delivery of such impulses from neurons to other cells, such as muscle cells or gland.

The pathway followed by the nerve impulse in the body is given below

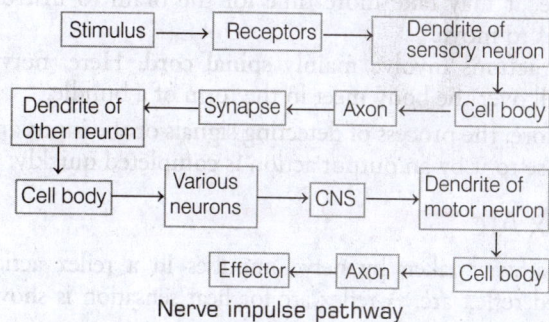
Nerve impulse pathway

Note Gustatory receptors will detect taste, while olfactory receptors will detect smell.

Neuromuscular Junction

The point where a muscle fibre comes in contact with a motor neuron carrying nerve impulses from the Central Nervous System (CNS). The neurotransmitter for the transmission of nerve impulse from neuron to the muscle fibre releases in the same way as impulses are transmitted across a synapse between two neurons.

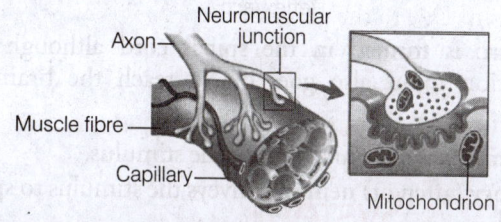
Neuromuscular junction

Limitations to the Use of Electrical Impulse

Electrical impulse is an excellent means to transmit information during fast responses to stimulus. But there are some limitations to the use of electrical impulses such as:
- (i) The electrical impulse will reach only those cells that are connected by nervous tissue, not each and every cell in the animal body.
- (ii) Once an electrical impulse is generated in a cell and transmitted, the cell will take some time to reset its mechanism before it can generate and transmit a new impulse.

Reflex Action

A reflex action is an **automatic** and **rapid response** to a stimulus, e.g. coughing, sneezing, blinking of eyes etc. It protects the body from damage and does not involve conscious thought. In reflex action, the message is passed straight to the motor neuron through a **relay neuron**.

Reflex actions are monitored and controlled through the spinal cord of nervous system, not by the brain. This is because, it may take more time for the brain to instruct muscles to move.

Reflex actions involve mainly **spinal cord**. Here, nerves from all over the body meet in the form of a bundle.

Therefore, the process of detecting signals or the input and response to it by an output action is completed quickly.

Reflex Arc

The pathway taken by nerve impulses in a reflex action is called reflex arc. A reflex arc for heat sensation is shown below:

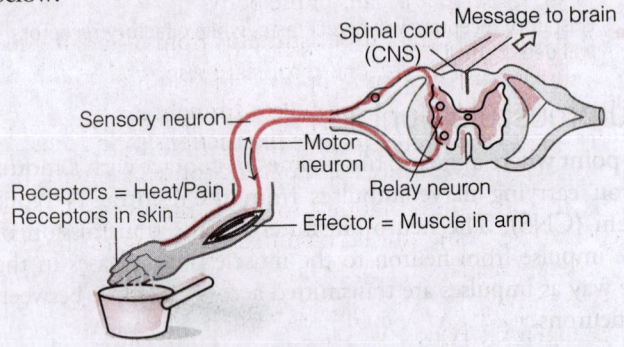

Reflex arc

Reflex arc is formed in the spinal cord although the information input also goes on to reach the brain. It involves :

(i) **Sense organs** which receive the stimulus.
(ii) **Sensory** (afferent) **neuron** conveys the stimulus to spinal cord.
(iii) **Spinal cord** interprets the stimulus and gives appropriate command to motor neurons.
(iv) **Motor** (efferent) **neuron** conveys motor command to effectors.
(v) **Effectors** or **muscles** execute the effect by neuromuscular movements.

Reflex arcs have not evolved in animals because the thinking process of the brain is not fast enough.

So, it is quite likely that reflex arcs have evolved as efficient ways of functioning in the absence of true thought processes, (performed by brain).

The flow chart showing reflex arc is given below:

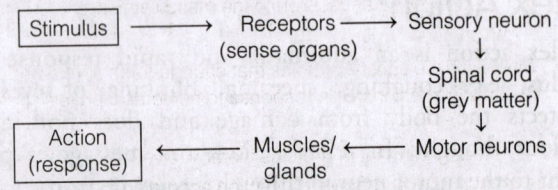

Note The relay neurons connect neurons with CNS.

Importance of Reflex Action

Reflex action is important in the following ways:

(i) It enables an organism for an **immediate response** to a harmful stimulus.
(ii) It reduces the overloading of brain.
(iii) It increases the chances of survival of an organism.

Check Point 01

1. Name the structural and functional unit of nervous system.
2. State True or False for the following statement:
   Gustatory receptors are meant to detect smell.
3. At which point information is acquired in the neuron?
4. Define reflex action.
5. Give two examples of reflexes.
6. Fill in the blank:
   A neuron which carries an impulse to the brain is called a .... neuron.

Divisions of Nervous System

The components of nervous system can be divided as follows:

1. **Central Nervous System** (CNS) It comprises of **brain** and **spinal cord**. It receives information from all parts of the body and integrate it.
2. **Peripheral Nervous System** (PNS) Communication between the central nervous system and the other parts of the body is facilitated by the peripheral nervous system. It consists of cranial nerves arising from the brain and spinal nerves arising from the spinal cord.

Central Nervous System (CNS)

It consists of the brain and the spinal cord.

I. Human Brain

Human brain is the **main coordinating centre** of the body, which enables an organism to think and take decisions. The thinking of the brain involves more complex mechanisms and neural connections. The human brain receives information from the sense organs, interprets it and sends instructions to the muscles or other effectors. The diagrammatic representation of human brain and its internal parts is as follows :

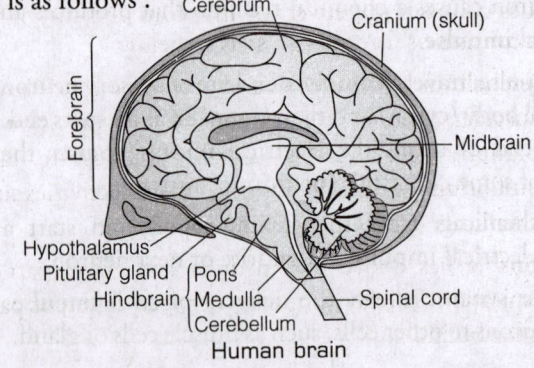

Human brain

The three main regions or parts found in the human brain are as follows:

1. Forebrain
It is the largest, most developed and main thinking part of the brain. It receives sensory impulses from various receptors. It comprises of

(i) **Cerebrum** It acts as the main **thinking part** of the brain. It is responsible for reasoning, speech, intelligence sight, hearing and usage of information.

There are separate areas of association, where sensory information is interpreted by combining the information from other receptors as well as with information that is already stored in the brain are found in the cerebrum itself, these are:

- **Sensory areas** Receive sensory impulses from various receptors in skin, muscles, eyes, ears and nose.
- **Association areas** Interpret sensory information by relating it to the previous experience and information from the other receptors.
- **Motor areas** Send impulses to muscles and glands. Also control the movement of voluntary muscles (leg muscles).

Note Voluntary actions are controlled by cerebrum, e.g. movement of muscles of limbs.

(ii) **Olfactory lobes** These are a pair of very small, solid, club-shaped bodies widely separated from each other. These are responsible for detecting smell from different receptors.

(iii) **Hypothalamus** This part controls the body temperature, urge of eating, drinking, etc.

2. Midbrain
It connects forebrain to the hindbrain. It controls the movement of head, neck and trunk to locate sounds and visual reflexes that are involved in focussing on the objects. It also controls reflex movements of eye muscles, pupil size etc.

3. Hindbrain
It provides connection between spinal cord and rest of the brain. It consists of three parts as given below

(i) **Cerebellum** It controls and coordinates different muscular actions. It is responsible for precision of voluntary actions. It maintains posture and equilibrium of the body during various activities such as walking, drinking, catching, riding etc.

(ii) **Pons** It lies above the medulla and takes part in respiration. It relays impulses between different parts of the brain.

(iii) **Medulla oblongata** It is found continuously with the spinal cord. It controls involuntary actions such as breathing, blood pressure (BP) etc., and regulates reflex responses like salivation and vomiting.

Note Midbrain and hindbrain form the brain stem, i.e. central trunk of the brain is connected to spinal cord.

Functions of Human Brain
Major functions of the human brain are

(i) It coordinates activities of the body so that mechanism and hormonal reactions of the body work together.

(ii) It receives information carrying nerve impulses from all the sensory organs of the body.

(iii) It correlates the various stimulus from different sense organs and produces appropriate response.

(iv) It responds to the impulses brought in by sensory organs by sending its own instructions to the muscles and glands causing them to function accordingly.

(v) It stores information, so that the behaviour of human being can be modified according to the past experiences.

II. Spinal Cord
It is a long, tubular bundle of nervous tissue arising from medulla oblongata. It functions primarily in the transmission of neural signals between brain and rest of the body.

Protection of Human Brain and Spinal Cord
Brain is a very delicate organ and is important for a variety of activities. The body is designed in such a way that the brain sits inside a **bony box**, inside which **fluid-filled balloon** provides further shock absorption. There are a hard, bumpy structure called **vertebral column** or **backbone**, present at the middle of the back, protects, spinal cord.

Mechanism of Nervous Tissue Action
The mechanism of nervous tissue action can be understood by the flow diagram given below

Nervous tissue receives informations from body parts and sends it to the brain.
↓
Brain processes informations and makes decisions based on that particular information.
↓
Conveys that decision to the muscular tissue.
↓
Muscles have special proteins that change both shape and arrangement in cell in response to nervous impulses.
↓
The new arrangement of proteins thereby, give the muscle cells a shorter form and move in direction according to the mind.

Peripheral Nervous System (PNS)

It consists of nerves that directly enter or leave the Central Nervous System (CNS) and connect different parts of the body. It consists of following types of nerves, which carry both sensory and motor neurons

(i) **Cranial nerves** These are the nerves, which emerge from brain and spread throughout the head.

(ii) **Spinal nerves** These are the nerves, which arise from spinal cord along most of its length and spreadthroughout the body (except the head).

(iii) **Visceral nerves** These are the special kind of nerves that mostly arise from the spinal cord and are connected to the internal organs of the body.

Note Autonomic nervous system is part of PNS that regulates the involuntary actions of our internal organs, e.g. BP, heart rate etc.

Check Point 02

1. What constitutes Central Nervous System (CNS)?
2. What is the role of Peripheral Nervous System (PNS)?
3. Mention the part of the brain involved in thinking. State one more function of this part.
4. Which part of the brain helps us to focus on the objects?
5. Blood pressure and heart rate will be regulated by which part of the brain?
6. Fill in the blank:
   .... protects the spinal cord.
7. Why do muscles change their shape in response to a nerve impulse?
8. State True or False for the following statement:
   Centre of hearing, smell, memory, sight, etc., are located in forebrain.

Coordination in Plants

Plants do not have nervous system or muscle tissue like animals. However, they still show movement and response. They use chemical means to convey information from one cell to another. The movements of plants are broadly classified into two main types—immediate response to stimulus and movement due to growth.

1. Immediate Response to Stimulus

It does not involve any growth. The plant rather moves its leaves in response to touch. Sensitive plants give immediate response to the stimulus. Movement of part of plant occurs at a point different from the point of touch. Plant communicates the information that a touch has occurred. This is done in the following manner:

(i) Plants use electrochemical means to convey the information from cell to cell. However, there are no specialised tissues for the conduction of information.

(ii) Plant cells change their shape by changing the amount of water in them. This happens due to swelling or shrinking of cell.

Sensitive plant (Mimosa pudica)

Note The movement of the sensitive plant in response to touch is very quick. The movement of sunflowers in response to day and night, on the other hand, is quite slow. Growth related movements of plants can be even slower.

2. Movement Due to Growth

Plants respond to stimuli by growing in a particular direction. This growth is directional due to which the plant appears moving.

Some plants like pea, pumpkin and cucumber climb up other plants or fences. This occurs by means of tendrils, which are sensitive to touch. When these tendrils come in contact with any support, the part of tendril in contact with the object does not grow as rapidly as the part of the tendril away from the object. This causes the tendril to circle around the object and thus, cling to it.

Tropic Movements

When the stimulus has a particular direction and movement of plant occurs in the direction of the stimulus (either towards the stimulus or in the opposite direction), this movement is called as **tropic movement**.

Types of Tropic Movements

These are based on environmental triggers like light, gravity of earth, water and certain chemicals.

(i) **Phototropic Movement** (stimulus–light)

The movement of the plant part in response to light is called **phototropic movement**. The phenomenon involved is called **phototropism**. The shoot grows towards light, while the growth of root is away from the light.

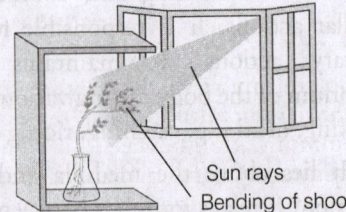

Response of the plant to the direction of light

Control and Coordination

(ii) **Geotropic Movement** (stimulus–gravity) The movement of plant part in response to gravity is called **geotropic movement**. The phenomenon involved is called **geotropism**. Roots always move towards centre of gravity (downward), while shoots usually grow upward and away from the earth.

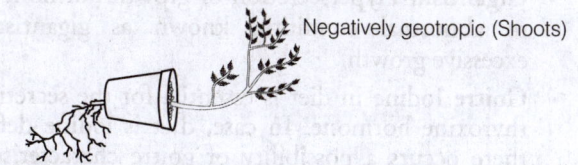
Plant showing geotropism

(iii) **Hydrotropic Movement** (stimulus–water) It is the growth of the plant in response to water. The phenomenon involved in this is called **hydrotropism**.

(iv) **Chemotropic Movement** (stimulus-chemical) It is the growth of the plant in response to a chemical stimulus. The phenomenon involved is called **chemotropism**, e.g. growth of pollen tube towards ovules during fertilisation.

Check Point 03

1. Plants do not have any nervous or muscle tissue, still they have the ability to sense touch. How?
2. 'Plants show tropism in response to stimuli'. Comment.
3. What is common in plants like pea, pumpkin and cucumber?
4. Match the following columns.

	Column I		Column II
1.	Geotropism	A.	Light
2.	Chemotropism	B.	Water
3.	Phototropism	C.	Gravity
4.	Hydrotropism	D.	Chemical

5. Observe the given figure. Identify A and B as types of tropism shown by plant.

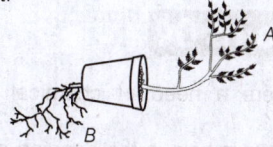

6. Fill in the blank:
In plants, the growth of pollen tube towards the chemicals produced by ovum during fertilisation shows ....

Chemical Communication

Cells cannot continuously create and transmit electrical impulses. Thus, most multicellular organisms use another means of communication between different cells, called the **chemical communication**. In this, instead of an electric impulse, a chemical compound is released, which would diffuse all around the original cells. Other cells around will detect the compound using special molecules. They can recognise and transmit the information carried by it. These compounds are called hormones.

Hormones

Hormones are released by the stimulated cells and diffuse all around the original cell.

Synthesis occurs at places away from the site of action from where they simply diffuse. Target cells detect this compound by the special molecules present on their surface.

There processing and transmittance are slower than electrical impulse. They reach all the cells of the body regardless of nervous connections and it is done steadily and persistently.

There are two types of hormones are follows

1. Plant Hormones

These chemical substances are naturally produced in plants. They are capable of regulating their important processes. Different plant hormones help to coordinate growth, development and responses to the environment.

Major classes of plant hormones and their effects are as follows

(i) **Auxins** These are usually synthesised in the tip of shoots. It helps them to grow longer. When plants are placed facing a light source, they show bending towards it. This is because the auxin diffuses towards the shady side of the shoot stimulating the cells to grow longer.

(ii) **Gibberellins** These are the hormones that help in the growth of the stem and flower.

(iii) **Cytokinins** These are the hormones, which promote cell division. Highest concentration of cytokinins occurs in fruits and seeds, i.e., areas of rapid cell division.

(iv) **Abscisic acid** It is a growth inhibitor. It is responsible for the wilting of leaves.

2. Animal Hormones

The chemical compounds or hormones are secreted in small amounts by endocrinez glands. These are poured directly in the blood. They are carried to specific organs with the help of circulatory system.

Major Hormones and their Functions

(i) **Adrenaline** It is secreted by **adrenal glands**. It works in stress situations. Its target organ is heart; which as a result, beats faster to supply more oxygen to the muscles. The blood to the digestive system and skin is reduced due to contraction of muscles around small arteries in their organs.

This diverts the blood to skeletal muscles. The breathing rate also increases because of the contractions of the diaphragm and the rib muscles. All these responses together enable the body to deal with the situation.

(ii) **Thyroxine** It is secreted by thyroid gland. It regulates carbohydrate, protein and fat metabolism in the body. Iodine is essential for its synthesis. Its deficiency leads to **goitre**.

(iii) **Growth hormone** It is secreted by pituitary, regulates growth and development in body. Its deficiency may cause **dwarfism** or **gigantism**.

(iv) **Testosterone and oestrogen** The changes associated with puberty are because of the secretion of testosterone in males and oestrogen in females.

(v) **Insulin** It is produced by pancreas and helps in regulating blood sugar level. Its deficiency may cause **diabetes**.

Endocrine Glands

These are **ductless glands**, which form a group of tissues or cells, acting at distant sites of the body known as **target organ** or **target cell**.

These include glands like the pituitary gland, thyroid gland, endocrine part of the pancreas, adrenal gland, gonads, etc., e.g. **adrenaline hormone** is secreted from adrenal gland directly into the blood and is carried to different parts of the body. It acts on target organs or specific tissues like heart. The endocrine gland distribution in human beings is given below

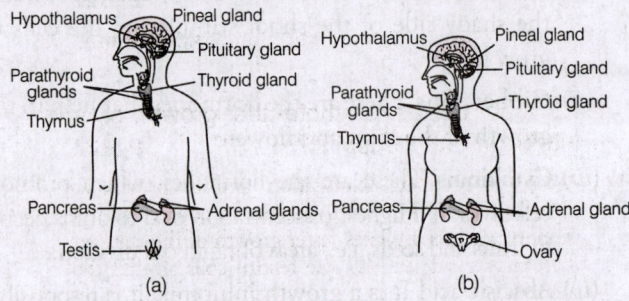

Endocrine glands in human beings; (a) Male (b) Female

Note • Pituitary or master gland controls the activity of other glands.
• Hypothalamus plays an important role in the release of many hormones. When the growth hormone level is low, hypothalamus releases growth hormone releasing factor which stimulates the pituitary gland to release growth hormone.

Hormonal Disorders

All hormones secreted in our body are required in specific amount. Even a slightly more (hypersecretion) or less (hyposecretion) secretion of any hormone can lead to different disorders.

Some common examples of hormonal disorders are given below:

- **Dwarfism** Deficiency of growth hormone in the human body (mainly in childhood), known as dwarfism.
- **Gigantism** Hypersecretion of growth hormone leads to abnormal condition known as gigantism or excessive growth.
- **Goitre** Iodine in diet is essential for the secretion of thyroxine hormone. In case, diet is iodine deficient there occurs a possibility of goitre characterised by swollen neck.
- **Diabetes mellitus** It occurs when reduced insulin is secreted by beta cells of pancreas. This leads to sugar accumulaion in the body. If it is not secreted in proper amounts, the sugar level in the blood rises causing many harmful effects. People with very high levels of blood sugar take insulin injections as a treatment.

Feedback Mechanism

Regulation of hormone secretion is controlled by a mechanism called the **feedback mechanism**. It keeps the secretion of hormones regulated, e.g. increased blood sugar levels are detected by the β-cells of pancreas, which respond by producing more insulin. The flowchart of feedback mechanism of blood glucose is given below:

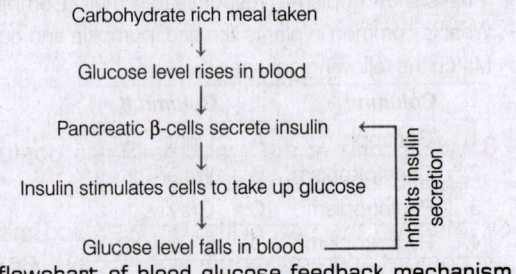

The flowchart of blood glucose feedback mechanism

Check Point 04

1. Why is there a need of chemical communication in organisms?
2. How does auxin help in the bending of shoots towards a light source?
3. The highest concentration of cytokinin is found in bud region. True of False
4. .... is a growth inhibiting hormone.
5. How does adrenaline prepare us for the stress situations?
6. What will happen if intake of iodine in our diet is low?
7. What is the significance of feedback mechanism in the control of hormonal secretions?

NCERT FOLDER

Intext Questions

1. What is the difference between a reflex action and walking? **Pg 119**

Sol. The differences between a reflex action and walking are as follows:

Reflex Action	Walking
It is an spontaneous and involuntary response to a stimulus.	It is acquired through learning and is a voluntary response.
It is regulated by spinal cord.	It is coordinated by the brain (hindbrain).
Its intensity cannot be changed.	Its intensity can be changed.
It increases the survival and protective values of an organism.	It is concerned with the locomotion.

2. What happens at the synapse between two neurons? **Pg 119**

Sol. Synapse is the small gap between two neurons. At the end of axon, the electrical impulse sets the release of some chemicals in a form of neurotransmitters (acetylcholine) which cross the gap (synapse) and start a similar electrical impulse in the dendrite of the next neuron. Synapse actually acts like a one way valve because the chemical substance is present only at one side of the gap.

3. Which part of the brain maintains posture and equilibrium of the body? **Pg 119**

Or Mention the part of the brain, which maintains posture and equilibrium of the body. **CBSE 2016**

Sol. **Cerebellum** is the part of hindbrain that maintains posture and equilibrium of the body.

4. How do we detect the smell of an agarbatti (incense stick)? **Pg 119**

Sol. The smell reaches the neurons of **olfactory receptor** of nose. It causes the generation of nerve impulses that reach the olfactory lobes of the forebrain to produce the sensation of smell.

5. What is the role of the brain in reflex action? **Pg 119**

Sol. Brain has limited role to play in reflex action. It is an extremely quick action, which does not involve any thinking by the brain. In this type of action, the stimulus is received by the spinal cord that sends a response, e.g. coughing. The action is registered in cerebral brain just for memory.

6. What are plant hormones? **Pg 122**

Sol. Plant hormones are organic substances produced naturally in higher plants. They control growth and other physiological functions of the plants. These are required in very small amounts.

7. How is the movement of leaves of sensitive plant different from the movement of a shoot towards light? **Pg 122**

Sol. Differences between movement of leaves and movement of shoot towards light are as follows:

Movement of Leaves (Sensitive Plant)	Movement of Shoot
This movement is independent of growth.	This movement is dependent on growth.
Stimulus is touch.	Stimulus is light.
Movement is not directional.	Movement is directional.
Movement is neither away nor towards the stimulus.	Movement is towards the stimulus.

8. Give an example of a plant hormone that promotes growth. **Pg 122**

Sol. **Auxin** is a plant hormone, which promotes growth in plants.

9. How do auxins promote the growth of a tendril around a support? **Pg 122**

Sol. Auxins promote cell elongation and are present at the shoot tip. When tendril comes in contact with a support, auxin stimulates faster growth of the cells on the opposite sides. Thus, the tendril coils around the support.

10. Design an experiment to demonstrate hydrotropism. **Pg 122**

Sol. The growth of plant parts towards or away from water is called **hydrotropism**. It is shown in the diagram given below:

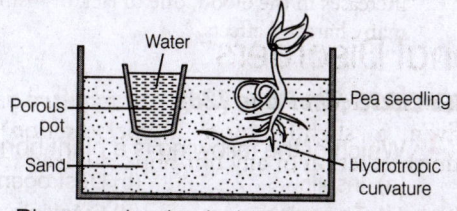

Diagram showing hydrotropic movement

To perform the experiment, take a plant (pea seedling) in a jar filled with sand. Place a porous pot filled with water in the wide jar. Roots of the plant will grow towards water and bend towards the water source showing positive hydrotropism.

11 How does chemical coordination take place in animals? **Pg 125**

Sol. Chemical coordination is **performed by hormones**, which are chemical messengers secreted by endocrine glands.

These hormones coordinate the activities of living organisms and also their growth.

The timing and the amount of hormones released are regulated by the feedback mechanism.

12 Why is it advised to use iodised salt in diet? **CBSE 2016**

Or Why is the use of iodised salt advisable? **Pg 125**

Sol. Iodised salt in diet is advisable because it contains iodine, which is essential element for the synthesis of thyroxine hormone by thyroid gland. In case, iodine is deficient in our diet, there is a possibility of suffering from goitre.

13 How does our body respond when adrenaline is secreted into the blood? **Pg 125**

Sol. Adrenaline hormone is secreted from adrenal gland into the blood and carried to different parts of the body. At the time of emergency, danger or stress, it is released in large quantities. As a result, it causes fast beating of heart, resulting in supply of more oxygen to muscles.

The blood supply to the digestive system and skin is reduced due to contraction of muscles around small arteries in these organs. The breathing rate also increases because of the contraction of diaphragm and rib muscles. All these responses together help the animal to deal with the emergency situation.

14 Why are some patients of diabetes treated by giving injections of insulin? **Pg 125**

Sol. Some diabetes patients are given injections of insulin to fulfil the requirement of insulin in their body. Insulin is a hormone produced by the pancreas and helps in regulating blood sugar levels in our body. If sugar level increases in the blood, due to lack of insulin, it leads to many harmful effects.

Exercises (On Page 126)

1 Which of the following is a plant hormone?
(a) Insulin (b) Oestrogen
(c) Thyroxine (d) Cytokinin

Sol. (d) Cytokinin is a plant hormone that promotes cell division in plants.

2 The gap between two neurons is called as
(a) dendrites (b) axon
(c) synapse (d) impulse

Sol. (c) Synapse is a gap between two neurons. It is a place, where information is transmitted from one neuron to the other neuron.

3 The brain is responsible for
(a) thinking (b) balancing the body
(c) regulating (d) All of the above

Sol. (d) Brain is the controlling centre of our body. It has different regions responsible for different functions of the body such as thinking, balancing, regulating, etc.

4 What is the function of receptors in our body? Think of situations, where receptors do not work properly. What problems are likely to arise?

Sol. The function of receptors in our body is very important as they **collect informations** about changes in the environment around us. Receptors then **pass the same information in the form of nerve impulse to the central nervous system**, where the information is processed and the ultimate response is given. Now, for example, if the gustatory receptors of our tongue do not work properly, we will not be able to know the taste of different types of foods (whether it is sweet, salty, sour or bitter, etc.)

5 Draw the structure of a neuron and explain its function.

Sol. For figure refer to Pg. 213 "Structure of a neuron".

Functions of a neuron The neuron receives information from receptors as electrical impulse, at its dendritic end. The impulse then travels from dendrite to the cell body and further along axon to its end. At the end of axon, electrical impulse leads to the release of some chemicals.

These chemicals cross the synapse and reach the next neuron. This is how nerve impulses travel through the body. Thus, neurons are important in receiving information from the surroundings and in sending it to the effector.

6 How does phototropism occur in plants?

Sol. The directional movement of the plant in response to light is called **phototropism**. The shoots respond by bending towards light and roots respond by bending away from the light.

This happens as follows:

(i) When sunlight falls straight on the plant, the auxin hormone synthesised at the tip of the stem spreads uniformly down the stem and due to equal concentration of auxin, stem grows straight.

(ii) When sunlight falls on only one side of the plant, the auxin diffuses towards the shady side of shoot. The concentration of auxin stimulates the cells to grow longer. Therefore, the stem appears to bend towards the source of light in the directional movement

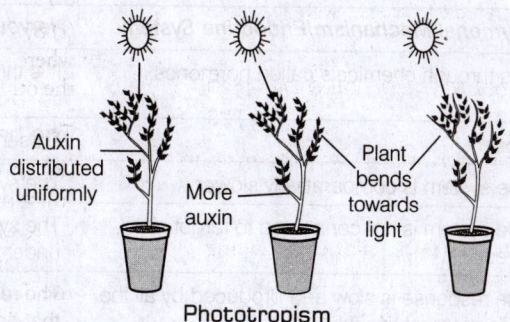

Phototropism

7 Which signals will get disrupted in case of a spinal cord injury?

Sol. In case of a spinal cord injury, **signals for reflex actions** and involuntary actions will get disrupted.

8 How does chemical coordination occur in plants?

Sol. Chemical coordination in plants is achieved by the **plant hormones**. Plant hormones are the chemical compounds, which help the plant to coordinate the growth, development and responses to the environment. Plant contains the following plant hormones :

(i) **Auxins** helps in cell elongation.
(ii) **Gibberellins** helps in the growth of the stem.
(iii) **Cytokinins** promotes cell division.
(iv) **Abscisic acid** inhibits plant growth.

9 What is the need for a system of control and coordination in an organism?

Sol. All the organisms need a well-organised system of control and coordination. Responding to stimuli is a characteristic property of all living organisms. On receiving a stimulus, the body responds in a manner that is most appropriate for its survival and functioning. The response that is given involves various organs (or parts) of body.

Thus, it is very necessary that all the organs work together in a proper coordinated way so as to provide the correct response. This working together of various organs in a systematic orderly way to provide proper control and response to stimulus is called coordination.

10 How are involuntary actions and reflex actions different from each other?

Sol. Differences between involuntary actions and reflex actions are as follows :

Basis	Involuntary Actions	Reflex Actions
System	They involve autonomic nervous system.	They involve all parts of voluntary nervous system though they are not under our control.
Activity	They involve functioning of the internal body parts.	They are concerned with emergency.
Divisions	The nervous system controlling involuntary actions has two divisions, sympathetic and parasympathetic.	There are no such divisions.
Stimuli	They occur in response to internal stimuli.	They commonly operate against harmful stimuli, which are generally external.
Occurrence	Most of the involuntary functions occur all the time.	Reflex actions occur occasionally.
Time	Sometimes gap occurs between stimulus and response.	They are almost instant.
Muscles	They are carried out by smooth muscles.	They are performed by striated muscles.
Examples	Beating of heart and peristalsis.	Closing of eyes when light is flashed on them.

11 Compare and contrast nervous and hormonal mechanisms for control and coordination in animals.

Sol. Comparison between hormonal mechanisms are as follows :

Basis	Hormonal Mechanism/Endocrine System	Nervous Mechanism
Passage of information	It is through chemicals called hormones	It is through electrical conduction.
Sensory receptors	Absent.	Present.
Rapidity	The system is comparatively slower	The system is rapid.
Connection	The system is not connected to target sites directly.	The system is directly connected to every part under its control.
Response	The response is slow and produced by all the cells of target tissues.	The response is quick and limited to those cells that are innervated with nerves.
Role in growth and development	The system controls growth and development.	It has little role in growth and development.
Components	It consists of glands and their secretions.	It consists of neurons, nerves and nervous organs.
Effects	The effect of chemical message lasts for longer period.	The effect of nervous message is for short duration.
Action	It is involuntary.	It can be voluntary or involuntary.

12 What is the difference between the manner in which movement takes place in a sensitive plant and the movement in our legs?

Sol. The differences between the movement in sensitive plant and our legs are as follows :

Movement in Sensitive Plant	Movement in Legs
It occurs in response to an external stimulus like touch.	It is a voluntary action performed and controlled by our will.
Plant cells change their shape by changing the amount of water (turgor changes) in them.	Movement of legs (voluntary action) is controlled by cerebellum, a part of hindbrain. It is due to change in special proteins of muscles.
No nerves are involved.	Nerves carry the message for movement of legs.

SUMMARY

- **Control and coordination** is the working together of various organs of a living organism in a systematic, controlled and efficient way to produce proper response to various stimuli.
- **Coordination in humans** is facilitated by the nervous system and hormones secreted by endocrine glands.
- **Nervous system** regulates voluntary and involuntary movements, collects and processes outside information, helps in reasoning, thinking, etc., and controls the reflex action occurring in our body.
- **Neurons** are the structural and functional unit of nervous system. These are the longest cell of the body. They consist of cell body, dendrites, axon and nerve endings. Functionally, neurons can be sensory, motor and mixed.
- **Synapse** is a small gap between neurons where nerve impulse passes from one neuron to the next.
- **Reflex action** is an automatic and rapid response to a stimuli that is controlled through the spinal cord *via* **relay neuron**.
- **Reflex arc** is the pathway taken by a nerve impulse during a reflex action.
- **Central nervous system** is comprised by the brain and spinal cord.
- **Brain** is the main coordinating centre of the body which enables an organism to think and take decisions. **Forebrain**, **midbrain** and **hindbrain** are the three parts of the brain.
- **Spinal cord** is a long, tubular bundle of nervous tissue arising from medulla oblongata and transmits neural signals between brain and body.
- **Peripheral nervous system** consists of all the nerves, i.e the cranial, spinal and visceral, connecting the central nervous system with different parts of the body.
- **Coordination in plants** occurs *via* electrochemical means which convey information from one cell to another.
- **Sensitivity of plants** refers to the ability of a plant to detect changes in water content and responding by changing their shapes.
- **Plant movements** occur in response to a stimuli. It can be of two types, i.e tropic or nastic.
- **Tropic movements** These movements of plants occur in the direction of stimulus, e.g. phototropism (stimulus-light), geotropism (stimulus-gravity), hydrotropism hydrotropism (stimulus-water) and chemotropism chemotropism (stimulus-chemicals).
- **Nastic movements** These movements occur irrespective of direction of stimulus, e.g. photonasty, thigmonasty, thermonasty and seismonasty.
- In **chemical coordination**, a chemical compound (hormones) is released for coordination.
- **Plant hormones** are the chemical substances naturally produced in plants for regulation of growth and development, responses, etc.
- **Auxins** help in cell elongation and division.
- **Gibberellins** help in stems and flower growth.
- **Cytokinins** promote cell division and delay ageing of leaves.
- **Abscisic acid** inhibits growth.
- **Ethylene** is a ripening hormone.
- **Animal hormones** are chemical compounds or messengers, secreted in small quantities by endocrine glands.
- **Endocrine glands** are ductless glands which act at distant sites from target organs. These include pituitary, thyroid, pancreas (mixed gland), adrenal glands and the gonads.
- **Pituitary gland** secretes tropic hormones, e.g. growth hormones, thyroid secretes thyroxine, pancreas secretes insulin and glucagon.
- **Hormonal disorders** occur when glands malfunction and hormone production is affected.
- **Dwarfism** occurs by hyposecretion of growth hormone.
- **Gigantism** is caused by hypersecretion of growth hormone.
- **Diabetes** Reduced amount of insulin is secreted by pancreas leads to high sugar level in blood.
- **Goitre** It is caused by the deficiency of iodine causing less secretion of thyroxine hormone.
- **Feedback mechanism** is the regulation of amount and the timing of hormonal secretion.

Exam Practice

Objective Type Questions

Multiple Choice Questions

1 In a neuron, conversion of electrical signal to a chemical signal occurs at/in **NCERT Exemplar**
 (a) cell body (b) axonal end
 (c) dendritic end (d) axon
Sol. (b) At the **axonal** end, the electrical impulse releases small amount of chemical substance (i.e. acetylcholine) into the synapse.

2 Which part of the human brain is most well-developed?
 (a) Forebrain (b) Hindbrain
 (c) Diencephalon (d) None of these
Sol. (a) Forebrain or cerebrum is the most well-developed part of the human brain.

3 Which part of the human brain controls body temperature?
 (a) Pituitary (b) Diencephalon
 (c) Hypothalamus (d) None of these
Sol. (c) Hypothalamus controls and regulates temperature of body, urge of eating, drinking, sleeping, etc.

4 Posture and balance of the body is controlled by **NCERT Exemplar**
 (a) cerebrum (b) cerebellum
 (c) medulla (d) pons
Sol. (b) Cerebellum controls the voluntary actions, e.g. posture.

5 Spinal cord originates from **NCERT Exemplar**
 (a) cerebrum (b) medulla
 (c) pons (d) cerebellum
Sol. (b) Spinal cord begins in continuation with medulla and extends downwards.

6 Growth of pollen tube towards ovule during fertilisation is an example of
 (a) phototropism (b) geotropism
 (c) chemotropism (d) hydrotropism
Sol. (c) Growth of pollen tube towards ovule during fertilisation is an example of chemotropism.

7 The main function of abscisic acid in plants is to **NCERT Exemplar**
 (a) increase the length of cells
 (b) promote cell division
 (c) inhibit growth
 (d) promote growth of stem
Sol. (c) The main function of abscisic acid in plants is to inhibit growth.

8 Iodine is necessary for the synthesis of which hormone? **NCERT Exemplar**
 (a) Adrenaline (b) Thyroxine
 (c) Auxin (d) Insulin
Sol. (b) Iodine is necessary for the synthesis of thyroxine hormone.

9 The hormone responsible for changes during puberty in male is **NCERT Exemplar**
 (a) oestrogen (b) testosterone
 (c) insulin (d) growth hormone
Sol. (b) Testosterone is the male sex hormone which controls the change associated with puberty in males.

10 Female sex hormone is termed as
 (a) androgen (b) insulin
 (c) oestrogen (d) None of these
Sol. (c) Oestrogen is a female sex hormone.

Fill in the Blanks

11 The sensitive plant .... folds up its leaflets on being touched.
Sol. *Mimosa pudica*

12 In animals, hormones are secreted by ....
Sol. endocrine glands.

13 Simple goitre is caused by the deficiency of .... in the diet.
Sol. iodine

14 .... promotes the development of secondary sexual characters in a female.
Sol. Oestrogen

15 The cell body of a neuron is called.......... .
Sol. cyton

True and False

16 Neurons are specialised for conducting the information through electrical impulse.
Sol. True

17 Dendrites or dendrons are protoplasmic branched processes which recieve and transmit stimulus.

Sol. True

18 Small gaps between the nerve endings where nerve impulses passes from one neuron to another are known as neurotransmitters.

Sol. False, Small gaps between the nerve endings where nerve impulses passes from one neuron to another are called synapses.

19 If the olfactory lobes of a person are removed, he will not be able to identify any smell.

Sol. True

20 Testosterone produces femaleness.

Sol. False, Testosterone produces maleness.

Match the Columns

21 Match the following columns.

	Column I		Column II
1.	Abscisic acid	A.	Synapse
2.	Junction	B.	Taste
3.	Gustatory	C.	Cranial nerves
4.	PNS	D.	Dwarfism
5.	Growth hormone	E.	Growth inhibitor

Sol. 1. → (E), 2. → (A), 3. → (B), 4. → (C), 5. → (D)

22 Match the following columns.

	Column I		Column II
1.	Insulin	A.	Endocrine glands
2.	Goitre	B.	Iodine
3.	Geotropism	C.	Cell division
4.	Cytokinin	D.	Gravity
5.	Hormones	E.	Diabetes mellitus

Sol. 1. → (E), 2. → (B), 3. → (D), 4. → (C), 5. → (A)

Assertion–Reason

Direction (Q. Nos. 23-27) *In each of the following questions, a statement of Assertion is given by the corresponding statement of Reason. Of the statements, mark the correct answer as*

(a) If both Assertion and Reason are true and Reason is the correct explanation of Assertion

(b) If both Assertion and Reason are true, but Reason is not the correct explanation of Assertion

(c) If Assertion is true, but Reason is false

(d) If Assertion is false, but Reason is true

23 Assertion Plants lack the nervous system, but they do coordinate.
Reason It is so because of hormones.

Sol. (a) Plants lack the nervous system, but coordinate *via* the hormones.

24 Assertion Reflex actions are automatic and rapid responses to stimuli.
Reason These actions are controlled by brain.

Sol. (c) Reflex actions are automatic and rapid response to stimuli. These actions are controlled by spinal cord, not by brain.

25 Assertion Gustatory receptors detect taste.
Reason Olfactory receptors are present in cerebellum.

Sol. (c) Gustatory receptors detect taste, while olfactory receptors detect smell. Assertion is true, but Reason is false.

26 Assertion Cytokinins are present in highest concentration in fruits and seeds.
Reason Cytokinins are responsible for promoting cell division.

Sol. (b) Cytokinins are the hormones, which promote cell division. Highest concentrations of cytokinins occurs in fruit and seeds, i.e., areas of rapid cell division.

27 Assertion Abscisic acid is responsible for wilting of leaves.
Reason It is a growth inhibitor.

Sol. (a) Abscisic acid is responsible for wilting of leaves because it is a growth inhibitor.

Case Based Questions

Direction (Q. Nos. 28-31) *Answer the questions on the basis of your understanding of the following passage and related studied concepts:*

Thyroid Stimulating Hormone (TSH) stimulates thyroid gland to produce thyroxine. Study the table given below.

Table: TSH levels during pregnancy

Stages of pregnancy	Normal (mU/L)	Low (mU/L)	High (mU/L)
First trimester	0.2-2.5	< 0.2	2.5-10
Second trimester	0.3-3.0	< 0.3	3.01-4.5
Third trimester	0.8-5.2	< 0.8	> 5.3

It is important to monitor TSH levels during pregnancy. High TSH levels and hypothyroidism can especially affect chances of miscarriage. Therefore, proper medication in consultation with a doctor is required to regulate/control the proper functioning of the thyroid gland. **CBSE 2020**

28 Give the full form of TSH.
Sol. TSH—Thyroid Stimulating Hormone.

29 State the main function of TSH.
Sol. It stimulates thyroid gland to secrete its hormone.

30 Why do TSH levels in pregnant women need to be monitored?
Sol. TSH imbalance can cause miscarriage.

31 A pregnant woman has TSH level of 8.95 mU/L. What care is needed for her?
Sol. The TSH level of pregnant women if 8.95 mU/L, she should be kept under medication in consultation of a doctor to regulate/control the proper functioning of thyroid gland.

Direction (Q. Nos. 32-35) *Study the table in which the levels of Thyroid Stimulating Hormone (TSH) in women are given and answer the questions that follow on the basis of understanding of the following paragraph and the related studied concepts.*

Age Range	Normal (mU/L)	Low (mU/L)
18-29 years	0.4-2.34 mU/L	< 0.4 mU/L
30-49 years	0.4-4.0 mU/L	< 0.4 mU/L
50-79 years	0.46-4.68 mU/L	< 0.46 mU/L

Women are at greater risk for developing abnormal TSH levels during menstruation, while giving birth and after going through menopause. Around 5% of women in the United States have some kinds of thyroid problem compared to 3% of men.

Despite claims that high TSH increases your risk for heart disease, a 2013 study found no link between high TSH and heart diseases. But a 2017 study showed that older women are especially at risk for developing thyroid cancer if they have high TSH levels along with thyroid nodules. **CBSE 2020**

32 A 35 year old woman has TSH level 6.03 mU/L. What change should she bring in her diet to control this level?
Sol. The woman who has TSH 6.03 mU/L should take iodine rich diet and should use iodised salt.

33 When do women face a greater risk of abnormal TSH level?
Sol. Women are at greater risk for developing abnormal TSH levels during menstruation, child bearing stage and through menopause.

34 State the consequence of low TSH level.
Sol. Low TSH level causes hypothyroidism disease.

35 Name the mineral that is responsible for synthesis of hormone secreted by thyroid gland.
Sol. Iodine mineral is required for synthesis of thyroxine by thyroid gland.

Direction (Q. Nos. 36-39) *Answer the questions on the basis of your understanding of the following table and related studied concepts:*

Hormone	Endocreine gland	Functions
Growth hormone	Pituitary gland	Stimulates growth in all organ
Thyroxin	Thyroid gland	Regulates metabolism for body growth
Testosterone	Testes	Development of male sex organs
Oestrogen	Ovaries	Development of female sex organs, regulation menstrual cycle.
Adrenaline	Adrenal gland	Helps in regulating stress situation
Releasing hormone	Hypothalamus	Stimulates pituitary gland to release hormones
Insulin	Pancreas	Regulates blood sugar level

36 Select the mismatched pair
 (a) Adrenaline : Pituitary gland
 (b) Testosterone : Testes
 (c) Oestrogen : Ovary
 (d) Thyroxin : Thyroid gland
Sol. (*a*) Pair in option (a) is incorrectly matched. Adrenaline is secreted by adrenal gland.

37 At the time of puberty both boys and girls show lets of changes in appearance. Name the hormones responsible for these changes.
Sol. Testosterone in males and oestrogen in females are responsible for the changes (secondary sexual characters) during puberty.

38 Name the endocrine gland associated with brain.
Sol. Hypothalamus and pituitary gland are associated with brain.

Control and Coordination

39 When we feel stressed or excited X hormone in secreted by Y site. What is X and Y?

	X	Y
(a)	melatonin	pineal gland
(b)	vasopressin	hypothalamus
(c)	adrenaline	adrenal gland
(d)	oxytoicn	adrenal gland

Sol. (c) X is adrenaline and Y is adrenal gland.

Direction (Q. Nos. 40-43) *Answer the questions on the basis of your understanding of the following passage and related studied concepts:*

The endocrine system regulates the body's processes by releasing chemical messengers (hormones) into the bloodstream. Hormones are potent chemical regulators; They are produced in minute quantities yet can have a large effect on metabolism.

The endocrine system comprises endocrine cells (organized into endocrine glands), and the hormones they produce. Unlike exocrine glands (e.g. sweat and salivary glands), endocrine glands are ductless glands, secreting hormones directly into the bloodstream rather than through a duct or tube.

Some organs (e.g. the pancreas) have both endocrine and exocrine regions, but these are structurally and functionally distinct.

The basis of hormonal control and the role of negative feedback mechanisms in regulating hormone levels are described below.

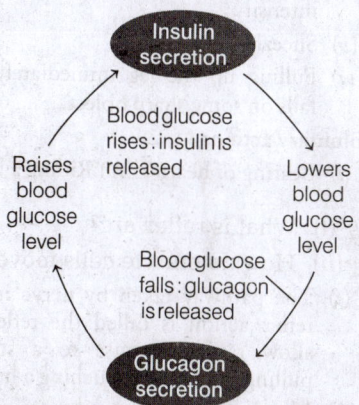

40 Why is the speed of hormonal responses slower?

Sol. The speed of hormonal responses is slower than nervous responses because the hormones diffuse and reach the target cell *via* blood.

41 What is common in both insulin and glucagon?

Sol. Insulin and glucagon both help in regulating the level of blood sugar (glucose). Insulin decreases blood glucose and glucagon raises it.

42 Among endocrine glands and exocrine, which have ducts?

Sol. Exocrine glands have ducts, but endocrine glands lack ducts and thus secrete hormone directly into the blood stream.

43 Hormones affect only specific target cells. State true or false.

Sol. True, endocrine cells produce hormones and secrete then into the blood stream where they are distributed throughout the body. Although hormones are broadcast throughout the body, they affect only specific target cells.

Very Short Answer Type Questions

44 All information about our environment is detected by specialised cells. Write the name given to such cells and also mention where are they located.

Sol. Such cells are called **receptors**. They are located in our various sense organs, e.g. olfactory receptors (for smell).

45 Name two components of central nervous system in humans. **CBSE 2015**

Sol. Two components of central nervous system are
(i) Brain   (ii) Spinal cord.

46 Name the sensory receptors found in the nose and on the tongue.

Sol. Olfactory receptors and gustatory receptors are the sensory receptors found in nose and on the tongue, respectively.

47 Identify the parts of brain concerned with
(i) memory, will and power
(ii) muscular coordination

Sol. (i) Cerebral hemisphere   (ii) Cerebellum

48 What is fluid present in between the meninges?

Sol. The fluid present in between meninges is cerebrospinal fluid.

49 Name the structure in which spinal cord is protected in human body?

Sol. Vertebral column. The structure in which spinal cord is protected in human body is vertebral column.

50 Name any two types of tropic movements.

Sol. Two types of tropic movements are:
  (i) **Geotropism**, i.e. response to gravity.
  (ii) **Chemotropism**, i.e. response to chemical substances.

51 What do we call the movement of shoot towards light?

Sol. The movement of shoot towards light is called **positive phototropism**.

52 A young green plant receives sunlight from one direction only. What will happen to its shoots and roots?

Sol. The shoots of the plant bend towards the light, whereas roots bend away from the light.

53 Name the plant hormones responsible for the following
  (a) Elongation of cells
  (b) Growth of stem
  (c) Promotion of cell division
  (d) Falling of senescent leaves

Sol. (a) Auxin
  (b) Gibberellin
  (c) Cytokinin
  (d) Abscisic acid

54 Why adrenaline is known as emergency hormone?

Sol. Adrenaline is the hormone secreted at the time of emergency or stress. It regulates heartbeat and oxygen level in the body in these conditions. Therefore, it is also known as emergency hormone.

55 Which hormone is responsible for the secondary sexual characters in male human beings?

Sol. **Testosterone** is responsible for the secondary sexual characters in male human beings.

56 Name the hormone which regulates sugar level in our body. Also, name the part of gland it is secreted from.

Sol. **Insulin** it is secreted by β-cells of pancreas gland.

57 What are inhibitory hormones?

Sol. Inhibitory hormones are the neurohormones secreted by the hypothalamus. They **inhibit the secretion** of certain hormones of pituitary gland.

58 Pituitary is also known as the master gland. Why?

Ans. Pituitary gland controls the activity of all other glands in our body. Therefore, it is called the master gland.

59 Endocrine glands are called ductless glands. Why?

Ans. These glands lack external ducts for discharging their secretions in blood.

Short Answer (SA) Type Questions

1 Draw a nerve cell and label on it the following: Nucleus, Dendrite, Axon **CBSE 2016**

Sol. Refer to figure on Pg. no. 213

2 Classify the following into reflex action and in voluntary actions of brain. **CBSE 2016**
  (i) Beating of heart
  (ii) Withdrawing your hand immediately on touching a hot object
  (iii) Change in size of pupil in response to intensity of light
  (iv) Riding a bicycle
  (v) Sneezing
  (vi) Pulling up the leg immediately when foot falls on some sharp object

Sol. Reflex actions
  (ii) Withdrawing your hand immediately on touching a hot object.
  (iii) Change in size of pupil in response to light intensity
  (v) Sneezing
  (vi) Pulling up the leg immediately when foot falls on some sharp object.

Voluntary actions
  (i) Beating of heart   (iv) Riding a bicycle

3 (i) What is reflex arc? **CBSE 2015**
  (ii) How do muscle cells move?

Sol. (i) The pathway taken by nerve impulses in a reflex action is called the reflex arc. They allow rapid response to a stimulus, e.g. pulling of hand on touching a hot object.
  (ii) Muscle cells have special proteins that change their shape and arrangement in the cell in response to electrical impulse. This forces the muscle cells to contract and relax, causing their movement.

All in one Control and Coordination 229

4 Why is the flow of signals in a synapse from axonal end of one neuron to dendritic end of another neuron, but not the reverse?
NCERT Exemplar

Sol. The synapse actually acts, like a one-way valve because the chemical substance is present only on one side of the gap. This chemical diffuses towards the dendrite end of next neuron where it generates an electrical signal.

Since, the chemicals are absent at the dendritic end of neuron, the nerve impulse can go across only from one side (which contains the chemical substance). In this way, it is ensured that nerve impulses travel in only one direction (through particular set of neurons).

5 (a) Plants do not have any nervous system but yet if we touch a sensitive plant, some observable changes take place in its leaves. Explain how could this plant respond to the external stimuli and how it is communicated.

(b) Name the hormone that needs to be administered to
   (i) increase the height of a dwarf plant.
   (ii) cause rapid cell division in fruits and seeds. **CBSE All India 2019**

Ans. Refer to text on Pg no. 216.

6 What are plant hormones? Name the plant hormones responsible for the following
   (i) Growth of stem
   (ii) Promotion of cell division
   (iii) Inhibition of growth
   (iv) Elongation of cells **CBSE Delhi 2019**

Sol. Refer to text on Pg no. 217.

7 Explain how the movement of leaves of a sensitive plant different from movements of shoots towards light.
CBSE 2016

Sol. Movements in *Mimosa pudica* (touch sensitive plant) occur in response to touch.

In such movements, plant cells change shape by changing the amount of water in them resulting in folding up and drooping of leaves. This movement is independent of growth.

Plants respond to a stimulus by growing in a particular direction and the movements due to growth. This growth is directional. Movement of shoots towards light indicates phototropism, i.e. movement occurs in response to light.

8 (i) State the function of the following plant hormones **CBSE 2016**
   (a) Abscisic acid   (b) Cytokinin

(ii) Define chemotropism

Sol. (i) (a) Abscisic acid
   • inhibits growth
   • causes dormancy of seeds, wilting of leaves
   • causes stomatal closure
(b) Cytokinin
   • promotes cell division
   • delays aging in leaves
   • reduces apical dominance

(ii) Chemotrophic movement is the growth of plant in response to a chemical stimulus, e.g growth of pollen tube towards ovules during fertilisation.

9 (i) Identify the endocrine glands A, B, C and D in the given diagram.
(ii) List the functions of parts D and E.

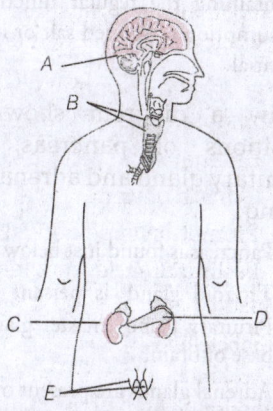

Sol. (i) A – Pituitary, B – Thyroid, C – Adrenal and D – Pancreas.
(ii) D – **Pancreas** secretes insulin, which controls the amount of sugar in blood.
E – **Testis** secrete testosterone, which controls sperm production and secondary sexual characters in males.

10 Answer the following **NCERT Exemplar**
(i) Which gland secretes digestive enzymes as well as hormones?
(ii) Name the endocrine gland associated with kidneys.
(iii) Which endocrine gland is present in males, but not in females?

Sol. (i) **Pancreas** It is called a mixed gland as it secretes pancreatic juice for digestion of food and hormones such as insulin.
(ii) **Adrenal gland** These glands are located one on top of each kidney.
(iii) **Testes** These are the glands, which are present only in males and secrete male sex hormone, testosterone.

11 If iodine is insufficient in one's diet, what might be the deficiency disease? How it can be present?

Or What will happen if intake of iodine in our diet is low? **NCERT Exemplar**

Sol. Iodine is essential for the synthesis of thyroxine hormone secreted by the thyroid gland. Thyroxine regulates the metabolism of carbohydrate, protein and fat in our body and is responsible for the growth and development of body.

Deficiency of iodine leads to hyposecretion of thyroxine hormone. It may disturb the metabolic and physical activities. The person might suffer from disorders like simple goitre. To avoid any disruption in the synthesis of thyroxine and maintaining the regular functioning of the body, consumption of iodised salt or iodine in food is very essential.

12 Draw a diagram showing the correct positions of pancreas, thyroid gland, pituitary gland and adrenal gland in human being. **CBSE 2016**

Sol. (a) Pancreas is found just below the stomach.
(b) Thyroid gland is persent just below the neck.
(c) Pituitary gland (master gland) is present at the base of brain.
(d) Adrenal glands are present on top of each kidney. Refer to figure on Pg no. 218

13 Some glands produce chemical substances that change the activity of target organs.
(a) Name these substance.
(b) Give the effect of the chemical produced by glands G and H given in the diagram below.

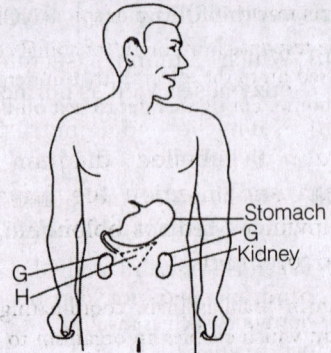

Sol. (a) Hormones
(b) G is adrenal gland. Its secretion adrenaline prepares the body for fight or flight response.

Example increased heart rate and breathing. Dilation of the eyes.
H is pancreas. It secretes hormones that control and maintain the blood sugar level.

14. Name the hormones secreted by the following endocrine glands and specify one function of each.
(i) Thyroid
(ii) Pituitary
(iii) Pancreas **CBSE 2018**

Sol. (i) **Thyroid gland** It secretes thyroxine hormone, which regulates the metabolism of carbohydrates, fats and proteins in body. Iodine is essential for the synthesis and secretion of throxine.
(ii) **Pituitary gland** It is known as the master gland of the human body as it controls the functioning and secretions of other glands.
It secretes many hormones, one of which is
Growth hormone that regulates growth and development of bones and muscles.
(iii) **Pancreas** (Both exocrine and endocrine, i.e. mixed gland) contains specialised cells which secrete two major hormones
(a) **Insulin**, which lowers the blood glucose level.
(b) **Glucagon**, which increases the blood glucose level.

15. Hormones are needed by our body in an appropriate amount, slightly more or less secretion causes disorders in our body. Illustrate this by using three examples. **CBSE 2015**

Sol. Hypersecretion (more secretion) or hyposecretion (less secretion) of different hormones lead to various disorders in our body. The three common examples are :
(i) **Goitre** Iodine acts as the necessary component for the synthesis of thyroxine hormone from thyroid gland. This disorder is caused due to the deficiency of iodine that leads to hyposecretion of thyroxine.
(ii) **Gigantism and dwarfism** Hypersecretion of growth hormone results in gigantism (very tall individual).
On the contrary, the hyposecretion or deficiency of growth hormone at an early stage of life makes the person very short, i.e. causes dwarfism.
(iii) **Diabetes mellitus** Insulin secreted by pancreas helps to lower the blood glucose level. When it is secreted in less amount, the body suffers from diabetes.)

Control and Coordination

16. What is feedback mechanism of hormone regulation? Take the example of insulin to explain this phenomenon. **CBSE Delhi 2019**

Sol. Refer to text on Pg. no. 218.

17. What will happen, if the pancreas of a person stop functioning?

Sol. Pancreas is an important endocrine gland in human body, which **helps** in **regulating** the **glucose level** in blood by **releasing** an important hormone called **insulin**. It also secretes digestive enzymes such as amylase, lipase etc., which help to breakdown various components of food. If pancreas will stop functioning, the person would need to administer insulin injections as well as required to take multiple digestive enzymes pills in order to help the breakdown of food.

18. Nervous and hormonal systems together perform the function of control and coordination in human beings. Justify this statement with the help of an example. **CBSE Delhi 2019**

Or A close coordination exists between the nerves and hormones. Discuss.

Ans. The endocrine and neural system works in tendem for the normal functioning of our body. The synthesis and release of certain hormones is regulated by the neural system. Also, the release of certain hormones influences the activity of nerves.

E.g. The presence of food in our stomach, distends the gastric wall. This results in secretion of gastric hormone which stimulates gastric juice secretion in stomach. Likewise, increase in the concentration of adrenaline stimulates the respiratory centre of the brain. This inturn leads to increase in the breathing rate of an individual.

Long Answer (LA) Type Questions

1. Some situations in our day to day life require quick response from our body. Illustrate the sentence with the help of suitable diagram and common examples.

Or What are reflex actions? Give two examples. Explain a reflex arc. **NCERT Exemplar**

Sol. **Sudden quick action in response to something occurring in environment is known as reflex action.**
Reflex action is a rapid, automatic response to a stimulus, which is not under the voluntary control of the brain, i.e. it is an involuntary action. It is a simple form of behaviour in which the same stimulus produces the same response every time, e.g.

(i) if we unknowingly touch a hot plate, we immediately move our hand away from it.

(ii) moving our foot away on stepping something sharp.

Other examples are knee jerk, coughing, yawning, sneezing, etc. For figure refer to text on Pg. 214.

Or

The pathway taken by nerve impulse in a reflex action is called the **reflex arc**.
Refer to flow chart on Pg. no. 214.

Reflex arcs have evolved in animals because the thinking process of brain was not fast enough during early stages of evolution. However, even after complex neuron networks have come into existence, reflex arc continues to be more efficient for quick responses.

2. With the help of labelled diagram explain the general scheme to illustrate how nervous impulses travel in the body? **CBSE 2016, 15**

Sol. All the information from the environment is detected by the receptors (sense organ) present in the body.

The stimulus received by the receptor is passed on in the form of electrical signals to dendrites and then to cyton of the neuron. The impulse then travels along the axon of the neuron.

On reaching the axonal end, it causes the nerve endings to release a chemical, which diffuses across a synapse and stimulates the presynaptic membranes of next neuron. In this way, the electrical signal reaches the brain or spinal cord.

The response from brain (or spinal cord) is similarly passed on to the effector, that undergoes the desired response. For figure refer to text on Pg. 214.

3. Draw a labelled diagram of human brain and mention the functions of the following: Medulla oblongata, cerebellum and forebrain. **CBSE 2015**

Sol. Human brain is main coordinating centre of the body, which enables an organism to think and take decisions.

For figure refer to text on Pg. 214.

Functions of different parts of the brain are:

Medulla oblongata It controls involuntary actions and regulates reflex responses. It also controls blood pressure, salivation and vomiting.

Cerebellum It controls and coordinates different muscular actions. It is responsible for voluntary actions and maintains equilibrium of the body during walking, drinking, catching, etc.

Forebrain It has following parts:

Cerebrum performs thinking, reasoning, speech, intelligence and usage of information.

Olfactory lobes are responsible for detecting smell from different receptors.

Hypothalamus controls body temperature, urge of eating, drinking, etc.

4 What are the major parts of the brain? Mention the functions of different parts.

NCERT Exemplar

Sol. Brain is the most important coordinating centre in the body. It has three major parts or regions namely the forebrain, midbrain and hindbrain.

Parts	Functions
Forebrain	
Cerebrum	Main thinking part of the brain.
Cerebral hemispheres	Intelligence and voluntary actions.
Olfactory lobes	Centres of smell.
Hypothalamus	Has centres of hunger, thirst etc.
Midbrain	Controls reflex movements of the neck, head and trunk in response to visual and auditory stimuli.
	Also controls the reflex movements of the eye muscles, changes in pupil size and shape of the eye lens.
Hindbrain Pons	Regulates respiration. Relays information between the cerebellum and the cerebrum.
Cerebellum	Maintains posture and balance the body. Enables us to make precise and accurate movements.
Medulla oblongata	Controls involuntary actions such as breathing etc. Controlling centre for reflexes such as swallowing, coughing, vomiting, etc.

5 List some functions of human brain.

Ans. Refer to text on Pg. 215 "Functions of Human brain".

6 'Plants also perform chemical coordination'. Elaborate.

Or Name various plant hormones. Also give their physiological effects on plant growth and development. **NCERT Exemplar**

Sol. Plants also perform chemical coordination for various activities with the help of hormones. These are the chemical compounds released by stimulated cells that diffuse to various locations in plants performing different functions. These hormones produced by plants are also called as phytohormones. Different types of hormones produced by plants are: Auxin, Gibberellins, Cytokinins, Abscisic acid, Ethylene.

Or

Plant Hormone	Physiological Effect
Auxin	• Synthesised in the young tip of roots and shoots. It diffuses towards the shady side of plant, which stimulates the cells to grow longer, resulting in bending of shoot towards light. • Promotes cell elongation and division • Plays important role in formation of roots and seedless fruits.
Gibberellins	• Helps in growth of stem and flower. • Helps in germination of seed.
Cytokinins	• Promote cell divsion and delay leaf aging. • Also stimulate leaf expansion.
Abscisic acid	• Growth inhibitor • Reverses the growth promoting effects of auxins and gibberellins.
Ethylene	• Promotes transverse growth. • Essential for fruit ripening, promotes senescence and abscission of leaves.

7 Why do we call pituitary gland as the master gland? Where is it located and what are its functions?

Sol. The pituitary gland secretes a number of hormones that regulate various functions of the body. It also controls the functioning of the other endocrine glands. Hence, called the master gland.

Location Pituitary gland is located just below the hypothalamus at the base of brain.

Pituitary gland secretes five important hormones, i.e.

(i) **Growth hormone** regulates the growth and development of bones and muscles.

Control and Coordination

(ii) **Tropic hormone** regulates the secretion from other endocrine glands.

(iii) **Prolactin hormone** regulates the function of mammary glands in females.

(iv) **Vasopressin hormone** regulates water and electrolyte balance in the body.

(v) **Oxytocin hormone** regulates the ejection of milk during lactation.

8. Name the hormone, which is secreted by the adrenal gland. How does this hormone help to deal with scary situations? **CBSE 2016**

Sol. Adrenal gland secretes adrenaline and corticoid hormones. Refer to Ans 13 Pg. 220 in NCERT Folder.

9. (i) What are animal hormones? List their two characteristics.

(ii) Name the hormone,
 (a) which brings change in male humans during the beginning of adolescence.
 (b) which coordinates the level of sugar in blood? **CBSE 2016**

Sol. (i) Hormones are the chemical substances, which control and coordinate the activities performed by organisms.

Characteristics of Hormones
(a) They are poured directly into the blood stream and are carried throughout the body by circulatory system.
(b) They act only on the specific target organs.

(ii) (a) Testosterone produced by testes regulates the changes in male during adolescence period.

(b) Insulin (decrease blood sugar) and glucagon (increase blood sugar), secreted by pancreas coordinates the sugar level in blood.

10. 'Nervous and hormonal systems together perform the function of control and coordination in human beings.' Justify the statement. **NCERT Exemplar**

Sol. The working together of various organs of human being in a systematic, controlled and efficient way to produce a proper response to various stimuli is known as coordination.

In humans, the nervous and hormonal systems together perform this control and coordination.

Nervous system consists of receptors that receive the stimulus from surrounding environment and send the message received by them to the spinal cord and brain in form of electrical impulses through the sensory nerves.

The motor nerves then transmit the response to the effector. The effectors are mainly the muscles and glands of our body. Thus, endocrine glands secreting hormones are directly or indirectly controlled by the nervous system.

Hence, control and coordination in humans (or animals) depend on two things for transmitting information, i.e. chemical signals of hormones and nerve impulses.

If they depended only on nerve impulses through nerve cells, only a limited range of tissues would be stimulated. Since, they get additional chemical signals as well, a large number of tissues are stimulated. This is why animals can show a wide range of response to stimulus.

CHAPTER EXERCISE

Multiple Choice Questions

1. Which of the following shows correct reflex arc?
   (a) Sensory organ → Spinal cord → Effector organ
   (b) Sensory organ → Brain → Effector organ
   (c) Effector organ → Brain → Sensory organ
   (d) Effector organ → Spinal cord → Sensory organ

2. Plant hormone responsible for phototropism is
   (a) gibberellin   (b) abscisic acid
   (c) cytokinin   (d) auxin

3. Chemically hormones are derivatives of
   (a) fat
   (b) protein
   (c) steroid
   (d) All of the above

4. Hypersecretion of growth hormone causes
   (a) gigantism   (b) dwarfism
   (c) sterility   (d) goitre

5. Deficiency of which hormone causes diabetes?
   (a) Insulin   (b) Thyroxine
   (c) Relaxin   (d) Oestrogen

Fill in the blanks

6. The pituitary gland lies on ....

7. ...... is plant's response to contact with hard surface.

8. .... is the master gland.

True and False

9. Human brain and spinal cord are solid.

10. Spinal cord arises from the medulla.

11. Sensory nerve connects the dorsal root of the spinal cord.

Match the columns

12. Match the following columns.

Column I		Column II
1. Auxin	A.	Brain box
2. Cranium	B.	Adrenaline
3. Anger	C.	Apical meristem
4. Gustatoreceptors	D.	Nose
5. Olfactoreceptors	E.	Tongue

Assertion–Reason

Direction (Q. Nos. 13-15) *In each of the following questions, a statement of Assertion is given by the corresponding statement of Reason. Of the statements, mark the correct answer as*

(a) If both Assertion and Reason are true and Reason is the correct explanation of Assertion
(b) If both Assertion and Reason are true, but Reason is not the correct explanation of Assertion.
(c) If Assertion is true, but Reason is false
(d) If Assertion is false, but Reason is true

13. **Assertion** Cerebrum acts as the main thinking part of the brain.
    Reason Cerebrum is responsible for reasoning, speech, intelligence, sight, hearing, usage of information, etc.

14. **Assertion** Thyroxine is secreted by thyroid gland.
    Reason Its deficiency leads to diabetes.

15. **Assertion** Endocrine glands are called ductless glands.
    Reason These glands direct pour their secretions into the blood.

Case Based Questions

Direction (Q. Nos. 16-19) *Answer the questions on the basis of your understanding of the following passage and related studied concepts:*

Plants respond to their environment they show sensitivity (irritability). Plant responses are rather slow compared with those of animals plants respond to stimuli (to changes in their environment) by changing their growth patterns. These growth responses enable a plant to make the most of the resources available in its environment.

Plants respond to many stimuli, but two are of particular importance: light (the photo stimulus) and gravity (the geo-stimulus). A growth response carried out by a plant in response to the direction of a stimulus is called a tropism.

16. When a response of plant or its part can be called a positive response?

17. Why roots are positively geotropic?

18. Define chemotropism.

19. Give an example where hydrotropic movements can be seen.

Control and Coordination

Answers

1. (a) 2. (d) 3. (d) 4. (a) 5. (a)
6. dienceophalon 7. Thigmotropism
8. Pituitary gland 9. False 10. True 11. False
12. 1.→(C), 2.→(A), 3.→(B), 4.→(E), 5.→(D)
13. (a) 14. (c) 15. (c)

Very Short Answer (VSA) Type Questions

20. Is reflex action the only function of spinal cord? Support your answer with a single statement.
21. The sensation of feeling fear or hunger is associated with which part of brain?
22. Give the exact location and function of cerebellum.
23. How is geotropism necessary for plant?
24. Write one function of each
    (i) Auxin (ii) Gibberellins
25. Name the source and target organs of adrenaline.

Short Answer (SA) Type Questions

26. What are receptors with reference to nervous system? List three types of receptors and mention their functions. How do receptors pass the information to brain?

27. Following are the two examples of plant movement.

(a) *Mimosa* plant

(b) Pea plant

(i) Which stimulus is common for movement in both the cases?
(ii) Does the movement take place towards the point where stimulus is received? Mention separately for both plants.
(iii) Give one reason for the movement in each case.

28. A plant in the laboratory is given increased dose of a hormone, which promotes the development of seedless fruits. Identify the hormone and write its other two functions.

29. A boy runs on seeing a stray dog. His breathing rate becomes very fast and blood pressure also increases.
    (i) Name the hormone found to be high in his blood and the gland which produces it.
    (ii) What other effects are caused by this hormone?

30. Adrenal glands are located on top of each kidney. What will happen if these glands do not secrete adrenaline?

31. Feedback mechanism is an important aspect of hormonal coordination. Explain.

Long Answer (LA) Type Questions

32.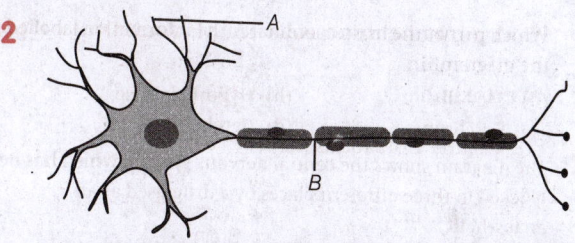

    (i) Name the parts labelled as A and B in the diagram given above.
    (ii) Which part acquires the information in the neuron?
    (iii) Through which part does the information travel?
    (iv) In what form does the information travel?
    (v) Where is the impulse converted into a chemical signal for onward transmission?

33. With the help of a labelled diagram, illustrate the pathway of response when someone pricks in your hand with a pin.

34. (i) A nerve input signal travelled only upto the spinal cord and gave output signal for a response. What type of action did the body show– voluntary or involuntary?
    (ii) Draw a nerve pathway for the above action and suggest specific terms for input nerve and output nerve.

35. Nerves and hormones both are used to control processes within the body. Using examples, show how nervous control and hormonal control (i) resemble and (ii) differ from one another.

36. (i) Suggest an explanation for the fact that the chemicals produced by endocrine glands are usually in the form of small molecules.
    (ii) Write any three endocrine glands and chemical produced by them.

Challengers*

1. The given diagrams shows some of the features of human skin.

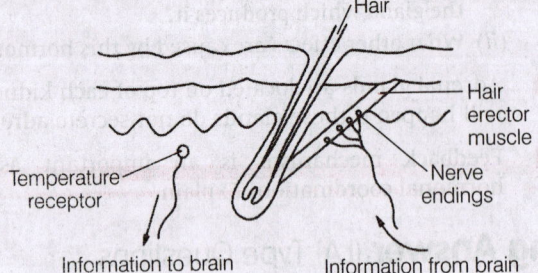

Which part of the brain coordinates the information labelled in the diagram?
   (a) Medulla
   (b) Hypothalamus
   (c) Cerebrum
   (d) Cerebellum

2. The diagram shows the central nervous system, which has been blocked in three different places by a drug used as an anaesthetic.

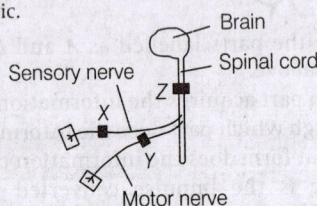

Three men had one anaesthetic block at X, Y or Z. One of the men can move his leg in response to a pinprick, but does not feel it. Where is the anaesthetic block in this man?
   (a) At X
   (b) At Y
   (c) At Z
   (d) No block

3. Observe the figure given below. In the figure, some parts are labelled as P, Q, R, S and T. Given below are functions associated with these parts.

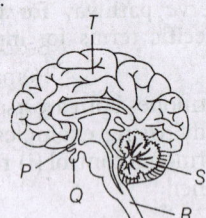

Parts of brain	Functions
P	Master hormone producers
Q	Controls body temperature
R	Controls unconscious activities
S	Helps to control balance
T	In conscious behaviour

Which part of the brain is matched with incorrect function?
   (a) P and S
   (b) P, Q and T
   (c) R and T
   (d) P, R and T

4. The diagram shows a reflex arc in which a bee sting causes the arm to be moved quickly.

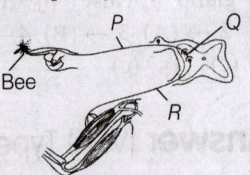

If the relay neurone is damaged, how will the transmission of nerve impulses in the reflex arc be affected?
   (a) Impulses cannot pass from P-Q
   (b) Impulses cannot pass from P-R
   (c) Impulses cannot pass from Q-P
   (d) Impulses cannot pass from R-Q

5. Adrenaline hormone is secreted in the body during emergency situations. What would be the effects of increased concentration of adrenaline on body?

	Concentration of glycogen in the liver	Concentration of glucose in the blood
(a)	Decrease	Increase
(b)	Increase	Increase
(c)	No effect	Decrease
(d)	Increase	No effect

6. A child is frightened by a loud noise and shouts for help. In which order, the different types of neurons involved will act?
   (a) Motor neurone → Relay neurone → Sensory neurone
   (b) Motor neurone → Sensory neurone → Relay neurone
   (c) Sensory neurone → Motor neurone → Relay neurone
   (d) Sensory neurone → Relay neurone → Motor neurone

7. Following are certain reflex actions occurring in our body.
   (I) Moving to the side of road when a speeding car approaches.
   (II) Closing of eyes in response to a sudden bright light.
   (III) Shouting when we are suddenly disturbed or get scared.
   (IV) Withdrawing hands on touching a hot surface. The reflex arc given below, will be occurring for,

   Receptors (sense organs) $\xrightarrow{\text{Sensory neurons}}$ Spinal cord $\xrightarrow{\text{Motor neurons}}$ Targets/effectors

   (a) I and II
   (b) I, II and III
   (c) I, II, III and IV
   (d) II and IV

Answer Key

| 1. | (b) | 2. | (c) | 3. | (b) | 4. | (b) | 5. | (a) |
| 6. | (d) | 7. | (c) | | | | | | |

*These questions may or may not be asked in the examination, have been given just for additional practice.

CHAPTER 07

How Do Organisms Reproduce?

Reproduction is the ability of a living organisms to produce new individuals similar to them. Like other essential life processes (nutrition, respiration, growth and excretion) reproduction is not essential to maintain life of an individual. It is essential for

- continuation of life on Earth.
- addition of new species.
- replacement of dead organisms.
- transfer of adaptations and variations from one generation to another.

The basic event in reproduction is the creation of a DNA copy and an additional cellular apparatus by the cell which are involved in this process.

Various organisms use different modes of reproduction depending on their body design. Mainly there are two modes of reproduction, i.e. asexual and sexual reproduction.

The Fundamentals of Reproduction

The reproducing organisms (parents) procreates new individuals. The individuals so produced are similar to each other and their parents. This similarity between siblings and offspring to their parents occurs because of the genes/DNA present in them. DNA is present in the nucleus of a cell in the form of a condensed structure called **chromosome**. Reproduction is most basic level involves making copies of the blueprints of its body design of an organism.

- With the help of biochemical reactions, cells build-up copies of their DNA during reproductive phase.
- DNA present in nucleus of the cell act as the information source. It helps in making different proteins and cellular machinery of cell, which makes up the different body designs of an organism.

Chapter Checklist

- The Fundamentals of Reproduction
- Types of Reproduction
- Modes of Asexual Reproduction
- Modes of Sexual Reproduction
- Sexual Reproduction in Flowering Plants
- Sexual Reproduction in Human Beings
- Significance of Sexual Reproduction
- Reproductive Health

Variation

DNA copying is accompanied by creation of an additional cellular apparatus. Afterwards, the cell divides effectively producing two new daughter cells. It always causes some or other type of variations in newly formed cell. This brings the differences found in the morphological and physiological features of an organism. Since no biochemical reaction is absolutely reliable, DNA copies generated are similar, but not absolutely identical.

The DNA copying should be perfectly accurate in reproduction process. The variations among the individuals will occur if not so. This may be beneficial or fatal for the individual. This inbuilt tendency for variations during reproduction is the basis for evolution.

Importance of Variation

Organisms occupy well-defined places or niches in the ecosystem, using their ability to reproduce. Those organisms which have the same body design occupies the same niche or place in the ecosystem.

The population tends to wipe out completely if a niche suitable for organisms of a particular population is drastically changed.

But, if variations occur in few individuals of these populations, there would be chances of survival of some individuals, e.g. in a population of bacteria living in temperate water. If the temperature increases due to the global warming, most of the bacteria would die. But, the variants which are resistant to heat would survive and grow further.

Thus, it shows that variations in a population are important for the survival of a species.

Types of Reproduction

There are mainly two types of reproduction, i.e. asexual and sexual.

1. Asexual Reproduction

This process is very common in unicellular organisms. It is said to be the simplest type of reproduction, e.g. binary fission in *Amoeba*, budding in *Hydra*, spore formation in *Rhizopus*, fungus and vegetative propagation in flowering plants like rose, etc.

Characteristics of asexual reproduction are
- It is a rapid mode of multiplication.
- Cell division takes place either mitotically or amitotically.
- The new individuals produced after cell divisions are always genetically identical or clone to their parents.
- A single parent is involved, i.e. opposite sexes are not involved.
- It does not involve the fusion of gametes.

2. Sexual Reproduction

This method is common in multicellular organisms. It involves male and female individuals to produce new generation by fusion of gametes produced by both the parents, e.g. in humans, dogs, cats, fishes, frogs, etc.

Characteristics of sexual reproduction are
- It is not a rapid mode of multiplication.
- Cell division involves meiosis at some stages, especially during gamete formation.
- The new individuals produced after cell division exhibit variation.
- Fusion of male gamete with the female gamete (sex cells) takes place.

Check Point 01

1. Fill in the blank:
   .... is the blueprint responsible for making all basic body designs.
2. Incorrect DNA copying can alter the reproduction process. List the effect of such a case.
3. What is the significance of body design in determining the habitat of an organism?
4. An existing population of birds was suddenly wiped out from an area. Give a suitable reason for the same.
5. How does the reproduction process can be classified on the basis of germ cells involved?
6. Give one advantage of asexual mode of reproduction.
7. State True or False for the following statement:
   Cell division involves mitosis during gamete formation.

Modes of Asexual Reproduction

Rapid mode of multiplication which involves only one parent. New individuals produced are genetically identical to parents (i.e. clone).

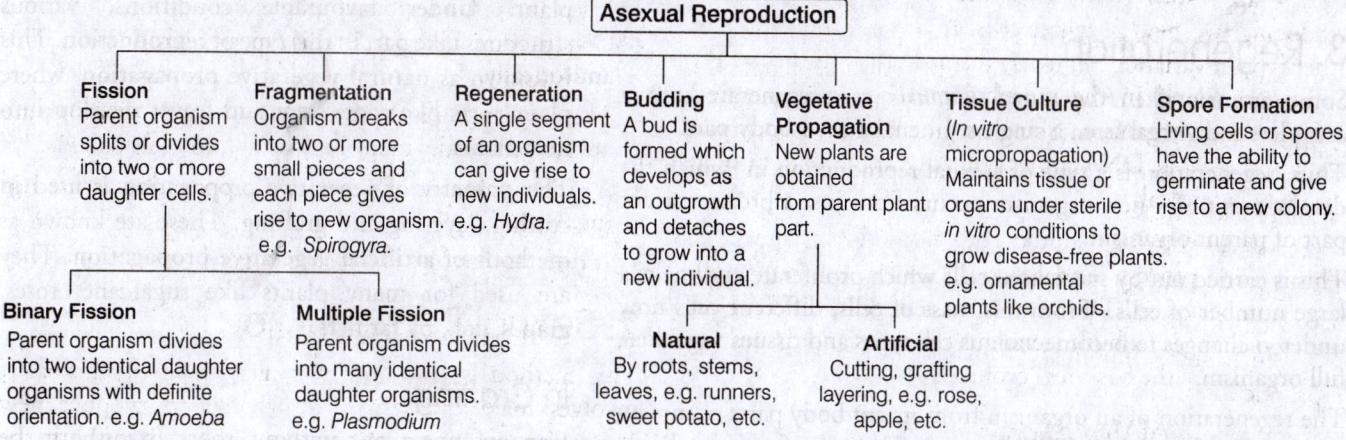

1. Fission

The process of reproduction by which a unicellular organism splits into two or more than two separate daughter cells is called fission.

It is the most common and simplest method of asexual reproduction in unicellular organisms, such as bacteria, protozoans and some fungi (yeast).

In this, cell division of the single-celled organism into two or more parts would lead to development of new organisms.

Generally, it is of two types, i.e. binary and multiple fission.

(i) Binary Fission

The type of fission where the parent organism divides into two identical daughter organisms with a definite orientation. At first the nucleus of cell divides into two. It is followed by division of the cytoplasm. Then, finally splitting of parent cell into two daughter cells occurs.

Some unicellular organisms show more organisation of their bodies. e.g. *Leishmania*, (causative agent of kala-azar) which have a whip-like structure at one end of the cell. In such organisms, binary fission occurs in a definite orientation in relation to their cell structure.

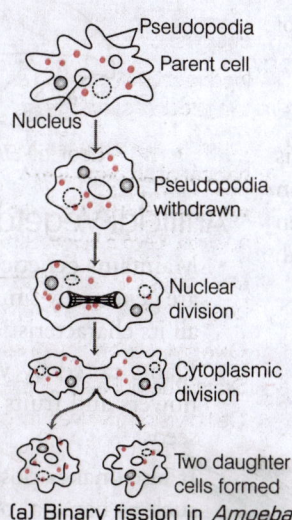

(a) Binary fission in *Amoeba*

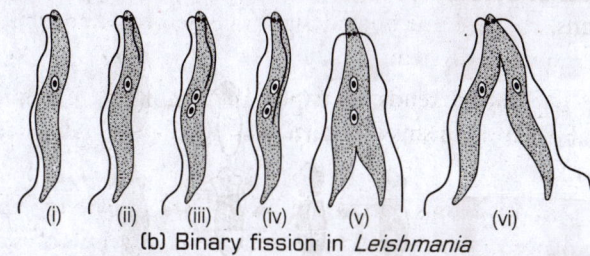

(b) Binary fission in *Leishmania*

(ii) Multiple Fission

The type of fission where the parent organism divides into many identical daughter organisms at the same time.

Multiple fission can be seen in organisms, such as *Plasmodium* (malarial parasite), *Monocystis* etc.

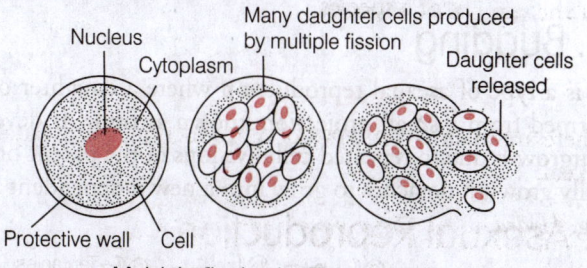

Multiple fission in *Plasmodium*

2. Fragmentation

It is a type of asexual reproduction observed in multicellular organisms like filamentous algae (*Spirogyra*) and sea animal called **sea anemone**. These organisms on maturation breakup into two or more small fragments or pieces. Each fragment subsequently grows to form a complete new organism.

This type of cell division is seen in multicellular organisms with a relatively simple body organisation. This process occurs under favourable conditions of moisture, temperature and nutrient availability.

3. Regeneration

Some animals like *Hydra* and *Planaria* can regenerate into a complete individual from a single segment of their body part.

Thus, regeneration is a type of asexual reproduction in which the development of a new organism occurs from just a broken or cut part of parent organism.

This is carried out by specialised cells which proliferate and make a large number of cells. From this mass of cells, different cells now undergo changes to become various cell types and tissues to make a full organism.

The regeneration of an organism from its cut body parts occurs by the process of growth and development. The cells of cut part divide and form mass of cells. These formed newly cells then change their shapes or become specialised to form different types of tissues and organs.

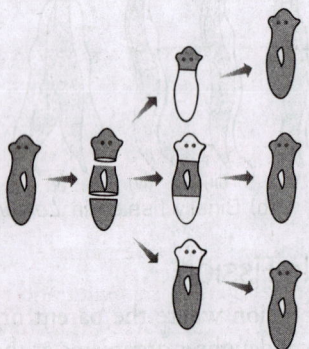

Regeneration in *Planaria*

Note Regeneration is not the same as reproduction. Most organisms do not normally depend on being cut up to be able to reproduce.

4. Budding

It is a type of asexual reproduction where a daughter organism is formed from a small projection known as bud. It develops as an outgrowth due to repeated cell divisions of the parent body. When fully grown it detaches to grow into a new independent individual, e.g. *Hydra*.

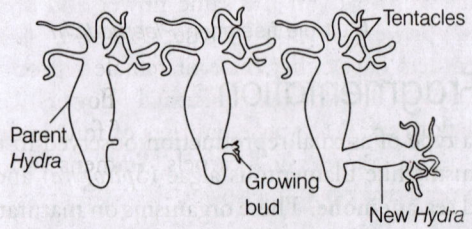

Budding in *Hydra*

5. Vegetative Propagation

It is a type of asexual plant reproduction in which, new plants are obtained from a part of the parent plant. Under favourable conditions, various structures take part in this type of reproduction. This is known as **natural vegetative propagation**, where plant parts like root, stem and leaves develop into new plants.

The property of vegetative propagation is used in cutting, layering and grafting. These are known as methods of **artificial vegetative propagation**. They are used for many plants like sugarcane, roses, grapes, etc., by farmers.

In Grafting

Piece of one plant without roots (scion) can be attached to the part with root (stock) of another plant.

Many apple varieties, lemon, grapes, mango, pear, etc., are grown through this method.

Organs of some plants are used for vegetative propagation, e.g.

- **Bud** of potato
- **Rhizome** of ginger
- **Bulb** of onion
- **Leaf buds** of *Bryophyllum*
- **Adventitious roots** of *Dahlia*.

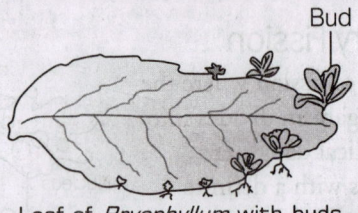

Leaf of *Bryophyllum* with buds

Artificial Vegetative Propagation

- Maintains genetic stability. The plants produced are genetically similar to the parent plant and have all its characteristics.
- Plants raised by vegetative propagation can bear flowers and fruits earlier than those produced by seeds.
- It also makes possible the propagation of plants such as banana, orange, rose and jasmine, which have less capacity to produce seeds.

Tissue Culture

In plant tissue culture new plants are grown by using living tissues. In this method, small pieces are cut from the plant, like flower buds, stem tissue, growing tips, leaves, etc. These are then transferred to an artificial nutrient medium where they divide rapidly to form a callus.

This callus is then transferred to fresh medium containing hormones for growth and differentiation, where it subsequently develops into plantlets.

After this, these are placed in soil to grow into a mature plant.

Various advantages of tissue culture are given below:

- It is possible to produce large number of plants from a single parent in a disease-free environment.
- Rapid production of ornamental plants like carnations, orchids, *Dahlia*, etc., is possible.

6. Spore Formation

In many multicellular organisms, blob-on-a-stick like structures are involved in reproduction. These blobs are known as sporangia, which contain spores as reproductive structures.

Thus, spore formation is also a type of asexual reproduction. Here living cells or spores have the ability to germinate and give rise to a new colony of daughter organism.

The spores are covered by thick walls that protect them in unfavourable conditions. When these spores come into contact with some moist surface like soil and can begin to grow.

The thread-like projections called **hyphae** develops on the bread, if a moist bread is kept in open for a few days. This is because the spores of *Rhizopus* present in the air settle down on the bread and germinate to form a new *Rhizopus* colony.

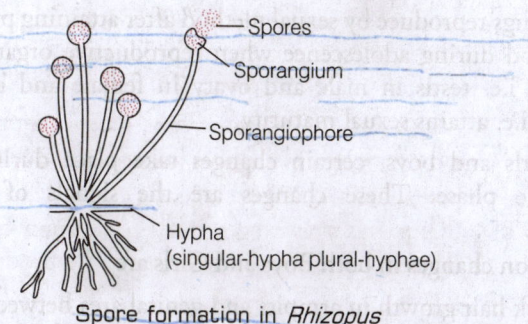

Spore formation in *Rhizopus*

Check Point 02

1. Fill in the blanks:
   (i) The mode of reproduction occurring in *Amoeba* is ....
   (ii) Propagation of plants such as banana, jasmine, rose. etc., can be achieved by ....

2. "Multicellular organisms can also reproduce asexually". Give an example to support the above statement.

3. A plant that has lost the capacity to produce seed. Name a process using which it can reproduce?

4. Indicate whether the given statement is true or false. *Hydra* can reproduce by spore formation.

5. Name two plants which are grown by the technique of tissue culture.

6. Why do spores remain viable during unfavourable conditions?

Modes of Sexual Reproduction

In this type of reproduction, both sexes, i.e. male and female are involved. Sex cell of one parent (male) fuses with the sex cell of another parent (female). This results in production of a new cell called zygote.

Thus, if the zygote has to grow and develop into an organism with highly specialised tissues and organs, then it has to have sufficient energy for doing this. Simple organisms have almost similar size of germ cells that are not very different from each other whereas, in complex organisms, the size of germ cells varies greatly. In these organisms, the germ cell with larger food stored is known as **female gamete**.

The other germ cell which is smaller and motile, is known as **male gamete**. Thus, the sexual mode of reproduction involves two major processes :

(i) Formation of gametes by meiosis
(ii) Fusion of gametes

Sexual Reproduction in Flowering Plants

Flowering plants are generally **angiosperm**s. They bear the reproductive parts within the flower and their seeds are enclosed in a fruit. Most plants have both male and female reproductive organs in the same flower and are known as **bisexual flowers**, e.g. lily, rose, *Hibiscus*, mustard, etc. While others have either male or female reproductive parts in a flower known as **unisexual flowers**, e.g. papaya, watermelon, etc. A flower comprises of four main parts, i.e. sepals, petals, stamens and carpels. Stamens and carpels are the reproductive parts of a flower.

- **Stamen** It is the male reproductive part of the flower. A single flower may have number of stamens in it.
- **Anther** It is a bilobed structure containing two pollen sacs present at tip of stamen. These produce pollen grains that are yellowish in colour.
- **Carpel** (Pistil) It is the female reproductive part, which is present in the centre of the flower.
  It comprises of mainly three parts:
  (i) **Stigma** It is the terminal part of carpel which may be sticky. It helps in receiving the pollen grains during pollination.
  (ii) **Style** It is the middle elongated part of carpel. It helps in the attachment of stigma to the ovary.
  (iii) **Ovary** It is the swollen bottom part of carpel. It contains ovules having an egg cell (female gamete).

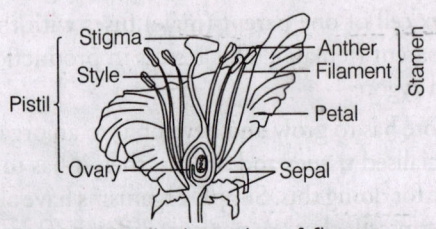

Longitudinal section of flower

The male germ cell must fuse with the female germ cell to initiate the process of reproduction in plants. The transfer of pollen grains from the anther of the stamen to the stigma of a flower is termed as **pollination**. The pollen grains can be transferred by various agents like wind, water, insects and animals. Pollination usually occurs in two ways:

(i) **Self-pollination** the pollen from the stamen of a flower is transferred to the stigma of the same flower.

(ii) **Cross-pollination** the pollen from the stamen of a flower is transferred to the stigma of different flower.

Fertilisation

Pollination is followed by fertilisation in plants. It is the process of fusion of male germ cells with the female gametes. It gives rise to a **zygote**. As soon as the pollen lands on suitable stigma, it reaches the female germ cells in ovary. This occurs *via* pollen tube. The pollen tube grows out of the pollen grain, travels through the style and finally reaches the ovary.

The fertilisation in the flowering plant is shown in the given figure.

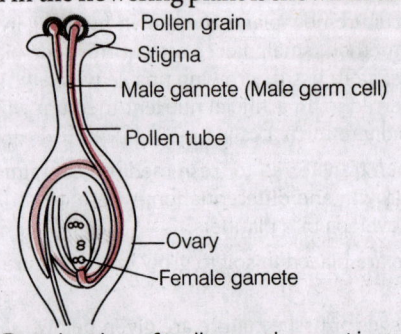

Germination of pollen grain on stigma

After fertilisation, the zygote divides many times and forms an embryo within the ovule. This ovule then develops a tough coat and gets converted into a seed. The ovary rapidly grows and ripens as fruit. The seed contains the future embryo that develops into a seedling under suitable conditions. This process is known as **germination**.

Check Point 03

1. Fill in the blank:
   The fusion of male and female gametes results in formation of ....
2. Indicate whether true or false. In bisexual flowers, either stamens or pistil is present.
3. What constitutes female reproductive part in a flower?
4. What are various agents of pollination?
5. State one reason why cross-pollination is preferred over self-pollination.
6. Where can zygote be found in the flower after fertilisation?
7. State True or False for the following statement:
   The seed contains the future plant.
8. The fruit is developed from which floral part?

Sexual Reproduction in Human Beings

Human beings reproduce by sexual method after attaining puberty. It is a period during adolescence when reproductive organ starts developing, i.e. testis in male and ovary in female and become functional, i.e. attains sexual maturity.

In both girls and boys, certain changes take place during this reproductive phase. These changes are the signals of sexual maturation.

(i) Common changes in both Boys and Girls are
  - Thick hair growth in armpits and genital area between the thighs.
  - Thinner hair appear on legs, arms and face.
  - Oily skin and appearance of pimples.

(ii) Specific changes in Boys and Girls are
   (a) **In Boys**
   - Thick facial hair growth.
   - Voice begins to crack or hoarse.
   - Penis occasionally begins to become enlarged and erect.
   (b) **In Girls**
   - Breast size begins to increase.
   - Darkening of nipple skin.
   - Start of menstruation.

All of these changes take place slowly, over a period of months and years. Also, each change does not complete quickly. All these changes take place differently in different people, i.e. every person has different patterns of hair growth or size and shape of breast and penis. All the changes discussed above are linked to reproductive process. Sexually mature male or female can produce gametes.

The male produces **sperm** and female produces **egg** or **ovum**. When the sperm fuses with the egg, then the developed organism is known as **offspring**.

However, an egg cell is genetically different from the sperm even though their chromosome numbers are the same. (we will study about this in detail in the chapter-4)

Significance of Sexual Reproduction

Some significance of sexual reproduction are as follows
(i) Sexual mode of reproduction involves the process of combining DNA from two different individuals. It does not disturbs the control of DNA over cellular apparatus.
(ii) It results in the re-establishment of the number of chromosomes and the DNA content in the new generation (through meiotic cell division).
(iii) It leads to new combinations of genes in gametes. Due to this reshuffling, genetic variation occurs.
(iv) It promotes diversity of traits/characters in the new generation.

Human Reproductive System

The actual transfer of germ cells between two people needs special organs for the sexual act. This include penis in males and vagina in females. The system of organs required for the process of sexual reproduction is called **reproductive system.**

1. Male Reproductive System

The male reproductive system consists of different parts. They produce the germ cells and deliver the germ cells to the site of fertilisation.

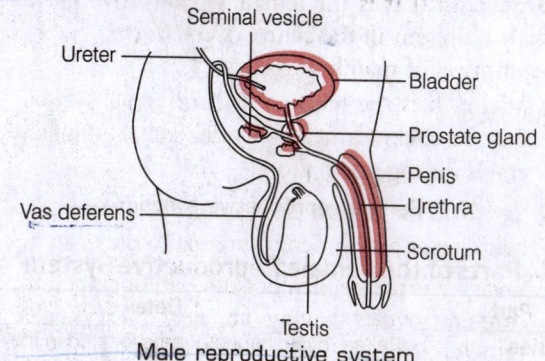

Male reproductive system

Parts of the Male Reproductive System

Part	Detail
Testis	• Paired, oval-shaped male sex organs. • Consist of seminiferous tubules, where the sperms are produced. • Produce a male sex hormone called **testosterone**. Which bring about changes in appearance of boys at puberty.
Scrotum	• Small pouch that contains testis. • Present outside the abdominal cavity. As sperms are formed here, this requires a lower temperature than the normal body temperature.
Vas deferens	• Tube-like structure which connects testis to the urethra in order to allow the passage of semen.
Urethra	• Common passage for both the sperms and urine. It never carries both of them at the same time. • Secretes seminal fluid and nutrients.
Prostate Gland and Seminal Vesicles	• Fluid and nutrients combine with sperm to form semen. Milky, viscous fluid contains fructose, proteins and other chemicals for nourishing and stimulating sperms.
Penis	• External male genital organ. • Transfers sperms into the vagina of the female during copulation.
Sperms	• Tiny and motile bodies that use their long tail to move through the female reproductive tract.

2. Female Reproductive System

The female germ cells or eggs are made in ovaries. They are also responsible for the production of some hormones.

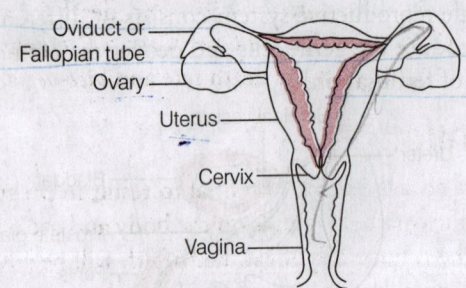

Female reproductive system

Parts of the Female Reproductive System

Part	Detail
Ovaries	• Paired, oval-shaped organs located in the abdominal cavity near the kidney. • Produce thousands of ova or egg cells. • Secrete female sex hormones like **oestrogen** and **progesterone**.
Oviduct (Fallopian tube)	• It has a funnel-shaped opening near the ovary. • Carries ova or egg from ovary to the uterus. • It is the site of fertilisation. • These open into the **uterus** from both the sides.
Uterus (womb)	• Hollow, pear-shaped, bag-like structure. • Here, the growth and development of foetus takes place.
Cervix	• It is the lower and the narrower portion of uterus which opens into the vagina.
Vagina	• Receives the sperms from the male partner. • Serves as a birth canal.

Fertilisation and Post-fertilisation Changes

The fusion of nucleus of the sperm (male gamete) and ovum (female gamete) is known as **fertilisation**. This process in human takes place in the following ways :

(i) The male gamete enters into the female genital tract (vagina) by the process of copulation or mating. This takes place in the **oviduct** or **Fallopian tube**.

(ii) The sperms are highly active and motile. They swim into the uterus through cervix and then pass into the oviduct.

(iii) Fertilisation only occurs, if an egg is present in the oviduct.

(iv) When a sperm reaches the egg, it penetrates inside the ovum. Syngamy or fusion of male and female nuclei occurs to form a zygote.

(v) The zygote undergoes various mitotic divisions to form an **embryo**.

(vi) The embryo sinks down and reaches into the soft and thick lining of the uterus. The embedding of the embryo in the thick lining of the uterus (known as **implantation**) and develops into a foetus.

During pregnancy, a special disc like tissue called **placenta** grows between the uterine wall and the embryo. Placenta forms finger-like projections called **villi** towards embryo. This create large surface area for the exchange of glucose and oxygen between the mother and the embryo.

The developing embryo also generates waste substances. These can be removed by transferring them into the mother's blood through the placenta. The development of the child inside the mother's body takes approximately nine months in human. Strong rhythmic muscular contractions in the uterus helps in the childbirth.

Menstruation

In females, ovaries release ovum or egg once every 28 days from the age of puberty. The uterus prepares itself every month to receive a fertilised egg. Thus, its lining becomes thick and spongy. If the egg is not fertilised it lives for about a day. Afterwards this lining of uterus is no longer required and menstruation occurs.

Menstruation is the phase of uterine bleeding in which an unfertilised egg and the thick uterine lining. It occurs through the vagina as blood and mucus. Menstruation lasts for about 3-5 days.

Check Point 04

1. What changes take place in boys during reproductive phase?
2. What is responsible for attainment of sexual maturity in both males and females?
3. Sperms are produced in testis, how do they reach the urethra for further passage into female reproductive tract?
4. What is the function of testosterone in males?
5. Fill in the blanks:
   (i) .... transfers the sperms into vagina of the female reproductive tract during copulation.
   (ii) .... forms villi towards the embryo, creating a large surface area for exchange of nutrients, gases, etc., between the mother and the embryo.
6. What is the function of Fallopian tube in female reproductive system?
7. What happens when fertilisation does not occur in female body?

Reproductive Health

It can be defined as the state of physical, mental and social fitness to lead a healthy reproductive life. Good reproductive health provides both male and female with
- the fertility control methods.
- awareness about how to limit their family size.
- protection from infection and sexually transmitted diseases.

A limited family size and no partial views about the sex of the unborn should be existed in our society. For this, we need to maintain sex ratio and population size.

Sex Ratio

It is the ratio of the number of females to the number of males in a population. The female-male sex ratio should be maintained in order to have a healthy society. Due to the reckless female foeticide, sex ratio is declining rapidly in some sections of our society. Therefore, prenatal sex-determination (determination of sex of child before birth) should be banned or prohibited by law.

Population Size

The size of the human population is a cause of concern because an expanding population makes it difficult to improve the standard of living. The rates of birth and death in a given population determine its size. The population size increases if the birth rate is higher than the death rate and *vice-versa*.

Birth Control

The sexual act always has the potential to result in pregnancy. Pregnancy makes major demands on the body and the mind of a woman. If she is not ready for it, her health will be adversely affected. Therefore, many ways have been devised to avoid pregnancy. The prevention of pregnancy is called contraception or birth control.

The methods used to prevent the occurrence of pregnancy are called contraceptive methods. These can be barrier, hormonal or chemical and surgical.

Surgery can also be used in order to remove unwanted pregnancies. These are sometimes used by people who do not want a child, e.g. illegal sex-selective abortion of female foetus.

Methods of Birth Control

Method	Example	Detail
Barrier	Condom	• Rubber sheath worn over the penis to stop sperm from entering the vagina. • Prevents transmission of Sexually Transmitted Diseases (STDs) and has no side effect.
	Diaphragm	• Rubber cup that is placed in the vagina over the cervix.
	Intra-Uterine Contraceptive Device (IUCD)	• Copper-T placed in uterus by doctor. • Used to prevent pregnancy. • Can cause side effects due to the irritation of uterus.
Hormonal	Oral contraceptive pills	• Contain hormones, which prevent release of ovum, so that fertilisation cannot occur. These disturb the hormonal balance of the body. • Can cause side effects also.
Chemical	Spermicide	• Applied in vagina. • Kills sperms. • Can only be used with condoms or diaphragm.
Surgical	Vasectomy	• Small portion of the sperm duct is cut or tied properly. Therefore, the sperm transfer will be prevented. • Prevents sperms from coming out. • An irreversible process.
	Tubectomy	• Small portion of oviduct is cut or tied properly. The Fallopian tube in the female gets blocked. The egg will not be able to reach the uterus and thus, fertilisation will not take place. • Prevents the egg from meeting the sperms. • An irreversible process.

Female Foeticide

The killing of unborn girl child is called female foeticide. It is happening because of misuse of ultrasound technique by which people get to know the sex of the child. It is female, they get it removed by surgery. This is reducing the number of girls drastically in some societies of our country.

Sexually Transmitted Diseases (STDs)

Sexually Transmitted Diseases (STDs) are caused by different pathogens transmitted by an intimate contact between a healthy person and an infected person. The most commonly transmitted sexual diseases include gonorrhoea and syphilis which are caused by bacteria. Viral infections such as warts and HIV-AIDS are also common.

Some Common STDs

Infection	Example	Causative Organism	Comment
Bacterial infections	Gonorrhoea	*Neisseria gonorrhoeae*	• Contracted on during unprotected sexual intercourse with an infected person. • Also passed by an infected mother to the developing foetus. • Infects ureter in men and cervix in women. • Treatment with antibiotics is effective. **Symptoms of gonorrhoea** • Discharge of pus from penis and vagina. • Burning sensation on urinating.
	Syphilis	*Treponema pallidum*	• Syphilis is transmitted from person to person by direct contact with syphilis sores These occur mainly on the external genitals, vagina, anus or in the rectum, can also occur on lips and mouth. • Syphilis can be transmitted during vaginal, anal or oral sexual contact. • Pregnant women with the disease can pass it to their unborn children. • Can be cured by antibiotics. **Symptoms of syphilis** • Appearance of sores on body parts. • Fever, ulcers, bone pain, liver disease and anaemia. These symptoms slow up during the tertiary stage of syphilis.
Viral infections	AIDS (Acquired Immuno Deficiency Syndrome)	HIV (Human Immunodeficiency Virus)	Incurable and fatal as it suppresses the immune system of the body. It can be transferred in following ways, • during unprotected sexual intercourse with an infected person. • sharing needles and transfusion of HIV unscreened blood. • from the mother to the child *via* placenta during pregnancy.
	Genital warts	HPV (Human Papilloma Virus)	• Causes warts over external genitalia and perianal area. • *Podophyllum* preparations are effective in treatment.

Check Point 05

1. Define reproductive health.
2. Give a reason for the declining balance in sex ratio.
3. Why expanding population is a matter of concern?
4. Fill in the blank:
   The most common method of birth control is ....
5. Name a method which acts as birth control and also protects from STDs.
6. State True or False for the following statement:
   Oral contraceptive measures help in birth control. True or False.
7. Name two STDs caused by bacteria.

NCERT FOLDER

Intext Questions

1. What is the importance of DNA copying in reproduction? *Pg 128*

Sol. The importance of DNA copying during reproduction are:
(i) It is responsible for the transmission of parental characteristics to the offsprings.
(ii) During DNA copying in reproduction, the changes occur due to the inheritance of traits from both the parents. This lead to certain genetic variations, which are useful for the evolution of species over a period of time.

2. Why is variation beneficial to the species, but not necessary for the individual? *Pg 128*

Sol. Variations allow organisms to exist in diverse habitats or niches. In its absence, a species may remain restricted to a particular area. If this area gets drastically altered due to various natural or man-made causes, the species may be wiped out. However, if some variations are present in few individuals, it would help them to colonise other habitats and survive. But, if variations are present in a single organism, there would be a very little chance for it to survive and species is lost forever.

3. How does binary fission differ from multiple fission? *Pg 133*

Sol. Differences between binary fission and multiple fission are given below

Binary Fission	Multiple Fission
The parent organism splits to form two new organisms.	The parent organism splits to form many new organisms at the same time.
It takes place during favourable environmental conditions.	It takes place during unfavourable environmental conditions.
It takes place in organisms like *Amoeba, Paramecium*, etc.	It takes place in organisms like *Plasmodium*.

4. How will an organism be benefitted, if it reproduces through spores? *Pg 133*

Sol. Spores are tiny, spherical, asexual reproductive bodies. They are covered with a hard protective wall. This enables them to survive in unfavourable conditions. They can only germinate and produce new plant under favourable conditions thereby benefitting the organism from dying out.

5. Can you think of reasons why more complex organisms cannot give rise to new individuals through regeneration? *Pg 133*

Sol. Multicellular organisms cannot reproduce cell-by-cell because they are not simply random collection of cells. They are formed of specialised cells organised as tissues and tissues into organs, which then have to be placed at different positions in the body. Multicellular organisms, therefore, require more complex ways of reproduction. Moreover, simple multicellular organisms can possess special type of cells which have the potential to grow into a new organism, but complex multicellular organisms have no such specialised cells.

6. Why is vegetative propagation practiced for growing some types of plants? *Pg 133*

Sol. Vegetative propagation is practiced for growing some types of plants because of the following reasons:
(i) Plants that have lost their capability to produce seeds can be propagated by this method.
(ii) It helps to grow plants bearing superior traits, as they are genetically identical to the parent plant.
(iii) It is used for growing plants which require a longer time to grow and become mature.

7. Why is DNA copying an essential part of the process of reproduction? *Pg 133*

Sol. Chromosomes in the nucleus of a cell contain information for inheritance of features from parents to the next generation in the form of DNA, which is the source of information for making proteins. Therefore, a basic event in reproduction is creation of DNA copy for transfer into the next generation.

8. How is the process of pollination different from fertilisation? *Pg 140*

Sol. Differences between pollination and fertilisation are

Pollination	Fertilisation
The transfer of pollen grains from anther to the stigma of a flower is called pollination.	The fusion of male and female gamete to form zygote is called fertilisation.
It involves only the male gamete (pollen grain).	It involves both male and female gamete.

9. What is the role of the seminal vesicles and the prostate gland? *Pg 140*

Sol. Secretions from seminal vesicles and prostate gland provide nutrition to the sperms. This makes transportation of sperms easier by providing them a fluid medium.

10. What are the changes seen in girls at the time of puberty? *Pg 140*

Sol. Changes seen in girls at the time of puberty are as follows:
(i) Growth of hairs in armpits and pubic region.
(ii) Mammary glands (breast) develop and hips broaden.
(iii) Uterus, vagina, Fallopian tube enlarge and pelvis widens.
(iv) Menstruation and ovulation also start.

11 How does the embryo get nourishment inside the mother's body? *Pg 140; CBSE 2015*

Sol. The embryo gets nutrition from the mother's blood with the help of a special tissue called **placenta**. This is a disc-like tissue which develops between the uterine wall and embryo. As mother eats, the food passes through the digestive system where the body breaks it down into small particles. These nutrients travel through the mother's blood stream and get exchanged with the blood stream of foetus through placenta.

12 If a woman is using a copper-T, will it help in protecting her from sexually transmitted diseases? *Pg 140 ; CBSE 2013*

Sol. No, copper-T does not prevent the transmission of sexually transmitted diseases. Copper-T only prevents implantation. The only safe method that can be used to prevent the transmission of sexually transmitted diseases is condoms.

Exercises *(On Page 141)*

1 Asexual reproduction takes place through budding in
  (a) *Amoeba* (b) Yeast
  (c) *Plasmodium* (d) *Leishmania*

Sol. (b) Asexual reproduction in *Hydra* and yeast takes place by budding.

2 Which of the following is not a part of the female reproductive system in human beings?
  (a) Ovary (b) Uterus
  (c) Vas deferens (d) Fallopian tube

Sol. (c) Vas deferens is a part of male reproductive system in humans.

3 The anther contains
  (a) sepals (b) ovules
  (c) carpels (d) pollen grains

Sol. (d) Anther is the male reproductive part in plants. It contains pollen grains, having male germ cells.

4 What are the advantages of sexual reproduction over asexual reproduction?

Sol. Sexual reproduction is considered to be superior over asexual reproduction as it brings about variations in the progeny. These variations allow organisms to live in diverse habitats with the help of adaptations. On the other hand, asexual reproduction does not bring about variations among progeny.

5 What are the functions performed by the testes in human beings?

Sol. Functions of testes in human beings include:
  (i) production of male sex cells–sperms.
  (ii) production of male sex hormone–testosterone.

6 Why does menstruation occur?

Sol. Menstruation occurs when the egg is not fertilised. Every month, uterus prepares itself to receive a fertilised egg. To nourish the embryo, its lining becomes thick and spongy. In case, egg is not fertilised, this lining breaks and discharges out of the body through the vagina in the form of blood. This is referred to as menstruation.

7 Draw a labelled diagram of the longitudinal section of a flower.

Sol. Refer to text on Pg. 242.

8 What are the different methods of contraception?

Sol. The different methods of contraception are:
  (i) **Barrier Methods** The devices such as condoms and diaphragm are physical barriers, which prevents sperms from meeting the egg.
  (ii) **Hormonal Methods** These contain hormonal preparations in the form of 'pills' which prevent the release of ovum.
  (iii) **Chemical Methods** The vaginal pills contain the chemicals called spermicides which kill the sperms.
  (iv) **Surgical Methods** In males, a small portion of sperm duct is cut by surgical method. The cut end is tied properly to prevent the sperms from coming out. In females, a small part of the Fallopian tube/oviduct is cut and tied to prevent the egg from entering the oviduct.

9 How are the modes of reproduction different in unicellular and multicellular organisms?

Sol. Unicellular organisms are made up of only a single cell, which performs all the functions necessary for life. So, reproduction is done by simple, asexual methods but in multicellular organisms various cells perform different functions.
So, production of all these specialised cells is required and simple methods for reproduction are insignificant. Thus, they reproduce by sexual reproduction.

10 How does reproduction help in providing stability to population of a species?

Sol. A species occupies a well-defined niche in an ecosystem, using its ability to reproduce. During reproduction, copies of DNA pass from one generation to the next. This copying of DNA takes place with consistency in reproducing organisms and This is important for the maintenance of body design features (physiological as well as structural) which allows the organism to use that particular niche. Reproduction is therefore, linked to the stability of population of a species.

11 What could be the reasons for adopting contraceptive methods?

Sol. The reasons for adopting contraceptive methods are:
  (i) To avoid frequent pregnancies, which in turn helps in population control.
  (ii) To prevent the spread of Sexually Transmitted Diseases (STDs).

SUMMARY

- **Reproduction** It is the process of producing new organisms from the existing organisms of the same species. It is vital for the existence and continuity of the species. Living organisms reproduce mainly through asexual reproduction or sexual reproduction.
- **Asexual Reproduction** It is the production of offspring by a single parent without the formation and fusion of gamete, e.g. binary fission in *Amoeba*, budding in *Hydra*, etc.
  - **Fragmentation** It is a form of asexual reproduction in which multicellular organisms break up into two or more small fragments or pieces, e.g. *Spirogyra*.
  - **Budding** In this, a daughter organism is formed from a small projection known as bud, which develops as an outgrowth due to repeated cell division on the parent body, e.g. yeast, *Hydra*.
  - **Regeneration** A fully differentiated organism can give rise to new individual organism from its body part, e.g. *Hydra*.
  - **Vegetative Propagation** New plants are obtained from a part of the parent plant like root, stem and leaves without the involvement of reproductive organs. The artificial method involves cutting, layering, grafting, tissue culture, etc.
  - **Spore Formation** Spores have the ability to germinate and give rise to a new colony, e.g. *Rhizopus*.
- **Sexual Reproduction** It is a type of reproduction in which the two sexes, i.e. male and female take part. It involves two major processes, i.e. formation of gametes and fusion of gametes (fertilisation).
- **Sexual Reproduction in Flowering Plants** The flowering plants or angiosperms bear special reproductive parts located in the flower and seeds enclosed in a fruit, formed after pollination and fertilisation.
- **Pollination** The transfer of pollen grains from the anther of the stamen to the stigma of a flower is termed as pollination.
- **Fertilisation in Plants** After pollination, one male gamete fuses with the female gamete to form a zygote. This fusion is called fertilisation.
- **Male Reproductive System** It includes :
  - (i) **Testes** A paired structure lying in scrotum. It produces sperms and hormone (testosterone).
  - (ii) **Vas Deferens** A duct arises from testes which brings sperms to urinary bladder.
  - (iii) **Urethra** Vas deferens opens into a common tube called urethra which carries sperms as well as urine, which runs through the penis.
  - (iv) **Penis** It is an external male genital organ with thick muscular walls to help in copulation.
  - (v) **Accessory Glands** Include paired seminal vesicles, prostate and urethral glands.
- **Female Reproductive System** It consists of :
  - (i) **Ovaries** Paired ovaries located in the abdominal cavity near the kidney which produce female gamete (ovum or egg) and hormones (oestrogen and progesterone).
  - (ii) **Fallopian Tube** It is a tube carrying the ovum (if not fertilised) or the zygote (if fertilised) to the uterus. It also acts as the site of fertilisation.
  - (iii) **Uterus** The two Fallopian tubes unite into an elastic bag-like structure known as uterus.
  - (iv) **Vagina** Uterus opens into the vagina through the cervix. It is also called the **birth canal**.
- **Fertilisation in Humans** After sexual act, the sperms reach the Fallopian tube where the ovum is present and fertilisation takes place to form a zygote which starts dividing for a period of nine months. Then a strong rhythmic muscular contraction in the uterus leads to childbirth.
- **Menstruation** If fertilisation does not take place then breakdown and removal of the thick, spongy lining of the uterus in the form of vaginal bleeding.
- **Reproductive Health in Humans** These are all those aspects of general health which help a person to lead a normal, safe and satisfying reproductive life.
- **Birth Control** A number of methods or techniques have been developed to prevent and control pregnancy. These methods are :
  - **Barrier** Condom, Diaphragm, Intrauterine Contraceptive Device (IUCD)
  - **Hormonal** Oral contraceptive pills
  - **Chemical** Spermicide
  - **Surgical** Vasectomy, tubectomy
- **Sexually Transmitted Diseases** (STDs) These are diseases which spread by sexual contact from an infected person to a healthy person. The most common ones are gonorrhoea, syphilis, genital warts and HIV-AIDS.

Exam Practice

Objective Type Questions

Multiple Choice Questions

1 Which of the following is not an outcome of variations present in population?
(a) Bacterial resistance to heat
(b) Different colour of eyes
(c) Maintenance of body design features
(d) Survival of species over time

Sol. (c) Variations are not responsible for maintenance of body design features. Rest others are outcome of variations present in a population.

2 Characters transmitted from parents to offsprings are present in **NCERT Exemplar**
(a) cytoplasm (b) ribosome
(c) Golgi bodies (d) genes

Sol. (d) Characters are transmitted from parents to their offsprings through genes.

3 The number of chromosomes in parents and offsprings of a particular species remains constant due to
(a) doubling of chromosomes after zygote formation
(b) halving of chromosomes during gamete formation
(c) doubling of chromosomes after gamete formation
(d) halving of chromosomes after gamete formation

Sol. (b) The number of chromosomes in parents and offsprings of a particular species remains constant due to halving of chromosomes during gamete formation (as a result of meiotic division).

4 Which of the following have buds on their leaves as vegetative reproducing structure?
(a) Rose (b) Strawberry
(c) *Bougainvillea* (d) *Bryophyllum*

Sol. (d) *Bryophyllum* reproduces by the buds present in their notches along the leaf margin of *Bryophyllum* which falls on the soil and develops into new plants.

5 In a flower, the parts that produce male and female gametes (germ cells) are
(a) stamen and anther
(b) filament and stigma
(c) anther and ovary
(d) stamen and style **NCERT Exemplar**

Sol. (c) In a flower, the parts that produce male and female gametes are anther and ovary, respectively.

6 The development of a seedling from an embryo under appropriate condition is called
(a) regeneration
(b) germination
(c) vegetative propagation
(d) pollination

Sol. (b) Germination is a process occurring in plants in which the embryo develops into a seedling under appropriate condition.

7 Which of the following helps in transport and nutrition of sperms?
(a) Mucus
(b) Blood
(c) Urine
(d) Glandular secretions

Sol. (d) Glands like prostate and seminal vesicles add their secretions to vas deferens so sperms are easily transported and nourished till maturation.

8 The correct sequence of organs in the male reproductive system for transport of sperms is
(a) Testis → Vas deferens → Urethra
(b) Testis → Ureter → Urethra
(c) Testis → Urethra → Ureter
(d) Testis → Vas deferens → Ureter
NCERT Exemplar

Sol. (a) Sperms formed in testis are delivered through the vas deferens which joins with another tube called urethra coming from the urinary bladder.

9 Which of the following is embedded in the uterine wall?
(a) Zygote (b) Embryo's head
(c) Placenta (d) Eggs

Sol. (c) Placenta is embedded in the uterine wall.

10 Which among the following diseases is not sexually transmitted?
(a) Syphilis (b) Hepatitis
(c) HIV-AIDS (d) Gonorrhoea
NCERT Exemplar

Sol. (b) Hepatitis is a water borne viral disease and not a sexually transmitted disease.

Fill in the Blanks

11 The main function of sperm is to reach the .... and fertilize it.
Sol. egg

12 Cutting and layering in plants are means of .... reproduction.
Sol. Vegetative

13 The gametes in humans are produced by the process called ....
Sol. Gametogenesis

14 In .... pollination, the pollen and stigma belongs to a flower on same plant.
Sol. Self pollination

15 Pollen grains of the flowers are also called ....
Sol. male gametophyte

True and False

16 Yeast regenerates into a complete individual from a single segment of its body.
Sol. False. Yeast reproduces by budding not by regeneration.

17 *Bryophyllum* reproduces by forming seeds.
Sol. False. *Bryophyllum* reproduces by means of vegetative buds which develop on the edge of leaves.

18 Shoe flower is a unisexual flower.
Sol. False, shoe flower is a bisexual flower.

19 Causal organism of dysantry is a virus
Sol. False. The causal organism of dysantry is *Entamoeba histolytica*.

20 Fission and regeneration are asexual method of reproduction.
Sol. True

Match the Columns

21 Match the following columns.

Column I	Column II
1. ovum	A. Germ cell produced by organism
2. Fertilisation	B. Female gamete
3. Zygote	C. Fusion of male and female gamete
4. Gamete	D. Cells resulting from union of male and female gamete

Sol. 1 → B, 2 → C, 3 → D, 4 → A

22 Match the following columns.

Column I	Column II
1. Budding	A. Rose
2. Grafting	B. *Amoeba*
3. Binary fission	C. *Hydra*
4. Zoospores	D. Algae

Sol. 1 → C, 2 → A, 3 → B, 4 → D

Assertion–Reason

Direction (Q. Nos. 23-27) *In each of the following questions, a statement of Assertion is given by the corresponding statement of Reason. Of the statements, mark the correct answer as*

(a) If both Assertion and Reason are true and Reason is the correct explanation of Assertion
(b) If both Assertion and Reason are true, but Reason is not the correct explanation of Assertion
(c) If Assertion is true, but Reason is false
(d) If Assertion is false, but Reason is true

23 Assertion Individuals produced by asexual reproduction are known as clones.
Reason They are known as clones because they are genetically identical.
Sol. (a) Both Assertion and Reason are true and Reason is the correct explanation of Assertion. The new individuals produced in asexual reproduction are always genetically identical to each other and their parents and are known as clones.

24 Assertion Scrotum is present outside the abdominal cavity.
Reason It stores sperms which require a lower temperature than the normal body temperature.
Sol. (a) Both Assertion and Reason are true and Reason is the correct explanation of Assertion. Scrotum, a pouch containing testis is present outside the abdominal cavity because sperms require temperature lower than the normal body temperature.

25 Assertion Vagina is also called as birth canal.
Reason During birth, the baby passes through the vagina.
Sol. (a) Both Assertion and Reason are true and Reason is the correct explanation of Assertion. Vagina is called as birth canal, because the fully natured baby passes through the vagina during birth.

26 **Assertion** Vasectomy is a surgical method of birth control.

Reason In vasectomy, small portion of oviduct is cut or tied properly.

Sol. (c) Assertion is true but Reason is false. The correct form of R is, Vasectomy is a surgical method of birth control, in which small portion of the sperm duct is cut or tied properly.

27 **Assertion** HIV-AIDS is a bacterial disease.

Reason It spreads through sharing of infected needles.

Sol. (d) Assertion is false but Reason is true. The correct form of Assertion is, HIV-AIDS is viral disease that is transmitted by a virus called HIV. It spreads through following routes,
- Unprotected sex
- Transfusion of HIV unscreened blood
- Sharing of needles, etc.
- It is one of the STDs.

Case Based Questions

Directions (Q. Nos. 28-31) *Answer the questions on the basis of your understanding of the following passage, table and related studied concepts:*

As soon as boys and girls reach adolescent age, certain changes start happening in their bodies under the influence of sex hormones produced in their bodies. These changes are mostly related to height, size, voice, pitch, physical attributes etc.

The table below shows the average height of boys and girls up to the age of 18 years.

Age/Years	Average Height / cm	
	Boys	Girls
0 (at birth)	52	51
1	76	75
2	88	88
3	97	97
4	103	103
5	110	110
6	118	117
7	125	122
8	131	128
9	135	133
10	141	140
11	145	146
12	150	153
13	156	158
14	164	161
15	169	162
16	172	162
17	174	162
18	175	162

28 State the changes happening in adolescent boys and girls.

Sol. The moustach starts appearing in boys and their voice becomes hoarse. There is onset of manstrual cycle in girls and their mammary glands starts developing.

29 When does the most rapid growth takes place?

Sol. Most rapid growth takes place within one year after birth of a baby.

30 The increase in height in girls almost ceases at age of
(a) 14 years (b) 15 years
(c) 16 years (d) 17 years

Sol. The increase in height of ceases at the age of 15 years.

31 Significant spurt in increase of height of boys occurs at the age of
(a) 11-12 years (b) 13-14 years
(c) 16-17 years (d) 17-18 years

Sol. In boys significant spurt in height occurs at the age of 11-12 yrs.

Directions (Q. Nos. 32-35) *Answer the questions on the basis of your understanding of the following passage and related studied concepts:*

The terms sexually transmitted disease (STDs) refers to a condition passed from one person to another through sexual contact. However it is not the only way STDs can be transmitted. An STD develops without any symptoms early on, or if any symptoms appear they are often dismissed as regular infections. It present there are several type of STDs known caused by different type of pathogens. Some of these STDs are curable while other are not. The only foot proof way of avoiding on STD is to practice safe sex.

32 State any two other methods of contracting an STD other than the sexual contact.

Sol. (i) Sharing needless with an infected person
(ii) Transfussion of STD unscreened blood.

33 Name any two STDs you have heard or read about recently.

Sol. (i) AIDS (Acquired Immuno Deficiency Syndrome)
(ii) Genital warts

How Do Organisms Reproduce?

34 How can people practice safe sex to avoid contracting an STD?
Sol. People can practice safe sex by using condoms.

35 Do you think like viruses, bacteria can also cause an STD? Give an example.
Sol. Yes bacteria is also known to cause STDs. For example syphillis is an STD caused by bacteria *Treponema pollidum*.

Very Short Answer Type Questions

36 State the method used for growing rose plants.z
Sol. Artificial method of vegetative propagation by stem cuttings and bud grafting.

37 Mention any one disadvantage of producing new plants by vegetative propagation.
Sol. There is no genetic variation, such plants are less adaptable to environmental changes.

38 Define sexual reproduction. **CBSE 2015**
Sol. Sexual reproduction is the method of reproduction involving fusion of gametes from both the parents, i.e. ovum (female) and sperm (male).

39 When does pollen tube develop in a flower?
Sol. During pollination, pollen grain falls over stigma. This pollen grain absorbs water and nutrients and produces a tube called pollen tube.

40 What is fertilisation and its product?
Sol. The fusion of sperm with the egg is called fertilisation. This leads to the formation of zygote, i.e. the product.

41 Why are testes located outside the abdominal cavity?
Sol. Testes are located outside the abdominal cavity because sperm formation requires a lower temperature than the normal body temperature.

42 List two functions of ovary of female reproductive system. **CBSE 2016**
Sol. Ovary in females is responsible for the production of female gamete (ova) and also produces hormones, i.e. oestrogen and progesterone.

43 What is the first sign of pregnancy in a woman?
Sol. The absence of menstrual cycle may be the first indication of pregnancy in a woman.

44 What is the function of the umbilical cord?
Sol. The umbilical cord contains blood vessels which supply blood between the foetus and the placenta.

45 How can pregnancy be prevented surgically?
Sol. When vas deferens in males are blocked surgically, sperm transfer is be prevented. Similarly, when Fallopian tubes are blocked in females the egg will not be able to reach the uterus thereby preventing pregnancy.

Short Answer (SA) Type Questions

1 Reproduction is linked to stability of population of a species. Justify the statement.
NCERT Exemplar; CBSE 2016
Sol. Refer to Ans 10 Exercises in NCERT Folder on Pg. 248.

2 Correlate the number of chromosomes with the size of the organism and answer the following questions.
  (i) Do larger organisms have more number of chromosomes/cells?
  (ii) Can an organism with fewer chromosomes reproduce more easily than organisms with more number of chromosomes?
  (iii) More the number of chromosomes/cells greater is the DNA content. Justify.
Sol. (i) No, there is no relationship between size of organism and its chromosome number.

(ii) No, the process of reproduction follows a common pattern and is not dependent on the number of chromosomes.)
(iii) Yes, since the major component of chromosome is DNA. If there are more chromosomes in a cell, the quantity of DNA will also be more.

3 Study the diagram given below:

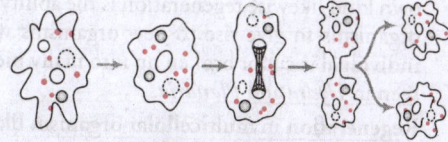

(i) Identify the process.
(ii) Which organism uses the above method for reproduction?
(iii) How is the above method different from the process of fragmentation?
CBSE 2015

Sol. (i) The process in the figure depicts binary fission in *Amoeba*, a method of asexual reproduction.
(ii) Binary fission also occurs in *Euglena* and *Paramecium*, etc.
(iii) Differences between fission and fragmentation are:

Fission	Fragmentation
It is the division of parent body into two identical daughter cells.	It is the division of parent body into two or more small fragments.
It occurs in unicellular organisms or multicellular organisms with simple body organisation.	It occurs only in multicellular organisms with complex cellular organisations.
e.g. *Amoeba*, *Plasmodium* (Protozoan).	e.g. *Spirogyra* (Algae).

4. (i) Identify whether budding as seen in *Hydra* is a type of sexual or asexual reproduction. Give reason for your answer.
(ii) How is this process different from fission? **CBSE 2015**

Sol. (i) Budding as seen in *Hydra* is a type of asexual reproduction which involves only a single parent. In this, a daughter organism is formed from a small projection called bud and it later detaches to grow into a new independent individual.
(ii) In budding, the new individuals develop from the parent as an extra outgrowth whereas in fission, parent's body divides into identical daughter cells.

5. Explain the term 'Regeneration' as used in relation to reproduction of organisms. Describe briefly how regeneration is carried out in multicellular organisms like *Hydra*? **CBSE 2016**

Sol. Regeneration is used in relation to reproduction because reproduction is the process by which a living organism is able to produce new individuals of its own kind likewise regeneration is the ability of some organisms to give rise to new organisms when the individual is cut or broken up into many pieces. It is seen in *Hydra* and *Planaria*.

Regeneration in multicellular organism like *Hydra*
(i) It is carried out by specialised cells.
(ii) When *Hydra* is cut or broken up into many pieces these specialised cells proliferate and make large number of cells.
(iii) From this mass of cells, different cells undergo changes to become various cell types and tissues.
(iv) These changes take place in an organised sequence referred to as development thereby making each piece to grow into a separate individual.

6. List any three advantages of vegetative propagation.

Sol. (i) The plants that cannot produce viable seeds such as banana, seedless grapes and oranges, etc., can be easily grown by vegetative propagation.
(ii) It is an easier, less expensive and a rapid method of propagation.
(iii) Genetically identical plants can be produced.

7. Ravi took three bread slices and kept them in the following conditions
(i) Slice 1 in a dry and dark place
(ii) Slice 2 in a moist and dark place
(iii) Slice 3 in moist and in refrigerator

What would he observe in each of the above conditions? Give reasons for your answer.

Sol. (i) In slice 1, no change will be observed or it will remain sterile because it lacks moisture.
(ii) A white cottony mass surrounded with black pin head-like structures are seen spreading on the surface of slice 2. This is because tiny spores of *Rhizopus* are always present in air which thrive in humid conditions. This is why on the slice 2 kept in moist and dark place, formation of sporangia and spores takes place, which are favourable for the growth of fungus.
(iii) In slice 3, also no change is observed (remains sterile) as it is kept at low temperature in the refrigerator.

8. Rajesh observed a patch of greenish black powdery mass on a stale piece of bread.
(i) Name the organism responsible for this and its specific mode of asexual reproduction.
(ii) Name its vegetative and reproductive parts. **CBSE SQP (Term-II)**

Sol. (i) The greenish black powdery mass on a stale piece of bread is due to bread mould, *Rhizopus*. It reproduces by the spore formation.
(ii) The vegetative part of *Rhizopus* is thread-like projections called hyphae and the reproductive part is tiny blob-like structures known as sporangia, which contain spores as reproductive structures.

9. Write one main difference between asexual and sexual mode of reproduction. Which species is likely to have comparatively better chances of survival, the one reproducing asexually or the one reproducing sexually? Give reason to justify your answer. **CBSE 2018**

Sol. The main difference between sexual and asexual reproduction involves the production and union of gametes in the process of fertilisation in sexually reproducting organisms which do not occur in asexual mode of reproduction.

Sexual reproduction is considered to be superior over asexual reproduction as it leads to variations, while asexual reproduction does not induce variations among progeny individuals.

Advantages of variations in individuals are
(i) It brings adaptation in individuals.
(ii) It helps in the survival of species.
(iii) It is the basis of evolution.

Hence, the species that reproduce through sexual reproduction have better chances of survival.

10 List six specific characteristics of sexual reproduction. **CBSE 2015**

Sol. Characteristics of sexual reproduction are
(i) It is biparental type of reproduction (two individuals are involved).
(ii) It takes place with the help of gametes.
(iii) It is a comparatively slower method of multiplication.
(iv) It is important for evolution.
(v) Abundant variations occur during this method.
(vi) It occurs in higher organisms along with some lower organisms.

11 Name the parts A, B and C shown in the following diagram and state one function of each.

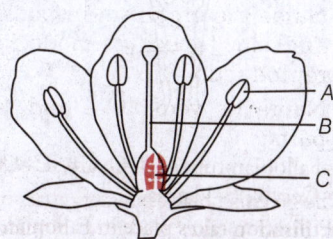

CBSE 2016

Sol.

Part	Function
A–Anther	Formation of pollen
B–Style	Lifting stigma to receive pollen
C–Ovary	Contains ovule which develop into seeds while ovary forms the fruit

12 (i) Define germination.
(ii) From the diagram given below identify the incorrectly labelled parts. **CBSE 2015**

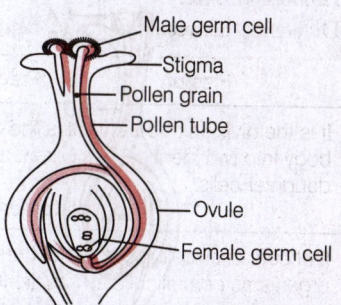

Sol. (i) The process by which a new plant grows and develops from a seed into a seedling under appropriate conditions is called germination. During germination various parts of seeds are formed that protect the growing embryo like seed coat.

(ii) The part labelled incorrectly are:
• Male germ cells – Should be pollen grain
• Pollen grain – Male germ cells
• Ovule – Should be the ovary

13 (i) Label the following diagram.

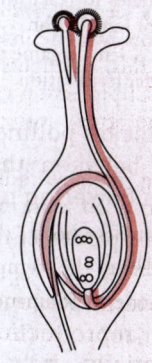

(ii) Which process is being shown in the diagram?

Sol. (i)

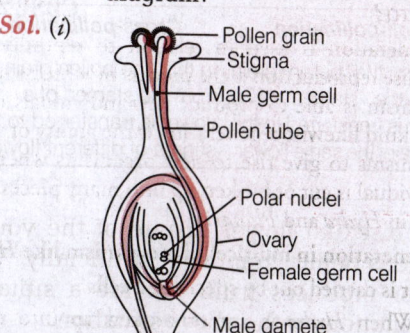

(ii) The diagram shows the process of pollination and germination of pollen grains on stigma of the flower.

14 (i) List two reasons for the appearance of variations among the progeny formed by sexual reproduction.

(ii)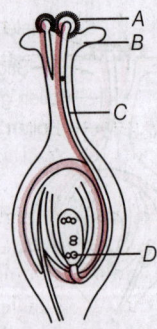

(a) Name the part marked A in the diagram.
(b) How does A reach part B?
(c) State the importance of the part C.
(d) What happens to the part marked D after fertilisation is over? **CBSE 2016**

Sol. (i) Refer to Ans 27 on Pg. 258.
(ii) (a) A–Pollen grain
(b) Pollen grain reaches part B, i.e. stigma by the process of pollination.
(c) Part C is pollen tube. It allows the passage for the male gametes to reach the ovary having female gamete for fertilisation.
(d) Part D, i.e. female gamete or egg cell that forms zygote after fertilisation.

15 What is meant by pollination? Name and differentiate between the two modes of pollination in flowering plants. **CBSE 2016**

Sol. Pollination is the process of the transfer of pollen grains from anther to the stigma of the flower.
There are two modes of pollination in flowering plants:
(i) Self-pollination (ii) Cross-pollination
Difference between self-pollination and cross-pollination are:

Self-pollination	Cross-pollination
In this, the pollen grain from the stamen of a flower is transferred to the stigma of the same flower.	In this, the pollen grain from the stamen of a flower is transferred to the stigma of different flower.

16 In a bisexual flower inspite of the young stamens being removed artificially, the flower produces fruit. Provide a suitable explanation for the above situation.
NCERT Exemplar

Sol. A bisexual flower has the male as well as female reproductive organs. If the young stamen (i.e. male unit) is removed artificially, the flower still has its pistil (i.e. female unit) intact. Therefore, cross-pollination can occur.

When the pollen grains from the anther of another flower are transferred to the stigma of this flower with the help of pollinating agents as insects, bees, wind and water, it causes cross-pollination.

After the pollen grains fall on stigma, the next step is fertilisation, followed by formation of fruits and seeds.

17 The sperms are tiny bodies that consist of mainly genetic material and a long tail
(i) Where are the sperms produced?
(ii) What is the role of the long tail?
(iii) How are the sperms delivered from the site of their production? **CBSE 2015**

Sol. (i) Sperms are produced in seminiferous tubules present in testes of male reproductive system.
(ii) The long tail of sperms helps in quick movement or motility of sperms through the female reproductive tract to reach egg cell.
(iii) Sperms are delivered from the site of their production by vas deferens, also known as sperm duct to the urethra in order to allow the passage of semen outside the body.

18 (i) Name the parts A to E of human female reproductive system.
(ii) Name the part in which fertilisation takes place in this system?

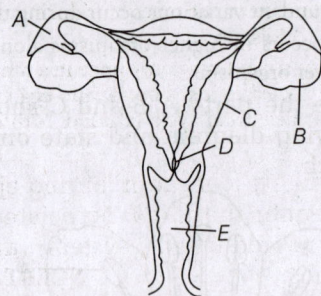

Sol. (i) A–Fallopian tube, B–Ovary, C–Uterus, D–Cervix, E–Vagina.
(ii) Fertilisation takes place in Fallopian tube.

19 Draw the human female reproductive system and label the following parts:
(i) Which produces ovum?
(ii) Where fertilisation takes place?

(iii) Where implantation of embryo takes place? **CBSE 2015, 2019**

Sol.

Female reproductive system (Oviduct or Fallopian tube, Ovary, Uterus, Cervix, Vagina)

(i) Ovum is produced by ovaries which are paired, oval-shaped organs.
(ii) Oviduct or Fallopian tubes are the site of fertilisation. Oviduct have funnel-shaped opening near ovary and carry ova or egg from ovary to uterus.
(iii) Implantation refers to embedding of the embryo in the thick lining of uterus.

20 How does fertilisation take place? Fertilisation occurs once in a month. Comment. **NCERT Exemplar**

Sol. Fertilisation In human beings, the sperms produced in the testis of males are introduced into the vagina of the woman through penis during copulation. The sperms are highly active and mobile and thus move up through cervix into the uterus.

From uterus, sperms pass into the oviducts. The oviduct contains an ovum released by the ovary during ovulation. Millions of sperms are released into the vagina at one time, but only one sperm fuses with the ovum in the oviduct to form a zygote. This is called fertilisation.

Fertilisation can occur only once in a month because the ovary releases just one mature egg every month during a menstrual cycle (around 14th day to 16th day).

21 Trace the path of sperm during ejaculation and mention the glands associated with the male reproductive system and their functions. **NCERT Exemplar**

Sol. Path of sperm during ejaculation Sperms come out from testis into the vas deferens. It then unites with another tube called urethra coming from the urinary bladder. Along the path of vas deferens, glands like the prostate and the seminal vesicle add their secretion, so that sperms are in fluid medium to make their transport easier. This fluid also provides nutrition.

Glands associated with male reproductive system are:
(i) **Testis** Secretes the hormone testosterone.
(ii) **Prostate gland and seminal vesicle** Add their secretion with the sperms.
(iii) **Cowper's gland** Secretion of this gland lubricates the urethra before ejaculation.

22 (i) Trace the path a male gamete takes to fertilise a female gamete after being released from the penis.
(ii) State the number of sets of chromosomes present in a zygote. **CBSE SQP (Term-II)**

Sol. (i) Male gamete (sperm) travel in the female reproductive tract after being released from the penis.
The sperms are highly active and motile. They swim into the uterus through vagina and then pass into the Fallopian tube (oviduct).
The fusion of male and female gamete results into the zygote.
(ii) A zygote is formed from the fusion of two gametes, the chromosome number is diploid ($2n$).

23 What changes are observed in the uterus if fertilisation does not occur? **NCERT Exemplar**

Sol. If the egg is not fertilised, it lives for about one day. Since, the ovary releases one egg every month, the uterus also prepares itself every month to receive a fertilised egg. Its lining becomes thick and spongy.
This would be required for nourishing the embryo if fertilisation had taken place. However, in absence of fertilisation, the lining slowly breaks and comes out through the vagina as blood and mucus. This cycle takes place roughly every month and is known as menstruation. It usually lasts for about 3-4 days.

24 Distinguish between a gamete and zygote. Explain their roles in sexual reproduction. **NCERT Exemplar**

Sol. Differences between a gamete and zygote are

Gamete	Zygote
The germ cells involved in sexual reproduction are called gametes, e.g. sperm in male and ova in female.	The fusion of male gamete and female gamete forms zygote during sexual reproduction.
Gametes are unfertilised reproductive cells.	Zygote is fertilised egg or fertilised ovum.
The fusion of sperm and egg forms a fertilised ovum or zygote.	Zygote undergoes development and forms a new organism.

Gamete formation is a prerequisite for the sexual reproduction to happen. Both sperm and ova unite to form a zygote. Zygote further develops and forms an embryo which becomes a baby.

25 What would be the ratio of chromosome number between an egg and its zygote? How is the sperm genetically different from the egg? **NCERT Exemplar**

Sol. The ratio of chromosome number between egg and its zygote is 1 : 2. An egg is a female gamete and it has haploid number of chromosomes. During fertilisation, it fuses with male gamete (also having haploid number of chromosomes) to form a zygote which now has diploid number of chromosomes.

Sperms and eggs are genetically different in terms of nature of sex chromosome. The sperm contains either X or Y-chromosome whereas, an egg will always have an X-chromosome.

26 What is placenta? Describe its structure. State its functions in case of pregnant human female.

Sol. Placenta is a special tissue that helps the developing human embryo (foetus) in obtaining nutrition from mother's blood.

Structure Placenta is a disc-like structure embedded in the uterine wall.

(i) It contains villi on the side of the embryo.
(ii) It contains blood spaces, on mother's side, which surround the villi.

Functions

(i) It provides a larger surface area for glucose other nutrients and O_2 to pass from mother's blood to the embryo.
(ii) It also removes metabolic wastes from the embryo.

27 Give two reasons for the appearance of variations among the progeny formed by sexual reproduction. **NCERT Exemplar**

Sol. Variations appear among the progeny formed by sexual reproduction due to the following reasons:

(i) Sexual reproduction results in new combinations of genes that are brought together during the formation of gametes by meiotic divisions (I and II). During meiosis-I crossing over between the homologous chromosome arms takes place. This reshuffling of genes in the gametes increases the chance of variation in offsprings.

(ii) The combination of two sets of chromosomes, one between the homologous chromosome arens set from each parent during zygote formation, leads to variation within a species.

28 What are the various ways to avoid pregnancy? Elaborate any one method.
NCERT Exemplar

Ans. Ways to avoid pregnancy are called contraceptive methods. It includes a number of ways such as:

(i) **Mechanical barrier**, e.g. condom
(ii) **Drugs** (oval pills for females)
(iii) **IUCD**, e.g. copper-T
(iv) **Surgical method** for permanent contraception.

Mechanical barrier There are a number of methods that create barrier between sperm and egg.

Some of them are as follows:

Condoms It is a fine rubber balloon-like structure worn over the penis during sexual intercourse. Semen is collected in it and not discharged into the vagina. This method also prevents the spread of STDs like AIDS, syphilis etc.

Diaphragms or Caps It can be fitted in the cervix of a woman to prevent semen from reaching the Fallopian tube.

29 What changes are observed in the uterus subsequent to implantation of young embryo?
NCERT Exemplar

Sol. After implantation of the embryo it gets nutrition from the mother's blood with the help of a special tissue called placenta. This is a disc, which is embedded in the uterine wall. It contains villi on the embryo's side of the tissue. On the mother's side are blood spaces, which surround the villi. This provides a large surface area for glucose and oxygen to pass from the mother to the embryo.

The developing embryo will also generate waste substances which can be removed by transferring them into the mother's blood through the placenta. The development of the child inside the mothers body takes approximately nine months after that the child is born as a result of rhythmic contractions of the uterine muscles.

Long Answer (LA) Type Questions

1 Reproduction is essentially a phenomenon that is not for the survival of an individual, but for the stability of a species. Justify.
NCERT Exemplar

Sol. All the living organisms need energy for their survival and growth. This energy is obtained from various life processes such as nutrition, excretion and respiration. Thus, these phenomena are essential for the survival of an individual. Compared to these life processes, reproduction may appear to be a waste of energy as it is not essential for survival of an individual.

It is basically important for continuity of the generation of an organism or species as DNA copying during reproduction helps to produce similar individuals as their parents to maintain stability of a species.

2 Why are budding, fragmentation and regeneration all considered as asexual types of reproduction? With neat diagrams explain the process of regeneration in *Planaria*.
NCERT Exemplar

Sol. Budding, fragmentation and regeneration are considered as asexual types of reproduction because all of them involve only one parent and sex or germ cells (gametes) are not involved in this type of reproduction.

Regeneration in *Planaria* It can be cut into any number of pieces and each piece grows into a complete organism. This is known as regeneration (see fig. below). Regeneration is carried out by specialised cells.

These cells proliferate and produce large numbers of cells. From this mass of cells, different cells undergo changes to become various cell types, tissues and organs. These changes take place in an organised manner referred to as development.

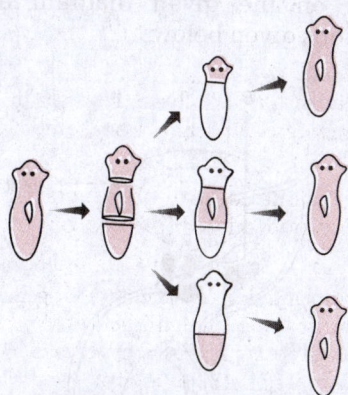

Regeneration in *Planaria*

3 (a) Name the mode of reproduction of the following organisms and state the important feature of each mode :
   (i) *Planaria*   (ii) *Hydra*
   (iii) *Rhizopus*
(b) We can develop new plants from the leaves of *Bryophyllum*. Comment.
(c) List two advantages of vegetative propagation over other modes of reproduction. **CBSE 2020**

Sol. (a) (i) *Planaria*—Regeneration
(ii) *Hydra*—Budding
(iii) *Rhizopus*—Sporulation
(b) The leaves of *Bryophyllum* bears vegetative adventitious buds which on separation can give rise to new plants.
(c) (i) Vegetative reproduction is easier and faster methods of reproduction.
(ii) It is useful in those plants/animals, which cannot reproduce sexually.

4 Answer the following questions:
(i) Name any three asexual modes of reproduction.
(ii) Explain with diagram the method by which *Amoeba* reproduces.
(iii) How is fission different from fragmentation? **CBSE 2015**

Sol. (i) Asexual reproduction process does not involve fusion of two different gametes from parents.
Three asexual modes of reproduction are:
(a) **Fission** The splitting of a unicellular organism into two or more separate, but identical daughter cells.
(b) **Budding** Division of parent organism by the formation of an outgrowth called bud. The daughter cells may remain attached or can separate from the parent body.
(c) **Fragmentation** The method in which multicellular organism breaks up into two or more smaller fragments.
(ii) *Amoeba* reproduces by binary fission.
Refer to figure on Pg. 239.
(iii) Refer to Short Ans. 3 (*iii*) on Pg. 254.

5 Define pollination. Explain the different types of pollination. List two agents of pollination? How does suitable pollination lead of fertilisation?
Delhi 2019

Sol. Refer to text on page no. 242.

6 (a) Draw a diagram showing germination of pollen on stigma of a flower and mark on it the following organs/parts:
   (i) Pollen grain   (ii) Pollen tube
   (iii) Stigma   (iv) Female germ cell
(b) State the significance of pollen tube.
(c) Name the parts of flower that develop after fertilisation into
   (i) Seed   (ii) Fruit   **CSBE 2020**

Sol. (a)

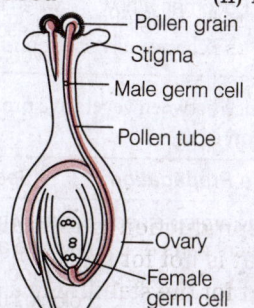

(b) The pollen tube takes its origin from intine of pollen grains. It grows through the style and reaches the micropyle of ovule. It carries male nuclei to the ovule for fertilisation.
(c) (i) Ovary develops into seed
(ii) Nature ovary develops into fruit.

7 Differentiate between the following:
  (i) Pollen tube and style
  (ii) Fission in *Amoeba* and *Plasmodium*
  (iii) Fragmentation and regeneration
  (iv) Bud of *Hydra* and *Bryophyllum*
  (v) Vegetative propagation and spore formation **CBSE 2015**

Sol. (i) Differences between pollen tube and style are:

Pollen Tube	Style
A tube growing out of pollen grain when it reaches stigma.	The middle elongated part of the carpel, i.e. female part of a flower.
It transports male gametes from pollen grains to ovules.	The attachment of stigma to the ovary.

(ii) Fission in *Amoeba* is binary and in *Plasmodium* is multiple. The difference is:

Binary Fission	Multiple Fission
The division of parental body into two identical daughter cells at a time.	The parental body divides into numerous daughter cells simultaneously.

(iii) Difference between fragmentation and regeneration is:

Fragmentation	Regeneration
The method in which multicellular organism breaks up into two or more smaller fragments.	The growth of a whole new organism from any of its body part, i.e. single segment forming new individual.

(iv) Difference between bud of *Hydra* and *Bryophyllum* is:

Bud of Hydra	Bud of Bryophyllum
It is seen during budding as an outgrowth on the body of *Hydra* which gets fully grown and then detaches from the body and becomes a new individual.	This is present on the leaf margins of leaf of *Bryophyllum* and develop into a new plant when it comes in contact with soil and other favourable conditions.

(v) Difference between vegetative propagation and spore formation is:

Vegetative Propagation	Spore Formation
New plants are obtained from different parts of parent body like leaves, stems, etc.	Spores when fall on land, have the ability to germinate and produce new fungal colonies under favourable conditions.

8 Draw the diagram of a flower and label the four whorls. Write the names of gamete producing organs in the female. **NCERT Exemplar**

Sol. Refer to the figure on Pg. 242.
The male gamete producing organ is anther while the female gamete producing organ is ovary in the flower.

9 Name the following
  (i) The body part in which the testes are present in a human male.
  (ii) The part from where the sperms are released out of the body.
  (iii) The part of female reproductive system containing a mature egg.
  (iv) The accessory fluid in human males, whose secretion activates the sperms.
  (v) The period of adolescence when the reproductive tissues begin to mature.

Sol. (i) Scrotum (scrotal sacs) (ii) Penis
  (iii) Ovary (iv) Semen (v) Puberty

10 Based on the given diagram answer the questions given below

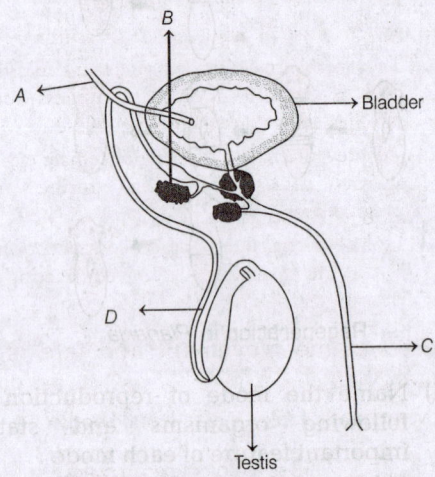

  (a) Label the parts *A*, *B*, *C* and *D*.
  (b) Name the hormone secreted by testis and mention its role.
  (c) State the functions of *B* and *C* in the process of reproduction. **CBSE 2020**

Sol. (a) *A*—Ureter
    B—Seminal Vesicle
    C—Urethra
    D—Vas deferens
  (b) Testosterone hormone is secreted by testis. It controls spermatogenesis (formation of sperm) and secondary sexual characters in male adolescents.
  (c) Seminal vesicle temporarily stores sperms.
    Urethra It transports and release urine and sperms outside the body.

11 (i) Identify the given diagram. Name the parts A to E. **CBSE (Delhi) 2019**

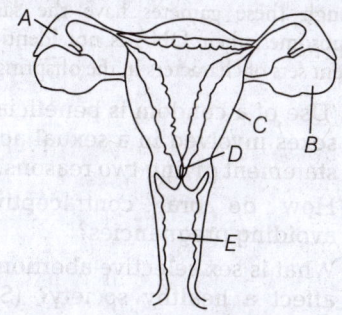

(ii) What is contraception? List three advantages of adopting contraceptive measures.

Sol. (i) The given figure represents the female reproductive system. Parts labelled A-E are
A. Oviduct or Fallopian tube   B. Ovary
C. Uterus   D. Cervix   E. Vagina

(ii) The prevention of pregnancies by using artificial method is called as contraception.

Advantage of using contraceptive measures are

(a) To control family size, population rise or birth rate. This is done by creating awareness about small families using contraceptive measures.

(b) To prevent chance meeting of female egg and male sperm thus, preventing future unwanted pregnancies.

(c) Use of barrier methods of contraception protects both the partners from contracting sexually transmitted diseases like AIDS.

12 Trace out the movement and fate of egg in female body.

Sol. Movement and fate of egg in female body

```
Eggs are produced in ovary
          ↓
Released in Fallopian tube
     ↓              ↓
If fertilised,    If unfertilised,
form zygote       degenerate
     ↓              ↓
Early embryo gets implanted    Passes out as
leading to pregnancy and       menstrual discharge
foetus starts to develop
```

13 (i) Write the function of following parts in human female reproductive system.
(a) Ovary   (b) Oviduct   (c) Uterus

(ii) Describe in brief the structure and function of placenta. **CBSE 2018**

Sol. (i)

Parts of female reproductive system	Functions
(a) Ovaries	Produce thousands of ova or egg cells. Secrete female sex hormones like oestrogen and progesterone.
(b) Oviduct (Fallopian tube)	Carries ova or egg from ovary to the uterus. It is the site of fertilisation.
(c) Uterus (Womb)	Here, the growth and development of foetus (embryo) take place. Rhythmic contractions of the muscles in the uterus cause labour pain and child birth.

(ii) **Structure of Placenta** Placenta is a disc between uterine wall and embryo which is embedded in the uterine wall. It contains villi on the embryo's side of the tissue. On the mother's side blood spaces are present, which surround the villi.

Functions of Placenta It provides a large surface area for glucose and oxygen to pass from the mother to the embryo. It also removes the waste generated by embryo, transferring it to mother's blood.

14 Give reasons:
(i) Placenta is extremely essential for foetal development.
(ii) Blocking of vas deferens prevents pregnancy.
(iii) Wind acts as a pollinating agent.
(iv) Use of condoms prevents pregnancy.
(v) Blocking of Fallopian tubes prevents pregnancy.

Sol. (i) Placenta is extremely essential for foetal development because it helps in nutrition, respiration, excretion, etc., of the foetus through the maternal supply.

(ii) Blocking of vas deferens prevents passage of sperms, hence, there is no fertilisation so it prevents pregnancy.

(iii) Wind acts as a pollinating agent because it helps in transfer of light weighted pollen grains from anther to stigma of a flower.

(iv) Condoms prevent entry of sperms into vagina, hence prevents pregnancy.

(v) If Fallopian tube is blocked, sperm and egg do not meet and fuse and fertilisation does not take place.

15 Describe the menstrual cycle.

Sol. In mature female, a cycle of events takes place in the uterus and vagina as described below

(i) In case fertilisation occurs, the inner wall of uterus thickens to receive the developing zygote.

(ii) In case fertilisation does not occur, the thickened wall along with the blood vessels breaks down and moves out of the vagina in the form of discharge called menstrual flow, which lasts for 2-8 days.

The cycle of events takes place in the ovaries and uterus in every twenty eight days and marked by menstrual flow is called menstrual cycle.

16 Write two points of difference between asexual and sexual type of reproduction. Describe why variations are observed in the offspring formed by sexual reproduction.

NCERT Exemplar

Sol. Differences between asexual and sexual reproduction are

Asexual Reproduction	Sexual Reproduction
It involves only one parent.	It often involves two parents.
Gametes are not produced.	Gametes are produced.
No fertilisation and zygote formation.	Fertilisation and zygote formation is observed.
Meiosis does not occur at anytime during reproduction.	Meiosis occurs at the time of gamete formation.

The reason why variations are observed in offsprings produced by sexual reproduction is that during sexual reproduction, two different types of gametes fuse. Although these gametes have the same number of chromosomes, their DNA is not identical. This brings different sets of characters in the offspring.

17 (a) 'Use of a condom is beneficial for both the sexes involved in a sexual act.' Justify this statement giving two reasons.

(b) How do oral contraceptives help in avoiding pregnancies?

(c) What is sex selective abortion? How does it affect a healthy society? (State any one consequence). *CBSE 2020*

Sol. (a) Use of a condom is beneficial for both the sexes involved in asexual act. It is because of the following facts

(i) It prevents pregnancy which is not desired by a couple.

(ii) It saves both the partners from sexually transmitted diseases like AIDS, etc.

(b) Oral contraceptives are the hormone pills which are taken by the females after their menstruation ends up. It is taken for 21 days daily. It changes the cyclic events of ovulation, etc. So, mature ovum is not available for fertilisation.

(c) Sex select abortion means if the factors is female, it is killed and extracted. This imbalanced the male and female ratio in the society.

CHAPTER EXERCISE

Multiple Type Questions

1. Reproduction is not essential for
   (a) continuation of life on Earth
   (b) addition of new species
   (c) transfer of variations to next generations
   (d) maintaining the life of an individual

2. The term pollination refers to
   (a) fusion of pollen grains and ovules
   (b) transfer of pollen grains to stigma
   (c) transfer of pollen grains to ovule
   (d) transfer of stamen to the carpels

3. The period during which reproductive organs in humans start developing and become functional is called
   (a) puberty   (b) adolescence
   (c) teenage   (d) maturity

4. Which of these is not a pubic character in human females?
   (a) Darkening of nipple skin
   (b) Increase in breast size
   (c) Enlargement of pelvic girdle
   (d) Voice begins to crack or hoarse

5. Which part of female reproductive tract is called birth canal?
   (a) Uterus   (b) Cervix
   (c) Vagina   (d) Fallopian tube

Fill in the Blanks

6. MTP is considered relationally safe till stands for ....

7. The method commonly used by Indian women for controlling the child birth is ....

8. Under unfavourable conditions of environment fungi refer reproduction using .... methods.

9. Union of male and female gametes is called ....

10. The full form of IUCD is ....

True or False

11. Living organisms can reproduce only by sexual methods.

12. Sexual reproduction involves the fusion of male and female gametes.

13. If no fertilisation takes place, the uterine wall disintegrates, resulting in menstruation.

14. The transfer of pollen grains from the anther of a stamen to the stigma of the pistil is called fertilisation.

15. AIDS primarily damages the body's immune system making it susceptible to other infections.

Match the Columns

16. Match the following columns.

	Column I		Column II
1.	Male primary sex organ	A.	Vas deference
2.	Structure through which sperm move out of the testis	B.	Seminal vesicle
3.	Paired glands which produce nutritive substance	C.	Testis
4.	Site of sperm maturation and storage	D.	Epididymis

Assertion–Reason

Direction (Q. Nos. 17-19) *In each of the following questions, a statement of Assertion is given by the corresponding statement of Reason. Of the statements, mark the correct answer as*
   (a) If both Assertion and Reason are true and Reason is the correct explanation of Assertion
   (b) If both Assertion and Reason are true, but Reason is not the correct explanation of Assertion
   (c) If assertion is true, but Reason is false
   (d) If assertion is false, but Reason is true
   (e) If both Assertion and Reason are false

17. **Assertion** DNA acts as the information source.
    Reason It helps in making different proteins and cellular machinery of the cell.

18. **Assertion** Menstruation is the regular discharge of blood from the thick uterine lining.
    Reason Menstruation occurs when egg is fertilised by sperm.

19. **Assertion** AIDS is an incurable and a fatal bacterial infection.
    Reason It suppresses the immune system of the body.

Case Based Questions

Direction (Q. Nos. 20-23) *Answer the questions on the basis of your understanding of the following passage and related studied concepts:*

Farmers, gardeners and horticulturists have developed various artificial methods of vegetative propagation for growing plants in gardens and nurseries. A very simple method of propagation involves a piece of the parent plants stem with nodes and internodes is placed in moist soil.

This grows into a new plant. In grafting the cutting of a plants are attached to the stem of a rooted plant.

The attached cutting becomes a part of the rooted plant, draws nutrition from it and grows roots at the joint. Now if it is separated, it grows into a new plant. In layering, one or more branches of the parent plant are bent close to the ground and covered with moist soil. The covered protions grow roots and develop into new plants.

20 Name any two artificial method of vegetative reproduction? In which method, cuttings from the parent plants are made to grow together? Name the cuttings involved in this process.

21 Name a plant in which layering produces a new plant.

22 Identify the method of artificial propagation used for
 (i) Rose (ii) Jasmine
 (iii) Apple

23 What is tissue culture?

Answers

1. (d) 2. (b) 3. (a) 4. (d) 5. (c)
6. 12 weeks
7. Condom/Oral pills   8. sexual
9. fertilisation
10. Intra Uterine Contraceptive Device
11. False   12. True   13. True   14. False
15. True   16. 1 → C, 2 → A, 3 → B, 4 → D
17. (a)   18. (c)   19. (d)

Very Short Answer Type Questions

24 Name the individual units of floral whorls.

25 What type of cell division occurs in *Plasmodium* during reproduction?

26 What will happen if *Hydra* is cut into many pieces?

27 Some of the fungal hyphae are aerial and bear black blobs. What are these blob-like structures on sticks called in *Rhizopus*?

28 Write the dual purposes served by urethra in males.

29 Delivery of sperms from where they are produced to urethra is facilitated by which part?

30 Which one is not STD among the following? AIDS, diarrhoea, genital warts, syphilis.

Short Answer (SA) Type Questions

31 Give a few characteristics of asexual reproduction.

32 When is vegetative propagation used? Name any three methods of vegetative propagation.

33 Draw a neat and labelled diagram showing longitudinal section of a bisexual flower.

34 What is implantation? Where does it take place? Mention the structure involved and its function.

35 Name the organ where ova are formed inside the body. Trace their pathway from formation to fertilisation.

36 What does HIV stand for? Is AIDS an infectious disease? List any four modes of spreading AIDS.

37 Explain
 (i) Population control
 (ii) Advantage of using contraceptives.

Long Answer (LA) Type Questions

38 'DNA copies generated will be similar, but may not be completely identical to the original'. Explain the statement with reference to asexually reproducing organisms.

39 Explain tissue culture technique. In which area this technique is finding its application?

40 Draw a neat diagram of fate of pollen after landing on stigma. Also label the following parts.
 (i) Female germ cell (ii) Pollen tube
 (iii) Pollen grain (iv) Male germ cell

41 What is the function of anther? How does fusion of male and female gametes take place in plants?

42 Give reasons why a woman should avoid frequent pregnancies. Explain the following methods of contraception giving one example of each.
 (i) Barrier method (ii) Chemical method.

Challengers*

1 The diagram shows the cross-section through the carpel of a flower just before fertilisation.

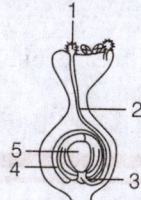

Where will the male and female gametes be just before fertilisation?

	Male gamete	Female gamete
(a)	1	5
(b)	1	4
(c)	2	4
(d)	3	5

2 Which conditions are necessary to activate enzymes when a seed germinates?

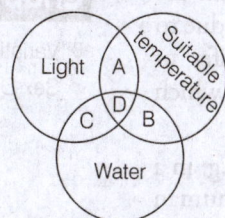

(a) C   (b) A   (c) D   (d) B

3 Given below are certain adaptations in fruits of certain plants. On the basis of information given below, identify the agent of pollination in both situations.

(i) Small, dry and light seeds with a parachute of fine hair.
(ii) Brightly-coloured, sweet and juicy but hard seeds.

(a) I-insects, II-animals   (b) I-water, II-insects
(c) I-wind, II-animals   (d) I-birds, II-insects

4 The diagram represents gametes P and Q fusing to give cell R. This cell then produces gametes S, T, U and V.

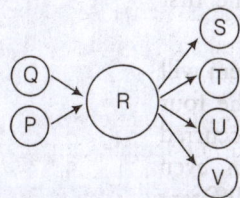

Which statement about the numbers of chromosomes in the cells and gametes is corrects.

(a) The numbers of chromosomes in P and Q are different
(b) The numbers of chromosomes in P and Q are same

(c) The numbers of chromosomes in S in one quarter of chromosomes in R
(d) The numbers of chromosomes in T is half the number of chromosomes in Q

5 Among all the methods of contraception, which one can prevent the implantation of the fertilised egg?

(a) Coil (mechanical)   (b) Condom (mechanical)
(c) Spermicide (chemical)   (d) Vasectomy (surgical)

6 The diagram shows the arrangement of blood vessels in the uterus wall and placenta of a pregnant women.

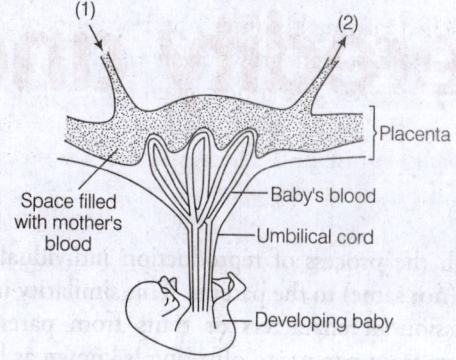

Which of the following will increase in concentration in the blood as it flows from 1 and 2?

(a) Amino acids   (b) Carbon dioxide
(c) Glucose   (d) Oxygen

7 The diagram show a section through the female reproductive system.

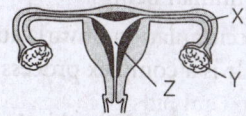

During pregnancy, where does mitosis occur in the cells of the embryo.

	X	Y	Z
(a)	✓	✓	✓
(b)	✓	✓	✗
(c)	✓	✗	✓
(d)	✗	✗	✓

key : ✓ = takes place, ✗ = does not take place

Answer Key

1.	(d)	2.	(d)	3.	(c)	4.	(b)	5.	(a)
6.	(b)	7.	(c)						

*These questions may or may not be asked in the examination, have been given just for additional practice.

CHAPTER 08

Heredity and Evolution

Through the process of reproduction individuals give rise to new individuals that are similar (not same) to the parents. This similarity in progeny or offspring or child is due to transmission of characters or traits from parents to their progeny. The transfer of characters from parents to offspring is known as **heredity** and the process through which characters or traits pass from one generation to another is called **inheritance**.

But, if we see closely we find that offspring are never a true copy of their parents, e.g. in a sugarcane field there are differences among individual plants, similarly in all human beings have different characteristics, complexion, height, eye colours, etc., these differences among the individuals of a species are called **variations**. Variations in plants are much lesser than human beings.

The long terms accumulation of variations lead to evolve a new species and the process is called **evolution**. It is a complex process and occurs over a long period of time.

Chapter Checklist
- Variation
- Sex-Determination

Accumulation of Variations During Reproduction

Inheritance from the previous generation provides both, a common body design and subtle changes in it, for the next generation. Now, when the new generation reproduces, the second generation produced will have variations that they inherit from the first generation, as well as newly created differences.

For example, if one bacterium divides and give rise to two individuals, each of them will divide again and give rise to two other individuals in the next generation. The four individual bacteria generated would be very similar with minor differences that occurred due to small inaccuracies in copying of DNA. However, in sexual reproduction, even greater diversity will be generated. Depending upon the nature of variations, different individuals would have different advantages the most important advantage of variation to a species is that it increases the chance of its survival in a changing environment.

Inheritance of Traits

Traits or characteristics, which are passed on from parents to their offspring generation to generation are controlled by **genes**. A gene is a unit of DNA which governs the synthesis of one protein that constants a specific character of the organism.

Heredity and Evolution

Genes are the units of heredity which transfer Characteristics (traits) from parents to their offsprings during reproduction. Due to the differences in genetic makeup, human population shows a great deal of variations in expression of various traits, e.g. height, skin colour, eye colour, shape of nose, lips and ears, blood groups, etc.

It has been observed that attached and free earlobes are two variants found in human population. The lowest part of the ear is called the **earlobe**.

In free earlobes, the earlobe is not attached to the side of the head, whereas, in attached earlobe, the earlobe is closely attached to the side of the head. This particularly trait is hereditary. The two variants of earlobes found in human population are schematically shown below

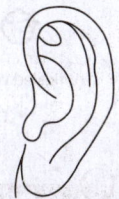 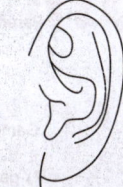

(a) Free earlobe   (b) Attached earlobe

Mendel's Contribution towards the Inheritance of Traits

The rules for inheritance of traits in human beings are related to the fact that both father and mother contribute equal amount of genetic material to the child. This means that each trait can be influenced by both paternal and maternal DNA. Thus, for each trait, there will be two versions in the child.

Mendel worked out the main rules of such inheritances. The heredity in most of the living organisms is found to be regulated by certain definite principles. Mendel opted for garden pea (*Pisum sativum*) to conduct his experiments. His experiments with garden pea along with the inferences drawn together constitute, the foundation of modern genetics. Mendel's contributions were unique because of the use of distinct variables and application of mathematics to the problem. He kept the record of each generation separately and studied the inheritance of only one pair of characters at a time.

Gregor Johann Mendel (1822-1884)

He was an Austrian Geneticist who, due to his knowledge of mathematics, was the first to keep count of individuals exhibiting a particular trait in each generation to study inheritance patterns in pea plants. Some of the basic laws of inheritance were proposed by him and now he is known to world as the Father of Genetics.

Important Terms and Definitions Used in Heredity

Term	Definition
Chromosome	A thread-like structure in the nucleus of the cell. It appears during cell division and it carries genes.
Gene	A functional unit of heredity. Present on chromosomes of cell nucleus. It is a piece of DNA that codes for one polynucleotide (protein). It determines a particular character (phenotype).
Character	The feature or characteristic of an individual like height, colour, shape, etc.
Trait	An inherited character, i.e. feature, which is normally inherited and has its detectable variant too. Here tall and dwarf are traits of a character, i.e. height.
Allele	One of the different forms of a particular gene, occupying the same position on a chromosome.
Hybrid	An individual having two different alleles for the same trait.
Dominant allele	An allele, whose phenotype will be expressed even in the presence of another allele of that gene. It is represented by a capital letter, e.g. T.
Recessive allele	An allele, which gets masked in the presence of dominant allele and can only affect the phenotype in the absence of a dominant gene. It is represented by a small letter, e.g. t.
Genotype	Genetic composition of an individual.
Phenotype	The expression of the genotype, which is an observable or measurable characteristic.
Monohybrid cross	A hybridisation cross in which inheritance of only one pair of contrasting characters is studied.
Dihybrid cross	A cross in which inheritance of two pairs of contrasting characters is simultaneously studied.
Homozygous	A condition in which an individual possesses a pair of identical genes controlling a given character and will breed true for this character (e.g. occurrence of two identical alleles for tallness in a P_1 tall pea plant).
Heterozygous	A condition in which an individual has a pair of contrasting genes for any one character and will not breed true for this character (e.g. existence of dominant and recessive alleles in F_1-hybrid tall pea plant).
Progeny	A descendant or offspring as a daughter organism.
Gametes	Reproductive cells containing only one set (haploid) of dissimilar chromosomes.

Experiment Conducted By Mendel

More than a century ago, Mendel worked out the main rules for inheritance. He performed following two experiments:

1. Inheritance of Traits for One Contrasting Character

- Mendel took pea plants with different characteristics such as height (tall and short plants).

- The progeny produced from them (F₁-generation plants) were all tall. Mendel then allowed F₁ progeny plants to undergo self-pollination.
- In the F₂-generation, he found that all plants were not tall, three quarter were tall and one quarter of them were short. This observation indicated that both the traits of shortness and tallness were inherited in F₁-generation. But only the tallness trait was expressed in F₁-generation.
- Two copies of the traits are inherited in each sexually reproducing organism.

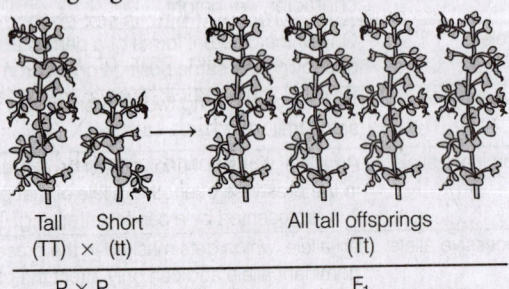

Mendel's experiment showing law of dominance

- TT and Tt are phenotypically tall plants, whereas tt is a short plant. For a plant to be tall, the single copy of 'T' is enough. Therefore, in traits Tt, 'T' is a dominant trait, while 't' is a recessive trait. In F₂-generation, both the characters are recovered, though one of these is not seen in F₁ stage. During gamete formation, the factor or allele of a pair segregate from each other.

Thus, the phenotypic ratio is 3 : 1 and the genotypic ratio is 1 : 2 : 1 for the inheritance of traits for one contrasting character.

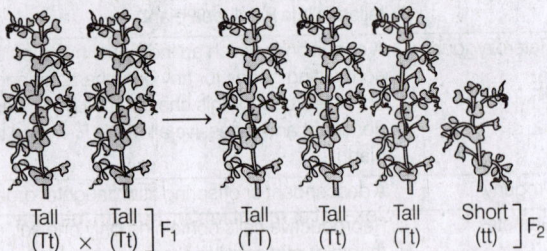

Mendel's experiment showing law of segregation

2. Inheritance of Traits for Two Visible Contrasting Characters

- Mendel took pea plants with two contrasting characters, i.e. one with a green round seed and the other one with a yellow wrinkled seed.
- When the F₁ progeny was obtained, they had round and yellow seeds, thus establishing that round and yellow are dominant traits.
- Mendel then allowed the F₁ progeny to be self-crossed (self-pollination) to obtain F₂ progeny. He found that seeds were round yellow, round green, wrinkled yellow and some were wrinkled green.
- The ratio of plants with above characteristics was 9 : 3 : 3 : 1, respectively (Mendel observed that two new combinations had appeared in F₂).
- In F₂-generation, all the four characters were assorted out independent of the others. Therefore, he said that a pair of alternating or contrasting characters behaves independently of the other pair. For example, seed colour is independent of seed coat. The independent inheritance of two separate traits shape and colour of seeds is schematically shown below

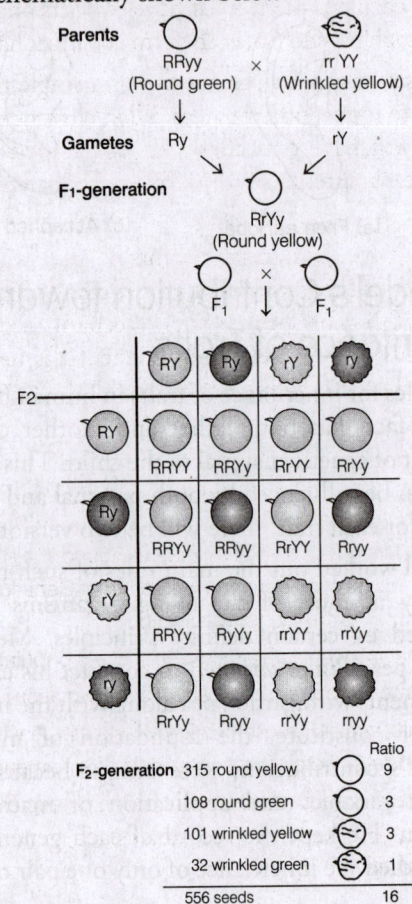

Independent inheritance of two separate traits, shape and colour of seeds.

Expression of Traits

Cellular DNA is the source of information for making proteins in the cell. A section of DNA that provides information for one particular protein is called **a gene** for that protein. As we know that plants have hormones that can trigger growth.

All in one Heredity and Evolution

Therefore, the amount of plant hormone formed will determine the plant's height. The amount of plant hormone made, will depend on the efficiency of the process for making it.

Consider an enzyme important for this process. If this enzyme works efficiently, a lot of hormones will be made (i.e. tall plant). If the gene for enzyme has an alteration, the enzyme will be less efficient.

Hence, the amount of hormone produced will be less (i.e. small plant).This proves that the traits (characters) are controlled by genes only.

Mechanism of Inheritance

If both parents help to determine the trait in the progeny, both parents must be contributing a copy of the same gene.

Thus, each pea plant must have two sets of all genes, one inherited from each parent. So, each germ cell must have only one gene set.

Each set of gene is present not as a single thread of DNA, but as separate independent pieces called **chromosomes**. Each cell of the body will have two copies of each chromosome, one inherited from each parent, i.e. one from male parent and one from female parent.

When two germ cells combine, they will restore the normal number of chromosomes in the progeny. This ensures the stability of the DNA of species. Such mechanism of inheritance explains the result of Mendel's experiments. It is used by all sexually and asexually reproducing organisms.

Check Point 01

1 Fill in the blanks:
   (i) The unit of hereditary material found in all living organisms is ....
   (ii) ...... is considered as the Father of Genetics.
   (iii) ...... is the monohybrid ratio.
2 What is meant by variations found in a population?
3 Name two human traits which show variation.
4 State True or False for the following statement:
   Mendel selected sugarcane for his experiments on genetics.
5 What is meant by pair of contrasting characters?
6 How is variation brought in the progeny in the sexually reproducing organisms?

Sex-Determination

A person can have either a male sex or a female sex. The process by which sex of a newborn individual is determined is called **sex-determination**. There are different strategies by which sex is determined in different species.

- In some species, **environmental factors** are important in determining the sex of the developing individual. For example, in few **reptiles**, the temperature at which the fertilised eggs are kept, determines the sex of the offspring. Incubation of the eggs of the lizard *Agama agama* at a high temperature produces males. However, incubation of the eggs of the turtle *Chrysema picta* at a high temperature produces females. In other animals, such as **snails**, individuals can change sex in different conditions, indicating that sex is not genetically determined.

- The determination of sex occurs largely by genetic control in **human beings**. In human beings, there are 23 pairs of chromosomes, out of which 22 pairs are **autosomes** and one pair is **sex chromosomes**.

- Females have a perfect pair of sex chromosome (homogametic) but males have a mismatched pair (heterogametic) in which one is X (normal sized) and the other is Y-chromosome (short in size).

Hence, an egg fertilised by X-chromosome carrying sperm results in a zygote with XX, which becomes a female and if an egg is fertilised by Y-chromosome carrying sperm, it results in a XY zygote that becomes male. Thus, the sex of the children will be determined by what they inherit from their father. A child who inherits an X-chromosome will be a girl and one who inherits a Y-chromosome will be a boy.

The inheritance of sex in humans is diagrammatically shown below

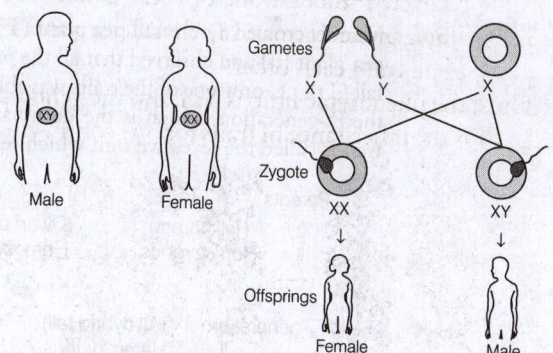

Sex-determination in human beings

Check Point 02

1 State True or False for the following statement:
   (i) In reptiles, individuals can change sex.
   (ii) The sex of the children will be determined by what they inherit from their mother.
2 Fill in the blanks:
   (i) ...... have a perfect pair of sex chromosome.
   (ii) In human beings, ... pairs are autosomes.
3 Write the sex of the baby that inherits Y-chromosome from the father.

NCERT FOLDER

Intext Questions

1 If a trait *A* exists in 10% of the population of an asexually reproducing species and a trait *B* exists in 60% of the same population, which trait is likely to have arisen earlier? **Pg 143**

Sol. In a population of asexually reproducing species, the chances of appearance of new traits due to variations are very low. And the trait which is already present in the population is likely to be in higher percentage and would have been arisen earlier. Therefore, the trait *B* present in 60% of the population is the trait which have arisen earlier.

2 How does the creation of variations in a species promote survival? **Pg 143**

Sol. During reproduction, copying of DNA takes place, which is not 100% accurate, thereby causing variations. If these variations are favourable, they help the individuals to survive and pass these variations to their progeny. Depending upon the nature of variations, different individuals have different advantages, which promotes their survival like bacteria which can withstand heat will survive better in a heat wave.

3 How do Mendel's experiments show that traits may be dominant or recessive? **Pg 147; CBSE 2016**

Sol. Mendel crossed a pure tall pea plant (TT) with pure dwarf pea plant (tt) and observed that all the progeny were hybrid tall (Tt), i.e. only one of the traits was able to express itself in the F_1-generation, which is the dominant trait. The other trait is called the recessive trait which remains suppressed.

```
Parents    ♀ TT        ×        ♂ tt
          (Tall parent)      (Dwarf parent)
          Homozygous    ↓     Homozygous
                       Tt
F₁-generation      (All hybrid tall)
                    Heterozygous
```

However, when he self-crossed plants of F_1-generation, he observed that one-fourth of the plants were dwarf and three-fourth were tall.

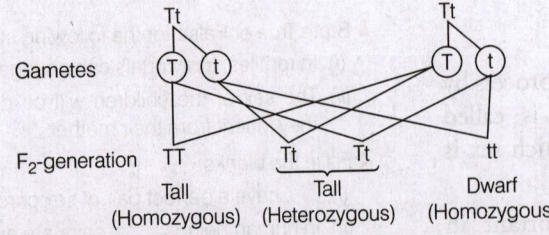

The expressed trait T for the tallness is dominant trait, while the trait 't' of dwarfness is recessive. Thus, Mendel's experiments show that trait may be dominant or recessive.

4 How do Mendel's experiments show that traits are inherited independently? **Pg 147; CBSE 2016**

Sol. Mendel performed a dihybrid cross between pure pea plants to show that traits are inherited independently. He selected a pea plant with round yellow (RRYY) and wrinkled green (rryy) seeds.

In the F_1 progeny, it was found that all plants were round yellow. But in F_2 progeny, some plants were round yellow and some were wrinkled green. However, there were plants which showed new combinations. Some of them were round with green seeds, while others were wrinkled with yellow seeds. Thus, the round/wrinkled trait and green/yellow seed trait and independently inherited.

5 A man with blood group 'A' married a woman with blood group 'O' and their daughter has blood group 'O'. Is this information enough to tell you which of the traits blood group 'A' or 'O' is dominant? Why or why not? **Pg 147**

Sol. The information is insufficient to tell whether the trait 'A' or 'O' is dominant. We can find out by assuming the following cases

In case I Let us assume that trait 'A' is dominant. Father may have $I^A I^A$ or $I^A I^O$ and mother $I^O I^O$.

In this case, 50% of the progeny will have blood group 'A' and 50% of the progenies will have blood group 'O', when father's blood group is $I^A I^O$ and mother is $I^O I^O$.

In case II Let us assume that 'O' is dominant. In this case, we see that the child may have blood group 'O'.

Since, in both the assumptions, the child can have blood group 'O', so we cannot infer which trait is dominant.

6 How is the sex of a child determined in human beings? **Pg 147**

Sol. A male germ cell which forms gametes carries one X and one Y-chromosome, while a female germ cell carries two X-chromosomes.

Therefore, sex of the child depends upon what happens during fertilisation.

(*i*) If a sperm carrying X-chromosome fertilises the egg, the child born will be a female (XX).

(*ii*) If a sperm carrying Y-chromosome fertilises the egg, the child born will be a male (XY).

All in one Heredity and Evolution

Thus, the sperm (the male gamete) determines the sex of the child.

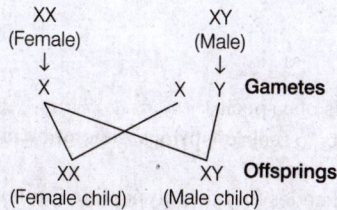

Exercises (On Page 159)

1 A Mendelian experiment consisted of breeding tall pea plants bearing violet flowers with short pea plants bearing white flowers. The progeny all bore violet flowers, but almost half of them were short. This suggests that the genetic makeup of the tall parent can be depicted as

(a) TTWW (b) TTww
(c) TtWW (d) TtWw

Sol. (c) The genetic makeup of the tall parent can be depicted as TtWW.

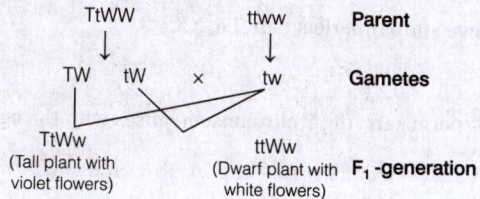

2 A study found that the children with light-coloured eyes are likely to have parents with light-coloured eyes. On this basis, can we say anything about whether the light eye colour trait is dominant or recessive? Why or why not?

Sol. From this study, we cannot make any inference whether light eye colour trait is recessive or dominant, because as both the parents have light colour eye, all the children will definitely have light colour eye (though certain variations may occur).

3 Outline a project which aims to find the dominant colour coat in dogs.

Sol. In order to find a dominant coat colour in dogs, homozygous black (BB) male dog and a homozygous white (bb) female dog are allowed to cross-breed in order to produce offsprings (F_1-generation).

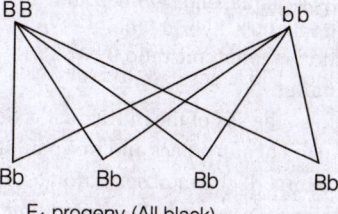

F_1 progeny (All black)

If all the offsprings in the F_1-generation are black, this concludes that black colour coat is dominant over white colour coat in dogs and if all the offsprings are white, the dominant colour will be white.

Note Questions related to deleted topics from CBSE Syllabus have not been covered in NCERT folder.

SUMMARY

- **Genetics** It is the branch of biology which deals with heredity and variations.
- **Variation** It refers to the differences in the characters or traits among the individuals of a species.
- **Inherited Traits** These are traits or characteristics, which are passed on from parents to their offsprings, generation after generation and are controlled by genes.
- **Gene** It is the basic unit of heredity present on chromosome, composed of DNA and codes for one polypeptide (protein).
- **Inheritance of Traits** (Mendelism) Gregor Johann Mendel (1822-1884) was the first one to keep count of individuals exhibiting a particular trait in each generation to study inheritance pattern in pea plants. He is regarded as the father of genetics. He used a number of contrasting, visible characters like round/wrinkled seeds, tall/short plants, white/violet flowers, etc.
- **Genetic Crosses Performed by Mendel**
- **Monohybrid Cross** It is a cross between two parents taking the alternative traits of one single character, e.g. a cross between tall and dwarf pea plant gives
  In F_1 -generation–100% hybrid
  In F_2 -generation–phenotypic ratio 3 : 1 and genotypic ratio 1 : 2 : 1.
- **Dihybrid Cross** It is a cross between two parents taking into consideration alternative trait of two different characters, e.g. a cross between two pea plants, one having round green seeds and other having wrinkled yellow seeds gives
  In F_1 -generation–100% hybrid type.
  In F_2 -generation–phenotypic ratio 9 : 3 : 3 : 1.
- **Sex-Determination**
- In human beings, the sex of the individual is determined genetically.
- There are 22 pairs of autosomes and one pair of sex chromosomes.
- Males have an imperfect pair of sex chromosomes, i.e. XY, while females have similar perfect pair, i.e. XX.
- In a woman, all eggs carry only X-chromosome.
- Sex of a child depends on the type of sperm which fuses with the egg.
- If the sperm carries X-chromosome, a girl child will be produced and if the sperm carrying Y chromosome fuses with the egg, it will result in birth of a baby boy.

Exam Practice

Objective Type Questions

Multiple Choice Questions

1 Exchange of genetic material takes place in
(a) vegetative reproduction
(b) asexual reproduction
(c) sexual reproduction
(d) budding **NCERT Exemplar**

Sol. (c) Exchange of genetic material takes place in sexual reproduction.

2 A cross between a tall plant (TT) and short pea plant (tt) resulted in progeny that were all tall plants because
(a) tallness is the dominant trait
(b) shortness is the dominant trait
(c) tallness is the recessive trait
(d) height of pea plant is not governed by gene 'T' or 't' **NCERT Exemplar**

Sol. (a) In F_1-generation, the cross between TT and tt will result into all tall plants. Thus, tallness is the dominant trait.

3 Which amongst the listed tools was used to study the law of inheritance in pea plant by Gregor J Mendel?
(a) Family tree (b) Pedigree chart
(c) Punnett square (d) Herbarium sheet

Sol. (c) Punnett square was used by GJ Mendel to determine the law of inheritance in his experiments with pea plants.

4 A trait in an organism is influenced by
(a) paternal DNA only
(b) maternal DNA only
(c) both maternal and paternal DNA
(d) neither by paternal nor by maternal DNA **NCERT Exemplar**

Sol. (c) A trait in an organism is influenced by both maternal and paternal DNA.

5 The number of pair(s) of sex chromosomes in the zygote of humans is
(a) one (b) two (c) three (d) four **NCERT Exemplar**

Sol. (a) The number of sex chromosomes in the zygote of humans is one pair.

6 The maleness of a child is determined by
(a) X-chromosome in the zygote
(b) Y-chromosome in the zygote
(c) cytoplasm of germ cell which determines the sex
(d) sex is determined by chance **NCERT Exemplar**

Sol. (b) The maleness of a child is determined by the Y-chromosome in zygote inherited from the father.

Fill in the Blanks

7 Allele is another name for ....
Sol. gene

8 Genes that are not expressed are called ....
Sol. recessive

9 In a monohybrid cross, one of the alleles is .... and another is ....
Sol. dominant; recessive

10 The number of autosomes in the human zygote is ....
Sol. 44

True and False

11 Genes assort the independently.
Sol. True

12 Most of the mutations are beneficial.
Sol. True

13 Free earlobes and attached earlobes are both recessive traits.
Sol. False; Free earlobes are dominant traits and attached earlobes are recessive traits.

14 A section of DNA that provides information for one particular protein is called an allele.
Sol. False; A section of DNA that provides information for one particular protein is called a gene.

Match the Columns

15 Match the following columns.

Column I		Column II	
A.	*Pisum sativum*	1.	Female gamete
B.	DNA	2.	Short sized
C.	X-chromosome	3.	Wings of bats and birds
D.	Y-chromosome	4.	Chromosome
E.	Analogy	5.	Garden pea

Sol. A → 1, B → 4, C → 1, D → 2, E → 5

Assertion-Reason

Direction (Q. Nos. 16-17) *In each of the following questions, a statement of Assertion is given by the corresponding statement of Reason. Of the statements, mark the correct answer as*

(a) If both Assertion and Reason are true and Reason is the correct explanation of Assertion

(b) If both Assertion and Reason are true, but Reason is not the correct explanation of Assertion

(c) If Assertion is true, but Reason is false

(d) If Assertion is false, but Reason is true

16 Assertion Dominant allele is an allele whose phenotype expresses even in the presence of another allele of that gene.

Reason It is represented by a capital letter, e.g. T.

Sol. (b) Dominant allele is an allele whose phenotype will be expressed even in the presence of another allele of that gene. It is represented by a capital letter, e.g. T.
Both Assertion and Reason are true, but Reason is not the correct explanation of Assertion.

17 Assertion The sex of the children will be determined by chromosome received from the father.

Reason A human male has one X and one Y-chromosome.

Sol. (a) If a child who inherits X-chromosome from the father will be a girl and one who inherits a Y-chromosome will be a boy.
Both Assertion and Reason are true and Reason is not the correct explanation of Assertion.

Case Based Questions

Direction (Q.Nos. 18-20) *Answer the questions on the basis of your understanding of the following table and related studied concepts.*

Sahil performed an experiment to study the inheritance pattern of genes. He crossed tall pea plants (TT) with short pea plants (tt) and obtained all tall plants in F_1-generation.

18 What will be set of genes present in the F_1-generation?

Sol. Tt is the set of genes present in F_1-generation.

19 Give reason why only tall plants are observed in F_1 progeny.

Sol. The cross between tall and short pea plants produces tall progeny.
The tall progeny is present in heterozygous condition in which 'T' (Tall plant) is a dominant trait and 't' is a recessive trait.

20 When F_1 plants were self-pollinated, a total of 800 plants were produced. How many of these would be tall, medium height or short plants? Give the genotype of F_2-generation.

Or

When F_1 plants were cross-pollinated with plants having tt genes, a total of 800 plants were produced. How many of these would be tall, medium height or short plants? Give the genotype of F_2-generation.

CBSE SQP (Term-II)

Sol. In the F_2-generation, the ratio of different character comes out to be

1 : 2 : 1
Tt Tt tt

If total 800 plants were produced, then 600 plants will be tall and 200 plants will be small.

Or

In the cross between Tt generation and tt genes, a total 800 plants were produced.
The cross is given below

F_1 generation   Tt   ×   tt
Gametes   T   t   t   t

F_2 generation Tt (Tall) → 1
                tt (Short) → 1   } Ratio

So, 400 tall plants and 400 short plants will be produced.

All in one Heredity and Evolution

275

Very Short Answer Type Questions

21 Reproduction leads to variation. How?

Sol. Sexual reproduction involves the fusion of male and female gametes, which leads to the mixing of characters of parents and thus, causes variations in characters.

22 In any population, no two individuals are absolutely similar. Why?

Sol. Variations occur in the genes of the organisms produced due to the mutations, reshuffling of genes and inheritance of acquired traits during the evolutionary process which make all individuals different from one another. Thus, in any population, no two individuals are absolutely similar.

23 What is the cause of variation in asexually reproducing organisms?

Sol. Environmental factors and mutations are the causes of variations in asexually reproducing organisms.

24 A Mendelian experiment consisted of breeding pea plants bearing violet flowers with pea plants bearing white flowers. What will be the result in F_1 progeny? **CBSE 2018**

Sol. Heterozygous pea plants with violet flowers will result in F_1-progeny.

25 Why is the progeny always tall when a tall pea plant is crossed with a short pea plant? **CBSE 2016**

Sol. The trait which represents the tallness in a pea plant is dominant over the another trait, shortness (dwarf). So progeny becomes tall when a tall pea plant is crossed with a short pea plant.

26 How many pairs of chromosomes are present in human beings? **CBSE 2016**

Sol. 23 pairs of chromosomes are present in human beings.

Short Answer (SA) Type Questions

1 A child questioned his teacher that why do organisms resemble their parents more as compared to grandparents. In which way will the teacher explain to the child? **CBSE 2015**

Sol. The two parents involved in sexual reproduction produce gametes which fuse together forming a zygote. It gradually develops into a young child showing certain similarities with the parents.

Since, a child inherits its characters from both the parents the resemblance with them is very close.

The grandparents and the child resemble less closely because a gap of gene pool is created by the parents of the child.

Variations of two generations mixing together and addition of new variations from parents, increases the difference between them to a greater extent. Hence, a child resembles more closely its parents than the grandparents.

2 Name the plant Mendel used for his experiments. What type of progeny was obtained by Mendel in F_1 and F_2-generations when he crossed the tall and short plants? Write the ratio he obtained in F_2-generation plants. **CBSE Delhi 2019**

Sol. Mendel used the pea plant for his experiments. He took pea plants with different characteristics such as height (tall and short plants). The progeny produced from them (F_1-generation) plants were all tall.

Mendel then allowed F_1 progeny plants to undergo self pollination. In the F_2-generation, he found that all plants were not tall, three quarter were tall and one quarter of them were short. The ratio he obtained in F_2-generation plants is 9 : 3 : 3 : 1.

3 In a pea plant, find the contrasting trait if
  (i) the position of flower is terminal
  (ii) the flower is white in colour
  (iii) shape of pod is constricted **CBSE 2015**

Sol. Contrasting traits were used by Mendel and were classified as dominant or recessive

	Character	Given Trait	Contrasting Trait
(i)	Position of flower	Terminal	Axial
(ii)	Colour of flower	White	Violet
(iii)	Shape of pod	Constricted	Full

4 Study the following cross and showing self-pollination in F_1, fill in the blank and answer the questions that follow.

RRYY × rryy Parents
(Round yellow) (Wrinkled green)
RrYy × …… F_1-generation
(Round yellow)

(i) In above question, what is the combination of characters in the F_2 progeny? What are the ratios?

(ii) Give reasons for the appearance of new combination of characters in the F₁ progeny. **NCERT Exemplar**

Sol.
RRYY × rryy   Parents
(Round yellow) (Wrinkled green)

RrYy × RrYy   F₁-generation
(Round yellow) (Round yellow)

(i) In F₂-generation, the combination of characters is
Round yellow = 9, Round green = 3
Wrinkled yellow = 3, Wrinkled green = 1
Thus, the ratio is 9 : 3 : 3 : 1

(ii) In F₁-generation, the production of all round yellow seeds explains that the round shape and yellow colour of the seeds were dominant traits over the wrinkled shape and green colour of the seeds which segregated during F₂-generation.

5 Mustard was growing in two fields A and B. While field A produced brown coloured seeds, field B produced yellow coloured seeds.

It was observed that in field A, the offspring showed only the parental trait for consecutive generations, whereas in field B, majority of the offspring showed a variation in the progeny.

What are the probable reasons for these?

Or In an asexually reproducing species, if a trait X exists in 5% of a population and trait Y exists in 70% of the same population, which of the two trait is likely to have arisen earlier? Give reason.
CBSE SQP (Term-II)

Sol. In field A, the reason for parental trait in consecutive generations of the offspring is self-pollination.

In field B, variation is seen to occur because of recombination of genes as cross-pollination is taking place.

Or

Trait Y which exists in 70% (larger fraction) of the population, is likely to have arisen earlier because in asexual reproduction, identical copies of DNA are produced and variations do not occur.

New traits come in the population due to sudden mutation and then are inherited.

70% of the population with trait Y is likely to have been replicating that trait for a longer period than 5% of population with trait X.

6 A green stemmed rose plant denoted by GG and a brown stemmed rose plant denoted by gg are allowed to undergo a cross with each other.

(a) List your observations regarding:
(i) Colour of stem in their F₁ progeny.
(ii) Percentage of brown stemmed plants in F₂ progeny, if F₁ plants are self-pollinated.
(iii) Ratio of GG and Gg in the F₂ progeny.

(b) Based on the finding of this cross, what conclusion can be drawn? **CBSE 2020**

Sol. GG × gg   Parents
(Green stem) (Brown stem)

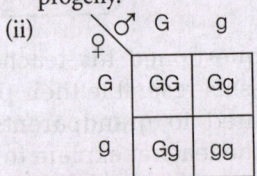

(a) (i) All the plants will be with green stem in F₁ progeny.

(ii)

	G	g
G	GG	Gg
g	Gg	gg

25% plants will be brown stemmed.
(iii) 25% GG
50% Gg

(b) 25%

7 Two pea plants - one with round yellow seeds (RRYY) and another with wrinkled green (rryy) seeds produce F₁ progeny that have round, yellow (RrYy) seeds.

When F₁ plants are self-pollinated, which new combination of characters is expected in F₂ progeny? How many seeds with these new combinations of characters will be produced when a total 160 seeds are produced in F₂ generation? Explain with reason.
CBSE SQP (Term-II)

Sol. When two pea plants one with round yellow seeds (RRYY) and another with wrinkled green (rryy) seeds produce F₁ progeny that have round, yellow seeds (RrYy).

When F₁ is self-pollinated, then

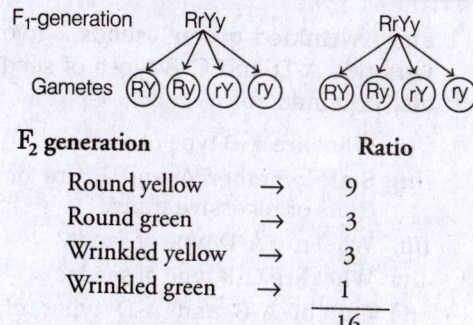

F₂ generation		Ratio
Round yellow	→	9
Round green	→	3
Wrinkled yellow	→	3
Wrinkled green	→	1
		16

The seeds with new combination of character will be

Round green–30
Wrinkled yellow–30
Wrinkled green–10

New combination are produced because of independent inheritance of seed shape and seed colour trait.

8 (a) Why is the F₁ progeny always tall plants, when a tall pea plant is crossed with a short pea plant?

(b) How is F₂ progeny obtained by self-pollination of F₁ progeny different from F₁ progeny? Give reason for this observation.

(c) State a conclusion that can be drawn on the basis of this observation.
CBSE 2020

Sol. (a) When tall plant (TT) is crossed with dwarf pea plant tt, every progeny is inherited with tall and dwarf gene together. Tall is dominant character, so plant becomes tall.

(b) The genotype of F₁ progeny is Tt.
The selfing between these plants is done in the follow way to obtain F₂ progeny

♀ \ ♂	T	t
T	TT Tall (Homozygous)	Tt Tall (Heterozygous)
t	Tt Tall (Heterozygous)	tt Dwarf (Homozygous)

Here, recessive and dominant gene get segregated we obtain one tall (homozygous), one dwarf (homozygous) and two tall (heterozygous) plants.

(c) This cross shows the law of segregation of character. It means character like tall and dwarf plant height do not mix while crossing them.

9 Does genetic combination of mother play a significant role in determining the sex of a newborn? **NCERT Exemplar**

Sol. No, the genetic combination of mother does not play any significant role in determining the sex of a newborn. This is because the female cell carries two X-chromosomes (XX). While the male cell carries one X and one Y-chromosome. The fusion of X-chromosome bearing sperm (of male cell) with X-chromosome of female egg produces a female child, while the fusion of Y-chromosome bearing sperm (of male cell) with X-chromosome of female egg produces a male child. Therefore it is the contribution of father which determines the sex of a newborn.

10 After self-pollination in pea plants with round, yellow seeds, following types of seeds were obtained by Mendel:
CBSE SQP 2020-21

Seeds	Numbers
Round, yellow	630
Round, green	216
Wrinkled, yellow	202
Wrinkled, greed	64

Analyse the result and describe the mechanism of inheritance which explains these results.

Or In humans, there is a 50% probability of the birth of a boy and 50% probability that a girl will be born. Justify the statement on the basis of the mechanism of sex-determination in human beings.

Sol. The ratio obtained is 9 : 3 : 3 : 1, which signifies dihybrid cross, in which parental as well as new combination are observed. This indicate that the progeny plants have not inherited a single whole gene set from each parent. Every germ cell takes one chromosome from the pair of maternal and paternal chromosome. When two germ cells combine, segregation one pair of characters is independent of other pair of characters.

Or

Determining the sex, humans have 23 pairs of chromosome. Both male and female carry two set of sex chromosome. Male has one X and one Y (XY) sex chromosome in which both are active. Female has both X (XX) sex chromosome in which one is active. All childrens will inherit an X chromosome from their mother regardless of whether they are boys or girls. Thus, the sex of the children will be determined by what they inherit from their father. A child who inherits an X chromosome from her father will be a girl and one who inherits a Y chromosome from him will be a boy.

Long Answer (LA) Type Questions

1 'A trait may be inherited, but may not be expressed'. Justify this statement with the help of a suitable example.

Sol. Let us take the following example to justify the above statement. Mendel crossed tall pea plants with dwarf pea plants.

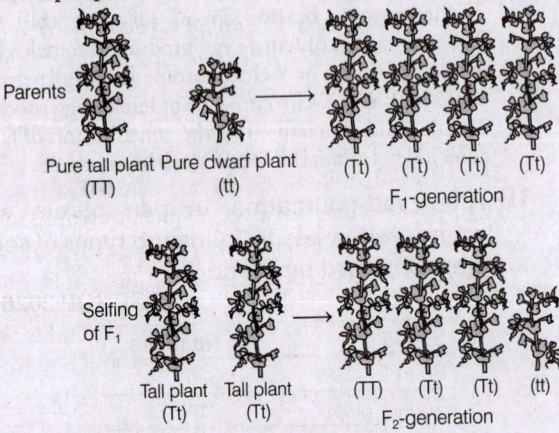

Mendel's observation F_1-generation contained all tall plants with genotype Tt, where 'T' represents a dominant trait and 't' represents a recessive trait. When F_1-generation underwent selfing, the trait that was unexpressed in F_1 (dwarf) was observed in some F_2-progeny. Thus, both traits, tall and dwarf, were expressed in F_2- generation in the ratio of 3 : 1.

2 Give reason for your choice.
A person first crossed pure-breed pea plants having round-yellow seeds with pure-breed pea plants having wrinkled-green seeds and found that only A-B type of seeds were produced in the F_1-generation. When F_1-generation pea plants having A-B type of seeds were cross-breed by self-pollination, then in addition to the original round yellow and wrinkled-green seeds, two new varieties A-D and C-B types of seeds were also obtained.

(i) What are A-B type of seeds?
(ii) State whether A and B are dominant traits or recessive traits.
(iii) What are A-D type of seeds?
(iv) What are C-B type of seeds?
(v) Out of A-B and A-D types of seeds, which one will be produced in (a) minimum number and (b) maximum number in the F_2-generation?

Sol. (i) A-B type of seeds are round in shape and yellow in colour as round and yellow both constitute the dominant character, hence expressed in F_1-generation.
(ii) A(round) and B(yellow) are dominant traits.
(iii) Round-green (A-D).
(iv) Wrinkled-yellow (C-B).
(v) (a) A-D in minimum number.
    (b) A-B in maximum number.

3 If we cross pure-breed tall (dominant) pea plants with pure-breed dwarf (recessive) pea plants, we get pea plants of F_1-generation. If we now self-cross the pea plant of F_1-generation, then we obtain pea plants of F_2-generation.

(a) What do the plants of F_1-generation look like?
(b) What is the ratio of tall plants to dwarf plants in F_2-generation?
(c) State the type of plants not found in F_1-generation but appeared in F_2-generation mentioning the reason for the same. **CBSE All India 2019**

Sol. Refer to text on Pg. no. 268.

CHAPTER EXERCISE

Multiple Type Questions

1 An inherited character which is normally inherited and has detectable variant is
   (a) trait (b) character
   (c) gene (d) allele

2 The law of dominance states that
   (a) a dominant trait always supresses the recessive trait
   (b) the recessive trait is always expressed
   (c) the dominant trait is always suppressed
   (d) the recessive trait dominates over dominant trait

3 Which Mendelian law states that inheritance of one character is always independent to the inheritance of other character within the same individual?
   (a) Law of dominance
   (b) Law of segregation
   (c) Law of independent assortment
   (d) Both (b) and (c)

Fill in the Blanks

4 The genetic composition of an individual is ....

5 The genotypic ratio of monohybrid cross is ....

6 .... is the development of one or more species from an existing species.

True and False

7 Each trait can be influenced by maternal DNA only.

8 Gamete is an individual having two different alleles for the same trait.

9 The determination of sex occurs largely by temperature control in human beings.

Match the Columns

10 Match the following columns.

Column A		Column B
A. Y-chromosome bearing male gamete	1.	Inherited trait
B. Colour of hair	2.	Natural selection
C. Speciation	3.	Tt
D. Heterozygous tall	4.	TT
E. Homozygous tall	5.	Male child

Assertion–Reason

Direction (Q. Nos. 11-12) *In each of the following questions, a statement of Assertion is given by the corresponding statement of Reason. Of the statements, mark the correct answer as*

(a) If both Assertion and Reason are true and Reason is the correct explanation of Assertion
(b) If both Assertion and Reason are true, but Reason is not the correct explanation of Assertion
(c) If Assertion is true, but Reason is false
(d) If Assertion is false, but Reason is true

11 Assertion The ratio of plants when Mendel took pea plants with two contrasting characters was 9 : 3 : 3 : 1.
Reason The ratio of plants when Mendel took pea plants with one contrasting character was 1 : 1.

12 Assertion All the human female gemetes will have only X-chromosome.
Reason Females are homogametic with two X chromosomes.

Direction (Q. Nos. 13-16) *Answer the questions on the basis of your understanding of the following passage, table and related studied concepts:*

Mendel selected Garden Pea for his experiments because he discovered for the first time the occurence of two types of seeds in Pea plants growing in the garden of his monastery. Mendel then used a number of contrasting visible characters of garden peas like.

	Character	Dominant	Recessive
1.	Plant height	Tall	Dwarf
2.	Flower position	Axial	Terminal
3.	Pod colour	Green	Yellow
4.	Pod shape	Full	Constricted
5.	Flower colour	Violet	White
6.	Seed shape	Round	Wrinkled
7.	Seed colour	Yellow	Green

Mendel's experiments were performed in three stages in selection of pure or true breeding parents, hybridisation and obtaining of F_1 generation of plants and self pollination of hybrid plants and raising of subsequent generations like F_2, F_3, F_4, etc.

13 How many contrasting traits were taken by Mendel in his monohybrid crosses?

14 Give a monohybrid cross to explain the F_1 generation formed by a plant with green pod colour and yellow pod colour.

15 State the first law of Mendel.

16 What do understand by homozyous tall plant and heterozygons tall plant?

Answers

1. (a)   2. (a)   3. (c)
4. genotype   5. 1 : 2 : 1   6. Speciation
7. False   8. False   9. False

Very Short Answer Type Questions

17 Variations are the basis of heredity. Explain.

18 Write the scientific term for 'Science of heredity and variation'.

19 When is a recessive trait able to show up?

20 What is the human being with XY pair of chromosomes called?

21 Which among the males and females are homogametic?

Short Answer (SA) Type Questions

22 What do you understand about independent inheritance of traits?

23 An animal (guinea pig) having black colour is crossed with guinea pig having same colour. They produced 100 offsprings, out of which 75 were black and 25 were white.
(i) What is the possible genotype?
(ii) Which trait is dominant and which is recessive?

24 A cross was made between pure breeding pea plants one with round and green seeds and the other with wrinkled and yellow seeds.
(i) Write the phenotype of F_1 progeny. Give reason for your answer.
(ii) Write the different types of F_2 progeny obtained along with their ratio when F_1 progeny was selfed.

25 A man having blood group 'O' ($I^O I^O$) marries a woman with blood group 'B' ($I^B I^O$). What will be the blood group of their children?

Long Answer (LA) Type Questions

26 How do variations occur in offsprings? Explain.

27 How do genes control the traits? Explain in detail.

Challengers*

1. What determines the sex of a child?
   (a) Chromosome content of the ovum
   (b) Chromosome content of the sperm
   (c) Number of days between ovulation and fertilisation
   (d) Number of days between fertilisation and implantation

2. When a breed of cattle with red coats is crossed with the same breed with white coats, all the offsprings have coats with a mixture of red and white hairs, a condition called roan.

   If roan cows were crossed with a red-coated bull, the theoretical ratio of the offsprings would be
   (a) all red
   (b) all roan
   (c) 1 red : 1 roan
   (d) 3 red : 1 roan

3. Which statement is true for a dominant allele?
   (a) It cannot undergo mutation
   (b) It gives a greater chance of survival than a recessive allele
   (c) It gives the same phenotype in heterozygotes and homozygotes
   (d) It is only responsible for male characteristics

4. Which statement about the genotypes of organisms is correct?
   (a) Dominant alleles are only found in homozygotes
   (b) One recessive allele always causes a recessive phenotype
   (c) Recessive phenotypes must be homozygous
   (d) The dominant phenotype must be heterozygous

5. A recessive homozygote is crossed with a heterozygote of the same gene. What will be the phenotype of the F_1-generation?
   (a) All dominant
   (b) 75% dominant, 25% recessive
   (c) 50% dominant, 50% recessive
   (d) 25% dominant, 50% heterozygous, 25% recessive

6. The genotype of the height of an organism is written as Tt. What conclusion may be drawn?
   (a) The allele for height has at least two different genes
   (b) There are atleast two different alleles for the gene for height
   (c) There are two different genes for height, each having a single allele
   (d) There is one allele for height with two different forms

Answer Key

1.	(b)	2.	(c)	3.	(c)	4.	(c)	5.	(c)
6.	(b)								

*These questions may or may not be asked in the examination, have been given just for additional practice.

CHAPTER 09

Light: Reflection and Refraction

Light is a form of energy that enables us to see. An object reflects the light rays that fall on it. These reflected light rays, when received by our eyes, make the object visible to us. We are able to see through a transparent medium as light is transmitted through it. The speed of light in vacuum or in air is $3 \times 10^8 \, ms^{-1}$. Light travels in a straight line.

Chapter Checklist

- Reflection of Light
- Mirror
- Image Formation by Spherical Mirrors
- Mirror Formula
- Refraction of Light
- Lens
- Image Formation in Lenses Using Ray Diagrams
- Lens Formula
- Power of a Lens

Reflection of Light

The phenomenon of bouncing back of light rays in the same medium on striking a smooth surface is called reflection of light.

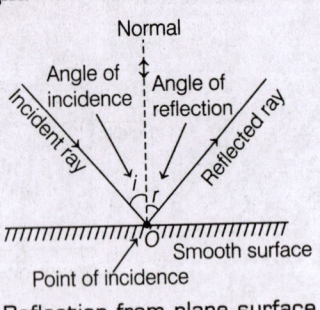

Reflection from plane surface

Laws of Reflection

There are two laws of reflection:
(i) Angle of incidence is always equal to the angle of reflection, i.e. $\angle i = \angle r$.
(ii) The incident ray, the reflected ray and the normal at the point of incidence, all lie in the same plane.

Regular and Diffuse Reflection of Light

If parallel beam of incident rays remain parallel even after reflection and go only in one direction is known as **regular reflection**. It takes place mostly in plane mirrors or highly polished metal surfaces.

Light : Reflection and Refraction

But if a parallel beam of incident rays is reflected in different directions is known as **diffused or irregular reflection** of light. It takes place in unpolished and rough surfaces.

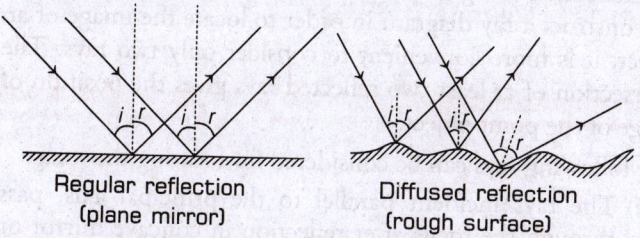

Regular reflection (plane mirror) | Diffused reflection (rough surface)

Note
- Silver metal is one of the best reflectors of light.
- A ray of light which is incident normally on a mirror is reflected back along its own path.
- Laws of reflection can be applied to all kinds of reflecting surface.

Image

If light rays coming from a point after reflection meet at another point or appear to meet at another point, then the second point is called the image of the first point.

Images are of two types:
1. **Real Image** If the light rays coming from a point actually, meet after reflection, then the image formed is called a real image.
2. **Virtual Image** If the light rays coming from a point, after reflection does not meet actually, but appear to meet at another point, then the image formed is called a virtual image.

Mirror

Mirror is a polished surface, which reflects almost all the light incident on it. Mirrors are of two types:

1. Plane Mirror

If the reflecting surface of a mirror is plane, then the mirror is called a plane mirror.

Image formed by a plane mirror has following properties:
- It is always virtual and erect.
- The size of image is equal to the size of the object.
- The distance between the image and the mirror is equal to the distance between the object and the mirror.
- The image is laterally inverted, i.e. left seems to be right and *vice-versa*.
- Focal length of a plane mirror is infinite.

Uses of Plane Mirrors

Plane mirrors are commonly used as looking glass, in making periscopes, kaleidoscopes etc.

2. Spherical Mirror

If the reflecting surface of the mirror is curved inwards or outwards, then the mirror is called a spherical mirror.

Spherical mirrors are of two types:
(a) The spherical mirror with inward curved reflecting surface is called **concave mirror**. A beam of light generally converges after reflection from such surfaces, hence it is also called **convergent mirror**.

e.g. The inner curved surface of a shining spoon can be considered as a concave mirror.

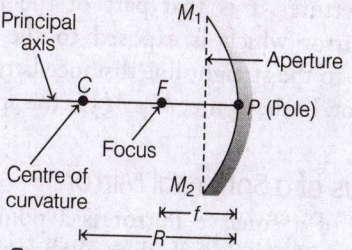

Concave or converging mirror

Here, f = focal length and R = radius of curvature.

(b) The spherical mirror with outward curved reflecting surface is called **convex mirror**. A beam of light generally diverges after reflection from this surface, hence it is also called **divergent mirror**.

e.g. The outer curved surface of a shining spoon can be treated or considered as convex mirror.

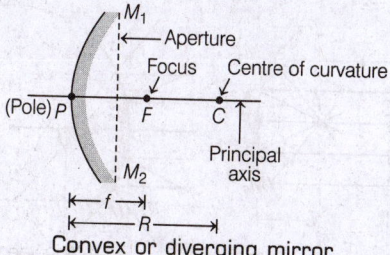

Convex or diverging mirror

Here, f = focal length and R = radius of curvature.

Some Definitions Related to Spherical Mirrors

Centre of Curvature

Centre of curvature of a spherical mirror is the centre of the imaginary sphere of which, the mirror is a part. In the above figures, it is marked by C. In case of concave mirror, the centre of curvature lies in front of it, while in case of convex mirror, the centre of curvature lies behind it.

Radius of Curvature
Radius of curvature of a spherical mirror is the radius of imaginary sphere of which, mirror is a part. In the above figure, it is shown by R.

Pole
Pole of the spherical mirror is the mid-point of its reflecting surface. In the above figure, it is shown by P.

Principal Axis
The principal axis of a spherical mirror is the line joining the pole and centre of curvature. In the figure, PC is the principal axis.

Aperture
The diameter of the reflecting surface of a spherical mirror is called its aperture. It is that part of the reflecting surface of a mirror which is exposed to the incident light. It is equal to the straight line distance between two ends of the mirror. In the figure, $M_1 M_2$ is the aperture of mirror.

Principal Focus of a Spherical Mirror
Principal focus of a concave mirror is a point on the principal axis of the mirror at which the light rays coming parallel to principal axis, after reflection actually meet.

Principal focus of a convex mirror is a point on its principal axis from which a beam of light rays parallel to axis, appears to diverge after being reflected from the mirror. It is represented by F.

For a concave mirror, the focus is in front of the mirror, while for a convex mirror, the focus is behind the mirror.

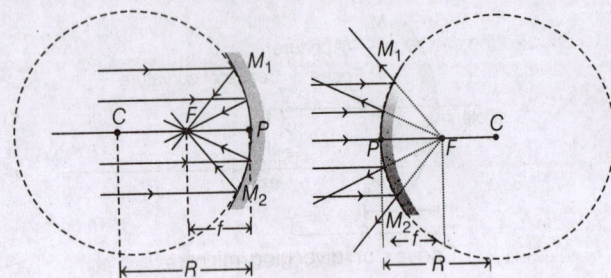

The focus of a concave mirror is real, while the focus of a convex mirror is virtual.

Focal Length
The distance between pole and principal focus of a spherical mirror is called its focal length. It is represented by f. If the aperture of the mirror is small, then $f = R/2$. It means that the principal focus of a spherical mirror lies midway between the pole and centre of curvature.

Representation of Images Formed by Spherical Mirrors Using Ray Diagrams
The reflection of light follows the same two laws everywhere. To construct a ray diagram in order to locate the image of an object, it is more convenient to consider only two rays. The intersection of at least two reflected rays gives the position of image of the point object.

The following rays can be considered for locating the image

(i) The rays incident parallel to the principal axis, pass through the focus after reflection in concave mirror or appear to come from focus in convex mirror.

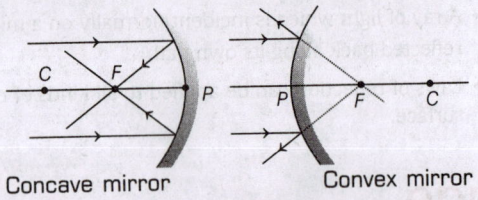

Concave mirror   Convex mirror

(ii) The rays passing through the focus of a concave mirror or passing towards focus of a convex mirror, become parallel to principal axis after reflection from the mirror.

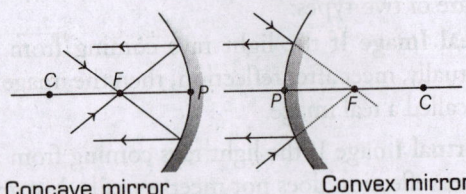

Concave mirror   Convex mirror

(iii) A ray passing through centre of curvature of a concave mirror or towards the direction of centre of curvature of a convex mirror, reflects back along the same path on striking the mirror surface.

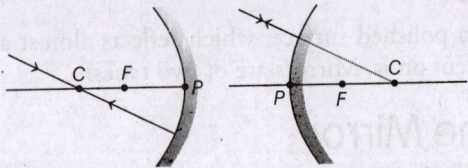

Concave mirror   Convex mirror

(iv) A ray incident obliquely to principal axis, towards a pole P of the concave or convex mirror is reflected obliquely, following the laws of reflection, i.e. $\angle i = \angle r$.

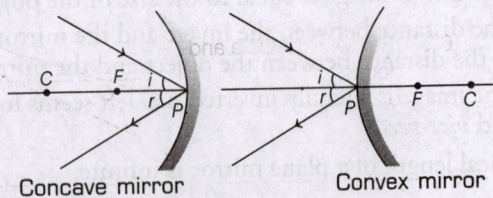

Concave mirror   Convex mirror

Image Formation by Spherical Mirrors

Image Formation by a Concave Mirror

The table given below illustrates the ray diagrams along with the position and nature of image, formed by a concave mirror for various positions of the object.

Formation of Image by Concave Mirror for Different Positions of Object

S. No.	Position of Object	Ray Diagram	Position of Image	Nature and Size of Image
1.	At infinity		At focus or in the focal plane	Real, inverted, extremely diminished in size
2.	Beyond the centre of curvature but at finite distance from mirror		Between focus and the centre of curvature	Real, inverted and diminished
3.	At the centre of curvature		At the centre of curvature	Real, inverted and same size as that of object
4.	Between focus and centre of curvature		Beyond the centre of curvature	Real, inverted and magnified
5.	At the focus		At infinity	Real, inverted and extremely magnified
6.	Between the pole and focus		Behind the mirror	Virtual, erect and magnified

Uses of Concave Mirrors
- Concave mirrors are commonly used in torches, search-lights and headlights of vehicles, to get powerful parallel beams of light.
- Concave mirrors are used as shaving mirrors to see larger image of the face.
- Dentists use concave mirrors to see large images of the teeth of patients.
- Large concave mirrors are used to converge sunrays on a point to produce large amount of concentrated heat in a solar furnace.

Image Formation by a Convex Mirror
For studying the image formed by a convex mirror, there are two positions of the object which are considered. Firstly, when the object is at infinity and the second position is, when the object is at a finite distance from the mirror. The table given below illustrates the ray diagrams along with the position and nature of image, formed by convex mirror for the following two positions of the object.

Formation of Image by Convex Mirror for Different Positions of Object

S. No.	Position of Object	Ray Diagram	Position of Image	Nature and Size of Image
1.	At infinity		At the principal focus, behind the mirror	Virtual, erect and extremely diminished
2.	Between infinity and the pole (i.e. at finite distance)		Between the principal focus and the pole, behind the mirror	Virtual, erect and diminished

Uses of Convex Mirrors
- Convex mirrors are commonly used as rear view mirrors in vehicles because they always give an erect image and have wider field of view as they are curved outward.
- Big convex mirrors are used as shop security mirrors, the shop owner can keep an eye on the customers to look for thieves and shoplifters among them.

Check Point 01
1. What kind of image is formed on a cinema screen?
2. If a ray of light is incident on a plane mirror such that it makes an angle of 30° with the mirror, then what will be the angle of reflection? [**Ans.** 60°]
3. What do you mean by laterally inverted?
4. Why does a ray of light passing through the centre of curvature of a concave mirror gets reflected along same path after reflection?
5. Fill in the blanks:
   (i) If the image formed by a convex mirror is observed to be virtual, erect and extremely diminished than the object, the position of the object is ....
   (ii) The type of spherical mirror which has a larger field of view is ....

Sign Convention for Reflection by Spherical Mirrors
While dealing with the reflection of light by spherical mirrors, we shall follow a set of sign convention called the new cartesian sign convention based on cartesian coordinates. In this convention, the pole (P) of the mirror is taken as the origin. The principal axis of the mirror is taken as X-axis of the coordinate system.

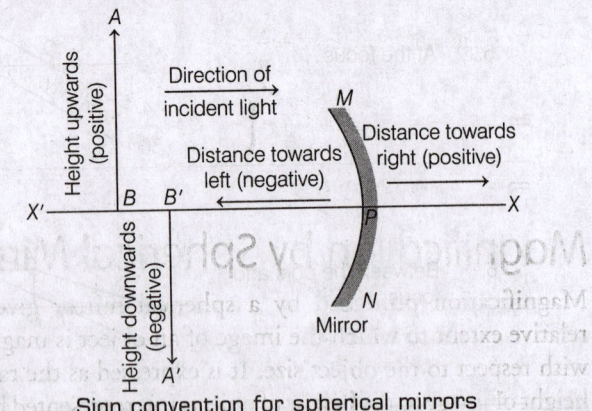

Sign convention for spherical mirrors

The conventions are as follows :
  (i) The object is always placed to the left of the mirror.
  (ii) All distances parallel to principal axis (X-axis) are measured from the pole of the mirror.
  (iii) Distances to the left of pole ($-$ve X-axis) are **negative**. Distances to the right of pole ($+$ve X-axis) are **positive**.
  (iv) Distances measured perpendicularly above the principal axis (along $+Y$-axis) are taken as **positive**.
  (v) Distances measured perpendicularly below the principal axis (along $-Y$-axis) are taken as **negative**.

Also, focal length of convex mirror is taken as **positive** whereas focal length of concave mirror is taken as **negative**.

Mirror Formula

In a spherical mirror, the distance of the object from its pole is called the **object distance** (u). The distance of the image from the pole of the mirror is called the **image distance** (v). The distance of the principal focus from the pole is called **focal length** (f). The relation between quantities u, v and f is called mirror formula.

It is expressed as
$$\frac{1}{v}+\frac{1}{u}=\frac{1}{f}$$

where, u, v and f are to be used according to their new cartesian sign convention.

This formula is valid in all situations for all spherical mirrors and for all positions of the object.

Example 1. *If an object is placed 10 cm from a convex mirror of radius of curvature 60 cm, then find the position of image.*

Sol. Given, object distance, $u = -10$ cm

Radius of curvature, $R = 60$ cm

$\therefore$ Focal length, $f = R/2 = \dfrac{60}{2} = 30$ cm

$\because$ By mirror formula, $\dfrac{1}{v}+\dfrac{1}{u}=\dfrac{1}{f}$

$\Rightarrow \dfrac{1}{v} = \dfrac{1}{f} - \dfrac{1}{u} = \dfrac{1}{30} - \left(-\dfrac{1}{10}\right) = \dfrac{4}{30}$

$\Rightarrow v = 7.5$ cm

Magnification by Spherical Mirror

Magnification produced by a spherical mirror gives the relative extent to which the image of an object is magnified with respect to the object size. It is expressed as the ratio of height of image to the height of object. It is represented by m.

i.e. Magnification, $m = -\dfrac{\text{Height of image }(h_i)}{\text{Height of object }(h_o)}$

or

Magnification is also related to the object distance (u) and image distance (v). It can be expressed as

$$m = \frac{\text{Image distance }(v)}{\text{Object distance }(u)} = \frac{-v}{u}$$

where, u and v are to be used with their appropriate sign. Magnitude of magnification of a mirror or a lens gives information about the size of the image relative to the object.

Magnification	Size of Image (h_i)
$m = 1$	$h_i = h_o$
$m < 1$	$h_i < h_o$
$m > 1$	$h_i > h_o$

Sign of magnification by mirror or lens gives information about nature of the image produced.

Sign of Magnification	Image
$-$ve	Real and inverted
$+$ve	Virtual and erect

Example 2. *An object is placed at a distance of 12 cm in front of a concave mirror. It forms a real image four times larger than the object. Calculate the distance of image from the mirror.*

Sol. Given, object distance, $u = -12$ cm

Magnification, $m = -4$

It is known that, $m = \dfrac{-v}{u}$

Therefore, we have

$-4 = \dfrac{-v}{-12} \Rightarrow v = -48$ cm

Identification of Mirrors

By observing the images produced by a mirror for different positions of object, its nature can be identified.

- If the image formed by the mirror is of same size as that of object for different positions of object, then the mirror is a plane mirror.
- If the image formed by the mirror is diminished for all positions of object, then the mirror is convex mirror.
- If the image formed behind the mirror is longer than the object, then the mirror is concave mirror.
- Focal length of a spherical mirror is independent of the medium in which it is placed.

Check Point 02

1. A spherical mirror has a focal length –10 cm. What type of mirror is it likely to be?
2. If the magnification of an image formed by a mirror is positive, what does it mean?
3. What is the magnification produced by a rear view mirror fitted in vehicles?
4. Rays from the sun converge at a point 15 cm in front of a concave mirror. Where should an object be placed, so that its image formed is equal to the size of the object?
5. An object is placed at a distance of 8 cm from a convex mirror of focal length 12 cm. Find the position of the image formed. [Ans. 4.8 cm]
6. If the object distance for a concave mirror is 24 cm and image distance is 12 cm in front of a mirror. Then, find the magnification of the mirror. [Ans. –1/2]

Refraction of Light

'Change in path of a light ray as it passes from one transparent medium to another transparent medium is called refraction of light.'

When light travels from a rarer medium to a denser one, it bends towards the normal ($i > r$) and when travels from a denser medium to a rarer one, it bends away from the normal ($i < r$).

where, i = angle of incidence
and r = angle of refraction.

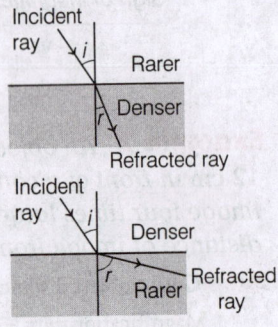
Refraction of light

Cause of Refraction

Speed of light is different in different media, i.e. more in rarer medium and comparatively less in denser medium. So, when light enters a denser medium, its speed reduces and it bends towards the normal and when it enters rarer medium, its speed increases and it bends away from the normal.

Examples of Refraction of Light

- The bottom of a pool or tank or pond containing water appears to be raised due to refraction of light which takes place when light rays pass from the pool of water into the air.
- The letters appear to be raised when viewed through a glass slab placed over the document because of refraction of light.
- A pencil partially immersed in water appears to be bent because of the refraction of light coming from the part of pencil that is immersed inside water.
- A lemon kept in water in a glass tumbler appears to be bigger than its actual size, when viewed from the sides.

Refraction through a Rectangular Glass Slab

When a light ray enters a glass slab, then the emergent ray is parallel to the incident ray but it is shifted sideward slightly.

In this case, refraction takes place twice, first when ray enters glass slab from air and second when exits from glass slab to air.

Both refractions have been shown in figure (here glass slab is denser medium and air is rarer medium).

The extent of bending of the ray of light at opposite parallel faces AB and CD of rectangular glass slab is equal and opposite. So, the ray emerging from face CD is parallel to incident ray but shifted sideward slightly.

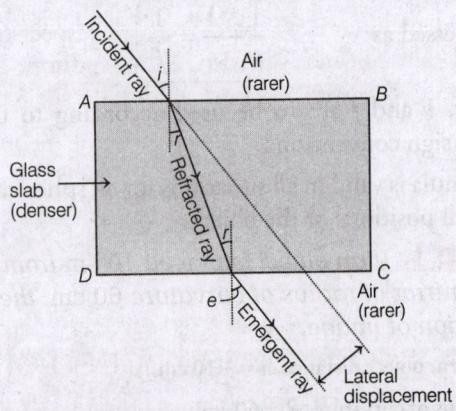
Refraction through a glass slab

where, i = angle of incidence,
r = angle of refraction
and e = angle of emergence.

Lateral Displacement The perpendicular distance between the emergent ray and incident ray when the light passes out of a glass slab is called lateral displacement.

Note
- Angle of incidence = Angle of emergence, i.e. $\angle i = \angle e$
- If the incident ray falls normally to the surface of glass slab, then there is no bending of the ray of light, it goes straight without any deviation.

Laws of Refraction

Refraction of light occurs according to the following laws:

(i) The incident ray, the refracted ray and the normal to the interface of two transparent media at the point of incidence, all lie in the same plane.

(ii) The ratio of sine of angle of incidence to the sine of angle of refraction for light of given colour is constant for a given pair of media (**Snell's law**). It is expressed as

$$\frac{\sin i}{\sin r} = \mu = \text{constant } (\mu \text{ or } n)$$

This constant is known as refractive index (μ).

Refractive Index

The extent of the change in direction of ray of light that takes place in a given pair of media is expressed in terms of the refractive index.

$_1\mu_2$ represents refractive index of medium 2 with respect to medium 1, when light is going from medium 1 to medium 2.

$$_1\mu_2 = \frac{\mu_2}{\mu_1} = \frac{\sin i}{\sin r}$$

The refractive index of a medium with respect to vacuum is called **absolute refractive index of the medium**. The absolute refractive index of a medium is simply called its refractive index.

For glass/water pair,

$$_w\mu_g = \frac{_a\mu_g}{_a\mu_w}$$

Note Refractive index of air is minimum and refractive index of diamond is maximum.

Refractive Index and Speed of Light

If c is the speed of light in air and v is the speed of light in medium, then the refractive index of the medium is

$$\mu = \frac{\text{Speed of light in vacuum /air}}{\text{Speed of light in medium}} = \frac{c}{v}$$

Hence, for any two media, the refractive index of the second medium with respect to first medium is equal to the ratio of the velocities of light in both the media.

Refractive index of glass with respect to air,

$$_a\mu_g = \frac{\text{Velocity of light in air}}{\text{Velocity of light in glass}} = \frac{c}{v_g} \quad \ldots(i)$$

Refractive index of water with respect to air,

$$_a\mu_w = \frac{\text{Velocity of light in air}}{\text{Velocity of light in water}} = \frac{c}{v_w} \quad \ldots(ii)$$

On dividing Eq. (ii) from Eq. (i), we get

$$\frac{_a\mu_w}{_a\mu_g} = \frac{v_g}{v_w} = {_g\mu_w}$$

Absolute Refractive index of some Material Media

Material Medium	Refractive Index	Material Medium	Refractive Index
Air	1.0003	Canada Balsam	1.53
Ice	1.31	Rock salt	1.54
Water	1.33	Carbon disulphide	1.63
Alcohol	1.36	Dense flint glass	1.65
Kerosene	1.44	Ruby	1.71
Fused quartz	1.46	Sapphire	1.77
Turpentine oil	1.47	Diamond	2.42
Benzene	1.50	Mustard oil	1.46
Crown glass	1.52	Glycerine	1.74

Example 3. *Light enters from air to diamond with refractive index 2.42. What is the speed of light in diamond? Given, speed of light in air is $3 \times 10^8 \text{ms}^{-1}$.*

Sol. Given, $_a\mu_d = 2.42$, $c = 3 \times 10^8 \text{ms}^{-1}$

Using, $_a\mu_d = \dfrac{\text{Speed of light in air }(c)}{\text{Speed of light in diamond }(v)}$

∴ Speed of light in diamond

$$(v) = \frac{c}{_a\mu_d} = \frac{3 \times 10^8}{2.42} = 1.24 \times 10^8 \text{ms}^{-1}$$

Check Point 03

1. The depth of a bucket filled with water seems to be less than its actual depth. Name the phenomenon responsible for this?

2. How is the refractive index of a medium related to the speed of light? Give an expression for refractive index of a medium with respect to another in terms of speed of light in these two media?

3. For the same angle of incidence, the angle of refraction in three different media A, B and C are 10°, 25° and 40°, respectively. In which medium the velocity of light will be maximum?

4. Fill up the blank :
The angle of incidence of light ray incident on surface of a plastic slab of refractive index $\sqrt{3}$ is ...., if the angle of refraction is 30°. **[Ans. 60°]**

5. If a ray of light enters from alcohol to air. The refractive index of alcohol is 1.36. Calculate the speed of light in alcohol with respect to air. **[Ans. $2.21 \times 10^8 \text{ ms}^{-1}$]**

6. The refractive index of glass with respect to air is $\dfrac{3}{2}$ and refractive index of water with respect to air is $\dfrac{4}{3}$. What will be the refractive index of water with respect to glass? **[Ans. $\dfrac{8}{9}$]**

Lens

Lens is a transparent medium bounded by two surfaces of which, one or both surfaces are spherical.

Lenses are of two types:

1. Convex or Converging Lens

A lens which is thicker at the centre and thinner at its ends is called convex lens. Convex lenses are of three types as shown below:

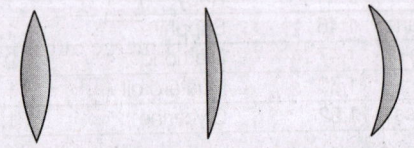

(i) Double convex lens (ii) Plano-convex lens (iii) Concavo-convex lens

A convex lens is also known as converging lens because it converges a parallel beam of light rays passing through it. A double convex lens is simply called **convex lens**.

2. Concave or Diverging Lens

A lens which is thinner at the centre and thicker at its ends is called a concave lens. Concave lenses are of three types as shown below:

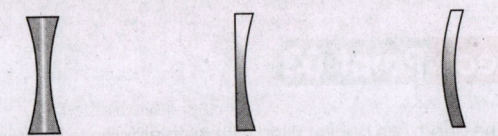

(i) Double concave lens (ii) Plano-concave lens (iii) Convexo-concave lens

A concave lens is also known as diverging lens because it diverges a parallel beam of light rays passing through it. A double concave lens is simply called concave lens.

Some Definitions Related to Lenses

Optical Centre

The centre point of a lens is known as its optical centre. It is represented by O. The optical centre is a point of the lens, directed to which incident rays refract without any deviation in the path.

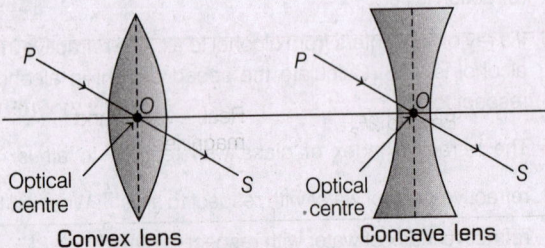

Centres of Curvature

The centres of the two imaginary spheres of which the lens is a part are called centres of curvature of the lens. It is represented by C. A lens has two centres of curvature with respect to its two curved surfaces.

Radii of Curvature

The radii of the two imaginary spheres of which the lens is a part are called radii of curvature of the lens. A lens has two radii of curvature. These may or may not be equal.

Principal Axis

The imaginary line joining the two centres of curvature is called principal axis of a lens. Principal axis also passes through the optical centre.

Principal Focus

Lens has two principal foci:

(i) **First Principal Focus** It is a point on the principal axis of lens, the rays starting from or directed to which, become parallel to principal axis after refraction.

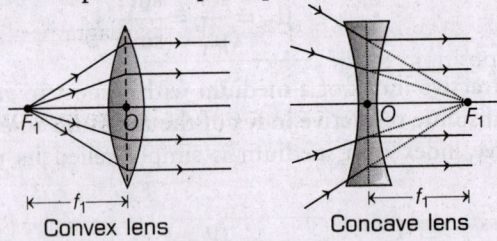

(ii) **Second Principal Focus** It is the point on the principal axis at which the rays coming parallel to the principal axis, converge on the other side of lens (convex) or appear to meet on the same side of lens (concave), after refraction from the lens.

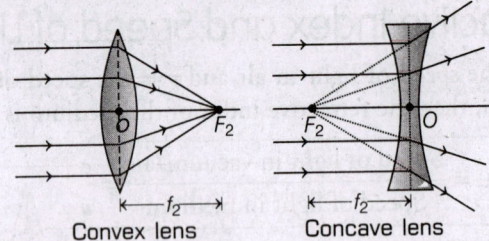

Both the foci of convex lens are real while that of concave lens are virtual.

Focal Length of Lens

The distance between focus and optical centre of lens is called focal length of lens.

Focal Plane

The plane passing through the focus and perpendicular to the principal axis is called focal plane.

Aperture

The effective diameter of the circular outline of a spherical lens is called its aperture.

Image Formation in Lenses Using Ray Diagrams

We can represent image formation by lenses using ray diagrams:

For drawing ray diagrams in lenses a like spherical mirrors, we consider any two of the following rays

(i) Rays which are parallel to the principal axis after refraction will pass through principal focus in case of convex lens and will appear to be coming from principal focus in case of concave lens.

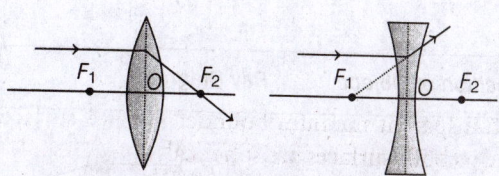

(ii) Ray passing through or directed to the focus will emerge parallel to the principal axis.

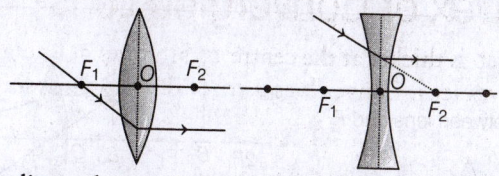

(iii) Ray directed to optical centre will emerge out undeviated.

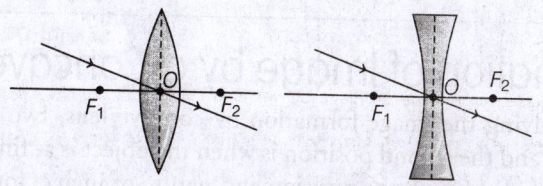

Formation of Image by a Convex Lens

The table given below illustrates the ray diagrams along with the position and nature of image, formed by convex lens for various positions of the object.

Formation of Image by Convex Lens for Different Positions of Object

S. No.	Position of Object	Ray Diagram	Position of Image	Nature and Size of Image
1.	At infinity		At F_2	Real, inverted and extremely diminished
2.	Beyond $2F_1$ (at finite distance)		Between F_2 and $2F_2$	Real, inverted and diminished
3.	At $2F_1$		At $2F_2$	Real, inverted and of same size as that of object
4.	Between F_1 and $2F_1$		Beyond $2F_2$	Real, inverted and magnified

S. No.	Position of Object	Ray Diagram	Position of Image	Nature and Size of Image
5.	At F_1		At infinity	Real, inverted and highly magnified
6.	Between lens and F_1		On same side of the lens as the object	Virtual, erect and magnified

Formation of Image by a Concave Lens

For studying the image formation by concave lens, two positions of object are considered. Firstly, when the object is at infinity and the second position is when the object is at finite distance from the lens. The table given below illustrates the ray diagrams along with the position and nature of image, formed by concave lens for the above two positions of the object.

Formation of Image by Concave Lens for Different Positions of Object

S. No.	Position of Object	Ray Diagram	Position of Image	Nature and Size of Image
1.	At infinity		At focus on same side of lens as object	Virtual, erect and highly diminished
2.	At finite distance		Between focus and optical centre, on the same side of lens as object	Virtual, erect and diminished

Check Point 04

1 Fill in the blank :
  (i) The lens which always forms a virtual image of an object, is ....
  (ii) Ray which are parallel to the principal axis after refraction will pass through .... in case of convex lens.
2 Which lens would you prefer to use while reading small letters from a dictionary?
3 What type of lens is an air bubble inside the water?
4 A convex lens is immersed in a liquid of refractive index greater than that of glass. How will the nature of lens change?
5 A convex lens of focal length 20 cm can produce a magnified virtual as well as real image. Is this a correct statement? If yes, where shall the object be placed in each case for obtaining these images?

Light : Reflection and Refraction

Sign Convention for Spherical Lenses

Sign convention for lenses is same as that for mirrors.
Also, focal length of convex lens is **positive** whereas focal length of concave lens is **negative**.

Lens Formula

This formula gives the relationship between object distance (u), image distance (v) and the focal length (f).

The lens formula is expressed as $\boxed{\dfrac{1}{v} - \dfrac{1}{u} = \dfrac{1}{f}}$

The lens formula is general and is valid in all situations for any spherical lens.

Example 4. *An object is placed 25 cm in front of a concave lens of focal length 25 cm. Find the location and nature of image.*

Sol. Given, object distance, $u = -25$ cm
Focal length, $f = -25$ cm and image distance, $v = ?$
From lens formula, $\dfrac{1}{v} - \dfrac{1}{u} = \dfrac{1}{f}$

So, $\dfrac{1}{v} = \dfrac{1}{f} + \dfrac{1}{u}$

$\Rightarrow \dfrac{1}{v} = \dfrac{u+f}{uf}$

$\Rightarrow v = \dfrac{uf}{u+f}$

$\Rightarrow v = \dfrac{-25 \times (-25)}{-25 - 25} = -12.5$ cm

Nature of image
(i) Virtual   (ii) Erect
(iii) On the same side of lens (iv) Diminished

Magnification by Lenses

The ratio of height of image (h_i) and the height of object (h_o) is called magnification (m).

Magnification, $\boxed{m = \dfrac{h_i}{h_o} \text{ or } m = \dfrac{v}{u}}$

Magnification is **positive**, when image formed is **virtual** and linear magnification is **negative**, when image formed is **real**.

Example 5. *A 5 cm tall object is placed perpendicular to the principal axis of a convex lens of focal length 20 cm. The distance of the object from lens is 30 cm. Determine the*
(i) position (ii) nature (iii) size of image formed.

Sol. Given, object size, $h_o = 5$ cm
Object distance, $u = -30$ cm

Focal length, $f = +20$ cm
Using lens formula, $\dfrac{1}{v} - \dfrac{1}{u} = \dfrac{1}{f}$

$\Rightarrow \dfrac{1}{v} = \dfrac{1}{u} + \dfrac{1}{f}$

$\Rightarrow \dfrac{1}{v} = -\dfrac{1}{30} + \dfrac{1}{20} = \dfrac{1}{60}$

$\Rightarrow v = 60$ cm

Since, magnification, $m = \dfrac{h_i}{h_o} = \dfrac{v}{u} \Rightarrow m = \dfrac{h_i}{5} = \dfrac{60}{-30}$

$\Rightarrow h_i = -10$ cm

Therefore, the image is real, inverted and magnified.

Power of a Lens

The ability of a lens to converge or diverge light rays is called power (P) of the lens. It is defined as the reciprocal of focal length,
i.e. $\boxed{P = 1/f \text{ (in metre)}}$

Its SI unit is dioptre (D) (1 D = 1 m^{-1}).

If f is expressed in metres, then power is expressed in dioptres. Thus, dioptre is the power of a lens whose focal length is 1 metre. If focal length is given in centimetre, then

$$\boxed{\text{Power} = \dfrac{100}{f \text{ (in cm)}}}$$

For concave lens, power and focal length are negative.
For convex lens, power and focal length are positive.

Power of Combination of Lenses

When two or more thin lenses are used in combination, the equivalent focal length (f) and power of the combination (P) can be calculated as

$\boxed{\dfrac{1}{f} = \dfrac{1}{f_1} + \dfrac{1}{f_2} + ...}$ and $\boxed{P = P_1 + P_2 + ...}$

Magnification of lens in combination (m) is given by
$\boxed{m = m_1 \times m_2 \times ....}$

Note
- The use of combination of lenses increases the sharpness of image, the image produced is also free from many defects.
- The additive property of the powers of the lenses can be used to design lens systems to minimise certain defects in images produced by a single lens. Such a lens system, consisting of several lenses in contact, is commonly used in designing of camera lenses and the objectives of microscopes and telescopes.

Example 6. *A convergent lens of power 8 D is combined with a divergent lens of power –10 D. Calculate*

(i) *power of combination.*
(ii) *focal length of combination.*

Sol. Given, power of convergent lens,
$$P_1 = 8 \text{ D}$$
Power of divergent lens,
$$P_2 = -10 \text{ D}$$
(i) Power of combination,
$$P = P_1 + P_2$$
$$= 8 - 10 = -2 \text{ D}$$
(ii) Focal length of combination
$$f = \frac{1}{P} = \frac{1}{-2} = -0.5 \text{ m}$$
$$= -50 \text{ cm}$$

Check Point 05

1. A student uses a lens of focal length –50 cm. What is the nature of the lens and its power? **[Ans. Concave lens, –2 D]**
2. You are provided with two lenses of focal length 20 cm and 30 cm, respectively. Which lens will you use to obtain more convergent light?
3. A lens has power 4 D. Find the focal length of the lens. **[Ans. 25 cm]**
4. Two lenses of power –3.5 D and +1 D are placed in contact. Find the total power of the combination of lens. Calculate the focal length of this combination. **[Ans. –2.5 D and 40 cm]**
5. If two lenses (convex) are in contact with each other, what happens to the ray after refraction?
6. A lens is cut into two equal halves
   (i) along the principal axis and
   (ii) perpendicular to principal axis. What will be the focal length of each half?

NCERT FOLDER

INTEXT QUESTIONS

1 Define principal focus of a concave mirror. **Pg 168**

Sol. Refer to the text on Pg 284.

2 The radius of curvature of spherical mirror is 20 cm. What is its focal length? **Pg 168**

Sol. Focal length, $f = \frac{R}{2} = \frac{20}{2} = 10$ cm

3 Name a mirror that can give an erect and enlarged image of an object. **Pg 168**

Sol. Concave mirror can give erect and enlarged image of an object.

4 Why do we prefer a convex mirror as rear view mirror in vehicles? **Pg 168**

Sol. The field of view of a convex mirror is wider than that of concave mirror and convex mirror always produces erect image of object, so we prefer convex mirror as rear view mirror for vehicles.

5 Find the focal length of a convex mirror whose radius of curvature is 32 cm. **Pg 171**

Sol. Given, radius of curvature, $R = 32$ cm

As we know, focal length, $f = \frac{\text{radius of curvature}}{2}$

So, $f = \frac{32}{2} = 16$ cm

6 A concave mirror produces three times magnified (enlarged) real image of object placed at 10 cm in front of it. Where is the image located? **Pg 171**

Sol. Real image is inverted. So, magnification is negative.

Thus, $m = -3 = \frac{\text{Image size}}{\text{Object size}}$

$$= \frac{h_i}{h_o} = -\frac{v}{u}$$

[where, v = image distance and u = object distance]

$$\Rightarrow -3 = \frac{-(v)}{(-10)} \quad [\because \text{object is placed in front of mirror}]$$

$$\Rightarrow -3 = \frac{v}{10}$$

Image distance, $v = -30$ cm

Negative sign shows that image is real, so it will be formed in front of the mirror.

7 A ray of light travelling in air enters obliquely into water. Does the light ray bend towards the normal or away from the normal? Why? **Pg 176**

Sol. Light bends towards the normal on entering water. It happens because water is an optically denser medium than air. When light travels from a rarer medium to denser medium, it bends towards the normal.

Light : Reflection and Refraction

8 Light enters from air to glass having refractive index 1.50. What is the speed of light in glass? The speed of light in vacuum is 3×10^8 ms^{-1}. **Pg 176**

Sol. Given, refractive index of glass $_a\mu_g = 1.50$
and speed of light in vacuum $= 3 \times 10^8$ ms^{-1}

$$_a\mu_g = \frac{\text{Velocity in air }(c)}{\text{Velocity in glass }(v)}$$

$$v = \frac{c}{_a\mu_g} = \frac{3 \times 10^8}{1.5} = 2 \times 10^8 \text{ ms}^{-1}$$

9 Find out from table given below, the medium having highest optical density. Also, find the medium with the lowest optical density. **Pg 176**

Absolute Refractive Index of Some Material Media

Material Medium	Refractive Index	Material Medium	Refractive Index
Air	1.0003	Canada Balsam	1.53
Ice	1.31	Rock salt	1.54
Water	1.33	Carbon disulphide	1.63
Alcohol	1.36	Dense flint glass	1.65
Kerosene	1.44	Ruby	1.71
Fused quartz	1.46	Sapphire	1.77
Turpentine oil	1.47	Diamond	2.42
Benzene	1.50		
Crown glass	1.52		

Sol. The medium with the highest refractive index will have the highest optical density. So, diamond has the highest optical density. The medium with the lowest refractive index will have the lowest optical density. So, air has the lowest optical density.

10 You are given kerosene, turpentine and water. In which of these does light travel the fastest? **Pg 176**

Sol. Given, $\mu_{\text{kerosene}} = 1.44$, $\mu_{\text{turpentine}} = 1.47$, $\mu_{\text{water}} = 1.33$
Light travels the fastest in a medium having minimum optical density or lowest refractive index.
Since, μ_{water} (= 1.33) is the lowest, speed of light is maximum in water.

11 The refractive index of diamond is 2.42. What is the meaning of this statement? **Pg 176**

Sol. Refractive index of any medium w.r.t. another indicates the extent to which light bends when it enters from first medium to the given medium. The given value of refractive index also states that speed of light in diamond is 1/2.42 times to the speed of light in vacuum.

12 Define 1D of power of lens. **Pg 184**

Sol. One dioptre is the SI unit of power of lens, whose focal length is 1 m.

13 A convex lens forms a real and inverted image of a needle at a distance of 50 cm from it. Where is the needle placed in front of convex lens, if the image is equal to the size of object? Also, find the power of the lens. **Pg 184**

Sol. Given, image distance, $v = +50$ cm
Magnification, $m = -1$ [∵ image is inverted]

$$m = \frac{v}{u} \Rightarrow u = \frac{v}{m} = \frac{50}{-1} = -50 \text{ cm}$$

So, needle is placed at 50 cm in front to the lens.

By lens formula, $\dfrac{1}{f} = \dfrac{1}{v} - \dfrac{1}{u} \Rightarrow \dfrac{1}{f} = \dfrac{1}{50} - \dfrac{1}{(-50)}$

$$\frac{1}{f} = \frac{1}{25} \Rightarrow f = 25 \text{ cm} = 0.25 \text{ m}$$

∴ Power, $P = \dfrac{1}{f} = \dfrac{1}{0.25} = 4$ D

14 Find the power of concave lens of focal length 2 m. **Pg 184**

Sol. ∴ Power $= \dfrac{1}{\text{Focal length}} = -\dfrac{1}{2} = -0.50$ D

Negative sign arises due to the divergent nature of concave lens.

EXERCISES
(On Pages 185 and 186)

1 Which one of the following materials cannot be used to make a lens?
(a) Water   (b) Glass
(c) Plastic   (d) Clay

Sol. (d) Clay can never be transparent, so it cannot be used to make lens.

2 The image formed by a concave mirror is observed to be virtual, erect and larger than the object. Where should be the position of the object?

(a) Between principal focus and centre of curvature
(b) At centre of curvature
(c) Beyond centre of curvature
(d) Between pole of the mirror and its principal focus

Sol. (d) If the object is placed between pole of the mirror and its principal focus virtual, erect and magnified image will be formed.

3 Where should an object be placed in front of a convex lens to get a real image of the size of the object?
(a) At the principal focus of the lens
(b) At twice the focal length
(c) At infinity
(d) Between the optical centre of the lens and its principal focus

Sol. (b) To get the real image of the size of the object, it should be placed at twice the focal length of a convex lens. Refer table (case 3) on page 291.

4 A spherical mirror and a thin spherical lens have each of a focal length −15 cm. The mirror and lens are likely to be
(a) both concave
(b) both convex
(c) mirror is concave and lens is convex
(d) mirror is convex and lens is concave

Sol. (a) The focal length is taken as negative for both concave mirror and concave lens.

5 No matter how far you stand from a mirror, your image appear erect. The mirror is likely to be
(a) plane   (b) concave
(c) convex   (d) either plane or convex

Sol. (d) Plane mirrors and convex mirrors always form the erect images.

6 Which of the following lenses would you prefer to use while reading small letters found in dictionary?
(a) A convex lens of focal length 50 cm
(b) A concave lens of focal length 50 cm
(c) A convex lens of focal length 5 cm
(d) A concave lens of focal length 5 cm

Sol. (c) Convex lens is used as magnifying glass.
As, focal length, $f = \dfrac{1}{P}$
Convex lens of focal length 50 cm has power 2 D, whereas convex lens of focal length 5 cm has power 20 D. Hence, better performance its focal length should be small.

7 We wish to obtain an erect image of an object, using a concave mirror of focal length 15 cm. What should be the range of distance of the object from the mirror? What is the nature of image? Is the image larger or smaller than the object? Draw a ray diagram to show the image formation in this case.

Sol. The object should be kept at a distance less than 15 cm from the mirror. The image is virtual and erect. The image is larger than the object.

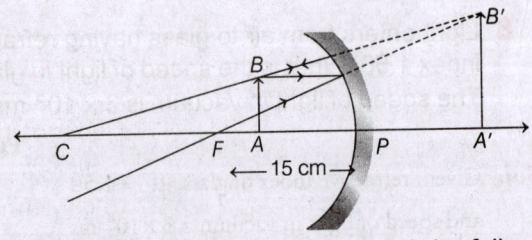

8 Name the type of mirror used in following situations:
(i) Headlight of car
(ii) Side/rear view mirror of vehicle
(iii) Solar furnace
Support your answer with a reason.

Sol. (i) Concave mirror, to get powerful beam of light.
(ii) Convex mirror to get larger field of view and erect image.
(iii) Concave mirror, as it can converge light rays of the sun in a small area.

9 One-half of a convex lens is covered with a black paper, will this lens produce a complete image of the object? Verify your answer experimentally.

Sol. The lens will produce a complete image, but the image will have lower intensity and brightness because in the lower part of the lens the rays are blocked.

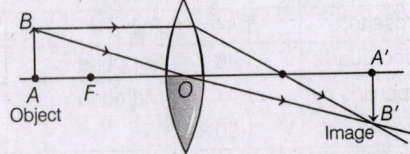

10 An object 5 cm in length is placed 25 cm away from a converging lens of focal length 10 cm. Draw the ray diagram and find position, size and nature of image formed.

Sol.

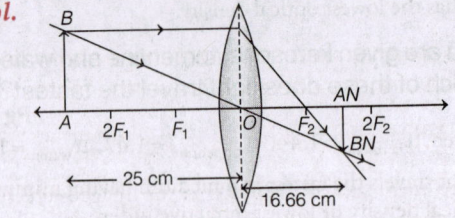

Given, object size, $h_o = 5$ cm; Image size, $h_i = ?$
Object distance, $u = -25$ cm; Image distance, $v = ?$
Focal length, $f = 10$ cm
From lens formula, $\dfrac{1}{f} = \dfrac{1}{v} - \dfrac{1}{u}$

or $\dfrac{1}{v} = \dfrac{1}{f} + \dfrac{1}{u} = \dfrac{1}{10} + \dfrac{1}{(-25)} = \dfrac{3}{50}$

or $v = \dfrac{50}{3} = 16.67$ cm from the lens

Size of image,
$$h_i = h_o \times \frac{v}{u} = 5 \times \frac{50}{3 \times (-25)} = -3.33 \text{ cm}$$
[diminished inverted image]
The image is real in nature.

11 A concave lens of focal length 15 cm forms an image 10 cm from the lens. How far is the object placed from the lens? Draw the ray diagram.

Sol. Given, focal length, $f = -15$ cm

Image distance, $v = -10$ cm

By lens formula, $\frac{1}{f} = \frac{1}{v} - \frac{1}{u}$

or $\frac{1}{u} = \frac{1}{v} - \frac{1}{f} = \frac{1}{-10} - \frac{1}{(-15)} = \frac{1}{15} - \frac{1}{10} = \frac{-1}{30}$

$u = -30$ cm from the lens.

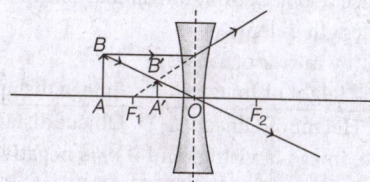

Thus, the object is placed at 30 cm from the concave lens.

12 An object is placed at a distance of 10 cm from a convex mirror of focal length 15 cm. Find the position and nature of image.

Sol. Given, object distance, $u = -10$ cm

Focal length, $f = 15$ cm

By mirror formula, $\frac{1}{v} = \frac{1}{f} - \frac{1}{u} = \frac{1}{15} - \frac{1}{(-10)} = \frac{5}{30}$

$v = 6$ cm from the mirror

Image is formed 6 cm behind the mirror.

So, image is virtual and erect.

13 The magnification produced by a plane mirror is +1. What does it mean?

Sol. If magnification is 1, the image size is same as that of object size.

Since, magnification is positive, the image is erect and virtual.

14 An object 5 cm in length is placed at a distance of 20 cm in front of a convex mirror of radius of curvature 30 cm. Find the position of image, its nature and size.

Sol. Given, object size, $h_o = 5$ cm

Object distance, $u = -20$ cm

Radius of curvature = 30 cm

Focal length, $f = \frac{30}{2} = 15$ cm

Position of image (by mirror formula)

$\frac{1}{f} = \frac{1}{u} + \frac{1}{v}$ or $\frac{1}{v} = \frac{1}{f} - \frac{1}{u} = \frac{1}{15} - \frac{1}{(-20)} = \frac{7}{60}$

$v = \frac{60}{7} = 8.57$ cm

Image is formed at 8.57 cm behind the mirror.

∴ Magnification, $m = \frac{h_i}{h_o} = -\frac{v}{u}$

⇒ $\frac{-60}{7 \times (-20)} = \frac{h_i}{5}$

$h_i = \frac{-60 \times 5}{-7 \times 20} = 2.14$ cm

Image is diminished, erect and hence virtual.

15 An object of size 7 cm is placed at 27 cm in front of a concave mirror of focal length 18 cm. At what distance from the mirror should the screen be placed, so that a sharp focussed image can be obtained? Find the size and nature of image.

Sol. Given, object size, $h_o = 7$ cm

Object distance, $u = -27$ cm

Focal length, $f = -18$ cm

By mirror formula, $\frac{1}{v} = \frac{1}{f} - \frac{1}{u} = \frac{1}{-18} - \frac{1}{(-27)} = \frac{-1}{54}$

Screen should be placed at 54 cm in front of the mirror.

Now, $\frac{h_i}{h_o} = -\frac{v}{u} \Rightarrow \frac{h_i}{7} = -\frac{(-54)}{(-27)}$ or $h_i = -14$ cm

So, image is double the size of object. Also, image is real and inverted (since, h_i is negative).

16 Find the focal length of a lens of power -2 D. What type of lens is this?

Sol. ∴ Focal length, $f = \frac{1}{\text{Power}} = \frac{1}{(-2)} = -0.5$ m

Since, f is negative, lens is concave.

17 A doctor has prescribed corrective lens of power +1.5 D. Find the focal length of the lens. Is the prescribed lens diverging or converging?

Sol. Given, power of lens, $P = +1.5$ D

It means the lens is convex

As power, $P = \frac{1}{f \text{ (in m)}}$

So, $f = \frac{1}{P} = \frac{1}{1.5} = \frac{10}{15} = 0.66$ m

⇒ $f = 0.66 \times 100 = 66$ cm

[It is a converging lens because its focal length is positive.]

SUMMARY

- **Light** is a form of energy that enables us to see.
- The phenomenon of bouncing back of light rays in the same medium on striking a smooth polished surface is known as **reflection of light**.
  Laws of Reflection
- Angle of incidence is always equal to angle of reflection, i.e. $\angle i = \angle r$.
- The incident ray, the reflected ray and the normal at the point of incidence, all lie in the same plane.
- **Concave mirror** is the spherical mirror with inward curved reflecting surface.
- **Convex mirror** is the spherical mirror with outward curved reflecting surface.
- The distance between the pole and the principal focus of a spherical mirror is known as its **focal length**.
- **Mirror formula** is given by $\dfrac{1}{v} + \dfrac{1}{u} = \dfrac{1}{f}$.

  where, u = distance of object from the pole of the mirror,
  v = distance of image from the pole of the mirror,
  and f = focal length of mirror.
- **Linear magnification**, $m = \dfrac{\text{Height of image }(h_i)}{\text{Height of object }(h_o)} = -\dfrac{v}{u}$

  If m is positive, image is virtual and if m is negative, image is real.
- Change in the path of a light ray as it passes from one medium to another medium is known as **refraction of light**.
  Laws of Refraction
- The incident ray, the refracted ray and the normal to the interface of two transparent media at the point of incidence, all lie in the same plane.
- The ratio of sine of angle of incidence to the sine of angle of refraction for light of given colour is constant for a given pair of media. $\mu = \dfrac{\sin i}{\sin r}$

This is known as **Snell's law** of refraction.
$$_1\mu_2 = \dfrac{\text{Speed of light in medium 1}}{\text{Speed of light in medium 2}}$$

- **Lens** is a transparent medium bounded by two surfaces in which, one or both surfaces are spherical.
- **Convex lens** is a lens which is thicker at the centre and thinner at its end.
- **Concave lens** is a lens which is thinner at the centre and thicker at its end.
  Lens Formula
  Lens formula is given by
  $$\dfrac{1}{v} - \dfrac{1}{u} = \dfrac{1}{f}$$

  where, v = distance of image from the optical centre of lens,
  u = distance of object from the optical centre of lens,
  and f = focal length of lens.
- Magnification, (by mirror or lenses)
  $$m = \dfrac{\text{Height of Image }(h_i)}{\text{Height of Object }(h_o)} = \dfrac{\text{Image distance }(v)}{\text{Object distance }(u)}$$

  If m is positive, image is virtual and if m is negative, image is real.
- The ability of a lens to converge or diverge light rays is known as **power of lens**. It is denoted by P.
- The SI unit of power is **dioptre (D)**.
  Power, $P = \dfrac{100}{\text{Focal length } f(\text{in cm})}$
- For concave lens, power and focal length are negative. For convex lens, power and focal length are positive.
- Power of combination of lenses is given by
  $$P = \dfrac{1}{f} = \dfrac{1}{f_1} + \dfrac{1}{f_2} + \ldots$$
  and $P = P_1 + P_2 + \ldots$

Exam Practice

Objective Type Questions

Multiple Choice Questions

1 Focal length of a plane mirror is
 (a) zero   (b) infinite
 (c) 25 cm   (d) – 25

Sol. (b) Focal length of a plane mirror is infinite, as the radius of curvature is ∞ (infinite).

2 An object is placed at a distance of 10 cm in front of a plane mirror, then the distance of image from mirror will be
 (a) 5 cm   (b) 10 cm
 (c) 20 cm   (d) 0

Sol. (b) The distance of image is equal to the distance of object from mirror. Therefore, the distance of image from mirror is 10 cm.

3 The image of an object placed in front of a convex mirror is formed at
 (a) the object itself
 (b) twice the distance of the object in front of the mirror
 (c) half the distance of the object in front of the mirror
 (d) behind the mirror

Sol. (d) behind the mirror.

4

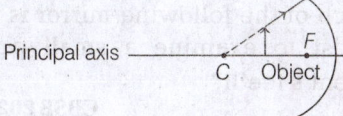

While looking at the above diagram, Nalini concluded the following?
 I. The image of the object will be a virtual one.
 II. The reflected ray will travel along the same path as the incident ray but in opposite direction.
 III. The image of the object will be inverted.
 IV. This is a concave mirror and hence the focal length will be negative.
CBSE SQP (Term-I)
Which of the above statements are correct?
 (a) I and II   (b) I and III
 (c) II, III and IV   (d) I, II, III and IV

Sol. (c) The light ray travelling through centre of curvature goes undeviated from the mirror after reflection or traces its path back. The image formed this way is inverted in nature. The focal length of concave mirror is always negative.

5 The radius of curvature of concave mirror is 12 cm. Then, the focal length will be
 (a) 12 cm   (b) 6 cm   (c) – 24 cm   (d) – 6 cm

Sol. (d) Given, radius of curvature, $R = 12$ cm.
We know that the focal length of concave mirror has negative value.
Hence, focal length, $f = \dfrac{-R}{2} = \dfrac{-12}{2} = -6$ cm

6 An object is placed 20 cm from the concave mirror of focal length 10 cm, then image is formed at
 (a) behind the mirror
 (b) between the mirror and focus
 (c) at focus
 (d) centre of curvature of mirror

Sol. (d) Given, focal length of concave mirror, $f = -10$ cm
Distance of object from concave mirror, $u = -20$ cm
From the mirror formula,

$\dfrac{1}{u} + \dfrac{1}{v} = \dfrac{1}{f} \Rightarrow \dfrac{1}{-20} + \dfrac{1}{v} = \dfrac{1}{-10}$

$\Rightarrow \dfrac{1}{v} = \dfrac{1}{-20} - \dfrac{1}{10}$

$\Rightarrow \dfrac{1}{v} = \dfrac{1-2}{20} \Rightarrow \dfrac{1}{v} = \dfrac{-1}{20}$

$\Rightarrow v = -20$ cm

Hence, the image is formed at the centre of curvature of mirror.

7 If the power of a lens is – 4.0 D, then it means that the lens is a
 (a) concave lens of focal length – 50 m
 (b) convex lens of focal length + 50 cm
 (c) concave lens of focal length – 25 cm
 (d) convex lens of focal length – 25 m
CBSE 2021 (Term-I)

Sol. (c) Given, power $P = -4.0$ D
Focal length, $f = \dfrac{1}{P} = -\dfrac{1}{4.0} = -25$ cm

8 Rays from Sun converge at a point 15 cm in front of a concave mirror. Where should an object be placed, so that size of its image is equal to the size of the object?
CBSE SQP (Term-I)
(a) 30 cm in front of the mirror
(b) 15 cm in front of the mirror
(c) Between 15 cm and 30 cm in front of the mirror
(d) More than 30 cm in front of the mirror

Sol. (a) At $u = 2F$ (or the centre of curvature), the concave mirror forms inverted and real image of the same size.

9 A 10 mm long alpin is placed vertically in front of a concave mirror. A 5 mm long image of the alpin is formed at 30 cm in front of the mirror. The focal length of this mirror is
(a) –30 cm   (b) –20 cm
(c) –40 cm   (d) –60 cm
NCERT Exemplar

Sol. (b) Given, object size, $h = +10.0$ mm
$(\because 1 \text{ cm} = 10 \text{ mm})$
$= +1.0$ cm
Image size, $h' = 5.0$ mm $= 0.5$ cm
Image distance, $v = -30$ cm (For real image)
Focal length, $f = ?$
As, magnification, $m = \dfrac{h' \text{ (image size)}}{h \text{ (object size)}}$
Also, magnification, $m = \dfrac{-v}{u} \Rightarrow \dfrac{h'}{h} = \dfrac{-v}{u}$
$\dfrac{0.5}{1} = \dfrac{-30}{u} \Rightarrow u = -60$ cm
Using mirror formula, $\dfrac{1}{f} = \dfrac{1}{v} + \dfrac{1}{u}$
$\Rightarrow \dfrac{1}{f} = \dfrac{1}{-30} - \dfrac{1}{60} = \dfrac{-2-1}{60} = \dfrac{-3}{60} \Rightarrow f = -20$ cm

10 The image of a candle flame formed by a lens is obtained on a screen placed on the other side of the lens. According to new cartesian sign convention, if the image is three times the size of the flame, then the lens is **CBSE SQP (Term-I)**
(a) concave and magnification is +3
(b) concave and magnification is –3
(c) convex and magnification is –3
(d) convex and magnification is +3

Sol. (b) A concave mirror forms real and inverted image of the object. Thus, from the given description option (b) is correct.

11 The image of an object placed in front of a concave mirror of focal length 15 cm is of the same size as the object. The distance between the object and its image is
CBSE SQP (Term-I)
(a) 15 cm   (b) 30 cm   (c) 60 cm   (d) zero

Sol. (b) When image height is equal to object height the object must be placed at centre of curvature i.e. $R = 2F = 2 \times 15 = 30$ cm.
Hence, object distance = 30 cm

12 Consider these indices of refraction: glass: 1.52; air: 1.0003; water: 1.333. Based on the refractive indices of three materials, arrange the speed of light through them in decreasing order.
CBSE 2021 (Term-I)
(a) The speed of light in water > the speed of light in air > the speed of light in glass
(b) The speed of light in glass > the speed of light in water > the speed of light in air
(c) The speed of light in air > the speed of light in water > the speed of light in glass
(d) The speed of light in glass > the speed of light in air > the speed of light in water

Sol. (c) Speed of light is maximum in rarer medium and speed of light is minimum in denser medium.
i.e. $v \propto \dfrac{1}{\mu}$, where μ is refractive index.

13 Which of the following mirror is used by a dentist to examine a small cavity in a patient's teeth?
CBSE 2021 (Term-I)
(a) Convex mirror
(b) Plane mirror
(c) Concave mirror
(d) Any spherical mirror

Sol. (c) Concave mirror forms enlaraged, erect image when object is placed between focus and pole. Therefore, concave mirror is used by a dentist to examine a small cavity in patient's teeth.

14 The relation $R = 2f$ is valid
(a) for concave mirrors but not for convex mirrors
(b) for convex mirrors but not for concave mirrors
(c) Neither for concave mirrors nor for convex mirrors
(d) for both concave and convex mirrors

Sol. (d) For all spherical mirrors, radius of curvature (R) is equal to twice the focal length. i.e. $R = 2f$

15 Velocity of light in air is 3×10^8 m/s. While its velocity in a medium is 1.5×10^8 m/s. Then, refractive index of this medium is
(a) 3 (b) 5
(c) 0.5 (d) 2

Sol. (d) Refractive index of medium with respect to air,
$$_a n_g = \frac{\text{Speed of light in air}}{\text{Speed of light in medium}}$$
$$_a n_g = \frac{3 \times 10^8}{1.5 \times 10^8} = 2$$

16 Figure shows a ray of light as it travels from medium A to medium B. Refractive index of the medium B relative to medium A is

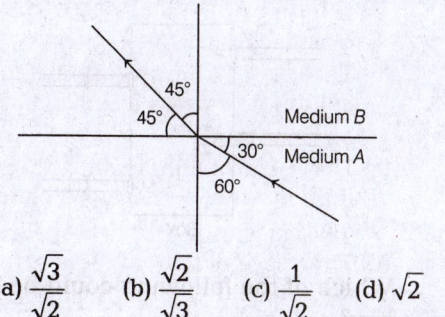

(a) $\frac{\sqrt{3}}{\sqrt{2}}$ (b) $\frac{\sqrt{2}}{\sqrt{3}}$ (c) $\frac{1}{\sqrt{2}}$ (d) $\sqrt{2}$

NCERT Exemplar

Sol. (a) Given, angle of incidence, $i = 60°$, angle of refraction, $r = 45°$
Refractive index of the medium B relative to medium A,
$$\mu_{BA} = \frac{\sin i}{\sin r} = \frac{\sin 60°}{\sin 45°} = \frac{\left(\frac{\sqrt{3}}{2}\right)}{\left(\frac{1}{\sqrt{2}}\right)} = \frac{\sqrt{3}}{\sqrt{2}}$$

17 A light ray enters from medium A to medium B as shown in the figure. The refractive index of medium B relative to A will be

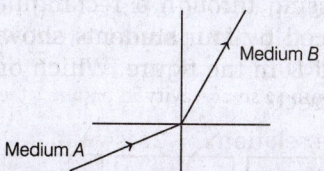

(a) greater than unity (b) less than unity
(c) equal to unity (d) zero

NCERT Exemplar

Sol. (a) Since light rays in the medium B goes towards normal. So it has greater refractive index and lesser velocity of light w.r.t. medium A. So refractive index of medium B w.r.t. medium A is greater than unity.

18

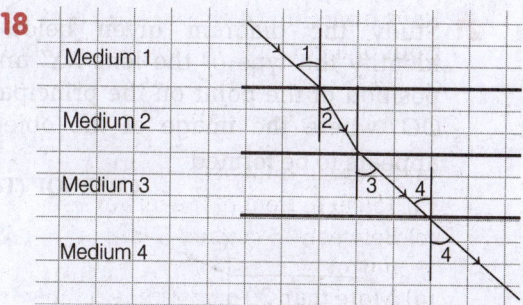

In the above diagram, light is travelling through different media. It is noted by a scientist that $\angle 1 = \angle 3 = \angle 4$ but $\angle 2 < \angle 1$. Which of the following statement would be correct? **CBSE SQP (Term-I)**

(a) Medium 1 is denser than medium 3 but its density is equal to medium 2
(b) Medium 2 is the rarest medium
(c) Medium 3 is denser than medium 1
(d) Medium 1 and 3 are essentially the same medium but medium 2 is denser than 1 and 3

Sol. (d) Medium 1, 3 and 4 are essentially the same medium as all the rays are parallel. The medium 2 is denser than 1, 3 and 4 as light ray bend towards the normal in medium 2.

19 The angle of incidence from air to glass at the point O on the hemispherical glass slab is **CBSE 2021 (Term-I)**

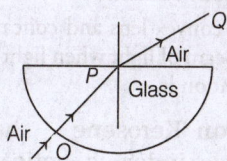

(a) 45° (b) 0°
(c) 90° (d) 180°

Sol. (b) Since light ray suffer no deviation thus the angle of incidence and refraction must be equal to zero.

20 When light is incident on a glass slab, the incident ray, refracted ray and the emergent ray are in three media A, B and C. If n_1, n_2 and n_3 are the refractive indices of A, B and C respectively and the emergent ray is parallel to the incident ray, which of the following is true? **CBSE 2021 (Term-I)**

(a) $n_1 < n_2 < n_3$
(b) $n_1 > n_2 > n_3$
(c) $n_1 < n_2 = n_3$
(d) $n_1 = n_3 < n_2$

Sol. (d) This is the case of a glass slab, where $\angle i = \angle e$, thus $n_1 = n_3$ and both are rarer than n_2.

21 Study the diagram given below and identify the type of the lens XX' and the position of the point on the principal axis OO' where the image of the object AB appears to be formed
   CBSE SQP (Term-I)

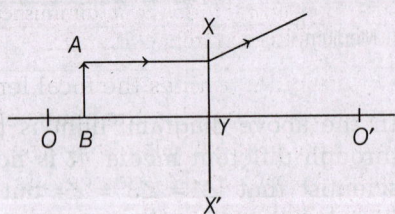

(a) concave; between O' and Y
(b) concave; between O and Y
(c) convex; between O' and Y
(d) convex; between O and Y

Sol. (b) The concave lens diverges light rays coming parallel to principal axis.

22 Which of the following can make a parallel beam of light when light from a point source is incident on it?
   CBSE SQP (Term-I)
(a) Concave mirror as well as convex lens
(b) Convex mirror as well as concave lens
(c) Two plane mirrors placed at 90° to each other
(d) Concave mirror as well as concave lens

Sol. (a) Both convex lens and concave mirror can make parallel beam of light when light from a point source is incident on it.

23 **Assertion** Kerosene having higher refractive index is optically denser than water, although its mass density is less than that of water.

Reason The speed of light decides whether a medium is optically rarer or optically denser. An optically denser medium may not possess greater mass density.

(a) Both Assertion and Reason are true and Reason is the correct explanation of Assertion.
(b) Both Assertion and Reason are true, but Reason is not the correct explanation of Assertion.
(c) Assertion is true, but Reason is false.
(d) Assertion is false, but Reason is true.

Sol. (a) The optical denser medium have greater electron density around a surrounding central atom, which decided optical property of medium. The optically denser medium may or may not be physically denser.

24 The refractive index of flint glass is 1.65 and that for alcohol is 1.36 with respect to air. What is the refractive index of the flint glass with respect to alcohol?
   CBSE SQP (Term-I)
(a) 0.82   (b) 1.21
(c) 1.11   (d) 1.01

Sol. (b) Given, $^{air}\mu_{glass} = 1.65$
$^{air}\mu_{alcohol} = 1.36$
$^{alcohol}\mu_{glass} = \dfrac{1.65}{1.36} = 1.21$

25 Beams of light are incident through the holes A and B and emerge out of box through the holes C and D respectively as shown in the figure.

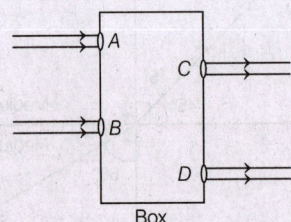

Which of the following could be inside the box?
(a) A rectangular glass slab
(b) A convex lens
(c) A concave lens
(d) A prism   **NCERT Exemplar**

Sol. (a) Here, the emergent rays are parallel to the direction of the incident ray. Therefore, a rectangular glass slab could be inside the box as the extent of bending of light ray at the opposite parallel faces AB (air-glass interface) and CD (glass-air interface) of the rectangular glass slab are equal and opposite. This is why the ray emerges parallel to the incident ray.

26 The path of a ray of light coming from air passing through a rectangular glass slab traced by four students shown as A, B, C and D in the figure. Which one of them is correct?

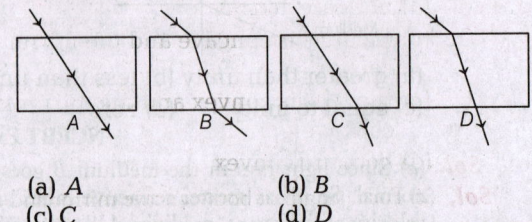

(a) A   (b) B
(c) C   (d) D
   NCERT Exemplar

Sol. (*b*) In a rectangular glass slab, the emergent rays are parallel to the direction of the incident rays, because the lateral deviation of bending of the ray of light at the opposite parallel faces (air-glass interface) and (glass-air interface) of the rectangular glass slab are equal and opposite. That is why the rays emerging out are parallel to the incident rays.

27 You are given water, mustard oil, glycerine and kerosene. In which of these media, a ray of light incident obliquely at same angle would bend the most?
(a) Kerosene
(b) Water
(c) Mustard oil
(d) Glycerine **NCERT Exemplar**

Sol. (*d*) The given material having their refractive index as kerosene is 1.44, water is 1.33, mustard oil is 1.46 and glycerine is 1.74. Thus, glycerine is most optically denser and hence have the largest refractive index. Therefore, ray of light bend most in glycerine.

28 An object of height 8 cm is placed at a distance of 40 cm infront of a convex lens of focal length 20 cm. The size of image is
(a) 12 cm (b) 4 cm (c) – 8 cm (d) 16 cm
NCERT Exemplar

Sol. (*c*) Given, object distance, $u = -40$ cm, focal length, $f = 20$ cm, size of object, $h_1 = 8$ cm
We know that,
$$\frac{1}{f} = \frac{1}{v} - \frac{1}{u} \Rightarrow \frac{1}{20} = \frac{1}{v} - \frac{1}{-40}$$
$$\Rightarrow \frac{1}{v} = \frac{1}{20} - \frac{1}{40} \Rightarrow v = 40 \text{ cm}$$
Thus, image distance, $v = 40$ cm
Now, magnification, $\frac{h_2}{h_1} = \frac{v}{u}$ [$h_2 \to$ size of image]
$$h_2 = \frac{40}{-40} \times h_1$$
$$= \frac{40}{-40} \times 8 = -8 \text{ cm}$$

29 If a lens and a spherical mirror both have a focal length of –15 cm, then it may be concluded that **CBSE SQP (Term-I)**
(a) both are concave
(b) the lens is concave and the mirror is convex
(c) the lens is convex and the mirror is concave
(d) both are convex

Sol. (*a*) Focal length of both concave mirror and concave lens is negative.

30 An optical device forms an erect image of an object placed in front of it. If the size of the image is one half that of the object, the optical device is a
(a) concave mirror (b) convex mirror
(c) plane mirror (d) convex lens

Sol. (*b*) Convex mirror forms erect, diminished image of the object placed in front of it.

31 A student determines the focal length of a device *A* by focussing the image of a far off object on a screen placed on the opposite side of the object. The device *A* is
(a) concave lens (b) concave mirror
(c) convex lens (d) convex mirror

Sol. (*d*) A convex mirror can focus or form an image at focus, the ray coming from far off distant object.

32 If the real image of a candle flame formed by a lens is three times the size of the flame and the distance between lens and image is 80 cm, at what distance should the candle be placed from the lens?
CBSE 2021 (Term-I)
(a) – 80 cm (b) – 40 cm
(c) $-\frac{40}{3}$ cm (d) $-\frac{80}{3}$ cm

Sol. (*d*) Given, magnification, $m = 3$
Image distance, $v = 80$ cm
We know that, magnification,
$$m = -\frac{\text{image distance}}{\text{object distance}}$$
$$3 = \frac{-80}{u} \Rightarrow u = -\frac{80}{3}$$

33 Which diagram shows image formation of an object on a screen by a converging lens?

(a)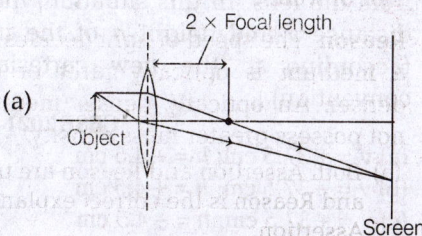

(b)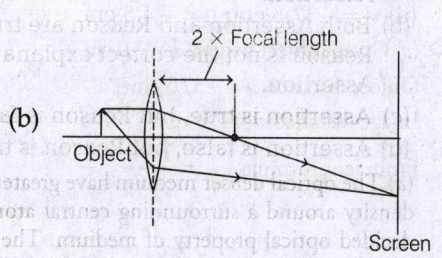

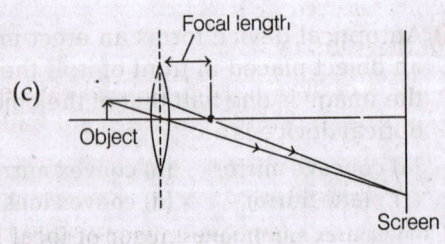

(c)

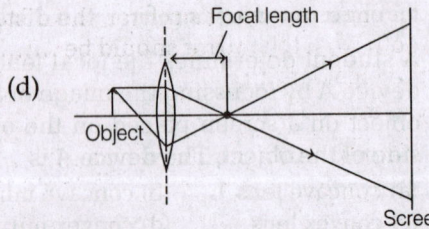

(d)

Sol. (c) Applying the laws of refraction through lenses, the rays travelling through optical centre must go undeviated. The rays travelling to principal axis must go through focus, we get the image formation by converging lens in diagram (c).

34 An object is placed in front of a concave lens. For all positions of the object, the image formed is always **CBSE SQP (Term-I)**
(a) real, diminished and inverted
(b) virtual, diminished and erect
(c) real, enlarged and erect
(d) virtual, erect and enlarged

Sol. (c) Concave lens always forms virtual, diminished and erect image of an object for any position.

35 An object of height 3.0 cm is placed vertically on the principal axis of a convex lens. When the object distance is −37.5 cm, an image of height −2.0 cm is formed at a distance of 25.0 cm from the lens. Next, the same object is placed vertically at 25.0 cm from the lens. In this situation, the image distance v and height h of the image is (according to the new cartesian sign convention) : **CBSE 2021 (Term-I)**
(a) $v = +37.5$ cm; $h = +4.5$ cm
(b) $v = -37.5$ cm; $h = +4.5$ cm
(c) $v = +37.5$ cm; $h = -4.5$ cm
(d) $v = -37.5$ cm; $h = -4.5$ cm

Sol. (c) Given, object height, $h = 3.0$ cm
Object distance, $u = -37.5$ cm
Image distance, $v = 25.0$ cm
From lens formula, $\dfrac{1}{f} = \dfrac{1}{v} - \dfrac{1}{u}$

$\dfrac{1}{f} = \dfrac{1}{25} + \dfrac{1}{37.5}$

$= \dfrac{3+2}{75} = \dfrac{5}{75} = \dfrac{1}{15}$

$f = 15$ cm

Now object distance, $u = -25$ cm
From lens formula, $\dfrac{1}{f} = \dfrac{1}{v} - \dfrac{1}{u}$

$\dfrac{1}{15} = \dfrac{1}{v} + \dfrac{1}{25}$

$\therefore \dfrac{1}{v} = \dfrac{1}{15} - \dfrac{1}{25}$

$= \dfrac{5-3}{75} = \dfrac{2}{75}$

$v = 37.5$ cm

Height of image $= -\dfrac{v}{u} \times$ Height of object

$= \dfrac{-37.5}{25} \times 3 = -4.5$ cm

36
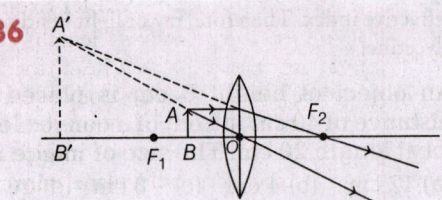

The above lens has a focal length of 10 cm. The object of height 2 mm is placed at a distance of 5 cm from the pole. Find the height of the image. **CBSE SQP (Term-I)**
(a) 4 cm (b) 6.67 mm
(c) 4 mm (d) 3.33 mm

Sol. (c) Given, focal length, $f = 10$ cm
Object height, $h = 2$ mm
Object distance, $u = 5$ cm
From lens formula, $\dfrac{1}{v} - \dfrac{1}{u} = \dfrac{1}{f}$

$\Rightarrow \dfrac{1}{v} = \dfrac{1}{f} + \dfrac{1}{u} = \dfrac{1}{10} - \dfrac{1}{5} = -\dfrac{1}{10}$

$\Rightarrow v = -10$ cm

Magnification, $m = -\dfrac{v}{u} = \dfrac{h'}{h}$

$\Rightarrow h' = -h \times \dfrac{v}{u} = 2 \times \dfrac{10}{5} = 4$ mm

37 Two thin lenses of power 3D and −2D are placed in contact, then power and focal length of the lens combination is
(a) +2D, +100 cm (b) +1D, +100 cm
(c) +5D, +20 cm (d) +1D, −100 cm
NCERT Exemplar

Light : Reflection and Refraction

Sol. (b) Given, power of lenses, $P_1 = 3D$, $P_2 = -2D$
Power of combination of the lens,
$$P = P_1 + P_2$$
$$= 3D - 2D = +1D$$
Combined focal length $= \dfrac{1}{P} \times 100$ cm
$$= \dfrac{1}{1} \times 100 = 100 \text{ cm}$$

38 A child is standing in front of a magic mirror. She finds the image of her head bigger, the middle portion of her body of the same size and that of the legs smaller. The following is the order of combinations for the magic mirror from the top.
(a) Plane, convex and concave
(b) Convex, concave and plane
(c) Concave, plane and convex
(d) Convex, plane and concave
NCERT Exemplar

Sol. (c) Concave mirrors (of large focal length) can be used to see a larger image of the head, the plane mirror for middle portion to see her body of the same size and convex mirror to see the diminished image of leg. Hence, the combinations for magic mirror from the top is concave mirror, plane mirror and convex mirror.

39 A lens has a power of + 4.0 D. It is
(a) a convex lens of focal length 4 m
(b) a concave lens of focal length 4 m
(c) a convex lens of focal length 0.25 m
(d) a concave lens of focal length 0.25 m
CBSE SQP (Term-I)

Sol. (b) Focal length and power of a convex lens is always positive. Thus, $f = \dfrac{1}{P} = \dfrac{1}{4} = 0.25$ m

40 The power of a combination of two lenses in contact is +1.0 D. If the focal length of one of the lenses of the combination is +20.0 cm, the focal length of the other lens would be
(a) – 120.0 cm   (b) + 80.0 cm
(c) – 25.0 cm   (d) – 20.0 cm

Sol. (c) From the combination of lenses, we have
$$\dfrac{1}{f} = \dfrac{1}{f_1} + \dfrac{1}{f_2}$$
$$\dfrac{1}{100} = \dfrac{1}{20} + \dfrac{1}{f_2}$$
$$\Rightarrow \dfrac{1}{f_2} = \dfrac{1}{100} - \dfrac{1}{20} = -\dfrac{4}{100}$$
$$\Rightarrow f_2 = -25.0 \text{ cm}$$

Fill in the Blanks

41 For a convex mirror, parallel rays of light appear to diverge from a point called the ……… .

Sol. Principal focus

42 If we use a concave mirror of focal length 2.5 cm as a dentist's mirror, the distance of tooth from the mirror should be ……… than the focal length.

Sol. Less than 2.5 cm

43 Magnification produced by a ……… lens is always less than 1.

Sol. Concave;
As concave lens always produces diminished image whenever an object is placed anywhere between optic centre (C) and infinity in front of a concave lens, hence magnification produced will less than 1.

44 The reciprocal of the ……… in metres gives you the power of the lens.

Sol. Focal length of lens;
As we know, power of lens $= \dfrac{1}{\text{focal length of lens}}$

45 For converging lenses, the power is ……… but for diverging lens the power is ……… .

Sol. Positive, negative

True and False

46 Nature of a mirror having a focal length +10 cm is converging in nature.

Sol. True

47 Nature of image formed by a concave lens is always real and erect.

Sol. False

48 The focal length of a spherical mirror is 10 cm, hence its radius of curvature will be 5 cm.

Sol. False;
As, $f = \dfrac{R}{2}$
Hence, $R = 2f = 2 \times 10 = 20$ cm

49 If a ray of light passes from denser to rarer medium, the angle of refraction will lesser than the angle of incidence.

Sol. False;
If a ray of light passes from denser to rarer medium, the refracted ray will bend away from the normal. Hence, angle of refraction will be more than the angle of incidence.

50 No refraction of light occurs if the ray of light hits the boundary of interface of medium at an angle of 90°.

Sol. True;
As $\angle i = 90°$, $\angle r = 90°$,
hence no refraction will take place.

Match the Columns

51 Match the Column A with Column B.

Column A		Column B
A. Lens formula	(i)	$\angle i \propto \angle r$
B. Snell's law	(ii)	$-\dfrac{v}{u}$
C. Refractive index	(iii)	$\dfrac{1}{v} - \dfrac{1}{u} = \dfrac{1}{f}$
D. Power of lens	(iv)	$\dfrac{c}{v}$
E. Magnification (spherical mirror)	(v)	$\dfrac{1}{f\text{(in metre)}}$

Sol. A → (iii), B → (i), C → (iv), D → (v) and E → (ii).

A → (iii) as formula of lens is the relation between object distance (u), image distance (v) and focal length (f) and represented as
$$\dfrac{1}{v} - \dfrac{1}{u} = \dfrac{1}{f}.$$

B → (i) According to Snell's law,
angle of incidence (i) ∝ angle of refraction (r)

C → (iv) Refractive index
$$(\mu) = \dfrac{\text{Speed of light in vacuum}}{\text{Speed of light in that medium}} = \dfrac{c}{v}$$

D → (v) Power of lens $(P) = \dfrac{1}{f \text{ (in cm)}}$

E → (ii) Magnification $(m) = -\dfrac{v}{u}$

Assertion-Reason

Direction (Q. Nos. 52-55) *In each of the following questions, a statement of Assertion is given by the corresponding statement of Reason. Of the statements, mark the correct answer as*

(a) If both Assertion and Reason are true and Reason is the correct explanation of Assertion.
(b) If both Assertion and Reason are true, but Reason is not the correct explanation of Assertion.
(c) If Assertion is true, but Reason is false.
(d) If Assertion is false, but Reason is true.

52 Assertion Large concave mirrors are used to concentrate sunlight to produce heat in solar cookers.

Reason Concave mirror converges the light rays falling on it to a point.

Sol. (a) Concave mirror converges the light rays falling on it to a point known as focus. So, large concave mirrors are used to concentrate sunlight to produce more heat in solar cookers.

53 Assertion A ray incident along normal to the mirror retraces its path.

Reason In reflection, angle of incidence is always equal to angle of reflection.

Sol. (a) When light ray incident along normal to the mirror, angle of incidence $\angle i = 0°$. According to law of reflection $\angle i = \angle r$, therefore angle of reflection $\angle r = 0°$, i.e. the incident ray retraces its path.

54 Assertion When a concave mirror is held under water, its focal length will increase.

Reason The focal length of a concave mirror is independent of the medium in which it is placed.

Sol. (d) Focal length is the property of mirror and is independent of the medium in which it is placed.

55 Assertion Higher is the refractive index of a medium or denser the medium, lesser is the velocity of light in that medium.

Reason Refractive index is inversely proportional to velcocity.

Sol. (a) According to Snell's law,
$$\dfrac{\sin i}{\sin r} = \dfrac{n_2}{n_1} = \dfrac{c/v_2}{c/v_1} = \dfrac{v_1}{v_2}$$
$$n_1 v_1 = n_2 v_2$$

This shows that higher is the refractive index of a medium or denser the medium, lesser is the velocity of light in that medium.

Case Based Questions

Direction (Q. Nos. 56-59) *Answers the questions on the basis of your understanding of the following passage and the related studied concepts :*

Magnification products like magnifying glass, compound microscope, telescope, etc., are important instruments for the daily activities of many individuals today. Whether the application is for commercial, professional or personal use, a magnifier enhances one's ability to perform or enjoy a task or hobby. A magnifying glass is a convex lens that is used to produce a magnified image of an object. The magnification of a magnifying glass depends upon whether it is placed between the user's eye and the object being viewed and the total distance between them. The highest magnifying power is obtained by putting the lens very close to the eye and moving the eye and the lens together to obtain the best focus.

56 What is magnifying glass?

Sol. A magnifying glass is a convex lens, i.e. used to produce a magnified image of an object.

57 The following diagram shows an experiment to measure the focal length of a lens. What is the focal length of the following lens?

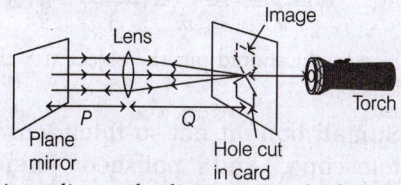

Sol. According to the diagram, Q is the focal length as it is the distance between focus and optic centre.

58 On what factors, magnification of a magnifying glass depends?

Sol. The magnification of magnifying glass depends upon whether it is placed between the users eye and the object being viewed and total distance between them.

59 Draw a diagram showing that the convex lens forms a virtual, erect, enlarged image of an object.

Sol.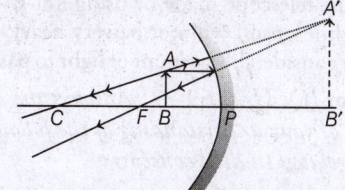

Direction (Q. Nos. 60-63) *Answers the questions on the basis of your understanding of the following table and the related studied concepts :*

Absolute refractive indices of some of the materials A, B, C and D are given in the following table :

Medium	Refractive index
A	1.54
B	1.33
C	2.42
D	1.65

60 What is the meaning of the statement that 'absolute refractive index of water is 1.33'?

Sol. Absolute refractive index of water is 1.33 means the ratio of the speed of light in vacuum and the speed of light in water is equal to 1.33.

61 How is absolute refractive index related to speed of light?

Sol. Absolute refractive index

$$= \frac{\text{Speed of light in vacuum}}{\text{Speed of light in that medium}}$$

62 In which of these materials, in the above table, light travels fastest?
(a) A   (b) B   (c) C   (d) D

Sol. (b) Light travels fastest in medium B. Since, B has the least refractive index it indicates that B is much optically rarer than all other medium hence light travels fastest in medium B.

63 The speed of light in air is $3 \times 10^8 \text{ ms}^{-1}$ and that in medium A is $1.5 \times 10^8 \text{ ms}^{-1}$. The refractive index of A will be
(a) 2   (b) 0.5
(c) 4.5   (d) 1.5

Sol. (a) Refractive index of A

$$= \frac{\text{Speed of light in air}}{\text{Speed of light in that medium}}$$

$$= \frac{3 \times 10^8}{1.5 \times 10^8} = 2$$

Direction (Q. Nos. 64-68) *Answers the questions on the basis of your understanding of the following table and the related studied concepts :*

Sumati wanted to see the stars of the night sky. She knows that she needs a telescope to see those distant stars. She finds out that the telescopes, which are made of lenses, are called refracting telescopes and the ones which are made of mirrors are called reflecting telescopes.

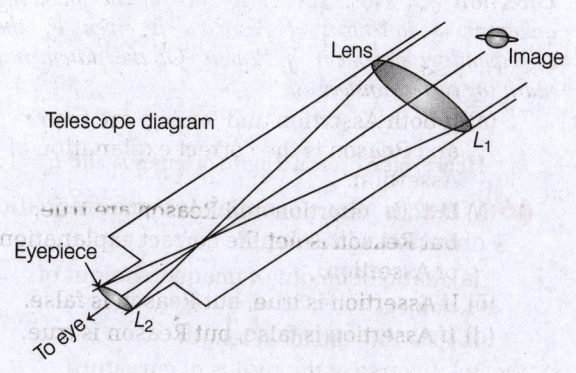
Telescope diagram

So, she decided to make a refracting telescope. She bought two lenses, L_1 and L_2 out of which L_1 was bigger and L_2 was smaller. The larger lens gathers and bends the light, while the smaller lens magnifies the image. Big, thick lenses are more powerful. So to see far away, she needed a big powerful lens. Unfortunately, she realised that a big lens is very heavy.

Heavy lenses are hard to make and difficult to hold in the right place. Also, since the light is passing through the lens, the surface of the lens has to be extremely smooth. Any flaws in the lens will change the image. It would be like looking through a dirty window. **CBSE SQP 2020-21**

64 Based on the diagram shown, what kind of lenses would Sumati need to make the telescope?
(a) Concave lenses
(b) Convex lenses
(c) Bi-focal lenses
(d) Flat lenses

Sol. (b) As shown in the given diagram, Sumati would need convex lenses in order to make the telescope.

65 If the powers of the lenses L_1 and L_2 are in the ratio of 4 : 1, what would be the ratio of the focal length of L_1 and L_2?
(a) 4 : 1   (b) 1 : 4   (c) 2 : 1   (d) 1 : 1

Sol. (b) Let f_1 and f_2 be the focal lengths of lenses L_1 and L_2, respectively.

As, power $= \dfrac{1}{\text{focal length}}$

Ratio of powers of lenses L_1 and L_2,

$\dfrac{P_1}{P_2} = \dfrac{4}{1}$ (given)

$\Rightarrow \dfrac{1/f_1}{1/f_2} = \dfrac{4}{1}$

$\Rightarrow \dfrac{f_2}{f_1} = \dfrac{4}{1}$

$\Rightarrow \dfrac{f_1}{f_2} = \dfrac{1}{4}$

Hence, ratio of focal lengths of lenses L_1 and L_2 = 1 : 4

66 What is the formula for magnification obtained with a lens?
(a) Ratio of height of image to height of object
(b) Double the focal length
(c) Inverse of the radius of curvature
(d) Inverse of the object distance

Sol. (a) Magnification obtained by a lens is the ratio of height of image h_i to the height of object h_o. i.e.,

Magnification, $m = \dfrac{h_i}{h_o}$

67 Sumati did some preliminary experiment with the lenses and found out that the magnification of the eyepiece (L_2) is 3. If in her experiment with L_2 she found an image at 24 cm from the lens, at what distance did she put the object?
(a) 72 cm   (b) 12 cm   (c) 8 cm   (d) 6 cm

Sol. (c) Given, magnification, $m = 3$

Image distance, $v = 24$ cm

Object distance, $u = ?$

As, $m = \dfrac{v}{u} \Rightarrow u = \dfrac{v}{m} = \dfrac{24 \text{ cm}}{3} = 8$ cm

Hence, she should put the object at 8 cm from the lens L_2.

68 Sumati bought not-so-thick lenses for the telescope and polished them. What advantages, if any, would she have with her choice of lenses?
(a) She will not have any advantage as even thicker lenses would give clearer images.
(b) Thicker lenses would have made the telescope easier to handle.
(c) Not-so-thick lenses would not make the telescope very heavy and also allow considerable amount of light to pass.
(d) Not-so-thick lenses will give her more magnification.

Sol. (c) The telescope made by using not-so-thick lenses (i.e. thin lenses) will not be very heavy. Also, it will allow considerable amount of light to pass through it.

Direction *(Q. Nos. 69-72) Answers the questions on the basis of your understanding of the following passage and the related studied concepts :*

Noor, a young student, was trying to demonstrate some properties of light in her Science project work. She kept 'X' inside the box (as shown in the figure) and with the help of a laser pointer made light rays pass through the holes on one side of the box. She had a small butter-paper screen to see the spots of light being cast as they emerged.

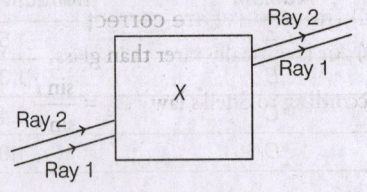

69 What could be the 'X' that she placed inside the box to make the rays behave as shown?
(a) a converging lens
(b) a parallel-sided glass block
(c) a plane mirror
(d) a triangular prism

Sol. (b) Since, incident rays are parallel to refracted ray, therefore parallel sided glass block is placed inside the box.

70 She measured the angles of incidence for both the rays on the left side of the box to be 48.6°. She knew the refractive index of the material 'X' inside the box was 1.5. What will be the approximate value of angle of refraction?
(a) 45° (b) 40° (c) 30° (d) 60°

Sol. (c) Given, angle of incidence, $i = 48.6°$
Refractive index, $\mu = 1.5$
From Snell's law refractive index, $\mu = \dfrac{\sin i}{\sin r}$
$\Rightarrow \quad 1.5 = \dfrac{\sin 48.6°}{\sin r}$
$\Rightarrow \quad \sin r = \dfrac{0.75}{1.5} = \dfrac{1}{2} \Rightarrow r = 30°$

71 Her friend noted the following observations from this demonstration:
(i) Glass is optically rarer than air.
(ii) Air and glass allow light to pass through them with the same velocity.
(iii) Air is optically rarer than glass.
(iv) Speed of light through a denser medium is faster than that of a rarer medium.
(v) The ratio of sine of angle of incidence in the first medium to the ratio of sine of angle of refraction in the second medium, gives the refractive index of the second medium with respect to the first one.

Which one of the combination of the above statements given below is correct?
(a) (ii), (iv) and (v) are correct
(b) (iii) and (iv) are correct
(c) (i), (iv) and (v) are correct
(d) (iii) and (v) are correct

Sol. (d) Air is optically rarer than glass.
According to Snell's law, $'\mu_2 = \dfrac{\sin i}{\sin r}$

or $\quad n_1 \sin i = n_2 \sin r$
Thus, $\dfrac{n_1}{n_2} = \dfrac{\sin i}{\sin r}$
which gives refractive index of a medium with respect to another medium.

72 If the object inside the box was made of a material with a refractive index less than 1.5, then
(a) lateral shift of the rays would have been less
(b) lateral shift of the rays would have been more
(c) lateral shift of the rays would remain the same as before
(d) there is not enough information to comment on any of the above statements

Sol. (a) If the refractive index is decreased, then the lateral shift decreases, as $d \propto \mu$.

Very Short Answer Type Questions

73 Due to which property of light, sharp shadows of opaque objects are obtained?

Sol. Since, light travels in straight line, any obstacle obstructing the path will cast its shadow. Hence, its the rectilinear propagation of light which helps in shadow formation.

74 What is the radius of curvature of plane mirror?

Sol. The radius of curvature of plane mirror is infinity.

75 A ray is incident on a plane mirror as shown in figure.

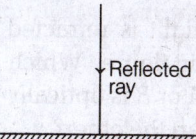

What is the angle of reflection for the above incident ray?

Sol. Since, the incident ray falls normally on the reflecting surface, the angle of incidence is zero and hence the angle of reflection is zero, according to the law of reflection.

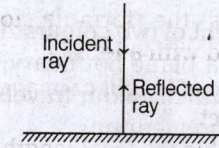

76 Where is the image formed when an object is at large distance from a concave mirror? **CBSE SQP 2020-21**

Sol. The image formed is at the focus of the mirror.

77 If you want to see an enlarged image of your face, which type of mirror will you use? Where will you place your face?

Sol. A concave mirror. The face should be placed between the pole and the focus of the mirror.

78 Write the relationship of object distance (u), image distance (v) and focal length (f).

Sol. $\dfrac{1}{u} + \dfrac{1}{v} = \dfrac{1}{f}$

79 The image formed by a concave mirror is observed to be real, inverted and larger than the object. Where is the object placed? **CBSE SQP 2020-21**

Sol. When the object is placed between the principal focus and the centre of curvature of concave mirror, the image formed will be real, inverted and larger than the object (as shown in figure).

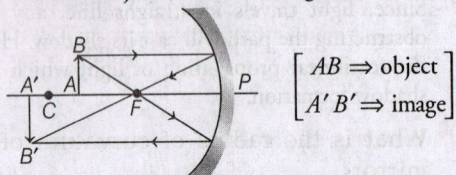

80 A ray of light is incident on a concave mirror after passing through the centre of curvature. What is the angle of incidence?

Sol. Zero degree

81 A ray of light is refracted as shown in figure. Which medium A or B is optically denser than the other?

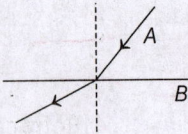

Sol. As the ray bends away from normal, medium A is optically denser than medium B.

82 Arrange air, glass and water in terms of descending order of refractive index.

Sol. The descending order is
glass (1.5) > water (1.33) > air (1.0003).

83 When light of two colours A and B is passed through a plane boundary; A is bent more than B. Which colour travels more slowly in the second medium?

Sol. Colour B travels slowly.

84 The refractive index of diamond is 2.42 and that of glass is 1.52. How much faster does light travel in glass than in diamond?

Sol. Given, $\mu_g = 1.52$, $\mu_d = 2.42$

But $\dfrac{v_g}{v_d} = \dfrac{\mu_d}{\mu_g} = \dfrac{2.42}{1.52} = 1.59$

Thus, light travels in glass 1.59 times faster than in diamond.

85 What is the minimum distance between an object and its real image formed by a convex lens?

Sol. The minimum distance is $4f$, i.e. when an object is placed at one of the two centres of curvature and the image is formed at the other centre of curvature, the image will be real.

86 If the magnification of a body of size 1 m is 2. What is the size of the image?

Sol. Given, $m = 2$, $h_o = 1$ m, $h_i = ?$

We know that, $m = \dfrac{h_i}{h_o}$

$\Rightarrow \quad h_i = m h_o = 2 \times 1 = 2$ m

87 Name the part of a lens through which a ray of light passes without suffering any deviation.

Sol. When a ray of light passes through optical centre of the lens (both concave and convex), it will emerge out undeviated (as shown in figure).

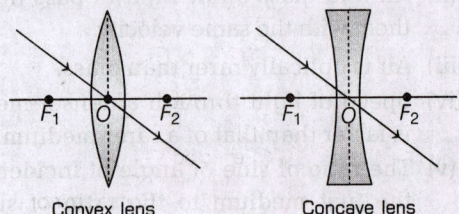

Convex lens   Concave lens

CBSE SQP 2020-21

88 Both a spherical mirror and a thin spherical lens have a focal length of (−15) cm. What type of mirror and lens are these? **CBSE SQP 2020-21**

Sol. Here, focal length = (−15) cm = negative

According to new cartesian sign conventions, the focal length of concave mirror and concave lens are negative. So, both spherical mirror and thin spherical lens will be concave in nature.

Short Answer (SA) Type Questions

1. Draw ray diagram in each of the following cases to show what happens after reflection to the incident ray when
  (a) it is parallel to the principal axis and falling on a convex mirror.
  (b) it is falling on a concave mirror while passing through its principal focus.
  (c) it is coming oblique to the principal axis and falling on the pole of a convex mirror. **CBSE 2020**

Sol. (a) Passes through focus of mirror after reflection.

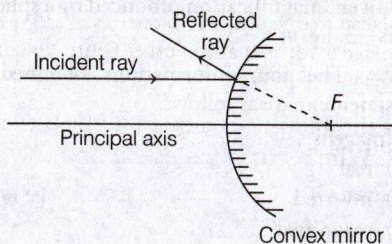

(b) Become parallel to principal axis.

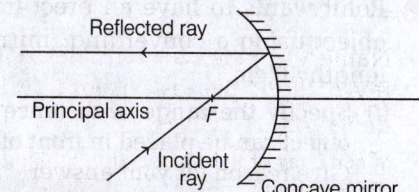

(c) Passes with $\angle i = \angle r$

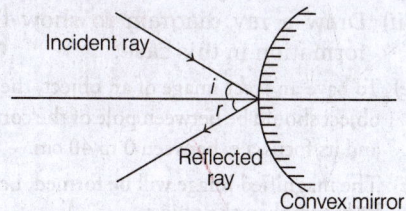

2. A child is standing in front of a magic mirror. She finds the image of her head bigger, the middle portion of her body of the same size and that of the legs smaller. Explain the construction of the magic mirror using different types of mirror. Also state the reasons in support of your answer. **CBSE 2020**

Sol. This mirror contains three types of mirror, i.e. concave mirror, plane mirror and convex mirror.

The upper most mirror is concave, so it forms bigger image of her head.

The middle mirror is plane, since it forms a image of same size of her body.

The lower mirror is convex, since it forms smaller image of her legs.

Thus, magic mirror is combination of 3 types of mirror.

3. (a) Water has refractive index 1.33 and alcohol has refractive index 1.36. Which of the two medium is optically denser? Give reason for your answer.
  (b) Draw a ray diagram to show the path of a ray of light passing obliquely from water to alcohol.
  (c) State the relationship between angle of incidence and angle of refraction in the above case. **CBSE 2020**

Sol. (a) Given, refractive index of water, $\mu_{water} = 1.33$
and refractive index of alcohol, $\mu_{alcohol} = 1.36$
$\therefore \quad \mu_{water} < \mu_{alcohol}$
Hence, alcohol is denser than water.

(b) Ray diagram is given below

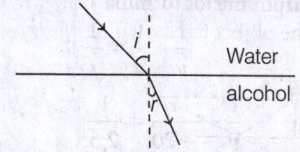

(c) Here, relation between angle of incidence and angle of refraction is $\dfrac{\sin i}{\sin r} = \dfrac{\mu_{alcohol}}{\mu_{water}} = \dfrac{1.36}{1.33}$
$\Rightarrow 1.33 \sin i = 1.36 \sin r$

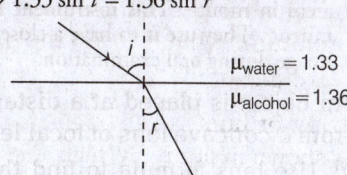

4. Refractive index of water with respect to air is 1.33 and that of diamond is 2.42.
  (i) In which medium does the light move faster, water or diamond?
  (ii) What is the refractive index of diamond with respect to water? **CBSE SQP 2020-21**

Sol. Given, refractive index of water, $\mu_w = 1.33$
and refractive index of diamond, $\mu_d = 2.42$

(i) As, refractive index $= \dfrac{\text{Speed of light in vacuum}}{\text{Speed of light in medium}}$

$\Rightarrow$ Refractive index $\propto \dfrac{1}{\text{Speed of light in medium}}$

$\therefore$ The refractive index of diamond is more than that of water, hence the speed of light is lesser in diamond as compared to in water.

Hence, light moves faster in water medium.

(ii) Now, refractive index of diamond w.r.t. water,
$$_w\mu_d = \frac{\mu_d}{\mu_w} = \frac{2.42}{1.33}$$
$$= 1.82 \text{ (approx)}$$

5 (a) A security mirror used in a big showroom has radius of curvature 5 m. If a customer is standing at a distance of 20 m from the cash counter, find the position, nature and size of the image formed in the security mirror.

(b) Neha visited a dentist in his clinic. She observed that the dentist was holding an instrument fitted with a mirror. State the nature of this mirror and reason for its use in the instrument used by dentist. **CBSE 2020**

Sol. (a) Given, radius of curvature, $R = 5$m,
$$f = \frac{R}{2} = 2.5 \text{ m}$$
Object distance, $u = -20$m
As, we know security mirror is convex mirror.
So, from mirror formula
$$\frac{1}{v} + \frac{1}{u} = \frac{1}{f}$$
$$\Rightarrow \frac{1}{v} + \frac{1}{-20} = \frac{1}{2.5}$$
$$\Rightarrow v = 2.22 \text{ m}$$
Since, object is beyond focus, hence image is behind the mirror, virtual, erect and small.

(b) Dentists use concave mirror to see teeth and other areas in mouth. This instrument is called 'mouth mirror'. They use it to have a closer and magnified image during oral examination.

6 An object is placed at a distance of 60 cm from a concave lens of focal length 30 cm.
(i) Use lens formula to find the distance of the image from the lens.
(ii) List four characteristics of the image (nature, position, size, erect/inverted) formed by the lens in this case.
(iii) Draw the ray diagram to justify your answer of part (ii). **CBSE 2019**

Sol. (i) Given, $u = -60$ cm, $f = -30$ cm
By lens formula, $\frac{1}{v} - \frac{1}{u} = \frac{1}{f}$
$$\Rightarrow \frac{1}{v} = \frac{1}{f} + \frac{1}{u} = \frac{1}{-30} + \frac{1}{-60}$$
$$= \frac{2+1}{-60} = -\frac{1}{20}$$
$$\Rightarrow v = -20 \text{ cm}$$

(ii) Since, v is negative, therefore image is formed at same side of object.
Nature of image is virtual, erect and diminished and image is formed between focus and optical centre.

(iii)
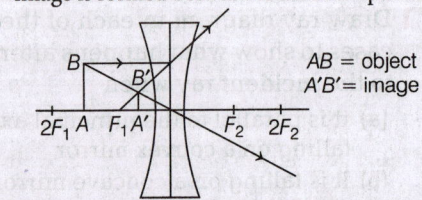
AB = object
A'B' = image

7 "The magnification produced by a spherical mirror is −3." List four informations you obtain from this statement about the mirror/image. **CBSE 2016**

Sol. Given, magnification produced by a spherical mirror is −3, i.e. $m = -3$.

∴ The four informations obtained from this statement are as follows:
Image is
(i) real
(ii) inverted   [∵ m is negative]
(iii) magnified   [$|m| > 1$]
(iv) spherical mirror used is concave mirror.

8 Rohit wants to have an erect image of an object using a converging mirror of focal length 40 cm.
(i) Specify the range of distance where the object can be placed in front of the mirror. Give reason for your answer.
(ii) Will the image be bigger or smaller than the object?
(iii) Draw a ray diagram to show the image formation in this case. **CBSE 2015**

Sol. (i) To have an erect image of an object, the position of object should be between pole of the concave mirror and its focus, i.e. between 0 to 40 cm.

(ii) The magnified image will be formed, i.e. image will be bigger than the object.

(iii)
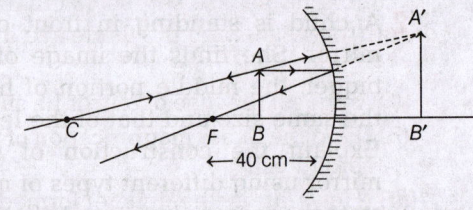

9 When a plane mirror is placed horizontally on levelled ground at a distance of 40 m from the foot of a tower, the top of the tower and its image in the mirror subtend an angle of 90° at the eye. What is the height of the tower?

Sol.

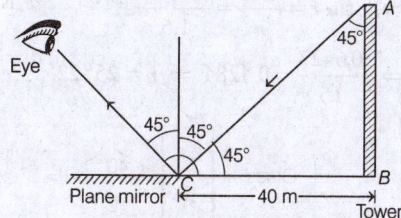

From geometry of figure, height of tower is 40 m.
As in right angled $\triangle ABC$,
$$\angle CAB = \angle BCA$$
$$\therefore CB = AB = 40 \text{ m}$$

10 If p, q and r denote the object distance, image distance and the radius of curvature respectively, of a spherical mirror, then find out the relation between them.

Sol. From mirror formula,
$$\frac{1}{f} = \frac{1}{v} + \frac{1}{u}$$

We have, $\dfrac{1}{\frac{r}{2}} = \dfrac{1}{q} + \dfrac{1}{p}$ $\left[\because f = \dfrac{r}{2}\right]$

or $\dfrac{2}{r} = \dfrac{p+q}{pq}$ or $\dfrac{r}{2} = \dfrac{pq}{p+q}$

$\therefore \quad r = \dfrac{2pq}{p+q}$

11 If the image formed by a mirror for all positions of the object placed in front of it is always erect and diminished, what type of mirror is it? Draw a ray diagram to justify your answer. Where and why do we generally use this type of mirror? **CBSE 2015**

Sol. The mirror is convex mirror.
Refer to text on Pg. 286.

12 A student wants to project the image of a candle flame on a screen 48 cm in front of a mirror by keeping the flame at a distance of 12 cm from its pole.
   (i) Suggest the type of mirror he should use.
   (ii) Find the linear magnification of the image produced.
   (iii) How far is the image formed from its object?
   (iv) Draw a ray diagram to show the image formation in this case. **CBSE 2014**

Sol. (i) He should use concave mirror, as it forms real images.
   (ii) Given, distance of object, $u = -12$ cm, distance of image, $v = -48$ cm

As, magnification, $m = \dfrac{-v}{u}$
$$= -\dfrac{(-48)}{(-12)} = -4$$

Negative sign indicates that image formed is real and inverted.
(iii) The image is formed at a distance of 48 cm from object.
(iv)

Real, inverted and enlarged image is formed beyond centre of curvature.

13 When an object is placed at a distance of 60 cm from a convex spherical mirror, the magnification produced is $\dfrac{1}{2}$. Where should the object be placed to get a magnification of $\dfrac{1}{3}$?

Sol. Given, distance of object, $u_1 = -60$ cm

Magnification, $m_1 = \dfrac{1}{2}$

Distance of object, $u_2 = ?$

Magnification, $m_2 = \dfrac{1}{3}$

$\therefore \qquad m_1 = \dfrac{-v_1}{u_1}$

$\Rightarrow v_1 = -m_1 u_1 = \dfrac{-1}{2} \times (-60) = 30$ cm

Using mirror formula,
$$\dfrac{1}{f_1} = \dfrac{1}{v_1} + \dfrac{1}{u_1} = \dfrac{1}{v_1} + \dfrac{1}{(-60)} = \dfrac{1}{30} - \dfrac{1}{60} = \dfrac{1}{60}$$
$$\Rightarrow f_1 = 60 \text{ cm}$$

Again $m_2 = \dfrac{-v_2}{u_2} \Rightarrow v_2 = \dfrac{-u_2}{3}$

Since, $f_1 = f_2$
[as the same mirror is used in both the cases]

$\therefore \quad \dfrac{1}{f_2} = \dfrac{1}{v_2} + \dfrac{1}{u_2} \Rightarrow \dfrac{1}{u_2} = \dfrac{1}{f_1} - \dfrac{1}{v_2}$

$\dfrac{1}{u_2} = \dfrac{1}{60} + \dfrac{3}{u_2}$

$\Rightarrow \dfrac{1}{u_2} - \dfrac{3}{u_2} = \dfrac{1}{60} \Rightarrow \dfrac{-2}{u_2} = \dfrac{1}{60}$

$\Rightarrow \qquad u_2 = -120 \text{ cm}$

14 A spherical mirror produces an image of magnification −1 on a screen placed at a distance of 50 cm from the mirror.

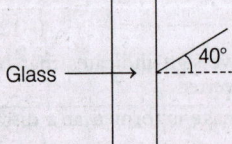

(i) Write the type of mirror.
(ii) Find the distance of the image from the object.
(iii) What is the focal length of the mirror?
(iv) Draw the ray diagram to show the image formation in this case. **CBSE 2014**

Sol. (i) The mirror is concave mirror.

(ii) Given, $m = -1$, $u = -50$ cm

∴ Magnification, $m = \dfrac{-v}{u} \Rightarrow -1 = \dfrac{-v}{-50}$

$\Rightarrow v = -50$ cm

Therefore, the image is real and inverted and of same size as that of the object.

Here, object is placed at centre of curvature, so the object distance is equal to the image distance, since screen is placed at distance of 50 cm from the mirror, therefore object distance = image distance = 50 cm.

The distance of the image from object is zero, i.e. the object is formed at $2f$.

(iii) Here $2f = 50$ cm $\Rightarrow f = \dfrac{50}{2} = 25$ cm

Object distance = image distance = 50 cm

(iv)

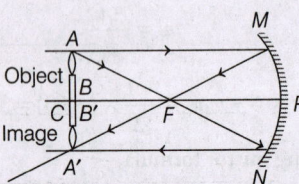

15 Figure shows a ray of light meeting the glass of the window of a car at an angle of incidence of 40°.

(i) Assuming that the refractive index of glass is 1.5, find the angle of refraction for this ray in the glass.
(ii) Complete the diagram by sketching the path of the ray through the glass and out on the other side.
(iii) Use the diagram to explain the effect of the glass on what is seen by the driver.

Sol. (i) Applying Snell's law, let r be the angle of refraction.

Given, $i = 40°$, $n = 1.5$

∴ Refractive index, $n = \dfrac{\sin i}{\sin r}$

$\Rightarrow \sin r = \dfrac{\sin i}{n} = \dfrac{\sin 40°}{1.5}$

$\Rightarrow \dfrac{0.6427}{1.5} = 0.4284 \Rightarrow r = 25°22'$

(ii)

(iii) The object is seen slightly displaced from its original position.

16 (i) "The refractive index of kerosene is 1.44." What is meant by this statement?

(ii) A ray of light strikes a glass slab at an angle of incidence equal to 30°. Find the refractive index of glass such that the angle of refraction is 19.5°. **CBSE 2015**

(Take, $\sin 19.5° = \dfrac{1}{3}$ and $\sin 30° = \dfrac{1}{2}$)

Sol. (i) Refractive index of kerosene is 1.44, this means that speed of light in kerosene oil is $\left(\dfrac{1}{1.44}\right)$ times the velocity of light in air.

(ii) Given, $i = 30°$ and $r = 19.5°$

From Snell's law,

$\mu_g = \dfrac{\sin i}{\sin r} = \dfrac{\sin 30°}{\sin 19.5°}$

$= \dfrac{1/2}{1/3} = \dfrac{3}{2} = 1.5$ $\left[\because \sin 30° = 1/2 \text{ and } \sin 19.5° = 1/3\right]$

17 (i) Draw a ray diagram to show the refraction of light through a glass slab and mark an angle of refraction and the lateral shift suffered by the ray of light while passing through the slab.

(ii) If the refractive index of glass for light going from air to glass is 3/2, find the refractive index of air for light going from glass to air. **CBSE 2016**

Sol. (i)

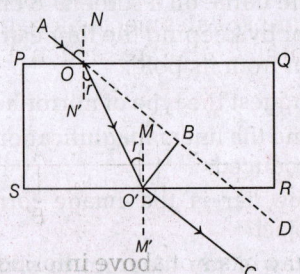

In the above figure,
∠$N'OO' = \angle r$ = angle of refraction
∠$MO'O = \angle r$ = angle of refraction
Distance, $O'B$ = lateral displacement

(ii) Given, refractive index from air to glass is $\frac{3}{2}$.

i.e. $_a\mu_g = \frac{\mu_g}{\mu_a} = \frac{3}{2}$.

$\because$ It is known that, $_1\mu_2 \times _2\mu_1 = 1$

$\Rightarrow \quad _a\mu_g \times _g\mu_a = 1 \Rightarrow _g\mu_a = \frac{1}{_a\mu_g}$

$\Rightarrow \quad _g\mu_a = \frac{1}{\left(\frac{3}{2}\right)} \Rightarrow _g\mu_a = \frac{2}{3}$

i.e. Refractive index of air for light going from glass to air is given by $_g\mu_a = \frac{2}{3}$.

18 The absolute refractive indices of glass and water are $\frac{4}{3}$ and $\frac{3}{2}$, respectively. If the speed of light in glass is 2×10^8 ms^{-1}, calculate the speed of light in

(i) vacuum   (ii) water   **CBSE 2015**

Sol. Given, $_a\mu_g = \frac{4}{3}$ and $_a\mu_w = \frac{3}{2}$

Speed of light in glass, $v_g = 2 \times 10^8$ ms^{-1}

(i) Speed of light in vacuum is given by

$c = _a\mu_g \times v_g \quad \left[\because _a\mu_g = \frac{c}{v_g}\right]$

$= \frac{4}{3} \times 2 \times 10^8 = \frac{8}{3} \times 10^8$ m s^{-1}

$= 2.67 \times 10^8$ m s^{-1}

(ii) Speed of light in water is given by

$v_w = \frac{c}{_a\mu_w} \quad \left[\because _a\mu_w = \frac{c}{v_w}\right]$

$= \frac{8}{3} \times 10^8 \times \frac{2}{3}$

$= \frac{16}{9} \times 10^8 = 1.78 \times 10^8$ m s^{-1}

19 Observe the following incomplete ray diagram of an object where the image $A'B'$ is formed after refraction from a convex lens.

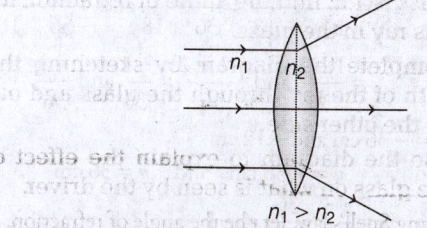

On the basis of above information fill in the blanks.

(i) The position of object AB would have been ..... .

(ii) Size of the object would have been ..... than the size of image.   **CBSE 2015**

Sol.(i) The position of object AB would have been beyond $2F_1$.

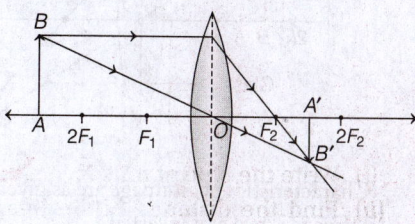

(ii) Size of the object would have been bigger than the size of image.

20 A convex lens made of a material of refractive index n_2 is kept in a medium of refractive index n_1. A parallel beam of light is incident on the lens. Draw the path of rays of light emerging from the convex lens, if

(i) $n_1 < n_2$ (ii) $n_1 = n_2$ (iii) $n_1 > n_2$

Sol.(i) When $n_1 < n_2$, light goes from rarer to denser medium. Thus, on passing through a convex lens, it converges.

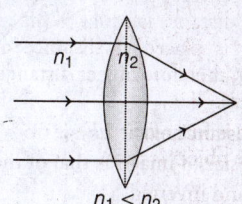

(ii) When $n_1 = n_2$, there is no change in medium. Therefore, no bending or refraction occurs.

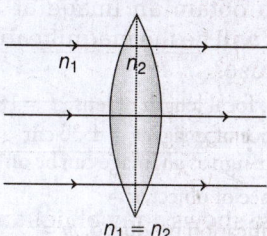

(iii) When $n_1 > n_2$, light goes from denser to rarer medium. Thus, on passing through a convex lens, it diverges.

21 Draw a labelled diagram showing how an image of a small size can be projected on large screen. State two characteristics of an image.

Sol.

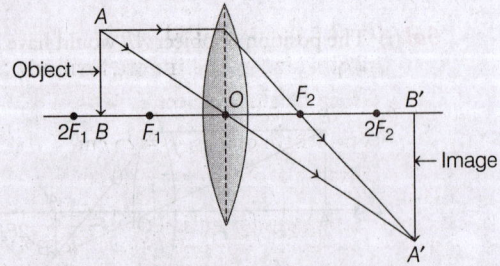

Characteristics of an image are as given below:
(i) Image is real and inverted.
(ii) Image is enlarged.

22 An object is placed at $2F_1$ in front of a convex lens. What is the
(i) position   (ii) size
(iii) nature of image?   **CBSE 2015**

Sol. When object is placed at $2F_1$,

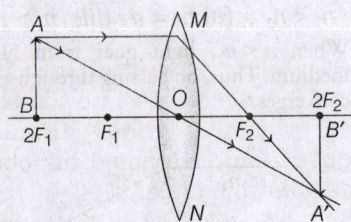

(i) Image is formed at $2F_2$.
(ii) Same size of image as that of the object.
(iii) Real and inverted.

23 At what distance should an object be placed from a convex lens of focal length 18 cm to obtain an image at 36 cm from it? What will be the magnification produced in this case?

Sol. Given, focal length of lens, $f = 18$ cm
Distance of image, $v = \pm 36$ cm
[∵ ± sign as an image can be on either side of lens]
Distance of object, $u = ?$
Magnification produced, $m = ?$
From lens formula, $\dfrac{1}{v} - \dfrac{1}{u} = \dfrac{1}{f} \Rightarrow \dfrac{1}{u} = \dfrac{1}{v} - \dfrac{1}{f}$

$= \dfrac{1}{\pm 36} - \dfrac{1}{18} = \dfrac{1}{36} - \dfrac{1}{18}$ and $\dfrac{1}{-36} - \dfrac{1}{18}$

$= \dfrac{1-2}{36}$ and $\dfrac{-1-2}{36} = \dfrac{-1}{36}$ and $\dfrac{-3}{36}$

∴ $u = -36$ cm and -12 cm
If $u = -36$ cm and $v = 36$ cm

Then, $m = \dfrac{v}{u} = \dfrac{36}{-36} = -1$

Image is real, inverted and same size.
If $u = -12$ cm and $v = -36$ cm

Then, $m = \dfrac{v}{u} = \dfrac{-36}{-12} = 3$

Image is virtual, erect and enlarged.

24 An object of height 5 cm is placed perpendicular to the principal axis of a concave lens of focal length 10 cm. If the distance of the object from the optical centre of the lens is 20 cm, determine the position, nature and size of the image formed using the lens formula.   **CBSE 2015**

Sol. Given, height of object, $h_o = 5$ cm
Focal length of the given concave lens, $f = -10$ cm,
distance of object, $u = -20$ cm, $v = ?$
Using lens formula, $\dfrac{1}{f} = \dfrac{1}{v} - \dfrac{1}{u}$

$\Rightarrow \dfrac{1}{v} = \dfrac{1}{f} + \dfrac{1}{u} = \dfrac{1}{(-10)} + \dfrac{1}{(-20)} = \dfrac{-1}{10} - \dfrac{1}{20}$

$= \dfrac{-2-1}{20} = \dfrac{-3}{20} \Rightarrow v = -6.67$ cm

Image is at 6.67 cm from concave lens.

As, magnification, $m = \dfrac{h_i}{h_o} = \dfrac{v}{u}$

$\Rightarrow h_i = h_o \times \dfrac{v}{u} = 5 \times \dfrac{-20}{3} \times \dfrac{1}{-20} = \dfrac{5}{3} = 1.67$ cm

Image is virtual, erect and diminished.

25 The image of an object formed by a lens is of magnification –1. If the distance between the object and its image is 60 cm, what is the focal length of the lens? If the object is moved 20 cm towards the lens, where would the image be formed? State reason and also draw a ray diagram in support of your answer.   **CBSE 2016**

Sol.

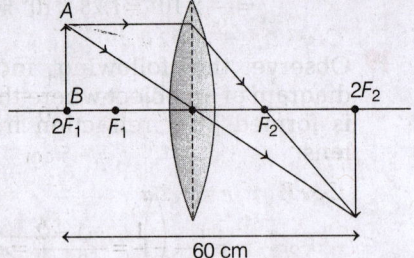

Given, $m = -1$, negative sign shows that image is real and inverted.
∴ $|m| = 1$, it means that $h_i = h_o$
and this is possible in convex lens.
It implies that object and image both will be at $2F$.
So, $v = u$.

Object distance, $u = -30$ cm
Image distance, $v = +30$ cm
∴ According to lens formula,
$$\frac{1}{f} = \frac{1}{v} - \frac{1}{u} \Rightarrow \frac{1}{f} = \frac{1}{30} - \left(\frac{-1}{30}\right)$$
$\Rightarrow \quad f = 15$ cm

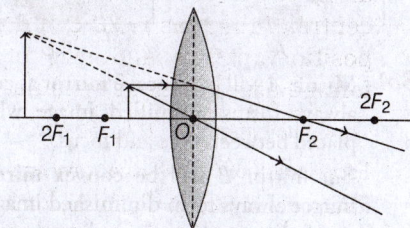

Now, object is moved 20 cm towards the lens.
∴ Object distance, $u = -10$ cm
Focal length, $f = +15$ cm
Again using lens formula,
$$\frac{1}{v} - \frac{1}{u} = \frac{1}{f} \Rightarrow \frac{1}{v} = \frac{1}{15} + \frac{1}{(-10)}$$
$$\Rightarrow \quad \frac{1}{v} = \frac{1}{15} - \frac{1}{10} = \frac{2-3}{30}$$
$\Rightarrow \quad v = -30$ cm

26 Find the distance at which an object should be placed in front of a convex lens of focal length 10 cm to obtain an image of double its size.

Sol. Given, focal length of lens, $f = 10$ cm
Distance of an object, $u = ?$
In convex lens, the image is real and virtual.
∴ Magnification, $m = \frac{v}{u} = \pm 2 \Rightarrow v = \pm 2u$
Using lens formula, $\frac{1}{f} = \frac{1}{v} - \frac{1}{u}$
Case I If $v = +2u$
$$\frac{1}{10} = \frac{1}{2u} - \frac{1}{u} \Rightarrow \frac{1}{10} = \frac{1-2}{2u} = \frac{-1}{2u}$$
$\Rightarrow \quad u = -5$ cm
Case II If $v = -2u$
$$\frac{1}{10} = \frac{1}{-2u} - \frac{1}{u} = \frac{-1-2}{2u} = \frac{-3}{2u}$$
$\Rightarrow \quad u = -15$ cm

27 A 6 cm tall object is placed perpendicular to the principal axis of a convex lens of focal length 25 cm. The distance of the object from the lens is 40 cm.
By calculation determine

(i) the position and
(ii) the size of the image formed.

Sol. Given, height of object, $h_o = 6$ cm
Focal length of lens, $f = 25$ cm
Distance of object, $u = -40$ cm
(i) Using lens formula, $\frac{1}{f} = \frac{1}{v} - \frac{1}{u}$
$$\Rightarrow \frac{1}{v} = \frac{1}{f} + \frac{1}{u} = \frac{1}{25} + \frac{1}{(-40)}$$
$$= \frac{8-5}{200} = \frac{3}{200}$$
$$v = \frac{200}{3} = 66.67 \text{ cm}$$
(ii) ∴ Magnification, $m = \frac{h_i}{h_o} = \frac{v}{u}$
$$\Rightarrow h_i = \frac{v}{u} \times h_o = \frac{200}{3 \times (-40)} \times 6 = -10 \text{ cm}$$

28 A student focussed the image of a candle flame on a white screen by placing the flame at various distances from a convex lens. He noted his observation in the following table.

S.No.	Distance of the Screen from Lens (cm)	Distance of the Flame from Lens (cm)
I	20	60
II	24	40
III	30	30
IV	40	24
V	70	12

Analyse the above table and give the answers of the following questions.
(i) What is the focal length of convex lens?
(ii) Which set of observation is incorrect and why?
(iii) Draw the ray diagram to show the image formation for any correct set of observation.

Sol. (i) We know that when object is placed at $2F$, the distance of an object from lens = distance of image from lens.
Therefore, from III observation, radius of curvature $R = 30$ cm
Thus, focal length, $f = \frac{R}{2} = \frac{30}{2} = 15$ cm

(ii) Last observation is incorrect because when an object is placed at a distance less than 15 cm away from convex lens, we will have virtual image, which cannot be taken on screen.

(iii) Refer to figure on Pg 291 and 292.

29 Ravi is given lenses with powers +5 D, −5 D, +10 D, −10 D and −20 D. Considering a pair of lenses at a time, which two lenses will he select to have a combination of total focal length when two lenses are kept in contact in each case.

(i) −10 cm   (ii) 20 cm   (iii) −20 cm

Sol. (i) When lenses of 10 D and −20 D are taken, total power, $P = 10\,D - 20\,D = -10\,D$ [$\because P = P_1 + P_2$]

Total focal length, $f = \dfrac{100}{-10} = -10$ cm

$\left[\because f\text{ (in cm)} = \dfrac{100}{P}\right]$

(ii) When lenses of 10 D and −5 D are taken, total power $P = 10\,D - 5\,D = 5\,D$

$\therefore$ Total focal length, $f = \dfrac{100}{5} = 20$ cm

(iii) When lenses of +5 D and −10 D are taken, total power, $P = +5\,D - 10\,D = -5\,D$

$\therefore$ Total focal length, $f = \dfrac{100}{-5} = -20$ cm

30 Two lenses of power −2.5 D and +1.5 D are placed in contact. Find the total power of the combination of lens. Calculate the focal length of this combination.

Sol. Given, $P_1 = -2.5\,D$ and $P_2 = +1.5\,D$

$\therefore$ Power of combination, $P = P_1 + P_2$

$= -2.5 + 1.5 = -1\,D$

We know that,

focal length of combination, $f = \dfrac{1}{P} = \dfrac{1}{-1}$ m

$= -100$ cm

31 According to the figures given below, identify the types of mirrors A and B.

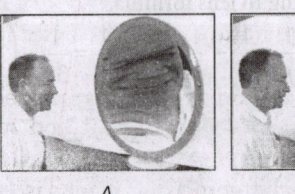

A   B

Sol. Mirror A will be **concave mirror** as concave mirror always forms magnified image when object is placed between pole and focus.

But mirror B will be **convex mirror** as convex mirror always form diminished image irrespective of the distance between pole and object.

32 An object is placed 15 cm in front of a lens A, the details of the image are given below. The process is repeated for a different lens B.

Lens A Real, inverted, magnified and at a great distance.

Lens B Real, inverted and same size as the object.

Estimate the focal length of each lens and state whether it is converging or diverging.

Sol. The focal length of lens B will be 7.5 cm because if an object is placed at $2f$, image will be formed at $2f$ only if its size is same as that of the object.

Since, $2f = 15$ cm $\Rightarrow f = \dfrac{15}{2} = 7.5$ cm

The focal length of lens A will be less than 15 cm (i.e. between 7 cm and 15 cm) because real, inverted magnified image is formed in convex lens only when the object is between f and $2f$.

Long Answer (LA) Type Questions

1 (a) Draw a labelled ray diagram to show the path of a ray of light incident obliquely on one face of a glass slab.

(b) Calculate the refractive index of the material of a glass slab. Given that the speed of light through the glass slab is 2×10^8 m/s and in air is 3×10^8 m/s.

(c) Calculate the focal length of a lens, if its power is −2.5 D.   **CBSE 2020**

Sol. (a) Refer to text on page 288.

(b) Given, speed of light through glass slab

$v = 2 \times 10^8$ m/s

and speed of light in air $c = 3 \times 10^8$.

As, refractive index, $\mu = \dfrac{c}{v} = \dfrac{3 \times 10^8}{2 \times 10^8} = 1.5$

(c) Given, power of lens $P = -2.5$ D

As, $P = \dfrac{1}{f}$

So, $f = \dfrac{1}{P} = \dfrac{1}{-2.5} = -0.4$ m

i.e. it is a concave lens.

All in one Light : Reflection and Refraction

2 Rishi went to a palmist to show his palm. The palmist used a special lens for this purpose.
  (a) State the nature of the lens and reason for its use.
  (b) Where should the palmist place/hold the lens so as to have a real and magnified image of an object?
  (c) If the focal length of this lens is 10 cm and the lens is held at a distance of 5 cm from the palm, use lens formula to find the position and size of the image. **CBSE 2020**

Sol. (a) A palmist uses convex lens to see the magnified image of palm lines.
  (b) The palmist will hold the lens where palm is in between the focus and pole of lens.
  (c) Given, focal length $f = 10$ cm
  and object distance, $u = -5$ cm
  From lens formula, $\dfrac{1}{v} - \dfrac{1}{u} = \dfrac{1}{f}$
  $\Rightarrow \dfrac{1}{v} = \dfrac{1}{10} + \dfrac{1}{-5} = \dfrac{1}{10} - \dfrac{1}{5}$
  $\Rightarrow v = -10$ cm
  Hence, the magnification
  $m = \dfrac{v}{u} = \dfrac{-10}{-5} = 2$
  Hence, the image is on same side of the lens as object (palm) and it is virtual erect and magnified.

3 (i) Define the following terms in context of spherical mirrors.
  (a) Pole (b) Centre of curvature
  (c) Principal axis (d) Principal focus
  (ii) Draw ray diagrams to show the principal focus of a
  (a) concave mirror and
  (b) convex mirror.
  (iii) Consider the following diagram in which M is a mirror and P is an object and Q is its magnified image formed by the mirror.

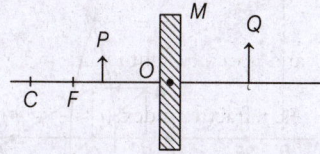

  State the type of the mirror M and one characteristic property of the image Q. **CBSE 2016**

Sol. (i) Refer to text on Pg. 283 and 284.
  (ii) Refer to text on Pg. 284.
  (iii) The given diagram in the question can be redrawn as

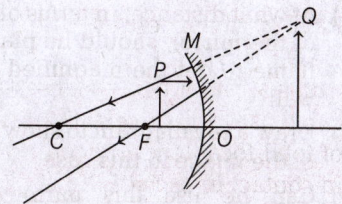

  So, M is a concave mirror and the image Q formed is enlarged.

4 A student has three concave mirrors A, B and C of focal lengths 20 cm, 15 cm and 10 cm, respectively. For each concave mirror, he performs the experiment of image formation for three values of object distance of 30 cm, 10 cm and 20 cm.
  Give reasons for the following:
  (i) For the three object distances, identify the mirror which will form an image equal in size to that of object. Find at least one value of object distance.
  (ii) Out of the three mirrors, identify the mirror which would be preferred to be used for shaving purpose.
  (iii) For the mirror B, draw ray diagram for image formation for any two given values of object distance. **CBSE 2015**

Sol. (i) When an object is placed at the centre of curvature (i.e. double the distance of focal length) of concave mirror, the image formed is equal in size to that of object. So, for object distance 20 cm, the mirror C with focal length 10 cm is used as
  $u = R = 2f = 2 \times 10$ cm $= 20$ cm.
  (ii) For shaving purpose, mirror B ($f = 15$ cm) would be preferred to form an enlarged and erect image of the face at distance 10 cm.
  (iii) (a) For $u = 30$ cm,

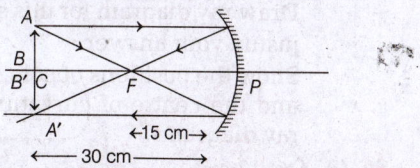

  (b) For $u = 10$ cm,

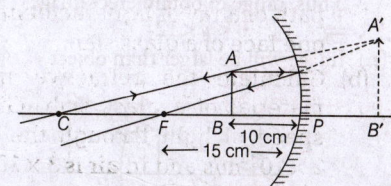

5 A student wants to project the image of a candle flame on the walls of the school laboratory by using a mirror.
  (i) Which type of mirror should he use and why?

(ii) At what distance, in terms of focal length f of the mirror, should he place the candle flame to get the magnified image on the wall?

(iii) Draw a ray diagram to show the formation of the image in this case.

(iv) Can he use this mirror to project a diminished image of the candle flame on the same wall? State 'how', if your answer is 'yes' and 'why not', if your answer is 'no'. **CBSE 2014**

Sol. (i) He should use a concave mirror. (1)

(ii) He should place the candle flame between focus and centre of curvature of the mirror to get the magnified image on the wall.

(iii) Formation of image

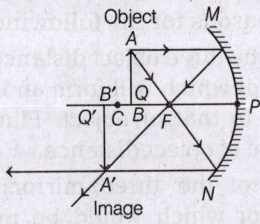

(iv) Yes, when object is located at infinity the diminished image is obtained.

6 It is desired to obtain an erect image of an object, using concave mirror of focal length of 12 cm.

(i) What should be the range of distance of an object placed in front of the mirror?

(ii) Will the image be smaller or larger than the object? Draw ray diagram to show the formation of image in this case.

(iii) Where will the image of this object be, if it is placed 24 cm in front of the mirror? Draw ray diagram for this situation also to justify your answer.

Show the positions of pole, principal focus and the centre of curvature in the above ray diagrams. **CBSE 2016**

Sol. (i) $f = -12$ cm,

Thus, range to obtain erect image
$\Rightarrow \quad 0 < u < 12$

(ii) Image will be larger than object

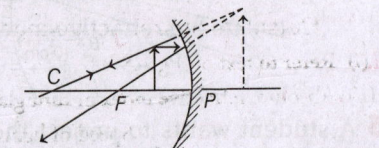

(iii) Position of image

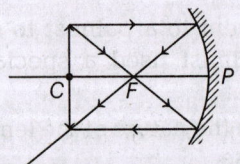

Here, $f = -12$ cm, $u = -24$ cm, $v = ?$
By using mirror formula,

$$\frac{1}{f} = \frac{1}{v} + \frac{1}{u} \Rightarrow \frac{1}{v} = \frac{1}{-12} - \frac{1}{(-24)}$$

$\Rightarrow \quad v = -24$ cm

7 A thin converging lens form a real magnified image and virtual magnified image of an object in front of it.

(i) Write the positions of the objects in each case.

(ii) Draw ray diagrams to show the image formation in each part.

(iii) How will the following be affected on cutting this lens into two halves along the principal axis?
(a) Focal length
(b) Intensity of the image formed by half lens.

Sol. (i) (a) Object is placed between F and $2F$.
(b) Object is placed between optical centre and F.

(ii) The ray diagrams are as follows:

Part (a)

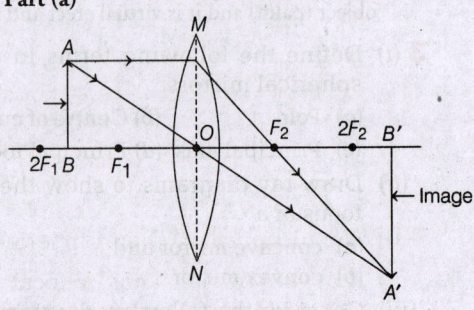

Part (b)

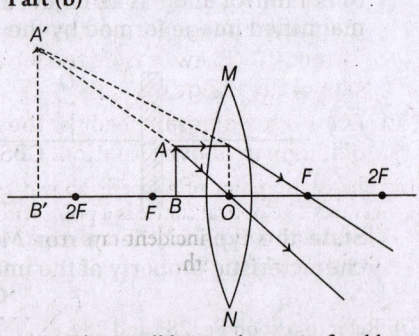

(iii) (a) There will be no change in focal length.
(b) Intensity will become one-fourth.

8 A student wants to project the image of a candle flame on the walls of school laboratory by using a lens.
  (i) Which type of lens should he use and why?
  (ii) At what distance in terms of focal length F of the lens should he place the candle flame, so as to get
    (a) a magnified and
    (b) a diminished image respectively, on the wall?
  (iii) Draw ray diagrams to show the formation of the image in each case. **CBSE 2014**

Sol. (i) He should use a convex lens as real images are formed by it.
  (ii) (a) For magnified image, he should place the candle flame between focus (F) and centre of curvature ($2F$) of lens.
  (b) To get diminished image, he should place the candle flame beyond centre of curvature ($2F$) of lens.
  (iii) (a) **For magnified image**

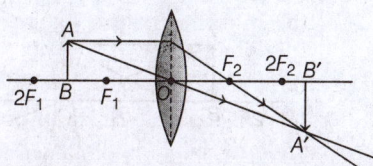

  (b) **For diminished image**

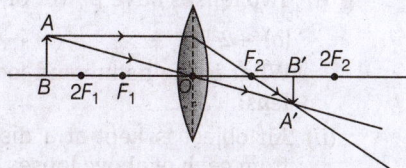

9 (i) Define optical centre of spherical lens.
  (ii) A divergent lens has a focal length of 20 cm. At what distance should an object of height 4 cm from the optical centre of the lens be placed, so that its image is formed 10 cm away from the lens. Find the size of the image also.
  (iii) Draw a ray diagram to show the formation of image in above situation. **CBSE 2016, 12**

Sol. (i) The centre point of a lens is known as its optical centre. The optical centre is a point within the lens, directed to which incident rays refract without any deviation in the path.

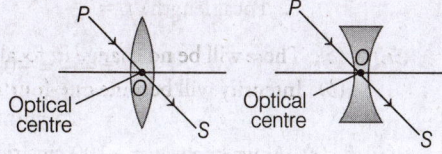

(ii) According to the question, the given lens is a divergent lens, i.e. concave lens.
Given, focal length, $f = -20$ cm
Height of object, $h_o = 4$ cm
Image distance, $v = -10$ cm
$\because$ By lens formula,
$$\frac{1}{v} - \frac{1}{u} = \frac{1}{f}$$
$$\Rightarrow \frac{-1}{10} - \frac{1}{u} = \frac{-1}{20}$$
$$\Rightarrow \frac{1}{u} = \frac{-1}{10} + \frac{1}{20}$$
$$\Rightarrow \frac{1}{u} = \frac{-2+1}{20}$$
$$\Rightarrow u = -20 \text{ cm}$$
$\therefore$ Magnification, $m = \dfrac{v}{u} = \dfrac{h_i}{h_o}$
$$\Rightarrow \frac{h_i}{4} = \frac{-10}{-20}$$
$$\Rightarrow h_i = 2 \text{ cm}$$
Size of the image, $h_i = 2$ cm

(iii)

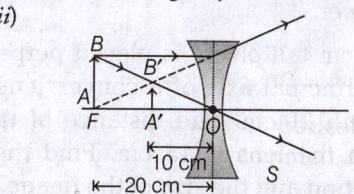

Thus, the object is placed at 20 cm from the concave lens.

10 (i) Define Snell's law of refraction.
  (ii) The speed of light in vacuum and in two different glasses are given in the following table:

Medium	Speed of light
Vacuum	3×10^8 m/s
Flint glass	1.86×10^8 m/s
Crown glass	1.97×10^8 m/s

Calculate the absolute refractive indices of flint glass and crown glass.
  (iii) Define refractive index of water. If the speed of light in air is 3×10^8 ms^{-1} and the speed of light in water is 2.2×10^8 ms^{-1}. Calculate the refractive index of water.

Sol. (i) Refer to text on Pg. 289.
  (ii) Absolute refractive index of flint glass
$$= \frac{\text{Speed of light in vacuum}}{\text{Speed of light in flint glass}}$$
$$= \frac{3 \times 10^8}{1.86 \times 10^8} = 1.61$$

Similarly, absolute refractive index of crown glass

$$= \frac{3 \times 10^8}{1.97 \times 10^8} = 1.52$$

(iii) Refractive index of water is defined as the ratio of the speed of light in a vacuum to the speed of light in water.

Speed of light in air, $v_a = 3 \times 10^8$ ms^{-1}

Speed of light in water, $v_w = 2.2 \times 10^8$ ms^{-1}

∴ Refractive index, $n = \dfrac{v_a}{v_w}$

$$= \frac{3 \times 10^8}{2.2 \times 10^8} = 1.4$$

11 One half of a convex lens of focal length 10 cm is covered with a black paper. Can such a lens produce an image of a complete object placed at a distance of 30 cm from the lens? Draw a ray diagram to justify your answer.

A 4 cm tall object is placed perpendicular to principal axis of a convex lens of focal length 20 cm. The distance of the object from the lens is 15 cm. Find the nature, position and the size of the image. **CBSE 2015**

Sol. Yes, a lens can form a complete image but of less intensity and brightness.

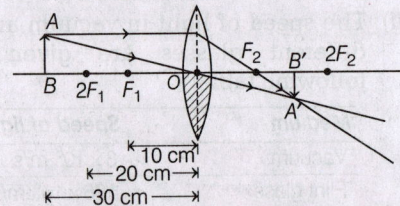

Given, height of object, $h_o = 4$ cm, focal length, $f = 20$ cm and distance of object, $u = -15$ cm

Using lens formula,

$$\frac{1}{f} = \frac{1}{v} - \frac{1}{u}$$

$$\Rightarrow \frac{1}{v} = \frac{1}{f} + \frac{1}{u} = \frac{1}{20} + \frac{1}{(-15)} = \frac{15 - 20}{300} = \frac{-5}{300}$$

∴ $v = -60$ cm

As, we know that magnification,

$$m = \frac{h_i}{h_o} = \frac{v}{u}$$

$$\Rightarrow h_i = h_o \times \frac{v}{u} = 4 \times \frac{-60}{-15} = 16 \text{ cm}$$

Image formed is virtual, erect and magnified.

12 (i) Define focal length of a spherical lens.

(ii) A divergent lens has a focal length of 30 cm. At what distance should an object of height 5 cm from the optical centre of the lens be placed, so that its image is formed 15 cm away the lens? Find the size of the image also.

(iii) Draw a ray diagram to show the formation of image in the above situation. **CBSE 2016**

Sol.(i) Refer to text on Pg. 290.

(ii) Given, divergent lens (concave lens) of $f = -30$ cm, $v = -15$ cm, $u = ?$, $h_o = 5$ cm

$$\frac{1}{f} = \frac{1}{v} - \frac{1}{u} \Rightarrow -\frac{1}{30} = -\frac{1}{15} - \left(\frac{1}{u}\right)$$

$$\Rightarrow u = -30 \text{ cm}$$

∴ Magnification, $m = \dfrac{v}{u} = \dfrac{h_i}{h_o}$

$$\Rightarrow \frac{15}{30} = \frac{h_i}{5} \Rightarrow h_i = \frac{5}{2} \Rightarrow h_i = 2.5 \text{ cm}$$

(iii)

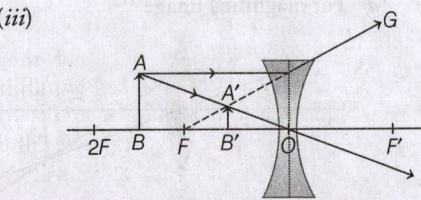

13 (i) Two lenses have power of

(a) +2 D (b) −4 D.

What is the nature and focal length of each lens? **CBSE 2012**

(ii) An object is kept at a distance of 100 cm from each of above lenses. Calculate

(a) image distance and

(b) magnification in each of the two cases.

Sol.(i) (a) Given, $P = +2$ D

Since, power is positive, so the lens is convex lens.

∴ Focal length, $f = \dfrac{1}{P} = \dfrac{1}{2} = 0.5$ m

$= 50$ cm

[where, P = power of lens]

(b) Given, $P = -4$ D

Since, power is negative, so the lens is concave lens.

∴ Focal length, $f = \dfrac{1}{P}$

$$= \frac{1}{-4} = -0.25 \text{ m}$$

$= -25$ cm

(ii) (a) As we know, $u = -100$ cm (sign convention)

Case I $f = 50$ cm

By using lens formula, $-\dfrac{1}{u}+\dfrac{1}{v}=\dfrac{1}{f}$, we get

$\dfrac{1}{v}=\dfrac{1}{f}+\dfrac{1}{u}=\dfrac{1}{50}-\dfrac{1}{100}=\dfrac{1}{100}$

or $v = 100$ cm

Case II $f = -25$ cm

Again using lens formula, $-\dfrac{1}{u}+\dfrac{1}{v}=\dfrac{1}{f}$, we get

$\dfrac{1}{v}=\dfrac{1}{f}+\dfrac{1}{u}$

$=-\dfrac{1}{25}-\dfrac{1}{100}=\dfrac{-5}{100}=-\dfrac{1}{20}$

$v = -20$ cm

(b) As, magnification, $m = \dfrac{v}{u}$

Case I $u = -100$ cm, $v = 100$ cm

$m = \dfrac{100 \text{ cm}}{-100 \text{ cm}} = -1$

Case II $u = -100$ cm, $v = -20$ cm

$m = \dfrac{-20 \text{ cm}}{-100 \text{ cm}} = \dfrac{1}{5} = 0.2$

14 *(i)* Draw a ray diagram to show the formation of image by a convex lens when an object is placed in front of the lens between its optical centre and principal focus.

(ii) In the above ray diagram mark the object distance (u) and the image distance (v) with their proper signs (+ ve or – ve as per the new cartesian sign convention) and state how these distances are related to the focal length (f) of the convex lens in this case.

(iii) Find the power of convex lens which forms a real and inverted image of magnification –1 of an object placed at a distance of 20 cm from its optical centre.   **CBSE 2016**

Sol. *(i)*

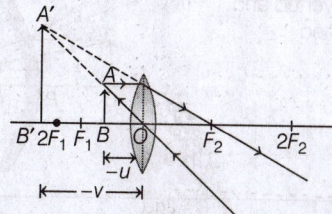

(ii) By using lens formula, we have $\dfrac{1}{v}-\dfrac{1}{u}=\dfrac{1}{f}$

$\Rightarrow$ $\dfrac{-1}{v}-\left(-\dfrac{1}{u}\right)=\dfrac{1}{f} \Rightarrow \dfrac{-1}{v}+\dfrac{1}{u}=\dfrac{1}{f}$

$\Rightarrow$ $\dfrac{-u+v}{uv}=\dfrac{1}{f}$

$\Rightarrow$ $f = \dfrac{uv}{v-u}$

This is a required relation between u, v and f in the case when object is placed between optical centre and principal focus of convex lens.

(iii) Given, magnification, $m = -1$

Object distance, $u = -20$ cm

$\therefore$ Magnification, $m = \dfrac{v}{u}$

$\Rightarrow$ $-1 = \dfrac{v}{-20}$

$\Rightarrow$ $v = 20$ cm

By using lens formula, $\dfrac{1}{v}-\dfrac{1}{u}=\dfrac{1}{f}$

$\Rightarrow \dfrac{1}{20}-\left(\dfrac{-1}{20}\right)=\dfrac{1}{f} \Rightarrow \dfrac{1}{20}+\dfrac{1}{20}=\dfrac{1}{f}$

$\Rightarrow$ $\dfrac{1}{10}=\dfrac{1}{f} \Rightarrow f = 10$ cm

$\therefore$ Power, $P = \dfrac{1}{f} = \dfrac{1}{10 \times 10^{-2}} = 10$ D

$\Rightarrow$ $P = 10$ D

15 What is meant by power of a lens? Define its SI unit.

You have two lenses A and B of focal lengths +10 cm and –10 cm, respectively. State the nature and power of each lens. Which of the two lenses will form a virtual and magnified image of an object placed 8 cm from the lens? Draw a ray diagram to justify your answer.   **CBSE 2015**

Sol. Refer to text Pg. 293.

Lens A of focal length +10 cm is convex lens

and power, $P = \dfrac{100}{f(\text{in cm})} = \dfrac{100}{10} = +10$ D

Lens B of focal length –10 cm is concave lens

and power, $P = \dfrac{100}{f(\text{in cm})} = \dfrac{100}{-10} = -10$ D

Lens A (i.e. convex lens) will form a virtual and magnified image of an object placed 8 cm from it, as shown.

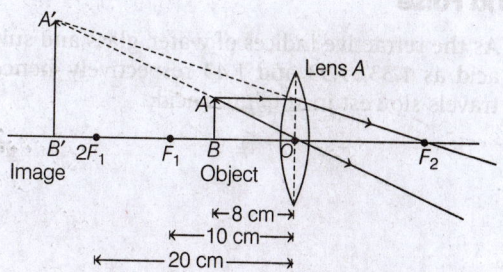

CHAPTER EXERCISE

Multiple Type Questions

1. A spherical mirror to be made from a cut portion of
   (a) hollow sphere of glass
   (b) solid sphere of plastic
   (c) solid sphere of glass
   (d) hollow sphere of metal

2. To determine the focal length of a concave mirror by forming image of a distant object, the screen should be placed
   (a) in any direction
   (b) inclined at angle of 45°
   (c) at right angle to the plane of mirror
   (d) parallel to the plane of mirror

3. An object is placed at a distance of 20 cm in front of concave mirror of focal length 10 cm. The image produced is
   (a) real, inverted and diminished
   (b) real, inverted and enlarged
   (c) real, inverted and same size
   (d) virtual, erect and enlarged

4. In order to determine focal length of a concave mirror by obtaining the image of distant object on screen, you need to measure the distance between
   (a) mirror and the screen
   (b) object and screen
   (c) mirror and object
   (d) mirror and screen also between object and screen

5. Which of the following lens will diverge the ray of light more?
   (a) 2 D   (b) 1 D
   (c) – 0.4 D   (d) – 0.8 D

Fill in the Blanks

6. The reciprocal of the .... in metres gives you the power of the lens.

7. For converging lenses, the power is .... but for diverging lens the power is ....

True and False

8. As the refractive indices of water, glass and sulphuric acid as 1.33, 1.53 and 1.43 respectively, hence light travels slowest in sulphuric acid.

9. A doctor has prescribed a corrective lens of power –1.5 D, hence the lens has a focal length is –66.6 cm.

Match the Columns

10. Match the Column A with Column B:

Column A (Magnification, m)	Column B (Nature of image)
(a) $m = 1$	(i) Inverted image
(b) $m < 1$	(ii) Diminished image
(c) $m > 0$	(iii) Erect image
(d) $m < 0$	(iv) Size of image = Size of object

11. Match the Column A with Column B:

Column A (Nature and size of image)	Column B (Ray diagram)
(a) Virtual, erect and diminished	(i) 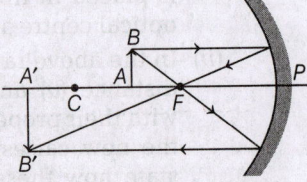
(b) Real, inverted and same size as that of object	(ii) 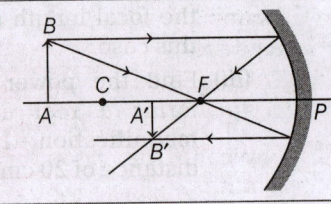
(c) Real, inverted and enlarged	(iii) 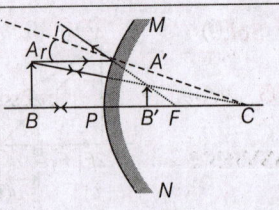
(d) Real, inverted and diminished	(iv)

Assertion-Reason

Direction (Q.Nos. 12-14) *In each of the following questions, a statement of Assertion is given by the corresponding statement of Reason. Of the statements, mark the correct answer as*

(a) If both Assertion and Reason are true and Reason is the correct explanation of Assertion.
(b) If both Assertion and Reason are true, but Reason is not the correct explanation of Assertion.
(c) If Assertion is true, but Reason is false.
(d) If Assertion is false, but Reason is true.

12. Assertion ENT specialist use a concave mirror as a head mirror to concentrate light on the body parts like eye, ear, nose etc.
Reason A concave mirror is more effective and easily available.

13. Assertion Keeping a point object fixed, if a plane mirror is moved, the image will also move.
Reason In case of a plane mirror, distance of object and its image is equal from any point on the mirror.

14. Assertion The speed of light in a rarer medium is greater than that in a denser medium.
Reason One light year equal to 9.5×10^{13} km.

Case Based Questions

Direction (Q.Nos. 15-18) *Answer the questions on the basis of your understanding of the following passage and the related studied concepts :*

Light is a form of energy which induces sensation of vision to our eyes. It becomes visible when it bounces off on surfaces and hits our eyes. Regular reflection takes place through a smooth polished surface. The mirror outside the driver side of a vehicle is usually a spherical mirror and printed on such a mirror is usually the warning "vehicles in this mirror are closer than they appear."

15. Name the type of spherical mirror used outside the driver side of a vehicle.

16. What is the reason for this warning written on the mirror?

17. Draw a ray diagram showing the image formation in such kind of mirror.

18. When light becomes visible?

Very Short Answer Type Questions

19. What is the radius of curvature of a plane mirror?

20. Does the value of speed of light change with medium?

21. Redraw the ray diagram given below in your answer book and complete the path of ray.

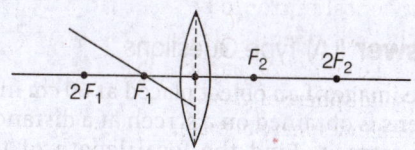

Short Answer (SA) Type Questions

22. An object of size 7.0 cm is placed at a distance of 27 cm in front of concave mirror of focal length 18 cm. At what distance from the mirror should a screen be placed, so that a sharp focussed image can be obtained? Find the size and the nature of the image.
[**Ans.** Screen be placed at -54 cm from the mirror
Size of image $= -14$ cm, real and interested]

23. Draw the ray diagram in your answer book and show the formation of image of object AB with suitable rays. Mention the position and nature of image.

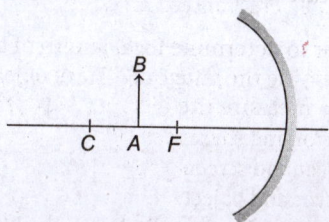

24. How far should an object be placed from a convex lens of focal length 20 cm to obtain its image at a distance of 30 cm from the lens? What will be the height of the image, if the object is 6 cm tall?
[**Ans.** Object distance, $u = -12$ cm
Height of the image, $h_i = -15$ cm]

25. A 5.0 cm tall object is placed perpendicular to the principal axis of a convex lens of focal length 20 cm. The distance of the object from the lens is 30 cm. By calculation determine
(i) the position and
(ii) the size of the image formed.
[**Ans.** Position of image $= 12$ cm
Size of image $= 2$ cm]

26. An object placed 45 cm from a lens forms an image on a screen placed 90 cm on the other side of the lens. Identify the type of the lens and find its focal length. [**Ans.** Convex lens, $+30$ cm]

Answers

1. (a) 2. (c) 3. (c) 4. (b) 5. (d)
6. focal length   7. positive, negative
8. False   9. True
10. (a) → (iv), (b) → (ii), (c) → (iii), (d) → (i)
11. (a) → (iv), (b) → (i), (c) → (ii), (d) → (iii)
12. (b)   13. (d)   14. (b)

27 Does the incident and emergent ray coincide in the process of refraction through glass slab? Give reason.

28 A ray of light enters a diamond from air. If the refractive index of diamond is 2.42, what % (percent) is speed of light in diamond with that of speed in air?

Long Answer (LA) Type Questions

29 The image of an object placed at 60 cm in front of a lens is obtained on a screen at a distance of 120 cm from it. Find the focal length of the lens. What would be the height of the image, if the object is 5 cm high?
[**Ans.** +120 cm, convex lens, Height of image is 10 cm]

30 (i) Two lenses have power of (a)+2D (b) −4D. What is the nature and focal length of each lens?
(ii) An object is kept at a distance of 100 cm from each of the above lenses.
Calculate the
(a) image distance and
(b) magnification in each of two cases.
[**Ans.** (i) (a) 50 cm, convex lens, (b) −25 cm, concave lens]

31 List the sign conventions for reflection of light by spherical mirrors. Draw a diagram and apply these conventions in the determination of focal length of a spherical mirror which forms a three times magnified real image of an object placed 16 cm in front of it.
[**Ans.** Focal length of concave mirror is −12 cm]

32 List the new cartesian sign convention for reflection of light by spherical mirrors. Draw a diagram and apply these conventions for calculating the focal length and nature of a spherical mirror which forms a 1/3 times magnified virtual image of an object placed 18 cm in front of it. [**Ans.** Focal length of convex mirror is + 9 cm]

33 (i) State and define the SI unit of power of a lens.
(ii) A convex lens of focal length 25 cm and a concave lens of focal length 10 cm are placed in close contact with each other. Calculate the lens power of this combination.

34 List the sign conventions that are followed in case of refraction of light through spherical lenses. Draw a diagram and apply these conventions in determining the nature and focal length of a spherical lens which forms three times magnified real image of an object placed 16 cm from the lens.
[**Ans.** Focal length of convex lens is + 12 cm]

Challengers*

1 A virtual image three times the size of the object is obtained with a concave mirror of radius of curvature 36 cm. The distance of the object from the mirror is
(a) 20 cm (b) 10 cm
(c) 12 cm (d) 5 cm

2 A convex mirror of focal length f produces an image $\frac{1}{n^{th}}$ of the size of the object. The distance of the object from the mirror is
(a) $\frac{n+1}{n}f$ (b) $(n+1)f$
(c) $(n-1)f$ (d) $\frac{n-1}{n}f$

3 A perfectly reflecting mirror has an area of $1\ cm^2$. Light energy is allowed to fall on it for an hour at the rate of $10\ Wcm^{-2}$. The force that acts on the mirror is
(a) $3.35 \times 10^{-7} N$ (b) $6.7 \times 10^{-7} N$
(c) $3.35 \times 10^{-8} N$ (d) $6.7 \times 10^{-8} N$

4 An object is placed at the centre of curvature of a concave mirror. The distance between its image and the pole is
(a) equal to f (b) between f and $2f$
(c) equal to $2f$ (d) greater than $2f$

5 The refractive index of dens flint glass is 1.65 and for alcohol, it is 1.36 with respect to air, then the refractive index of the dens flint glass with respect to alcohol is
(a) 1.31 (b) 1.21
(c) 1.11 (d) 1.01

6 Refractive index of diamond with respect to glass is 1.6. If the absolute refractive index of glass is 1.5, then the absolute refractive index of diamond is
(a) 1.4 (b) 2.4
(c) 3.4 (d) 4.4

7 A ray of light from a denser medium strikes a rarer medium at an angle of incidence as shown in figure. The reflected and refracted rays make an angle of 90° with each other. The angles of reflection and refraction are r and r'. The critical angle is

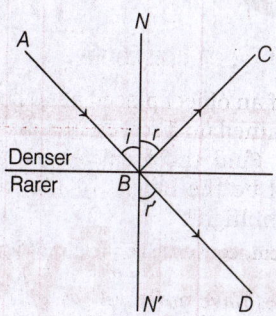

(a) $\sin^{-1}(\tan r)$ (b) $\sin^{-1}(\tan i)$
(c) $\sin^{-1}(\tan r')$ (d) $\tan^{-1}(\tan i)$

8 A convex lens A of focal length 20 cm and a concave lens B of focal length 5 cm are kept along the same axis with a distance d between them. If a parallel beam of light falling on A leaves B as a parallel beam, then the distance d in cm will be
(a) 25 (b) 15
(c) 30 (d) 50

9 A thick plane convex lens made of crown glass (refractive index 1.5) has thickness of 3 cm at its centre.
An ink mark made at the centre of its plane face, when viewed normal through the curved face, appears to be at a distance x from the curved face. Then, x is equal to
(a) 2 cm (b) 2.1 cm
(c) 2.3 cm (d) 2.5 cm

10 An object is placed in front of a screen and a convex lens is placed at a position such that the size of the image formed is 9 cm. When the lens is shifted through a distance of 20 cm, the size of the image becomes 1 cm. The focal length of the lens and the size of the object are respectively.
(a) 7.5 cm and 3.5 cm (b) 7.5 cm and 4.5 cm
(c) 6 cm and 3 cm (d) 7.5 cm and 3 cm

Answer Key

1.	(c)	2.	(c)	3.	(d)	4.	(c)	5.	(b)
6.	(b)	7.	(a)	8.	(b)	9.	(d)	10.	(d)

*These questions may or may not be asked in the examination, have been given just for additional practice.

CHAPTER 10

Human Eye and The Colourful World

The human eye uses light and enables us to see the objects around us. It works on the phenomenon of refraction of light through a natural convex lens made of transparent living material (tissues) and enables us to see things around us. Using different properties of light, many spectacular optical phenomena occur in nature. Few of them, like rainbow formation, blue colour of sky, twinkling of stars, based on dispersion, scattering and atmospheric refraction are discussed in this chapter.

The Human Eye

The human eye is one of the most valuable and sensitive sense organs in the human body like camera. It enables us to see the wonderful world and colours around us. The human eye is like a camera, its lens system forms an image on a light-sensitive screen called retina.

Structure of Human Eye

The human eye has the following main parts:

- **Cornea** It is the transparent bulged out spherical membrane covering the front of the eye. Light enters the eye through this membrane. Most of the refraction of light rays entering the eye occurs at the outer surface of the cornea.
- **Crystalline Lens** The eye lens is a convex lens made of a transparent, soft and flexible jelly-like material made of proteins. The eye-lens is held in position by suspensory ligaments.
- **Iris** It is a dark muscular diaphragm between the **cornea** and the **lens**. It controls the size of the **pupil**. It is the colour of the **iris** that we call as the colour of the eye.
- **Pupil** It is a small hole between the **iris** through which light enters the eye. In dim light, it opens up completely due to expansion of eye muscles, but in bright light it becomes very small due to contraction of eye muscles.

Chapter Checklist

- The Human Eye
- Defects of Vision and their Correction
- Refraction of Light through a Prism
- Dispersion of White Light by a Glass Prism
- Atmospheric Refraction
- Scattering of Light

Human Eye and the Colourful World

- **Ciliary Muscles**: They hold the lens in position and help in modifying the curvature of the eye lens.
- **Retina**: It is the light-sensitive surface of the eye on which the image is formed. It contains light-sensitive cells known as **rods** and **cones**. Rod cells respond to the intensity of light and cone cells respond to the illumination. i.e. primary colours. Number of rod cells is greater than number of cone cells. These cells generate signals which are transmitted to the brain through optic nerves.

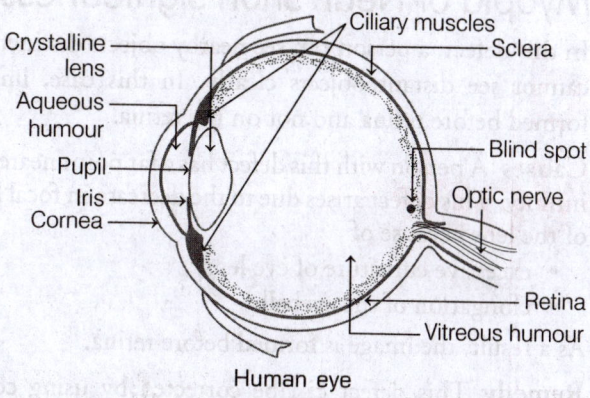

Human eye

- **Optic Nerve**: It transmits visual informations from the **retina** to the **brain**.
- **Sclera**: It is an opaque, fibrous, protective, outer layer of an eye containing **collagen** and **elastic fibre**. It is also known as **white of the eye**.
- **Blind Spot**: It is the point at which the optic nerve leaves the eye. It contains no rods and cones, so an image formed at this point is not sent to the brain.
- **Aqueous Humour**: Between the cornea and eye lens, we have a space filled with a transparent liquid called the aqueous humour which helps the refracted light to be focussed on retina. It also maintains intraocular pressure.
- **Vitreous Humour**: The space between the eye lens and retina is filled with another liquid known as vitreous humour.

Note
- Iris regulates the amount of light entering the eye by adjusting the size of the pupil.
- The pupil appears black because no light is reflected by it.
- The eye ball is nearly spherical in shape with a diameter of 2.3 cm.
- If cornea, pupil, eye lens, retina, optic nerves, aqueous humour and vitreous humour malfunction or get damaged it will result in visual impairment.

Formation of an Image

An image is formed on the retina by successive refractions at the cornea, the aqueous humour, lens and vitreous humour. It is real, diminished and inverted in nature.

The light-sensitive cells of retina get activated upon illumination and generate electrical signals. These signals are then sent to the brain *via* the **optic nerve**. The brain interprets these signals and finally processes the informations, so that we perceive objects as they are.

Colour of Objects

The rod shaped cells of retina respond to the intensity of light, i.e. the degree of brightness or darkness but do not respond to colours. The cone cells are sensitive to the different extent of primary colours such as red, blue and green.

Note Eyesight of Bees The retinal cones of bees are sensitive to the ultraviolet light which we cannot see with our eyes.
Eyesight of Chicks Chicks wake up earlier in the morning than humans because their retina have mostly cones which are very sensitive to bright light and rods are very few.

Terms Related to Human Eye

(i) **Accommodation** It is the ability or the property of the eye lens to focus both near and distant objects by adjusting its focal length. However, the focal length cannot be decreased or increased beyond a certain limit, due to which a healthy person cannot view clearly, if the object is held too close (i.e. less than 25 cm) or too far from the eye.

For distant objects

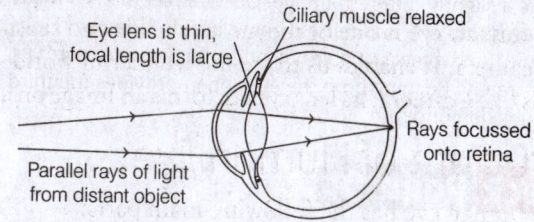

For near objects

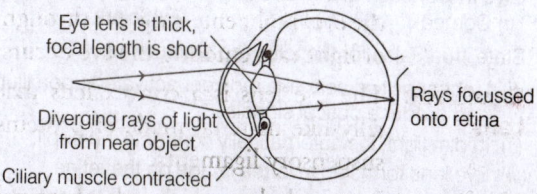

Power of accommodation of eye

The ciliary muscles help in changing the curvature of the eye lens. When muscles are relaxed, the lens becomes thin and its focal length is increased. This enables us to see distant objects clearly.

While viewing nearby objects, the ciliary muscles contract. So, the lens becomes thicker and its focal length decreases.

(ii) **Power of accommodation** It is the maximum variation in power of eye lens for focussing near by or far objects, clearly at retina. For a young adult with normal vision, the power of accommodation is about 4D. The eye loses its power of accommodation at old age.

(iii) **Far point of the eye** It is the farthest point up to which the eye can see clearly. It is infinity for normal eye.

(iv) **Near point of the eye** The minimum distance, at which an object can be seen most distinctly without any strain is called the **least distance** of distinct vision. For a normal eye of an adult, it is 25 cm. It is also called near point of the eye.

(v) **Persistence of vision** The time for which impression or sensation of an object continues to remain in the eye is called persistence of vision. It is about 1/16 th of a second which means that the minimum time for which we should view an object, so that its clear image is formed on retina is 1/16 th of a second.

Note When the eye is looking at the nearby objects, eye lens becomes more convex (i.e. focal length decreases).

Why do We Have Two Eyes for Vision and Not Just One?

A human being has a horizontal field of view of about 150° with one eye and of about 180° with two eyes. So, two eyes give a wider field of view. The ability to detect faint objects is enhanced with two eyes.

Our eyes are separated by a few centimetres and each eye sees a slightly different image. Our brain combines the two images into one and tells us how close or far away things are. Thus, the two eyes enables to judge the distance more accurately. Keeping both the eyes open provides the third dimension of depth.

Check Point 01

1. Give the function of the following
 (i) Cornea   (ii) Iris   (iii) Sclera
2. State True/False for the following statements:
 (i) Light-sensitive cells like rods get activated upon illumination and produce optical signals.
 (ii) In dim light, iris automatically contracts the pupil.
 (iii) Eye lens forms an inverted image on the retina.
 (iv) Iris is a transparent spherical membrane which covers the front of the eye.
3. Fill in the blank:
 The cells which respond only to the intensity of light are called ....
4. Name the cells which are responsible for the colour determination.

Defects of Vision and their Correction

The defects due to which a person cannot see the object distinctly and comfortably are called defects of vision.

The main defects of vision are :
 (i) Myopia or near/short sightedness
 (ii) Hypermetropia or far/long sightedness
 (iii) Presbyopia

Myopia or Near/Short Sightedness

In this defect, a person can see nearby objects distinctly but cannot see distant objects clearly. In this case, image is formed before retina and not on the retina.

Causes A person with this defect has a far point nearer than infinity. This defect arises due to the decrease in focal length of the lens because of
- excessive curvature of eye lens,
- elongation of the eyeball.

As a result, the image is formed before retina.

Remedy This defect can be corrected by using concave lens. A concave lens of suitable power will bring back the image on retina.

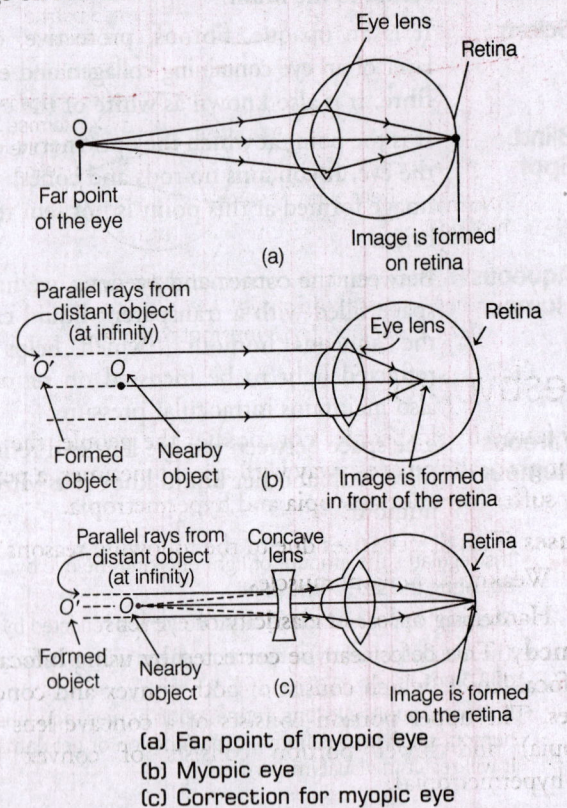

(a) Far point of myopic eye
(b) Myopic eye
(c) Correction for myopic eye

Hypermetropia or Far/Long Sightedness

In this defect, a person can see distant objects clearly but cannot see nearby objects clearly. A person with this defect has the near point farther away from normal near point (25 cm). In this case, the image is formed beyond retina.

Causes This defect arises due to following reasons:
- Focal length of eye lens becomes large.
- Eyeball becomes too short, so that the image is formed behind retina.

Remedy This defect can be corrected by using a convex lens of suitable power. This will bring the image back on retina.

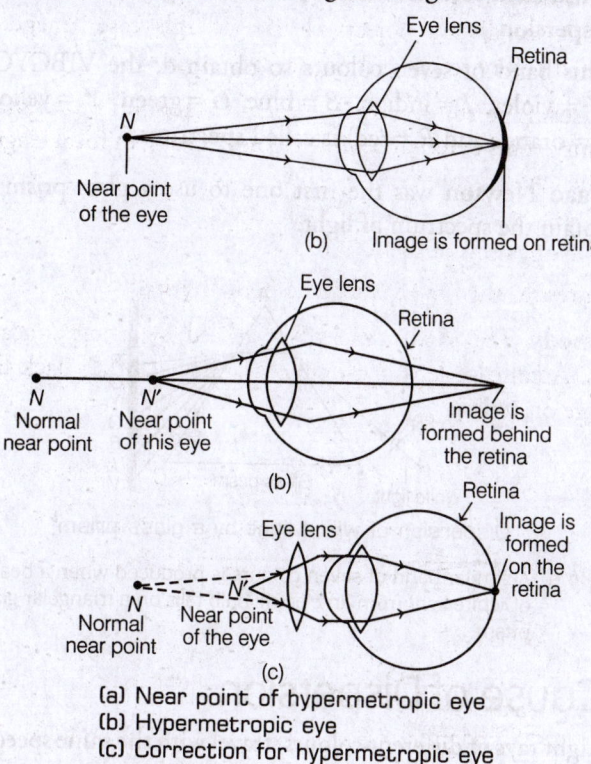

(a) Near point of hypermetropic eye
(b) Hypermetropic eye
(c) Correction for hypermetropic eye

Presbyopia

It is found in old people. For most of the people, the near point gradually recedes away with age. Sometimes, a person may suffer from both myopia and hypermetropia.

Causes This defect arises due to the following reasons:
- Weakness of ciliary muscles.
- Hardening or loss of elasticity of eye lens.

Remedy This defect can be corrected by using bifocal or varifocal lenses which consist of both convex and concave lenses. The upper portion consists of a concave lens (for myopia) and lower portion consists of convex lens (for hypermetropia).

Cataract

It is a condition in which crystalline lens of eye becomes milky and cloudy due to growth of membrane over it. It generally occurs among people at old age. This causes partial or complete loss of vision. It is possible to restore vision through a cataract surgery.

Note
- These days, it is possible to correct the eye defects with contact lenses or through surgical interventions.
- Contact lenses are small lenses placed in contact with the eye which is a replacement for the traditional spectacles.

Numerical Problems

There are many numerical problems which are generally based on myopia and hypermetropia on finding the focal length and power of the lens which are used to correct the defect. These problems are solved by using lens formula,

$$\frac{1}{f} = \frac{1}{v} - \frac{1}{u}$$

where, f = focal length of the lens (if f is +ve, then lens is convex and if f is −ve, then lens is concave lens.)

v = image distance and u = object distance.

In these problems, always remember that for healthy human eye, the far point is infinity and near point is least distance of distinct vision, i.e. 25 cm.

Example 1. *A person cannot see the object beyond 3 m distinctly. State the nature and focal length of the lens required to correct this defect of vision.*

Sol. Here, a person cannot see the object beyond 3 m. That means that he is suffering from myopia. To correct this defect, a concave lens of will be used which can form the image of an object which is at infinite distance at 3m from eye.

Given, object distance, $u = -\infty$

Image distance, $v = -3$ m $= -300$ cm (far point)

Focal length, $f = ?$

From lens formula,

$$\frac{1}{v} - \frac{1}{u} = \frac{1}{f}$$

i.e. $\quad \dfrac{1}{-300} - \dfrac{1}{(-\infty)} = \dfrac{1}{f}$

$\Rightarrow \quad \dfrac{1}{f} = \dfrac{1}{-300}$

$\Rightarrow \quad f = -300$ cm
$\quad \quad \quad = -3$ m

According to the sign of given focal length, the lens is diverging in nature, i.e. it is a concave lens.

Check Point 02

1. Name the defect of vision for which (i) far point of an eye is less than infinity (ii) near point of an eye is more than 25 cm.
2. When we look nearby objects, what happens to the focal length of our eye?
3. Name the type of lens used to correct
   (i) myopia   (ii) presbyopia
4. State True/False for the following statements :
   (i) The defect which is caused when a person's eye lens hardens is known as Myopia.
   (ii) Herdening or loss of elasticity of eye lens is main cause of presbyopia.
5. Fill in the blank :
   If a milky or cloudy membrane grow over the eye lens, then the person is suffering from the defect of ....

Refraction of Light through a Prism

Prism is a transparent refracting medium bounded by at least two lateral surfaces, inclined to each other at a certain angle. It has two triangular bases and three rectangular lateral surfaces. The angle between two lateral surfaces is called **angle of prism** (A).

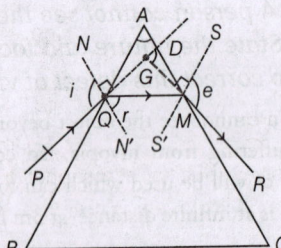

Refraction of light through a triangular glass prism

In the diagram given above, a ray of light PQ is entering from air to glass at the first surface AB. The light ray on refraction is bent towards the normal. At the second surface AC, the light ray enters from glass to air, so it bents away from the normal. The above diagram shows refraction through a prism, where

PQ = incident ray, QM = refracted ray,
MR = emergent ray, $\angle A$ = angle of prism,
$\angle i$ = angle of incidence, $\angle r$ = angle of refraction,
$\angle e$ = angle of emergence, $\angle D$ = angle of deviation.

Angle of Deviation (D)

It is the angle at which the emergent ray (extended backward) makes with the incident ray (extended forward). It depends upon angle of prism, i.e. ($\angle A$), angle of incidence ($\angle i$) and angle of emergence ($\angle e$) and is given by

$$\angle D = \angle i + \angle e - \angle A$$

Dispersion of White Light by a Glass Prism

The phenomenon of splitting of white light into its constituent colours, when it passes through a prism is called **dispersion**.

This band of seven colours so obtained, the VIBGYOR (V = violet, I = indigo, B = blue, G = green, Y = yellow, O = orange and R = red) is called **spectrum**.

Isaac Newton was the first one to use a glass prism to obtain the spectrum of light.

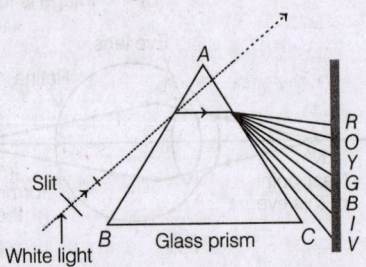

Dispersion of white light by a glass prism

Note A similar band of seven colours is produced when a beam of white light from an electric bulb falls on a triangular glass prism.

Cause of Dispersion

Light rays of different colours, travel with the same speed in vacuum and air but in any other medium, they travel with different speeds and bend through different angles, which leads to the dispersion of light.

Red light has the maximum wavelength and **violet light** has the minimum wavelength. So in any medium, red light travels fastest and deviates least, while violet light travels slowest and deviates maximum, i.e.

$$\text{Wavelength} \propto \text{Velocity} \propto \frac{1}{\text{Deviation}}$$

Recombination of White Light

Newton showed that the reverse of dispersion of light is also possible. He kept two prisms close to each other, one in erect position and the other in an inverted position. The light gets dispersed when passes through the first prism.

The second prism receives all the seven coloured rays from first prism and recombines them into original white light. This observation shows that sunlight is made up of seven colours. Any light that gives spectrum similar to that of sunlight is called **white light**.

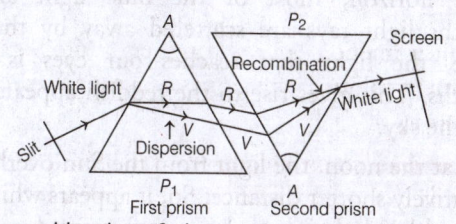

Recombination of the spectrum of white light

Rainbow

A rainbow is a natural spectrum appearing in the sky after a rain shower. It is caused by dispersion of sunlight by tiny water droplets, present in the atmosphere. A rainbow is always formed in a direction opposite to that of the Sun. The water droplets act like small prisms. They refract and disperse the incident sunlight, then reflect it internally and finally, refract it again when it comes out of the raindrop. Due to the dispersion of light and internal reflection, different colours reach the observer's eye. A rainbow can also be seen on a sunny day by looking at the sky through a waterfall or through a water fountain, with the Sun behind you.

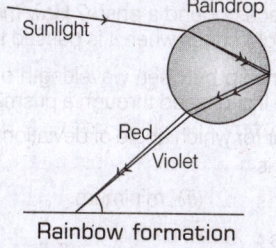

Rainbow formation

Note Red colour appears on the upper side of the rainbow and violet on the lower side, in case of primary rainbow.

Atmospheric Refraction

The Earth's atmosphere is not uniform throughout, its density goes on changing as we move up or down. It can be considered to be consisting of layers of different densities, which act as rarer or denser medium with respect to each other. Due to this, when the light rays pass through the earth's atmosphere, they undergo refraction. The refraction of light caused by these layers is called **atmospheric refraction**.

Some Phenomena Based on Atmospheric Refraction

Twinkling of Stars

The twinkling of a star is due to atmospheric refraction of starlight. As the light from the star enters the earth's atmosphere, it undergoes refraction due to varying optical densities of air at various altitudes. The continuously changing atmosphere refracts the light by different amounts. In this way, the starlight reaching our eyes increases and decreases continuously and the star appears to twinkle at night.

The Stars Seem Higher than They Actually Are

As the light from a star enters the Earth's atmosphere, it undergoes refraction and bends towards the normal each time due to the atmospheric refraction. Therefore, the apparent position of the star is slightly different from its actual position. The star appears to be slightly higher than its actual position, when viewed near the horizon.

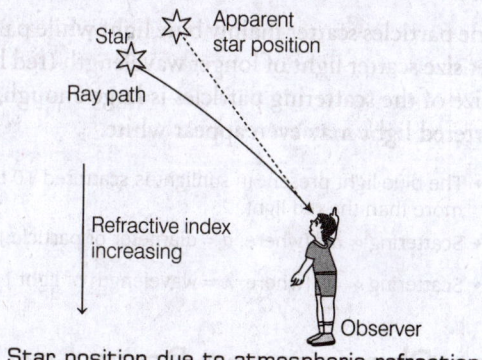

Star position due to atmospheric refraction

Planets do not Twinkle

As planets are of larger size and much closer to the earth, than stars they can be considered as a collection of large number of point sized sources of light. The total variation in the amount of light entering our eye from all these individual point sized sources will average out to zero which nullify the twinkling effect of each other. Therefore, planets do not twinkle.

Advance Sunrise and Delayed Sunset

The Sun is visible to us about two minutes before the actual sunrise and about two minutes after the actual sunset. This is because of atmospheric refraction. When the Sun is slightly below the horizon, the sunlight coming from the less dense to more dense air, is refracted downwards. Because of this, the Sun appears to be raised above the horizon and so the Sun can be seen about two minutes before actual sunrise.

Similarly, due to atmospheric refraction, the Sun can be seen for about two minutes even after the Sun has set below horizon.

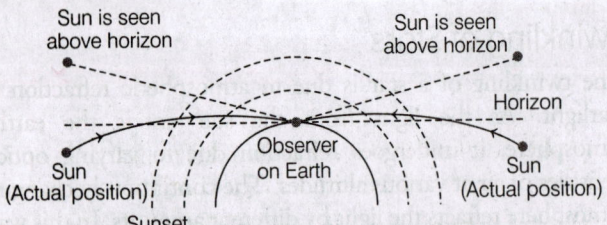

Atmospheric refraction effect at sunrise and sunset

Note At sunrise and sunset, the Sun appears flattened. This apparent flattening of the Sun's disc is also due to atmospheric refraction.

Scattering of Light

The reflection of light from an object in all directions is called scattering of light. The colour of scattered light depends on the size of scattering particles and wavelength of light.

Very fine particles scatter mainly blue light while particles of larger size scatter light of longer wavelength (red light). If the size of the scattering particles is large enough, then the scattered light may even appear white.

Note
- The blue light present in sunlight is scattered 10 times more than the red light.
- Scattering $\propto d^6$ [where, d = diameter of particle.]
- Scattering $\propto \dfrac{1}{\lambda^4}$ [where, λ = wavelength of light.]

Some Phenomena Based on Scattering of Light

Tyndall Effect

A beam of light passing through a true solution is not scattered. The scattering of light when it passes through a colloidal solution is called Tyndall effect. The earth's atmosphere is a heterogeneous mixture of minute particles of smoke, tiny water droplets, suspended particles of dust and molecules of air which becomes visible due to scattering of light.

Why the Colour of the Sky is Blue?

During the day time, sky appears blue. This is because the size of the particles in the atmosphere is smaller than the wavelength of visible light, so they scatter the light of shorter wavelengths.

The scattered blue light enters our eye. It should be noted that the sky appears black to the passengers flying at higher altitudes because scattering of light is not prominent at such height due to the absence of particles.

Colour of Sun at Sunrise and Sunset

At sunrise and sunset, the Sun and the sky appear red. Light from the Sun near the horizon passes through thicker layers of air and covers larger distance in the atmosphere before reaching our eyes.

Near the horizon, most of the blue light and shorter wavelengths light rays are scattered away by the particles. Therefore, the light that reaches our eyes is of longer wavelengths. This gives rise to the reddish appearance of the Sun and the sky.

However at the noon, the light from the Sun overhead would travel relatively shorter distance. So, it appears white as only a little of the blue and violet colours are scattered.

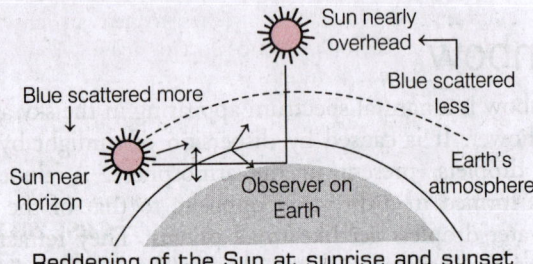

Reddening of the Sun at sunrise and sunset

Note If the Earth had no atmosphere, then sky would have appeared dark and black.

Check Point 03

1. How many surfaces bound a prism? How many refractions does a beam of white light suffer, when it is passed through a prism?
2. Give the relationship between wavelength of light and its angle of deviation, when it is passed through a prism.
3. Name the colour for which angle of deviation while passing through the glass prism is
   (i) maximum   (ii) minimum.
4. Fill in the blanks :
   (i) The colour of light which has minimum speed in glass is ....
   (ii) The colour of light which has minimum frequency is ....
5. State True/False for the following statements :
   (i) To observe Tyndall effect size of the scatteres should be greater than the wavelength of light.
   (ii) Rainbow is caused by dispersion of sunlight by tiny water droplets, present in the atmosphere.
6. For which colour, a glass has larger refractive index, violet or green?
7. Water in deep sea is blue in colour. Why?

NCERT FOLDER

Intext Questions

1 What is meant by power of accommodation of the eye? **pg 190**

Sol. Power of accommodation of eye is the maximum variation in power of eye lens for focussing nearby or distant objects clearly on retina.

2 A person with a myopic eye cannot see objects beyond 1.2 m distinctly. What should be the type of the corrective lens used to restore proper vision? **pg 190**

Sol. The person is suffering from myopia or short sightedness. To correct this defect of vision, concave lens of suitable focal length is used.

3 What is the far point and near point of the human eye with normal vision? **pg 190**

Or What is the range of vision of a normal eye? **CBSE 2011**

Sol. The near and far points for a normal eye are 25 cm and infinity respectively.

4 A student has difficulty in reading the blackboard while sitting in the last row. What could be the defect the child is suffering from? How can it be corrected? **pg 190**

Sol. Since, the child cannot see distant objects, it means that he is suffering from myopia. The image is formed before the retina in case of myopic eye. It can be corrected by using concave lens of suitable focal length.

Exercises
(On Pages 197 and 198)

1 The human eye can focus objects at different distances by adjusting the focal length of eye lens. This is due to
(a) presbyopia (b) accommodation
(c) near sightedness (d) far sightedness

Sol. (b) Accommodation is the ability of eye lens to focus both near and distant objects by adjusting its focal length.

2 The human eye forms the image of an object at its
(a) cornea (b) iris
(c) pupil (d) retina

Sol. (d) Retina is the light sensitive surface of eye which acts like screen on which the image is formed.

3 The least distance of distinct vision for a young adult with normal vision is about
(a) 25 m (b) 2.5 cm
(c) 25 cm (d) 2.5 m

Sol. (c) The minimum distance at which an object can be seen most distinctly without any strain is 25 cm.

4 The change in focal length of eye lens is caused by action of
(a) pupil (b) retina
(c) ciliary muscles (d) iris

Sol. (c) Ciliary muscles contract and expand in order to change the lens shape for focussing image at retina.

5 A person needs a lens of power − 5.5 D for correcting his distant vision. For correcting his near vision he needs a lens of power + 1.5 D. What is the focal length of the lens required for correcting (i) distant vision and (ii) near vision?

Sol. (i) We know that,

Focal length $= \dfrac{1}{\text{Power}} = -\dfrac{1}{5.5}$

[given, power, $P = -5.5$ D]

$= -0.18$ m
$= -18$ cm   [concave lens]

(ii) Focal length $= \dfrac{1}{\text{Power}} = +\dfrac{1}{1.5} = 0.67$ m

[given, power, $P = +1.5$ D]

$= 67$ cm   [convex lens]

6 The far point of a myopic person is 80 cm in front of the eye. What is the nature and power of the lens required to correct the problem?

Sol. For correcting myopia, concave lens is required. The image of a distant object should be formed at 80 cm by the concave lens.

$\therefore u = -\infty, v = -80$ cm

By lens formula, $\dfrac{1}{f} = \dfrac{1}{v} - \dfrac{1}{u}$

$= \dfrac{1}{-80} - \dfrac{1}{\infty} = \dfrac{-1}{80}$

Power $= \dfrac{1}{f \text{ (in metre)}} = \dfrac{-100}{80} = -1.25$ D

7 Make a diagram to show how hypermetropia is corrected. The near point of a hypermetropic eye is 1 m. What is the power of lens required to correct this defect? Assume that near point of the normal eye is 25 cm.

Sol. Hypermetropia is corrected by convex lens.
The ray diagram is as follows:

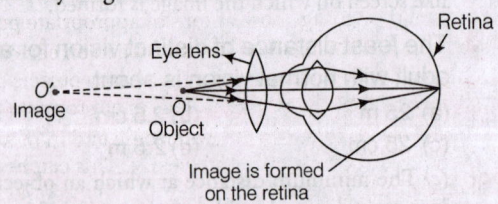

Now, according to the question,
Given values are,
Image distance, $v = -1$ m $= -100$ cm
Object distance, $u = -25$ cm
[For correction, image should be at 1m]
From lens formula,
$$\frac{1}{v} - \frac{1}{u} = \frac{1}{f}$$
$$\Rightarrow \frac{1}{f} = \frac{u-v}{uv}$$
$$\Rightarrow f = \frac{uv}{u-v} = \frac{-25 \times (-100)}{-25 + 100} = \frac{100 \times 25}{75}$$
So, $f = \frac{100}{3}$ cm $= \frac{1}{3}$ m

Power of the lens, $P = \frac{1}{f \text{ (in metre)}} = 3$ D

8 Why is a normal eye not able to see clearly the objects placed closer than 25 cm?

Sol. As our eye cannot focus the objects placed closer than 25 cm on the retina, we are unable to see the objects clearly.

9 What happens to the image distance in the eye when we increase the distance of an object from the eye?

Sol. The image distance remains the same because the focal length of the eye lens gradually changes to maintain the position of image on the retina of the eye.

10 Why do stars twinkle?

Sol. Stars twinkle due to atmospheric refraction of starlight. The starlight passes through different layers of atmospheric medium of gradually changing refractive index. So, it is refracted multiple times. As the apparent position of star and the physical condition of the earth's atmosphere are not constant the amount of starlight entering the eye flickers and gives a twinkling effect.

11 Explain, why the planets do not twinkle?

Sol. Planets are very close to the earth as compared to the stars. They also act as extended source of light. The total variation in the amount of light entering our eyes from all the individual point sized sources will average out to zero, which nullify the twinkling effect of each other. So, planets do not twinkle.

12 Why does the Sun appear reddish early in the morning?

Sol. In the morning, Sun near the horizon is far away from us. So, light has to travel a longer distance through the atmosphere to reach our eyes. So, near the horizon most of the blue light would be scattered away. Therefore, the light that reaches our eyes would be red in colour. Hence, the Sun appears red early in the morning.

13 Why does the sky appear to be dark instead of blue to an astronaut?

Sol. Sky appears dark to the astronauts because there is no atmosphere and hence no scattering of light takes place in the space.

SUMMARY

- The human eye is one of the most valuable and sensitive sense organs in the human body which enables us to see the wonderful world and colours around us.

Structure of Human Eye

- **Cornea** It is the transparent spherical membrane covering the front of the eye. It provides 67% of eye's focussing power.
- **Crystalline Lens** It is the central part of the eye that facilitates the image formation.
- **Iris** It is the dark muscular diaphragm between **cornea** and **lens**. It controls the size of the **pupil**.
- **Pupil** It is a small hole between the **iris** through which light enters the eye.
- **Ciliary muscles** They hold the lens in position and help in modifying the curvature of the lens.
- **Retina** It is the light sensitive surface of eye on which image is formed. It captures the light rays formed by the lens and sends impulses to the brain *via* optic nerves.
- **Optic nerve** It transmits the visual information from retina to the brain.
- **Sclera** It is an outer coat which protects the eye.
- **Blind spot** It is the point insensitive to eye at which the optic nerve leaves the eye.
- **Aqueous humour** It is a aqueous and present between the cornea and maintains intraocular pressure.
- **Vitreous humour** The space between the eye lens and retina is filled with another liquid known as vitreous humour.

- The ability or the property of the eye lens to focus both near and distant objects by adjusting its focal length is known as **accommodation**.
- The maximum variation in power of eye lens for focusing near or far objects, clearly at retina is known as **power of accommodation**.
- The farthest point up to which the eye can see clearly is known as far point of eye. It is infinity for normal eye.
- The minimum distance at which an object can be seen most distinctly without any strain is known as the **least distance of distinct vision**. For normal eye of an adult, it is 25 cm. It is also known as **near point** of eye.

Defects of Vision
The main defects of vision are:

- **Myopia** Due to this defect a person can see near by objects clearly but cannot see distant objects clearly. This can be corrected by using concave lens of appropriate power.
- **Hypermetropia** Due to this defect a person can see distant objects clearly but cannot see the nearby objects clearly. This can be corrected by using convex lens of appropriate power.
- **Presbyopia** is found in old age people and in this defect, one cannot read comfortably and clearly. This can be corrected by using bifocal lenses.

- **Prism** is a transparent refracting medium with two triangular bases and three rectangular lateral surfaces, inclined to each other at a certain angle.
- When a ray of light passes through a prism, it bends towards the thicker part of the prism.
- The angle which the emergent ray makes with the incident ray is known as **angle of deviation** (D).
- The phenomenon of splitting of white light into its constituent colours, when it passes through a prism is known as **dispersion**.
- This band of seven colours, so obtained, the VIBGYOR (V = violet, I = indigo, B = blue, G = green, Y = yellow, O = orange and R = red) is known as **spectrum**.
- Isaac Newton was the first one to use a glass prism to obtain the spectrum of light.
- Red light has maximum wavelength and violet light has the minimum wavelength.
- **Rainbow** is caused by dispersion of sunlight by tiny water droplets, present in the atmosphere.
- The refraction of light due to the layers present in the atmosphere is known as **atmospheric refraction**.

Phenomena based on Atmospheric Refraction
- Twinkling of stars
- The stars seem higher than they actually are.
- Advance sunrise and delayed sunset

- The reflection of light from an object in all directions is known as **scattering of light**.

Phenomena based on Scattering of Light
- Tyndall effect
- Blue colour of the sky
- Colour of Sun at sunrise and sunset

Exam Practice

Objective Type Questions

Multiple Choice Questions

1 The size of the pupil of the eye is adjusted by
(a) cornea   (b) retina
(c) iris   (d) blind spot

Sol. (c) Iris is a dark muscular diaphragm that controls the size of the pupil.

2. When ciliary muscles are relaxed, focal length of eye lens is
(a) maximum
(b) minimum
(c) Neither maximum nor minimum
(d) Cannot say

Sol. (a) When we are looking at distant objects, the ciliary muscles are relaxed and the eye lens becomes thin. Consequently, the focal length of the eye lens becomes maximum.

3. To focus the image of a nearby object on the retina of an eye
(a) the distance between eye-lens and retina is increased
(b) the distance between eye-lens and retina is decreased
(c) the thickness of eye-lens is decreased
(d) the thickness of eye-lens is increased

Sol. (d) To look at the near by objects the eye-lens has to be thick or more convex to increase its converging power.

4. The far point of eye of a person is 2m. The type of the lens needed in spectacles to increase the far point to infinity is
(a) concave lens   (b) convex lens
(c) cylindrical lens (d) bifocal lens

Sol. (a) Concave lens is needed in spectacles to increase the far point to infinity.

5 A person with a myopic eye cannot see object beyond −1.2 m distinctly. The power of the corrective lens used to restore proper vision is
(a) − 0.83 D   (b) − 0.92 D
(c) + 0.21 D   (d) + 0.91 D

Sol. (a) The corrective lens should form the image of far off object at the far point of the myopic person.

By lens formula,
$$\frac{1}{f} = \frac{1}{v} - \frac{1}{u} = \frac{1}{-1.2} - \frac{1}{\infty} = \frac{-1}{1.2} \Rightarrow f = -1.2 \text{ m}$$

∴ Power of a lens, $P = \frac{-1}{1.2} = -0.83$ D

6 A person uses a lens of power + 3D to normalise vision. Near point of hypermetropic eye is
(a) 1.66 m   (b) 0.66 m   (c) 0.33 m   (d) − 1 m

Sol. (d) Focal length of lens, $f = \frac{1}{P}$

$= \frac{1}{3} \times 100 = \frac{100}{3}$ cm

By lens formula, $\frac{1}{f} = \frac{1}{v} - \frac{1}{u} \Rightarrow \frac{1}{\frac{100}{3}} = \frac{1}{v} - \frac{1}{(-25)}$

$\Rightarrow v = -100$ cm $= -1$ m

7 A student sitting on the last bench can read the letters written on the blackboard but is not able to read the letters written in his text book. Which of the following statements is correct?
(a) The near point of his eyes has receded away
(b) The near point of his eyes has come closer to him
(c) The far point of his eyes has come closer to him
(d) The far point of his eyes has receded away   **NCERT Exemplar**

Sol. (a) According to given condition the student suffering from hypermetropia or far sightedness. He can see distant objects clearly but cannot see nearby objects distinctly, i.e. the near point of his eyes has receded away.

8 When a ray of light passes through a glass prism, it suffers two refractions. During these refractions, the ray bends
CBSE 2021 (Term-I)
(a) away from the base in both cases
(b) towards the base in both cases
(c) towards the base in first case and away from the base in second case
(d) away from the base in first case and towards the base in second case

Human Eye and the Colourful World

Sol. (b) In the refraction through prism, the refracted ray bends towards the base.

9 Splitting of white light into seven colours on passing through a glass prism is due to
(a) dispersion (b) refraction
(c) scattering (d) reflection
NCERT Exemplar

Sol. (a) The splitting of white light into its component colours on passing through a glass is called dispersion.

10 A prism ABC (with BC as base) is placed in different orientations. A narrow beam of white light is incident on the prism as shown in figure. In which of the following cases, after dispersion, the sixth colour from the top corresponds to the colour of the sun? **CBSE SQP (Term-I)**

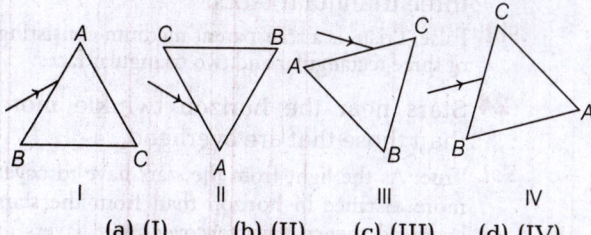

(a) (I) (b) (II) (c) (III) (d) (IV)

Sol. (b) Generally, in case of a prism (II), the formation of spectrum is shown below

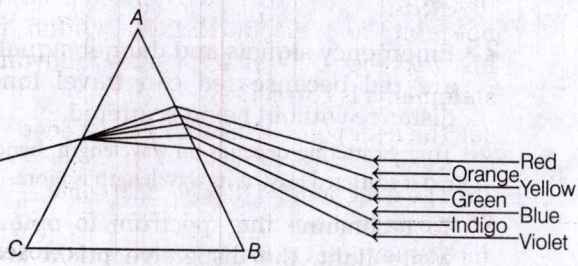

In the above figure, from top the sixth colour is Indigo. But we can see that from bottom the sixth colour is orange which is the colour of sun. So, we can obtain the correct situation by inverting the prism. Thus, the required orientations can be bound in case II.

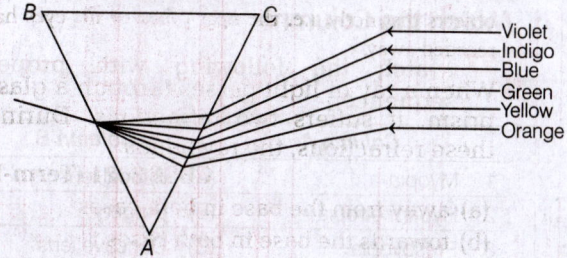

11 If a beam of red light and a beam of violet light are incident at the same angle on the inclined surface of a prism from air medium and produce angles of refraction r and v respectively, which of the following is correct? **CBSE 2021 (Term-I)**
(a) $r = v$ (b) $r > v$
(c) $r = \dfrac{1}{v}$ (d) $r < v$

Sol. (d) Since, red light deviates the least, therefore refracting angle for the red light will also be minimum. Hence, $r < v$.

12 At noon the Sun appears white as
(a) light is least scattered
(b) all the colours of the white light are scattered away
(c) blue colour is scattered the most
(d) red colour is scattered the most
NCERT Exemplar

Sol. (a) At noon the Sun appears white because the light from the sun is directly over head and travel relatively shorter distance. The sun appears white as only a little of the blue and violet colours are scattered.

13 To an astronaut the sky on the moon appears dark because
(a) there is no light on the moon
(b) there is no atmosphere on the surface of the moon
(c) moon is a non-luminous object
(d) the surface of the moon absorbs all the sunlight

Sol. (b) There is no atmosphere on the moon. Thus, light rays are not scattered and hence sky appears dark.

14 Which of the following phenomena of light are involved in the formation of a rainbow?
(a) Reflection, refraction and dispersion
(b) Refraction, dispersion and total internal reflection
(c) Refraction, dispersion and internal reflection
(d) Dispersion, scattering and total internal reflection
NCERT Exemplar

Sol. (c) A rainbow is caused by dispersion, refraction and internal reflection of sunlight by tiny water droplets, present in the atmosphere and always formed in a direction opposite to that of the sun. The water droplets act like small prisms. They refract and disperse the incident sunlight, then reflect it internally and finally refract it again when it comes out of the raindrop.

15 Twinkling of stars is due to atmospheric
(a) dispersion of light by water droplets
(b) refraction of light by different layers of varying refractive indices
(c) scattering of light by dust particles
(d) internal reflection of light by clouds
NCERT Exemplar, CBSE 2021 (Term-I)

Sol. (b) The twinkling of a star is due to atmospheric refraction of lights of stars. These lights, on entering the earth's atmosphere, undergoes refraction continuously before it reaches the earth.

The path of rays of light coming from the distant star goes on varying slightly, the apparent position of the star fluctuates and the amount of starlight entering the eye flickers. The star sometimes appears brighter and at some other time, fainter gives us the twinkling effect.

16 Which of the following statements is correct regarding the propagation of light of different colours of white light in air?
(a) Red light moves fastest
(b) Blue light moves faster than green light
(c) All the colours of the white light move with the same speed
(d) Yellow light moves with the mean speed as that of the red and the violet light
NCERT Exemplar

Sol. (c) Different colours of white light in air or vacuum move with the same speed but different wavelengths and frequencies.

17 The danger signals installed at the top of tall buildings are red in colour. These can be easily seen from a distance because among all other colours, the red light
(a) is scattered the most by smoke or fog
(b) is scattered the least by smoke or fog
(c) is absorbed the most by smoke or fog
(d) moves fastest in air **NCERT Exemplar**

Sol. (b) The danger signals installed at the top of tall buildings are red in colour because among all other colours, red colour is scattered the least by smoke or fog. Thus it can be easily seen from long distance.

Scattering is inversely proportional to the fourth power of wavelength. As wavelength of red is most, hence red colour is scattered the least.

Fill in the Blanks

18 The defect caused due to increase in the focal length of eye-lens is known as ....

Sol. Hypermetropia (long-sightedness)

19 Short-sightedness can be corrected by using .... lenses.

Sol. Concave

20 The colour of the white light deviated through the largest angle by a prism is ....

Sol. Violet

21 The orange-reddish appearance of the sun during sunrise and sunset is because of ....

Sol. Atmospheric refraction

True and False

22 Myopia and long-sightedness are the same eye-defects.

Sol. False; Myopia and short-sightedness are the same eye-defects.

23 Prism is a homogeneous transparent medium consisting two rectangular and three triangular faces.

Sol. False; Prism is a transparent medium consisting of three rectangular and two triangular faces.

24 Stars near the horizon twinkle more than those that are overhead.

Sol. True; As the light from the stars have to cover more distance in horizon than from the stars overhead, hence have to cover more layers of atmosphere, having different optical densities and refractive index, hence more twinkling effects.

25 Emergency signals and danger signals are red because red can travel long distance without being scattered.

Sol. True; Scattering depends on wavelength, hence red is scattered least as its wavelength is more.

26 To recombine the spectrum to obtain white light, the dispersive prism and recombination prism should be in same position.

Sol. False; To recombine the spectrum to obtain white light, the recombination prism should be in inverted position with dispersive prism.

Match the Columns

27 Match the following with proper sequence:

	Column A		Column B
1.	Myopia	(A)	Bifocal lens
2.	Hypermetropia	(B)	Surgery
3.	Presbyopia	(C)	Concave lens
4.	Cataract	(D)	Convex lens

Sol. (1) → (C), (2) → (D), (3) → (A), (4) → (B)

Assertion-Reason

Direction (Q. Nos. 28-34) *In each of the following questions, a statement of Assertion is given by the corresponding statement of Reason. Of the statements, mark the correct answer as*

(a) If both Assertion and Reason are true and Reason is the correct explanation of Assertion.
(b) If both Assertion and Reason are true, but Reason is not the correct explanation of Assertion.
(c) If Assertion is true, but Reason is false.
(d) If Assertion is false, but Reason is true.

28 Assertion Myopia is due to the increased converging power of the eye lens.

Reason Myopia can be corrected by using spectacles made from concave lenses.

Sol. (b) In Myopia eye due to the increased converging power of eye lens, the image of a far off object is formed in front of the retina.
Myopia can be corrected by using spectacles made from concave lens.

29 Assertion The light of violet colour deviates the most and the light of red colour the least, while passing through a prism.

Reason For a prism material, refractive index is highest for red light and lowest for the violet light.

Sol. (b) The light of violet colour deviates most and the light of red colour the least, while passing through a prism. For a prism material refractive index is highest for violet light and lowest for the red light.

30 Assertion The given diagram is of correction of a myopic eye.

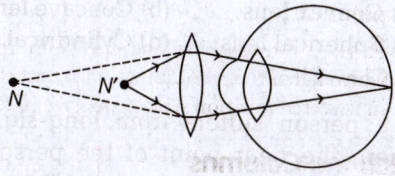

Reason Myopia arises due to excessive curvature of the eye lens or elongation of the eyeball.

Sol. (d) The given diagram is of correction of hypermetropic eye, hence Assertion is false as concave lens is used for myopic eye but Reason is true as myopic arises due to excessive curvature of eye lens or the elongation of the eye-ball.

31 Assertion Refraction of white light through prism gives rise to dispersion.

Reason Both the refracting surfaces of glass slab are parallel to each other. But the refracting surfaces of prism are inclined to an angle called angle of prism.

Sol. (b) Both Assertion and Reason are true, but Reason is not the correct explanation of Assertion. Light rays of different colours travel with different speeds and bend through different angles when pass through different media which is the cause of dispersion.

32 Assertion The stars twinkle while the planet do not.

Reason The stars are much bigger in size than the planets.

Sol. (b) As planets are of larger size and much closer to the earth than stars, planets can be considered as a collection of large number of point sized sources of light. The total variation in the amount of light entering our eye from all these individual point sized sources will average out to zero which nullify the twinkling effect of each other. Therefore, planets do not twinkle.

33 Assertion Blue colour of sky appears due to scattering of blue colour.

Reason Blue colour has shortest wave length in visible spectrum.

Sol. (a) During the day time, sky appears blue. This is because the size of the particles in the atmosphere is smaller than the wavelength of visible light, so they scatter the light of shorter wavelengths. The scattered blue light enters our eye, as according to Rayleigh' scattering,

$$\text{scattering} \propto \frac{1}{(\text{wavelength})^4}$$

34 Assertion Sky appears blue in the day time.

Reason White light is composed of seven colours. **CBSE SQP (Term-I)**

Sol. (b) Both A and R are true because sky appears blue in the day time as blue light is scattered the most. It is due to the scattering.

Case Based Questions

Direction (Q. Nos. 35-38) *Answer the questions on the basis of your understanding of the following table, figure and related studied concepts:*

After tracing the ray of path of light through a glass prism, a student measures the angle of incidence ∠i, angle of refraction ∠r, prism angle ∠A, angle of emergence (∠e) and angle of deviation (∠D).

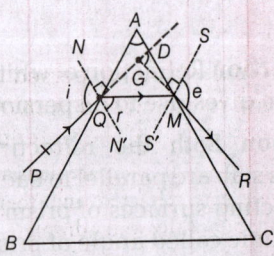

Observation table based on the above experiment done by student is as follows:

Number of observations	Angle of incidence ($\angle i$)	Angle of emergence ($\angle e$)	Angle of deviation ($\angle D$)
(1)	30°	60°	30°
(2)	35°	55°	30°
(3)	40°	50°	30°
(4)	45°	45°	30°
(5)	50°	40°	30°

On analysing his measurements based on the following diagram as well as table, answer the following questions:

35 From the given ray diagram, name the ray that represented by the (i) PQ (ii) QM

Sol. (i) Incident ray of light represented by *PQ*
(ii) Refracted ray represented by *QM*

36 Name the phenomena associated with the splitting of white light into band of seven colours or spectrum.

Sol. Dispersion of light

37 Select the correct option from the following based on the analysis of his measurements:
(a) $\angle A + \angle D = \angle i$
(b) $\angle A + \angle D = \angle i + \angle e$
(c) $\angle A + \angle e = \angle i + \angle D$
(d) $\angle i + \angle D = \angle A + \angle e$

Sol. (b) From the above table, it is clear that
$\angle A + \angle D = \angle i + \angle e$

38 Which of the following is the correct set-up of protractor for tracing the path of ray of light through a glass prism, for measuring the angle of incidence?

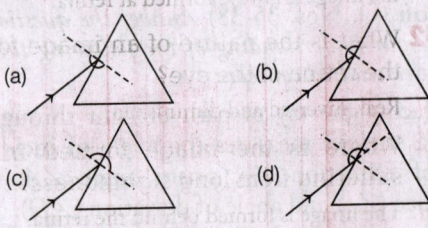

Sol. (a) As angle of incidence is the angle between the incident ray and normal drawn on the refracting surface.

Direction (Q. Nos. 39-42) *Answer the questions on the basis of your understanding of the following passage and related studied concepts:*

The human eye has a converging lens system that produces an image just like a camera. If the eye views a distant object, real, inverted, diminished image is produced. When you wear glasses, you see the images of the objects not the objects themselves. The images you see are upright and on the same side of the lens as the objects therefore the image you see is virtual. In order to see clearly the image has to be within your range of clear vision, i.e. between your near and far points. The lenses make the image of the object placed at the near point appear to be at the person's actual near point. e.g. if a person has an unaided near point of 0.60 m they need a converging lens in their glasses to make them able to see clearly an object that is only 25 cm from their eyes.

39 Write the nature and size of the image produced in human eye when it views a distant object.

Sol. The image produced in human eye will be real, inverted and diminished in size.

40 If the near point of an eye has been shifted to 80 cm, the person must be suffering from some refractive defect of eye. Name the defect and the cause of the defect.

Sol. Hypermetropia, because the near point of eye shifts from 25 cm to 80 cm, i.e. the image is formed behind the retina. The cause of this defect is low converging power of eye-lens or shortening of eye-ball.

41 In order to correct the vision of above condition which type of lens should the person use in his spectacles?
(a) Convex lens   (b) Concave lens
(c) Spherical lens   (d) Cylindrical lens

Sol. (a) Convex lens

42 If a person suffers from long-sightedness. Then, the near point of the person who is using a spectacle of power + 1 D is
(a) 33.33 cm   (b) 33.33 m
(c) 3.33 cm   (d) 3.33 m

Sol. (a) As. $P = +1$ D

$\therefore \quad f = \dfrac{1}{P} = \dfrac{100}{1}$ cm

Applying lens formula,

$\Rightarrow \quad \dfrac{1}{v} - \dfrac{1}{u} = \dfrac{1}{f} \Rightarrow \dfrac{1}{v} - \dfrac{1}{u} = \dfrac{1}{100}$

Human Eye and the Colourful World

$$\frac{1}{v} - \frac{1}{-25} = \frac{1}{100}$$

$$\frac{1}{v} = \frac{1}{100} - \frac{1}{25} = \frac{1-4}{100} = \frac{-3}{100}$$

$$v = -\frac{100}{3} = -33.33 \text{ cm}$$

Thus, the near point of the person is 33.33 cm.

Direction (Q. Nos. 43-46) *Answer the questions on the basis of your understanding of the following passage and related studied concepts:*

On a sunny day, Krish looked at the sky through a water fountain and was surprised to see a rainbow in the sky.

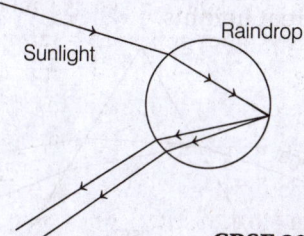

CBSE 2021 (Term-I)

43 The location of the Sun when Krish observed a rainbow was
(a) behind him
(b) in front of him
(c) overhead
(d) on his left side

Sol. (a) The rainbow appears opposite side of the Sun in sky.

44 The phenomena of light involved in the formation of a rainbow are
(a) reflection, refraction, dispersion
(b) refraction, dispersion, internal reflection
(c) refraction, dispersion, scattering
(d) dispersion, scattering, internal reflection

Sol. (b) Refraction, dispersion, persion and total internal reflection are the phenomenon involved in the formation of rainbow.

45 In the formation of a rainbow, the role of water droplets present in the water fountain is to act as a
(a) glass slab   (b) convex lens
(c) concave lens   (d) prism

Sol. (d) Tiny water droplets act as prism in formation of rainbow.

46 While entering a water droplet, the sunlight gets
(a) refracted only
(b) reflected internally
(c) refracted and dispersed
(d) first refracted and then dispersed while coming out of the water droplet

Sol. (d) The water droplets are denser than air, therefore sunlight gets refracted and then dispersed, while coming out of the water droplet.

Very Short Answer Type Questions

47 Name the part of an eye which is equivalent to
(i) diaphragm and
(ii) photographic plate, in a camera.

Sol. (i) Iris of an eye is equivalent to the diaphragm in a camera.
(ii) Retina is equivalent to a photographic plate in a camera.

48 How is the sense of vision carried from the eye to the brain?

Sol. Sense of vision is carried by optic nerves from eye to brain.

49 Why is blind spot so called?

Sol. Blind spot is a point at which the optic nerve leaves the eye. It contains no rods or cones, so when an image is formed at this point, it is not sent to the brain.

50 What happens to the lens and the ciliary muscles when you are looking at nearby objects?

Sol. The ciliary muscles contract and the lens becomes thick. Hence, its focal length decreases.

51 When we increase the distance of an object from the eye, the image distance from the eye lens in the normal eye   **CBSE 2020**
(a) increases
(b) decreases
(c) remains unchanged
(d) depends on the size of the eyeball

Sol. (c) There is no change to the image distance in the eye when we increase the distance of an object from the eye to see closer or distant object clearly. The eyes, due to its ability of accommodation can increase or decrease focal length of its lens, so that the image is always formed at retina.

52 What is the nature of an image formed on the retina of the eye?

Sol. Real, inverted and diminished.

53 Where is the image formed in an eye suffering from long sightedness?

Sol. The image is formed behind the retina.

54 Where do we see
(i) concave lens and
(ii) convex lens in a bifocal spectacle?

Sol. (i) Concave lens is in upper part.
(ii) Convex lens is in lower part.

55 Which phenomenon is responsible for increasing the apparent length of the day by 4 min?

Sol. Atmospheric refraction.

56 What is the twinkling of stars due to?

Sol. It is due to refraction of star light by earth's atmosphere.

57 What is the relation between intensity of scattered light and its amplitude?

Sol. Intensity of scattered light is directly proportional to the square of the amplitude (a) of scattered light, i.e. $I \propto a^2$

58 How can you identify the type of defect of vision a person is suffering from by physically touching his spectacles?

Sol. When you touch the spectacles, if the lens is bulging out, it is a convex lens.
Hence, the person is suffering from hypermetropia. And if the lens is thinner from centre, it means it is concave lens. Hence, the person is suffering from myopia.

59 Bees are able to see ultraviolet light. Comment.

Sol. The retina of bees contains cone cells that are sensitive to ultraviolet light. So the bees are able to see ultraviolet light.

60 A piece of cloth appears red in sunlight. How will it appears when held in the blue portion of a spectrum?

Sol. It will appear black in the spectrum.

61 Why does the Sun appear white at noon?
CBSE SQP 2020-21

Sol. At noon, the Sun appears white because the light from the Sun is directly over head and travel relatively shorter distance. The Sun appears white as only a little of the blue and violet colours are scattered at noon.

62 The sky appears dark to passengers flying at very high altitudes mainly because
(a) scattering of light is not enough at such heights
(b) there is no atmosphere at great heights
(c) the size of molecules is smaller than the wavelength of visible light
(d) the light gets scattered towards the earth **CBSE 2020**

Sol. The sky appears dark to passengers flying at very high altitudes because there is no atmosphere at great heights. Due to absence of minute particles, there is no scattering of light. Thus, sky appears dark at great heights.

63

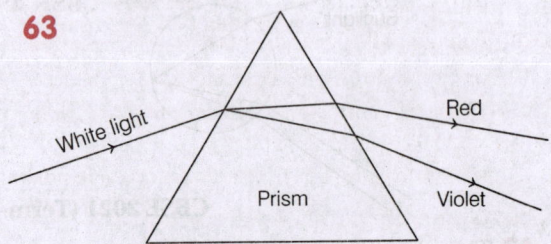

A student observes the above phenomenon in the lab as a white light passes through a prism. Among many other colours, he observed the position of the two colours red and violet.

What is the phenomenon called? What is the reason for the violet light to bend more than the red light? **CBSE SQP 2020-21**

Sol. The phenomenon is called dispersion, which is defined as the splitting of white light into its constituent colours, when it passes through a prism.

Red light has the maximum wavelength and violet light has the minimum wavelength. As, wavelength is directly proportional to speed. So, in any medium, red light travels fastest and deviates least, while violet light travels slowest and deviates the most, i.e.,

Wavelength $\propto$ Velocity $\propto \dfrac{1}{\text{Deviation}}$

All in one Human Eye and the Colourful World

Short Answer (SA) Type Questions

1 Trace the sequence of events which occur when a bright light is focused on your eyes. **CBSE 2019**

Sol. Refer to text on page 328 and 329.

2 Draw a labelled diagram of human eye. What is the significance of the blind spot?

Sol. Refer to diagram on Pg. 329.

The **blind spot** is the least sensitive spot on the retina. And an image formed there is not seen by the eye. It contains no rods or cones.

3 State one main function each of iris, pupil, and cornea. **CBSE 2015**

Sol. Function of
(i) **Iris** controls the size of pupil.
(ii) **Pupil** controls the amount of light entering the eye.
(iii) **Cornea** provides 67% of eye's focussing power.

4 Name the parts of the eye that
(i) controls the amount of light entering the eye.
(ii) determine the colours of a person's eye.
(iii) focus objects at different distances on the retina.

Sol. (i) Pupil
(ii) Iris
(iii) The combination of cornea, aqueous humour, the crystalline lens, ciliary muscles and vitreous humour.

5 How do we see objects erect when the eye forms a real, inverted image of them on its retina?

Sol. The light sensitive cells of retina converts the image formed on it into electrical signals. These electrical signals are transmitted to the brain through optic nerve. The brain, while interpreting and processing these signals, reinvert the image formed and we see the object erect.

6 How can change of size of eyeball be one of the reason for
(i) myopic and (ii) hypermetropic eye?
Compare the size of eyeball with that of a normal eye in each case. How does this change of size affect the position of image in each case? **CBSE 2015**

Sol. (i) The eye suffering from myopia, has long eyeball than that of normal eye due to which the retina is at a larger distance from the eye lens. This results in the formation of the image before retina.

(ii) The eye suffering from hypermetropia has short eyeball than that of normal eye due to which the retina is at smaller distance from the eye lens. This results in the formation of the image behind the retina.

7 A person suffering from myopia (near-sightedness) was advised to wear corrective lens of power – 2.5 D. A spherical lens of same focal length was taken in the laboratory. At what distance should a student place an object from this lens, so that it forms an image at a distance of 10 cm from the lens?

Sol. Given, $P = -2.5$ D, $v = 10$ cm

Case I
When $v = +10$ cm (in the direction opposite to object),

As, we know, $P = \dfrac{1}{f}$

So, $f = \dfrac{1}{P} = \dfrac{1}{-2.5} = -0.4$ m $= -40$ cm

$\therefore \quad \dfrac{1}{v} - \dfrac{1}{u} = \dfrac{1}{f}$

$\Rightarrow \quad \dfrac{1}{10} - \dfrac{1}{u} = -\dfrac{1}{40}$

$\Rightarrow \quad u = 8$ cm

(It is not taken, since u should be + ive)

Case II
When, $v = -10$ cm (in the direction of object),

$\dfrac{1}{v} - \dfrac{1}{u} = \dfrac{1}{f} \Rightarrow \dfrac{1}{-10} - \dfrac{1}{u} = -\dfrac{1}{40}$

$u = -13.33$ cm

8 A student uses spectacles of focal length – 2.5 m. **CBSE 2020**
(a) Name the defect of vision he is suffering from.
(b) Which lens is used for the correction of this defect?
(c) List two main causes of developing this defect.
(d) Compute the power of this lens.

Sol. Given, $f = -2.5$ m, i.e., a concave lens, since focal length is negative.
(a) He is suffering from myopia because the focal length required for the lens is negative.
(b) Concave lens

345

(c) This defect arises due to the decrease in focal length of the lens because of
  (i) excessive curvature of eye lens
  (ii) elongation of the eyeball
(d) As we know, power, $P = \dfrac{1}{f}$

$\Rightarrow \quad P = \dfrac{1}{-2.5} = -0.4\,D$

9 What happens to the image distance in the normal human eye when we decrease the distance of an object say 10 m to 1 m? Justify your answer. **CBSE 2019**

Sol. The image distance remains the same because the focal length of the eye lens gradually changes to maintain the position of image on the retina of the eye.

10 List two main causes of a person developing near sightedness. Show with the help of a ray diagram how this defect can be corrected. **CBSE 2015**

Sol. Two main causes of a person developing near sightedness are
  (i) Excessive curvature of eye lens
  (ii) Elongation of eyeball
Correction by concave lens

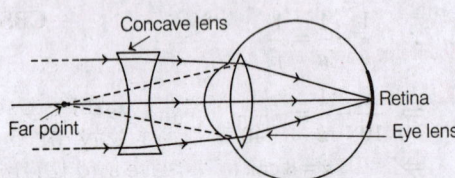

11 Study the diagram given below and answer the questions that follows:

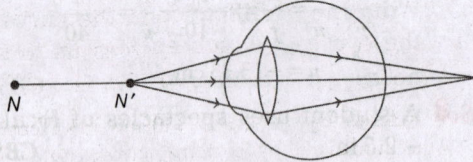

  (i) Which defect of vision is represented in this case? Give reason for your answer.
  (ii) What could be the two causes of this defect?
  (iii) With the help of a diagram show how this defect can be corrected by the use of a suitable lens?

Sol. (i) This defect is hypermetropia as the image of near point is formed beyond retina.
  (ii) The two causes of the defect are follows:
    (a) Size of eyeball decreases.
    (b) Focal length of the lens increases.

(iii) This defect can be corrected by using a convex lens of suitable focal length.

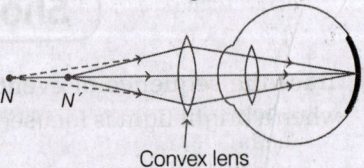

12 (a) A person is suffering from both myopia and hypermetropia.
  (i) What kind of lenses can correct this defect?
  (ii) How are these lenses prepared?
(b) A person needs a lens of power + 3D for correcting his near vision and − 3D for correcting his distant vision. Calculate the focal lengths of the lenses required to correct these defects. **CBSE 2020**

Sol. (a) (i) Refer to text on page 331.
  (ii) Lenses are made from materials like glass or plastic and are around and polished or molded to a desired shape.

(b) As, we know, power of lens, $P = \dfrac{1}{f} \Rightarrow f = \dfrac{1}{P}$

Hence, for first lens, focal length $f = \dfrac{1}{+3}$

$= +0.33$ or $+33.33$ cm (convex lens)
Similarly, for second lens focal length

$f = \dfrac{1}{-3} = -0.33$ m or -33.33 cm

(concave lens)

13 A beam of white light falling on a glass prism gets split up into seven colours marked 1 to 7 as shown in the diagram.

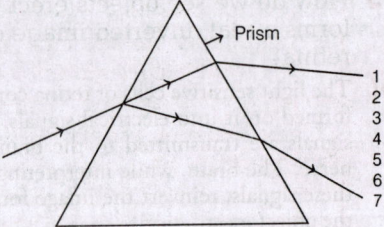

  (i) The colour at position marked 3 and 5 are similar to the colour of the sky and the colour of gold metal, respectively. Is the above statement made by the student correct or incorrect justify?
  (ii) Which of the above shown positions corresponds approximately to the colour of (a) a brinjal, (b) danger signal, (c) neel which is applied to clothes, (d) orange. **CBSE 2012**

Sol. (i) No, because 3 refers to yellow and 5 to blue colours of the spectrum.

(ii) (a) 7   (b) 1   (c) 6   (d) 2

14 (a) With the help of labelled ray diagram, show the path followed by a narrow beam of monochromatic light when it passes through a glass prism.

(b) What would happen if this beam is replaced by a narrow beam of white light? **CBSE 2020**

Sol. (a) When a monchromatic light passed through a glass prism, it get deviated from its original path.

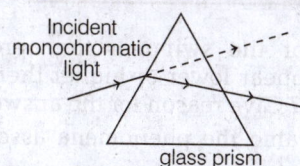

(b) When a white light passed through a prism, it splits out in a band of seven colours, which is called spectrum.

15 A narrow beam PQ of white light is passing through a glass prism ABC as shown in the diagram.

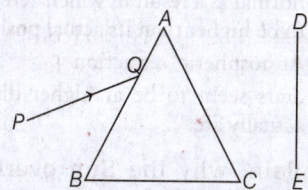

Trace it on your answer sheet and show the path of the emergent beam as observed on the screen DE.

(i) Write the name and cause of the phenomenon observed.

(ii) Where else in nature is this phenomenon observed?

(iii) Based on this observation, state the conclusion which can be drawn about the constituents of white light. **CBSE 2014**

Sol.

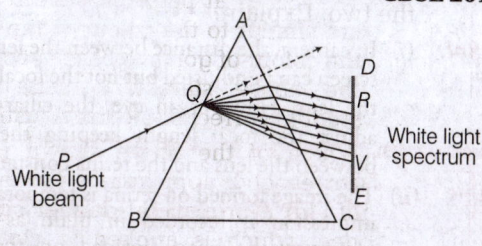

(i) The phenomenon of splitting of white light into its constituent colours is called dispersion of light. It is caused because different constituent colours of light travel with different speeds in the medium other than air/vacuum and bend through different angles.

(ii) In nature, this phenomenon is observed in formation of rainbow.

(iii) Based on phenomenon of dispersion, we can conclude that
(a) White light consists of seven colours.
(b) Violet light suffers maximum deviation and red light suffers minimum deviation.

16 What is rainbow? Draw a labelled diagram to show the formation of a rainbow. **CBSE 2019**

Sol. Refer to text on Pg. 333.

17 What is the cause of dispersion of white light through a glass prism? Draw a ray diagram to show the path of light when two identical glass prisms are arranged together in inverted position with respect to each other and a narrow beam of white light is allowed to fall obliquely on one of the faces of the prisms. **CBSE 2019**

Sol. Refer to text on Pg. 332-333.

18 What is scattering of light? Use this phenomenon to explain why (i) the Sun appears reddish at sunrise and (ii) the clear sky appears blue? **CBSE 2019**

Sol. Refer to text on Pg. 334.

19 Define the term power of accommodation. Write the modification in the curvature of the eye lens which enables us to see the nearby objects clearly? **CBSE 2019**

Sol. Refer to text on Pg. 329, 330 and 331 [Terms related to human eye, hypermetropia (Remedy)].

20 Write the structure of eye lens and state the role of ciliary muscles in the human eye. **CBSE 2019**

Sol. Refer to text on Pg. 328 and 329 (Structure of human eye).

21 When a beam of white light is passed through a triangular glass prism, it gets dispersed into its seven colour components. Why do we get these colours? In the given figure, the colours X and Y represent the extreme components of the spectrum. Identify X and Y.

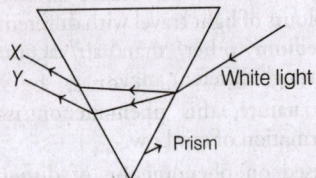

CBSE 2012

Sol. (i) Different colours of light bend through different angles with respect to the incident ray as they travel with different speeds while passing through a prism, which leads to the dispersion of light.
(ii) X = violet, Y = red

22 State the cause of dispersion of white light passing through a glass prism. How did Newton show that white light of Sun contains seven colours using two identical glass prisms?

Draw a ray diagram to show the path of light when two identical glass prisms are arranged together in inverted position with respect to each other and a narrow beam of white light is allowed to fall obliquely on one of the prisms. **CBSE 2016**

Sol. Light rays of different colours travel with the same speed in vacuum and air. But in any other medium, they travel with the different speeds and bend through the different angles, which leads to the dispersion of light. This occurs as both the prisms behave like a single rectangular glass slab of parallel sides.

Newton showed that the reverse of dispersion of light is also possible. He kept two prisms close to each other one in erect position and the other in an inverted position. The light gets dispersed when it passes through the first prism. The second prism receives all the seven coloured rays from first prism and recombines them into the original white light. This observation shows that sunlight is made up of seven colours.

Any light that gives spectrum similar to that of sunlight is called **white light**.

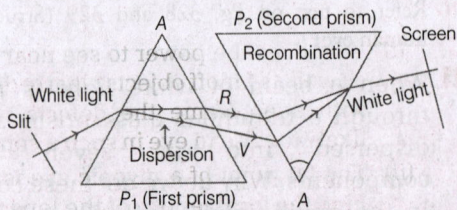

Recombination of the spectrum of white light

23 In the picture given below, a swimmer inside the water in a swimming pool looks at an aeroplane flying the sky.

(i) For the swimmer the aeroplane will appear lower or higher then it actually is? Give reason for the answer.
(ii) Name the phenomena associated with it.
(iii) Name any other phenomena associated with it.

Sol. (i) For the swimmer the aeroplane will appear to be higher then it actually is. As water is a denser medium, so when light travels from water to air, i.e. denser to rarer, it will bend away from the normal as a result of which aeroplane will appear to be higher than its actual position.
(ii) Atmospheric refraction
(iii) Stars seem to be at higher distance than they actually are.

24 Explain, why the Sun overhead at noon, appears white?

Sol. When the Sun is overhead at noon, the light coming from the Sun has to travel a relatively shorter distance through the atmosphere to reach us. Hence only a little of the blue colour of the white light is scattered. Since, the light is coming from the overhead, the Sun has almost all its component colours in the right proportion. Therefore, the Sun in the sky overhead appears white to us.

25 A camera in many ways is similar to the human eye, still there are some basic differences in image formation between the two. Explain.

Sol. (i) In camera, the distance between the lens and the screen can be adjusted but not the focal length of the lens. However, in eye, the ciliary muscles adjust the focal length keeping the distance between the lens and the retina constant.
(ii) The image formed on retina is temporary and its impression is recorded in brain as memory. However, the image formed on the film of camera is a permanent record.

26 Sun is visible two minutes before actual sunrise and two minutes after sunset. Give reason.

Sol. It is because of atmospheric refraction. When the Sun is slightly below the horizon, the light coming from it travels from less dense to more dense air and is refracted downwards. Thus, the Sun appears to be raised and can be seen two minutes before actual sunrise and two minutes after actual sunset.
Refer diagram on page 334.

27 Explain, how scattering of light depends up on particle size?

Sol. Since, scattering $\propto d$, where d is diameter of the particle also, scattering $\propto \dfrac{1}{\text{wavelength}}$.

This means, very fine particles scatter mainly blue light while particles of larger size scatter light of longer wavelength. If the size of the scattering particles is very large, the scattered light may appear white.

28 (a) A narrow beam of white light is incident on three glass objects as shown below. Comment on the nature of behaviour of the emergent beam in all three cases.

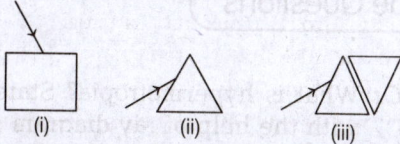

(b) There is a similarity between two of the emergent beam. Identify the two.

Sol. (a) (i) The incident beam of light after refraction through glass slab emerges out parallel to the incident beam but laterally shifted. But no dispersion takes place in this case.
(ii) The incident beam of light after refraction through prism splits into a band of seven colours which are violet, indigo, blue, green, yellow, orange and red. These coloured rays emerge out of the prism along different directions and become distinct. Therefore, dispersion of white light takes place.
(iii) When the incident beam passes through the first prism, it gets splitted into the band of seven colours. But those coloured rays are incident on an identical inverted prism. Then recombination of the coloured rays takes place. This emergent light is parallel to the incident beam but slightly shifted outward.
(b) The emergent beam in the case (i) and (iii) are similar. As in both the cases, the beams emerging are parallel to the incident beam and are slightly shifted.

29 Give reasons:
(a) Red colour is selected for danger signals.
(b) The sky appears dark in space.
(c) The time difference between actual sunset and apparent sunset is about 2 min.

Sol. (a) Scattering of red light is minimum, so danger signals can be seen from far distances.
(b) Sky appears dark in space because there is no atmosphere and hence no scattering of light in space.
(c) We are able to see the Sun 2 minutes before the actual sunrise and 2 minutes after the actual sunset due to refraction of light by the atmosphere.

30 A doctor has prescribed a corrective lens of power – 1.2 D to a person suffering from defect of vision.
(i) Identify the defect from which he is suffering.
(ii) Find the focal length of the lens.
(iii) Is the prescribed lens diverging or converging? Show the nature of this lens with the help of a ray diagram.
CBSE 2012

Sol. (i) He is suffering from myopia because the focal length required for the lens is negative.
(ii) Given, $P = -1.2$ D
$\therefore \quad f = \dfrac{1}{P} \quad \left[\text{where, } P = \text{power of lens and } f = \text{focal length}\right]$
$= \dfrac{1}{-1.2} = \dfrac{-10}{12} = -0.83$ m

(iii) The lens will be diverging because power is negative.

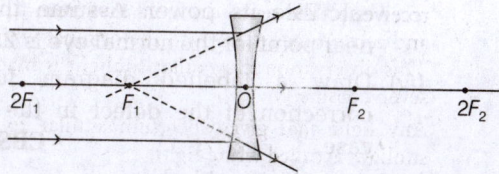

31 (i) Why does the power to see near objects as well as far off objects clearly diminish with age? Name the defects that are likely to arise in eye in such a condition.
(ii) The far point of a myopic eye is 60 cm. Find the focal length of the lens used to correct it. **CBSE 2012**

Sol. (i) The defects arise due to the gradual weakening of the ciliary muscles and diminishing flexibility of the eye lens.

Sometimes, a person may suffer from both myopia and hypermetropia. This condition of defect is called presbyopia. Such people often require bi-focal lenses to correct this defect.

(ii) Using lens formula, $\dfrac{1}{v} - \dfrac{1}{u} = \dfrac{1}{f} \Rightarrow \dfrac{1}{(-60)} = \dfrac{1}{f}$

[given, $v = -60$ cm, $u = \infty$]

$f = -60$ cm

32. (i) Ravi kept a book at a distance of 10 cm from the eyes of his friend Hari. Hari is not able to read anything written on the book. Explain, why?

(ii) A lens of focal length 5 cm is being used by a student in the laboratory as a magnifying glass. His least distance of distinct vision is 25 cm. What magnification is the student getting? **CBSE 2011**

Sol. (i) It happens because the least distance of distinct vision is 25 cm.

(ii) Given, $v = -25$ cm, $f = 5$ cm, $m = ?$

From lens formula,

$\dfrac{1}{f} = \dfrac{1}{v} - \dfrac{1}{u}$

$\Rightarrow \dfrac{1}{u} = \dfrac{1}{v} - \dfrac{1}{f}$

$\Rightarrow \dfrac{1}{u} = \dfrac{1}{-25} - \dfrac{1}{5}$

$= \dfrac{-1-5}{25} = \dfrac{-6}{25}$

$\Rightarrow u = \dfrac{-25}{6}$ cm

We know that, $m = \dfrac{v}{u} = \dfrac{-25 \times 6}{-25}$

$\Rightarrow m = 6$

Long Answer (LA) Type Questions

1. A person is unable to see objects distinctly placed within 50 cm from his eyes.

(i) Name the defect of vision the person is suffering from and list its two possible causes.

(ii) Draw a ray diagram to show the defect in the above case.

(iii) Mention the type of lens used by him for the correction of the defect and calculate its power. Assume that the near point for the normal eye is 25 cm.

(iv) Draw a labelled diagram for the correction of the defect in the above case. **CBSE 2019**

Sol. (i) Person suffering with myopia.

Myopia occurs due to

(a) excessive curvature of eye lens.

(b) elongation of the eye ball.

[(ii), (iii), (iv)] Refer to text on page no. 330 Topic (Myopia or near/short sightedness)

2. What is hypermetropia? List two causes for the development of this defect. Explain the method of correcting this defect with the help of ray diagrams.

Or What is hypermetropia? State two causes with the help of ray diagram show (a) eye defect (b) correction of hypermetropia.

Sol. Refer to text on Pg. 331.

3. (i) Demonstrate an activity with a well labelled diagram to prove that white light is made up of seven colours.

(ii) Which colour of light bends least and which one the most while passing out from the prism? Also state the reason for the same. **CBSE 2015**

Sol. (i) To understand how white light of the Sun is made of seven colours, let us take a thick sheet of cardboard and make a small hole or narrow slit in its middle. Allow sunlight to fall on the slit. This gives a narrow beam of white light. Now, take a glass prism and allow this white light to fall on one of its faces as shown in figure.

Turn the prism slowly until the light that comes out of it appears on a nearby screen. We see a beautiful band of seven colours on a screen called visible spectrum. The sequence of colours seen from the lower part of the screen is violet (V), indigo (I), blue (B), green (G), yellow (Y), orange (O) and red (R). The acronym for this is VIBGYOR.

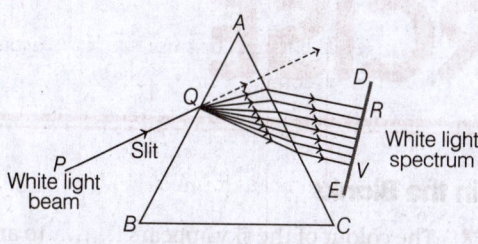

(ii) Red light has the maximum wavelength and violet light has the minimum wavelength, so in any medium, red light bends least while violet light bends the most.

As, wavelength $\propto \dfrac{1}{\text{deviation (or bending)}}$

4 What is atmospheric refraction? Use this phenomenon to explain the following natural events.
   (i) Twinkling of stars.
   (ii) Advanced sunrise and delayed sunset.
Draw diagrams to illustrate your answers.
CBSE 2016

Sol. Refer to text on Pg. 333 (Atmospheric refraction)
   (i) Refer to text on Pg. 333 (Twinkling of stars).
   (ii) Refer to text on Pg. 333 and 334 (Advance sunrise and delayed sunset).

5 What is meant by scattering of light? Mention the factor on which it depends. Explain, why the colour of the clear sky is blue? An astronaut in space finds sky to be dark. Explain reason for this observation.
CBSE 2015

Sol. (i) The reflection of light from an object in all directions is called scattering of light.
The colour of scattered light depends on the size of scattering particles and wavelength of light.
i.e. Scattering $\propto d^6$

[where, d = diameter of particle]

and scattering $\propto \dfrac{1}{\lambda^4}$

[where, λ = wavelength of particle]

(ii) During the day time, sky appears blue. This is because the size of particles in the atmosphere is smaller than the wavelength of visible light, so they are more effective in scattering the light of shorter wavelengths, i.e. blue light.

(iii) For an astronaut, sky appears dark because there is no scattering of light in space due to absence of particles.

6 (i) A student is unable to see clearly the words written on the black board placed at a distance of approximately 3m from him. Name the defect of vision the boy is suffering from. State the possible causes of this defect and explain the method of correcting it.
   (ii) Why do stars twinkle? Explain.
CBSE 2018

Sol. (i) The student is suffering from myopia/near or short sightedness.
Near sightedness is caused due to
   (a) too high converging power of the eye lens.
   (b) eyeball being too long.
To correct this defect of vision, he must use a concave lens. The concave lens of suitable focal length will bring the image back to the retina as shown in the given figure.

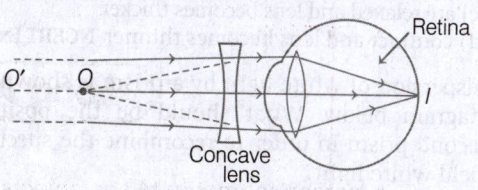

(ii) Refer to text on page 6 (Twinkling of stars).

7 (i) Write the function of each of the following parts of human eye
   (a) Cornea
   (b) Iris
   (c) Crystalline lens
   (d) Ciliary muscles
(ii) Why does the sun appear raddish early in the morning? Will this phenomenon be observed by an astronaut on the moon? Give reason to justify your answer.
CBSE 2018

Sol. (i) [(a), (b), (c) and (d)] Refer to text on Pg. 328 and 329 (Structure of human eye).
(ii) Refer to text on Pg. 334 (Colour of sun at sunrise and sunset).

CHAPTER EXERCISE

Multiple Choice Questions

1. An image is formed on the retina. This is due to
   (a) successive refraction at the retina
   (b) successive refraction at the cornea
   (c) reflection at the cornea
   (d) reflection at the retina

2. When light rays enter the eye, most of the refraction occurs at the
   (a) crystalline lens
   (b) outer surface of the cornea
   (c) iris
   (d) pupil **NCERT Exampler**

3. The focal length of the eye lens increases when eye muscles
   (a) are relaxed and lens becomes thinner
   (b) contract and lens becomes thicker
   (c) are relaxed and lens becomes thicker
   (d) contract and lens becomes thinner **NCERT Exampler**

4. Dispersion of white light by a prism is shown in the diagram below. What should be the position of second prism in order to recombine the spectra and yield white light?

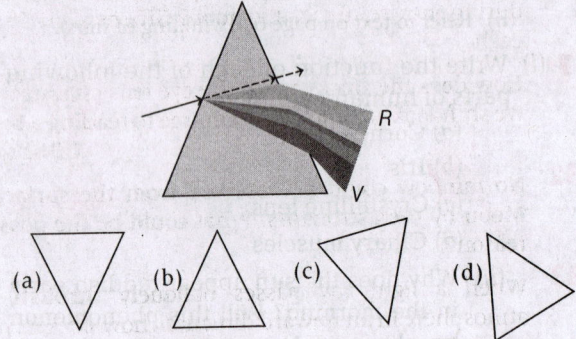

5. Which of the following phenomena is based on atmospheric refraction?
   (a) Tyndall effect
   (b) Colour of sun at sunrise
   (c) Twinkling of stars
   (d) None of the above

6. The colour of scattered light depends on
   (a) size of scattering particles
   (b) wavelength of light
   (c) Both (a) and (b)
   (d) None of the above

Fill in the Blanks

7. The colour of the sky appears .... to an astronaut.

8. The .... controls the amount of light entering the eye.

True and False

9. Colour of eye is determined by the colour of iris.

10. The greyish appearance of sky is due to the presence of smoke and dust particles in the atmosphere.

11. To observe tyndall effect. The size of the scatterer smaller than the wavelength of light.

Match the Columns

12. Match the following with proper sequence:

Column A		Column B
A. Twinkling of stars	p.	Dispersion
B. Rainbow formation	q.	Refraction
C. White colour of clouds	r.	Atmospheric refraction
D. Glittering of diamond	s.	Scattering

Assertion-Reason

Direction (Q. Nos. 13-16) *In each of the following questions, a statement of Assertion is given by the corresponding statement of Reason. Of the statements, mark the correct answer as*
(a) If both Assertion and Reason are true and Reason is the correct explanation of Assertion.
(b) If both Assertion and Reason are true, but Reason is not the correct explanation of Assertion.
(c) If Assertion is true, but Reason is false.
(d) If Assertion is false, but Reason is true.

13. **Assertion** Rainbow is an example of the dispersion of sunlight by the water droplets.
    Reason Light of shorter wavelength is scattered much more than light of larger wavelength.

14. **Assertion** An image formed on retina is real, diminished and inverted in nature.
    Reason The eye lens is convex lens.

15. **Assertion** Red light has the maximum wavelength and violet light has the minimum wavelength.
    Reason Red light deviates least, while violet light deviates maximum.

Human Eye and the Colourful World

16. Assertion A normal eye can see objects clearly, which are at a distance between 25 cm and infinity.

Reason The ability of eye lens to adjust its focal length is called accommodation.

Case Based Questions

Direction (Q.Nos. 17-20) Answers the questions on the basis of your understanding of the following passage and the related studied concepts:

A mirage is a naturally occuring optical phenomenon in which light rays are bent to produce a displaced image of distant objects on the sky. The fluctuations in the refractive index of the earth's atmosphere is responsible for atmospheric refraction. Mirage is one of the example of atmospheric refraction.

In contrast to hallucination, a mirage is a real optical phenomenon that can be captured on camera, since light rays are actually refracted to form the false image at the observer's location, e.g. inferior images on land are very easily mistaken for the reflections from a small water body. Heat-haze, also known as heat swimmer, refers to the inferior which can be experienced when viewing objects through a mirage layer of heated air. A superior mirage occurs when the air below the line of sight is colder than the air above it.

17. How superior and inferior mirage occurs?

18. What is the cause of atmospheric refraction?

19. When light travels from hot air to cold air, then blends
  (a) towards the normal
  (b) away from the normal
  (c) towards the normal and scatter
  (d) away from the normal and scatter

20. Mirage is formed because of
  (a) bending of light because of multiple layers of atmosphere having different densities
  (b) bending of light because of temperature difference of air
  (c) dispersion of light because of temperature difference of air
  (d) scattering of light because of temperature difference of air

Very Short Answer Type Questions

21. Which part of eye acts as a cable which connects the eye with the brain?

22. What will be the focal length of eye lens when eye muscles are relaxed?

23. Name the condition of the eye lens becoming cloudy. **CBSE 2012**

24. Our eye is sensitive for which range of wavelength of light?

Short Answer (SA) Type Questions

25. Name the part of the eye where image is formed by the eye lens. What is the nature of the image formed? How is this image sent to the brain?

26. State the role of ciliary muscles in accommodation. **CBSE 2012**

27. Why we have two eyes to view the objects?

28. A boy uses spectacles of focal length – 60 cm. Name the defect of vision he is suffering from. Which lens is used for the correction of this defect? Compute the power of this lens.

[Ans. Myopia, (–5/3) D]

29. What is the result of dispersion of white light?

30. What is the difference in colours of the Sun observed during sunrise/sunset and noon? Give explanation for each.

31. How does the thickness of the eye lens change when we shift looking from a distant tree to reading a book? **CBSE 2012**

32. No rainbow could be observed from the surface of Moon by the astronauts. What could be the possible reason?

33. When a light ray passes obliquely through the atmosphere in an upward direction, how does its path generally change?

34. The minimum power of eye lens is 40 D. If the far point of normal eye is infinity, find the size of the eye ball. **CBSE 2012**

35. A person got his eyes tested. The optician prescription for the spectacles read.

Left eye = –3 D and right eye = –3.5 D

Discuss the defects from which person is suffering.

36. The power of a lens is +1.5 D. Name the type of defects of vision that can be corrected by using this lens. Find the focal length of the lens.

Answers

1. (b) 2. (b) 3. (a) 4. (a) 5. (c) 6. (c)
7. black 8. iris 9. True 10. True 11. False
12. (A) → (r), (B) → (p), (C) → (s), (D) → (q)
13. (b) 14. (b) 15. (a) 16. (a)
19. (a) 20. (b)

354

37 If the far point of eye lens is 10 m, find power of the lens required to correct the defect.

38 Mention the position where image is focussed in the eye of a person having hypermetropia. **CBSE 2012**

39 A person is able to see objects clearly only when these are lying at distance between 50 cm and 300 cm from his eyes. Name the kind of defects of vision he is suffering from. **CBSE 2012**

40 What will be the angle of deviation through a prism angle 60°, when angles of incidence and emergence are 45° each? [**Ans.** 30°.]

Long Answer (LA) Type Questions

41 (i) List the parts of the human eye that control the amount of light entering into it. Explain, how they perform this function?
(ii) Write the function of retina in human eye.

(iii) Do you know that the corneal-impairment can be cured by replacing the defective cornea with the cornea of the donated eye? How and why should we organise groups to motivate the community members to donate their eyes after death? **CBSE 2014**

42 A student finds the writing on the blackboard as blurred and unclear when sitting on the last desk of the classroom. He however sees clearly when sitting on the front desk at an approximate distance 2 m from the blackboard.
(i) Draw the ray diagram to illustrate the formation of image of the blackboard writing by his eye lens when he sits at the (a) last desk, (b) front desk.
(ii) Name the defect of vision the student is suffering from. Also, list two causes of this defect.
(iii) Name the kind of lens that would enable him to see clearly when he is seated at the last desk. Draw the ray diagram to illustrate how this lens helps him to see clearly. **CBSE 2011**

Challengers*

1 For a healthy eye, the rays of light entering the eye form a sharp image on retina. For a myopic eye, the rays from distant objects focus in front of the retina forming a blurred image. Which of the following lenses shown below will help to correct myopia?

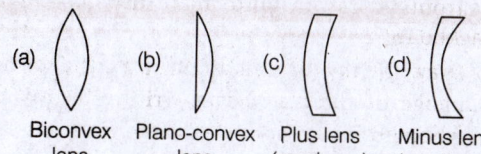

(a) Biconvex lens (b) Plano-convex lens (c) Plus lens (meniscus) (d) Minus lens (meniscus)

2 A near sighted person wears eye glass of power 5.5D for distant vision. His doctor prescribes a correction of + 1D in near vision part of his bi-focals, which is measured relative to the main part of the lens. Then, the focal length of his near vision part of the lens is

(a) −18.18 cm   (b) −20 cm
(c) −22.22 cm   (d) +20.22 cm

3 In given figure, a light ray AB is incident normally on one face PQ of an equilateral glass prism.
Find out the angles at faces PQ and PR.

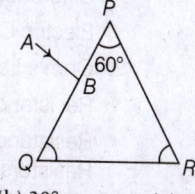

(a) 60°   (b) 30°   (c) 45°   (d) 90°

4 A thin prism P_1 with angle 4° and made from glass of refractive index 1.54 is combined with another prism P_2 made from glass of refractive index 1.92 to produce dispersion without deviation. Then, the angle of the prism P_2 is

(a) 2.3°   (b) 4.3°   (c) 3.2°   (d) 2.0°

5 Light rays are deviated by a prism

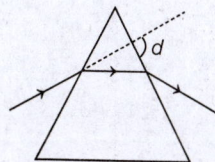

The deviation angle d is measured for light rays of different frequency, including blue light and red light. Which graph is correct?

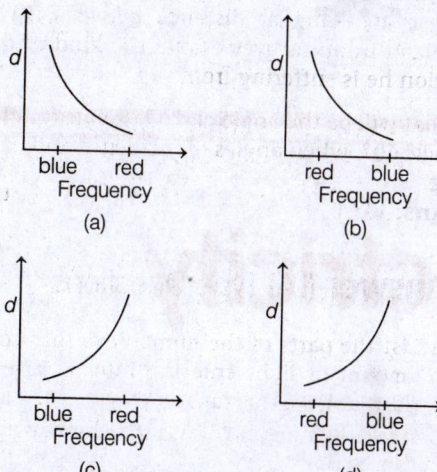

6 Even in absolutely clear water, a diver cannot see very clearly because

(a) rays of lights get diffused
(b) velocity of light is reduced in water
(c) ray of light passing through the water makes it turbid.
(d) the focal length of the eye lens in water gets changed and the image is no longer focussed sharply on the retina.

7 A glass slab is placed over a page on which the word VIBGYOR is printed with each letter in corresponding colour. Then, which of the following is correct?

(a) The images of all the letters will be in the same place as that on paper
(b) Letter V is raised more
(c) Letter R is raised more
(d) None of the above

8 Which amongst the given radiation is preferred for taking photographs in fog?

(a) Ordinary visible light   (b) Infrared
(c) Microwave   (d) X-rays

Answer Key

1.	(d)	2.	(c)	3.	(a)	4.	(a)	5.	(d)
6.	(d)	7.	(b)	8.	(b)				

*These questions may or may not be asked in the examination, have been given just for additional practice.

CHAPTER 11

Electricity

One of the most essential part of life in today's world is **electricity**. It is a controllable and convenient form of energy. It is being used in almost every sector of modern society like households, commercial, transport and industry, etc., to make life faster and easier.

Chapter Checklist

- Electric Charge and Current
- Electric Potential and Potential Difference
- Electric Circuit
- Ohm's Law
- Resistance
- Resistance of a System of Resistors
- Heating Effect of Electric Current
- Electric Power

Electric Charge and Current

Electric Charge

A charge is a physical entity which is defined by excess or deficiency of electrons on a body.

A body is said to be **negatively charged**, if it **gains** electrons. e.g. An ebonite rod rubbed with fur acquires negative charge. A body is said to be **positively charged**, if it **loses** electrons. e.g. A glass rod rubbed with a silk cloth acquires positive charge.

The SI unit of electric charge is **coulomb** (C), which is equivalent to the charged contained in nearly 6×10^{18} electrons.

The total charge acquired by a body is an integral multiple of magnitude of charge on a single electron. This principle is called **quantisation of charge**.

- Magnitude of charge on one electron, $e = -1.6 \times 10^{-19}$ C.
- Charge on n electrons, $q = ne = n \times 1.6 \times 10^{-19}$ C.
- Magnitude of charge on one proton, $e = +1.6 \times 10^{-19}$ C.

Electric Current

It is defined as the rate of flow of electric charge through any cross-section of a conductor in unit time.

If q amount of charges flows through a conductor in t time, then

$$\text{Electric current } (I) = \frac{\text{Charge } (q)}{\text{Time } (t)} = \frac{ne}{t} \qquad [\because q = ne]$$

where, n = number of electrons flowing through the conductor.

All in one Electricity

The SI unit of electric current is **ampere** (A), named in honour of French scientist Andre-Marie Ampere (1775-1836). It is a scalar quantity.

When 1 coulomb of charge flows through any cross-section of a conductor in 1 second, then the electric current flowing through it is said to be 1 ampere.

i.e. $1 \text{ ampere} = \dfrac{1 \text{ coulomb}}{1 \text{ second}} \Rightarrow 1\text{A} = \dfrac{1\text{ C}}{1\text{s}}$

Smaller units of current are **milliampere** (1 mA = 10^{-3} A) and **microampere** (1 μA = 10^{-6} A).

Direction of Electric Current

The direction of electric current is taken as opposite to the direction of the flow of electrons (negative charges). In an electric circuit the current flows from positive terminal of the cell to the negative terminal.

Flow of Charges Inside a Wire

Inside a solid, the atoms are packed together very closely to each other but electrons are able to travel through the solid crystal as if they were in vacuum. When a steady current flows in a conductor, then the electrons in it move with a certain average **drift speed** (the constant speed of the electrons inside the conductor with which they move under the effect of external electric supply) of the order of 10^{-4} m/s. Thus, flow of charges (i.e. electrons) produces current in a wire.

Ammeter
Electric current is measured by a device called ammeter. It is a low resistance device which is always connected in series with the device through which the current is to be measured.

Example 1. *A current of 150 mA flows through a circuit for 2 min. Find the amount of charge that flows through the circuit.*

Sol. Given, Current, $I = 150 \text{ mA} = 150 \times 10^{-3}$ A
Time, $t = 2 \text{ min} = 2 \times 60 = 120$ s
Amount of charge, $q = ?$
We know that, $q = I \times t$
$\Rightarrow \quad q = 150 \times 10^{-3} \times 120$
$\Rightarrow \quad q = 18$ C
So, 18 C of charge flows around the circuit.

Example 2. *A total of 6×10^{46} electrons flow through a current carrying conductor when connected through an external power supply for 20 s. Find the value of current in the conductor.*

Sol. Given, Total number of electrons, $n = 6 \times 10^{46}$ electrons
Time, $t = 20$ s, Current, $I = ?$
We know that, $q = ne$ ...(i)
[from the principle of quantisation of electric charge]
and $I = \dfrac{q}{t}$ ...(ii)

From Eqs. (i) and (ii), we get
$I = \dfrac{ne}{t} = \dfrac{6 \times 10^{46} \times 1.6 \times 10^{-19}}{20}$ [∵ $e = 1.6 \times 10^{-19}$ C]
$= 0.48 \times 10^{27}$ A $= 4.8 \times 10^{26}$ A

Thus, the current through the conductor is 4.8×10^{26} A.

Electric Potential and Potential Difference

Electric Potential

It is defined as the amount of work done when a unit positive charge is moved from infinity to a point.

If work done in moving a positive charge q from infinity to a point is W, then electric potential V of that point is

$$V = \dfrac{W}{q}$$

The SI unit of electric potential is **volt** (V) and is named after Italian physicist Alessandro Volta (1745-1827). It is a scalar quantity.

Electric Potential Difference (ΔV)

The electric potential difference between two points is defined as the work done in moving a unit positive charge from one point to other point.

The electric potential difference between two points in a current carrying conductor is said to be **1 volt**, if 1 joule of work is done in moving 1 coulomb of electric charge from one point to other point.

Thus, $1 \text{ volt} = \dfrac{1 \text{ joule}}{1 \text{ coulomb}}$

$\Rightarrow \quad 1\text{V} = \dfrac{1\text{J}}{1\text{C}}$

$\Rightarrow \quad 1\text{V} = 1\text{J/C} = 1\text{JC}^{-1}$

Smaller units of electric potential,
$1 \text{ mV} = 10^{-3}$ V, $1 \text{μV} = 10^{-6}$ V

Larger units of electric potential,
$1 \text{ kV} = 10^3$ V, $1 \text{ MV} = 10^6$ V

Voltmeter

The electric potential difference between two points in a circuit is measured using a device called voltmeter. It is a high resistance device which is always connected in parallel with the component(s) through which potential difference is to be measured.

Example 3. *How much work is done in moving a charge of 3 C across two points having a potential difference 15 V?*

Sol. Given, Charge, $q = 3C$ and Potential difference, $\Delta V = 15V$

The amount of work done in moving the charge
$$W = Vq = 15 \times 3 = 45 \text{ J}$$

Example 4. *Calculate the potential difference between two terminals of a battery, if 100 J of work is required to transfer the charge of 20 C from one terminal of the battery to the other.*

Sol. Given, Work done, $W = 100$ J; Charge, $q = 20$ C
Potential difference, $\Delta V = ?$
We know that, $\Delta V = \dfrac{W}{q} = \dfrac{100}{20} = 5$ V

The potential difference between two points is 5 V.

Example 5. *How much work is done in moving a charge of 2 C from a point of 118 V to a point at 128 V?*

Sol. Given, Charge, $q = 2$ C;
Potential at point A, $V_A = 118$ V;
Potential at point B, $V_B = 128$ V; Work done, $W = ?$
We know that,
Potential difference, $\Delta V = V_B - V_A = 128 - 118 = 10$ V
$\therefore$ Work done, $W = \Delta V \times q = 10 \times 2 = 20$ J
So, the work done in moving the charge is 20 J.

Check Point 01

1. Fill in the blanks:
   (i) The electric potential difference between two points in a circuit is measured using a device called ....
   (ii) Direction of flow of electric current in conductor is taken in opposite direction of movement of ....
2. True and False for the following statements:
   (i) Ammeter is a high resistance device which is always connected in parallel.
   (ii) The SI unit of electric potential difference is J/C.
3. If a body has positive charge, then what does it mean?
4. In which direction does current flow in an electric circuit?
5. The charge on an electron is 1.6×10^{-19} C. Find the number of electrons that will flow per second to constitute a current of 2A.
6. If work done in moving a charge of 20 mC from infinity to a point O in an electric field is 15 J, then what is the electric potential at this point?

Electric Circuit

A closed and continuous path through which electric current flows is known as electric circuit. It has various components including a **source of current** (say a cell or battery), **a load** (say a bulb or any other appliance), a **switch/key** (to open or close a circuit), **a fuse**, all connected through connecting wires. These wires are generally made of copper.

When the key is closed, then the circuit is called **closed circuit**. This means that current would flow through the circuit to operate the device. When the key is open, then the circuit is called **open circuit**. This means that current would not flow through the circuit.

Circuit Diagram

It is a schematic diagram which represents the relative positions and connections of various circuit components represented by their symbols.

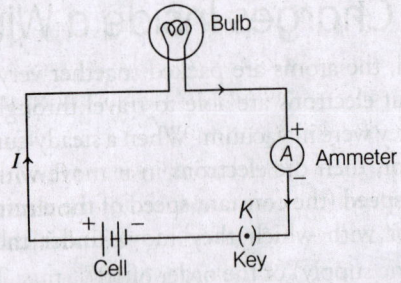

A schematic diagram of an electric circuit having cell, electric bulb, ammeter and plug key

Symbols used in Electric Circuits

Circuit Components	Descriptions	Symbols
An electric cell	Provides constant potential difference between two points	
Battery	Combination of two or more cells connected in series	
Switch or Plug key (open)	Open the circuit	—( )— or
Switch or Plug key (closed)	Close the circuit	—(•)— or
Wires joint	—	
Wires crossing without joining (or touching)	—	

Circuit Components	Descriptions	Symbols
Electric bulb	Circuit components	—⊗— or —⊗—
Resistor or resistance	Controls current flowing through the circuit	—⟋⟍⟋⟍—
Rheostat or variable resistance	Provides variable resistance or potential divider	—⟋⟍⟋⟍— or —⟋⟍⟋⟍—
Ammeter	Measures current flowing through circuit	—(A)—
Voltmeter	Measures potential difference between two points	—(V)—
Fuse	Safety device	—o o—

Ohm's Law

This law was given by a German Physicist **Georg Simon Ohm** (1787-1854) in the year 1827. It gives a relationship between **current** I, flowing in a metallic wire and **potential difference** V, across its terminals.

According to this law, the electric current flowing through a conductor is directly proportional to the potential difference applied across its ends, providing the physical conditions (such as temperature) remain unchanged.

If V is the potential difference applied across the ends of a conductor through which current I flows, then according to Ohm's law,

$$V \propto I \quad \text{[at constant temperature]}$$

or $\boxed{V = IR}$ or $\boxed{I = \dfrac{V}{R}}$

where, R is the constant of proportionality called **resistance of the conductor** at a given temperature.

From the above formula, it is clear that current is inversely proportional to resistance. If resistance is doubled, then current gets halved and if resistance is halved, then current gets doubled.

Note The conductors which obey Ohm's law are called ohmic conductors while the conductors which do not obey Ohm's law are called non-ohmic conductors.

V-I Graph

The graph between the potential difference V and the corresponding current I is found to be a straight line passing through the origin for ohmic (metallic) conductors.

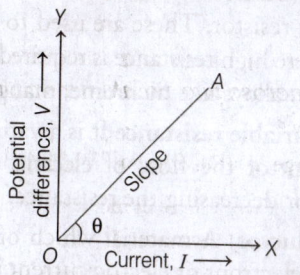

V-I graph for metallic conductor

Resistance

It is that property of a conductor by virtue of which it opposes/resists the flow of charges/flow of current through it. Its SI unit is **ohm** and is represented by the Greek letter Ω.

Resistance of a conductor is given by $R = \dfrac{V}{I}$.

It is said to be 1 ohm, if a potential difference of 1 volt across the ends of the conductor makes a current of 1 ampere to flow through it.

i.e. $\quad 1 \text{ ohm} = \dfrac{1 \text{ volt}}{1 \text{ ampere}}$

$\Rightarrow \quad 1\Omega = \dfrac{1 \text{ V}}{1 \text{ A}} = 1 \text{ VA}^{-1}$

Example 6. *The potential difference between the terminals of an electric heater is 75 V when it draws a current of 5 A from the source. What current will the heater draw, if the potential difference is increased to 150 V?*

Sol. Given, Potential difference, $V = 75$ V
Current, $I = 5$ A
We know that, $R = \dfrac{V}{I} \Rightarrow R = \dfrac{75}{5} = 15 \, \Omega$

When potential difference is increased to 150 V, then current is

$$I' = \dfrac{I}{R} = \dfrac{150}{15} = 10 \text{ A}$$

So, the current through the heater becomes 10 A.

Some Important Terms Related to Resistance

Some important terms related to resistance are as follows:

- **Resistor** A component in an electric circuit which offers resistance to the flow of electrons constituting electric current is known as resistor. These are used to make those electrical devices, where high resistance is required. It reduces current in a circuit, e.g. alloys like nichrome, manganin and constantan.
- **Rheostat/variable resistance** It is a variable resistor, which is used to control the flow of electric current by manually increasing or decreasing the resistance.
- **Good conductor** A material which offers low resistance to the flow of electrons or electric current in an electric circuit is known as a good conductor, e.g. silver, copper, aluminium. Amongst these, silver is the best conductor of electricity.
- **Poor conductor** A material which offers higher resistance than conductors to the flow of electrons or electric current in an electric circuit is known as poor conductor, e.g. mercury, lead, stainless steel, alloys of iron and chromium.
- **Insulator** A material which offers very high resistance to the flow of electrons or electric current in an electric circuit is known as insulator, e.g. rubber, dry wood and plastic. Electric current does not flow through them.

Factors on which the Resistance of a Conductor Depends

The electrical resistance of a conductor depends on the following factors:

(i) **Length of the conductor** The resistance of a conductor R is directly proportional to its length l.

i.e. $$\boxed{R \propto l} \qquad \ldots(i)$$

Since, the resistance of a wire is directly proportional to its length, i.e. when the length of a wire is doubled/halved, then its resistance also gets doubled/halved.

(ii) **Area of cross-section of the conductor** The resistance of a conductor R is inversely proportional to its area of cross-section A.

i.e. $$\boxed{R \propto \frac{1}{A}} \qquad \ldots(ii)$$

Since, the resistance of a wire is inversely proportional to its area of cross-section, i.e. when the area of cross-section of wire is doubled, then its resistance gets halved and if area of cross-section of wire is halved, then its resistance will get doubled.

Note When a conductor is stretched (increased its length), then its area of cross-section decreases accordingly but the volume (i.e. area × length) of the conductor remains the same.

(iii) **Nature of the material of the conductor** The resistance of a conductor depends on the nature of the material of which it is made. Some materials have low resistance, whereas others have high resistance.

Therefore, from Eqs. (i) and (ii), we can write

$$R \propto \frac{l}{A} \quad \text{or} \quad \boxed{R = \rho \frac{l}{A}}$$

where, ρ is the constant of proportionality and is called **electric resistivity** or **specific resistance** of the material of the conductor.

Resistivity

It is defined as the resistance of a conductor of unit length and unit area of cross-section. Its SI unit is **ohm-metre** (Ω-m).

The resistivity of a material does not depend on its length or thickness but depends on the nature of the substance and temperature. It is a characteristic property of the material of the conductor and varies only, if its temperature changes.

Insulators such as glass, rubber, ebonite, etc., have a very high resistivity (10^{12} to 10^{17} Ω-m), while conductors have a very low resistivity (10^{-8} to 10^{-6} Ω-m).

Alloys have higher resistivity than that of their constituent metals. They do not oxidise easily at high temperatures, this is why they are used to make heating elements of divices such as electric iron, heaters, etc. Tungsten is almost used exclusively for filaments of electric bulbs, whereas copper and aluminium are generally used for electrical transmission lines.

Example 7. *A wire of given material having length l and area of cross-section A has a resistance of 10 Ω. What would be the resistance of another wire of the same material having length l/4 and area of cross-section 2.5 A?*

Sol. For first wire, Length = l, Area of cross-section = A
and Resistance, $R_1 = 10\ \Omega$,

i.e. $$R_1 = \frac{\rho l}{A} = 10\ \Omega \Rightarrow \rho = \frac{10A}{l} \qquad \ldots(i)$$

For second wire, length = $l/4$, area of cross-section = $2.5 A$

$\therefore$ Resistance, $R_2 = \rho \frac{l/4}{2.5 A} = \frac{10A}{l} \cdot \frac{l}{4 \times 2.5 A}$ [from Eq. (i)]

$$= 1\ \Omega$$

So, the resistance of that wire is 1 Ω.

Alli∩one Electricity

Example 8. *Resistance of a metal wire of length 2 m is 30 Ω at temperature 25°C. If the diameter of the wire is 0.6 mm, then what will be the resistivity of the metal at that temperature?*

Sol. Given, Length of wire, $l = 2$ m

Resistance, $R = 30\ \Omega$,
Temperature, $T = 25°C$
Diameter of wire, $d = 0.6$ mm $= 6 \times 10^{-4}$ m
Resistivity of the wire, $\rho = ?$

We know that, $\rho = \dfrac{RA}{l} = \dfrac{R\pi d^2}{4l}$ $\left[\because A = \dfrac{\pi d^2}{4}\right]$

$= \dfrac{30 \times \pi \times (6 \times 10^{-4})^2}{4 \times 2}$

$= 4.24 \times 10^{-6}$ Ω-m

The resistivity of the metal at 25°C is 4.24×10^{-6} Ω-m.

Check Point 02

1. Fill in the blanks:
    (i) When the length of a conductor is increased to double, then its resistivity ....
    (ii) The resistance of conducting wire is .... proportional to its length.

2. True and False for the following statements:
    (i) If the length of wire is halved and its cross-sectional area is doubled, then its resistance would be decreased to one fourth.
    (ii) The ratio of electric current flowing through the conductor to potential difference applied across the conductor at constant temperature is called resistance of conductor.

3. What does it mean a circuit is closed or open?

4. A student made an electric circuit as shown below

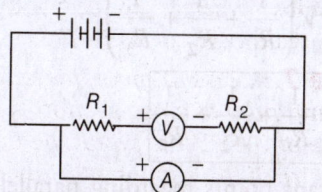

   Is there any mistake in this circuit? If any then correct it.

5. Define the electric resistance of a wire and also write its SI unit.

6. Keeping the potential difference constant, the resistance of a circuit is halved. Then, how much does the current changes?

7. What is the difference between a good conductor and a poor conductor? Give two examples of each.

8. The potential difference across a wire is 75V and its electric resistance is 30 Ω. Find out the electric current through the wire. **[Ans. 2.5A]**

Resistance of a System of Resistors

Two or more resistors can be connected with each other by different combinational methods in order to achieve the desired equivalent resistance in a particular circuit. There are two methods of joining the resistors together which are as given below:

Resistors in Series

When two or more resistors are connected end to end to each other, then they are said to be **connected in series**. The following figure shows the connection of resistors in series.

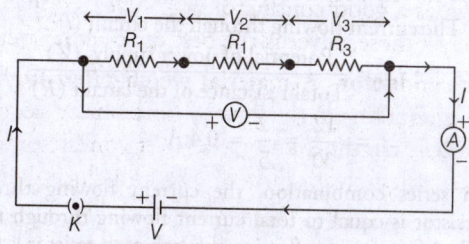

Series Combination of Resistors

An applied potential V produces current I in the resistors and R_1, R_2 and R_3 causing a potential drop V_1, V_2 and V_3 respectively, through each resistor.

Total potential, $\quad V = V_1 + V_2 + V_3$

By Ohm's law, $\quad V_1 = IR_1$,
$\quad V_2 = IR_2$ and $V_3 = IR_3$

Thus, $V = V_1 + V_2 + V_3 = IR_1 + IR_2 + IR_3$

$\Rightarrow \quad V = I(R_1 + R_2 + R_3)$

If R is the equivalent resistance and $V = IR$

Hence, $\quad IR = I(R_1 + R_2 + R_3)$

$\Rightarrow \quad \boxed{R = R_1 + R_2 + R_3}$

Some important points regarding series combination of resistors are as follows:

- The equivalent resistance is equal to the sum of the all individual resistances.
- The equivalent resistance is thus greater than the resistances of either resistor. This is also known as **maximum effective resistance**.
- The current through each resistor is same.
- The potential difference across each resistor is different.

Example 9. *Three resistors of 5 Ω, 10 Ω and 15 Ω are connected in series with a 12 V power supply. Calculate their combined resistance, the current that flows in the circuit and in each resistor and the potential difference across each resistor.*

Sol. Given, $R_1 = 5\Omega$, $R_2 = 10\Omega$, $R_3 = 15\Omega$, $V = 12V$,
$R = ?$, $I = ?$ and $V_1, V_2, V_3 = ?$

According to question, the three resistors are connected in series combination, then equivalent resistance,
$R = R_1 + R_2 + R_3 = 5 + 10 + 15 = 30 \Omega$

∴ The current flowing through the circuit (I)
$= \dfrac{\text{Potential of power supply }(V)}{\text{Total resistance of the circuit }(R)}$
$= \dfrac{12}{30} = \dfrac{2}{5} = 0.4$ A

In series combination, the current flowing through each resistor is equal to total current flowing through the circuit. Therefore, current flowing through each resistor is 0.4 A.

∴ Potential difference across first resistor,
$V_1 = IR_1 = 0.4 \times 5 = 2$ V
Potential difference across second resistor,
$V_2 = IR_2 = 0.4 \times 10 = 4$ V
and potential difference across third resistor,
$V_3 = IR_3 = 0.4 \times 15 = 6$ V

Example 10. *Study the following electric circuit. Find the readings of (i) the ammeter and (ii) the voltmeter.*

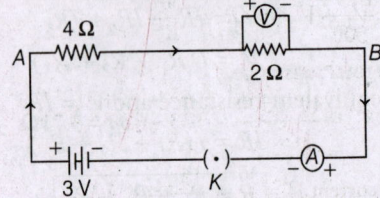

Sol. In the given circuit, the resistance of 4 Ω and bulb resistance of 2 Ω are connected in series, so equivalent resistance of the circuit,
$R = R_1 + R_2 = 4\Omega + 2\Omega = 6\Omega$

(i) Total current flowing in the circuit, (I)
$= \dfrac{\text{Potential difference }(V)}{\text{Total resistance }(R)} = \dfrac{3}{6} = 0.5$ A

In series combination, current flowing through each component of the circuit is same and is equal to the total current flowing in the circuit. So, 0.5 A current will flow through the ammeter, so its reading will be 0.5 A.

(ii) Reading of voltmeter = Potential difference across 2 Ω bulb
∴ $V = IR = 0.5 \times 2 = 1$ V
[∵ current flowing through the bulb is 0.5 A]

Disadvantages of Series Combination

(i) In this combination, if any of the component fails to work, then the circuit will break and none of the components will work.

(ii) It is not possible to connect a bulb and a heater in series simultaneously because they need different values of current to operate properly.

Resistors in Parallel

When two or more resistors are connected simultaneously between two points to each other, then they are said to be connected in parallel combination. The following figure shows the connection of resistors in parallel

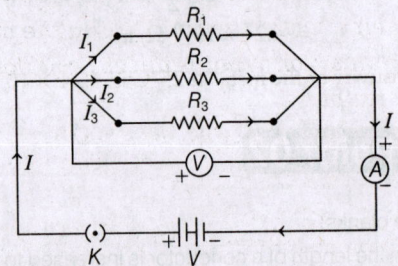

An applied potential difference V produces current I_1 in R_1, I_2 in R_2 and I_3 in R_3.

Total current, $I = I_1 + I_2 + I_3$ ...(i)

By Ohm's law, $I_1 = \dfrac{V}{R_1}$, $I_2 = \dfrac{V}{R_2}$ and $I_3 = \dfrac{V}{R_3}$

If R is the equivalent resistance, then $I = \dfrac{V}{R}$

Thus, $\dfrac{V}{R} = \dfrac{V}{R_1} + \dfrac{V}{R_2} + \dfrac{V}{R_3}$ [from Eq. (i)]

$\Rightarrow \dfrac{V}{R} = V\left(\dfrac{1}{R_1} + \dfrac{1}{R_2} + \dfrac{1}{R_3}\right)$

$\Rightarrow \boxed{\dfrac{1}{R} = \dfrac{1}{R_1} + \dfrac{1}{R_2} + \dfrac{1}{R_3}}$

Some important points regarding parallel combination of resistors are as follows:

- The reciprocal of equivalent resistance is equal to the sum of the reciprocal of individual resistances.
- The equivalent resistance is less than the resistance of either resistor. This is also known as **minimum effective resistance**.
- The current from the source is greater than the current through either resistor.
- The potential difference across each resistor is same.

Applications of Parallel Combination in Daily Life

Parallel combination of resistances is highly useful in circuits used in daily life, as the circuits used have components of different resistances requiring different amounts of current.

This type of combination in a circuit divides the current among the components (electrical gadgets), so that they can have necessary amount of current to operate properly. This is the reason of connecting electrical appliances in parallel combination in household circuit.

Example 11. *Two 40 Ω resistors and a 20 Ω resistor are all connected in parallel with a 12 V power supply. Calculate their effective resistance and the current through each resistor. What is the current flowing through the supply?*

Sol. Given, $R_1 = 40\Omega$, $R_2 = 40\Omega$, $R_3 = 20\Omega$,
$V = 12V, R = ?, I, I_1, I_2, I_3 = ?$

According to circuit, the three resistors are connected in parallel combination, then effective resistance,

$$\frac{1}{R} = \frac{1}{R_1} + \frac{1}{R_2} + \frac{1}{R_3} = \frac{1}{40} + \frac{1}{40} + \frac{1}{20}$$

$$= \frac{1+1+2}{40} = \frac{4}{40} = \frac{1}{10}$$

$$\Rightarrow R = 10 \Omega$$

So, the three resistors together have an effective resistance of 10 Ω. Each resistor has a potential difference of 12 V across it. Because in parallel combination, the potential difference across each resistance is equal to the total potential difference applied on the combination.

We know that,

$$\text{Current}(I) = \frac{\text{Potential difference }(V)}{\text{Resistance }(R)}$$

We get the following results for the current:

Current through 40 Ω resistor, $I_1 = \frac{12}{40} = 0.3$ A

Also, $I_2 = 0.3$ A

Current through 20 Ω resistor, $I_3 = \frac{12}{20} = 0.6$ A

∴ Current, $I = I_1 + I_2 + I_3 = 0.3$ A $+ 0.3$ A $+ 0.6$ A
$= 1.2$ A

Problem Based on Combination of Resistors (Series and Parallel Both)

In this combination, circuit has some resistances connected in **series combination** and some in **parallel combination**. This type of combination is also called **complex circuit**. The following are some examples which will help you to solve questions on combination of resistances in series and parallel both.

Example 12. *In the given figure, $R_1 = 5 \Omega$, $R_2 = 10 \Omega$, $R_3 = 15 \Omega$, $R_4 = 20 \Omega$, $R_5 = 25 \Omega$ and a 15V battery is connected to the arrangement. Calculate*
(i) the total resistance in the circuit, and
(ii) the total current flowing in the circuit.

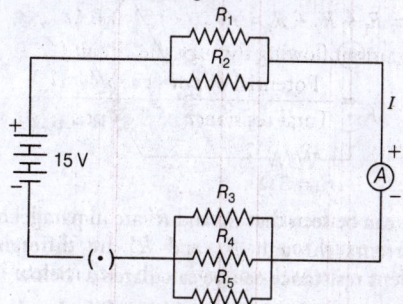

Sol. Resistors R_1 and R_2 are in parallel.

So, $\frac{1}{R'} = \frac{1}{R_1} + \frac{1}{R_2} \Rightarrow \frac{1}{R'} = \frac{1}{5} + \frac{1}{10} \Rightarrow R' = \frac{10}{3} \Omega$

Similarly, R_3, R_4 and R_5 are in parallel

$\Rightarrow \frac{1}{R''} = \frac{1}{R_3} + \frac{1}{R_4} + \frac{1}{R_5} = \frac{1}{15} + \frac{1}{20} + \frac{1}{25}$

$\frac{1}{R''} = \frac{20+15+12}{300} \Rightarrow R'' = \frac{300}{47}$

Thus, the total resistance,

$R = R' + R'' = \frac{10}{3} + \frac{300}{47} = 3.33 + 6.38 = 9.71 \Omega$

The total current, $I = \frac{V}{R} = \frac{15}{9.71} = 1.54$ A

Example 13. *Consider the circuit diagram as given below*

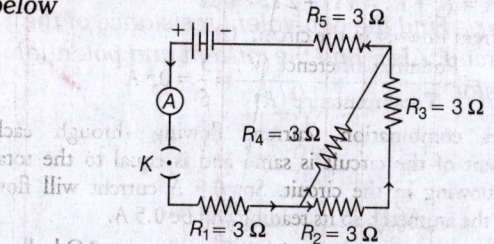

If $R_1 = R_2 = R_3 = R_4 = R_5 = 3 \Omega$, then find the equivalent resistance of the circuit.

Sol. From the combination, it can be observed that R_2 and R_3 are in series order.

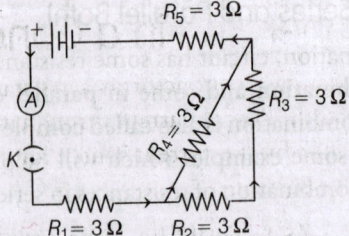

As current through R_2 and R_3 is same. So, their equivalent resistance is $R' = R_2 + R_3 = 3\,\Omega + 3\,\Omega = 6\,\Omega$

Now, the given circuit can be redrawn as shown below

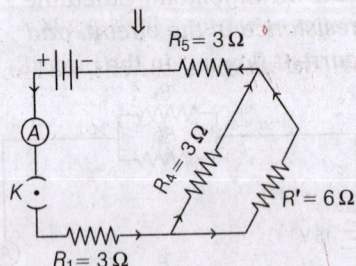

Now, it can be seen that R_4 and R' are in parallel combination. As, currents through R_4 and R' are different. So, their equivalent resistance can be calculated as below

$$\frac{1}{R''} = \frac{1}{R'} + \frac{1}{R_4} = \frac{1}{6} + \frac{1}{3} = \frac{1+2}{6} = \frac{3}{6} = \frac{1}{2}$$

$$\therefore \quad R'' = 2\,\Omega$$

Now, the given circuit can be redrawn as shown below

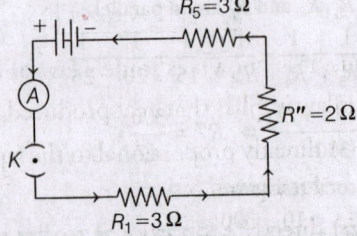

Now, it is clear from the above circuit that all the resistances R_5, R'' and R_1 are in series combination.

As, current through R_1, R'' and R_5 is same.

∴ Equivalent resistance of the circuit is

$$R = R_5 + R'' + R_1 = 3\,\Omega + 2\,\Omega + 3\,\Omega = 8\,\Omega$$

Example 14. *Find the equivalent resistance of the following circuit. Also, find the current and potential at each resistor.*

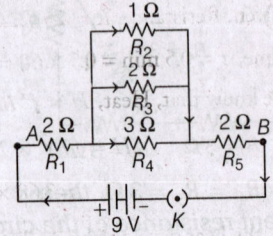

Sol. In the given circuit, R_2, R_3 and R_4 are in parallel combination. As, currents through R_2, R_3 and R_4 are different. So, their equivalent resistance R is

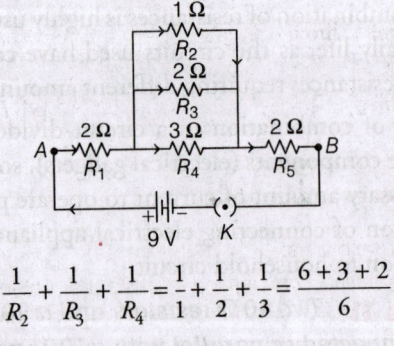

$$\frac{1}{R'} = \frac{1}{R_2} + \frac{1}{R_3} + \frac{1}{R_4} = \frac{1}{1} + \frac{1}{2} + \frac{1}{3} = \frac{6+3+2}{6} = \frac{11}{6}$$

$$\Rightarrow R' = \frac{6}{11}\,\Omega$$

Now, the given circuit can be redrawn as shown below

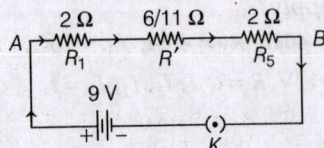

Now, R_1, R' and R_5 are in series combination. As, current through R_1, R' and R_5 is same.

So, equivalent resistance of the whole circuit is

$$R = R_1 + R' + R_5 = 2 + \frac{6}{11} + 2 = \frac{22 + 6 + 22}{11} = \frac{50}{11}\,\Omega$$

Now, total current flowing through the circuit,

$$I = \frac{V}{R} = \frac{9}{\frac{50}{11}} = \frac{99}{50} \approx 2\,A$$

Current through R_1 and R_5 will be same as these are in series combination and will be equal to the total current flowing through the circuit.

$$\therefore \qquad I = I_1 = I_5 = 2\,A$$

Potential drop at R_1, $V_1 = I_1 R_1 = 2 \times 2 = 4\,V$

Potential drop at R_5, $V_5 = I_5 R_5 = 2 \times 2 = 4\,V$

Now, potential drop at R', V' can be calculated as

$$V = V_1 + V_5 + V'$$

$$\Rightarrow 9 = 4 + 4 + V'$$

$$\Rightarrow V' = 1\,V$$

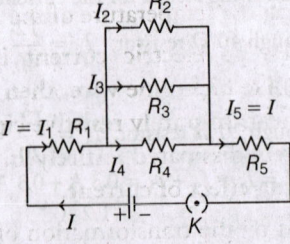

As R_2, R_3 and R_4 are in parallel combination, so potential drop at all resistances will be same as 1 V.

$$V_2 = V_3 = V_4 = V' = 1V$$

Current through R_2, $I_2 = \dfrac{V_2}{R_2} = \dfrac{V'}{R_2} = \dfrac{1}{1} = 1A$

Similarly, $I_3 = \dfrac{V_3}{R_3} = \dfrac{V'}{R_3} = \dfrac{1}{2} = 0.5 A$ and $I_4 = \dfrac{V_4}{R_4} = \dfrac{V'}{R_4} = \dfrac{1}{3} = 0.33 A$

Check Point 03

1. Fill in the blanks:
   (i) In series combination of resistors, potential difference across each resistor is .... while electric current through each resistor is ....
   (ii) If two resistors of equal resistance R are connected in parallel, then equivalent resistance will be ....
2. True and False for the following statements:
   (i) In parallel combination of resistors, the equivalent resistance is less than the resistance of either resistor.
   (ii) The potential difference across each resistor in parallel combination is same.
3. If different resistors have same value of electric potential across them, in which way they are connected to each other?
4. Why, we do not use series combination of connecting electric appliances in household circuit?
5. What do you understand by mixed combination of resistances?
6. In the circuit shown below, calculate the net resistance of the circuit.

   [Ans. 12.5 Ω]

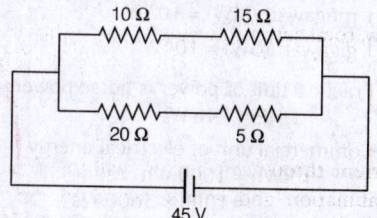

Heating Effect of Electric Current

A cell or a battery is the source of electrical energy. Due to the chemical reactions inside them a potential difference is setup which is responsible for the flow of current through any electrical circuit. So, to maintain this flow, the source continuously has to provide the energy. But only a part of this energy helps in maintaining the current consumed into useful work. Rest of it may be consumed in the form of heat by raising the temperature of the appliances.

Therefore, **when an electric current is passed through a high resistance wire like nichrome wire, then the wire becomes very hot and produces heat. In purely resistive circuits, the source of energy continuously gets dissipated entirely in the form of heat. This is called the heating effect of current.**

This is obtained by the transformation of electrical energy into heat energy. e.g. electric heater, electric iron, etc.

Calculation of Heat Generated in a Conductor

Assuming a conductor as a resistance wire which resists the flow of current through it. So, work must be done by the current source for continuous flow of the current.

Now, we calculate the work done by the source when the current I flows through a wire of resistance R. When an electric charge q moves against a potential difference V. Then,

Amount of work, $W = q \times V$ ...(i)

From definition of current, we know that,

$$I = \dfrac{q}{t} \text{ or } q = I \times t \quad \text{...(ii)}$$

From Ohm's law,

$$\dfrac{V}{I} = R \text{ or } V = IR \quad \text{...(iii)}$$

Substituting the values of q and V in Eq. (i), we get

$$W = (I \times t) \times IR = I^2 Rt$$

Assuming that all electrical work done or electrical energy consumed is converted into heat energy, i.e. heat produced. So, heat produced is given by

$$\boxed{H = I^2 \times R \times t}$$

Thus, it is known as **Joule's law of heating**.

This law implies that heat produced in a resistor is

(i) directly proportional to the square of current for a given resistance.

(ii) directly proportional to the resistance for a given current.

(iii) directly proportional to the time for which the current flows through the resistor.

Example 15. *An electric iron of resistance 25 Ω takes a current of 7 A. Calculate the heat developed in 0.5 min.*

Sol. Given, Resistance, $R = 25 \, \Omega$; Current, $I = 7 A$;

Time, $t = 0.5$ min $= 0.5 \times 60 = 30$ s; Heat, $H = ?$

We know that, Heat, $H = I^2 Rt$

$H = (7)^2 \times 25 \times 30 = 36750$ J

$= 3.68 \times 10^4$ J

So, the heat developed is 3.68×10^4 J.

Example 16. *200 J of heat is produced 10 s in a 5Ω resistance. Find the potential difference across the resistor.*

Sol. Given, Heat, $H = 200$ J, Resistance, $R = 5$ Ω
Time, $t = 10$ s, Potential difference, $V = ?$
We know that,
Heat, $H = I^2 Rt$
$\Rightarrow$ Current, $I = \sqrt{\dfrac{H}{Rt}} = \sqrt{\dfrac{200}{5 \times 10}} = 2$ A

So, the potential difference across the resistor is
$V = IR$ [by Ohm's law]
$= 2 \times 5 = 10$ V

Practical Applications of Heating Effect of Electric Current

Although heating effect of electric current causes undesirable loss of electrical energy still there are some useful applications of it. Some of them are given below

Electric Bulb

It has a filament made of tungsten. So, most of the power consumed by this, is **dissipated** in the form of heat and some part is converted into light because it has high resistivity and high melting point.

The filament is thermally isolated and the bulb is filled with chemically inactive nitrogen and argon gas to prolong the life of filament.

Electric Fuse

It is used as a safety device in household circuits. It protects the circuits, by stopping the flow of any unduly high electric current. It is connected in series with the mains supply. It consists of an alloy of **lead** and **tin** which has appropriate melting point.

When the current flowing through the circuit exceeds the safe limit, the temperature of the fuse wire increases and hence, the fuse wire melts and breaks the circuit. This helps to protect the other circuit elements from hazards caused by heavy current.

Fuses are always rated for different current values such as 1 A, 2 A, 5 A, 10 A, 15 A, etc.

Electric Power

It is defined as the amount of electric energy consumed in a circuit per unit time.

If W be the amount of electric energy consumed in a circuit in t seconds, then the electric power is given by

$$P = \dfrac{W}{t}$$

But W = electric energy = $Vq = VIt$ [$\because q = It$]

$\therefore$ $P = \dfrac{VIt}{t}$ $\Rightarrow$ $\boxed{P = VI}$

According to Ohm's law, $V = IR$

$\therefore$ $P = IR \times I = I^2 R$

$\Rightarrow$ $= \dfrac{V^2}{R}$ $\left[\text{putting } I = \dfrac{V}{R}\right]$

The SI unit of electric power is **watt** (W).

It is said to be 1 watt, if 1 ampere current flows through a circuit having 1 volt potential difference.

i.e.   1 watt = 1 volt × 1 ampere = 1 VA

Note
- Bigger units of power are as given below:
  1 kilowatt (kW) = 10^3 W
  1 megawatt (MW) = 10^6 W
  1 gigawatt (GW) = 10^9 W
- Practical unit of power is horse power.
  1 HP = 746 W
- Commercial unit of electrical energy
  1 kWh = 1000 Wh
  $= 1000 \times 3600$ Ws
  $= 3.6 \times 10^6$ Ws $= 3.6 \times 10^6$ J
- Number of units consumed by electric appliances is
  $= \dfrac{\text{watt} \times \text{hours}}{1000}$

Are electrons already consumed in an electric circuit?

No, electrons are not consumed in an electric circuit. We pay the electricity board or electric company to provide energy to move electrons through all the electric gadgets like fan, bulb, refrigerator, etc., installed in our homes. We pay for the electrical energy that we use.

Example 17. *An electric fan runs from the 220 V mains. The current flowing through it is 0.6 A. At what rate is the electrical energy transformed by the fan? How much energy is transformed in 2 min?*

Sol. Given, Potential difference, $V = 220$ V
Current, $I = 0.6$ A,
Time, $t = 2$ min $= 120$ s,
Power, $P = ?$
We know that,
Power, $P = VI = 220 \times 0.6 = 132$ W
and $E = Pt = 132 \times 120 = 15840$ J
So, the power of fan is 132 W and it transforms 15840 J of energy.

Example 18. *An electric refrigerator rated 500 W operates 6 hours/day. What is the cost of the energy to operate it for 30 days at ₹4.5 per kWh?*

Sol. Energy consumed by refrigerator in 30 days
$$= 500 \text{ W} \times 6 \frac{\text{hours}}{\text{day}} \times 30 \text{ days}$$
$$= 90000 \text{ Wh} = 90 \text{ kWh}$$
∴ Cost of energy to operate the refrigerator for 30 days
$$= 90 \text{ kWh} \times ₹ 4.5 \text{ per kWh}$$
$$= ₹ 405$$

Example 19. *An electric iron consumes energy at a rate of 880W, when heating is at the maximum rate and 340W, when the heating is at the minimum. The voltage is 220V. What are the current and the resistance is each case?*

Sol. Given, $P_{max} = 880$ W
$P_{min} = 340$ W
$V = 200$ V
Power, $P = VI$, Current, $I = P/V$

(i) When heating is at the maximum rate
$$I = \frac{P_{max}}{V} = \frac{880}{220} = 4\text{A}$$
Resistance of the electric iron
$$R = \frac{V}{I} = \frac{220}{4} = 55 \, \Omega$$

(ii) When heating is at the minimum rate
$$I = \frac{P_{min}}{V} = \frac{340}{220} = 1.54\text{A}$$
Resistance of the electric iron
$$R = \frac{V}{I} = \frac{220}{1.54} = 142.85 \, \Omega$$

Check Point 04

1 Fill in the blanks:
  (i) Heat produced in a resistor is .... proportional to the square of current for a given resistor.
  (ii) The filament of electric bulb is made of ....

2 True and False:
  (i) 1 kilowatt hour is equal to one unit.
  (ii) Electric fuse is connected in series with the main supply.

3 What is the heating effect of electric current?

4 State the factors on which the heat produced in a current conductor depends. Give one practical application of this effect.

5 A fuse wire consists of an alloy of lead and tin. Why?

6 An electric heater of resistance 500 Ω is connected to a mains supply for 30 min. If 15A current flows through the filament of the heater, then calculate the heat energy produced in the heater. [**Ans.** 20.25×10^7 J]

7 Why are electric bulbs filled with chemically inactive nitrogen and argon?

8 What is the maximum power in kilowatts of the appliance that can be connected safely to a 13A, 230V mains socket? [**Ans.** 2.99 kW]

9 Power of a lamp is 60W. Find the energy in joules consumed by it in 1 s. [**Ans.** 60 J]

NCERT FOLDER

Intext Questions

1 What does an electric circuit mean? **Pg 200**

Sol. A closed and continuous path of electric current is known as electric circuit.

2 Define the unit of electric current. **Pg 200**

Sol. The SI unit of electric current is ampere (A).

The current flowing through a conductor is said to be 1A, if a charge of 1 coulomb (C) flows through it in 1 second (s)

or $\quad 1A = \dfrac{1C}{1s}$

3 Calculate the number of electrons constituting one coulomb of charge. **Pg 200**

Sol. We know that, charge on one electron $= 1.6 \times 10^{-19}$ C

$\Rightarrow 1.6 \times 10^{-19}$ coulomb charge = 1 electron.

$\therefore$ 1 coulomb charge $= \dfrac{1}{1.6 \times 10^{-19}} = 6.25 \times 10^{18}$ electrons

4 Name a device that helps to maintain a potential difference across a conductor. **Pg 202**

Sol. Electric cell or battery is a device that helps to maintain a potential difference across a conductor.

5 What is meant by saying that the potential difference between two points is 1 V? **Pg 202**

Sol. The potential difference between two points is said to be 1 V if 1 J of work is done in moving 1 coulomb of electric charge from one point to other point.

6 How much energy is given to each coulomb of charge passing through a 6 V battery? **Pg 202**

Sol. Given, charge, $q = 1$ C, potential, $V = 6$ V, $W = ?$

As we know, $W = qV = 1 \times 6 = 6$ J

6 J is given to each coulomb of charge passing through a 6V battery.

7 On what factors does the resistance of a conductor depend? **Pg 209**

Sol. The resistance of a conductor depends on following factors:
(i) Length of the conductor.
(ii) Area of cross-section of the conductor.
(iii) Nature of material of the conductor.

8 Will current flow more easily through a thick wire or a thin wire of the same material, when connected to the same source? Why? **Pg 209**

Sol. Resistance is inversely proportional to the area of cross-section of the wire. Since, thick wire has a large area of cross-section, its resistance will be less. Thus, current will flow more easily through the thick wire.

9 Let the resistance of an electrical component remains constant while the potential difference across the two ends of the component decreases to half of its former value. What change will occur in the current through it? **Pg 209**

Sol. Let resistance be R. Potential difference V across the two ends becomes $V/2$. Since, $I = V/R$

As $V \to V/2$, $\quad I = \dfrac{V}{2R} = \dfrac{1}{2}I$

In other words, current through the component becomes half of its original value.

10 Why are coils of electric toasters and electric irons made of alloy rather than a pure metal? **Pg 209**

Sol. Alloys have a higher resistivity than their constituent metals. They do not oxidise or burn at higher temperatures as they have high melting point. Thus, they are used to make coils of electrical toasters and electric irons rather than pure metals.

11 Use the given table to answer the questions.

Electrical Resistivity of Some Substances at 20° C

	Material	Resistivity (Ω-m)
Conductors	Silver	1.60×10^{-8}
	Copper	1.62×10^{-8}
	Aluminium	2.63×10^{-8}
	Tungsten	5.20×10^{-8}
	Nickel	6.84×10^{-8}
	Iron	10.0×10^{-8}
	Chromium	12.9×10^{-8}
	Mercury	94.0×10^{-8}
	Manganese	1.84×10^{-6}
Alloys	Constantan (Cu + Ni)	49×10^{-6}
	Manganin (Cu + Mn + Ni)	44×10^{-6}
	Nichrome (Ni + Cr + Mn + Fe)	100×10^{-6}
Insulators	Glass	10^{10}-10^{14}
	Hard rubber	10^{13}-10^{16}
	Ebonite	10^{15}-10^{17}
	Diamond	10^{12}-10^{13}
	Dry paper	10^{12}

(i) Which among iron and mercury is a better conductor?
(ii) Which material is the best conductor? **Pg 209**

Sol. The substance which has less resistivity is a better conductor.
(i) Iron is a better conductor than mercury.
(ii) Silver is the best conductor as it has the least resistivity.

12 Draw a schematic diagram of a circuit consisting of a battery of three cells of 2 V each, a 5 Ω resistor, a 8 Ω resistor and a 12 Ω resistor and a plug key, all connected in series. **Pg 213**

Sol. The schematic diagram is shown as below:

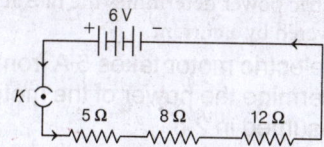

13 Redraw the above circuit, putting in an ammeter to measure the current through the resistors and a voltmeter to measure the potential difference across 12 Ω resistor. What would be the readings in ammeter and voltmeter? **Pg 213**

Sol.

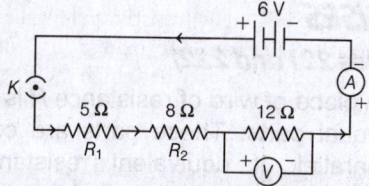

Equivalent resistance of the circuit,
$R = R_1 + R_2 + R_3 = 5 + 8 + 12 = 25\,\Omega$
[∵ R_1, R_2 and R_3 are connected in series]
In series combination, current flowing through all the resistances is same and equal to the total current flowing through the circuit.
∴ Current in the resistors, $I = \dfrac{V}{R} = \dfrac{6}{25} = 0.24\,\text{A}$
∴ Ammeter reading = 0.24 A
Potential across 12 Ω resistance,
$V = IR = 0.24 \times 12 = 2.88\,\text{V}$
∴ Voltmeter reading is 2.88 V.

14 Judge the equivalent resistance when the following are connected in parallel
(i) 1 Ω and 10^6 Ω
(ii) 1 Ω, 10^3 Ω and 10^6 Ω. **Pg 216**

Sol. (i) 1 Ω (ii) 1 Ω
When resistors are connected in parallel, then the equivalent resistance is less than the least resistance connected in the combination. In both the above cases, the equivalent resistance is less than 1 Ω but is approximately 1 Ω.

15 An electric lamp of 100 Ω, a toaster of 50 Ω and a water filter of resistance 500 Ω are connected in parallel to a 220 V source. What is the resistance of an electric iron connected to the same source that takes as much current as all the three appliances and what is the current through it? **Pg 216**

Sol. Let resistance of lamp, $R_1 = 100\,\Omega$
Resistance of toaster, $R_2 = 50\,\Omega$
Resistance of filter, $R_3 = 500\,\Omega$

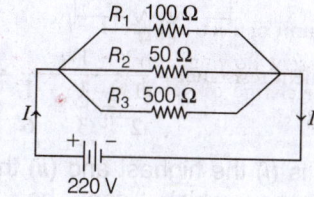

Net resistance,
$\dfrac{1}{R} = \dfrac{1}{R_1} + \dfrac{1}{R_2} + \dfrac{1}{R_3}$
[∵ R_1, R_2 and R_3 are connected in parallel]
$\dfrac{1}{R} = \dfrac{1}{100} + \dfrac{1}{50} + \dfrac{1}{500} = \dfrac{16}{500}$ or $R = \dfrac{500}{16} = 31.25\,\Omega$
So, resistance of iron to take same current as much current drawn by all the appliances should be 31.25 Ω.
Current through circuit,
$I = \dfrac{V}{R} = \dfrac{220}{31.25} = 7.04\,\text{A}$
Thus, current through iron is 7.04 A.

16 What are the advantages of connecting electrical appliances in parallel with the battery instead of connecting them in series? **Pg 216**

Sol. Following are the advantages of connecting electrical devices in parallel with the battery:
(i) Parallel circuits divides the current among the electrical devices, so that they can have necessary amount of current to operate properly.
(ii) If one of the devices in a parallel combination fuses or fails, then the other devices keep working without being affected.

17 How can three resistors of resistances 2 Ω, 3 Ω and 6 Ω be connected to give a total resistance of
(i) 4 Ω (ii) 1 Ω? **Pg 216**

Sol. (i) If 3 Ω and 6 Ω are connected in parallel, thus equivalent resistance of parallel combination
$= \dfrac{1}{1/3 + 1/6} = 2\,\Omega$
If this combination is connected in series with 2 Ω resistance, then total equivalent resistance
$= 2\,\Omega + 2\,\Omega = 4\,\Omega$.

The resistor connections are as shown below:

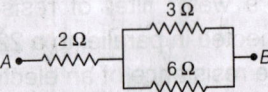

(ii) Since, equivalent resistance is less than the least value of resistance (i.e. 2 Ω), it means that all three resistors are connected in parallel.

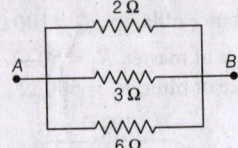

Equivalent resistance $= \dfrac{1}{\frac{1}{2}+\frac{1}{3}+\frac{1}{6}} = 1\ \Omega$

18 What is (i) the highest and (ii) the lowest total resistance which can be secured by combinations of four coils of resistances 4 Ω, 8 Ω, 12 Ω and 24 Ω? **Pg 216**

Sol. (i) Resistance is maximum when resistors are connected in series.

A •—[4Ω]—[8Ω]—[12Ω]—[24Ω]—• B

$R_{max} = 4+8+12+24 = 48\ \Omega$

(ii) Resistance is minimum when resistors are connected in parallel.

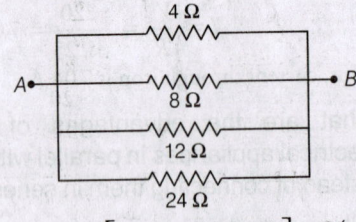

$R_{min} = 1/\left[\dfrac{1}{4}+\dfrac{1}{8}+\dfrac{1}{12}+\dfrac{1}{24}\right] = \dfrac{24}{12}\ \Omega = 2\ \Omega$

19 Why does the cord of an electric heater not glow while heating element does? **Pg 218**

Sol. The cord of an electric heater has lesser resistance than its heating element. So, more heat is produced in the heating element than the cord and it glows.

20 Compute the heat generated while transferring 96000 C of charge in one hour through a potential difference of 50 V? **Pg 218**

Sol. Given, Charge, $q = 96000$ C, Time, $t = 1$ h $= 3600$ s
Potential difference, $V = 50$ V
We know that,
Heat generated, $H = VIt = \dfrac{Vqt}{t}$ $\left[\because I = \dfrac{q}{t}\right]$
$= Vq = 50 \times 96000 = 4800000$ J $= 4800$ kJ
4800 kJ is generated while transferring 96000 C of charge.

21 An electric iron of resistance 20 Ω takes a current 5 A. Calculate the heat developed in 30 s. **Pg 218**

Sol. Given, Resistance, $R = 20\ \Omega$,
Current, $I = 5$ A, Time, $t = 30$ s
We know that,
Heat developed, $H = I^2 Rt$
$= (5)^2 \times 20 \times 30 = 5 \times 5 \times 20 \times 30 = 15000$ J $= 15$ kJ
15 kJ heat is developed in 30 s.

22 What determines the rate at which energy is delivered by a current? **Pg 220**

Sol. Electric power determines the rate at which energy is delivered by a current.

23 An electric motor takes 5 A from a 220 V line. Determine the power of the motor and energy consumed in 2 h. **Pg 220**

Sol. Given, $I = 5$ A, $V = 220$ V, $t = 2$ h
∴ Power of motor,
$P = VI = 220 \times 5 = 1100$ W $= 1.1$ kW
∴ Energy consumed $= Pt = 1.1 \times 2 = 2.2$ kWh
Thus, the power of the motor is 1.1 kW and energy consumed is 2.2 kWh.

EXERCISES
(On Pages 221 and 222)

1 A piece of wire of resistance R is cut into five equal parts. These parts are connected in parallel. If equivalent resistance of this combination is R', then find the ratio R/R' is

(a) $\dfrac{1}{25}$ (b) $\dfrac{1}{5}$ (c) 5 (d) 25

Sol. (d) Resistance of complete wire is R. If it is cut into 5 equal parts, then resistance of each part will be $\dfrac{R}{5}$.

Five parts of resistance $\dfrac{R}{5}$ each are connected in parallel as shown in the figure

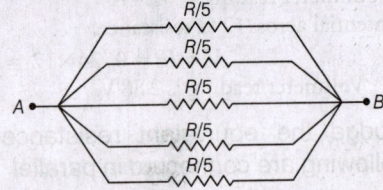

Equivalent resistance,
$R' = \dfrac{1}{\left(\dfrac{1}{R/5}\right)+\left(\dfrac{1}{R/5}\right)+\left(\dfrac{1}{R/5}\right)+\left(\dfrac{1}{R/5}\right)+\left(\dfrac{1}{R/5}\right)} = \dfrac{1}{\dfrac{25}{R}} = \dfrac{R}{25}$

∴ Ratio, $\dfrac{R}{R'} = \dfrac{R}{\dfrac{R}{25}} = 25$

All in one Electricity

2 Which of the following terms does not represent electric power in a circuit?
(a) I^2R (b) IR^2 (c) VI (d) V^2/R

Sol. (b) ∴ Electric power $= VI = IR \times I = I^2 R$ [∵ $V = IR$]
$$= \left(\frac{V}{R}\right)^2 \cdot R = \frac{V^2}{R} \quad \left[\because I = \frac{V}{R}\right]$$
So, IR^2 does not represent electric power.

3 An electric bulb is rated 220 V and 100 W. When it is operated on 110 V, the power consumed will be
(a) 100 W (b) 75 W (c) 50 W (d) 25 W

Sol. (d) Given, $V = 220$ V, $P = 100$ W
∴ Resistance of bulb, $R = V^2/P$
$$= \frac{220 \times 220}{100} = 484 \, \Omega$$
Now, when $V = 110$ V,
then power consumed,
$$P = \frac{V^2}{R} = \frac{110 \times 110}{484} = 25 \, W$$

4 Two conducting wires of same material and of equal lengths and equal diameters are first connected in series and then parallel in a circuit across the same potential difference, the ratio of heat produced in series and parallel combinations would be
(a) 1 : 2 (b) 2 : 1 (c) 1 : 4 (d) 4 : 1

Sol. (c) Let R be the resistance of each wire. The resistance of both the wires will be same because they are of same material and have same length and same cross-sectional area. Equivalent resistance in series
$$= R + R = 2R$$
Heat produced, $H = \frac{V^2 t}{R}$
If wires are connected in series, then $H_S = \frac{V^2 t}{2R}$
Equivalent resistance in parallel $= \frac{R}{2}$
Heat produced, $H_P = \frac{2V^2 t}{R}$
∴ Ratio of heat produced,
$$\frac{H_S}{H_P} = \frac{\frac{V^2 t}{2R}}{\frac{2V^2 t}{R}} = 1 : 4$$
Thus, the ratio of H_S and H_P is 1:4.

5 How is voltmeter connected in circuit to measure the potential difference between the two points?

Sol. A voltmeter is always connected in parallel in the circuit to measure the potential difference between two points.

6 A copper wire has diameter 0.5 mm and resistivity $\rho = 1.6 \times 10^{-8}$ Ω-m. What will be the length of its wire to make its resistance 10 Ω? How much does the resistance change, if diameter is doubled? **CBSE 2014**

Sol. Given, radius of wire = diameter / 2
$$= \frac{0.5}{2} = 0.25 \, mm = 0.25 \times 10^{-3} \, m,$$
$\rho = 1.6 \times 10^{-8}$ Ω-m and $R = 10$ Ω
(i) We know that, resistance,
$$R = \frac{\rho l}{A} = \frac{\rho l}{\pi r^2} \quad [\because A = \pi r^2]$$
or $l = \frac{R \pi r^2}{\rho} = \frac{10 \times 3.14 \times 0.25 \times 0.25 \times 10^{-6}}{1.6 \times 10^{-8}}$
$= 122.66$ m

(ii) Resistance, $R \propto \frac{1}{d^2}$

If diameter is doubled, then resistance becomes one-fourth of its original value.

7 The values of current I flowing in a given resistor for the corresponding values of potential difference V across the resistor are as given below:

I (amperes)	0.5	1.0	2.0	3.0	4.0
V (volts)	1.6	3.4	6.7	10.2	13.2

Plot a graph between V and I and also calculate the resistance of that resistor.

Sol.

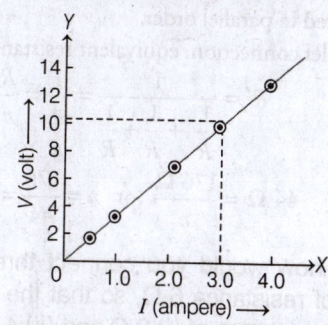

Resistance = Slope of graph
$$= \frac{Y\text{-intercept}}{X\text{-intercept}} = \frac{(10.2 - 0) \, V}{(3.0 - 0) \, A} = 3.4 \, \Omega$$
Thus, the resistance of the resistor is 3.4 Ω.

8 When a 12 V battery is connected across an unknown resistor, there is a current of 2.5 mA in the circuit. Find the value of resistance of resistor.

Sol. Given, $V = 12$ V, $I = 2.5$ mA $= 2.5 \times 10^{-3}$ A, $R = ?$
∴ Resistance, $R = \frac{V}{I}$ [by Ohm's law]
$\Rightarrow R = \frac{12}{2.5 \times 10^{-3}} = 4.8 \times 10^3 \, \Omega$

9 A battery of 9 V is connected in series with resistors of 0.2 Ω, 0.3 Ω, 0.4 Ω, 0.5 Ω and 12 Ω, respectively. How much current would flow through the 12 Ω resistor?

Sol. The circuit diagram for the given system of resistors can be drawn as below

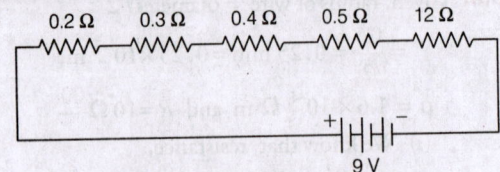

∴ Total resistance, $R = R_1 + R_2 + R_3 + R_4 + R_5$
$= 0.2\ \Omega + 0.3\ \Omega + 0.4\ \Omega + 0.5\ \Omega + 12\ \Omega$
$= 13.4\ \Omega$

Current through all resistors in series is the same.

∴ Current through 12 Ω resistor $= \dfrac{V}{R}$

$= \dfrac{9\ V}{13.4\ \Omega} = 0.67\ A$

10 How many 176 Ω resistors (in parallel) are required to carry 5 A on a 220 V line? **CBSE 2014**

Sol. Given, $V = 220$ V, $I = 5$ A

∴ Resistance of the wire, $R' = \dfrac{V}{I} = \dfrac{220}{5} = 44\ \Omega$

The net resistance 44 Ω is less than the individual resistance 176 Ω, so individual resistances are to be connected in parallel order.

In parallel connection, equivalent resistance

$R' = \dfrac{1}{\dfrac{1}{R} + \dfrac{1}{R} + \dfrac{1}{R}} = \dfrac{1}{\dfrac{n}{R}} = \dfrac{R}{n}$

∴ $44\ \Omega = \dfrac{176\ \Omega}{n}$ or $n = \dfrac{176}{44} = 4$ resistors

11 Show how would you connect three resistors, each of resistance 6 Ω, so that the combination has a resistance of (i) 9 Ω and (ii) 4 Ω?

Sol. (i) If two 6 Ω resistors are connected in parallel, then the equivalent resistance is $\left(\dfrac{6}{2}\right) = 3\ \Omega$.

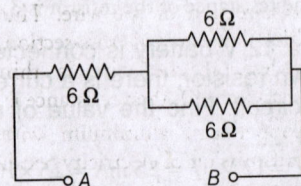

This combination is connected in series with a 6 Ω resistor to get overall equivalent resistance of $(6 + 3) = 9\ \Omega$.

(ii) Equivalent resistance of two resistances connected in series,

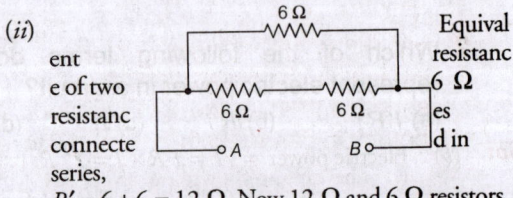

$R' = 6 + 6 = 12\ \Omega$. Now, 12 Ω and 6 Ω resistors are connected in parallel.

Equivalent resistance, $R_{eq} = \dfrac{12 \times 6}{12 + 6} = \dfrac{72}{18} = 4\ \Omega$

12 Several electric bulb designed to be used on a 220 V electric supply line are rated at 10 W. How many lamps are connected in parallel with each other across two wires 220 V line, if the maximum allowable current is 5 A?

Sol. Given, Potential difference, $V = 220$ V
Power, $P = 10$ W; Current, $I = 5$ A

∴ Resistance of bulb,

$R' = \dfrac{V^2}{P} = \dfrac{220 \times 220}{10} = 4840\ \Omega$

Since, bulbs are connected in parallel,

Equivalent resistance $(R) = \dfrac{\text{Individual resistance }(R')}{\text{Number of bulbs }(n)}$

$\Rightarrow R = \dfrac{4840}{n}\ \Omega,\ V = IR$

$\Rightarrow 220 = \dfrac{5 \times 4840}{n}$

$\Rightarrow n = \dfrac{5 \times 4840}{220} = 110$ bulbs

13 A hot plate of an electric oven connected to a 220 V line has two resistance coils A and B, each of 24 Ω resistance, which may be used separately in series or in parallel. What are the currents in three cases?

Sol. Given, $V = 220$ V, $R_A = R_B = 24\ \Omega$

(i) Current in plates when used separately,

$I = \dfrac{V}{R_A} = \dfrac{V}{R_B} = \dfrac{220}{24} = 9.16\ A$

(ii) Current in plates when connected in series.
Equivalent resistance in series,

$R = R_A + R_B = 24 + 24 = 48\ \Omega$

∴ Current flowing, $I = \dfrac{V}{R} = \dfrac{220}{48} = 4.58\ A$

(iii) Current in plates when connected in parallel.
Equivalent resistance in parallel,

$R = \dfrac{R_A R_B}{R_A + R_B} = \dfrac{24 \times 24}{48} = 12\ \Omega$

∴ Current flowing, $I = \dfrac{V}{R} = \dfrac{220}{12} = 18.32\ A$

14 Compare the power used in 2 Ω resistor in each of the following circuits (i) a 6 V battery in series with 1 Ω and 2 Ω resistors, (ii) a 4 V battery in parallel with 12 Ω and 2 Ω resistors.

Sol. (i) The circuit shown right has resistance connected in series combination:

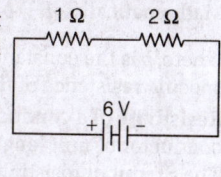

Current in the circuit,
$$I = \frac{V}{R_1 + R_2} = \frac{6}{3} = 2\,A$$

∴ Power used $= I^2 R = 2^2 \times 2$
$$= 2 \times 2 \times 2 = 8\,W$$

(ii) The circuit is shown as right :

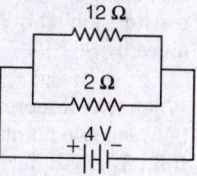

In parallel combination, potential across each resistor is same and equal to the potential applied to the circuit.

Potential across 2 Ω resistor,
$$V = 4\,V$$

Power used, $\dfrac{V^2}{R} = \dfrac{4 \times 4}{2} = 8\,W$

Power used in both the cases is same.

15 Two lamps, one rated at 100 W-220 V and other 60 W-220 V are connected in parallel to electric mains supply. What current is drawn from the line, if supply voltage is 220 V?

Sol. Given, potential, $V = 220\,V$
Power, $P_1 = 100\,W$
Power, $P_2 = 60\,W$

∴ Current, $I_1 = \dfrac{P_1}{V}$
$$= \frac{100}{220} = 0.45\,A$$

Current, $I_2 = \dfrac{P_2}{V} = \dfrac{60}{220} = 0.27\,A$

∴ Total current drawn,
$$I = I_1 + I_2$$
$$= 0.45 + 0.27$$
$$= 0.72\,A$$

16 Which uses more energy, a 250 W TV set in 1 h or a 1200 W toaster in 10 min?

Sol. Given, $P_1 = 250\,W,\qquad P_2 = 1200\,W,$
$t_1 = 1\,h = 3600\,s,\quad t_2 = 10\,min = 600\,s$

∴ Energy,
$Q_1 = P_1 t_1 = 250 \times 3600 = 900000\,J = 900\,kJ$
and $Q_2 = P_2 t_2 = 1200 \times 600 = 720000\,J = 720\,kJ$
Thus, TV set uses more energy.

17 An electric heater of resistance 8 Ω draws 15 A from the mains for 2 h. Calculate the rate at which heat is developed in the heater.

Sol. Given, Resistance, $R = 8\,\Omega$, Current, $I = 15\,A$
Time, $t = 2\,h = 7200\,s$

∴ Heat developed, $H = I^2 Rt$
$$= 15 \times 15 \times 8 \times 7200\,J$$

∴ Rate of heat developed,
$$P = \frac{H}{t} = \frac{15 \times 15 \times 8 \times 7200}{7200}$$
$$= 1800\,W \text{ or } 1800\,J/s$$

Thus, the rate at which heat is developed in the heater is 1800 joule per second.

18 Explain the following questions
(i) Why is tungsten used almost exclusively for filament of electric lamps?
(ii) Why are the conductors of electric heating devices such as bread toasters and electric irons made of alloys rather than pure metals?
(iii) Why is the series arrangement not for used domestic circuits?
(iv) How does the resistance of a wire vary with its area of cross-section?
(v) Why are copper and aluminium wires usually employed for electricity transmission?

CBSE 2015, 14

Sol. (i) Tungsten has a high melting point (3380 °C). It does not melt at high temperature. It retains as much of heat generated, so that it becomes very hot and emits light. That is the reason why tungsten is used as filament of electric lamps.

(ii) Conductors of electric heating devices are made of alloys because alloys do not oxidise (burn) readily at high temperature unlike metals. Also, alloys have a greater resistivity (generally) as compared to their constituent pure metals.

(iii) There are 2 reasons for not using series connections for domestic circuits.
  I. Devices of different current ratings cannot be connected as the current is constant in series circuit.
  II. If one device fails, the circuit is broken and all devices stop working.

(iv) Resistance is inversely proportional to the area of cross-section of the wire. Thus, if the wire is thick (large area of cross-section), then resistance is less. If the wire is thin (less area of cross-section), then resistance is large.

(v) Copper and aluminium wires are used for transmission of electricity because they have low resistivity. So, they conduct the electric current without heavy heat losses. Also, they are quite cost effective, as compared to silver.

SUMMARY

- **Electricity** is one of the most convenient and widely used form of energy in today's world.
- An **electric charge** is a physical entity which is defined by excess or deficiency of electrons on a body. The SI unit of electric charge is **coulomb** (C).
- The total charge acquired by a body is an integral multiple of magnitude of charge on a single electron. This principle is called **quantisation of charge**.
- **Electric current** is defined as the rate of flow of electric charge through any cross-section of a conductor in unit time.

  Electric current $(I) = \dfrac{\text{Charge }(q)}{\text{Time }(t)}$

  The SI unit of electric current is **ampere** (A).
- **Electric potential** is defined as the amount of work done when a unit positive charge is moved from infinity to a point in an electric field.

  Electric potential $(V) = \dfrac{\text{Work done }(W)}{\text{Charge moved }(q)}$

  The SI unit of electric potential is **volt** (V).
- **Electric potential difference** is defined as the work done per unit charge in moving a unit positive charge from one point to other point.
- A closed and continuous path through which electric current flows is known as **electric circuit**.
- George Simon Ohm established a relationship between the electric current I, flowing in a metallic wire and potential difference V, across its terminals.
- According to Ohm's law, the electric current flowing through a conductor is directly proportional to the potential difference applied across its ends, provided the temperature remains unchanged.

  $V \propto I$

  or $V = IR$

  where, R is the constant of proportionality called resistance of the conductor at a given temperature.
- **Resistance** is the property of a conductor due to which it opposes the flow of electric current through it.

  Mathematically, Resistance $(R) = \dfrac{\text{Potential difference }(V)}{\text{Electric current }(I)}$

  The SI unit of resistance is **ohm** (Ω).
- At a given temperature resistance of a conductor depends on its (i) length l, (ii) cross-section area A, and (iii) nature of the material of the conductor.

  It is found that $R \propto l$ and $R \propto \dfrac{1}{A}$

  Mathematically, $R = \rho \dfrac{l}{A}$

  where, ρ is the constant of proportionality called resistivity or specific resistance of the conductor.
- **Resistivity** of a conductor is defined as the resistance of a conductor of unit length and unit area of cross-section. The SI unit of resistivity is **ohm-metre** (Ω - m).
- In an electric circuit resistors may be connected (i) series (ii) parallel arrangement.
- When two or more resistors are connected end to end, they are said to be connected in series. If R_1, R_2 and R_3 be three resistors joined in series then the equivalent resistor R_S is given by

  $R_S = R_1 + R_2 + R_3$
- When two or more resistors are connected simultaneously between two points, then they form a parallel arrangement. If R_1, R_2 and R_3 be the individual resistors joined in parallel then the equivalent resistor R_P is given by

  $\dfrac{1}{R_P} = \dfrac{1}{R_1} + \dfrac{1}{R_2} + \dfrac{1}{R_3}$
- Practical electrical circuits may involve the combination of basic series and parallel circuits.
- When an electric current is passed through a high resistance wire like nichrome wire, then the wire becomes very hot and produces heat. This is called the **heating effect of current**.
- When a current is passed through a resistance wire, heat is produced. Amount of heat produced depends on (i) current flowing I, (ii) resistance R of that wire, and (iii) time t for which current is being flown.
- If on applying, a potential difference V across the ends of a conductor of resistance R, the current I flows for a time t, then as per Joule's law of heating the electric energy consumed is given by

  $W = qV = VIt = I^2Rt = \dfrac{V^2 t}{R}$

  The dissipated electrical energy appears as heat. Thus, heat produced

  $H = VIt = I^2Rt = \dfrac{V^2 t}{R}$
- **Electric power** is defined as the amount of electric energy consumed in a circuit per unit time.

  Electric Power $(P) = \dfrac{W}{t}$

  The SI unit of electric power is **watt** (W).

Exam Practice

Objective Type Questions

Multiple Choice Questions

1 A current of 4.8 A is flowing in a conductor. The number of electrons passing per second through the conductor will be
(a) 3×10^{20} (b) 76.8×10^{20}
(c) 7.68×10^{-19} (d) 3×10^{19}

Sol. (d) Given, current, $I = 4.8\,A$, $e = 1.6 \times 10^{-19} C$

We know that, $I = \dfrac{q}{t} = \dfrac{ne}{t}$

$\therefore \quad \dfrac{n}{t} = \dfrac{I}{e} = \dfrac{4.8}{1.6 \times 10^{-19}} = 3 \times 10^{19}$

2 Which one of the following is the correct set-up for studying the dependence of the current on the potential difference across a resistor and why? **CBSE 2019**

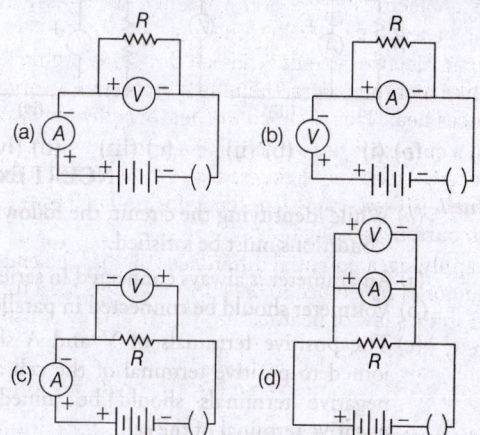

Sol. (c) Option (c) represents correct set-up for studing the dependence of the current on the potential difference across a resistor because ammeter A is connected in series while voltmeter V is connected across parallel of resistor R.

3. The values of mA and μA are
CBSE (All India) 2020
(a) 10^{-6} A and 10^{-9} A respectively
(b) 10^{-3} A and 10^{-6} A respectively
(c) 10^{-3} A and 10^{-9} A respectively
(d) 10^{-6} A and 10^{-3} A respectively

Sol. (b) As, $1\,mA = 10^{-3}$ A and $1\,\mu A = 10^{-6}$ A
Since, $1\,m = 10^{-3}$
and $1\,\mu = 10^{-6}$
Thus, option (b) is correct.

4. A cylindrical conductor of length l and uniform area of cross-section A has resistance R. Another conductor of length $2.5\,l$ and resistance $0.5\,R$ of the same material has area of cross-section
CBSE (All India) 2020
(a) $5A$ (b) $2.5A$ (c) $0.5A$ (d) $\dfrac{1}{5}A$

Sol. (a) As, resistance of a conductor
$R = \rho \dfrac{l}{A} \Rightarrow A = \rho \dfrac{l}{R}$ ...(i)

Given, conductor of length $2.5l$ and resistance $0.5R$.

$\therefore \quad 0.5R = \rho \dfrac{2.5l}{A'}$

$\Rightarrow \quad A' = \rho \dfrac{2.5l}{0.5R}$ ...(ii)

From Eqs. (i) and (ii), we get

$\dfrac{A'}{A} = \dfrac{\rho\left(\dfrac{2.5\,l}{0.5\,R}\right)}{\rho\left(\dfrac{l}{R}\right)} \Rightarrow A' = 5A$

5 If a wire of resistance R is melted and recast to half of its length, the new resistance of the wire will be
(a) $\dfrac{R}{4}$ (b) $\dfrac{R}{2}$ (c) R (d) $2R$

Sol. (a) Volume of the wire does not change when the wire is melted and recast. If l and A are the original length and area of cross-section and l' and A' are their corresponding values on recastion

$Al = A'l'$

$\dfrac{l'}{l} = \dfrac{A}{A'}$

$\therefore \quad \dfrac{l'}{l} = \dfrac{1}{2}$ (Given)

$\therefore \quad \dfrac{A}{A'} = \dfrac{1}{2}$

New resistance, $R' = \dfrac{\rho l'}{A'}$

$R = \dfrac{\rho l}{A}$

$\dfrac{R'}{R} = \dfrac{\rho l'/A'}{\rho l/A} = \left(\dfrac{l'}{l}\right)\left(\dfrac{A}{A'}\right) = \left(\dfrac{1}{2}\right)\left(\dfrac{1}{2}\right) = \dfrac{1}{4}$

$R' = R/4$

6. A cylindrical conductor of length l and uniform area of cross section A has resistance R. The area of cross-section of another conductor of same material and same resistance but of length $2l$ is

CBSE (All India) 2020

(a) $\dfrac{A}{2}$ (b) $\dfrac{3A}{2}$
(c) $2A$ (d) $3A$

Sol. (c) As resistance of a conductor

$$R = \rho \dfrac{l}{A} \Rightarrow A = \rho \dfrac{l}{R} \quad ...(i)$$

Given, another conductor of $R' = R$, $l' = 2l$ and $\rho' = \rho$

Then, $R' = \rho' \dfrac{l'}{A'} \Rightarrow R = \rho \dfrac{2l}{A'}$

Hence, $A' = \rho \dfrac{2l}{R}$ ...(ii)

From Eq. (i) and (ii), we get

$$\dfrac{A'}{A} = \dfrac{\rho \dfrac{2l}{R}}{\rho \dfrac{l}{R}} \Rightarrow A' = 2A$$

7. The maximum resistance which can be made using four resistors each of resistance $\dfrac{1}{2}\Omega$ is

CBSE (All India) 2020

(a) 2Ω (b) 1Ω (c) 2.5Ω (d) 8Ω

Sol. (a) Given 4 resistors, each of resistance $1/2\Omega$

As, we know, equivalent resistance in series,
$R_{eq_1} = R_1 + R_2 + R_3 + R_4$
$= \dfrac{1}{2} + \dfrac{1}{2} + \dfrac{1}{2} + \dfrac{1}{2} = 2\Omega$

and parallel, $\dfrac{1}{R_{eq_2}} = \dfrac{1}{R_1} + \dfrac{1}{R_2} + \dfrac{1}{R_3} + \dfrac{1}{R_4}$

$= \dfrac{1}{\dfrac{1}{2}} + \dfrac{1}{\dfrac{1}{2}} + \dfrac{1}{\dfrac{1}{2}} + \dfrac{1}{\dfrac{1}{2}}$

$\Rightarrow R_{eq_2} = \dfrac{1}{8}$ or $0.125\,\Omega$

Hence, maximum resistance is 2Ω, when all 4 resistors are connected in series.

8. What is the minimum resistance which can be made using five resistors each of $1/5\,\Omega$?

NCERT Exemplar

(a) $(1/5)\,\Omega$ (b) $(1/25)\,\Omega$
(c) $(1/10)\,\Omega$ (d) $(25)\,\Omega$

Sol. (b) The minimum resistance is obtained when resistors are connected in parallel combination.

Thus, equivalent resistance, $R_P = \dfrac{R}{n} = \dfrac{1/5}{5} = \dfrac{1}{25}\,\Omega$,

R_P = equivalent resistance for parallel combination.

9. What is the maximum resistance which can be made using five resistors each of $(1/5)\,\Omega$?

(a) $(1/5)\,\Omega$ (b) $10\,\Omega$ (c) $5\,\Omega$ (d) $1\,\Omega$

NCERT Exemplar

Sol. (d) The maximum resistance is obtained when resistors are connected in series combination. Thus equivalent resistance $R_s = n \times R = 5 \times \dfrac{1}{5} = 1\Omega$,

R_s = equivalent resistance for series combination.

10. Identify the circuit in which the electrical components have been properly connected.

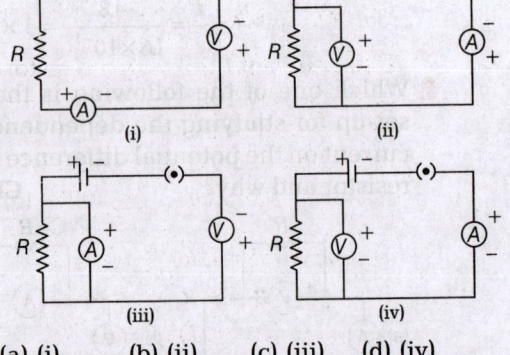

(a) (i) (b) (ii) (c) (iii) (d) (iv)

NCERT Exemplar

Sol. (b) While identifying the circuit, the following conditions must be satisfied.

(a) An ammeter is always connected in series.
(b) Voltmeter should be connected in parallel.
(c) The positive terminals of V and A should be joined to positive terminal of the cell and their negative terminals should be joined to the negative terminal of the cell.

Thus, the above conditions are satisfied in case (ii).

11. A student carries out an experiment and plots the V-I graph of three samples of nichrome wire with resistances R_1, R_2 and R_3 respectively as shown in figure. Which of the following is true?

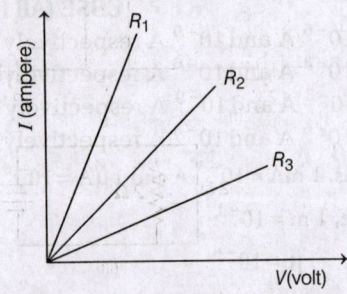

Electricity

(a) $R_1 = R_2 = R_3$ (b) $R_1 > R_2 > R_3$
(c) $R_3 > R_2 > R_1$ (d) $R_2 > R_3 > R_1$

NCERT Exemplar

Sol. (c) We know that slope of V and I tells about the resistance and (slope of V and I) $\propto \dfrac{1}{\text{Resistance}}$

i.e.

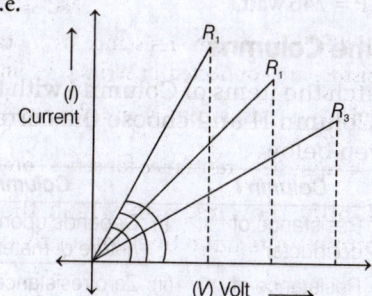

So, $R_3 > R_2 > R_1$

12 If the current I through a resistor is increased by 100% (assume that temperature remains unchanged), the increase in power dissipated will be
(a) 100%   (b) 200%   (c) 300%   (d) 400%

NCERT Exemplar

Sol. (c) Power, $P = I^2 R$
$P_1 = I^2 R$
and $P_2 = (2I)^2 R = 4I^2 R$
[∵ 100% increase in current means that current becomes $2I$]

∴ Increase in power dissipated $= P_2 - P_1$
$= 4I^2 R - I^2 R$
$= 3I^2 R$ [∵ $I^2 R = P_1$]
$= 3P_1$

Percentage increase in power dissipated $= \dfrac{3P_1}{P_1} \times 100$
$= 300\%$

13 In the following circuits, heat produced in the resistor or combination of resistors connected to a 12 V battery will be

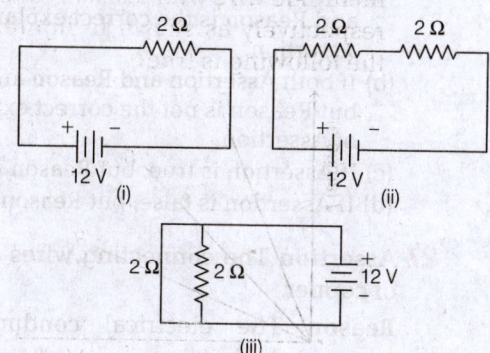

(a) same in all the cases
(b) maximum in case (i)
(c) maximum in case (ii)
(d) maximum in case (iii) **NCERT Exemplar**

Sol. (d) In Case (i), $R = 2\,\Omega$
Case (ii), $R = 2 + 2 = 4\,\Omega$
Case (iii), $\dfrac{1}{R} = \dfrac{1}{2} + \dfrac{1}{2} = 1 \Rightarrow R = 1\,\Omega$

Since, $H = \dfrac{V^2}{R} \times t$.

As voltage in the three cases for equivalent resistance is same, so $H \propto \dfrac{1}{R}$. Hence, heat produced is maximum in case (iii).

14 100 J of heat is produced each second in a 4 Ω resistance. The potential difference across the resistor is
(a) 20 V   (b) 10 V
(c) 5 V   (d) 15 V

Sol. (a) Given, heat, $H = 100\,J$
Resistance, $R = 4\,\Omega$
Time, $t = 1\,s$
We know that, $H = I^2 Rt$

$I = \sqrt{\dfrac{H}{Rt}} = \sqrt{\dfrac{100}{4 \times 1}} = 5\,A$

Potential difference across the resistor,
$V = IR = 5 \times 4 = 20\,V$

15 Two bulbs have the following ratings:
(i) 40 W, 220 V   (ii) 20 W, 110 V
The ratio of their resistances is
(a) 1:2   (b) 2:1   (c) 1:1   (d) 1:3

Sol. (b) Given, $P_1 = 40\,W$, $P_2 = 20\,W$, $V_1 = 220\,V$, $V_2 = 110\,V$

We know that, $P = \dfrac{V^2}{R}$

$\Rightarrow R = \dfrac{V^2}{P}$

∴ $\dfrac{R_1}{R_2} = \dfrac{V_1^2}{V_2^2} \times \dfrac{P_2}{P_1}$

$= \dfrac{(220)^2}{(110)^2} \times \dfrac{20}{40} = \dfrac{2}{1}$

$R_1 : R_2 = 2 : 1$

16 An electric kettle consumes 1 kW of electric power when operated at 220 V. A fuse wire of what rating must be used for it?
(a) 1 A   (b) 2 A   (c) 4 A   (d) 5 A

NCERT Exemplar

377

Sol. (d) Given, power, $P = 1$ kW $= 1000$ W

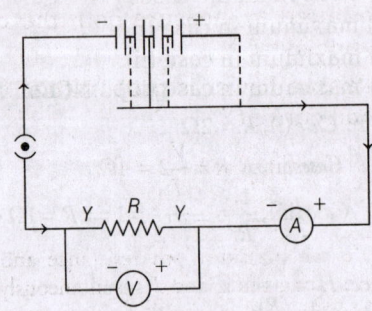

Voltage, $V = 220$ V
Current, $I = ?$

$$I = \frac{P}{V} = \frac{1000}{220} = 4.5 \text{ A}$$

Thus, the rating of fuse-wire is 5 A which is greater than 4.5 A.

Fill in the Blanks

17 Electric current is the rate of flow of ....

Sol. Charge

18 Alloy of metals usually has greatest resistivity than their constituent ....

Sol. Metals

19 Ohm's law is the relation between .... and ....

Sol. Electric current and potential difference.

20 1 kilowatt hour = ... J

Sol. 1 kilowatt hour = 1 kilowatt × 1 hour
= 1000 watt × 3600 s = 3.6×10^6 J

True and False

21 When one electron is removed from a metal specimen, then it becomes negative.

Sol. False; When one electron is removed from a metal specimen, then it becomes positive.

22 Ammeter is a device used to measure potential difference between two point in the electric circuit.

Sol. False; Ammeter is a low resistance device used to measure electric current in the electric circuit.

23 Ohm's law is valid in the electric circuit for which V-I graph is obtained as straight line.

Sol. True; The electric circuit in which Ohm's law is valid, the electric current flowing through the conductor is directly proportional to the potential difference applied across its ends, providing the physical conditions remains unchanged.
Hence, V-I graph obtained is straight line.

24 Specific resistance of a conductor increases on increasing its temperature.

Sol. True; Specific resistance a resistivity of a conductor increases on increasing its temperature.

25 Horse power is the unit of power.

Sol. True; Horse power is the large unit of power.
1 HP = 746 watt

Match the Columns

26 Match the items of Column I with the items of Column II and choose the correct codes given below.

Column I	Column II
A. Resistance of conductor	(i) Depends upon the nature of material
B. Resistance of semiconductor	(ii) Zero resistance
C. Resistivity	(iii) Increases with increase of temperature
D. Super conductor	(iv) Decreases with decrease of temperature

Codes
(a) A→(ii), B→(iii), C→(iv), D→(i)
(b) A→(iii), B→(iv), C→(i), D→(ii)
(c) A→(iii), B→(i), C→(iv), D→(ii)
(d) A→(iv), B→(iii), C→(i), D→(ii)

Sol. (b) A→ (iii) Resistance of conductor increases with increase of temperature.
B→ (iv) Resistance of semiconductor decreases with decrease of temperature.
C→ (i) Resistivity of a material depends upon the nature of material. It does not depend on the dimensions of material.
D→ (ii) Resistance of superconductor is zero.

Assertion-Reason

Direction (Q. Nos. 27-33) *In each of the following questions, a statement of Assertion is given by the corresponding statement of Reason. Of the statements, mark the correct answer as*
(a) If both Assertion and Reason are true and Reason is the correct explanation of Assertion.
(b) If both Assertion and Reason are true, but Reason is not the correct explanation of Assertion.
(c) If Assertion is true, but Reason is false.
(d) If Assertion is false, but Reason is true.

27 Assertion The connecting wires are made of copper.

Reason The electrical conductivity of copper is high.

Sol. (a) Copper conducts the current without offering much resistance due to high electrical conductivity. Hence, conducting wires are made of copper.

28 Assertion When the length of a wire is doubled, then its resistance also gets doubled.

Reason The resistance of a wire is directly proportional to its length.

Sol. (a) The resistance of wire, $R = \rho \dfrac{l}{A}$
i.e. $R \propto l$
Since, the resistance of a wire is directly proportional to its length, i.e. when the length of a wire is doubled/halved then its resistance also gets doubled/halved.

29. Assertion Alloys are commonly used in electrical heating devices like electric iron and heater.

Reason Resistivity of an alloy is generally higher than that of its constituent metals but the alloys have lower melting points than their constituent metals.

CBSE (All India) 2020

Sol. (c) As the resistivity and melting point of alloys are higher than their constituent metals. So, alloys are commonly used in electrical heating devices like electric iron and heater.

30. Assertion At high temperatures, metal wires have a greater chance of short circuiting.

Reason Both resistance and resistivity of a material vary with temperature.

CBSE (All India) 2020

Sol. (a) Both assertion and reason are correct and reason is correct explanation of the assertion.
At high temperature, chances of short circuiting increase due to increase in resistance and resistivity of material.

31 Assertion The 200 W bulbs glow with more brightness than 100 W bulbs.

Reason A 100 W bulb has more resistance than 200 W bulb.

Sol. (a) The resistance, $R = \dfrac{V^2}{P}$
$R \propto \dfrac{1}{P}$
i.e. Higher the wattage of a bulb, lesser is the resistance and so it will glow bright.

32 Assertion A voltmeter and ammeter can be used to measure both the resistance and power.

Reason Power is proportional to voltage and current.

Sol. (b) Resistance, $R = \dfrac{V}{I}$
Power, $P = VI$
We can measure both resistance and power by measuring the V and I simultaneously in circuit. So, option (b) is correct.

33 Assertion Heater wire must have high resistance and high melting point.

Reason If resistance is high, the electric conductivity will be less.

Sol. (a) Heater wire must have high resistance and high melting point, because in series current remains same, therefore according to Joule's law, $H = I^2 Rt$, heat produced is high if R is high, therefore melting point must be high, so that wire may not melt with increase in temperature.

Case Based Questions

Direction (Q. Nos. 34-37) *Answers the questions on the basis of your understanding of the following passage and the related studied concepts.*

How does a metal conductor conduct electricity? You would think that a low energy electron have great difficulty passing through a solid conductor. Inside a solid, the atoms are packed together with very little spacing between them. But it turns out electrons are able to 'travel' through a perfect solid crystal smoothly and easily, almost as if they were in a vacuum. The motion of electrons in a conductor, however is very different from that of charges in empty space. When a steady current flows through a conductor, the electrons in it move with a certain average 'drift speed'.

One can calculate this drift speed of electrons for a typical copper wire carrying a small current and it is found to be actually very small of the order of 1 mms^{-1}. How is it then that an electric bulb lights up as soon as we turn the switch ON? It cannot be that a current starts only when an electron from one terminal of the electric supply physically reaches the other terminal through the bulb, because the physical drift of electrons in the conducting wires is a very show process.

34 The electrons move with a certain speed inside the conductor when a battery is connected across it, is called
(a) average speed
(b) thermal speed
(c) drift speed
(d) efflux speed

Sol. (c) When battery is connected across the conductor, then a steady current flows through the conductor and the electrons in it moves with certain average speed called drift speed.

35 The order of drift speed of electrons in copper wire is
(a) 10^{-3} m/s
(b) 10^{-4} m/s
(c) 10^{4} m/s
(d) 10^{3} m/s

Sol. (a) Drift speed of electrons for a typical copper wire, is found to be the order of $1 \text{ mms}^{-1} = 10^{-3}$ m/s.

36 Does drift speed and thermal speed of electrons inside a metal conductor remain same?

Sol. No, drift speed of electrons inside the conductor is much smaller than its thermal velocity.

37 How does an electric bulb light up as soon as we turn the switch ON?

Sol. When we turn the switch ON, then free electrons near the electric bulb start drifting due to electric field inside the conductor, hence electric current starts flowing through the bulb as soon as we turn the switch ON.

Very Short Answer Type Questions

38 Define resistance. Give its SI unit. **CBSE 2019**

Sol. Refer to text on Pg. 359.

39 Name and define the SI unit of current. **CBSE 2019**

Sol. Refer to text on Pg. 356 and 357.

40 Some work is done to move a charge Q from infinity to a point A in space. The potential of the point A is given as V. What is the work done to move this charge from infinity in terms of Q and V?

Sol. Work done to move charge Q from infinity to a point A in space is given by
Work done = Charge × Potential of point A
i.e. $W = QV$

41 Write the function of voltmeter in an electric circuit. **CBSE 2019**

Sol. Voltmeter is used to measure potential difference between two points in electric circuit.

42 What is the function of a galvanometer in a circuit?

Sol. Galvanometer is an instrument that can measure the small electrical current by deflection in a circuit.

43 When two ends of a metallic wire are connected across the terminals of a cell, then some potential difference is set up between its ends. In which direction electrons are flowing through the conductors?

Sol. Electrons are flowing through the conductors from its higher potential end to its lower potential end.

44 Draw a circuit diagram using a battery of two cells, two resistors of 3Ω each connected in series, a plug key and a rheostat.

Sol. The required circuit diagram is given as below:

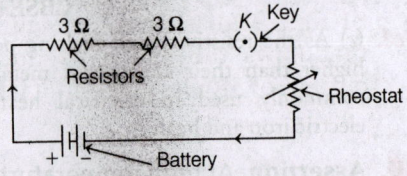

45 Draw the V-I graph for ohmic and non-ohmic conductors.

Sol. V-I graph for ohmic conductor is given as below:

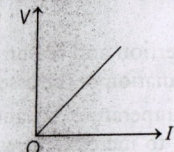

V-I graph for non-ohmic conductor is given as below:

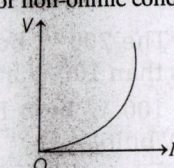

46 Out of the two wires P and Q shown below, which one has greater resistance? Justify it.

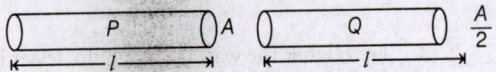

Sol. Smaller the area of cross-section, greater will be resistance as

$$R \propto \frac{1}{A} \quad \text{[since, lengths are same]}$$

So, wire Q has greater resistance.

47 Find the minimum resistance that can be made using five resistors each of $(1/5)\Omega$.
NCERT Exemplar

Sol. Minimum resistance can be obtained by connecting resistors in parallel, $R_{eq} = \frac{R}{n} = \frac{1/5}{5} = \frac{1}{25} \Omega$

48 Two unequal resistances are connected in parallel. If you are not provided with any other parameters (e.g., Numerical values of I and R), what can be said about the voltage drop across the two resistors?
CBSE SQP 2020-21

Sol. In parallel combination of resistors, the voltage drop across each resistor is same. So, for the two unequal resistances connected in parallel, the voltage drop across both the resistors will be same.

49 Give two examples for application of heating effect of electric current.

Sol. Electric iron and electric bulb are two examples for application of heating effect of electric current.

50 Nichrome is used to make the element of electric heater. Why?

Sol. Nichrome is used to make the element of electric heater because it is an alloy with high resistivity and high melting point.

51 What do you understand by the term fuse in an electric circuit?

Sol. Fuse is a safety device connected in series in an electric circuit which melts when the circuit gets overloaded or short circuited.

Short Answer (SA) Type Questions

1 What is meant by electric current? Write its SI unit. Calculate the amount of charge that flows through a conductor when a current of 5A flows through it for 2 min.
CBSE 2015

Sol. Electric current is defined as the rate of flow of electric charge through any cross-section of a conductor.
SI unit of electric current is ampere(A).
Given, $I = 5A$, $t = 2$ min $= 2 \times 60$ s $= 120$ s, $q = ?$
We know that, charge, $q = I \times t$
$\Rightarrow \quad q = 5 \times 120 = 600$ C
Thus, the amount of charge flowing through conductor is 600 C.

2 (i) State the relation between potential difference, work done and charge moved.

(ii) Calculate the work done in moving a charge of 4 C from a point at 220 V to a point at 230 V.

Sol. (i) The relation between potential difference, work done and charge moved is given by

$$\text{Potential difference} = \frac{\text{Work done}}{\text{Charge moved}}$$

$$\Rightarrow \quad V = \frac{W}{q}$$

(ii) Given, charge, $q = 4$ C
Potential at point A, $V_A = 220$ V
Potential at point B, $V_B = 230$ V
Work done, $W = ?$
∴ Potential difference, $V = V_B - V_A$
$= 230 - 220 = 10$ V
We know that, work done,
$W = V \times q$
$= 10 \times 4 = 40$ J

3 What is meant by "electrical resistance" of a conductor? State how resistance of a conductor is affected when

(i) a low current passes through it for a short duration,

(ii) a heavy current passes through it for about 30 s.
CBSE 2016

Sol. Electrical resistance of a conductor may be defined as the property of any substance to oppose the flow of current through it.

(i) The resistance of the conductor will increase when a low current pass through it for a short duration.

(ii) The resistance of the conductor will decrease when a heavy current pass through it.

4 Read the following informations :

(i) Resistivity of copper is lower than that of aluminium which in turn is lower than that of constantan.

(ii) Six wires labelled as A, B, C, D, E and F have been designed as per the following parameters:

Wire	Length	Diameter	Material	Resistance
A	l	$2d$	Aluminium	R_1
B	$2l$	$d/2$	Constantan	R_2
C	$3l$	$d/2$	Constantan	R_3
D	$l/2$	$3d$	Copper	R_4
E	$2l$	$2d$	Aluminium	R_5
F	$l/2$	$4d$	Copper	R_6

Answer the following questions using the above data:

(a) Which of the wires has maximum resistance and why?

(b) Which of the wires has minimum resistance and why?

(c) Arrange R_1, R_3 and R_5 in ascending order of their values. Justify your answer.

Sol. (a) Wire C has maximum resistance because it has maximum length, least thickness and highest resistivity.

(b) Wire F has the minimum resistance, since it has least length, maximum thickness and least resistivity. $\left[\text{using, } R = \rho\dfrac{l}{A}\right]$

(c) $R_3 > R_5 > R_1$

[using relation, $R = \rho\dfrac{l}{A}$ and comparison]

5 A student carries out an experiment and plots the V-I graph of a sample of nichrome wire at three temperature T_1, T_2 and T_3 as shown in the figure.

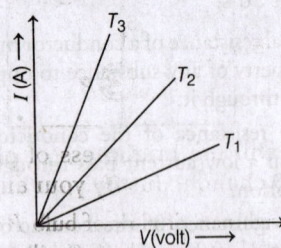

(i) Which of the following relation among temperatures T_1, T_2 and T_3 is correct?
(a) $T_1 > T_2 > T_3$ (b) $T_3 > T_2 > T_1$
(c) $T_1 = T_2 = T_3$ (d) $T_2 = \dfrac{T_1 + T_3}{2}$

(ii) At which temperature, the resistance of nichrome wire is minimum?
(a) T_1 (b) T_2
(c) T_3 (d) None of these

(iii) At which temperature, V-I graph obeys Ohm's law?
(a) T_1 (b) T_2
(c) T_3 (d) None of these

Sol. (i) (b) Slope of V-I graph for nichrome wire is directly proportional to its temperature. Hence, correct relation among T_1, T_2 and T_3 is given as
$$T_3 > T_2 > T_1$$

(ii) (a) Resistance of nichrome wire is directly proportional to temperature. Since, $T_1 < T_2 < T_3$, hence resistance of nichrome wire is minimum at temperature T_1.

(iii) (d) Because each V-I curve is a straight line i.e. $V \propto I$

6 A metal wire has diameter of 0.25 mm and electrical resistivity of 0.8×10^{-8} Ω-m.

(i) What will be the length of this wire to make a resistance 5 Ω?

(ii) How much will the resistance change, if the diameter of the wire is doubled? **CBSE 2016**

Sol. Given, diameter = 0.25 mm

Resistivity, $\rho = 0.8 \times 10^{-8}$ Ω-m

(i) Resistance, $R = 5\,\Omega$

We know that, $R = \dfrac{\rho l}{A}$

$\Rightarrow l = \dfrac{RA}{\rho} = \dfrac{5 \times \pi \times \left[\dfrac{0.25}{2} \times 10^{-3}\right]^2}{0.8 \times 10^{-8}}$

$\left[\because A = \pi r^2 \text{ and } r = \dfrac{D}{2}\right]$

$= \dfrac{5 \times \pi \times 1.56 \times 10^{-8}}{0.8 \times 10^{-8}} = 30.62$ m

(1½)

(ii) ∴ Resistance, $R = \dfrac{\rho l}{A} = \dfrac{\rho l}{\pi \left(\dfrac{D}{2}\right)^2} = \dfrac{\rho l}{\pi} \times \dfrac{4}{D^2}$

$\left[\because A = \pi r^2 \text{ and } r = \dfrac{D}{2}\right]$

$R' = \dfrac{\rho l}{A} = \dfrac{\rho l}{\pi \left(\dfrac{2D}{2}\right)^2}$ [∵ D has become 2D]

$= \dfrac{\rho l}{\pi D^2}$

All in one Electricity

Now, $\dfrac{R'}{R} = \dfrac{\rho l}{\pi D^2} \div \dfrac{\rho l \times 4}{\pi D^2}$

$= \dfrac{\rho l}{\pi D^2} \times \dfrac{\pi D^2}{\rho l \times 4} = \dfrac{1}{4}$

$\therefore \quad R' = \dfrac{R}{4}$

Thus, resistance will decrease by 4 times.

7 Show how would you join three resistors, each of resistance 9 Ω, so that the equivalent resistance of the combination is

(i) 13.5 Ω (ii) 6 Ω? **CBSE 2018**

Sol. To get an equivalent resistance of 13.5Ω, we connect resistors as

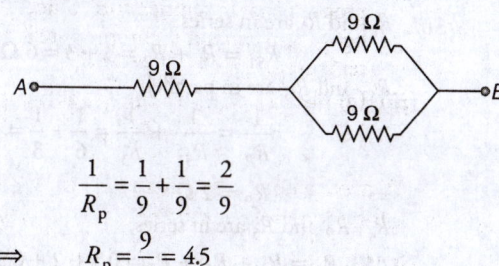

$\dfrac{1}{R_p} = \dfrac{1}{9} + \dfrac{1}{9} = \dfrac{2}{9}$

$\Rightarrow \quad R_p = \dfrac{9}{2} = 4.5$

$\therefore \quad R_{eq} = 9 + 4.5 = 13.5\,\Omega$

To get an equivalent a resistance of 6Ω, we connect resistors as

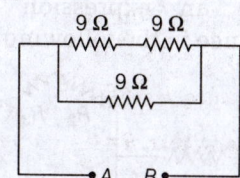

Here, $R_s = 9 + 9 = 18\,\Omega$

$\therefore \quad \dfrac{1}{R_{eq}} = \dfrac{1}{9} + \dfrac{1}{18} = \dfrac{3}{18}$

$\Rightarrow \quad R_{eq} = 6\,\Omega$

8

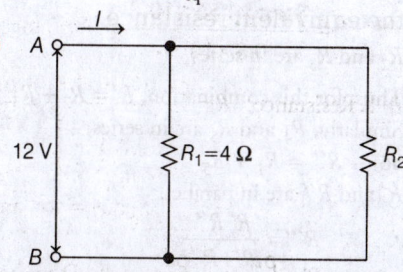

A student has two resistors 2 Ω and 3 Ω. She has to put one of them in place of R_2 as shown in the circuit. The current that she needs in the entire circuit is exactly 9 A. Show by calculation which of the two resistors she should choose?

Sol. The given circuit is shown below

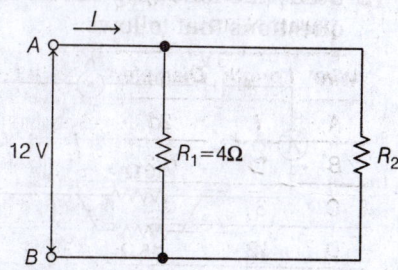

Let R be the resistance of the entire circuit.
Given, overall current needed, I = 9 A
Voltage, V = 12 V
Using Ohm's law, V = IR

$\Rightarrow \quad R = \dfrac{V}{I} = \dfrac{12}{9} = \dfrac{4}{3}\,\Omega$

Now, the resistors R_1 and R_2 are in parallel combination.

$\therefore \quad \dfrac{1}{R} = \dfrac{1}{R_1} + \dfrac{1}{R_2}$

$\Rightarrow \quad \dfrac{1}{R} = \dfrac{1}{4} + \dfrac{1}{R_2}$

$\Rightarrow \quad \dfrac{3}{4} = \dfrac{1}{4} + \dfrac{1}{R_2}$ $\left[\because R = \dfrac{4}{3}\,\Omega\right]$

$\Rightarrow \quad \dfrac{1}{R_2} = \dfrac{3}{4} - \dfrac{1}{4} = \dfrac{2}{4} = \dfrac{1}{2}$

$\Rightarrow \quad R_2 = 2\,\Omega$

So, the student should choose 2Ω resistor.

9 A battery E is connected to three identical lamps P, Q and R as shown in figure. Initially, the switch S is kept open and the lamp P and Q are observed to glow with same brightness. Then, switch S is closed.

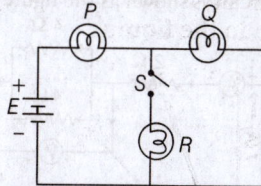

How will the brightness of glow of bulbs P and Q change? Justify your answer.

Sol. The brightness of glow of bulb P will increase and brightness of glow of bulb Q will decrease.

This is because, on closing S, bulbs Q and R will be in parallel and the combination will be in series with bulb P. Hence, the total resistance of the circuit will decrease and the current flowing in the circuit will increase. Therefore, the glow of bulb P will increase.

Also, bulbs Q and R will be in parallel in this case. So, the current gets divided and lesser current flows through Q and hence the glow of bulb Q decreases.)

10 Study the following circuit and answer the questions that follows:

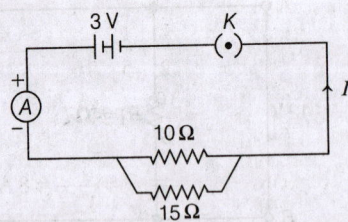

(i) State the type of combination of two resistors in the circuit.
(ii) How much current is flowing through
   (a) 10 Ω and   (b) 15 Ω resistor?
(iii) What is the ammeter reading?

Sol. (i) Two resistors are in parallel combination.
(ii) Current through
   (a) 10 Ω resistor, $I_1 = \dfrac{V}{R} = \dfrac{3}{10} = 0.3$ A
   (b) 15 Ω resistor, $I_2 = \dfrac{V}{R} = \dfrac{3}{15} = 0.2$ A
(iii) Ammeter reading = Total current flowing through the circuit
   $= 0.3 + 0.2 = 0.5$ A

11 Draw a circuit diagram of an electric circuit containing a cell, a key, an ammeter, a resistor of 2 Ω in series with a combination of two resistors (4 Ω each) in parallel and a voltmeter across the parallel combination. Will the potential difference across the 2 Ω resistor be the same as that across the parallel combination of 4 Ω resistors? Give reasons.   **NCERT Exemplar**

Sol. The circuit is shown as the figure

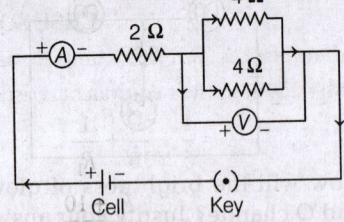

Effective resistance of combination of two resistors (4 Ω each) in parallel is
$$R_{\text{eff}} = \dfrac{4 \times 4}{4+4} = 2 \, \Omega$$
Since, the resistor of 2 Ω and parallel combination of two 4 Ω resistors are in series, same current will flow through these. Hence, the potential difference across 2 Ω resistor is same as that across the parallel combination of two resistors.

12 Five resistors are connected in a circuit as shown in figure. Find the ammeter reading when the circuit is closed.

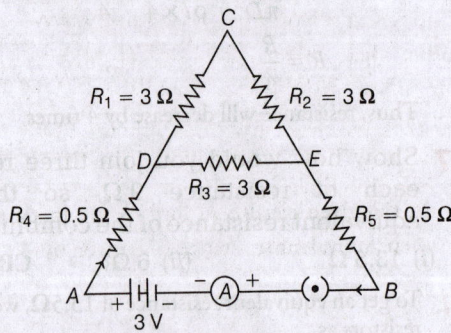

Sol. R_1 and R_2 are in series,
$$R_{S1} = R_1 + R_2 = 3 + 3 = 6 \, \Omega$$
R_{S1} and R_3 are in parallel.
$$\therefore \quad \dfrac{1}{R_P} = \dfrac{1}{R_{S1}} + \dfrac{1}{R_3} = \dfrac{1}{6} + \dfrac{1}{3} = \dfrac{1}{2}$$
$$\Rightarrow \quad R_P = 2 \, \Omega$$
R_4, R_P and R_5 are in series,
$$\therefore \quad R_S = R_4 + R_P + R_5 = 0.5 + 2 + 0.5 = 3 \, \Omega$$
Then, current, $I = \dfrac{V}{R_S} = \dfrac{3}{3} = 1$ A

13 Derive an expression for equivalent resistance in the following case

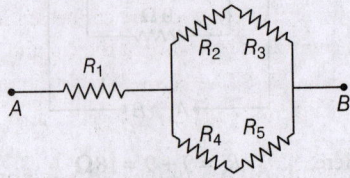

Decide which resistances are in series and parallel. Solve for series and then for parallel. Combine both the results to get the equivalent resistance.

Sol. R_2 and R_3 are in series.
Thus, for this combination, $R' = R_2 + R_3$
Similarly, R_4 and R_5 are in series,
So, $R'' = R_4 + R_5$
R' and R'' are in parallel.
$$\therefore \quad R''' = \dfrac{R'R''}{R'+R''}$$
$$= \dfrac{(R_2 + R_3)(R_4 + R_5)}{R_2 + R_3 + R_4 + R_5}$$
R_1 and R''' are in series.
$$\therefore \quad R_{eq} = R_1 + \dfrac{(R_2 + R_3)(R_4 + R_5)}{R_2 + R_3 + R_4 + R_5}$$

14 Find the equivalent resistance in the following circuit.

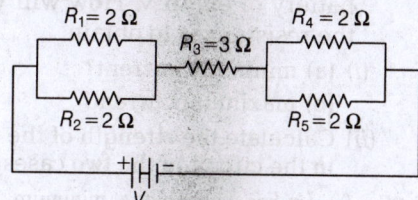

Sol. In the given circuit, R_1 and R_2 are in parallel. So, their equivalent resistance R' is given by

$$\frac{1}{R'} = \frac{1}{R_1} + \frac{1}{R_2}$$

$$= \frac{1}{2} + \frac{1}{2} = \frac{2}{2} = 1$$

$$\Rightarrow \quad R' = 1\,\Omega$$

Similarly, equivalent resistance R'' of R_4 and R_5 is given by

$$\frac{1}{R''} = \frac{1}{R_4} + \frac{1}{R_5} = \frac{1}{2} + \frac{1}{2} = \frac{2}{2}$$

$$\Rightarrow \quad R'' = 1\,\Omega$$

The circuit can be redrawn as

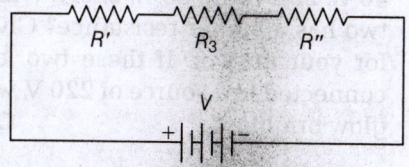

Now, all the resistances are connected in series.
So, equivalent resistance of the circuit,

$$R = R' + R_3 + R''$$
$$= 1 + 3 + 1 = 5\,\Omega$$

15 A circuit diagram is given as shown below:

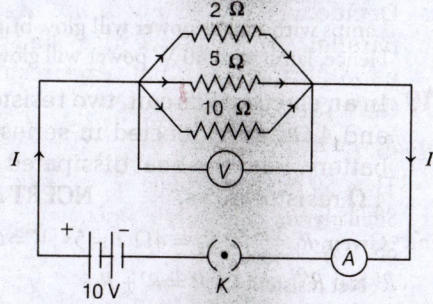

Calculate
(i) the total effective resistance of the circuit.
(ii) the total current in the circuit.
(iii) the current through each resistor.

Sol. Given, $R_1 = 2\,\Omega$, $R_2 = 5\,\Omega$,
$R_3 = 10\,\Omega$, $V = 10\,V$

(i) Total effective resistance as the combination is in parallel,

$$\frac{1}{R_{\text{eff}}} = \frac{1}{R_1} + \frac{1}{R_2} + \frac{1}{R_3}$$

$$= \frac{1}{2} + \frac{1}{5} + \frac{1}{10} = \frac{5+2+1}{10} = \frac{8}{10}$$

$$\Rightarrow \quad R_{\text{eff}} = \frac{10}{8} = 1.25\,\Omega$$

(ii) Total current, $I = \dfrac{V}{R_{\text{eff}}} = \dfrac{10}{1.25} = 8\,A$

$$= 5 + 2 + 1 = 8\,A$$

(iii) Current through each resistor,

$$I_1 = \frac{V}{R_1} = \frac{10}{2} = 5\,A, \quad I_2 = \frac{V}{R_2} = \frac{10}{5} = 2\,A$$

and $\quad I_3 = \dfrac{V}{R_3} = \dfrac{10}{10} = 1\,A$

16

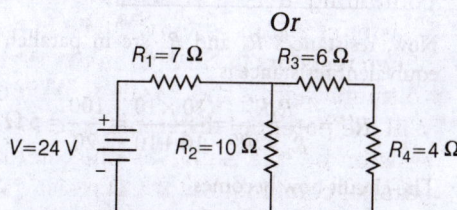

In the above circuit, if the current reading in the ammeter A is 2A, what would be the value of R_1?

Or

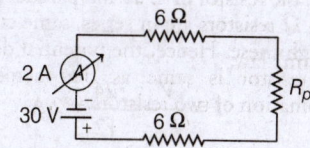

Calculate the total resistance and the total current in the circuit.

CBSE SQP (Term-II)

Sol. The resistances $5\,\Omega$, $10\,\Omega$ and R_1 are in parallel combination, so their equivalent resistance is

$$\frac{1}{R_p} = \frac{1}{5} + \frac{1}{10} + \frac{1}{R_1}$$

$$= \frac{2R_1 + R_1 + 10}{10 R_1}$$

$$\Rightarrow \quad R_p = \frac{10 R_1}{3 R_1 + 10} \qquad \ldots(i)$$

The circuit now becomes

Here, resistances 6Ω, R_p and 6Ω are in series, so equivalent resistance of the circuit becomes

$R_{eq} = 6 + 6 + R_p$
$= 12 + \dfrac{10R_1}{3R_1 + 10}$ [From Eq. (i)]
$= \dfrac{46R_1 + 120}{3R_1 + 10}$

∴ Current drawn, $I = V/R_{eq}$

$\Rightarrow R_{eq} = \dfrac{V}{I}$

$\Rightarrow \dfrac{46R_1 + 120}{3R_1 + 10} = \dfrac{30}{2}$

$\Rightarrow 92R_1 + 240 = 90R_1 + 300$

$\Rightarrow R_1 = \dfrac{60}{2} = 30\,\Omega$

Or

Here, resistances R_3 and R_4 are in series, so their is equivalent resistance is $R' = R_3 + R_4 = 6 + 4 = 10\,\Omega$
The circuit is reduced to

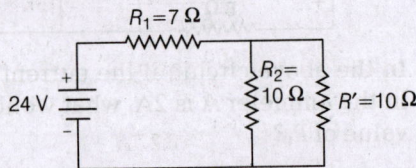

Now, resistances R_2 and R' are in parallel, so their equivalent resistance is

$R'' = \dfrac{R_2 R'}{R_2 + R'} = \dfrac{10 \times 10}{10 + 10} = \dfrac{100}{20} = 5\,\Omega$

The circuit now becomes

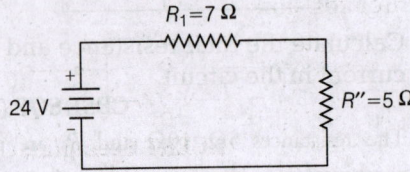

The resistances R_1 and R'' are in series, so their equivalent or total resistance of circuit is

$R_{eq} = R_1 + R'' = 7 + 5 = 12\,\Omega$

The final circuit is as shown

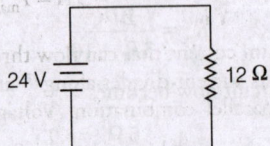

By Ohm's law,

$I = \dfrac{V}{R_{eq}} = \dfrac{24}{12} = 2\,A$

17 Two resistors with resistances 5 Ω and 10 Ω respectively, are to be connected to a battery of emf 6 V. How will you connect the resistances to obtain

(i) (a) minimum current?
(b) maximum current?

(ii) Calculate the strength of the total current in the circuit in the two cases.

Sol. (i) (a) For obtaining minimum current, the two resistors should be connected in series.

(b) For obtaining maximum current, the two resistors should be connected in parallel.

(ii) ∴ Total current in the circuit,
(parallel combination)

$I = \dfrac{V}{R} = \dfrac{6 \times 3}{10} = 1.8\,A$

∴ Total current in the circuit,
(series combination)

$I = \dfrac{V}{R} = \dfrac{6}{15} = 0.4\,A$

18 You have two electric lamps having rating 40 W, 220 V and 60 W, 220 V. Which of the two has a higher resistance? Give reason for your answer. If these two lamps are connected to a source of 220 V, which will glow brighter? **CBSE 2016**

Sol. We know that, power, $P = \dfrac{V^2}{R}$

Thus, resistance is inversely proportional to power, i.e. higher power less will be resistance and vice-versa. So, the electric lamp with power rating 40 W will have a higher resistance as compared to 60 W lamp.

Lamps with higher power will glow brighter. Hence, lamp with 60 W power will glow brighter.

19 In an electrical circuit, two resistors of 2 Ω and 4 Ω are connected in series to a 6 V battery. Find the heat dissipated by the 4 Ω resistor in 5 s. **NCERT Exemplar**

Sol. Given, $R_1 = 2\Omega, R_2 = 4\Omega, t = 5\,s, V = 6\,V$

∴ Net resistance, $R = R_1 + R_2$
$= 2\Omega + 4\Omega = 6\Omega$

∴ Current, $I = \dfrac{V}{R} = \dfrac{6V}{6\Omega} = 1\,A$

In series, same 1A current passes through both resistors.

∴ Heat dissipated, $H = I^2 R_1 \times t$
$= (1)^2 \times 4 \times 5$
$= 20\,J$

20 (i) It would cost a man ₹ 3.50 to buy 1.0 kWh of electrical energy from the main electricity board. His generator has a maximum power of 2.0 kW. The generator produces energy at this maximum power for 3 h. Calculate how much it would cost to buy the same amount of energy from the main electricity board.

(ii) A student boils water in an electric kettle for 20 min. Using the same mains supply, he wants to reduce the boiling time of water. To do so should he increase or decrease the length of the heating element? Justify your answer. **CBSE SQP (Term-II)**

Sol. (i) Given, power of generator, $P = 2$ kW

Time, $t = 3$ h

∴ Energy consumed, $E = P \times t$
$= 2 \times 3 = 6$ kWh

Since, cost of 1 kWh of electrical energy is ₹ 3.50.

∴ Cost of 6 kWh of electrical energy $= 6 \times 3.50$
$= ₹ 21.0$

(ii) As we know that
Heat, $H = I^2 Rt$

Here, I is constant, so to reduce the boiling time (t), the R should be decreased.

Since, $R = \rho \dfrac{l}{A}$ or $R \propto l$

So, the length of the heating element should be decreased.

21 The potential difference between two terminals of an electric iron is 220V and the current flowing through its element is 5A. Calculate the resistance and wattage of the electric iron. **CBSE 2016**

Sol. The potential difference between two terminals of an electric iron $(V) = 220$V, current flowing through its element $(I) = 5$ A.

Therefore, resistance, $R = \dfrac{V}{I} = \dfrac{220}{5} \Omega = 44 \Omega$

We know that, power, $P = V \times I$
$= 220 \times 5 = 1100$ W

22 (i) Write Joule's law of heating.

(ii) Two lamps, one rated 100W, 220V and the other 60W, 220V are connected in parallel to electric main supply. Find the current drawn by two bulbs from the line, if the supply voltage is 220V. **CBSE 2018**

Sol. (i) According to Joule's law of heating, amount of heat produced in a resistor is

(a) directly proportional to square of current flowing through the resistor.
∴ $H \propto I^2$

(b) directly proportional to resistance of the resistor.
∴ $H \propto R$

(c) directly proportional to time for which the current flows through the resistor.
∴ $H \propto t$

Hence, $H = I^2 Rt$

(ii)
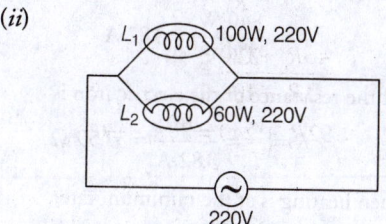

Here, potential, $V = 220$ V
Power, $P_1 = 100$ W, $P_2 = 60$ W
As, current drawn is given by

$I = \dfrac{\text{Power }(P)}{\text{Voltage }(V)}$ [From $P = VI$]

So, $I_1 = \dfrac{100}{220} = 0.45$ A

and $I_2 = \dfrac{60}{220} = 0.27$ A

23 Three 2 Ω resistors, A, B and C are connected as shown in figure. Each of them dissipates energy and can withstand a maximum power of 18 W without melting. Find the maximum current that can flow through the three resistors.

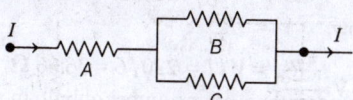

NCERT Exemplar; CBSE 2010

Sol. Given, resistance, $R = 2 \Omega$
Maximum power, $P_{max} = 18$ W
Maximum current, $I_{max} = ?$
As we know, $P = I^2 R$

$\Rightarrow I = \sqrt{\dfrac{P}{R}} = \sqrt{\dfrac{18}{2}} = 3 \text{ A} = I_{max}$

Maximum current that can flow through 2Ω resistor is 3 A. This current divides along B and C because they are in parallel combination. Voltage across B and C remain same and hence $I \propto \dfrac{1}{R}$. Since, B and C have same resistance same current flows through them.

i.e. $\dfrac{3}{2} = 1.5$ A flows through B and C.

24 An electric iron consumes energy at a rate of 840 W when heating is at the maximum rate and 360 W when the heating is at the minimum rate. The applied voltage is 220 V. What is the value of current and the resistance in each case?

Sol. We know that the power input is $P = VI$

Thus, the current, $I = \dfrac{P}{V}$

When heating is at the maximum rate,
$$I = \dfrac{840 \text{ W}}{220 \text{ V}} = 3.82 \text{ A}$$

and the resistance of the electric iron is
$$R = \dfrac{V}{I} = \dfrac{220 \text{ V}}{3.82 \text{ A}} = 57.59 \; \Omega$$

When heating is at the minimum rate,
$$I = \dfrac{360 \text{ W}}{220 \text{ V}} = 1.64 \text{ A}$$

and the resistance of the electric iron is
$$R = \dfrac{V}{I} = \dfrac{220 \text{ V}}{1.64 \text{ A}} = 134.15 \; \Omega$$

25 An electrical bulb is rated 40 W, 220 V. How many bulbs can be connected in parallel with each other across the two wires of 220 V line, if the maximum allowable current is 6 A? **CBSE 2016**

Sol. Given, $P = 40$ W, $V = 220$ V, $I = 6$ A

We know that, $R = V^2 / P$
$= (220)^2 / 40$
$= 48400 / 40$
$= 1210 \; \Omega$

Now, $V = IR_{eq}$
$\Rightarrow R_{eq} = V/I = 220/6 = 36.66 \; \Omega$

Suppose, there are x number of bulb in parallel
$36.66 = 1210/x$
$\therefore \quad x = 1210/36.66 = 33.006 = 33$

26 (i) List the factors on which the resistance of a conductor in the shape of a wire depends.

(ii) Why are metals good conductors of electricity, whereas glass is a bad conductor of electricity? Give reason.

(iii) Why are alloys commonly used in electrical heating devices? Give reason. **CBSE 2018**

Sol. (i) Resistance of a wire depends on,

(a) length of wire : $R \propto l$

(b) area of cross-section of wire : $R \propto \dfrac{1}{A}$

(c) resistivity of material of wire : $R \propto \rho$
$$\therefore \quad R = \rho \dfrac{l}{A}$$

(ii) Metals are good conductor as their resistivity is very low whereas glass is a bad conductor as its resistivity is very high.

(iii) Alloys are used as heating elements as their resistivity and melting points both are very high.

27 The value of current (I) flowing through a given resistor of resistance (R). For the corresponding values of potential difference (V) across the resistor are as given below

V (Volts)	0.5	1.0	1.5	2.0	2.5	3.0	4.0	5.0
I (Ampere)	0.1	0.2	0.3	0.4	0.5	0.6	0.8	1.0

Plot a graph between current (I) and potential difference (V) and determine the resistance (R) of the resistor. **CBSE 2018**

Sol. Scale, At x axis, 1 div (1 cm) = 0.1 A
At y axis, 1 div (1 cm) = 0.5 V

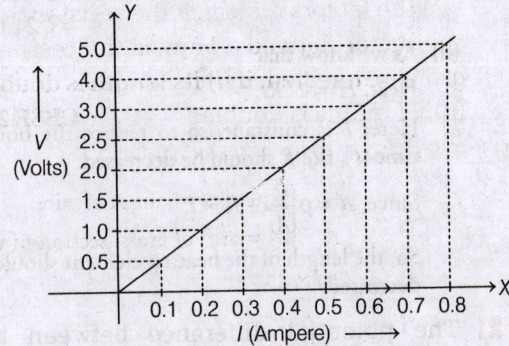

$\therefore$ Resistance = R = Slope of graph = $\dfrac{V}{I}$

$\therefore \quad R = \dfrac{y_2 - y_1}{x_2 - x_1} = \dfrac{1.5 - 1.0}{0.3 - 0.2} = \dfrac{0.5}{0.1} = 5 \; \Omega$

28 An electric geyser rated at 1500 W, 250 V is connected to a 250 V line mains. Solve

(i) the electric current drawn by it.

(ii) energy consumed by it in 50 h.

(iii) cost of energy consumed, if each unit costs ₹ 6.

Sol. Given, power, $P = 1500$ W,
voltage, $V = 250$ V

(i) $\therefore$ Electric current drawn,
$$I = \dfrac{P}{V} = \dfrac{1500}{250} = 6 \text{ A}$$

Electricity

(ii) ∴ Energy consumed, $E = \text{Power} \times \text{Time}$
$= 1500 \times 50$ [∵ $t = 50$ h]
$= 75000$ Wh $= 75$ kWh
[∵ 1 kW = 1000 W]
$= 75$ unit [∵ 1 unit = 1 kWh] (1)

(iii) ∵ Cost of energy consumed
$= 75 \times 6 = ₹450$

29 A heater coil connected to 200 V has a resistance of 80 Ω. If the heater is plugged in for the time t such that 1 kg of water at 20°C attains a temperature of 60°C. Find
(i) the power of heater.
(ii) the heat absorbed by water.
(iii) the value of t in seconds.

Sol. (i) ∴ Power of heater,
$$P = \frac{V^2}{R}$$
$= \frac{200 \times 200}{80} = 500$ W

(ii) ∴ Heat absorbed by water, $H = mC\theta_R$
$= 1 \times 4200 \times 40$
[∵ $\theta_R = 60° - 20° = 40°C, C = 4200$ J/kg °C]
$= 168000$ J
$= 168$ kJ

(iii) ∴ Energy consumed by heater, $H = P \times t$
$168000 = 500 \times t$
$\Rightarrow t = \frac{168000}{500} = 336$ s

Long Answer (LA) Type Questions

1 What is meant by resistance of a conductor? Name and define its SI unit. List the factors on which the resistance of a conductor depends. How is the resistance of a wire affected, if (i) its length is doubled, (ii) its radius is doubled? **CBSE 2016**

Sol. Refer to text on Pg. 359 and 360.

(i) ∴ $R = \dfrac{\rho l}{A}$ $\begin{bmatrix} \text{where, } l = \text{length of wire,} \\ A = \text{area of cross-section of wire} \end{bmatrix}$

$R' = \dfrac{\rho l \times 2}{A}$

∴ $R' = 2R$

i.e. resistance will be doubled, if length of the wire is doubled.

(ii) ∴ $R = \dfrac{\rho l}{A} \Rightarrow R = \dfrac{\rho l}{\pi r^2}$ [∵ $A = \pi r^2$]

$R' = \dfrac{\rho l}{\pi (2r)^2} = \dfrac{\rho l}{\pi r^2} \times \dfrac{1}{4} = \dfrac{R}{4}$

Thus, resistance will decrease by four times, if radius of wire is doubled.

2 (i) Distinguish between the terms electrical resistance and resistivity of conductor.

(ii) A copper wire of resistivity 1.63×10^{-8} Ω-m has cross-section area of 10.3×10^{-4} cm². Calculate the length of the wire required to make a 20 Ω coil. **CBSE 2016**

Sol. (i) Refer to text on Pg. 359 and 360 for definitions of R and ρ.

Resistance depends on the length and area of a substance.
Resistivity depends on the nature and temperature of the substance.

(ii) Given, $\rho = 1.63 \times 10^{-8}$ Ω-m
$A = 10.3 \times 10^{-4}$ cm² $= 10.3 \times 10^{-4} \times 10^{-4}$ m²
$R = 20$ Ω, $l = ?$

We know that, Resistance, $R = \dfrac{\rho l}{A}$

$\Rightarrow l = \dfrac{RA}{\rho} = \dfrac{20 \times 10.3 \times 10^{-4} \times 10^{-4} \text{ m}^2}{1.63 \times 10^{-8} \text{ Ω-m}}$

$= \dfrac{20 \times 10.3 \times 10^{-8}}{1.63 \times 10^{-8}} = 126.38$ m

3 (a) State Ohm's law.
(b) How is an ammeter connected in an electric circuit?
(c) The power of a lamp is 100 W. Find the energy consumed by it in 1 min.
(d) A wire of resistance 5Ω is bent in the form of a closed circle. Find the resistance between two points at the ends of any diameter of the circle.
CBSE (All India) 2020

Sol. (a) Refer to text on page 359.
(b) An ammeter is connected in series in a circuit.
(c) Given, $P = 100$ W and time $t = 1$ minute $= 60$ s.
As, energy $E = Pt$
$= 100 \times 60 = 6000$ J

(d) Given, a wire with resistance 5Ω. Now, wire is converted into a ring as shown below

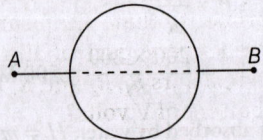

The equivalent circuit,

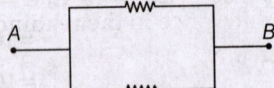

Hence, $R_{eq} = R_{AB} = \dfrac{2.5 \times 2.5}{2.5 + 2.5} = 1.25\ W$

4 (i) Heating elements of electrical heating devices is made up of an alloy rather than a pure metal. Give two reasons.

(ii) Four resistors of 4Ω each are joined end to end to form a square. Calculate the equivalent resistance of the combination between two adjacent corner? **CBSE 2016**

Sol. (i) Alloys are used for making electrical heating devices due to the following reasons:
(a) They have a higher resistivity as compared to pure metals.
(b) They do not oxidise readily at high temperatures.

(ii) The resistance between points A and B is given by

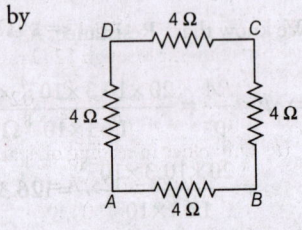

$R = \dfrac{1}{\dfrac{1}{4} + \dfrac{1}{4+4+4}} = \dfrac{1}{\dfrac{1}{4} + \dfrac{1}{12}} = \dfrac{1}{\dfrac{3+1}{12}} = \dfrac{4}{12}$

$= 3\ \Omega$

5 (i) Define electric power. An electrical device of resistance R is connected across a source of voltage V and draws a current I. Derive an expression for power in terms of current and resistance.

(b) Two electric bulbs rated 100 W, 220 V and 60 W, 220 V are connected in parallel to an electric mains of 220 V. Find the current drawn by the bulbs from the mains.
CBSE 2019

Sol. (i) Refer to text on page. 366.
Topic (Electric power)

(ii) For first bulb, $P_1 = 100\ W, V_1 = 220\ V$

$\therefore R_1 = \dfrac{V_1^2}{P_1} = \dfrac{220 \times 200}{100} = 484\ \Omega$

For second bulb, $P_2 = 60\ W, V_2 = 220\ V$

$\therefore R_2 = \dfrac{V_2^2}{P_2} = \dfrac{220 \times 220}{60} = 806.6\ \Omega$

Since, both bulbs are connected in parallel combination.
Hence, equivalent resistance,

$R = \dfrac{R_1 R_2}{R_1 + R_2}$

$R = \dfrac{484 \times 806.6}{484 + 806.6} = 302.5$

Current drawn by the bulbs,

$I = \dfrac{V}{R} = \dfrac{220}{302.5} = 0.73\ A$

6 (a) Define power and state its SI unit.

(b) A torch bulb is rated 5V and 500 mA. Calculate its
(i) power
(ii) resistances
(iii) energy consumed when it is lighted for $2\dfrac{1}{2}$ hours.
CBSE (All India) 2020

Sol. (a) Refer to text on page 366.

(b) Given, voltage rating, V = 5 V and current rating I = 500 mA

(i) As, we know power of bulb
$P = VI = 5 \times 500 \times 10^{-3}$
[∵ A = 10 mA⁻³]
$= 2.5\ W = 2.5 \times 10^{-3}\ kW$

(ii) Resistance of bulb,
$R = \dfrac{V}{I}$ (ohm's law)

$\Rightarrow R = \dfrac{5}{500 \times 10^{-3}} = 10\ \Omega$

(iii) Energy consumed in $2\dfrac{1}{2}$ hour
$E = P \cdot t = \dfrac{2.5 \times 2.5}{1000}$
$[2\dfrac{1}{2} h = 2.5\ h]$

$= \dfrac{6.25}{1000} = 0.00625\ kWh$

7. (a) Two lamps rated 100 W, 220 V and 10 W, 220 V are connected in parallel to 220 V supply. Calculate the total current through the circuit.

(b) Two resistors X and Y of resistances 2 Ω and 3 Ω respectively are first joined in parallel and then in series. In each case, the supplied voltage is 5 V.

(i) Draw circuit diagrams to show the combination of resistors in each case.

(ii) Calculate the voltage across the 3 Ω resistor in the series combination of resistors.
CBSE (All India) 2020

Sol. (a) Given, rating of two lamps, $P_1 = 100$ W, $V_1 = 220$ V, $P_2 = 10$ W and $V_2 = 220$ V
The circuit is shown below

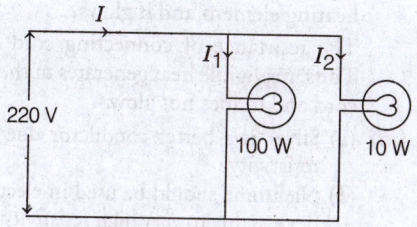

Current in 1st lamp,
$$I = \frac{P}{V} \quad [\because \text{power} = \text{current} \times \text{voltage}]$$
$$\Rightarrow I_1 = \frac{100}{220} = 0.45 \text{ A}$$

Current in 2nd lamp,
$$\Rightarrow I_2 = \frac{P_2}{V_2} = \frac{10}{220} = 0.045 \text{ A}$$

As, net current from source
$$I = I_1 + I_2 = 0.45 + 0.045 = 0.49 \text{ A}.$$

(b) Given, $X = 2\,\Omega, Y = 3\,\Omega$ and $V = 5$ V
(i) Circuits are given below

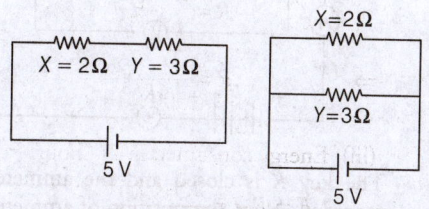

(ii) Current in series combination circuit,
$$I = \frac{V}{R_{eq}} = \frac{V}{X+Y} = \frac{5}{2+3} = 1 \text{ A}$$

Since, current in series circuit is same through all resistors, so potential drop across 3Ω resistance
$$V_Y = IY = 1 \times 3 = 3 \text{ V}$$

8 (i) How will you infer with the help of an experiment that the same current flows through every part of the circuit containing three resistors R_1, R_2 and R_3 in series connected to a battery of V volts?

(ii) Study the following circuit and find out the
(a) current in 12 Ω resistor.
(b) difference in the reading of A_1 and A_2, if any.

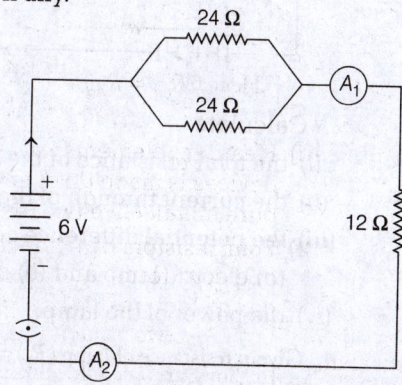

CBSE 2019

Sol. (i) Refer to text on page 361 (Resistors in series).

(ii) (a) Equivalent resistance of given circuit is R, then
$$R = (24 \parallel 24) + 12 = \frac{24 \times 24}{24+24} + 12$$
$$= 12 + 12 = 24\,\Omega$$
$\therefore$ Current through 12 Ω resistor,
$$I = \frac{V}{R} = \frac{6}{24} = 0.25 \text{ A}$$

(b) Difference in reading of A_1 and A_2
$(0.25 - 0.25)$ A = 0 A

9 (i) With the help of suitable circuit diagram, prove that the reciprocal of the equivalent resistance of a group of resistances joined in parallel is equal to the sum of the reciprocals of the individual resistances.

(ii) In an electric circuit two resistors of 12 Ω each are joined in parallel to a 6 V battery. Find the current drawn from the battery. **CBSE 2019**

Sol. (i) Refer to text on page 362 (Resistors in parallel).

(ii) 12 Ω and 12 Ω resistors are connected in parallel, hence equivalent resistance.
$$R = \frac{12 \times 12}{12+12} = 6\,\Omega$$
Potential difference $(V) = 6$ V
$\therefore$ Current drawn $(I) = \dfrac{V}{R} = \dfrac{6}{6} = 1 \text{ A}$

10 An electric lamp of resistance 20 Ω and a conductor of resistance 4 Ω are connected to a 6 V battery as shown in the circuit given below.

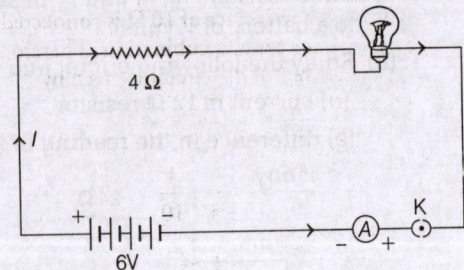

Calculate

(i) the total resistance of the circuit.
(ii) the current through of the circuit.
(iii) the potential difference across the
 (a) electric lamp and (b) conductor.
(iv) the power of the lamp.   **CBSE 2019**

Sol. Given, resistance of lamp $(R_1) = 20\ \Omega$
Resistance of conductor $(R_2) = 4$
Potential difference of battery $(V) = 6\ V$

(i) Total resistance, $R = R_1 + R_2 = 20 + 4 = 24\ \Omega$

(ii) Current through the circuit
$$I = \frac{V}{R} = \frac{6}{24} = 0.25\ A$$

(iii) (a) Potential difference across electric lamp $= IR_1$
$= 0.25 \times 20 = 5\ V$

(b) Potential difference across conductor
$= IR_2 = 0.25 \times 4 = 1\ V$

(iv) Power of lamp $= I^2 R_1$
$= (0.25)^2 \times 20 = 0.0625 \times 20 = 1.25\ W$

11 (i) The potential difference between two points in an electric circuit is 1 V. What does it mean? Name a device that helps to measure the potential difference across a conductor.

(ii) Why does the connecting cord of an electric heater not glow while the heating element does?

(iii) Electrical resistivities of some substances at 20 °C are given as below:

Silver	: $1.60 \times 10^{-8}\ \Omega\text{-m}$
Copper	: $1.62 \times 10^{-8}\ \Omega\text{-m}$
Tungsten	: $5.2 \times 10^{-8}\ \Omega\text{-m}$
Iron	: $10.0 \times 10^{-8}\ \Omega\text{-m}$
Mercury	: $94.0 \times 10^{-8}\ \Omega\text{-m}$
Nichrome	: $100 \times 10^{-6}\ \Omega\text{-m}$

Answer the following questions using above data:

(a) Among silver and copper, which one is a better conductor and why?

(b) Which material would you advise to be used in electrical heating devices and why?   **CBSE 2014, 12**

Sol. (i) If the potential difference between two points is 1 V, it means that if a charge of 1 C is moved from one point to the other, then 1 J of work is done.

The potential difference across a conductor is measured by means of an instrument called the voltmeter.

(ii) The electric power P is given by
$$P = I^2 R$$

The resistance of the heating element is very high. Large amount of heat generates in the heating element and it glows.

The resistance of connecting cord is very low. Thus, negligible heat generates in the connecting cord and it does not glow.

(iii) (a) Silver is a better conductor due to its lower resistivity.

(b) Nichrome should be used in electrical heating devices due to very high resistivity.

12 How will you infer with the help of an experiment that the same current flows through every part of the circuit containing three resistance in series connected to a battery?   **NCERT Exemplar**

Sol. The experimental set up comprise three resistors R_1, R_2 and R_3 of three different values such as $1\Omega, 2\Omega$ and 3Ω which are connected in series. Connect them with a battery of 6V, an ammeter and plug key, as shown in figure,

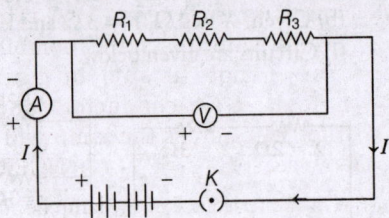

The key K is closed and the ammeter reading is recorded. Now, the position of ammeter is changed to anywhere in between the resistors again, the ammeter reading is recorded each time. It's observed that there was identical reading each time, which shows that same current flows through every part of the circuit containing three resistances in series connected to a battery.

13 (i) Which is the better way to connect lights and other appliances in domestic circuit, series connection or parallel connection? Justify your answer.

(ii) An electrician has made electric circuit of a house in such a way that, if a lamp gets fused in a room of the house, then all the lamps in other rooms of the house stop working. What is the defect in this type of circuit wiring? Give reason.   **CBSE 2015**

Sol. (i) Parallel connection is a better way to connect lights and other appliances in domestic circuit.
It is because
(a) when we connect a number of devices in parallel combination, each device gets the same potential as provided by the battery and it keeps on working even, if other devices stop working.
(b) parallel connection is helpful when each device has different resistances and requires different current for its operation as in this case the current divides itself through different devices unlike series connection.

(ii) Electrician has made series connection of all the lamps in electric circuit of house because of which, if one lamp gets fused, all the other lamps stop working.
This is due to the fact that when devices are connected in series, then if one device fails, the circuit gets broken and all the devices in that circuit stop working.

14 (i) A current of 1 A flows in a series circuit having an electric lamp and a conductor of 5 Ω when connected to a 10 V battery. Calculate the resistance of the electric lamp.

(ii) Now, if a resistance of 10 Ω is connected in parallel with this series combination, then what change (if any) in current flowing through 5 Ω conductor and potential difference across the lamp will take place? Give reason.   **NCERT Exemplar**

Sol. (i) Let the resistance of the lamp be R_1 and resistance of conductor be $R_2 = 5$ Ω

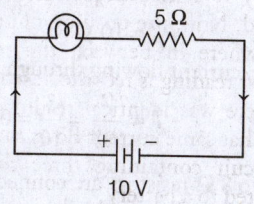

∴ Total resistance in series,
$R_S = R_1 + R_2 = R_1 + 5$

Current, $I = 1$ A, voltage, $V = 10$ V
Using Ohm's law, $V = IR_S$
$10 = 1(R_1 + 5) \Rightarrow R_1 = 5$ Ω
Thus, the resistance of electric lamp is 5 Ω.

(ii) Now, a resistance of 10 Ω is connected in parallel with the series combination. Therefore, the total resistance of the circuit is given by
$\dfrac{1}{R_P} = \dfrac{1}{R_1 + 5} + \dfrac{1}{10}$

$\Rightarrow \dfrac{1}{R_P} = \dfrac{1}{5+5} + \dfrac{1}{10}$

$\Rightarrow \dfrac{1}{R_P} = \dfrac{1}{10} + \dfrac{1}{10}$

∴ $R_P = 5$ Ω

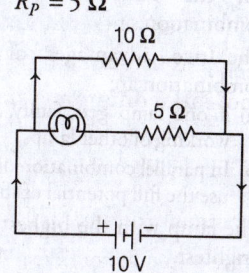

Hence, current flowing in the circuit,
$I = \dfrac{V}{R} = \dfrac{10}{5} = 2$ A

Thus, 1 A current will flow through 10 Ω resistor and 1 A will flow through the lamp and conductor of 5 Ω resistance. Hence, there will be no change in current flowing through 5 Ω conductor. Also, there will be no change in potential difference across the lamp.

15. In the given circuit, A, B, C and D are four lamps connected with a battery of 60 V.

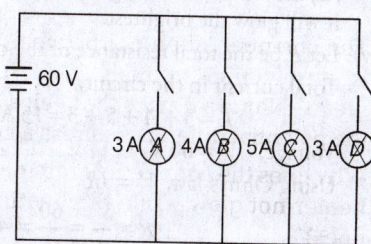

Analyse the circuit to answer the following questions.

(i) What kind of combination are the lamps arranged in (series or parallel)?

(ii) Explain with reference to your above answer, what are the advantages (any two) of this combination of lamps?

(iii) Explain with proper calculations which lamp glows the brightest?

(iv) Find out the total resistance of the circuit.
CBSE SQP 2020-21

Sol. The given circuit is shown below.

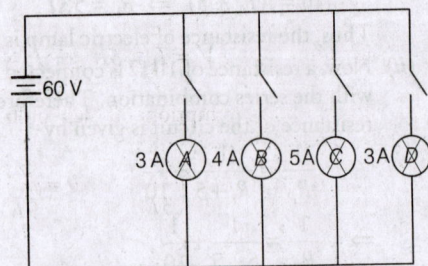

(i) In the circuit, all the lamps have same voltage i.e., 60 V but each lamp is having different current. So, the lamps are arranged in parallel combination.

(ii) The two advantages of lamps in parallel combination are
(a) if one lamp gets faulty, it will not affect the working of other lamps.
(b) In parallel combination of lamps, each lamp will use the full potential of the battery.

(iii) The lamp with the highest power will glow the brightest.
As, power = Voltage × Current
In this case, all the lamps have same voltage i.e., 60 V.
For lamp A, current = 3 A
∴ Power = 60 × 3 = 180 W
For lamp B, current = 4 A
∴ Power = 60 × 4 = 240 W
For lamp C, current = 5 A
∴ Power = 60 × 5 = 300 W
For lamp D, current = 3 A
∴ Power = 60 × 3 = 180 W
As, the lamp C is having the maximum power, so it will glow the brightest.

(iv) Let R be the total resistance of the circuit.
Total current in the circuit,
$I = 3 + 4 + 5 + 3 = 15$ A
Voltage, $V = 60$ V
Using Ohm's law, $V = IR$
⇒ $R = \dfrac{V}{I} = \dfrac{60}{15} = 4\,\Omega$

16 Two resistances when connected in parallel give resultant value of 2 Ω, when connected in series the value becomes 9 Ω. Calculate the value of each resistance.

Sol. We know that two resistances are in parallel and hence
$\dfrac{1}{R_P} = \dfrac{1}{R_1} + \dfrac{1}{R_2}$

⇒ $R_P = \dfrac{R_1 R_2}{R_1 + R_2}$

Given, $R_P = 2\,\Omega$
⇒ $2 = \dfrac{R_1 R_2}{R_1 + R_2}$
∴ $2(R_1 + R_2) = R_1 R_2$ ...(i)

Now, same resistances are in series, $R_S = R_1 + R_2$
Given, $R_S = 9\,\Omega$
⇒ $9 = R_1 + R_2$ ...(ii)

From Eqs. (i) and (ii), we get
$R_1 R_2 = 18$
Again, using Eq. (ii), we get
$R_2 = 9 - R_1$
∴ $R_1(9 - R_1) = 18$
⇒ $R_1^2 - 9R_1 + 18 = 0$
⇒ $(R_1 - 6)(R_1 - 3) = 0$
Either, $R_1 = 6$ or $R_1 = 3$
$R_2 = 3\,\Omega$ or $R_2 = 6\,\Omega$

Thus, two resistances are 3 Ω and 6 Ω.

17 (i) Find the value of current I in the circuit given as below:

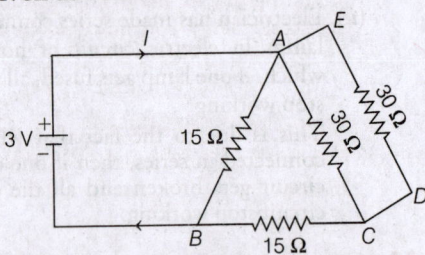

(ii) You have four resistors of 8 Ω each. Show how would you connect these resistors to have effective resistance of 8 Ω?

Sol. (i) R_{AC} and R_{ED} are in parallel, so
$\dfrac{1}{R'_P} = \dfrac{1}{R_{AC}} + \dfrac{1}{R_{ED}} = \dfrac{1}{30} + \dfrac{1}{30} = \dfrac{1}{15}$
⇒ $R'_P = 15\,\Omega$

Now, R'_P and R_{BC} are in series, so
$R'_S = R'_P + R_{BC} = 15 + 15 = 30\,\Omega$

Again, R_{AB} and R'_S are in parallel, so
$\dfrac{1}{R''_P} = \dfrac{1}{R_{AB}} + \dfrac{1}{R'_S} = \dfrac{1}{15} + \dfrac{1}{30} = \dfrac{1}{10}$
∴ $R''_P = 10\,\Omega$

So, current flowing through the circuit is
$I = \dfrac{V}{R''_P} = \dfrac{3}{10} = 0.3$ A

(ii) Two 8 Ω resistors are connected in parallel. Two such parallel combination must be connected in series to get effective resistance of 8 Ω.

Such combination is shown as below:

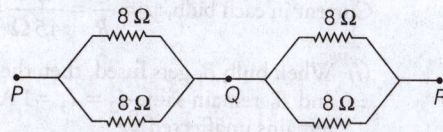

18 Obtain an expression for the heat produced in a conductor when a voltage V is applied across it. Heating effect of electric current is desirable as well as undesirable. Explain this statement. **CBSE 2016**

Sol. When an electric charge Q moves against a potential difference V, then the amount of work done is given by
$$W = Q \times V \qquad ...(i)$$
We also know that, $I = Q/t$
So, $\qquad Q = I \times t \qquad ...(ii)$
and from Ohm's law, $V = IR \qquad ...(iii)$
Putting the values of Eqs. (ii) and (iii) in Eq. (i), we get
$$W = I \times t \times I \times R$$
∴ Work done, $\quad W = I^2 Rt$

Assuming that all the electrical work done or all the electrical energy consumed is converted into heat energy.
∴ $\qquad W = H = I^2 Rt$

Heating effect of electric current is desirable because it as useful for the functioning of electrical bulbs, etc., and undesirable because it leads to unnecessary loss of energy in the form of heat.

19 Three incandescent bulbs of 100 W each are connected in series in an electric circuit. In another set of three bulbs of the same wattage are connected in parallel to the source.

(i) Will the bulb in the two circuits glow with the same brightness? Justify your answer.

(ii) Now, let one bulb in both the circuits get fused. Will the rest of the bulbs continue to glow in each circuit? Give reason.
NCERT Exemplar

Sol. (i) Let us assume that the resistance of each bulb be R. The circuit diagram in two cases may be drawn as given below:

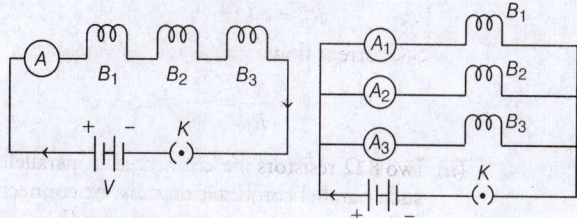

Equivalent resistance in series combination
$$R_S = R + R + R = 3R, \text{voltage} = V$$
Let current through each bulb in series combination be I_1.

By Ohm's law, $V = I_1 \times 3R \Rightarrow I_1 = \dfrac{V}{3R}$

∴ Power consumption of each bulb in series combination,
$$P_1 = I_1^2(3R) = \left(\dfrac{V}{3R}\right)^2 \times 3R = \dfrac{V^2}{9R^2} \times 3R$$
$$= \dfrac{V^2}{3R} \qquad ...(i)$$

For parallel circuit,
the resistance of each bulb = R
Voltage across each bulb = V
[∵ same voltage in parallel combination]

∴ Power consumption of each bulb in parallel combination is given by
$$P_2 = \dfrac{V^2}{R} \qquad ...(ii)$$

From Eqs. (i) and (ii), we get
$$\dfrac{P_2}{P_1} = \dfrac{(V^2/R)}{(V^2/3R)}$$
$$\Rightarrow \qquad \dfrac{V^2}{R} \times \dfrac{3R}{V^2} = 3 \Rightarrow P_2 = 3P_1$$

Therefore, each bulb in parallel combination glows 3 times brighter than that of each bulb in series combination.

(ii) When one bulb gets fused then in series combination, the circuit gets broken and current stops flowing, whereas in parallel combination, same voltage continues to act on the remaining bulbs and hence other bulbs continues to glow with same brightness.

20 B_1, B_2 and B_3 are three identical bulbs connected as shown in figure. Ammeters A_1, A_2 and A_3 are connected as shown in figure.

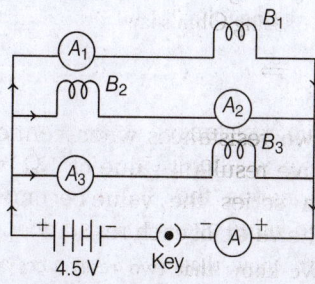

When all the bulbs glow, then the current of 3 A is recorded by ammeter A.

(i) What happens to the glow of the other two bulbs when bulb B_1 gets fused?

(ii) What happens to the reading of A_1, A_2, A_3 and A when the bulb B_2 gets fused?

(iii) How much power is dissipated in the circuit when all the three bulbs glow together? **NCERT Exemplar**

Sol. Resistance of combination of three bulbs in parallel,

$$R_{eq} = \frac{V}{I} = \frac{4.5}{3} = 1.5\,\Omega$$

If R is the resistance of each wire, then

$$\frac{1}{R_{eq}} = \frac{1}{R} + \frac{1}{R} + \frac{1}{R}$$

or $\quad \dfrac{1}{R_{eq}} = \dfrac{3}{R}$

or $\quad R = 3R_{eq} = 3 \times 1.5 = 4.5\,\Omega$

Current in each bulb, $I = \dfrac{V}{R} = \dfrac{4.5\,V}{4.5\,\Omega} = 1\,A$

(i) When bulb B_1 gets fused, then the currents in B_2 and B_3 remain same $I_2 = I_3 = 1\,A$, so their glow remains unaffected.

(ii) When bulb B_2 gets fused, then the current in B_2 becomes zero and currents in B_1 and B_3 remain 1 A.

∴ Total current, $I = I_1 + I_2 + I_3$
$= 1 + 0 + 1 = 2\,A$

Current in ammeter $A_1, I_1 = 1\,A$
Current in ammeter $A_2, I_2 = 0$
Current in ammeter $A_3, I_3 = 1\,A$
Current in ammeter $A, I = 2\,A$

(iii) When all the three bulbs are connected, then power dissipated,

$$P = \frac{V^2}{R_{eq}} = \frac{(4.5)^2}{1.5} = 13.5\,W$$

CHAPTER EXERCISE

Multiple Type Questions

1. Three 2Ω resistances are connected so as to make a triangle. The resistance between any two vertices is
   (a) 6Ω
   (b) 2Ω
   (c) $\frac{3}{4}$Ω
   (d) $\frac{4}{3}$Ω

2. Two wires of same metal have the same length but their cross-sectional area in the ratio 3 : 1. They are joined in series. The resistance of the thicker wire is 10 Ω. The total resistance of the combination will be
   (a) 40 Ω
   (b) $\frac{40}{3}$ Ω
   (c) $\frac{5}{2}$ Ω
   (d) 100 Ω

3. An electric refrigerator rated 400 W operates 8 hours/day. The cost of the energy to operate it for 30 days at ₹ 3 per kWh is
   (a) ₹ 288
   (b) ₹ 320
   (c) ₹ 430
   (d) ₹ 190

4. Two resistors of resistance 2Ω and 4Ω when connected to a battery will have **NCERT Exemplar**
   (a) same current flowing through them when connected in parallel
   (b) same current flowing through them when connected in series
   (c) same potential difference across them when connected in series
   (d) different potential difference across them when connected in parallel

5. An electric heater is rated 100 W and 220 V. If it is operated on 110 V. The power consumption will be
   (a) 10 W
   (b) 25 W
   (c) 15 W
   (d) 100 W

Fill in the Blanks

6. Kilowatt hour is the unit of ....

7. In parallel combination of resistors, potential difference across each resistor is ....

True and False

8. Ohm's law is valid for conductor and semiconductor both.

9. Fuse wire is made up of an alloy of tin and lead.

Match the Columns

10. Match the items of Column I with items of Column II and choose the correct codes given below.

Column I (Circuit components)	Column II (Symbols)
A. Rheostat	(i) —o—o—
B. Fuse	(ii) —(•)—
C. Open switch	(iii) —WWW—
D. Closed switch	(iv) —( )—

    Codes
    (a) A →(iii), B → (i), C →(iv), D →(ii)
    (b) A →(iii), B → (iv), C →(i), D →(ii)
    (c) A →(i), B → (iii), C →(iv), D →(ii)
    (d) A →(ii), B → (iii), C →(iv), D →(i)

Assertion-Reason

Direction (Q. Nos. 11-13) *In each of the following questions, a statement of Assertion is given by the corresponding statement of Reason. Of the statements, mark the correct answer as*

(a) If both Assertion and Reason are true and Reason is the correct explanation of Assertion.
(b) If both Assertion and Reason are true, but Reason is not the correct explanation of Assertion.
(c) If Assertion is true, but Reason is false.
(d) If Assertion is false, but Reason is true.
(e) If Assertion and Reason both are false.

11. **Assertion** Electric current will not flow between two charged bodies when connected, if their charges are same.
    Reason Current is the rate of flow of charge.

12. **Assertion** Fuse wire must have high resistance and low melting point.
    Reason Fuse is used to protect the circuit.

13. **Assertion** Alloys are used to make heating elements of devices such as electric iron, heater etc.
    Reason Alloys do not oxidise easily at high temperature.

Case Based Questions

Direction (Q.Nos. 14-17) Answer the questions on the basis of your understanding of the following passage and related studied concepts:

Light bulbs can be connected together in an electric circuit in two different ways. If the light bulbs are connected one after another as shown in figure. They are connected in series.

If one of the light bulb burns out, all the light bulbs in series to it will go out because the pathway for the electricity flow is broken.

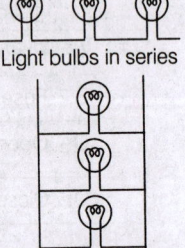
Light bulbs in series

Light bulbs in parallel

If the light bulbs are connected on separate branches as shown in figure, they are connected in parallel. If one of the light bulbs burns out, the other light bulbs will continue to work because there is a separate pathway for the electricity to flow around the burned-out light bulb.

14 In series combination of bulbs
(a) current through each bulb is same
(b) current through each bulb is different
(c) current is maximum in either of the ends bulbs
(d) current is minimum in either of the ends bulbs

15 In parallel combination of bulbs, if one of the light bulb burns out then other light bulbs
(a) will go out also
(b) will continue to work
(c) will continue of glow with increased brightness
(d) will continue to glow with decreased brightness

16 Write any two advantage of series combination of bulbs over parallel combination of bulbs.

17 In which combination of bulbs, brightness is greater, when they are connected with battery of same potential?

Answers
1. (d) 2. (a) 3. (a) 4. (b) 5. (b)
6. Energy 7. Same 8. False 9. True
10. (a) 11. (d) 12. (a) 13. (b) 14. (a) 15. (b)

Very Short Answer (VSA) Type Questions

18 Electric fuse is an important component of all domestic circuits. Why? **CBSE 2011**

19 State the law which governs the amount of heat produced in a metallic conductor when current is passed through it for a given time. Express this law mathematically. **CBSE 2007**

20 You are given three bulbs of 40 W, 60 W and 100 W. Which of them has lower resistance? **[Ans.** 100 W**]**

Short Answer (SA) Type Questions

21 What kind of graph is obtained by plotting values of V and I? Why?

22 Aluminium wire has radius 0.25 mm and length of 75 m. If the resistance of the wire is 10 Ω. Calculate the resistivity of aluminium. **[Ans.** 2.62×10^{-8} Ω-m**]**

23 Write the advantages of connecting electrical appliances in parallel and disadvantages of connecting them in series in a household circuit.

24 It is possible to replace resistors joined in series by an equivalent single resistor of resistance. How?

25 You are given three resistors each of 3 Ω and you are asked to get all possible values of resistance when you connect them in different combinations. How many values of resistance can you get?

26 Find the current drawn from the battery by network of four resistors shown in the figure.
[Ans. 0.3 A**]** **CBSE 2015**

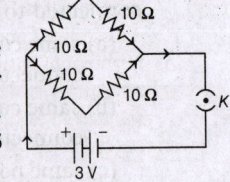

Long Answer (LA) Type Questions

27 A wire is cut into three equal parts and then connected in parallel with the same source. How will its **CBSE 2011**
(i) resistance and resistivity gets affected?
(ii) How would the total current and the current through the parts change?

28 How will you conclude that the same potential difference (voltage) exists across three resistors connected in a parallel arrangement to a battery?

29 What will be the length of a nichrome wire of resistance 5.0 Ω, if the length of similar wire of 120 cm has resistance of 2.5 Ω? Why? **[Ans.** 240 cm**]**

Challengers*

1. Three different circuits (I, II and III) are constructed using identical batteries and resistors of R and $2R$ ohm. What can be said about current I in arm AB of each circuit?

   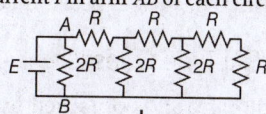
   I

   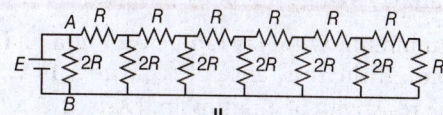
   II

   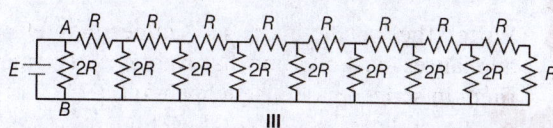
   III

   (a) $I_I > I_{II} > I_{III}$
   (b) $I_I < I_{II} < I_{III}$
   (c) $I_{II} < I_I < I_{III}$
   (d) $I_I = I_{II} = I_{III}$

2. Two cells of 3V each are connected in parallel. An external resistance of $0.5\,\Omega$ is connected in series to the junction of two parallel resistors of $4\,\Omega$ and $2\,\Omega$ and then to common terminal of battery through each resistor as shown in figure. What is the current flowing through $4\,\Omega$ resistor?

   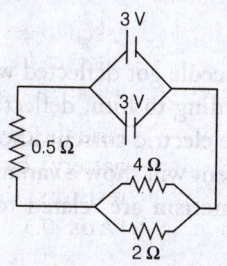

   (a) 0.25 A   (b) 0.55 A
   (c) 0.35 A   (d) 1.50 A

3. The current flowing through a wire of resistance $2\,\Omega$ varies with time as shown in figure alongside. The amount of heat produced (in J) in 3 s would be

   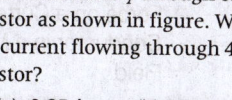

   (a) 2 J
   (b) 18 J
   (c) 28 J
   (d) 10 J

4. In the movie *Tango and Cash*, Kurt Russell and Sylvester Stallone escape from a prison by jumping off the top of a tall wall through the air and onto a high voltage power line. Before the jump, Stallone objects to the idea, telling Russell "We are going to fry." Russell responds with "You did not take high school Physics. Did you? As long as you are only touching one wire and your feet are not touching the ground, you do not get electrocuted." Is this a correct statement?

5. Two wires A and B with circular cross-sections having identical lengths and are made of the same material. Yet, wire A has four times the resistance of wire B. How many times greater is the diameter of wire B than wire A?

6. Calculate the equivalent resistance of the network across the points A and B shown in figure.

   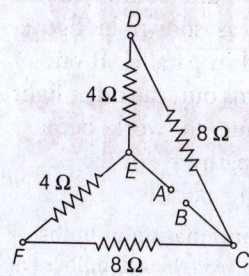

7. The amount of energy transferred when 10 C of charge passes through a potential difference of 20 V is the same as the energy needed to raise a 2 kg mass through a distance x. Find the value of x, take the value of g as $10\,m/s^2$.

8. The diagram shows a cell connected in series with an ammeter and three resistors ($10\,\Omega$, $20\,\Omega$, $30\,\Omega$). The circuit can be completed by a movable constant M. When M is connected to X, then ammeter reads 0.6 A. What is the ammeter reading when M is connected to Y?

9. The circuit diagram is for a fan dryer that blows either hot air or cold air. Both switches R and S are as shown often. Which switch (s) is/are to be closed to obtain either hot or cold air?

   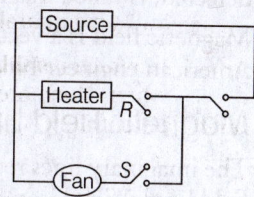

Answer Key

1.	(d)	2.	(b)	3.	(c)

---

* These questions may or may not be asked in the examination, have been given just for additional practice.

CHAPTER 12

Magnetic Effects of Electric Current

Hans Christian Oersted in 1820, discovered that a compass needle got deflected when a current carrying metallic conductor is placed nearby it. According to him, deflection of compass needle was due to the magnetic field produced by the electric current known as **magnetic effect of current**. Any change in the direction of current will show a variation in deflection. Thus, it was concluded that, **electricity** and **magnetism** are related to each other.

Chapter Checklist
- Magnetic Field
- Force on a Current Carrying Conductor in a Magnetic Field
- Domestic Electric Circuits

Magnetic Field
The space around a magnet, in which its effect can be experienced, i.e. its force can be detected, is called magnetic field.

Magnetic field is a **vector** quantity. The SI unit of magnetic field is **tesla** named after the American engineer **Nikola Tesla**. The smaller unit of magnetic field is **gauss**.

Magnetic Field Lines
The imaginary lines representing magnetic field around a magnet are known as magnetic field lines. When iron filings are kept near a magnet, they get arranged in a pattern which represent the magnetic field lines.

The lines are drawn along the direction in which a magnetic North pole of the compass needle would move under the influence of the field produced by a bar magnet. It is taken by convention that the field lines emerge from North pole and merge at the South pole.

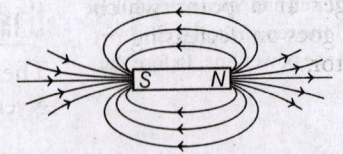
Field lines around a bar magnet

Note A compass needle behave as a small bar magnet whose one end points approximately towards North called North seeking or North pole and other end points towards South called South seeking or South pole.

Properties of Magnetic Field Lines

The magnetic field lines have the following properties:
(i) They originate from North pole of a magnet and end at its South pole, by convention.
(ii) These lines are closed and continuous curves.
(iii) They are crowded near the poles, where the magnetic field is strong and separated far from the poles, where the magnetic field is weak.
(iv) Field lines never intersect with each other. If they do, that would mean that there are two directions of the magnetic field at the point of intersection, which is impossible.

Magnetic Field due to a Current Carrying Conductor

When electric current flows through a metallic conductor, a magnetic field is produced around it. The pattern of magnetic field produced by a current carrying conductor depends on its shape.

Different magnetic field patterns are produced by current carrying conductors of different shapes.

Magnetic Field due to a Current through a Straight Conductor

The magnetic field lines around a current carrying straight conductor are concentric circles whose centres lie on the wire. The magnitude of magnetic field B produced by a straight current carrying wire at a given point is

(i) **Directly proportional** to the current I passing through the wire,

i.e. $\boxed{B \propto I}$ ...(i)

If current is increased, then the magnetic field produced is stronger and *vice-versa*.

(ii) **Inversely proportional** to the distance r from the current carrying conductor,

i.e. $\boxed{B \propto \dfrac{1}{r}}$ ...(ii)

The magnetic field is stronger at a point which is nearer to the conductor and goes on decreasing on moving away from the conductor.

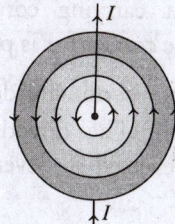

Concentric field lines around a straight conductor

By using Eqs. (i) and (ii), we get

$\boxed{B \propto \dfrac{I}{r}}$

If the direction of current in a straight wire is known, then the direction of magnetic field produced by it is obtained by **Maxwell's right hand thumb rule**.

Maxwell's Right Hand Thumb Rule

It's a convenient way of finding the direction of magnetic field associated with a current carrying conductor. It states that, if you hold the current carrying straight wire in the grip of your right hand in such a way that the stretched thumb points in the direction of current, then the direction of the curl of the fingers will give the direction of the magnetic field. This rule is also called Maxwell's corkscrew rule.

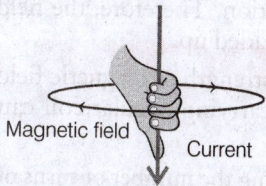

Maxwell's Right Hand Thumb Rule

Check Point 01

1. What is the SI unit of magnetic field?
2. State True and False for the following statements:
   (i) The direction of magnetic field inside a bar magnet is from North pole to South pole.
   (ii) Magnetic field lines are closed and continuous curves.
3. Why cannot two field lines intersect each other?
4. Fill in the blanks:
   (i) The magnetic field produced in a straight current carrying conductor .... as the distance from it increases.
   (ii) The lines of force round a straight current carrying conductor are in the shape of ....
5. Where is the magnetic field due to a straight current carrying wire
   (i) stronger   (ii) weaker?

Magnetic Field due to a Current through a Circular Loop

The magnetic field lines due to a circular coil is shown in the given figure.

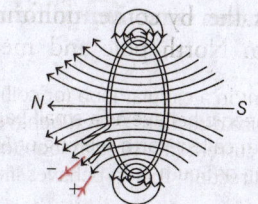

Magnetic field lines due to a current through a circular loop

At every point on a current carrying circular loop, the magnetic field is in the form of concentric circles around it. As we move away from it, the circles would become larger and larger. When we reach the centre of loop, the field appears to be a straight line.

The magnetic field produced by current carrying circular wire at a given point is

(i) **Directly proportional** to the amount of current (I) passing through it,

i.e. $\boxed{B \propto I}$ ... (i)

(ii) **Directly proportional** to the number of turns (N) of the wire,

i.e. $\boxed{B \propto N}$ ... (ii)

This is because the current in each turn is in the same direction. Therefore, the field due to these turns get added up.

Thus, the strength of magnetic field produced by a current carrying circular coil can be increased by

(a) increasing the number of turns of the coil.

(b) increasing the current flowing through the coil.

Magnetic Field due to a Current in a Solenoid

A **solenoid** is defined as a coil consisting of a large number of circular turns of insulated copper wire. These turns are wrapped closely to form a cylinder.

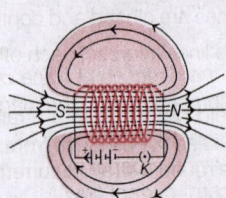

Magnetic field lines of force due to a current carrying solenoid

The field lines around a current carrying solenoid are similar to that produced by a bar magnet. This means that a current carrying solenoid behaves as if it has North pole and South pole. The field lines inside the solenoid are parallel to each other. Thus, the strength of magnetic field is the same, i.e. uniform at all points inside a solenoid.

Note If the current in a circular loop (or coil) is in anti-clockwise direction, then it behaves like a North pole. If the current in a circular loop (or coil) is in clockwise direction, then it behaves like South pole.

Electromagnet

The strong magnetic field produced inside a solenoid can be used to magnetise a piece of magnetic material like soft iron when placed inside the coil. The magnet so formed is called electromagnet. The magnetic effect remains only till the current is flowing through the solenoid. An electromagnet is used in electric bells, electric motors, telephone diaphragms, loudspeakers and for sorting scrap metal.

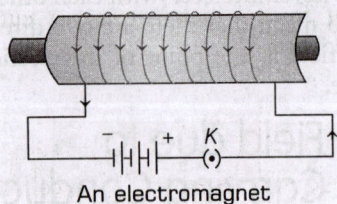

An electromagnet

Check Point 02

1. Fill in the blank:
   The strength of the magnetic field ...., if the number of turns is increased in a solenoid.

2. State True and False for the following statements:
   (i) The magnetic lines of force inside a solenoid are in the form of parallel straight lines indicating that field is .... at all points inside the solenoid.
   (ii) The magnetic field pattern obtained using solenoid is same as the magnetic field pattern obtained using a ....

3. A circular loop carrying a current is placed on a horizontal surface (current is in the clockwise direction). What is the direction of its magnetic field at the centre? What is the direction of the magnetic field at a point outside the surface of the loop?

4. What is the difference in the pattern of magnetic field due to a circular loop and inside a solenoid?

5. What is the principle of an electromagnet?

Force on a Current Carrying Conductor in a Magnetic Field

When a current carrying conductor is placed in a magnetic field, it experiences a force except when it is placed parallel to the magnetic field. The force acting on a current carrying conductor in a magnetic field is due to interaction between magnetic field produced by the current carrying conductor and external magnetic field in which the conductor is placed.

The direction of force on the conductor depends on:

(i) **Direction of current** The direction of force on the conductor can be reversed by reversing the direction of current.

Magnetic Effects of Electric Current

(ii) **Direction of magnetic field** The direction of force on the conductor can be reversed by reversing the direction of magnetic field by interchanging the position of poles.

Force on the conductor is maximum when the direction of current is at right angles to the direction of magnetic field.

Fleming's Left Hand Rule

The direction of force which acts on a current carrying conductor placed in a magnetic field is given by Fleming's left hand rule.

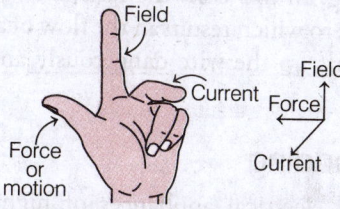
Fleming's left hand rule

It states that, if the forefinger, thumb and middle finger of left hand are stretched mutually perpendicular to each other, such that the forefinger points along the direction of external magnetic field, middle finger indicates the direction of current, then the thumb points towards the direction of force acting on the conductor.

Magnetism in Medicine

An electric current always produces a magnetic field. Extremely weak electric currents are produced in human body by the movement of the charged particles and are called ionic currents. This weak ionic current flowing along the nerve cells produces magnetic field in our body.

Our nerves carry electric impulse to the muscles which produces temporary magnetic field. These fields are weak and one-billionth of the earth's magnetic field. The heart and the brain are the two main organs of human body, where magnetic field produced is significant. This magnetic field inside the body forms the basis of obtaining the images of different body parts and it is done by using a technique called MRI (Magnetic Resonance Imaging). Analysis of these images helps in medical diagnosis. Thus, magnetism has important uses in medicine.

Example 1. *A current carrying conductor enters a magnetic field at right angles to it as shown in figure. What will be the direction of force acting on the conductor?*

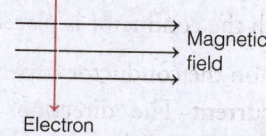

Sol. According to Fleming's left hand rule, the direction of force on the conductor is perpendicular to the direction of magnetic field and current. Since, the direction of current is taken opposite to the direction of motion of electrons, therefore the force on electron is directed into the page.

Direct Current and Alternating Current

Direct Current (DC)

An electric current whose magnitude is either constant or variable but the direction remains the same is called direct current. It is denoted by DC. Sources of DC are voltaic cell, a dry cell, battery, DC generator, etc.

Alternating Current (AC)

An electric current whose magnitude changes with time and direction reverses periodically is called alternating current. It is denoted by AC. Sources of AC are hydro-electric generators, thermal power generators and nuclear power generators, etc. The number of cycles completed by the AC in one second is called the **frequency of AC**. The frequency of AC in India is 50 Hz which means that AC changes its direction after $\frac{1}{100}$ second.

The major difference between AC and DC is that DC always flows in one direction, while AC reverses its direction periodically. The advantage of AC over DC is that electric power can be transmitted over long distances without much loss of energy.

Check Point 03

1. When is the force on a current carrying wire
   (i) maximum   (ii) minimum?

2. Fill in the blanks:
   The rule that gives the direction of force on a current carrying conductor placed perpendicular to the magnetic field is ....

3. The direction of magnetic field at a place is coming out of the paper. A wire whose direction of current flow is as shown in the figure is placed there. In which direction is the force due to the magnetic field experienced by the wire?
   [Ans. South-East direction]

4. What is the cause of magnetic field inside a human body?

5. Differentiate between the time varying and constant currents.

Domestic Electric Circuits

Electricity generated at power stations is brought to our homes by two thick copper or aluminium wires. One of these is called **live wire** (in red insulation cover), which is at a potential of 220 V with a frequency of 50 Hz and the other is called **neutral wire** (in black insulation cover), which is at zero potential.

These wires (live and neutral) pass into an **electricity meter** (connected in homes) through a main fuse. They are connected to the line wires in the home through a main switch. Usually, there are two separate circuits in a house, the **lighting circuit** with a 5 A fuse (bulbs, fans, etc.) and the **power circuit** with a 15 A fuse (geysers, air coolers, etc.).

Each **distribution circuit** is provided with a separate fuse. If a fault like short circuiting occurs in one circuit, its corresponding fuse blows off but the other circuit remains unaffected. Various distribution circuits are connected in parallel. All the electrical appliances like bulbs, fans and sockets, etc., are connected in parallel across the live wire and neutral wire.

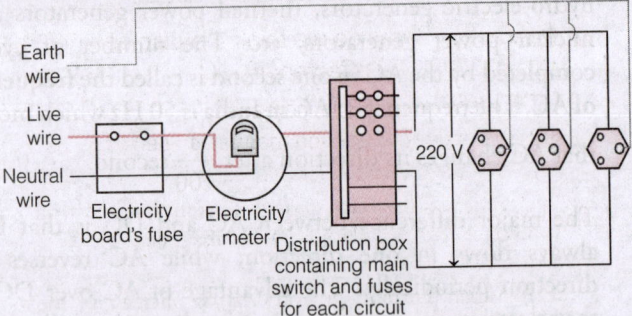

A schematic diagram of the common domestic circuits

Faults and Safety Measures in Domestic Electric Circuit

Earth Wire

To avoid risk of electrical shock, the metal body of appliances is earthed. The metal case of the appliance is connected to the earth (i.e. zero potential) by means of a metal wire called **earth wire** (in green insulation cover). One end of the metal wire is buried in the earth.

The appliances are connected to the earth by using the top pin of a 3-pin plug. Earthing saves us from electrical shocks.

Fuse

It is a safety device. It is a thin wire made of **tin and lead** alloy having low melting point around 200 °C. It is used to prevent the possible damage caused by overloading and short circuiting.

Short Circuiting

If the live wire and neutral wire come in contact either directly or *via* conducting wire, then it is called short circuiting. In this case, the resistance of the circuit is almost zero which results in the flow of a large current. This heats up the wire dangerously and may lead to fire.

Overloading

If many electrical appliances of high power rating are switched on at the same time, then they draw a large current from the circuit. This is called overloading. The large amount of current flowing through the wire excessively heats up the wire and may lead to fire.

Check Point 04

1. At what potential and frequency are the domestic electric circuits operated?
2. Fill in the blanks:
   (i) Usually, three insulated wires of different colours are used in an electrical appliance. Colours of live, neutral and earth wires are ...., ... and ....
   (ii) When many electrical appliances of high power rating are switched on at the same time it causes ....
3. Why should a fuse wire of defined rating not be replaced by one with a larger rating?
4. What do you mean by short circuit?

NCERT FOLDER

INTEXT QUESTIONS

1 Why does a compass needle get deflected when brought near a bar magnet? **(Pg 224)**

Sol The compass needle gets deflected due to the magnetic field around a bar magnet.

2 Draw magnetic field lines around a bar magnet. **(Pg 228)**

Sol. Refer to figure on Pg. 400.

3 List the properties of magnetic lines of force. **(Pg 228)**

Sol. Refer to text on Pg. 401.

4 Why do not two magnetic lines of force intersect with each other? **(Pg 228)**

Sol. If two magnetic lines of force intersect each other, it would mean that there are two directions of the magnetic field at the point of intersection, which is not possible.

5 Consider a circular loop of wire lying in the plane of table. Let a current passes through the loop in clockwise direction. Apply the right hand thumb rule to find out the direction of the magnetic field inside and outside the loop. **(Pg 229)**

Sol. Applying the right hand thumb rule, the magnetic field inside the loop is in vertically downward direction and outside the loop, it is in vertically upward direction.

6 The magnetic field in a given region is uniform. Draw a diagram to represent it. **(Pg 229)**

Sol. In a uniform magnetic field, the magnetic field lines of force are parallel and equidistant from each other as shown in the diagram.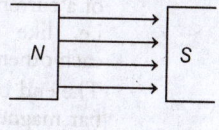

7 Choose the correct option.
The magnetic field inside a long straight solenoid carrying current **(Pg 229)**
(a) is zero
(b) decreases as we move towards its end
(c) increases as we move towards its end
(d) is the same at all points

Sol. (d) Magnetic field inside a solenoid is same at all the points.

8 Which of the following properties of a proton can change while it moves freely in a magnetic field? **(Pg 231)**
(a) Mass (b) Speed
(c) Velocity (d) Momentum

Sol. (d) Proton is a charged particle. When it moves in a magnetic field, a magnetic force is applied due to its velocity and hence the momentum changes.

9 In Activity 7, how do we think the displacement of rod AB will be affected, if
(i) current in rod AB is increased,
(ii) a stronger horse-shoe magnet is used and
(iii) length of the rod AB is increased? **(Pg 232)**

Sol. In Activity 7, the force acting on a current carrying conductor when placed in a magnetic field is illustrated.
(i) When current in rod AB is increased, the displacement of rod is increased, as force acting on rod is directly proportional to the current flowing through it. On increasing the current, force on the conductor increases.
(ii) If a stronger horse-shoe magnet is used, then the strength of magnetic field will increase leading to greater force on the rod. Due to this, the displacement of rod will increase.
(iii) Displacement of conductor is increased with an increase in length of the conductor. On increasing the length, more force will act on the conductor.

10 A positively charged particle (α-particle) projected towards West is deflected towards North by a magnetic field. The direction of magnetic field is **(Pg 232)**
(a) towards South
(b) towards East
(c) downward
(d) upward

Sol. (d) The positively charged particle is moving towards West, i.e. the direction of current is towards West (current flows in the direction of the motion of positive charge). The particle is deflected towards North, so the direction of force is towards North. Thus, from Fleming's left hand rule, the direction of magnetic field is in upward direction.

11 State Fleming left hand rule. **(Pg 233)**

Sol. Refer to text on Pg. 403.

12 Name some sources of direct current. **(Pg 237)**

Sol. Some sources of direct current are electrochemical dry cells, solar cells, lead acid accumulator batteries, DC generators, etc.

13 Which sources produce alternating current? **(Pg 237)**

Sol. Some sources that produce alternating current are AC generators, thermal power stations, car alternators, etc.

14 Name two safety measures commonly used in electric circuits and appliances. **(Pg 238)**

Sol. Electric fuse and earth wire are two safety measures commonly used in electric circuits.

15 An electric oven of 2 kW power rating is operated in a domestic circuit (220 V) that has a current rating of 5 A. What result do you expect? Explain. **(Pg 238)**

Sol. $\therefore$ Current, $I = \dfrac{P}{V} = \dfrac{2000 \text{ W}}{220 \text{ V}} > 5 \text{ A}$

Since, current drawn by oven is greater than the rated value of current, which may cause overloading and excessive heating of the circuit.

16 What precautions should be taken to avoid the overloading of domestic electric circuits? **(Pg 238)**

Sol. The following precautions should be taken to avoid the overloading of domestic electric circuits as given below:
(i) The circuits should be of proper current rating and appliances should be connected accordingly.
(ii) Wires should be checked from time-to-time and those wires whose insulation is worn, should be immediately replaced.
(iii) Connection of too many appliances in a single socket must be avoided.

EXERCISES (On Pages 240 and 241)

1 Which of the following correctly describes the magnetic field near a long straight wire?
(a) The field consists of straight lines perpendicular to the wire
(b) The field consists of straight lines parallel to the wire
(c) The field consists of radial lines originating from the wire
(d) The field consists of concentric circles centred on the wire

Sol. (d) The magnetic field lines due to a straight current carrying wire are concentric circles with centre on the wire.

2 The essential difference between AC generator and DC generator is that
(a) AC generator has electromagnet while DC generator has permanent magnet
(b) DC generator generates higher voltage
(c) AC generator generates higher voltage
(d) AC generator has slip rings while DC generator has commutator

Sol. (d) AC generator has slip rings while DC generator has split rings as commutator. Due to slip rings, the current produced by AC generator flows in both directions while current produced by DC generator flows in single direction.

3 At the time of short circuit, the current in the circuit
(a) reduces substantially   (b) does not change
(c) increases heavily   (d) vary continuously

Sol. (c) Increases heavily.

4 State whether the following statements are true or false.
(i) The field at the centre of a long circular coil carrying current will be parallel straight lines.
(ii) A wire with a green insulation is usually the live wire of an electric supply.

Sol. (i) True
(ii) False, the wire with green insulation is the earth wire not the live wire.

5 List three methods of producing magnetic fields.

Sol. Three methods of producing magnetic field are as given below:
(i) Passing electric current through a straight conductor/circuit.
(ii) Passing electric current through a circular loop.
(iii) Passing electric current through a solenoid.

6 How does a solenoid behave like a magnet? Can you determine the North and South poles of a current carrying solenoid using a bar magnet? Explain.

Sol. A solenoid behaves like a magnet when electric current passes through it.
One end of a solenoid behaves as a North pole and the other end behaves as a South pole. We can use a bar magnet to determine the North and South poles of a current carrying solenoid by using the property, i.e. like poles repel and unlike poles attract each other.
The end of solenoid which attracts North pole of a bar magnet is magnetic South pole of the solenoid. The end of solenoid which repels the North pole of a bar magnet is the magnetic North pole of the solenoid.

7 When is the force experienced by a current carrying conductor placed in a magnetic field largest?

Sol. The force experienced by a current carrying conductor placed in a magnetic field is the largest when conductor is kept perpendicular to the direction of the magnetic field.

Magnetic Effects of Electric Current

8 Imagine that you are sitting in a chamber with your back to one wall. An electron beam moving horizontally from back wall towards the front wall is deflected by a strong magnetic field to your right side. What is the direction of magnetic field?

Sol. According to Fleming's left hand rule, the direction of magnetic field is vertically downward.

9 State the rule to determine the direction of a
  (i) magnetic field produced around a straight conductor carrying current,
  (ii) force experienced by a current carrying straight conductor placed in a magnetic field which is perpendicular to it,

Sol. (i) Refer to text on Pg. 401 (Maxwell's right hand thumb rule).

(ii) Refer to text on Pg. 403 (Fleming's left hand rule).

10 When does an electric short circuit occur?

Sol. An electric short circuit occurs when the insulation of wires is damaged or there is a fault in the appliance. Due to this, the live wire and neutral wire come in direct contact and the current in the circuit increases abruptly.

11 What is the function of an earth wire? Why is it necessary to earth metallic appliances?

Sol. The earth wire is connected to a metallic plate buried deep inside the earth. In this way, the metallic body of appliance is connected to the earth, which provides a low resistance conducting path for electric current. Hence, any leakage of current to the metallic body of appliance flows to the earth through the earth wire. The user might not get a severe electric shock on touching such an appliance in case of a fault.

Note Questions related to deleted topics from CBSE Syllabus have not been covered in NCERT folder.

SUMMARY

- Oersted experimentally proved that magnetic field is produced around a conductor when an electric current is passed through it.
- The region around a magnet, in which the force of magnet can be detected, is called its **magnetic field**.
- The imaginary lines representing magnetic field around a magnet are known as **magnetic field lines**.
- Magnetic field lines form closed paths.
- The magnitude of the magnetic field (B) produced at a given point near a current carrying straight conductor is
  (i) $B \propto I$ [where, I is the current]
  (ii) $B \propto \dfrac{1}{r}$ [where, r = distance from the wire]
- The direction of the magnetic field produced by a current carrying conductor is given by Maxwell's right hand thumb rule.
- According to **right hand thumb rule**, hold the current carrying wire in your right-hand such that the thumb is stretched along the direction of current, then the fingers will wrap around the wire in the direction of the magnetic field.
- The magnetic field produced by current carrying circular wire at a given point depends on the following factors:
  (i) Directly proportional to the current I passing through the wire, i.e. $B \propto I$
  (ii) Directly proportional to the number of turns (N) of the wire, i.e. $B \propto N$
- A **solenoid** is defined as a coil consisting a large number of circular turns of insulated copper wire.
- The strength of magnetic field produced by a current carrying solenoid depends on the following factors:
  (i) The number of turns of solenoid ($B \propto N$).
  (ii) The strength of current ($B \propto I$).
  (iii) The nature of core material used to make solenoid.
- An **electromagnet** is a solenoid coil that gets magnetised, i.e. it becomes a magnet due to flow of current.
- When a current carrying conductor is placed in a magnetic field, it experiences a force except when it is placed parallel to the magnetic field.
- The direction of force which acts on a current carrying conductor placed in a magnetic field is given by Fleming's left hand rule.
- **Fleming's left hand rule** states that, if the forefinger, thumb and middle finger of left hand are stretched mutually perpendicular and the forefinger points along the direction of external magnetic field, middle finger indicates the direction of current, then thumb points the direction of force acting on the conductor.
- An electric current whose magnitude is either constant or variable but the direction of flow in a conductor remains the same is called **direct current**. It is denoted by **DC**.
- An electric current whose magnitude changes with time and direction reverses periodically is called **alternating current**. It is denoted by **AC**.
- The **domestic supply circuit** consists of three types of wires, namely (i) live wire having red insulation, (ii) neutral wire having black insulation and (iii) earth wire having green insulation.
- If the live wire and neutral wire come in contact either directly or *via* conducting wire, then the situation is called **short circuiting**.
- If many electrical appliances of high power rating are switched on at the same time, then they draw large current from the circuit. This is called **overloading**.
- **Fuse** is the most important safety device used in domestic power supply circuits which prevents the possible damage caused by overloading and short circuiting.

Exam Practice

Objective Type Questions

Multiple Choice Questions

1 Choose the incorrect statement from the following regarding magnetic lines of field
(a) The direction of magnetic field at a point is taken to be the direction in which the North pole of a magnetic compass needle points
(b) Magnetic field lines are closed curves
(c) If magnetic field lines are parallel and equidistant, they represent zero field strength
(d) Relative strength of magnetic field is shown by the degree of closeness of the field lines **NCERT Exemplar**

Sol. (c) Options (a), (b) and (d) are correct but option (c) is incorrect as, the parallel lines of magnetic field represent the uniform magnetic field.

2 A constant current flows in a horizontal wire in the plane of the paper from East to West as shown in figure. The direction of magnetic field at a point will be North to South

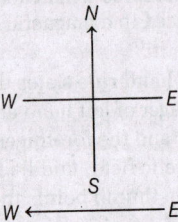

(a) directly above the wire
(b) directly below the wire
(c) at a point located in the plane of the paper on the North side of the wire
(d) at a point located in the plane of the paper on the South side of the wire
NCERT Exemplar

Sol. (b) According to right hand thumb rule, when conductor is held in right hand, keeping thumb from East to West as shown in the figure, the curve of the finger will be from North to South at a point lying directly below the wire.

3 Magnetic field due to a current through a straight conductor depends on
(a) current
(b) distance from the wire
(c) Both (a) and (b)
(d) cross-sectional area of wire

Sol. (c) Magnetic field (B) due to a current (I) through a straight conductor depends on the current and distance from the wire (r), i.e.

$$B \propto I \Rightarrow B \propto \frac{1}{r}$$

$$B \propto \frac{I}{r}$$

4 The magnetic field at a distance r from a long wire carrying current I is 0.4 T. The value of magnetic field at a distance $2r$ is
(a) 0.2 T (b) 0.1 T (c) 0.15 T (d) 1 T

Sol. (a) As, $B \propto \dfrac{1}{r}$

$$\therefore \quad \frac{B_1}{B_2} = \frac{2r}{r}$$

[where, B_1 and B_2 are magnetic fields at a distances r and $2r$]

$$\Rightarrow B_2 = \frac{B_1}{2} = \frac{0.4}{2} = 0.2 \text{ T}$$

5 A circular loop placed in a plane perpendicular to the plane of paper carries a current when the key is on. The current as seen from points A and B (in the plane of paper and on the axis of the coil) is anti-clockwise and clockwise, respectively. The magnetic field lines point from B to A. The N-pole of the resultant magnet is on the face close to

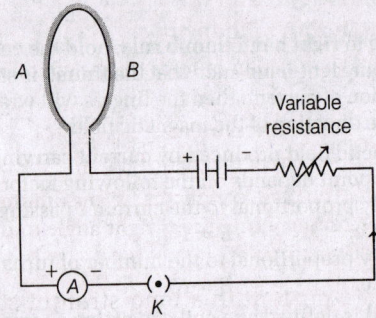

(a) A
(b) B
(c) A, if the current is small and B, if the current is large
(d) B, if the current is small and A, if the current is large **NCERT Exemplar**

Sol. (a) The N-pole of the resultant magnet is on the face close to A, because the magnetic field lines enter in loop from B and come out from A. Also, as a matter of fact magnetic lines come out of the N-pole of magnet. Therefore, face close to A represents N-pole. The currents in A and B are same.

6 In a horizontal conductor, the direction of current is from East to West. Then, the direction of magnetic field to a point directly above, it will be
(a) clockwise
(b) anti-clockwise
(c) clockwise, if viewed from East end
(d) anti-clockwise, if viewed from East end

Sol. (c) If we apply right hand thumb rule, then direction of magnetic field will be clockwise, if viewed from East end and anti-clockwise, if viewed from West end.

7 The strength of magnetic field inside a long current carrying straight solenoid is
(a) more at the ends than at the centre
(b) minimum in the middle
(c) same at all points
(d) found to increase from one end to the other **NCERT Exemplar**

Sol. (c) The strength of magnetic field lines inside a long current carrying straight solenoid is same at all points, because the magnetic field lines are straight, equi-spaced and parallel to the axis of solenoid and hence uniform magnetic field exist inside the solenoid.

8 Force on a current carrying conductor in a magnetic field depends on
(a) direction of current
(b) direction of magnetic field
(c) Both (a) and (b)
(d) length of the wire

Sol. (c) The direction of force on the conductor depends on
(i) direction of current
(ii) direction of magnetic field
Force on the conductor is maximum when the direction of current is at right angle to the direction of magnetic field.

9 For a current in a long straight solenoid N and S-poles are created at the two ends. Among the following statements, the incorrect statement is
(a) The field lines inside the solenoid are in the form of straight lines, which indicates that the magnetic field is the same at all points inside the solenoid.
(b) The strong magnetic field produced inside the solenoid can be used to magnetise a piece of magnetic material like soft iron when placed inside the coil.
(c) The pattern of the magnetic field associated with the solenoid is different from the pattern of the magnetic field around a bar magnet.
(d) The N and S-poles exchange position when the direction of current through the solenoid is reversed. **NCERT Exemplar**

Sol. (c) Here, option (c) is incorrect as the pattern of magnetic field inside a solenoid is uniform and similar to that of bar magnet.

10 The most important safety method used for protecting home appliances from short circuiting or overloading is
(a) earthing
(b) use of fuse
(c) use of stabilizers
(d) use of electric meter **NCERT Exemplar**

Sol. (b) The most important safety method used for protecting home appliances from short circuiting or overloading is the electric fuse. This is a safety device having thin wire of short length made of tin (25%) and lead (75%) alloy having low melting point around 200°C and always connected in series to limit the current in the circuit.
Whenever current through the fuse exceeds the set limit, the fuse wire melts and breaks the circuit. This saves the main circuit components from damage.

11 To avoid risk of electrical shock, which phenomena is used?
(a) Over loading (b) Short circuiting
(c) Earthing (d) None of these

Sol. (c) To avoid risk of electrical shock, the metal body of appliance is earthed. Earthing means to connect the metal case of the appliance to earth by means of a metal wire called earth wire. One end of the metal wire is buried in the earth.

Fill in the Blanks

12 A fuse wire should always connected in .... in the electrical circuits.
Sol. series

13 Fuse used in domestic circuits is to prevent the damage to the appliances due to overloading and ....
Sol. short circuiting

True and False

14 The magnetic effect of current was discovered by Fleming.

Sol. False; The magnetic effect of current was discovered by Oersted.

15 In order to provide a strong magnetic field in a small region, an electromagnet can be made in U-shape.

Sol. True

16 Fleming's left hand rule gives the direction of force of conductor.

Sol. True

17 The magnetic field lines in the middle of the current carrying solenoid are spirals.

Sol. False; The magnetic field lines in the middle of the current carrying solenoid are parallel to the axis of the tube.

18 If the front face of a circular wire carrying current behaves like a North pole, the direction of current in this face of the circular wire is anti-clockwise.

Sol. True

19 The frequency of direct current is 50 Hz.

Sol. False; Frequency of direct current is 0.

Match the Columns

20 Match the following columns.

Column A	Column B
A. Direction of force	p. Direction of magnetic force on a North pole
B. Direction of magnetic field produced by straight current carrying conductor	q. Fleming's left hand rule
C. Direction of magnetic field lines at a point in a magnet	r. Maxwell's right hand thumb rule

Sol. (A) → (q), (B) → (r), (C) → (p)

Assertion-Reason

Direction (Q. Nos. 21-24) *In each of the following questions, a statement of Assertion is given by the corresponding statement of Reason. Of the statements, mark the correct answer as.*

(a) If both Assertion and Reason are true and Reason is the correct explanation of Assertion.
(b) If both Assertion and Reason are true, but Reason is not the correct explanation of Assertion.
(c) If Assertion is true, but Reason is false.
(d) If Assertion is false, but Reason is true.

21 Assertion The magnetic field produced by a current carrying solenoid is independent of its length and cross-section area.

Reason The magnetic field inside the solenoid is uniform.

Sol. (b) The magnetic field is independent of length and area. It is uniform inside the solenoid.

22 Assertion The magnetic field is stronger at a point which is nearer to the conductor and goes on decreasing on moving away from the conductor.

Reason The magnetic field B produced by a straight current carrying wire is inversely proportional to the distance from the wire.

Sol. (a) The magnitude of magnetic field is
 (i) directly proportional to the current I passing through the wire.
 (ii) Inversely proportional to the distance r from the wire.
The magnetic field is stronger at a point which is nearer to the conductor and goes on decreasing on moving away from the conductor.

23 Assertion Electric appliances with metallic body have three connections, whereas an electric bulb has two pin connections.

Reason Three pin connections reduce heating of connecting wires.

Sol. (b) The metallic body of the electrical appliance is connected to the third pin which is connected to the earth. This is a safety precaution and avoids eventual electric shock. By doing this, the extra charge flowing through the metallic body is passed to earth and avoid shocks. There is nothing such as reducing the heating of connecting wires by three pin connections.

24 Assertion A current carrying conductor experiences a force in a magnetic field.

Reason The force acting on a current carrying conductor in a magnetic field is due to interaction between magnetic field produced by the current carrying conductor and external magnetic field in which the conductor is placed.

Sol. (b) When a current carrying conductor is placed in a magnetic field, it experiences a force except when it is placed parallel to the magnetic field. The force acting on a current carrying conductor in a magnetic field is due to interaction between magnetic field produced by the current carrying conductor and external magnetic field in which the conductor is placed.

Magnetic Effects of Electric Current

Case Based Questions

Direction (Q. Nos. 25-28) *Answer the questions on the basis of your understanding of the following table and related studied concepts:*

Name of the appliances	Power
Television	230W
Light bulbs	60 W, 100 W
Amplifier	180 W
Refrigerator	150 W
Electric iron	750 W
Electric kettle	2 kW
Immersion heater	3 kW
Cooker	8 kW

25 The current required by the cooker at 230 V is given by
 (a) 40 A   (b) 45 A   (c) 35 A   (d) 50 A

Sol. (c) Power, $P = 8$ kW $= 8000$ W   (from given table)
Voltage, $V = 230$ V
The current (I) required by a cooker of power 8 kW is given by
$$I = \frac{P}{V} = \frac{8000}{230} = 35 \text{ A}$$

26 What is the maximum number of 60 W bulbs that can be run from the mains supply of 220 volts, if you do not want to overload a 5A fuse?
 (a) 12 bulbs   (b) 18 bulbs
 (c) 20 bulbs   (d) 14 bulbs

Sol. (b) Suppose x numbers of bulbs can be used safely.
Power of 1 bulb = 60 W
So, power of x bulbs, $P = 60 \times x$
Potential difference, $V = 220$ V
∴ $P = V \times I$
$60 \times x = 220 \times 5$
$\Rightarrow x = \frac{220 \times 5}{60} = 18$

27 For an electric iron, calculate the maximum amount of current and the number of units of electricity, it would use in 30 min from above table.

Sol. From the table, power of electric iron = P
For electric iron, $P = 750$ W
Voltage, $V = 230$ V
Hence, current, $I = \frac{P}{V} = \frac{750}{230} = 3.26$ A

Energy = $P \times t = \frac{750}{1000} \times \frac{30}{60}$ kWh
= 0.375 kWh = 0.375 units

28 What current is taken by electric immersion heater working on 240 V mains? Take data from above table.

Sol. From the table, power, $P = 3$ kW, voltage, $V = 240$ V
∴ $P = V \times I$
$\Rightarrow$ Current, $I = \frac{P}{V} = \frac{3 \times 1000}{240}$
$= 12.5$ A

Very Short Answer Type Questions

29 What is the function of a galvanometer in a circuit? **CBSE 2019**

Sol. The function of a galvanometer is to detect the presence of current in an electric circuit.

30 What is meant by magnetic field? **CBSE 2016**

Sol. Magnetic field is a region around a magnetic material or a moving electric charge in which the force of magnetism acts.

31 Draw a diagram to show magnetic field due to a bar magnet in a given region. **CBSE 2016**

Sol.

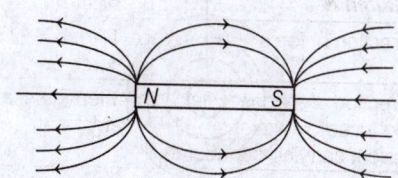

32 A constant current flows in a horizontal wire in the plane of the paper from East to West as shown in figure. At what point, the direction of magnetic field will be North to South? **NCERT Exemplar**

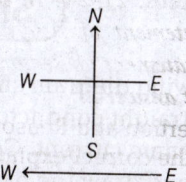

Sol. According to right hand thumb rule, when conductor is held in right hand, keeping thumb from East to West as shown in the figure, then the curve of the finger will be from North to South at a point lying directly below the wire.

33 Draw the magnetic field lines around a straight current carrying conductor.
CBSE SQP 2020-21

Sol. The observations that can be noted from the galvanometer reading are :
(i) There are momentary galvanometer deflections that die out shortly.
(ii) The deflections are in opposite directions.

34 In the arrangement shown in figure there are two coils wound on a non-conducting cylindrical rod. Initially the key is not inserted in the circuit. Later the key is inserted and then removed shortly after.

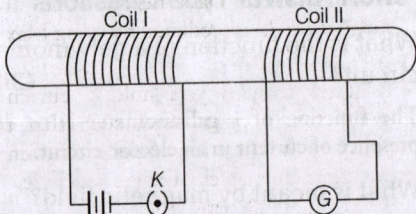

What are the two observations that can be noted from the galvanometer reading?
Latest CBSE Sample paper

Sol. The magnetic field lines around a straight current carrying conductor are concentric circles whose centres lie on the wire (as shown in figure).

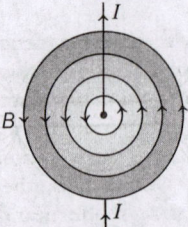

In the above figure, I and B represent the current and magnetic field, respectively.

35 What does the divergence of magnetic field lines near the ends of a current carrying straight solenoid indicate? **NCERT Exemplar**

Sol. The divergence of magnetic field lines indicates the increase in strength of magnetic field near the ends of a current carrying solenoid.

36 How is the type of current that we receive in domestic circuit different from one that runs a clock? **CBSE 2015**

Sol. The current that we receive in domestic circuit is alternating current (AC), while that which runs a clock is direct current (DC).

37 How can it be shown that a magnetic field exists around a wire through which a direct current is passing?

Sol. By this placing, a compass near the wire, the current starts to flow through the wire, the needle gets deflected. This shows that a magnetic field exists, around a wire through which direct current is passing.

38 How should the electric lamps in a building be connected, so that the switching on or off in a room has no effect on other lamps in the same building?

Sol. The electric lamps in a building should be connected in parallel, so that if one lamp stops working due to some fault, then all other appliances keep working.

39 Which is the most important safety method used for protecting home appliances from short circuiting or overloading?
NCERT Exemplar

Sol. The use of fuse is the most important safety method used for protecting home appliances from short circuiting or overloading.

Short Answer (SA) Type Questions

1 The following diagram shows two parallel straight conductors carrying same current. Copy the diagram and draw the pattern of the magnetic field lines around them showing their directions. What is the magnitude of magnetic field at a point X which is equidistant from the conductors? Give justification for your answer.
CBSE 2019

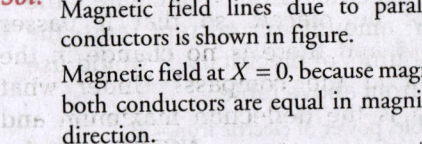

Sol. Magnetic field lines due to parallel current carrying conductors is shown in figure.

Magnetic field at $X = 0$, because magnetic field at X due to both conductors are equal in magnitude but opposite in direction.

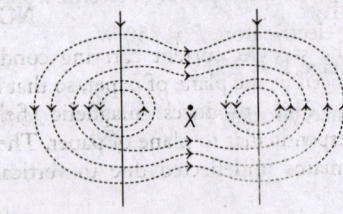

Magnetic Effects of Electric Current

2 State right hand thumb rule to determine the direction of magnetic field around a current carrying conductor. Apply this rule to find the direction of magnetic field inside and outside a circular loop of wire lying in the plane of a table and current is flowing through it clockwise. **CBSE 2019**

Sol. Refer to text on Pg. 401 and 402.

3 What are magnetic field lines? How is the direction of magnetic field at a point determined? Mention two important properties of magnetic field lines.

Sol. The imaginary lines representing magnetic field around a magnet are known as magnetic field lines.

The direction of the magnetic field at a point can determined using Maxwell's right hand thumb rule.

Two important properties of magnetic field lines are:
(i) The magnetic field lines are closed and continuous curves.
(ii) They never intersect each other.

4 What are magnetic field lines? Justify the following statements. **CBSE 2015**
(i) Two magnetic field lines never intersect each other.
(ii) Magnetic field lines are closed curves.

Sol. The imaginary lines representing magnetic field around a magnet are known as magnetic field lines.
(i) If two field lines intersect each other, this would mean that at the point of intersection, the direction of magnetic field is in two directions, which is not possible.
(ii) The direction of field lines outside a magnet is from North pole to South pole while it is from South to North pole inside the magnet and thus forms closed curves.

5 A magnetic compass needle is placed in the plane of paper near point A as shown in the figure. In which plane should a straight current carrying conductor be placed, so that it passes through A and there is no change in the deflection of the compass? Under what condition is the deflection maximum and why? **NCERT Exemplar**

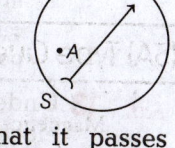

Sol. The straight current carrying conductor should be placed in the plane of paper, so that it passes through A. This produces magnetic field in a plane perpendicular to plane of paper. The compass needle remains undeflected due to vertical magnetic field produced by wire, since compass needle is free to rotate only in horizontal plane.

The deflection in compass needle is maximum when the conductor through A is perpendicular to the plane of paper and the magnetic field due to straight current carrying conductor lies in the plane of paper.

6 The flow of current in a circular wire creates a magnetic field at its centre. How can existence of this field be detected? State the rule which helps to predict the direction of magnetic field.

Sol. The existence of this field can be detected by using a magnetic compass needle. The direction of magnetic field is predicted by using Maxwell's right hand thumb rule.

It states that, if you hold a current carrying conductor in right hand, such that the thumb points in the direction of electric current, then the direction in which fingers encircle, gives the direction of magnetic field.

7 Meena draws magnetic field lines of field close to the axis of a current carrying circular loop. As she moves away from the centre of the circular loop, she observes that the lines keep on diverging. How will you explain her observation?
NCERT Exemplar

Sol. We know that the magnetic field is stronger near the current carrying conductor and weaker as we move away from the conductor. In case of a current carrying circular loop, the magnetic field is weaker near the outer edge but stronger near the centre of the loop. Due to this, the magnetic field lines appear as straight lines near the centre.

As we move towards the outer edge of the circular loop, the magnetic field lines appear to be diverging, so that they can be circular around the wire of the loop.

8 Find the direction of magnetic field due to a current carrying circular coil held
(i) Vertically in North-South plane and an observer looking it from East sees the current to flow in anti-clockwise direction.
(ii) Vertically in East-West plane and an observer looking it from South sees the current to flow in anti-clockwise direction.
(iii) Horizontally and an observer looking at it from below sees current to flow in clockwise direction. **CBSE 2016**

Sol. (i) When the coil is kept in the North-South plane and the current is flowing in the anti-clockwise through the loop, then the magnetic field is in the East to West direction.

(ii) When the coil is in vertically East-West plane and current through the coil is in anti-clockwise direction, then the magnetic field is in the South to North direction.

(iii) When a circular coil carrying current is placed horizontally and the direction of the current is clockwise, then the direction of the field for the observer positioned below the coil is in the downward direction.

9 A horizontal power line carries a current from East to West direction. What is the direction of the magnetic field due to the current in the power line at a point above and at a point below the power line?

Sol. According to right hand thumb rule,

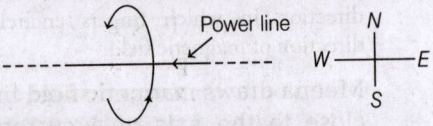

(i) The direction of magnetic field at a point above the power line is from South to North.

(ii) The direction of magnetic field at a point below the power line is from North to South.

10 AB is a current carrying conductor in the plane of the paper as shown in figure. What are the directions of magnetic fields produced by it at points P and Q?

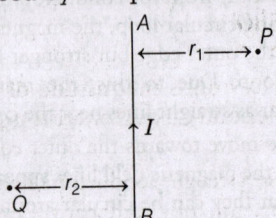

Given $r_1 > r_2$, where will the strength of the magnetic field be larger? **NCERT Exemplar**

Sol. According to the right hand thumb rule, magnetic field at P is into the plane of paper and at Q, it is out of the plane of paper.

The strength of the magnetic field at Q will be larger as strength of the field $\propto \dfrac{1}{r \text{ (distance)}}$.

11 Diagram shows the lengthwise section of a current carrying solenoid.

⊗ Indicates current entering into the page,

⊙ indicates current emerging out of the page.

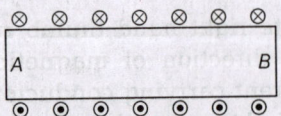

Decide which end of the solenoid A or B, will behave as North pole. Give reason for your answer. Also, draw field lines inside the solenoid. **CBSE 2016**

Sol. From diagram, we can see that current is entering from A and emerging out from B.

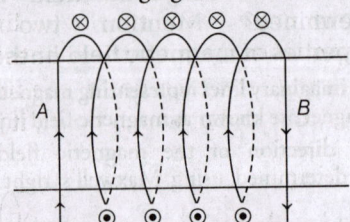

Thus, using right hand thumb rule, direction of magnetic field lines is from B to A. We know that, magnetic field lines move from North to South direction. Thus, B represents North pole or A represents South pole.

12 Give reasons for the following:

(a) There is either a convergence or a divergence of magnetic field lines near the ends of a current carrying straight solenoid.

(b) The current carrying solenoid when suspended freely rests alone a particular direction.

CBSE (All India) 2020

Sol. (a) The magnetic field lines are crowded (convergent) near the poles of solenoid. Hence, the magnetic field is strong and divergent, where the magnetic field is weak.

(b) A freely suspended current carrying solenoid always points in the north-south direction even in the absence of any other magnet. Because the earth itself behave as a magnet or solenoid to point always in a particular direction.

13 Under what conditions permanent electromagnet is obtained, if a current carrying solenoid is used? Support your answer with the help of a labelled circuit diagram. **NCERT Exemplar**

Sol. The conditions to obtain permanent electromagnet, if a current carrying solenoid is used are given as

(i) The current through the solenoid should be direct current.

(ii) The rod inside is made up of a magnetic material such as steel.

All in one Magnetic Effects of Electric Current

(iii) The magnetic material should be of high retentivity and should not lose its magnetic property easily.

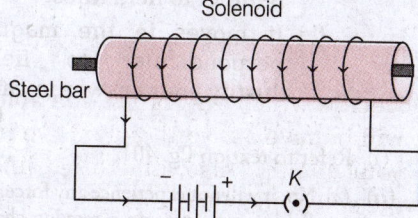

14 For the current carrying solenoid as shown below, draw magnetic field lines and give reason to explain that out of the three points A, B and C at which point, the field strength is maximum and at which point, it is minimum.

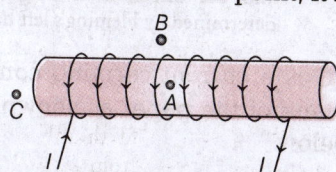

CBSE 2015

Sol. Magnetic field lines due to a solenoid

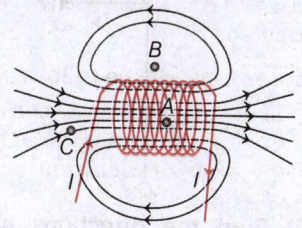

In case of an ideal solenoid, magnetic field strength is maximum at point A and is minimum or zero at point B. This is because the magnetic field is strong, where magnetic field lines are crowded and is weak, where magnetic field lines are far apart. At the point C, the density of the field lines is less than that of point A but greater than that of point B. So, the order of magnetic field at points A, B and C is

$$B_B < B_C < B_A$$

15 List two distinguishing features between overloading and short circuiting. **CBSE 2014**

Sol. Refer to text on Pg. 404.

16 What is an electric fuse? What is its role in electric circuits? Should it be placed on neutral wire or on live wire? Justify your answer. **CBSE 2015**

Sol. Refer to text on Pg. 404 (Fuse).

Fuse should be placed in series with the live wire because the live wire carries large current. During short circuit or overloading, if a large current is produced, then the fuse needs to be in this part of the circuit, so that it can blow off. If the fuse was connected on neutral wire and a fault occurred on the line, would not be sensed by the fuse and circuit does not blow off. Hence, severe damage may be caused.

Long Answer (LA) Type Questions

1 (i) Draw magnetic field lines produced around a current carrying straight conductor passing through a cardboard. Name, state and apply the rule to mark the direction of these field lines.

(ii) How will the strength of the magnetic field change when the point, where magnetic field is to be determined is moved away from the straight wire carrying constant current? Justify your answer. **CBSE 2019**

Sol. (i) Refer to text on Pg. 401.
(ii) Refer to text on Pg. 401 and 402.

2 (i) Describe an activity to obtain magnetic field line around current carrying straight conductor.
(ii) State the rule used to find the direction of this magnetic field.

(iii) How does magnitude of magnetic field depend on current through a conductor? **CBSE 2016**

Sol. (i) Take a straight conductor XY and pass it through the centre of a cardboard. Connect the ends of the conductor to the terminals of a battery through a rheostat R_h, a key K and ammeter A, so that the current flows from Y to X as shown in the figure below.

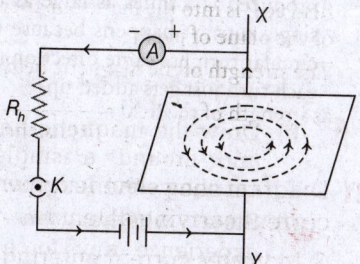

Sprinkle some iron filing on the cardboard. When the cardboard is tapped, then the iron filings will arrange themselves in concentric circles. These concentric circles represent the magnetic field lines. This shows that around a straight current carrying conductor, there exist a magnetic field. Also, it is in the form of concentric circles with the conductor as the centre.

(ii) The direction of magnetic field lines can be given by the right hand thumb rule. According to this rule, if we imagine the linear wire (conductor) to be held in the grip of the right hand, so that the thumb points in the direction of current, then the curvature of the fingers around the conductor will represent the direction of magnetic field lines. If the current flows from Y to X in the straight conductor, then the direction of magnetic field lines will be anti-clockwise and if the current flows from X to Y in the straight conductor, then the direction of magnetic field will be clockwise.

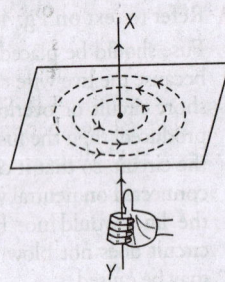

(iii) The magnitude of the magnetic field is directly proportional to the current through the conductor.

3 Explain with the help of a labelled diagram, the distribution of magnetic field due to a current through a circular loop. Why is it that, if a current carrying coil has n turns, the field produced at any point is n times as large as that produced by a single turn? **NCERT Exemplar**

Sol. Refer to text on Pg. 401 and 402.
If there is a circular coil having n turns, then the field produced is n times as large as that produced by a single turn. It happens because the current in each circular turn has same direction and the field due to each turn just gets added up.

4 (i) Draw the magnetic field lines through and around a single loop of wire carrying electric current.
(ii) State whether an α-particle will experience any force in a magnetic field, if (α-particles are positively charged particles).

(a) It is placed in the field at rest.
(b) It moves in the magnetic field parallel to field lines.
(c) It moves in the magnetic field perpendicular to field lines. Justify your answer in each case. **CBSE 2015**

Sol. (i) Refer to text on Pg. 401.
(ii) (a) No, it will not experience any force. As, magnetic field exerts force on a moving charged particle only.
(b) No, it will not experience any force because magnetic field exerts a force in perpendicular direction to motion of the particle.
(c) Yes, it will experience a force in a direction perpendicular to the direction of its own motion and the direction of magnetic field can be determined by Fleming's left hand rule.

5 PQ is a current carrying conductor in the plane of the paper as shown in the figure below.

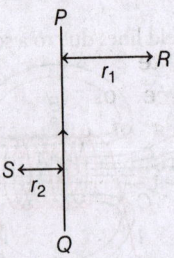

(i) Find the directions of the magnetic fields produced by it at points R and S.
(ii) Given $r_1 > r_2$, where will the strength of the magnetic field be larger? Give reasons.
(iii) If the polarity of the battery connected to the wire is reversed, how would the direction of the magnetic field be changed?
(iv) Explain the rule that is used to find the direction of the magnetic field for a straight current carrying conductor.
CBSE SQP 2020-21

Sol. (i) According to right hand thumb rule, the magnetic field produced by PQ at point R is into the plane of the paper and at point S is out of the plane of paper.
(ii) Here, $r_1 > r_2$
The magnetic field will be larger at point S as compared to that at point R.
This is because the magnetic field produced by a straight current-carrying conductor is inversely proportional to the distance from the wire. So, the magnetic field will be larger at the point which is nearer to the conductor.

As, point S is nearer to the conductor as compared to point R.

So, field at S > field at R

(iii) If the polarity of the battery is reversed, the current will be going from top to bottom in the wire and the magnetic field lines will now be in the clockwise direction on the plane which is perpendicular to the wire carrying current.

(iv) Maxwell's right hand thumb rule is used to find the direction of the magnetic field for a straight current carrying conductor.

This law states that, if you hold the current carrying straight wire in the grip of your right hand in such a way that the stretched thumb points in the direction of current, then the direction of the curl of the fingers will give the direction of the magnetic field.

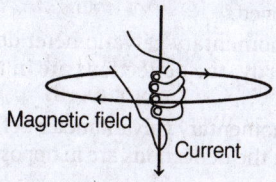

6 Differentiate between AC and DC. Name one source of each. Write any two advantages of alternating current over direct current. **CBSE 2016**

Sol. Refer to the text on Pg. 403.

Source of DC   —   Batteries
Source of AC   —   Power plants

Advantages of alternating current over direct current are as follows:

(i) Alternating voltages can be stepped up or stepped down as per requirement, using a transformer.

(ii) Alternating voltages can be transmitted over long distances with small loss of power.

7 Explain, why electric power transmitted at high voltages and low currents to distant places? **CBSE 2016**

Sol. Wire resistance causes losses in electric power transmission. If you keep resistance constant, losses are directly proportional to voltage and the square of the current.

If you double the voltage, for the same power, the current is halved and power dissipation is effectively halved for the same power.

Another reason is that cable required for transmitting low currents has less cross-sectional area and are lighter. So, it is less expensive than heavier cable. Also, the number of towers required a certain distance is also reduced.

CHAPTER EXERCISE

Multiple Type Questions

1. Which of the following is the properties of magnetic field lines?
   (a) Magnetic field lines are closed and continuous curves
   (b) Magnetic field lines never intersect with each other
   (c) Magnetic field lines are crowded near the poles
   (d) All of the above

2. A uniform magnetic field exists in the plane of paper pointing from left to right as shown in the figure. In the field, an electron and a proton move as shown in the figure. The electron and the proton experience

   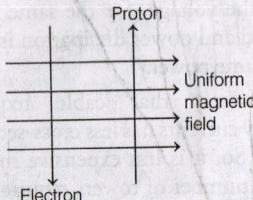

   NCERT Exemplar
   (a) Forces both pointing into the plane of paper
   (b) Forces both pointing out of the plane of paper
   (c) Forces pointing into the plane of paper and out of the plane of paper, respectively
   (d) Force pointing opposite and along the direction of the uniform magnetic field, respectively

3. The strength of magnetic field produced by current carrying solenoid depends on
   (a) the number of turns in solenoid
   (b) the strength of current
   (c) the nature of core material
   (d) All of the above

4. Choose the incorrect statement. **NCERT Exemplar**
   (a) Fleming's right hand rule is a simple rule to know the direction of induced current.
   (b) The right hand thumb rule is used to find the direction of magnetic fields due to current carrying conductors.
   (c) The difference between the direct and alternating currents is that the direct current always flows in one direction, where as the alternating current reverses its direction periodically.
   (d) In India, the AC changes direction after every $\frac{1}{50}$ s.

5. In the arrangement shown in figure below, there are two coils wound on a non-conducting cylindrical rod. Initially, the key is not inserted. Then, the key is inserted and later removed. Then,

   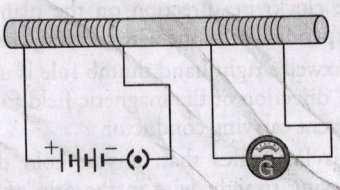

   (a) the deflection in the galvanometer remains zero throughout.
   (b) there is a momentary deflection in the galvanometer but it dies out shortly and there is no effect when the key is removed.
   (c) there are momentary galvanometer deflections that die out shortly; the deflections are in the same direction.
   (d) there are momentary galvanometer deflections that die out shortly; the deflections are in opposite directions.

Fill in the Blanks

6. When an electric current is passed through a ...., a magnetic field is produced which is very similar to that of a bar magnet.

7. The space around a magnet in which its magnetic force is exerted is called a ....

True and False

8. A TV set consumes an electric power of 230 W and 230 V mains supply, hence the correct fuse for TV set is 5A.

Match the Columns

9. Match the following columns

Column A	Column B
A. Dynamo	p. Gauss
B. Fuse	q. Tree system
C. House wiring	r. Fleming's right hand rule
D. Magnetic field	s. MCB

Assertion-Reason

Direction (Q. Nos. 10-11) *In each of the following questions, a statement of Assertion is given by the corresponding statement of Reason. Of the statements, mark the correct answer as.*
   (a) If both Assertion and Reason are true and Reason is the correct explanation of Assertion.
   (b) If both Assertion and Reason are true, but Reason is not the correct explanation of Assertion.
   (c) If Assertion is true, but Reason is false.
   (d) If Assertion is false, but Reason is true.

10 Assertion To avoid risk of electrical shock, the metal body of electric appliances is earthed.

Reason Earthing saves us from electrical shocks.

11 Assertion When current passes through a solenoid, then it tends to contract.

Reason The current flowing through two parallel wires in the same direction give rise to force of attraction on each other.

Case Based Questions

Direction (Q. Nos. 12-16) Answer the questions on the basis of your understanding of the following passage, table and related studied concepts:

A solenoid is a long helical coil of wire through which a current is run in order to create a magnetic field. The magnetic field of the solenoid is the superposition of the fields due to the current through each coil. It is nearly uniform inside the solenoid and close to zero outside and is similar to the field of a bar magnet having a North pole at one end and a South pole at the other depending upon the direction of current flow. The magnetic field produced in the solenoid is dependent on a few factors such as, the current in the coil, number of turns per unit length etc.

The following graph is obtained by a researcher, while doing an experiment to see the variation of the magnetic field with respect to the current in the solenoid.

The unit of magnetic field as given in the graph attached is in (mT) and the current is given in (A).

CBSE SQP 2020-21

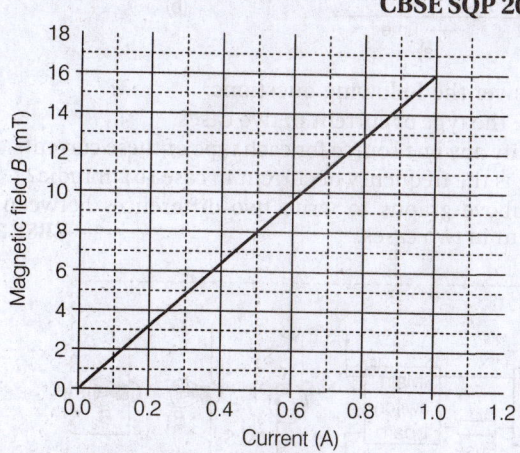

12 What type of energy conversion is observed in a linear solenoid?
(a) Mechanical to magnetic
(b) Electrical to magnetic
(c) Electrical to mechanical
(d) Magnetic to mechanical

Sol. (c) A linear solenoid is an electromagnetic device that converts electrical energy into mechanical energy.

13 What will happen, if a soft iron bar is placed inside the solenoid?
(a) The bar will be electrocuted resulting in short-circuit
(b) The bar will be magnetised as long as there is current in the circuit
(c) The bar will be magnetised permanently
(d) The bar will not be affected by any means

Sol. (b) When a soft iron bar is placed inside the solenoid, it will magnetise the iron bar as long as there is current in the circuit. Hence, the strength of the magnetic field inside the solenoid will also increase.

14 The magnetic field lines produced inside the solenoid are similar to that of
(a) a bar magnet
(b) a straight current carrying conductor
(c) a circular current carrying loop
(d) electromagnet of any shape

Sol. (a) The magnetic field lines produced inside the solenoid are similar to that produced by a bar magnet. This means that a current carrying solenoid behaves as if it has North pole and South pole. The field lines inside the solenoid are parallel to each other. The magnetic field lines due to a current carrying solenoid and bar magnet are shown below

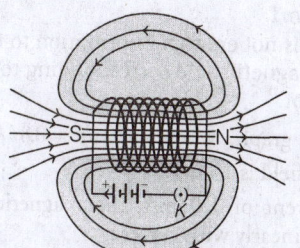

Field lines produces by a current carrying solenoid

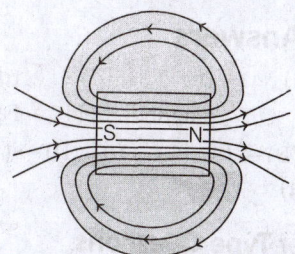

Field lines produced by a bar magnet

15 After analysing the graph, a student writes the following statements.
I. The magnetic field produced by the solenoid is inversely proportional to the current.

II. The magnetic field produced by the solenoid is directly proportional to the current.
III. The magnetic field produced by the solenoid is directly proportional to square of the current.
IV. The magnetic field produced by the solenoid is independent of the current.

Choose from the following which of the following would be the correct statement(s).
(a) Only IV (b) I, III and IV
(c) Both I and II (d) Only II

Sol. (d) The given magnetic field versus current graph is linear graph. It is clear from the graph that magnetic field increases with increase in current. Hence, the magnetic field produced by the solenoid is directly proportional to the current.

16 From the graph, deduce which of the following statements is correct?
(a) For a current of 0.8 A, the magnetic field is 13 mT.
(b) For larger currents, the magnetic field increases non-linearly.
(c) For a current of 0.8 A, the magnetic field is 1.3 mT.
(d) There is not enough information to find the magnetic field corresponding to 0.8 A current.

Sol. (a) From graph, when current = 0.8 A, the magnetic field is 13 mT.
Upto current of 1.0 mA, the magnetic field increases linearly with current.
For larger values of current (>1A), the graph does not depict any information.

Answers
1. (d) 2. (a) 3. (d) 4. (d) 5. (d)
6. solenoid 7. magnetic field 8. False
9. (A) → (r), (B) → (s), (C) → (q), (D) → (p),
10. (a) 11. (a)

Very Short Answer Type Questions
17 What name is given to the device which automatically cut-off the electrical supply during short circuiting in household wiring?

18 In which wire in an AC housing circuit, is the switch introduced to operate the light?

19 The diagram shows a coil of wire wound on a soft iron core forming an electromagnet. A current is passed through the coil in the direction indicated by the arrows.
Mark the N and S-poles produced in the iron core.

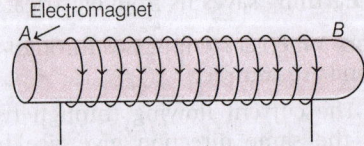

20 Why is an alternating current considered to be advantageous over direct current for long range transmission of electric energy? **CBSE 2014**

Short Answer (SA) Type Questions
21 Why does a magnetic compass needle pointing North and South in the absence of a nearby magnet gets deflected when a bar magnet or a current carrying loop is brought near it. Describe some salient features of magnetic field lines concept.

22 With the help of a labelled circuit diagram illustrate the pattern of field lines of the magnetic field around a long current carrying straight conducting wire. How is the right hand thumb rule useful to find direction of magnetic field associated with a current carrying conductor?

Long Answer (LA) Type Questions
23 You are given the following current-time graphs from two different sources:

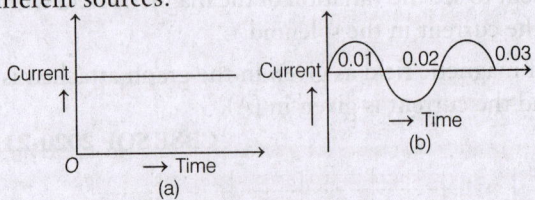

Now, answer the following questions:
(i) Name the type of current in two cases.
(ii) Identify any one source for each type of these currents.
(iii) What is the frequency of current in case (b) in India?
(iv) Use above graphs to write two differences between the current in two cases. **CBSE 2010**

24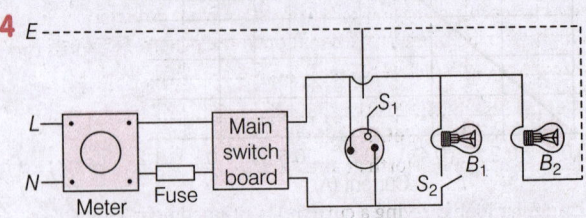

(i) The figure shows a domestic electric circuit. Study this circuit carefully and list any three errors in the circuit and justify your answer.
(ii) Give one difference between the wires used in the element of an electric heater and in a fuse.
(iii) List two advantages of parallel connection over series connection.

Challengers*

1 Which of the following figures shows the correct magnetic field lines?

2 If the key in the arrangement as shown below is taken out (the circuit is made open) and magnetic field lines are drawn over the horizontal plane ABCD, the lines are

NCERT Exemplar

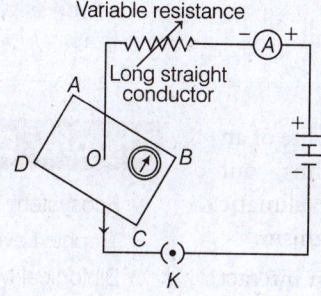

(a) concentric circles
(b) elliptical in shape
(c) straight lines parallel to each other
(d) concentric circles near the point O but of elliptical shapes as we go away from it

3 Three plotting compasses are placed close to a solenoid carrying a current. How many of the compass needles will change direction, if the current through the solenoid is increased? (Ignore the effect of the earth's magnetic field.)

(a) Only 1 compass needle
(b) 2 compass needle
(c) 3 compass needle
(d) None of the above

4 A ship is to reach a place 8° South of West. In what direction should the ship be steered, if declination at the place is 18° West?

(a) West of magnetic North at angle 64°
(b) East of magnetic South at angle 64°
(c) West of magnetic South at angle 50°
(d) East of magnetic North at angle 18°

5 A rectangular loop carrying a current i is situated near a long straight wire such that the wires is parallel to one of the sides of the loop and is in the plane of the loop. If a steady current i is created in wire as shown in figure below, then the loop will

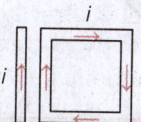

(a) rotate about an axis parallel to the wire
(b) move towards the wire
(c) move away from the wire or towards right
(d) remain stationary

6 Four metal rods are placed, in turn, inside a coil of copper wire.

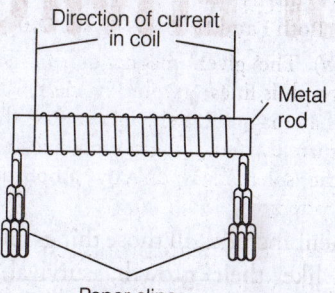

The table below gives the results of the experiment. Which rod would be the most suitable to use for the case of a coil in a circuit breaker?

Metal rod	Number of paper clips picket up when there is a current in the coil	Number of paper clips still attracted when the current is switched off
(a)	1	0
(b)	20	2
(c)	35	0
(d)	35	30

7 A copper wire is held between the poles of a magnet.

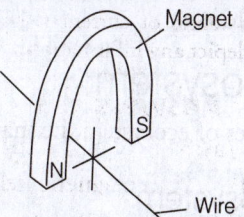

The current in the wire can be reversed. The pole of the magnet can also be changed over. In how many of the four directions shown can the force act on the wire?

(a) 1   (b) 2   (c) 3   (d) 4

Answer Key

1.	(a)	2.	(c)	3.	(d)	4.	(a)	5.	(b)
6.	(c)	7.	(b)

*These questions may or may not be asked in the examination, have been given just for additional practice.

CHAPTER 13

Our Environment

Environment includes all those things and set of conditions which influences the life of an organism like their growth, survival, development and reproduction. Thus, our environment is composed of the physical surroundings, living beings and climatic conditions of the region. A change in any of these conditions can affect the organism.

To understand how, we need to look at the different ways in which an organism interact with others and with its surroundings. In this chapter, we will look at the interactions between the organisms of an ecosystem.

Ecosystem

It is the structural and functional unit of biosphere. It is a stable ecological unit where regular input of energy and circulation of matter takes place. The term ecosystem was coined by **AG Tansley** (in 1935). All the interacting organisms in an area together with the non-living constituents (abiotic components) of the environment form an ecosystem, e.g. a lake, a field or a forest.

Types of Ecosystem

There are two types of ecosystem, i.e. natural and artificial ecosystem.

1. Natural Ecosystem

The naturally existing ecosystem without any human support is called as **natural ecosystem**. Depending upon the habitats, natural ecosystem may be terrestrial (desert, grassland and forest) and aquatic (ponds, lakes, estuaries and marine).

2. Artificial Ecosystem

An ecosystem which is created and maintained by humans is called as **artificial** or **man-made ecosystem**. These rely on human efforts to sustain. It does not possess a self-regulating mechanism.

Note Agro-ecosystem is the largest man-made ecosystem. Other examples are aquariums, botanical gardens, parks, field crops, etc.

Chapter Checklist

- Ecosystem
- Trophic Levels
- Biological Magnification or Biomagnification
- Human Impact on the Natural Environment
- Managing the Garbage We Produce
- Waste Types and Their Effects on Our Environment

Components of Ecosystem

Since, the environment refers to both physical and biological conditions, it encompasses both living (biotic) and non-living (abiotic) components of the earth.

1. Biotic Components

These include all the living organisms present in the ecosystem, i.e. plants, animals and microorganisms.

The living organisms are interconnected with one another by various mechanisms and show interdependence on each other. These are primarily classified into different groups on the basis of their nutritional relationships.

On the basis of food they consume, the different living organisms can be categorised into three groups. These are as follows

(i) **Producers** All green plants and certain blue-green algae which can produce food by the process of photosynthesis are producers. These are also called **autotrophs**. These absorb radiant energy of sun and produce organic compounds (i.e. carbohydrates). These convert solar energy into chemical energy and thus called **autotrophic**, e.g. plants and blue-green algae.

These are the source of nutrition for rest of ecosystem. They take up CO_2 and release oxygen in turn into environment, thus balance the composition of air.

(ii) **Consumers** These are dependent on producers for their nutritional requirement and consume food prepared by producers. These are also called **heterotrophs**. Consumers can be further divided into the following three categories

- **Herbivores** These are primary or **first order consumers** which feed directly on the producers, i.e. plants. e.g. grazing animals like zebra, goat, horse, sheep, etc.

- **Carnivores** These are the animals that feed on other animals. The carnivores which feed on herbivores are called **second order consumers**.
  Some carnivores may be **predators** (like lions, hawks and wolves which attack and kill their prey and feed on their bodies). Some may be **scavengers** (like jackals that feed on dead animals that they find). These are called **third order consumers**.

- **Omnivores** These are animals that feed on both plants and animals, e.g. humans and bears.

(iii) **Decomposers** These are microorganisms which feed on decaying and dead organic matter. These breakdown the remains of dead animals and plants, to releases various substances that can be used by other members of the ecosystem, e.g. bacteria and fungi.

These are useful in decomposing waste from ecosystem. These help in recycling of materials, cleaning of waste and creating space for the growth of new organisms. If these organisms are removed from any ecosystem, recycling of nutrients will stop and balance in the ecosystem will be lost.

2. Abiotic Components

The abiotic components of an ecosystem are the non-living components on which living organisms are dependent. Each abiotic component influences the number and variety of plants and animals present in an ecosystem. This inturn influence the biodiversity of an area. These components are light, temperature, water, atmospheric gases, wind, etc.

- **Light** Light energy (sunlight) is the primary source of energy in nearly all ecosystems. It is used by green plants (which contain chlorophyll). During photosynthesis plants manufacture organic substances by combining inorganic substances.

- **Temperature** The distribution of plants and animals is greatly influenced by extremes in temperature. The pattern of rain also affects the growth of the plant. This plant growth determines the overall variety of animals living in that place.

- **Atmospheric Gases** Oxygen is required for respiration and carbon dioxide for photosynthesis. Nitrogen is made available to plants by certain bacteria and through the action of lightening.

- **Wind** It helps in pollination and seed dispersal of some plants. It can remove and redistribute top soil, especially where vegetation has been reduced.

- **Water** It is essential for life. Plant and animal habitats vary from entirely aquatic environments to very dry deserts.

Check Point 01

1. In what way, the biotic components of an ecosystem are different from abiotic components?
2. State True or False for the following statements.
   (i) Producers are also referred to as the autotrophs.
   (ii) Herbivores also known as first order consumers.
4. Zebra, jackals, lions, goat, horse, wolves and sheep. Identify the first order consumers from those given above. Give a reason to support your answer.
5. Based on their feeding habits, differentiate between parasites and decomposers.

Trophic Levels

The transfer of food or energy takes place through various steps or levels in the food chain known as **trophic levels**. The producers (autotrophs) are present at the **first trophic level**. They fix solar energy, making it available for consumers (heterotrophs). The herbivores or the primary consumers are found at the **second trophic level**. Small carnivores or secondary consumers are present at the **third trophic level**. The large or the tertiary consumers form the **fourth trophic level**.

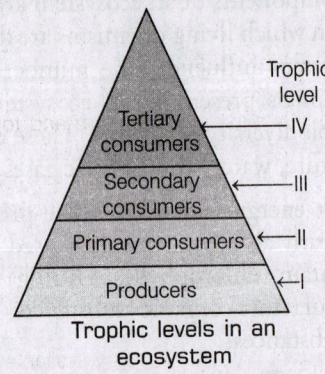
Trophic levels in an ecosystem

Food Chain

It is a linear network of living organisms in a community through which energy is transferred in the form of food. It describes relationship of organisms about 'who eats whom'.

The simplest food chains operating in nature are represented in given below

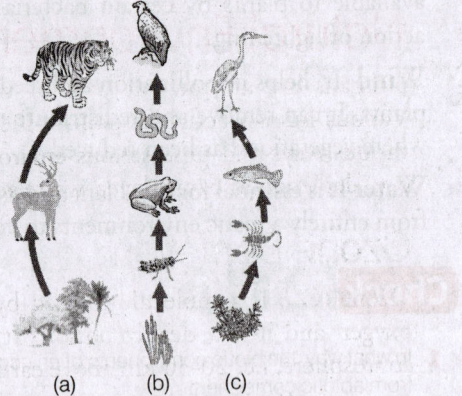
Food chain in nature; (a) in forest, (b) in grassland and (c) in a pond

On the basis of choice of habitat, food chains are of two types
 (i) **Terrestrial food chain** It is the food chain present on land.
    e.g. Grass → Insects → Snake → Hawk.
 (ii) **Aquatic food chain** It is the food chain in different water bodies.
    e.g. Phytoplankton → Zooplankton → Fish → Shark.

Significance of Food Chain

- Food chain involves the transfer of energy, materials and nutrients.
- The organisms of food chain serves as the vehicles of transfer of energy from one level to another.
- The knowledge of food chain helps in understanding the feeding relationship as well as the interaction between organisms in an ecosystem.
- In addition to the above points, it also helps to understand the movement of toxic substances and the problems associated with biological magnification in the ecosystem.

Food Web

It is the interconnection of different food chains, which correlate at various trophic levels operating in an ecosystem. Each organism is generally eaten by two or more other kinds of organisms. They in turn are eaten by several other organisms.

So, instead of a straight line, the relationship is shown as a series of branching lines hence, creating a food web.

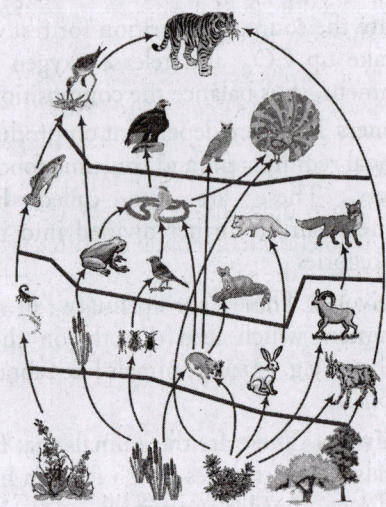
Food web consisting of many interlinked food chains

Energy Flow

Energy is accumulated by the primary producers and it is transferred through food chain to different **trophic levels**. This phenomenon is called energy flow.

It is unidirectional and there is no recycling or going back to previous level, whenever energy is transferred from one form to another, some energy is always lost.

The flow of energy in an ecosystem can be understood in the following steps
- The green plants in a terrestrial ecosystem capture about 1% of the energy of sunlight (light energy). They convert it into food (chemical energy).
- The green plants are eaten by primary consumers. Due to this, a major amount of energy is lost as heat. Some amount goes into digestion and in doing work and rest goes towards growth and reproduction.

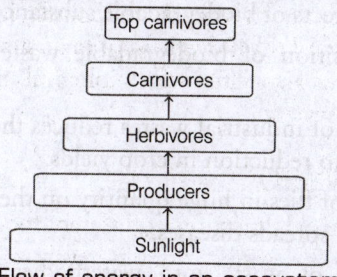
Flow of energy in an ecosystem

- An average of 10% of the energy of food eaten by an organism is turned back into its own body and made available for the next level of consumers. This is known as the **10% law** (Lindemann in 1942).
- Therefore, 10% can be taken as the average value for the amount of organic matter that is present at each step and reaches to the next trophic level.
- Since, only a little energy is available for the next level of consumers, food chains generally consist of three or four steps. The loss of energy at each step is very large. So, little usable energy is left after four trophic levels.
- From the above diagram, it is clear that flow of energy is unidirectional. The energy that is captured by autotrophs, does not revert back to the solar input. Also, the energy which passes to the herbivores, does not come back to autotrophs.

Biological Magnification or Biomagnification

It is the phenomenon of progressive increase in the concentration of non-biodegradable toxicants in organisms at each successive trophic level. It is also called **bioconcentration**.

Causes of Biomagnification

Harmful chemicals and pesticides like DDT, etc., are sprinkled on crop plants to protect them from pests and diseases. These chemicals either wash down into soil or into waterbodies. From the soil, these are absorbed by plants and from waterbodies, these are taken by aquatic plants and animals. This is why our food grains, such as wheat, rice, fruits and vegetables contain varying amount of pesticides residues. In this manner, the toxic chemicals enter the food chain.

As these chemicals are non-biodegradable, they get accumulated in organisms body. Their concentration keeps on increasing at each trophic level. The maximum concentration of these chemicals gets accumulated in human body. This is because they occupy the topmost place in any food chain.

Check Point 02

1. In three words, describe the relationship of organisms working in a food chain.
2. Fill in the blanks:
   Members present at the bottom and top of a terrestrial food chain are .... and ....
3. Consider a food chain of the following : Fish, crab, phytoplankton, shark. Arrange the above chain in the proper order of trophic level.
4. State True or False for the following statements:
   Percentage of solar radiation is absorbed by green plants for photosynthesis is 10%.
5. In which form is the 10% energy available for transfer?
6. Fertilisers and other chemicals used in agriculture are harmful to us. Give reason.
7. Identify the organisms from the following food chain which will respectively have maximum and minimum concentration of chemicals in its body. Peacock, frog, snake, grasshopper.

Human Impact on the Natural Environment

Humans are an integral part of the environment. Various human activities pollute the environment in various ways and pose serious environmental threats, e.g. depletion of ozone layer, waste accumulation, etc.

Ozone Depletion

Ozone (O_3) is a molecule formed by three atoms of oxygen and it is a deadly poison. It is found in the stratosphere, i.e. 20-30 km above earth.

Ozone at the higher levels of the atmosphere is a product of UV radiations acting on oxygen (O_2) molecule. The high energy UV radiations split apart some molecular oxygen (O_2) into free oxygen (O) atoms. These atoms are very reactive and combine with the molecular oxygen to form ozone.

$$O_2 \xrightarrow{UV} O + O$$
$$O + O_2 \longrightarrow O_3 \text{ (Ozone)}$$

Ozone Layer and its Importance

The layer of atmosphere in which most of the atmosphere's ozone is concentrated is called **ozone layer**.

- It shields the surface of the earth from harmful ultraviolet (UV) radiations of the sun.
- These radiations are highly damaging to organisms. They can cause skin cancer in human beings, damage eyes (cause disease called **cataract**), decrease crop yield, disturb global rainfall, etc.

Depletion of Ozone Layer

Due to environmental pollution, ozone layer has began to deplete in the 1980s. This was mainly due to the increasing use synthetic chemicals like **Chlorofluorocarbons** (CFCs). These are used in refrigerants as coolant and in fire extinguishers.

CFCs are very stable. These are found to persist in the atmosphere. Being stable, they do not degrade easily and rise high up in the atmosphere. In the atmosphere, UV radiations breakdown CFCs molecules and release chlorine atom. These atoms on reacting with ozone, dissociates ozone molecules into oxygen.

Thus, decreasing amount of ozone results in the depletion of ozone layer. An example of ozone layer depletion can be observed in Antarctica.

The United Nations Environment Programme (UNEP) succeeded in forming an agreement to freeze CFCs production at 1986 levels.

Managing the Garbage We Produce

The household waste is called **garbage**. Every household produces a lot of garbage on daily basis. Improvements in our lifestyle have resulted in greater amounts of waste material generation. These waste substances can be divided into two main groups

1. Biodegradable substances
2. Non-biodegradable substances

1. Biodegradable Substances

The substances which can be disposed off naturally by the action of microorganisms like bacteria, fungi, etc., are called biodegradable substances. These organisms secrete enzyme which causes breakdown of biodegradable substances into simple forms.

Biodegradable waste can also be put to treatment by waste management plants. They can be used as manure or compost to increase soil fertility, e.g. garbage, sewage, livestock waste, used tea leaves, waste papers, left-over food articles, etc.

These act as pollutants only when their quantity becomes large. The effects of biodegradable substances are as follows

- Decomposition of biodegradable wastes leads to foul smell.
- Dumping of industrial wastes reduces the fertility of soil and leads to reduction in crop yields.
- Breeding of flies in huge quantity on these wastes carries germs and spreads diseases.
- Dumping of waste into waterbodies leads to water pollution. This results in the spread of various water borne diseases.

2. Non-Biodegradable Substances

The substances that cannot be converted into harmless simpler forms by the action of microorganisms are called non-biodegradable substances.

These are toxic, harmful, may be inert and accumulate in the environment. These account for the major pollutants of the environment. Most of the non-biodegradable wastes result from human activities, e.g. radioactive wastes, plastic, insecticides, heavy metals such as lead, arsenic, aluminium, etc.

The effects of non-biodegradable substances are as follows

- Substances like radioactive wastes, lead, mercury, etc., accumulate in the environment and causes life threatening diseases in humans and other living beings.
- They pollute water and harm the aquatic plants and animals.

Methods of Waste Disposal

Garbage management practices include method of disposing garbage with least effect on the environment.

Disposal of waste means to get rid of waste. This practice should be done in a scientific way.

Firstly the wastes should be segregated as biodegradable or non-biodegradable and recyclable material. This enables application of proper disposal treatment.

Our Environment

There are various methods of waste disposal are as given below

(i) **Recycling** It is the processing of waste materials to form new products. Materials like tin, cans, metallic articles, rags, paper, glass, polythene, etc., are recyclable.

(ii) **Composting** Biodegradable domestic wastes, such as left-over food, fruit and vegetable peels, etc., can be buried in a pit, dug into ground. They are converted into compost and used as manure.

(iii) **Incineration** It is burning of a substance at high temperature to form ash. It reduces the volume of the waste considerably. It is commonly used to dispose hospital waste.

(iv) **Landfills** Solid waste is dumped into a low lying area and covered with soil. A big landfill site can be used to dispose waste materials for a considerable time.

(v) **Sewage Treatment** Sewage is carried over to Sewage Treatment Plants (STPs). Here, the sewage is filtered. Organic material in the sewage is allowed to settle down and decompose in large tanks. The water from these tanks is cleaned and is released into waterbodies.

(vi) **Biogas Production** In some places, sewage is decomposed anaerobically to yield biogas and manure.

Use of Disposable Paper Cups in Trains

Some years back, tea used to be served in reusable glasses in trains. But for the reasons of hygiene, reusable glasses were replaced by disposable plastic cups. However, disposal of millions of these cups on a daily basis was not easy as plastic cups. These are non-biodegradable, i.e. they cannot be disposed off completely. So, they caused problem to the environment.

The railways as an alternative, used kulhads (disposable cups made of clay), but the production of these cups at a large scale resulted in the loss of top fertile soil.

Therefore, to circumvent this problem, disposable paper cups are now being used which are biodegradable. These can be disposed off completely without any harm to the environment.

Check Point 03

1. Ozone present in the atmosphere is very important for sustenance of life on Earth. Justify.
2. Fill in the blank:
   The ultraviolet radiations are damaging to .... components of the environment.
3. Efforts are being made for substituting the chemicals like CFCs. Why?
4. In what way can biogegradable substances be used by farmers?
5. Why is plastic bag called non-biodegradable while paper is not?
6. State True or False for the following statement.
   The process in which wastes are burned at high temperature is called incineration.
7. Untreated sewage being disposed in waste bodies leads to water pollution. Suggest the practices that can be included for better disposal of sewage waste.
8. What best method can be used for the safe disposal of hospital wastes?

NCERT FOLDER

Intext Questions

1 Which of the following groups contain only biodegradable items?
  (a) Grass, flowers and leather
  (b) Grass, wood and plastic
  (c) Fruit-peels, cake and lime-juice
  (d) Cake, wood and grass

Sol. (c) Fruit-peels, cake and lime-juice are only biodegradable item.

2 Which of the following constitute a food chain?
  (a) Grass, wheat and mango
  (b) Grass, goat and human
  (c) Goat, cow and elephant
  (d) Grass, fish and goat

Sol. (b) Grass → Goat → Human make a food chain

3 Which of the following are environment-friendly practices?
  (a) Carrying cloth-bags to put purchases in while shopping
  (b) Switching off unnecessary lights and fans
  (c) Walking to school instead of getting your mother to drop you on her scooter
  (d) All of the above

Sol. (d) All the practices given in question are environment friendly.

4 Why are some substances biodegradable and some non-biodegradable? **Pg 257**

Sol. Certain substances are easily acted upon by the action of enzymes of saprophytes and get converted into simpler substances, hence are called biodegradable. Whereas certain substances like plastic, etc., cannot be degraded by the action of enzymes and thus, are called non-biodegradable.

5 Give any two ways in which biodegradable substances would affect the environment. **Pg 257**

Sol. The two ways in which biodegradable substances would affect the environment are
  (i) Their degradation may release certain gases in the atmosphere thereby, polluting the environment.
  (ii) They may become breeding places of flies and many other pests, thus causing diseases.

6 Give any two ways in which non-biodegradable substances would affect the environment. **Pg 257**

Sol. The two ways in which non-biodegradable substances would affect the environment are
  (i) They make the environment poisonous and unfit for survival of living forms of life.
  (ii) They block the transfer of energy and minerals in the ecosystem.

7 What are trophic levels? Give an example of a food chain and state the different trophic levels in it. **Pg 261**

Sol. The transfer of food or energy takes place through various levels in the food chain, which are known as trophic levels, e.g.

Trees →	Rabbit →	Snake →	Hawk
(First trophic level)	(Second trophic level)	(Third trophic level)	(Fourth trophic level)
[Producers]	[I consumer]	[II consumer]	[III consumer]

8 What is the role of decomposers in the ecosystem? **Pg 261**

Sol. Organisms that feed on dead plants and animals are called decomposers, e.g. bacteria, fungi, etc. They breakdown the complex organic compounds present in the dead remains into simpler substances and obtain nutrition from them. These substances are released into the soil and the atmosphere.
Thus, they play the following roles
  (i) They help in recycling of materials, replenishment of the soil's nutrients, etc.
  (ii) They clean our surroundings by decomposing dead organisms and organic wastes.

9 What is ozone and how does it affect any ecosystem? **Pg 264**

Sol. Ozone is a triatomic molecule, i.e. made up of three atoms of oxygen joined together. Its molecular formula is O_3. It can affect any ecosystem in the following ways
  (i) It protects against ultraviolet rays if, present in stratosphere.
  (ii) Ozone dissipates the energy of UV rays by undergoing dissociation followed by reassociation.
  $$2O_3 \longrightarrow 3O_2 + \text{Energy}$$
  (iii) In atmosphere, it is highly toxic and cause injury to mucous membranes, eye irritation and internal haemorrhages in animals and humans.

10 How can you help in reducing the problem of waste disposal? Give any two methods. **Pg 264**

Sol. Refer to text 'methods of waste disposal' on Pg. 426 and 427.

Exercises (On Page 99)

1 What will happen if we kill all the organisms in one trophic level?

Sol. If we kill all the organisms in one trophic level, the lower trophic level will grow more in number and the higher trophic level will not survive. Hence, flow of energy from one trophic level to other will not take place.

2 (i) Will the impact of removing all the organisms in a trophic level be different for different trophic levels?
(ii) Can the organisms of any trophic level be removed without causing any damage to the ecosystem?

Sol. (i) Yes, the impact of removing all the organisms in a trophic level will be different for different trophic levels. The lower trophic level of an ecosystem has a greater number of individuals than the higher trophic levels. Removal of producers will affect all the organisms of successive trophic levels and it will threat their survival. The removal of higher trophic level will lead to increase in organisms of lower trophic level and the organisms of higher trophic level will die due to the shortage of food.

(ii) No, removal of all organisms of a trophic level will disturb the ecosystem. Killing of higher trophic level organisms will cause explosion in the population of lower level organisms. This will adversely affect the ecosystem and thus environment.

3 What is biological magnification? Will the levels of this magnification be different at different levels of the ecosystem?

Sol. Biological magnification refers to the increase in the concentration of certain toxicants at each successive trophic level.

No, the levels of magnification will not be same in all trophic levels. When the chemicals do not get degraded and get accumulated progressively at each trophic level, it leads to biomagnification. Biomagnification is more in organisms of higher trophic levels.

4 What are the problems caused by non-biodegradable waste that we generate?

Sol. Refer to ans. on Pg. 428 of Intext Questions 6.

5 If all the waste we generate is biodegradable, will this have no impact on the environment?

Sol. If all the waste is biodegradable, then there will be no accumulation of waste and the Earth would be a cleaner place to live. But if, this biodegradable waste is too large in amount then its slow degradation may lead to air pollution (due to release of gases) as well as water and land pollution.

6 Why is damage to the ozone layer a cause for cancer? What steps are being taken to limit this damage?

Sol. Thinning of ozone layer present in stratosphere is called depletion of ozone layer. Due to depletion of ozone layer, harmful ultraviolet radiations can reach the surface of Earth, which may lead to skin diseases, cancer, etc. To reduce the depletion of ozone layer, use of chlorofluorocarbons has been minimised. In 1987, the UNEP has passed an agreement to freeze CFC production at 1986 levels.

SUMMARY

- **Environment** It is the physical and biological conditions of the surroundings of an organism.
- **Ecosystem** All the interacting organisms in an area together with their non-living components of the environment constitute a system called ecosystem.
  Ecosystems are of two types
  (i) Natural ecosystem (ii) Artificial ecosystem
  - **Components of Ecosystem** An ecosystem is made up of two main components
    (i) **Abiotic Components** It is the non-living parts of an ecosystem on which an organism depends. It includes physical factors as light, temperature, wind, soil, etc.
    (ii) **Biotic Components** It include all the living orgainsms present in the ecosystem. It includes mainly three categories of organisms.
    - **Producers** make their own food, e.g. plants.
    - **Consumers** depend on producers for their nutritional requirements, e.g. grazing animals, humans.
    - **Decomposers** The microorganisms which feed on decaying and dead matter, e.g. bacteria, fungi.
- **Food Chain** It is the linear network of organisms through which energy is transferred in the form of food by the process of one organism consuming the other. There is unidirectional flow of energy from one organism to another.
- **Trophic Levels** The transfer of food or energy in the various steps in the food chain forms trophic level. Each food chain is composed of three to four trophic levels
  (i) **First Trophic Level** Autotrophs/producers
  (ii) **Second Trophic Level** Herbivores/primary consumers
  (iii) **Third Trophic Level** Small carnivores/secondary consumers
  (iv) **Fourth Trophic Level** Large carnivores/tertiary consumers.
- **Food Web** Each organism is generally eaten by two or more other kinds of organisms, which in turn are eaten by several other organisms. So, a food web consists of a series of branching networks of various food chains being interconnected at various trophic levels.
- **Energy Flow** It is unidirectional. Food chain shows how food and energy pass from one organism to another in a habitat. Also only 10% energy is available to the next trophic level in a food chain.
- **Biological Magnification** It is a phenomenon of progressive increase in the concentration of a toxicant at each successive trophic level, e.g. pesticides like DDT sprinkled on plants enter the body of human beings through the food chain.
- **Ozone depletion**
  (i) Ozone (O_3) is a molecule formed by three atoms of oxygen.
  (a) $O_2 \xrightarrow{UV} O + O$ (b) $O + O_2 \longrightarrow O_3$ (Ozone)
  (ii) It shields the surface of the Earth from harmful UV rays of the Sun.
  (iii) Use of CFCs causes the depletion of ozone layer.
- **Waste Substances** The left over or discarded substance is called waste. It can be in solid, liquid or gaseous form.
- **Biodegradable Substances** These are the materials which can be broken down into simple harmless forms naturally by the microbial action. These pollute environment when present in huge quantities, e.g. livestock waste, left-over food articles, etc.
- **Non-biodegradable Substances** These are the materials which cannot be broken down into simpler harmless forms by action of microorganisms. These pollute the environment, e.g. plastic, heavy metals, etc.
- **Waste Disposal** The household waste is called garbage. The waste should be disposed off in a scientific way by segregating waste into biodegradable and non-biodegradable materials. Methods of waste disposal include recycling, composting, incineration, landfills, sewage treatment, biogas production, etc.

Exam Practice

Objective Type Questions

Multiple Choice Questions

1 Which of the following is not a functional component of an ecosystem?
 (a) Communities (b) Decomposers
 (c) Sunlight (d) Energy flow

Sol. (d) The flow of energy is not a functional component of an ecosystem.

2 Which one of the following is an artificial ecosystem?
 (a) Pond (b) Crop field
 (c) Lake (d) Forest
   NCERT Exemplar

Sol. (b) Crop field is an artificial ecosystem. It is an agricultural land created by man.
Pond, lake and forests are natural ecosystem, as they are self-sustainable and do not need human interference for their maintenance.

3 Organisms which synthesise carbohydrates from inorganic compounds using radiant energy are called
 (a) decomposers (b) producers
 (c) herbivores (d) carnivores
   NCERT Exemplar

Sol. (b) Organisms which synthesise carbohydrates from inorganic compounds using radiant energy are called producers, e.g. all green plants, blue-green algae.

4 Food web is the
 (a) food that a spider collects using its web
 (b) network of interlinked trophic levels
 (c) network of interlinked food chains
 (d) display of food items on a website

Sol. (c) A food web is a network of inter-linked food chains operating at various trophic levels.

5 Flow of energy in an ecosystem is always
 (a) unidirectional (b) bidirectional
 (c) multidirectional (d) no specific direction
   NCERT Exemplar

Sol. (a) Flow of energy in an ecosystem is always unidirectional.

6 In a food chain, the snake predated as rabbit which fed on fresh green bushes. What percentage amount of the energy accumulated by rabbit, would be acquired by snakes?

 (a) 90% (b) 10%
 (c) 50% (d) 25%

Sol. (b) According to Lindemann's 10% energy law, only 10% of the energy is transferred from one trophic level to the subsequent trophic level.

7 Accumulation of non-biodegradable pesticides in the food chain in increasing amount at each higher trophic level is known as
 (a) eutrophication
 (b) pollution
 (c) biomagnification
 (d) accumulation   **NCERT Exemplar**

Sol. (c) Bio-magnification is the accumulation of non-biodegradable pesticides in the food chain in increasing amount at each higher trophic level.

8 Depletion of ozone is mainly due to
 (a) chlorofluorocarbon compounds
 (b) carbon monoxide
 (c) methane
 (d) pesticides   **NCERT Exemplar**

Sol. (a) Depletion of ozone is mainly due to Chlorofluorocarbons (CFCs).

9 Burning of waste products at high temperature to form ash, reduces waste considerably. This method of waste disposal is called
 (a) composting
 (b) sewage treatment
 (c) recycling
 (d) incineration

Sol. (d) Incinerators involve degradation of wastes by burning them at high temperatures.

10 Replacing of plastic cups by the paper cups for selling tea on train is preferred because
 (a) paper cups are more aesthetic
 (b) paper cups are more hygienic
 (c) paper cups are cheaper
 (d) paper cups are biodegradable and eco-friendly

Sol. (d) The paper cups are preferred over plastic cups because being biodegradable they are not potential wastes.

Fill in the Blanks

11 Green plants of terrestrial ecosystem capture only ...... of solar energy.

Sol. 1-2%

12 UNEP has made it mendatory for companies to make....... free refrigerators.

Sol. CFC

13 Leaves, papers can be decomposed by decomposers so are called .... substances.

Sol. Biodegradable

14 Grass → Grasshopper, → Birds. It is an example of ....

Sol. Food chain

True and False

15 Biotic components of an ecosystem include temperature, bacteria, soil and minerals.

Sol. False; Temperature is not a biotic component.

16 Aquarium is a man-made ecosystem.

Sol. True

17 All decomposers include algae and fungi.

Sol. False; All decomposers include bacteria and fungi but not algae.

18 Only green plants can make use of radiant solar energy.

Sol. True

19 Ozone is a toxic gas composed of three oxygen molecule.

Sol. True

20 CFC takes its origin from spray foams and coolants of refrigerators.

Sol. True

21 Human made plastics can be degraded by bacterial actions.

Sol. False. Plastics cannot be degraded by action of bacteria or fungi.

22 Kulhads (disposable cups) are made of sandy loam soils.

Sol. False; Kulhads are made up of clay soils.

Match the Columns

23 Match the following columns.

	Column I		Column II
1.	Autotrophs	A.	Soil
2.	Heterotrophs	B.	Lion
3.	Decomposers	C.	Bacteria
4.	Abiotic	D.	Algae

Sol. 1 → D, 2 → B, 3 → C, 4 → A

24 Match the following columns.

	Column I		Column II
1.	Trees	A.	Primary consumer
2.	Deers	B.	Secondary consumers
3.	Birds	C.	Top consumers
4.	Lion	D.	Producers

Sol. 1 → D, 2 → A, 3 → B, 4 → C

Assertion–Reason

Direction (Q. Nos. 25-28) *In each of the following questions, a statement of Assertion is given by the corresponding statement of Reason. Of the statements, mark the correct answer as*

(a) If both Assertion and Reason are true and Reason is the correct explanation of Assertion

(b) If both Assertion and Reason are true, but Reason is not the correct explanation of Assertion

(c) If Assertion is true, but Reason is false

(d) If Assertion is false, but Reason is true

(e) If Assertion and Reason both are false

25 Assertion Aquariums are known as the man-made ecosystems.

Reason Aquariums are created and maintained by humans.

Sol. (*a*) Aquariums are known as the man-made ecosystems because these are created and maintained by humans.

26 Assertion Consumers are present at the first trophic level.

Reason Consumers or heterotrophs fix energy making it available for autotrophs.

Sol. (*e*) Autotrophs are present at the first trophic level because they fix solar energy, making it available for consumers or heterotrophs.

27 Assertion Aquatic food chain is the food chain present in water bodies.

Reason The example of aquatic food chain is phytoplankton → zooplankton → fish → shark.

Sol. (*a*) Aquatic food chain is the food chain present in water bodies, e.g. phytoplankton → zooplankton → fish → shark.

28 Assertion Biomagnification is caused due to the accumulation of non-biodegradable toxicants in organisms at each successive trophic level.

Reason Biomagnification leads to the maximum accumulation of chemicals in small fishes.

Sol. (e) Biomagnification is caused due to the accumulation of non-biodegradable toxic chemicals like DDT in organisms at each successive trophic level. The maximum concentration of these chemicals gets accumulated in human body because they occupy the topmost place in any food chain.

Case Based Questions

Direction (Q. Nos. 29-33) *Answer the questions on the basis of your understanding of the following passage and related studied concepts:*

Food chains are very important for the survival of most species. When only one element is removed from the food chain it can result in extinction of a species in some cases. The foundation of the food chain consists of primary producers.

Primary producers or autotrophs can use either solar energy or chemical energy to create complex organic compounds, whereas species at higher trophic levels cannot and so must consume producers or other life that itself consumes producers.

Because the Sun's light is necessary for photosynthesis, most life could not exist if the Sun disappeared. Even so, it has recently been discovered that there are some forms of life, chemotrophs, that appear to gain all their metabolic energy from chemosynthesis driven by hydrothermal vents thus showing that some life may not require solar energy to thrive.
CBSE Question Bank

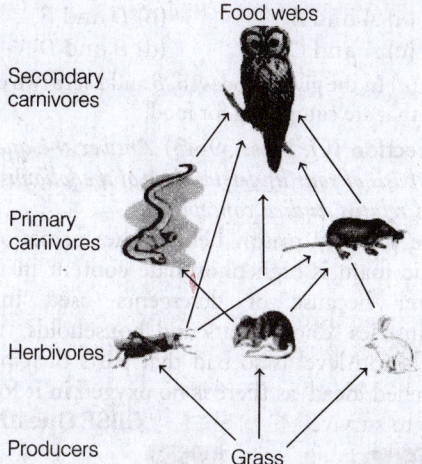

29. If 10,000 J solar energy falls on green plants in a terrestrial ecosystem, what percentage of solar energy will be converted into food energy?
    (a) 10,000 J
    (b) 100 J
    (c) 1000 J
    (d) It will depend on the type of the terrestrial plant.

Sol. (b) According to the 10% law, only 10% of the energy is transferred to each trophic level from its lower trophic level. Therefore, if 10,000 J solar energy falls on green plants in a terrestrial ecosystem, 100 J of solar energy will be converted into food energy.

30. Mr. X is eating curd/yogurt. For this food intake in a food chain he should be considered as occupying
    (a) first trophic level (b) second trophic level
    (c) third trophic level (d) fourth trophic level

Sol. (c) First trophic level is occupied by producers or green plants.
Producers are consumed by herbivores which are present at the second trophic level. Curd or yogurt is consumed by third trophic level organism such as Ravi.

31. The decomposers are not included in the food chain. The correct reason for the same is because decomposers :
    (a) act at every trophic level of the food chain
    (b) do not breakdown organic compounds
    (c) convert organic material to inorganic forms
    (d) release enzymes outside their body to convert organic material to inorganic forms

Sol. (a) As the decomposers (bacteria and fungi) decompose every organism at each trophic level, so it is impossible to place the decomposers in food chain.

32. Matter and energy are two fundamental inputs of an ecosystem. Movement of
    (a) energy is bidirectional and matter is repeatedly circulating.
    (b) energy is repeatedly circulation and matter is unidirectional.
    (c) energy is unidirectional and matter is repeatedly circulating.
    (d) energy is multidirectional and matter is bidirectional.

Sol. (c) Energy flow through an ecosystem in only one direction. Energy is passed from organisms at one trophic level or energy level to organisms in the next trophic level. Unlike energy, matter is recycled in ecosystem.

33. Which of the following limits the number of trophic levels in a food chain?
    (a) Decrease in energy at higher trophic levels
    (b) Less availability of food
    (c) Polluted air
    (d) Water

Sol. (a) Decrease in energy at higher trophic levels limits the number of trophic levels in a food chain. At each trophic level, a large proportion of energy is utilised for the maintenance of organisms occurring at that structure trophic level. Organisms get less and less energy at successive level.

Direction (Q. Nos. 34-38) *Answer the questions on the basis of your understanding of the following passage and related studied concepts:*

Observe the food web and answer the questions given below

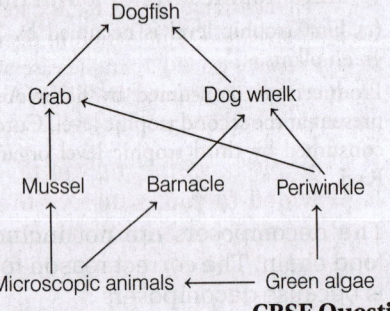

CBSE Question Bank

34 The mussel can be described as
(a) producer
(b) primary consumer
(c) secondary consumer
(d) decomposer

Sol. (c) The trophic level of secondary consumer represented by mussels filtering particle (mainly microalgae) out of the water.

35 Which trophic level is incorrectly defined?
(a) Carnivores - secondary or tertiary consumers
(b) Decomposers - microbial heterotrophs
(c) Herbivores - primary consumers
(d) Omnivores - molds, yeast and mushrooms

Sol. (d) Omnivores — molds, yeast and mushrooms. Omnivores can be primary or secondary consumers, whereas molds, yeast and mushrooms are example of decomposers.

36 The given figure best represents

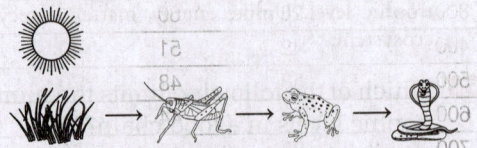

(a) Grassland food chain
(b) Parasitic food chain
(c) Forest food chain
(d) Aquatic food chain

Sol. (a) A food chain in a grassland ecosystem starts with grass being the primary producer by trapping energy from sunlight.

Insects like grasshoppers are primary consumers because they directly depend on the green plant for their food. The frog is secondary consumer because it eats insect and snake is tertiary consumer because it eats frog.

37 Why do all food chains start with plants?
(a) Because plants are easily grown
(b) Because plants are nutritious
(c) Because plants can produce its own energy
(d) Because plants do not require energy

Sol. (c) A food chain always starts with a producer. This is an organism that makes its own food. Most food chain start with green plants because plants can make their food by photosynthesis.

38 In the food web, what two organisms are competing for food?

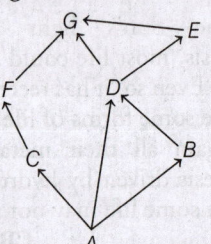

(a) A and B (b) D and F
(c) A and C (d) B and D

Sol. (d) In the given food web, B and D are two organisms that are competing for food.

Direction (Q. Nos. 39-43) *Answer the questions on the basis of your understanding of the following passage and related studied concepts:*

The primary reason behind the formation of the toxic foam is high phosphate content in the waste water because of detergents used in dyeing industries, dhobi ghats and households. Yamuna's pollution level is so bad that parts of it have been labelled 'dead' as there is no oxygen in it for aquatic life to survive. **CBSE Question Bank**

39 Predict the pH value of the water of river Yamuna if the reason for froth is high content of detergents dissolved in it.
(a) 10-11 (b) 5-7
(c) 2-5 (d) 7

Sol. (a) If high content of detergent dissolved in water of river Yamuna then the value of pH of water will be 10-11. Because nature of detergent is basic. So, water becomes basic and pH of basic water may be 7-14.

40 Which of the following statements is correct for the water with detergents dissolved in it?
(a) Low concentration of hydroxide ion (OH^-) and high concentration of hydronium ion (H_3O^+).
(b) High concentration of hydroxide ion (OH^-) and low concentration of hydronium ion (H_3O^+).
(c) High concentration of hydroxide ion (OH^-) as well as hydronium ion (H_3O^+).
(d) Equal concentration of both hydroxide ion (OH^-) and hydronium ion (H_3O^+).

Sol. (b) Almost all detergents have NaOH which is basic in nature and gives OH^- ion in water. When they dissolved in water then the concentration of hydroxide ion (OH^-) increases and the concentration of hydronium ion (H_3O^+) decreases.

41 The table provides the pH value of four solutions P, Q, R and S.

Solutions	pH value
P	2
Q	9
R	5
S	11

Which of the following correctly represents the solutions in increasing order of their hydronium ion concentration?
(a) $P > Q > R > S$
(b) $P > S > Q > R$
(c) $S < Q < R < P$
(d) $S < P < Q < R$

Sol. (c) The value of pH of solution depends on hydronium ion concentration. Lower the value of pH it means higher the hydronium ion concentration.
Hence, according to given pH values the increasing order of hydronium ion concentration will be $S < Q < R < P$. (11 < 9 < 5 < 2).

42 High content of phosphate ion in river Yamuna may lead to
(a) decreased level of dissolved oxygen and increased growth of algae.
(b) decreased level of dissolved oxygen and no effect of growth of algae.
(c) increased level of dissolved oxygen and increased growth of algae.
(d) decreased level of dissolved oxygen and decreased growth of algae.

Sol. (a) Phosphorus is an essential element for plant life but when there is too much of it in water, it can speed up eutrophication (a reduction in dissolved oxygen in water bodies caused by an increase of mineral and organic nutrients) of river and lakes. A sign of this is excess algae in the lake.

43 If a sample of water containing detergents is provided to you, which of the following methods will you adopt to neutralise it?
(a) Treating the water with baking soda
(b) Treating the water with vinegar
(c) Treating the water with caustic soda
(d) Treating the water with washing soda

Sol. (b) Detergents are basic in nature.
So, for neutralise it, acid is required. Because vinegar is an acid, it can neutralise detergents.

Direction (Q. Nos. 44-47) *Answer the questions on the basis of your understanding of the following passage and related studied concepts:*

Untreated human sewage should not enter river water, but occasionally an overflow from a water treatment plant occurs. The table below contain information on the changes that occurred in river water downstream from a sewage overflow.

Distance downstream/m	Concentration of dissolved oxygen/percentage of maximum	Number /arbitrary units of			
		Bacteria	Algae	Fish
(point of sewage entry)	95	88	20	20
100	30	79	8	6
200	20	74	7	1
300	28	60	21	0
400	42	51	40	0
500	58	48	70	0
600	70	44	83	0
700	80	42	90	0
800	89	39	84	0
900	95	36	68	4
1000	100	35	55	20

Study the data given above and answer the following questions.

44 What is the percentage of oxygen at the distance of 300 metres from source disposal of sewage water?

Sol. 28 percent.

45 At what distance from waste disposal the number of fishes becomes zero?

Sol. 300 metres.

46 Give reason why the number of algae grows upto the distance of 700 metre.

Sol. The level of dissolved oxygen increases as water moves away from the point of disposal of water.

47 Suggest one method by which this type of pollution can be avoided.

Sol. The untreated industrial waste/sewage water should be taken to treatment plant to remove its harmful elements/chemicals.

Direction (Q. Nos. 48-51) *Answer the questions on the basis of your understanding of the following passage and related studied concepts:*

Certain substances in the environment are harmful when absorbed in high concentrations. Substances, such as pesticides, radioactive isotopes, heavy metals and industrial chemicals such as PCBs can be taken up by organisms *via* their food or simply absorbed from the surrounding medium.

The toxicity of a pesticide is a measure of how poisonous the chemical is, not only to the target organisms, but to non-target species as well. The specificity (broad or narrow spectrum) of a pesticide describes how selective it is in targeting a pest. an important issue relating to the use of a pesticide is its persistence; how long it remains in the environment.

A pesticide may be biodegradable or resistant to biological breakdown. Many highly persistent pesticides cannot be metabolised or excreted.

48 Name few environment dyrading substances.

Sol. Industrial wastes, chemical fertilisers

49 What is toxicity?

Sol. Toxicity is the measure of harming effect of any chemical to the target organisms.

50 Which among the following is non-bio-degradable substances?
(a) Rubber (b) Wood
(c) Leaves (d) Paper

Sol. Rubber

51 Which amongst the following is not hazardous for the environment?
(a) Pesticides
(b) Fertilizers
(c) Heavy metals
(d) Manures

Sol. Manures

Very Short Answer Type Questions

52 Name some abiotic components of an ecosystem.

Sol. Temperature, rainfall, wind, soil and minerals are some abiotic components of ecosystem.

53 What do you mean by artificial ecosystem.

Sol. Those ecosystem which are made and maintained by man are called artificial ecosystem.

54 Draw a food chain most likely to be a part of a forest ecosystem.

Sol. Grass → Deer → Lion.

55 Which of the following belongs to the first trophic level?

Grasshopper, rose plant, cockroach, vulture, neem plant.

Sol. Rose plant and neem plant.

56 Among all four types of animals, i.e. carnivores, decomposers, herbivores and producers, how does energy flow in an ecosystem, occur through these organisms?

Sol. The energy flow through these organisms will follow a typical food chain pattern, i.e. producers → herbivores → carnivores → decomposers.

57 Now a days, our government is stressing upon the use of jute or paper bags instead of plastic bags. What purpose is supposed to be achieved by the government?

Sol. Jute bags or paper bags are prepared from biodegradable materials thus, lowering the environmental pollution. Plastic bags are non-biodegradable and affect the environment adversely.

58 If a harmful chemical enters in food chain comprising snakes, peacock, mice and plants, which of these organisms is likely to have the maximum concentration of this chemical in its body?

Sol. Peacock.

59 Why did United Nations act to control the production of CFCs used in refrigerators?

Sol. CFCs deplete the ozone layer around the Earth, hence United Nations act to control its production.

60 List two items which can be easily recycled, but we generally throw them in the dustbins?

Sol. Steel, cans and paper can be easily recycled, but we generally throw them in dustbins.

61 A lake has been polluted by sewage. On comparison with the sample of unpolluted water, the water in the lake is found to have increased contents of some components. Identify these components.

Sol. Sewage usually contains organic substances. The decomposition of these substances by decomposers increases nitrogenous compounds in water.

62 Why should biodegradable and non-biodegradable wastes be discarded in two separate dustbins?

Sol. Biodegradable materials are broken down by microorganisms in nature into simple harmless substances. Non-biodegradable materials need a different treatment like heat and temperature for disposal and hence, both should be discarded in two different dustbins.

63 Write one negative effect of affluent life style of few persons of a society on the environment. **CBSE 2016**

Sol. Affluent people use resources recklessly, which leads to their depletion and generation of excess waste. Due to their high living standards, such an affluence has terrible consequences on the environment.

Short Answer (SA) Type Questions

1 (a) Define ecosystem.
(b) Autotrophs are at the first level of food chain. Give reason.
(c) In a food chain of frogs, grass, insects and snakes assign trophic level to frogs. To which category of consumers do they belong to? **CBSE 2020**

Sol. (a) Ecosystem is the structural and functional unit of biosphere and is a stable ecological unit where regular input of energy and circulation matter takes place.
(b) Autotrophs are the producers, i.e. green plants. They can make up of solar radiation for photosynthesis and prepare food materials for themselves and thus also make first trophic level for herbivores.
(c) They will belong to category of primary consumers.

2 Why are crop fields known as artificial ecosystem? **NCERT Exemplar**

Sol. Artificial ecosystems are those ecosystems which are modified and managed by human beings.
Crop fields are man-made. Here plants do not grow naturally rather most of the plants are grown by humans according to the season, type of soil, etc. Crop fields are not like wild forest area, which is left to the care of nature and can sustain itself.
In crop fields, the land is managed, soil is prepared for sowing seeds, then irrigated and further progress is also kept under observation for getting good yield. This is why, crop fields are known as artificial ecosystem.)

3 Complete the following flowchart based on ecosystem and its components. **CBSE 2020**

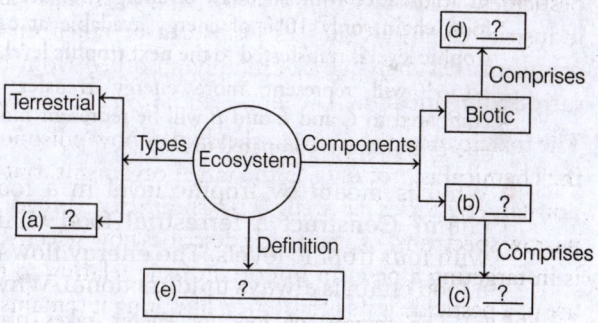

Sol. (a) Aquatic
(b) Abiotic
(c) Water
(d) Plants
(e) Ecosystem is the structural and functional unit of biosphere.

4 We do not clean ponds or lakes, but an aquarium needs to be cleaned, Why? **NCERT Exemplar**

Sol. A pond or lake is a natural ecosystem. They are self-sustaining and complete. In them, all the organisms of food chain are available.
If any organism dies, there are microbes like bacteria and fungi to decompose their bodies into simpler

substances. An aquarium, on the contrary is an artificial and incomplete ecosystem.

Abiotic components are not supplied naturally to it. It may not have all the biotic components in it. If a fish dies in an aquarium in the absence of decomposer, it will lie there as a rotten body, polluting the water of aquarium. Thus, an aquarium needs regular cleaning.

5 In the following food chain, vertical arrows indicate the energy lost to the environment and horizontal arrows indicate energy transferred to the next trophic level. Which one of the three vertical arrows (A, C and E) and which one of the two horizontal arrows (B and D) will represent more energy transfer? Give reason for your answer.
CBSE SQP (Term-II)

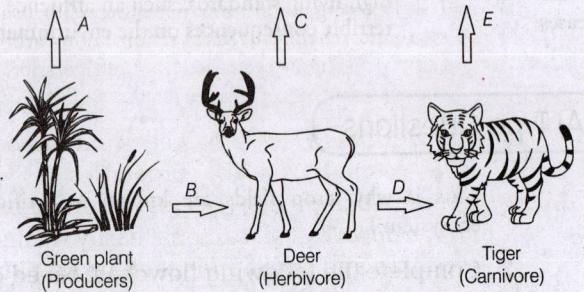

Green plant (Producers)   Deer (Herbivore)   Tiger (Carnivore)

Sol. In accordance with 10% law of energy transfer in food chain, only 10% of energy available at one trophic level is transferred to the next trophic level.

So, A will represent more energy transfer as compared to C and E and B will be represent more energy transfer as compared to D.

6 What is meant by trophic level in a food chain? Construct a terrestrial food chain with four trophic levels. The energy flow in a food chain is always unidirectional. Why?

Sol. (a) The transfer of food or energy takes place through various steps or levels in the food chain known as trophic levels.
(b) Grass → Insect → Frog → Snake → Kite.
(c) Energy is accumulated by the producers to consumers at different trophic levels and is unidirectional always.

7 Write the common food chain of a pond ecosystem. *NCERT Exemplar*

Sol. In a freshwater aquatic ecosystem like a pond, the following organisms are included

Producers Rooted or large floating plants and the minute floating plants, usually algae called phytoplankton.

Herbivores The algae are eaten up by protozoans, (zooplankton).

Carnivores The protozoans are eaten up by small fish.

Large carnivores Big fishes and fish-eating bird or animal eat small fishes.

Algae (Producer) → Protozoan (Herbivore) → Small fish (Carnivore) → Large fish/bird/animal (Large carnivore)

Food chain of a pond ecosystem

8 State 10% law. Explain with an example how energy flows through different trophic levels?

Sol. According to 10% law, only 10% of the energy entering a particular trophic level of organisms is available for transfer to the next higher trophic level.

The flow of energy through a food chain is unidirectional and it moves progressively through various trophic levels as follows

(i) Green plants capture 1% of energy of the sunlight that falls on their leaves and convert it into food energy.

(ii) When green plants are eaten by primary consumers, a great deal of energy is lost as heat to the environment. On an average only 10% of food eaten is turned into its own body and made available for the next level of consumers.

(iii) Thus, 10% can be taken as average value of the amount of organic matter present at each step and reaches the next level of consumers.

9 Indicate the flow of energy in an ecosystem. Why it is unidirectional?
NCERT Exemplar

Sol. The flow of energy in an ecosystem occurs in the following sequence

Sun ⟶ Producer ⟶ Herbivore (Primary consumer) ⟶ Carnivore (Secondary consumer)

The flow of energy is unidirectional because of the reasons given below

(i) Energy flows progressively from one trophic level to another and cannot revert back. Energy given out as heat is lost to the environment and does not return to be used again.

(ii) The available energy decreases at higher trophic level. Out of the total energy available at a particular trophic level, only 10% is passed on to the next trophic level, making it impossible for energy to flow in the reverse direction.

10 With the help of an example, involving four organisms, describe how energy flows through different trophic levels?

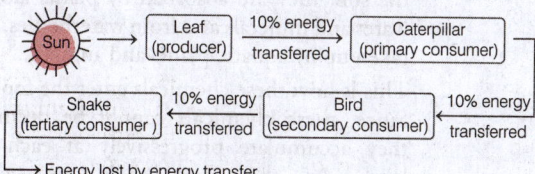

Sol. Leaf captures the Sun's energy and uses it to make organic compounds through photosynthesis but, only 1% of the energy is converted into glucose during photosynthesis. When these leaves are eaten by caterpillar most of the energy (90%) is lost as heat. Only 10% of the energy reaches to the next level of the consumers.

11 DDT was sprayed in a lake to regulate breeding of mosquitoes. How would it affect the trophic levels in the following food chain associated with a lake? Justify your answer. **CBSE SQP (Term-II)**

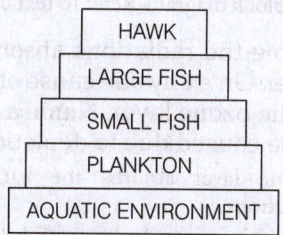

Sol. DDT is a non-biodegradable pesticide will enter the food chain from the first trophic level i.e. plankton and from plankton, these are taken up a small fishes and large fishes.

In this manner, this toxic chemical enter the food chain. Their concentration keeps on increasing at each trophic level. This phenomenon is called as biological magnification.

So, the hawk will have the highest level of pesticide because they occupy the topmost place in the given food chain.

12 Gas A, found in the upper layer of the atmosphere, is a deadly poison but is essential for all living beings. The amount of this gas started declining sharply in the 1980s.

  (i) Identify gas A. How is it formed at higher levels of the atmosphere?

  (ii) Why is it essential for all living beings? State the cause for the depletion of this gas. **CBSE SQP (Term-II)**

Sol. (i) Gas A is ozone (O_3).

Ozone at higher levels of the atmosphere is a product of UV radiations acting on oxygen (O_2 molecule).

The high energy UV radiation split apart some molecular oxygen (O_2) into free oxygen (O) atoms. These atoms are very reactive and combine with the molecular oxygen to form ozone.

$$O_2 \xrightarrow{UV} O + O$$
$$O + O_2 \longrightarrow O_3 \text{ (Ozone)}$$

(ii) In ozone layer shields, the surface of the Earth from harmful ultraviolet (UV) radiation of the Sun. These radiation cause skin cancer in human beings, damage eyes, disturb global rainfall, etc.

It is depleting mainly due to the increasing use of synthetic chemicals like chlorofluorocarbons (CFCs). These are used in refrigerants as coolants and in fire extinguishers.

13 A modern insecticide has been introduced with certain new properties like, accumulation in the bodies of predators, broken down by soil bacteria, easily washed into lakes and rivers and taken up by plant roots. Among all these properties which one will help in reducing or keeping the level of environment pollution to lowest.

Sol. Insecticides are non-biodegradable chemicals added to crop fields to stop the growth of insects infecting the crops. Modern insecticides are being developed keeping in mind, the harm they cause to the environment and its components. Biodegradable insecticides can be decomposed into harmless substances, which will subsequently be dispersed in their specific pathways and cause no pollution.

Non-biodegradable insecticides build up in the fat tissues of the body and pass on to organisms that feed on it.

Hence, they accumulate along the food chain resulting in significant amounts in the tissues of consumers at the highest trophic level.

The property of newly developed insecticide includes that it can easily get decomposed into simpler components by soil bacteria. Thus, it will help in the reduction of environmental pollution.

14 (i) Natural water bodies are not regularly cleaned whereas an aquarium needs regular cleaning. Why?

  (ii) What are decomposers? What will be the consequence if the decomposers are completely eradicated from an ecosystem? Give justification in support of your answer. **CBSE (All India) 2019**

Sol. (i) Refer to text on page no. 422 (Types of Ecosystem)
(ii) Refer to text on page no. 423 (Decomposer)

15 Give reason to justify the following
(i) The existence of decomposers is essential in a biosphere.
(ii) Flow of energy in a food chain is unidirectional. **CBSE 2016**

Sol. (i) Decomposers are essential in a biosphere as they breakdown dead complex organic matter into recyclable simpler compounds. Also, they help in returning the nutrients to the nutrient pool.
(ii) The flow of energy through different steps in the food chain is unidirectional. The energy captured by autotrophs (plants) does not revert back to the solar input and it passes to the herbivores and moves progressively through various trophic levels.

16 Correct the explanation given for the terms if wrong.
(i) **Biomagnification** Decrease of chemicals at the successive trophic levels of a food chain.
(ii) **Ecosystem** Interaction between biotic components of environment.
(iii) **Aquarium** Natural ecosystem.

Sol. (i) **Biomagnification** Increase of chemicals at the successive trophic levels of a food chain.
(ii) **Ecosystem** Interaction between abiotic and biotic components of environment.
(iii) **Aquarium** Artificial ecosystem.

17 Select the mis-matched pair in the following and correct it. **NCERT Exemplar**

(i) Biomagnification	Accumulation of toxic chemicals at the successive trophic levels of a food chain.
(ii) Ecosystem	Biotic components of environment.
(iii) Aquarium	A man-made ecosystem.
(iv) Parasites	Organisms which obtain food from other living organisms.

Sol. (ii) is mis-matched. An ecosystem consists of biotic components (comprising living organisms) and abiotic components (comprising physical factors like temperature, water, wind, etc) of environment.

18 How can we help in reducing the problem of waste disposal? Suggest any three methods. **Delhi 2019**

Sol. Refer to text on Pg. no. 427.

19 Our food grains, such as wheat and rice, the vegetables and fruits and even meat are found to contain varying amounts of pesticide residues. State the reason to explain how and why it happens? **CBSE 2014**

Sol. A large number of pesticides and chemicals are used to protect our crops from pests and diseases. Some of these chemicals are washed down into the soil, while some enter in the waterbodies. From the soil, they are absorbed by plants along with water and minerals and from waterbodies, they are taken up by aquatic plants and animals.

This is how these chemicals enter the food chain. Since, these chemicals cannot be decomposed, they accumulate progressively at each trophic level. As the food chain proceeds, the concentration of pesticides also increases. This increase in the concentration of harmful chemicals at each step of the food chain is called biomagnification. That is why food grains, such as wheat and rice, vegetables, fruits and even meat are found to contain pesticide residues.

20 Define an ecosystem. Draw a block diagram to show the flow of energy in an ecosystem. **Delhi 2019**

Sol. Ecosystem is defined as the structural and functional unit of biosphere. It is a stable ecological unit where continuous input of energy and circulation of matter occurs.
For block diagram-Refer to text on page no. 425.

21 Name the radiations absorbed by ozone layer. Give any one cause of the depletion of the ozone layer. Name a disease likely to be caused due to depletion.

Sol. Ozone layer absorbs the harmful ultraviolet radiations.
One cause of the depletion of the ozone layer is the use of Chlorofluorocarbons (CFCs). Ozone layer depletion may lead to skin cancer in human beings.

22 (i) What harm is caused to skin by ultraviolet rays?
(ii) At which level, pesticides enter the food chain?
(iii) How are most of the solid wastes in urban areas disposed of?

Sol. (i) Ultraviolet rays can cause skin cancer.
(ii) Pesticides enter the food chain at the producer level.
(iii) Landfilling is done to decompose solid wastes in urban areas.

23 How is ozone formed in the upper atmosphere? State its importance. What is responsible for its depletion? Write one harmful effect of ozone depletion. **All India 2019**

Sol. Refer to text on page no. 425 and 426.

24 How would you dispose the following wastes
   (i) Domestic wastes like vegetable peels?
   (ii) Industrial wastes like metallic cans?
   (iii) Plastic material?

Sol. (i) Landfill
   (ii) Recycling
   (iii) Recycling.

25 What are the advantages of cloth bags over plastic bags during shopping?
NCERT Exemplar

Sol. Advantages of cloth bags over plastic bags during shopping are
   (i) Cloth bags are biodegradable thus can be easily decomposed by microorganisms.
   (ii) Cloth bags can be used again, can be washed and do not cause any harm to the environment.
   (iii) Plastic bags are non-biodegradable and hence can pollute the environment.

26 Why is Government of India imposing a ban on the use of polythene bags? Suggest two alternatives to these bags and explain how this ban is likely to improve the environment? **CBSE 2014**

Sol. Government of India is imposing a ban on the use of polythene bags because they cannot be degraded naturally by the action of microorganisms. Because of their non-biodegradability, they stay in the soil for a long time and continue to poison it with toxic byproducts that keep leaching from them.

Also, they do not allow water to seep in, as they are waterproof. These polythene bags, when accidentally eaten by stray animals, can harm them and can even lead to their death. Jute and cloth bags can be used in place of polythene bags. The advantages of using cloth and jute bags are as follows
   (i) They are environment-friendly as they are biodegradable.
   (ii) They are renewable and can be easily recycled.
   (iii) They have more strength than polythene bags because they are thick and can be used again and again.

Thus, use of jute and cloth bags can help to reduce pollution.

27 Draw a sequence of suitable methods of disposal of waste produced at your home to minimise environmental pollution. **CBSE 2015**

Or

What is meant by garbage management? Suggest four methods to manage the garbage.

Sol. The household waste produced from various activities is called garbage and its proper disposal is done in such a way that it does not affect the environment. This is called garbage management.

Methods of waste disposal include
   (i) **Recycling** The processing of certain wastes to form new products is called recycling, e.g. paper, glass, polythene, etc., are recyclable. They can be used to make cards, decorative items, etc.
   (ii) **Composting** It is the process of collecting biodegradable wastes like leftovers of food items, peels, etc. and burying them in a pit. The product is used as manure.
   (iii) **Incineration** It is burning of a substance at high temperature to form ash.
   (iv) **Landfills** Dumping of waste in low lying areas is called landfill.
   (v) **Sewage treatment** In sewage treatment plants, the sewage is processed and decomposed.

28 It is the responsibility of the government to arrange for the management and disposal of waste. As an individual you have no role to play. Do you agree. Support your answers with two reasons.

Sol. I do not agree with the above statement. As an individual, I also have a role to play in waste management and I can contribute in the following ways
   (i) Cut down waste generation.
   (ii) Make compost pit for biodegradable waste.
   (iii) Recycle non-biodegradable waste.

Long Answer (LA) Type Questions

1 (i) How do food chains get shortened? How does the shortening of food chain affect the biosphere?

(ii) How will you justify that vegetarian food habits give us more calories?

Sol. (i) Undesirable activities of man eliminate growth of organisms belonging to one or more trophic levels in a food chain. Thus, the food chain gets shortened, e.g. hunting tigers for their skin, etc.

It causes imbalance in the functioning of ecosystem and biosphere. If organisms of one trophic level are eliminated, the organisms prior to that trophic level will flourish and increase in number. Also, the organisms of the subsequent trophic level will sharply decrease, thereby creating an imbalance.

(ii) Vegetarian food chain is advantageous in terms of energy because it has less number of trophic levels. As we know, only 10% of the energy is transferred to the next trophic level in a food chain, so if a person is vegetarian then, he would have maximum amount of energy by consuming producers or plants in a food chain. Vegetarian food chain gives ten times more energy than the non-vegetarian food chain.

2 (i) Energy flow in a food chain is unidirectional. Justify this statement.

(ii) Explain how the pesticides enter a food chain and subsequently get into our body.

CBSE 2014

Sol. (i) The producers convert solar energy into chemical energy in the form of organic compounds. The primary consumers (herbivores) derive their nutrition from the producers. According to the energy transfer law, only 10% of energy is transferred from one trophic level to the other.

So, the energy that is captured by the producers does not revert back to the Sun and the energy transferred to the herbivores does not come back to the producers. It just keeps on moving to the next trophic level in one direction. That is why the flow of energy in the food chain is always unidirectional.

(ii) A large number of pesticides and chemicals are used to protect our crops from pests and diseases. Some of these chemicals are washed down from the soil, while some enter the waterbodies. From the soil, they are absorbed by plants along with water and minerals, and from the waterbodies, they are taken up by aquatic plants and animals. This is how these chemicals enter the food chain.

As these chemicals cannot decompose, they accumulate progressively at each trophic level. This increase in the concentration of harmful chemicals with each step of the food chain is called biomagnification. As human beings occupy the top level in any food chain, these chemicals get accumulated in our bodies in considerably high amount causing diseases.

3 What are decomposers? What will be the consequence of their absence in an ecosystem? **NCERT Exemplar**

Sol. Organisms which breakdown the complex organic compounds present in dead and decaying matter are called **decomposers**, e.g. certain bacteria and fungi.

Decomposers act as cleaning agents of environment by decomposing dead bodies of plants and animals. They also help in recycling of materials, replenishment of soil's nutrients, etc.

The consequence of their absence in an ecosystem can be disastrous as discussed. The dead bodies would persist for long, leading to their accumulation and thus, polluting the environment. The biogenetic nutrients associated with these remains will not be returned back to the environment. As a result, all the nutrients present in soil, air and water would soon be exhausted and the whole life cycle of organisms will be disrupted.

4 Explain some harmful effects of agricultural practices on the environment. **NCERT Exemplar**

Sol. Some harmful effects of agricultural practices on the environment are as follows

(i) **Soil degradation** Extensive cropping causes loss of soil fertility. Also, over the time it can lead to soil erosion and finally to desertification.

(ii) **Pollution** Use of synthetic chemical fertilisers and pesticides leads to soil, water and air pollution.

(iii) **Water shortage** Excess use of ground water for agriculture lowers the water level. This results in acute water shortage at many places.

(iv) **Biomagnification** The chemical pesticides, being non-biodegradable accumulate in organisms in increasing amounts at each trophic level.

(v) **Deforestation** Indiscriminate cutting of trees for agriculture has resulted in loss of habitat for wildlife. Thus, it also causes damage to natural ecosystem.

5 Suggest suitable mechanism(s) for waste management in fertiliser industries. **NCERT Exemplar**

Sol. **Effluents** and **harmful gases** are the main wastes, which are produced in a fertiliser factory. Suitable mechanism for waste management are

(i) For the control of gaseous pollutants combustion equipments are used which can be oxidised. The pollutants are exposed to a high temperature in the process. Air pollutants, such as certain gases, vapour and inflammable compounds are controlled through the use of adsorption equipments. Adsorption is a surface phenomenon that needs the presence of a large solid surface area. Toxic and odoriferous compounds are efficiently removed by this process.

(ii) Three options available for controlling the effluents are

(a) Control can take place at the point of generation within the factory.

(b) Waste water can be pre-treated before discharge in municipal treatment systems.

(c) Waste water can be treated completely in a factory and either reused or discharged directly into running water bodies like canals, rivers, etc.

6 What are the byproducts of fertiliser industries? How do they affect the environment? **NCERT Exemplar**

Sol. The byproducts of fertiliser industries are the oxides of nitrogen, sulphur and phosphorus, etc., which are released by the breakdown of the pesticides and some chemical fertilisers.

These oxides along with residual chemicals persists in the environment as they are non-biodegradable. They are oxides of sulphur and nitrogen which are released into atmosphere where they cause air pollution and acid rain. They cause harmful effects in living beings, on crops and other organisms. Also, the pesticides get mixed with soil and water. From there, these are absorbed by the growing plants along with water and minerals and pass into their bodies through the food chain.

The pesticides enter the food chain at the producer level and in the process of transfer of food through food chains, these harmful chemicals get concentrated at each trophic level.

7 Write in detail about garbage management.

Sol. Garbage management can be done in following ways

(i) Household left-out garbage should be used to produce biogas which can be used for cooking.

(ii) Sewage can be very well-treated and turned into water. It can be used for cleaning utensils by primary, tertiary and quaternary treatment in water treatment plants.

(iii) Volume of hospital wastes can be reduced by incineration.

(iv) Radioactive wastes can be landfilled or taken away from habitable area, so that no radiation leaks can cause any abnormality in organisms living in nearby areas.

(v) Heavy metals, such as lead and mercury should be separated and destroyed as these are responsible for causing various health hazards in human beings.

8 Suggest any five activities in daily life, which are eco-friendly. **NCERT Exemplar**

Sol. Some daily life eco-friendly activities are

(i) **Save a Tree, use Less paper** You can buy 'tree-free' 100% post-consumer recycled paper for everything from greeting cards to toilet paper.

Paper with a high post-consumer waste content uses less pulp and keeps more waste paper out of landfills.

(ii) **Opt Bamboo for Hardwood Floors** Bamboo is considered as an environmental-friendly flooring material due to its high yield and the relatively fast rate at which it replenishes itself. It takes just 4-6 years for bamboo to mature, compared to 50-100 years for typical hardwoods. Just be sure to look for sources that use formaldehyde-free glues.

(iii) **Reduce Plastics, Reduce Global Warming** Each year, Americans throw away some 100 billion polyethylene plastic bags being used as grocery and trash bags. Unfortunately, plastics are made from petroleum, the processing and burning of which is considered one of the main contributors to global warming, according to the EPA. In addition, sending plastics to the landfill also increases greenhouse gases. Reduce, reuse and recycle your plastics are one of the best ways to combat global warming.

(iv) **Use Healthier Paints** Conventional paints contain solvents, toxic metals and Volatile Organic Compounds (VOCs) that can cause smog, ozone pollution and indoor air quality problems with negative health effects, according to the EPA. These unhealthy ingredients are released into the air, while you are painting, drying of paint and even after the paints are completely dry. Opt for zero or low VOC paint, made by major paint manufacturers today.

(v) **Use Compost** Instead of using synthetic fertilisers, compost provides a full complement of soil organisms and the balance of nutrients needed to maintain the soil's health. Healthy soil minimises the population of weeds. It is a key to produce good quality plants, which in turn can prevent many pest problems from developing.

CHAPTER EXERCISE

Multiple Type Questions

1. Which of the following is an example of man-made ecosystem?
   (a) Herbarium
   (b) Aquarium
   (c) Tissue culture
   (d) Forest

2. Which of the following is the most stable ecosystem?
   (a) Mountain
   (b) Desert
   (c) Forest
   (d) Oceans

3. The 10% law for energy transfer in food chain was given by
   (a) Stanley
   (b) Tansley
   (c) Lindemann
   (d) Weismann

4. Biomagnification is highest in
   (a) producer
   (b) primary consumer
   (c) secondary consumer
   (d) decomposer

5. Bad ozone is formed in
   (a) atmosphere
   (b) ionosphere
   (c) stratosphere
   (d) troposphere

Fill in the blanks

6. Gardens and crops are .... ecosystems.
7. Lions are top level consumers of a .... ecosystem.
8. Accumulation of toxic substances at every level of food chain is called ....

True and False

9. Algae are chief producers in an aquatic ecosystem.
10. Herbivores are secondary consumers.
11. Green plants in a terrestrial ecosystem capture 10% of solar radiation.
12. Flow of energy in an ecosystem is always unidirection.

Match the Columns

13. Match the following

Column I		Column II
A. Pond	1.	Artificial ecosystem
B. Crop land	2.	Biomagnification
C. DDT	3.	Natural ecosystem
D. Decomposers	4.	Fungi

Assertion–Reason

Direction (Q. Nos. 14-16) *In each of the following questions, a statement of Assertion is given by the corresponding statement of Reason. Of the statements, mark the correct answer as*

(a) If both Assertion and Reason are true and Reason is the correct explanation of Assertion
(b) If both Assertion and Reason are true, but Reason is not the correct explanation of Assertion
(c) If Assertion is true, but Reason is false
(d) If Assertion is false, but Reason is true
(e) If Assertion and Reason both are false

14. **Assertion** Biotic components of an ecosystem include all the living organisms present in that ecosystem.
    Reason Biotic components also include wind, gases, light, etc.

15. **Assertion** Light is the primary source of energy in nearly all ecosystems.
    Reason Light is used by autotrophs to synthesise their food.

16. **Assertion** Ozone layer shields the surface of Earth from UV radiations.
    Reason The UV radiations are highly damaging to organisms.

Answers

1. (b) 2. (d) 3. (c) 4. (c) 5. (d)
6. man made 7. terrestrial/forest
8. biomagnification 9. True 10. False 11. False
12. True 13. A→(3), B→(1), C→(2), D→(4)
14. (c) 15. (a) 16. (a)

Case Based Questions

Direction (Q.Nos. 17-20) *Answer the questions on the basis of your understanding of the following passage and related studied concepts:*

Depletion in the concentration of ozone over a restricted area as over antaritica is called ozone hole. During 1956-1970 period, springtime thickness of ozone over antarctica was 280-325 dobson units (DU = 1 ppb). During 1979 it was 225 DV, 136 DU in 1985 and 94 DV in 1994. Springtime depletion of ozone is due to action of sunlight over pollutants which release chemicals (e.g. chlorine) that destroy ozone. An ozone hole was discovered over Antarctica by Farman et al, 1985 who also coined the term. It is quite large (23 million square km in 1992 and 28.3 million sq km in 2000). A small ozone hole also occur over North pole. It was discovered in 1990. Thinning of ozone shield has also been reported else where (e.g. 8% between 30°-50°N). In the period in between 1997-2001 the global average ozone column has declined by 3% below pre-1980 level. This thinning of ozone shield will increase the amount of UV-radiations reaching the earth which will result in more persons catching skin cancer and more persons becoming blind.

17. What do you understand by a ozone hole?
18. Where was the first ozone hole discovered? Also write its area.
19. Describe how continuous thinning of ozone layer is harmful to humans.
20. What is the cause of springtime ozone depletion?

Direction (Q.Nos. 21-24) *Answer the questions on the basis of your understanding of the following passage and related studied concepts:*

The most obvious interaction between different organisms in an ecosystem is feeding. During feeding, one organism is obtaining food, energy and raw materials from another one. Usually one organism eats another, but then may itself be food for a third species.

The feeding relationships of the different organisms in the ecosystem can be shown in a food chain, as in the given below

$$\text{Grass} \to \text{Deer} \to \text{Lion}$$

Since so little energy is transferred from the base to the top of a food chain, a top carnivore must eat many herbivores. These herbivores are probably not all of the same species. In turn, each herbivore is likely to feed on many different plants species. All these different feeding relationships can be shown in a food web.

21. How does an organisms specially animals derive their energy and minerals.
22. Write an example of food chain.
23. What is common ween mice, rat and a squirrels.
24. How is food web more complex than the food chain?

Very Short Answer Type Questions

25. Which biological factor is responsible for poor vegetation in deserts?
26. Which group of organisms convert organic materials to inorganic forms?
27. Are plants actually producers of energy?
28. What do we call the various steps involved in the food chain?
29. Why is straight line food chain not common in the natural ecosystem?
30. How many trophic levels does a food chain normally have?
31. How is being a vegetarian advantageous in terms of energy?
32. State one reason to justify the position of man at the apex of most food chains.
33. What term is given to the phenomenon where a harmful chemical enters a food chain and starts accumulating?
34. Does change in lifestyle add waste to the environment?

Short Answer (SA) Type Questions

35. Draw a pond ecosystem showing its different components.
36. 'Man is only a consumer'. Justify the statement.
37. How much energy will be available to hawks in the food chain comprising hawk, snake, paddy and mice if 10,000 J of energy is available to paddy from the Sun?
38. Number of trophic levels is limited to 3-4 in a food chain. Give reason.
39. Look at the following figures. Choose the correct one and give reason for your choice.

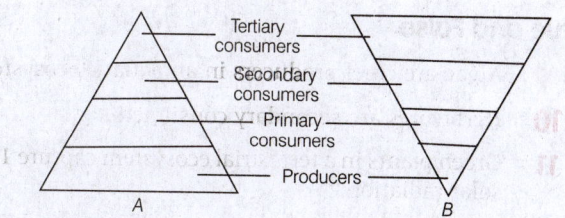

40 Make an aquatic food chain upto tertiary consumer level. State the trophic level at which concentration of pesticides is maximum and why?

41 Why are bacteria and fungi called decomposers? List advantages of decomposers to the environment.

42 How is Earth kept warm by nature? Describe in detail.

43 How do human activities affect the environment?

44 (i) Which part of waste is changed into agricultural resource?
(ii) How can pesticides be allowed in beverages?
(iii) On recycling, waste paper is converted into which product?

45 Why do harmful chemicals concentrate as we go up in a food chain?

46 State any three environmental problems caused by man.

Long Answer (LA) Type Questions

47 Divide the wastes generated from your house into biodegradable and non-biodegradable categories. Suggest methods for their disposal.

48 Categorise some of the activities performed by you as an eco-friendly person. Suggest some more eco-friendly activities which we should adopt in day-to-day life.

49 What is environment? What type of substances are the major pollutants of the environment?

50 Make two food chains and a food web from the following set of living organisms : Grass, vulture, deer, insect, snake. Identify the tertiary consumers in both the food chains.

51 What happens once the Sun's energy reaches the Earth? Explain with the help of diagram.

52 (i) If the primary consumer has 400 J of energy. What would be the energy trapped by the producer and also write the energy present at the quaternary consumer level?
(ii) State the 10 % law, associated with flow of energy in trophic levels of organisms.

53 An industry is being established near a town. How can the wastes generated from this industry affect the local environment?

54 Give a detailed account of ozone layer depletion and the harm ozone layer depletion has caused to the ecosystem.

55 Identify a deadly poisonous gas X found at the higher levels of atmosphere. Write its chemical formula and equation of its formation. Why is damage to X layer a cause of concern?

Challengers*

1 The diagram shows part of a river into which sewage is being pumped. Some of the effects of adding sewage to the river are shown in the graph. At which point in the river are decomposers most active?

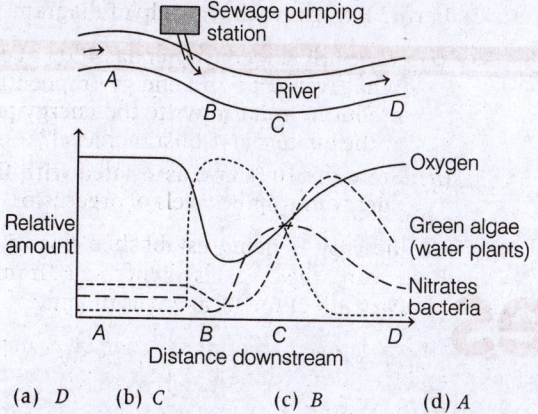

(a) D (b) C (c) B (d) A

2 The diagram shows the flow of energy through an ecosystem.

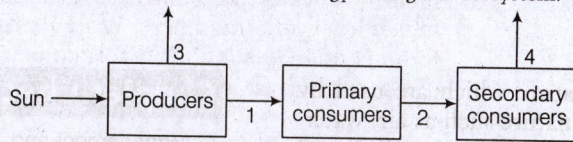

The smallest amount of energy transferred between organisms and the largest amount of energy lost to the ecosystem is represented by which arrows?

	Smallest energy transfer	Largest energy loss
(a)	4	3
(b)	2	1
(c)	2	3
(d)	1	4

3 The following graph shows the concentration of oxygen in a river, measured at stations 1-5, each 100 m apart. A sewage outflow is observed just after station 1. At which stations will the concentration of organic matter be lowest?

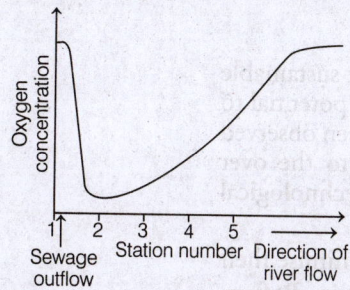

(a) 1 and 5 (b) 2 and 3
(c) 3 and 4 (d) 4 and 5

4. Fertilisers are used on farmlands to increase the nutritive quality of soil and thus, the crop productivity. However, they greatly impact our environment in negative ways. A fertiliser industry is planning to release nitrate-free or reduced nitrate containing fertiliser to make it more environment-freindly. This control of nitrate rich fertilisers is necessary because

(a) nitrates cause acid rain, killing trees and fishes when released in the environment
(b) they decrease the natural fertility of the soil
(c) nitrates may lead to excessive growth of water plants
(d) it poisons different crop plants

5. The diagram shows the organisms in a habitat.

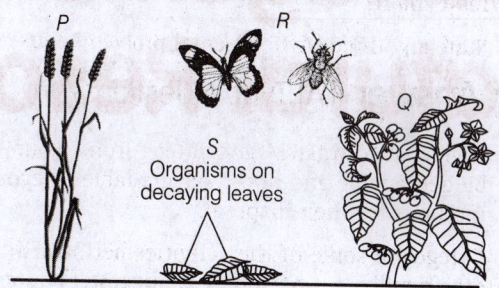

Which of the following indicates the feeding relationships of these organisms?

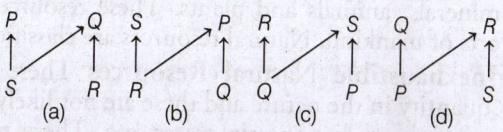

6. The diagram represents the flow of substances within a balanced ecosystem. The boxes are various trophic levels. Which box represents the producers?

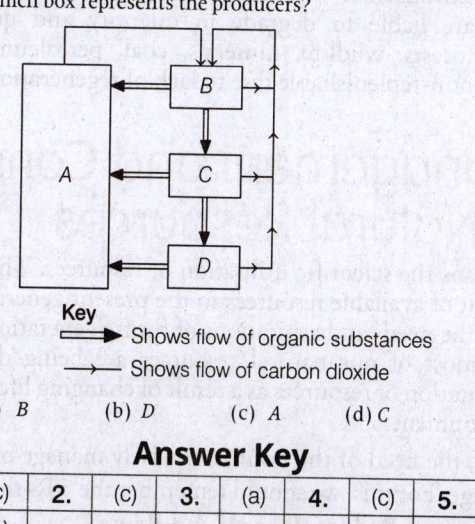

(a) B (b) D (c) A (d) C

Answer Key

1.	(c)	2.	(c)	3.	(a)	4.	(c)	5.	(c)
6.	(a)								

*These questions have been given just for additional practice. These may or may not be asked in the examination.

CHAPTER 14

Management of Natural Resources

Natural resources are living and non-living components of nature which are used by humans to meet their requirements. These are the stock of the nature such as air, water, soil, minerals, animals and plants. These resources contribute to meet necessities and comforts of mankind. Natural resources are classified into following two categories

(i) **Inexhaustible Natural Resources** These resources are present in unlimited quantity in the nature and these are not likely to be exhausted by human activities, e.g. solar radiation, air, water, etc. These resources are renewable and thus are replenished naturally.

(ii) **Exhaustible Natural Resources** These resources are limited in nature and are liable to degrade in quantity and quality by human activities, e.g. soil, forests, wildlife, minerals, coal, petroleum, etc. These are non-renewable and non-replenishable due to lack of regeneration.

Management and Conservation of Natural Resources

It means the scientific utilisation of resources. This method yield the greatest sustainable benefit of available resources to the present generation, while maintaining its potential to meet the needs and aspirations of future generations. In recent years, it has been observed that most of our natural resources are being depleted. It is mainly due to the over exploitation of resources as a result of changing lifestyle, over population and technological development.

Thus, the need of the hour is to wisely manage our natural resources and minimise their wastage. For this, we should remember the 5 Rs that can save the environment, i.e. **Refuse, Repurpose, Reduce, Recycle and Reuse.**

1. **Refuse** This mean to buy or accept product that can harm you and your environment, e.g. we should say no to single use plastic carry bags and should prefer jute carry bags or paper carry bags.

Chapter Checklist

- Management and Conservation of Natural Resources
- Forests
- Water for All
- Coal and Petroleum
- An Overview of Natural Resource Management

Management of Natural Resources

2. **Repurpose** This means to use a product for some other useful purpose when it can no more be used for the original purpose, e.g., we should use cracked crockery or cups with broken handles to grow small plants and as feeding vessels for birds.

3. **Reduce** This means to minimise the use of various products which are obtained directly or indirectly from natural resources. For example, we should save electricity by switching off unnecessary lights and fans. We should also save water by repairing leaky taps. Moreover, food should not be wasted on several occasions like marriages, parties, etc.

4. **Recycle** This involves the processing of things that are considered waste and turns them into useful products. The articles made of recycled plastic, glass, paper or metal can be used instead of using fresh plastic, paper, etc.

5. **Reuse** This means to use things again and again, e.g. use of cloth napkin instead of paper napkins, used envelopes can be reversed and used again, the empty plastic bottles of jams or pickle can be used to store things in kitchen. This method is actually better than recycling because the process of recycling uses some amount of energy, reduces stress on environment and things are maximally utilised.

Concept of Sustainable Development

It is the process of development that sustains natural systems and their yields, which can be maintained for a long time without any damage to the environment.

The concept of sustainable development encourages growth that meet the current basic human needs, while preserving the resources for the needs of the future generations.

Sustainable development implies a change in all aspects of life. It depends upon the willingness of the people to change their perceptions of the socio-economic and environmental conditions around them and the readiness of each individual to alter their present use of natural resources.

We need to manage our natural resources carefully because:

- Natural resources are limited and with the current increasing rate of human population due to improvement in health-care, the demand for all the resources is increasing expotentially.
- Natural resources requires a long term perspective, so that they can last for the generations to come and will not merely be exploited for short term gains.
- To ensure equitable distribution of resource, so that all people but not just a handful of rich and powerful people, benefit from the development of these resources.
- To control the damage caused to the environment, while resources are extracted or used, e.g. mining causes pollution. Hence, sustainable natural resource management demands the planning for the safe disposal of wastes.

Note
- Principles of conservation and sustainable management were well established in the pre-historic India. Our ancient literature is full of such examples where valves and sensitivity of humans towards nature was glorified.
- Both productive as well as protective aspect of forest vegetation were emphasised, during the Vedic period. During the later Vedic period, agriculture emerged as a dominant economic activity.

Pollution of the Ganga and Ganga Action Plan (GAP)

Ganga is one of the most important river of India. It runs over 2500 km from Gangotri in the Himalayas to the Ganga Sagar in Bay of Bengal. It is being polluted by more than hundred cities and towns in Uttar Pradesh, Bihar and West Bengal.

- Several human activities like washing of clothes, immersion of ashes, chemical effluents of industries are also responsible for the pollution of Ganga.
- Ganga Action Plan (GAP) was a programme launched by Government of India in April 1985 in order to reduce the pollution load on the river.
- Namami Gange Programme is an Integrated Conservation Mission approved as a Flagship Programme by the Union Government in June, 2014. It was launched to accomplish the twin objectives of effective abatement of pollution conservation and rejuvenation of River Ganga. The National Mission for clean Ganga is the implementation wing set up in October, 2016.
- Coliform is a group of bacteria, found in human intestines. Its presence in water indicates contamination by disease causing microorganisms which was found to be very high in Ganga during 1993-1994 indicating it as a reservoir of many water borne diseases.

Check Point 01

1. .... is an exhaustible natural resource.
2. Why should we use the exhaustible natural resources judiciously?
3. Name the 5 Rs' that will help us to conserve natural resources for long term use.
4. The strategy of 5 Rs' have become profound in environment management programme. Give reason.
5. Concept of sustainable development has been adopted to limit the damage being incurred to the environment. True or False.
6. The two measures that can be adopted by anyone to conserve our natural resources are .... and ....

Forests

These are an extensive area of land covered with trees and other plants. These are plant communities made of trees, shrubs, herbs, etc. They grow in almost all parts of the Earth from cold polar areas to hot equatorial areas, from high mountains to low plains and from wet areas to dry deserts of the world. Forests are the **hotspots** of **biodiversity** because of presence of large number of species.

Forests need to be conserved because

- They preserve the biodiversity found in the forest (loss of diversity may lead to the loss of ecological stability).
- They provide **habitat to numerous species** of plants and animals. All inhabitants get food and protection from the forests.
- They help in protecting the soil from **erosion**.
- They store a large amount of water which acts as buffer for ecosystem during dry periods.
- They play a vital role in the atmospheric circulation and thus, control the global climate.
- The leaves of trees absorb carbon dioxide and release oxygen, the phenomenon (photosynthesis) that is vital for all life on the Earth.
- They provide timber to man for various activities like construction.
- They are the major source of edible fruits and nuts. Numerous waxes and oils are also obtained from forests. Sap of many trees is used as a raw material to manufacture variety of goods.
- Bark of some trees are used to make cork and medicines. A variety of chemicals are produced from forests for their use in tanning of leather, inks, dyes, medicines, alcohol, etc.

Note Forests are the most rapidly depleting natural resource because of their multiple products.

Stakeholders

A stakeholder can be a person, a group or an organisation that may be affected or have any kind of interest in the project or in the project's outcome either directly or indirectly. All stakeholders are not equal, every stakeholder has his own expectations and requirements and they should be handled the way he expects.

When we consider the conservation of forests, we need to look at the stakeholders who are

1. **The Local People** These people live in or around forests and are dependent on forest products for various aspects of their life. They need large quantities of firewood, small timber and thatch (craft for building roof). Bamboo is used to make slats for huts and baskets for collecting and storing food materials. Implements for agriculture, fishing and hunting are largely made of wood. Forests are also the sites for fishing and hunting.

   In addition to people, gathering fruits, nuts and medicines from the forests, their cattle also graze in forest areas or feed on other fodder which is collected from forests.

2. **The Forest Department** It is India's biggest landlord and controls the resources from forests. The officials of this department tend to ignore both local knowledge and local needs in their management practices. Thus, vast tracts of forests have been converted to monocultures of pine or *Eucalyptus*.

   In order to plant these trees, huge areas are first cleared of all vegetation. This destroys a large amount of biodiversity in the area. Not only this, the varied needs of the local people, leaves for fodder, herbs for medicines, fruits and nuts for food, can no longer be met from such forests. Such plantations are useful for the industries to access specific products and are an important source of revenue for the Forest Department.

3. **Industry** It considers the forest as merely a source of raw material for its factories. And huge interest groups seek to influence the government for access to these raw materials at artificially low rates, e.g. after cutting down all teak trees in one area, they will get their teak from a forest farther away.

   They do not have any stake in ensuring that one particular area should yield an optimal amount of some produce for all generations to come.

4. **Nature and Wildlife Enthusiasts** These are one who want to conserve nature in its pristine form. They are not dependent on the forests.

   The conservationists first started conserving large animals like lions, tigers, elephants and rhinoceros. But, they now recognise the need to preserve biodiversity as a whole.

   There have been enough instances of local people working traditionally for the conservation of forest, e.g. the great **Himalayan National Park** contains within its reserved area alpine meadows which were grazed by sheep in summer. When this national park was formed, this practice was put to an end. Now, it is seen that without the regular grazing by sheep, the grass first grows very tall and then falls over preventing fresh growth.

Amrita Devi Bishnoi Award

For Bishnoi community in Rajasthan, the conservation of forest and wildlife had been a religious tenet. In 1731, Amrita Devi Bishnoi, sacrificed her life along with 363 others for the protection of Khejri trees in Khejrali village near Jodhpur in Rajasthan. In the memory of "Amrita Devi Bishnoi," the Government of India has recently instituted an "Amrita Devi Bishnoi National Award for Wildlife Conservation."

Sustainable Management

The controlled use of a natural resource in such a way that its present availability and continuous flow to the future generation is ensured without any disturbance to the environment is known as **sustainable management**. The resources should be used in such a way that it does not hinder the present progress and also does not put at stake, the future availability of the resources.

Forest resources need to be used in a manner, which is **environmentally** and **developmentally sound**. The benefits of the controlled exploitation should go to the local people.

If the resource exploitation will be too high, then the economic and social development will be faster, but the environment will further deteriorate. So, natural resources should be used continuously in such a way that economic growth and ecological conservation should go hand in hand.

Chipko Andolan (Hug the Trees Movement)

This movement was started in early 1970s from Reni village, in Garhwal. A logging contractor was allowed to cut trees in a forest close to the village.

On a particular day, the contractor's workers appeared in the forest to cut the trees while the men folk were absent. The women of the village reached the forest and huged the tree trunks preventing the workers from cutting trees. Thus thwarted, the contractor had to withdraw.

People's Participation

The Chipko Movement quickly spread across communities and media. It forced the government to whom the forest belongs, to rethink their priorities in the use of forest produce. Experience has taught people that the destruction of forest affects not just the availability of forest products, but also the quality of soil and the sources of water.

Participation of the local people can indeed lead to the efficient management of forests. A programme named **"Silviculture"** had also been started to replenish the depleting forests, so as to meet the diverse needs of various sectors and maintain balance in ecosystem and its functions.

An Example of People's Participation in the Management of Forests

In 1972, the sal forests in the South Western districts of West Bengal degraded alarmingly. Traditional methods like policing and surveillance employed by forest department resulted in frequent clashes between forest officials and villagers.

AK Banerjee, an officer of forest department changed the strategy by making a beginning in the Arabari forest range of Midnapore district. Villagers were involved in the protection of sal forests, in return villagers were given employment and were allowed to collect fuel, wood and fodder on payment of a nominal fee. With the active and willing participation of the villagers, the sal forests showed a remarkable recovery by 1983.

Wildlife and Its Conservation

The depleting forests not only reduce the availability of natural resourecs, but also cause the loss of wildlife present in them. The poaching or killing of wild animals present in forests for commercial benefits is also an increasing threat.

The animals are killed for their skin, teeth, fur, feathers, tusks, etc., used in commercial production of many products. This practice disturbs the existing food chains and food webs in an ecosystem and thus, the ecological balance.

The measures for conservation of wildlife are as follow

- The **poaching** should be made a punishable offence.
- Monitoring/surveillance by the forest department should be increased.
- Conservation strategies for endangered animals is vital.
- The number of national parks and sanctuaries should be increased with adequate security.

Check Point 02

1. Forests are also called………. .
2. Why government established Amrita Devi Bishnoi award?
3. Local people are not included in the stakeholders. True or False.
4. Name the forest department officer, who had initiated people's participation in the management of forests?
5. In our country, vast tracts of forests are cleared and a single species of plant is cultivated. What does this practice promote?
6. Two measures for the conservation of wildlife are ……… and ………. .

Water for All

It is a basic necessity for all forms of terrestrial and aquatic life. It is available in the form of several waterbodies like oceans, rivers, lakes and ponds.

Rain is a very important source of water. In India, it largely occurs during the monsoons. This means that most of the rain falls in few months of the year and replenishes the waterbodies.

Inspite of good rains, the failure to sustain availabilies of underground water is due to

- Lack of sufficient vegetative cover on the ground because of which, only little rainwater seeps into the ground and get stored as groundwater.
- The high yielding varieties of crops require much more amount of water for irrigation.
- Untreated sewage and industrial wastes discharged into the rivers and lakes reduce the availability of usable water.

Following practices have been made to manage the water resources

- Dams, tanks and canals are used since many years to meet the minimum requirements for both agriculture and daily needs.
- Regulation of use of water stored in dams.
- Optimum cropping pattern based on water availability.

Mismanagement of water distribution are as follows

- Mismanagement of water distribution has largely led to the benefits being taken by a few people only. There is no equal distribution of water.
- People close to the water reservoirs grow water intensive crops like sugarcane and rice, while people farther downstream do not get any water.
- The natives who have been promised benefits that never arrived are added to discontented list of people who have been displaced for building of the dam and its canal network.

Kulhs of Himachal Pradesh

Parts of Himachal Pradesh had evolved a local system of canal irrigation called Kulhs over four hundred years ago. The water in streams was diverted to the fields in the villages farthest from the source of Kulh, then to villages progressively higher up.

In this way, water was shared between many villages, but the Kulhs were taken over by the Irrigation Department. Most of them became non-functional and there was no peaceful sharing of water as before.

Dams

These are the barriers constructed across the rivers to hold the water. These are large reservoirs of water that ensure the storage of adequate water for different uses.

Water stored in dams can be used for different purposes as given below

- For irrigation.
- For the generation of electricity (hydroelectric power).
- To control floods as dams store water during rainy season.
- Supply of water to great distance (to the place where required) through the canal system, e.g. Indira Gandhi Canal has brought greenery to considerable areas of Rajasthan.

Narmada Bachao Andolan

Narmada Bachao Andolan (Save the Narmada movement) was a protest against raising the height of the Sardar Sarovar Dam on the river Narmada.

Criticisms about Large Dams

Large dams cause following three problems in particular

(i) **Social Problems** Because they displace large number of peasants and tribals without enough compensation or rehabilitation.

(ii) **Economic Problems** Because they utilise large amount of public money without the generation of proportionate benefits.

(iii) **Environmental Problems** Because they contribute enormously to deforestation which leads to the loss of biological diversity.

Water Harvesting

It means storing rainwater where it falls or storing the run-off water in a local area for reuse.

Watershed management aims at scientific conservation of soil and water in order to increase the biomass production. The aim is to develop primary resources of land and water to increase the production of secondary resources of plants and animals for their use in a way that will not result in ecological imbalance. The advantages of watershed management are that it increases the production and income of watershed community, reduces droughts and floods and increases the life of downstream dam and reservoirs.

Conventional Methods of Water Harvesting

In India, different communities use hundreds of indigenous water saving methods to capture every trickle of water that had fallen on their land.

Management of Natural Resources

These methods are
- Digging of small pits and lakes.
- Placing simple watershed systems.
- Building small earthen dams.
- Constructing dykes, sand and limestone reservoirs.
- Setting up rooftop water collecting units.

Traditional Water Harvesting System

In largely level terrain, the water harvesting structures are mainly crescent-shaped earthen embankments or low, straight concrete and rubble check dams built across seasonally flooded gullies. Monsoon rains fill ponds behind the structures. Only the largest structures hold water year round and others usually get dry in six months or less after the monsoons.

Their main purpose, is not to hold surface water, but to recharge the ground water beneath. The various advantages of water stored in the ground are

- It does not evaporate, but spreads out to recharge wells.
- It provides moisture for vegetation over a wide area.
- It does not provide breeding grounds for mosquitoes like stagnant water collected in ponds or artificial lakes.
- The groundwater is also relatively protected from contamination by human and animal waste.
- Dark coloured, viscous and foul smelling crvde oil. It is a mixture of several solid, requid and gaseous hydrocarbons.

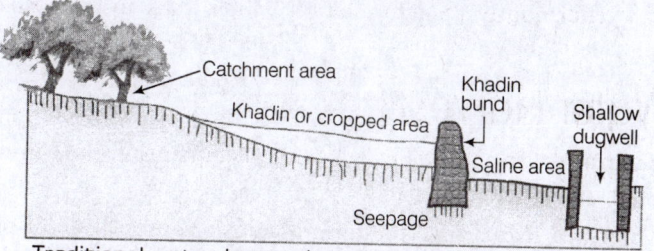

Traditional water harvesting system–an ideal setting of the Khadins system

Some of the ancient water harvesting structures are as follows

Region	Ancient Water Harvesting Structures
Rajasthan	Khadins, tanks and nadis
Maharashtra	Bandharas and tals
Madhya Pradesh and Uttar Pradesh	Bundhis
Bihar	Ahars and pynes
Himachal Pradesh	Kulhs
Jammu	Ponds in the Kandi belt
Tamil Nadu	Eris (tanks)
Kerala	Surangams
Karnataka	Kattas

Note In 2015, Dr. Rajendra Singh won the Stockholm Water Prize. In 20 years of efforts, 8,600 Johads (Pokhars or percolation ponds) and other structures have been built in Rajasthan to collect water. Also, water had been brought back to a 1000 villages across the state.

Check Point 03

1. Parts of Himachal Pradesh had evolved a local system of canal irrigation called..........
2. For what purpose (any one) were the dams constructed? Do you think dams are serving their purpose completely?
3. The aim behind Narmada Bachao Andolan is ....
4. Underground water is very essential component of water conservation programme. True or False.
5. Despite nature's bounty, why is there a failure in sustaining the underground water sources?

Coal and Petroleum

These are the most important source of energy. These are the largest conventional fossil fuels. In addition to carbon, these also contain hydrogen, nitrogen and sulphur.

Coal It is a combustible organic fuel that occurs inside the Earth.

Petroleum (*Petro* = rocks and *oleum* = oil) It is a naturally occurring dark coloured, viscous and foul smelling crude oil. It is a mixture of several solid, liquid and gasous hydrocarbons.

Coal and petroleum were formed from the degradation of biomass millions of years ago and hence, these are the resources that will be exhausted in the future. As per an estimation, our known petroleum resources will last for about forty years and the coal resources will last for another two hundred years.

Uses of Coal and Petroleum

Coal and petroleum both are used as energy source for different purposes. Coal is used in thermal power plants, steam engine, etc.

Petroleum and its products like diesel, petrol, kerosene, LPG are used in vehicles, ships, aircrafts and household purposes like cooking.

Pollution caused by Coal and Petroleum

When coal and petroleum are burnt, the products like carbon dioxide, water, oxides of nitrogen and oxides of sulphur are released into air.

When combustion takes place in insufficient air (oxygen), carbon monoxide is formed instead of carbon dioxide.

The oxides of sulphur, nitrogen and carbon monoxide are poisonous at high concentrations among these products. Carbon dioxide is a greenhouse gas. The increase in amount of carbon dioxide in the atmosphere will lead to intense global warming. Thus, we need to use these resources judiciously.

Conservation of Coal and Petroleum

General practices to reduce the consumption of coal and petroleum are as follows:

- Switch off the lights, fans, television and other electrical appliances when not in use.
- Use energy efficient appliances to save electricity like CFL as they consume less energy.
- Use stairs to climb at least upto three floors of a building.
- Public transport system needs to be improved, so that people can use them instead of using their personal vehicles.
- On cold days, an extra sweater can be used instead of heating device like heater or sigri.

An Overview of Natural Resource Management

Sustainable management of natural resources is a difficult task. In addressing this issue, we need to keep an open mind with regard to the interests of various stakeholders. People act with their own best interests as the priority, but it leads to misery for a large number of people and a total destruction of our environment is slowly occurring.

Going beyond laws, rules and regulations, we need to minimise our requirements individually and collectively, so that the benefits of development can reach to everyone and to all generations to come.

Check Point 04

1. Coal and petroleum are .... type of resources.
2. What is the ultimate source of energy for the fossil fuels?
3. Burning of fossil fuel causes pollution. True or false?
4. Gases released from the combustion of petroleum and coal are?
5. Suggest a general practice which will help in reduction of coal and petroleum use.

NCERT FOLDER

Intext Questions

1. What changes can you make in your habits to become more environment friendly? Pg 271

Sol. We should try and know about how our choices of using natural resources affect the environment. Use of renewable resources and biodegradable materials should be promoted, e.g.
 (i) Use of paper bags instead of single use plastic bags.
 (ii) Use of energy sources like LPG, solar energy, etc. which do not cause much pollution.
 (iii) Use of substances which can be recycled or can be reused.

2. What would be the advantages of exploiting resources with short term aims? How would these advantages differ from the advantages of using a long term perspective in managing our resources? Pg 271

Or List the advantages each of
 (i) Exploiting resources with short term aims, and
 (ii) Using a long term perspective in managing our natural resources. **CBSE Delhi 2019**

Sol. Exploiting natural resources with short term aims has some advantages. First of all, it take millions of years for the formation of natural resources and it is not possible to renew them.
Hence, the aims with long termed perspective are that these resources must last for the generations to come. For this, short term aim must be avoided. Our current basic needs can be fulfilled only by awareness.
The expenditure for short term requirements will be less and there will be full utilisation of resources and the wastage will be very low.

3. Why do you think there should be equitable distribution of resources? What forces would be working against an equitable distribution of our resources? (CBSE Delhi 2019) Pg 271

Sol. There should be equitable distribution of resources among all people–rich and poor, so that all are benefitted from the development of these resources.
Such an even distribution of resources restrict the exploitation, wastage and misuse of these resources. The poor will also get a chance to get benefit for himself and this way the society will improve. Unfortunately, it has been observed that mainly the rich and the powerful people take the full advantage of these resources and the poor are devoid of its pleasure. The following forces work against an equitable distribution of resources
 (i) Lack of natural resources (due to improper management of resources.
 (ii) Profit agenda by people over using resources.
 (iii) Excessive utilisation by rich people and corruption.

4. Why should we conserve forests and wildlife? Pg 275

Sol. We must conserve our forests as they are of great value because
 (i) forests help in protection of land and retaining sub-soil water.
 (ii) forests check floods and maintain ecosystem.
Wildlife is important for us because:
 (i) They provide great aesthetic value for human beings.
 (ii) They help in maintaining the ecological balance.

5. Suggest some approaches towards the conservation of forests. Pg 275

Sol. Various approaches are required for the conservation of forests. Afforestation is one of the most important approach.
Besides this approach, following steps should be taken:
 (i) Deforestation should be banned.
 (ii) People should be made more aware about importance of forests.
 (iii) The protected areas should be managed by local people which would be quite efficient.
 (iv) More National parks and sanctuaries should be formed to conserve the biodiversity.
 (v) Hunting should be banned and laws should be formulated against hunting.
 (vi) There should be proper laws for exploitation of forest resources.

6. Find out about the traditional systems of water harvesting/management in your region. Pg 278

Sol. There are many traditional methods of water harvesting or management. These are khadins, ponds, tals, etc. Also, wells have been dugged for drinking water and irrigation purposes. Canals have been developed and water reservoirs are made by the government for providing proper drinking water.

7. Compare the traditional system of water with the probable system in hilly/mountainous areas or plains or plateau regions. Pg 278

Sol. In hilly/mountainous areas, most of the rainwater flows fast downwards and thus, people have more opportunity of water harvesting, while in plains and plateau, the water flows with slow speed and most of it is percolated down in the soil.

8. Find out the source of water in your region/ locality. Is water from this source available to all people living in that area? Pg 278

Sol. There are mainly two sources of water in our locality
(i) Handpumps (ii) Municipality supply
The water from handpumps is available to all people, but access to municipality water is restricted to developed colonies only.

Exercises (On Page 280)

1 What changes would you suggest in your home in order to be environment-friendly?

Sol. Certain changes can be incorporated in our daily routine at home to make it more eco-friendly.
(i) We should plant different kinds of shady plants, fruit and vegetable bearing trees.
(ii) We should use water and electricity efficiently in routine activities.
(iii) Food should be properly stored to avoid any spoilage, thereby preventing its wastage.
(iv) There should be proper drainage system for the water to pass in the drains.
(v) There should be proper disposal of water.
(vi) Dustbins and other waste products should be properly covered and the garbage should not be dumped around the houses.
(vii) Proper sanitary and hygiene methods must be adopted.

2. Can you suggest some changes in your school which would make it environment-friendly?

Sol. (i) To make our school environment-friendly, it is essential to plant different kinds of shady and fruity trees. Different flowering plants should also be planted.
(ii) Waste material such as used paper, foil, empty packets should be properly thrown into the dustbin.
(iii) Solar panels must be fitted in school premises in order to save electricity.
(iv) Rainwater harvesting in school ground can help to recharge ground water.

3. We saw in this chapter that there are four main stakeholders when it comes to forests and wildlife. Which among these should have the authority to decide the management of forest produce? Why do you think so?

Sol. Out of the four categories of stakeholders, the local people living around the forest areas should be given the authority to decide the management of forest produce. This is because the traditional methods of exploitation of natural resources employed by the local people ensure that the sustainability of resources is maintained and they remain conserved in sufficient amount to meet the needs of future generations.

Their traditional methods ensure the recovery and regrowth of resources after they have used them, e.g. in the reserved area of great Himalayan National Park, when nomadic shepherds were allowed to graze their sheep in the alpine meadows during summers, the grass regrew naturally after grazing.

But, without the regular grazing by sheep today in that area the grass first grows very tall and then falls over there, preventing fresh growth.

There are also some examples of local people that have been working traditionally for conservation of forests like Bishnoi community in Rajasthan. So, the local people can manage the use of forest resources efficiently.

4 How can you as an individual contribute or make a difference to the management of
(i) forests and wildlife
(ii) water resources and
(iii) coal and petroleum?

Sol. (i) Contributions of an individual to the management of **forest** and **wildlife** are
(a) We should judiciously use the forest products.
(b) Cutting of trees for paper, timber, etc., should be strictly controlled.
(c) Killing of wild animals for their skin, horns, etc., should be banned.
(d) Afforestation should be more and more practised.
(e) Management of the forest should be given to local people.
(ii) Contributions of an individual to the management of **water resources** are
(a) Leaking taps should be repaired.
(b) Water from industries should not be directly dumped in the riverwater, thus reducing water pollution.
(c) Use of insecticides and pesticides should be minimised, which are usually washed away with rain. They contaminate river water and underground water.
(d) Methods like rainwater harvesting, construction of canals should be promoted. Construction of dams may also prove beneficial.

Management of Natural Resources

(iii) Contributions of an individual to the management of **coal and petroleum** are
  (a) Use of coal and petroleum as a source of energy should be minimised.
  (b) Use of CNG or LPG as fuels in automobiles should be promoted.
  (c) Renewable resources of energy like solar power, hydropower, wind energy, tidal energy, etc., should be used. It is better to walk over a short distance or use a bicycle rather than going by car or scooter.

5 What can you do as an individual to reduce your consumption of the various natural resources?

Sol. The following activities can help in reducing consumption of the various natural resources:
  (i) Use of solar cooker and minimum use of cooking gas.
  (ii) Closing all taps when not in use.
  (iii) Switching off electric appliances when not in use.
  (iv) Making minimum use of auto-vehicles and more of public transport vehicles.
  (v) Minimum use of air conditioners in summers and electric heaters in winters.
  (vi) Avoid wastage of food.

6 List five things you have done over the last one week to
  (i) conserve our natural resources.
  (ii) increase the pressure on our natural resources.

Sol. (i) **For conserving natural resources**
  (a) Limited use of water
  (b) Plantation in free areas
  (c) Irrigation of plants
  (d) Limited use of petrol/diesel
  (e) Smokeless fuel utilisation

(ii) **Increase the pressure on our natural resources**
  (a) Extra use of water
  (b) Day and night lighting
  (c) Unnecessary traffic due to use of car
  (d) Burning of polythene and wastes
  (e) Destroying the plants

7. On the basis of the issues raised in this chapter, what changes would you incorporate in your lifestyle in a move towards a sustainable use of our resources?

Sol. On the basis of issues raised in this chapter, we would incorporate the 5 Rs' in our lifestyle and a move towards limited use of petrol/diesel, water conservation, more plantation, use of LPG in homes, use of biodegradable products, etc. We will work towards the sustainable utilisation of resources.

SUMMARY

- **Natural resources** are the stock of nature such as air, water, soil, minerals, animal and plants. They are of two types: Inexhaustible natural resources and Exhaustible natural resources.
- One should keep in mind the 5 Rs to save the environment:
- **Refuse** It means to say no to things people offers you that are not needed.
- **Repurpose** It means to use a product again which cannot be used for the original purpose.
  - **Reduce** It means to minimise the use of various products obtained directly or indirectly from natural resources.
  - **Recycle** This involves the processing of things that are considered waste and turning them into useful products.
  - **Reuse** It means to use things again and again. It is better than recycling because the process of recycling uses some energy.
- **Sustainable development** It is the process of development to sustain natural systems and their yields which can be maintained for a long time without any damage to the environment.
- If the conservation of forest is considered, then we need to look at the stakeholders who are:
  - A stakeholder can be person, a group or an organisation that may be affected or have any kind of interest in the project or in the project's outcome either directly or indirectly.
  - **Sustainable management** The controlled use of a resource in such a way that its present availability and continuous flow to the future generation is ensured without any disturbance to the environment.
- **Chipko Andolan** was started in early 1970 from Reni village, in Garhwal.
- Rain is a very important source of water. Rain in India largely occurs during the monsoons.
- The failure to sustain underground water availability is due to the high yielding varieties of crops which require much more amount of water for irrigation than the traditional varieties.
- **Dams** are the barriers constructed across rivers to hold the water. These are large reservoirs of water that ensures storage of adequate water for different uses.
- Narmada Bachao Andolan (save the Narmada) was a protest against raising the height of the Sardar Sarovar dam on the river Narmada.
- Large dams cause following three problems:
  (i) Social problems (ii) Economic problems
  (iii) Environmental problems
- Water harvesting means storing rainwater where it falls or storing the run-off water in a local area for reuse.
- The advantages of watershed management are that it increases the production and income of watershed management community, reduces droughts and floods.
- Parts of Himachal Pradesh had evolved a local system of canal irrigation called **kulhs** over four hundred years ago.
- Coal is a combustible organic fuel that occurs inside the Earth.
- Petroleum is a naturally occurring liquid composed of organic molecules. It is found in large quantities below the Earth surface.
- When coal and petroleum are burnt, the products like carbon dioxide, water, oxides of nitrogen and oxides of sulphur are released into air thus, pollutes the environment.

Exam Practice

Objective Type Questions

Multiple Choice Questions

1 The most rapidly dwindling natural resource in the world is
(a) water (b) forests (c) wind (d) sunlight
NCERT Exemplar
Sol. (b) Forests are the most rapidly dwindling natural resource in the world.

2 Which of the following is not a natural resource?
(a) Mango tree (b) Snake
(c) Wind (d) Wooden house
NCERT Exemplar
Sol. (d) Wooden house is not a natural resource.

3 Select the eco-friendly activity among the following.
(a) Using car for transportation
(b) Using polybags for shopping
(c) Using dyes for colouring clothes
(d) Switching off unnecessary lights and fans
NCERT Exemplar
Sol. (d) To minimise the use of various resources like electricity by switching off unnecessary lights and fans when not needed is an eco-friendly activity.

4 Ganga Action Plan was started in
(a) 1975   (b) 1985
(c) 2004   (d) 1982
Sol. (b) Ganga Action Plan (GAP) was a programme launched by Government of India in April 1985 in order to reduce the pollution load on the river Ganga.

5 Expand the abbreviation GAP
(a) Governmental Agency for Pollution Control
(b) Gross Assimilation by Photosynthesis
(c) Ganga Action Plan
(d) Governmental Agency for Animal Protection **NCERT Exemplar**
Sol. (c) GAP is the abbreviation for Ganga Action Plan.

6 Destruction of forest can cause
(a) habitat loss
(b) floods and droughts
(c) soil erosion and degradation
(d) All of the above

Sol. (d) The indiscriminate destruction of forest cover leads to problems like habitat loss, ecological imbalance that cause floods and draughts, soil erosion and degradation, etc.

7 Select the incorrect statement.
NCERT Exemplar
(a) Economic development is linked to environmental conservation
(b) Sustainable development encourages development for current generation and conservation for resources for future generations
(c) Sustainable development does not consider the view points of stakeholders
(d) Sustainable development is a long planned and persistent development
Sol. (c) Statement in option (c) is incorrect and can be corrected as follows: Sustainable development considers the view points of stakeholders. It is a process in which decentralised economic growth and ecological conservation go hand in hand. Rest statements are correct.

8 How many Rs' are there to save the environment?
(a) Five (b) Four (c) Three (d) six
Sol. (a) There are five Rs' to save the environment. These are Refuse, Reduce, Reuse, Repurpose and Recycle.

9 Opposition to the construction of large dams is due to
(a) social reasons
(b) economic reasons
(c) environmental reasons
(d) All of the above
Sol. (d) Opposition to the construction of large dams by local people is due to social, economic and environmental problems.

10 Ground water will not be depleted due to
(a) afforestation
(b) untreated sewage and industrial waste discharge
(c) loss of forest and decreased rainfall
(d) cropping of high water demanding crops
Sol. (a) Ground water will not be depleted due to afforestation (i.e. plantation of trees). This is because forests help in conserving ground water.

Fill in the Blanks

11 Forests are .... hotspots.
Sol. biodiversity

12 .... prevents flooding because they store water during rainy season.
Sol. Dam

13 Removal, decrease or deterioration of the forest cover of an area is called ....
Sol. deforestation

14 .... is the processing of the waste materials to form new products.
Sol. Recycle

15 .... resources are likely to diminish and get exhausted with continuous exploitation.
Sol. Natural

True and False

16 An environmental friendly decision is to reuse jam and pickle bottles.
Sol. True

17 The pH of water can be tested by using universal indicator.
Sol. True

18 Presence of coliform bacteria in a water body indicates contamination by industrial effluents.
Sol. Presence of coliform bacteria in a water body indicates contamination by disease causing microorganisms.

19 Narmada Bachao Andolan was a protest against raising the height of the Sardar Sarovar Dam on the river Ganga.
Sol. False; Narmada Bachao Andolan was a protest against raising the height of the Sardar Sarovar Dam on the river Narmada.

20 Ground water does not evaporate, but spreads out to recharge wells.
Sol. True

Match the Columns

21 Match the following.

	Column I		Column II
A.	Kulhs	1.	Johads
B.	Tehri Dam	2.	Himachal Pradesh
C.	Dr. Rajendra Singh	3.	Biomass
D.	Coal and petroleum	4.	Forests
E.	Stakeholders	5.	Ganga

Sol. A → 2, B → 5, C → 1, D → 3, E → 4

22 Match the following.

	Column A		Column B
A.	Surangams	1.	Timber industries
B.	Forests	2.	Khejri tress
C.	Non-renewable energy	3.	Solar radiation
D.	Renewable energy	4.	Coal
E.	Amrita Devi Bishnoi	5.	Kerala

Sol. A → 5, B → 1, C → 4, D → 3, E → 2

Assertion-Reason

Direction (Q. Nos. 23-27) *In each of the following questions, a statement of Assertion is given by the corresponding statement of Reason. Of the statements, mark the correct answer as*

(a) If both Assertion and Reason are true and Reason is the correct explanation of Assertion
(b) If both Assertion and Reason are true, but Reason is not the correct explanation of Assertion
(c) If Assertion is true, but Reason is false
(d) If Assertion is false, but Reason is true

23 Assertion Inexhaustible natural resources are present in abundant amount in nature.
Reason Inexhaustible natural resources are non-renewable and non-replenishable.
Sol. (c) Inexhaustible natural resources are present in unlimited quantity in the nature and these are not likely to be exhausted by human activities. These resources are renewable and thus replenishable.
Thus, Assertion is true, but Reason is false.

24 Assertion Dams are the barriers constructed across the rivers to hold the water.
Reason These dams ensure the storage of adequate water for different uses.
Sol. (a) Dams are the barriers constructed across the rivers to hold the water. They ensure the storage of adequate water for different uses.
Therefore, both Assertion and Reason are true and Reason is the correct explanation of Assertion.

25 Assertion Coal is a combustible organic fuel.
Reason It occurs inside the volcanoes.
Sol. (c) Coal is a combustible organic fuel that occurs inside the earth. Thus, Assertion is true, but Reason is false.

26 Assertion Consumption of coal and petroleum can be reduced by many ways.
Reason One of them is to switch off the lights, fans, etc.

Sol. (a) Consumption of coal and petroleum can be reduced by many ways. One of them is to switch off the lights, fans, television, etc. Therefore, both Assertion and Reason are true and Reason is the correct explanation of Assertion.

27 Assertion The gases released by burning of coal and petroleum are poisonous.
Reason The oxides of sulphur, nitrogen and carbon monoxide are poisonous at high concentrations.

Sol. (a) The gases released by burning of coal and petroleum (oxides of sulphur, nitrogen and carbon monoxide) are poisonous at high concentrations. Therefore, both Assertion and Reason are true and Reason is the correct explanation of Assertion.

Case Based Questions

Direction (Q. Nos. 28-31) *Answer the questions based on the two tables given below. Study these tables related to motor fuels and answer the questions that follow*

Ethanol

A. Advantages	Disadvantages
Reduces air pollution	Increases the tendency of fuels of evaporate
Can disperse through the ground water	May corrode some parts of some vehicles
Improves octane rating	May make engines hard to start in cold weather
Rapidly biodegradable	Mar separate form the petrol reducing power output

B. Methyl Tert-Butyl Ether (MTBE)

Reduces air pollution	Contaminates ground water
Improves the octane rating of the fuel	Gives drinking water an unpleasant taste
Reduces carbon dioxide emissions	Is a possible carcinogen to humans
Does not corrode engine parts	Resists biological decomposition

28 Refer to table A and table B. Identify the reason why ethanol is preferred over MTBE as a motor fuel?

Sol. Ethanol is favoured over MTBE because it is rapidly decomposed by soil bacteria while MTBE is not.

29 Why there is a need to search for alternative fuels?

Sol. Coal and petroleum are exhaustible resources which will be exhausted in the future. Thus, we want alternative fuels to sustain natural resources and to minimise harmful effects on the environment.

30 Which of the following is used in vehicles, ships, aircrafts and household purposes the cooking?

(a) LPG (b) CO_2 (c) O_3 (d) Coal

Sol. (a) LPG is used in vehicles, ships, aircrafts, household purposes like cooking, etc.

31 Why will coal and petroleum get exhausted in the future?
(a) These were formed from the degradation of biomass millions of years ago.
(b) They will be depleted soon
(c) They will get depleted and then will be formed again.
(d) None of the above

Sol. (a) Coal and petroleum will get exhausted in the future because these were formed from the degradation of biomass millions of years ago.

Direction (Q. Nos. 32-35) *Answer the questions on the basis of your understanding of the following paragraph and the related studied concepts.*

In rural areas (villages areas), most of the ground has open soil due to which rainwater can seep into the ground naturally to make up for the loss in groundwater due to excessive use. In urban areas (city areas), however, most of the ground is covered with buildings, concrete, pavements and metalled roads due to which only very little rainwater seeps into the ground naturally. Most of the rainwater which falls in cities flows into dirty water drains and goes away. So, rainwater harvesting is necessary in city areas.

32 Why is rainwater harvesting necessary in city areas?

Sol. Rainwater harvesting is necessary in city areas because most of the rainwater which fells in cities flows into dirty water drains and goes away.

33 Write any two advantages of rainwater harvesting in rural areas.

Sol. Rainwater harvesting in rural areas not only increases the agricultural production and income of the farmers and also mitigates the effect of droughts and floods.

34 What is the main purpose of water harvesting?

Sol. The main purpose of water harvesting is not to hold rainwater on the surface of the Earth, but to make rainwater peridate under the ground so as to recharge ground water.

35 Write two advantages of rainwater harvesting in urban areas.

Sol. The rainwater harvesting in urban areas increases the availability of ground water and helps in overcoming water shortage.

Very Short Answer Type Questions

36 How is the increase in demand for energy affecting atmosphere?

Sol. Increased consumption of fossil fuels releases a lot of polluting gases, some of which are causing global warming and also producing acid rain.

37 Instead of using gas, an alternative 'A' can be used to cook food which does not require any fuel. However, this alternative cannot work at night. Identify A.

Sol. Solar cooker is the alternative of using gas or any fuels for cooking. It can easily cook pulses, vegetables and rice, but requires the presence of sun light.

38 Give an example to show that exploitation of resources lead to pollution.

Sol. Mining causes pollution because of the large amount of slag formed, which is discarded for every tonne of metal extracted. This discarded material being toxic in nature highly pollutes the environment.

39 Make a list of few industries that are dependent on forest products.

Sol. Timber, paper, lac and sports equipment industries are dependent on forest products.

40 Why did Amrita Devi Bishnoi sacrificed her life?

Sol. In 1731, Amrita Devi Bishnoi along with 363 other people sacrificed their life for the protection of Khejri trees in Khejrali village near Jodhpur in Rajasthan.

41 Where was Chipko Andolan started and by whom?

Sol. Chipko Andolan was started in Reni village in Garhwal. It was initiated by Gaura Devi.

42 Suggest some consequences due to the loss of biodiversity?

Sol. Loss of biodiversity will lead to ecological crisis. The food chains and food webs will get disturbed and resources will not be available for the upcoming future generations.

43 Large waterbodies, i.e. oceans are present on the Earth yet there is scarcity of water. Explain.

Sol. Oceans are the largest bodies of water, but the water present in them is salty and thus, cannot be used without processing.

44 To test the level of water quality, study of which parameters can be done?

Sol. To test the level of water quality, pH of water (it can be checked by using universal indicator), BOD and biological testing are done.

45 Is water conservation necessary? Give reason. **NCERT Exemplar**

Sol. The water available on Earth is more than enough for all. But, due to its uneven distribution, wide seasonal fluctuations in rainfall and poor quality of available water, it is necessary to conserve water.

Short Answer (SA) Type Questions

1 Distinguish between inexhaustible and exhaustible resources.

Sol. Differences between inexhaustible and exhaustible resources are:

Inexhaustible Resources	Exhaustible Resources
These resources have an ability to renew themselves in a given period of time.	These resources cannot be renewed after exhaustion.
These are renewable or replenishable resources.	These are non-renewable or non-replenishable resources.
They do not require conservation steps to be taken as they can be renewed, e.g. sunlight, water, etc.	They require conservation steps to be taken, so that they can be used in future also, e.g. iron, coal, etc.

2 In the context of conservation of natural resources, explain the terms reduce, recycle and reuse. From among the materials that we use in daily life, identify two materials for each category.
NCERT Exemplar

Sol. **Reduce** This means to use a material/commodity in lesser quantity e.g. using electricity and water efficiently.

Recycle It means a material that is used once is collected and sent back to a manufacturer, so that they can make some other useful materials from it, e.g. used paper, plastic bottles, metal objects can be recycled.

Management of Natural Resources

Reuse It means using a thing over and over again instead of throwing it away. This is actually even better than recycling because the process of recycling uses some energy.

3. Reuse is better than recycling of materials. Give reason to justify this statement.
CBSE 2016

Sol. Reuse of materials is the better one in 3 Rs to save the environment because
(i) reuse of material does not use any energy.
(ii) it reduces the stress on environment.
(iii) things are maximally utilised, as they are used again and again, instead of being thrown away.

4. What is exploitation of resources with short term aims? List its four advantages.
CBSE (All India) 2019

Sol. Exploitation of resources with short term aims means consumption of resources for immediate requirement without conservation for future.
Its four advantages are
(i) It fulfils the requirements of mass population.
(ii) It provides the industrial growth.
(iii) It provides economic growth and development.
(iv) It makes life comfortable.

5. List three rules of forests in conserving the environment. How do the forests get depleted? State two consequences of deforestation on the environment.
CBSE (All India) 2019

Sol. Forests need to be conserved because
(i) They provide habitat to numerous species of plants and animals.
(ii) They help in protecting the soil from erosion.
(iii) They store a large amount of water which acts as buffer for ecosystem in dry periods.
Forests are getting depleted because of industrial needs and for development projects like building roads or dens.
The consequences of deforestation on the environment are
(i) Loss of wildlife which further cause ecological imbalance.
(ii) Due to not forests soil erosion become the dominating factor.
(iii) Ground water level is not recharged.

6. List few activities that have led to the contamination of the river Ganga.

Sol. Activities that have led to the contamination of the river Ganga are:
(i) Largely untreated sewage is dumped into the Ganga everyday.
(ii) Other human activities like bathing, washing of clothes, immersion of ashes or unburnt dead bodies have also lead to the contamination of Ganga.
(iii) Toxic chemical effluents are also added to Ganga and their toxicity kill large number of fishes.

7. What important message is conveyed by Amrita Devi Bishnoi Award for wildlife conservation?

Sol. Amrita Devi Bishnoi Award encourages the people to promote wildlife conservation as the lady sacrificed her life along with 363 other people for the protection of Khejri trees.
Conservation of wildlife and forests is crucial to our own welfare as it has both economic and ecological benefits.
Economic Benefits Source of food, fodder, timber, industrial raw materials and medicines.
Ecological Benefits It regulates climate, prevents soil erosion and floods, retains rainwater, supplies to streams and springs. It acts as gene bank for improvement of domesticated plants and animals.

8. What was the cause behind the Chipko Andolan and what happened during it? What was the result of the movement?

Sol. The cause behind the Chipko Andolan was to stop the plan of cutting down the forest trees near Reni village by logging contractors.
During Hug the Trees Movement, when the contractor's workers appeared in the forest, the women of the village hugged the tree trunks, thus preventing the workers from felling the trees.
The result was that the contractor had to withdraw ultimately and the government of India was forced to give a fresh thought to the proper use of forest produce.

9. (i) Locate and name the water reservoirs in Figures (A) and (B). **NCERT Exemplar**
(ii) Which has an advantage over the other and why?

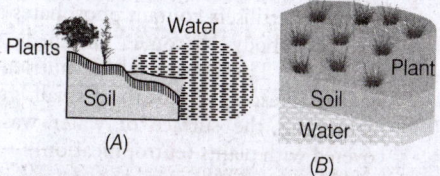

Sol. (i) The water reservoir is a pond in Fig. (A) and underground waterbody in Fig. (B).
(ii) Underground waterbody has more advantage over water reservoir. There are many advantages of water stored in the ground. Some of these are:
(a) It does not evaporate.
(b) It spreads out to recharge wells and provides moisture for crops over a wide area.
(c) It does not promote breeding of mosquitoes (unlike stagnant water collected in ponds, etc.).
(d) It is free from contamination by human and animal wastes.
(d) It is utilised for the benefit of local population.

10. What is water harvesting? List two main advantages associated with water harvesting, at the community level. Write two causes for the failure of sustained availability of ground water.
CBSE Delhi 2019

Sol. Water harvesting is defined as the process of collecting and conserving run-off water from the run-off area into an area where the collected water is either used directly or stored in the soil profile.

The two main advantages associated with water harvesting at the community level are as follows

(i) The ground water level increases due to recharging of wells.

(ii) The water can be stored during rainy season and can be used when required.

The causes of the failure of sustained availability of groundwater are pumping out too much water through deep tube wells and lack of sufficient vegetation cover on the ground due to which only a little rainwater seeps into the ground.

11. In a village in Karnataka, people started cultivating crops all around a lake which was always filled with water. They added fertilisers to their field in order to enhance the yield. Soon, they discovered that the waterbody was completely covered with green floating plants and fishes started dying in large numbers. Analyse the situation and give reasons for excessive growth of plants and death of fish in the lake.
NCERT Exemplar

Sol. Use of fertilisers adds nutrients to the waterbody leading to eutrophication and thus, results in loss of fishes in lake. Since, people used excessive fertilisers in the fields, these added fertilisers flow away with rain into the waterbody.

As many fertilisers contain phosphates and nitrates, the waterbody become enriched with these chemicals. This enriches the nutrients in water leading to excessive growth of small, green, aquatic plants and the surface of water was completely covered with plants (eutrophication).

These small plants consume most of the dissolved oxygen of the water leading to its deficiency. Due to this, the fishes and other aquatic organisms in the lake die because of oxygen starvation and depletion of light.

12. What is a dam? Why do we seek to build large dams?

While building large dams which three main problems should particularly be addressed to maintain peace among local people? Mention them. *CBSE 2018*

Sol. Dam is huge structure (barrier) usually constructed on rivers to hold water and store it in reservoirs. It is further connected to a hydro-power plant to generate electricity.

As a large dam can store more amount of water in its reservoir, hence more potential energy of water can be converted into electrical energy with using turbines, hence we seek to build large dams.

While building large dams following problems are addressed to maintain peace among people.

(i) Construction of dams leads to ecological damage.

(ii) A large variety of plants, animals and their habitats gets submerged in water.

(iii) It creates the problem of satisfactory rehabilation of displaced people.

13. What does watershed management mean and aim at? What are the advantages of watershed management?

Sol. Watershed management aims at scientific conservation of primary resources of land and water to increase the production of secondary resources of plants and animals for their use in a way that will not result in ecological imbalance.

The advantages of watershed management include increase in the production and income of watershed community, reduces droughts and floods and increases the life of downstream dam and reservoirs.

14. Suggest some precautionary measures which should be taken while harvesting rainwater.

Sol. Harvested rainwater is used for direct usage or for recharging underground water table. It is most important to ensure that the rainwater caught is free from pollutants. Following measures should be taken while harvesting rainwater:

(i) Roof or terraces used for harvesting should be clean, free from dust, etc.

(ii) Do not keep or store chemicals, detergents, etc., where the water is being harvested.

(iii) The whole system should be checked before and after each rain.

15. Although coal and petroleum are produced by degradation of biomass, yet we need to conserve them. Why? *NCERT Exemplar*

Sol. Coal and petroleum were formed from the degradation of biomass millions of years ago. As these resources are being utilised at a much faster rate than their formation, they will be exhausted in the near future. And then we would need to look for alternative sources of energy.

This is the reason why we need to conserve them, although these resources are produced by degradation of biomass.

Management of Natural Resources

16 What measures would you take to conserve electricity in your house? **NCERT Exemplar**

Sol. The following measures can be taken to conserve electricity in our house:
(i) Switch off the fans and lights in unoccupied rooms when they are not required.
(ii) Maximise use of solar radiation. It is a pollution-free and cost-free resource that is easily available.
(iii) During winters, instead of electric geysers, solar water heating system should be used.
(iv) Fluorescent tubes like CFL should be used instead of electric bulbs as the former consume less electricity.

17 Why do we need to manage our resources carefully? Also, explain how do we need to manage our resources?

Sol. We need to manage our resources carefully because these are limited and due to exponentially increasing population, the demand for these resources keeps on increasing, but these resources also need to be preserved for future generations.

The resources need to be managed and used in a manner such that these are equitably distributed amongst the rich and the poor. Their use does not cause damage to the environment. The wastes generated during their use need to be disposed off safely.

18 Carbon dioxide is considered as toxic to mankind. Explain.

Sol. Carbon dioxide (CO_2) is a greenhouse gas and its concentration in atmosphere more than the normal range is considered toxic to mankind due to the following reasons:
(i) Being a greenhouse gas, it is actively responsible for increasing the temperature of Earth's atmosphere that results in melting of glaciers.
(ii) Too much carbon dioxide can have a negative effect on some food crops.
(iii) Burning of more and more fossils is increasing the amount of carbon dioxide in the atmosphere causing increased greenhouse effect leading to global warming.

Long Answer (LA) Type Questions

1 What direct value does a forest have for man?

Sol. Forests contribute to the economic development of our country by providing goods and services to the people and industry. They are intimately linked with our culture and civilisation.

Forests are useful to human for the following reasons
(i) They provide timber for building and furniture.
(ii) They provide raw materials for the paper industry, board industry, plywood industry, etc.
(iii) They yield bamboos, which is called poor man's timber. Industrially, bamboos are used as a raw material in paper and rayon industry.
(iv) They provide fuel energy, which is needed by villagers staying in the vicinity. They also provide fodder and grazing grounds for animals.
(v) They also provide various animal products such as musk, honey, wax, tusser or mooga silk, etc.

2 What is the importance of forests as a resource? **NCERT Exemplar**

Sol. Forests are renewable natural resource. They are important as a resource due to the following reasons:
(i) Provide habitat, food and protection to wildlife.
(ii) Help in balancing CO_2 and O_2 in atmosphere.
(iii) Improve water holding capacity of soil.
(iv) Regulate water cycle.
(v) For human beings, they are the source of various essential commodities like-fuel, wood, timber, fruits, resins, etc.

Forests help in the conservation of biodiversity as a large number of species of plants and animals inhabit these areas.

3 Suggest your views on the traditional systems of water harvesting.

Sol. In recent years, many parts of our country have been facing crisis of groundwater availability. Thus, there is a greater need of surface water collection, storage, treatment and supply at household level for domestic use.

Many indigenous water saving methods have been used by local communities to capture water wherever it falls on their land, like digging small pits and lakes, building small earthen dams and reservoirs and setting up roof top rainwater harvesting units.

In different parts of our country, rainwater harvesting was practised in different ways. In Madhya Pradesh, check dams, tanks and community lift irrigation schemes were used to overcome drought. As a result, food production got increased by 38% in between 1990 and 1995.

In Andhra Pradesh also, percolation tanks and checkdams were constructed to overcome drought. Even in Maharashtra, percolation tanks were used to convert drought prone areas into green lands.

In Jodhpur (Rajasthan), Gramin Vigyan Vikas Samiti motivated people to build storage tanks. Water harvesting techniques are highly specific for specific areas and the benefits are also localised.

These days, rooftop rainwater harvesting is practiced. It is a method of direct collection of rainwater on the rooftop of buildings, houses as well as those of industries buildings.

The rainwater collected can be stored for direct use or can be allowed to reach under the ground. Once the water reaches the groundwater table is raised. It is thus, a solution to the problem of depleting groundwater.

4 Suggest a few measures for controlling carbon dioxide levels in the atmosphere. **NCERT Exemplar**

Sol. Few measures for controlling carbon dioxide levels in the atmosphere are as follow

(i) Reduce the consumption of petrol in automobiles. Using of car-pools and public transport helps in reducing petrol usage.

(ii) Use alternative fuels such as CNG (clean fuel) instead of coal and petroleum.

(iii) Manure should be prepared out of litter instead of burning it.

(iv) The smoke coming out of the thermal power stations and other industries should be well-treated to remove harmful gases, before discharging it into atmosphere.

(v) Planting more trees in the polluted area.

5 On the environment day, i.e. 5th June, every year, your school organises various activities related to Earth, ecosystem and environment, etc., like best out of waste, paper machetes and several others.

What purpose do you think is served by this measure?

Sol. 5th June is celebrated as the World Environment Day all over the world run by UNEP. It is celebrated to raise global awareness for taking initiatives to protect nature and the planet Earth.

At national and international levels various activities, projects, seminar, etc., take place to bring awareness amongst people.

At school level, various activities are planned and organised to draw the interest of students and parents. Environment theme topics are incorporated in activities like arts and drawing on save Earth, save tigers, go green, save electricity, global warming, etc.

- **Slogan writing** Students have to write attractive slogans on various environment related topics.
- **Best out of waste** Using their parents help, students create different designs by using waste products like used paper, straws, cans, bottles, etc.
- **Theatre** Enacting of some serious environmental issues through plays.
- **Debates/Discussion** Children debate on various issues of environment.

All these activities create awareness among the students and parents about our environment and how can we protect it. The students participate in these activities and spread the message as far and wide as possible.

6 Prepare a list of five activities that you perform daily in which natural resources can be conserved or energy utilisation can be minimised. **NCERT Exemplar**

Sol. Refer to Ans. 5 in NCERT Folder Exercises.

7 What are fossil fuels? How are coal and petroleum formed? Why fossil fuel should be used judiciously?

Sol. Refer to text 'Coal and Petroleum' on Pg 453 and 454.

CHAPTER EXERCISE

Multiple Type Questions

1. The three Rs that will help us to conserve natural resources and minimise their wastage are
   (a) recycle, regenerate, reuse
   (b) reduce, regenerate, reuse
   (c) reduce, reuse, redistribute
   (d) reduce, recycle, reuse

2. The main cause for abundant coliform bacteria in the river Ganga is
   (a) discharge of industrial effluents
   (b) disposal of half or unburnt corpses into water
   (c) immersion of ashes
   (d) All of the above

3. Reforestation is useful for
   (a) increasing the fertility of soils
   (b) reducing floods
   (c) preventing soil erosion
   (d) All of the above

4. The best measures for water resource management is/are
   (a) rainwater harvesting
   (b) construction of dams
   (c) Both (a) and (b)
   (d) None of the above

5. The poisonous gas released in the environment due to incomplete combustion of fossil fuels is
   (a) CO_2 (b) CO
   (c) H_2S (d) All of these

Fill in the Blanks

6. The 5Rs' are Reuse, Repurpose, ..., Recycle and ....

7. The killing of wild animals is also called ....

8. In India, rain largely occurs during ....

True and False

9. Monoculture destroys a large amount of biodiversity in the area.

10. The ground water is not protected from contamination by human and animal waste.

11. The forest Department is India's biggest land lord and controls the resources from forests.

Match the column

12. Match the following.

	Column I		Column II
A.	Chipko Andolan	1.	Reni Village
B.	Arabari forest	2.	Poaching
C.	Wild life	3.	Biodiversity hotspots
D.	Forests	4.	Coliform
E.	GAP	5.	Mindapore district

Assertion–Reason

Direction (Q. Nos. 13-15) *In each of the following questions, a statement of Assertion is given by the corresponding statement of Reason. Of the statements, mark the correct answer as*

(a) If both Assertion and Reason are true and Reason is the correct explanation of Assertion
(b) If both Assertion and Reason are true, but Reason is not the correct explanation of Assertion
(c) If Assertion is true, but Reason is false
(d) If Assertion is false, but Reason is true

13. **Assertion** Forests are the hotspots of biodiversity.
    Reason They provide habitat to numerous species of plants and animals.

14. **Assertion** Wild animals have increased greatly in number.
    Reason These wild animals are killed by poaching.

15. **Assertion** Petroleum is used for household purposes like cooking.
    Reason Petroleum is used in thermal power plants.

Case Based Questions (Q.Nos. 16-18)

International Union of conservation of Nature and Natural Resources. (IUCN) which is now called World Conservation Union (WCU). It has its head quarters at Morges, Switzerland. It maintains a red data book or red list which is a catelogue of taxa facing risk of extinction. Threatened species is the one which is liable to become extinct if not allowed to realise its full biotic potential by providing protection from exotic species/human exploitation/habitat deterioration/ depletion of food. Red data book or red list was initiated in 1963. The red light has eight categories of species few of which are given below

Category	Percentage			
	Critically endangered	Endangered	Vulnerable	Lower risk
Angiosperms	16	19	51	14
Amphibians	14	22	48	16
Reptiles	15	21	43	21
Birds	9	17	36	38
Mammals	10	19	34	37

The purpose of red list is to provide the degree of awareness of threat of biodiversity; provide global index about already decline of biodiversity; identification and documentation of species at higher risk of extinction and preparing conservation priorities to help in conservation action.

16 What is Red Data book?

17 According to the Table given which species has the maximum population in critically endangered category and which has the least?

18 What are the purpose of preparing Red List?

Case Based Questions

Direction (Q. Nos. 19-22) *Read the passage and answer the question that follow*

Coal and petroleum were formed from the degradation of biomass of plants and animals respectively buried deep under the earth millions of years ago. We obtain coal from the 'coal mines' dug into the earth and petroleum is obtained by digging 'oil wells' deep in the Earth.

The crude petroleum oil obtained from oil wells is then separated into fuels such as LPG, petrol, diesel and kerosene. We have been using coal and petroleum resources at such a rapid rate in the past the they will get exhausted in the near future. It has been estimated that at the present rate of consumption the known petroleum reserves of the Earth will last us for just about 40 years more and the coal will last for about another 200 years only.

Once exhausted, coal and petroleum will not be available to us in near future (because they are formed extremely slowly over a very, very long time). It is therefore, necessary to conserve (or save) coal and petroleum resources of the Earth by reducing their consumption so that they may last for as long, as possible.

19 How were coal and petroleum formed?

20 Why will coal and petroleum not be available in near future?

21 How can we reduce the consumption of coal and petroleum?

22 State one problem caused by coal as a fuel.

Answers

1. (d)   2. (b)   3. (d)   4. (c)   5. (b)
12. (1) → (E), (2) → (A), (3) → (B), (4) → (C), (5) → (D)
13. (a)   14. (d)   15. (c)

Very Short Answer (VSA) Type Questions

23 Name the prominent ecologist, who is responsible for Chipko Andolan and the lady behind the success of the movement.

24 In which region of India, Bundhis are used for water harvesting?

25 What is the main purpose of rainwater harvesting?

26 Name the most common practice of recharging groundwater.

27 Which country has the world's strictest standards for the control of water and air pollution?

28 How can we prevent floods?

29 Name a clean gaseous fuel other than LPG and natural gas.

30 Name the only resource which is not obtained from the Earth.

31 Why is it necessary to conserve our environment?

Short Answer (SA) Type Questions

32 How local people can be used for successful forest management?

33 What is water harvesting? Write any two advantages of it.

34 Construction of a dam on a river often results in the reduction of fish catch. Why is it so?

35 State the advantages of constructing dams across the rivers.

36 Why is water considered as the most valuable natural resource?

37 What is petroleum? Which other substances are derived from crude petroleum?

38 Write a few steps to reduce consumption of coal and petroleum.

39 In what ways damages are caused to the environment?

Management of Natural Resources

Long Answer (LA) Type Questions

40 Forest resources ought to be used in a manner that is both environmentally and developmentally sound. Explain this briefly.

41 Quote some instances where human intervention saved the forest from destruction.

42 Explain "industrialisation is one of the main causes of deterioration of environment."

43 How can an individual contribute or make a difference to the management of
(i) Forest? (ii) Fossil fuels

44 Why are environmentalists insisting upon sustainable natural resource management? Give reasons.

45 CFL is costly as compared to incandescent electric bulb. Even, then it is advised that incandescent bulbs should be replaced by CFLs. Why so?

46 Give reasons for switching over from fossil fuels to other sources of energy.

Challengers*

1 Which of the following statement(s) is/are correct about the renewable natural resource?
(a) It gets exhausted soon
(b) It requires millions of years to replenish
(c) It reappears at the rate it is used
(d) It cannot be replenished within a short period

2 Which of the following statements about the construction of a dam are incorrect?
(a) It provides an eco-friendly environment
(b) It is used to generate electricity
(c) It displaces the largely poor tribals that do not get any benefit
(d) It prevents the occurrence of floods in the river

3 'Narmada Bacho Andolan' has been organised under the leadership of
(a) Ravi Shankar Maharaj
(b) Medha Patekar
(c) Amrita Devi Bishnoi
(d) Baba Ramdev

4 Which of the following causes imbalance in the environment?
(a) Excess growing of green plants
(b) Using more renewable resources
(c) Biodiversity
(d) Increasing human population

5 Consider the following system of water harvesting

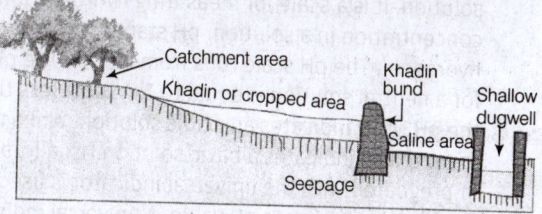

Which of the following systems is depicted by the given figure?
(a) Kulh system (b) Khadin system
(c) Tals (d) Both (b) and (c)

6 Which of the following movements means 'Hug the trees movement'?
(a) Narmada Bachao Andolan (b) Chipko Andolan
(c) Tehri Andolan (d) Biodiversity movement

7 Complete the following by choosing the correct option.
In 1972, the West Bengal Forest Department recognised its failures in reviving the degraded .... forests in the South-Western districts of the state.
(a) Teak (b) Bamboo (c) Sal (d) Rosewood

Answer Key

1.	(c)	2.	(a)	3.	(b)	4.	(d)	5.	(b)
6.	(b)	7.	(c)						

*These questions may or may not be asked in the examination, have been given just for additional practice.

EXPERIMENTS

EXPERIMENT 1

Objective

To determine the pH of the following samples by using pH paper/universal indicator.

(i) Dilute hydrochloric acid
(ii) Dilute sodium hydroxide solution
(iii) Dilute ethanoic acid solution
(iv) Lemon juice
(v) Water
(vi) Dilute hydrogen carbonate solution

Materials Required

Six test tubes, a test tube stand, pH papers, a glass rod, test solution of dil. HCl, dil. NaOH, dil. CH_3COOH, lemon juice, water and dil. HCO_3^-.

Theory

The pH is the measure of the acidic or basic strength of a solution. It is a scale for measuring hydrogen ion concentration in a solution. pH stands for 'power of hydrogen'. The pH scale runs from 0 to 14. The pH value for a neutral solution is equal to 7. A value less than 7 on the pH scale indicates an acidic solution. While the value more than 7 indicates a basic solution. Usually, a paper impregnated with the universal indicator is used for finding the proximate pH value. A universal indicator is a collectively mixture of indicators which show a colour change in a solution, thereby, interpreting how acidic or basic a solution is. In other words, it shows different colours at different pH.

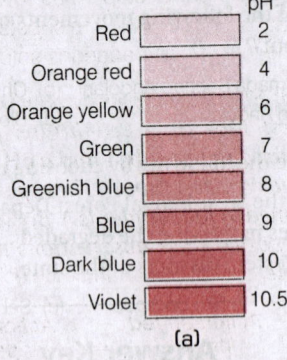

Colour	pH
Red	2
Orange red	4
Orange yellow	6
Green	7
Greenish blue	8
Blue	9
Dark blue	10
Violet	10.5

(a)

Procedure

1. Place six clean test tubes in a test tube stand.
2. Take the solutions of dilute HCl, dilute NaOH, dilute CH_3COOH, lemon juice, water and dilute HCO_3^- separately in five test tubes and label them.
3. Put one or two drops of each test solution on different strips of pH papers, using a glass rod as shown in figure (b). Glass rod used for one sample must be washed with water before used for the other sample.

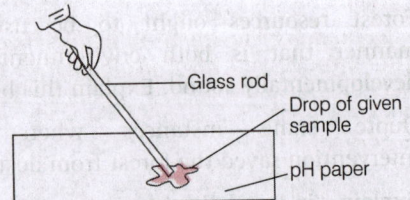

(b) Testing the pH of a sample by putting a drop on pH paper by glass rod

4. Note the pH by comparing the colour appeared on pH paper with those on colour chart as shown in figure (a). Write the colour and pH in the observation table.

Observation Table

S.No.	Sample	Colour produced	Approximate pH	Inference
1.	Dilute HCl			
2.	Dilute NaOH			
3.	Dilute CH_3COOH			
4.	Lemon juice			
5.	Water			
6.	Dilute HCO_3^-			

Results/Conclusions

1. pH of dilute HCl is .... and solution is ....
2. pH of dilute NaOH is .... and solution is ....
3. pH of dilute CH_3COOH is .... and solution is ....
4. pH of lemon juice is .... and it is .... in nature.
5. pH of water is .... and it is......................... .
6. pH of dilute HCO_3^- is .... and its solution is ....

Precautions

1. The test sample solutions should be freshly prepared.
2. Extract fresh juice from lemon in a clean test tube. Use the dilute solution of lemon juice.
3. Glass rod used for one sample should be used for other sample only after washing it with tap or clean water.
4. Do not touch or taste any of the solution.
5. Use separate pH paper for testing different solutions.
6. Match the colour developed on pH paper with the pH chart carefully.

QUESTIONS

1. *A student adds few drops of the universal indicator to a solution of dilute hydrochloric acid in the way shown here.*

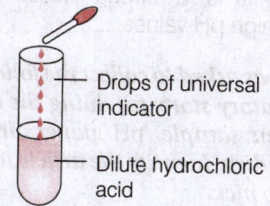

What colour student would observed after the addition of universal indicator?

Ans. The student would observed that the colour of acid changes to red after the addition of universal indicator. This shows that hydrochloric acid is a strong acid with an approximate pH of 2.

2. *In an experiment to test the pH of a given samples using pH paper, four students recorded the following observations:*

Sample taken	pH paper colour turned to
(a) Water	Blue
(b) Dil. HCl	Red
(c) Dil. NaOH	Blue
(d) Dil. ethanoic acid	Orange

Which one of the above observations is incorrect?

Ans. The observation (a) is incorrect as water being neutral in nature, i.e. water is neither acidic nor basic and has a pH value equals 7 at 25°C. So, water does not change the colour of pH paper to blue.

3. *A student observed that the colour of pH paper changes to green, when she dipped it in water. She added a few drops of concentrated hydrochloric acid to the water. Will she observe any change in pH paper? Justify your answer. Change in colour she would observe on the pH paper is*

Ans. Yes, the colour of pH paper would turn to light red.

Reason The colour of pH paper is green in neutral medium, while it is red in acidic medium.

4. *On adding a few drops of universal indicator to three unknown colourless solutions P, Q and R taken separately in three test tubes shown in the following diagrams, a student observed the changes in colour as green in P, red in Q and violet in R.*

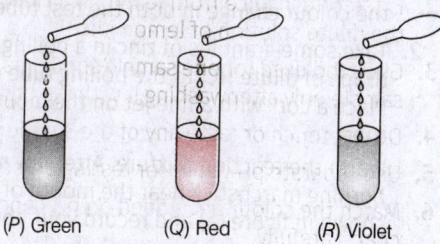

(P) Green (Q) Red (R) Violet

Arrange the solutions in decreasing order of their pH values.

Ans. The approximate pH of solutions are $P = 7$, $Q = 1$ and $R = 14$. Therefore, the decreasing order of pH of the solutions is $R > P > Q$.

5. *Four students were asked to test the pH of four samples as shown under.*

Student	H_2O	CH_3COOH	HCl	NaOH
A	7	1	1	1
B	7	3	1	1
C	7	1	1	13
D	7	3	1	13

Whose result is reported correctly?

Ans. The result reported by student D is correct because H_2O is neutral, its pH will be 7, CH_3COOH is weak acid, its pH will be nearly 3, HCl is strong acid, its pH will be 1 and NaOH is strong base, therefore, its pH will be 13.

6. *Solid sodium bicarbonate was placed on a strip of pH paper. What colour would you observe on a strip of pH paper?*

Ans. The colour of pH paper strip would not change.

Reason pH paper shows colour depending on the hydrogen ion concentration present in solution. As sodium bicarbonate is in a solid state, therefore, it does not contain any hydrogen ions. Hence, it does not give any colour on pH paper strip. Thus to observe the colour on pH paper strip, the substance should be in the form of their aqueons solution.

7. *2 mL of ethanoic acid was taken in test tube I and test tube II. A red litmus paper was introduced in test tube I and a pH paper was introduced in test tube II. The experiment was performed by four students A, B, C and D; and they reported their observations as given in the table.*

Student	Action on red litmus	Action on pH paper
A	Turned blue	Turned pink
B	Remains unchanged	Turned green
C	Turned blue	Turned blue
D	Remains unchanged	Turned pink

Which set of observations are correct?

Ans. The correct observations were given by student D. Red litmus paper remains unchanged in ethanoic acid, while pH paper turns pink in acidic solution.

8. **Test tube I contains bicarbonate solution while test tube II contains lemon juice. On introducing pH paper strips in both of them. What change would be observed?**

Ans. pH paper strip would show blue colour in test tube I and red colour in test tube II.

9. **A sample of soil is mixed with water and allowed to settle. The clear supernatant solution turns the pH paper yellowish orange. What would you add to change the colour of this pH paper to greenish blue?**

Ans. The pH paper shows greenish blue colour for weak bases. Thus, to change the colour of pH paper to greenish blue, aqueous solution of weak bases like magnesium hydroxide would be added to the pH paper.

10. **Four students took the following samples of solution of equal in the laboratory and find their pH. Dilute NaOH solution, dilute HCl, dilute CH_3COOH solution.**

Ans. The pH value would be highest for dilute NaOH solution as it is a strong base. Strong bases possesses high pH values.

11. **A student was asked to collect the following articles from laboratory store, for doing the experiment of pH of given sample. pH paper, dropper, litmus paper, petridish. Identify the article which he is not supposed to pick.**

Ans. Petridish is not supposed to use.

EXPERIMENT 2

Objective
To study the properties of acids and bases (HCl and NaOH) by their reaction with
   (i) litmus solution (blue/red)   (ii) zinc metal
   (iii) solid sodium carbonate

Materials Required
Test tubes, test tube stand, test tube holder, cork, droppers, boiling tubes, burner, flat bottom flask, thistle funnel, beaker, litmus solution (red and blue), zinc granules, solid sodium carbonate, dil. HCl and dil. NaOH.

Theory
- Acids turn blue litmus solution red and do not affect the red litmus solution. As HCl is an acid, it will turn blue litmus solution red.
- HCl reacts with zinc metal, to form a salt, zinc chloride ($ZnCl_2$) and liberates hydrogen (H_2) gas is liberated.

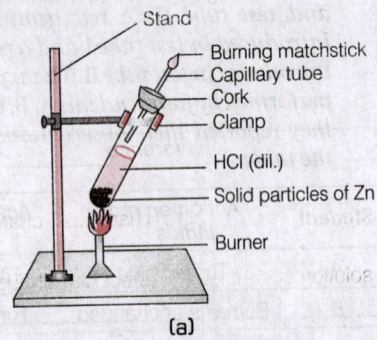

(a)

$$Zn(s) + 2HCl(aq) \longrightarrow ZnCl_2(aq) + H_2(g)\uparrow$$
Zinc Hydrochloric acid Zinc chloride Hydrogen

- Hydrogen gas burns in air with a pop sound.
$$2H_2(g) + O_2(g) \longrightarrow 2H_2O(l)$$

- HCl reacts with sodium carbonate (aqueous/solid) to liberate carbon dioxide (CO_2) gas, which turns lime water milky. When excess of CO_2 is passed through the solution, then the milkiness disappears.

$$Na_2CO_3(s/aq) + 2HCl(aq) \longrightarrow 2NaCl(aq) + H_2O(l) + CO_2(g)$$

$$Ca(OH)_2(aq) + CO_2(g) \longrightarrow \underset{\substack{\text{(milky white ppt.)}\\ \text{Calcium carbonate}}}{CaCO_3(s)} + H_2O(l)$$

$$CaCO_3(s) + H_2O(l) + \underset{\text{in excess amounts}}{CO_2(g)} \longrightarrow$$
$$\underset{\substack{\text{(soluble)}\\ \text{Calcium hydrogen carbonate}\\ \text{(milkiness disappears)}}}{Ca(HCO_3)_2(aq)}$$

- Bases turn red litmus solution blue and do not affect the blue litmus. As NaOH is a base, it will turn red litmus solution blue.
- NaOH reacts with zinc metal, to form sodium zincate and hydrogen gas is liberated, which burns with a pop sound.

$$Zn(s) + 2NaOH(aq) \longrightarrow \underset{\text{Sodium zincate}}{Na_2ZnO_2(aq)} + H_2(g)\uparrow$$

- NaOH does not react with solid or aqueous Na_2CO_3.

Procedure
1. Take 1 mL dilute HCl in two test tubes each. Label them as A and B, and keep them in a test tube stand. Add blue litmus solution with the help of dropper in test tube A and red litmus solution in test tube B. Observe the colour change in both the test tubes.

2. Take some granules of zinc in a boiling tube. Add few drops of dilute HCl to the boiling tube using a dropper. Place a cork with a fine jet on the mouth of the boiling tube.
   Warm the reaction mixture. After few minutes, bring a burning matchstick near the mouth of the fine jet as shown in figure (a) and record your observation.

3. Take a small amount of sodium carbonate (solid or aqueous solution) in a flat bottom flask. (You can also do the experiment in a poly carbonate tube).

   Add dilute HCl to it with the help of a thistle funnel (figures (b) and (c)). Pass the gas evolved through lime water and observe the change in colour of the lime water.

4. Take 1 mL dilute NaOH solution in two test tubes each Label them as C and D and keep them in a test tube stand. Add red litmus solution in test tube D. Observe the change in colour in both the test tubes.

5. Repeat the same procedure from step 2 to step 3 with dilute NaOH and record your observations in observation table.

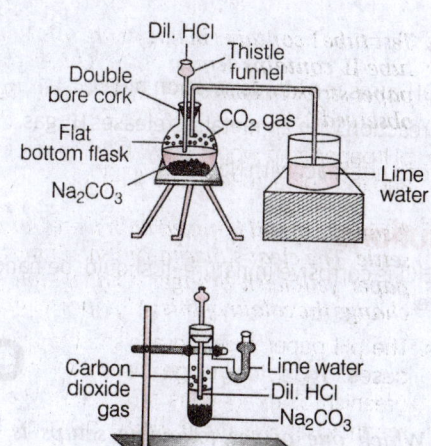

Observation Table for HCl

Experiment	Observation	Inference
Litmus test Add blue litmus solution to test tube A containing dilute HCl. Add red litmus solution to test tube B containing dilute HCl.	Blue litmus solution turns .... in colour of red litmus solution.	HCl has .... character. HCl .... affect red litmus solution.
Reaction with Zn metal Add dilute HCl to Zn granules and warm the contents. Bring a burning matchstick near the jet.	.... gas evolved. The gas evolved burns with a .... sound	Zn reacts with dilute HCl and liberates .... gas.
Na_2CO_3 test Add few drops of dilute HCl to Na_2CO_3.	A colourless, odourless gas is evolved, which turns lime water milky. On passing the gas in excess in lime water, the milkiness disappears.	CO_2 gas is liberated dilute HCl reacts with Na_2CO_3. $2HCl + Na_2CO_3 \longrightarrow 2NaCl + CO_2 + H_2O$

Result

1. HCl turns blue litmus solution red.
2. It releases H_2 gas on reaction with Zn metal.

Observation Table for NaOH

Experiment	Observation	Inference
Litmus test Add red litmus solution to test tube A containing dilute NaOH. Add blue litmus solution to another test tube B containing dilute NaOH.	Red litmus solution turns .... in colour of blue litmus solution.	NaOH has .... character. It .... affect blue litmus solution.
Reaction with Zn metal Add Bring dilute NaOH to Zn granules and warm the reaction mixture. Bring a burning matchstick near the jet.	.... gas evolved. The gas evolved burns with a sound.	Zn reacts with dilute. NaOH and liberates .... gas.
Na_2CO_3 test Add few drops of dilute NaOH to Na_2CO_3.	.... change is observed.	NaOH and Na_2CO_3 does not react.

Result
1. NaOH turns red litmus solution blue.
2. On reaction with Zn metal, it releases H_2 gas.
3. It does not react with Na_2CO_3.

Precautions
1. As HCl is corrosive in nature, it should be handled with care.
2. Use small quantities of Zn and HCl, otherwise large amount of H_2 will be formed, which may cause explosion.
3. Use clean zinc metal, otherwise the reaction will occur very slowly.
4. The apparatus must be airtight in reaction of Zn with HCl, Zn with NaOH and Na_2CO_3 with HCl.
5. Do not touch or taste NaOH, HCl and Na_2CO_3.

QUESTIONS

1. Which one of the following setups is the most appropriate for the evolution of hydrogen gas and its identification?

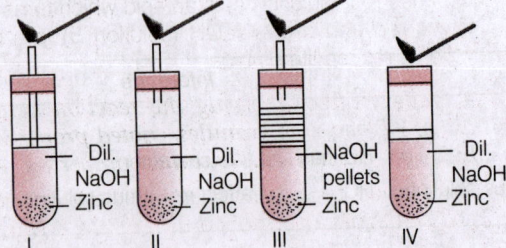

Ans. Set up II

$$Zn(s) + 2NaOH\ (aq) \longrightarrow \underset{\text{Sodium zincate}}{Na_2ZnO_2(aq)} + H_2\uparrow$$

The gas evolved is tested properly such that delivery tube does not dip in the solution.

2. When Zn metal reacts with hydrochloric acid. Which gas is evolved? How would you identify the evolved gas?

Ans. Hydrogen gas is evolved. The gas can be identified by bringing the burning matchstick near the jet, the gas burns with a pop sound.

$$Zn(s) + 2HCl\ (aq) \longrightarrow ZnCl_2(aq) + H_2\uparrow$$

3. Four students were asked by their teacher to arrange the set ups I-IV as given below and identify the gas evolved in each case, if any.

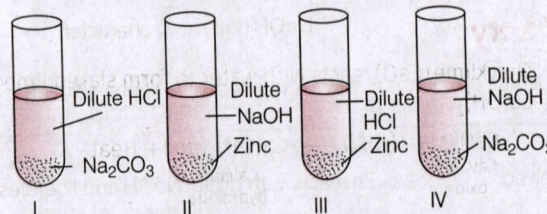

Ans. The gas would be evolved in set ups I to III except in IV. In set up 1, evolved gas is CO_2. In set up 2 and set up, evolved gas is H_2.

4. When dilute hydrochloric acid is added to solid sodium carbonate in a test tube then, what would be observed? Write if any chemical reaction takes place?

Ans. Brisk effervescence takes place due to the evolution of CO_2 gas. The chemical reaction taking place is

$$Na_2CO_3 + 2HCl \longrightarrow 2NaCl + H_2O + CO_2\uparrow$$

5. Four students I, II, III and IV were asked to examine the changes for blue and red litmus paper strips with dil. HCl (solution A) and dil. NaOH (solution B). The following observations were reported by the four students. The sign (–) indicating no colour change.

I

Litmus	A	B
Blue	–	Red
Red	–	Blue

II

Litmus	A	B
Blue	Red	–
Red	–	Blue

III

Litmus	A	B
Blue	Red	Red
Red	Blue	Blue

IV

Litmus	A	B
Blue	Blue	Blue
Red	Red	Red

Which of the above observations is correct?

Ans. The correct observation is observed by Student II.

6. Given below are certain chemical properties of substances:
 I. It turns blue litmus to red.
 II. It turns red litmus to blue.
 III. It reacts with zinc and a gas evolves.
 IV. It reacts with solid sodium carbonate to give brisk effervescence.

Out of these properties, which are shown by dilute hydrochloric acid?

Ans. Properties I, III and IV are shown by dilute hydrochloric acid.

(I) Dilute hydrochloric acid will turn blue litmus to red.

(III) $Zn(s) + 2HCl(aq) \longrightarrow ZnCl_2(aq) + H_2(g)\uparrow$

(IV) $Na_2CO_3(s) + 2HCl(aq) \longrightarrow 2NaCl(aq) + CO_2(g)\uparrow + H_2O(l)$

7. The following pairs of substances are available in the laboratory:

I. *Zinc and dilute hydrochloric acid.*

II. *Zinc and dilute sodium hydroxide solution.*

III. *Sodium bicarbonate and dilute hydrochloric acid.*

Which of these can be used to produce a colourless and odourless gas, which gives a pop sound on burning?

Ans. H_2 gas is evolved in (I) and (II). It is colourless, odourless gas and gives pop sound on burning.

$Zn(s) + 2HCl(aq) \longrightarrow ZnCl_2(aq) + H_2(g)$

Zn will react with sodium hydroxide to form sodium zincate. In this reaction, zinc will not displace sodium from sodium hydroxide, but will displace hydrogen.

$Zn(s) + 2NaOH \longrightarrow \underset{\text{Sodium zincate}}{Na_2ZnO_2} + H_2(g)$

8. *A teacher gave two test tubes, one containing water and the other containing sodium hydroxide solution, to the students and asked them to identify the test tube containing sodium hydroxide solution. How does the students would identify the sodium hydroxide solution?*

Ans. Red litmus paper can be used as red litmus paper turns blue in sodium hydroxide solution potassium hydroxide solution.

9. *Four students I, II, III and IV were asked to examine the changes for blue and red litmus paper strips with dilute HCl (solution A) and dilute NaOH (solution B). The following observations were reported by the 4 students. The sign ...... indicates no colour change.*

	Litmus	A	B	Litmus	A	B
I	Blue	......	red	Blue	red	......
II	Red	......	blue	Red	......	blue
III	Blue	red	red	Blue	blue	blue
IV	Red	blue	blue	Red	red	red

Which student would report the correct observation?

Ans. The correct observation is taken by student III because HCl (solution A) is an acid which turns blue litmus red and dilute NaOH (solution B) is a base which turns red litmus blue.

10. *A student after observing the reaction between dilute HCl on zinc granules, noted properties of hydrogen gas evolved. Write these properties.*

Ans. The evolved hydrogen gas is colourless, odourless and burns with a pop sound.

11. *Which one of the following would you need to identify the gas that evolve when you heat NaOH solution with zinc metal?*

Ans. When a base like NaOH treated with any active metal like Zn, it produces H_2 gas. And the presence of the hydrogen gas can be tested by bringing a burning splinter/matchstick near the gas produced. The gas will burn with a pop sound confirming the presence of hydrogen gas.

$2HaOH(aq) + Zn(s) \longrightarrow Na_2ZnO_2(aq) + H_2\uparrow$

EXPERIMENT 3

Objective

To perform and observe the following reactions and classify them into :
  (i) Combination reaction
  (ii) Decomposition reaction
  (iii) Displacement reaction
  (iv) Double displacement reaction

A. Action of water on quicklime.
B. Action of heat on ferrous sulphate crystals.
C. Iron nails kept in copper sulphate solution.
D. Reaction between sodium sulphate and barium chloride solution.

Materials Required

Quicklime, water, beaker, $FeSO_4$, hard glass tube, two iron nails, $CuSO_4(aq)$, thread, laboratory stand with a clamp, sand paper, single bored cork, sodium sulphate solution, barium chloride solution, test tubes, burner, iron container, boiling tube and test tube holder.

Theory

- Quicklime (CaO) reacts with water to form slaked lime $Ca(OH)_2$.

$\underset{\text{Calcium oxide}}{CaO(s)} + H_2O(l) \longrightarrow \underset{\text{Calcium hydroxide}}{Ca(OH)_2(aq)} + \text{Heat}$

It is a combination reaction as calcium oxide combines with water to form a single product calcium hydroxide solution. A large amount of heat is released during the reaction showing that the reaction is exothermic in nature.

- Ferrous sulphate crystal on heating, gives ferric oxide, sulphur dioxide and sulphur trioxide.

$$2FeSO_4(s) \xrightarrow{Heat} Fe_2O_3(s) + SO_2(g) + SO_3(g)$$
Iron (II) sulphate (light green) — Ferric oxide (reddish brown) — Sulphur dioxide — Sulphur trioxide

It is a decomposition reaction as calcium. As a single reactant breaks down to give simpler products.

- When iron nails are placed in blue coloured copper sulphate solution, then iron displaces copper ions from solution of an aqueous $CuSO_4$ to form $FeSO_4$ and reddish brown copper metal gets deposited.

$$Fe(s) + CuSO_4(aq) \longrightarrow FeSO_4(aq) + Cu(s)$$
Iron — Copper sulphate — Iron (II) sulphate — Copper

It is a single displacement reaction of metal by another metal. Iron is placed above copper in the activity series. Elements placed above in this series are more reactive than those placed below them. Thus, iron is more reactive than copper.

- When sodium sulphate solution is mixed with barium chloride solution, then white precipitate of $BaSO_4(s)$ is formed.

$$BaCl_2(aq) + Na_2SO_4(aq) \longrightarrow BaSO_4 \downarrow + 2NaCl(aq)$$
Barium chloride — Sodium sulphate — Barium sulphate (white ppt.) — Sodium chloride

It is a double displacement reaction. In this reaction, SO_4^{2-} ions from Na_2SO_4 solution are displaced by Cl^- ions and Cl^- ion in $BaCl_2$ are displaced by SO_4^{2-} ions. Therefore, $BaSO_4$ is formed and NaCl remains in the solution.

Procedure
Experiment A
1. Take calcium oxide in an iron container.
2. Slowly add water to it.
3. Observe what happens. Touch the container.

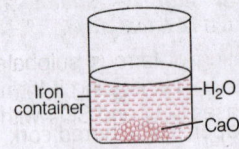

Action of water on quicklime

Experiment B
1. Take 2 g of $FeSO_4$ in a dry boiling tube. Note the colour of ferrous sulphate crystals.
2. Hold the boiling tube with the test tube holder.
3. Heat the boiling tube over the flame of a burner as shown in figure (b) observe the odour of gases evolved and the colour of the crystals after heating..
4. Classify the reaction.

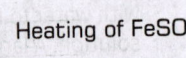

Heating of FeSO

Experiment C
1. Take two test tubes, mark them as A and B. To each test tube, pour about 10 mL of $CuSO_4$ solution.
2. Take two iron nails and clean them with a sand paper.
3. Tie one iron nail with a thread on a laboratory stand and immerse this carefully in $CuSO_4$ solution in test tube A through a bored cork [as shown in fig. [c] for about 15 minutes keep one nail aside for comparison.
4. After 15 minutes, take out the nail from $CuSO_4$ solution and compare the intensity of blue colour of copper sulphate solution before and after the experiments in test tubes A and B.
5. Record your observations and classify the reaction.
   Also, compare the colour of iron nail dipped in copper sulphate solution with one kept a side.

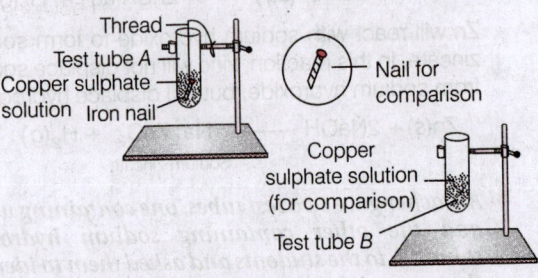

To perform and observe the reaction between iron nail and copper sulphate solution

Experiment D
1. Take 3 mL of sodium sulphate (Na_2SO_4) solution in a test tube and mark it as A. In another test tube, take 3 mL of barium chloride ($BaCl_2$) solution and mark it as B.
2. Transfer the (Na_2SO_4) solution from test tube A to the test tube B containing $BaCl_2$ solution.
3. Mix the two solutions with gentle shaking and leave the mixture undisturbed for some time.
4. Observe the changes in colours of the solutions and record the observation.
5. Classify the type of reaction.

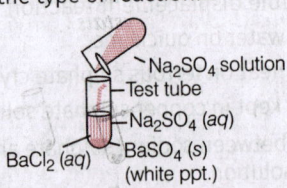

Double displacement reaction between sodium sulphate and barium chloride solutions

All in one Experiments

477

Observation Table

S.No.	Experiment	Observation	Inference
A	Take calcium oxide in an iron container and slowly add water to this.	The hissing sound is produced and solution becomes hot.	$CaO(s) + H_2O(l) \longrightarrow Ca(OH)_2(aq)$ It is a combination reaction.
B	Heat ferrous sulphate solid in a dry boiling tube.	The gases with suffocating smell of burning sulphur are produced and residue is reddish brown.	$2FeSO_4(s) \xrightarrow{\Delta} Fe_2O_3(s) + SO_2(g)\uparrow + SO_3(g)\uparrow$ It is a decomposition reaction.
C	Take aqueous $CuSO_4$ solution in a test tube and immerse iron nail in it with the help of thread.	The colour of solution changes from blue to pale green and reddish brown copper metal is deposited at the nail.	$Fe(s) + CuSO_4(aq) \longrightarrow FeSO_4(aq) + Cu(s)$ It is a displacement reaction.
D	Add sodium sulphate solution taken in a test tube A and add to the barium chloride solution taken in test tube B. Mix and shake the solution mixture gently.	White precipitate is formed.	$Na_2SO_4(aq) + BaCl_2(aq) \longrightarrow BaSO_4(s) + 2NaCl(aq)$ It is a double displacement reaction.

Result

1. Reaction of CaO with H_2O is a combination reaction.
2. Heating of $FeSO_4$ crystals is a decomposition reaction.
3. Reaction of iron nails with $CuSO_4(aq)$ is a displacement reaction.
4. Reaction of $Na_2SO_4(aq)$ solution with $BaCl_2(aq)$ solution is a double displacement reaction.

Precautions

1. Do not touch iron container for long time as the container is very hot to touch.
2. Do not touch the boiling tube, while heating $FeSO_4$.
3. Do not touch or taste $CuSO_4$ solution.
4. Do not touch or taste $BaCl_2$ or Na_2SO_4 solution.
5. Clean the iron nails properly by using sand paper before dipping them in copper sulphate solution.

QUESTIONS

1. What will happen when CO_2 gas is through the product formed by the reaction between CaO and H_2O?

Ans. $\underset{\text{Calcium oxide}}{CaO} + \underset{\text{Water}}{H_2O} \longrightarrow \underset{\substack{\text{Calcium hydroxide}\\\text{(milky)}}}{Ca(OH)_2}$

$\underset{\substack{\text{Calcium hydroxide}\\\text{(milky)}}}{Ca(OH)_2} + \underset{\text{Carbon dioxide}}{CO_2(g)} \longrightarrow \underset{\substack{\text{Calcium carbonate}\\\text{(white)}}}{CaCO_3} + H_2O$

2. Why does the container become hot when water is added to calcium oxide?

Ans. The reaction between calcium oxide and water is highly exothermic in nature, thus during reaction, the container becomes hot.

3. Which is the correct way to observe the effect of heat on ferrous sulphate crystals? Why?

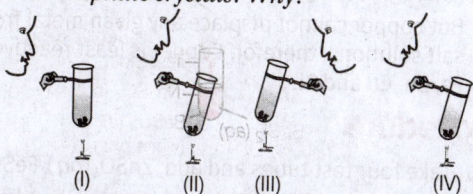

Ans. II is the correct way to observe the effect of heat on $FeSO_4$ crystals. Test tube should be towards the sink, so that the poisonous gases are not inhaled and heating should be done at the tip of flame, which is hottest.

4. What happens when ferrous sulphate are heated in a test tube?

Ans. Heating of ferrous sulphate is a decomposition reaction. On heating it forms a solid Fe_2SO_3 and releases SO_2 and SO_3 with an odour of burning sulphur.

$\underset{\text{Ferrous sulphate}}{2FeSO_4(s)} \xrightarrow{\text{Heat}} \underset{\text{Ferric oxide}}{Fe_2O_3(s)} + \underset{\substack{\text{Sulphur}\\\text{dioxide}}}{SO_2(g)} + \underset{\substack{\text{Sulphur}\\\text{trioxide}}}{SO_3(g)}$

5. Four groups of students were assigned separately the experiment of interaction of iron nail with a solution of copper sulphate. Each group recorded the observations as given below in the table. Which group of students recorded all the observations correctly?

Group of students	Initial colour of solution	Final colour of solution	Change in the iron nail
A	Blue	Colourless	Grey coat
B	Green	Green	Brown coat
C	Blue	Blue	Brown coat
D	Blue	Light green	Brown coat

Ans. The students of group D recorded all the observations correctly.

6. *What type of reaction occurs, when zinc granules are added to blue coloured in copper sulphate solution?*

Ans. When zinc granules added to blue coloured copper sulphate solution, zinc being more reactive than copper displaces copper from copper sulphate solution and forms colourless zinc sulphate solution. It is a displacement reaction.

7. *Identify the following reactions.*
  (i) Reaction of zinc metal with copper sulphate solution.
  (ii) Heating to lead nitrate.
  (iii) Reaction between silver nitrate and sodium chloride.
  (iv) Burning of magnesium in air.

Ans. (i) Reaction of zinc metal with copper sulphate solution is a displacement reaction.
$$Zn(s) + CuSO_4(aq) \longrightarrow ZnSO_4(aq) + Cu(s)$$
(ii) Heating of lead nitrate is a decomposition reaction.
$$2Pb(NO_3)_2(s) \xrightarrow{\Delta} 2PbO(s) + 4NO_2(g) + O_2(g)$$
(iii) Reaction between silver nitrate and sodium chloride is a double displacement reaction.
$$2AgNO_3(aq) + 2NaCl \longrightarrow 2AgCl + 2NaNO_3$$
(iv) Burning of magnesium in air is a combination reaction.
$$2Mg + O_2 \longrightarrow 2MgO(s)$$

8. *Four students were asked to study the reaction between barium chloride and sodium sulphate. They reported their experiments as follows.*
  (i) On mixing the powder of barium chloride and sodium sulphate, the colour of the mixture changes to brown
  (ii) On adding powdered sodium sulphate to barium chloride solution, solution becomes white
  (iii) On adding the powder of barium chloride to sodium sulphate solution, solution turns white
  (iv) On mixing solution of barium chloride and sodium sulphate, white solid substance is formed

  Which of the above a correct report?

Ans. The correct report is of (iv) because on mixing the solutions of both barium chloride and sodium sulphate, white precipitate is formed.
$$BaCl_2(aq) + Na_2SO_4(aq) \longrightarrow \underset{\text{White ppt.}}{BaSO_4(s)} + 2NaCl(aq)$$

EXPERIMENT 4

Objective
(i) To observe the action of Zn, Fe, Cu and Al metals on the following salt solutions
  (a) $ZnSO_4(aq)$ (b) $FeSO_4(aq)$
  (c) $CuSO_4(aq)$ (d) $Al_2(SO_4)_3(aq)$

(ii) To arrange Zn, Fe, Cu and Al metals in the decreasing order of reactivity based on the above results.

Materials Required
Aluminium foil, copper turnings, zinc granules, iron filings, ferrous sulphate solution, copper sulphate solution, zinc sulphate solution, aluminium sulphate solution, test tubes, test tube stand and a piece of sand paper.

Theory
- Different metals have different reactivities towards chemical reagents. Some metals are more reactive than others. The metals which can lose electrons more readily to form positive ions are more reactive. Displacement reactions can be used to find out the relative reactivities of metals. More reactive metals can displace less reactive metals from their salt solutions.

- For example, amongst metals, Zn, Fe, Cu and Al, can displace Zn, Fe, Cu from their salt solutions, therefore it is the most reactive among the metals, Zn, Fe, Cu and Al.
$$2Al(s) + 3ZnSO_4(aq) \longrightarrow Al_2(SO_4)_3(aq) + 3Zn(s)$$
$$2Al(s) + 3FeSO_4(aq) \longrightarrow Al_2(SO_4)_3(aq) + 3Fe(s)$$
$$2Al(s) + 3CuSO_4(aq) \longrightarrow Al_2(SO_4)_3(aq) + 3Cu(s)$$

- Zn can displace Fe and Cu from their salt solutions, therefore zinc is more reactive than Fe and Cu.
$$Zn(s) + CuSO_4(aq) \longrightarrow ZnSO_4(aq) + Cu(s)$$
$$Zn(s) + FeSO_4(aq) \longrightarrow ZnSO_4(aq) + Fe(s)$$

- Fe can displace copper from copper sulphate solution, therefore it is more reactive than copper.
$$Fe(s) + CuSO_4(aq) \longrightarrow FeSO_4(aq) + Cu(s)$$

- But copper cannot displace any given metal from their salt solutions, therefor, Copper is least reactive among Fe, Zn, Cu and Al.

Procedure
1. Take four test tubes and add $ZnSO_4(aq)$, $FeSO_4(aq)$, $CuSO_4(aq)$ and $Al_2(SO_4)_3(aq)$ in to then and mark them as A, B, C and keep them in a test tube stand.
2. Add a piece of aluminium foil in all of them.

3. Observe the changes in colour, metal deposited and record the observation in observation table.
4. Repeat the procedure from steps 1 to 3 for zinc granules, iron filings and copper turnings separately by dipping them in fresh salt solutions of metals and observe for displacement reactions.

(iii) Fe is unable to displace Zn from its salt solution, whereas Zn is able to displace Fe from its salt solution, therefore Zn is more reactive than Fe.

2. The decreasing order of reactivity for these metals is

$$\underset{\text{Most reactive}}{Al} > Zn > Fe > \underset{\text{Least reactive}}{Cu}$$

Result

1. The action of Zn, Fe, Cu and Al metals on $ZnSO_4(aq)$, $FeSO_4(aq)$, $CuSO_4(aq)$ and $Al_2(SO_4)_3(aq)$ solutions are as follows:
   (i) Al is able to displace Fe, Cu and Zn from their salt solutions, therefore Al is most reactive among these.
   (ii) Cu is unable to displace any metal among Al, Fe and Zn from their salt solutions, therefore Cu is least reactive.

Precautions

1. Clean all metals with sand paper.
2. Some may react slowly, therefore observe the changes carefully.
3. Do not touch or taste the chemicals.
4. Wash the test tubes after every set of observation of interacting of a particular metal with four salt solutions.
5. Wash your hands with soap, if you touch any solution.

Observation Table

Experiment	Observation	Inference
Add Al metal in $ZnSO_4$ solution.	No change in colour of the solution and greyish Zn metal got deposited on Al metal.	Al is more reactive than Zn. (Al displaces Zn from its salt solution.)
Add Al metal in $FeSO_4$ solution.	The pale green colour of solution becomes colourless and greyish black iron metal got deposited on Al metal.	Al is more reactive than Fe. (Al displaces Fe from its salt solution.)
Add Al metal in $CuSO_4$ solution.	The blue colour of solution becomes colourless and reddish brown copper metal got deposited on Al metal.	Al is more reactive than Cu. (Al displaces Cu from its salt solution.)
Add Al metal in $Al_2(SO_4)_3$ solution.	No reaction takes place.	Al cannot react with $Al_2(SO_4)_3$. (A metal cannot displace itself from its salt solution.)
Add Zn metal in $ZnSO_4$ solution.	No reaction takes place.	Zn does not react with $ZnSO_4$ solution.
Add Zn metal in $FeSO_4$ solution.	The pale green colour of solution becomes colourless and greyish black Fe metal got deposited on Zn metal.	Zn is more reactive than iron. (Zn displaces Fe from its salt solution.)
Add Zn metal in $CuSO_4$ solution.	Blue solution becomes colourless and copper metal (reddish brown) got deposited on Zn metal.	Zn is more reactive than Cu. (Zn displaces Cu from its salt solution.)
Add Zn metal in $Al_2(SO_4)_3$ solution.	No reaction takes place.	Zn is less reactive than Al.
Add Fe metal in $FeSO_4(aq)$ solution.	No reaction takes place.	Iron does not react with $FeSO_4$.
Add Fe metal in $ZnSO_4(aq)$ solution.	No reaction takes place.	Iron is less reactive than Zn.
Add Fe metal in $CuSO_4(aq)$ solution.	Reddish brown copper metal got deposited and blue colour of solution becomes light green.	Iron is more reactive than copper.
Add Fe metal in $Al_2(SO_4)_3$ solution.	No reaction takes place.	Iron is less reactive than Al.
Add Cu metal in $CuSO_4$ solution.	No reaction takes place.	Copper does not react with $CuSO_4$.
Add Cu metal in $FeSO_4$ solution.	No reaction takes place.	Copper is less reactive than iron.
Add Cu metal in $ZnSO_4$ solution.	No reaction takes place.	Copper is less reactive than Zn.
Add Cu metal in $Al_2(SO_4)_3$ solution.	No reaction takes place.	Copper is less reactive than Al.

QUESTIONS

1. *Zinc granules were added to zinc sulphate, copper sulphate, aluminium sulphate and iron sulphate solution as shown below.*

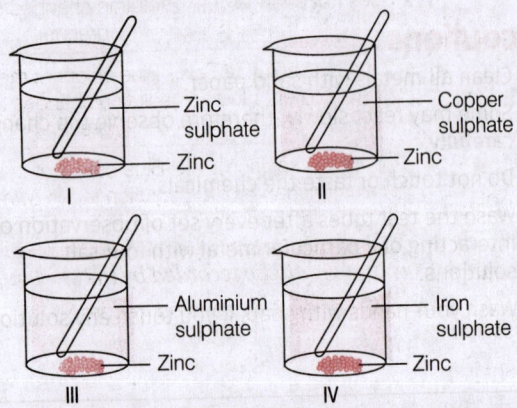

In which beakers would you observe the deposition of metal on zinc?

Ans. In beakers II and IV, zinc will displace copper from copper sulphate solution and iron from iron sulphate solution respectively, as zinc is more reactive than copper and iron.

2. *A student puts one iron nail each in four test tubes containing solutions of zinc sulphate, aluminium sulphate, copper sulphate and iron sulphate. In which solution, a reddish brown coating was observed on the surface of iron nail?*

Ans. Reddish brown coating is formed due to the formation of copper metal, which is possible when iron nail is dipped in $CuSO_4(aq)$ because iron is more reactive than copper (based on reactivity series of metal).

$$Fe(s) + CuSO_4(aq) \longrightarrow FeSO_4(aq) + Cu(s)$$
Iron   Blue   Pale green   Reddish brown

3. *A student takes four test tubes containing solutions of different colours marked I, II, III and IV as shown below. Which test tubes could be containing copper sulphate solution and ferrous sulphate solution?*

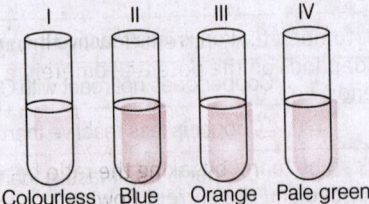

Ans. Test tubes II and IV, respectively.

4. *A student performed the following four experiments:*

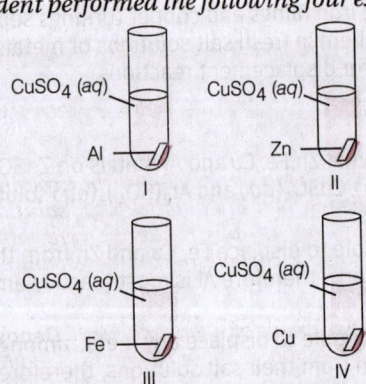

In which experiment(s) would he find the formation of a solid deposition?

Ans. In experiments I, II and III, he would observe the solid deposition because Al, Zn and Fe are more reactive than Cu.

5. *A more reactive metal displaces a less reactive metal from the aqueous solution of the latter. From the following sets tell which one represents a correct picture of both the possible (✓) reactions and impossible (✗) reactions between metals and the solutions of different salts?*

Metal	$Al_2(SO_4)_3$	$CuSO_4$	$FeSO_4$	$ZnSO_4$
Al	✗	✓	✓	✓
Cu	✓	✗	✗	✗
Fe	✓	✓	✗	✗
Zn	✗	✓	✗	✓

Ans. Al represents the correct picture of possible and impossible reactions.

6. *Zinc pieces were placed in each of the four test tubes containing different salt solutions as shown below:*

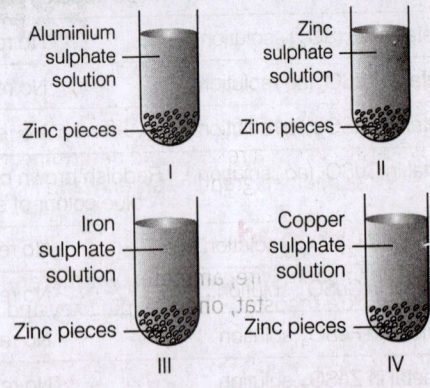

In which solutions, a change in colour would be observed?

Ans. The colour change will take place in test tubes III and IV as zinc is more reactive than iron as well as copper.

$$Zn(s) + \underset{\text{(Pale green)}}{FeSO_4(aq)} \longrightarrow \underset{\text{(Colourless)}}{ZnSO_4(aq)} + Fe(s)$$

$$Zn(s) + \underset{\text{(Blue)}}{CuSO_4(aq)} \longrightarrow \underset{\text{(Colourless)}}{ZnSO_4(aq)} + Cu(s)$$

7. *Students in a lab were assigned the experiment to study the reaction of Zn with FeSO₄ solution. The following set of observations were obtained. Identify the set, where all the observations were correct.*

Set	Initial colour of solution	Final colour of solution	Deposits if any
(a)	Colourless	Pale green	Black
(b)	Pale green	Colourless	Black
(c)	Colourless	Colourless	Red
(d)	Pale green	Blue	Black

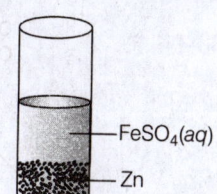

Ans. FeSO₄ is pale green in colour, when Zn is added (which is more reactive than Fe), then it displaces Fe as black precipitates and the solution becomes colourless due to the formation of ZnSO₄.

8. *Aluminium sulphate and copper sulphate solutions were taken in two test tubes I and II, respectively. A few pieces of iron filings were then added to both the solutions. The four students A, B, C and D recorded their observations in the form of a table as given.*

Student	Aluminium sulphate solution (I)	Copper sulphate solution (II)
A	Colourless solution changes to light green.	Blue colour of the solution is retained.
B	Colourless solution does not change.	Blue colour of the solution changes to green.
C	Colourless solution changes to light blue.	Blue colour of the solution changes to green.
D	Colourless solution remains unchanged.	Blue colour of the solution fades away.

Which of the above represents the correct set of observations that would be recorded by the student?

Ans. The correct set of observations is recorded by the student B.

Reason

(i) Iron does not react with aluminium sulphate, $Al_2(SO_4)_3$ solution because Fe is less reactive than Al.

(ii) Blue colour of copper sulphate solution changes to green colour of iron sulphate because Fe is more reactive than Cu.

$$\underset{\text{(Blue)}}{Fe + CuSO_4} \longrightarrow \underset{\text{(Green)}}{FeSO_4 + Cu}$$

9. *Iron nails were dipped in a blue coloured solution kept in a test tube. After half hour, it was observed that the colour of the solution had changed. Identify the solution in the test tube that of*

Ans. The blue colour of the solution is of CuSO₄ and its colour is changed because iron is more reactive than copper therefore, it can displace Cu from CuSO₄ solution.

$$\underset{\substack{\text{(blue)}\\\text{Copper sulphate}}}{Fe(s) + CuSO_4(aq)} \longrightarrow \underset{\substack{\text{(pale green)}\\\text{Iron sulphate}}}{FeSO_4(aq)} + \underset{\substack{\text{(reddish brown)}\\\text{Copper}}}{Cu(s)}$$

EXPERIMENT 5

Objective

To study the dependence of potential difference (V) on current (I) flowing across a resistor and determine its resistance (R). Also, plot a graph between V and I.

Apparatus Required

Nichrome or manganin wire, ammeter, voltmeter, battery eliminator, rheostat, one-way plug key and connecting wires.

Specific Objective

1. To learn how to define the steady current.
2. To understand the need for a battery to have current.
3. To learn about the opposition to the flow of current.
4. To learn how to use eliminator, rheostat, voltmeter and ammeter.
5. To draw V-I graph to find resistance.

Theory

At constant temperature, current flowing through a conductor depends on the potential difference applied across its ends, i.e.

$$I \propto V \Rightarrow V = IR$$

Resistance can be found by taking the ratio between the potential applied and the current flowing as a result of it. Potential difference and current can be measured by using voltmeter and ammeter in volt and ampere respectively.

Procedure

1. Set up the circuit arrangement as shown in circuit diagram or apparatus arrangement.
2. Note the least count of the ammeter and voltmeter.
3. Find zero error, if any of the ammeter and voltmeter have record it in the Table A.
4. Before switching on the battery eliminator, you should ensure that the positive terminals of ammeter and voltmeter must be connected to the positive terminal of the battery eliminator and rheostat, respectively. Nichrome/manganin wire is connected between the two negative terminals of the voltmeter, i.e. parallel across voltmeter.
5. Plug the key/switch on the battery eliminator and adjust the rheostat by sliding its variable terminal till the ammeter shows a reading. Ammeter shows the current passing through the nichrome wire, whereas voltmeter shows the potential difference across the nichrome wire.
6. Record your observation in table B, i.e. readings of ammeter and voltmeter. Switch off the battery eliminator for a moment.
7. Repeat the steps 5 and 6 for the different values of current.
8. Tabulate all the observations in the observation Table B and find the ratio of $\frac{V}{I}$ for each set of observations. Find mean value of R.
9. Plot a graph by taking I along X-axis and V along Y-axis.

Circuit Diagram

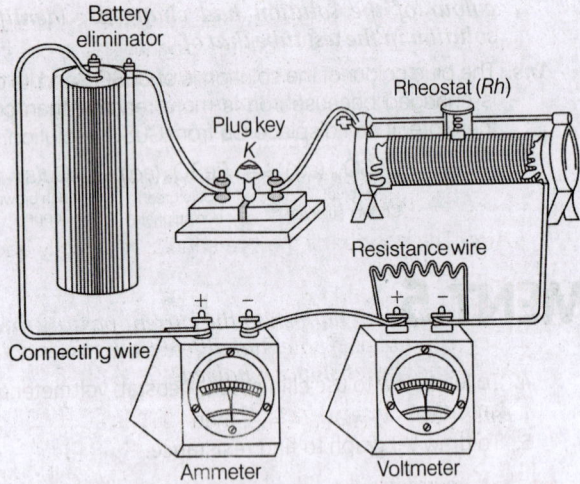
Diagram of apparatus arrangement

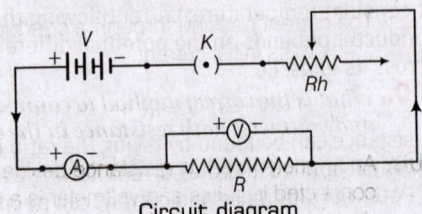
Circuit diagram

Observation Table

Table A for ammeter and voltmeter

	Ammeter (A)	Voltmeter (V)
1. Range	....	....
2. Least count	....	....
3. Zero error	...... e_1	.... e_2 ....
4. Zero correction	$-e_1$	$-e_2$

Table B for reading of ammeter and voltmeter

S.No.	Voltmeter reading V in volt (V)	Ammeter reading I in ampere (A)	$R = \frac{V}{I}$ in ohm (Ω)

Mean value of R = ... Ω.

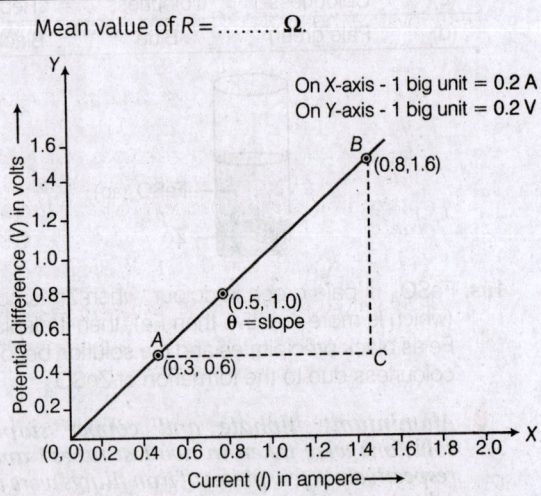
Graph between potential difference and current

Calculation

1. Find the ratio of V and I for each corrected set of observation. Mean value of R = ... Ω.
2. Plot the graph as shown between the potential difference V along Y-axis (scale: 10 small divisions = 0.2 V) and the current I along X-axis (scale: 10 small divisions = 0.2 A) as shown.
3. Find the slope of line.
   Slope of line $AB = \frac{BC}{AC} = \frac{V_2 - V_1}{I_2 - I_1}$.

   ∴ Resistance of nichrome wire is given by
   Slope of line $AB = \tan\theta = ... \Omega$.

   Inverse of the slope of V - I curve gives conductance (σ).

Result

1. Straight line nature of the *V-I* graph shows that as the current flowing through the resistance (nichrome wire) increases, the potential difference across it increases linearly, i.e. both are directly proportional to each other. This proves the Ohm's law graphically.
2. The resistance of nichrome (or manganin) wire obtained from the graph is equal (or approximately equal) to the mean value of the slope of *V-I* graph in different situations. It also verifies the Ohm's law.
3. The resistance of the given wire = ... Ω.

Precautions

1. The ends of connecting wires should be neat and clean.
2. All connections should be tight.
3. Never allow the current to flow in the resistance wire for a longer time, to avoid heating effect (as $R \propto T$).
4. Range of voltmeter should be greater than the applied voltage.
5. A low resistance ranged rheostat must be used.
6. The area of cross-section of the connecting wire should be large because it offers negligible resistance.

QUESTIONS

1. *In Ohm's law experiment, what are the physical quantity/quantities which is/are to be kept constant while doing experiment?*

Ans. Physical quantities like temperature and pressure should remain constant.

2. *Three students X, Y and Z while performing the experiment to study the dependence of current on the potential difference across a resistor, connects the ammeter (A), the battery (B), the key (K) and the resistor (R) in series, in the following three different orders.* **CBSE 2012**
$X \to B, K, R, A, B$; $Y \to B, A, K, R, B$; $Z \to B, R, K, A, B$
Who has connected them in the correct order?

Ans. Ammeter, resistor and the key are always connected in any order in series with the battery.

3. *What is the use of rheostat in a circuit to verify ohm's law?*

Ans. The rheostat is used in the circuit to change the magnitude of the current.

4. *Name the device which is used to maintain constant potential difference between two points of a conductor.*

Ans. When the cell is connected to a conducting circuit element, then the potential difference sets the charge in motion in the conductor.

5. *You are given four voltmeters of given ranges. These are voltmeter with range of 0-1 V, voltmeter with range of 0-3 V, voltmeter with range of 0-4 V, voltmeter with range of 0-5 V. What is the correct choice of voltmeter for doing the experiment with a battery of 4.5 V?*

Ans. The correct choice is 0-5 V as the battery reading is 4.5 V and it should lie in this range.

6. *The voltmeter, ammeter and resistance shown in the circuit have been checked to be correct. On plugging the key, the ammeter reads 0.9 A but the voltmeter reads zero. What could be the reason for this?*

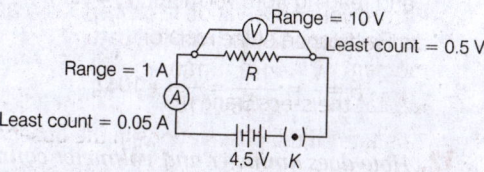

Ans. It is so because of the loose connections of the voltmeter.

7. *In this experiment, it is advised to take out the key from the plug when the observations are not being taken. Why?*

Ans. To avoid unnecessary heating of wire, it is advised to take out the key from the plug when the observations are not being taken because current produces heating effect and the resistance increases with the increase in temperature.

8. *While taking the reading of meter, what should be the position of eye?*

Ans. The position of the eye should be directly above the pointer.

9. *What will happen to the current passing through a conductor, if potential difference across it is doubled and the resistance is halved?*

Ans. As $V' = 2V, R' = \dfrac{R}{2}$, then

current, $I' = \dfrac{V'}{R'} = \dfrac{2V}{R/2} = 4I$ $\left[\because \dfrac{V}{R} = I\right]$

The current passing through a conductor will be four times to its initial current.

10. *What is the correct method to connect the ammeter and voltmeter with resistance in the circuit?*

Ans. An ammeter is a low resistance device, so it is always connected in series and voltmeter is a high resistance device, so it is connected in parallel.

11. The current flowing through a resistor connected in an electric circuit and the potential difference applied across its ends are shown in figure below.

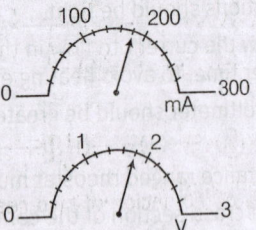

What will be the value of the resistance of the resistor?

Ans. Reading from ammeter (I) = 180 mA = 0.18 A,

and reading from voltmeter (V) = 1.8 V

∴ Resistance of the resistor,

$$R = \frac{V}{I} = \frac{1.8}{0.18} = \frac{180}{18} = 10\, \Omega$$

12. How does ammeter and voltmeter connected with resistance in the circuit to verify Ohm's law?

Ans. In a circuit, ammeter should be connected in series, while voltmeter in parallel.

13. In an experiment on studying the dependence of the current I flowing through a given resistor on the potential difference V applied across it, a student has to change the value of the current. For doing this, what should he change?

Ans. If we change the number of cells in electric circuit, the potential difference will change and as a result current flowing in the circuit changes.

14. If a student while studying the dependence of current on the potential difference keeps the circuit closed for a long time to measure the current and potential difference, then how will resistance affected?

Ans. If the circuit is closed for a long time, then current flows in it for a long time which results that the resistor is heated.

15. Draw a circuit diagram to show experimental set up for verification of Ohm's law.

Ans. Circuit diagram to show experimental set up for verification of Ohm's law is shown below:

16. The rest positions of the pointers of a milliammeter and voltmeter not in use are as shown in Fig A. When a student uses these in his experiment, then the reading of pointers are in position shown in Fig B. Calculate the corrected value of current and voltage in this experiment.

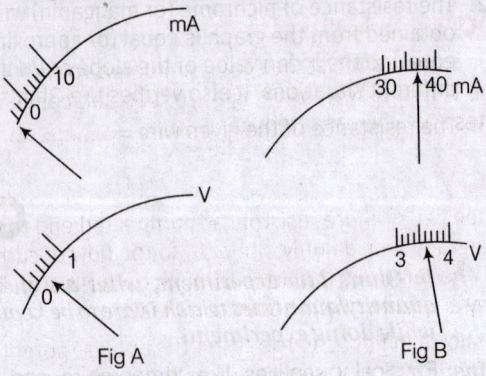

Fig A Fig B

Ans. ∵ Current, I = 30.4 mA

Voltage, $V = 3.3 - 0.2 = 3.1$ V

[∵ there is an error of 0.2 V at rest]

17. Electric current I and potential difference V are shown in the following figures across a resistor
(i) What are the reading of voltmeter and ammeter in the given figure.
(ii) Calculate resistance

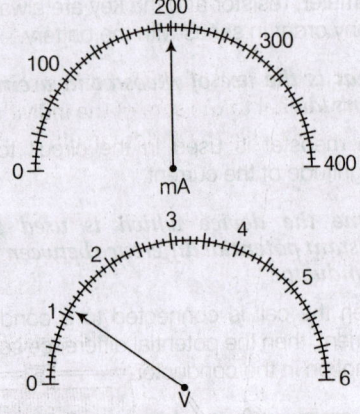

Ans. (i) ∵ Reading of volmeter = 1.1 V

and reading of ammeter = 200 mA

(ii) ∴ Resistance, $R = \frac{V}{I}$

$$= \frac{1.1\, V}{200\, mA}$$

$$= \frac{1.1\, V}{200 \times 10^{-3}\, A}$$

$$= \frac{1.1}{0.2}\, \Omega = 5.5\, \Omega$$

All in one Experiments

EXPERIMENT 6

Objective
To determine the equivalent resistance of two resistors when connected in series.

Apparatus Required
Two standard resistance coils, ammeter, voltmeter, one-way plug key, low resistance rheostat, connecting wires and cell or battery eliminator.

Theory
When two or more resistors are connected end to end, then they provide only one path to the flow of current, i.e. the same current flows through each resistor. Then, they are said to be in series combination.

As shown in figure. (b), let V be the applied potential difference by a DC source across the combination of unknown resistors R_1 and R_2.

If V_1 and V_2 be the potential differences measured by the voltmeters across each resistor, then

$$V = V_1 + V_2 \quad \ldots(i)$$

According to Ohm's law, for each resistor,

$$V_1 = IR_1, V_2 = IR_2$$

and

$$V = IR_S \quad \ldots(ii)$$

From Eqs. (i) and (ii), we get

$$IR_S = IR_1 + IR_2$$

$$\Rightarrow R_S = R_1 + R_2$$

Thus, the equivalent resistance (R_S) of the series combination is equal to the sum of the individual resistance connected in the series circuit.

Circuit Diagram

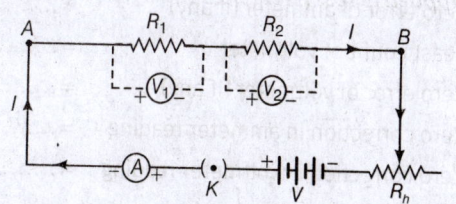

(b) Series combination of two resistors

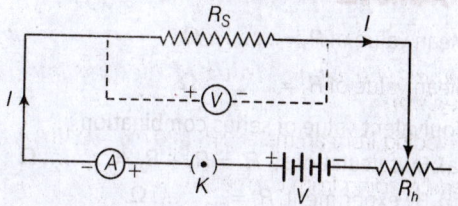

(c) Equivalent resistance in series combination

Procedure
1. Connect the circuit in a similar manner as shown in circuit diagram in figure (b) or apparatus arrangement in figure (a) with one of the unknown resistors.
2. Find the values of two given unknown resistors one by one.
3. Tabulate atleast three readings of the ammeter and voltmeter separately for the given unknown resistors by changing the sliding contact of the rheostat.
4. By using Ohm's law, find the value of each resistance, let it be R_1 and R_2.
5. Connect both the resistors in series combination between the two terminals of the voltmeter as shown in figure (b).
6. Plug the key and take the readings of ammeter and voltmeter.
7. Repeat the step 6 three times by changing the position of the sliding contact of the rheostat.
8. Tabulate the readings and find the ratio of V and I. It will give the equivalent resistance of the combination as shown in figure (c).

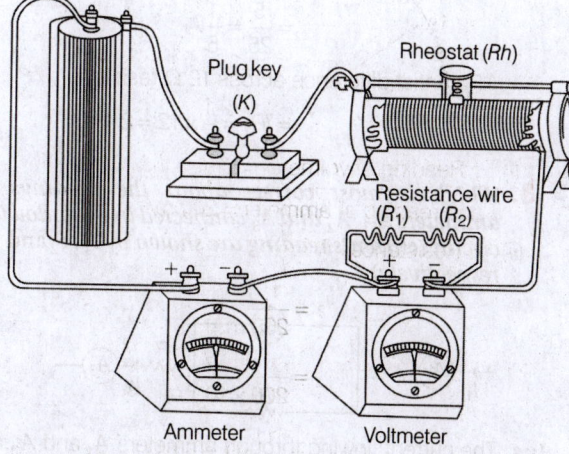

(a) Arrangement diagram of apparatus

Observation Table

Resistor used	Number of observations	Voltmeter reading (volt)	Ammeter reading (ampere)	$R = \dfrac{V}{I}$ (ohm)	Mean value of resistance (ohm)
R_1	(a)				
	(b)				
	(c)				
R_2	(a)				
	(b)				
	(c)				
$R_S = R_1 + R_2$	(a)				
	(b)				
	(c)				

485

Observations

1. Least count of ammeter = ... A
2. Zero error of ammeter (if any) = ... A
3. Least count of voltmeter = ... V
4. Zero error of voltmeter (if any) = ... V
5. Zero correction in ammeter reading = ... A
6. Zero correction in voltmeter reading = ... V

Calculations

1. Mean value of R_1 = ... Ω
2. Mean value of R_2 = ... Ω

   Equivalent value of series combination
   (a) By calculations, $R'_S = R_1 + R_2$ = ... Ω
   (b) By experiment, R_S = ... Ω.
   Difference in both values
   $= R_S - R'_S$ = ... Ω

Result

1. There is a close agreement between the calculated values and the value obtained by the experiment. Hence, $R_S = R_1 + R_2$ is verified.
2. The equivalent resistance R_S = ... Ω.

Percentage Error

It can be found by using the following relation:

Percentage error

$$= \frac{\text{Experimental value} - \text{Calculated value}}{\text{Calculated value}} \times 100$$

$$= \frac{R_S - R'_S}{R'_S} \times 100 = ...\%$$

It shows percentage error is within experimental error.

Precautions

1. Remove the dust and other insulating particles from the ends of connecting wire by rubbing it with sand paper.
2. All the connections should be tight and properly done as per circuit diagram.
3. Take out the plug from the plug key in between the two observations.
4. A low resistance rheostat should be used in the circuit to obtain a large variation in current.
5. A thick copper connecting wire should be used in the circuit.
6. The positive terminals of the ammeter and voltmeter must be connected to the positive terminal of the battery or battery eliminator.
7. Never connect the two terminals of the cell without any resistance.

QUESTIONS

1. *While doing the experiment, on finding the equivalent resistance of two resistors connected in series, three students A, B and C set up their circuits as shown below:*

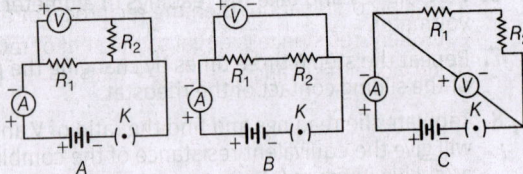

Which of the figure(s) shows a correct set-up?

Ans. Students B and C are correctly connected.

2. *Two resistors are connected in series as shown in the diagram.*

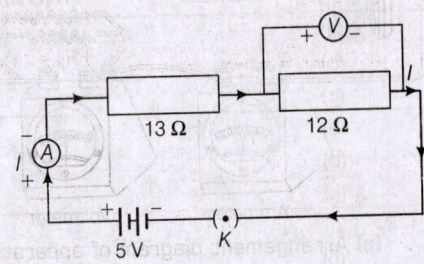

What will be the potential difference across 12 Ω resistor? **CBSE 2015**

Ans. Equivalent resistance of two resistors of resistances 13 Ω and 12 Ω is
$R = R_1 + R_2 = 13 + 12 = 25\ \Omega$

According to Ohm's law, current in circuit is

$$I = \frac{V}{R}$$

$$= \frac{5}{25} = \frac{1}{5}\ A$$

$\therefore$ Potential difference across 12 Ω resistor

$$= IR_2 = \frac{1}{5} \times 12 = 2.4\ V$$

3. *Which is most correct about the readings of ammeters A_1, A_2 and A_3 connected in the following circuit (currents reading are shown by I_1, I_2 and I_3, respectively)*

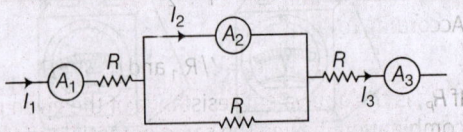

Ans. The current flowing through ammeters A_1 and A_3 are same.

4. The diagram shows a network of four resistors which is connected to an electric source. Identify the resistors which are connected in series in this network.

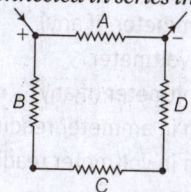

Ans. The resistors B, C and D are connected in series.

5. To determine the equivalent resistance of two resistors when connected in series, a student arranged the circuit components as shown in the diagram. But he did not succeed to achieve the objective.

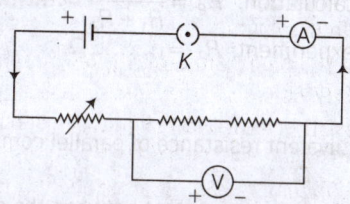

What mistake has been committed by him in setting up the circuit?

Ans. Because positive terminal of ammeter must be connected with positive terminal of cell and negative terminal of an ammeter must be connected to negative terminal of a cell.

6. A student arranges the following circuit to get equivalent resistance of a series combination of two resistors R_1 and R_2.

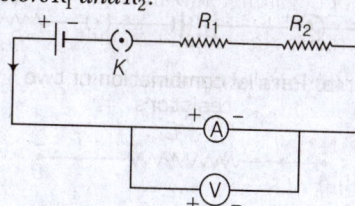

Does ammeter and voltmeter give correct reading?

Ans. The voltmeter should be connected across the components of R_1 and R_2 to give correct reading for potential difference.

7. What will be the total voltages across the series combination of resistor?

Ans. Total voltages across the series combination of resistor is sum of the voltage drop across each resistor.

EXPERIMENT 7

Objective
To determine the equivalent resistance of two resistors when connected in parallel.

Apparatus Required
Two standard resistance coils, ammeters, voltmeter, one-way plug key, a low resistance rheostat, connecting wires and cell or battery eliminator.

Theory
An arrangement of the resistors in which number of resistances are connected between two common points in such a way that the potential difference across each resistance is equal to the applied voltage, then such an arrangement is called parallel combination.

As shown in figure (b), two resistances R_1 and R_2 are connected between two points A and B in parallel combination. Let the potential difference applied by the DC source to this combination be V. Let I_1 and I_2 be the currents measured by ammeters, connected in series with each resistor, R_1 and R_2 respectively, then

$$I = I_1 + I_2 \quad \ldots(i)$$

According to Ohm's law,

$$I_1 = V/R_1 \text{ and } I_2 = V/R_2 \quad \ldots(ii)$$

If R_P, is the equivalent resistance of the given parallel combination, having the same potential difference as the applied potential, then

$$I = V/R_P \quad \ldots(iii)$$

From Eq. (i), we get

$$\frac{V}{R_P} = \frac{V}{R_1} + \frac{V}{R_2}$$

$$\Rightarrow \frac{1}{R_P} = \frac{1}{R_1} + \frac{1}{R_2} \Rightarrow R_P = \frac{R_1 R_2}{R_1 + R_2}$$

Therefore, when a number of resistances are connected in a parallel combination, then the reciprocal of the equivalent resistance is equal to the sum of reciprocals of individual resistance.

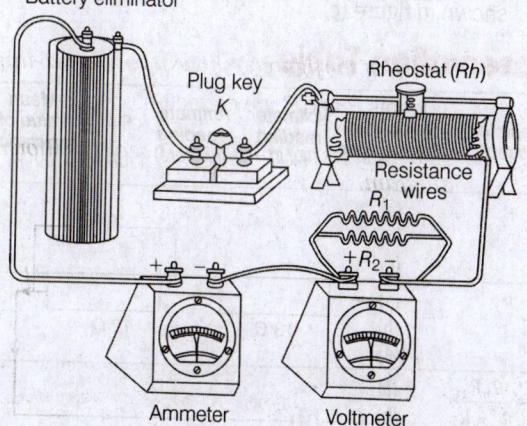

(a) Arrangement diagram of apparatus

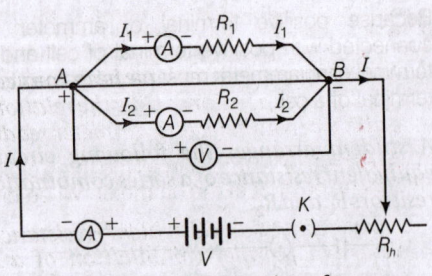

(b) Parallel combination of two resistors

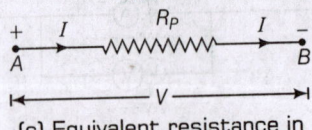

(c) Equivalent resistance in parallel combination

Procedure

1. Connect the circuit in a similar manner as shown in circuit diagram in figure (b) or apparatus arrangement in figure (a) with one of the unknown resistors.
2. Find the values of all given unknown resistors by adopting the procedure of experiment to determine the equivalent resistance of two resistors when connected in series.
3. Tabulate atleast three readings of the ammeter and voltmeter separately for the given unknown resistors by changing the sliding contact of the rheostat.
4. By using Ohm's law, find the value of each resistance let it be R_1 and R_2.
5. Connect the given resistors in parallel combination between the two terminals of the voltmeter as shown in figure (b).
6. Plug the key and take the readings of ammeter and voltmeter.
7. Repeat the step 6 three times by changing the position of the sliding contact of the rheostat.
8. Tabulate the readings and find the ratio of V and I. It will give the equivalent resistance of the combination as shown in figure (c).

Observation Table

Resistor used	Number of observations	Voltmeter reading (volt)	Ammeter reading (ampere)	$R = \dfrac{V}{I}$ (ohm)	Mean value of resistance (ohm)
R_1	(a) (b) (c)				
R_2	(a) (b) (c)				
$R_P = \dfrac{R_1 R_2}{R_1 + R_2}$	(a) (b) (c)				

Observations

1. Least count of ammeter = ...A
2. Zero error of ammeter (if any) = ...A
3. Least count of voltmeter = ...V
4. Zero error of voltmeter (if any) = ...V
5. Zero correction in ammeter reading = ...A
6. Zero correction in voltmeter reading = ...V

Calculations

1. Mean value of R_1 = ... Ω.
2. Mean value of R_2 = ... Ω.

Equivalent value of parallel combination:

(a) By calculation, $R'_P = \dfrac{R_1 R_2}{R_1 + R_2} = ...\Omega$.

(b) By experiment, $R_P = ...\Omega$.

Results

1. The equivalent resistance of parallel combination = ...Ω
2. There is a close agreement between the calculated value and the value obtained by the experiment.
Hence, $\dfrac{1}{R_P} = \dfrac{1}{R_1} + \dfrac{1}{R_2}$ is verified.

Percentage Error

Percentage error

$= \dfrac{\text{Experimental value} - \text{Calculated value}}{\text{Calculated value}} \times 100$

$= \dfrac{R_P - R'_P}{R'_P} \times 100 = ...\%$

It shows that percentage error is within the experimental error.

Precautions

1. Remove the dust and other insulating particles from the ends of connecting wire by rubbing it with sand paper.
2. All the connections should be tight and properly done as per circuit diagram.
3. Take out the plug from the plug key in between the two observations.
4. A low resistance rheostat should be used in the circuit to obtain a large variation in current.
5. A thick copper connecting wire should be used in the circuit.
6. The positive terminals of the ammeter and voltmeter must be connected to the positive terminal of the battery or battery eliminator.
7. Never connect the two terminals of the cell without any resistance.

QUESTIONS

1. *A student uses a battery of adjustable voltage 0-6 V. She has to perform an experiment to determine the equivalent resistance of two resistors when connected in parallel. Two resistors are of values $3\,\Omega$ and $5\,\Omega$. What will be the best choice of combination of voltmeter and ammeter to be used in the experiment?* **CBSE 2015**

Ans. Applied voltage of range 0-6 V lies within the voltmeter range 0-10 V and current through each resistor lies in the ammeter range 0-2 A.

2. *Four ammeters A_1, A_2, A_3 and A_4 are connected to different resistors in a circuit as shown in the following figure. Minimum current will be recorded in which ammeter?*

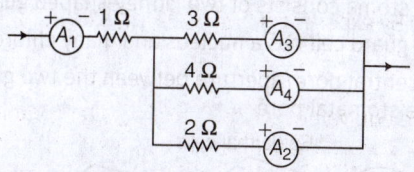

Ans. Current is divided in parallel combination, more the resistance, lesser will be the current.

3. *Three students draw the following circuit diagrams to find resistance of parallel combination of two resistors. Which amongst following is/are correct circuit diagram/ diagrams?*

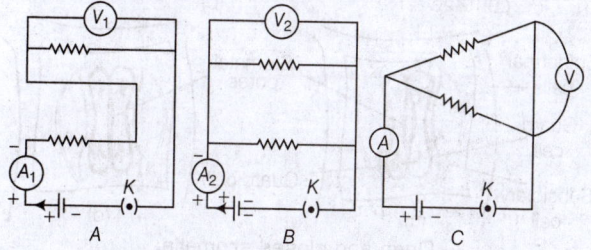

Ans. The voltmeter should be connected in parallel to both the resistors, so only circuit diagram B is correct.

4. *For the three circuits shown below:*

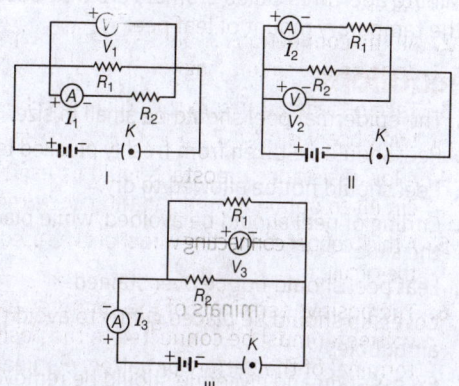

The same two resistors R_1 and R_2 have been connected in parallel in all the circuits but the voltmeter and ammeter have been connected in the three different positions. Give the relation between the all three voltmeter and ammeter readings?

Ans. The reading of voltmeter in all the three circuits will be the same but that of the ammeter will be different.

5. *To determine the equivalent resistance of two resistors in parallel combination of a circuit is shown below. In the given circuit which terminals are wrongly connected?*

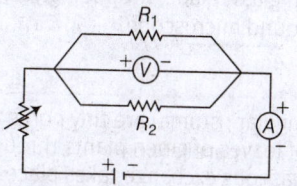

Ans. In the given circuit, ammeter is wrongly connected.

6. *Study the combination of resistors given below and find the two resistors in parallel combination.*

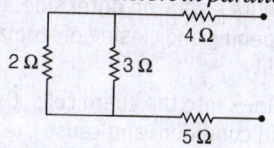

Ans. The two resistors 2Ω and 3Ω are connected in parallel.

7. *In parallel combination of resistors, two students connected the ammeter in two different ways as shown in given circuits A and B. In which circuit, the ammeter has been correctly connected?*

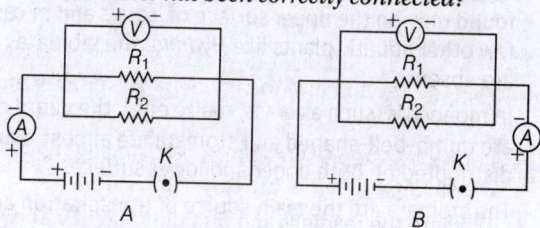

Ans. Ammeter is connected in series having its terminals connected in accordance to that of the cell. So, it is connected correctly only in circuit A.

8. *For the given circuit, name the components which are connected in parallel.*

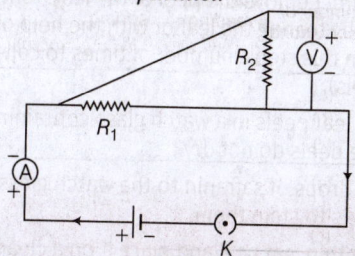

Ans. The components R_1, R_2 and V are connected in parallel combination. Because terminals of the resistance and voltmeter are connected together.

EXPERIMENT 8

Objective
To prepare a temporary mount of a leaf peel to show stomata.

Materials Required
Leaf of *Tradescantia* or *Periwinkle* or *Balsam*, slides, coverslip, forceps, needles, cotton cloth, brush, blotting paper, watch glass, blade, dropper, glycerine, safranin and a compound microscope.

Theory
Stomata (singular : stoma) are tiny pores found in the epidermis of leaves of green plants through which the process of gaseous exchange takes place. Each stoma is bounded by two guard cells, which unlike the other epidermal cells, possess chloroplasts.

The walls of guard cells are thicker on inner side and thinner and more elastic on outer side. The guard cells control the opening and closing of stomata by changes in their turgidity.

When water flows into the guard cells, they swell, expand (turgid condition) and cause the stomatal pore to open. On the contrary, when they lose water they shrink (flaccid condition) and close the stomatal pore.

In case of dicot plants (such as *Petunia*), the guard cells are **kidney-shaped** and the distribution of stomata is more on lower surface than upper surface of leaves, whereas in case of plants like water lily, stomata are found only on the upper surface of leaves and in case of few other aquatic plants like *Hydrilla*, the stomata are absent.

In monocots (such as grass, maize etc.), the guard cells are **dumb-bell-shaped** and stomata are almost equally distributed on both upper and lower surfaces.

The stomata are the main source of transpiration and they also help in exchange of oxygen, carbon dioxide and water vapours with air.

Procedure
1. Take a freshly plucked leaf of *Tradescantia* or *Periwinkle* or *Balsam*. Remove the peel of the leaf from its lower surface by tearing the leaf or with the help of forceps (perform this step a number of times to collect 5-6 leaf peels).
2. Put the leaf peels in a watch glass containing water, so that the peels do not dry.
3. Add 1-2 drops of safranin to the watch glass containing leaf peels to stain them.
4. Select a thin leaf peel and place it on a clean slide with the help of brush (leaf peel should be placed in centre of slide).
5. Put a drop of glycerine on the slide over the peel.
6. Now, with the help of a needle, gently place a coverslip over the peel.
7. Remove the excess stain and glycerine with a blotting paper. Care should be taken while cleaning, as the peel should not be disturbed.
8. First, observe the slide under the lower magnification (i.e. 10x) of a compound microscope and then, under higher magnification (i.e. 45x).

Observations
1. Epidermal peel consists of stomata embedded in a single layer of epidermal cells, which are irregular in outline with no intercellular spaces.
2. Each stoma consists of two kidney-shaped guard cells.
3. Each guard cell has a nucleus and many chloroplasts.
4. The central pore/aperture between the two guard cells is the stomatal pore.

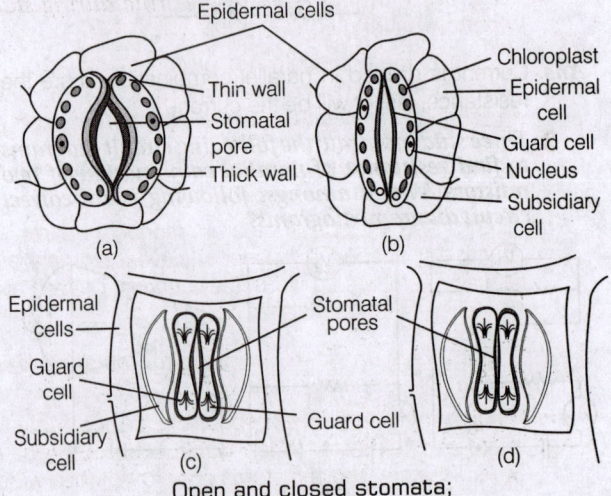

Open and closed stomata; Dicots (a,b) and Monocots (c,d)

Result
Minute apertures called stomata are well-observed in the temporary mount of leaf peel.

Precautions
1. The epidermal peel should be small in size.
2. Peel should be taken from freshly plucked leaf.
3. Peel should not be allowed to dry.
4. Curling of peel should be avoided, while placing it on the slide.
5. Leaf peel should not be over stained.
6. Coverslip should be placed gently to avoid the entry of air bubbles.
7. Excess stain and glycerine should be removed carefully with a blotting paper without disturbing the peel on glass slide.

QUESTIONS

1. Which pigment is responsible for the green colour of leaf. Give its location and function also.

Ans. Green colour of leaf is due to the pigment called chlorophyll. It is present in the chloroplast of plants. It allows plant to absorb light and use the energy to synthesise carbohydrates from CO_2 and H_2O.

2. Name a plant in which stomata are usually absent.

Ans. Stomata are usually absent in *Hydrilla*. It is a submerged plant that grows under water. Its narrow leaves have no stomata at all. They breathe through their body surface.

3. A student focused on the leaf epidermal peel under a low power microscope, but could not see all parts. What should he do to for correct observation?

Ans. To observe all parts of a leaf peel epidermis, the student should focus under high power using the fine adjustment knob.

4. Leaf peels are mounted in glycerine during slide preparation why?

Ans. Leaf peels are mounted in glycerine to prevent it from drying. Glycerine is a hygroscopic compound which forms a layer of moisture over the leaf peel.

5. Identify the shape of guard cells in monocot and dicot plants.

Ans. The shape of guard cells in monocot plants is dumb-bell-shaped. In monocot leaves, stomata are equally distributed on both the surfaces. Dicots have kidney-shaped guard cells.

6. Which pressure is responsible for opening and closing of stomata?

Ans. Turgor Pressure (TP) is responsible for opening and closing of stomata. When water enters the guard cells, TP increases and stoma opens and when water exits, TP decreases, stoma closes.

7. A figure of plant at 18:00 hours on a day is given alongside.

(i) Name the condition of stomata during this stage in plant.

(ii) Draw and label the guard cells and stomata as they would appear in the leaves of the plant.

Ans. (i) Placcid

(ii)
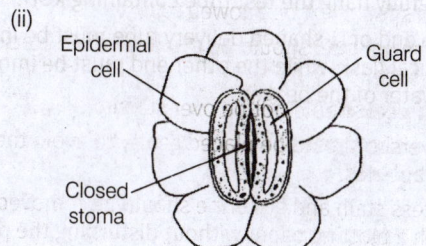

8. What happens to the guard cells, when they are stretched?

Ans. The guard cells become turgid when they are stretched. This results in widening of space between two guard cells, thereby opening the stomata.

9. To prepare a temporary mount for observing stomata, the peel should is isolated from which part?

Ans. Stomata are present in leaves on both the surfaces as photosynthesis, respiration and all other processes occur through leaves. Roots are underground, hence stomata is not present in them.

10. Identify parts shown A and B in the given diagram are

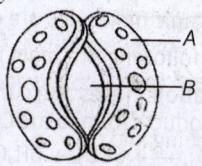

Ans. A is the guard cell, which regulates the opening and closing of B, i.e. the stomatal pore.

11. A student prepared the temporary mount of stained leaf peel. After observing the slide under microscope, he draw the following sketch. Correct the parts A, B, C and D labelled by him.

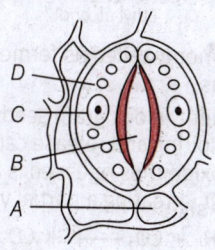

Ans. A. Guard cell   B. Stomatal aperture
C. Nucleus   D. Chloroplast

12. In an experiment to prepare temporary stained mount of a leaf epidermal peel, how can extra stain be removed? What possible outcome would be observed if it is removed with cotton wool?

Ans. Extra stain can be wiped off using a piece of blotting paper with gentle press of thumb. Tilting the slide a little can remove excess stain.

Cotton wool fibres can stick the wet slide, this will cause incorrect observation of the slide.

13. Explain, why only turgid leaf is selected for the preparation of temporary mount of a leaf peel?

Ans. When guard cells are turgid, the stomatal cells will be in open state. Hence, a turgid and freshly plucked leaf is selected to ensure that guard cells are turgid and stomata are open.

EXPERIMENT 9

Objective
To show experimentally that carbon dioxide is given out during respiration.

Materials Required
Conical flask, U-shaped delivery tube (tube bent twice at right angles), cotton wool or moist blotting paper, water, thread, beaker, test tube, rubber cork with one hole, 20% freshly prepared KOH solution, vaseline and soaked gram seeds.

Theory
Respiration is a catabolic process that liberates chemical energy, when organic molecules are oxidised.

Respiration is of following two main types:

1. **Aerobic respiration** Takes place in the presence of oxygen. The products formed are CO_2 and H_2O.
$$\underset{\text{Glucose}}{C_6H_{12}O_6} + 6O_2 \longrightarrow 6CO_2 + 6H_2O + \underset{\text{(38 ATP)}}{\text{Energy}}$$

2. **Anaerobic respiration** Takes place in the absence of molecular oxygen. It is incomplete oxidation of substrates. The end products are carbon dioxide and ethyl alcohol.
$$\underset{\text{Glucose}}{C_6H_{12}O_6} \xrightarrow{\text{Yeast}} 2\underset{\text{Ethyl alcohol}}{C_2H_5OH} + 2CO_2 + \underset{\text{(2 ATP)}}{\text{Energy}}$$

It is more commonly called as fermentation in microorganisms.

In this experiment, moist gram seeds are taken as they are actively respiring and release carbon dioxide. The carbon dioxide thus released is absorbed by KOH and forms K_2CO_3, creating a partial vacuum.

$$\underset{\substack{\text{Potassium} \\ \text{hydroxide}}}{2KOH} + CO_2 \longrightarrow \underset{\substack{\text{Potassium} \\ \text{carbonate}}}{K_2CO_3} + H_2O$$

Procedure
1. Take about 25-30 gram seeds and germinate them for about 3-4 days by placing them on moist cotton wool or moist blotting paper.
2. Place the germinated seeds into a conical flask and sprinkle little water in flask to moisten the seeds.
3. Take freshly prepared 20% KOH solution in a test tube and hang it in conical flask with the help of thread.
4. Close the mouth of conical flask by placing a rubber cork with a single hole in it to insert the U-shaped glass delivery tube in it.
5. Place the other end of U-shaped delivery tube into a beaker filled with water.
6. Seal all the connections of the experimental setup with vaseline so as to make it airtight.
7. Now, mark the initial level of water in the U-shaped delivery tube.
8. Keep the apparatus undisturbed for about 1-2 hours. Note the change in the level of water in delivery tube, immersed in water of the beaker.

Observations
After sometime the level of water will rise in the U-shaped delivery tube dipped in beaker.

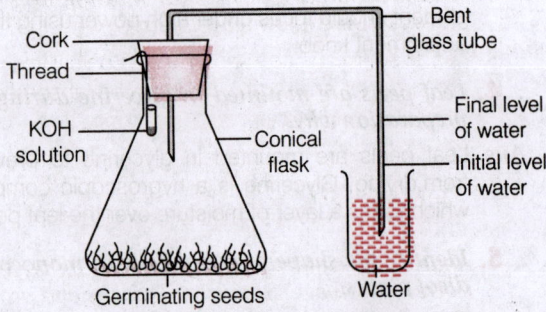

Experiment to show that carbon dioxide is given out during respiration

Result
Germinated gram seeds in conical flask release carbon dioxide during respiration. The CO_2 in turn is absorbed by the KOH present in hanging test tube in conical flask. This creates a vacuum in conical flask, which causes upward movement of water in U-shaped delivery tube. It leads to change in level of water in delivery tube.

Precautions
1. Germinating seeds should be moist.
2. All connections of the setup must be airtight.
3. Only freshly prepared KOH solution must be used.
4. Carefully hang the test tube containing KOH.
5. One end of U-shaped delivery tube must be in the conical flask, while the other end must be immersed in water of the beaker.

QUESTIONS

1. *(i) What is the reason for using germinating seeds in the experiment?*

(ii) If instead of moist seeds, boiled seeds are used, what will happen?

Ans. (i) Germination occurs only in hiring seeds. It will not occurs in boiled seeds because these seeds do not respire.

(ii) Germinating seeds are used for the experiment because they reprise actively at faster rate.

2. *What is the purpose of adding KOH to the experimental setup?*

Ans. KOH is commonly used to absorb the CO_2 released by germinating seeds during respiration.

3. *What will happen if the KOH solution will not be placed in the experimental setup?*

Ans. If KOH solution is not placed in the conical flask of the experimental setup, CO_2 will not be absorbed and water level will not rise in the bent tube.

KOH absorbs the CO_2, which creates a partial vacuum in the conical flask. This causes a rise in water level in the U-shaped delivery tube.

4. *Anaerobic respiration is also called as glycolysis. Correct the above statement. Epic the end products formed by anaerobic respiration.*

Ans. Anaerobic respiration is also called as fermentation in microorganisms such as yeast. The common products formed in this process are ethyl alcohol or lactic acid.

5. *Give an alternative to the experimental setup for testing that CO_2 is released during resperation.*

Ans. (d) The alternative setup for the experiment is to use lime water instead of plain water in the beaker. Lime water turns milky when it comes in contact with CO_2. Also, KOH solution should be removed from the setup. NaOH can be used instead of KOH.

6. *Mona set an apparatus to perform that CO_2 is essential for respiration, but failed to obtain the results. What is the mistake in her setup?*

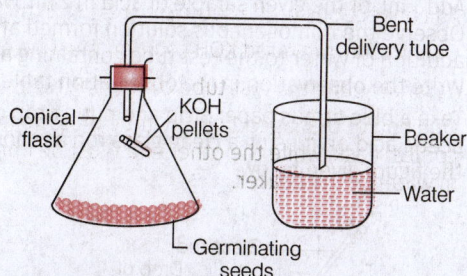

Ans. The mistake in the setup is that bent tube is above the water level. The longer end of the glass tube is supposed to be dipped inside water.

7. *The following experimental setups were kept in the laboratory to show that CO_2 is given out during respiration.*

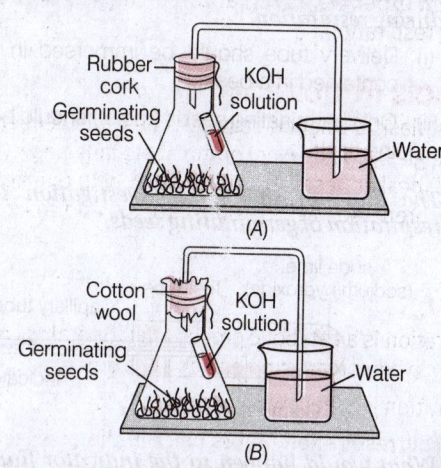

After 2hr, students observed that water rises in which delivery tube?

Ans. Only setup A is airtight because a rubber stopper has been used. So, partial vacuum due to absorption of CO_2 by KOH will be created here, leading to rise in water. In setup B, cotton wool is not effective to create a partial vacuum.

8. *What does the following experimental setup indicates?*

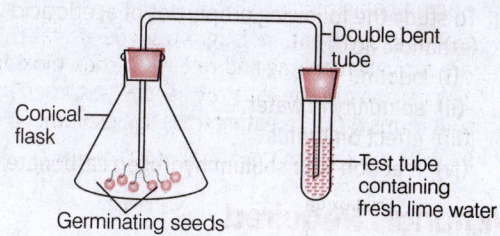

Ans. The experiment indicates that the germinating seeds respire and produce carbon dioxide due to which lime water has turned milky.

9. *The diagram shows apparatus used to investigate respiration.*

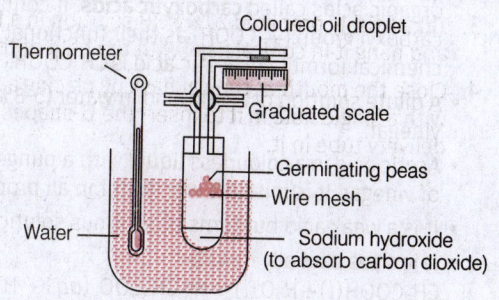

Ans. Amount of oxygen used can be measured as oxygen is absorbed for respiration to produce energy for the germination of embryo in the seeds.

10. *Give any two precautions to be taken while setting up the experiment to show that CO_2 is evolved during respiration.*

Ans. (i) Delivery tube should be immersed in a water contained in a beaker.
(ii) Only germinating seeds (moist) should be kept in the flask.

11. *The diagram shows an investigation into the respiration of germinating seeds.*

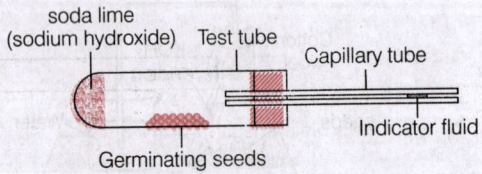

What would happen to the indicator fluid in the capillary tube shown in the diagram?

Ans. The germinating seeds use O_2 for respiration. This CO_2 is absorbed by NaOH solution. This causes further uptake of O_2 by the seeds from air moving the indicator fluid towards the test tube.

12. *In the test tube A and B shown below, yeast was kept in sugar solution. Which products of respiration would you expect in test tubes A and B?*

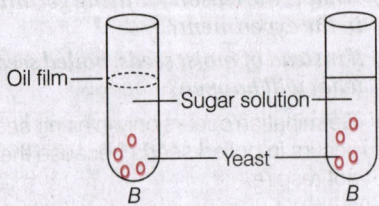

Ans. Test tube A The product formed in A will be ethanol, carbon dioxide and energy. Oil prevents oxygen to enter the solution. So, it undergoes anaerobic respiration.

Test tube B In the presence of oxygen, yeast shows aerobic respiration due to which carbon dioxide, water and energy are produced.

13. *In the experiment to show respiration in germinating seeds, which chemical is used in the small tube and which gas is released by seeds.*

Ans. Germinating seeds respire aerobically to product CO_2 as end producer.

KOH pellets in small tube absorb the CO_2 released by germinating seeds.

EXPERIMENT 10

Aim
To study the following properties of acetic acid (ethanoic acid):
(i) odour
(ii) solubility in water
(iii) effect on litmus
(iv) reaction with sodium hydrogen carbonate

Materials Required
Test tubes, test tube stand, litmus paper strips (blue and red), glass rod, sodium hydrogen carbonate and acetic acid.

Theory
- Acetic acid (ethanoic acid) belongs to a class of organic acids called **carboxylic acids**. It contains a carboxyl group (—COOH) as their functional group. The chemical formula of acetic acid is CH_3COOH.
- A dilute solution of acetic acid in water (5-8%) is called vinegar.
- Acetic acid is a colourless liquid with a pungent odour of vinegar. It is miscible with water in all proportions.
- It is a weak acid but turns blue litmus solution red.
- It ionises partially in water,
$CH_3COOH(l) + H_2O(l) \rightleftharpoons CH_3COO^-(aq) + H_3O^+(aq)$
- Acetic acid reacts with sodium hydrogen carbonate (bicarbonate) to evolve carbon dioxide gas with a brisk effervescence and produces salt and water.

$$\underset{\text{Acetic acid}}{CH_3COOH(l)} + \underset{\text{Sodium hydrogen carbonate}}{NaHCO_3(s)} \longrightarrow \underset{\text{Sodium acetate (salt)}}{CH_3COO^-Na^+(aq)}$$
$$+ \underset{\text{Carbon dioxide}}{CO_2\uparrow} + \underset{\text{Water}}{H_2O(l)}$$

Procedure
1. Take a clean test tube and add a given sample of 1 mL acetic acid into the test tube.
2. Smell the odour of the sample of the acid taken in the test tube by wafting.
3. Add 1 mL of the given sample of acid in 2 mL water. Observe the homogeneous solution formed after the addition of water to the test tube containing acid. Write the observation in the observation table.
4. Take a blue litmus paper strip and put a drop of acetic acid on it using a clean glass rod as shown in the figure given below.

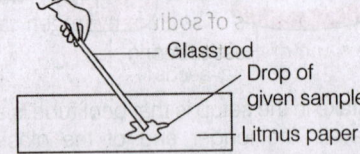

Testing the colour change of the litmus paper

5. Note the colour change of the litmus paper and write the colour in the observation table.
6. Add a drop of acetic acid on a red litmus paper strip using a clean glass rod as shown in the figure.
7. Note the colour change of the litmus paper and write the colour in the observation table.
8. Take another clean test tube and add 1 mL of acetic acid to it. Add a pinch of sodium bicarbonate (sodium hydrogen carbonate —$NaHCO_3$) to the test tube containing acetic acid. Pass the evolved gas through the lime water and observe the changes.

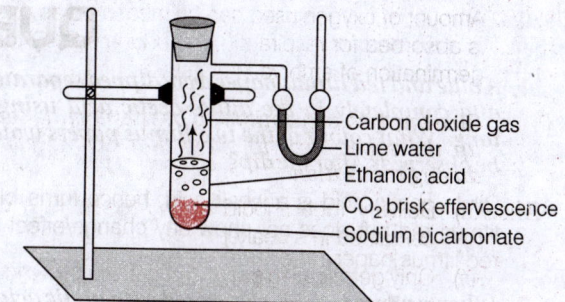

Fig. 2 Set up for the reaction of sodium bicarbonate with acetic acid

Observation Table

S. No.	Experiment	Observation	Inference
1.	**Odour** Smell the sample of acetic acid taken in a test tube by wafting.	It gives a pungent smell of vinegar.	Acetic acid smells like a vinegar.
2.	**Solubility test** Add acid to a test tube containing the water.	A homogeneous solution is formed.	Acetic acid is soluble in water.
3.	**Effect on litmus** Put a drop of ethanoic acid on a (i) blue litmus paper (ii) red litmus paper	(i) Blue litmus paper turns red. (ii) No change in red litmus paper.	Acetic acid is acidic in nature.
4.	**Reaction with sodium hydrogen carbonate** Add a pinch of sodium hydrogen carbonate to the test tube containing acetic acid.	A colourless, odourless gas is evolved which with a brisk effervescence turns lime water milky. On passing excess of this gas in lime water, the milkiness disappears.	CO_2 gas is liberated in the reaction between acetic acid and sodium hydrogen carbonate. $CH_3COOH\ (aq) + NaHCO_3(s) \longrightarrow CH_3COONa\ (aq) + CO_2(g)\uparrow + H_2O\ (e)$ The lime water turns milky due to the formation of a white precipitate $CaCO_3$ which dissolves when excess of CO_2 is passed. Hence, the milkness of lime water disappears. $\underset{\text{calcium hydroxide}}{Ca(OH)_2(aq)} + \underset{\text{carbon dioxide}}{CO_2(g)} \longrightarrow \underset{\text{Calcium carbonate}}{CaCO_3(s)\downarrow} + \underset{\text{Water}}{H_2O(l)}$

Results

1. Acetic acid has a pungent odour of vinegar.
2. Acetic acid is completely soluble in water.
3. It turns blue litmus paper to red.
4. It evolves CO_2 gas, when reacts with sodium hydrogen carbonate.
   $CH_3COOH\ (aq) + NaHCO_3(s) \longrightarrow CH_3COONa\ (aq) + H_2O\ (l) + CO_2(g)$

Precautions

1. Ethanoic acid should be handled carefully.
2. Do not taste or touch ethanoic acid.
3. Do not taste or touch sodium hydrogen carbonate.
4. Use small quantities of sodium hydrogen carbonate, to control the intensity of CO_2 evolved.
5. Use clean and dry test tubes.

QUESTIONS

1. *A blue and red litmus paper were dipped separately and completely in the dilute acetic acid using a tong. What colour of the two litmus papers would be observed? After the dip?*

Ans. Dilute acetic acid is a weak acid, hence turns blue litmus red but does not show any change/effect on red litmus paper.

2. *When a white powder was mixed with acetic acid, a colourless and odourless gas was produced which turns lime water milky. What is this white powder?*

Ans. White powder is sodium hydrogen carbonate (bicarbonate) which evolves CO_2 on reaction with acetic acid and CO_2 gas turns lime water milky.

3. *What is the common name of ethanoic acid as sold in the market in the form of 5-8% dilute solution?*

Ans. The common name of 5-8% solution of ethanoic acid is vinegar as sold in the market.

4. *Lime water turns milky upon reaction with carbon dioxide gas due to formation of white precipitate. Identify the white precipitate which gives milky colour to the solution.*

Ans. Reaction of $NaHCO_3$ with CH_3COOH releases CO_2 gas which reacts with lime water (calcium hydroxide) to produce calcium carbonate ($CaCO_3$), a white precipitate. This white precipitate gives milky colour to the solution.

$$NaHCO_3(s) + CH_3COOH(aq) \longrightarrow CH_3COONa(aq) + H_2O(l) + CO_2\uparrow(g)$$
(Sodium bicarbonate) (Acetic acid)

$$CO_2(g) + Ca(OH)_2(aq) \longrightarrow CaCO_3(s)\downarrow + H_2O(l)$$
(Lime water) (white ppt.)

5. *7 mL of acetic acid was added to equal volume of water and the mixture was shaken well for one minute and allowed to settle. Which of the following figure represents the correct observation?*

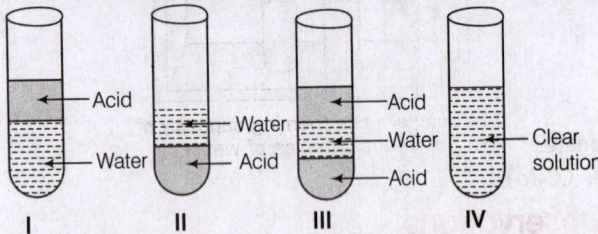

Ans. Figure (iv) represents the correct observation as acetic acid dissolves in water to form a clear solution.

6. *When Shweta smells a colourless liquid and observed that the it smells like vinegar which is used for preserving pickles. What is this the colourless liquid called?*

Ans. Vinegar is a 5-8% aqueous solution of acetic acid.

7. *When Ram adds a pinch of sodium hydrogen carbonate powder to acetic acid solution, a brisk effervescence is observed.*

Ans. Explain CO_2 gas is evolved with brisk effervescence when sodium hydrogen carbonate reacts with acetic acid.

$$\underset{\text{Acetic acid}}{CH_3COOH(aq)} + \underset{\text{Sodium hydrogen carbonate}}{NaHCO_3(s)} \longrightarrow$$
$$CH_3COONa(s) + H_2O(l) + \underset{\text{Carbon dioxide}}{CO_2(g)\uparrow}$$

8. *By name the type of the reaction that occurs between ethanoic acid and sodium hydrogen carbonate?*

Ans. The reaction between ethanoic acid and sodium hydrocarbonate involves the loss of carbon dioxide molecule, thus, the reaction is termed as decarboxylation.

9. *How does acetic acid reacts with sodium hydrogen carbonate?*

Ans. Acetic acid reacts with sodium hydrogen carbonate vigorously releasing effervescence of CO_2.

10. *Acetic acid is added to a solid X kept in a test tube. A colourless, odourless gas Y evolves. The gas is passed through lime water which turned milky. What could be X and Y possibly?*

Ans. X is sodium hydrogen carbonate $NaHCO_3$ which reacts with acetic acid to release a colourless, odourless CO_2 gas Y which turns lime water milky. The chemical reaction taking place is

$$NaHCO_3(s) + CH_3COOH(aq) \longrightarrow$$
$$\underset{x}{CH_3COONa(aq)} + H_2O(l) + \underset{Y}{CO_2(g)\uparrow}$$

11. *Why carbon dioxide gas is passed through lime water for a short duration only?*

Ans. When carbon dioxide gas is passed through lime water for a short duration, a precipitate of $CaCO_3$ is formed, which gives the lime water a milky appearance.

$$Ca(OH)_2(aq) + CO_2(g) \longrightarrow \underset{\text{(white ppt.)}}{CaCO_3(s)} + H_2O(l)$$

When excess of CO_2 is passed through lime water, the $CaCO_3$ precipitate dissolves to form soluble calcium bicarbonate.

$$CaCO_3(s) + CO_2(g) + H_2O(l) \longrightarrow Ca(HCO_3)_2(aq)$$

Thus, the milky lime water becomes clear again.

12. *Name three commerical uses of acetic acid.*

Ans. (i) 5-8% aqueous solution of ethanoic acid (vinegar) is used to preserve pickles.
(ii) It is used in the manufacture of rubber.
(iii) It is used in the manufacture of various dyes.

13. *Which salt of carboxylic acid is commonly used as food preservative?*

Ans. Sodium benzoate is used as a food preservative.

EXPERIMENT 11

Aim
To study the comparative cleaning capacity of a sample of soap in soft and hard water.

Materials Required
Tap water (or well water), distilled water, calcium hydrogen carbonate or calcium sulphate, soap sample, test tubes, test tube stand, glass rod, measuring cylinder (50 mL) and a measuring scale.

Theory
- Hardness of water is due to the presence of salts of calcium and magnesium (hydrogen carbonates, chlorides and sulphates) in water. These salts are soluble in water.
- When soap is added to hard water, it forms scum by reacting with the salts of magnesium and calcium ions. This scum is insoluble and floats on the top surface of water.
- The scum is formed due to the formation of insoluble calcium and magnesium salts of fatty acids.

$$2C_{17}H_{35}COONa + CaCl_2 \longrightarrow (C_{17}H_{35}COO)_2Ca + 2NaCl$$
Soluble sodium stearate (soap) + Calcium chloride (in hard water) → Insoluble calcium stearate (scum)

$$2C_{17}H_{35}COONa + MgSO_4 \longrightarrow (C_{17}H_{35}COO)_2Mg + Na_2SO_4$$
Soluble sodium stearate (soap) + Magnesium sulphate (in hard water) → Insoluble magnesium stearate (scum)

- Therefore, the presence of calcium and magnesium salts in water precipitates the soap thereby reducing its cleaning power and hence, foaming capacity.

Procedure
1. Take three beakers and mark them as A, B and C.
2. Add 20 mL of distilled water in beaker A, 20 mL of tap water in beaker B and 20 mL of distilled water in beaker C.
3. Add 2 g of calcium sulphate (or calcium hydrogen carbonate) to 20 mL of distilled water taken in beaker C.
4. Stir the contents of beaker C with the help of clean glass rod till calcium sulphate (or calcium hydrogen carbonate) dissolves in water.
5. Add equal amount of weighed soap to all the three beakers A, B and C.
6. Stir the contents of the three beakers with separate clean glass rods.
7. Place three tubes in a test tube stand and mark them as A, B and C.
8. Pour 3 mL of the above prepared soap solution from the beakers in the corresponding test tubes.

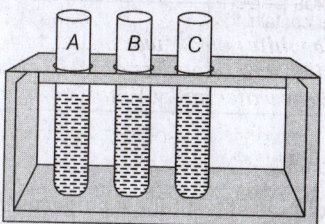

Test tubes containing different soap solutions

9. Take test tube A and shake it ten times by placing thumb on its mouth.

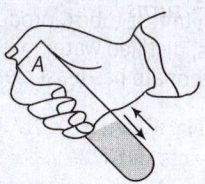

Shaking the test tube

10. On shaking the test tube, foam or lather will be formed. Measure the length of foam produced immediately with the help of a measuring scale.
11. Similarly, repeat steps 9 and 10 with the remaining two samples.

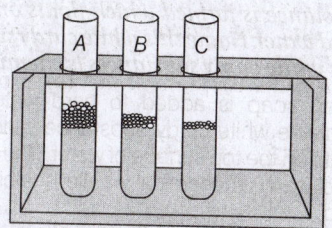

To compare the foaming capacity of different samples of water

Observations
1. Mass of sample of soap taken in each beaker = ... g.
2. Volume of distilled water and tap water added in each beaker = ... mL.
3. Volume of soap sample taken in each test tube = ... mL.
4. Number of times each test tube is shaken = ...

Calculations

S.No.	Mixture mL [water + soap]	Test tube reading Initial length before shaking, I (solution) (cm)	Test tube reading Final length after shaking, F [solution + foam] (cm)	Length of the foam produced in cm = [F − I]
1.	A. Tap water + soap			
2.	B. Distilled water + soap			
3.	C. Water containing CaSO$_4$ [or Ca(HCO$_3$)$_2$ + soap]			

Results

1. Soap solution in test tube A produces the maximum length of foam. Thus, distilled water (soft water) has the most cleansing capacity.
2. Soap solution in test tube B produces smaller length of foam as compare to test tube A. Thus, tap water has less cleansing capacity than soft water.
3. Soap solution in test tube C produces minimum length of foam. Thus, distilled water mixed with calcium hydrogen carbonate has least cleansing capacity.

For cleaning and washing purposes, the foam produced depends upon the free availability of hydrophobic portion of soap [i.e. hydrocarbon part]. In hard water, foam is trapped due to scum or precipitation of salts, thereby making hard water unsuitable for washing. Therefore, more the length of foam produced, more would be the cleaning capacity of the soap.

Precautions

1. Use similar soap sample for both soft and hard water.
2. Stir the mixture carefully while dissolving soap in water for avoiding spilling of soap solution.
3. The quantity of soap sample taken in all solutions should be same.
4. The amount of distilled water taken in each beaker should be same.
5. The mass of the soap sample must be determined very carefully using a physical balance.
6. Shake every test tube for equal number of times in a similar manner in order to avoid any disparity.
7. Measure the length of the foam produced immediately after its production.

QUESTIONS

1. *What happens when calcium hydrogen carbonate is added to beaker containing soap solution?*

Ans. When calcium hydrogen carbonate is added to soap solution, calcium ions react with soap thereby reducing the lather forming capacity of soap due to the formation of scum.

2. *When soap is added to hard water, a white curdy substance is formed which floats on the surface of hard water. Name this white curdy substance. What this white curdy substances is chemically called?*

Ans. When soap is added to hard water, it forms an insoluble white curdy substance called **scum** which floats on the top surface of water. The scum formed in hard water is chemically called calcium salt of fatty acid.

3. *Tanu tried to dissolve the soap in water but the soap does not dissolve and gives no lather or foam. What conclusion can you draw from this observation?*

Ans. If soap does not dissolve in water, this suggest that the water taken by Tanu is hard, i.e. it contains salts of calcium and magnesium (generally bicarbonates, chlorides or sulphates).

4. *Sometimes soap partially dissolves in water while sometimes it does not. State the reason behind this observation.*

Ans. CaSO$_4$ causes permanent hardness of water making soap insoluble in water, while Ca(HCO$_3$)$_2$ causes temporary hardness of water making soap partially soluble in water.

5. *On what factors, the amount of foam produced by the soap depends?*

Ans. It depends on free availability of hydrophobic portion of soaps (alkyl group of non-polar end).

6. *In hard water, ... portion of soap is trapped due to formation of scum.*

Ans. Hydrophobic portion (alkyl groups) are trapped due to formation of scum.

7. *Washing clothes will be more difficult in ground water. Why?*

Ans. Among the given options, ground water consists of higher concentration of hardening agents [Ca(HCO$_3$)$_2$, CaSO$_4$ etc.] making soap difficult to form lather hence, reducing its cleansing efficiency.

8. *Sodium carbonate (Na$_2$CO$_3$) is added to some soap. Why?*

Ans. Na$_2$CO$_3$ reacts with hardening agents and precipitate them down making water soft.

9. *Neha takes about 10 mL of distilled water in four boiling tubes marked A, B, C and D. She dissolves sodium sulphate in A, potassium sulphate in B, calcium sulphate in C and magnesium sulphate in D. After that she adds equal amount of soap solution in each boiling tube. After shaking, in which boiling tube she would observe a good amount of lather.*

Ans. In boiling tube A and B, she would observe a good amount of lather.

EXPERIMENT 12

Aim
To determine the focal length of
A. concave mirror
B. convex lens
by obtaining the image of a distant object.

[A] For Concave Mirror

Apparatus Required
A concave mirror, a mirror holder, a small screen fixed on a stand and a measuring scale.

Theory
- A spherical mirror whose reflecting surface is curved inwards, i.e. faces towards the centre of the sphere is called a concave mirror.
- It also obeys the laws of reflection of light like a plane mirror.
- Thus, the rays of light coming from a distant object such as the Sun or a building or a tree can be considered to be parallel to each other as given in the figure.

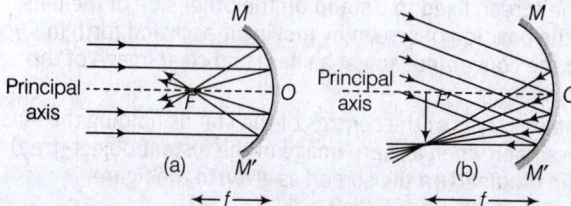

Image formation of a distant object by a concave mirror when (a) incident parallel rays of light are parallel to the principal axis (b) incident parallel rays of light are not parallel to the principal axis

- When parallel rays of light fall on a concave mirror along its axis, the rays meet at a point in front of the mirror after reflection from it. This point is the focus of the mirror.
- When a parallel beam of light comes from a distant object, then a real, inverted and very small image is formed at the focus of the mirror.
- Since, the image formed by the mirror is real, so it can be obtained on a screen.
- The distance between the pole O of the concave mirror and the focus F, is the focal length of the concave mirror.
- Thus, the focal length of a concave mirror can be estimated by obtaining a real image of a distant object at its focus.

Procedure
1. Fix a concave mirror in the mirror holder and place it on the table near an open window. Turn the face of mirror towards a distant object (suppose a tree).
2. Place the screen fitted to a stand in front of the concave mirror. Adjust the distance of screen, so that the image of the distant object is formed on it as given in the figure below.

   We can infer from the figure that a clear and bright image could be obtained, if the distant object (a tree), is illuminated with sunlight and the screen is placed in the shade. A bright image of the Sun could also be obtained, if the sunlight is made to fall directly on the concave mirror.
3. When a sharp image of the distant object is obtained, then mark the position of the centre of the stand holding the mirror and the screen as a and b, respectively (see figure).

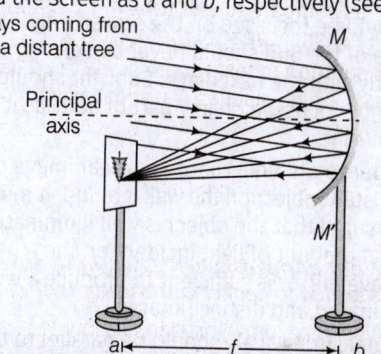

Determination of focal length of a concave mirror

4. Measure the horizontal distance between the centre of the concave mirror and the screen with the help of a measuring scale.
5. Record the observations in the observation table.
6. Repeat the experiment two more times by obtaining the images of two different distant objects and measure the distances between the concave mirror and the screen in each case. Record them in the observation table.
7. Find the mean value of the focal length for all the observations for different objects.

Observations and Calculations

S.No.	Name of the distant object	Distance between the concave mirror and the screen, i.e. (f) in (cm)	in (m)	Mean focal length of the concave mirror, (f) in (m)
1.				
2.				
3.				

- Focal length for first object $(f_1) = \ldots$ m
- Focal length for second object $(f_2) = \ldots$ m
- Focal length for third object $(f_3) = \ldots$ m

Mean focal length $= \dfrac{f_1 + f_2 + f_3}{3} = \ldots$ m

Result

The approximate value of focal length of the given concave mirror is ………m.

Precautions

1. Concave mirror should be placed near an open window through which sufficient sunlight enters with its polished surface facing the distant object.
2. There should not be any obstacle in the path of rays of light incident on the concave mirror.
3. If the image of the Sun has to be formed, then it should be focussed on the screen only. The image of the Sun should never be seen directly with the naked eye. Sunlight should never be focussed on any part of body as it can burn it.
4. In order to obtain a sharp and clear image of the distant object on the wall/ground, it must be ensured that the object is well illuminated, so that amount of light incident on the concave mirror is sufficient to produce a well illuminated and distinct image.
5. The measuring scale should be parallel to the base of both the stands.
6. The mirror holder along with the mirror should be kept perpendicular to the measuring scale for precise measurements.

(B) For Convex Lens

Apparatus Required

A thin convex lens, a lens holder, a small screen fixed to a stand and a measuring scale.

Theory

- A lens whose both the spherical surfaces are bulging outwards is called convex lens.
- When the parallel beam of light coming from a distant object (such as the Sun, a building, a tree, etc.) falls on a convex lens, the rays after refraction, converge at a point on its other side. This point is one of the two foci of the lens.
- If the parallel beam of light comes from a distant object, then a real, inverted image of very small size is formed at the focus of the lens as given in the figure.

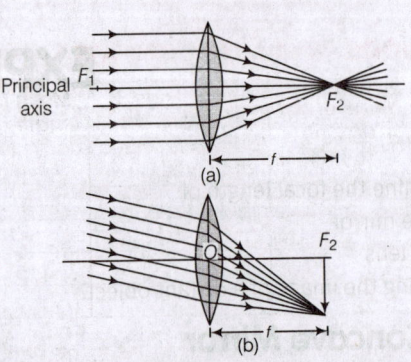

Image formation of a distant object by a convex lens
(a) The beam of light incident on the lens is parallel to the principal axis
(b) The beam of light incident on the convex lens is not parallel to the principal axis

- Since, the image formed by the lens is real, so it can also be obtained on a screen as that of concave mirror.
- The distance between the optical centre O of the convex lens and the focus F_1 or F_2 is its focal length.
- Thus, the focal length of a convex lens can be estimated by obtaining a real image of a distant object at its focus.

Procedure

1. Fix a thin convex lens on the lens holder and place it on the table same as that done in the case of concave mirror.
2. Place the screen fixed to a stand on the other side of the lens. Adjust the position of screen by moving it back and forth in front of the convex lens to get a sharp and clear image of the distant object.
3. Mark the positions of the centres of the stands holding the lens and the screen when a sharp image of the distant object (tree) has been obtained on the screen as given in the figure.

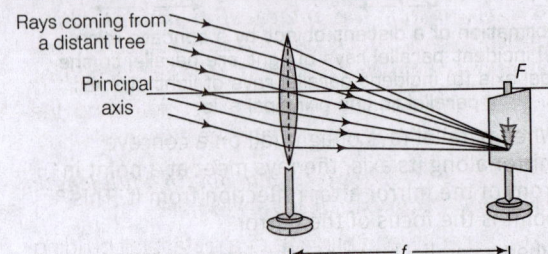

Determination of focal length of a thin convex lens

4. Now, measure the horizontal distance between the centres of the convex lens and the screen with the help of a measuring scale.
5. Record the observations in the corresponding column of the observation table.
6. Repeat this experiment two more times by obtaining the images of two different distant objects. Measure the distance between the convex lens and the screen in each case. Record them in the observation table.
7. Find the average or mean value of the focal length observed for different objects.

Observations and Calculations

S. No.	Name of the distant object	Distance between the convex lens and the screen, i.e. in (cm)	in (m)	Mean focal length of the convex lens, (f) (m)
1.				
2.				
3.				

- Focal length for first object (f_1) = ... m
- Focal length for second object (f_2) = ... m
- focal length for third object (f_3) = ... m
- Mean focal length = $\dfrac{f_1 + f_2 + f_3}{3}$ = ... m

Result

The approximate value of focal length of the given convex lens is .... m.

Precautions

1. The principal axis of the convex lens should be horizontal, i.e. the lens should be placed vertically.
2. There should be no obstacle in the path of rays of light from the distant object incident on the convex lens.
3. The image of the Sun formed by the lens should be focussed only on the screen. The image of the Sun should never be seen directly with the naked eye or it should never be focussed with a convex lens on any part of the body, paper or any inflammable materials as it can burn.
4. Sometimes, the parallel rays of light originating from a distant object and incident on a convex lens may not be parallel to its principal axis. The image in such situation might be formed slightly away from the principal axis of the lens.
5. The base of the stands of the convex lens and screen should be parallel to measuring scale. To determine the focal length, the distance between the convex lens and the screen should be measured horizontally.

QUESTIONS

1. All the rays, after reflection, from a concave mirror, meet at a point in front of the mirror. Name this point.

Ans. When parallel rays of light fall on a concave mirror along its axis, the rays meet at a point in front of the mirror after reflection from it. This point is called focal point of the mirror.

2. In an experiment to determine the focal length of concave mirror, the image of a distant object formed by a mirror is obtained on a screen. What distance is measured to estimate the focal length?

Ans. Focal length can be estimated by measuring the distance between the mirror and the screen.

3. Which type of mirror is used to obtain a full length image of a distant tall building or tree?

Ans. To obtain a full length image of a distant tall building or tree, a concave mirror must be used.

4. In an experiment to obtain a virtual, erect and magnified image of an object, using a concave mirror, where should the object be placed?

Ans. To obtain a virtual, erect and magnified image by using a concave mirror, object should be placed between focus and pole of the mirror.

5. Your school laboratory has a large window. To determine the focal length of a concave mirror using one of the walls as the screen, the experiment must be performed by the student on which of the wall?

Ans. The image obtained from a concave mirror can be focussed on the same wall as the window.

6. In an experiment to determine the focal length of a concave mirror, a student obtained a sharp image of a distant building on the screen. To obtain the sharp image of a window grill of the laboratory on the same screen, in which direction should he move the screen?

Ans. To obtain a sharp image of a window grill of the laboratory, the student should move the screen slightly away from the mirror.

7. Radha has to do an experiment on determining the focal length of a given concave mirror by using a distant object. Out of the following set ups (I, II, III and IV) available to her, the set up that is likely to give her the best result is

  I. A mirror holder, a screen holder and a scale.
  II. A screen, a mirror holder and a scale.
  III. A screen holder and a scale.
  IV. A mirror holder and a screen holder.

Ans. Radha requires a screen, a mirror holder and a scale to determine the focal length of a given concave mirror by using a distant object. So setup II will give her the best result.

8. What happens to the ray of light passing through the optical centre of the convex lens?

Ans. A ray of light passing through the optical centre of the lens passes without suffering any deviation.

9. In an experiment to determine the focal length of a convex lens by using the Sun as an object at infinity, Ram could not find a screen with a stand. Which method is the most appropriate and safe to be used by him as a screen.

Ans. The image of the Sun should never be focused on an inflammable object, as it can burn it. So, he can use the wall of the room.

10. *A student obtained a sharp inverted image of a distant building on the screen behind the convex lens. Then, he removed the screen and looked through the lens directly in the direction of the object. What will he observed?*

Ans. Placing a screen is just a method to observe the real image formed by a convex lens. Therefore, the image of a distant object continues to form at the focus of the convex lens even when the screen has been removed. Thus, an inverted image of the building at the focus of the lens will be observed.

11. *In an experiment to determine the focal length of a convex lens, a student obtained a sharp image of a grill of a window on a screen. To obtain the sharp image of a distant building instead of grill, in which direction should he move the lens?*

Ans. He should move the lens towards the screen, so as to bring the focus of lens on screen for image formation of distant object at focus.

12. *Rohit performs an experiment on determining the focal length of a convex lens. He kept a lighted candle at one end of table, a screen on its other end and the lens between them as shown in figure below. The positions of the three are adjusted to get a sharp image of the flame of candle on the screen.*

If now the flame of candle were to be replaced by a distant lamp on a far away electric pole, by moving the screen in which direction, Rohit would be able to get a sharp image of this distant lamp on the screen?

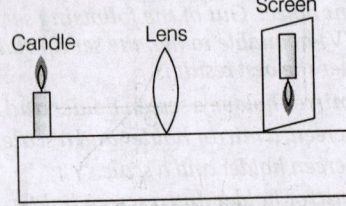

Ans. The image of a nearby object will be focussed either between F and $2F$ or at $2F$ or beyond $2F$. In order to bring the focus of lens on the screen, for the image formation of distant object at F, the lens has to be moved towards the screen or the screen towards the lens.

13. *A student was asked to select one concave mirror and one convex lens from a lot of mirrors and lenses of different kinds. What can be the correct method adopted by him?*

Ans. A concave mirror and a convex lens can only form an enlarged, virtual and erect image of an object.

14. *A student obtained a sharp image of a candle flame placed at the distant end of the laboratory table on a screen using a concave mirror to determine its focal length. The teacher suggested him to focus a distant building about 1 km far from the laboratory, for getting more correct value of the focal length. What will he do, in order to focus the distant building on the same screen?*

Ans. In order to focus the distant building on the same screen, the student should slightly move the screen towards the building. It is because more the distance of the object, image will be sharply seen at focus.

15. *To determine the approximate focal length of the given convex lens by focussing a distant object (say, a sign board), you try to focus the image of the object on a screen. What are the characteristics of image?*

Ans. On focussing the distant object through convex lens, the image we will obtain on the screen is always inverted and diminished.

16. *Suppose you have focussed on a screen the image of candle flame placed at the farthest end of the laboratory table using a convex lens. If your teacher suggests you to focus the parallel rays of the Sun, reaching your laboratory table, on the same screen, then what are you expected to do?*

Ans. The image will be closer to the focus as the distance of the object is larger. So, in this case, we will be able to get a sharp image of Sun on the screen by moving the screen in the direction of lens or the lens in the direction of screen.

17. *In the figure given below, S is the position of the screen on which a clear image of a distant object is formed by the mirror M. The object is now moved closer towards the mirror by same distance d. If $d \ll f$. How will you get a clear image?*

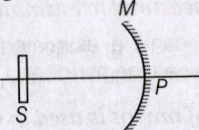

Ans. For $d \ll f$, the image is formed behind the mirror. i.e. A virtual image is formed. Since, a virtual image cannot be obtained on the screen, therefore there is no need to move the screen.

18. *A student obtains a sharp image of the distant window (W) of the school laboratory on the screen (S) using the given concave mirror (M). To determine its focal length, what distance should he measure to get the focal length of the mirror?*

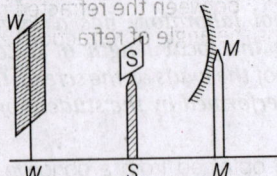

Ans. He should measure the distance between the screen (S) and the mirror, i.e. *MS*.

As the image of a distant object is obtained at the focus of concave mirror.

19. *A student used a device (X) to obtain/focus the image of a well illuminated distant building on a screen (S) as shown below in the figure. Name the device used and its focal length.*

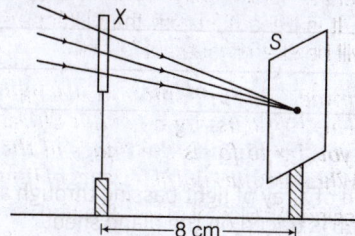

Ans. Device *X* is a convex lens of focal length 8 cm. As the rays coming from a distant building through the convex lens converges at its focus.

20. *Four students I, II, III and IV carried out measurement of focal length of a concave mirror as shown in the four diagrams.*

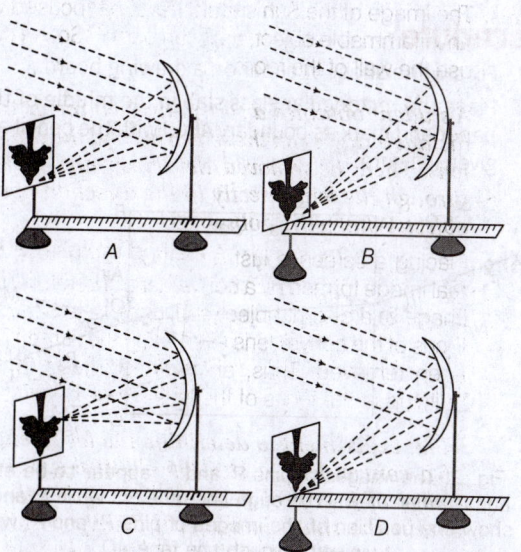

The best result will be obtained by which student?

Ans. Student *A* will obtain the best result for correct measurement of focal length, sharp image must be obtained on the screen and the meter scale must be correctly placed between screen and centre of concave mirror.

EXPERIMENT 13

Aim

To trace the path of a ray of light passing through a rectangular glass slab for different angles of incidence. Measure the angle of incidence, angle of refraction, angle of emergence and interpret the result.

Apparatus Required

A rectangular glass slab, drawing board, white sheet of paper, protractor, a measuring scale, pins and drawing pins or adhesive tape.

Theory

1. When a ray of light passes from air to glass through a rectangular glass slab, it bends towards the normal at the surface of the air-glass boundary *AD* as shown in the Fig. 1. This phenomenon is called "refraction of light".
2. Here, in this figure, the angle *XON* between the incident ray *XO* and normal *NOM* at the point of incidence *O* is the angle of incidence ($\angle i$).
3. The angle *MOO'* between the refracted ray *OO'* and the normal *NOM* is the angle of refraction ($\angle r$). Then, the refracted ray *OO'* strikes the face *BC* of the glass slab, that forms the glass air boundary at the opposite face of the glass slab *ABCD*. It undergoes refraction again.

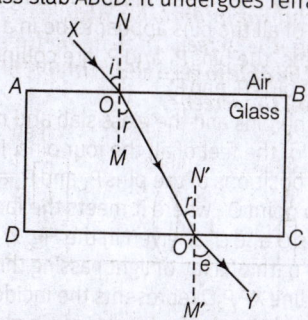

Fig. 1. Incident and emergent rays in the case of refraction through a glass slab

4. The deviation of the ray of light this time is away from the normal *M'O'N'* at the point of incidence *O'*.
5. The refracted ray *O'Y* is known as the emergent ray with respect to the incident ray *XO*, incident at the face *AD*.
6. The angle between the emergent ray *O'Y* and the normal *M'O'N'* to the face *BC*, i.e. $\angle M'O'Y$ is known as angle of emergence ($\angle e$).

Procedure

1. Fix a white sheet of paper on a drawing board.
2. Place the rectangular glass slab in the middle of the paper and mark its boundary ABCD with the pencil as given in figure.

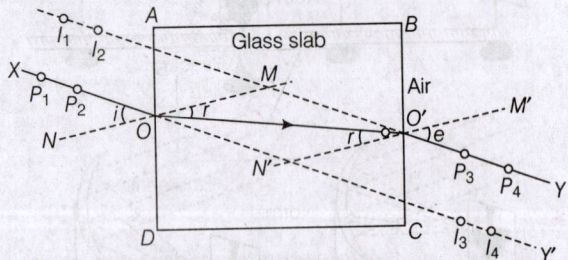

Fig. 2. The images of pins P and P appear to be at I and I when viewed through the face BC while I and I show the position of the images of pins P and P when viewed through the face AD

3. Remove the rectangular glass slab. Draw a thin line XO directing towards O and inclined to the face AD of the glass slab at any angle preferably between 30° and 60°. It is advisable to take point O in the middle of the face AD. Replace the glass slab exactly over the boundary marked on the paper.
4. Fix two pins P_1 and P_2 vertically about 5 cm apart by gently pressing their heads with thumb on the line XO.
5. Observe the images of pins P_1 and P_2 through the face BC of the rectangular glass slab. While observing the images of the pins P_1 and P_2 through the face BC of the glass slab, fix two more pins at points P_3 and P_4 such that, feet of all the pins appear to be in a straight line. In other words, the pins P_3 and P_4 are collinear with the images of pins P_1 and P_2.
6. Remove the pins and the glass slab and mark the positions of the feet of all the four pins. Join points that mark the positions of the pins P_3 and P_4 and extend the line up to point O', where it meets the face BC. Also, join the points O and O' as given in the Fig. 2, where XOO'Y show the path of a ray of light passing through the glass slab. The line XP_1P_2O represents the incident ray. Line OO' shows the path of refracted ray in glass slab while line O' P_3P_4Y shows the emergent ray.
7. Draw the normal NOM to the face AD at the point of incidence O and similarly, the normal M'ON', to the face BC at point O'. Measure the angle of incidence XON ($\angle i$), angle of refraction MOO' ($\angle r$) and angle of emergence M'O'Y ($\angle e$).
8. Record the values of $\angle i$, $\angle r$ and $\angle e$ in the observation table.
9. Repeat the experiment for two more angles of incidence in the range 30° to 60° and record the values of angles r and e in each case.

Observation Table

S. No.	Angle of incidence $\angle i = (\angle XON)$	Angle of refraction $\angle r = (\angle MOO')$	Angle of emergence $\angle e = (\angle M'O'Y)$	Deviation $\angle i - \angle e$
1.				
2.				
3.				

Results

1. The path of a ray of light passing through a rectangular glass slab is traced on the plane sheet.
2. The relation between the angle of incidence, angle of refraction and angle of emergence are obtained through different observations.
3. From observations, $\angle r < \angle i$ in each case, thus the ray entering from air to glass bends towards the normal.
4. From observation, $\angle i = \angle e$, the emergent ray emerging out of the rectangular glass slab, is parallel to, but laterally displaced with respect to the incident ray.
5. Angle of refraction $\angle r$ increases with increase in angle of incidence $\angle i$.

Precautions

1. The glass slab should be perfectly rectangular with all its faces smooth.
2. The tips of pins P_1, P_2, P_3 and P_4 should be sharp. These pins fixed on the sheet of paper may not be exactly perpendicular to the plane of paper. Thus, if their heads appear to be collinear, their feet may not be so. It must, therefore be important to look at the feet of pins and their images while ascertaining collinearity between them. The mark of the pointed end or the foot of a pin on the paper must be considered while marking its position.
3. The distance of 5 cm between the pins P_1 and P_2 or P_3 and P_4 must be carefully maintained to obtain an accurate direction of incident ray and that of emergent ray with greater accuracy.
4. Take, the angle of incidence preferably between 30° and 60°.
5. Thin lines should be drawn using a sharp pencil to obtain accuracy.
6. The angles should be measured accurately using a good quality protractor having clear markings by keeping the eye above the marking.

QUESTIONS

1. *What should be the range of angle of incidence while performing the experiment of tracing the path of ray of light passing through the glass slab, to get the best result?*

Ans. The angle of incidence, while performing this experiment to get the best result must be in the range 30° to 60°.

2. *What is the relation between angle of incidence $\angle i$, angle of refraction $\angle r$ and angle of emergence $\angle e$ in the glass slab experiment?*

Ans. As the ray enters from air to glass, therefore it bends towards the normal such that $\angle r < \angle i$. Also, the emergent ray, emerging from glass slab, is parallel to, but laterally displaced with respect to the incident ray such that $\angle i = \angle e$.

3. *What happens to the ray of light, when it emerges out from glass slab to air in the glass slab experiment?*

Ans. When a ray of light travels from a denser medium to a rarer medium, it bends away from the normal. Hence, it bends away from the normal at glass-air interface.

4. *When a ray of light is incident on a glass slab perpendicularly in glass slab experiment, then what will happen to the ray of light?*

Ans. When a ray of light is incident on a glass slab perpendicularly, then the ray of light passes undeviated through it.

5. *In an experiment to trace the path of a ray of light passing through a rectangular glass slab, the correct markings of angle of incidence (i), angle of refraction (r) and angle of emergence (e) is shown below in which diagram?*

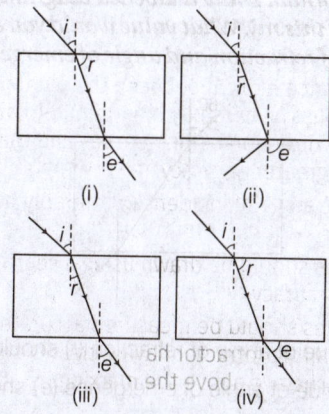

Ans. The angle of incidence (i) is the angle between the incident ray and the normal at the air-glass interface, the angle of refraction (r) is the angle between the refracted ray and the normal at air-glass interface and the angle of emergence is the angle between the emergent ray and the normal at the glass-air interface as shown below:

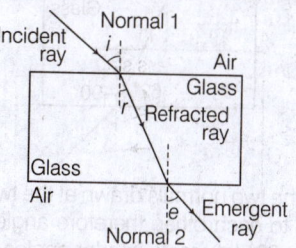

6. *Ram while performing an experiment on tracing the path of a light ray passing through a rectangular glass slab, measured three angles marked as θ_1, θ_2 and θ_3 in the figure. How θ_1, θ_2 and θ_3 related?*

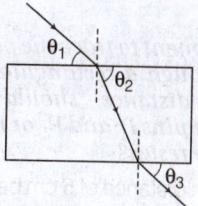

Ans. Since, in glass slab experiment,

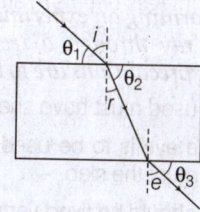

$\angle i > \angle r$ but $\angle e = \angle i$
$\Rightarrow \quad \theta_1 < \theta_2$ but $\theta_1 = \theta_3$

7. *Mohit performed the glass slab experiment using different angles of incidences. He measured the angles of refraction and emergence in each case and recorded them as given in the table.*

S.No.	Angle of incidence ($\angle i$)	Angle of refraction ($\angle r$)	Angle of emergence ($\angle e$)
1.	30°	25°	30°
2.	40°	45°	40°
3.	50°	52°	54°
4.	60°	58°	64°

Which of the observation made by him is correct?

Ans. In glass slab experiment,
$$\angle i > \angle r \text{ and } \angle e = \angle i$$
So, observation 1 is correct.

8. A ray of light is incident on a glass slab as shown in the figure below. What will be the angle of refraction for this ray of light?

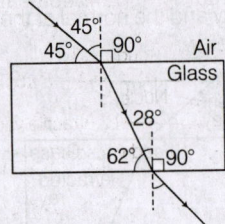

Ans. Since, the two normals drawn at the two interfaces are parallel to each other, therefore angle of refraction is equal to 28° (alternate interior angles are equal).

9. What happens to the refraction angle, when angle of incidence increases in the experiment to trace the path of a ray of light passing through a glass slab?

Ans. Angle of refraction increases with increase in angle of incidence.

10. In an experiment to trace the path of a ray of light passing through a rectangular glass slab, what minimum distance should be maintained between the pins P_1 and P_2 or P_3 and P_4 to obtain the accurate result?

Ans. The minimum distance of 5 cm between pins P_1 and P_2 or P_3 and P_4 must be carefully maintained to obtain an accurate result.

11. While performing an experiment, to trace the path of a light ray through a rectangular glass slab, which four precautions are to be taken?

Ans. (i) all pins used must have sharp points.

(ii) only one eye is to be used in fixing two pins on other side of the slab.

(iii) all pins should be fixed vertically.

(iv) The first two pins for incident ray are fixed such that the line joining the pins is inclined to the edge of the glass slab.
However, the two pins on the other side of the slab are fixed by looking through the glass slab.

12. A student performs an experiment on finding the focal length of a convex lens by keeping a lighted candle on one end of laboratory table, a screen on its other end and the lens between them as shown in the figure.

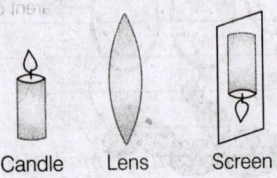

Candle　　Lens　　Screen

The positions of the three are adjusted to get a sharp image of the candle flame on the screen. If now the candle flame were to be replaced by a distant lamp on a far away electric pole, how would the student be able to get a sharp image of this distant lamp on the screen? Explain.

Ans. The image will be closer to focus as the distance of the object is larger. So, the student would be able to get a sharp image of distant object on the screen by moving the screen in the direction of the lens or the lens in the direction of screen, i.e. by bringing the lens and screen closer.

13. While tracing the path of ray of light through a glass slab, the angle of incidence is generally taken between 30° and 60°. Explain, the reason on the basis of your performing this experiment of different angles of incidence.

Ans. On the basis of experiment, it is observed that

(i) the angle of emergence also increases with the increase in angle of incidence or vice-versa.

(ii) if the angle of incidence is less than 30°, very less bending occurs at the emergent glass-air interface.

(iii) if the angle of incidence is greater than 60°, the emergent ray may emerge from the side surface of the rectangular glass slab instead of opposite parallel surface.

Hence, angle of incidence should be taken between 30° and 60° for tracing the path of ray of light through a glass slab.

14. In an experiment with a rectangular glass slab, a student observed that a ray of light incident at an angle of 60° with the normal on one face of the slab, after refraction strikes the opposite face of the slab before emerging out into air making an angle of 42° with normal. Draw a labelled diagram to show the path of this ray. What value would you assign to the angle of refraction and angle of emergence?

Ans.

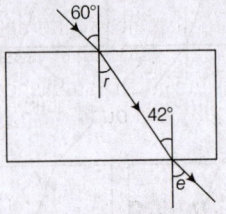

The value of angle of refraction (r) should be 42°.
The value of angle of emergence (e) should be 60°.

EXPERIMENT 14

Aim
To study (a) binary fission in *Amoeba* and (b) budding in yeast and *Hydra* with the help of prepared permanent slides.

Materials Required
Permanent slides showing binary fission in *Amoeba* and budding in yeast and *Hydra*, compound, microscope, worksheets, pencil, eraser, sharpener, etc.

Theory
- Reproduction is one of the basic characteristic feature of living organisms.
- An organism reproduces, in order to form individuals of its own kind.
- Reproduction may be either asexual or sexual in living organisms.
- The type of reproduction taking place without fusion of gametes is called asexual reproduction.
- Sexual reproduction is a type of reproduction in which male and female gametes are involved.
- Asexual reproduction involves only one parent cell and is common in lower organisms. It is the process of rapid multiplication in which the new organisms produced are genetically identical to the parent.
- Asexual reproduction may be of various types, such as binary fission, multiple fission, budding, fragmentation, sporulation and vegetative propagation.

Procedure
1. Take a permanent slide showing binary fission in *Amoeba* and budding in yeast and *Hydra*.
2. Carefully observe the various stages of binary fission of *Amoeba* and budding in yeast and *Hydra* with the help of a compound microscope.
3. Observe each permanent slide first under lower magnification and then under higher magnification of compound microscope.
4. Draw well-labelled diagram of different stages of binary fission in *Amoeba* and budding in yeast and *Hydra*.
5. Compare the features with established characteristics of fission in *Amoeba* and budding in yeast and *Hydra*.

Observations

Binary Fission in *Amoeba*
- *Amoeba* reproduces by binary fission method where division of parent cell and its components occurs by stretching.
- Nucleus breaks into two daughter nuclei (karyokinesis) slowly followed by division of cytoplasm (cytokinesis).
- Two identical daughter cells (Amoebae) are formed at the end of division.
- Thus, two new daughter Amoebae are formed from a single parent.

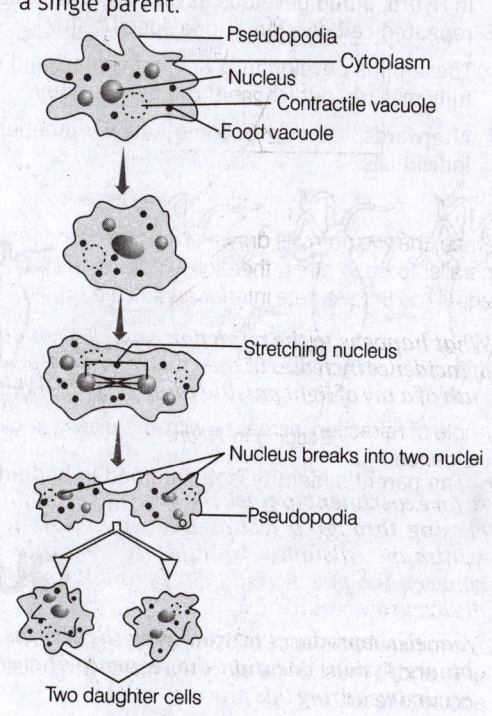

Binary fission in *Amoeba*

Budding in Yeast
- Yeast cells are larger and spherical or oval in shape.
- In asexual reproduction of yeast, there is a bulb-like projection (cytoplasmic extensions) also called as bud. It arises from the parent cell.
- Nucleus starts dividing first by stretching followed by cytokinesis.
- Then the nucleus of the parent cell divides by mitosis and later forms two daughter nuclei.
- One of the two daughter nuclei migrates into the enlarging bud forming a daughter cell.

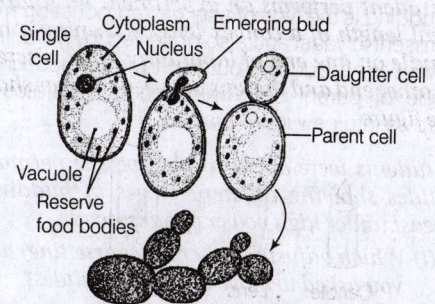

Budding in *Yeast*

- The bud is finally separated from the parent body (cell). They grows into a new individual.
- The parent's identity is maintained in budding.

Budding in *Hydra*

- Organisms such as *Hydra* use regenerative cells for reproduction in the process of budding.
- In *Hydra*, a bud develops as an outgrowth due to repeated cell division at one specific site.
- These buds develop into tiny individuals and when fully mature, detach from the parent body.
- Afterwards, they become new independent individuals.

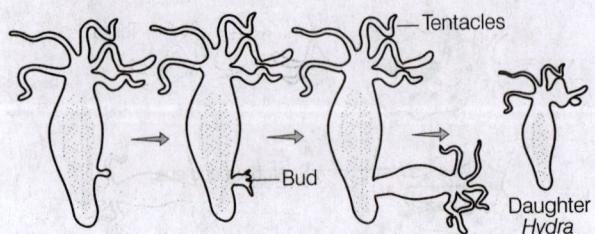

Budding in *Hydra*

- The parent's identity is maintained in budding.

Result and Discussion

The prepared slides show asexual reproduction in which only one individual is involved in the formation of new individuals.

Precautions

1. Slides should be handled carefully.
2. Clean the stage of microscope before and after the use.
3. Do not tilt the microscope and hold it vertically.
4. Slide should be firmly clipped on the stage.
5. Focus the slides properly.
6. First observe under low power of objective and than change to high power lens for better and detailed study.
7. Draw the detailed diagram of structures seen under the microscope.
8. Keep microscope in box carefully when not in use.

QUESTIONS

1. *Amoeba reproduces asexually by the process of binary fission. Mention the sequence of events occurring during this process.*

Ans. The correct sequence of events in binary fission of *Amoeba* is

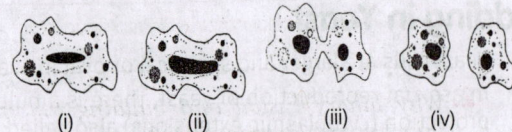

(i) duplication of cellular contents
(ii) appearance of pseudopodia
(iii) stretching of nucleus
(iv) separated daughter nuclei.

2. *Asexual reproduction by budding occurs in which organisms?*

Ans. Budding is the type of asexual reproduction mainly present in yeast and also observed in *Hydra*. In this process, a bud-like outgrowth is formed on one side of parent cell, which soon separates and grows into new individual.

3. *Students were asked to observe the permanent slides showing different stages of budding in yeast under high power of microscope.*
(i) *Which adjustment screw (coarse/fine) were you asked to move to focus the slides?*
(ii) *Draw three diagrams in correct sequence showing budding in yeast.*

Ans. (i) Fine adjustment screw is to be used to focus on the movement of yeast under high power of a microscope.
(ii) The correct sequence A-D shows the budding in yeast.

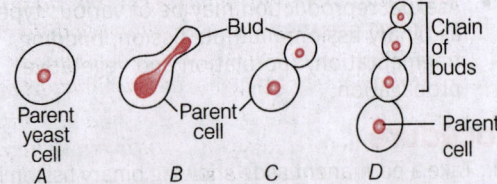

4. *The figure given below demonstrates which process of division in Amoeba?*

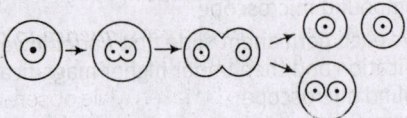

Ans. Amitosis is the process by which a cell directly separates, as the nucleus and cytoplasm are directly cut into two. During binary fission in *Amoeba* the nucleus divides amitotically into two, which is followed by the division of cytoplasm.

5. *During the process of binary fission, the organism undergoes 3-4 stages of division. Which type of cell division occurs during this process? Name the first division of amoebic cell.*

Ans. Mitosis during binary fission division of nucleus, i.e. karyokinesis occurs first. It is followed by cytoplasmic division.

6. *From the following diagrams, identify the correct sequence of binary fission in Amoeba:*

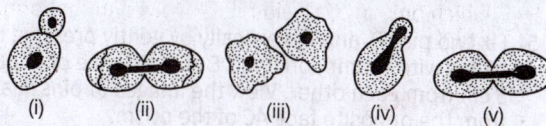

(i)   (ii)   (iii)   (iv)   (v)

Ans. The correct stages of binary fission are shown in the figures (ii), (v) and (iii). In the figures (ii) and (v) there is stretching of nucleus is seen and in figure (iii) there are two daughter amoebae formed after fission. The stages (i) and (iv) represent budding.

7. *Following diagrams were drawn by different students on having seen prepared slides of budding in yeast.*

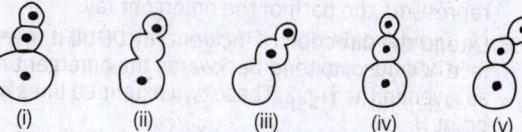

(i)   (ii)   (iii)   (iv)   (v)

Which of these are correct diagrams?

Ans. From the diagrams drawn in the question only (i), (iv) and (v) represent the correct diagrams of budding in yeast. As in the other two figures (ii) and (iii) either the parent is lacking nucleus or the bud is lacking nucleus, which does not occur in the case of budding.

8. *A student has to focus his compound microscope to observe a prepared slide showing different stages of binary fission in Amoeba. The steps, he is likely to follow are listed below in a haphazard manner:*

  I. *Adjust the diaphragm and the mirror of the microscope so, that sufficient light may enter to illuminate the slide.*
  II. *Fix the slide on the stage carefully.*
  III. *Adjust the microscope to high power and focus.*
  IV. *Adjust the microscope to low power and focus.*

Arrange them into correct sequence to observe the slide under the microscope.

Ans. The correct steps to be taken while observing different stages of binary fission in *Amoeba* are

II ⟶ I ⟶ IV ⟶ III.

9. *You are given two slides, one with binary fission in Amoeba and other with budding in Hydra. How would you identify which of the given slide is showing binary fission on the basis of the number of nuclei present?*

Ans. The slide showing two nuclei in the centrally constricted organism is binary fission in *Amoeba*, the other slide would be showing one nuclei in the parent cell body and another one in the bud, thus proving budding in *Hydra*.

10. *A student is observing a permanent slide showing sequentially the different stages of asexual reproduction taking place in Hydra. Name this process and draw diagrams of what he observes in a proper sequence.*

Ans. *Hydra* shows budding, a type of asexual reproduction in which a daughter organism is formed from a small projection known as bud, which develops as an outgrowth due to repeated cell divisions on the parent body.

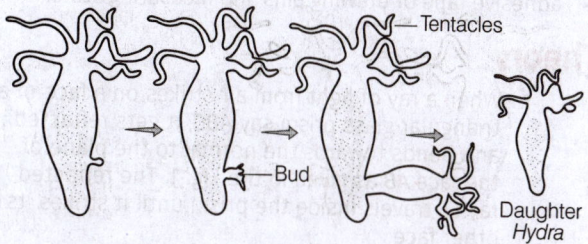

11. *Write down the differences between reproduction in yeast and reproduction in Amoeba.*

Ans.

Reproduction in Yeast	Reproduction in Amoeba
Yeast reproduces through the process of regeneration called budding.	*Amoeba* reproduces through binary fission.
In yeast, buds develop on the parent body and grow into tiny individuals and may detach from it after maturity.	In *Amoeba*, nucleus divides into two daughter nuclei followed by cytoplasmic division.
Cell division does not occur during reproduction in yeast.	In reproduction of *Amoeba*, cell division occurs.

12. *Why binary fission and budding are included under asexual reproduction?*

Ans. In both these processes, only one parent is involved in reproduction process. There is no formation and fusion of male and female gametes.

13. *Draw a labelled diagram to show that particular stage of binary fission in Amoeba in which its nucleus elongates and divides into two and a constriction appears in its cell membrane.*

Ans. The stage of binary fission in *Amoeba* in which its nucleus elongates and divides into two and a constriction appears in its cells membrane is given below:

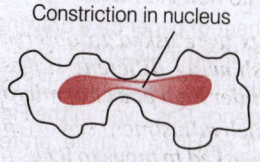

Amoeba dividing

EXPERIMENT 15

Aim
To trace the path of the rays of light through a glass prism.

Apparatus Required
A glass prism, drawing board, white paper, pins, adhesive tape or drawing pins and measuring scale.

Theory
- When a ray of light from air strikes on a face of a triangular glass prism say ABC, it gets refracted and bends towards the normal to the plane of the face AB as given in the Fig. 1. The refracted ray EF travels inside the prism until it strikes its other face.

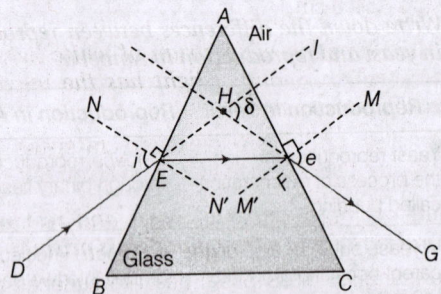

Fig. 1. Refraction of light through a prism

- Here again, the ray from glass gets refracted into air but bends away from the normal towards the face BC.
- Here, the ray FG is the ray that emerges out of the glass prism at the glass-air boundary face AC.
- The ray FG that emerges out of the glass prism at the face AC after successive refractions is the emergent ray.
- Usually, the emergent ray is bent towards the base BC of the prism as shown in Fig. 1.
- The angle ∠IHG between the incident ray DE, when extended and the emergent ray FG, when produced backwards to meet at a point H is known as the angle of deviation (∠δ).

Procedure
1. Fix a white sheet of paper on a drawing board. Draw a thin line XY at the middle of the paper.
2. Draw a thin line NEN' perpendicular to the line XY at point of incidence E as given in the Fig. 2, below. Also, draw a line DE making any angle, preferably between 30° and 60°.
3. Place the prism with one of its refracting surfaces AB along the line XY.
4. Mark the boundary ABC of the glass prism holding it firmly with your hand.

5. Fix two pins P_1 and P_2 vertically by gently pressing their heads with thumb, on line DE at a distance of about 5 cm from each other. View the images of pins P_1 and P_2 from the opposite face AC of the prism.
6. Fix two more pins P_3 and P_4 vertically such that the feet of pins P_3 and P_4 appear to be on the same straight line as the feet of the images of the pins P_1 and P_2 as viewed through the face AC of the prism.
7. Remove the pins and prism. Mark the positions of feet of pins P_3 and P_4 on the sheet of paper.
8. Draw a straight line joining the points that mark the positions of pins P_3 and P_4. Extend this line, so that it meets the face AC of the prism at point F. The line FG represents the path of the emergent ray.
9. Extend the direction of incident ray DE till it meets the face AFC. Also, extend backwards the emergent ray FG as given in the Fig. 2. These two extended lines meet at point H.

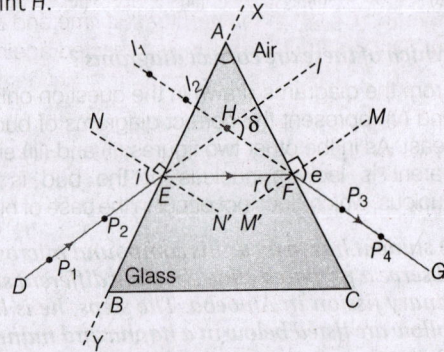

Fig. 2. The images of pins P_1 and P_2 appear to be at I_1 and I_2 when viewed through the face AC of the glass prism. Rays DE, EF and FG represent the incident, refracted and emergent rays, respectively. ∠DEN is the angle of incidence (∠i) and ∠FHI is the angle of deviation (∠δ).

Result
The path of a ray of light incident on one face of a glass prism is shown by the ray DEFG in Fig. 2.

Precautions
1. While viewing the collinearity of pins and images, the eye should be kept at a distance from the pins, so that all of them can be seen simultaneously.
2. The pins P_1, P_2, P_3 and P_4 fixed on the paper may not be exactly perpendicular to the plane of paper. It is, therefore desirable to look at the feet of the pins or their images while establishing their collinearity. Thus, the position of each pin is marked with pointed tip of the pins on the paper.
3. In order to locate the direction of incident ray and refracted ray with a greater accuracy, the distance between the pins P_1 and P_2 and that between P_3 and P_4 should not be too short or too large. A separation of nearly 5 cm between the pins would be sufficient.
4. The angle of incidence should preferably be taken between 30° and 60°.

QUESTIONS

1. *In an experiment to trace the path of the rays of light through a glass prism, what happens to the ray of light striking on a face of prism?*

Ans. When a ray of light from air strikes on a face of a triangular glass prism, it gets refracted and bends towards the normal to the plane.

2. *In an experiment to trace the path of the rays of light through a glass prism, what happens to the ray of light emerging from a prism?*

Ans. When a ray of light emerges from a prism, it gets refracted and bends away from the normal.

3. *Tell about the number of times a ray of light gets refracted while passing through a triangular glass prism?*

Ans. When a ray of light strikes on the first face of triangular glass prism, it gets refracted for first time and bends towards the normal, which gets refracted again from the second face and bends away from the normal.

4. *In an experiment to trace the path of a light through a glass prism, four students traced the path of ray of light refracted through prism as shown below.*

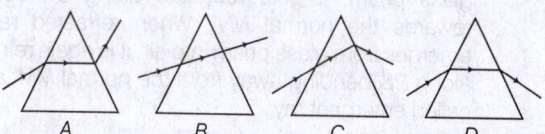

Which one of them traced the correct path?

Ans. When a ray of light strikes a glass prism, it gets refracted and bends towards the normal, which gets refracted again from the other face of prism and bends away from the normal. So, student D traced the correct path.

5. *Why does a prism splits a beam of white light passing through it into seven colours?*

Ans. Splitting of white light into its component colours on passing through the prism is due to the difference in velocities of colours.

6. *A ray of light passes through a prism of angle 60° in the minimum deviation position. Find the angle of refraction inside the prism.*

Ans. When the prism is placed in minimum deviation position, the angle of refraction is, $r = \dfrac{A}{2} = \dfrac{60°}{2} = 30°$
where, A = angle of prism.

7. *In the formation of spectrum of white light by a prism, which of the colours are deviated the least and the most?*

Ans. The red colour which has the maximum wavelength is deviated the least and the violet colour which has the minimum wavelength is deviated the most.

8. *When a ray of light incident on a glass prism suffers minimum deviation, give the relations between A and r?*

Ans. (c) For a prism in minimum deviation position, relations between A and r are $i = \dfrac{A + \delta_m}{2}$, $i = e$ and $r = A/2$.

9. *In glass prism experiment, give the sufficient distance between the pins to get accuracy for the direction of incident ray and emergent ray.*

Ans. The sufficient distance between the pins P_1 and P_2 or P_3 and P_4 is 5 cm.

10. *In the formation of spectrum of white light by a prism, which colour of light has the maximum speed in glass prism?*

Ans. The yellow colour has the maximum speed in the glass prism among the other given colours.

11. *What are the number of bases and rectangular lateral surfaces in a triangular glass prism?*

Ans. The triangular glass prism has five surfaces out of which two are triangular bases and three are rectangular lateral surfaces.

12. *State the relation between angle of incidence (i), angle of emergence (e), angle of prism (A) and angle of deviation (δ).*

Ans. The relation is given by
$$i + e = A + \delta$$

13. *In a glass prism experiment, if a ray of light is incident normally on one of the faces of the prism, then what will be the angle of refraction?*

Ans. For a normally incident ray, both the angle of incidence and angle of refraction are zero.

14. *For the following ray diagram, which of the angles are correctly marked?*

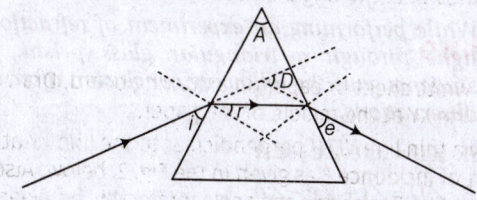

Ans. From the figure, the correctly marked angles are
A = Angle of prism, D = angle of deviation
r = Angle of refraction

15. Study the following diagrams in which the path of a ray of light passing through a glass prism as traced by four students P, Q, R and S are shown below

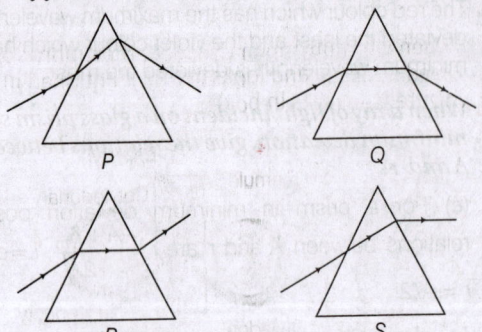

Which student who has traced the path correctly?

Ans. Student Q has traced the path correctly. When a ray of light travels from a rarer (air) to a denser medium of prism, it bends towards the normal to the first surface and when a ray of light travels from a denser medium of prism to a rarer medium (air), it bends away from the normal to the second surface.

16. A student traces the path of a ray of light through a triangular glass prism for different values of angle of incidence. On analysing the ray diagrams, how will emergent angle behave?

Ans. The peculiar shape of the prism makes the emergent ray bend at an angle to the direction of the incident ray.

17. While doing experiment to trace the path of a ray of light through a triangular glass prism, a student is not getting emergent ray in straight line. The probable reason for that may be
 (i) he did not mark the boundary of prism
 (ii) while performing experiment, prism got displaced from its original position
 (iii) pins used to trace the path were not exactly vertical
 (iv) pins used to trace the path were not in straight line

Ans. All the reasons are correct for not getting the emergent ray in a straight line.

18. While performing an experiment of refraction of light through a triangular glass prism, four students gave the following conclusion after their observations.
  A. $\angle D = \angle i - \angle e + \angle A$
  B. $\angle D = \angle i + \angle e - \angle A$
  C. $\angle D = \angle i - \angle e - \angle A$
  D. $\angle D = \angle i + \angle e + \angle A$

Which student gave the correct conclusion?

Ans. The conclusion given by student B is correct, i.e.
$\angle D = \angle i + \angle e - \angle A$
where, $\angle D$ = angle of deviation
$\angle i$ = angle of incidence
$\angle e$ = angle of emergence
$\angle A$ = angle of prism

19. A student while doing the experiment of tracing the path of ray of light through a triangular glass prism is not able to see the image of object (pins) properly. What may be the possible reason behind this?

Ans. In order to see the clear image of an object (pins), prism should be placed on white paper.

20. An experiment of tracing the path of light rays through a triangular glass prism was set up in the laboratory and ray diagram was drawn as shown.

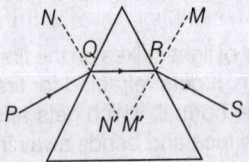

Identify refracted ray.

Ans. When an incident ray of light PQ enters from air into glass prism, it gets refracted along QR bending towards the normal NN'. When refracted ray QR emerges from glass prism into air, it is again refracted along RS bending away from the normal MM' and is called emergent ray.

21. Mention some precautions that should be taken while doing the experiment on tracing the path of the rays of light through a glass prism.

Ans. Following precautions should be taken:
 (i) Prism should be within the boundary made all through the experimentation.
 (ii) Pins should be fixed vertically to the plane of the paper.
 (iii) The distance between the pins should be at least 5 cm.
 (iv) Protractor should be used correctly to measure the angles.
 (v) Angle of incidence should be taken between 30° and 60° to observe the refraction clearly.

22. Why does the white light not split into different colours when it passes through a glass slab?

Ans. A glass slab may be considered to be made up of two prism kept inverted with respect to each other. So, when a beam of white light passes through one prism, it gets dispersed, but on passing through second inverted prism, the spectrum recombines to form a beam of white light again.

EXPERIMENT 16

Aim
To identify the different parts of an embryo of a dicot seed.

Materials Required
Whole gram seeds (Dicot seed), petridish, forceps, needles, hand lens or dissecting microscope and cotton cloth/wool.

Theory
- A seed is a ripened ovule with a small embryonic plant enclosed in a covering called seed coat, usually with some stored food.
- The gram seed is formed within a small pod or legume.
- It is light brown in colour.
- Its surface may be smooth or wrinkled.
- The furrow in the middle of seed bears an oval dark patch called chalaza.
- A seed has following parts, i.e. hilum, seed coat, an embryo and an endosperm.
- The small oval scar present on seed coat is called hilum.
- In between the hilum and pointed end, a small pore called micropyle is present.
- The seeds soak water through the micropyle during seed germination.

Procedure
1. Take about 25-30 seeds of gram (*Cicer arietinum*).
2. Put these seeds for germination for 3-4 days by placing them on moist cotton wool or moist blotting paper.
3. After 3-4 days, take/select well-germinated seeds.
4. Swiftly remove the seed coat of seeds.
5. Gently separate/open the two parts of the seeds.
6. Study the different parts of seeds using a hand lens and record your observations.

Observations
When we split open the germinated seeds, the following observations can be easily made on the seeds.
1. Gram seed has a brown covering, which is called seed coat, easily separable from germinated seeds. It provides protection to underlying parts of the seed.
2. Micropyle is a pore present at the grooved side of the seeds. Water enters the seed through this pore, seed imbibes water, becomes activated and starts germination process.
3. When we gently open the seed, the embryo of the seed is visible and looks like as mentioned in the figure (see parts in box).

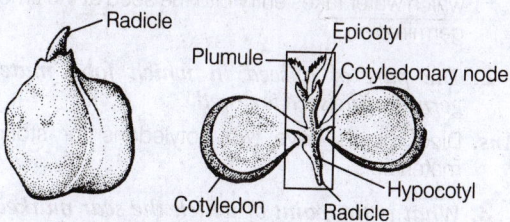

4. The middle portion of the seed is called embryonal axis.
5. It bears epicotyl and hypocotyl.
6. Epicotyl gives rise to plumule, whereas hypocotyl gives rise to radicle.
7. Attached with embryonal axis are two broad leaf-like structures called cotyledons.

Result and Discussion
The seed is a miniature plant. It is a dormant stage, but is a living entity. When given optimum conditions (water, temperature, soil, proper aeration), it germinates.

The embryo of dicot seed is easily seen in the germinated seed. Embryo of a dicot seed includes two cotyledons and tigellum.

Cotyledons are leaf of the embryo having reserve food material.

Tigellum is main axis of the embryo having epicotyl and hypocotyl.

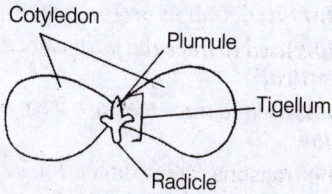

Precautions
1. Healthy seeds should be choosen for this study.
2. These should be properly placed for germination (provide all necessary conditions for seed germination).
3. Well-germinated gram seed should be selected for study.
4. Gentle and soft handling of the germinated seed is required otherwise embryonal axis gets broken easily.

QUESTIONS

1. **Identify the opening present in a seed through which seed absorbs water at the time of seed germination.**

   Ans. The micropyle is a small opening of a seed through which water takes entry into the seed at the time of seed germination.

2. **The part of a seed in which food material for germinating seed is stored.**

   Ans. Dicot plants have two cotyledons for storing food material.

3. **What is the point of which the scar marked on the seed present near the micropyle?**

   Ans. Hilum is that point of seed by which it is attached to the ovary. It remains in the form of a scar on the seed.

4. **What do you call the food laiden tissue present in the developing seed?**

   Ans. The food laiden tissue, either present on one side of the embryo or surrounding the embryo on either sides is endosperm.

5. **In a germinating seed, the radicle emerges before the plumule, why?**

   Ans. The radicle emerges before the plumule because it needs to penetrate into the soil to facilitate water absorption for the growing embryo.

6. **A seed is covered by a hard coat on its outside surface, what purpose is served by this seed coat?**

   Ans. (i) Protection of embryo present inside the seed.

   (ii) Prevent any type of physical harm.

   (iii) Dehydration of embryo is prevented by the seed coat.

7. **Suggest a reason for overnight soaking of the seeds before the start of experiment.**

   Ans. During soaking, the cotyledons absorb water from the container and become actively germinating.

PERIODIC TESTS

Pre-Mid Term Tests
{Chapters covered—Chemistry (1, 2), Physics (9, 10), Biology (5, 6) }

TEST 1

1. Two solutions A and B have pH values 6 and 8, respectively. Which of the following statements is correct?
   (a) Solution A having pH 6 is basic
   (b) Solution B having pH 8 is acidic
   (c) Solution A and B, both are acidic
   (d) Solution B having pH 8 is basic

2. .... is the part of brain, which controls posture and balance of the body.
   (a) Cerebrum   (b) Cerebellum
   (c) Brain stem   (d) Medulla

3. The human eye can focus objects at different distance by adjusting the focal length of the eye lens. This is due to
   (a) accommodation   (b) far sightedness
   (c) near-sightedness (d) presbyopia

4. Which phenomenon is responsible for increasing the apparent length of the day by 4 min?

5. Write the functions of two upper chambers of human heart.

6. Identify the reducing agent in the following reaction:
   $Fe_2O_3 + 3CO \longrightarrow 2Fe + 3CO_2$

7. A real image, one-fifth the size of object is formed at a distance of 18 cm from a mirror. What is the nature of mirror? Calculate its focal length. [**Ans.** $f = -15$ cm]

8. A brown substance X on heating in air forms a substance Y. When hydrogen gas is passed over heated Y, it again changes back into X. Name the substance X and Y.

9. What are the end products formed during fermentation in yeast? Under what conditions a similar process takes place in our body that leads to muscle cramps?

Test 2

1. Which of the following reactions is a type of single displacement reaction?
   (a) $Fe(s) + CuSO_4(aq) \longrightarrow FeSO_4(aq) + Cu(s)$
   (b) $3Fe + 4H_2O \longrightarrow Fe_3O_4 + 4H_2$
   (c) $CH_4 + 2O_2 \xrightarrow{\Delta} CO_2 + 2H_2O$
   (d) $AgNO_3 + NaBr \longrightarrow AgBr + NaNO_3$

2. Which one of the following organelles is the site where photosynthesis occurs?
   (a) Vacuole   (b) Chromoplast
   (c) Chloroplast   (d) Cytoplasm

3. The plant hormone whose function is to inhibits growth and also promotes wilting of leaves is ....

   (a) abscisic acid   (b) auxin
   (c) ethylene   (d) cytokinin)

4. The image formed by a pin hole camera is sharpest when the
   (a) camera is used in a dark room
   (b) object is brightly illuminated
   (c) distance from the pin hole to the object is small
   (d) hole is very small

5. Why does the sky appear to be dark instead of blue to an astronaut?

6. Two solutions A and B have pH values of 5 and 8, respectively. Which solution will be basic in nature?

7. Write balanced chemical equation for the following reactions
   (i) Silver bromide on exposure to sunlight decomposes into silver and bromine.
   (ii) Sodium metal reacts with water to form sodium hydroxide and hydrogen gas.

8. Explain why transportation of materials is necessary in animals.

9. Describe the formation of rainbow in the sky with the help of a diagram.

Test 3

1. The common name of the compound $CaOCl_2$ is
   (a) baking soda
   (b) caustic soda
   (c) slaked lime
   (d) bleaching powder

2. The process of slow oxidation of oil and fat present in food materials resulting in the change of smell and taste in them is called as
   (a) precipitation
   (b) rancidity
   (c) corrosion
   (d) Both (a) and (b)

3. Which one of the following substances is oxidised in body during respiration?
   (a) Starch   (b) Glucose
   (c) Carbon dioxide (d) All of these

4. A virtual image, larger than the object can be produced by
   (a) plane mirror   (b) concave lens
   (c) convex mirror   (d) concave mirror

5. State the laws of reflection of light.

6. How do auxins promote the growth of a tendril around a support?

7. How would you distinguish between baking powder and washing soda by heating?

8. State in brief the role of lungs in the exchange of gases.

9. Light enters from air to diamond with refractive index 2.42. What is the speed of light in diamond? (Given, speed of light in air is 3×10^8 ms^{-1}) [Ans. 1.24×10^8 ms^{-1}]

TEST 4

1. Aluminium reacts with ferric oxide. Which of the following is the correct a balanced chemical equation for the above reaction?
   (a) $2Al + 2FeO \longrightarrow Al_2O_3 + 2Fe$
   (b) $Al + Fe_2O_3 \longrightarrow Al_2O_3 + Fe$
   (c) $Fe_2O_3 + 2Al \longrightarrow Al_2O_3 + 2Fe$
   (d) $Al_2O_3 + Fe \longrightarrow Fe_2O_3 + 2Al$

2. In the chlor alkali process, the gases which liberate at anode and cathode are respectively
   (a) H_2 and Cl_2 (b) O_2 and H_2
   (c) N_2 and H_2 (d) Cl_2 and H_2

3. A person standing in front of a mirror finds his image larger than himself. This implies that the mirror is
   (a) concave
   (b) cylindrical with bulging side outwards
   (c) plane
   (d) convex

4. Justify the statement, 'plants and animals are pH sensitive.'

5. Why does a ray of light passing through the centre of curvature of a concave mirror, gets reflected along the same path?

6. How can you identify regarding the type of defect a person is suffering from by physically touching his spectacles?

7. Alveoli are called functional unit of lungs. Give reason.

8. A plant hormone X causes stomatal closure. Name X. Give any two hormones which can reverse the effect of X on plant growth.

9. Havi-like structures called Ilia are formed in the trachea of living organisms. What is the function of Ilia in the tracheal tube?

TEST 5

1. The reaction between an acid and salt is termed as
   (a) precipitation reaction
   (b) single displacement reaction
   (c) neutralisation reaction
   (d) decomposition reaction

2. Which of the following is a redox reaction?
   (a) $BaCl_2 + PbSO_4 \longrightarrow BaSO_4 + PbCl_2$
   (b) $CuSO_4 \cdot 5H_2O \xrightarrow{Heat} CuSO_4 + 5H_2O$
   (c) $CaO + H_2O \longrightarrow Ca(OH)_2 + Heat$
   (d) $CuO + H_2 \xrightarrow{\Delta} Cu + H_2O$

3. A piece of cloth looks red in sunlight. It is held in the blue portion of solar spectrum, it will appear
   (a) white (b) black (c) blue (d) red

4. Name the gas evolved when dilute hydrochloric acid reacts with sodium carbonate. How is it recognised?

5. A person suffering from an eye defect uses lenses of power –1D. Name the defect he is suffering from and nature of lens used.

6. If the magnification of a body of size 1m is 2, what is the size of the image?

7. State the equation for anerobic respiration in yeast.

8. In emergency situations, gland A produces X hormone. Identify A and X. Also, suggest any two responses which occur due to the release of X in the body.

9. Why is chlorophyll pigment essential in green plants?

Mid Term Tests

{Chapters covered—Chemistry (1, 2, 3 and 4), Physics (9, 10, 11 and 12), Biology (5, 6, 7 and 8)}

Test 1

1. Which of the following combinations of sex chromosomes produces a male child?
   (a) XX   (b) XY
   (c) XO   (d) YO

2. Detergents are usually
   (a) sodium or potassium salts of long chain carboxylic acids
   (b) ammonium or sulphonate salts of long chain carboxylic acids
   (c) sodium or potassium salts of long chain of esters
   (d) ammonium or sulphonate salts of long chain of esters

3. If n equal resistance are first connected in series and then connected in parallel, the ratio of the maximum to the minimum resistance is
   (a) $\dfrac{1}{n}$ (b) n^2 (c) $\dfrac{1}{n^2}$ (d) n

4. Although metals form basic oxides, name one metal which forms an amphoteric oxide.

5. A piece of granulated zinc was dropped into copper sulphate solution. After some time, the colour of the solution changed from blue to colourless. Why?

6. When we breathe out, why does the air passage not collapse?

7. Explain the nature of the covalent bond using the bond formation in CH_3Cl.

8. Two electric bulbs P and Q have their resistances in the ratio of 1: 2. They are connected in series across a battery. Find the ratio of power dissipation in these bulbs.

9. List out the basic features of reproduction.

Test 2

1. .... mode of reproduction involves fusion of gametes.
   (a) Sexual (b) Asexual
   (c) Both (a) and (b) (d) Neither (a) nor (b)
2. Which of the following alloys contains a non-metal as one of its constituents?
   (a) Zinc amalgam (b) Steel
   (c) Brass (d) Bronze
3. Which metal is the best reflector of light?
   (a) Iron (b) Silver
   (c) Copper (d) None of these
4. Determine the rate at which energy is delivered by a current.
5. A wire of resistivity is pulled to double its length. What will be its new resistivity?
6. What will happen if platelets were absent in the blood?
7. Mention four differences between saturated and unsaturated hydrocarbons.
8. Magnetic field lines can be entirely confined within the core of toroid, but not within a straight solenoid. Why?
9. Explain Mendel's observation when he crossed a homozygous tall (TT) plant with homozygous dwarf (tt) plant followed by self-cross.

Test 3

1. The metal which reacts violently with cold water is
   (a) sodium (b) potassium
   (c) aluminium (d) Both (a) and (b)
2. Which one of the following organisms reproduces asexually by budding?
   (a) *Hydra* (b) *Amoeba*
   (c) *Paramecium* (d) All of these
3. Which hormone is responsible for the secondary sexual characters in male human beings?
   (a) Oestrogen (b) Progesterone
   (c) Testosterone (d) Oxytocin
4. In electrical wires copper is used for electrical conduction mainly because
   (a) it has low resistivity
   (b) it is cheaper
   (c) it has a higher melting point
   (d) None of these above
5. List two characteristics of covalent compounds.
6. What happens to the pupil of the eye when the light is very bright?
7. Which type of organisms will have more variations—sexually or asexually reproducing organisms? Justify.
8. How does the strength of magnetic field due to a current carrying conductor depend upon
   (i) distance from the conductor?
   (ii) current flowing through the conductor?
9. Name a metal which
   (i) is the good conductor of heat
   (ii) has a very low melting point
   (iii) does not react with oxygen even at high temperature.
   (iv) is most ductile.

TEST 4

1. The process in which a carbonate ore is heated below its melting point in the absence of air to convert it into metal oxide is called
   (a) roasting
   (b) electrolytic reduction
   (c) calcination
   (d) electrolytic refining
2. Consider the following reaction :
   $CH_3CH_2OH \xrightarrow[\text{or acidified } K_2Cr_2O_7 + \text{Heat}]{\text{Alkaline } KMnO_4 + \text{Heat}} X$
   X is
   (a) acetic acid
   (b) ethyl acetate
   (c) ethanol
   (d) ethene

All in one Periodic Tests

3. The magnetic field lines inside a current carrying solenoid are
   (a) circular (b) straight
   (c) curved   (d) parabolic

4. An ore gives carbon dioxide on treatment with a dilute acid. What steps will you take to convert such an ore into a free metal?

5. Suggest one way of discriminating a wire carrying current from a wire carrying no current.

6. Why is an ammeter likely to be burnt, if you connect it in parallel?

7. A man has blood group A, his wife has blood group AB. Suggest the possible blood of their children.

8. Does evaporation play a role in the occurrence of transpiration? If yes, explain how.

9. Differentiate between asexual and sexual reproduction.

TEST 5

1. Which of the following represents the general formula of a saturated hydrocarbon?
   (a) C_nH_{2n} (b) C_nH_{2n-2}
   (c) C_nH_{2n+2} (d) C_nH_{2n+1}

2. The set of metals which do not react with dilute sulphuric acid to produce salt and hydrogen gas is
   (a) Zn, Cu, Au   (b) Ag, Pt, Zn
   (c) Na, Zn, Hg   (d) Hg, Ag, Pt

3. The power of source of energy producing 600 J energy in 20 sec is
   (a) 300 W (b) 1800 W (c) 30 W (d) 100 W

4. Arrange the following in the increasing order of their pH values:
   Acetic acid, sodium carbonate solution, hydrochloric acid

5. State the difference between the wire used in the element of an electric heater and in a fuse wire.

6. What will be the frequency of an alternating current if its direction changes after every 0.013?

7. Name a hormonal method which prevents contraception in females.

8. How will you describe the evolutionary link between the forelimbs of vertebrates and leaves in plants?

9. How does the response generated by hormonal mechanism differ from neural mechanism?

Post-Mid Term Tests

{Chapters covered—Chemistry (1, 2, 3, 4), Physics (9, 10, 11, 12), Biology (5, 6, 7, 8, 13 and 14)}

Test 1

1. The phenomenon in which non-biodegradable chemicals get accumulated at each trophic level of a food chain is known as ....
   (a) eutrophication   (b) biomagnification
   (c) decomposition   (d) energy transfer

2. Atomic size refers to the radius of an atom. It generally increases down the group because
   (a) nuclear charge increases
   (b) new shells are being added
   (c) valency increases
   (d) increase in chemical reactivity

3. In general, salts
   (a) contain hydrogen ions
   (b) contain hydroxide ions
   (c) are ionic compounds
   (d) turn litmus red

4. A ray of light is incident on a plane mirror at an angle of incidence of 20°. The deviation produced by the mirror is
   (a) 140°   (b) 120°   (c) 60°   (d) 30°

5. Name the sensory receptors found in the nose and on the tongue.

6. Name two activities in our daily lives in which solar energy is used.

7. How is the process of pollination different from fertilisation?

8. Why respiration and decomposition processes are considered to be an exothermic process? Explain.

9. The strategy of 3Rs have become profound in environment management programme. Explain.

Test 2

1. Which one of the following does not relate to the solar energy?
   (a) Tidal energy   (b) Wave energy
   (c) Nuclear energy   (d) Wind energy

2. Which of the following describes the artificial removal of wastes from the body?
   (a) Haemodialysis
   (b) Haemoglobin removal
   (c) Excretion
   (d) None of the above

3. Which of the following contains oxalic acid?
   (a) Tomato   (b) Sour milk
   (c) Pineapple   (d) Orange

4. Name the group of chemical compounds which adversely affect the ozone layer.

5. Define 1 D of power of a lens.

6. State one difference between autotrophs and heterotrophs.

7. Why sodium chloride has high melting point?

8. Biogas is considered to be a boon to the farmers. Give reasons.

9. Why do we need alternative sources of energy?

Test 3

1. What is the technical term for the graphical representation of the trophic structures in food chain?
   (a) Food web   (b) Food cycle
   (c) Energy web   (d) Food assimilation

2. IUPAC name of HCOOH is
   (a) methanoic acid   (b) ethanoic acid
   (d) propanoic acid   (d) methanol

3. When we use biomass to generate electricity we convert ...... energy locked in the biomass to electrical energy.
   (a) chemical   (b) kinetic
   (c) nuclear   (d) None of these

4. Three elements B, Si and Ge are known by which name?

5. Mention one drawback of monoculture.

6. Write the name and chemical formula of the products formed by heating gypsum at 373K.

7. Why does the cord of an electric heater not glow while heating element does?

8. Explain the concept of sustainable development.

9. How does tooth enamel get damaged? What should be done to prevent it?

TEST 4

1. Method used for the purification of metals of high reactivity is
   (a) galvanisation
   (b) alloying
   (c) chromium plating
   (d) electrolytic refining)

2. An element reacts with oxygen to give a compound with a high melting point. This compound is also soluble in water, the element is likely to be
   (a) zinc   (b) silicon   (c) calcium   (d) iodine

3. A convex mirror is used to form an image of a real object. Then, the incorrect statement is
   (a) the image is real
   (b) the image is erect
   (c) the image lies between pole and focus
   (d) the image is diminished

4. (i) Name the bond formed when X_7^{14} combines with Y_9^{18}.
   (ii) Write the chemical formula of the compound formed when X_7^{14} combines with Y_9^{18}.

5. When a battery is connected to a closed circuit, charge flows in the circuit almost instantaneously. Why?

6. Why are the coal, petroleum and natural gas called fossil fuels?

7. The biomass of the successive trophic level generally decreases as it moves up. Give reason.

8. When does anaerobic respiration occur in our body? Give an example.

9. What is the purpose of segregation of chestbins into blue and green colour?

TEST 5

1. The class of organic compounds which gives effervescence with $NaHCO_3$ solution is
   (a) ketones
   (b) esters
   (c) alkynes
   (d) alkanes

2. Which of the following metals does not show the property of malleability?
   (a) Iron   (b) Graphite
   (c) Aluminium   (d) Silver

3. A soft iron bar is introduced inside a current carrying solenoid. The magnetic field inside the solenoid.
   (a) will increase   (b) will become zero
   (c) will decrease   (d) will remain same

4. Justify that the hydropower is a renewable source of energy.

5. Why the bulb gets fused, if it is operated at a higher potential than its power rating?

6. In the second generation, the dwarf trait reappears during Mendel's experiment in monohybrid cross. Why so?

7. What is the purpose of 3Rs in the environment management programme?

8. The blood pressure, salivation, pupil movement, etc. are all the involuntary movements. Which part of the brain is responsible for controlling these actions?

9. Write the harmful effects of using plastic bags on the environment. Suggest ten alternatives to plastic bags.

Sample Papers
(1-3)

SAMPLE QUESTION PAPER 1
A Highly Simulated Sample Question Paper for CBSE Class Xth Examination

SCIENCE

General Instructions

- The question paper comprises four Sections A, B, C and D. There are 36 questions in the question paper. All questions are compulsory.
- **Section A** Qns. 1 to 20 all questions and parts there of are of one mark each. These questions contain multiple choice questions (MCQs), very short answer questions and assertion-reason type questions. Answers to these should be given in one word or one sentence.
- **Section B** Qns. 21 to 26 are short answer type questions, carrying 2 marks each. Answers to these questions should be in the range of 30 to 50 words.
- **Section C** Qns. 27 to 33 are short answer type questions, carrying 3 marks each. Answers to these questions should be in the range of 50 to 80 words.
- **Section D** Qns. 34 to 36 are long answer type question carrying 5 marks each. Answer to these questions should be in the range of 80 to 120 words.
- There is no overall choice. However, internal choices have been provided in some questions. A student has to attempt only one of the alternatives in such questions.
- Wherever necessary, neat and properly labelled diagrams should be drawn.

Time : 3 hours   Max. Marks : 80

Section A

1. Oxalic acid is an organic acid while hydrochloric acid is an inorganic acid. On what basis, they are classified into different type of acids?

   Or Given an example of both monobasic and dibasic acids.

2. In a food chain, 20,000 J of energy is available to the producer. How much energy will be transferred from the secondary consumer to the tertiary consumer?

3. Where should an object be placed infront of a convex lens to obtain a real image of same size as that of the object?

   Or The image formed by a concave mirror is observed to be virtual, erect and larger than the object. Where should be the position of the object?

4. List two advantages of vegetative reproduction practised in case of an orange plant.

   Or How does AIDS spread from one person to another?

5. Define second order consumers.

   Or Why we feel burning in the stomach when we overeat?

6. What is the filteration unit of kidney?

   Or From where does the oxygen liberated during photosynthesis?

7. Define optical centre of spherical lens.

8. Define centre of curvature of spherical lens.

9. In the following reaction,
   $$CuO(s) + H_2(g) \longrightarrow Cu(s) + H_2O(l)$$
   Which substance is oxidised and reduced ?

10. A star sometimes appears brighter and some other times fainter. What is this effect called?

11. The flow of current in a circular wire creates a magnetic field at its centre. How can existance of this field can be detected? Name the rule which helps to predict the direction of magnetic field.

12. Define scattering of light.

13. Electrolysis of water is a decomposition reactions. The mole ratio of hydrogen and oxygen gases liberated during electrolysis of water is

Assertion-Reason Questions (Q. Nos. 14-16)
In each of the following questions, a statement of Assertion is given by the corresponding statement of Reason. Out of the given statements, choose the correct one.
(a) If both Assertion and Reason are true and Reason is the correct explanation of Assertion.
(b) If both Assertion and Reason are true, but Reason is not the correct explanation of Assertion.
(c) If Assertion is true, but Reason is false.
(d) If Assertion is false, but Reason is true.

14. **Assertion** Arteries are thick walled and elastic in nature.
    Reason Arteries have to transport blood.

15. **Assertion** Diamond does not conduct electricity.
    Reason Diamond has high refractive index.

16. **Assertion** Carbon can form a variety of compounds that are exceptionally stable.
    Reason Due to its small size carbon has tendency to form multiple bonds.

Answer Q. Nos. 17-20 *Contain five sub-parts each. You are expected to answer any four sub-parts in these questions.*

17. *Read the following and answer any four questions from 17 (i) to 17 (v).*

    The general requirement for energy and materials is common in all organisms, but it is fulfilled in different ways. Organisms use simple food material obtained from inorganic sources in the form of carbon dioxide and water, these organisms, called as autotrophs, include green plants and some bacteria other organisms utilise complex substances, known as heterotroph. The process by which green plants make their food is called photosynthesis which occurs in chloroplast, after that food and minerals are transported to all parts of the plants with the help of xylem and pholem tissue and from various processes like translocation, absorption, osmosis, etc.

    (i) The diagram shows the arrangement of cells inside the leaf of a green plant. Which cells normally contain chloroplast?

    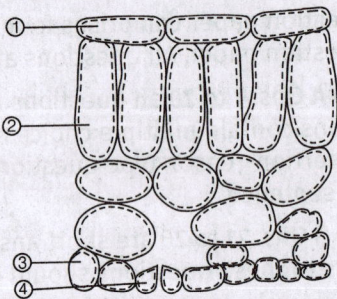

    (a) 1, 3 (b) 2, 4
    (c) 1, 4, 3 (d) All of these

    (ii) A plant shoot is left in ink solution for several hours.
    A section is cut through the stem. What would you see?

    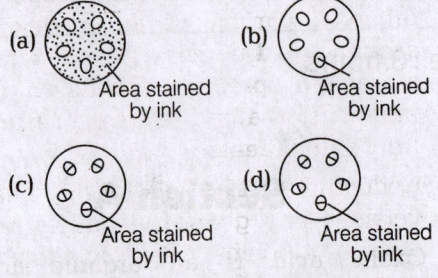

    (iii) The diagram shows a transverse section from the middle of a root of a dicotyledonous plant.
    In which tissue are sugars and amino acids transported?

    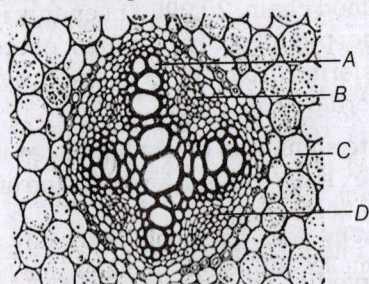

    (a) Tissue marked as A
    (b) Tissue marked as B

Sample Question Paper 1

(c) Tissue marked as *C*

(d) Tissue marked as *D*

(iv) A young plant may wilt when dig up and re-planted in another place. What causes this?

(a) The leaves lose less water

(b) The roots cannot take up mineral salts

(c) The stem cannot transport water

(d) The surface area of the root is reduced

(v) What causes water to enter plant roots from the soil?

(a) Water potential in root hairs and soil is equal

(b) Water potential in root hairs and xylem is equal

(c) Water potential in roots hair is higher than in the soil

(d) Water potential in root hairs is lower than in the soil

18. *Read the following and answer any four questions from 18 (i) to 18 (v).*

Heterozygoes is a state of living inherited different forms of a particular gene from each one your biological parents. Now by, different forms we generally mean that there are different portion of the gene where the sequence is different whereas homozygous is a genetic condition where an individual, inherits the same allele for a particular gene from both parents.

Codominance is a relationship between two versions of a gene. Individuals receive one version of a gene, called an allele from each parent. If the allele are different the dominant allele usually will be expressed, while the effect of the other allele called recessive.

In birds, the male is the homogametic sex. A male bird showing the recessive trait was mated with a female showing the dominant trait of a characteristic governed by a pair of alleles which are sex linked.

(i) What is the probability that the male offspring will show the dominat trait?

(a) zero   (b) 0.25

(c) 0.50   (d) 1.00

(ii) Why does haemophilia usually affect only males, although females may carry the gene responsible for the disease?

(a) The gene is inactive in the female

(b) The gene is dominant only in males

(c) The gene is carried on the X chromosome

(d) The gene is carried on the Y chromosome

(iii) A red-flowered plant crossed with a white-flowered plant of the same species, produced F_1 plants which all had pink flowers.

Self-pollination of the F_1 plants produced an F_2 generation in which 39 plants had red flowers, 83 had pink flowers and 40 had white flowers.

What does this experiment demonstrate?

(a) codominance

(b) continuous variation

(c) a dihybrid cross

(d) linkage

(iv) The pie chart shows the results of a survey of the incidence of blood groups A, B, AB and O amongst people im Britain.

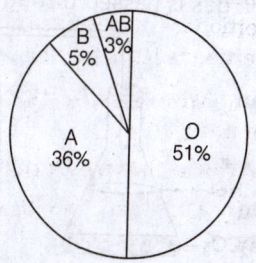

Which of the following conclusions can be deduced from the diagram?

(a) Only 5% of individuals are heterozygous for blood group alleles.

(b) Group O is the most common as it is the homozygous recessive group.

(c) Group O is most common because it has the selective advantage of being the universal donor.

(d) Any individual, selected at random from the sample population, has a 1 in 20 chance of being blood group AB.

(v) In the human ABO blood group system, there are six possible genotypes but only four pheontypes. An explanation of this is that the ABO blood groups are controlled by

(a) one gene locus with three codominant alleles

(b) one gene locus with two codominant alleles and two recessive alleles

(c) one gene locus with two codominant alleles and one recessive allele

(d) two unlinked gene loci each with two alleles, one dominant and one recessive

19. *Read the following and answer any four questions from 19 (i) to 19 (v).*

Acids are those substances which are sour in taste. They turn blue litmus red. Acids react with metals to liberate H_2 gas.

(i) Bases are
   (a) bitter in taste and soapy to touch
   (b) sour in taste
   (c) tasteless
   (d) salty in taste

(ii) In the figure given below, name the gas envolved and what happens to lime water, when gas is passed through it.

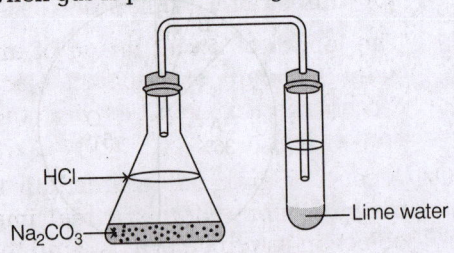

   (a) The gas envolved is H_2 and there is no effect on lime water
   (b) The gas evolved is CO_2 and it turns lime water milky
   (c) The gas evolved in CO_2 and there is no effect on lime water
   (d) The gas envolved is SO_2 and it turns lime water milky

(iii) In reaction,
$Zn(s) + 2HCl(aq) \longrightarrow X + H_2(g)$, X is
   (a) $ZnSO_4$ (b) $ZnCl_2$
   (c) ZnH_2 (d) $Zn(OH)_2$

(iv) What happens when Zn metal reacts with NaOH solution?
   (a) The solution becomes colourless and no gas is evolved
   (b) The solution becomes colourless, and a colourless and odourless gas is evolved

   (c) The solution becomes colourless, and a pungent smelling gas is evolved
   (d) The solution becomes blue and a colourless gas comes out

(v) The correct sequence of increasing order of pH of substance 0.1 M HCl, 0.1 M NaOH, Pure water, NaCl solution
   (a) 0.1 M HCl < Pure water = NaCl solution < 0.1 M NaOH
   (b) 0.1 M HCl < 0.1 M NaOH < Pure water < NaCl solution
   (c) 0.1 M NaOH < NaCl solution = Pure water < 0.1 M HCl
   (d) Pure water < NaCl solution < 0.1 M HCl < 0.1 M NaOH

20. *Read the following and answer any four questions from 20 (i) to 20 (v).*

Two students *A* and *B* performed an experiment on finding the image formation by a concave mirror. They performed the experiment for different positions of object and obtained different positions of image.

(i) If the object is placed between focus and centre of curvature, the position of image will be
   (a) at focus
   (b) between focus and pole
   (c) beyond centre of curvature
   (d) None of the above

(ii) The image of a bright object is brought on a screen with the help of a concave mirror. If the upper half of the concave mirror is covered, then
   (a) the size of the image will become half
   (b) the image will get disappeared
   (c) the brightness of the image will get reduced
   (d) the image will change its position

(iii) *CD* is an image of an object *AB* formed by an optical device X. Identify X.

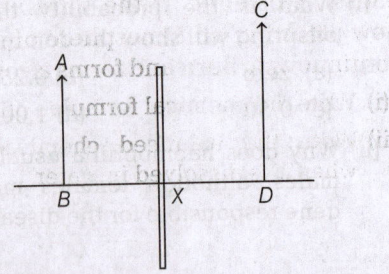

Sample Question Paper 1

529

(a) Concave lens (b) Convex lens
(c) Concave mirror (d) Convex mirror

(iv) If the object is placed at a distance of 10 cm in front of the mirror, the image will be formed at a distance of [Take, magnification to be (–3)]

(a) 20 cm (b) – 20 cm
(c) 30 cm (d) – 30 cm

(v) For the given data showing the focal lengths of three concave mirrors A, B and C and the respective distances of different objects from these mirrors.

Concave mirrors	Object distance (in cm)	Focal length (in cm)
A	45	20
B	30	15
C	20	30

In the given positions of objects from the mirrors, the mirror(s) which will form diminished image(s) of the object(s) is/are

(a) only A (b) only B
(c) only C (d) Both A and B

Section B

21. (a) Draw a neat diagram of the stomatal apparatus found in the epidermis of leaves. Label the stomatal aperture, guard cells, chloroplast and epidermal cells in the diagram.
    (b) What is the shape of the guard cells?

22. (i) A current of 150 mA flows through a circuit for 2 minutes. Find the amount of charge that flows through the circuit.
    (ii) An electric fan runs from the 220V mains. The current flowing through it is 0.5A. At what rate is the electrical energy transformed by the fan? How much energy is transformed in 2 minutes?

23. A magnesium ribbon is burnt in oxygen to give a white compound X accompanied by emission of light. If the burning ribbon is now placed in an atmosphere of nitrogen, it continuous to burn and forms a compound Y.
    (i) Write the chemical formulae of X and Y.
    (ii) Write the balanced chemical equation when X is dissolved in water.

Or Solid calcium oxide was taken in a container and water was added slowly to it.
    (i) State the two observations made in the experiment.
    (ii) Write the name and chemical formulae of the product formed.

24. List four properties of magnetic field lines.

25. Explain the action of dil. HCl on the following along with chemical equation.
    (i) Magnesium ribbon (ii) Sodium hydroxide

26. The anaerobic respiration in muscle leads to the formation of an end product. Name this product.

Or Differentiate between fermentation in yeast and aerobic respiration on the basis of the end products formed.

Section C

27. Explain the following by giving reasons.
    (a) In mammals separation of oxygenated and deoxygenated blood is necessary.
    (b) Arteries form capillaries.

28. The length of a real image of an object is twice the length of the object, placed at 25 cm from a convex lens. Find the power of convex lens.

Or A concave mirror of focal length 18 cm and magnification 2 forms a real image of an object on its principal axis. Find the position of image.

29. Explain various methods of waste disposal.

30. What happens to the rate of photosynthesis, in each of the following situations?
    (a) Good manuring in the area
    (b) No rainfall in the area
    (c) Stomata gets blocked by dust

31. Write a balanced chemical equation for each of the following reactions and also classify them.
    (i) A piece of sodium metal is added to absolute ethanol to form sodium ethoxide and hydrogen gas.
    (ii) Hydrogen sulphide gas reacts with oxygen gas to form solid sulphur and liquid water.

UNSOLVED

32. (i) State three factors on which the heat produced by an electric current depends.
(ii) Calculate the heat produced when 96000 C of charge is transferred in 1 h through a potential difference of 50 V.

33. The pH of a salt used to make tasty and crispy pakoras is 14. Examine the salt and write a chemical equation for its formation. List its two uses.

Section D

34. 'Double circulation plays an essential role in the maintenance of homeostasis in human beings.' Validate the above point giving suitable explanation.

Or Describe the process of digestion of food in humans with the help of a well-labelled diagram.

35. (i) Define resistance and 1 ohm.
(ii) In the circuit diagram given below, find the
(a) total resistance of the circuit,
(b) total current flowing in the circuit and
(c) potential difference across R_1.

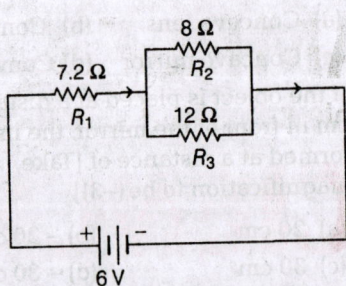

36. You are given two containers made up of copper and aluminium. You are also given solutions of dil. HCl, dil. HNO_3, $ZnCl_2$ and H_2O. In which of the above containers, these solutions can be kept?

Or Given reasons for the following statements.
(a) Zinc oxide acts as an amphoteric oxide.
(b) Non-metals generally do not displace hydrogen from dilute acids.
(c) Aluminium easily combines with oxygen but it still can be sued for manufacturing utensils.
(d) Hydrogen reduces cupric oxide to red copper metal.
(e) Na, K and Ca metals form hydrides by combination with hydrogen gas, but most of the other metals do not.

Answers

14. (b)   **15.** (b)   **16.** (a)
17. (i) (b), (ii) (c), (iii) (b), (iv) (d), (v) (d)
18. (i) (d), (ii) (c), (iii) (a), (iv) (d), (v) (c)
19. (i) (a), (ii) (b), (iii) (b), (iv) (b), (v) (a)
20. (i) (c), (ii) (c), (iii) (c), (iv) (d), (v) (a)

22. (i) 18 C   (ii) 13200 J
28. 2 D or −54 cm
32. (ii) 4788.4 kJ
35. (ii) (a) 12 Ω,   (b) 0.5 A,   (c) 3.6 V

SAMPLE QUESTION PAPER 2
A Highly Simulated Sample Question Paper for CBSE Class Xth Examination

SCIENCE

General Instructions
See Sample Paper 1

Section A

1. In an experiment, saliva is added to a test tube containing fine powdered bread pieces. Comment on the result obtained from this experiment?

2. Define lateral inversion.

Or What is the angle of an equilateral prism?

3. What will be the phenotypic expression of dominant character in the F_1-generation in Mendel experiment?

4. Define one ampere.

5. What type of material should be used for making a strong electromagnet?

6. From where the developing embryo gets its nourishment from the mother?

Or Malarial parasite exhibit which type of asexual reproduction?

7. What will be the colour of the sky when it is observed from a place in the absence of any atmosphere?

8. Write the chemical formula of plaster of paris and gypsum.

9. List two difference between 'holozoic nutrition' and 'saprophytic nutrition.' Give two examples of each.

Or Point out two differences between an artery and a vein.

10. Why sodium carbonate is a basic salt?

11. Give an example, which represents a chemical change and not a physical change?

Or Define combination reaction.

12. Define the term bioconcentration.

13. Give an example of a phenomenon, where Tyndall effect can be observed.

Or The extent of deviation of a ray of light on passing through a prism depends on the colour. Give reason.

Assertion-Reason Questions (Q. Nos. 14-16)
In each of the following questions, a statement of Assertion is given by the corresponding statement of Reason. Out of the given statements, choose the correct one.

(a) If both Assertion and Reason are true and Reason is the correct explanation of Assertion.
(b) If both Assertion and Reason are true, but Reason is not the correct explanation of Assertion.
(c) If Assertion is true, but Reason is false.
(d) If Assertion is false, but Reason is true.

14. **Assertion** Phosphorus is kept in water.
    Reason Non-metals do not react with water.

15. **Assertion** Ozone present in the higher levels of atmosphere is a product of UV-radiations acting on oxygen.
    Reason Ozone molecules are reactive and combine with free oxygen atoms to form more ozone molecules.

16. **Assertion** Heater wire must have high resistance and high melting point.
    Reason Heating element of electric heater made of nichrome.

Answer Q. Nos. 17-20 Contain five sub-parts each. You are expected to answer any four sub-parts in these questions.

17. Read the following and answer any four questions from 17 (i) to 17 (v).

The sample pieces of five metals A, B, C, D and E are added to the tabulated salt solutions separately.

The results observed are shown in the table given below

Metal	Salt solutions		
	FeSO₄	ZnSO₄	CuSO₄
A	No change	No change	No change
B	Grey deposit	No change	Brown coating
C	No change	No change	No change
D	No change	No change	—
E	Brownish-red deposit	Grey coating	Brown coating

Read the observations carefully and give the answer of the following.

(i) Which is the most reactive metal?
(a) A   (b) B
(c) D   (d) E

(ii) Which is the least ractive metal?
(a) A   (b) C
(c) D   (d) E

(iii) What will happen when metal B reacts with acid ?
(a) Salt will formed along with CO_2 gas
(b) Salt will formed along with H_2 gas
(c) Metal oxide will formed along with water
(d) Metal oxide will formed along with hydrogen gas

(iv) Which type of reaction is observed in the given data ?
(a) Decomposition reaction
(b) Displacement reaction
(c) Neutralisation reaction
(d) Endothermic reaction

(v) What will happen if metal C reacts with $AgNO_3$?
(a) No change   (b) Grey coating
(c) Brown coating   (d) Red coating

18. Read the following and answer any four questions from 18(i) to 18(v).

The following table gives different positions of images and their sizes for different positions of objects in case of image formation by convex lens.

Position of object	Position of image	Relative size of image
At infinity	At focus F_2	Highly diminished and point-sized
Beyond $2F_1$	Between F_2 and $2F_2$	Diminished
At $2F_1$	At $2F_2$	Same size
Between F_1 and $2F_1$	Beyond $2F_2$	Enlarged
At focus F_1	At infinity	Infinitely large or highly enlarged
Between focus F_1 and optical centre O	On the same side of the lens as the object	Enlarged

(i) The nature of the image, if an object is placed at infinity is
(a) real and erect
(b) real and inverted
(c) virtual and erect
(d) virtual and inverted

(ii) If the magnification of converging lens is + 1, then the image formed is
(a) real, inverted and of the same size as that of the object
(b) virtual, erect and of the same size as that of the object
(c) real, inverted and bigger than the size of the object
(d) virtual, erect and bigger than the size of the object

(iii) Prachi determined the focal length of a device X by focusing a distant object on the screen as shown in the following diagram.

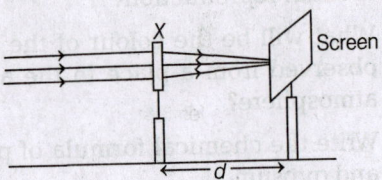

Select the correct statement from the following:
(a) Device X is a concave mirror and distance d is its focal length.
(b) Device X is a concave mirror and distance d is its radius of curvature.
(c) Device X is a convex lens and distance d is its radius of curvature.
(d) Device X is a convex lens and distance d is its focal length.

(iv) The focal length of a lens for an object placed 50 cm from the lens producing virtual image at a distance of 10 cm in front of the lens will be

Sample Question Paper 2

(a) 12 cm (b) −12.5 cm
(c) 5 cm (d) −5 cm

(v) The lower half of a convex lens is covered with black paper (as shown in figure). The effect on the image on the screen would be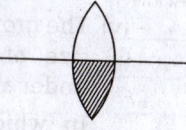
(a) the lower half of the image disappears
(b) the upper half of the image disappears
(c) the image remains same
(d) the image becomes less brighter than before

19. *Read the following and answer any four questions from 19 (i) to 19 (v).*

Gregor Mendel, conducted the hybridisation experiments by applying statistical analysis and mathematical logic. The confirmation of his inferences from experiments on successive generations of his test plants, proved that his results pointed to general rules of inheritance. Mendel investigated characters in garden pea plant that were manifested as two opposing traits, e.g. tall and dwarf plants, yellow and green seeds, etc. He conducted his cross-pollination experiments using several true breeding pea lines, i.e. the ones that have undergone continuous self-pollination and shows stable trait inheritance and expression for several generations.

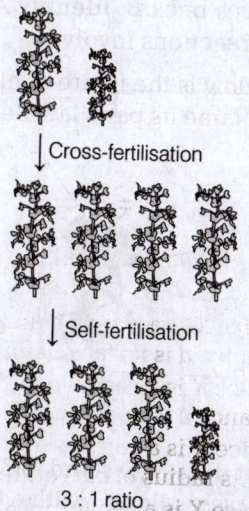

(i) The characteristic of true breeding is
(a) self-pollination

(b) stable trait inheritance
(c) expression for several generation
(d) All of the above

(ii) Which of the following are genetically identical?
(a) brothers and sisters in the same
(b) cuttings taken from the same
(c) gametes from the same parent
(d) seeds produced by the same tree

(iii) Two heterozygotes are crossed. Some of the offspring show the recessive characteristic.
What is the probability that the offspring that show the recessive characteristic are homozygous?
(a) 0.00 (b) 0.5
(c) 0.25 (d) 1.00

(iv) In the spotted leopard, coat colour is controlled by a single gene with two alleles, H and h. The black panther is a variety of spotted leopard. The diagram shows a cross between a spotted leopard and a black panther. All the offspring in the F_1 generation were spotted leopards. The results of a cross between two animals of the F_1 generation are also shown.

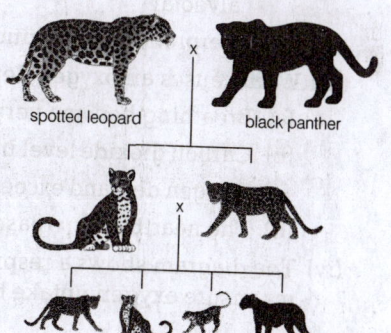

What are the genotypes of the original two parents?

	Spotted leopard	Black panther
(a)	HH	hh
(b)	HH	Hh
(c)	Hh	hh
(d)	Hh	Hh

(v) The diagram shows the inheritance of flower colour in pure breeding roses.

Which flower is heterozygous for colour?

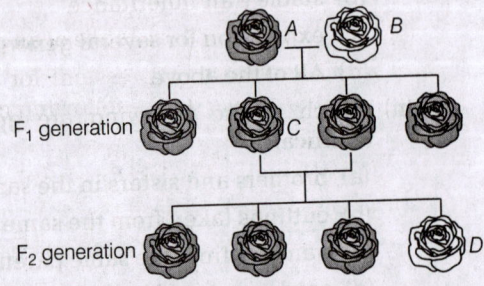

20. Read the following and answer any four questions from 20(i) to 20(v).

The human respiratory system is composed of a pair of lungs. These are attached to a system of tubes which open on the outside nostrils. Choose the correct option with respect to the function.

(i) The correct passage of air is
   (a) Pharynx → Larynx → Trachea
   (b) Brochioles → Lungs → Bronchi
   (c) Nasal passage → Trachea → Bronchi
   (d) Larynx → Pharynx → Trachea

(ii) What causes emphysema?
   (a) Blockage of the bronchioles
   (b) Destruction of the alveolar walls
   (c) Inflammation of the walls of the alveolar
   (d) Overproduction of mucus debt.

(iii) What causes an oxygen dept to develop?
   (a) Breathing become very rapid
   (b) Carbon dioxide level in the blood rises
   (c) Oxygen demand exceed oxygen supply
   (d) The heartbeat increases

(iv) The diagram shows a respirometer used to meansure oxygen uptake by woodice.

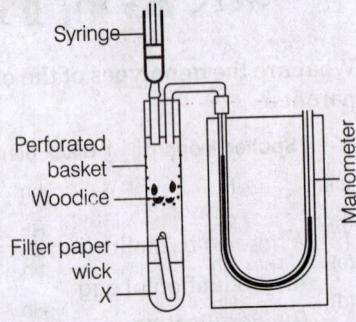

What is X?
   (a) Buffer solution to control the pH
   (b) Lime water to indicate the presence of carbon dioxide
   (c) Potassium hydroxide solution to absorb carbon dioxide
   (d) Water to control the humidity

(v) The growth curve shows the change in the size of a yeast population maintained under anaerobic conditions.

In which stage of growth is there the greatest mean rate of ethanol production per cell?

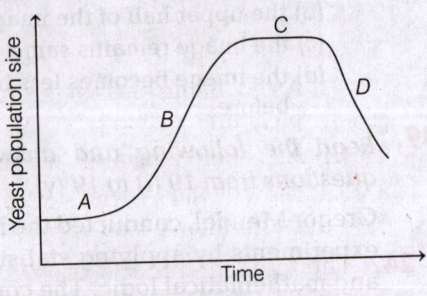

Section B

21. An alkali metal A gives a compound B (molecular mass = 40) on reacting with water. The compound B gives a soluble compound C on treatment with aluminium oxide. Identify A, B and C and give the reactions involved.

Or An element A reacts with water to form a compound B which is used in white-washing. The compound B on heating forms an oxide C which on treatment with water gives back B. Identify A, B and C and give the reactions involved.

22. Given below is the figure of human excretory system. Name its parts labelled as A to H.

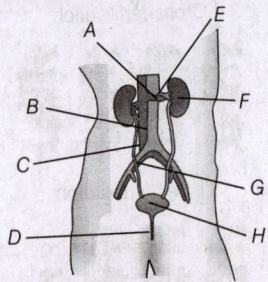

Or (i) What does STD stand for? Name two such diseases along with their causative organisms.

(ii) Name the causative organism of AIDS. What are the modes of transmission of AIDS?

Sample Question Paper 2

23. Consider the following figure.

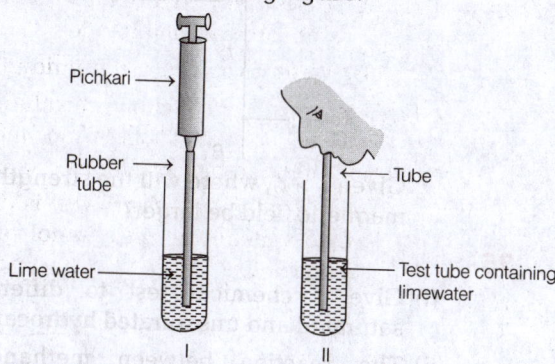

(I) Air is being passed into limewater with a pichkari.

(II) Air is being exhaled into limewater.

Draw your own conclusions from the information given and describe it step wise.

24. The focal length of a convex lens is 10 cm. A candle of height 12 cm is placed at a distance of 20 cm from that lens. Find the position, nature and height of image of candle.

25. Draw a circuit diagram of an electric circuit containing a cell, a key an ammeter, a resistor of 2Ω in series with a combination of two resistors (4Ω each) in parallel and a voltmeter across the parallel combination. Will the potential difference across the 2Ω resistor be the same as that across the parallel combination of 4Ω resistors? Explain.

26. Draw a labelled diagram of human eye. What is the significance of the blind spot?

Section C

27. A student wants to get the image of a candle flame on the walls of school laboratory by using a lens.

(i) Which type of lens should be use and why?

(ii) At what distance in terms of focal length F of the lens should he place the candle flame, so as to get

(a) a magnified?

(b) a diminished image respectively, on the wall?

28. (i) A wire of resistivity ρ is stretched to double its length. How does it affect the

(a) resistance

(b) and resistivity?

(ii) Draw a circuit diagram which depicts two resistors R_1 and R_2 connected in parallel with the source, ammeter, voltmeter, key and rheostat.

Or

(i) What is the resistance of an air gap?

(ii) Derive an expression for equivalent resistance for the following circuit :

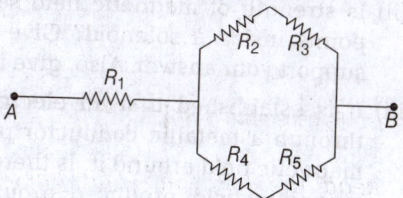

29. An element of group 14 has two common allotropes A and B. A is very hard and is bad conductor of electricity. While, B is soft to touch and good conductor of electricity. Identify the element and its allotropes. Explain reasons for their different properties?

30. List points of significance of reproductive health in a society. Name any two areas related to reproductive health which have improved over the past 50 years in our country.

31. Name the two reproductive parts of a bisexual flower which contain the germ cells. State the location and function of its female reproductive part.

32. Give two examples of covalent compounds which you have studied. State any four properties in which covalent compounds differ from ionic compounds.

33. (i) Name the parts labelled A to E in the figure of the human female reproductive system given below.

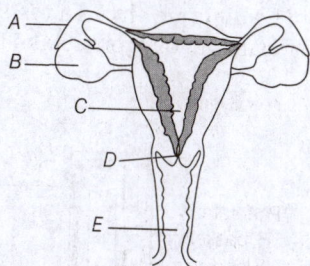

(ii) Where do the following events occur?

(a) Production of egg

(b) Fertilisation

(c) Implantation of the zygote

(d) Entry of the sperms

(iii) What is ovum?

Section D

34. (i) State the factors on which strength of magnetic field produced by a solenoid depends.

(ii) Is strength of magnetic field same at all points inside a solenoid? Give reason to support your answer. Also, give it use.

(iii) It is established that an electric current through a metallic conductor produces a magnetic field around it. Is there a similar magnetic field produced around a thin beam of moving

(a) α - particles, (b) neutrons?

Justify your answer.

Or (i) When is the force experienced by a current carrying conductor placed in a magnetic field largest?

(ii) (a) What conclusion do you get from the observation that a current carrying wire deflects a compass needle placed near it?

(b) How this deflection can be increased?

(iii) AB is a current carrying conductor in the plane of the paper as shown in figure. What are the directions of magnetic fields produced by it at points P and Q?

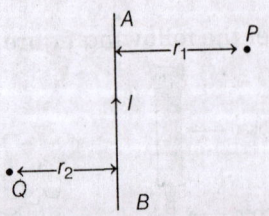

Given $r_1 > r_2$, where will the strength of the magnetic field be larger?

35. (i) Give a chemical test to differentiate saturated and unsaturated hydrocarbons.

(ii) The reaction between methane and chlorine considered as a substitution reaction. Explain.

(iii) Why are the covalent compounds weaker than ionic compounds?

Or (i) Name the products formed when ethanol reacts with oxygen.

(ii) Define saturated and unsaturated hydrocarbons with examples.

(iii) Draw the structure of ethanoic acid.

(iv) Name the following functional groups.

(a) —COOH   (b) — CHO

36. How are raw materials such as water and minerals transported from the roots to the rest of the parts in highly organised plants?

Answers

14. (a)   15. (c)   16. (a)

17. (i) (d), (ii) (b), (iii) (b), (iv) (b), (v) (a)

18. (i) (b), (ii) (b), (iii) (d), (iv) (b), (v) (d)

19. (i) (d), (ii) (b), (iii) (b), (iv) (a)

20. (i) (b), (ii) (b), (iii) (c), (iv) (c)

24. −12 cm   25. 2 Ω

SAMPLE QUESTION PAPER 3
A Highly Simulated Sample Question Paper for CBSE Class Xth Examination

SCIENCE

General Instructions
See Sample Paper 1

Section A

1. Catenation is the ability of an atom to form bonds with other atoms of the same element. Compare the catenation property of carbon and silicon.

2. A positive charge is moving upwards in a magnetic field directed towards North. In which direction will the particle be deflected?

3. What is the function of the umbilical cord?

4. If a round, green seeded pea plant (RRyy) is crossed with a wrinkled, yellow seeded plant (rrYY), what will be the phenotype of seed produced in F_1?

5. Diamond is a poor conductor of electricity while graphite is a good conductor. Assign reason.

6. Where is the image of an object placed in front of a convex mirror formed?

Or Why is rainbow seen in the sky during rainy season?

7. Why cannot fertilisation take place in flowers if pollination does not occurs?

Or Where is the zygote located in the flower after fertilisation?

8. Why is fullerence so called?

9. By what, plaster of Paris get hardens?

10. What is the ratio of the resistance, if two bulbs have ratings of 40 W, 220 V and 20 W, 110 V?

Or Why does the connecting cord of an electric heater not glow while the heating element does?

11. Explain the term genotype and phenotype.

Or State principle of segregation.

12. Arrange the following metals in the decreasing order of reactivity.

Na, Cu, Ag, Fe

Or The atomic numbers of four elements P, Q, R and S are 6, 10, 12 and 17 respectively. A covalent bond is formed by which elements?

13. How are the alveoli designed to maximise the exchange of gases?

Assertion-Reason Questions (Q. Nos. 14-16)
In each of the following questions, a statement of Assertion is given by the corresponding statement of Reason. Out of the given statements, choose the correct one.

(a) If both Assertion and Reason are true and Reason is the correct explanation of Assertion.
(b) If both Assertion and Reason are true, but Reason is not the correct explanation of Assertion.
(c) If Assertion is true, but Reason is false.
(d) If Assertion is false, but Reason is true.

14. **Assertion** Photosynthesis is considered as an endothermic reaction.
   Reason Energy gets released in the process of photosynthesis.

15. **Assertion** When zinc is added to a solution of iron (II) sulphate, no change is observed.
   Reason Zinc is more reactive than iron.

16. **Assertion** To an astronaut, sky appears dark.
   Reason Scattering of light depends on the wavelength of light.

Answer Q. Nos. 17-20 Contain five sub-parts each. You are expected to answer any four sub-parts in these questions.

17. Read the following and answer any four questions from 17 (i) to 17 (v).

When food comes in contact with the surface area of the cell of *Amoeba*, pseudopodia encircle the food by making good cap. Then the food is engulf by the process of phagocytosis.

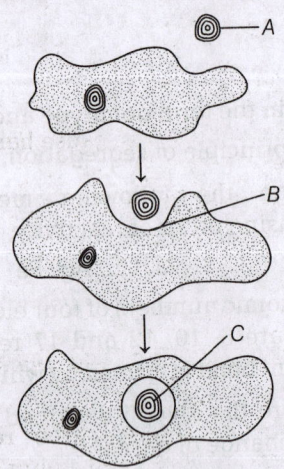

(i) In diagram label A, B and C indicates
(a) food particle, food cup, food alveoli
(b) food cup, food particle, food alveoli
(c) food cup, food alveoli, food particle
(d) food particle, food alveoli, food cup

(ii) In which form *Amoeba* ingest food?
(a) Ingestion of whole animal
(b) Fully digested food
(c) Animal of class Crustacea
(d) None of the above

(iii) The diagram shows part of the human alimentary canal.

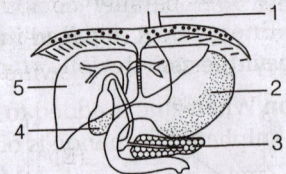

Which two structures produce substances involved in the digestion of fat?
(a) 1 and 5   (b) 2 and 3
(c) 3 and 4   (d) 4 and 5

(iv) What are the functions of the colon?

	Water absorbed	Enzymes secreted
(a)	no	no
(b)	no	yes
(c)	yes	no
(d)	yes	yes

(v)

Product of digestion	Absorption in the presence of oxygen/arbitrary units	Absorption in the absence of oxygen/arbitrary units
amino acids	5.3	1.7
fatty acids	1.9	2.0
glucose	6.4	2.3
glycerol	4.8	4.7

The table shows the results of an investigation into the absorption of products of digestion in the presence and absence of oxygen.

Which conclusion can be drawn from these results?

(a) All products of digestion are absorbed by both active transport and diffusion.
(b) All products of digestion are absorbed by diffusion only.
(c) Amino acids and glucose are absorbed by active transport only.
(d) Fatty acids and glycerol are absorbed mainly by diffusion.

18. Read the following and answer any four questions from 18(i) to 18(v).

A metal M reacts vigorously with water to form a solution (S) and a gas (G). The solution (S) turns red litmus to blue whereas gas (G), which is lighter than air, burns with a pop sound. Metal (M) has a low melting point and is used as a coolant in nuclear reactors.

(i) Name the metal (M)?
(a) Sodium   (b) Magnesium
(c) Calcium   (d) Potassium

(ii) Which of the following statement about metal 'M' is true?
(I) It can be cut with knife.
(II) It is present in first group of periodic table.
(III) It's valency is +2.

Sample Question Paper 3

(IV) It is a stable element.
(a) I, II
(b) II, III, IV
(c) I, II, III
(d) IV

(iii) The gas (G) evolved is
(a) Colourless and odourless
(b) It is used as fuel in rockets
(c) It exists in free state
(d) Both (a) and (b)

(iv) If we add phenolphthalein in 'S', what will happen?
(a) The solution turns pink
(b) The solution remains colourless
(c) The solution becomes green
(d) The solution becomes blue

(v) What happens when Na_2CO_3 is added to 'S'?
(a) CO_2 gas is evolved
(b) No reaction takes place
(c) Sodium bicarbonate is formed
(d) None of these

19. Read the following and answer any four questions from 19 (i) to 19 (v).

Nature provided us well-balanced environment in which there was a perfect harmony among the living organism in regard to food chain and the ecosystem was so well regulated that every organism was enjoying its full quota of a biotic factors with the advancement of mental ability, man become most dominant form of life or Earth, to fulfill the requirement of ever increasing human population, man began to exploit natural resources through deforestation unplanned, profit oriented, capitalism and technological advancement. This led to slow degradation of environment and different problem also, e.g. solid waste, disposal, ozone depletion, other pollution related problems.

(i) Ozone layer of upper atmosphere is being destroyed by
(a) Ozone
(b) PAN
(c) Aldehyde
(d) All of these

(ii) Which of the following causes imbalance in the environment?
(a) Excess growing of green plants
(b) Using more renewable resources
(c) Biodiversity
(d) Increasing human population

(iii) Which of the following is not an abiotic component?
(a) Light
(b) Temperature
(c) Carnivore
(d) Water

(iv) In an ecosystem, which are recycled?

	Carbon	Energy	Nitrogen
(a)	✓	✓	✓
(b)	✓	✓	✗
(c)	✓	✗	✓
(d)	✗	✓	✓

(v) UV radiations can cause harmful diseases like
(a) Skin cancer
(b) Pneumonia
(c) Cataract
(d) Both (a) and (c)

20. Read the following and answer any four questions from 20 (i) to 20 (v).

A student arranged three resistors, two ammeters, a battery and a plug key as shown in the given figure.

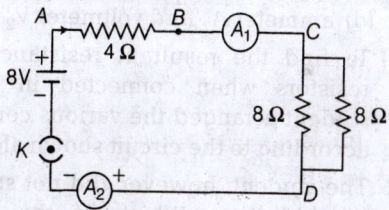

(i) The effective resistance of two 8 Ω resistors combination is
(a) 1Ω
(b) 2Ω
(c) 4Ω
(d) 8Ω

(ii) Four students performed experiments on series and parallel combination of two given resistors R_1 and R_2 which obey Ohm's law and plotted the following I-V graphs

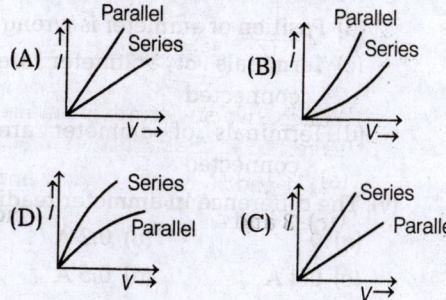

Which of the graphs is correctly labelled in terms of 'series' and 'parallel'?
(a) Graph A (b) Graph B
(c) Graph C (d) Graph D

(iii) The following apparatus is available in the school laboratory

Battery : 4.5 V
Rheostat : Varies battery voltage from 0 to 4.5 V
Resistors : 1 Ω and 2 Ω
Ammeters : A_1 of range 0 to 1 A; Least count 0.05 A
: A_2 of range 0 to 3 A; Least count 0.1 A
Voltmeters : V_1 of range 0 to 5 V; Least count 0.1 V
: V_2 of range 0 to 10 V; Least count 0.5 V

The best combination of ammeter and voltmeter for finding the resultant resistance of the two given resistors connected in series would be
(a) ammeter A_1 and voltmeter V_1
(b) ammeter A_1 and voltmeter V_2
(c) ammeter A_2 and voltmeter V_1
(d) ammeter A_2 and voltmeter V_2

(iv) To find the resultant resistance of two resistors when connected in series, a student arranged the various components according to the circuit shown alongside. The student, however, did not succeed in his objective. Which of the following mistake has been made by the student in setting up the circuit?

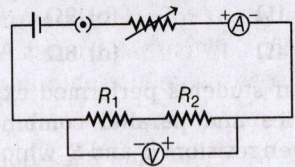

(a) Position of voltmeter is wrong
(b) Position of ammeter is wrong
(c) Terminals of voltmeter are wrongly connected
(d) Terminals of ammeter are wrongly connected

(v) The difference in ammeter readings is
(a) 0   (b) 0.2 A
(c) 0.4 A   (d) 0.5 A

Section B

21. Identify and state the rule to determine the direction of a
    (i) magnetic field produced around a straight current carrying conductor.
    (ii) force experienced by a straight current carrying conductor placed in a magnetic field.

Or If you have three resistors each of resistance 6 Ω, then how would you connect these resistors so that the combination has a resistance of
(i) 9 Ω,   (ii) 4 Ω ?

22. Differentiate between
    (i) Urea and urine
    (ii) Excretion and egestion

23. There are three resistors R_1, R_2 and R_3 connected in parallel as shown in the following figure.

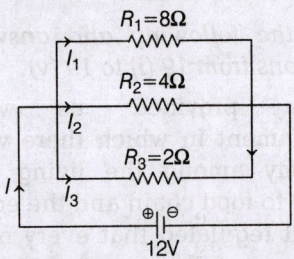

Find the total current drawn from the source of 12V.

24. Balance and name the reducing agent in the following reaction.
$MnO_2 + Al \longrightarrow Mn + Al_2O_3$

Or Write the chemical equations for the following
(i) Iron reacts with steam
(ii) Magnesium reacts with dil. HCl

25. Name the properties of metals used in the following cases :
(a) Aluminium foil
(b) Metal jewellery
(c) Cable wires
(d) Bells

26. Define the following terms
(i) Lateral displacement
(ii) Principle of reversibility of light.

Section C

27. There are two lens of focal lengths 50 cm and −25 cm. An object is kept at a distance of 100 cm from each of the lenses. Calculate
    (i) image distance and
    (ii) magnification in each of the two cases.

28. Consider the following figure.

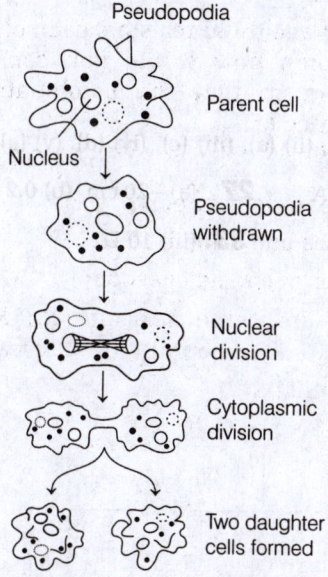

Analyse and recompile the information in your own words.

Or Explain the process of breakdown of glucose in a cell.
    (i) In the absence of oxygen
    (ii) In the presence of oxygen

29. Three 2 Ω resistors, A, B and C are connected as shown in figure. Each of them dissipates energy and can withstand a maximum power of 18 W without melting. Find the maximum current that can flow through the three resistors.

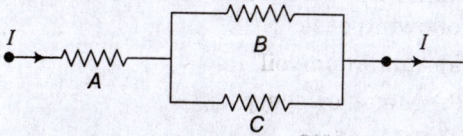

30. What are trophic levels? Describe its types.

31. (i) Why iron corrodes but aluminium does not?
    (ii) Write chemical name and the formula of the brown gas produced during thermal decomposition of lead nitrate.
    (iii) What is the general name of the chemicals which are added to fat and oil containing foods to prevent the development of rancidity?

32. Describe the raw materials required for photosynthesis.

Section D

33. (i) Draw a ray diagram to show the formation of image by a convex lens when an object is placed in front of the lens between its optical centre and principal focus.
    (ii) In the ray diagram mark the object distance u and the image distance v with their proper signs (+ ve or − ve as per the new cartesian sign convention) and state how these distances are related to the focal length f of the convex lens in this case.
    (iii) Find the power of convex lens which forms a real and inverted image of magnification −1 of an object placed at a distance of 20 cm from its optical centre.

34. A couple is expecting their first child. What are the chances that the child born would be a boy or a girl?

Or A person first crossed pure breed pea plants having round yellow seeds with pure breed pea plants having wrinkled-green seeds and found that only A-B type of seeds were produced in the F_1-generation. When F_1-generation pea plants having A-B type of seeds were self-pollinated, then in addition to the original round yellow and wrinkled green seeds, two new varieties A-D and C-B types of seeds were also obtained.
    (i) What are A-B type of seeds?
    (ii) State whether A and B are dominant traits or recessive traits.
    (iii) What are A-D and C-B type of seeds?
    (iv) Out of A-B and A-D types of seeds, which one will be produced in (a) minimum number and (b) maximum number in the F_2-generation?
    (v) Give reason for the appearance of new combination of characters in the F_2 progeny.

35. (i) Why does 1 M HCl solution have a higher concentration of H^+ ions than 1 M CH_3COOH solution?
(ii) How does the flow of acid, rain water into a river makes the survival of aquatic life in the river difficult?
(iii) Which acid is stinging hair of nettle leaves?

Or

(i) How does a strong acid differ from a concentrated acid?
(ii) Account for the following
  (a) Antacid tablets are used by a person suffering from acidity.
  (b) Toothpaste is used for cleaning teeth.

Answers

14. (a) or (c)   **15.** (d)   **16.** (b)
17. (i) (a), (ii) (b), (iii) (c), (iv) (c), (v) (d)
18. (i) (a), (ii) (a), (iii) (a), (iv) (a), (v) (b)
19. (i) (c), (ii) (d), (iii) (c), (iv) (c), (v) (d)
20. (i) (c), (ii) (a), (iii) (c), (iv) (d), (v) (a)
23. 10.5 A   **27.** (a) −20 cm (b) 0.2
29. 1.5 A   **33.** (iii) 10 D

STATEWISE NTSE QUESTIONS

Chemical Reactions and Equations

1. Identify the correct statement(s) in relation to the following reaction

$$Zn + 2HCl \longrightarrow ZnCl_2 + H_2$$

1. Zinc is acting as an oxidant
2. Chlorine is acting as a reductant
3. Hydrogen ion is acting as an oxidant
4. Zinc is acting as a reductant **(Kerala)**

(a) 1 and 4   (b) 2 and 3
(c) 3 and 4   (d) 1 and 3

2. Which of the following reactions is displacement reaction? **(Odisha)**

(a) $CH_4 + 2O_2 \longrightarrow CO_2 + 2H_2O$
(b) $Cr_2O_3 + 2Al \longrightarrow Al_2O_3 + 2Cr$
(c) $2H_2O_2 \longrightarrow 2H_2O + O_2$
(d) $P_4 + NaOH \longrightarrow PH_3 + NaHPO_2$

3. $Fe_2O_3 + 2Al \longrightarrow Al_2O_3 + 2Fe$

The type of the above reaction is **(UP)**

(a) addition reaction
(b) double displacement reaction
(c) dissociation reaction
(d) displacement reaction

4. A solid compound 'X' on heating gives CO_2 gas and a residue. The residue mixed with water forms 'Y'. On passing an excess of CO_2 through 'Y' in water, a clear solution 'Z' is obtained. On boiling Z, compound 'X' is formed. The compound 'X' is …… **(Goa)**

(a) Na_2CO_3 (b) $CaCO_3$
(c) K_2CO_3 (d) $Ca(HCO_3)_2$

Acids, Bases and Salts

5. Which of the following contain five molecule of water of crystallisation? **(Haryana)**

(a) Blue vitriol   (b) White vitriol
(c) Epsom salt   (d) Green vitriol

6. Which of the following is an acid? **(Odisha)**

(a) NaOH   (b) NH_4NO_3 (c) $Mg(OH)_2$ (d) $B(OH)_3$

7. The pH value of pure water is **(UP)**

(a) 0   (b) 14   (c) 1   (d) 7

8. Which of the following oxalic acid is found naturally? **(UP)**

(a) Curd   (b) Tamarind
(c) Tomato   (d) Lemon

9. The chemical formulae of baking soda is **(UP)**

(a) NH_4Cl (b) $NaHCO_3$
(c) Na_2CO_3 (d) $NaCl$

10. The nature of calcium phosphate present in tooth enamel is **(Uttarakhand)**

(a) basic   (b) amphoteric
(c) acidic   (d) neutral

11. Which is weak acid? **(Gujarat)**

(a) Oxalic acid   (b) Hydrochloric acid
(c) Nitric acid   (d) Sulphuric acid

12. What is chemical formula of milk of magnesia? **(Gujarat)**

(a) $MgNO_3$ (b) $MgSO_4$
(c) $Mg(OH)_3$ (d) $Mg(OH)_2$

13. ……… is not an example of aerosol. **(Gujarat)**

(a) Fog   (b) Clouds
(c) Mist   (d) Shaving cream

14. Which of these can be used as olfactory indicator? **(Delhi)**

(a) Vanila   (b) Onion
(c) Clove   (d) All of these

Metals and Non-Metals

15. Which of the following is an oxide ore?

(a) Calcite   (b) Zincite **(Haryana)**
(c) Magnesite   (d) Calamine

16. Rekha dropped a metal piece A in the solution of another metal B. After some time a new colourless compound C is formed. A, B, C respectively can be **(Haryana)**

(a) Cu, $ZnSO_4$, $CuSO_4$ (b) Mg, NaCl, $MgCl_2$
(c) Mg, $CuSO_4$, $MgSO_4$ (d) Fe, $ZnSO_4$, $FeSO_4$

FULLY SOLVED

17. Which of the following element react with oxygen to form a compound with high melting point, which is soluble in water? (Odisha)
(a) Calcium (b) Carbon
(c) Silicon (d) Iron

18. The alloy containing a non-metal is (Odisha)
(a) brass (b) bronze
(c) steel (d) white metal

19. Cinnabar is an ore of which metal? (UP)
(a) Al (b) Cu
(c) Hg (d) Zn

20. Which is not correct? (Gujarat)
(a) Acid + Base ⟶ Salt + Water
(b) Acid + Metaloxide ⟶ Salt + Water
(c) Non-Metal oxide + Water ⟶ Base
(d) Base + Metal ⟶ Salt + Hydrogen + Water

21. Which is not a step of metallurgy? (Gujarat)
(a) Reduction (b) Roasting
(c) Corrosion (d) Concentration of ore

22. What will be the products when acid reacts with metals? (Delhi)
(a) Water and hydrogen gas
(b) Acid and hydrogen gas
(c) Salt and hydrogen gas
(d) Base and hydrogen gas

Carbon and Its Compounds

23. The correct IUPAC name for
$CH_2 = C(CH_3) - CH = CH_2$ is (Kerala)
(a) 2-methylbutane
(b) 2-methyl, 1, 3-butadiene
(c) 1, 3-pentadiene
(d) 2-methylbutene

24. Which of the following is main ingredient of biogas and CNG? (Odisha)
(a) Ethyne (b) Propane
(c) Methane (d) Butane

25. Which one of the following is functional group of propanone? (Odisha)
(a) Carboxylic acid (b) Aldehyde
(c) Ketone (d) Alcohol

26. The by product of soap industry is (Odisha)
(a) glycol (b) glucose
(c) glycerol (d) ethanol

27. The functional group of ethanal is (UP)
(a) >C=O (b) —CHO
(c) —OH (d) —COOH

28. The IUPAC name of C_2H_5OH is (UP)
(a) ethanol (b) methanol
(c) methanal (d) ethanal

29. The general formula of cycloalkane is (Goa)
(a) C_nH_{2n} (b) C_nH_{2n-1}
(c) C_nH_{2n+1} (d) C_nH_{2n-2}

30. According to IUPAC system, which type of compound is shown by the given structure?

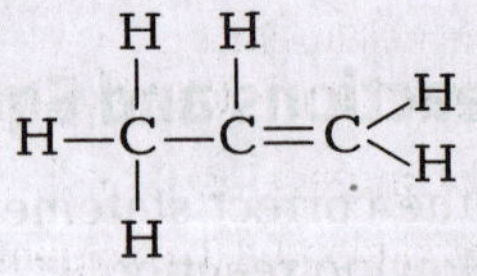

$$H-\underset{H}{\overset{H}{C}}-\underset{H}{\overset{H}{C}}=C\underset{H}{\overset{H}{<}}$$

(Uttarakhand)
(a) Ketone (b) Alkene
(c) Alkyne (d) Aldehyde

31. In water purification, fullerene is used as (Maharashtra)
(a) fuel (b) insulator
(c) catalyst (d) reductant

32. What is the condensed structured formula of alcohol? (Maharshtra)
(a) —OH (b) —CHO
(c) —COOH (d) —NH_2

Life Processes

33. .... respires through lungs. (Gujarat)
(a) Crabs (b) Lizard
(c) Sepia (d) Prawns

34. Anaerobic respiration takes place only in .... (Gujarat)
(a) mitochondria (b) glands
(c) lungs (d) cytoplasm

35. The small intestine receives the secretion from .... (Gujarat)
(a) salivary glands
(b) stomach and liver
(c) liver and salivary glands
(d) liver and pancreas

36. Wherein do the pulmonary veins open? (Gujarat)
(a) Left auricle
(b) Left ventricle
(c) Lungs
(d) Right auricle

37. Salivary glands secrete which of these enzymes? (Goa)
(a) Amylase (b) Lipase
(c) Pepsin (d) Trypsin

Statewise NTSE Questions

38. Breakdown of pyruvate to yield CO_2, H_2O and energy takes place in **(Goa)**
(a) cytoplasm (b) mitochondrion
(c) chloroplast (d) nucleus

39. Which of the following is NOT the purpose of transpiration? **(Delhi)**
(a) Help in absorption and transportation in plants
(b) Prevents loss of water
(c) Maintains the shape and structure of plants by keeping the cell turgid
(d) Supplies water for photosynthesis

40. Pulmonary vein carries **(Delhi)**
(a) deoxygenated blood (b) oxygenated blood
(c) mixed blood (d) None of these

41. Loop of Henle is found in **(Delhi)**
(a) lungs (b) liver (c) nephron (d) neuron

42. Glycolysis takes place in **(MP)**
(a) mitochondria (b) cytoplasm
(c) nucleus (d) chloroplast

43. When ATP is converted into ADP it releases **(MP)**
(a) enzymes (b) secretions
(c) energy (d) hormones

44. Saliva contains an enzyme called **(AP)**
(a) trypsin (b) ptyalin
(c) lipase (d) pepsin

45. What happens to the inhaled air as it passes through the nasal cavity? **(AP)**
(a) Warmed to the body temperature
(b) Moistened by mucus
(c) Filtered in the nasal cavity
(d) All of the above

46. Identify the correct sequence for the process of energy production from carbohydrates. **(Maharashtra)**
(a) Carbohydrates → Glycolysis → Pyruvic acid → Acetyl Co-A → Krebs cycle → CO_2 + H_2O + Energy
(b) Carbohydrates → Glycolysis → Pyruvic acid → Krebs cycle → CO_2 + H_2O + Energy
(c) Carbohydrates → Glycolysis → Acetyl Co-A → CO_2 + H_2O + Energy
(d) Carbohydrates → Glycolysis → Acetyl Co-A → Krebs cycle → Pyruvic acid → CO_2 + H_2O + Energy

47. Mode of nutrition in *Cuscuta* is **(Haryana)**
(a) saprophytic (b) autotrophic
(c) parasitic (d) insectivorous

48. Structural and functional unit of kidney is **(Haryana)**
(a) nephron (b) ureter (c) neuron (d) urethra

49. Exchange of gases in human occurs in **(Haryana)**
(a) trachea (b) pleura
(c) bronchi (d) alveoli

50. Choose the incorrect statement about glycolysis. **(Kerala)**
(a) Glucose is converted to carbon dioxide and water
(b) Takes place in cytoplasm
(c) Does not require oxygen
(d) The first phase of cellular respiration

51. The products of light reaction are **(Kerala)**
(a) oxygen, ATP, NADPH (b) ATP, CO_2, NADPH
(c) CO_2, oxygen, ATP (d) ADP, oxygen, NADPH

52. Which one of the following is correct about vein? **(Kerala)**
(a) Valves are present
(b) Thick-walled
(c) Carries blood in high speed and high pressure
(d) Carries blood from the heart

53. A person was found to have reduced level of reabsorption of water and glucose due to kidney damage. The following labelled parts would be the site of damage for this patient.

Karnataka
(a) Q (b) P (c) S (d) R

54. Identify the correct statements about blood.
A. Platelets are produced in the bone marrow.
B. When haemoglobin combines with oxygen forms carboxyhaemoglobin.
C. Calcium ions play an important role in clotting of blood.
D. Fibrins are formed by the conversion of fibrinogen by the enzyme thrombin.
(Karnataka)
(a) A and B (b) B, C and D
(c) B and D (d) A, C and D

55. The primary source of the synthesis of carbohydrates in plants is **(Goa)**
(a) atmospheric CO_2 (b) lipids
(c) fats (d) proteins

Control and Coordination

56. It is found as four small glands. **(Gujarat)**
(a) Parathyroid gland (b) Adrenal gland
(c) Pituitary gland (d) Thyroid gland

57. Which of the following is not a component of respiratory system in humans? **(Goa)**
(a) Pharynx (b) Larynx
(c) Hypothalamus (d) Trachea

58. Cell division in plants is promoted by **(Delhi)**
(a) abscisic acid (b) gibberellin
(c) ethylene (d) cytokinin

59. Flight and fight hormone is **(Delhi)**
(a) adrenaline (b) thyroxine
(c) oxytocin (d) insulin

60. The number of pairs of nerves which arise from spinal cord is **(Delhi)**
(a) 21 (b) 31 (c) 41 (d) 51

61. Identify the adrenal gland from the following figure. **(Maharashtra)**

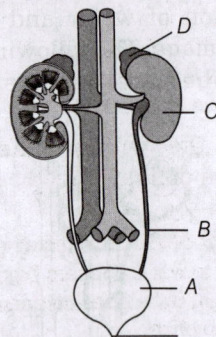

(a) A (b) B (c) C (d) D

62. Lateral ventricles are found in **(Haryana)**
(a) cerebellum (b) cerebral hemisphere
(c) diencephalon (d) medulla oblongata

63. A plant hormone known as stress hormone is **(Kerala)**
(a) gibberellin (b) cytokinin
(c) auxin (d) abscisic acid

How do Organisms Reproduce?

64. Exchange of genetic material takes place in **(Goa)**
(a) vegetative reproduction
(b) asexual reproduction
(c) sexual reproduction
(d) budding

65. The main method of reproduction in yeast is **(Rajasthan)**
(a) budding (b) sporogenesis
(c) cutting (d) grafting

66. Which of the following is not a secondary reproductive organ? **(Rajasthan)**
(a) Fallopian tube (b) Uterus
(c) Ovary (d) Vagina

67. Choose the correct statement from the below: Each human cell contains **(AP)**
(a) one pair of autosome and 22 pairs of allosomes
(b) only 23 pairs of allosomes
(c) only 23 pairs of autosomes
(d) 22 pairs of autosomes and one pair of allosome

68. Which is the sequence of four whorls of flower from outside to inside? **(Maharashtra)**
(a) Calyx → Corolla → Androecium → Gynoecium
(b) Gynoecium → Androecium → Corolla → Calyx
(c) Calyx → Androecium → Corolla → Gynoecium
(d) Gynoecium → Corolla → Androecium → Calyx

Heredity and Evolution

69. Chemical composition of chromosome is **(MP)**
(a) DNA and lipids
(b) DNA and carbohydrates
(c) proteins and lipids
(d) DNA and proteins

70. The recessive character in pea plant in the following is **(Karnataka)**
(a) violet flower
(b) axillary flower
(c) round seed
(d) green seed

Light : Reflection and Refraction

71. Linear magnification (m) produced by a rear view mirror fitted in vehicles **(Chandigarh)**
(a) is equal to one
(b) is infinity
(c) is more than one
(d) is less than one

72. Which of the following ray diagrams, show the correct refraction of ray of light? **(Chandigarh)**

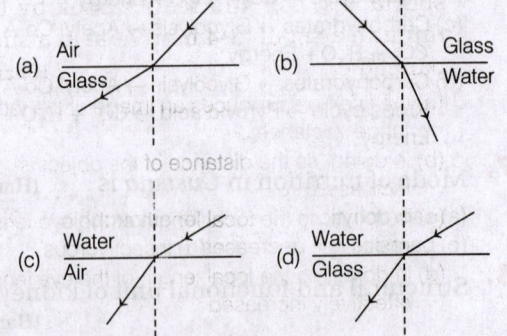

Statewise NTSE Questions

73. If a symmetrical convex lens of focal length f is cut into two parts along the principal axis as shown in the figure, the focal length of each part will be **(Chandigarh)**

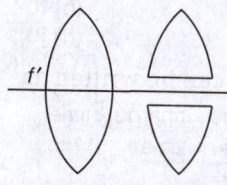

(a) $\dfrac{f}{2}$ (b) $\dfrac{f}{4}$
(c) f (d) ∞

74. What is speed of light in glass? **(Gujarat)**
(a) 2×10^8 ms^{-1} (b) 2.25×10^8 ms^{-1}
(c) 3×10^8 ms^{-1} (d) 1.75×10^8 ms^{-1}

75. Which equation not represent Snell's law? **(Gujarat)**
(a) $\dfrac{n_2}{n_1} = \dfrac{\sin\theta_1}{\sin\theta_2}$ (b) $\dfrac{n_1}{n_2} = \dfrac{\sin\theta_2}{\sin\theta_1}$
(c) $n_1 \sin\theta_1 = n_2 \sin\theta_2$ (d) $n_1 \sin\theta_2 = n_2 \sin\theta_1$

76. A lady is standing in front of a magic mirror. She finds the image of her head bigger, the middle portion of her body of same size and that of legs smaller. Which of the following is the correct order of combination for the magic mirror from the top? **(Punjab)**
(a) Plane, convex, concave
(b) Convex, plane, concave
(c) Plane, concave, convex
(d) Concave, plane, convex

77. The refractive index of the material of a double convex lens is 1.5 and its focal length is 5 cm. If the radii of curvature are equal, then the value of the radius of curvature is .... cm. **(AP)**
(a) 6.5   (b) 5
(c) 8   (d) 5.6

Human Eye and Colourful World

78. Far sighted people, who have lost their spectacles, can still read a book by looking through a small (3-4 mm) hole in a sheet of a panel, because **(Chandigarh)**
(a) the fine hole produces an image of the letters at a longer distance
(b) in doing, so the distance of the object is increased
(c) in doing, so the focal length of the eye lens is effectively decreased
(d) in doing, so the focal length of the eye lens is effectively increased

79. Which statement is true for an eye donor?
  (i) Eye donor can belong to any age group or gender.
  (ii) People who use spectacles cannot donate eye.
  (iii) Eye must be removed within 4-6 h after death.
  (iv) Eye removal process takes only 10-15 min.
(Chandigarh)
(a) i, ii, iii   (b) i, iii, iv
(c) i, ii, iv   (d) ii, iii, iv

80. When a milky and cloudy layer is formed on the eye lens of old age person, they lose their vision partially or completely. This type of situation is called **(Gujarat)**
(a) myopia   (b) cataract
(c) hypermetropia   (d) presbyopia

81. A person cannot see objects distinctly kept beyond 2m. This defect can be corrected by the which type of lens and of what power of its? **(Punjab)**
(a) Convex lens, + 0.5 D
(b) Concave lens, + 0.5 D
(c) Convex lens, – 0.2 D
(d) Concave lens, – 0.5 D

82. Choose the wrong statement related to refraction of light. **(Maharashtra)**
(a) Twinkling of stars
(b) Oval shape of sun in morning and evening
(c) Object in water appears bigger in size
(d) Red light undergoes dispersion, while passing through prism

83. The size of an object as perceived by an eye depends primarily on **(Telangana)**
(a) actual size of the object
(b) distance of the object from the eye
(c) aperture of the pupil
(d) size of the image formed on the retina

84. The process of re-emission of absorbed light in all directions with different intensities by the atom or molecule is called **(Telangana)**
(a) scattering of light
(b) dispersion of light
(c) reflection of light
(d) refraction of light

Electricity

85. The equivalent resistance of network of three 2Ω resistors cannot be **(Chandigarh)**
(a) 0.67   (b) 2Ω
(c) 3Ω (d) 6Ω

547

FULLY SOLVED

86. Electric bulb B_1 (100 W - 250 V) and electric bulb B_2 (100 W - 200 V) are connected across source of 250 V as shown in figure, what is the potential drop across electric bulb B_2?
(Chandigarh)

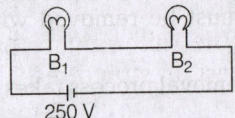

(a) 200 V (b) 250 V
(c) 98 V (d) 48 V

87. Determine the equivalent resistance between points X and Y in the following circuit. (Gujarat)

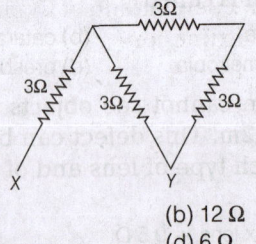

(a) 5 Ω (b) 12 Ω
(c) 9 Ω (d) 6 Ω

88. Which formula is not correct for R? (where, R = resistance) (Gujarat)
(a) $R = \dfrac{W}{I^2 t}$ (b) $R = \dfrac{V^2}{P}$
(c) $R = I^2 t$ (d) $R = \dfrac{P}{I^2}$

89. The unit of electric potential difference is (Gujarat)
(a) JC (b) J/C
(c) J (d) C/J

90. What is the equivalent resistance between A and B? (Punjab)

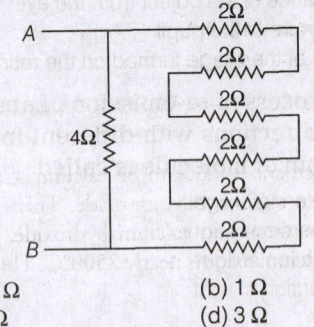

(a) 16 Ω (b) 1 Ω
(c) 7 Ω (d) 3 Ω

91. An electric kettle consumes 1 kW of electric power when operated at 220 V. A fuse wire of what rating must be used for it? (Punjab)
(a) 1 A (b) 2 A
(c) 5 A (d) 4 A

92. A current of 2 A is drawn by a filament by an electric bulb. Number of electrons passing through a cross-section of the filament in 8 s would be approximately (Punjab)
(a) 10^{20} (b) 10^{27}
(c) 10^{32} (d) 10^{40}

93. The voltage can be written as (Punjab)
(a) work done × charge × time
(b) $\dfrac{\text{work done} \times \text{time}}{\text{current}}$
(c) $\dfrac{\text{work done}}{\text{current} \times \text{time}}$
(d) work done × charge

Magnetic Effect of Current

94. A beam of α-particles moving towards east is deflected towards south by magnetic field. The direction of magnetic field is (Chandigarh)
(a) towards south
(b) towards east
(c) downward
(d) upward

95. The strength of magnetic field inside a long current carrying straight solenoid is (Punjab)
(a) minimum in the middle
(b) more at the ends than at the centre
(c) same at all points
(d) found to increase from one end to the other

Our Environment

96. Which of the following groups have only non-biodegradable components?
 1. Wood, Paper, Leather
 2. Polythene, Detergent, PVC
 3. Plastic, Detergent, Glass
 4. Plastic, Glass, Animal dung (Gujarat)
(a) 1 and 4 (b) Only 3
(c) 2 and 3 (d) 1 and 3

97. Which of the following is an abiotic component? (Goa)
(a) Animals (b) Plants
(c) Microorganisms (d) Soil

98. In our country, vast tracts of forests and a single species of plants is cultivated. This practice promotes .... (Goa)
(a) biodiversity in that area
(b) growth of natural forest
(c) monoculture in that area
(d) preserve the natural ecosystem in the area

Statewise NTSE Questions

99. In the food chain given below, if the amount of energy available at fourth trophic level is 5 kJ, what was the energy available at the producer level?

Grass → Grasshopper → Frog → Snake → Hawk **(Delhi)**

(a) 5000 kJ
(b) 500 kJ
(c) 50 kJ
(d) 5 kJ

100. Which wavelength of harmful UV-radiations is prevented by ozone layer in entering the earth atmosphere? **(Gujarat)**

(a) 210-300 nm
(b) 200-310 nm
(c) 120-210 nm
(d) 400-700 nm

101. Which gas is not responsible for global warming? **(MP)**

(a) CO_2 (b) O_3 (c) NO_2 (d) N_2

Management of Natural Resources

102. Which of the following is not an ancient water harvesting structure? **(Delhi)**

(a) Kattas (b) Sargam
(c) Kulhs (d) Surangam

103. The number of biosphere reserves established in India is **(Rajasthan)**

(a) 18 (b) 118
(c) 142 (d) 669

104. About what percentage of living species is in danger of extinction? **(Haryana)**

(a) 20% (b) 10% (c) 30% (d) 1%

Answers

1. (c) Loss in electrons (oxidation)

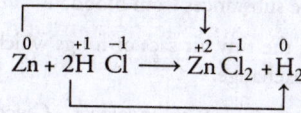

Gain in electrons (reduction)

Therefore, Zn is acting as an reductant or reducing agent and HCl and H^+ ion is acting as an oxidant or oxidising agent.

2. (b) $Cr_2O_3 + 2Al \longrightarrow Al_2O_3 + 2Cr$

The above equation is an example of displacement reaction as aluminium being more reactive than chromins, displaces it from its compounds.

3. (d) Displacement reaction Al is more reactive than Fe, so displaces Fe in its compound.

4. (b) $\underset{X}{CaCO_3} \xrightarrow{\Delta} \underset{Residue}{CaO} + CO_2 \uparrow$

$\underset{Residue}{CaO} + H_2O \longrightarrow \underset{Y}{Ca(OH)_2} + H_2O + CO_2$

$\longrightarrow \underset{Z}{Ca(HCO_3)_2}$

$\underset{Z}{Ca(HCO_3)_2} \xrightarrow{\Delta} \underset{X}{CaCO_3} + H_2O + CO_2$

5. (a) Blue vitriol — $CuSO_4 \cdot 5H_2O$

6. (d) $B(OH)_3$, H_3BO_3 is acid. Its chemical name is boric acid.

7. (d) Pure water is neutral, so its pH will be 7.

8. (c) Curd → Lactic acid, Tamarind → Tartaric acid Tomato → Oxalic acid, Lemon → Citric acid

9. (b) Baking soda → $NaHCO_3$ (Sodium bicarbonate).

10. (a) Enamel is a calcium hydroxy pactite

$Ca_5(PO_4)_3OH$

As it contains OH^- ions so it is basic in nature.

11. (a) Oxalic acid $(H_2C_2O_4)$ is a weak acid as it does not dissociate completely in aqueous solution to produce H^+ ions.

12. (d) $Mg(OH)_2$: Milk of magnesia acts as a strong antacid.

13. (d) Shaving cream is a form not an aerosol.

14. (d) Vanilla, onion and clove are olfactory indicators.

15. (b) Oxide ore : Zincite — ZnO
→ Calcite : $CaCO_3$
→ Calamine : $ZnCO_3$
→ Magnesite : $MgCO_3$

16. (c) $Mg + CuSO_4 \longrightarrow \underset{(Colourless)}{MgSO_4} + Cu$

17. (a) The element is likely to be calcium. Calcium reacts with oxygen to form calcium oxide. This calcium oxide dissolves in water and calcium hydroxide. The melting point of calcium oxide is nearly 2500°C. Thus, answer (a) is correct.

18. (c) The alloy containing a non-metal is steel. It is an alloy of iron (metal) and carbon (non-metal).

19. (c) Cinnabar is HgS which is an ore of Hg.

20. (c) Non-metal oxide + water ⟶ Base

$CO_2 + H_2O \longrightarrow H_2CO_3$

21. (c) Corrosion it is an oxidative process.

22. (c) Acid + Metal ⟶ Salt + Hydrogen gas↑

23. (b) $\overset{1}{CH_2}=\overset{2}{\underset{\underset{CH_3}{|}}{C}}-\overset{3}{CH}=\overset{4}{CH_2}$

    2-methylbut-1, 3-diene or 2-methyl-1, 3-butadiene

24. (c) Methane (CH_4) is the main ingredient of biogas and CNG. It is a flammable gas.

25. (c) Propanone has structure ; $CH_3-\overset{\overset{O}{\|}}{C}-CH_3$.

    Therefore it contains ketone ($>C=O$) as a functional group.

26. (c) The by product of soap industry is glycerol

    Fat or Oil + Alkali $\xrightarrow{Heat}$ Soap + Glycerol
    (Ester)   (Sodium   (Sodium   An alcohol
               hydroxide)   salt of
                                    fatty acid)

27. (b) Formula of ethanal is CH_3CHO.
    So, functional group is —CHO.

28. (a) IUPAC name of C_2H_5OH is ethanol.

29. (a) e.g., Cyclohexane (C_6H_{12}).

30. (b) The hydrocarbons which contain atleast one double bond are called alkene. These have general formula, C_nH_{2n}.

31. (c) Catalyst

32. (a) Alcohols contain —OH functional group.

33. (b) Reptiles (land dwellers) respire through lungs, e.g. lizard.

34. (d) Aerobic respiration takes place in mitochondria while, anaerobic respiration takes place in the cell cytoplasm.

35. (d) Small intestine receives secretions from two glands, i.e. liver (bile juice) and pancreas (pancreatic juice).

36. (a) Pulmonary vein brings oxygenated blood from lungs to the left auricle

37. (a) Salivary gland secretes ptyalin, also called salivary amylase which acts on starch to form maltose sugar.

38. (b) Breakdown of pyruvate to yield CO_2, water and energy is termed as citric acid or Krebs cycle. It takes place in mitochondria.

39. (b) Transpiration helps in the absorption and upward movement of water and minerals dissolved in it. It maintains the shape and structure of plants and causes loss of water.

40. (b) Pulmonary vein supplies oxygenated blood from lungs to the left atrium.

41. (c) Loop of Henle is a part of nephron. Its main function is to reabsorb water and sodium chloride from filtrate. This conserves water for the organisms producing concentrate urine.

42. (b) Breakdown of glucose into pyruvic acid in cytoplasm during respiration is termed as glycolysis.

43. (c) ATP is the energy currency for most cellular processes. Its hydrolysis releases fixed amount of energy which is used to drive endothermic reactions taking place in the cell.

44. (b) Ptyalin is a form of amylase found in the saliva of humans which helps in the digestion of starch.

45. (d) As air passes through nasal cavities, it is warmed and humidified, so that air that reaches lungs is warm and moist. The combination of cilia and mucus helps to filtre out solid particles from air.

46. (a) During respiration, following sequence takes place.
    Glucose (Carbohydrates) → Glycolysis → Pyruvic acid → Acetyl Co-A → Krebs cycle → CO_2 + H_2O + Energy.

47. (c) *Cuscuta* is also known as dodder plant or Amarbel which is parasitic in nature and enters inside xylem and phloem of host plant to acquire nutrition.

48. (a) Nephron is the structural and functional unit of kidney which actually produces urine in the process of removing waste substances from blood.

49. (d) Alveoli are the tiny air sacs of lungs which allow for rapid gaseous exchange.

50. (a) The statement (a) is incorrect. Glycolysis is a metabolic pathway that converts glucose into pyruvate. It occurs in the cytoplasm and requires no oxygen.

51. (a) ATP and NADPH are the products of light reaction of photosynthesis. These are later used in dark reaction to synthesise glucose. Oxygen is a byproduct.

52. (a) Veins are blood vessels that carry deoxygenated blood towards the heart. Most veins are equipped with valves to prevent blood flowing in the reverse direction.

53. (a) *P* is Malpighian corpuscle
    Q is PCT
    R is Henle' loop
    S is collecting duct
    PCT helps in the absorption of glucose and water.

54. (d) When carbon monoxide combines with haemoglobin, it forms carboxyhaemoglobin, hence B is incorrect and A, C, D is correct, i.e. option (d).

55. (a) Atmospheric CO_2 is fixed to form glucose in the dark reaction of photosynthesis performed by plants.

56. (a) The parathyroid glands are small pea sized glands located in the neck just behind the thyroid gland. They are four in number.

57. (c) Hypothalamus is a part of forebrain. Pharynx, larynx and trachea are component of respiratory system in humans.

Statewise NTSE Questions

58. (d) Cytokinin promotes cell division and is present in greater concentration in areas of rapid cell division such as in fruits and seeds.

59. (a) Adrenal glands located on the top of the kidneys secrete two hormones, i.e. adrenaline and noradrenaline. These hormones are released during stress of any kind or emergency and are called emergency hormones. These hormones prepare body during the flight, fright and fight.

60. (b) Nerves that arise from spinal cord are called spinal nerves. Humans have 31 pairs of spinal nerves.

61. (d) Adrenal glands are small, triangular-shaped glands located on top of both kidneys.

62. (b) Lateral ventricles are two largest cavities of ventricular system of human brain. Each cerebral hemisphere contains a lateral ventricle known as left and right ventricle, respectively.

63. (d) Abscisic acid is called stress hormone as it induces various responses in plants against stress conditions.

64. (c) In sexual reproduction, two parents are involved. So, at the time of gamete formation through meiosis, exchange of genetic material takes place between homologous chromosomes.

65. (a) The method by which yeast commonly reproduces is budding.

66. (c) Ovary produces female gamete (ova/egg), hence known as female primary sexual organ.

67. (d) Human cell contains 22 pairs of autosomes and the other two chromosomes are sex chromosomes, also called allosomes.

68. (a) The sequence of four whorls of flower (from outside to inside) is as follows

$$\text{Calyx} \to \text{Corolla} \to \text{Androecium} \to \text{Gynoecium}$$

69. (d) Chromosomes are thread-like structures of nucleic acid (DNA) and protein called histones, found in the nucleus of most living cells, carrying genetic information in the form of genes.

70. (d) Out of the given options, green seed is a recessive trait in pea plant.

71. (d) Rear view mirror is convex mirror, which always form image reduced in size, so $m<1$.

72. (d) In refraction, a ray from rarer medium to denser medium bends towards normal.

73. (c) Focal length does not change, because no change in the radii of curvature occurs.

74. (a) As, $\mu = \dfrac{c}{v}$ $\left(\because c = 3 \times 10^8 \text{ and } \mu_{glass} = \dfrac{3}{2}\right)$

$\Rightarrow v_{glass} = \dfrac{c}{\mu_{glass}} = \dfrac{3 \times 10^8}{3/2}$

$= 2 \times 10^8$ m/s

75. (d) From Snell's law,

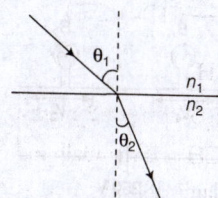

$\dfrac{n_2}{n_1} = \dfrac{\sin \theta_2}{\sin \theta_1}$

$\Rightarrow \quad n_2 \sin \theta_1 = n_1 \sin \theta_2$

76. (d) As, magnified image is formed only by concave mirror.

∴ Correct combination is concave, plane and convex (plane has same size image).

77. (b) Applying lens maker's formula,

$\dfrac{1}{f} = (\mu - 1)\left(\dfrac{2}{R}\right)$

$\Rightarrow \quad R = 5$

$[\because f = 5 \text{ and } \mu = 1.5]$

78. (c) Focal length of eye decreases by looking from a small hole.

79. (a) Statements (i), (ii) and (iii) are correct.

80. (b) Cataract-eye lens becomes cloudy and lose of vision.

81. (d) To correct myopia, concave lens used

$P = -\dfrac{1}{2} = -0.5$ D

82. (d) Statement (d) has no relation to refraction.

83. (a) It depends primarily on actual size of the object.

84. (a) Definition of scattering of light.

85. (b) Possible combination and their $R_{equivalent}$

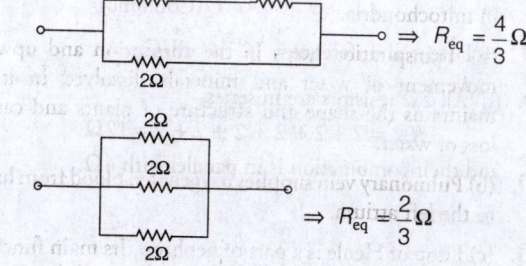

86. (c) As, $R = \dfrac{V^2}{W}$

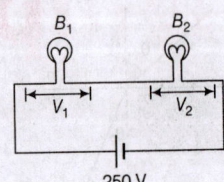

$R_1 = \dfrac{(250)^2}{100} = 625\,\Omega$

and $R_2 = \dfrac{(200)^2}{100} = 400\,\Omega \Rightarrow I = \dfrac{V}{R_1 + R_2} = \dfrac{250}{1025}$

So, $V_2 = IR_2 = \dfrac{250}{1025} \times 400 \approx 98\,V$

87. (a) As, R_{eq}

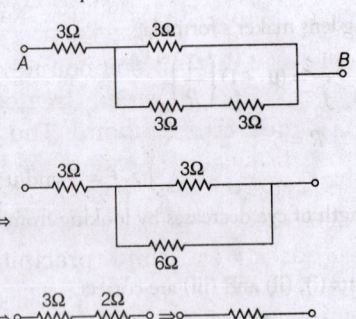

88. (c) (a) $R = \dfrac{W}{I^2 t} = \dfrac{\text{Work done}}{I \times (I \times t)} = \dfrac{W}{IQ} = \dfrac{V}{I}$ $\left[\because \dfrac{W}{Q} = V\right]$

[where, Q = charge]

(b) $R = \dfrac{V^2}{P} = \dfrac{V^2}{V \cdot I} = \dfrac{V}{I}$ [$\because$ Power, $P = VI$]

(c) $R = I^2 t = IQ$ [wrong]

(d) $R = \dfrac{P}{I^2} = \dfrac{VI}{I^2} = \dfrac{V}{I}$

So, option (c) is wrong.

89. (b) As, potential difference $= \dfrac{\text{work done}}{\text{charge}}$

$= \dfrac{W\,(\text{Joule})}{Q\,(\text{Coulomb})}$

$\Rightarrow$ Potential difference $= JC^{-1}$ or J/C

90. (d) All $2\,\Omega$ resistors are in series,

$R_{eq} = 2 + 2 + 2 + 2 + 2 + 2 = 12\,\Omega$

and their combination is in parallel with $4\,\Omega$.

So, $R_{eq} = \dfrac{4 \times 12}{4 + 12} = 3\,\Omega$

91. (c) As, power, $P = VI$

$\Rightarrow I = \dfrac{P}{V} = \dfrac{1000}{220} = 4.6\,A$

Fuse rating should be 5 A, it is safe upto 4.6 A current.

92. (a) As, current, $I = \dfrac{Q}{t} = \dfrac{ne}{t}$

[$\because e$ = charge of electron $= 1.6 \times 10^{-19}$ C]

$\Rightarrow n = \dfrac{It}{e} = \dfrac{2 \times 8}{1.6 \times 10^{-19}} = 10^{20}$ electrons

93. (c) $\therefore$ Voltage $= \dfrac{\text{Work done}}{\text{Charge}}$

$= \dfrac{\text{Work done}}{\text{Current} \times \text{Time}}$

[$\because$ Charge = Current $\times$ Time]

94. (d) α-particle feels a force in upward direction.

95. (c) For a long straight solenoid, magnetic field inside is nearly uniform and constant.

96. (c) A type of substances which cannot be broken down by natural organisms and acts as a source of pollution is called non-biodegradable components, e.g. plastic, polythene, PVC, detergent, etc.

97. (d) Soil is the abiotic component of ecosystem while rest are biotic components.

98. (c) Monoculture is the cultivation of a single crop in a given area.

99. (a) When the plants are eaten by an animal, about 10% of the energy stored in the food is fixed into animal flesh. Similarly, only 10% energy is transferred at each trophic level. Therefore, the energy available at the producer level is 5000 kJ.

100. (b) Ozone layer absorbs harmful UV-radiations of range 200-310 nm (approx.) and prevent them from entering earth's atmosphere.

101. (d) Nitrogen is inert in nature, so they do not absorb infrared radiations emitted by the earth surface.

102. (b) Sargam is not an ancient water harvesting structure while Kattas, Kulhs and Surangams are ancient water harvesting structures found in Karnataka, Himachal Pradesh and Kerala, respectively.

103. (a) Biosphere reserves established in India by government are 18.

104. (c) 30% of living species is in danger of extinction.

Junior Science Olympiad
Chapterwise Questions

Chemical Reactions and Equations

1. Which are the entities that are oxidised and reduced respectively in the following reaction?

   $2\,Pb(NO_3)_2 \xrightarrow{\Delta} 2PbO + 4NO_2 + O_2$ (2016)

   (a) Pb and O
   (b) N and O
   (c) Pb and N
   (d) O and N

2. On thermal decomposition, which of the following substances will give oxygen gas?

   I. NH_4NO_3 II. NH_4ClO_3
   III. $(NH_4)_2Cr_2O_7$ IV. $(NH_4)_2SO_4$ (2016)

   (a) I and II
   (b) II and III
   (c) III and IV
   (d) I and IV

3. Which of the following is an oxidation–reduction reaction? (2014)

   (a) $H_3O^+(aq) + CO_3^{2-}(aq) \longrightarrow HCO_3^-(aq) + H_2O$
   (b) $HNO_3(aq) + NH_3(aq) \longrightarrow NH_4^+(aq) + NO_3^-(aq)$
   (c) $Mg(s) + F_2(g) \longrightarrow MgF_2(s)$
   (d) $Pb(NO_3)_2(aq) + 2\,NaCl(aq) \longrightarrow PbCl_2(s) + 2NaNO_3(aq)$

Acids, Bases and Salts

4. P, Q, R are different colourless solids, while S is a colourless solution. They are (in random order) sodium chloride (NaCl), calcium carbonate ($CaCO_3$), acetic acid (CH_3COOH) and phenolphthalein indicator (Phph). Small amount of the above substances were added in pairs (e.g. P with Q; P with R etc.) to a small amount of water in a test tube. They give the following results as shown in the observation table (2017)

   Observations table:

	P	Q	R
Q	No reaction	–	No reaction
R	Dark pink colour	No reaction	–
S	No reaction	No reaction	Effervescence

   Then the chemicals are

	P	Q	R	S
(a)	NaCl	$CaCO_3$	CH_3COOH	Phph
(b)	$C_{20}H_{14}O_4$	NaCl	$CaCO_3$	CH_3COOH
(c)	CH_3COOH	Phph	NaCl	$CaCO_3$
(d)	$CaCO_3$	CH_3COOH	Phph	NaCl

5. A colourless solution of compound A gives white precipitate, B, when treated with sodium hydroxide solution. The white precipitate dissolves in excess of sodium hydroxide solution. The clear solution thus obtained when treated with hydrogen sulphide gas gives white precipitate C. Identify A, B and C. (2016)

   (a) $MgSO_4$, $Mg(OH)_2$, MgS
   (b) $Al_2(SO_4)_3$, $Al(OH)_3$, Al_2S_3
   (c) $ZnSO_4$, $Zn(OH)_2$, ZnS
   (d) $(NH_4)_2SO_4$, NH_4OH, $(NH_4)_2S$

6. There are 3 containers X, Y and Z. X contains 10mL of water and Z contains 10mL of milk. Y contains 5mL of milk (same as in container Z) mixed with 5 mL of water. All three containers have pH value of 6.5. P amount of acetic acid is added to container X, Q amount to Y and R amount to Z. Such that the final pH value in each container is 5.5. Then, which of the following is true? (2014)

   (a) $P < Q < R$
   (b) $P < R = Q$
   (c) $P = Q = R$
   (d) $P < R < Q$

7. A white crystalline salt P reacts with dilute HCl to liberate a suffocating gas Q and also forms a yellow precipitate. The gas Q turns potassium dichromate acidified with H_2SO_4 to a green colored solution R, P, Q and R are? (2014)

	P	Q	R
(a)	$Na_2S_2O_3$	SO_2	$Cr_2(SO_4)_3$
(b)	Na_2SO_3	Cl_2	$Cr(SO_4)_3$
(c)	Na_2SO_4	SO_3	$Cr_2(SO_4)_3$
(d)	Na_2S	Cl_2	$Cr_2(SO_4)_3$

FULLY SOLVED

Metals and Non-Metals

8. Observe the following diagram carefully. Concentration of solution in each test tube is 0.1M. The test tube in which a chemical reaction occurs is (2018)

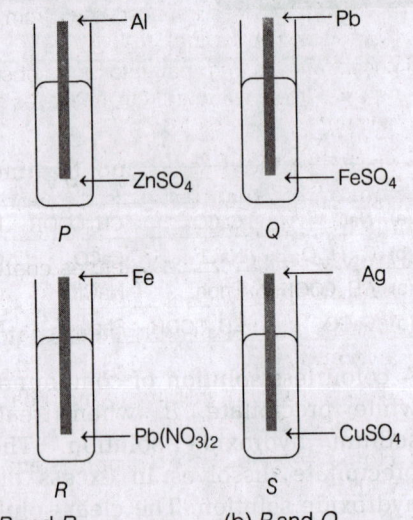

(a) P and R
(b) P and Q
(c) Q and R
(d) P and S

9. You are provided with 4 metal ores at different levels of activity series, extraction of these metals from their ores involves oxidation and reductions. Match the metal ores with their extraction processes. (2017)

	Metal ores		Processes
1.	Cinnabar	I.	Oxidation and reduction
2.	Zincblende	II.	Oxidation
3	Haematite	III.	Electrolysis
4.	Galena	IV.	Reduction

(a) 1-I, 2-II, 3-IV, 4-II
(b) 1-II, 2-I, 3-IV, 4-I
(c) 1-I, 2-III, 3-II, 4-IV
(d) 1-IV, 2-II, 3-III, 4-I

10. Following experiments were carried out separately in chemistry laboratory in different test tubes, labelled as (I), (II), (III) and (IV)

I. Mg + dil. HCl   II. Al + dil. H_2SO_4
III. Cu + dil. HCl   IV. Mn + dil. HNO_3

She observed hydrogen gas is not produced in (2017)

(a) only test tube (IV)
(b) both test tubes (III) and (IV)
(c) only test tube (III)
(d) both test tubes (II) and (III)

11. Sunanda was experimenting with an electrolytic cell. She took an aqueous solution of sodium chloride and added some zinc sulphate into it. When she dipped platinum electrodes in the electrolyte and passed electric current through the solution the species discharged at cathode and anode respectively were (2015)

(a) zinc and chlorine
(b) sodium and oxygen
(c) hydrogen and chlorine
(d) zinc and oxygen

12. The electrolysis of aqueous NaOH solution yields (2014)

(a) Na at cathode, O_2 at anode
(b) H_2 at cathode, O_2 at anode
(c) H_2 at anode, O_2 at cathode
(d) H_2 at anode, Na at cathode

Carbon and Its Compounds

13. Soaps (sodium salt of fatty acid) are the molecules in which the two ends have differing properties; one is hydrophilic whereas other is hydrophobic. Hydrophobic part refers to tail of the soap which is always out of water.

Which of the following statement is true about soap? (2015)

	Hydrophilic	Hydrophobic
(a)	Sodium	Fatty acid
(b)	Fatty acid	Sodium
(c)	Glycerine	Sodium
(d)	Sodium	Ester

14. Alkaline potassium permagnate or acidified potassium dichromate is used to convert alcohol to acid. Choose the correct option from the following if methanol (CH_3OH) is treated with acidified potassium dichromate solution. (2015)

	Formula of acid formed	Potassium dichromate is undergoing	Methanol is undergoing
(a)	CH_3COOH	Reduction	oxidation
(b)	HCOOH	Oxidation	Reduction
(c)	CH_3COOH	Oxidation	Reduction
(d)	HCOOH	Reduction	oxidation

Life Processes

Direction (Ques 19-22) *Read passage carefully and answer the questions given below.*

Some experiments were carried out using *Croton* sp. plants to understand the process of photosynthesis. It was observed that the leaves of the plant exposed to light for longer duration accumulated more starch. However, due to the presence of pre-formed starch in the leaves, it was difficult to find the net productivity on a fixed exposure to light source. Therefore, it was necessary to obtain starch-free leaves in the plant before starting the experiment. **(2018)**

15. Which of the following would help obtain starch-free leaves in the plant?
(a) Expose the leaves to blue light for 48 hours before starting the experiment
(b) Keep the plant in dark for about 48 hours before starting the experiment
(c) Remove starch from the leaves by exosmosis, 48 hours before starting the experiment
(d) Keep the leaves to red light for 48 hours before starting the experiment

16. After a period of illumination, the leaves were boiled in alcohol to make them colourless. Which of the following could be used to test the end product stored in the leaves?
(a) Cobalt chloride paper   (b) Litmus paper
(c) Iodine solution
(d) Copper sulphate solution

17. Some of the starch-free leaves were coated with wax on both the surfaces. The plant was maintained under normal environmental conditions. At the end of the experiment, the wax coated leaves are likely to show ....
(a) accumulation of more water
(b) wilting of the wax coated leaves
(c) increase in sucrose accumulation
(d) decrease in number of chloroplasts

18. During the morning hours, using a fine blade, an incision was made to the leaves such that the phloem tissue was cut open. Analysis of the liquid oozing out was found to contain high amount of
(a) xylose   (b) ribose
(c) sucrose   (d) galactose

19. In a hypothetical experiment, the outer tissues of the woody part of the stem of a dicotyledonous plant are removed in the form of a ring, leaving only the xylem and pith intact. Which one of the statements is most likely to be correct? **(2017)**

(a) Water transport from the root to leaves will be obstructed but food transport from leaves to stem will be unhindered
(b) Water transport from root to leaves will not be obstructed but food transport from stem to leaves will be hindered
(c) Water transport from root to leaves will not be obstructed but food transport down from the leaves stops at the ring
(d) Water transport from leaves to root is obstructed but food transport down from the leaves stops at the ring

20. In an experiment involving treatments to demonstrate transpiration, six experimental setups were as follows

I. Woody plant with only leaves coated with vaseline jelly.
II. Woody plant with only stem coated with vaseline jelly.
III. Woody plant without any coating of vaseline jelly.
IV. Herbaceous plant with only stem coated with vaseline jelly.
V. Herbaceous plant with only leaves coated with vaseline jelly.
VI. Herbaceous plant without any coating of vaseline jelly.

Cobalt chloride ($CoCl_2$) paper (changes from blue to pink when wet) was attached to the leaves and stem. The plants were well-watered and kept under adequate sunlight. The following were proposed. **(2017)**

Plants	Colour change of $CoCl_2$ paper on Leaves	Stem
I	Blue	Blue
II	Pink	Pink
III	Pink	Blue
IV	Blue	Blue
V	Blue	Pink
VI	Pink	Blue

Which of the above is/are correct?
(a) I, II and V   (b) Only II
(c) III, IV and VI   (d) Only V

21. Ingestion, digestion, absorption, assimilation and egestion are the steps in food processing in our body. Majority of absorption takes place in small intestine (villi) and which is transported to different organs through the circulatory system. Starting with villi, which of the following is the correct sequence of organs that the absorbed food passes through? **(2016)**

(a) Liver → Other organs → Heart
(b) Heart → Liver → Other organs
(c) Heart → Other organs → Liver
(d) Liver → Heart → Other organs

22. The 'chief cells' of stomach secrete hydrochloric acid. Consider a hypothetical situation in which the 'chief cells' are destroyed resulting in complete inhibition of acid secretion in stomach. In comparison to a normal person, which one of the following is most likely to happen in the stomach during the above condition? **(2016)**
(a) Digestion of proteins will increase
(b) Digestion of fats will start
(c) Digestion of carbohydrates will continue
(d) Digestion of fat will decrease

Directions (Ques 23-27) *Read passage carefully and answer the questions given below.*

The nephron is a basic unit of kidney which is made of Bowman's capsule, proximal convoluted tubule, loop of Henle and distal convoluted tubule. The proximal convoluted tubule absorbs major amount of water, glucose, other essential elements from the filtrate but still around 180 litres of filtrate passes through loop of Henle daily, out of which only 1-2 litres is thrown out of body in the form of concentrated urine. Hence, loop of Henle plays a crucial role in reabsorption of water and salts. The loop of Henle is located in medulla part of kidney and consists of descending and ascending limb. The ascending one has thicker walls which are non-permeable to water. It is important factor for creating concentration gradient throughout the loop's length. The filtrate entering the loop has 300 units concentration and it keeps on changing as shown in the figure due to reabsorption process. Study the diagram and answer the following questions.

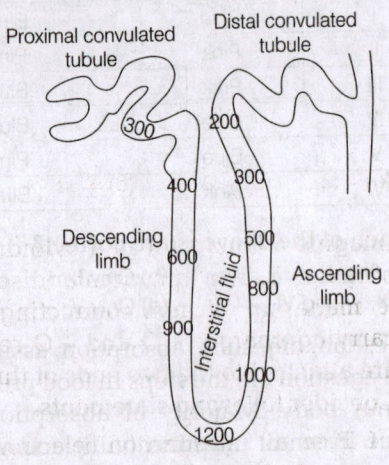

(2016)

23. The concentration of filtrate increases as it passes down the descending tubule due to reabsorption of .... in the interstitial fluid.
(a) NaCl
(b) water
(c) amino acids
(d) glucose

24. In ascending tubule, the filtrate shows decrease in concentration as it reaches distal convoluted tubule. This is because of
(a) active transport of water from interstitial fluid to ascending tubule
(b) active transport of salts from ascending tubule to interstitial fluid
(c) passive transport of salts from interstitial fluid to ascending tubule
(d) passive transport of water from interstitial fluid to ascending tubule

25. In an animal X, loop of Henle is shorter than normal length. The result would be
(a) it will excrete lesser amount of concentrated urine
(b) it will excrete same amount of urine without any difference
(c) it will excrete large amount of dilute urine
(d) it will excrete lesser amount of dilute urine

26. What is the likely habitat of such animal X?
(a) Aquatic
(b) Hot, arid desert
(c) Polar
(d) Grasslands

27. An artificial kidney is a device to remove nitrogenous waste products from the blood during dialysis. The device contains tubes that are suspended in a tank filled with dialysing fluid. The patient's blood is passed through these tubes. During this passage, waste products from the blood pass into the dialysing fluid.

Pick the correct options given below to fill the blanks in the following statements.

'The tubes of the artificial kidney are ...., while the dialysing fluid is .... to the blood. The waste products from the blood pass into the dialysing fluid by .... transport.'
(a) semipermeable, isotonic, passive
(b) permeable, hypotonic, active
(c) permeable, isotonic, passive
(d) semipermeable, hypotonic, active

Junior Science Olympiad Chapterwise Questions

28. The actual path followed by a glucose molecule in the process of aerobic respiration for the production of 36 or 38 ATP would be (2014)
    (a) Cytoplasm – Mitochondrial matrix – Oxysomes
    (b) Cytoplasm – Oxysomes – F_1-particles
    (c) Mitochondrial matrix – F_1-particles – Oxysomes
    (d) Mitochondrial matrix – Oxysomes – Cytoplasm

How do Organisms Reproduce

29. Which type of reproduction from the following, gives evidence that the genetic information needed for the complete development of an individual is contained actually in haploid set of chromosomes? (2014)
    (a) Budding in *Hydra*
    (b) Multiple fission in *Amoeba*
    (c) Development of male honeybee (drone) from egg
    (d) Binary fission in *Paramecium*

Light : Reflection and Refraction

30. A ray of light passes through a thick glass sheet with some angle of incidence θ as shown in the figre. The refractive index of glass is (2018)

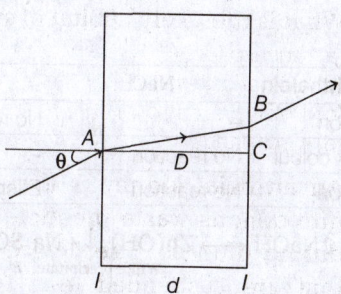

    (a) Exactly d/DC.
    (b) Approximately d/DC
    (c) Approximately d/DC
    (d) Approximately AD/AC

31. Focal length of a concave mirror is f. In terms of f, the separation between an object and its doubly magnified real image by this mirror is (2016)
    (a) 9f/2 (b) 5f/2 (c) 4f (d) 3f/2

Human Eye and Colourful World

32. Some people face problems seeing distant objects clearly. They, however, have no problem seeing nearby objects. A person wears a spectacle with concave lenses to see distant objects. He is able to see nearby object clearly without using lenses. When this person is reading without using the spectacles the image will be formed (2018)
    (a) on the blind spot
    (b) behind the retina
    (c) in front of the retina
    (d) in the fovea region on the retina

Electricity

33. Five polyester balls labelled P, Q, R, S and T are suspended from insulating threads. Several experiments are performed on the balls and the following observations are made.

    I. Ball P repels R and attracts Q
    II. Ball S attracts Q and has no effect on T
    III. A negatively charged rod attracts both P and T

    Which one of the following options correctly describes the nature of charges on the respective balls (0 refers to uncharged)? (2018)

	P	Q	R	S	T
(a)	+	−	+	0	+
(b)	+	−	+	+	0
(c)	−	+	−	0	0
(d)	+	−	+	0	0

34. Seven 1 Ω resistances are connected as shown in the figure. Resistance of the conducting wires is negligible. Effective resistance between A and B is (2017)

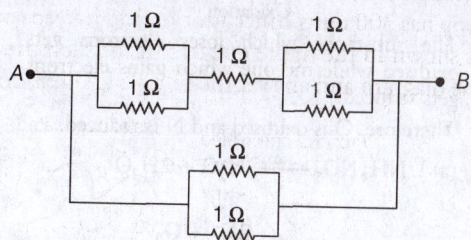

    (a) $\frac{2}{5}\Omega$ (b) $\frac{3}{7}\Omega$ (c) $\frac{19}{7}\Omega$ (d) $\frac{5}{7}\Omega$

35. Imagine a conductor in a cylindrical shape of radius R. Two thin circular discs of radius R made up of non-conducting material, carrying charge $+Q$ and $-Q$ respectively, are attached to the two ends of this cylinder. Consider following statements.

    I. Free or conduction electrons in the conducting cylinder will drift towards $+Q$.
    II. A constant current will be set up through cylinder.

557

III. Constant current will flow for very short duration of time. (2016)
(a) Only I is true (b) Only II is true
(c) Only III is true (d) Only I and III are true

36. Three filament bulbs made from a metal of low thermal coefficient of resistivity are arranged as shown in the figure. The wattage rating of each bulb is the power output, if it is connected independently across 240V. The bulb that glows brightest and least bright are respectively (2015)

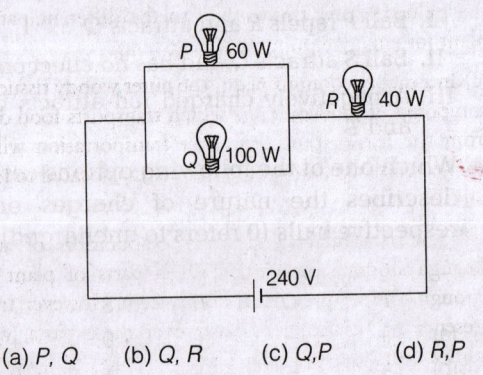

(a) P, Q (b) Q, R (c) Q, P (d) R, P

Our Environment

37. Which of the following can be categorised as a parasite in true sense? (2014)
(a) The female *Anopheles* mosquito sucks blood from human
(b) Human foetus developing in uterus draws nourishment from mother
(c) Head louse lives on human scalp and lays eggs on hair
(d) The cuckoo lays eggs in crow's nest for subsequent parental care

Management of Natural Resources

38. To overcome the problem of water shortage, most urban cities in India promote the concept of 'rainwater harvesting'. Although the harvested water can be used variously, the main purpose of water harvesting is to
(a) directly collect water for household purposes (2016)
(b) use surface water for irrigation
(c) recharge ground water
(d) refill lakes and other water bodies

Answers

1. (d)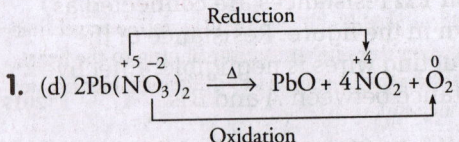

The substance which loses electrons gets oxidised while the one which gains electrons gets reduced.
Therefore, O is oxidised and N is reduced.

2. (a) I. $NH_4NO_3 \xrightarrow{\Delta} N_2O + 2H_2O$
$\downarrow$
$2N_2 + O_2$

II. $2NH_4ClO_3 \xrightarrow{\Delta}$
$N_2 + O_2 + Cl_2 + 4H_2O$

3. (c) $\overset{0}{Mg} + \overset{0}{F_2} \xrightarrow{\Delta} \overset{+2}{Mg}\overset{-1}{F_2}$ (Oxidation / Reduction)

Therefore, the reaction given in option (c) is an oxidation-reduction reaction and such reactions are called redox reactions.

4. (b) P : phenophthalein (Indicator)
Q : NaCl (Neutral salt)
R : CaCO₃ (Basic salt)
S : CH₃COOH (Acid)

	Phenolphthalein	NaCl	CaCO₃
NaCl	No reaction	–	No reaction
CaCO₃	Dark pink colour	No reaction	–
CH₃COOH	No reaction	No reaction	Effervescence

5. (c) $\underset{\underset{Zinc\ sulphate}{'A'}}{ZnSO_4} + 2NaOH \longrightarrow \underset{\underset{White\ precipitate,\ 'B'}{}}{Zn(OH)_2\downarrow} + Na_2SO_4$

$\underset{'B'}{Zn(OH)_2} + \underset{(Excess)}{2NaOH} \longrightarrow \underset{\underset{(Soluble)}{Sodium\ zincate}}{Na_2ZnO_2} + 2H_2O$

$Na_2ZnO_2 + H_2S \longrightarrow \underset{\underset{'C'}{White\ precipitate,}}{ZnS} + 2NaOH$

6. (a) The container X require least amount of acetic acid, container Y require more amount of acetic acid than container X while container Z requires maximum amount of acetic acid. Therefore, $P < Q < R$.

7. (a) $\underset{\underset{Sodium\ thiosulphate}{'P'}}{Na_2S_2O_3(s)} + \underset{Dil.}{HCl(l)} \longrightarrow$

$\underset{\underset{Sulphur\ dioxide\ (Suffocating\ gas)}{'Q'}}{SO_2(g)} + \underset{\underset{of\ sulphur}{yellow\ precipitates}}{S(s)} + H_2O(l) + 2NaCl(aq)$

$\underset{Acidified}{K_2Cr_2O_7} + 3SO_2 \xrightarrow{H_2SO_4}$

$K_2SO_4 + \underset{\underset{coloured\ solution)}{'R',\ Chromium\ sulphate\ (green}}{Cr_2(SO_4)_3} + H_2O$

Junior Science Olympiad Chapterwise Questions

8. (a) Al is more reactive than Zn and thus displace Zn from its compound.

   $2Al(s) + 3ZnSO_4(aq) \longrightarrow Al_2(SO_4)_3 + 3Zn(s)$

   Similarly Fe is more reactive than Pb and thus displace Pb from its compound.

   $Fe(s) + Pb(NO_3)_2(aq) \longrightarrow Fe(NO_3)_2(aq) + Pb(s)$

9. (b) 1. Cinnabar (HgS) is extracted through oxidation.

   2. Zincblende (ZnS) is extracted through both oxidation and reduction.

   3. Haematite (Fe_2O_3) is extracted through reduction.

   4. Galena (PbS) is extracted through oxidation and reduction.

10. (c) Cu being a less reactive metal does not liberate hydrogen gas on reaction with dilute HCl.

    $Mg + \underset{(Dilute)}{2HCl} \longrightarrow MgCl_2 + H_2 \uparrow$

    $2Al + \underset{(Dilute)}{3H_2SO_4} \longrightarrow Al_2(SO_4)_3 + 3H_2 \uparrow$

    Only Mn and Mg on reaction with HNO_3(dil.) gives H_2 gas.

    $Mn + \underset{(Dilute)}{2HNO_3} \longrightarrow Mg(NO_3)_2 + H_2 \uparrow$

11. (c) Electrolysis of aqueons solution of sodium chloride gives hydrogen and chloride at cathode and anode respectively. Reactions of electrolysis of *eq* NaCl are given below.

    At cathode : $2H^+ + \bar{e} \longrightarrow H_2$ (Reduction)

    At anode : $2Cl^- \longrightarrow Cl_2 + 2\bar{e}$ (Oxidation)

12. (d) Electrolysis of aqueous NaOH solution yeilds, O_2 at anode and H_2 at cathode. Reactions are given below:

    At anode : $OH^-(aq) \longrightarrow OH + \bar{e}$

    $4OH \longrightarrow 2H_2O + O_2$

    At cathode : $2H^+ + 2e^- \longrightarrow 2H$ or H_2

13. (a) Soap molecule is made up of two parts-a long hydrocarbon part (or non-ionic part) or fatty acid part and a short ionic part containing —COO^-Na^+.

    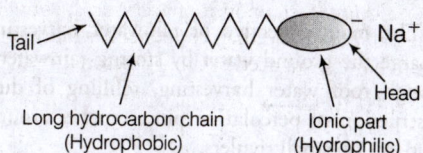

14. (d) $\underset{Methanol}{CH_3OH} \xrightarrow[+ \text{ Heat}]{\text{Alkaline } K_2Cr_2O_7} \underset{\text{Formic acid}}{HCOOH}$

    In this reaction, $K_2Cr_2O_7$ is reduced to Cr^{3+} and CH_3OH is oxidised to HCOOH (Formic acid).

15. (b) The correct option is (b), i.e. keep the plant in dark for about 48 hours before starting the experiment, because it will lead to consumption of synthesised food by the plant during respiration.

16. (c) The correct option is (c), iodine solution turns violet in colour due to the presence of starch. Thus, it is used to test starch.

17. (a) The correct option is (a), i.e. accumulation of more water. Because of transpiration water moves upward to the stomata, but due to the coating of wax, the water cannot ooze out through stomata, thus, water gets accumulated in leaves.

18. (c) The correct option is (c), i.e. sucrose is transported in the phloem fibres from leaves to the different parts of plant for energy requirement and storage.

19. (c) In a dicotyledonous plant, the outer woody tissues are composed of phloem tissue which transports food down from the leaves, thus the water transportation will be unaffected while food would not be translocated to lower parts of plant.

20. (d) The transpiration involves evaporation of water through stomata present on green parts of plant and through lenticels present on woody stem. However, in the presence of vaseline jelly layer over these parts, water cannot transpirate.

    Thus, in plant specimen V, transpiration occurring through stem changes cobalt chloride paper to pink, but due to the presence of vaseline jelly, the paper on leaves remains blue as transpiration does not occur at leaves.

21. (d) Substances absorbed in the small intestine travel first to the liver for processing before continuing to the heart, from where it is get distributed to different target organs through a network of arteries.

22. (c) Hydrochloric acid (HCl) is involved in the activation of inactive pepsinogen enzyme into active pepsin enzyme which catalyses the digestion of protein, thus its absence will affect protein metabolism. However, digestion of carbohydrate will continue as there will be no HCl (acidic medium) to stop action of salivary amylase.

    Digestion of fat will not be influenced as it begins, when food enters into the small intestine.

23. (b) The descending limb of Henle's loop is permeable to water, which results in the reabsorption of water from filtrate.

24. (b) The ascending limb of Henle's loop is impermeable to water, but it allows active transport of salts to the interstitial fluid.

25. (c) It will excrete large amount of dilute urine as the shorter Henle's loop is not efficient in effective reabsorption of water, thus the urine will be dilute and in excess.

26. (a) Fresh water aquatic animals pass excess of dilute urine.

27. (a) Semipermeable, isotonic, passive.

28. (a) During cellular respiration, a glucose molecule is gradually broken down into carbon dioxide and water to produce energy in the form of ATP. This process occurs

in three main stages at three different locations, first is glycolysis which occurs in cytoplasm, next is Krebs cycle which takes place in mitochondrial matrix and final stage, electron transport and ATP formation occurs across inner mitochondrial membrane and oxysomes.

29. (c) A drone is a male honeybee that is the product of an unfertilised egg, having haploid set of chromosomes. They are themselves haploid males, such type of development is termed as arrhenotokous parthenogenesis or simply arrhenotoky.

30. (b) From Snell's law,
$$\mu = \frac{\sin\theta}{\sin r}$$
From ΔABC and ΔDBC,
$$\mu = \frac{BC}{BD} \times \frac{AB}{BC} = \frac{AB}{BD}$$

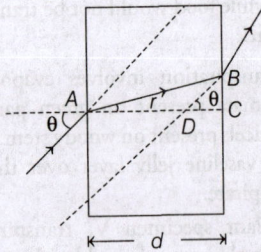

As BC is very small, then
$$\mu = \frac{AC}{DC} = \frac{d}{DC}$$

31. (d) ∴ Magnification, $m = \frac{-v}{u}$
$$\Rightarrow 2 = \frac{-v}{u} \Rightarrow v = -2u$$
By using lens formula,
$$\frac{1}{v} + \frac{1}{u} = \frac{1}{f}$$
$$\frac{1}{+2u} + \frac{1}{(-u)} = \frac{1}{f}$$
$$\Rightarrow -\frac{1}{2u} = \frac{1}{f} \text{ or } u = -\frac{f}{2}$$
$$\Rightarrow v = f$$
Thus, separation between object and image
$$= f + \frac{f}{2} = \frac{3f}{2}$$

32. (d) As the person is suffering from near sightedness. So, he does not have any problem to see nearby objects. Thus, the image of nearby object will be formed in the fovea region on the retina for clear vision.

33. (d) From I observation → P and R are of same charge and Q is of opposite charge.
From II observation → S and T have no effect, so they are neutral or uncharged.
From III observation → P should be of the charge.
Thus, option (d) is correct.

34. (a) Modified circuit diagram as shown below.

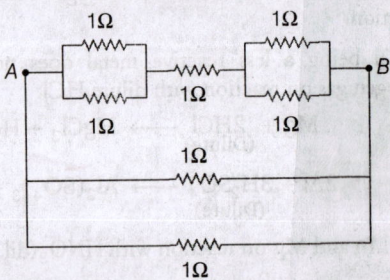

So, now $R_{eq} = 2 \| 1 \| 1 = \frac{2}{5} \Omega$

35. (a) When circular discs of charge $+Q$ and $-Q$ are connected across cylindrical conductor, the free or conduction electron starts moving from higher potential disc to lower potential disc. But as the circuit is not closed, so no current will flow in the conductor.

36. (d) Equivalent power for same rated voltage,
$$P_{eq} = (100 + 60) \| 40 = \frac{160 \times 40}{160 + 40} = 32 \text{ W}$$
∵ For series connected bulbs, the bulb which has least wattage glow brighters and for parallel connection, it is opposite to series So, R get most brighter and P get least.

37. (c) Parasite is an organism which lives in or on another organism (its host) and benefits by deriving nutrients at the other's expense. Head louse is a true parasite as it lives permanently on human scalp and sucks blood to get nutrition.

38. (c) The main objective of rainwater harvesting is to recharge the ground water by storing rainwater locally, through roof water harvesting, refilling of dug wells, construction of percolation pits, trenches around fields and dams on small rivulets.